GREETING

Priest: The Lord be with you.
Assembly: And with your spirit.

PENITENTIAL ACT A

I confess to almighty God
and to you, my brothers and sisters,
that I have greatly sinned,
in my thoughts and in my words,
in what I have done
    and in what I have failed to do,
All strike their breast as they say:
through my fault, through my fault,
through my most grievous fault;
therefore I ask Blessed Mary ever-Virgin,
all the Angels and Saints,
and you, my brothers and sisters,
to pray for me to the Lord our God.

PENITENTIAL ACT B

Priest: Have mercy on us, O Lord.
Assembly: For we have sinned against you.
Priest: Show us, O Lord, your mercy.
Assembly: And grant us your salvation.

GLORIA

Glory to God in the highest,
and on earth peace to people of good will.

We praise you,
we bless you,
we adore you,
we glorify you,
we give you thanks for your great glory,
Lord God, heavenly King,
O God, almighty Father.

Lord Jesus Christ, Only Begotten Son,
Lord God, Lamb of God, Son of the Father,
you take away the sins of the world,
    have mercy on us;
you take away the sins of the world,
    receive our prayer;
you are seated at the right hand of the Father,
    have mercy on us.

For you alone are the Holy One,
you alone are the Lord,
you alone are the Most High,
Jesus Christ,
with the Holy Spirit,
in the glory of God the Father. Amen.

DIALOGUE AT THE GOSPEL

Deacon or Priest: The Lord be with you.
Assembly: And with your spirit.
Deacon or Priest: A reading from the holy
    Gospel according to N.
Assembly: Glory to you, O Lord.

NICENE CREED

I believe in one God,
the Father almighty,
maker of heaven and earth,
of all things visible and invisible.

I believe in one Lord Jesus Christ,
the Only Begotten Son of God,
born of the Father before all ages.
God from God, Light from Light,
true God from true God,
begotten, not made,
    consubstantial with the Father;
through him all things were made.
For us men and for our salvation
he came down from heaven,
All bow at the following words up to:
    and became man.
and by the Holy Spirit was incarnate
    of the Virgin Mary,
and became man.

For our sake he was crucified under Pontius
    Pilate,
he suffered death and was buried,
and rose again on the third day
in accordance with the Scriptures.
He ascended into heaven
and is seated at the right hand of the Father.
He will come again in glory
to judge the living and the dead
and his kingdom will have no end.

I believe in the Holy Spirit, the Lord,
    the giver of life,
who proceeds from the Father and the Son,
who with the Father and the Son
    is adored and glorified,
who has spoken through the prophets.

I believe in one, holy, catholic and apostolic
    Church.
I confess one Baptism for the forgiveness of sins
and I look forward to the resurrection of the dead
and the

APOSTLES' CREED

May replace the Nicene Creed
I believe in God,
the Father almighty,
Creator of heaven and earth,
and in Jesus Christ, his only Son, our Lord,
All bow at the following words up to:
    the Virgin Mary,
who was conceived by the Holy Spirit,
born of the Virgin Mary,
suffered under Pontius Pilate,
was crucified, died and was buried;
he descended into hell;
on the third day he rose again from the dead;
he ascended into heaven,
and is seated at the right hand
    of God the Father almighty;
from there he will come to judge
    the living and the dead.

I believe in the Holy Spirit,
the holy catholic Church,
the communion of saints,
the forgiveness of sins,
the resurrection of the body,
and life everlasting. Amen.

INVITATION TO PRAYER

Priest: Pray... the almighty Father.
Assembly: May the Lord accept the
        sacrifice at your hands
        for the praise and glory of his name,
        for our good
        and the good of all his holy Church.

PREFACE DIALOGUE

Priest: The Lord be with you.
Assembly: And with your spirit.
Priest: Lift up your hearts.
Assembly: We lift them up to the Lord.
Priest: Let us give thanks to the Lord
        our God.
Assembly: It is right and just.

HOLY, HOLY, HOLY

Holy, Holy, Holy Lord God of hosts.
Heaven and earth are full of your glory.
Hosanna in the highest.
Blessed is he who comes
    in the name of the Lord.
Hosanna in the highest.

MEMORIAL ACCLAMATION A

We proclaim your Death, O Lord,
and profess your Resurrection
until you come again.

MEMORIAL ACCLAMATION B

When we eat this Bread and drink this Cup,
we proclaim your Death, O Lord,
until you come again.

MEMORIAL ACCLAMATION C

Save us, Savior of the world,
for by your Cross and Resurrection
you have set us free.

SIGN OF PEACE

Priest: The peace of the Lord be with you
        always.
Assembly: And with your spirit.

INVITATION TO COMMUNION

Priest: Behold... supper of the Lamb.
Assembly: Lord, I am not worthy
        that you should enter under my roof,
        but only say the word
        and my soul shall be healed.

DISMISSAL

Priest: The Lord be with you.
Assembly: And with your spirit.

WORSHIP

FOURTH EDITION

GIA PUBLICATIONS, INC.
CHICAGO

PREFACE

Twenty-five years have passed since the publication of the third edition of GIA's flagship hymnal, *Worship*. Those years have witnessed the development and refinement of the practice of full, conscious, and active participation in the public prayer life of the Roman Catholic Church in the United States of America. *Worship—Fourth Edition* endeavors to continue the tradition of supporting the people of God in their sung and spoken prayer.

The hymnal committee of five chosen for *Worship—Fourth Edition* boasts over two hundred combined years of experience as pastoral musicians in parish, cathedral, and seminary settings, with additional experience as pastors and teachers; diocesan liturgy and music directors; staff to the liturgy secretariat of the National Conference of Catholic Bishops; composers, writers, editors, and publishers; and members, presenters, and leaders in organizations such as the National Association of Pastoral Musicians and the Hymn Society in the United States and Canada.

The organization of this hymnal, like its predecessor, reflects the liturgical life of the Church. The book begins with the Liturgy of the Hours, the daily prayer of the Church, edited in such a way as to enable parishes to celebrate the approved rite on Sundays and most solemnities. A separate volume, *Worship: Liturgy of the Hours Leaders Edition* (1986), is compatible with the new edition and contains proper antiphons, readings, intercessions, and prayers for each day.

Following the Liturgy of the Hours, the section of Psalms and Canticles is expanded to include psalmody for the rites and psalmody for the Liturgy of the Hours—specifically, all the psalms and canticles for Morning Prayer and Evening Prayer II for all Sundays of the four-week cycle (as well as most solemnities) and for Morning Prayer from the Office for the Dead, and the nine psalms for Night Prayer. It includes psalms for general use, among them settings that may be used as entrance, offertory, or communion processionals. Most of these are complete psalms from *The Revised Grail Psalms*—approved for liturgical use in the United States in 2008—and are set to the psalm tones of Joseph Gelineau, SJ. In each case, an alternate Conception Abbey psalm tone by Gregory Polan, OSB, is also provided. The pointing of the psalm verses applies to both the Gelineau tones and the Conception Abbey tones. For the latter, the penultimate note in each phrase of the psalm tone corresponds to the syllable before the final accent in each line of text.

The most widely used psalm settings from the piano/guitar-based repertoire are present, along with a number of additional psalms for major feasts; many of these can be used as seasonal psalms. For the growing number of multicultural parishes, bilingual (English and Spanish) psalms are provided for major feasts, specifically those for which a single parish celebration is normative, such as the liturgies of the Triduum, Christmas Midnight Mass, and even Thanksgiving Day. The translations include *The Revised Grail Psalms*, New American Bible, and paraphrases. An index of psalms and canticles provides extensive information on liturgical use.

The section of Rites of the Church presents the sacramental rituals with an outline of each rite, ritual commentary, and musical elements such as responsorial psalms and acclamations—material intended to enable the average worshiper to participate fully in these liturgies.

The 2011 implementation of the *Roman Missal, Third Edition* is a significant factor in the development of this fourth edition of *Worship*. Following the recommendation of the United States Conference of Catholic Bishops, the Order of Mass is presented with the chants from the *Roman Missal*. Eight complete Mass settings in varying styles and degrees of solemnity follow, including a bilingual, English-Spanish Mass. Individual service music items conclude the section, with eucharistic acclamations from the same source grouped together. For the complete Masses the emphasis is on new settings, while for the individual service music items the emphasis is on revised versions of previously published works.

At the heart of the committee's work on the hymns and songs was the task of further developing the "hymn of the day" feature from *Worship—Third Edition*. The world of hymnody has expanded dramatically in the past twenty-five years, producing an unprecedented number of new texts for worship, with many based on the Scriptures of the three-year lectionary. An index of hymns for the Church year specifies hymns that relate directly to the gospel for each Sunday, and sometimes offers additional suggestions related to the other readings. This group of hymns is not in a single section of the book; rather these hymns fall into their appropriate liturgical and topical categories.

To facilitate their most immediate use, the hymns of the day are generally set to familiar tunes—this being a departure from the previous edition, which had included many unfamiliar tunes. A few lesser-known tunes have been chosen to avoid overusing a tune, or when the editors felt strongly about a certain pairing of words with music; in these cases, a second hymn is often suggested. When introducing new tunes, the committee intentionally used them more than once, so that the work of learning a new tune reaps multiple opportunities for its use. In the instances when a tune for a hymn of the day is unfamiliar, the metrical index of tunes is instrumental in choosing other pairings.

Perhaps the single most defining feature of *Worship—Fourth Edition* is the effort the committee put into choosing high-quality hymn texts. The result is a body of hymns that are theologically sound, poetically substantive, and attuned to the needs of the rites and liturgical calendar. Each text has undergone the scrutiny of a newly formed English Text Review Committee. Hymns having more than a century of use were compared to their original versions as well as to their versions in contemporary hymnals. Some previously omitted verses were added, some original wording was restored, and other edits were made according to the best judgment of the committee. Alterations made to copyrighted texts were done with permission.

Believing that most Catholic parishes in the United States use an eclectic repertoire, the committee strove to make this hymnal more diverse than the previous edition. It includes the most widely used titles from the piano/guitar-based repertoire, with piano accompaniments provided; throughout, guitar chords are provided when practical.

While this is clearly a hymnal for English-speaking communities, Spanish and other foreign language hymns and songs are included in order to enable those communities to recognize, in a small way, the increasingly multicultural nature of many assemblies. Short songs from Taizé, Iona, and other sources have been chosen—songs intended to be repeated for as long as the liturgical action requires. Many of these pieces are presented with additional languages, both European and Asian. Staples from the Church's heritage of chant are included, many with Latin and English texts. An index of foreign language settings is provided.

The assembly books are published in two editions: with and without lectionary readings. Both include responsorial psalm refrains, which consist of those that are newly composed as well as those taken from *Worship—Third Edition*. For the first time in a volume of Lectionary Psalms, each refrain can be joined to verses sung to either Gelineau tones or those of Michel Guimont. This separate volume of Lectionary Psalms uses the revised Grail translation.

Special recognition is given to Jeffry Mickus (hymnal coordinator, editing, typesetting, book layout), Michael Boschert (permissions editor), Joshua Evanovich (book layout), Gail Gillespie (typesetting, proofreading), Clarence Reiels (proofreading), and Phil Roberts (typesetting, book layout). Acknowledgment is given to the text review committee members: Neil Borgstrom, Michael Boschert, Kelly Dobbs-Mickus, Ronald Krisman, and Randall Sensmeier; to Br. Michael Marcotte, OSB, for his help in assigning Conception Abbey psalm tones; and to Gabe Huck and Ronald Krisman for the ritual commentary. Special thanks is given to individuals who responded to early inquiries and a survey, and to those who offered feedback during the process. The committee as a whole wishes to single out individual members for their unique contributions: Ronald Krisman for his extensive editorial work, including heading the text review committee, Spanish and other foreign language editing, and compiling the scriptural index and the psalms and canticles index; to Ronald Krisman and Kelly Dobbs-Mickus for the liturgical and topical indexes; to James Chepponis for editorial help and proofreading; and to Robert Batastini for his expertise and his guidance at every step of the way. Finally, acknowledgment is given to Alec Harris, GIA's president, and to David Anderson, vice president, for their constant support.

Worship—Fourth Edition Committee
Kelly Dobbs-Mickus
   General Editor and Project Director
Rev. Ronald F. Krisman
Robert J. Batastini
Rev. James J. Chepponis
Charles Gardner

Contents

Liturgy of the Hours

Psalms and Canticles

Rites of the Church

Mass

Hymns and Songs

Lectionary

Indexes

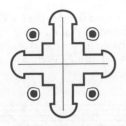

Liturgy of the Hours

When darkness gives way before the sun's light and a new day begins, people of all religions have had their rites of morning: words and songs and gestures with which to pray. It has been the same at the end of the day's light, and again in the last moments before sleep.

Christians, following the example of their Jewish ancestors, continued to pray at morning and evening and night. These moments are the hinges of daily life. As they came round each day they have been occasions to repeat what every child has learned by heart: words to praise God for a new morning, to thank the Father for Christ who is our light as evening comes, to invoke God's strong protection through the hours of night.

The daily prayers of Christians were fashioned at first from very simple things: the sign of the cross, the Lord's Prayer, a few verses and songs and short psalms, intercessions. And for most Christians morning and night remain times for such simple prayers always said by heart.

The pages of this section offer a form of daily prayer that grew from this same tradition. When Christians have gathered in the early morning, at day's end, just before retiring, the simple prayers for the individual have grown more elaborate. The daily assemblies of Christians gave shape to what became known as the divine office or "liturgy of the hours." In recent times, these prayers have been restored to some of their original simplicity and are again being prayed in parish churches and Christian households.

In using and in adapting the forms of morning, evening and night prayer given below, two things are especially important. First, these are not to be prayers which could be prayed any time. Rather, they are prayers (in word, song, gesture, silence) which are prompted by the morning itself, by the evening, by the night. Their content and pace should reflect what is unique to each of these moments. Second, the assembly's parts in these prayers should be gradually learned by heart. Simplicity, repetition and care for times of silence make it possible for these prayers to belong fully to those who assemble.

Worship—Fourth Edition contains the proper psalms and canticles for all Sundays, most solemnities, morning prayer from the Office for the Dead, and night prayer; consult the Index of Psalms and Canticles. Proper antiphons, readings, intercessions, and prayers for each day are found in *Worship—Liturgy of the Hours, Leaders' Edition* (1986) or *Christian Prayer*.

2 INVITATORY

The invitatory belongs at the very beginning of each day's prayer. It precedes either the Office of Readings or Morning Prayer. It consists of the dialogue below followed by Psalm 24, 67, 95, or 100. A bilingual setting of Psalm 67 is found at no. 61; settings of Psalm 95 are found at nos. 71 and 72 (with seasonal antiphons); settings of Psalm 100 are found at nos. 77 and 78.

Stand. All make the sign of the cross on their lips.

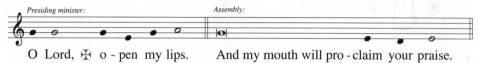

O Lord, ✠ o - pen my lips.   And my mouth will pro - claim your praise.

3 Morning Prayer / Lauds

The Church's sense for how to pray in the morning comes from our Jewish heritage. Whatever the day, whatever the difficulties, the tradition has been to begin the day with praise for the Creator. The sign of the cross, first traced on the Christian at baptism, is again made to begin the new day and its prayer. In the hymn and the psalms, in the scripture and intercessions, each one who prays and the community together finds what it is to stand at the beginning of a new day as a Christian. The morning's prayer gives the day its meaning when, through the years, these prayers become one's own.

The following verse and response are omitted when the hour begins with the invitatory.

Stand. All make the sign of the cross.

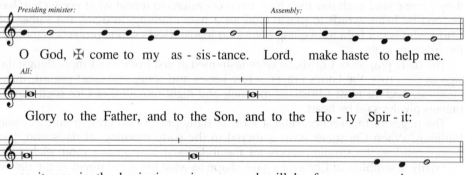

O God, ✠ come to my as - sis - tance.   Lord,   make haste to help me.

Glory to the Father, and to the Son, and to the Ho - ly Spir - it:

as it was in the beginning, is now, and will be for ev - er. A - men.

Added outside Lent:

Al - le - lu - ia.

Text: ICEL, © 1974

4 HYMN

This or another morning hymn (see nos. 846 to 851), or one related to the season or feast, may be sung.

1. Fa - ther, we   praise you,   now   the night is   o - ver;
2. Rul - er of   all things,   fit   us for your   man-sions;
3. All - ho - ly   Fa - ther,   Son, and e - qual Spir - it,

Ac - tive and watch - ful, stand we all be - fore you;
Ban - ish our weak - ness, health and whole - ness send - ing;
Trin - i - ty bless - ed, send us your sal - va - tion;

Sing - ing, we of - fer prayer and med - i -
Bring us to heav - en, with your saints u -
Yours is the glo - ry, gleam - ing and re -

ta - tion: Thus we a - dore you.
nit - ed; Joy with - out end - ing.
sound - ing Through all cre - a - tion.

Text: *Nocte surgentes;* attr. to St. Gregory the Great, 540–604; tr. by Percy Dearmer, 1867–1936, alt.
Tune: CHRISTE SANCTORUM, 11 11 11 5; Paris *Antiphoner*, 1681

PSALMODY

The singing of one or more psalms is a central part of morning prayer. Psalm 63 is one of the premier morning psalms. Psalm 51 is commonly substituted for Psalm 63 on Wednesday and Friday, as well as during Lent. Other appropriate psalms for morning are Psalms 5, 8, 33, 42, 47, 66, 72, 80, 85, 93, 95, 98, 100, 118, 148, 149, and 150.

Sit

PSALM PRAYER

After each psalm a moment of silence is observed. This may be followed by a psalm prayer, to which all respond: **Amen.**

WORD OF GOD

A period of silence may follow the reading.

RESPONSE TO THE WORD OF GOD

A. ADVENT

5

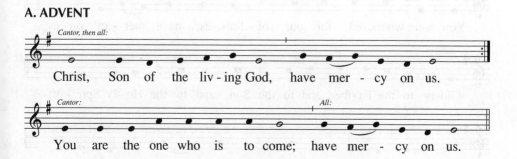

Cantor, then all:

Christ, Son of the liv - ing God, have mer - cy on us.

Cantor: *All:*

You are the one who is to come; have mer - cy on us.

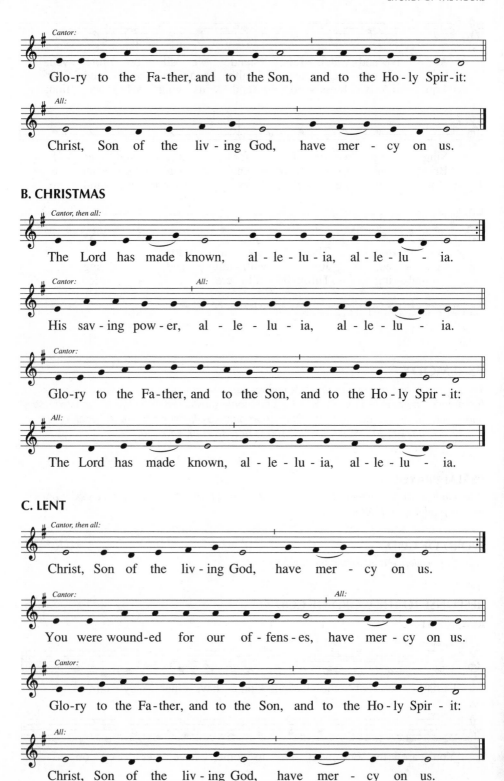

Cantor:
Glo-ry to the Fa-ther, and to the Son, and to the Ho-ly Spir-it:

All:
Christ, Son of the liv-ing God, have mer - cy on us.

B. CHRISTMAS

Cantor, then all:
The Lord has made known, al - le - lu - ia, al - le - lu - ia.

Cantor: *All:*
His sav - ing pow - er, al - le - lu - ia, al - le - lu - ia.

Cantor:
Glo-ry to the Fa-ther, and to the Son, and to the Ho - ly Spir - it:

All:
The Lord has made known, al - le - lu - ia, al - le - lu - ia.

C. LENT

Cantor, then all:
Christ, Son of the liv - ing God, have mer - cy on us.

Cantor: *All:*
You were wound-ed for our of - fens - es, have mer - cy on us.

Cantor:
Glo-ry to the Fa-ther, and to the Son, and to the Ho - ly Spir - it:

All:
Christ, Son of the liv - ing God, have mer - cy on us.

D. EASTER

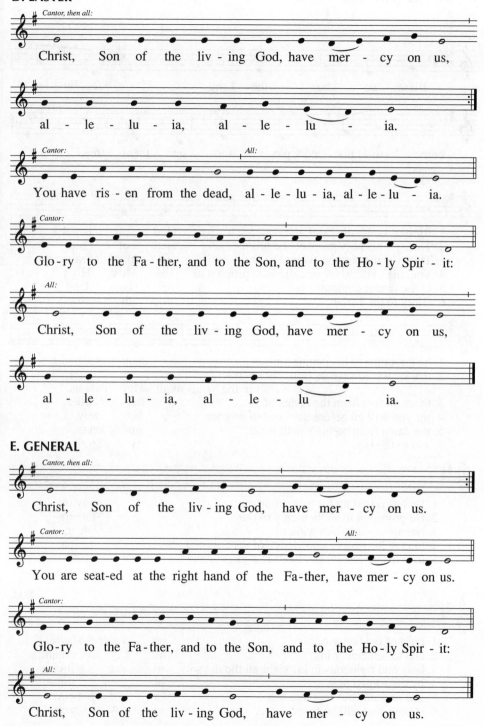

Cantor, then all:
Christ, Son of the liv - ing God, have mer - cy on us,
al - le - lu - ia, al - le - lu - ia.

Cantor: You have ris - en from the dead, *All:* al - le - lu - ia, al - le - lu - ia.

Cantor: Glo - ry to the Fa - ther, and to the Son, and to the Ho - ly Spir - it:

All: Christ, Son of the liv - ing God, have mer - cy on us,
al - le - lu - ia, al - le - lu - ia.

E. GENERAL

Cantor, then all:
Christ, Son of the liv - ing God, have mer - cy on us.

Cantor: You are seat-ed at the right hand of the Fa-ther, *All:* have mer - cy on us.

Cantor: Glo - ry to the Fa-ther, and to the Son, and to the Ho-ly Spir - it:

All: Christ, Son of the liv - ing God, have mer - cy on us.

Text: *Liturgy of the Hours,* © 1974, ICEL
Tune: Robert LeBlanc, © 1986, GIA Publications, Inc.

6 GOSPEL CANTICLE

Stand

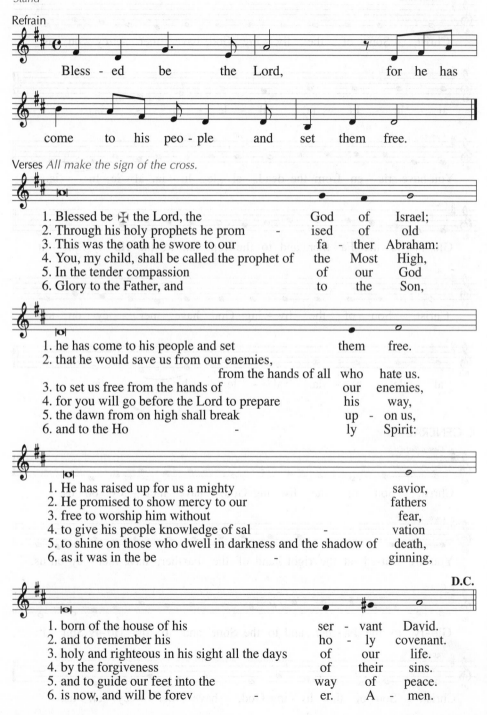

Refrain

Bless - ed be the Lord, for he has
come to his peo - ple and set them free.

Verses *All make the sign of the cross.*

1. Blessed be ✠ the Lord, the God of Israel;
2. Through his holy prophets he prom - ised of old
3. This was the oath he swore to our fa - ther Abraham:
4. You, my child, shall be called the prophet of the Most High,
5. In the tender compassion of our God
6. Glory to the Father, and to the Son,

1. he has come to his people and set them free.
2. that he would save us from our enemies,
   from the hands of all who hate us.
3. to set us free from the hands of our enemies,
4. for you will go before the Lord to prepare his way,
5. the dawn from on high shall break up - on us,
6. and to the Ho - ly Spirit:

1. He has raised up for us a mighty savior,
2. He promised to show mercy to our fathers
3. free to worship him without fear,
4. to give his people knowledge of sal - vation
5. to shine on those who dwell in darkness and the shadow of death,
6. as it was in the be - ginning,

D.C.

1. born of the house of his ser - vant David.
2. and to remember his ho - ly covenant.
3. holy and righteous in his sight all the days of our life.
4. by the forgiveness of their sins.
5. and to guide our feet into the way of peace.
6. is now, and will be forev - er. A - men.

Text: Luke 1:68–79; *International Consultation on English Texts*
Music: Refrain, Ronald F. Krisman, © 2011, GIA Publications, Inc.; verses, Michel Guimont, © 1994, 1998, GIA Publications, Inc.

INTERCESSIONS 7

The following intercessions or similar ones may be used.

Cantor or presiding minister:

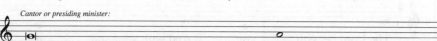

1. Show us your mercy, O   Lord;
2. Clothe your ministers with   righteousness;
3. Give peace, O Lord, in all the   world;
4. Lord, keep this nation under your   care;
5. Let your way be known upon   earth;
6. Let not the needy, O Lord, be for - gotten;
7. Create in us clean hearts, O   God;

All:

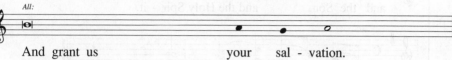

And grant us   your   sal - vation.
Let your people   sing   for   joy.
For only in you can we   live   in   safety.
And guide us in the way of jus - tice   and   truth.
Your saving health a   -   mong   all   nations.
Nor the hope of the poor be tak - en   a -   way.
And sustain us with your   Ho   -   ly   Spirit.

Text: *The Book of Common Prayer*
Music: *Praise God in Song,* © 1979, GIA Publications, Inc.

THE LORD'S PRAYER 8

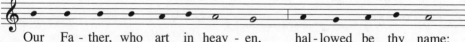

Our Fa - ther, who art in heav - en,   hal - lowed be thy name;

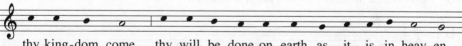

thy king-dom come,   thy will be done on earth as it is in heav-en.

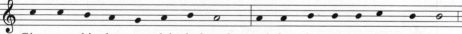

Give us this day our dai - ly bread,   and for-give us our tres-pass-es,

as we for-give those who tres - pass a - gainst us;   and lead us not

in - to temp - ta - tion,   but de - liv - er us from e - vil.

Music: Traditional chant, adapt. by Robert Snow, 1964; acc. by Robert J. Batastini, © 1975, 1993, GIA Publications, Inc.

CONCLUDING PRAYER
All respond: **Amen.**

9 DISMISSAL

Priest or deacon:
The Lord be with you.

Assembly:
And with your spir - it.

Priest or deacon:
May almight - y God bless you, the Fa - ther,

and the Son, and the Holy Spir - it.

All:
A - men! A - men!

Priest or deacon:
Go in peace.

Assembly:
Thanks be to God.

Text: ICEL, © 2010
Music: Amen, Michael Joncas, © 1979, GIA Publications, Inc.

10 *Dismissal, if the leader is not a priest or deacon:*

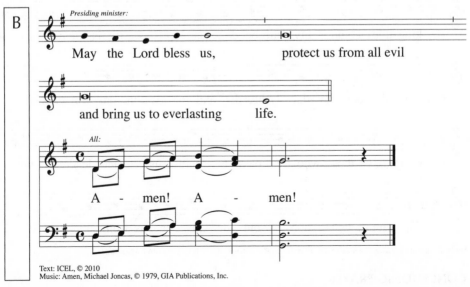

Presiding minister:
May the Lord bless us, protect us from all evil

and bring us to everlasting life.

All:
A - men! A - men!

Text: ICEL, © 2010
Music: Amen, Michael Joncas, © 1979, GIA Publications, Inc.

All may conclude the celebration by exchanging a sign of peace.

Evening Prayer / Vespers   11

The Church gathers in the evening to give thanks for the day that is ending. In the earliest tradition, this began with the lighting of the lamps as darkness fell and with the hymn of praise of Christ who is "radiant Light . . . of God the Father's deathless face." The evening psalms and the Magnificat bring the day just past to focus for the Christian: "God has cast down the mighty from their thrones, and has lifted up the lowly"; "God has remembered the promise of mercy, the promise made to our ancestors." Prayers of intercession are almost always part of the Church's liturgy, but those which conclude evening prayer are especially important. As day ends, the Church again and again lifts up to God the needs and sorrows and failures of all the world. Such intercession is the daily task and joy of the baptized.

Stand. All make the sign of the cross.

A

Presiding minister: *Assembly:*

O God, ✠ come to my as-sis-tance. Lord, make haste to help me.

All:

Glory to the Father, and to the Son, and to the Ho - ly Spir - it:

as it was in the beginning, is now, and will be for ev - er. A-men.

Added outside Lent:

Al - le - lu - ia.

Text: ICEL, © 1974

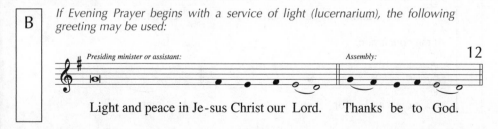

B

If Evening Prayer begins with a service of light (lucernarium), the following greeting may be used:

Presiding minister or assistant: *Assembly:*   12

Light and peace in Je-sus Christ our Lord. Thanks be to God.

13 HYMN

This or another evening hymn (see nos. 852 to 855), or one related to the season or feast, may be sung.

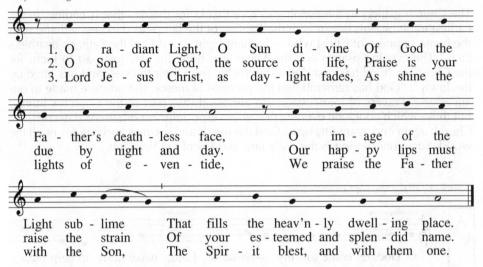

1. O   ra - diant Light, O   Sun   di - vine Of   God   the
2. O   Son   of   God,   the   source   of   life,   Praise is   your
3. Lord Je - sus   Christ, as   day - light   fades, As   shine   the

Fa - ther's   death - less   face,   O   im - age   of   the
due   by   night   and   day.   Our   hap - py   lips   must
lights   of   e - ven - tide,   We   praise   the   Fa - ther

Light   sub - lime   That   fills   the   heav'n - ly   dwell - ing   place.
raise   the   strain   Of   your   es - teemed and   splen - did   name.
with   the   Son,   The   Spir - it   blest, and   with   them   one.

Text: *Phos Hilaron*, Greek, c.200; tr. by William G. Storey, ©
Music: JESU DULCIS MEMORIA, LM; Mode I; acc. by Richard Proulx, © 1975, GIA Publications, Inc.

14   *If the lucernarium is celebrated, the evening thanksgiving may be sung:*

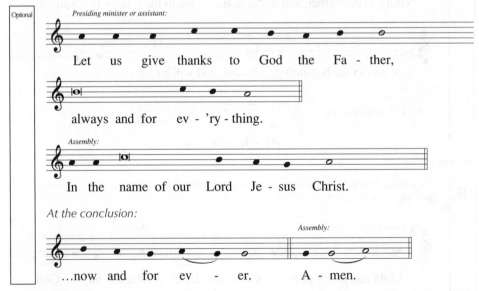

Optional

Presiding minister or assistant:

Let   us   give   thanks   to   God   the   Fa - ther,

always and for   ev - 'ry - thing.

Assembly:

In   the   name of our   Lord   Je - sus   Christ.

At the conclusion:

Assembly:

...now   and   for   ev - er.   A - men.

PSALMODY

The singing of one or more psalms is a central part of evening prayer. Psalm 141 is one of the premier evening psalms. It is customary to use incense as it is sung. Other appropriate psalms for evening are Psalms 4, 19, 23, 27, 84, 91, 104, 110, 111, 112, 114, 115, 117, 118, 121, 122, 130, 136, 139, and 145.

Sit

PSALM PRAYER

After each psalm a moment of silence is observed. This may be followed by a psalm prayer, to which all respond: **Amen.**

WORD OF GOD

A period of silence may follow the reading.

RESPONSE TO THE WORD OF GOD   15

A. ADVENT

Cantor, then all:

Lord, show us your mer-cy and love. Cantor: And grant us your sal - va - tion,

All: your mer - cy and love. Cantor: Glo-ry to the Fa-ther, and to the Son,

and to the Ho-ly Spir - it: All: Lord, show us your mer - cy and love.

B. CHRISTMAS

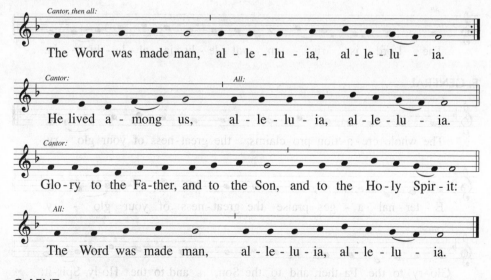

Cantor, then all:

The Word was made man, al - le - lu - ia, al - le - lu - ia.

Cantor: He lived a - mong us, All: al - le - lu - ia, al - le - lu - ia.

Cantor: Glo - ry to the Fa-ther, and to the Son, and to the Ho - ly Spir - it:

All: The Word was made man, al - le - lu - ia, al - le - lu - ia.

C. LENT

Cantor, then all:

Listen to us, O Lord, and have mer-cy, for we have sinned a-gainst you.

Cantor: ... *All:*

Christ Jesus, hear our hum-ble pe-ti - tions for we have sinned a-gainst you.

Cantor:

Glo-ry to the Fa-ther, and to the Son, and to the Ho-ly Spir-it:

All:

Listen to us, O Lord, and have mer-cy, for we have sinned a-gainst you.

D. EASTER

Cantor, then all:

The Lord is ris - en, al - le - lu - ia, al - le - lu - ia.

Cantor: ... *All:*

He has ap - peared to Si - mon, al - le - lu - ia, al - le - lu - ia.

Cantor:

Glo-ry to the Fa-ther, and to the Son, and to the Ho-ly Spir-it:

All:

The Lord is ris - en, al - le - lu - ia, al - le - lu - ia.

E. GENERAL

Cantor, then all:

The whole cre-a-tion pro-claims the great-ness of your glo-ry.

Cantor: ... *All:*

E-ter-nal a-ges praise the great-ness of your glo-ry.

Cantor:

Glo-ry to the Fa-ther, and to the Son, and to the Ho-ly Spir-it:

All:

The whole cre-a-tion pro-claims the great-ness of your glo-ry.

Text: *Liturgy of the Hours,* © 1974, ICEL
Music: Robert LeBlanc, © 1986, GIA Publications, Inc.

GOSPEL CANTICLE

16

Stand

Refrain

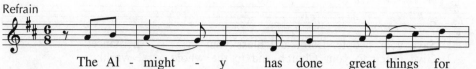

The Al - might - y has done great things for

me, and ho - ly is his Name.

Verses *All make the sign of the cross.*

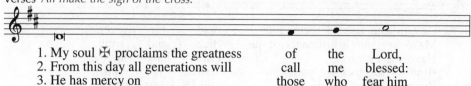

1. My soul ✠ proclaims the greatness of the Lord,
2. From this day all generations will call me blessed:
3. He has mercy on those who fear him
4. He has cast down the mighty from their thrones,
5. He has come to the help of his ser - vant Israel
6. Glory to the Father, and to the Son,

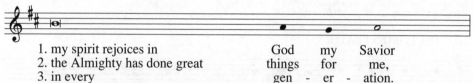

1. my spirit rejoices in God my Savior
2. the Almighty has done great things for me,
3. in every gen - er - ation.
4. and has lifted up the lowly.
5. for he has remembered his prom - ise of mercy,
6. and to the Ho - ly Spirit:

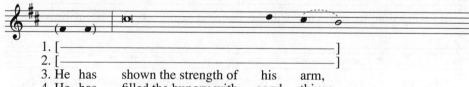

1. [————————————————]
2. [————————————————]
3. He has shown the strength of his arm,
4. He has filled the hungry with good things,
5. the promise he made to our fa - thers,
6. as it was in the beginning, is now,

D.C.

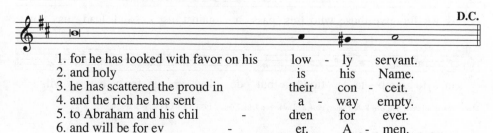

1. for he has looked with favor on his low - ly servant.
2. and holy is his Name.
3. he has scattered the proud in their con - ceit.
4. and the rich he has sent a - way empty.
5. to Abraham and his chil - dren for ever.
6. and will be for ev - er. A - men.

Text: Luke 1:46–55; *International Consultation on English Texts*
Music: Refrain, Ronald F. Krisman, © 2011, GIA Publications, Inc.; verses, Michel Guimont, © 1994, 1998, GIA Publications, Inc.

17 INTERCESSIONS

The following intercessions or similar ones may be used.

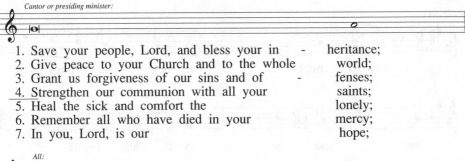

Cantor or presiding minister:

1. Save your people, Lord, and bless your in - heritance;
2. Give peace to your Church and to the whole world;
3. Grant us forgiveness of our sins and of - fenses;
4. Strengthen our communion with all your saints;
5. Heal the sick and comfort the lonely;
6. Remember all who have died in your mercy;
7. In you, Lord, is our hope;

All:

Govern and uphold them, now and for - ever.
Make us your instruments of jus - tice and truth.
Have mercy on us, Lord, have mercy.
Bind us together by your Ho - ly Spirit.
Relieve the sufferings of all your people.
Welcome them into the light of your kingdom.
And we shall never hope in vain.

Text: Adapted from *The Book of Common Prayer*
Music: *Praise God in Song*, © 1979, GIA Publications, Inc.

18 THE LORD'S PRAYER

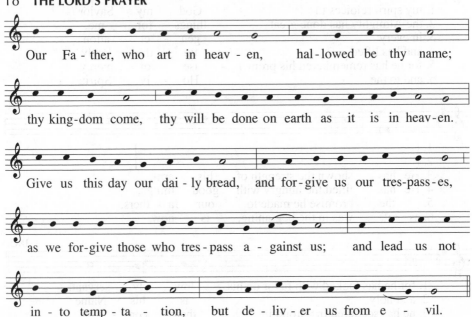

Our Fa - ther, who art in heav - en, hal - lowed be thy name;

thy king-dom come, thy will be done on earth as it is in heav-en.

Give us this day our dai - ly bread, and for-give us our tres-pass-es,

as we for-give those who tres-pass a - gainst us; and lead us not

in - to temp - ta - tion, but de - liv - er us from e - vil.

Music: Traditional chant, adapt. by Robert Snow, 1964; acc. by Robert J. Batastini, © 1975, 1993, GIA Publications, Inc.

CONCLUDING PRAYER

All respond: **Amen.**

DISMISSAL

Priest or deacon: The Lord be with you. *Assembly:* And with your spir - it.

Priest or deacon: May almight - y God bless you, the Fa - ther,

and the Son, and the Holy Spir - it.

All: A - men! A - men!

Priest or deacon: Go in peace. *Assembly:* Thanks be to God.

Text: ICEL, © 2010
Music: Amen, Michael Joncas, © 1979, GIA Publications, Inc.

Dismissal, if the leader is not a priest or deacon:

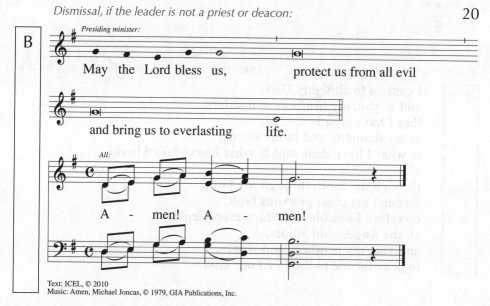

Presiding minister: May the Lord bless us, protect us from all evil

and bring us to everlasting life.

All: A - men! A - men!

Text: ICEL, © 2010
Music: Amen, Michael Joncas, © 1979, GIA Publications, Inc.

All may conclude the celebration by exchanging a sign of peace.

21 Night Prayer / Compline

The Church's prayers at night are direct and simple. The Christian remembers with sorrow the day's evil and failure, and places this before the mercy of God. Before surrendering to sleep, there is prayer for God's protection through the night and an expression of acceptance: "Now, Lord, you may dismiss your servant." The night prayer concludes by binding together the sleep of this night with the final falling asleep in the Lord: "May the all-powerful Lord grant us a restful night and a peaceful death." Night's last words are often a gentle invocation of our mother, "When this exile is ended, show us your womb's blessed fruit, Jesus."

Stand. All make the sign of the cross.

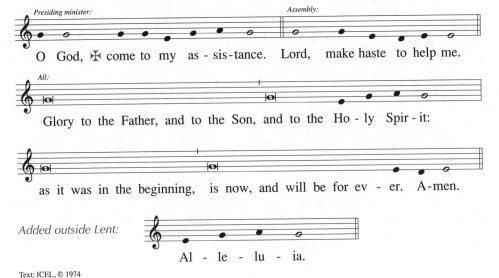

Presiding minister:

O God, ✠ come to my as - sis - tance.

Assembly:

Lord, make haste to help me.

All:

Glory to the Father, and to the Son, and to the Ho - ly Spir - it:

as it was in the beginning, is now, and will be for ev - er. A-men.

Added outside Lent:

Al - le - lu - ia.

Text: ICEL, © 1974

A brief examination of conscience may be made. At its conclusion, the following may be said:

Optional

**I confess to almighty God
and to you, my brothers and sisters,
that I have greatly sinned,
in my thoughts and in my words,
in what I have done and in what I have failed to do,**
All strike their breast as they say:
**through my fault, through my fault,
through my most grievous fault;
therefore I ask blessed Mary ever-Virgin,
all the Angels and Saints,
and you, my brothers and sisters,
to pray for me to the Lord our God.**

HYMN

22

This or another evening hymn (see nos. 852 to 855), or one related to the season or feast, may be sung.

1. Be - fore the end - ing of the day, Cre - a - tor
2. Let ev - 'ry heart rest free from fear, At peace, to
3. Let peace - ful rest the strength re - new Of all who
4. Al - might - y Fa - ther, hear our cry Through Je - sus

of the world, we pray: Pro - tect us by your
feel your pres - ence near; Our souls, through night hours
place their trust in you; Let e - vil nev - er
Christ, our Lord most high, And with the Spir - it,

love and might, And keep us safe through - out the night.
veiled in sleep, In your blest light, their vig - il keep.
have its way; Pre - serve us for an - oth - er day.
Par - a - clete, Whose reign the end - less a - ges greet.

Text: *Te lucis ante terminum*, 7th C.; tr. by Peter Scagnelli, ©
Music: TE LUCIS ANTE TERMINUM, LM; adapt. by Howard Hughes, SM, © 1982, GIA Publications, Inc.

PSALMODY

The proper psalms for Night Prayer are: Sunday, Psalm 91; Monday, Psalm 86; Tuesday, Psalm 143; Wednesday, Psalms 31 and 130; Thursday, Psalm 16; Friday, Psalm 88; and Saturday, Psalms 4 and 134.

Sit

After the psalm a moment of silence is observed.

WORD OF GOD

A period of silence may follow the reading.

RESPONSORY

23

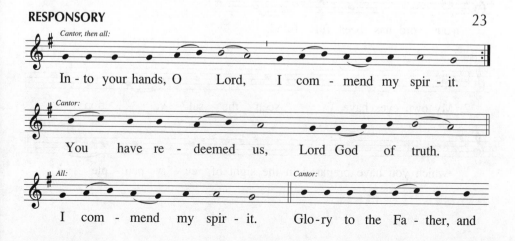

Cantor, then all:

In - to your hands, O Lord, I com - mend my spir - it.

Cantor:

You have re - deemed us, Lord God of truth.

All:

I com - mend my spir - it.

Cantor:

Glo - ry to the Fa - ther, and

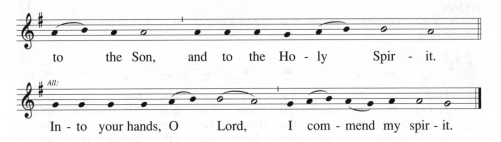

to the Son, and to the Ho - ly Spir - it.

All:
In - to your hands, O Lord, I com - mend my spir - it.

Text: *Liturgy of the Hours,* © 1974, ICEL
Music: Sarum tone, adapt. by Richard Proulx, © 1986, GIA Publications, Inc.

24 GOSPEL CANTICLE

Stand

Antiphon

Pro - tect us, Lord, as we stay a - wake; watch o - ver us

as we sleep, that a - wake we may keep watch with Christ,

and, a - sleep, rest in his peace.

Verse 1 *All make the sign of the cross.*

1. Lord, ✠ now you let your ser - vant go in peace:

D.C.

your word has been ful - filled.

Verse 2

2. My own eyes have seen the sal - va - tion

D.C.

which you have prepared in the sight of ev - 'ry peo - ple.

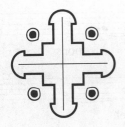

Psalms and Canticles

Verse 3

3. A light to re - veal you to the na - tions

D.C.

and the glory of your peo - ple Is - ra - el.

Verse 4

4. Glory to the Fa - ther, and to the Son and to the

Ho - ly Spir - it: as it was in the be - gin - ning,

D.C.

is now, and will be for ev - er. A - men.

Text: Antiphon from *Liturgy of the Hours*, © 1974, ICEL; verses, Luke 2:29–32; *International Consultation on English Texts*
Music: Sarum tone, adapt. by Richard Proulx, © 1986, GIA Publications, Inc.

CONCLUDING PRAYER
All respond: **Amen.**

CONCLUSION

25

Presiding minister:

May the all-powerful Lord grant us a restful night and a peaceful death.

All:

A - men! A - men!

Text: ICEL, © 1974
Music: Amen, Michael Joncas, © 1979, GIA Publications, Inc.

The Marian antiphon, "Salve Regina," no. 882, or during Easter season, "Regina Caeli," no. 519, may follow.

27 Psalm 6

Antiphon I

Re - turn, O Lord, and res - cue my soul.

Text: Psalm 6:5, The Grail, © 1963, The Grail, GIA Publications, Inc., agent
Music: Richard Proulx, © 1986, GIA Publications, Inc.

Antiphon II

Have mer - cy on me, Lord; my strength is gone.

Text: *Lectionary for Mass*, © 1969, 1981, 1997, ICEL
Music: Robert J. Batastini, © 1975, GIA Publications, Inc.

Conception Abbey Tone

Music: Gregory J. Polan, OSB, © 2010, Conception Abbey, admin. by GIA Publications, Inc.

Gelineau Tone

Music: Joseph Gelineau, SJ, © 1963, The Grail, GIA Publications, Inc., agent

Domine ne in furore tuo

1. ² O LORD, do not rebúke me in your
   ánger;
   repróve me nót in your ráge.
   ³ Have mércy on me, LORD, for I
   lánguish.
   LORD, héal me; my bónes are sháking,
   ⁴ and my sóul is gréatly sháken.

2. But yóu, O LORD, how lóng?
   ⁵ Retúrn, LORD, réscue my sóul.
   Sáve me in your mérciful lóve.
   ⁶ For in déath there is no remémbrance
   of yóu;
   from the gráve, whó can give you
   práise?

3. ⁷ Í am exháusted with my gróaning;
   every níght I drench my béd with téars,
   I bedéw my cóuch with wéeping.
   ⁸ My éyes waste awáy with gríef;
   I have grown óld surrounded bý all my
   fóes.

4. ⁹ Léave me, áll who do évil,
   for the LORD heeds the sóund of my
   wéeping.
   ¹⁰ The LORD has héard my pléa;
   the LORD will recéive my práyer.
   ¹¹ All my fóes will be shámed and
   greatly sháken,
   súddenly pút to sháme.

5. Give práise to the Fáther Almíghty,
   to his Són, Jesus Chríst the Lórd,
   to the Spírit who dwélls in our héarts,
   both nów and for éver. Amén.

Text: Psalm 6; *The Revised Grail Psalms*; © 2010, Conception Abbey and The Grail, admin. by GIA Publications, Inc., agent

Psalm 4   26

Antiphon

Have mer - cy, Lord, and hear my prayer.

Text: *Liturgy of the Hours,* © 1974, ICEL
Music: Eugene Englert, © 1986, GIA Publications, Inc.

Conception Abbey Tone

Music: Gregory J. Polan, OSB, © 2010, Conception Abbey, admin. by GIA Publications, Inc.

Gelineau Tone

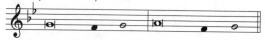

Music: Joseph Gelineau, SJ, © 1963, The Grail, GIA Publications, Inc., agent

Cum invocarem

1. ² I cálled, the God of jústice gáve me ánswer;
   from ánguish you reléased me, have mércy and héar me!

2. ³ Children of mán, how lóng will my glóry be dishónored,
   will you lóve what is fútile and séek what is fálse?

3. ⁴ Knów that the LÓRD works wónders for his fáithful one;
   the LÓRD will héar me whenéver I cáll him.

4. ⁵ Tremble, do not sín: pónder on your béd and be stíll.
   ⁶ Óffer right sácrifice, and trúst in the LÓRD.

5. ⁷ "Whát can bring us háppiness?" mány sáy.
   Líft up the líght of your fáce on us, O LÓRD.

6. ⁸ You have pút into my héart a gréater jóy
   than abúndance of gráin and new wíne can províde.

7. ⁹ In péace I will lie dówn and fáll asléep,
   for yóu alone, O LÓRD, make me dwéll in sáfety.

8. Give práise to the Fáther, the Són and Holy Spírit,
   both nów and for áges unénding. Amén.

Text: Psalm 4; *The Revised Grail Psalms*; © 2010, Conception Abbey and The Grail, admin. by GIA Publications, Inc., agent

Psalm 8 28

Antiphon I

How great is your name, O Lord our God, through all the earth!

Text: The Grail
Music: A. Gregory Murray, OSB
© 1963, The Grail, GIA Publications, Inc., agent

Antiphon II

From the voic-es of chil - dren, Lord, comes the sound of your praise.

Text: The Grail
Music: A. Gregory Murray, OSB
© 1963, The Grail, GIA Publications, Inc., agent

Conception Abbey Tone

Music: Gregory J. Polan, OSB, © 2010, Conception Abbey, admin. by GIA Publications, Inc.

Gelineau Tone

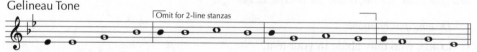

Music: Joseph Gelineau, SJ, © 1963, The Grail, GIA Publications, Inc., agent

Domine, Dominus noster

1. *²O LORD, our Lórd, how majéstic
   is your náme through áll the éarth!

2. Your májesty is sét above the héavens.
   ³From the móuths of children and of bábes
   you fáshioned praise to fóil your énemy,
   to sílence the fóe and the rébel.

3. ⁴When I see the héavens, the wórk of your fíngers,
   the móon and the stárs which you arránged,
   ⁵what is mán that you should kéep him in mínd,
   the son of mán that you cáre for hím?

4. ⁶Yet you have máde him little lówer than the ángels;
   with glóry and hónor you crówned him,
   ⁷gave him pówer over the wórks of your hánds:
   you put áll things únder his féet,

5. ⁸Áll of them, shéep and óxen,
   yes, éven the cáttle of the fíelds,
   ⁹birds of the áir, and físh of the séa
   that máke their wáy through the wáters.

6. *¹⁰O LORD, our Lórd, how majéstic
   is your náme through áll the éarth!

7. Give glóry to the Fáther Almíghty,
   to his Són, Jesus Chríst the Lórd,
   to the Spírit who dwélls in our héarts,
   both nów and for éver. Amén.

Omitted when Antiphon I is used.

Text: Psalm 8; *The Revised Grail Psalms*; © 2010, Conception Abbey and The Grail, admin. by GIA Publications, Inc., agent

Psalm 16: You Will Show Me the Path of Life   30

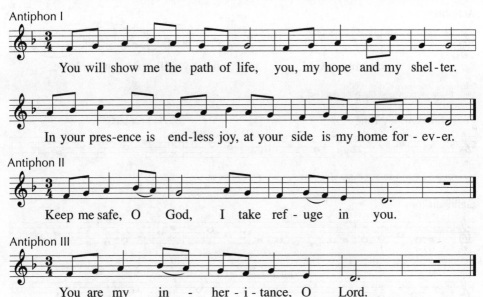

Antiphon I

You will show me the path of life,   you, my hope and my shel-ter.

In your pres-ence is   end-less joy, at your side is my home for - ev-er.

Antiphon II

Keep me safe, O   God,   I take ref - uge   in   you.

Antiphon III

You are my   in - her - i - tance, O   Lord.

Verses

1. Faithful God, I look to you, you alone my life and fortune,
   never shall I look to other gods, you shall be my one hope.

2. From of old you are my heritage, you my wisdom and my safety,
   through the night you speak within my heart, silently you teach me.

3. So my heart shall sing for joy, in your arms I rest securely,
   you will not abandon me to death, you shall not desert me.

Text: Psalm 16:1–2, 6–8, 9–10; Marty Haugen, © 1988, GIA Publications, Inc.; antiphon III, *Lectionary for Mass*, © 1969, 1981, 1997, ICEL
Music: Marty Haugen; antiphons II and III adapt. by Diana Kodner, © 1988, 1994, GIA Publications, Inc.

31 Psalm 16

Antiphon

In you, my God,   my bod-y will rest in   hope.

Text: *Liturgy of the Hours,* © 1974, ICEL
Music: Eugene Englert, © 1986, GIA Publications, Inc.

Conception Abbey Tone

Music: Gregory J. Polan, OSB, © 2010, Conception Abbey, admin. by GIA Publications, Inc.

Gelineau Tone

Music: Joseph Gelineau, SJ, © 1963, The Grail, GIA Publications, Inc., agent

Conserva me Domine

1. Presérve me, O Gód, for in yóu I take
   réfuge.
   [2] I sáy to the LORD, "Yóu are my Lórd.
   My háppiness líes in yóu alóne."

2. [3] Ás for the hóly ones who dwéll in the
   lánd,
   they are nóble, and in thém is áll my
   delíght.
   [4] Those who chóose other góds incréase
   their sórrows.
   I will nót take párt in their ófferings of
   blóod.
   Nór will I táke their námes upon my
   líps.

3. [5] O LORD, it is yóu who are my pórtion
   and cúp;
   yóu yoursélf who secúre my lót.
   [6] Pléasant pláces are márked out for mé:
   a pléasing héritage indéed is míne!

4. [7] I will bléss the LORD who gíves me
   cóunsel,
   who éven at níght dirécts my héart.
   [8] I kéep the LORD befóre me álways;
   with hím at my ríght hand, Í shall not
   be móved.

5. [9] And so, my héart rejóices, my sóul is
   glád;
   éven my flésh shall rést in hópe.
   [10] For yóu will not abándon my sóul
   to héll,
   nor lét your hóly one sée corrúption.

6. [11] You will shów me the páth of lífe,
   the fúllness of jóy in your présence,
   at your ríght hand, blíss foréver.

7. Give práise to the Fáther Almíghty,
   to his Són, Jesus Chríst the Lórd,
   to the Spírit who dwélls in our héarts,
   both nów and for éver. Amén.

Text: Psalm 16; *The Revised Grail Psalms*; © 2010, Conception Abbey and The Grail, admin. by GIA Publications, Inc., agent

Psalm 19: Lord, You Have the Words   32

Antiphon

Lord, you have the words of ev-er-last-ing life.

Verses

1. The law of the Lord is perfect, refreshing the soul;
   the Lord's rule is to be trusted, the simple find wisdom.

2. The fear of the Lord is holy, abiding for ever;
   the decrees of the Lord are true, all of them just.

3. The precepts of the Lord are right, they gladden the heart,
   the command of the Lord is clear, giving light to the eye.

4. They are worth more than gold, than the finest gold,
   sweeter than honey, than honey from the comb.

Text: Psalm 19:8, 9, 10, 11; David Haas, © 1983, GIA Publications, Inc.; antiphon, *Lectionary for Mass*, © 1969, 1981, 1997, ICEL
Music: David Haas, © 1983, GIA Publications, Inc.

33 Psalm 19

Antiphon I

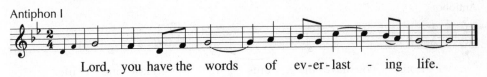

Lord, you have the words of ev-er-last - ing life.

Text: *Lectionary for Mass*, © 1969, 1981, 1997, ICEL
Music: Richard Proulx, © 1975, GIA Publications, Inc.

Antiphon II

The pre-cepts of the Lord give joy to the heart.

Text: *Lectionary for Mass*, © 1969, 1981, 1997, ICEL
Music: Randolph Currie, © 1986, GIA Publications, Inc.

Antiphon III

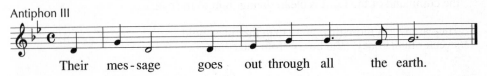

Their mes-sage goes out through all the earth.

Text: *Lectionary for Mass*, © 1969, 1981, 1997, ICEL
Music: James J. Chepponis, © 1986, GIA Publications, Inc.

Antiphon IV

Let the clouds rain down the just one; and the earth bring forth a Sav-ior.

Text: *Simple Gradual*, © 1968, ICEL
Music: Alan Rees, OSB, alt., © 1969, Geoffrey Chapman Ltd.

Conception Abbey Tone

Omit for 3-line stanzas

Music: Gregory J. Polan, OSB, © 2010, Conception Abbey, admin. by GIA Publications, Inc.

Gelineau Tone

Sts. 1–4   Omit for 3-line stanzas

Sts. 5–12

Music: Joseph Gelineau, SJ, © 1963, The Grail, GIA Publications, Inc., agent

Caeli enarrant gloriam Dei

1. ² The héavens decláre the glóry of Gód,
   and the fírmament procláims the wórk of his hánds.
   ³ Dáy unto dáy convéys the méssage,
   and níght unto níght impárts the knówledge.

29 Psalm 15

Antiphon

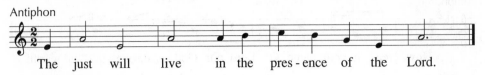

The just will live in the pres - ence of the Lord.

Text: *Lectionary for Mass*, © 1969, 1981, 1997, ICEL
Music: Robert J. Batastini, © 1995, GIA Publications, Inc.

Conception Abbey Tone

Omit for 4-line stanzas

Music: Gregory J. Polan, OSB, © 2010, Conception Abbey, admin. by GIA Publications, Inc.

Gelineau Tone

Omit for 4-line stanzas

Music: Joseph Gelineau, SJ, © 1963, The Grail, GIA Publications, Inc., agent

Domine quis habitabit

1. LORD, whó may abíde in your tént,
   and dwéll on your hóly móuntain?
   ²Whoéver wálks without fáult;
   who dóes whát is júst,
   and spéaks the trúth from his héart.

2. ³Whoéver does not slánder with his tóngue,
   who dóes no wróng to a néighbor,
   who cásts no slúr on a fríend,
   ⁴who lóoks with scórn on the wícked,
   but hónors those who féar the LÓRD.

3. Who keeps an óath, whatéver the cóst,
   ⁵who lénds no móney at ínterest,
   and accépts no bríbes against the ínnocent.
   Súch a one shall néver be sháken.

4. Give práise to the Fáther Almíghty,
   to his Són, Jesus Chríst the Lórd,
   to the Spírit who dwélls in our héarts,
   both nów and for éver. Amén.

Text: Psalm 15; *The Revised Grail Psalms*; © 2010, Conception Abbey and The Grail, admin. by GIA Publications, Inc., agent

2. ⁴No spéech, no wórd, whose vóice goes unhéeded;
    ⁵their sóund goes fórth through áll the éarth,
    their méssage to the útmost bóunds of the wórld.

3. ⁶Thére he has pláced a tént for the sún;
    it comes fórth like a brídegroom cóming from his tént,
    rejóices like a chámpion to rún his cóurse.

4. ⁷At one énd of the héavens is the rísing of the sún;
    to its fúrthest énd it rúns its cóurse.
    There is nóthing concéaled from its búrning héat.

5. ⁸The láw of the LÓRD is pérfect;
    it revíves the sóul.
    The decrées of the LÓRD are stéadfast;
    they give wísdom to the símple.

6. ⁹The précepts of the LÓRD are ríght;
    they gládden the héart.
    The commánd of the LÓRD is cléar;
    it gives líght to the éyes.

7. ¹⁰The féar of the LÓRD is púre,
    abíding foréver.
    The júdgments of the LÓRD are trúe;
    they are, áll of them, júst.

8. ¹¹They are móre to be desíred than góld,
    than quántities of góld.
    And swéeter are théy than hóney,
    than honey flówing from the cómb.

9. ¹²So in thém your sérvant finds instrúction;
    great rewárd is in their kéeping.
    ¹³But whó can detéct their own érrors?
    From hídden faults acquít me.

10. ¹⁴From presúmption restráin your sérvant;
    máy it not rúle me.
    Thén shall Í be blámeless,
    cléan from grave sín.

11. ¹⁵May the spóken wórds of my móuth,
    the thóughts of my héart,
    win fávor in your síght, O LÓRD,
    my róck and my redéemer!

12. Praise the Fáther, the Són and Holy Spírit,
    both nów and for éver,
    the God who ís, who wás, and who wíll be,
    wórld without énd.

Text: Psalm 19; *The Revised Grail Psalms*; © 2010, Conception Abbey and The Grail, admin. by GIA Publications, Inc., agent

34   Psalm 22

Antiphon I

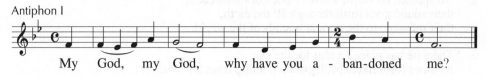

My God, my God, why have you a - ban-doned me?

Text: *Lectionary for Mass*, © 1969, 1981, 1997, ICEL
Music: Frank Schoen, © 1975, GIA Publications, Inc.

Antiphon II

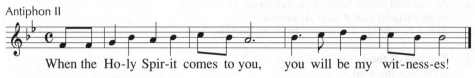

When the Ho-ly Spir-it comes to you, you will be my wit-ness-es!

Text: *Lectionary for Mass*, © 1969, 1981, 1997, ICEL
Music: Marty Haugen, © 1986, GIA Publications, Inc.

Conception Abbey Tone

Music: Gregory J. Polan, OSB, © 2010, Conception Abbey, admin. by GIA Publications, Inc.

Gelineau Tone

Music: Joseph Gelineau, SJ, © 1963, The Grail, GIA Publications, Inc., agent

Deus, Deus meus respice

1. ²My Gód, my Gód, whý have you forsáken me?
   Whý are you fár from sáving me,
   só fár from my wórds of ánguish?
   ³O my Gód, I call by dáy and you dó not ánswer;
   I cáll by níght and I fínd no repriéve.

2. ⁴Yet yóu, O Gód, are hóly,
   enthróned on the práises of Ísrael.
   ⁵In you our fórebears pút their trúst;
   they trústed and you sét them frée.
   ⁶When they críed to yóu, they escáped;
   in you they trústed and were nót put to sháme.

3. ⁷But Í am a wórm and no mán,
   scorned by éveryone, despísed by the péople.
   ⁸Áll who sée me deríde me;
   they curl their líps, they tóss their héads:
   ⁹"He trústed in the LÓRD, let him sáve him;
   let him reléase him, for in hím he delíghts."

4. [10] Yes, it was yóu who tóok me from the wómb,
    entrústed me to my móther's bréast.
    [11] To yóu I was commítted from bírth;
    from my móther's womb, yóu have been my Gód.
    [12] Stáy not fár from mé;
    trouble is néar, and there is nó one to hélp.

5. [13] Mány búlls have surróunded me,
    fierce búlls of Báshan close me ín.
    [14] Agáinst me they ópen wide their móuths,
    like a líon, rénding and róaring.

6. [15] Like wáter Í am poured óut,
    disjóinted are áll my bónes.
    My héart has becóme like wáx,
    it is mélted withín my bréast.

7. [16] Párched as burnt cláy is my thróat,
    my tóngue cléaves to my jáws.
    You láy me in the dúst of déath.
    [17] For dógs háve surróunded me;
    a bánd of the wícked beséts me.
    They tear hóles in my hánds and my féet;

8. [18] I can cóunt every óne of my bónes.
    They stáre at mé and glóat.
    [19] They divíde my clóthing amóng them,
    they cást lóts for my róbe.

9. [20] But you, O LÓRD, do not stáy afar óff;
    my stréngth, make háste to hélp me!
    [23] Réscue my sóul from the swórd,
    my lífe from the gríp of the dóg.
    [22] Save my lífe from the jáws of the líon,
    my poor sóul from the hórns of wild búlls.

10. [23] I will téll of your náme to my kín,
    and práise you in the mídst of the assémbly;
    [24] "Yóu who fear the LÓRD, give him práise;
    all descéndants of Jácob, give him glóry;
    revére him, all you descéndants of Ísrael.

11. [25] For hé has néver despísed
    nor scórned the póverty of the póor.
    From hím he has not hídden his fáce,
    but he héard him whenéver he críed."

12. [26] Yóu are my práise in the gréat assémbly.
    My vóws I will páy before thóse who féar him.
    [27] The póor shall éat and shall háve their fíll.
    They shall práise the LÓRD, thóse who séek him.
    May their héarts live ón foréver and éver!

13. [28] All the éarth shall remémber and retúrn to the LORD,
 all fámilies of the nátions wórship befóre him,
 [29] for the kíngdom is the LORD's, he is rúler of the nátions.
 [30] They shall wórship him, áll the míghty of the éarth;
 befóre him shall bów all who go dówn to the dúst.

14. [31] And my sóul shall live for hím, my descéndants sérve him.
 They shall téll of the LORD to generátions yet to cóme,
 [32] decláre his saving jústice to péoples yet unbórn:
 "Thése are the thíngs the LORD has dóne."

15. Give práise to the Fáther, the Són and Holy Spírit,
 both nów and for áges unénding. Amén.

Text: Psalm 22; *The Revised Grail Psalms*; © 2010, Conception Abbey and The Grail, admin. by GIA Publications, Inc., agent

35 Psalm 22: My God, My God

Antiphon

My God, my God, O why have you a - ban - doned me?

Verses

1. All who see me laugh at me, they mock me and they shake their heads:
 "He relied on the Lord, let the Lord be his refuge."

2. As dogs around me, they circle me about.
 Wounded me and pierced me, I can number all my bones.

3. My clothing they divided, for my garments casting lots,
 O Lord, do not desert me, but hasten to my aid.

4. I will praise you to my people, and proclaim you in their midst,
 O fear the Lord, my people, give glory to God's name.

Text: Psalm 22:8–9, 17–18, 19–20, 23–24; Marty Haugen, © 1983, GIA Publications, Inc.; antiphon, *Lectionary for Mass*, © 1969, 1981, 1997, ICEL
Music: Marty Haugen, © 1983, GIA Publications, Inc.

Psalm 23: Shepherd Me, O God   36

Antiphon

Shep-herd me, O God, be - yond my wants, be -
yond my fears, from death in - to life.

Verses

1. God is my shepherd, so nothing shall I want;
   I rest in the meadows of faithfulness and love;
   I walk by the quiet waters of peace.

2. Gently you raise me and heal my weary soul;
   you lead me by pathways of righteousness and truth;
   my spirit shall sing the music of your name.

3. Though I should wander the valley of death,
   I fear no evil, for you are at my side;
   your rod and your staff, my comfort and my hope.

4. You have set me a banquet of love in the face of hatred,
   crowning me with love beyond my pow'r to hold.

5. Surely your kindness and mercy follow me all the days of my life;
   I will dwell in the house of my God forevermore.

Text: Psalm 23; Marty Haugen
Music: Marty Haugen
© 1986, GIA Publications, Inc.

37 Psalm 23

Antiphon I

My shep-herd is the Lord, noth-ing in-deed shall I want.

Text: Psalm 23; The Grail
Music: Joseph Gelineau, SJ
© 1963, The Grail, GIA Publications, Inc., agent

Antiphon II

His good-ness shall fol-low me al-ways to the end of my days.

Text: Psalm 23; The Grail
Music: A. Gregory Murray, OSB
© 1963, The Grail, GIA Publications, Inc., agent

Antiphon III

The Lord is my shep-herd, noth-ing shall I want: he

leads me by safe paths, noth-ing shall I fear.

Text: Psalm 23; The Grail
Music: A. Gregory Murray, OSB
© 1963, The Grail, GIA Publications, Inc., agent

Antiphon IV

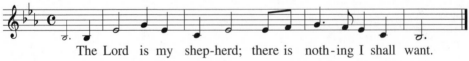

The Lord is my shep-herd; there is noth-ing I shall want.

Text: Psalm 23; The Grail, © 1963, The Grail, GIA Publications, Inc., agent
Music: Richard Proulx, © 1975, GIA Publications, Inc.

Antiphon V

Though I walk in the val-ley of dark - ness, I

fear no e - vil, for you are with me.

Text: *Lectionary for Mass*, © 1969, 1981, 1997, ICEL
Music: Robert J. Batastini, © 2011, GIA Publications, Inc.

Antiphon VI

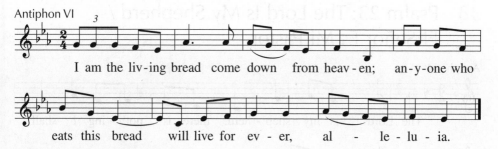

I am the liv-ing bread come down from heav-en; an-y-one who

eats this bread will live for ev - er, al - le - lu - ia.

Text: *Liturgy of the Hours,* © 1974, ICEL
Music: Ronald F. Krisman, © 2011, GIA Publications, Inc.

Conception Abbey Tone

Omit for 4-line stanzas

Music: Gregory J. Polan, OSB, © 2010, Conception Abbey, admin. by GIA Publications, Inc.

Gelineau Tone

Omit for 4-line stanzas

Music: Joseph Gelineau, SJ, © 1963, The Grail, GIA Publications, Inc., agent

Dominus pascit me

1. The LORD is my shépherd;
   there is nóthing I shall wánt.
   ² Frésh and gréen are the pástures
   where he gíves me repóse.
   Near réstful wáters he léads me;
   ³ hé revíves my sóul.

2. He guídes me alóng the right páth,
   for the sáke of his náme.
   ⁴ Thóugh I should wálk in the válley
   of the shádow of déath,
   no évil would I féar, for you are
   with me.
   Your cróok and your stáff will give
   me cómfort.

3. ⁵ You have prepáred a táble befóre me
   in the síght of my fóes.
   My héad you have anóinted with óil;
   my cúp is overflówing.

4. ⁶ Surely góodness and mércy shall
   fóllow me
   all the dáys of my lífe.
   In the LORD's own hóuse shall I dwéll
   for léngth of days unénding.

5. To the Fáther and Són give glóry,
   give glóry to the Spírit.
   To God who ís, who wás, and who wíll
   be,
   for éver and évér.

Text: Psalm 23; *The Revised Grail Psalms,* © 2010, Conception Abbey and The Grail, admin. by GIA Publications, Inc.

38 Psalm 23: The Lord Is My Shepherd / El Señor Es Mi Pastor

Antiphon I*

The Lord is my shep - herd; there is noth - ing I shall want. The Lord is my shep-herd; noth - ing shall I fear.

Antiphon II*

El Se-ñor es mi pas-tor, na - da me fal - ta.

El Se-ñor es mi pas-tor, na - da me fal - ta.

Verses

1. The LORD is my shepherd;
   there is nothing I shall want.
   Fresh and green are the pastures
   where he gives me repose.
   Near restful waters he leads me;
   he revives my soul.

2. He guides me along the right path,
   for the sake of his name.
   Though I should walk in the valley of the
      shadow of death,
   no evil would I fear, for you are with me.
   Your crook and your staff will give
      me comfort.

3. You have prepared a table before me
   in the sight of my foes.
   My head you have anointed with oil;
   my cup is overflowing.

4. Surely goodness and mercy shall
      follow me
   all the days of my life.
   In the LORD's own house shall I dwell
   for length of days unending.

1. El Señor es mi pastor, nada me falta:
   en verdes praderas me hace recostar;
   me conduce hacia fuentes tranquilas
   y repara mis fuerzas.

2. Me guía por el sendero justo,
   por el honor de su nombre.
   Aunque camine por cañadas oscuras,
   nada temo, porque tú vas conmigo:
   tu vara y tu cayado
   me sosiegan.

3. Preparas una mesa ante mí,
   enfrente de mis enemigos;
   me unges la cabeza con perfume,
   y mi copa rebosa.

4. Tu bondad y tu misericordia
      me acompañan
   todos los días de mi vida,
   y habitaré en la casa del Señor
   por años sin término.

Antiphons I and II may be sung simultaneously.

Text: Psalm 23; English antiphon, *Lectionary for Mass*, © 1969, 1981, 1997, ICEL; verses, *The Revised Grail Psalms*, © 2010, Conception Abbey and The Grail, admin. by GIA Publication, Inc.; Spanish text, *Leccionario, Edición Hispanoamérica*, © 1970, 1972, Conferencia Episcopal Española
Music: Antiphons, Ronald F. Krisman, © 2004, GIA Publications, Inc.; verses, Michel Guimont, © 1994, 1998, GIA Publications, Inc.

Psalm 25: To You, O Lord   39

Antiphon

To you, O Lord, I lift my soul, to you, I lift my soul.

Verses

1. Lord, make me know your ways, teach me your paths
   and keep me in the way of your truth, for you are God, my Savior.

2. For the Lord is good and righteous, revealing the way to those who wander,
   gently leading the poor and the humble.

3. To the ones who seek the Lord, who look to God's word, who live God's love,
   God will always be near, and will show them mercy.

Text: Psalm 25:4–5, 8–9, 12–14; Marty Haugen, © 1982, GIA Publications, Inc.; antiphon, *Lectionary for Mass*, © 1969, 1981, 1997, ICEL
Music: Marty Haugen, © 1982, GIA Publications, Inc.

40 Psalm 25

Antiphon I

To you, O Lord, I lift my soul.

Text: *Lectionary for Mass*, © 1969, 1981, 1997, ICEL
Music: Robert J. Thompson, © 1975, GIA Publications, Inc.

Antiphon II

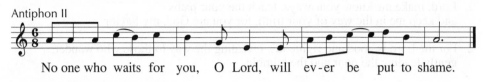

No one who waits for you, O Lord, will ev-er be put to shame.

Text: *Lectionary for Mass*, © 1969, 1981, 1997, ICEL
Music: Ronald F. Krisman, © 2004, GIA Publications, Inc.

Antiphon III

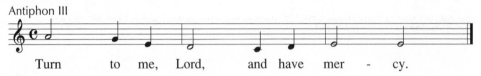

Turn to me, Lord, and have mer - cy.

Text: *Rite of Penance*, © 1975, ICEL
Music: Ronald F. Krisman, © 2011, GIA Publications, Inc.

Conception Abbey Tone

Music: Gregory J. Polan, OSB, © 2010, Conception Abbey, admin. by GIA Publications, Inc.

Gelineau Tone

Music: Joseph Gelineau, SJ, © 1963, The Grail, GIA Publications, Inc., agent

Ad te Domine levavi

1. To you, O LORD, I líft up my sóul.
    ² In yóu, O my Gód, I have trústed;
    let me nót be pút to sháme;
    let not my énemies exúlt over mé.
    ³ Let none who hópe in yóu be put to sháme;
    but shámed are those who wántonly break fáith.

2. ⁴ O LORD, make me knów your wáys.
    Téach mé your páths.
    ⁵ Guíde me in your trúth, and téach me;
    for yóu are the Gód of my salvátion.

3. I have hóped in yóu all day lóng.
    ⁶ Remémber your compássion, O LORD,
    ánd your mérciful lóve,
    for théy are fróm of óld.

Psalm 31: Father, into Your Hands / 43
Padre, a Tus Manos

Antiphon I*

Fa - ther, in-to your hands I com - mend my spir - it.

Antiphon II*

Pa - dre, a tus ma -nos en-co-mien-do mi_es - pí-ri-tu.

Verses

1. In you, O LORD, I take refuge.
Let me never be put to shame.
In your justice, set me free.
Into your hands I commend my spirit.
You will redeem me, O LORD, O
faithful God.

2. Because of all my foes I have become
a reproach,
an object of scorn to my neighbors
and of fear to my friends.
Those who see me in the street flee
from me.
I am forgotten, like someone dead,
and have become like a broken vessel.

3. But as for me, I trust in you, O LORD;
I say, "You are my God.
My lot is in your hands, deliver me
from the hands of my enemies and
those who pursue me."

4. Let your face shine on your servant.
Save me in your merciful love.
Be strong, let your heart take courage,
all who hope in the LORD.

1. A ti, Señor, me_acojo:
no quede yo nunca defraudado;
tú, que eres justo, ponme a salvo.
A tus manos encomiendo mi_espíritu:
tú, el Dios leal, me librarás.

2. Soy la burla de todos mis enemigos,
la irrisión de mis vecinos,
el espanto de mis conocidos:
me ven por la calle, y escapan de mí.
Me han olvidado como a un muerto,
me han desechado como a un cacharro
inútil.

3. Pero yo confío en ti, Señor,
te digo: "Tú eres mi Dios."
En tu mano están mis azares:
líbrame de los enemigos que me
persiguen.

4. Haz brillar tu rostro sobre tu siervo,
sálvame por tu misericordia.
Sean fuertes y valientes de corazón,
los que esperan en el Señor.

*For a bilingual setting, sing an entire antiphon in one language, followed by the
other language.

Text: Psalm 31:2 and 6, 12–13, 15–16, 17 and 25; English antiphon, *Lectionary for Mass*, © 1969, 1981, 1997, ICEL; verses, *The Revised Grail
Psalms*, © 2010, Conception Abbey and The Grail, admin. by GIA Publication, Inc.; Spanish text, *Leccionario, Edición Hispanoamérica*, © 1970,
1972, Conferencia Episcopal Española
Music: Antiphons, Ronald F. Krisman, © 2004, GIA Publications, Inc.; verses, Michel Guimont, © 1994, 1998, GIA Publications, Inc.

44   Psalm 31

Antiphon I

Lord God, be my ref - uge and my strength.

Text: *Liturgy of the Hours,* © 1974, ICEL
Music: Randolph Currie, © 1986, GIA Publications, Inc.

Antiphon II

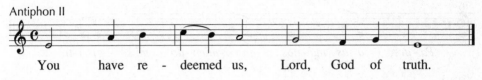

You have re - deemed us, Lord, God of truth.

Text: *Rite of Penance,* © 1975, ICEL
Music: Ronald F. Krisman, © 2011, GIA Publications, Inc.

Conception Abbey Tone

Music: Gregory J. Polan, OSB, © 2010, Conception Abbey, admin. by GIA Publications, Inc.

Gelineau Tone

Music: Joseph Gelineau, SJ, © 1963, The Grail, GIA Publications, Inc., agent

In te Domine speravi

1. ² In yóu, O LÓRD, I take réfuge.
    Let me néver be pút to sháme.
    In your jústice, sét me frée;
    ³ incline your éar to me, and spéedily réscue me.

2. Be a róck of réfuge for mé,
    a míghty strónghold to sáve me.
    ⁴ For yóu are my róck, my strónghold!
    Lead me, guíde me, for the sáke of your náme.

3. ⁵ Reléase me from the snáre they have hídden,
    for yóu indeed are my réfuge.
    ⁶ Into your hánds I comménd my spírit.
    You will redéem me, O LÓRD, O faithful Gód.

4. ⁷ You detést those who sérve empty ídols.
    As for mé, I trúst in the LÓRD.

5. [8] Let me be glád and rejóice in your
 mércy,
 for yóu who have séen my afflíction
 and taken héed of my sóul's distréss,
 [9] have not léft me in the hánds of the
 énemy,
 but sét my féet at lárge.

6. [10] Have mércy on mé, O LÓRD,
 for Í am in distréss.
 My éyes are wásted with gríef,
 my sóul and my bódy.

7. [11] For my lífe is spént with sórrow,
 and my yéars with síghs.
 Afflíction has bróken down my
 stréngth,
 and my bónes waste awáy.

8. [12] Becáuse of áll my fóes
 I have becóme a repróach,
 an óbject of scórn to my néighbors
 and of féar to my fríends.

9. Those who sée me in the stréet
 flee from mé.
 [13] I am forgótten, like sómeone déad,
 and have becóme like a bróken
 véssel.

10. [14] I have héard the slánder of the
 crówd;
 térror all aróund me,
 as they plót togéther agáinst me,
 as they plán to take my lífe.

11. [15] But as for mé, I trúst in you, O
 LÓRD;
 I say, "Yóu are my Gód.
 [16] My lót is in your hánds, delíver me
 from the hánds of my énemies
 and thóse who pursúe me.

12. [17] "Let your fáce shíne on your sérvant.
 Sáve me in your mérciful lóve.
 [18] Let me nót be put to sháme, O LÓRD,
 for Í cáll on yóu;
 lét the wícked be shámed!

13. [19] "Lét them be sílenced in the gráve!
 Let lýing líps be stílled,
 that speak háughtily agáinst the júst man
 with príde ánd contémpt."

14. [20] How gréat is the góodness, LÓRD,
 that you kéep for thóse who féar you,
 that you shów to thóse who trúst you
 in the síght of the chíldren of mén.

15. [21] You híde them in the shélter of
 your présence,
 secúre from human schéming;
 you kéep them sáfe within your tént
 from dispúting tóngues.

16. [22] Blest be the LÓRD for he has
 wóndrously shówn me
 his merciful lóve in a fórtified cíty!

17. [23] "I am fár remóved from your síght,"
 I sáid in my alárm.
 Yet you héard the vóice of my pléa
 when I críed to you for hélp.

18. [24] Lóve the LÓRD, all you his sáints.
 The LÓRD guards the fáithful.
 But the LÓRD will repáy to the fúll
 the óne who acts with príde.

19. [25] Be stróng, let your héart take cóurage,
 all who hópe in the LÓRD.
 Praise the Fáther, the Són and Holy Spírit,
 for éver and éver.

Text: Psalm 31; *The Revised Grail Psalms*; © 2010, Conception Abbey and The Grail, admin. by GIA Publications, Inc., agent

45   Psalm 33: Let Your Mercy Be on Us / Señor, Que Tu Misericordia

Antiphon I

Let your mer - cy   be   on   us,   O   God,
Se - ñor, que   tu   mi - se - ri - cor - dia

To verses

as   we   place   our   trust   in   you.
ven - ga   so   -   bre   no - so - tros.

Antiphon II

The   earth   is   full   of   the   good-ness   of
La   mi - se - ri - cor - dia   de   nues - tro

To verses

God,   the   good - ness   of   our   God.
Dios   lle - na   la   tie - rra.

Antiphon III

Hap - py   are   the   peo - ple   the   Lord   has
Di - cho - so   el   pue - blo que_el Se - ñor   se_es - co -

To verses

cho - sen,   cho - sen   to   be   his   own.
gió   co - mo   he - re - dad.

Verses

1. Your words, O God, are truth indeed, and all your works are ever faithful;
   you love justice and right, your compassion fills all creation.

2. See how the eye of God is watching, ever guarding all who wait in hope,
   to deliver them from death and sustain them in time of famine.

3. Exult, you just, in the Lord, for praise is the song of the righteous!
   How happy the people of God, the ones whom God has chosen!

4. Our soul is waiting for God, for God is our help and our shield.
   May your kindness, O God, be upon us who place our hope in you.

1. *La palabra del Señor es recta, y todas sus acciones son leales;*
   la justicia él ama, y la tierra su gracia llena.

2. *Los ojos de Dios ven a sus fieles, los que_esperan su misericordia;*
   los rescata de la muerte y sacia en tiempo de_hambre.

3. *Festejen, justos, al Señor, es propio de los buenos alabarlo.*
   Dichoso el pueblo de Dios, que él se_escogió como_heredad.

4. *Aguardamos al Señor: él es nuestro auxilio y_escudo;*
   que tu_amor, Señor, esté con nosotros, como lo_esperamos de ti.

Text: Psalm 33:4–5, 12, 18–19, 20, 22; Marty Haugen; Spanish tr. by Ronald F. Krisman, © 1987, 2011, GIA Publications, Inc.;
English antiphon III, *Lectionary for Mass*, © 1969, 1981, 1997, ICEL
Music: Marty Haugen, © 1987, 1994, GIA Publications, Inc.

Psalm 34: The Cry of the Poor 46

Antiphon

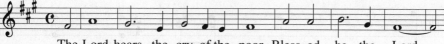

The Lord hears the cry of the poor. Bless-ed be the Lord.

Verses

1. I will bless the Lord at all times, with praise ever in my mouth.
   Let my soul glory in the Lord, who will hear the cry of the poor.

2. Let the lowly hear and be glad: the Lord listens to their pleas;
   and to hearts broken, God is near, who will hear the cry of the poor.

3. Every spirit crushed, God will save; will be ransom for their lives;
   will be safe shelter for their fears, and will hear the cry of the poor.

4. We proclaim your greatness, O God, your praise ever in our mouth;
   every face brightened in your light, for you hear the cry of the poor.

Text: Psalm 34:2–3, 6–7, 18–19, 23; John Foley, SJ
Music: John Foley, SJ
© 1978, 1991, John B. Foley, SJ, and OCP

47 Psalm 34: Look to God / Qui Regarde vers Dieu

Refrain — A

Look to God and be filled with ra-diant joy. Lift up your
French: Qui re - gar - de vers Dieu res-plen - di - ra, sur son vi -
Spanish: Los que mi - ran a Dios re - ful - gi - rán. So - bre sus

heads for God hears our prayer, lift up your
sa - ge, plus d'a - mer - tu - me, sur son vi -
ros - tros no ha - brá a-mar - gu - ra. So - bre sus

heads for God hears our prayer.
sa - ge, plus d'a - mer - tu - me.
ros - tros no ha - brá a-mar - gu - ra.

Verses — B

O Look to
Qui re -
Los que

Text: Psalm 34, *The Revised Grail Psalms*, © 2010, Conception Abbey and The Grail, admin. by GIA Publications, Inc.; Spanish tr. © 1970, 1972, Conferencia Episcopal Española; refrain, Taizé Community, © 2007, Les Presses de Taizé, GIA Publications, Inc., agent
Music: Taizé Community, © 2007, Les Presses de Taizé, GIA Publications, Inc., agent

Psalm 34: Taste and See   48

Antiphon

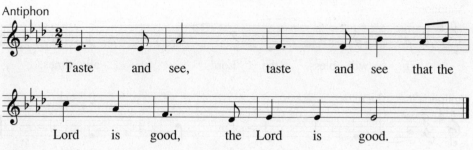

Taste and see, taste and see that the
Lord is good, the Lord is good.

Verses

1. I will bless the Lord at all times,
   his praise always on my lips.
   The Lord shall be the glory of my soul;
   the humble shall hear and be glad.

2. Glorify the Lord with me,
   together let us praise his name.
   I sought the Lord: he answered me;
   he set me free from all my fear.

3. Look upon the Lord and be radiant;
   hide not your face from the Lord.
   He heard the cry of the poor;
   he rescued them from all their woes.

4. The angel of the Lord is with his people
   to rescue those who trust in him.
   Taste and see the goodness of the Lord;
   seek refuge in him and be glad.

5. Saints of the Lord, revere him;
   those who fear him lack nothing.
   Lions suffer want and go hungry,
   but those who seek him lack no blessing.

6. Children of the Lord, come and hear,
   and learn the fear of the Lord.
   Who is he who longs for life,
   whose only love is for his wealth?

7. Keep evil words from your tongue,
   your lips from speaking deceit.
   Turn aside from evil and do good;
   seek and strive after peace.

Text: Psalm 34:2–15; Stephen Dean
Music: Stephen Dean
© 1981, Stephen Dean. Published by OCP.

49 Psalm 34: I Will Bless the Lord

Antiphon I

I will bless the Lord at all times.

Antiphon II

Taste and see the good - ness of the Lord.

Antiphon III

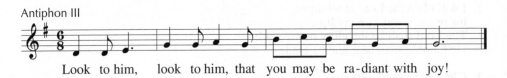

Look to him, look to him, that you may be ra-diant with joy!

Antiphon IV

The Lord is close to the bro - ken - heart - ed.

Antiphon V

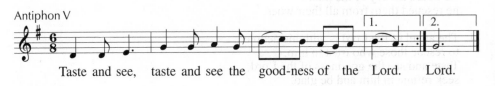

Taste and see, taste and see the good-ness of the Lord. Lord.

Guimont Tone

Benedicam Dominum

1. ² I will bless the LORD at àll times;
   praise of him is always in mý mouth.
   ³ In the LORD my soul shall make ìts boast;
   the humble shall hear ánd be glad.

2. ⁴ Glorify the LORD wìth me;
   together let us praise hís name.
   ⁵ I sought the LORD, and hè answered me;
   from all my terrors he sét me free.

3. ⁶Look toward him and bè radiant;
   let your faces not be ábashed.
   ⁷This lowly one called; the LÒRD heard,
   and rescued him from all hís distress.

4. ⁸The angel of the LORD is èncamped
   around those who fear him, tó rescue them.
   ⁹Taste and see that the LORD ìs good.
   Blessed the man who seeks refúge in him.

5. ¹⁰Fear the LORD, you hìs holy ones.
   They lack nothing, those whó fear him.
   ¹¹The rich suffer want and gò hungry,
   but those who seek the LORD láck no blessing.

6. ¹²Come, children, ànd hear me,
   that I may teach you the fear of thé LORD.
   ¹³Who is it that desìres life
   and longs to see prospérous days?

7. ¹⁴Guard your tongue fròm evil,
   and your lips from speaking déceit.
   ¹⁵Turn aside from evil and dò good.
   Seek after peace, ánd pursue it.

8. ¹⁶The LORD turns his eyes to thè just,
   and his ears are open to théir cry.
   ¹⁷The LORD turns his face against thè wicked
   to destroy their remembrance fróm the earth.

9. ¹⁸When the just cry out, the LÒRD hears,
   and rescues them in all their dístress.
   ¹⁹The LORD is close to the brokènhearted;
   those whose spirit is crushed hé will save.

10. ²⁰Many are the trials of thè just man,
    but from them all the LORD wíll rescue him.
    ²¹He will keep guard over all hìs bones;
    not one of his bones sháll be broken.

11. ²²Evil brings death to thè wicked;
    those who hate the just man áre doomed.
    ²³The LORD ransoms the souls of hìs servants.
    All who trust in him shall not bé condemned.

12. Give praise to the Father Àlmighty,
    to his Son, Jesus Christ thé Lord,
    to the Spirit who dwells in òur hearts
    both now and for evér. Amen.

Text: Psalm 34; *The Revised Grail Psalms*, © 2010, Conception Abbey and The Grail, admin. by GIA Publications, Inc.; antiphons, *Lectionary for Mass*, © 1969, 1981, 1997, ICEL
Music: Michel Guimont, antiphon II and verses, © 1995, and antiphons I, III, IV, V, © 2011, GIA Publications, Inc.

50 Psalm 42

Antiphon I

Like a deer that longs for run-ning streams,

my soul longs for you, my God.

Text: *Lectionary for Mass*, © 1969, 1981, 1997, ICEL
Music: Richard Proulx, © 1986, GIA Publications, Inc.

Antiphon II

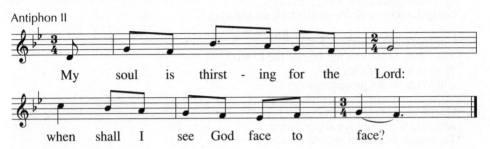

My soul is thirst-ing for the Lord:

when shall I see God face to face?

Text: Psalm 42:3, The Grail
Music: Joseph Gelineau, SJ
© 1963, 1993, The Grail, GIA Publications, Inc. agent

Conception Abbey Tone

Omit for 2-line stanza

Omit for 4-line stanzas

Music: Gregory J. Polan, OSB, © 2010, Conception Abbey, admin. by GIA Publications, Inc.

Gelineau Tone

Omit for 2-line stanza

Repeat for 5-line stanza

(St. 5)

Music: Joseph Gelineau, SJ, © 1963, The Grail, GIA Publications, Inc., agent

Quemadmodum desiderat

1. [2] Líke the déer that yéarns
   for rúnning stréams,
   só my sóul is yéarning
   for yóu, my Gód.

2. [3] My sóul is thírsting for Gód,
   the líving Gód;
   whén can I énter and appéar
   before the fáce of Gód?

3. [4] My téars have becóme my bréad,
   by dáy, by níght,
   as they sáy to me áll the day lóng,
   "Whére is your Gód?"

4. [5] These thíngs will Í remémber
   as I póur out my sóul:

5. For Í would gó to the pláce
   of your wóndrous tént,
   all the wáy to the hóuse of Gód,
   amid críes of gládness and thanksgíving,
   the thróng keeping jóyful féstival.

6. ⁶ Whý are you cast dówn, my sóul;
   why gróan withín me?
   Hope in Gód; I will práise him yet agáin,
   my saving présence and my Gód.

7. ⁷ My sóul is cast dówn withín me,
   thérefore I remémber you
   from the lánd of Jórdan and Mount Hérmon,
   from the Híll of Mízar.

8. ⁸ Déep is cálling on déep,
   in the róar of your tórrents;
   your bíllows and áll your wáves
   swépt over mé.

9. ⁹ By dáy the LÓRD decrées
   his mérciful lóve;
   by níght his sóng is with mé,
   prayer to the Gód of my lífe.

10. ¹⁰ I will sáy to Gód, my róck,
    "Whý have you forgótten me?
    Whý do Í go móurning
    oppréssed by the fóe?"

11. ¹¹ With a déadly wóund in my bónes,
    my énemies revíle me,
    sáying to me áll the day lóng,
    "Whére is your Gód?"

12. ¹² Whý are you cast dówn, my sóul;
    why gróan withín me?
    Hope in Gód; I will práise him yet agáin,
    my saving présence and my Gód.

13. Praise the Fáther, the Són and Holy Spírit,
    both nów and for éver,
    the God who ís, who wás and who wíll be,
    wórld without énd.

Text: Psalm 42; *The Revised Grail Psalms*; © 2010, Conception Abbey and The Grail, admin. by GIA Publications, Inc., agent

51 Psalm 46

Antiphon

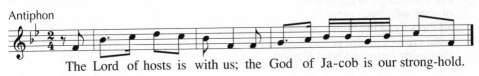

The Lord of hosts is with us; the God of Ja-cob is our strong-hold.

Text: Psalm 46; The Grail
Music: A. Gregory Murray, OSB
© 1963, The Grail, GIA Publications, Inc., agent

Conception Abbey Tone

Music: Gregory J. Polan, OSB, © 2010, Conception Abbey, admin. by GIA Publications, Inc.

Gelineau Tone

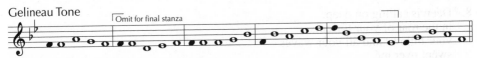

Music: Joseph Gelineau, SJ, © 1963, The Grail, GIA Publications, Inc., agent

Deus noster refugium

1. ² Gód is for ús a réfuge and stréngth,
   an éver-present hélp in tíme of distréss:
   ³ so wé shall not féar though the éarth should róck,
   though the móuntains quáke to the héart of the séa;
   ⁴ éven though its wáters ráge and fóam,
   éven though the móuntains be sháken by its túmult.

2. ⁵ The wáters of a ríver give jóy to God's cíty,
   the hóly place, the dwélling of the Móst Hígh.
   ⁶ Gód is withín, it cánnot be sháken;
   Gód will hélp it at the dáwning of the dáy.
   ⁷ Nátions are in túmult, kíngdoms are sháken:
   he lífts his vóice, the éarth melts awáy.

3. ⁹ Cóme and behóld the wórks of the LÓRD,
   the áwesome déeds he has dóne on the éarth.
   ¹⁰ He puts an énd to wárs over áll the éarth;
   the bow he bréaks, the spear he snáps, the shíelds he burns with fíre:
   ¹¹ "Be stíll and knów that Í am Gód,
   exálted over nátions, exálted over éarth!"

4. Give práise to the Fáther, the Són and Holy Spírit
   both nów and for áges unénding. Amén.

Text: Psalm 46; *The Revised Grail Psalms;* © 2010, Conception Abbey and The Grail, admin. by GIA Publications, Inc., agent

Psalm 47: God Mounts His Throne 52

Antiphon

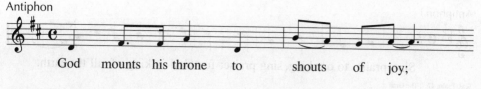

God mounts his throne to shouts of joy;

a blare of trum - pets for the Lord.

Verses

1. All peoples, clap your hands.
   Cry to God with shouts of joy!
   For the LORD, the Most High, is awesome,
   the great King over all the earth.

2. God goes up with shouts of joy.
   The LORD goes up with trumpet blast.
   Sing praise for God; sing praise!
   Sing praise to our king; sing praise!

3. God is King of all the earth.
   Sing praise with all your skill.
   God reigns over the nations.
   God sits upon his holy throne.

Text: Psalm 47:2–3, 6–7, 8–9, *The Revised Grail Psalms*, © 2010, Conception Abbey and The Grail, admin. GIA Publications, Inc.; antiphon, *Lectionary for Mass*, © 1969, 1981, 1997, ICEL
Music: James J. Chepponis, © 1994, 2011, GIA Publications, Inc.

53 Psalm 47

Antiphon I

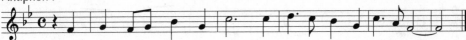

Sing praise to our king, sing praise: for God is king of all the earth.

Text: Psalm 47:7; The Grail
Music: A. Gregory Murray, OSB
© 1963, The Grail, GIA Publications, Inc., agent

Antiphon II

God mounts his throne to shouts of joy, to shouts, to shouts of joy.

Text: *Lectionary for Mass,* © 1969, 1981, 1997, ICEL
Music: Richard Proulx, © 1975, GIA Publications, Inc.

Antiphon III

Christ is the light of the na - tions, to bring sal - va - tion to the ends of the earth.

Text: *Simple Gradual,* © 1968, ICEL
Music: John R. Ainslie, © 1969, Geoffrey Chapman Ltd.

Conception Abbey Tone

Music: Gregory J. Polan, OSB, © 2010, Conception Abbey, admin. by GIA Publications, Inc.

Gelineau Tone

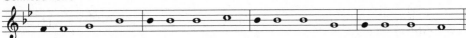

Music: Joseph Gelineau, SJ, © 1963, The Grail, GIA Publications, Inc., agent

Omnes gentes plaudite

1. ² All péoples, cláp your hánds.
   Cry to Gód with shóuts of jóy!
   ³ For the LORD, the Most Hígh, is
   áwesome,
   the great kíng over áll the éarth.

2. ⁴ He húmbles péoples únder us
   and nátions únder our féet.
   ⁵ Our héritage he chóse for ús,
   the príde of Jácob whom he lóves.

3. ⁶God goes úp with shóuts of jóy.
The LORD goes úp with trúmpet blást.
⁷Sing práise for Gód; sing práise!
Sing práise to our kíng; sing práise!

4. ⁸God is kíng of áll the éarth.
Sing práise with áll your skíll.
⁹Gód reigns óver the nátions.
God síts upon his hóly thróne.

5. ¹⁰The prínces of the péoples are assémbled
with the péople of the Gód of Ábraham.
The rúlers of the éarth belong to Gód,
whó is gréatly exálted.

6. Give práise to the Fáther Almíghty,
to his Són, Jesus Chríst the Lórd,
to the Spírit who dwélls in our héarts,
both nów and for éver. Amén.

Text: Psalm 47; *The Revised Grail Psalms*; © 2010, Conception Abbey and The Grail, admin. by GIA Publications, Inc., agent

Psalm 51: Be Merciful, O Lord 54

Antiphon

Be mer-ci-ful, O Lord, for we have sinned; be
mer-ci-ful, O Lord, for we have sinned.

Verses

1. Have mercy on me, God, in your kindness,
in your compassion, blot out my offense.
O wash me more and more from my guilt and my sorrow,
and cleanse me from all of my sin.

2. My offenses, truly I know them, and my sins are always before me;
against you alone have I sinned, O Lord, what is evil in your sight I have done.

3. Create in me a clean heart, O God, put your steadfast spirit in my soul.
Cast me not away from your presence, O Lord, and take not your spirit from me.

4. Give back to me the joy of your salvation, let your willing spirit bear me up
and I shall teach your way to the ones who have wandered,
and bring them all home to your side.

Text: Psalm 51:3–4, 5–6, 12–13, 14–15; Marty Haugen, © 1983, GIA Publications, Inc.; antiphon, *Lectionary for Mass*, © 1969, 1981, 1997, ICEL
Music: Marty Haugen, © 1983, GIA Publications, Inc.

55 Psalm 51

Antiphon I

Have mer - cy, Lord; cleanse me from all my sins.

Text: Psalm 51; The Grail
Music: Joseph Gelineau, SJ
© 1963, The Grail, GIA Publications, Inc., agent

Antiphon II

Lord, if you will, you can make me clean.

Text: A. Gregory Murray, OSB
Music: A. Gregory Murray, OSB
© 1963, The Grail, GIA Publications, Inc., agent

Antiphon III

Give back to me the joy of your sal - va - tion.

Text: *Rite of Penance,* © 1975, ICEL
Music: Howard Hughes, SM, © 1975, GIA Publications, Inc.

Conception Abbey Tone

Omit for 5-line sts.
Omit for 4-line stanzas

Music: Gregory J. Polan, OSB, © 2010, Conception Abbey, admin. by GIA Publications, Inc.

Gelineau Tone

Omit for 5-line sts.
Omit for 4-line stanzas

Music: Joseph Gelineau, SJ, © 1963, The Grail, GIA Publications, Inc., agent

Miserere mei Deus

1. ³ Have mércy on mé, O Gód,
   accórding to your mérciful lóve;
   accórding to your gréat compássion,
   blót out mý transgréssions.
   ⁴ Wash me complétely fróm my iníquity,
   and cléanse me fróm my sín.

2. ⁵ My transgréssions, trúly I knów them;
   my sín is álways befóre me.
   ⁶ Against yóu, you alóne, have I sínned;
   what is évil in your síght I have dóne.
   So yóu are júst in your séntence,
   withóut repróach in your júdgment.

3. ⁷ O sée, in guílt I was bórn,
  a sínner when my móther concéived me.
  ⁸ Yes, you delíght in sincérity of héart;
  in sécret you téach me wísdom.
  ⁹ Cleanse me with hýssop, and Í shall be púre;
  wash me, and Í shall be whíter than snów.

4. ¹⁰ Let me héar rejóicing and gládness,
  that the bónes you have crúshed may exúlt.
  ¹¹ Túrn away your fáce from my síns,
  and blót out áll my guílt.

5. ¹² Creáte a pure héart for me, O Gód;
  renew a stéadfast spírit withín me.
  ¹³ Do not cást me awáy from your présence;
  take not your hóly spírit from mé.

6. ¹⁴ Restóre in me the jóy of your salvátion;
  sustáin in me a wílling spírit.
  ¹⁵ I will téach transgréssors your wáys,
  that sínners may retúrn to yóu.

7. ¹⁶ Réscue me from blóodshed, O Gód,
  Gód of mý salvátion,
  and then my tóngue shall ring óut your jústice.
  ¹⁷ O Lórd, ópen my líps
  and my móuth shall procláim your práise.

8. ¹⁸ For in sácrifice you táke no delíght;
  burnt óffering from mé would not pléase you.
  ¹⁹ My sácrifice to Gód, a broken spírit:
  a bróken and húmbled héart,
  O Gód, you wíll not spúrn.

9. ²⁰ In your good pléasure, show fávor to Síon;
  rebuíld the wálls of Jerúsalem.
  ²¹ Thén you will delíght in right sácrifice,
  burnt ófferings whólly consúmed.
  Then you will be óffered young búlls on your áltar.

10. Give práise to the Fáther Almíghty,
  to his Són, Jesus Chríst the Lórd,
  to the Spírit who dwélls in our héarts,
  both nów and for éver. Amén.

Text: Psalm 51; *The Revised Grail Psalms*; © 2010, Conception Abbey and The Grail, admin. by GIA Publications, Inc., agent

56 Psalm 51: Misericordia, Señor / Be Merciful, O Lord

Antiphon

Mi-se-ri - cor - dia,   Se - ñor,   he-mos pe - ca - do.

Be mer-ci -ful, O Lord,   for we have sinned.

Verses

1. Misericordia, Dios mío, por tu bondad; por tu inmensa compasión borra mi culpa.
   Lava del todo mi delito, todo mi delito, limpia mi pecado.

2. Pues la culpa que he hecho reconozco, tengo siempre presente mi pecado;
   contra ti sólo pequé, contra ti, Señor, contra ti, cometí la maldad que aborreces.

3. Oh Dios, crea en mí un corazón puro, renuévame con espíritu firme;
   no me arrojes lejos de tu rostro, no me quites tu santo espíritu.

4. Dame tu salvación que regocija, mantén en mí un alma generosa;
   líbrame de la muerte, mi Salvador, y mi boca cantará tu alabanza.

1. O God, have mercy on me in your goodness;
   in your compassion wipe out my offense.
   Thoroughly wash me from my guilt,
   wash me from my guilt; cleanse me of all my sin.

2. I acknowledge my sin and my offenses for they are always before me.
   Against you alone have I sinned, against you alone have I sinned.
   I have done what is evil in your sight.

3. O God, create for me a clean heart, renew in me a steadfast spirit.
   Cast me not out from your presence, my God, do not take from me your holy spirit.

4. Restore my joy in your salvation; sustain a willing spirit within me!
   Rescue me from death, my saving God, and my mouth will proclaim your praise!

Text: Psalm 51:3–4, 5–6, 12–13, 14 and 17; English antiphon, *Lectionary for Mass*, © 1969, 1981, 1997, ICEL; English verses and Spanish verses 2 and 4 adapt. by Paul A. Tate, © 2005, GIA Publications, Inc.; Spanish antiphon and verses 1 and 3, *Leccionario, Edición Hispanoamérica*, © 1970, 1972, Conferencia Episcopal Española
Music: Paul A. Tate, © 2005, GIA Publications, Inc.

Psalm 63: My Soul Is Thirsting   57

Antiphon

My soul is thirst - ing, my soul is thirst - ing,

my soul is thirst - ing for you, O Lord my God.

Verses

1. O God, you are my God whom I seek;
   O God, you are my God whom I seek;
   for you my flesh pines, my soul thirsts like the earth,
   parched, lifeless, without water.

2. Thus have I gazed toward you in your holy place
   to see your power and your glory.
   Your kindness is a greater good than life itself;
   my lips will glorify you.

3. Thus will I bless you while I live;
   lifting up my hands I will call upon your name.
   As with a banquet shall my soul be satisfied;
   with exultant lips my mouth shall praise you.

4. For you have been my help, you have been my help;
   in the shadow of your wings I shout for joy.
   My soul clings fast to you; your right hand holds me firm;
   in the shadow of your wings I sing for joy.

Text: Psalm 63:2, 3–4, 5–6, 8–9; verses adapt. © 1970, Confraternity of Christian Doctrine, Washington, D.C.; antiphon by Michael Joncas, © 1987, GIA Publications, Inc.
Music: Michael Joncas, © 1987, GIA Publications, Inc.

58 Psalm 63:2–9

Antiphon I

My soul is thirst-ing for you, O

Lord, thirst-ing for you, my God.

Text: *Lectionary for Mass*, © 1969, 1981, 1997, ICEL
Music: Richard Proulx, © 1975, GIA Publications, Inc.

Antiphon II

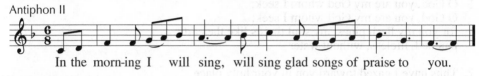

In the morn-ing I will sing, will sing glad songs of praise to you.

Text: *Praise God in Song*
Music: David Clark Isele
© 1979, GIA Publications, Inc.

Conception Abbey Tone

Omit for 4-line stanza

Music: Gregory J. Polan, OSB, © 2010, Conception Abbey, admin. by GIA Publications, Inc.

Gelineau Tone

Omit for 4-line stanza

Music: Joseph Gelineau, SJ, © 1963, The Grail, GIA Publications, Inc., agent

Deus, Deus meus, ad te

1. ² O Gód, you are my Gód; at dawn I
      séek you;
   for yóu my sóul is thírsting.
   For yóu my flésh is píning,
      like a drý, weary lánd without wáter.
   ³ I have cóme before yóu in the
      sánctuary,
   to behóld your stréngth and your glóry.

2. ⁴ Your loving mércy is bétter than lífe;
      my líps will spéak your práise.
   ⁵ I will bléss you áll my lífe;
      in your náme I will líft up my hánds.
   ⁶ My sóul shall be fílled as with a
      bánquet;
   with joyful líps, my móuth shall
      práise you.

3. ⁷ When I remémber yóu upon my béd,
      I muse on yóu through the wátches
      of the níght.
   ⁸ For yóu have béen my stréngth;
      in the shádow of your wíngs I rejóice.
   ⁹ My sóul clings fást to yóu;
      yóur right hánd uphólds me.

4. Give práise to the Fáther Almíghty,
   to his Són, Jesus Chríst the Lórd,
   to the Spírit who dwélls in our héarts,
   both nów and for éver. Amén.

Text: Psalm 63:2–9; *The Revised Grail Psalms*; © 2010, Conception Abbey and The Grail, admin. by GIA Publications, Inc., agent

Psalm 64   59

Antiphon

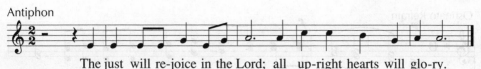

The just will re-joice in the Lord; all up-right hearts will glo-ry.

Text: Psalm 64:11; The Grail, © 1963, The Grail, GIA Publications, Inc., agent
Music: Suzanne Toolan, RSM, © 1986, GIA Publications, Inc.

Conception Abbey Tone

Music: Gregory J. Polan, OSB, © 2010, Conception Abbey, admin. by GIA Publications, Inc.

Gelineau Tone

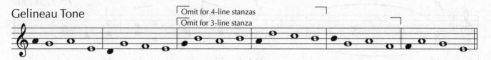

Music: Joseph Gelineau, SJ, © 1963, The Grail, GIA Publications, Inc., agent

Exaudi Deus orationem meam

1. [2]Hear, O Gód, the vóice of my
    compláint;
    guard my lífe from dréad of the fóe.
  [3]From the assémbly of the wícked,
    híde me,
    from the thróng of thóse who do évil.

2. [4]They shárpen their tóngues like swórds.
    They áim bitter wórds like árrows,
  [5]to shóot at the ínnocent from ámbush,
    shóoting súddenly and féarlessly.

3. [6]Holding fírm in their évil cóurse,
    they conspíre to lay sécret snáres.
    They sáy, "Whó will sée us?
  [7]Whó can séarch out our crímes?"

4. They have hátched their wícked plóts,
    and bróught them tó perféction.
    How profóund the dépths of the héart!

5. [8]Gód will shóot them with his árrow,
    and déal them súdden wóunds.
  [9]Their ówn tongue bríngs them to rúin;
    all who sée them sháke their héads.

6. [10]Thén will áll be afráid;
    they will téll what Gód has dóne.
    Théy will pónder God's déeds.
  [11]The júst one will rejóice in the LORD;
    and flý to hím for réfuge.
    All úpright héarts will glóry.

7. Give práise to the Fáther Almíghty,
    to his Són, Jesus Chríst the Lórd,
    to the Spírit who dwélls in our héarts,
    both nów and for éver. Amén.

Text: Psalm 64; *The Revised Grail Psalms*; © 2010, Conception Abbey and The Grail, admin. by GIA Publications, Inc., agent

60   Psalm 66: Jubiláte, Allelúia

Ostinato Refrain

O

Ju - bi - lá - te   De - o   om - nis ter - ra!
Shout to God with joy, all   peo-ples of the earth!

O

Al-le - lú - ia,   al-le - lú - ia!

Text: Psalm 66; Taizé Community
Music: Taizé Community
© 2007, Les Presses de Taizé, GIA Publications, Inc., agent

Psalm 67: The Earth Has Yielded Its Fruit / 61
La Tierra Ha Dado Su Fruto

Antiphon I

The earth has yield - ed its fruit; the
La tie - rra_ha da - do su fru - to,

Lord our God has blessed us.
nos ben - di - ce_el Se - ñor, nues - tro Dios.

Antiphon II

O God, let all the na - tions praise you! O
Oh Dios, que te_a - la - ben los pue - blos, que

God, let all the na - tions praise you!
to - dos los pue - blos te_a - la - ben.

Verses

1. O God, be gracious and bless us
and let your face shed its light upon us.
So will your ways be known upon earth
and all nations learn your salvation.

2. Let the nations be glad and shout for joy,
with uprightness you rule the peoples;
you guide the nations on earth.

3. Let the peoples praise you, O God;
let all the peoples praise you.
May God still give us his blessing
that all the ends of the earth may
revere him.

1. *El Señor tenga piedad y nos
bendiga,
ilumine su rostro sobre nosotros;
conozca la tierra tus caminos,
todos los pueblos tu salvación.*

2. *Que canten de alegría las naciones,
porque riges el mundo con justicia,
riges los pueblos con rectitud
y gobiernas las naciones de la tierra.*

3. *Oh Dios, que te alaben los pueblos,
que todos los pueblos te_alaben.
Que Dios nos bendiga;
que le teman hasta los confines del
orbe.*

Text: Psalm 67:2–3, 5, 6 and 8; English antiphon, *Lectionary for Mass*, © 1969, 1981, 1997, ICEL; verses, *The Revised Grail Psalms*, © 2010, Conception Abbey and The Grail, admin. by GIA Publication, Inc.; Spanish text, *Leccionario, Edición Hispanoamérica*, © 1970, 1972, Conferencia Episcopal Española
Music: Antiphon I, Ronald F. Krisman, and antiphon II, Tony E. Alonso, © 2004, GIA Publications, Inc.; verses, Michel Guimont, © 1994, 1998, GIA Publications, Inc.

62 Psalm 71

Antiphon I

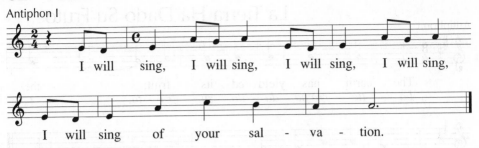

I will sing, I will sing, I will sing, I will sing,
I will sing of your sal - va - tion.

Text: *Lectionary for Mass,* © 1969, 1981, 1997, ICEL
Music: Robert J. Batastini, © 2011, GIA Publications, Inc.

Antiphon II

My God, my God, come quick-ly to help me.

Text: *Lectionary for Mass,* © 1969, 1981, 1997, ICEL
Music: Ronald F. Krisman, © 2011, GIA Publications, Inc.

Conception Abbey Tone

Omit for 5-line sts.
Omit for 4-line stanzas

Music: Gregory J. Polan, OSB, © 2010, Conception Abbey, admin. by GIA Publications, Inc.

Gelineau Tone

Omit for 5-line sts.
Omit for 4-line stanzas

Music: Joseph Gelineau, SJ, © 1963, The Grail, GIA Publications, Inc., agent

In te Domine speravi

1. ¹In yóu, O LÓRD, I take réfuge;
   let me néver be pút to sháme.
   ²In your jústice, réscue me, frée me;
   inclíne your éar to me and sáve me.

2. ³Be my róck, my cónstant réfuge,
   a míghty strónghold to sáve me,
   for yóu are my róck, my strónghold.
   ⁴My God, frée me from the hánd of the wícked,
   from the gríp of the unjúst, of the oppréssor.

3. ⁵It is yóu, O Lórd, who are my hópe,
   my trúst, O LÓRD, from my yóuth.
   ⁶On yóu I have léaned from my bírth;
   from my mother's wómb, you have béen my hélp.
   At all tímes I gíve you práise.

4. [7] My fáte has filled mány with áwe,
but yóu are my míghty réfuge.
[8] My móuth is fílled with your práise,
with your glóry, áll the day lóng.
[9] Do not rejéct me nów that I am óld;
when my stréngth fails dó not forsáke
me.

5. [10] For my énemies are spéaking abóut me;
those who wátch me take cóunsel
togéther,
[11] saying: "Gód has forsáken him; fóllow
him.
Séize him; there is nó one to sáve him."
[12] O Gód, do not stáy afar óff;
O my Gód, make háste to hélp me!

6. [13] Let them be pút to sháme and destróyed,
thóse who séek my lífe.
Let them be cóvered with sháme and
confúsion,
thóse who séek to hárm me.

7. [14] But as for mé, I will álways hópe,
and práise you móre and móre.
[15] My móuth will téll of your jústice,
and áll the day lóng of your salvátion,
though I can néver téll it áll.

8. [16] I will come with práise of your míght,
O Lórd;
I will cáll to mínd your jústice,
yóurs, O LÓRD, alóne.
[17] O Gód, you have táught me from my
yóuth,
and I procláim your wónders stíll.

9. [18] Even tíll I am óld and gray-héaded,
dó not forsáke me, O Gód.
Let me téll of your míghty árm
to évery cóming generátion;

10. [19] Your stréngth and your jústice, O
Gód,
réach to the híghest héavens.
It is yóu who have wórked such
wónders.
O Gód, whó is like yóu?

11. [20] You have made me wítness many
tróubles and évils,
but you will gíve me báck my lífe.
You will ráise me from the dépths
of the éarth;
[21] you will exált me and consóle me
agáin.

12. [22] So I will gíve you thánks on the
lýre
for your fáithfulness, Ó my Gód.
To yóu will I síng with the hárp,
to yóu, the Hóly One of Ísrael.
[23] When I síng to you, my líps shall
shout for jóy,
and my sóul, which yóu have
redéemed.

13. [24] And áll the day lóng my tóngue
shall téll the tále of your jústice,
for they are pút to sháme and
disgráced,
thóse who séek to hárm me.

14. Give práise to the Fáther Almíghty,
to his Són, Jesus Chríst the Lórd,
to the Spírit who dwélls in our
héarts,
both nów and for éver. Amén.

Text: Psalm 71; *The Revised Grail Psalms*; © 2010, Conception Abbey and The Grail, admin. by GIA Publications, Inc., agent

63 Psalm 84

Antiphon I

How love-ly is your dwell-ing place, O Lord of hosts.

Text: Psalm 84:2, The Grail
Music: A. Gregory Murray, OSB
© 1963, The Grail, GIA Publications, Inc., agent

Antiphon II

Bless-ed, bless-ed are they who dwell in your house, O Lord.

Text: *Lectionary for Mass*, © 1969, 1981, 1997, ICEL
Music: Robert J. Batastini, © 1998, GIA Publications, Inc.

Antiphon III

During Lent

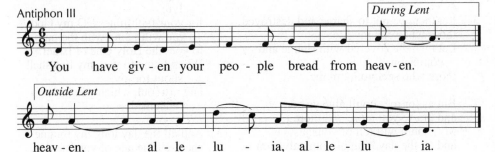

You have giv-en your peo-ple bread from heav-en.

Outside Lent

heav-en, al-le-lu-ia, al-le-lu-ia.

Text: *Simple Gradual*, © 1968, ICEL
Music: Ronald F. Krisman, © 2011, GIA Publications, Inc.

Conception Abbey Tone

Omit for 4-line stanzas

Omit for 2-line stanzas

Music: Gregory J. Polan, OSB, © 2010, Conception Abbey, admin. by GIA Publications, Inc.

Gelineau Tone

Repeat for 5-line stanza
Omit for 2-line stanzas

Music: Joseph Gelineau, SJ, © 1963, The Grail, GIA Publications, Inc., agent

Quam dilecta

1. ² How lóvely is your dwélling pláce,
   Ó LÓRD of hósts.

2. ³ My sóul is lónging and yéarning
   fór the cóurts of the LÓRD.
   My héart and my flésh cry óut
   tó the líving Gód.

3. [4] Éven the spárrow finds a hóme,
   and the swállow a nést for hersélf
   in which she séts her yóung, at your áltars,
   O LORD of hósts, my kíng and my Gód.

4. [5] Blessed are théy who dwéll in your hóuse,
   foréver sínging your práise.
   [6] Blessed the péople whose stréngth is in yóu,
   whose héart is sét on pilgrim wáys.

5. [7] As they gó through the Báca Válley,
   they máke it a pláce of spríngs;
   the áutumn rain cóvers it with póols.
   [8] They wálk with éver-growing stréngth;
   the God of góds will appéar in Síon.

6. [9] O LORD Gód of hósts, hear my práyer;
   give éar, O Gód of Jácob.
   [10] Turn your éyes, O Gód, our shíeld;
   lóok on the fáce of your anóinted.

7. [11] One dáy withín your cóurts
   is bétter than a thóusand élsewhere.
   The thréshold of the hóuse of Gód
   I prefér to the dwéllings of the wícked.

8. [12] For the LORD Gód is a sún, a shíeld;
   the LORD will gíve us his fávor and glóry.
   He will nót withhóld any góod
   to thóse who wálk without bláme.

9. [13] O LÓRD of hósts, how bléssed
   is the mán who trústs in yóu!

10. Give práise to the Fáther Almíghty,
    to his Són, Jesus Chríst the Lórd,
    to the Spírit who dwélls in our héarts,
    both nów and for éver. Amén.

Text: Psalm 84; *The Revised Grail Psalms*; © 2010, Conception Abbey and The Grail, admin. by GIA Publications, Inc., agent

64 Psalm 86

Antiphon I

In - cline your ear, O Lord, and an - swer me.

Text: *Lectionary for Mass,* © 1969, 1981, 1997, ICEL
Music: Ronald F. Krisman, © 2011, GIA Publications, Inc.

Antiphon II

O Lord, our God, un - wea - ried is your love for us.

Text: *Liturgy of the Hours,* © 1974, ICEL
Music: John Schiavone, © 1986, GIA Publications, Inc.

Antiphon III

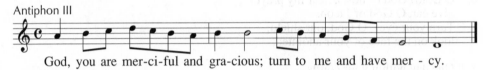

God, you are mer - ci - ful and gra - cious; turn to me and have mer - cy.

Text: *Lectionary for Mass,* © 1969, 1981, 1997, ICEL
Music: Robert J. Batastini, © 1975, GIA Publications, Inc.

Antiphon IV

Lord, you are great and do mar - vel - ous deeds: you a - lone are God.

Text: *Simple Gradual,* © 1968, ICEL
Music: Paul Inwood, © 1969, Geoffrey Chapman Ltd.

Conception Abbey Tone

Music: Gregory J. Polan, OSB, © 2010, Conception Abbey, admin. by GIA Publications, Inc.

Gelineau Tone

Music: Joseph Gelineau, SJ, © 1963, The Grail, GIA Publications, Inc., agent

Inclina Domine aurem tuam

1. Turn your éar, O LÓRD, and ánswer me,
   for Í am póor and néedy.
   ²Presérve my sóul, for I am fáithful;
   save the sérvant who trústs in you, my Gód.

2. ³ Have mércy on mé, O Lórd,
 for I crý to you áll the day lóng.
 ⁴ Gládden the sóul of your sérvant,
 for I líft up my sóul to you, O Lórd.

3. ⁵ O Lórd, you are góod and forgíving,
 full of mércy to áll who call to yóu.
 ⁶ Give éar, O LORD, to my práyer,
 and atténd to my vóice in supplicátion.

4. ⁷ In the dáy of distréss, I will cáll to you,
 and súrely yóu will ánswer me.
 ⁸ Among the góds there is nóne like you, O Lórd,
 nor wórks to compáre with yóurs.

5. ⁹ All the nátions you have máde shall cóme;
 they will bow dówn befóre you, O Lórd,
 and glórifý your náme,
 ¹⁰ for you are gréat and do márvelous déeds,
 yóu who alóne are Gód.

6. ¹¹ Téach me, O LORD, your wáy,
 so that Í may wálk in your trúth,
 single-héarted to féar your náme.

7. ¹² I will práise you, Lord my Gód, with all my héart,
 and glórify your náme foréver.
 ¹³ Your mércy to mé has been gréat;
 you have sáved me from the dépths of the gráve.

8. ¹⁴ The proud have rísen agáinst me, O Gód;
 a bánd of the rúthless seeks my lífe.
 To yóu they páy no héed.

9. ¹⁵ But you, O Gód, are compássionate and grácious,
 slów to ánger, O Lórd,
 abúndant in mércy and fidélity;
 ¹⁶ túrn and take píty on mé.

10. O gíve your stréngth to your sérvant,
 and sáve the són of your hándmaid.
 ¹⁷ Shów me the sígn of your fávor,
 that my fóes may sée to their sháme
 that you, O LORD, give me cómfort and hélp.

11. Give práise to the Fáther Almíghty,
 to his Són, Jesus Chríst the Lórd,
 to the Spírit who dwélls in our héarts,
 both nów and for éver. Amén.

Text: Psalm 86; *The Revised Grail Psalms*; © 2010, Conception Abbey and The Grail, admin. by GIA Publications, Inc., agent

65 Psalm 88

Antiphon

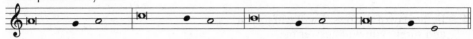

Day and night I cry to you, my God.

Text: *Liturgy of the Hours,* © 1974, ICEL
Music: Suzanne Toolan, RSM, © 1986, GIA Publications, Inc.

Conception Abbey Tone

Music: Gregory J. Polan, OSB, © 2010, Conception Abbey, admin. by GIA Publications, Inc.

Gelineau Tone

Music: Joseph Gelineau, SJ, © 1963, The Grail, GIA Publications, Inc., agent

Domine Deus salutis meae

1. ²O LORD and Gód of my salvátion,
   I crý before you dáy and níght.
   ³Let my práyer cóme into your présence.
   Inclíne your éar to my crý.

2. ⁴For my sóul is fílled with évils;
   my lífe is on the brínk of the gráve.
   ⁵I am réckoned as óne in the tómb;
   Í am like a wárrior without stréngth,

3. ⁶Like one róaming amóng the déad,
   like the sláin lýing in their gráves,
   like thóse you remémber no móre,
   cut óff, as they áre, from your hánd.

4. ⁷You have láid me in the dépths of the pít,
   in régions that are dárk and déep.
   ⁸Your ánger wéighs down upón me;
   I am drówned benéath your wáves.

5. ⁹You have táken awáy my fríends;
   to thém you have máde me háteful.
   Imprísoned, I cannót escápe;
   ¹⁰my éyes are súnken with gríef.

6. I cáll to you, LORD, all day lóng;
   to yóu I strétch out my hánds.
   ¹¹Will you wórk your wónders for the déad?
   Will the shádes rise úp to práise you?

7. [12] Will your mércy be tóld in the gráve,
   or your fáithfulness in the pláce of perdítion?
   [13] Will your wónders be knówn in the dárk,
   your jústice in the lánd of oblívion?

8. [14] But Í, O LORD, crý out to yóu;
   in the mórning my práyer comes befóre you.
   [15] Whý do you rejéct me, O LÓRD?
   Why do you híde your fáce from mé?

9. [16] I am wrétched, close to déath from my yóuth.
   I have bórne your tríals; I am númb.
   [17] Your fúry has swept dówn upón me;
   your térrors have útterly destróyed me.

10. [18] They surróund me all the dáy like a flóod;
    togéther they clóse in agáinst me.
    [19] Friend and néighbor you have táken awáy:
    my óne compánion is dárkness.

11. Give práise to the Fáther Almíghty,
    to his Són, Jesus Chríst the Lórd,
    to the Spírit who dwélls in our héarts,
    both nów and for éver. Amén.

66 Psalm 89: For Ever I Will Sing / Cantaré Eternamente

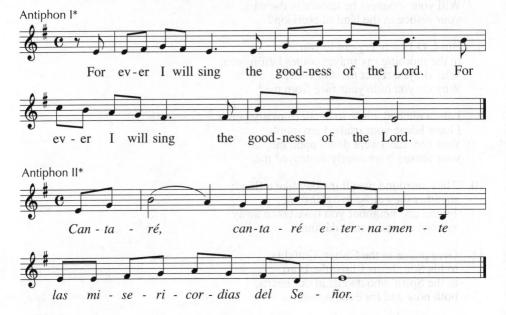

Antiphon I*

For ev-er I will sing the good-ness of the Lord. For

ev-er I will sing the good-ness of the Lord.

Antiphon II*

Can - ta - ré, can-ta - ré e - ter - na - men - te

las mi - se - ri - cor - dias del Se - ñor.

Verses

1. I will sing forever of your mercies, O LORD;
   through all ages my mouth will proclaim your fidelity.
   I have declared your mercy is established forever;
   your fidelity stands firm as the heavens.

2. "With my chosen one I have made a covenant;
   I have sworn to David my servant:
   I will establish your descendants forever,
   and set up your throne through all ages."

3. How blessed the people who know your praise,
   who walk, O LORD, in the light of your face,
   who find their joy every day in your name,
   who make your justice their joyful acclaim.

4. For you are the glory of their strength;
   by your favor it is that our might is exalted.
   Behold, the LORD is our shield;
   he is the Holy One of Israel, our king.

5. "I have found my servant David,
   and with my holy oil anointed him.
   My hand shall always be with him,
   and my arm shall make him strong."

Antiphons I and II may be sung simultaneously.

6. "My mercy and my faithfulness shall be with him;
   by my name his might shall be exalted.
   He will call out to me, 'You are my father,
   my God, the rock of my salvation.'"

7. "He will call out to me, 'You are my father,
   my God, the rock of my salvation.'
   I will keep my faithful love for him always;
   with him my covenant shall last."

1. *Cantaré eternamente las misericordias del Señor,*
   anunciaré tu fidelidad por todas las edades.
   Porque dije: Tu misericordia es un edificio eterno,
   más que el cielo has afianzado tu fidelidad.

2. *"Sellé una alianza con mi elegido,*
   jurando a David, mi siervo:
   'Te fundaré un linaje perpetuo,
   edificaré tu trono para todas las edades.'"

3. *Dichoso el pueblo que sabe aclamarte:*
   caminará, oh Señor, a la luz de tu rostro;
   tu nombre es su gozo cada día,
   tu justicia es su orgullo.

4. *Porque tú eres su honor y su fuerza,*
   y con tu favor realzas nuestro poder.
   Porque el Señor es nuestro escudo,
   y el Santo de Israel nuestro rey.

5. *"Encontré a David, mi siervo,*
   y lo he ungido con óleo sagrado;
   para que mi mano esté siempre con él
   y mi brazo lo haga valeroso."

6. *"Mi fidelidad y misericordia lo acompañarán,*
   por mi nombre crecerá su poder.
   Él me invocará: 'Tú eres mi padre,
   mi Dios, mi Roca salvadora.'"

7. *"Él me invocará: 'Tú eres mi padre,*
   mi Dios, mi Roca salvadora.'
   Le mantendré eternamente mi favor,
   y mi alianza con él será estable."

Text: Psalm 89:2–3, 4–5, 16–17, 18–19, 21–22, 25 and 27, 27 and 29; English antiphon, *Lectionary for Mass*, © 1969, 1981, 1997, ICEL; verses, *The Revised Grail Psalms*, © 2010, Conception Abbey and The Grail, admin. by GIA Publication, Inc.; Spanish text, *Leccionario, Edición Hispanoamérica*, © 1970, 1972, Conferencia Episcopal Española
Music: Antiphons, Ronald F. Krisman, © 2004, GIA Publications, Inc.; verses, Michel Guimont, © 1994, 1998, GIA Publications, Inc.

67 Psalm 90

Antiphon I

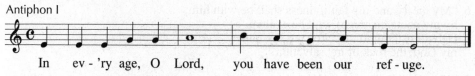

In ev - 'ry age, O Lord, you have been our ref - uge.

Text: *Lectionary for Mass,* © 1969, 1981, 1997, ICEL
Music: C. Alexander Peloquin, © 1975, GIA Publications, Inc.

Antiphon II

Fill us with your love, O Lord, and we will sing for joy!

Text: *Lectionary for Mass,* © 1969, 1981, 1997, ICEL
Music: Robert J. Batastini, © 1975, 1995, GIA Publications, Inc.

Conception Abbey Tone

Music: Gregory J. Polan, OSB, © 2010, Conception Abbey, admin. by GIA Publications, Inc.

Gelineau Tone

Music: Joseph Gelineau, SJ, © 1963, The Grail, GIA Publications, Inc., agent

Domine refugium factus es

1. O Lórd, yóu have been our réfuge,
   from generátion tó generátion.
   ² Befóre the móuntains were bórn,
   or the éarth or the wórld were brought fórth,
   you are Gód, from áge to áge.

2. ³ You túrn man báck to dúst,
   and say, "Retúrn, O chíldren of mén."
   ⁴ To your éyes a thóusand yéars
   are like yésterday, cóme and góne,
   or líke a wátch in the níght.

3. ⁵ You swéep them awáy like a dréam,
   like gráss which is frésh in the mórning.
   ⁶ In the mórning it spróuts and is frésh;
   by évening it wíthers and fádes.

4. ⁷ Indéed, we are consúmed by your ánger;
   we are strúck with térror at your fúry.
   ⁸ You have sét our guílt befóre you,
   our sécrets in the líght of your fáce.

5. [9] All our dáys pass awáy in your ánger.
Our yéars are consúmed like a sígh.
[10] Seventy yéars is the spán of our dáys,
or éighty if wé are stróng.
And móst of these are tóil and páin.
They pass swíftly and wé are góne.

6. [11] Who understánds the pówer of your ánger?
Your fúry mátches the féar of you.
[12] Then téach us to númber our dáys,
that wé may gain wísdom of héart.

7. [13] Turn báck, O LÓRD! How lóng?
Show píty tó your sérvants.
[14] At dawn, fíll us with your mérciful lóve;
we shall exúlt and rejóice all our dáys.
[15] Give us jóy for the dáys of our afflíction,
for the yéars when we lóoked upon évil.

8. [16] Let your déed be séen by your sérvants,
and your glórious pówer by their chíldren.
[17] Let the fávor of the Lórd our God be upón us;
give succéss to the wórk of our hánds.
O give succéss to the wórk of our hánds.

9. Give práise to the Fáther Almíghty,
to his Són, Jesus Chríst the Lórd,
to the Spírit who dwélls in our héarts,
both nów and for éver. Amén.

Text: Psalm 90; *The Revised Grail Psalms*; © 2010, Conception Abbey and The Grail, admin. by GIA Publications, Inc., agent

Psalm 91: Be with Me, Lord 68

Antiphon

Be with me, Lord, when I am in trou-ble, be with me, Lord, I   pray.

Verses

1. You who dwell in the shelter of the Lord, Most High,
   who abide in the shadow of our God,
   say to the Lord: "My refuge and fortress, the God in whom I trust."

2. No evil shall befall you, no pain come near,
   for the angels stand close by your side,
   guarding you always and bearing you gently, watching over your life.

3. Those who cling to the Lord live secure in God's love,
   lifted high, those who trust in God's name.
   Call on the Lord, who will never forsake you.
   God will bring you salvation and joy.

Text: Psalm 91:1-2, 10-11, 14-15; Marty Haugen
Music: Marty Haugen
© 1980, GIA Publications, Inc.

69 Psalm 91

Antiphon I

My ref-uge, my strong-hold, my God in whom I trust!

Text: The Grail
Music: A. Gregory Murray, OSB
© 1963, The Grail, GIA Publications, Inc., agent

Antiphon II

Call up - on the Lord and he will hear you.

Text: The Grail
Music: Joseph Gelineau, SJ
© 1963, The Grail, GIA Publications, Inc., agent

Antiphon III

Night holds no ter-rors for me sleep-ing un-der God's wings.

Text: *Liturgy of the Hours*, © 1974, ICEL
Music: Peter Hallock, acc. by Michael Connolly, © 1986, GIA Publications, Inc.

Antiphon IV

Be with me, Lord, when I am in trou - ble.

Text: *Lectionary for Mass*, © 1969, 1981, 1997, ICEL
Music: C. Alexander Peloquin, © 1975, GIA Publications, Inc.

Conception Abbey Tone

Music: Gregory J. Polan, OSB, © 2010, Conception Abbey, admin. by GIA Publications, Inc.

Gelineau Tone

Music: Joseph Gelineau, SJ, © 1963, The Grail, GIA Publications, Inc., agent

Qui habitat in adiutorio

1. ¹ He who dwélls in the shélter of the Most Hígh,
    and abídes in the sháde of the Almíghty,
    ² sáys to the LÓRD, "My réfuge,
    my strónghold, my Gód in whom I trúst!"

2. ³ He will frée you from the snáre of the fówler,
    fróm the destrúctive plágue;
    ⁴ hé will concéal you with his pínions,
    and únder his wíngs you will find réfuge.
    His fáithfulness is búckler and shíeld.

3. ⁵ You will not féar the térror of the níght,
    nor the árrow that flíes by dáy,
    ⁶ nor the plágue that prówls in the dárkness,
    nor the scóurge that lays wáste at nóon.

4. ⁷ A thóusand may fáll at your síde,
    ten thóusand fáll at your ríght:
    yóu it will néver appróach.

5. ⁸ Your éyes have ónly to lóok
    to sée how the wícked are repáid.
    ⁹ For yóu, O LÓRD, are my réfuge.
    You have máde the Most Hígh your dwélling.

6. ¹⁰ Upon yóu no évil shall fáll,
    no plágue appróach your tént.
    ¹¹ For yóu has he commánded his ángels
    to kéep you in áll your wáys.

7. ¹² They shall béar you upón their hánds,
    lest you stríke your fóot against a stóne.
    ¹³ On the líon and the víper you will tréad,
    and trámple the young líon and the sérpent.

8. ¹⁴ Since he clíngs to me in lóve, I will frée him,
    protéct him, for he knóws my náme.
    ¹⁵ When he cálls on mé, I will ánswer him;
    I will bé with hím in distréss;
    I will delíver him, and gíve him glóry.

9. ¹⁶ With léngth of dáys I will contént him;
    I will shów him my sáving pówer.
    To the Fáther, the Són and Holy Spírit
    give práise for éver. Amén.

Text: Psalm 91; *The Revised Grail Psalms*; © 2010, Conception Abbey and The Grail, admin. by GIA Publications, Inc., agent

70   Psalm 93

Antiphon I

The Lord is King for ev - er - more.

Text: Psalm 93; The Grail
Music: A. Gregory Murray, OSB
© 1963, The Grail, GIA Publications, Inc., agent

Antiphon II

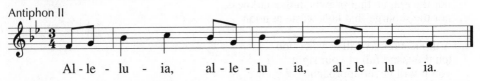

Al - le - lu - ia,   al - le - lu - ia,   al - le - lu - ia.

Music: A. Gregory Murray, OSB, © 1963, The Grail, GIA Publications, Inc., agent

Conception Abbey Tone

Music: Gregory J. Polan, OSB, © 2010, Conception Abbey, admin. by GIA Publications, Inc.

Gelineau Tone

Music: Joseph Gelineau, SJ, © 1963, The Grail, GIA Publications, Inc., agent

Dominus regnavit

1. [1] The LORD is kíng, with májesty enróbed.
   The LORD has róbed himsélf with míght;
   he has gírded himsélf with pówer.

2. The wórld you made fírm, not to be móved;
   [2] your thróne has stood fírm from of óld.
   From all etérnity, O LÓRD, you áre.

3. [3] The flóods have lífted up, O LÓRD,
   the flóods have lífted up their vóice;
   the flóods have lífted up their thúnder.

4. [4] Gréater than the róar of mighty wáters,
   more glórious than the súrgings of the séa,
   the LÓRD is glórious on hígh.

5. [5] Trúly your decrées are to be trústed.
   Hóliness is fítting to your hóuse,
   O LÓRD, until the énd of tíme.

6. Give glóry to the Fáther Almíghty,
   to his Són, Jesus Chríst the Lórd,
   to the Spírit who dwélls in our héarts.

Text: Psalm 93; *The Revised Grail Psalms*; © 2010, Conception Abbey and The Grail, admin. by GIA Publications, Inc., agent

Psalm 95: Let Us Come before the Lord   71

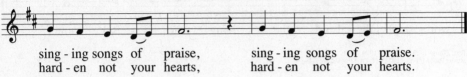

Antiphons I, II

I Let us   come   be - fore   the   Lord   our   God
II If   to - day   you   hear   the   voice   of   God,

sing - ing songs of   praise,   sing - ing songs of   praise.
hard - en not your hearts,   hard - en not your hearts.

Verses

1. O come, let us sing with joy before the Lord;
   let us acclaim the Rock of our salvation.
   Let us greet God with thanksgiving;
   with songs let us hail the Lord.

2. A great king is God, far greater than all gods;
   the depths of earth, the hills are in God's hands.
   To our maker belongs the sea;
   the dry land was shaped by God's hands.

3. O come, let us bow, bow down in worship;
   let us kneel before the Lord who made us.
   For the Lord is God and shepherd,
   and we are the sheep of God's flock.

4. O that today you would listen to God's voice:
   "Harden not your hearts as at Meribah and Massah,
   where your forebears tested me although they had seen my works."

Text: Psalm 95:1–2, 3–5, 6–7c, 7d–9; James J. Chepponis
Music: James J. Chepponis
© 2004, GIA Publications, Inc.

72   Psalm 95

Antiphon I: Advent

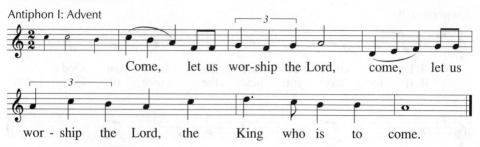

Come, let us wor-ship the Lord, come, let us
wor-ship the Lord, the King who is to come.

Text: *Liturgy of the Hours,* © 1974, ICEL
Music: Paul M. French, © 2011, GIA Publications, Inc.

Antiphon II: Christmas

Christ is born for us;
Christ is born for us; come, let us a-dore him.

Text: *Liturgy of the Hours,* © 1974, ICEL
Music: Paul M. French, © 2011, GIA Publications, Inc.

Antiphon III: Lent

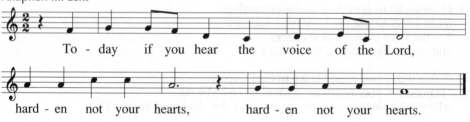

To-day if you hear the voice of the Lord,
hard-en not your hearts, hard-en not your hearts.

Text: *Liturgy of the Hours,* © 1974, ICEL
Music: Paul M. French, © 2011, GIA Publications, Inc.

Antiphon IV: Easter

The Lord is ris-en, the Lord is ris-en, al-le-
lu - ia, al-le-lu - ia.

Text: *Liturgy of the Hours,* © 1974, ICEL
Music: Paul M. French, © 2011, GIA Publications, Inc.

Antiphon V: General

Cry out with joy to the Lord, all the earth;

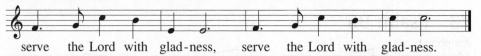

serve the Lord with glad-ness, serve the Lord with glad-ness.

Text: *Liturgy of the Hours,* © 1974, ICEL
Music: Paul M. French, © 2011, GIA Publications, Inc.

Antiphon VI: General

O come, let us wor - ship the Lord.

Text: The Grail
Music: Joseph Gelineau, SJ
© 1963, The Grail, GIA Publications, Inc., agent

Antiphon VII: General

Let us bow down be-fore the Lord, the God who made us.

Text: The Grail
Music: A. Gregory Murray, OSB
© 1963, The Grail, GIA Publications, Inc., agent

Conception Abbey Tone

Music: Gregory J. Polan, OSB, © 2010, Conception Abbey, admin. by GIA Publications, Inc.

Gelineau Tone

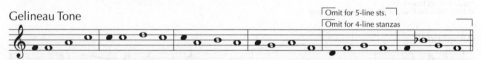

Music: Joseph Gelineau, SJ, © 1963, The Grail, GIA Publications, Inc., agent

Venite, exultemus

1. ¹Come, let us ríng out our jóy to the
   LÓRD;
   háil the róck who sáves us.
   ²Let us cóme into his présence, giving
   thánks;
   let us háil him with a sóng of práise.

2. ³A míghty Gód is the LÓRD,
   a great kíng abóve all góds.
   ⁴In his hánds are the dépths of the éarth;
   the héights of the móuntains are hís.
   ⁵To hím belongs the séa, for he máde it,
   and the drý land that he sháped by his
   hánds.

3. ⁶O cóme; let us bów and bend lów.
   Let us knéel before the Gód who máde
   us,
   ⁷for hé is our Gód and wé
   the péople who belóng to his pásture,
   the flóck that is léd by his hánd.

4. O that todáy you would lísten to his
   vóice!
   ⁸"Hárden not your héarts as at Méribah,
   as on that dáy at Mássah in the désert
   ⁹when your fórebears pút me to the tést;
   when they tríed me, though they sáw
   my wórk.

5. ¹⁰"For forty yéars I wearied of thát
   generátion,
   and I sáid, 'Their héarts are astráy;
   this péople does not knów my wáys.'
   ¹¹Thén I took an óath in my ánger,
   'Néver shall they énter my rést.'"

6. Give práise to the Fáther Almíghty,
   to his Són, Jesus Chríst the Lórd,
   to the Spírit who dwélls in our héarts,
   both nów and for éver. Amén.

Text: Psalm 95; *The Revised Grail Psalms;* © 2010, Conception Abbey and The Grail, admin. by GIA Publications, Inc., agent

73   Psalm 96

Antiphon I

Great is the Lord, wor-thy of praise; tell all the na-tions

"God is King"; spread the news of his love.

Text: Psalm 96:3–4; The Grail
Music: Joseph Gelineau, SJ
© 1963, The Grail, GIA Publications, Inc., agent

Antiphon II

Bring an of-fer-ing and en-ter God's courts:

in his tem - ple wor-ship the Lord.

Text: Psalm 96:6; The Grail
Music: Clifford Howell, SJ
© 1963, 1993, The Grail, GIA Publications, Inc., agent

Antiphon III

Pro - claim God's mar - vel-ous deeds to all the na - tions.

Text: *Lectionary for Mass,* © 1969, 1981, 1997, ICEL
Music: Randolph Currie, © 1986, GIA Publications, Inc.

Antiphon IV

Let heav-en re-joice and earth be glad: the Lord has come.

Text: *Simple Gradual,* 1968, ICEL
Music: A. Gregory Murray, OSB, © 1969, Geoffrey Chapman Ltd.

Antiphon V

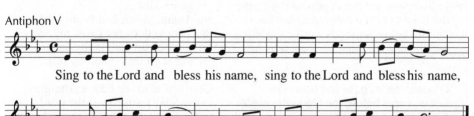

Sing to the Lord and bless his name, sing to the Lord and bless his name,

al - le - lu - ia. Al-le - lu - ia, al - le - lu - ia.

Text: *Simple Gradual,* 1968, ICEL
Music: Ronald F. Krisman, © 2011 GIA Publications, Inc.

Conception Abbey Tone

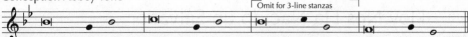

Omit for 3-line stanzas

Music: Gregory J. Polan, OSB, © 2010, Conception Abbey, admin. by GIA Publications, Inc.

Gelineau Tone

For 3-line stanzas

For 4-line stanzas

Music: Joseph Gelineau, SJ, © 1963, The Grail, GIA Publications, Inc., agent

Cantate Domino canticum novum, cantate

1. ¹ O síng a new sóng to the LÓRD;
   síng to the LÓRD, all the éarth.
   ² O síng to the LÓRD; bless his náme.

2. Procláim his salvátion day by dáy.
   ³ Téll among the nátions his glóry,
   and his wónders amóng all the péoples.

3. ⁴ For the LÓRD is great and híghly to
   be práised,
   to be féared abóve all góds.
   ⁵ For the góds of the nátions are náught.

4. It was the LÓRD who máde the
   héavens.
   ⁶ In his présence are májesty and
   spléndor,
   stréngth and hónor in his hóly place.

5. ⁷ Give the LÓRD, you fámilies of
   péoples,
   give the LÓRD glóry and pówer;
   ⁸ give the LÓRD the glóry of his náme.

6. Bring an óffering and énter his cóurts;
   ⁹ wórship the LÓRD in holy spléndor.
   O trémble befóre him, all the éarth.

7. ¹⁰ Say to the nátions, "The LÓRD is kíng."
   The wórld he made fírm in its pláce;
   he will júdge the péoples in fáirness.

8. ¹¹ Let the héavens rejóice and earth be
   glád;
   let the séa and all withín it thunder
   práise.
   ¹² Let the lánd and all it béars rejóice.
   Then will all the trées of the wóod
   shout for jóy.

9. ¹³ At the présence of the LÓRD, for he
   cómes,
   he cómes to júdge the éarth.
   He will júdge the wórld with jústice;
   he will góvern the péoples with his trúth.

10. Give práise to the Fáther Almíghty,
    to his Són, Jesus Chríst the Lórd,
    to the Spírit who dwélls in our héarts,
    both nów and for éver. Amén.

Text: Psalm 96; *The Revised Grail Psalms*; © 2010, Conception Abbey and The Grail, admin. by GIA Publications, Inc., agent

74   Psalm 96: Today Is Born Our Savior / Hoy Nos Ha Nacido un Salvador

Antiphon

To - day   is   born our   Sav - ior, Christ the   Lord.

Hoy   nos   ha na - ci - do un Sal - va - dor.   Born our

Sav - ior,   Christ the Lord.   *El Me - sí - as,   el Se - ñor.*

Verses

1. O sing a new song to the LORD;
   sing to the LORD, all the earth.
   O sing to the LORD; bless his name.

2. Proclaim his salvation day by day.
   Tell among the nations his glory,
   and his wonders among all the peoples.

3. Let the heavens rejoice and earth be glad;
   let the sea and all within it thunder praise.
   Let the land and all it bears rejoice.
   Then will all the trees of the wood shout for joy.

4. At the presence of the LORD, for he comes,
   he comes to judge the earth.
   He will judge the world with justice;
   he will govern the peoples with his truth.

1. *Canten al Señor un cántico nuevo,*
   canten al Señor, toda la tierra;
   canten al Señor, bendigan su nombre.

2. *Proclamen día tras día su victoria.*
   Cuenten a los pueblos su gloria,
   sus maravillas a todas las naciones.

3. *Alégrese el cielo, goce la tierra,*
   retumbe el mar y cuanto lo llena;
   vitoreen los campos y cuanto hay en ellos,
   aclamen los árboles del bosque.

4. *Delante del Señor, que ya llega,*
   ya llega a regir la tierra:
   regirá el orbe con justicia
   y los pueblos con fidelidad.

Text: Psalm 96:1–2a, 2b–3, 11–12, 13; English antiphon, *Lectionary for Mass*, © 1969, 1981, 1997, ICEL; verses, *The Revised Grail Psalms*, ©
2010, Conception Abbey and The Grail, admin. by GIA Publication, Inc.; Spanish text, *Leccionario, Edición Hispanoamérica*, © 1970, 1972,
Conferencia Episcopal Española
Music: Antiphon, Ronald F. Krisman, © 2004, GIA Publications, Inc.; verses, Michel Guimont, © 1994, 1998, GIA Publications, Inc.

Psalm 98: All the Ends of the Earth   75

Antiphon I

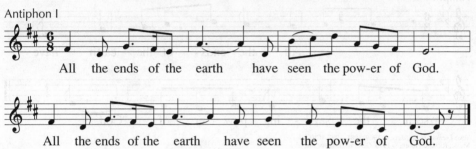

All the ends of the earth have seen the pow-er of God.

All the ends of the earth have seen the pow-er of God.

Antiphon II

Sing to the Lord a new song, for God has done won-der-ful deeds.

Sing to the Lord a new song, for God has done won-der-ful deeds.

Verses

1. Sing to the Lord a new song, for God has done wondrous deeds;
   whose right hand has won the victory for us, God's holy arm.

2. The Lord has made salvation known, and justice revealed to all,
   remembering kindness and faithfulness to Israel.

3. All of the ends of earth have seen salvation by our God.
   Joyfully sing out, all you lands; break forth in song.

4. Sing to the Lord with harp and song, with trumpet and with horn.
   Sing in your joy before the king, the king, our Lord.

Text: Psalm 98:1, 2–3b, 3c–4, 5–6; David Haas, Marty Haugen
Music: David Haas, Marty Haugen; antiphon II adapt. by Diana Kodner
© 1983, 1994, GIA Publications, Inc.

76 Psalm 98

Antiphon I

Sing a new song to the Lord, sing a new song to the Lord: praise him from the ends of the earth, al - le - lu - ia, al - le - lu - ia.

Text: *Simple Gradual*, © 1968, ICEL
Music: Ronald F. Krisman, © 2011, GIA Publications, Inc.

Antiphon II

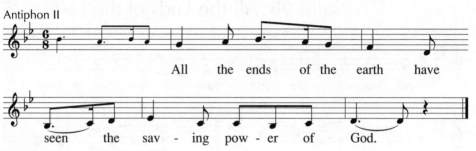

All the ends of the earth have seen the sav - ing pow - er of God.

Text: *Lectionary for Mass*, © 1969, 1981, 1997, ICEL
Music: Richard Proulx, © 1975, GIA Publications, Inc.

Conception Abbey Tone

Music: Gregory J. Polan, OSB, © 2010, Conception Abbey, admin. by GIA Publications, Inc.

Gelineau Tone

Music: Joseph Gelineau, SJ, © 1963, The Grail, GIA Publications, Inc., agent

Cantate Domino canticum novum, quia mirabilia

1. O síng a new sóng to the LÓRD,
   for hé has worked wónders.
   His right hánd and his hóly árm
   have bróught salvátion.

2. ² The LÓRD has made knówn his salvátion,
   has shówn his delíverance to the nátions.
   ³ He has remémbered his mérciful lóve
   and his trúth for the hóuse of Ísrael.

3. All the énds of the éarth have séen
   the salvátion of our Gód.
   ⁴ Shóut to the LÓRD, all the éarth;
   break fórth into jóyous sóng,
   and síng out your práise.

4. ⁵Sing psálms to the LÓRD with the hárp,
   with the hárp and the sóund of sóng.
   ⁶With trúmpets and the sóund of the hórn,
   raise a shóut before the Kíng, the LÓRD.

5. ⁷Let the séa and all withín it thúnder;
   the wórld, and thóse who dwéll in it.
   ⁸Let the rívers cláp their hánds,
   and the hílls ring out their jóy

6. ⁹At the présence of the LÓRD, for he cómes,
   he comes to júdge the éarth.
   He will júdge the wórld with jústice,
   and the péoples with fáirness.

7. Give práise to the Fáther Almíghty,
   to his Són, Jesus Chríst the Lórd,
   to the Spírit who dwélls in our héarts,
   both nów and for éver. Amén.

Text: Psalm 98; *The Revised Grail Psalms*; © 2010, Conception Abbey and The Grail, admin. by GIA Publications, Inc., agent

77   Psalm 100

Antiphon I

A - rise, come to your God, sing him your songs of re - joic - ing.

Text: Joseph Gelineau, SJ
Music: Joseph Gelineau, SJ
© 1963, The Grail, GIA Publications, Inc., agent

Antiphon II

Al - le - lu - ia,   al - le - lu - ia,   al - le - lu - ia.

Music: A. Gregory Murray, OSB, © 1963, The Grail, GIA Publications, Inc., agent

Conception Abbey Tone

Music: Gregory J. Polan, OSB, © 2010, Conception Abbey, admin. by GIA Publications, Inc.

Gelineau Tone

Music: Joseph Gelineau, SJ, © 1963, The Grail, GIA Publications, Inc., agent

Jubilate Deo

1. Cry out with jóy to the LORD, all the éarth.
   ² Sérve the LORD with gládness.
   Come befóre him, sínging for jóy.

2. ³ Know that hé, the LORD, is Gód.
   He máde us; we belóng to hím.
   We are his péople, the shéep of his flóck.

3. ⁴ Énter his gátes with thanksgíving
   and his cóurts with sóngs of práise.
   Give thánks to him, and bléss his náme.

4. ⁵ Indéed, how góod is the LORD,
   etérnal his mérciful lóve.
   He is fáithful from áge to áge.

5. Give práise to the Fáther Almíghty,
   to his Són, Jesus Chríst the Lórd,
   to the Spírit who dwélls in our héarts.

Text: Psalm 100; *The Revised Grail Psalms*, © 2010, Conception Abbey and The Grail, admin. by GIA Publications, Inc., agent

Psalm 100: We Are God's People   78

Ostinato Refrain

We are God's peo - ple, the flock of the Lord.

Verses

1. Cry out with joy to the Lord, all you lands, all you lands.
   Serve the Lord now with gladness, come before God singing for joy!

2. Know that the Lord is God! Know that the Lord is God,
   who made us, to God we belong, God's people, the sheep of the flock!

3. Go, now within the gates giving thanks, giving thanks.
   Enter the courts singing praise, give thanks and bless God's name!

4. Indeed, how good is the Lord, whose mercy endures for ever,
   for the Lord is faithful, is faithful from age to age!

Text: Psalm 100:1–2, 3, 4, 5; David Haas
Music: David Haas
© 1983, GIA Publications, Inc.

79 Psalm 103

Antiphon I

O bless the Lord, O bless the Lord, my soul.

Text: *Lectionary for Mass*, © 1969, 1981, 1997, ICEL
Music: John Schiavone, © 1986, GIA Publications, Inc.

Antiphon II

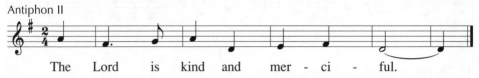

The Lord is kind and mer - ci - ful.

Text: *Lectionary for Mass*, © 1969, 1981, 1997, ICEL
Music: David Haas, © 1986, GIA Publications, Inc.

Antiphon III

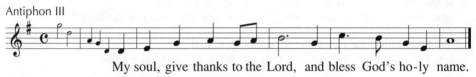

My soul, give thanks to the Lord, and bless God's ho-ly name.

Text: Psalm 103:1; © 1963, 1993, The Grail, GIA Publications, Inc., agent
Music: Richard Proulx, © 1975, GIA Publications, Inc.

Antiphon IV

The Lord is kind and mer - ci - ful,

slow to an - ger, and rich in com - pas - sion.

Text: *Lectionary for Mass*, © 1969, 1981, 1997, ICEL
Music: Norah Duncan IV, © 2011, GIA Publications, Inc.

Conception Abbey Tone

Music: Gregory J. Polan, OSB, © 2010, Conception Abbey, admin. by GIA Publications, Inc.

Gelineau Tone

Music: Joseph Gelineau, SJ, © 1963, The Grail, GIA Publications, Inc., agent

Benedic anima mea, et omnia

1. Bléss the LORD, O my sóul,
    and all withín me, his hóly náme.
   ² Bléss the LORD, O my sóul,
    and néver forgét all his bénefits.

2. ³It is the Lórd who forgíves all your
    síns,
  who héals every óne of your ílls,
  ⁴who redéems your lífe from the gráve,
  who crówns you with mércy and
    compássion,
  ⁵who fílls your life with good thíngs,
  renéwing your yóuth like an éagle's.

3. ⁶The LÓRD does júst déeds,
  gives full jústice to áll who are
    oppréssed.
  ⁷He made knówn his wáys to Móses,
  and his déeds to the chíldren of Ísrael.

4. ⁸The LÓRD is compássionate and
    grácious,
  slow to ánger and rích in mércy.
  ⁹Hé will not álways find fáult;
  nor persíst in his ánger foréver.
  ¹⁰He does not tréat us accórding to
    our síns,
  nor repáy us accórding to our fáults.

5. ¹¹For as the héavens are hígh above
    the éarth,
  so strong his mércy for thóse who
    féar him.
  ¹²As fár as the éast is from the wést,
  so far from ús does he remóve our
    transgréssions.

6. ¹³As a fáther has compássion on his
    chíldren,
  the LORD's compássion is on thóse who
    féar him.
  ¹⁴For he knóws of whát we are máde;
  he remémbers that wé are dúst.

7. ¹⁵Mán, his dáys are like gráss;
  he flówers like the flówer of the field.
  ¹⁶The wind blóws, and it ís no móre,
  and its pláce never sées it agáin.

8. ¹⁷But the mércy of the LÓRD is
    everlásting
  upon thóse who hóld him in féar,
  upon chíldren's chíldren his jústice,
  ¹⁸for thóse who kéep his cóvenant,
  and remémber to fulfíll his commánds.

9. ¹⁹The LÓRD has fixed his thróne in
    héaven,
  and his kíngdom is rúling over áll.
  ²⁰Bless the LÓRD, all yóu his ángels,
  mighty in pówer, fulfílling his wórd,
  who héed the vóice of his wórd.

10. ²¹Bléss the LÓRD, all his hósts,
  his sérvants, who dó his wíll.
  ²²Bléss the LÓRD, all his wórks,
  in évery pláce where he rúles.
  Bléss the LÓRD, O my sóul!

11. Give práise to the Fáther Almíghty,
  to his Són, Jesus Chríst the Lórd,
  to the Spírit who dwélls in our héarts,
  both nów and for éver. Amén.

Text: Psalm 103; *The Revised Grail Psalms*; © 2010, Conception Abbey and The Grail, admin. by GIA Publications, Inc., agent

80 Psalm 103: The Lord Is Kind and Merciful

Antiphon

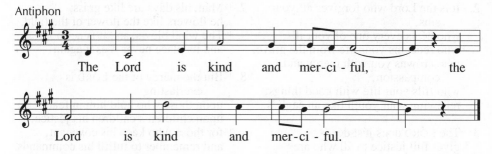

The Lord is kind and mer-ci - ful, the

Lord is kind and mer-ci - ful.

Verses

1. Bless the Lord, O my soul, and all my being bless God's name;
   bless the Lord, and forget not God's benefits.

2. God pardons all your iniquities, and comforts your sorrows,
   redeems your life from destruction and crowns you with kindness.

3. Merciful, merciful and gracious is our God;
   slow to anger, abounding in kindness.

Text: Psalm 103:1–2, 3–4, 8; para. by Marty Haugen, © 1983, GIA Publications, Inc.; antiphon, *Lectionary for Mass*, © 1969, 1981, 1997, ICEL
Music: Marty Haugen, © 1983, GIA Publications, Inc.

81 Psalm 104: Lord, Send Out Your Spirit on Us

Antiphon

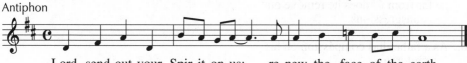

Lord, send out your Spir-it on us; re-new the face of the earth.

Verses

1. Bless the LORD, O my soul!
   O LORD my God, how great you are!
   How many are your works, O LORD!
   The earth is full of your creatures.

2. You take away their breath, they die,
   returning to the dust from which they came.
   You send forth your spirit, and they are created,
   and you renew the face of the earth.

3. May the glory of the LORD last forever!
   May the LORD rejoice in his works!
   May my thoughts be pleasing to him.
   I will rejoice in the LORD.

Text: Psalm 104:1, 24, 29–30, 31, 34, *The Revised Grail Psalms,* © 2010, Conception Abbey and The Grail, admin. GIA Publications, Inc.
Music: James J. Chepponis, © 1994, 2011, GIA Publications, Inc.

Psalm 104: Lord, Send Out Your Spirit 82

Antiphon

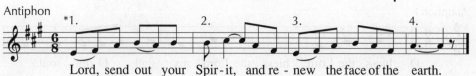

Lord, send out your Spir-it, and re-new the face of the earth.

Verses

1. Bless the Lord, O my soul; O Lord, my God, you are great indeed!
   How manifold are your works, O Lord! The earth is full of your creatures!

2. If you take away their breath, they die and they return to their dust.
   When you send forth your spirit of life, they are created in your sight!

3. May his glory last for all time; may the Lord be glad in his works.
   Pleasing to him will be my theme; I will be glad in the Lord!

May be sung as a canon.

Text: Psalm 104:1, 24, 29–30, 31, 34; Paul Lisicky, © 1985, GIA Publications, Inc.; antiphon, *Lectionary for Mass,* © 1969, 1981, 1997, ICEL
Music: Paul Lisicky, © 1985, GIA Publications, Inc.

83 Psalm 104

Antiphon I

O bless the Lord, bless the Lord, my soul, O my soul.

Text: *Lectionary for Mass,* © 1969, 1981, 1997, ICEL
Music: Robert J. Batastini, © 1998, GIA Publications, Inc.

Antiphon II

The whole world is filled with the Spir-it of the Lord, al-le - lu - ia.

Text: *Simple Gradual,* © 1968, ICEL
Music: John R. Ainslie, © 1969, Geoffrey Chapman Ltd.

Conception Abbey Tone

Music: Gregory J. Polan, OSB, © 2010, Conception Abbey, admin. by GIA Publications, Inc.

Gelineau Tone

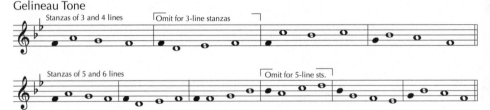

Music: Joseph Gelineau, SJ, © 1963, The Grail, GIA Publications, Inc., agent

Benedic anima mea Domino

1. ¹ Bléss the LÓRD, O my sóul!
   O LORD my Gód, how gréat you áre,
   clóthed in májesty and hónor,
   ² wrápped in líght as with a róbe!

2. You strétch out the héavens like a tént.
   ³ On the wáters you estáblish your
   dwélling.
   You máke the clóuds your cháriot;
   you ríde on the wíngs of the wínd.
   ⁴ You máke the wínds your méssengers,
   fláme and fíre your sérvants.

3. ⁵ You sét the éarth on its foundátion,
   immóvable from áge to áge.
   ⁶ You wrápped it with the dépths like a
   clóak;
   the wáters stood hígher than the
   móuntains.
   ⁷ At your thréat they tóok to flíght;
   at the vóice of your thúnder they fléd.

4. ⁸ The mountains róse, the válleys
   descénded,
   to the pláce which yóu had appóinted
   them.
   ⁹ You set límits they míght not páss,
   lest they retúrn to cóver the éarth.

5. ¹⁰ You make spríngs gush fórth in the
   válleys;
   they flów in betwéen the hílls.
   ¹¹ They give drínk to all the béasts of the
   fíeld;
   the wild ásses quénch their thírst.
   ¹² There the bírds of héaven build their
   nésts;
   from the bránches they síng their sóng.

6. ¹³ From your dwélling you wáter the hílls;
   by your wórks the éarth has its fíll.
   ¹⁴ You máke the grass grów for the cáttle
   and plánts to sérve mankind's néed.

7. That he may bríng forth bréad from
     the éarth
   [15] and wíne to chéer the héart;
   óil, to máke faces shíne,
   and bread to stréngthen the héart of
     mán.

8. [16] The trées of the LÓRD drink their fíll,
   the cédars he plánted on Lébanon;
   [17] thére the bírds build their nésts;
   on the tréetop the stórk has her hóme.
   [18] For the góats the lófty móuntains,
   for the rábbits the rócks are a réfuge.

9. [19] You made the móon to márk the
     mónths;
   the sún knows the tíme for its sétting.
   [20] You spréad the dárkness, it is níght,
   and all the béasts of the fórest creep
     fórth.
   [21] The young líons róar for their préy,
   and séek their fóod from Gód.

10. [22] At the rísing of the sún they gáther;
    and they gó to lie dówn in their déns.
    [23] Mán goes fórth to his wórk,
    to lábor till évening fálls.

11. [24] How mány are your wórks, O LÓRD!
    In wísdom you have máde them áll.
    The éarth is fúll of your créatures.

12. [25] Vast and wíde is the spán of the séa,
    with its créeping thíngs past cóunting,
    líving things gréat and smáll.
    [26] The shíps are móving thére,
    and Levíathan you máde to pláy with.

13. [27] Áll of these lóok to yóu
    to gíve them their fóod in due séason.
    [28] You gíve it, they gáther it úp;
    you ópen wide your hánd, they are
      well fílled.

14. [29] You híde your fáce, they are
      dismáyed;
    you táke away their bréath, they díe,
    retúrning to the dúst from which
      they cáme.
    [30] You send forth your spírit, and théy
      are creáted,
    and you renéw the fáce of the éarth.

15. [31] May the glóry of the LÓRD last
      foréver!
    May the LÓRD rejóice in his wórks!
    [32] He lóoks on the éarth and it trémbles;
    he tóuches the móuntains and they
      smóke.

16. [33] I will síng to the LÓRD all my lífe,
    sing psálms to my Gód while I líve.
    [34] May my thóughts be pléasing to hím.
    Í will rejóice in the LÓRD.

17. [35] Let sínners vánish from the éarth,
    and the wícked exíst no móre.
    Bléss the LÓRD, O my sóul.

18. Give práise to the Fáther Almíghty,
    to his Són, Jesus Chríst the Lórd,
    to the Spírit who dwélls in our héarts,
    both nów and for éver. Amén.

Text: Psalm 104; *The Revised Grail Psalms*; © 2010, Conception Abbey and The Grail, admin. by GIA Publications, Inc., agent

84 Psalm 110:1–5, 7

Antiphon I

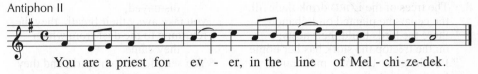

The Lord said to my lord: "Sit at my right hand."

Text: Psalm 110:1
Music: James J. Chepponis, © 2011, GIA Publications, Inc.

Antiphon II

You are a priest for ev - er, in the line of Mel - chi - ze - dek.

Text: *Lectionary for Mass*, © 1969, 1981, 1997, ICEL
Music: John Schiavone, © 1986, GIA Publications, Inc.

Conception Abbey Tone

Music: Gregory J. Polan, OSB, © 2010, Conception Abbey, admin. by GIA Publications, Inc.

Gelineau Tone

Music: Joseph Gelineau, SJ, © 1963, The Grail, GIA Publications, Inc., agent

Dixit Dominus

1. The LORD's revelátion to my lórd:
   "Sít at my right hánd,
   until I máke your fóes your fóotstool."

2. ² The LORD will sénd from Síon
   your scépter of pówer:
   rúle in the mídst of your fóes.

3. ³ With yóu is príncely rúle
   on the dáy of your pówer.
   In holy spléndor, from the wómb before the dáwn,
   Í have begótten yóu.

4. ⁴ The LORD has sworn an óath he will not chánge:
   "You áre a príest foréver,
   in the líne of Melchízedék."

5. ⁵ The Lórd, stánding at your ríght,
   shatters kíngs in the dáy of his wráth.

6. ⁷ He shall drínk from the stréam by the wáyside,
   and thérefore he shall líft up his héad.

7. To the Fáther and Són give práise,
   and tó the Holy Spírit,
   both nów and for éver. Amén.

Text: Psalm 110:1–5, 7; *The Revised Grail Psalms*; © 2010, Conception Abbey and The Grail, admin. by GIA Publications, Inc., agent

Antiphon

I thank you, Lord,   for your   faith - ful - ness and   love.

Text: The Grail, © 1963, The Grail, GIA Publications, Inc., agent
Music: Randolph Currie, © 1986, GIA Publications, Inc.

Conception Abbey Tone

Omit for 3-line stanzas

Music: Gregory J. Polan, OSB, © 2010, Conception Abbey, admin. by GIA Publications, Inc.

Gelineau Tone

Omit for 3-line stanzas

Music: Joseph Gelineau, SJ, © 1963, The Grail, GIA Publications, Inc., agent

Confitebor tibi

1. I will práise the LÓRD with all my
   héart,
   in the méeting of the júst and the
   assémbly.
   ² Gréat are the wórks of the LÓRD,
   to be póndered by áll who delíght in
   them.

2. ³ Majéstic and glórious his wórk;
   his jústice stands fírm foréver.
   ⁴ He has gíven us a memórial of his
   wónders.
   The LÓRD is grácious and mérciful.

3. ⁵ He gives fóod to thóse who féar him;
   keeps his cóvenant éver in mínd.
   ⁶ His mighty wórks he has shówn to his
   péople
   by gíving them the héritage of nátions.

4. ⁷ His hándiwork is jústice and trúth;
   his précepts are áll of them súre,
   ⁸ standing fírm foréver and éver,
   wróught in úprightness and trúth.

5. ⁹ He has sént redémption to his péople,
   and estáblished his cóvenant foréver.
   Hóly his náme, to be féared.

6. ¹⁰ The fear of the LÓRD is the begínning
   of wísdom;
   understánding marks áll who attáin it.
   His práise endúres foréver!

7. Give práise to the Fáther Almíghty,
   to his Són, Jesus Chríst the Lórd,
   to the Spírit who dwélls in our héarts,
   both nów and for éver. Amén.

Text: Psalm 111; *The Revised Grail Psalms*; © 2010, Conception Abbey and The Grail, admin. by GIA Publications, Inc., agent

86   Psalm 112

Antiphon

Hap-py   are those   who   do   what the Lord   com - mands.

Text: *Lectionary for Mass,* © 1969, 1981, 1997, ICEL
Music: Ronald F. Krisman and Kelly Dobbs-Mickus, © 2011, GIA Publications, Inc.

Conception Abbey Tone

Music: Gregory J. Polan, OSB, © 2010, Conception Abbey, admin. by GIA Publications, Inc.

Gelineau Tone

Music: Joseph Gelineau, SJ, © 1963, The Grail, GIA Publications, Inc., agent

Beatus vir qui timet

1. Bléssed the mán who fears the LORD,
   who tákes great delíght in his
      commándments.
   2 His descéndants shall be pówerful
   on éarth;
   the generátion of the úpright will be
      blést.

2. 3 Ríches and wéalth are in his hóuse;
   his jústice stands fírm foréver.
   4 A light ríses in the dárkness for the
      úpright;
   he is génerous, mérciful, and júst.

3. 5 Ít goes wéll for the mán
   who déals génerously and lénds,
   who condúcts his affáirs with jústice.
   6 Hé will néver be móved;
   foréver shall the júst be remémbered.

4. 7 He hás no féar of evil néws;
   with a fírm heart, he trústs in the
      LORD.
   8 With a stéadfast héart he will not féar;
   he will sée the dównfall of his fóes.

5. 9 Open-hánded, he gíves to the póor;
   his jústice stands fírm foréver.
   His míght shall be exálted in glóry.

6. 10 The wícked sées and is ángry,
   grinds his téeth and fádes awáy;
   the desíre of the wícked leads to
      dóom.

7. Give práise to the Fáther Almíghty,
   to his Són, Jesus Chríst the Lórd,
   to the Spírit who dwélls in our héarts,
   both nów and for éver. Amén.

Text: Psalm 112; *The Revised Grail Psalms;* © 2010, Conception Abbey and The Grail, admin. by GIA Publications, Inc., agent

87   Psalm 113: Sit Nomen Dómini

Ostinato Refrain

Sit   no - men   Dó - mi - ni   sit   be - ne - dí - ctum.
Now and for - ev - er-more God's   name be ex - alt - ed.

Nunc   et   in   saé - cu - la   be - ne - dí - ctum.
Praised be   God's   ho - ly name,   Al - le - lu - ia.

Text: Psalm 113:1–2, 3, 4–5, 6–7; Taizé Community
Music: Taizé Community
© 2007, Les Presses de Taizé, GIA Publications, Inc., agent

Psalm 114   88

Antiphon

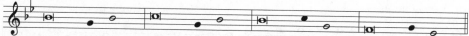

God has freed us and re-deemed us with his might - y   arm.

Text: The Grail, © 1963, The Grail, GIA Publications, Inc., agent
Music: Richard Proulx, © 1986, GIA Publications, Inc.

Conception Abbey Tone

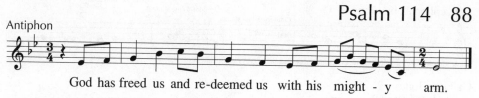

Music: Gregory J. Polan, OSB, © 2010, Conception Abbey, admin. by GIA Publications, Inc.

Gelineau Tone

Music: Joseph Gelineau, SJ, © 1963, The Grail, GIA Publications, Inc., agent

In exitu Israel

1. When Ísrael came fórth from Égypt,
   the house of Jácob from a fóreign
      péople,
   [2] Júdah becáme his témple,
   Ísrael becáme his domáin.

2. [3] The séa behéld them and fléd;
   the Jórdan turned báck on its cóurse.
   [4] The móuntans léapt like ráms,
   and the hílls like yéarling shéep.

3. [5] Whý was it, séa, that you fléd;
   that you túrned back, Jórdan, on your
      cóurse?
   [6] O móuntains, that you léapt like ráms;
   O hílls, like yéarling shéep?

4. [7] Trémble, O éarth, before the Lórd,
   in the présence of the Gód of Jácob,
   [8] who túrns the róck into a póol,
   and flínt into a spríng of wáter.

5. Give práise to the Fáther Almíghty,
   to his Són, Jesus Chríst the Lórd,
   to the Spírit who dwélls in our héarts,
   both nów and for éver. Amén.

Text: Psalm 114; *The Revised Grail Psalms*; © 2010, Conception Abbey and The Grail, admin. by GIA Publications, Inc., agent

89 Psalm 115

Antiphon

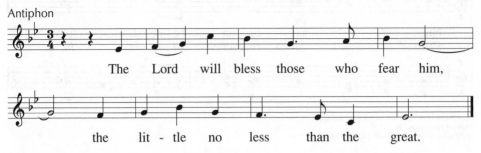

The Lord will bless those who fear him, the lit - tle no less than the great.

Text: Psalm 115:13; The Grail, © 1963, The Grail, GIA Publications, Inc., agent
Music: Richard Proulx, © 1986, GIA Publications, Inc.

Conception Abbey Tone

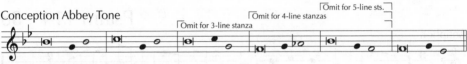

Omit for 5-line sts.
Omit for 4-line stanzas
Omit for 3-line stanza

Music: Gregory J. Polan, OSB, © 2010, Conception Abbey, admin. by GIA Publications, Inc.

Gelineau Tone

For 3- and 4-line stanzas

Omit for 3-line stanza

(St. 8)   (St. 8)

For 5- and 6-line stanzas

Omit for 5-line sts.

Music: Joseph Gelineau, SJ, © 1963, The Grail, GIA Publications, Inc., agent

Non nobis Domine

1. ¹ Not to ús, O LÓRD, not to ús,
   but to yóur name gíve the glory,
   for your mérciful lóve and fidélity.
   ² Whý should the nátions sáy:
   "Whére ís their Gód?"

2. ³ But our Gód is ín the héavens;
   he dóes whatéver he wílls.
   ⁴ Their ídols are sílver and góld,
   the wórk of húman hánds.

3. ⁵ They have móuths but they cánnot spéak;
   they have éyes but they cánnot sée.
   ⁶ They have éars but they cánnot héar;
   they have nóstrils but they cánnot sméll.

4. ⁷ They have hánds but they cánnot féel;
   they have féet but they cánnot wálk.
   They máke no sóund from their thróats.
   ⁸ Their mákers will cóme to be líke them,
   as will áll who trúst in thém.

5. [9]House of Ísrael, trúst in the LORD;
   hé is their hélp and their shíeld.
   [10]House of Áaron, trúst in the LORD;
   hé is their hélp and their shíeld.
   [11]Those who féar the LORD, trúst in the LORD;
   hé is their hélp and their shíeld.

6. [12]The LORD remémbers us, and hé will bléss us;
   he will bléss the hóuse of Ísrael.
   He will bléss the hóuse of Áaron.

7. [13]He will bléss those who féar the LORD,
   the líttle no léss than the gréat.
   [14]To yóu may the LORD grant íncrease,
   to yóu and áll your chíldren.

8. [15]Máy you be blést by the LORD,
   the máker of héaven and éarth.
   [16]The héavens, the héavens belóng to the LORD,
   but to the chíldren of mén, he has gíven the éarth.

9. [17]The déad shall not práise the LORD,
   nor thóse who go dówn into the sílence.
   [18]But wé who líve bless the LORD
   both nów and forévermóre.

10. Give práise to the Fáther Almíghty,
    to his Són, Jesus Chríst the Lórd,
    to the Spírit who dwélls in our héarts,
    both nów and for éver. Amén.

90 Psalm 116

Antiphon I

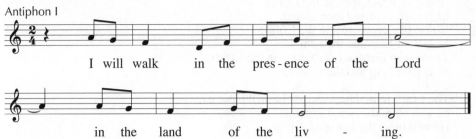

I will walk in the pres-ence of the Lord in the land of the liv - ing.

Text: Psalm 116:9; The Grail, © 1963, The Grail, GIA Publications, Inc., agent
Music: Richard Proulx, © 1975, GIA Publications, Inc.

Antiphons II, III

II How can I re-pay the Lord for his good-ness to me?
III Pre-cious in the eyes of the Lord is the death of his friends.

Text: Psalm 116:12, 15; The Grail
Music: A. Gregory Murray, OSB
© 1963, The Grail, GIA Publications, Inc., agent

Conception Abbey Tone

Music: Gregory J. Polan, OSB, © 2010, Conception Abbey, admin. by GIA Publications, Inc.

Gelineau Tone

Music: Joseph Gelineau, SJ, © 1963, The Grail, GIA Publications, Inc., agent

Dilexi

1. ¹I lóve the LORD, for he has héard
   my vóice, my appéal;
   ²for he has túrned his éar to mé
   whenéver I cáll.

2. ³They surróunded me, the snáres of déath;
   the ánguish of the gráve has fóund me;
   ánguish and sórrow I fóund.
   ⁴I cálled on the náme of the LORD:
   "Delíver my sóul, O LORD!"

3. ⁵ How grácious is the LORD, and júst;
   our Gód has compássion.
   ⁶ The LORD protécts the símple;
   I was brought lów, and he sáved mé.

4. ⁷ Turn báck, my sóul, to your rést,
   for the LORD has been góod to yóu;
   ⁸ he has képt my sóul from déath,
   my eyes from téars, and my féet from stúmbling.

5. ⁹ I will wálk in the présence of the LORD
   in the lánd of the lívíng.

6. ¹⁰ I trústed, éven when I sáid,
   "I am sórely afflícted,"
   ¹¹ and whén I sáid in my alárm,
   "These péople are all líárs."

7. ¹² How cán I repáy the LORD
   for áll his góodness to mé?
   ¹³ The cúp of salvátion I will ráise;
   I will cáll on the náme of the LORD.
   ¹⁴ My vóws to the LORD I will fulfíll
   befóre all his péoplé.

8. ¹⁵ How précious in the éyes of the LORD
   is the déath of his fáithful.
   ¹⁶ Your sérvant, LORD, your sérvant am Í,
   the són óf your hándmaid;
   you have lóosened my <u>bónds</u>.

9. ¹⁷ A thánksgiving sácrifice I máke;
   I will cáll on the náme of the LORD.
   ¹⁸ My vóws to the LORD I will fulfíll
   befóre all his péoplé,
   ¹⁹ in the cóurts of the hóuse of the LORD,
   in your mídst, O Jerúsalém.

10. Praise the Fáther, the Són, and Holy Spírit,
    both nów and for éver,
    the God who ís, who wás and is to cóme
    at the énd of the áges.

Text: Psalm 116; *The Revised Grail Psalms*; © 2010, Conception Abbey and The Grail, admin. by GIA Publications, Inc., agent

91 Psalm 116: Our Blessing-Cup / El Cáliz Que Bendecimos

Antiphon I*

Our bless-ing-cup is a com-mun-ion with the Blood of Christ. Our bless-ing-cup is a com-mun-ion with the Blood of Christ.

Antiphon II*

El cá-liz que ben-de-ci-mos es la co-mu-nión de la san-gre de Cris-to. El cá-liz que ben-de-ci-mos es la co-mu-nión de la san-gre de Cris-to.

Verses

1. How can I repay the LORD
for all his goodness to me?
The cup of salvation I will raise;
I will call on the name of the LORD.

2. How precious in the eyes of the LORD
is the death of his faithful.
Your servant, LORD, your servant am I,
the son of your handmaid;
you have loosened my bonds.

3. A thanksgiving sacrifice I make;
I will call on the name of the LORD.
My vows to the LORD I will fulfill
before all his people.

1. *¿Cómo pagaré al Señor
todo el bien que me ha hecho?
Alzaré la copa de la salvación,
invocando su nombre.*

2. *Mucho le cuesta al Señor
la muerte de sus fieles.
Señor, yo soy tu siervo, hijo de
tu esclava:
rompiste mis cadenas.*

3. *Te ofreceré un sacrificio
de alabanza,
invocando tu nombre, Señor.
Cumpliré al Señor mis votos
en presencia de todo el pueblo.*

For a bilingual setting, sing the first half of the antiphon in one language, followed by the second half in the other.

Text: Psalm 116:12–13, 15–16, 17–18; English antiphon, *Lectionary for Mass*, © 1969, 1981, 1997, ICEL; verses, *The Revised Grail Psalms*, © 2010, Conception Abbey and The Grail, admin. by GIA Publication, Inc.; Spanish text, *Leccionario, Edición Hispanoamérica*, © 1970, 1972, Conferencia Episcopal Española
Music: Antiphons, Ronald F. Krisman, © 2004, GIA Publications, Inc.; verses, Michel Guimont, © 1994, 1998, GIA Publications, Inc.

Psalm 118: Let Us Rejoice   92

Antiphon

This is the day   the Lord has   made;   let   us re-
Or: Al - le - lu - ia,   al - le - lu - ia!   Al   - le -

joice and be   glad.   This is the   day   the Lord has
lu   -   ia!   Al - le - lu - ia,   al - le - lu -

made;   let   us re - joice and be   glad.
ia!   Al   - le - lu   -   ia!

Verses

1. Give thanks to the Lord, for God is good; God's mercy endures for ever.
   Let the house of Israel say: "God's mercy endures for ever."

2. The hand of the Lord has struck with power; God's right hand is exalted.
   I shall not die, but live anew, declaring the works of the Lord.

3. The stone which the builders rejected has become the cornerstone.
   The Lord of love and mercy has brought wonder to our eyes!

Text: Psalm 118:1–2, 16–17, 22–23; Marty Haugen, © 1983, GIA Publications, Inc.; antiphon, *Lectionary for Mass,* © 1969, 1981, 1997, ICEL
Music: Marty Haugen, © 1983, GIA Publications, Inc.

Psalm 118: This Is the Day   93

Antiphon

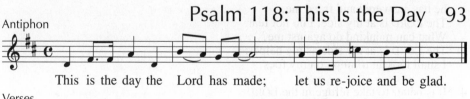

This is the day the   Lord has made;   let us re-joice and be glad.

Verses

1. Give praise to the LORD, for he is good;
   his mercy endures forever.
   Let the house of Israel say,
   "His mercy endures forever."

2. "The LORD's right hand has done
      mighty deeds;
   his right hand is exalted."
   I shall not die, I shall live
   and recount the deeds of the LORD.

3. The stone that the builders rejected
   has become the cornerstone.
   By the LORD has this been done,
   a marvel in our eyes.

Text: Psalm 118:1–2, 16–17, 22–23, *The Revised Grail Psalms,* © 2010, Conception Abbey and The Grail, admin. GIA Publications, Inc.;
   antiphon, *Lectionary for Mass,* © 1969, 1981, 1997, ICEL
Music: James J. Chepponis, © 1994, 2011, GIA Publications, Inc.

94 Psalm 118

Antiphon

Give thanks to the Lord for he is good, his love is ev-er-last-ing.

Text: *Lectionary for Mass,* © 1969, 1981, 1997, ICEL
Music: Chrysogonus Waddell, OCSO, © 1986, GIA Publications, Inc.

Conception Abbey Tone

Music: Gregory J. Polan, OSB, © 2010, Conception Abbey, admin. by GIA Publications, Inc.

Gelineau Tone

Music: Joseph Gelineau, SJ, © 1963, The Grail, GIA Publications, Inc., agent

Confitemini Domino

1. ¹ Give práise to the LÓRD, for he is góod;
    his mércy endúres foréver.

2. ² Let the hóuse of Ísrael sáy,
    "His mércy endúres foréver."
    ³ Let the hóuse of Áaron sáy,
    "His mércy endúres foréver."
    ⁴ Let thóse who féar the LORD sáy,
    "His mércy endúres foréver."

3. ⁵ I cálled to the LÓRD in my distréss;
    he has ánswered and fréed me.
    ⁶ The LÓRD is at my síde; I do not féar.
    What can mánkind do agáinst me?
    ⁷ The LÓRD is at my síde as my hélper;
    I shall lóok in tríumph on my fóes.

4. ⁸ It is bétter to take réfuge in the LÓRD
    than to trúst in mán;
    ⁹ it is bétter to take réfuge in the LÓRD
    than to trúst in prínces.

5. ¹⁰ The nátions áll encírcled me;
    in the náme of the LÓRD I cut them óff.
    ¹¹ They encírcled me áll aróund;
    in the náme of the LÓRD I cut them óff.
    ¹² They encírcled me abóut like bées;
    they blázed like a fíre among thórns.
    In the náme of the LÓRD I cut them óff.

6. [13] I was thrust dówn, thrust dówn and fálling,
    but the LÓRD was my hélper.
  [14] The LÓRD is my stréngth and my sóng;
    hé was my sávior.
  [15] There are shóuts of jóy and salvátion
    in the ténts of the júst.

7.   "The LORD's right hánd has done míghty déeds;
  [16] his ríght hand is exálted.
    The LÓRD's ríght hánd
    has done míghty déeds."
  [17] I shall not díe, I shall líve
    and recóunt the déeds of the LÓRD.

8. [18] The LORD púnished me, púnished me sevérely,
    but did nót hand me óver to déath.

9. [19] Open to mé the gátes of jústice:
    I will énter and thánk the LÓRD.
  [20] Thís is the LÓRD's own gáte,
    where the júst énter.
  [21] I will thánk you, for yóu have ánswered,
    and yóu are my sávior.

10. [22] The stóne that the buílders rejécted
    has becóme the córnerstone.
  [23] By the LÓRD has thís been dóne,
    a márvel in our éyes.
  [24] This is the dáy the LÓRD has máde;
    let us rejóice in ít and be glád.

11. [25] O LÓRD, gránt salvátion;
    O LÓRD, grant succéss.
  [26] Blést is hé who cómes
    in the náme of the LÓRD.
    We bléss you from the hóuse of the LÓRD;
  [27] the LORD is Gód, and has gíven us líght.

12.   Go fórward in procéssion with bránches,
    as fár as the hórns of the áltar.
  [28] Yóu are my Gód, I práise you.
    My Gód, I exált you.
  [29] Give práise to the LÓRD, for he is góod;
    his mércy endúres foréver.

13.   Praise the Fáther, the Són and Holy Spírit,
    both nów and for éver,
    the God who ís, who wás, and who wíll be,
    wórld without énd.

95 Psalm 121

Antiphon

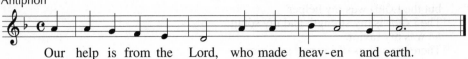

Our help is from the Lord, who made heav-en and earth.

Text: *Lectionary for Mass,* © 1969, 1981, 1997, ICEL
Music: John Schiavone, © 1975, GIA Publications, Inc.

Conception Abbey Tone

Music: Gregory J. Polan, OSB, © 2010, Conception Abbey, admin. by GIA Publications, Inc.

Gelineau Tone

Music: Joseph Gelineau, SJ, © 1963, The Grail, GIA Publications, Inc., agent

Levavi oculos meos

1. I líft up my éyes to the móuntains;
   from whére shall come my hélp?
   ²My hélp shall cóme from the LÓRD,
   who made héaven and éarth.

2. ³He will kéep your fóot from stúmbling.
   Your guárd will never slúmber.
   ⁴Nó, he sléeps not nor slúmbers,
   Ísrael's guárd.

3. ⁵The LORD your guárd, the LÓRD your sháde
   at yóur right hánd.
   ⁶By dáy the sún shall not smíte you,
   nor the móon in the níght.

4. ⁷The LÓRD will guárd you from évil;
   he will guárd your sóul.
   ⁸The LORD will guárd your góing and cóming,
   both nów and foréver.

5. Praise the Fáther, the Són and Holy Spírit,
   both nów and for éver,
   the God who ís, who wás and who wíll be,
   wórld without énd.

Text: Psalm 121; *The Revised Grail Psalms*; © 2010, Conception Abbey and The Grail, admin. by GIA Publications, Inc., agent

Psalm 122: Let Us Go Rejoicing 96

Antiphon

Let us go re - joic-ing to the house of the Lord.

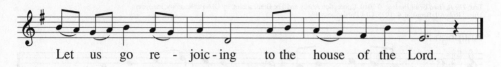

Let us go re - joic-ing to the house of the Lord.

Verses

1. I rejoiced when I heard them say: "Let us go to the house of the Lord."
   And now our feet are standing within your gates, O Jerusalem.

2. Jerusalem is a city built with unity and strength.
   It is there, it is there that the tribes go up, the tribes of the Lord.

3. For Israel's law is to praise God's name and there to give God thanks.
   There are set the judgment thrones for all of David's house.

4. Pray for the peace of Jerusalem! "May those who love you prosper.
   May peace ever reign within your walls, and wealth within your buildings!"

5. For love of my family and love of my friends, I pray that peace be yours.
   For love of the house of the Lord our God I pray for your good.

Text: Psalm 122; Michael Joncas, © 1987, GIA Publications, Inc.; antiphon, *Lectionary for Mass*, © 1969, 1981, 1997, ICEL
Music: Michael Joncas, © 1987, GIA Publications, Inc.

97 Psalm 122

Antiphon I

I re-joiced when they said to me, "Let us go to the house of the Lord."

Text: *The Revised Grail Psalms*; © 2010, Conception Abbey and The Grail, admin. by GIA Publications, Inc., agent
Music: Robert J. Batastini, © 1975, GIA Publications, Inc.

Antiphon II

We shall go up with joy to the house of our God.

Text: Psalm 122; The Grail
Music: A. Gregory Murray, OSB
© 1963, The Grail, GIA Publications, Inc., agent

Antiphon III

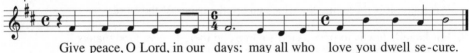

Give peace, O Lord, in our days; may all who love you dwell se-cure.

Text: *Simple Gradual*, © 1968, ICEL
Music: Clifford Howell, SJ, © 1969, Geoffrey Chapman Ltd.

Conception Abbey Tone

Music: Gregory J. Polan, OSB, © 2010, Conception Abbey, admin. by GIA Publications, Inc.

Gelineau Tone

(St. 5)

Music: Joseph Gelineau, SJ, © 1963, The Grail, GIA Publications, Inc., agent

Laetatus sum

1. I rejoiced when they sáid to mé,
   "Let us gó to the hóuse of the LORD."
   ²And nów our féet are stánding
   withín your gátes, O Jerúsalem.

2. ³Jerúsalem is buílt as a cíty
   bónded as óne togéther.
   ⁴It is thére that the tríbes go úp,
   the tríbes óf the LORD.

3. For Ísrael's wítness it ís
   to práise the náme of the LORD.
   ⁵Thére were set the thrónes for
   júdgment,
   the thrónes of the hóuse of Dávid.

4. ⁶For the péace of Jerúsalem práy,
   "May they prósper, thóse who lóve you."
   ⁷May péace abíde in your wálls,
   and secúrity bé in your tówers.

5. ⁸For the sáke of my fámily and fríends,
   let me sáy, "Péace upon yóu."
   ⁹For the sáke of the hóuse of the LORD,
   our Gód,
   I will séek good thíngs for yóu.

6. Praise the Fáther, the Són and Holy Spírit,
   both nów ánd for éver,
   the God who ís, who wás and is to cóme
   át the énd of the áges.

Text: Psalm 122; *The Revised Grail Psalms*; © 2010, Conception Abbey and The Grail, admin. by GIA Publications, Inc., agent

Psalm 123 98

Antiphon

Our eyes are fixed on the Lord, plead-ing for his mer-cy.

Text: *Lectionary for Mass*, © 1969, 1981, 1997, ICEL
Music: James J. Chepponis, © 2011, GIA Publications, Inc.

Conception Abbey Tone

Omit for 4-line stanzas

Music: Gregory J. Polan, OSB, © 2010, Conception Abbey, admin. by GIA Publications, Inc.

Gelineau Tone

Repeat for 5-line stanza

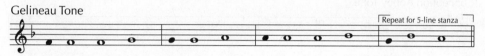

Music: Joseph Gelineau, SJ, © 1963, The Grail, GIA Publications, Inc., agent

Ad te levavi oculos meos

1. To yóu have I lífted up my éyes,
   you who dwéll in the héavens.
   ² Behóld, like the éyes of sláves
   on the hánd of their lórds,

2. Líke the éyes of a sérvant
   on the hánd of her místress,
   so our éyes are on the LÓRD our Gód,
   till he shów us his mércy.

3. ³ Have mércy on us, LÓRD, have mércy.
   We are fílled with contémpt.
   ⁴ Indéed, all too fúll is our sóul
   with the scórn of the árrogant,
   the disdáin of the próud.

4. Praise the Fáther, the Són and Holy Spírit,
   both nów and for éver,
   the God who ís, who wás and who wíll be,
   wórld without énd.

Text: Psalm 123; *The Revised Grail Psalms*; © 2010, Conception Abbey and The Grail, admin. by GIA Publications, Inc., agent

99 Psalm 126

Antiphon

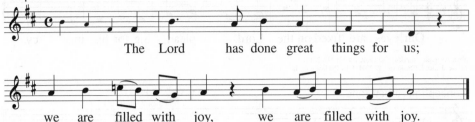

The Lord has done great things for us; we are filled with joy, we are filled with joy.

Text: *Lectionary for Mass*, © 1969, 1981, 1997, ICEL
Music: Richard Proulx, © 1975, GIA Publications, Inc.

Conception Abbey Tone

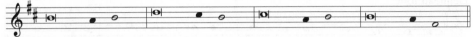

Music: Gregory J. Polan, OSB, © 2010, Conception Abbey, admin. by GIA Publications, Inc.

Gelineau Tone

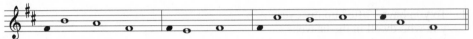

Music: Joseph Gelineau, SJ, © 1963, The Grail, GIA Publications, Inc., agent

In convertendo

1. When the LORD brought back the éxiles of Síon,
   we thóught we were dréaming.
   ² Thén was our móuth filled with láughter;
   on our tóngues, songs of jóy.

2. Then the nátions themsélves said, "What great déeds
   the LORD worked for thém!"
   ³ What great déeds the LORD worked for ús!
   Indéed, we were glád.

3. ⁴ Bring báck our éxiles, O LORD,
   as stréams in the sóuth.
   ⁵ Thóse who are sówing in téars
   will síng when they réap.

4. ⁶ They go óut, they go óut, full of téars,
   bearing séed for the sówing;
   they come báck, they come báck with a sóng,
   béaring their shéaves.

5. Praise the Fáther, the Són and Holy Spírit,
   both nów and for éver,
   the God who ís, who wás and who wíll be,
   wórld without énd.

Text: Psalm 126; *The Revised Grail Psalms*; © 2010, Conception Abbey and The Grail, admin. by GIA Publications, Inc., agent

Antiphon

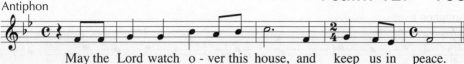

May the Lord watch o - ver this house, and keep us in peace.

Text: The Grail
Music: A. Gregory Murray, OSB
© 1963, The Grail, GIA Publications, Inc., agent

Conception Abbey Tone

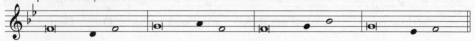

Music: Gregory J. Polan, OSB, © 2010, Conception Abbey, admin. by GIA Publications, Inc.

Gelineau Tone

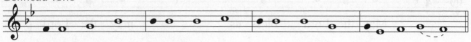

Music: Joseph Gelineau, SJ, © 1963, The Grail, GIA Publications, Inc., agent

Nisi Dominus

1. If the LORD does not build the house,
   in vain do its builders labor;
   if the LORD does not guard the city,
   in vain does the guard keep <u>watch</u>.

2. ² In vain is your earlier rising,
   your going later to rest,
   you who toil for the bread you eat,
   when he pours gifts on his beloved while they slumber.

3. ³ Yes, children are a gift from the LORD,
   a blessing, the fruit of the womb.
   ⁴ Indeed, the sons of youth
   are like arrows in the hand of a warrior.

4. ⁵ Blessed is the warrior
   who has filled his quiver with these arrows!
   He will have no cause for shame,
   when he disputes with his foes in the gateways.

5. Give praise to the Father Almighty,
   to his Son, Jesus Christ the Lord,
   to the Spirit who dwells in our hearts,
   both now and for ever. Amen.

Text: Psalm 127; *The Revised Grail Psalms*; © 2010, Conception Abbey and The Grail, admin. by GIA Publications, Inc., agent

101   Psalm 128: Blest Are Those Who Love You

Antiphon I

Blest are those who love you, hap - py those who
fol-low you, blest are those who seek you, O God.

Antiphon II

May the Lord bless us, may the Lord pro -
tect us, all the days, all the days of our life.

Verses

1. Happy all those who fear the Lord, and walk in God's pathway;
   you will find what you long for: the riches of our God.

2. Your spouse shall be like a fruitful vine in the midst of your home,
   your children flourish like olive plants rejoicing at your table.

3. May the blessings of God be yours all the days of your life,
   may the peace and the love of God live always in your heart.

Text: Psalm 128:1–2, 3, 5; Marty Haugen
Music: Marty Haugen; antiphon II adapt. by Diana Kodner
© 1987, 1993, GIA Publications, Inc.

Psalm 130: With the Lord There Is Mercy   102

Antiphon

With the Lord there is mer - cy and the
full - ness of re - demp - tion, call to him in your
tri - als, he will an - swer when - ev - er you call.

Verses

1. Out of the depths I cry to you,
   I cry to you, O Lord.
   Lord, open your ears and hear my voice,
   attend to the sound of my plea.

2. If you, O Lord, should mark our guilt,
   then, Lord, who could hope to survive?
   But with you is found forgiveness of sin,
   and mercy that we might revere you.

3. Trust in the Lord, count on his word,
   wait for the Lord, my soul.
   I will wait for the Lord all the days of my life
   as sentinels wait for the dawn.

4. More than the sentinels wait for the dawn,
   let Israel wait for the Lord.
   For kindness is his, redemption for all,
   forgiveness of sins for his people.

Text: Psalm 130; Michael Joncas
Music: Michael Joncas
© 1983, OCP

103 Psalm 130

Antiphon I

Out of the depths I cry to you, O Lord.

Text: *Lectionary for Mass*, © 1969, 1981, 1997, ICEL
Music: Randolph Currie, © 1986, GIA Publications, Inc.

Antiphon II

If you, O Lord, should mark our sins, Lord, who would sur-vive?

Text: Psalm 130:3; The Grail
Music: Clifford W. Howell, SJ
© 1963, The Grail, GIA Publications, Inc., agent

Antiphon III

I place all my trust in you, my God; all my hope is in your

sav - ing word.

Text: Joseph Gelineau, SJ
Music: Joseph Gelineau, SJ
© 1963, The Grail, GIA Publications, Inc., agent

Antiphon IV

I hope in the Lord, I trust in his word.

Text: *Lectionary for Mass*, © 1969, 1981, 1997, ICEL
Music: J. Robert Carroll, © 1975, GIA Publications, Inc.

Antiphon V

With the Lord there is mer-cy, and full-ness of re - demp-tion.

Text: *Lectionary for Mass*, © 1969, 1981, 1997, ICEL
Music: J. Robert Carroll, © 1975, GIA Publications, Inc.

Conception Abbey Tone

Music: Gregory J. Polan, OSB, © 2010, Conception Abbey, admin. by GIA Publications, Inc.

Gelineau Tone

Music: Joseph Gelineau, SJ, © 1963, The Grail, GIA Publications, Inc., agent

De profundis

1. Out of the dépths I crý to you, O LÓRD;
   [2] Lórd, hear my vóice!
   O lét your éars be atténtive
   to the sóund of my pléadings.

2. [3] If you, O LÓRD, should márk iníquities,
   Lórd, who could stánd?
   [4] But with yóu is fóund forgíveness,
   that yóu may be re<u>vé</u>red.

3. [5] I lóng for yóu, O LÓRD,
   my soul lóngs for his wórd.
   [6] My sóul hópes in the Lórd
   more than wátchmen for dáybreak.

4. Móre than wátchmen for dáybreak,
   [7] let Israel hópe for the LÓRD.
   For wíth the LÓRD there is mércy,
   in him is pléntiful redémption.
   [8] It is hé who will redéem Israel
   from áll its iníquities.

5. To the Fáther Almíghty give glóry,
   give glóry to his Són,
   to the Spírit most Hóly give práise,
   whose réign is for éver.

Text: Psalm 130; *The Revised Grail Psalms*; © 2010, Conception Abbey and The Grail, admin. by GIA Publications, Inc., agent

104   Psalm 134

Antiphon

In the si - lent hours of night, bless the Lord.

Ecce nunc benedicite

Verse 1

1. O come, bless the LORD, all you ser - vants of the LORD,

D.C.

who stand by night in the courts of the house of the LORD.

Verse 2

D.C.

2. Lift up your hands to the ho - ly place, and bless the LORD.

Verse 3

D.C.

3. May the Lord bless you from Si-on, he who made both heav-en and earth.

Verse 4

4. Glory to the Father, and to the Son, and to the Ho - ly Spir - it:

D.C.

as it was in the be - gin - ning, is now, and will be for ev-er. A-men.

Text: Psalm 134; *The Revised Grail Psalms,* © 2010, Conception Abbey and The Grail, admin. by GIA Publications, Inc.; antiphon from *Liturgy of the Hours,* © 1974, ICEL
Music: Howard Hughes, SM, © 1979, GIA Publications, Inc.

Psalm 141 105

Antiphon

My prayers rise like in-cense, my hands like the eve-ning of-f'ring.

Text: *Praise God in Song,* © 1979, GIA Publications, Inc.
Music: Robert J. Batastini, © 1986, GIA Publications, Inc.

Conception Abbey Tone

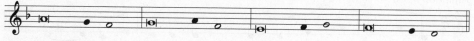

Music: Gregory J. Polan, OSB, © 2010, Conception Abbey, admin. by GIA Publications, Inc.

Gelineau Tone

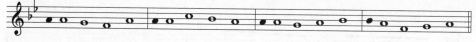

Music: Joseph Gelineau, SJ, © 1963, The Grail, GIA Publications, Inc., agent

Domine clamavi ad te

1. I have cálled to you, LORD; hásten to hélp me!
    Héar my vóice when I crý to yóu.
    ²Let my práyer be accépted as íncense befóre you,
    the ráising of my hánds like an évening oblátion.

2. ³Sét, O LORD, a guárd on my móuth;
    kéep wátch at the dóor of my líps!
    ⁴Do not túrn my héart to thíngs that are évil,
    to wícked déeds with thóse who are sínners.

3. Néver allów me to sháre in their féasting.
    ⁵If a góod man stríkes me ít is kíndness;
    but let the óil of the wícked not anóint my héad.
    Let my práyer be éver agáinst their málice.

4. ⁶If they fáll into the mérciless hánds of their júdges,
    théy will grásp how kínd are my wórds.
    ⁷As clóds of éarth plowed úp on the gróund,
    so their bónes were stréwn at the móuth of the gráve.

5. ⁸To you my éyes are túrned, O LORD, my Lórd.
    In yóu I take réfuge; spáre my sóul!
    ⁹From the tráp they have láid for me, kéep me sáfe;
    kéep me from the snáres of thóse who do évil.

6. ¹⁰Let the wícked togéther fáll into their tráps,
    while Í pursúe my wáy unhármed.
    Give práise to the Fáther, the Són and Holy Spírit,
    both nów and for áges unénding. Amén.

Text: Psalm 141; *The Revised Grail Psalms*; © 2010, Conception Abbey and The Grail, admin. by GIA Publications, Inc., agent

106 Psalm 143

Antiphon I

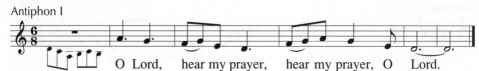

O Lord, hear my prayer, hear my prayer, O Lord.

Text: *Lectionary for Mass*, © 1969, 1981, 1997, ICEL
Music: Richard Proulx, © 1975, GIA Publications, Inc.

Antiphon II

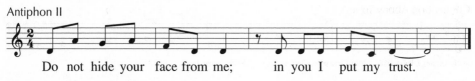

Do not hide your face from me; in you I put my trust.

Text: *Liturgy of the Hours*, © 1974, ICEL
Music: Randolph Currie, © 1986, GIA Publications, Inc.

Antiphon III

Teach me to do your will, my God.

Text: *Rite of Penance*, © 1975, ICEL
Music: Kelly Dobbs-Mickus, © 2011, GIA Publications, Inc.

Antiphon IV

For the sake of your name, O Lord, save my life.

Text: *Lectionary for Mass*, © 1969, 1981, 1997, ICEL
Music: Robert J. Batastini, © 1975, GIA Publications, Inc.

Conception Abbey Tone

Music: Gregory J. Polan, OSB, © 2010, Conception Abbey, admin. by GIA Publications, Inc.

Gelineau Tone

Music: Joseph Gelineau, SJ, © 1963, The Grail, GIA Publications, Inc., agent

Domine exaudi

1. O LÓRD, lísten to my práyer;
   túrn your éar to my appéal.
   You are fáithful, you are júst; give ánswer.
   ² Do not cáll your sérvant to júdgment,
   for in your síght no one líving is jústified.

2. ³ The énemy pursúes my sóul;
   he has crúshed my lífe to the grónd.
   He has máde me dwéll in dárkness,
   like the déad, lóng forgótten.
   ⁴ Thérefore my spírit fáils;
   my héart is désolate withín me.

3. ⁵ I remémber the dáys that are pást;
   I pónder áll your wórks.
   I múse on what your hánd has wróught,
   ⁶ and to yóu I strétch out my hánds.
   Like a párched land my sóul thirsts for yóu.

4. ⁷ O LÓRD, make háste and ánswer me,
   for my spírit fáils withín me.
   Do not híde your fáce from mé,
   lest Í becóme like thóse
   who gó down ínto the gráve.

5. ⁸ In the mórning, let me knów your loving mércy,
   for in yóu I pláce my trúst.
   Make me knów the wáy I should wálk;
   to yóu I líft up my sóul.

6. ⁹ Réscue me, O LÓRD, from my fóes;
   to yóu have I fléd for réfuge.
   ¹⁰ Téach me to dó your wíll,
   for yóu áre my Gód.

7. ¹¹ Lét your good spírit guíde me
   upón gróund that is lével.
   LORD, save my lífe for the sáke of your náme;
   in your jústice, lead my sóul out of distréss.

8. Give práise to the Fáther Almíghty,
   to his Són, Jesus Chríst the Lórd,
   to the Spírit who dwélls in our héarts,
   both nów and for éver. Amén.

107 Psalm 145: I Will Praise Your Name for Ever

Antiphon I

I will praise your name for ev - er, my king and my God.

Antiphon II

The hand of the Lord feeds us; God

an - swers all our needs.

Antiphon III

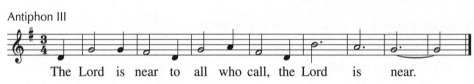

The Lord is near to all who call, the Lord is near.

Antiphon IV

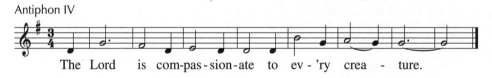

The Lord is com-pas - sion-ate to ev - 'ry crea - ture.

Verses

1. I will exalt you, God my king, for ever bless your holy name.
   I will exalt you ev'ry day, and evermore your praise proclaim.

2. For I will bless you at all times, and praise your name through all my days.
   The Lord is great beyond all thought, the Lord is worthy of high praise.

3. Each generation speaks your praise, proclaims your deeds to ev'ry land.
   They praise the splendor of your works, the mighty power of your hand.

4. They tell the power of your deeds, and always speak of you with awe.
   They spread the news of your great love, and sing the justice of your law.

5. The Lord is merciful and kind, so slow to anger when we fall.
   The Lord is good in ev'ry way, and is compassionate to all.

6. Let all your works give thanks, O Lord, and may your faithful ones sing praise.
   May they proclaim your glorious reign, may they affirm your mighty ways.

7. May all proclaim your power, Lord, the glorious might of your domain.
   Your rule endures for evermore, for endless ages you will reign.

8. The Lord is faithful in each word, and hears the cry of all who call.
   The Lord upraises those bowed down, the Lord supports all those who fall.

9. The eyes of all look up to you for food and drink, which you supply.
   You open wide your gracious hand, and ev'ry need you satisfy.

10. The Lord is just in ev'ry way, forever loving in each deed.
    The Lord is near to those who call, who call with truth in time of need.

11. The Lord fulfills our hearts' desires, with saving power hears our cry.
    The Lord protects all those who love, but all the wicked surely die.

12. My mouth will sing the praise of God, the God whom heav'n and earth adore.
    Let ev'ry creature bless God's name for ever and for evermore.

Text: Psalm 145: James J. Chepponis, © 1999, GIA Publications, Inc.; antiphon 1, *Lectionary for Mass*, © 1969, 1981, 1997, ICEL
Music: James J. Chepponis, © 1999, GIA Publications, Inc.

108 Psalm 145

Antiphon I

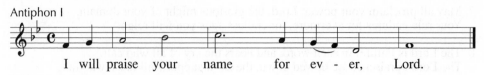

I will praise your name for ev - er, Lord.

Text: *Lectionary for Mass*, © 1969, 1981, 1997, ICEL
Music: Donald J. Reagan, © 1986, GIA Publications, Inc.

Antiphon II

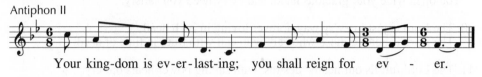

Your king-dom is ev-er-last-ing; you shall reign for ev - er.

Text: Psalm 145:13
Music: Randolph Currie, © 1986, GIA Publications, Inc.

Antiphon III

The Lord is com-pas - sion-ate toward all his works.

Text: *Lectionary for Mass*, © 1969, 1981, 1997, ICEL
Music: J. Robert Carroll, © 1975, GIA Publications, Inc.

Conception Abbey Tone

Music: Gregory J. Polan, OSB, © 2010, Conception Abbey, admin. by GIA Publications, Inc.

Gelineau Tone

Music: Joseph Gelineau, SJ, © 1963, The Grail, GIA Publications, Inc., agent

Exaltabo te Deus

1. I will extól you, my Gód and kíng,
    and bless your náme foréver and éver.
    ² I will bléss you dáy after dáy,
    and praise your náme foréver and éver.
    ³ The LORD is gréat and híghly to be práised;
    his gréatness cánnot be méasured.

2. ⁴ Age to áge shall procláim your wórks,
    shall decláre your míghty déeds.
    ⁵ They will téll of your great glóry and spléndor,
    and recóunt your wónderful wórks.

3. ⁶They will spéak of your áwesome déeds,
   recóunt your gréatness and míght.
   ⁷They will recáll your abúndant góodness,
   and síng of your just déeds with jóy.

4. ⁸The LORD is kínd and fúll of compássion,
   slow to ánger, abóunding in mércy.
   ⁹How góod is the LÓRD to áll,
   compássionate to áll his créatures.

5. ¹⁰All your wórks shall thánk you, O LÓRD,
   and áll your fáithful ones bléss you.
   ¹¹They shall spéak of the glóry of your réign,
   and decláre your míghty déeds,

6. ¹²To make known your míght to the chíldren of mén,
   and the glórious spléndor of your réign.
   ¹³Your kíngdom is an éverlasting kíngdom;
   your rule endúres for áll generátions.

7. The LORD is fáithful in áll his wórds,
   and hóly in áll his déeds.
   ¹⁴The LÓRD suppórts all who fáll,
   and ráises up áll who are bowed dówn.

8. ¹⁵The éyes of áll look to yóu,
   and you gíve them their fóod in due séason.
   ¹⁶You ópen your hánd and sátisfy
   the desíre of every líving thíng.

9. ¹⁷The LORD is júst in áll his wáys,
   and hóly in áll his déeds.
   ¹⁸The LORD is clóse to áll who cáll him,
   who cáll on hím in trúth.

10. ¹⁹He fulfílls the desíres of those who féar him;
    he héars their crý and he sáves them.
    ²⁰The LORD keeps wátch over áll who lóve him;
    the wícked he will útterly destróy.

11. ²¹Let my móuth speak the práise of the LÓRD;
    let all flésh bless his hóly náme
    foréver, for áges unénding.

12. Give práise to the Fáther Almíghty,
    to his Són, Jesus Chríst the Lórd,
    to the Spírit who dwélls in our héarts,
    both nów and for éver. Amén.

Text: Psalm 145; *The Revised Grail Psalms*; © 2010, Conception Abbey and The Grail, admin. by GIA Publications, Inc., agent

109 Psalm 146

Antiphon

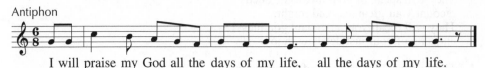

I will praise my God all the days of my life,   all the days of my life.

Text: *Liturgy of the Hours*, © 1974, ICEL
Music: James J. Chepponis, © 2011, GIA Publications, Inc.

Conception Abbey Tone

Music: Gregory J. Polan, OSB, © 2010, Conception Abbey, admin. by GIA Publications, Inc.

Gelineau Tone

Music: Joseph Gelineau, SJ, © 1963, The Grail, GIA Publications, Inc., agent

Lauda anima mea

1. My sóul, give práise to the LÓRD;
   2 I will práise the LÓRD all my lífe,
   sing práise to my GÓd while I líve.

2. 3 Pút no trúst in prínces,
   in mortal mán who cánnot sáve.
   4 Take their bréath, they retúrn to the
   éarth,
   and their pláns that dáy come to
   nóthing.

3. 5 Blessed is hé who is hélped by
   Jacob's Gód,
   6 whose hópe is in the LÓRD his Gód,
   who máde the héavens and the éarth,
   the séas and áll they contáin,
   7 who presérves fidélity foréver,
   who does jústice to thóse who are
   oppréssed.

4. It is hé who gives bréad to the húngry,
   the LÓRD who sets prísoners frée,
   8 the LORD who ópens the éyes of the
   blínd,
   the LORD who ráises up thóse who
   are bowed dówn.

5. It is the LÓRD who lóves the júst,
   9 the LÓRD who protécts the stránger
   and uphólds the órphan and the wídow,
   but thwárts the páth of the wícked.
   10 The LÓRD will réign foréver,
   the God of Síon from áge to áge.

6. Give práise to the Fáther Almíghty,
   to his Són, Jesus Chríst the Lórd,
   to the Spírit who dwélls in our héarts,
   both nów and for éver. Amén.

Text: Psalm 146; *The Revised Grail Psalms*; © 2010, Conception Abbey and The Grail, admin. by GIA Publications, Inc., agent

Psalm 147:12–20   110

Antiphon

O praise the Lord, Je - ru-sa-lem! Si-on, praise your God!

Text: Psalm 147:12, The Grail, © 1963, The Grail, GIA Publications, Inc., agent
Music: Thomas S. Savoy, © 1986, GIA Publications, Inc.

Conception Abbey Tone

Music: Gregory J. Polan, OSB, © 2010, Conception Abbey, admin. by GIA Publications, Inc.

Gelineau Tone

Music: Joseph Gelineau, SJ, © 1963, The Grail, GIA Publications, Inc., agent

Lauda Jerusalem

1. [12] O Jerúsalem, glórify the LÓRD!
   O Síon, práise your Gód!
   [13] He has stréngthened the bárs of your gátes;
   he has bléssed your chíldren withín you.
   [14] He estáblished péace on your bórders;
   he gíves you your fíll of finest whéat.

2. [15] He sénds out his wórd to the éarth,
   and swíftly rúns his commánd.
   [16] He shówers down snów like wóol;
   he scátters hóarfrost like áshes.

3. [17] He húrls down háilstones like crúmbs;
   befóre such cóld, who can stánd?
   [18] He sénds forth his wórd and it mélts them;
   at the blówing of his bréath the waters flów.

4. [19] He revéals his wórd to Jácob;
   to Ísrael, his decrées and júdgments.
   [20] He has nót dealt thús with other nátions;
   he has nót táught them his júdgments.

5. Give práise to the Fáther Almíghty,
   to his Són, Jesus Chríst the Lórd,
   to the Spírit who dwélls in our héarts,
   both nów and for éver. Amén.

Text: Psalm 147:12–20; *The Revised Grail Psalms*; © 2010, Conception Abbey and The Grail, admin. by GIA Publications, Inc., agent

111 Psalm 148

Antiphon

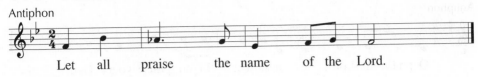

Let all praise the name of the Lord.

Text: *Lectionary for Mass,* © 1969, 1981, 1997, ICEL
Music: Robert J. Batastini; acc. by Richard Proulx, © 1975, 1986, GIA Publications, Inc.

Conception Abbey Tone

Music: Gregory J. Polan, OSB, © 2010, Conception Abbey, admin. by GIA Publications, Inc.

Gelineau Tone

Music: Joseph Gelineau, SJ, © 1963, The Grail, GIA Publications, Inc., agent

Laudate Dominum de caelis

1. Práise the LÓRD from the héavens;
   práise him ín the héights.
   ² Práise him, áll his ángels;
   práise him, áll his hósts.

2. ³ Práise him, sún and móon;
   práise him, all shíning stárs.
   ⁴ Práise him, híghest héavens,
   and the wáters abóve the héavens.

3. ⁵ Let them práise the náme of the LÓRD.
   He commánded: théy were creáted.
   ⁶ He estáblished them foréver and éver,
   gave a láw which shall nót pass awáy.

4. ⁷ Práise the LÓRD from the éarth,
   sea créatures and all ócean dépths,
   ⁸ fire and háil, snów and míst,
   stormy wínds that fulfíll his commánd;

5. ⁹ Móuntains ánd all híllls,
   frúit trees ánd all cédars,
   ¹⁰ béasts, both wíld and táme,
   réptiles and bírds on the wíng;

6. ¹¹ Kíngs of the éarth and all péoples,
   prínces and all júdges of the éarth,
   ¹² young mén and máidens as wéll,
   the óld and the yóung togéther.

7. ¹³ Let them práise the náme of the LÓRD,
   for his náme alóne is exálted,
   his spléndor above héaven and éarth.

8. ¹⁴ He exálts the stréngth of his péople.
   He is the práise of áll his fáithful,
   the práise of the chíldren of Ísrael,
   of the péople to whóm he is clóse.

9. Give práise to the Fáther Almíghty,
   to his Són, Jesus Chríst the Lórd,
   to the Spírit who dwélls in our héarts,
   both nów and for éver. Amén.

Text: Psalm 148; *The Revised Grail Psalms*; © 2010, Conception Abbey and The Grail, admin. by GIA Publications, Inc., agent

Psalm 149   112

Antiphon

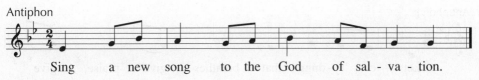

Sing   a   new   song   to   the   God   of   sal - va - tion.

Text: Psalm 149:1 and 4
Music: Eugene Englert, © 1986, GIA Publications, Inc.

Conception Abbey Tone

Omit for 4-line stanza

Music: Gregory J. Polan, OSB, © 2010, Conception Abbey, admin. by GIA Publications, Inc.

Gelineau Tone

Omit for 4-line stanza

Music: Joseph Gelineau, SJ, © 1963, The Grail, GIA Publications, Inc., agent

Cantate Domino

1. Síng a new sóng to the LÓRD,
   his práise in the assémbly of the fáithful.
   ² Let Ísrael rejóice in its Máker;
   let Sion's chíldren exúlt in their kíng.
   ³ Let them práise his náme with dáncing,
   and make músic with tímbrel and hárp.

2. ⁴ For the LÓRD takes delíght in his péople;
   he crówns the póor with salvátion.
   ⁵ Let the fáithful exúlt in glóry,
   and rejóice as they táke their rést.
   ⁶ Let the práise of Gód be in their móuths
   and a twó-edged swórd in their hánd,

3. ⁷ To déal out véngeance to the nátions
   and púnishment upón the péoples;
   ⁸ to bínd their kíngs in cháins
   and their nóbles in fétters of íron;
   ⁹ to cárry out the júdgment decréed.
   This is an hónor for áll his fáithful.

4. Give práise to the Fáther Almíghty,
   to his Són, Jesus Chríst the Lórd,
   to the Spírit who dwélls in our héarts,
   both nów and for éver. Amén.

Text: Psalm 149; *The Revised Grail Psalms*; © 2010, Conception Abbey and The Grail, admin. by GIA Publications, Inc., agent

113 Psalm 150

Antiphon I

Let ev - 'ry-thing that breathes give praise, give praise, give praise to the Lord.

Text: *Liturgy of the Hours,* © 1974, ICEL
Music: Ronald F. Krisman, © 2011, GIA Publications, Inc.

Antiphon II

Al - le - lu - ia, al - le - lu - ia, al - le - lu - ia.

Music: Ronald F. Krisman, © 2011, GIA Publications, Inc.

Conception Abbey Tone

Omit for 3-line stanza

Music: Gregory J. Polan, OSB, © 2010, Conception Abbey, admin. by GIA Publications, Inc.

Gelineau Tone

Omit for 3-line stanza

Music: Joseph Gelineau, SJ, © 1963, The Grail, GIA Publications, Inc., agent

Laudate Dominum in sanctis eius

1. Praise Gód in his hóly pláce;
   práise him in his míghty fírmament.
   ² Práise him for his pówerful déeds;
   práise him for his bóundless grándeur.

2. ³ O práise him with sóund of trúmpet;
   práise him with lúte and hárp.
   ⁴ Práise him with tímbrel and dánce;
   práise him with stríngs and pípes.

3. ⁵ O práise him with resóunding cýmbals;
   práise him with cláshing of cýmbals.
   ⁶ Let éverything that bréathes praise the LÓRD!

4. Give práise to the Fáther Almíghty,
   to his Són, Jesus Chríst the Lórd,
   to the Spírit who dwélls in our héarts,
   both nów and for éver. Amén.

Text: Psalm 150; *The Revised Grail Psalms*; © 2010, Conception Abbey and The Grail, admin. by GIA Publications, Inc., agent

Exodus 15: Song of Moses 114

Antiphon

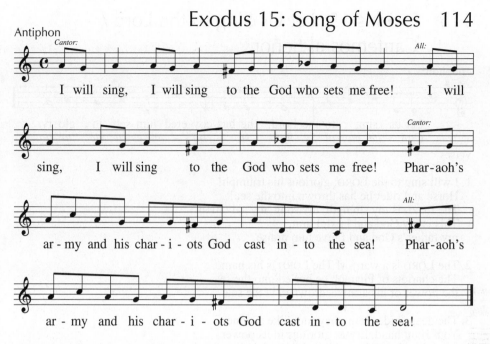

Verses

1. The Lord is my strength, my protection and my shield;
   Pharaoh's army and his chariots God cast into the sea.
   Our God is a warrior whose name is "the Lord,"
   God of might, God of victory!

2. The brave and the mighty, the pride of Pharaoh's army,
   God plunged them to the bottom of the sea like a stone.
   The hand of the Lord is magnificent in power;
   the Lord has crushed our foes!

3. O God who redeems, who delivers us from slavery,
   you set us on the mountain of your holy place.
   Your throne and your temple shall endure for all time;
   your reign shall never end!

Text: Exodus 15; Scott Soper
Music: Scott Soper
© 1997, GIA Publications, Inc.

115   Exodus 15: Let Us Sing to the Lord / Cantemos al Señor

Antiphon*

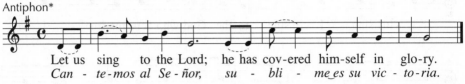

Let us sing to the Lord; he has cov-ered him-self in glo-ry.
Can - te-mos al Se-ñor, su - bli - me_es su vic - to-ria.

Verses

1. I will sing to the LORD; glorious his triumph!
Horse and rider he has thrown into the sea!
The LORD is my strength, my song, my salvation.
This is my God and I extol him,
my father's God and I give him praise.

2. The LORD is a warrior! The LORD is his name.
The chariots of Pharaoh he hurled into the sea,
the flower of his army is drowned in the sea.

3. The deeps hide them; they sank like a stone.
Your right hand, LORD, glorious in its power,
your right hand, LORD, has shattered the enemy.

4. The people you have redeemed pass by.
You will lead them and plant them on your mountain,
the place, O LORD, where you have made your home,
the sanctuary, LORD, which your hands have made.
The LORD will reign for ever and ever!

1. *Cantaré al Señor, sublime es su victoria,*
caballo y carros ha arrojado en el mar.
Mi fuerza y mi poder es el Señor, él fue mi salvación.
Él es mi Dios: yo lo alabaré;
el Dios de mis padres: yo lo ensalzaré.

2. *El Señor es un guerrero, su nombre es "el Señor."*
Los carros del Faraón los lanzó al mar,
ahogó en el mar Rojo a sus mejores capitanes.

3. *Las olas los cubrieron, bajaron hasta el fondo como piedras.*
Tu diestra, Señor, es fuerte_y terrible,
tu diestra, Señor, tritura al enemigo.

4. *Los introduces y los plantas en el monte de tu heredad,*
lugar del que hiciste tu trono, Señor;
santuario, Señor, que fundaron tus manos.
El Señor reina por siempre jamás.

For a bilingual setting, sing the antiphon in one language and repeat in the other.

Text: Exodus 15:1–6, 17–18; The Grail, © 1963, The Grail, GIA Publications, Inc., agent; English antiphon, *Lectionary for Mass*, © 1969, 1981,
1997, ICEL; Spanish text, *Leccionario, Edición Hispanoamérica*, © 1970, 1972, Conferencia Episcopal Española
Music: Antiphon, Ronald F. Krisman, © 2004, GIA Publications, Inc.; verses, Michel Guimont, © 1994, 1998, GIA Publications, Inc.

Isaiah 38:10–14, 17–20   116

Antiphon

I will sing to the Lord all the days of my life.

Text: Isaiah 38:20
Music: Michael E. Young, © 1986, GIA Publications, Inc.

Psalm Tone

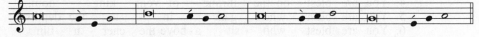

Music: A. Gregory Murray, OSB, © L. J. Carey and Co., Ltd.

Gelineau Tone

Music: Joseph Gelineau, SJ, © 1963, The Grail, GIA Publications, Inc., agent

Ego dixi

1. I **said**: So I must **gò away**,
   my **life** half **spent**,
   as**signed** to the **wòrld** be**low**
   for the **rest** óf my **years**.

2. I said: No **more** shall I **sèe** the **LORD**
   in the **land** óf the **living**,
   no **more** shall I **look** ùpon **men**
   with**ín** this **world**.

3. My **home** is pulled **up** ànd re**moved**
   like a **shép**herd's **tent**.
   Like a **weav**er you have **rolled** ùp my
   life,
   you **cut** it fróm the **loom**.

4. Between **even**ing and **mornìng** you
   finish it.
   I cry for **help** úntil **dawn**.
   I **suffer** as **thòugh** a **lion**
   were **breakíng** my **bones**.

5. I **cry** out in **grief** lìke a **swallow**,
   I **moan** líke a **dove**.
   My **eyes** look **wearilỳ** to **heav**en.
   Take **care** óf me, **Lord**!

6. **You** have held **bàck** my **life**
   from the **pít** of **doom**.
   You have cast **far** fròm your **sight**
   every **one** óf my **sins**.

7. For the **world** below cànnot **thank**
   you,
   nor **death** gíve you **praise**.
   Those who go **down** tò the **grave**
   cannot **hope** fór your **mer**cy.

8. The **living**, the **livìng** man **thanks** you,
   as **I** dó this **day**;
   the **fa**ther shall **tèll** his **chil**dren
   of your **fáith**ful **mer**cy.

9. O **LORD**, **come** tò our **res**cue,
   and **we** shàll sing **psalms**,
   sing **psalms** all the **days** òf our **life**
   in the **house** óf the **LORD**.

10. Praise the **Father**, the **Son** and **Hòly**
    Spirit,
    both **now** ánd for **ever**,
    the God who **is**, who **was** and ìs to
    come
    at the **end** óf the **ages**.

Text: Isaiah 38:10–14, 17–20; The Grail, © 1963, The Grail, GIA Publications, Inc., agent

117 Daniel 3:52–57 / You Are Blest, Lord God

Benedictus es Domine

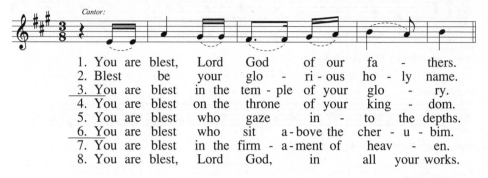

1. You are blest, Lord God of our fa - thers.
2. Blest be your glo - ri - ous ho - ly name.
3. You are blest in the tem - ple of your glo - ry.
4. You are blest on the throne of your king - dom.
5. You are blest who gaze in - to the depths.
6. You are blest who sit a - bove the cher - u - bim.
7. You are blest in the firm - a-ment of heav - en.
8. You are blest, Lord God, in all your works.

To you glo - ry and praise for ev - er - more.

Text: Daniel 3:52–57; The Grail
Music: Joseph Gelineau, SJ
© 1963, The Grail, GIA Publications, Inc., agent

Daniel 3:57–88 / O All You Works of the Lord   118

Benedicite omnia opera Domini

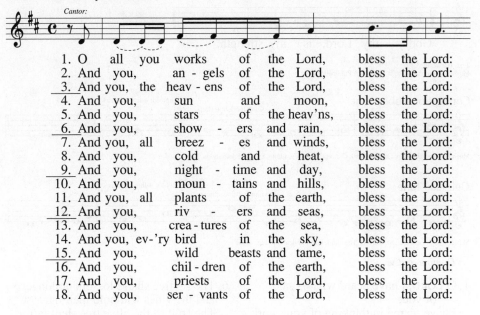

1. O all you works of the Lord, bless the Lord:
2. And you, an - gels of the Lord, bless the Lord:
3. And you, the heav - ens of the Lord, bless the Lord:
4. And you, sun and moon, bless the Lord:
5. And you, stars of the heav'ns, bless the Lord:
6. And you, show - ers and rain, bless the Lord:
7. And you, all breez - es and winds, bless the Lord:
8. And you, cold and heat, bless the Lord:
9. And you, night - time and day, bless the Lord:
10. And you, moun - tains and hills, bless the Lord:
11. And you, all plants of the earth, bless the Lord:
12. And you, riv - ers and seas, bless the Lord:
13. And you, crea - tures of the sea, bless the Lord:
14. And you, ev-'ry bird in the sky, bless the Lord:
15. And you, wild beasts and tame, bless the Lord:
16. And you, chil - dren of the earth, bless the Lord:
17. And you, priests of the Lord, bless the Lord:
18. And you, ser - vants of the Lord, bless the Lord:

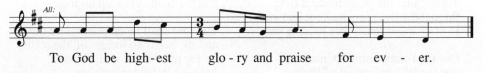

To God be high-est glo - ry and praise for ev - er.

Text: Daniel 3:57–88; The Grail
Music: A. Gregory Murray, OSB
© 1963, The Grail, GIA Publications, Inc., agent

119 Habakkuk 3:2–4, 13a, 15–19

Antiphon

God, my Lord, is my strength.

Text: Habakkuk 3:19a
Music: Randolph Currie, © 1986, GIA Publications, Inc.

Conception Abbey Tone

Music: Gregory J. Polan, OSB, © 2010, Conception Abbey, admin. by GIA Publications, Inc.

Gelineau Tone

Music: Joseph Gelineau, SJ, © 1963, The Grail, GIA Publications, Inc., agent

Domine audivi

1. O LÓRD, I have héard what is sáid
   of you;
   I have féared in thínking of your wórk.
   Throughóut the yéars make it líve;
   throughóut the yéars make it knówn.
   In your ánger remémber to have mércy.

2. Our Gód cáme from Théman
   and the hóly móuntain of Pháran.
   His májesty cóvers the héavens,
   and the éarth is fílled with his glóry.

3. His bríghtness is líke the líght.
   Hórns of stréngth are in his hánds:
   thére his pówer is hídden.
   You went fórth to sáve your péople,
   to sáve your Anóinted, your Chríst.

4. You dróve his hórses in the séa,
   in the múd of ínfinite wáters.
   I have héard and was fílled with féar:
   at the sóund my líps have trémbled.

5. A wéakness énters my bónes,
   and féar takes stréngth from my límbs.
   I am cónfident in the dáy of tribulátion
   which is sét against the péople who
   bínd us.

6. The fíg tree shall blóssom no lónger,
   and the vínes withhóld their hárvest.
   The frúit of the ólive tree shall fáil,
   and the fíelds yield úp no fóod.

7. The fóld shall be émptied of its shéep,
   and the hérds no longer fíll the stálls.
   As for mé, I exúlt in the LÓRD;
   I rejóice in Gód my sávior.

8. The Lórd my GÓD is my stréngth:
   he makes my féet as nímble as the
   déer's
   and béars my fóotsteps on hígh.

9. Glóry to the Fáther, and to the Són,
   and tó the Hóly Spírit,
   as it wás in the begínning, is nów,
   and wíll be for éver. Amén.

Text: Habakkuk 3:2–4, 13a, 15–19; The Grail, © 1963, The Grail, GIA Publications, Inc., agent

Luke 1:46–53 / My Soul Gives Glory   120

1. My soul gives glo - ry to my God, Who reach - es
2. God's mer - cy com - forts all who fear, Em - brac - ing
3. God's jus - tice sends the rich a - way, But feeds the

down with lov - ing grace To lift me from my
with a stead - fast arm That casts the might - y
poor with lav - ish things. Each hun - gry soul now

low es - tate And set me in the high - est place.
from their thrones, But keeps the hum - ble safe from harm.
fills with joy And joins the song that Mar - y sings:

Ma - gní - fi - cat, ma - gní - fi - cat! With all my heart, I
Ma - gní - fi - cat, ma - gní - fi - cat! The weak find strength; the
Ma - gní - fi - cat, ma - gní - fi - cat! To God, Cre - a - tor,

an - swer Yes When God an - noun - ces won - drous
wea - ry, rest. God's prom - ise sounds from age to
Christ, the Son; And Ho - ly Spir - it— tri - une

news. And ev - 'ry age shall call me blest.
age: The need - y of the world are blest.
God: All prais - es to the Three in One.

Text: Luke 1:46–53; Mary Louise Bringle, © 2004, GIA Publications, Inc.
Tune: MAGNIFICAT, LMD; Michael Joncas, © 1979, 1988, GIA Publications, Inc.

121 Luke 1:46–55 / Canticle of Mary

Antiphon I

My soul re-joic-es, my soul re-joic-es in my God.

Text: *Lectionary for Mass,* © 1969, 1981, 1997, ICEL
Music: Robert J. Batastini, © 1972, GIA Publications, Inc.

Antiphon II

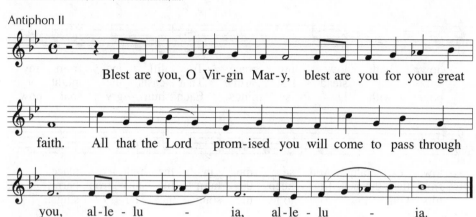

Blest are you, O Vir-gin Mar-y, blest are you for your great

faith. All that the Lord prom-ised you will come to pass through

you, al-le-lu - ia, al-le-lu - ia.

Text: *Liturgy of the Hours,* © 1974, ICEL
Music: John Schiavone, © 2011, GIA Publications, Inc.

Antiphon III

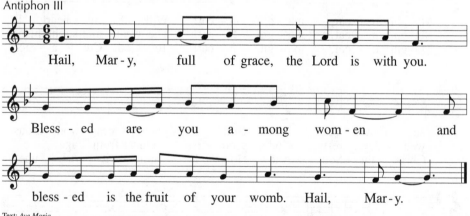

Hail, Mar-y, full of grace, the Lord is with you.

Bless - ed are you a - mong wom-en and

bless - ed is the fruit of your womb. Hail, Mar-y.

Text: *Ave Maria*
Music: John Schiavone, © 2011, GIA Publications, Inc.

Conception Abbey Tone

Music: Gregory J. Polan, OSB, © 2010, Conception Abbey, admin. by GIA Publications, Inc.

Gelineau Tone

Stanzas 1, 2, 9, 10   Stanzas 3–8

Music: Joseph Gelineau, SJ, © 1963, The Grail, GIA Publications, Inc., agent

Magnificat anima mea

1. My sóul glórifies the Lórd,
   my spírit rejóices in Gód, my Sávior.

2. He lóoks on his sérvant in her nóthingness;
   hencefórth all áges will cáll me bléssed.

3. The Almíghty works márvels for mé.
   Hóly his náme!

4. His mércy is from áge to áge,
   on thóse who féar him.

5. He púts forth his árm in stréngth
   and scátters the proudhéarted.

6. He cásts the míghty from their thrónes
   and ráises the lówly.

7. He fílls the stárving with good thíngs,
   sends the rích away émpty.

8. He protécts Ísrael his sérvant,
   remémberíng his mércy,

9. The mércy prómised to our fáthers,
   for Ábrahám and his sóns for éver.

10. Praise the Fáther, the Són and Holy Spírit,
    both nów and for áges unénding. Amén.

Text: Luke 1:46–55; The Grail, © 1963, The Grail, GIA Publications, Inc., agent

122 Luke 1:46–55 / Holy Is Your Name

Verse 1

1. My soul is filled with joy as I sing to God my savior:
   you have looked upon your servant, you have visited your people.

Antiphon

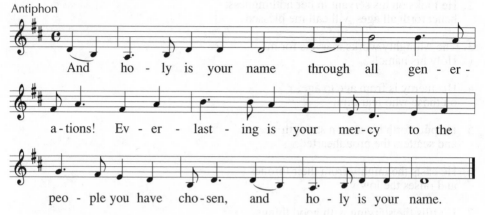

And ho-ly is your name through all gen-er-a-tions! Ev-er-last-ing is your mer-cy to the peo-ple you have cho-sen, and ho-ly is your name.

Verses 2–5

2. I am lowly as a child, but I know from this day forward
   that my name will be remembered, for all will call me blessed.

3. I proclaim the pow'r of God, you do marvels for your servants;
   though you scatter the proud hearted, and destroy the might of princes.

4. To the hungry you give food, send the rich away empty.
   In your mercy you are mindful of the people you have chosen.

5. In your love you now fulfill what you promised to your people.
   I will praise you Lord, my savior, everlasting is your mercy.

Text: Luke 1:46–55, David Haas
Music: WILD MOUNTAIN THYME, Irregular; Irish traditional; arr. by David Haas
© 1989, GIA Publications, Inc.

123 Luke 1:46–55 / Proclaim the Greatness of God

Antiphon

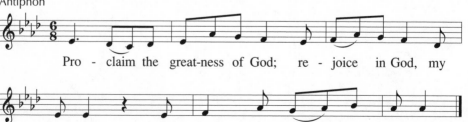

Pro-claim the great-ness of God; re-joice in God, my Sav-ior! Re-joice in God, my Sav-ior!

Verses

1. For he has favored his lowly one, and all shall call me blessed.
The almighty has done great things for me, and holy is his name.

2. He favors those who fear his name, in ev'ry generation.
He has shown the might and strength of his arm,
and scattered the proud of heart.

3. He has cast the mighty from their thrones, and lifted up the lowly.
He has filled the hungry with all good gifts, and sent the rich away.

4. He has helped his servant Israel, remembering his mercy.
He promised his mercy to Abraham and his children for evermore.

Text: Luke 1:46–55; James J. Chepponis
Music: James J. Chepponis
© 1980, GIA Publications, Inc.

Luke 1:46–55 / Magníficat 3 124

Refrain

Ma - gní - fi - cat á - ni - ma me - a, ma - gní - fi - cat á - ni - ma
My spir - it ex-ults and re - joic - es, my spir - it ex-ults and re -
Pro - cla - ma mi ser la gran - de - za, pro - cla - ma mi ser la gran-

me - a, ma - gní - fi - cat á - ni - ma me - a Dó - mi - num.
joic - es, my spir - it ex-ults and re - joic - es in the Lord.
de - za, pro - cla - ma mi ser la gran - de - za del Se - ñor.

Verses

O

Text: Luke 1:46–55; Taizé Community
Tune: Taizé Community
© 2007, Les Presses de Taizé, GIA Publications, Inc., agent

125 Luke 1:68–79 / Now Bless the God of Israel

1. Now bless the God of Is - ra - el, Who
2. Re - mem - ber - ing the cov - e - nant, God
3. In ten - der mer - cy, God will send The

comes in love and pow'r, Who rais - es from the
res - cues us from fear, That we might serve in
day - spring from on high, Our ris - ing sun, the

roy - al house De - liv - 'rance in this hour. Through
ho - li - ness And peace from year to year; And
light of life For those who sit and sigh. God

ho - ly proph - ets God has sworn To
you, my child, shall go be - fore To
comes to guide our way to peace, That

free us from a - larm, To save us from the
preach, to proph - e - sy, That all may know the
death shall reign no more. Sing prais - es to the

heav - y hand Of all who wish us harm.
ten - der love, The grace of God most high.
Ho - ly One! O wor - ship and a - dore!

Text: *Benedictus*, Luke 1:68–79; Ruth Duck, © 1992, GIA Publications, Inc.
Tune: FOREST GREEN, CMD; English melody; harm. by Ralph Vaughan Williams, 1872–1958, alt.

Luke 2:29 / Nunc Dimíttis   126

Ostinato Refrain

Nunc di - mít - tis ser - vum tu - um, Dó - mi -
Let your ser - vant now go in peace, O

ne, se - cún - dum ver - bum
Lord, now go in peace ac -

ne, Dó - mi - ne,
Lord, O Lord,

pa - ce.
word.

Last time

tu - um in pa - ce, Dó - mi - ne. Nunc di -
cord - ing to your word, to your word. Let your

Last time

Text: Luke 2:29; Taizé Community, 1980
Tune: Jacques Berthier, 1923–1994

127 Luke 2:29–32 / Canticle of Simeon

Antiphon

Guard us, O Lord,   while we sleep, and keep us in peace.

Text: The Grail
Music: Guy Weitz and A. Gregory Murray, OSB
© 1963, The Grail, GIA Publications, Inc., agent

Conception Abbey Tone

Music: Gregory J. Polan, OSB, © 2010, Conception Abbey, admin. by GIA Publications, Inc.

Gelineau Tone

Music: Joseph Gelineau, SJ, © 1963, The Grail, GIA Publications, Inc., agent

Nunc dimittis

1. At lást all-pówerful Máster,
   you give léave to your sérvant to gó
   in péace, accórding to your prómise.

2. For my éyes have séen your salvátion
   which yóu have prepáred for all nátions,
   the líght to enlíghten the Géntiles
   and give glóry to Ísrael, your péople.

3. Give práise to the Fáther Almíghty,
   to his Són, Jesus Chríst the Lórd,
   to the Spírit who dwélls in our héarts,
   both nów and for éver. Amén.

Text: Luke 2:29–32; The Grail, © 1963, The Grail, GIA Publications, Inc., agent

Ephesians 1:3–10   128

Antiphon

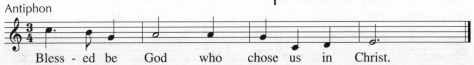

Bless - ed be God who chose us in Christ.

Psalm Tone

Benedictus Deus

1. Praised be the God and Father of our Lord Jesus Chrìst,
   who bestowed on ús in Christ
   every spiritual blessing ín the heavens.

2. God chose us in hìm
   before the wórld began
   to be holy and blameless ín his sight.

3. He predestined us to be his adopted children through Jesus Chrìst,
   such was his will and pleasure, that all might praise the glórious favor
   he has bestowed on us in hís beloved.

4. In him and through his blood, we have been redèemed,
   and our síns forgiven,
   so immeasurably generous is God's favór to us.

5. God has given us the wìsdom
   to understand fullý the mystery,
   the plan he was pleased to decrée in Christ.

6. A plan to be carried out in Christ, in the fullness of tìme,
   to bring all things into óne in him,
   in the heavens and ón the earth.

7. Glory to the Father, and to the Son, and to the Holy Spìrit:
   as it was in thé beginning,
   is now, and will be for evér. Amen.

Text: Antiphon, *Liturgy of the Hours*, © 1974, ICEL; verses, Ephesians 1:3–10; *New American Bible*, © 1970, Confraternity of Christian Doctrine, Inc.
Music: Eugene Englert, © 1986, GIA Publications, Inc.

129 Philippians 2:6–11

Qui cum in forma Dei

Cantor:
1. Though he was in the form of God, Jesus did not deem equality with God

some - thing to be grasped at. JE-SUS CHRIST IS LORD!

Assembly:
JE-SUS CHRIST IS LORD! **Cantor:** 2. Rather, he emptied him - self

and took the form of a slave, being born in the like - ness of men.

JE-SUS CHRIST IS LORD! **Assembly:** JE-SUS CHRIST IS LORD!

Cantor:
3. He was known to be of hu - man es - tate, and it was thus that he hum -

bled him-self, obediently accepting e - ven death, death on a cross!

JE-SUS CHRIST IS LORD! **Assembly:** JE-SUS CHRIST IS LORD!

Cantor:
4. Be - cause of this, God high - ly ex - alt - ed him

and bestowed on him the name a - bove ev - 'ry oth - er name,

Assembly:

JE-SUS CHRIST IS LORD! JE-SUS CHRIST IS LORD!

Cantor:

5. so that at Je - sus' name ev - 'ry knee must bend

in the heav'ns, on the earth, and un - der the earth,

and every tongue pro - claim to the glo-ry of God the Fa - ther:

Assembly:

JE-SUS CHRIST IS LORD! JE-SUS CHRIST IS LORD!

Cantor:

6. Glo - ry to the Fa - ther, and to the Son,

and to the Ho - ly Spir - it: as it was in the be - gin-ning, is

now, and will be for ev - er. A - men.

Assembly:

JE-SUS CHRIST IS LORD! JE-SUS CHRIST IS LORD!

Text: Philippians 2:6–11; *New American Bible*, © 1970, Confraternity of Christian Doctrine, Inc.
Music: Howard Hughes, SM, © 1985, GIA Publications, Inc.

130 1 Peter 2:21–24

Antiphon

By your wounds, O Christ, we have been healed.

Psalm Tone

Omit for stanza 1

In hoc enim

1. Christ suf-fèred for you, and left you án ex-am-ple,

to have you fol-low in hís foot-steps. 2. He dìd no wrong,

no de-ceit was found in hís mouth. When he was ìn-sult-ed,

he re-turned nó in-sult. 3. When he was màde to suf-fer,

he did not coun-ter with threats. In-stead he de-liv-ered him-sèlf up

to the One who judg-és just-ly. 4. In his own bod-y

he brought your sins tò the Cross, so that all of us, dead tó sin,

could live in ac-cord with Gòd's will. By his wounds you áre healed.

Text: 1 Peter 2:21–24; *New American Bible*, © 1970, Confraternity of Christian Doctrine, Inc.
Music: Richard Proulx, © 1986, GIA Publications, Inc.

Revelation 19: All Power Is Yours   131

Antiphon

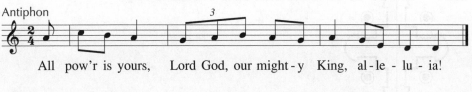

All pow'r is yours,   Lord God, our might-y King, al-le-lu-ia!

Refrain I

Al - le - lu -   ia,   al - le - lu -   ia!

Verses

Cantor: Refrain II

Al - le - lu -   ia!

Cantor: Refrain I

Al - le - lu -   ia,   al - le - lu -   ia!

Salus et gloria

1. Salvation, glory and pòwer to our Gód: (Alleluia!)
   his judgments are hònest and trúe. (Alleluia, alleluia!)

2. Sing praise to our God, àll you his sérvants, (Alleluia!)
   all who worship him reverently, greàt and smáll. (Alleluia, alleluia!)

3. The Lord our all-powerful Gòd is Kíng; (Alleluia!)
   let us rejoice, sing pràise, and give him glóry. (Alleluia, alleluia!)

4. The wedding feast of the Làmb has begún, (Alleluia!)
   and his bride is prepàred to wélcome him. (Alleluia, alleluia!)

5. Glory to the Father, and to the Sòn, and to the Holy Spírit, (Alleluia!)
   as it was in the beginning, is now, and will be for èver. Amén. (Alleluia, alleluia!)

Text: Revelation 19:1–7; *The Liturgy of the Hours,* © 1974, ICEL
Music: Howard Hughes, SM, © 1976, 1978, ICEL

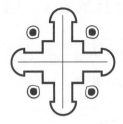

Rites of the Church

132 Christian Initiation of Adults

The passage of an adult into the Christian community takes place over an extended period of time. The members of the local Church, the catechists and sponsors, the clergy and the diocesan bishop take part in the journey from inquiry through the catechumenate to baptism, confirmation and eucharist. With their example the candidates are invited to pray, to reflect on the word of God, to fast and to join in the community's practice of charity. They are to learn the way of Jesus from the members of the Church.

This journey of the candidates and community is marked by liturgical rites; thus the community publicly acknowledges, encourages and strengthens the candidates. The first of these is the rite of becoming catechumens. It concludes the sometimes lengthy period during which those who have come to ask about the way of the Church and the life of a Christian have heard the gospel proclaimed and seen it practiced. Those who then feel called to walk in this way of Christ's Church ask to begin the journey toward baptism. If the Church judges the inquirers ready, they are accepted into the order of catechumens.

Those who have entered the catechumenate are already part of the household of Christ. During this time the catechumens are to hear and reflect on God's word, to learn the teachings and practices of the Church, to become gradually accustomed to the ways of prayer and discipline in the Church, to observe and to join in the good works of Christians. Ordinarily the catechumens are present on Sunday for the liturgy of the word and may be dismissed after the homily—to continue prayer and study with their catechists—since they cannot join in the Eucharist.

Rites of exorcism and blessing may be celebrated during the catechumenate. Through such rites the Church prays that the catechumens will be purified, strengthened against all evil and thus eagerly grow in faith and good works. The very presence of the catechumens—at the Sunday liturgy, in these special rites and in everyday life—is itself a source of strength and blessing to the faithful.

Each year as Lent begins, the bishop, with the help of the local pastor and others involved with the catechumens, is to call those catechumens who are judged ready to prepare themselves for baptism at the Easter Vigil. Thus the catechumens become the "elect," the chosen, and for the forty days of Lent they make preparations: praying, fasting, doing good works. All the faithful join them in this. On several Sundays in Lent the rites of scrutiny take place when the assembled Church prays over the elect. During Lent also the catechumens may publicly receive the words of the Church's creed and of the Lord's Prayer.

Good Friday and Holy Saturday are days of prayer, fasting and preparation for the rites of the Easter Vigil. On the night between Saturday and Sunday, the Church assembles to keep vigil and listen to many readings from Scripture. Then the catechumens are called forward for baptism and confirmation. These rites are found in the Easter Vigil.

The newly baptized, now called neophytes, take a special place in the Sunday Eucharist throughout the fifty days of Eastertime. This is a time for deepening their incorporation into the Church.

All of these stages of initiation take place in the midst of the community. In various rites, the faithful show the Christian life to the inquirers and catechumens. In turn, the faithful are strengthened and challenged in their faith by the presence of the catechumens.

Those who seek to belong to the Roman Catholic Church and who are already baptized may participate in the catechesis and in some of the rites of the catechumenate but they are not baptized again. Rather, they are received into the full communion of the Roman Catholic Church.

ACCEPTANCE INTO THE ORDER OF CATECHUMENS   133

INTRODUCTORY RITES

The following, or another appropriate song or psalm, may be sung as the priest goes to meet the candidates and their sponsors.

134

How great the sign of God's love for us: Je - sus Christ our Lord.

Text: *Rite of Christian Initiation of Adults*, © 1985, ICEL
Music: Paul M. French, © 2011, GIA Publications, Inc.

The priest greets the assembly: candidates, sponsors, members of the parish. The candidates are asked what it is that they seek from God's Church, and each replies.

CANDIDATES' FIRST ACCEPTANCE OF THE GOSPEL

The priest solemnly asks if the candidates are ready to begin walking the way of the gospel. The sponsors and all present are asked if they stand ready to assist the candidates as they strive to know and follow Christ. All respond: **We are.**

After a brief prayer, all may sing the following acclamation: 135

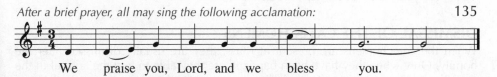

We praise you, Lord, and we bless you.

Text: *Rite of Christian Initiation of Adults*, © 1985, ICEL
Music: Paul M. French, © 2011, GIA Publications, Inc.

136 SIGNING OF THE CANDIDATES WITH THE CROSS

The sign of the cross marks the candidates for their new way of life. The priest signs each on the forehead saying:

N., receive the cross on your forehead.
It is Christ himself who now strengthens you
with this sign of his love.
Learn now to know him and follow him.

All sing the following or another suitable acclamation:

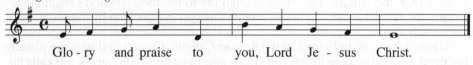

Glo - ry and praise to you, Lord Je - sus Christ.

Text: *Rite of Christian Initiation of Adults*, © 1985, ICEL
Music: Marty Haugen, © 1995, GIA Publications, Inc.

Sponsors and others also sign the candidates. Ears and eyes and other senses may also be signed. The priest prays that the catechumens may share in the saving power of the cross. The acclamation above may be repeated as necessary.

INVITATION TO THE CELEBRATION OF THE WORD OF GOD

If the assembly processes to the place for the liturgy of the word, an appropriate psalm or hymn may be sung.

137 LITURGY OF THE WORD

There may be one or more readings from Scripture, together with a responsorial psalm. After the homily, a Bible may be given to the new catechumens for their study and prayer throughout the time of the catechumenate.

INTERCESSIONS FOR THE CATECHUMENS

All join in prayer for the new catechumens.

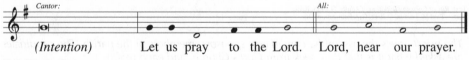

(Intention) Let us pray to the Lord. Lord, hear our prayer.

Music: Byzantine chant

If the Eucharist is to be celebrated, the catechumens are first dismissed. For music to accompany the dismissal, see below.

138 RITES OF THE CATECHUMENATE

DISMISSAL OF THE CATECHUMENS

When the catechumens are present at Mass, they are usually dismissed after the homily. Only when they have been baptized are they able to join the faithful in the reception of the eucharist. After their dismissal, the catechumens remain together and are joined by their catechists or others to pray and reflect on the scripture readings.

The following may be sung to accompany the dismissal:

Priest: Go in peace, and may the Lord remain with you always.

All: Go now in peace, go now in peace, Christ will be your way, your truth, your life.

Text: *Rite of Christian Initiation of Adults*, © 1985, ICEL
Music: Lynn Trapp, © 1991, MorningStar Music Publishers

CELEBRATIONS OF THE WORD OF GOD

On Sundays, after the catechetical sessions, before the beginning of a new liturgical season, and at other times the catechumens and others may join for liturgy: song, reading of Scripture, psalmody, prayer and silence are normally part of such a service.

MINOR EXORCISMS

At appropriate times during the catechumenate, the catechists or other approved ministers may lead the community in prayers of exorcism over the catechumens. These prayers acknowledge the struggle against evil and ask that God strengthen the catechumens.

BLESSINGS OF THE CATECHUMENS

Prayers of blessing and the laying on of hands may take place whenever the catechumens gather for instruction or other purposes. Catechists or other approved ministers ask these blessings over the catechumens.

ANOINTINGS AND PRESENTATIONS

During the catechumenate or during Lent, the candidates may be anointed with the oil of catechumens as a sign of strength given for their struggle to live the gospel. At some point in this time they are publicly presented with the Church's treasury of prayer and faith, the Lord's Prayer and the Creed.

RITE OF ELECTION OR ENROLLMENT OF NAMES

At the beginning of Lent, it is the responsibility of the bishop to call those who are judged ready to prepare for the sacraments of initiation at Easter. The bishop is to consult first with the pastors, catechists and others. The rite of election may take place at the cathedral. If the rite takes place in the parish church, the bishop may designate the pastor to act in his place.

This rite is also called the "Enrollment of Names." Each candidate now gives his/her name, or writes it down. When all have been enrolled, the bishop says: "You have been chosen to be initiated into the sacred mysteries at the Easter Vigil." He then speaks to them and to their sponsors about their lenten preparation for baptism.

While or immediately after the candidates have signed their names, an appropriate hymn or acclamation may be sung, for example, Blessed Be God, Who Chose You in Christ, *no. 917.*

139 SCRUTINIES

The scrutinies occur on the Third, Fourth and Fifth Sundays of Lent. The elect are called before the community for exorcism and prayer. If the Intercessions for the Elect are chanted, the assembly may respond with:

Ký-ri-e, e - lé-i-son, Ký-ri-e, e - lé-i-son.

Music: Jacques Berthier, © 1998, Les Presses de Taizé, GIA Publications, Inc., agent

PREPARATORY RITES

Various preparation rites take place during the day on Holy Saturday. These include prayer, recitation of the Creed, and the rite of Ephphetha (opening of ears and mouth).

SACRAMENTS OF INITIATION

The sacraments of initiation take place at the Easter Vigil.

PERIOD OF MYSTAGOGIA

"Mystagogia" refers to the fifty-day period of postbaptismal catechesis and celebration when the newly baptized are gradually drawn by the community into the fullness of Christian life and prayer. The newly baptized retain a special place in the assembly and are mentioned in the prayers of intercession. A special celebration, on Pentecost or just before, may mark the conclusion of the whole period of initiation.

Baptism of Children

Children are baptized in the faith of the Church: of parents, godparents, the local parish, the Church throughout the world, the saints. Bringing their children for baptism, the parents profess their commitment to make a home where the gospel is lived. And the godparents and all members of the community promise to support the parents in this. Thus the children enter the waters of baptism and so are joined to this people, all baptized into the death and resurrection of Christ.

Baptism is celebrated above all at the Easter Vigil, but also on other Sundays, for Sunday is the Lord's Day, the day when the Church gathers to proclaim the paschal mystery. Baptism is always celebrated in an assembly of members of the Church and may take place at Sunday Mass.

RECEPTION OF THE CHILDREN   141

The people may sing a psalm or hymn suitable for the occasion as the priest/deacon goes to meet the parents and godparents at the entrance of the church, or as all process into the church.

The parents and godparents are welcomed by all. The priest/deacon asks the names of the children and questions the parents about their own expectations and willingness to take on the responsibilities this baptism brings. The godparents are asked if they are ready to assist the parents in their responsibilities as Christian mothers and fathers.

With joy, then, the priest/deacon, the parents and godparents make the sign of the cross on the child's forehead as the priest or deacon says: "I claim you for Christ our Savior by the sign of his cross."

If there is to be a procession to the place where Scripture will be read, the following antiphon, or a hymn, may be sung:

Cantor, then all:

There is one God, one Fa-ther of all.

Text: *Rite of Baptism for Children,* © 1969, ICEL
Music: Robert J. Batastini, © 2011, GIA Publications, Inc.

LITURGY OF THE WORD   142

FIRST READINGS

One or more passages from Scripture are read. At the conclusion of each:

Reader: The word of the Lord.
Assembly: **Thanks be to God.**

RESPONSORIAL PSALM

The following psalm may follow the first reading:

Refrain

The Lord is my light and my sal - va - tion.

Text: *Lectionary for Mass,* © 1969, ICEL
Music: Howard Hughes, SM, © 1985, GIA Publications, Inc.

Verses

The Lord is my light and my salvation;
whom shall I fear?

The Lord is the stronghold of my life;
whom should I dread? ℞.

There is one thing I ask of the LORD,
only this do I seek:
to live in the house of the LORD
all the days of my life,
to gaze on the beauty of the LORD,
to inquire at his temple. ℟.

I believe I shall see the LORD's goodness
in the land of the living.
Wait for the LORD; be strong;
be stouthearted, and wait for the LORD! ℟.

Text: Psalm 27:1, 4, 13–14, *The Revised Grail Psalms*, © 2010, Conception Abbey and The Grail, admin. by GIA Publications, Inc.
Music: Michel Guimont, © 1995, GIA Publications, Inc.

Additional responsorial psalms for Baptism of Children are listed in the Index of Psalms and Canticles, no. 1233.

143 GOSPEL

Before the gospel reading, an acclamation is sung:

Al - le - lu - ia, al - le - lu - ia, al - le - lu - ia.

Music: Chant Mode VI; acc. by Richard Proulx, © 1985, GIA Publications, Inc.

During Lent:

Praise to you, Lord Je - sus Christ, king of end - less glo - ry!

Text: ICEL, © 1969
Music: Frank Schoen, © 1970, GIA Publications, Inc.

Deacon (or priest): The Lord be with you.
  Assembly: **And with your spirit.**
   Deacon: A reading from the holy Gospel according to N.
  Assembly: **Glory to you, O Lord.**

After the reading:

   Deacon: The Gospel of the Lord.
  Assembly: **Praise to you, Lord Jesus Christ.**

144 INTERCESSIONS

All join in prayer for the Church, the needs of the world, the poor, the children to be baptized and their parents.

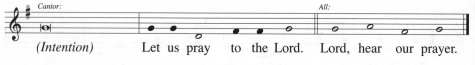

(Intention) Let us pray to the Lord. Lord, hear our prayer.

Music: Byzantine chant

This prayer concludes with the litany of the saints, which may include the patron saints of the children and of the local Church.

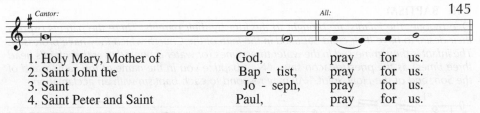

145

1. Holy Mary, Mother of God, pray for us.
2. Saint John the Bap - tist, pray for us.
3. Saint Jo - seph, pray for us.
4. Saint Peter and Saint Paul, pray for us.

The names of other saints may be added here. The litany concludes:

5. All holy men and women, Saints of God, pray for us.

PRAYER OF EXORCISM AND ANOINTING

146

The priest/deacon stands before the parents with their infants and prays that God deliver these children from the power of evil. The children may be anointed with the oil of catechumens, an anointing which makes them strong for their struggle against evil in their lives. Or, the priest/deacon may lay hands on each child to show the love and concern the Church has for them. If there is a procession to the baptistry, the following may be sung:

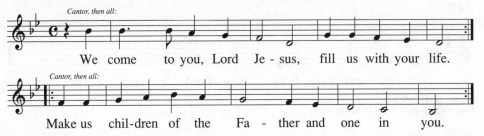

We come to you, Lord Je - sus, fill us with your life.

Make us chil-dren of the Fa - ther and one in you.

Text: *Rite of Baptism for Children*, © 1969, ICEL
Music: Ronald Arnatt, © 1984, GIA Publications, Inc.

SACRAMENT OF BAPTISM

147

BLESSING AND INVOCATION OF GOD OVER BAPTISMAL WATER

When all are gathered at the font, the priest/deacon leads a blessing of the water, unless the baptismal water has already been blessed.

RENUNCIATION OF SIN AND PROFESSION OF FAITH

The priest/deacon then questions the parents and godparents, and they make a renunciation of sin and evil and profess their faith. The assembly listens to their responses. The priest/deacon then invites all to give their assent to this profession of faith, using the following formulary, a similar one (no. 916), or a suitable song by which the community expresses its faith with a single voice.

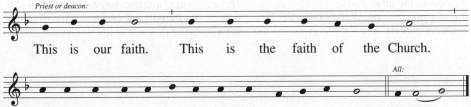

This is our faith. This is the faith of the Church.

We are proud to pro-fess it in Christ Je - sus our Lord. A - men.

Text: *Rite of Baptism for Children*, © 1969, ICEL

148 BAPTISM

One by one, the infants are brought to the font by their parents. There the parents express their desire to have their child baptized in the faith of the Church which they have professed. The infant is then immersed in the water three times (or water is poured over the infant's head three times) as the priest/deacon says: "N., I baptize you in the name of the Father, and of the Son, and of the Holy Spirit." All may respond to each baptism with an acclamation.

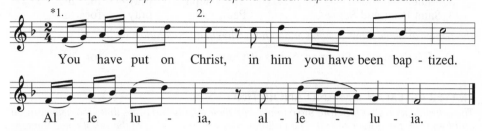

*May be sung in canon.

Text: *Rite of Baptism for Children,* © 1969, ICEL
Music: Howard Hughes, SM, © 1977, ICEL

149

During Lent:

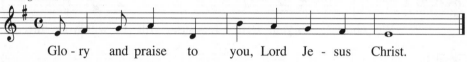

Text: *Rite of Christian Initiation of Adults,* © 1985, ICEL
Music: Marty Haugen, © 1995, GIA Publications, Inc.

150 ANOINTING WITH CHRISM

The priest/deacon anoints each child on the crown of the head with holy chrism, a mixture of oil and perfume. The word "Christ" means "anointed." The baptized child has been "Christed" and the sweet smell of the anointing reminds all of this.

CLOTHING WITH THE BAPTISMAL GARMENT AND GIVING OF THE CANDLE

The infants are then clothed in baptismal garments and a candle for each of the newly baptized is lighted from the paschal candle.

(Optional) EPHPHETHA

The priest/deacon may touch the ears and mouth of each child: "May Jesus soon touch your ears to receive his word, and your mouth to proclaim his faith."

CONCLUSION AND BLESSING

If baptism is celebrated at Mass, the liturgy continues with the Eucharist. Otherwise, all process to the altar, carrying lighted candles. The above acclamation may be sung again during this procession. All then pray the Lord's Prayer, the parents are blessed, after which all respond: **Amen***, and the liturgy concludes with a hymn of praise and thanksgiving.*

Confirmation

Along with baptism and eucharist, confirmation is a sacrament of Christian initiation. It is the seal of baptism, the giving of the Holy Spirit. Adults are confirmed immediately after their baptism at the Easter Vigil. Children who have been baptized as infants are confirmed some years later. The bishop or his delegate presides over the celebration. The rite is usually celebrated within Mass; the introductory rites are done in the usual way.

LITURGY OF THE WORD

FIRST READINGS

One or more passages from Scripture are read. At the conclusion of each:

Reader: The word of the Lord.
Assembly: **Thanks be to God.**

RESPONSORIAL PSALM

The following psalm may follow the first reading:

Refrain

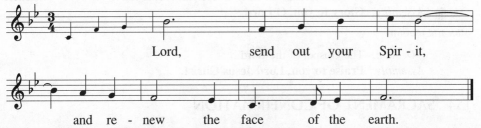

Lord, send out your Spir - it, and re - new the face of the earth.

Text: *Lectionary for Mass,* © 1969, ICEL
Music: Richard Proulx, © 1975, GIA Publications, Inc.

Verses

Bless the LORD, O my soul!
O LORD my God, how great you are.
How many are your works, O LORD!
In wisdom you have made them all.
The earth is full of your creatures. ℟.

All of these look to you
to give them their food in due season.
You give it, they gather it up;
you open wide your hand, they are well
    filled. ℟.

You send forth your spirit, and they
    are created,
and you renew the face of the earth.
May the glory of the LORD last forever!
May the LORD rejoice in his works! ℟.

I will sing to the LORD all my life,
sing psalms to my God while I live.
May my thoughts be pleasing to him.
I will rejoice in the LORD. ℟.

Text: Psalm 104:1 and 24, 27–28, 30–31, 33–34, *The Revised Grail Psalms,* © 2010, Conception Abbey and The Grail, admin. by
    GIA Publications, Inc.
Music: Joseph Gelineau, SJ, © 1963, The Grail, GIA Publications, Inc., agent

Additional responsorial psalms for Confirmation are listed in the Index of Psalms and Canticles, no. 1233.

153 GOSPEL

Before the gospel reading, an acclamation is sung:

Cantor, then all:

Al - le - lu - ia, al - le - lu - ia, al - le - lu - ia.

Music: Chant Mode VI; acc. by Richard Proulx, © 1985, GIA Publications, Inc.

During Lent:

Cantor, then all:

Praise to you, Lord Je - sus Christ, king of end - less glo - ry!

Text: ICEL, © 1969
Music: Frank Schoen, © 1970, GIA Publications, Inc.

Deacon (or priest): The Lord be with you.
    Assembly: **And with your spirit.**
      Deacon: A reading from the holy Gospel according to N.
    Assembly: **Glory to you, O Lord.**

After the reading:

      Deacon: The Gospel of the Lord.
    Assembly: **Praise to you, Lord Jesus Christ.**

154 SACRAMENT OF CONFIRMATION

PRESENTATION OF THE CANDIDATES
The pastor or another minister calls the candidates by name to come forward. Sponsors may accompany candidates.

HOMILY

RENEWAL OF BAPTISMAL PROMISES
The bishop leads the candidates in the renunciation of sin and evil and the profession of their faith. When the candidates have responded, the bishop invites all to give their assent to this profession of faith, using the following formulary, a similar one (no. 916), or a suitable song by which the community expresses its faith with a single voice.

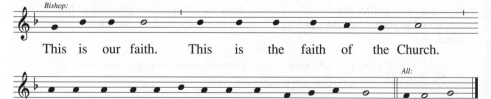

Bishop:

This is our faith. This is the faith of the Church.

All:

We are proud to pro-fess it in Christ Je - sus our Lord. A - men.

Text: *Rite of Confirmation,* © 1975, ICEL

LAYING ON OF HANDS

Over and over the Church makes this gesture in the sacraments as a blessing, a sign of solidarity and love. Here the bishop prays for the coming of the Holy Spirit on those confirmed.

ANOINTING WITH CHRISM

Chrism is a mixture of olive oil and perfume that has been consecrated by the bishop at the end of Lent. The meaning of "Christ" is "the anointed," so in this gesture the candidate is anointed, sealed, to follow in the way of Christ. The bishop rubs the chrism into the forehead of each candidate and says: "N., be sealed with the gift of the Holy Spirit," and the newly confirmed person responds, "Amen." The bishop then says, "Peace be with you," and the newly confirmed person responds, "And with your spirit." The assembly may join in song during the anointing.

After the anointing the liturgy continues with the prayer of the faithful and the liturgy of the eucharist. If confirmation is celebrated apart from Mass, the intercessions are followed by the Lord's Prayer (see no. 219), the blessing, and the concluding hymn.

155 Holy Communion outside Mass

When for good reason Communion cannot be received at Mass, the faithful may share in the paschal mystery through the liturgy of the word and the reception of Holy Communion.

156 INTRODUCTORY RITES

An appropriate hymn or psalm may be sung.

GREETING

If the minister is a priest or deacon, the usual form of greeting is used:

Assembly: **And with your spirit.**

If the minister is not a priest or deacon, another form of greeting may be used:

Assembly: **Blessed be God for ever.**

PENITENTIAL ACT

The minister invites silent reflection and repentance. After some silence:

Assembly: **I confess to almighty God**
and to you, my brothers and sisters,
that I have greatly sinned,
in my thoughts and in my words,
in what I have done and in what I have failed to do,
All strike their breast as they say:
through my fault, through my fault,
through my most grievous fault;
therefore I ask blessed Mary ever-Virgin,
all the Angels and Saints,
and you, my brothers and sisters,
to pray for me to the Lord our God.

The forms found at nos. 204 and 205 may also be used.

157 CELEBRATION OF THE WORD OF GOD

FIRST READINGS

One or more passages from Scripture are read. At the conclusion of each:

Reader: The word of the Lord.
Assembly: **Thanks be to God.**

RESPONSORIAL PSALM

An appropriate psalm may follow the first reading.

GOSPEL

158

Before the gospel reading, an alleluia or Lenten acclamation is sung.

[*Deacon (or priest):* The Lord be with you.]
           Assembly: **And with your spirit.**
            Reader: A reading from the holy Gospel according to N.
      Assembly: **Glory to you, O Lord.**

After the reading:

            Reader: The Gospel of the Lord.
      Assembly: **Praise to you, Lord Jesus Christ.**

INTERCESSIONS

159

The assembly joins in prayer for the needs of the world, of the poor, and of the Church.

HOLY COMMUNION

160

The minister invites all to join in the Lord's Prayer, then to exchange a sign of peace. The minister then raises the eucharistic bread and all respond to the invitation.

Assembly: **Lord, I am not worthy**
        that you should enter under my roof,
        but only say the word
        and my soul shall be healed.

A psalm or hymn may be sung during Communion. Afterwards, there may be a period of silence or the singing of a psalm or hymn. The minister then recites a concluding prayer.

CONCLUDING RITE

All are blessed and dismissed.

Presiding minister: Go in the peace of Christ.

      Assembly: **Thanks be to God.**

161 Eucharistic Exposition and Benediction

"Exposition of the holy eucharist . . . is intended to acknowledge Christ's marvelous presence in the sacrament. Exposition invites us to the spiritual union with him that culminates in sacramental communion. Thus it fosters very well the worship which is due to Christ in spirit and in truth.

This kind of exposition must clearly express the cult of the blessed sacrament in its relationship to the Mass. The plan of the exposition should carefully avoid anything which might somehow obscure the principal desire of Christ in instituting the eucharist, namely, to be with us as food, medicine, and comfort" (*Holy Communion and Worship of the Eucharist outside of Mass*, #82).

162 EXPOSITION

As the priest or deacon prepares the holy eucharist for adoration, the following or another suitable song is sung:

1. O Sav - ing Vic - tim, o - p'ning wide The
2. To your great name be end - less praise, Im -
1. O sa - lu - tá - ris hó - sti - a, Quae
2. U - ni tri - nó - que Dó - mi - no Sit

gate of heav'n to us be - low! Our foes press on from
mor - tal God - head, One in Three; O grant us end - less
cae - li pan - dis ó - sti - um: Bel - la pre - munt ho -
sem - pi - tér - na gló - ri - a: Qui vi - tam si - ne

ev - 'ry side: Your aid sup - ply, your strength be - stow.
length of days When our true na - tive land we see.
stí - li - a, Da ro - bur fer au - xí - li - um.
tér - mi - no No - bis do - net in pá - tri - a.

Text: Thomas Aquinas, c.1225–1274; tr. by Edward Caswall, 1814–1878 and John Mason Neale, 1818–1866, alt.
Tune: DUGUET, LM; Dieudonné Duguet, 1794–1849

163 ADORATION

During the adoration there are prayers, songs, scripture readings, and possibly a homily to develop a better understanding of the eucharistic mystery. Silent prayer is also encouraged. If time allows, the Liturgy of the Hours may be celebrated here.

164 BENEDICTION

As the priest or deacon incenses the Blessed Sacrament, the following or another appropriate hymn or song may be sung:

1. Come a - dore this won - drous pres - ence; Bow to Christ, the
2. Glo - ry be to God the Fa - ther, Praise to his co -
1. *Tan - tum er - go Sa - cra - mén - tum Ve - ne - ré - mur*
2. *Ge - ni - tó - ri, Ge - ni - tó - que Laus et ju - bi -*

source of grace! Here is kept the an - cient prom - ise
e - qual Son, Ad - o - ra - tion to the Spir - it,
cér - nu - i: Et an - tí - quum do - cu - mén - tum
lá - ti - o, Sa - lus, ho - nor, vir - tus quo - que

Of God's earth - ly dwell - ing - place. Sight is blind be -
Bond of love, in God - head one. Blest be God by
No - vo ce - dat rí - tu - i: Prae - stet fi - des
Sit et be - ne - dí - cti - o: Pro - ce - dén - ti

fore God's glo - ry. Faith a - lone may see his face.
all cre - a - tion Joy - ous - ly while a - ges run!
sup - ple - mén - tum Sén - su - um de - fé - ctu - i.
ab u - tró - que Com - par sit lau - dá - ti - o.

Text: Thomas Aquinas, c.1225–1274; tr. by James Quinn, SJ, 1919–2010, © 1969. Used by permission of Selah Publishing Co., Inc.
Tune: ST. THOMAS (Wade), 8 7 8 7 8 7; John F. Wade, 1711–1786

After a prayer, the priest or deacon blesses the assembly with the Blessed Sacrament.

REPOSITION 165

As the priest or deacon replaces the Sacrament in the tabernacle, the assembly may sing or say the following acclamations:

Blessed be God.
Blessed be his holy name.
Blessed be Jesus Christ, true God and true man.
Blessed be the name of Jesus.
Blessed be his most sacred heart.
Blessed be his most precious blood.
Blessed be Jesus in the most holy sacrament of the altar.
Blessed be the Holy Spirit, the Paraclete.
Blessed be the great Mother of God, Mary most holy.
Blessed be her holy and immaculate conception.
Blessed be her glorious assumption.
Blessed be the name of Mary, virgin and mother.
Blessed be Saint Joseph, her most chaste spouse.
Blessed be God in his angels and in his saints.

166 Reconciliation of Several Penitents

The sacrament of penance, also called the sacrament of reconciliation, may be celebrated with one penitent or with many. The latter form, the communal penance service, is a gathering of a few or a large number of Christians. Together they listen to Scripture, sing psalms and hymns, pray, individually confess their sins and receive absolution, then praise God whose mercy and love are greater than our evil. In the rite of penance, the members of the Church confront the struggle that was entered at baptism. There has been failure, evil done and good undone, but the penitent Church comes again and again to name and renounce its sins and to return to the way of the Lord.

167 INTRODUCTORY RITES

An appropriate hymn or psalm may be sung (see nos. 957–971).

GREETING

The priest greets the assembly, using these or other words:

> *Priest:* Grace to you and peace from God our Father
> and the Lord Jesus Christ.
>
> *Assembly:* **And with your spirit.**

OPENING PRAYER

After silent prayer, the priest concludes the gathering rite with a solemn prayer.

168 CELEBRATION OF THE WORD OF GOD

FIRST READINGS

One or more passages from Scripture are read. At the conclusion of each:

> *Reader:* The word of the Lord.
>
> *Assembly:* **Thanks be to God.**

RESPONSORIAL PSALM

The following psalm may follow the first reading:

Refrain

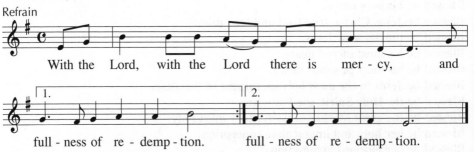

With the Lord, with the Lord there is mer - cy, and

1. full - ness of re - demp - tion.

2. full - ness of re - demp - tion.

Text: *Lectionary for Mass*, © 1969, 1981, 1997, ICEL
Music: Ronald F. Krisman, © 2004, GIA Publications, Inc.

Verses

Out of the depths I cry to you, O Lᴏʀᴅ;
Lord, hear my voice!
O let your ears be attentive
to the sound of my pleadings. ℞.

If you, O Lᴏʀᴅ, should mark iniquities,
Lord, who could stand?
But with you is found forgiveness,
that you may be revered. ℞.

I long for you, O Lᴏʀᴅ,
my soul longs for his word.
My soul hopes in the Lord
more than watchmen for daybreak. ℞.

For with the Lᴏʀᴅ there is mercy,
in him is plentiful redemption.
It is he who will redeem Israel
from all its iniquities. ℞.

Text: Psalm 130:1–2, 3–4, 5–6, 7–8; *The Revised Grail Psalms*, © 2010, Conception Abbey and The Grail, admin. by GIA Publications, Inc.;
Music: Michel Guimont, © 1995, GIA Publications, Inc.

Additional responsorial psalms for Reconciliation of Several Penitents are listed in the Index of Psalms and Canticles, no. 1233.

GOSPEL 169

Before the gospel reading, an acclamation is sung:

Al - le - lu - ia,   al - le - lu - ia,   al - le - lu - ia.

Music: Chant Mode VI; acc. by Richard Proulx, © 1985, GIA Publications, Inc.

During Lent:

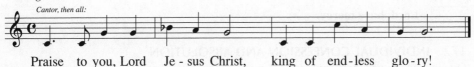

Praise to you, Lord Je - sus Christ,   king of end - less glo - ry!

Text: ICEL, © 1969
Music: Frank Schoen, © 1970, GIA Publications, Inc.

Deacon (or priest): The Lord be with you.
    Assembly: **And with your spirit.**
      Deacon: A reading from the holy Gospel according to N.
    Assembly: **Glory to you, O Lord.**

After the reading:

      Deacon: The Gospel of the Lord.
    Assembly: **Praise to you, Lord Jesus Christ.**

HOMILY

EXAMINATION OF CONSCIENCE

In silence or through some other manner all reflect on their lives with sorrow for their sins.

170   SACRAMENT OF PENANCE

GENERAL CONFESSION OF SINS

*Kneeling (or with another posture that expresses sorrow), all join in confession.
This form may be used:*

Assembly: **I confess to almighty God
and to you, my brothers and sisters,
that I have greatly sinned,
in my thoughts and in my words,
in what I have done and in what I have failed to do,**
All strike their breast as they say:
**through my fault, through my fault,
through my most grievous fault;
therefore I ask blessed Mary ever-Virgin,
all the Angels and Saints,
and you, my brothers and sisters,
to pray for me to the Lord our God.**

171

*Standing, all join in a litany using one of the following responses, or a song asking God's
mercy. The Lord's Prayer is then recited or sung. (See no. 219)*

A   **We pray you, hear us.**

B   **Lord, be merciful to me, a sinner.**

C   **Lord, have mercy.**

172   INDIVIDUAL CONFESSION AND ABSOLUTION

*One by one the penitents approach the priest confessors. All confess their sins, accept some
fitting act of satisfaction and the counsel of the confessor. Then the priest extends his hands
over the penitent's head and speaks the prayer of absolution, concluding: "Through the ministry of the Church may God give you pardon and peace, and I absolve you from your sins
in the name of the Father, and of the Son, and of the Holy Spirit." The penitent responds,
"Amen." (Note: On those occasions when general absolution is permitted, the rest of the rite
remains the same.)*

173   PROCLAMATION OF PRAISE FOR GOD'S MERCY

*The priest invites all to give thanks and to show by their lives—and in the life of the whole
community—the grace of repentance. A psalm, canticle or hymn may be sung to proclaim
God's mercy.*

Refrain

Praise   the   Lord   and   call   up - on   his   name.

Verses
I thank you, Lord, you were angry with me
but your anger has passed and you give me comfort. ℟.

Truly, God is my salvation,
I trust, I shall not fear.
For the Lord is my strength, my song,
he became my savior.
With joy you will draw water
from the wells of salvation. ℟.

Give thanks to the Lord, give praise to his name!
Make his mighty deeds known to the peoples!
Declare the greatness of his name,
sing a psalm to the Lord!
For he has done glorious deeds,
make them known to all the earth! ℟.

People of Zion, sing and shout for joy
for great in your midst is the Holy One of Israel. ℟.

Text: Isaiah 12:1–6; The Grail, © 1963, The Grail, GIA Publications, Inc., agent
Music: Michel Guimont, © 1995, GIA Publications, Inc.

CONCLUDING PRAYER OF THANKSGIVING
This prayer is spoken by the priest.

BLESSING AND DISMISSAL
The priest blesses all present and the deacon or other minister dismisses the assembly.
All respond: **Thanks be to God.**

174 Anointing of the Sick

The sacrament of the anointing of the sick is celebrated when a Christian's health is seriously impaired by sickness or old age. Through the anointing with the blessed oil of the sick, the Church supports those who struggle against illness or injury and continues the healing work of Christ. The anointing is intended to bring hope and comfort to those anointed and, to the gathered assembly of family and friends, a spirit of support and sharing in the sufferings of their brothers and sisters.

The anointing may be celebrated within Mass or outside Mass. In either case a liturgy of the word precedes the anointing. Following is the rite of anointing within Mass.

175 INTRODUCTORY RITES

An appropriate hymn or psalm may be sung (see nos. 972–981).

GREETING

After all make the sign of the cross, the priest greets the assembly, using these or other words.

> *Priest:* The grace of our Lord Jesus Christ,
> and the love of God,
> and the communion of the Holy Spirit
> be with you all.
>
> *Assembly:* **And with your spirit.**

The priest introduces the celebration, and the penitential act may follow (see Order of Mass, nos. 204 and 205). Then, after a period of silence, he says the opening prayer, to which all respond: **Amen**.

176 LITURGY OF THE WORD

FIRST READINGS

One or more passages from Scripture are read. At the conclusion of each:

> *Reader:* The word of the Lord.
> *Assembly:* **Thanks be to God.**

RESPONSORIAL PSALM

The following psalm may follow the first reading:

Refrain

My God, my God, come quick-ly to help me.

Text: *Pastoral Care of the Sick: Rites of Anointing and Viaticum*, © 1982, ICEL
Music: Ronald F. Krisman, © 2011, GIA Publications, Inc.

Verses

In you, O LORD, I take refuge;
let me never be put to shame.
In your justice, rescue me, free me;
incline your ear to me and save me. ℟.

It is you, O Lord, who are my hope,
my trust, O LORD, from my youth.
On you I have leaned from my birth;
from my mother's womb, you have
been my help. ℟.

My mouth is filled with your praise,
with your glory, all the day long.
Do not reject me now that I am old;
when my strength fails do not forsake me. ℟.

But as for me, I will always hope,
and praise you more and more.
My mouth will tell of your justice,
and all the day long of your salvation. ℟.

Text: Psalm 71:1–2, 5–6, 8–9, 14–15, *The Revised Grail Psalms*, © 2010, Conception Abbey and The Grail, admin. by GIA Publications, Inc.
Music: A. Gregory Murray, OSB, © L. J. Carey and Co., Ltd.

Additional responsorial psalms for Anointing of the Sick are listed in the Index of Psalms and Canticles, no. 1233.

GOSPEL 177

Before the gospel reading, an acclamation is sung:

Al - le - lu - ia, al - le - lu - ia, al - le - lu - ia.

Music: Chant Mode VI; acc. by Richard Proulx, © 1985, GIA Publications, Inc.

During Lent:

Praise to you, Lord Je - sus Christ, king of end - less glo - ry!

Text: ICEL, © 1969
Music: Frank Schoen, © 1970, GIA Publications, Inc.

Deacon (or priest): The Lord be with you.
 Assembly: **And with your spirit.**
  Deacon: A reading from the holy Gospel according to N.
 Assembly: **Glory to you, O Lord.**

After the reading:

  Deacon: The Gospel of the Lord.
 Assembly: **Praise to you, Lord Jesus Christ.**

HOMILY

LITURGY OF ANOINTING 178

LITANY

The assembly joins in prayers for the sick and for those who care for them. Each petition concludes with "Lord, have mercy," and all repeat:

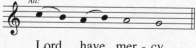

Lord, have mer - cy.

LAYING ON OF HANDS

The priest silently lays hands on the head of each sick person in a gesture of prayer, healing and solidarity.

179 PRAYER OVER THE OIL

If the oil is already blessed, the priest leads a prayer of thanksgiving over it.
After each invocation:

Bless-ed be God who heals us in Christ.

Text: *Pastoral Care of the Sick: Rites of Anointing and Viaticum,* © 1982, ICEL
Music: Paul M. French, © 2011, GIA Publications, Inc.

If the oil is not blessed, the priest says the prayer of blessing.

180 ANOINTING

The priest anoints each sick person on the forehead, saying:

Through this holy anointing may the Lord in his love and mercy help you with the grace of the Holy Spirit.

Assembly: **Amen.**

The priest anoints the hands of each sick person, saying:

May the Lord who frees you from sin save you and raise you up.

Assembly: **Amen.**

The priest may anoint other parts of the body.

PRAYER AFTER ANOINTING

The priest prays for those who have been anointed. Then the liturgy of the eucharist is celebrated with special prayers for the sick (see Order of Mass, no. 212).

If the rite of anointing is celebrated outside Mass, the liturgy begins with the greeting, introduction, and penitential act (or sacrament of penance). After the scripture readings a period of silence is observed, or the priest gives a brief homily. The liturgy of anointing is celebrated as above. Then the Lord's Prayer is recited or sung, the liturgy of Holy Communion may follow, and a final blessing is given.

Marriage

The mutual and lifelong commitment of a man and a woman in marriage is viewed by the Church as a sacred covenant. When two Christians marry, it is also a sacrament, an effective sign of the presence of God in the world and a symbol of Christ's love for his Church. In the sacrament of matrimony God's special graces are given to the couple to live out "in mutual and lasting fidelity" the vows they make to each other and to God in the presence of the Christian community.

At their wedding the bride and groom themselves are the ministers of the sacrament to each other; the priest or deacon who presides over the wedding serves as the authorized witness of the Church and prays the nuptial blessing of the Church over the spouses.

The rite of marriage may be celebrated at Mass or outside of Mass. In either case the rite begins with a liturgy of the word: the proclamation of God's faithful love by means of readings from Scripture and a reflection on them (the homily). The following elements are included in all celebrations.

INTRODUCTORY RITES

An appropriate hymn or psalm may be sung during the procession or immediately after it (see nos. 982–987).

GREETING

After all make the sign of the cross, the priest or deacon greets the assembly, using these or other words.

> *Priest:* The grace of our Lord Jesus Christ,
> and the love of God,
> and the communion of the Holy Spirit
> be with you all.

Assembly: **And with your spirit.**

OPENING PRAYER

The priest or deacon introduces the celebration and, after a period of silence, says the opening prayer, to which all respond: **Amen**. *All then sit.*

LITURGY OF THE WORD

FIRST READINGS

One or more passages from Scripture are read. At the conclusion of each:

> *Reader:* The word of the Lord.
> *Assembly:* **Thanks be to God.**

RESPONSORIAL PSALM

The following psalm may follow the first reading:

Refrain

Taste and see the good - ness of the Lord.

Verses

I will bless the Lord at all times;
praise of him is always in my mouth.
In the Lord my soul shall make its boast;
the humble shall hear and be glad. ℟.

Look toward him and be radiant;
let your faces not be abashed.
This lowly one called; the Lord heard,
and rescued him from all his distress. ℟.

Glorify the Lord with me;
together let us praise his name.
I sought the Lord, and he answered me;
from all my terrors he set me free. ℟.

The angel of the Lord is encamped
around those who fear him, to rescue them.
Taste and see that the Lord is good.
Blessed the man who seeks refuge in
him. ℟.

Text: Psalm 34:2–9, *The Revised Grail Psalms*, © 2010, Conception Abbey and The Grail, admin. by GIA Publications, Inc.; refrain trans. © 1969, ICEL
Music: Michel Guimont, © 2004, GIA Publications, Inc.

Additional responsorial psalms for Marriage are listed in the Index of Psalms and Canticles, no. 1233.

184 GOSPEL

Before the gospel reading, all stand as an acclamation is sung:

Al - le - lu - ia, al - le - lu - ia, al - le - lu - ia.

Music: Chant Mode VI; acc. by Richard Proulx, © 1985, GIA Publications, Inc.

During Lent:

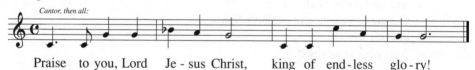

Praise to you, Lord Je - sus Christ, king of end - less glo - ry!

Text: ICEL, © 1969
Music: Frank Schoen, © 1970, GIA Publications, Inc.

Deacon (or priest): The Lord be with you.
     Assembly: **And with your spirit.**
     Deacon: A reading from the holy Gospel according to N.
     Assembly: **Glory to you, O Lord.**

After the reading:

     Deacon: The Gospel of the Lord.
     Assembly: **Praise to you, Lord Jesus Christ.**

HOMILY *(All sit)*

RITE OF MARRIAGE 185

After the homily all stand. The priest or deacon invites the couple to declare to each other their consent to enter into marriage, and receives the couple's vows in the name of the Church. Wedding rings, a sign of love and fidelity, may be blessed and exchanged and, according to particular customs, other rituals expressing the couple's union may be added.

In the prayer of the faithful the Church prays for the needs of the world, the local community, and the newly married couple. A common response to each petition is: **Lord, hear our prayer.**

If the liturgy of the eucharist does not follow the rite of marriage, the priest or deacon prays the nuptial blessing at the end of the prayer of the faithful. The celebration concludes with the Lord's Prayer and a final blessing.

When the liturgy of the eucharist follows the rite of marriage, the nuptial blessing is given after the Lord's Prayer before Holy Communion. Everything else follows the Order of Mass, beginning with the presentation and preparation of the gifts. The bride and groom may bring the bread and wine to the altar. See Order of Mass, no. 212.

THE LORD'S PRAYER 186

Assembly: **Our Father, who art in heaven,**
hallowed be thy name;
thy kingdom come,
thy will be done
on earth as it is in heaven.
Give us this day our daily bread,
and forgive us our trespasses,
as we forgive those who trespass against us;
and lead us not into temptation,
but deliver us from evil.

BLESSING AND DISMISSAL

All respond to each part of the blessing: **Amen.**

Deacon or priest: Go in peace.
Assembly: **Thanks be to God.**

A hymn or instrumental music may follow.

187 Holy Orders

From the time of the apostles, God has called some members of the Church to minister to the others through the diaconate and the priesthood. In the sacrament of Holy Orders a man accepts this call from God which is expressed through the Church's representative, the bishop.

Ordained bishops, presbyters (priests) and deacons have a unique role within the Catholic community and exercise this service by teaching, leading worship and offering pastoral care and guidance.

The sacrament of Holy Orders has distinct rites for the ordination of bishops, priests and deacons. A bishop always presides over the celebration. Common to each rite is an imposition of hands by the bishop on the head of the one being ordained, signifying the outpouring of the gifts of the Holy Spirit for ministry, and a prayer of consecration.

Rites of ordination are celebrated within Mass and usually at the cathedral church of the diocese; the introductory rites are done in the usual way.

188 LITURGY OF THE WORD

FIRST READINGS

One or more passages from Scripture are read. At the conclusion of each:

   Reader: The word of the Lord.
   Assembly: **Thanks be to God.**

RESPONSORIAL PSALM

The following psalm may follow the first reading:
Refrain

Go out to the world and teach all na - tions.

Go out to the world. Al-le - lu - ia, al-le - lu - ia.

Text: *Lectionary for Mass,* © 1969, 1981, 1997, ICEL
Music: Ronald F. Krisman, © 1982, GIA Publications, Inc.

Verses

O sing a new song to the Lord;
sing to the Lord, all the earth.
O sing to the Lord; bless his name. ℟.

Proclaim his salvation day by day.
Tell among the nations his glory,

and his wonders among all the peoples. ℟.

Say to the nations, "The Lord is king."
The world he made firm in its place;
he will judge the peoples in fairness. ℟.

Text: Psalm 96:1–2, 2–3, 10, *The Revised Grail Psalms,* © 2010, Conception Abbey and The Grail, admin. by GIA Publications, Inc.
Music: Michel Guimont, © 1995, GIA Publications, Inc.

Additional responsorial psalms for Holy Orders are listed in the Index of Psalms and Canticles, no. 1233.

GOSPEL

Before the gospel reading, all stand as an acclamation is sung:

Al - le - lu - ia,   al - le - lu - ia,   al - le - lu - ia.

Music: Chant Mode VI; acc. by Richard Proulx, © 1985, GIA Publications, Inc.

During Lent:

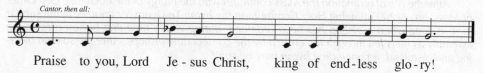

Praise to you, Lord Je - sus Christ,   king of end - less glo - ry!

Text: ICEL, © 1969
Music: Frank Schoen, © 1970, GIA Publications, Inc.

Deacon (or priest): The Lord be with you.
    Assembly: **And with your spirit.**
      Deacon: A reading from the holy Gospel according to N.
    Assembly: **Glory to you, O Lord.**

After the reading:

    Deacon: The Gospel of the Lord.
    Assembly: **Praise to you, Lord Jesus Christ.**

RITE OF ORDINATION

After the Gospel has been proclaimed, the rite begins with the calling, presentation and election of the candidate(s) by the bishop and the consent of the people. In the ordination of bishops the hymn Veni, Creator Spiritus *is then sung (see nos. 537, 543, and 546).*

HOMILY

EXAMINATION OF CANDIDATE(S) AND PROMISE OF OBEDIENCE

Each candidate is questioned about his readiness to assume the responsibilities of the order to which he is being ordained. He then makes a promise of obedience to his lawful superior. Unmarried candidates for the diaconate also make a promise to live a celibate life.

LITANY OF SAINTS

After an invitation to prayer, the Litany of Saints is chanted. (See no. 1070.)

LAYING ON OF HANDS AND PRAYER OF CONSECRATION

In silence the ordaining bishop prays for the coming of the Holy Spirit on those ordained through a laying on of hands. For those being ordained priests, all members of the order of presbyters who are present repeat this solemn gesture. Similarly all bishops present lay their hands on those who are being ordained as bishops. An open Book of the Gospels is also placed on the heads of those being ordained bishops. Then the ordaining bishop prays the prayer of consecration.

INVESTITURE AND ANOINTING WITH CHRISM

Those newly ordained are clothed with the liturgical vestments of their order. While newly ordained priests are vested, the hymn Veni Creator, Spiritus or another appropriate hymn similar to it is sung (see nos. 537, 543, and 546). The hands of newly ordained priests and the heads of newly ordained bishops are anointed with sacred Chrism, the mixture of olive oil and perfume consecrated at the annual diocesan Chrism Mass. All the newly ordained are presented with the Book of the Gospels. Priests are presented with the bread, wine and water used for the celebration of Mass, while bishops are invested with ring, miter, and pastoral staff. All the newly ordained then receive the kiss of peace from the ordaining bishop and from the members of their respective order who are present. The assembly may join in song during these rituals.

After the rite of ordination the Mass continues with the liturgy of the eucharist. (See Order of Mass, no. 212.) Following Holy Communion the hymn Te Deum, or another hymn similar to it, is sung when a bishop has been ordained, during which time that bishop blesses the assembly as he is led through the church by the consecrating bishops. After the solemn blessing and dismissal, a concluding hymn may be sung.

Funerals

The rites which surround the death of a Christian extend from Viaticum (the last Holy Communion) and final prayers before death through the wake service and funeral liturgy to the burial of the body or cremated remains. In all of this the community affirms its faith in the communion of saints and the resurrection of the dead. The family and friends are helped in their time of sorrow with prayer and song. Thus they express present grief even as they hold to the Church's lasting hope.

The funeral liturgy may be celebrated within Mass or outside Mass. In either case the rite begins with a liturgy of the word. The following elements are included in all celebrations.

INTRODUCTORY RITES

GREETING   192

All stand as the priest (or deacon) greets the assembly at the door, using these or other words.

> *Priest:* Grace to you and peace from God our Father
> and the Lord Jesus Christ.

> *Assembly:* **And with your spirit.**

The body is sprinkled with holy water, a reminder of baptism. The family or pall bearers spread the pall, a garment like that which the Christian received at baptism, over the body. The funeral procession then moves into the church accompanied by an appropriate hymn or psalm.

Refrain   193

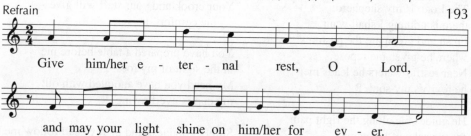

Give him/her e - ter - nal rest, O Lord,
and may your light shine on him/her for ev - er.

Text: *Order of Christian Funerals,* © 1985, ICEL
Music: Robert J. Batastini, © 1986, GIA Publications, Inc.

Verses

I love the LORD, for he has heard
my voice, my appeal;
for he has turned his ear to me
whenever I call. ℟.

They surrounded me, the snares of death;
the anguish of the grave has found me;
anguish and sorrow I found.
I called on the name of the LORD:
"Deliver my soul, O LORD!" ℟.

How gracious is the LORD, and just;
our God has compassion.

The LORD protects the simple;
I was brought low, and he saved me. ℟.

Turn back, my soul, to your rest,
for the LORD has been good to you;
he has kept my soul from death,
my eyes from tears, and my feet from
stumbling. ℟.

I will walk in the presence of the LORD
in the land of the living.
Praise the Father, the Son and Holy Spirit,
for ever and ever. ℟.

Text: Psalm 116A, *The Revised Grail Psalms,* © 2010, Conception Abbey and The Grail, admin. by GIA Publications, Inc.
Music: Joseph Gelineau, SJ, © 1963, The Grail, GIA Publications, Inc., agent

OPENING PRAYER

After silent prayer, the priest concludes the introductory rites with a solemn prayer, to which all respond: **Amen.**

194 LITURGY OF THE WORD

FIRST READINGS

One or more passages from Scripture are read. At the conclusion of each:

Reader: The word of the Lord.
Assembly: **Thanks be to God.**

RESPONSORIAL PSALM

The following psalm may follow the first reading:

Refrain

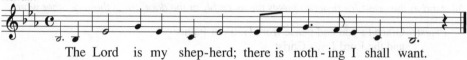

The Lord   is   my   shep-herd; there is   noth-ing I   shall   want.

Text: *Lectionary for Mass*, © 1969, 1981, 1997, ICEL
Music: Richard Proulx, © 1975, GIA Publications, Inc.

Verses

The LORD is my shepherd;
there is nothing I shall want.
Fresh and green are the pastures
where he gives me repose.
Near restful waters he leads me;
he revives my soul. ℟.

He guides me along the right path,
for the sake of his name.
Though I should walk in the valley
   of the shadow of death,
no evil would I fear, for you are with me.

Your crook and your staff will give
   me comfort. ℟.

You have prepared a table before me
in the sight of my foes.
My head you have anointed with oil;
my cup is overflowing. ℟.

Surely goodness and mercy shall follow me
all the days of my life.
In the LORD's own house shall I dwell
for length of days unending. ℟.

Text: Psalm 23, *The Revised Grail Psalms*, © 2010, Conception Abbey and The Grail, admin. by GIA Publications, Inc.
Music: Joseph Gelineau, SJ, © 1963, The Grail, GIA Publications, Inc., agent

Additional responsorial psalms for Funerals are listed in the Index of Psalms and Canticles, no. 1233.

195 GOSPEL

Before the gospel reading, all stand as an acclamation is sung:

Al - le - lu - ia,   al - le - lu - ia,   al - le - lu - ia.

Music: Chant Mode VI; acc. by Richard Proulx, © 1985, GIA Publications, Inc.

During Lent:

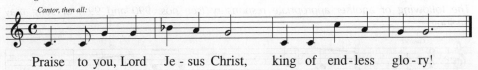

Praise to you, Lord Je - sus Christ, king of end-less glo-ry!

Text: ICEL, © 1969
Music: Frank Schoen, © 1970, GIA Publications, Inc.

Deacon (or priest): The Lord be with you.
Assembly: **And with your spirit.**
Deacon: A reading from the holy Gospel according to N.
Assembly: **Glory to you, O Lord.**

After the reading:

Deacon: The Gospel of the Lord.
Assembly: **Praise to you, Lord Jesus Christ.**

HOMILY *(All sit)*

PRAYER OF THE FAITHFUL 196
All join in prayer for the deceased, for grieving family members and friends, and for the needs of the Church and the world.

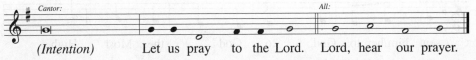

(Intention) Let us pray to the Lord. Lord, hear our prayer.

Music: Byzantine chant

If the funeral liturgy is celebrated within Mass, the liturgy of the eucharist follows (see Order of Mass, no. 212). During the eucharistic prayer, special remembrance is made of the deceased. Following the prayer after communion, the funeral liturgy concludes with the final commendation (below).

When the funeral liturgy is celebrated outside Mass, the final commendation follows the prayer of the faithful.

FINAL COMMENDATION 197
The ministers and assembly gather around the body of the deceased. After an invitation to prayer, all pray silently. The coffin may then be sprinkled with holy water and incensed, or this may take place during or after the song of farewell.

198 SONG OF FAREWELL

The following or another appropriate responsory (see nos. 990 and 994) or song may be sung.

1. Saints of God, come to his/her aid!
2. May Christ who called you, take you to him - self;
3. Give him/her e - ter - nal rest, O Lord,

Come to meet him,/her, an - gels of the
may an - gels lead you to A - bra - ham's
and may your light shine on him/her for

Lord!
side. Re - ceive his/her soul and pre -
ev - er.

sent him/her to God, to God the Most High.

All:

Re - ceive his/her soul and pre - sent him/her to

God, to God the Most High.

Text: *Order of Christian Funerals*; alt. by Richard Proulx
Music: Richard Proulx
© 1975, GIA Publications, Inc.

199 PRAYER OF COMMENDATION

At the conclusion of the prayer all respond: **Amen.**

PROCESSION TO THE PLACE OF COMMITTAL

The deacon or priest says: In peace let us take our brother/sister to his/her place of rest.

SONG

As the assembly leaves the church, one of the following or another appropriate responsory (see no. 991) or song may be sung.

200

In pa-ra-dí-sum de-dú-cant te án-ge-li:
May choirs of an-gels es-cort you in-to par-a-dise:

in tu-o ad-vén-tu su - scí-pi-ant te
and at your ar-ri-val may the mar-tyrs re-ceive

már-ty - res, et per-dú-cant te in
and wel-come you; may they bring you home in -

ci-vi-tá-tem san - ctam Je - rú-sa-lem.
to the ho-ly cit - y, Je - ru-sa-lem.

Cho - rus an - ge-ló - rum te su -
May the ho - ly an - gels wel -

scí-pi-at, et cum Lá - za-ro quon-dam
come you, and with Laz - a-rus, who lived in

páu-pe-re ae-tér - nam
pov-er-ty, may you have

há-be-as ré-qui-em.
ev - er - last - ing rest.

Text: *In paradisum* and *Chorus angelorum,* tr. © 1986, GIA Publications, Inc.
Tune: Mode VII; acc. by Richard Proulx, 1937–2010, © 1986, GIA Publications, Inc.

201

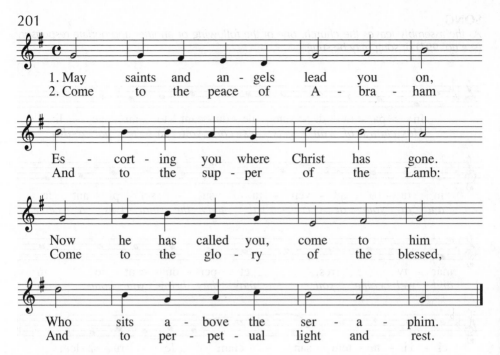

1. May saints and an - gels lead you on,
2. Come to the peace of A - bra - ham

Es - cort - ing you where Christ has gone.
And to the sup - per of the Lamb:

Now he has called you, come to him
Come to the glo - ry of the blessed,

Who sits a - bove the ser - a - phim.
And to per - pet - ual light and rest.

Text: *In paradisum*, tr. © 1985, ICEL
Tune: OLD HUNDREDTH, LM; Louis Bourgeois, c.1510–1561

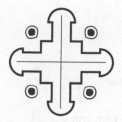

Mass

Order of Mass 202

The Church gathers on the Lord's Day to listen to Scripture, to offer prayers, to give thanks and praise to God while recalling God's gifts in creation and saving deeds in Jesus, and to share in Holy Communion.

In these rites of word and eucharist, the Church keeps Sunday as the Lord's Day, the day of creation and resurrection, the "eighth day" when the fullness of God's kingdom is anticipated. The Mass or eucharistic celebration of the Christian community has rites of gathering, of word, of eucharist, of dismissal. All those who gather constitute the assembly. One member of this assembly who has been ordained to the presbyterate or episcopate, the priesthood, leads the opening and closing prayers and the eucharistic prayer, and presides over the whole assembly. A member ordained to the diaconate may assist, read the gospel, and preach. Other members of the assembly are chosen and trained for various ministries: These are the readers, servers, ushers, musicians, communion ministers. All of these assist the assembly. It is the assembly itself, all those present, that does the liturgy.

The Order of Mass which follows is familiar to all who regularly join in this assembly. It is learned through repetition. This Order of Mass leaves many decisions to the local community, and others are determined by the various seasons of the liturgical year.

INTRODUCTORY RITES
The rites which precede the liturgy of the word assist the assembly to gather as a community. They prepare that community to listen to Scripture and to celebrate the Eucharist together. The procession and entrance song are ways of expressing the unity and spirit of the assembly.

GREETING
All make the sign of the cross.

Priest: In the name of the Father, and of the Son, and of the Holy Spirit.

A - men.

After the sign of the cross one of the greetings is given.

A   *Priest:*   The grace of our Lord Jesus Christ,
                           and the love of God,
                           and the communion of the Holy Spirit
                           be with you all.

B   *Priest:*   Grace to you and peace from God our Father
                           and the Lord Jesus Christ.

C   *Priest:*   The Lord be with you. (*Bishop:* Peace be with you.)

Assembly:

And   with   your   spir - it.

203   BLESSING AND SPRINKLING OF HOLY WATER

On Sundays, especially during the season of Easter, instead of the penitential act below, the blessing and sprinkling of holy water may take place.

204   PENITENTIAL ACT

The priest invites all to be mindful of their sins and of the great mercy of God. After a time of silence, one of the following forms is used.

A   *Assembly:*   **I confess to almighty God
                           and to you, my brothers and sisters,
                           that I have greatly sinned,
                           in my thoughts and in my words,
                           in what I have done and in what I have failed to do,**
                           All strike their breast as they say:
                           **through my fault, through my fault,
                           through my most grievous fault;
                           therefore I ask blessed Mary ever-Virgin,
                           all the Angels and Saints,
                           and you, my brothers and sisters,
                           to pray for me to the Lord our God.**

B

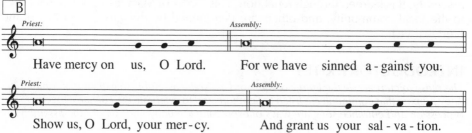

Priest: Have mercy on us, O Lord.   *Assembly:* For we have sinned a - gainst you.

Priest: Show us, O Lord, your mer - cy.   *Assembly:* And grant us your sal - va - tion.

C

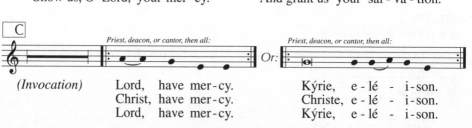

Priest, deacon, or cantor, then all: *Or:*   *Priest, deacon, or cantor, then all:*

(*Invocation*)   Lord,   have mer - cy.   Kýrie,   e - lé - i - son.
                Christ,   have mer - cy.   Christe,   e - lé - i - son.
                Lord,   have mer - cy.   Kýrie,   e - lé - i - son.

Priest: May almighty God…everlasting life.

A - men.

KYRIE 205

Unless form C of the penitential act has been used, the Kyrie follows.

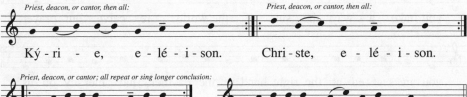

Ký - ri - e, e - lé - i - son. Chri - ste, e - lé - i - son.

Ký - ri - e, e - lé - i - son. Ký - ri - e, e - lé - i - son.

Or:

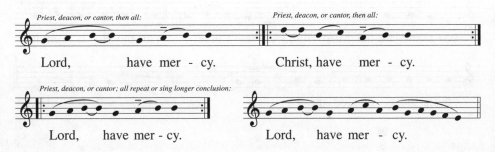

Lord, have mer - cy. Christ, have mer - cy.

Lord, have mer - cy. Lord, have mer - cy.

GLORIA 206

The Gloria is omitted during Advent, Lent, and most weekdays.

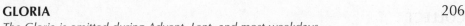

Glo - ry to God in the high - est, and on earth peace to peo - ple

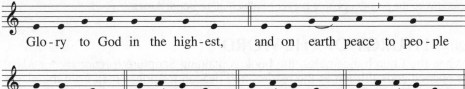

of good will. We praise you, we bless you, we a - dore you,

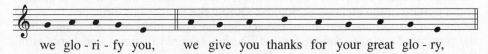

we glo - ri - fy you, we give you thanks for your great glo - ry,

Lord God, heav - en - ly King, O God, al - might - y Fa - ther.

Lord Je-sus Christ, On-ly Be-got-ten Son, Lord God, Lamb of God,

Son of the Fa-ther, you take a-way the sins of the world, have mer-cy on us;

you take a-way the sins of the world, re-ceive our prayer;

you are seat-ed at the right hand of the Fa-ther, have mer-cy on us.

For you a-lone are the Ho-ly One, you a-lone are the Lord,

you a-lone are the Most High, Je-sus Christ, with the Ho-ly Spir-it,

in the glo-ry of God the Fa - ther. A - men.

COLLECT

After the invitation from the priest, all pray in silence for a while. The introductory rites conclude with the proper opening prayer to which all respond: **Amen.**

207 LITURGY OF THE WORD

When the Church assembles, the book containing Scripture (*Lectionary for Mass*) is opened and all listen as the readers and deacon (or priest) read from the places assigned. The first reading is normally from the Hebrew Scriptures (Old Testament), the second from the letters of the New Testament, and the third from the Book of Gospels. Over a three-year cycle, the Church reads through the letters and gospels and a portion of the Hebrew Scriptures. During the Sundays of Ordinary Time, the letters and gospels are read in order, each Sunday continuing near the place where the previous Sunday's readings ended. During Advent/Christmas and Lent/Easter, the readings are those which are traditional and appropriate to these seasons.

The Church listens to and—through the weeks and years—is shaped by the word of God. Those who have gathered for the Sunday liturgy are to give their full attention to the words of the reader. A time of silence and reflection follows each of the first two readings. After the first reading, this reflection continues in the singing of the psalm. A homily, bringing together the scripture readings and the life of the community, follows the gospel. The liturgy of the word concludes with the dismissal of the catechumens, the creed and the prayers of intercession. In the latter, the assembly continues its constant work of recalling and praying for the universal Church and all those in need.

This reading and hearing of the word—simple things that they are—are the foundation of the liturgical celebration. The public reading of Scripture and the rituals which surround this—silence and psalm and acclamation, posture and gesture, preaching and litany of intercession—gather the Church generation after generation. They gather and sustain and gradually make of us the image of Christ.

FIRST READING

After the reading:

The word of the Lord. Thanks be to God.

After a period of silence, the responsorial psalm is sung.

SECOND READING

After the reading:

The word of the Lord. Thanks be to God.

A time of silence follows the reading.

GOSPEL

208

Before the gospel, an acclamation is sung.

Al - le - lú - ia, al - le - lú - ia, al - le - lú - ia.

During Lent:

Praise and hon - or to you, O Lord Je - sus Christ.

Before the gospel:

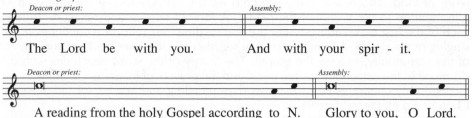

Deacon or priest: The Lord be with you. *Assembly:* And with your spir - it.

Deacon or priest: A reading from the holy Gospel according to N. *Assembly:* Glory to you, O Lord.

After the reading:

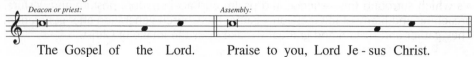

Deacon or priest: The Gospel of the Lord. *Assembly:* Praise to you, Lord Je - sus Christ.

HOMILY

209 PROFESSION OF FAITH
Musical settings can be found at nos. 226 and 341.

**I believe in one God,
the Father almighty,
maker of heaven and earth,
of all things visible and invisible.**

**I believe in one Lord Jesus Christ,
the Only Begotten Son of God,
born of the Father before all ages.
God from God, Light from Light,
true God from true God,
begotten, not made, consubstantial with the Father;
through him all things were made.
For us men and for our salvation
he came down from heaven,**
All bow at the following words up to: and became man.
**and by the Holy Spirit was incarnate of the Virgin Mary,
and became man.**

**For our sake he was crucified under Pontius Pilate,
he suffered death and was buried,
and rose again on the third day
in accordance with the Scriptures.
He ascended into heaven
and is seated at the right hand of the Father.
He will come again in glory
to judge the living and the dead
and his kingdom will have no end.**

I believe in the Holy Spirit, the Lord, the giver of life,
who proceeds from the Father and the Son,
who with the Father and the Son is adored and glorified,
who has spoken through the prophets.

I believe in one, holy, catholic and apostolic Church.
I confess one Baptism for the forgiveness of sins
and I look forward to the resurrection of the dead
and the life of the world to come. Amen.

Instead of the Nicene Creed, especially during Lent and the Easter season, **210**
the Apostles' Creed may be used:

I believe in God,
the Father almighty,
Creator of heaven and earth,
and in Jesus Christ, his only Son, our Lord,
All bow at the following words up to: the Virgin Mary.
who was conceived by the Holy Spirit,
born of the Virgin Mary,
suffered under Pontius Pilate,
was crucified, died and was buried;
he descended into hell;
on the third day he rose again from the dead;
he ascended into heaven,
and is seated at the right hand of God the Father almighty;
from there he will come to judge the living and the dead.

I believe in the Holy Spirit,
the holy catholic Church,
the communion of saints,
the forgiveness of sins,
the resurrection of the body,
and life everlasting. Amen.

PRAYER OF THE FAITHFUL 211

The people respond to each petition as follows, or according to local practice.

Deacon or cantor: Let us pray to the Lord.

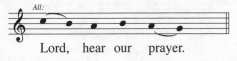

Lord, hear our prayer.

Or:

Lord, have mer - cy.

212 **LITURGY OF THE EUCHARIST**

To celebrate the Eucharist means to give God thanks and praise. When the altar has been prepared with the bread and wine, the assembly joins the priest in remembering the gracious gifts of God in creation and God's saving deeds. The center of this is the paschal mystery, the death of our Lord Jesus Christ which destroyed the power of death and his rising which brings us life. That mystery into which we were baptized we proclaim each Sunday at the Eucharist. It is the very shape of Christian life. We find this in the simple bread and wine which stir our remembering and draw forth our prayer of thanksgiving. "Fruit of the earth and work of human hands," the bread and wine become our Holy Communion in the Body and Blood of the Lord. We eat and drink and so proclaim that we belong to one another and to the Lord.

The members of the assembly quietly prepare themselves even as the table is prepared. The priest then invites all to lift up their hearts and join in the eucharistic prayer. All do this by giving their full attention and by singing the acclamations from the "Holy, Holy, Holy" to the great "Amen." Then the assembly joins in the Lord's Prayer, the sign of peace and the "Lamb of God" litany which accompanies the breaking of bread. Ministers of communion assist the assembly to share the Body and Blood of Christ. A time of silence and prayer concludes the liturgy of the eucharist.

PRESENTATION AND PREPARATION OF THE GIFTS

Bread and wine are brought to the altar and the deacon or priest prepares these gifts. If there is no music, the prayers may be said aloud, and all may respond: **Blessed be God for ever.** *The priest then invites all to pray.*

Priest: Pray, brethren (brothers and sisters),
        that my sacrifice and yours
        may be acceptable to God, the almighty Father.

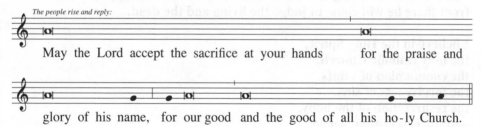

The people rise and reply:

May the Lord accept the sacrifice at your hands   for the praise and glory of his name, for our good and the good of all his ho-ly Church.

The priest says the prayer over the offerings and all respond: **Amen.**

213 **EUCHARISTIC PRAYER**

The central prayer of the Mass begins with this dialogue between priest and assembly.

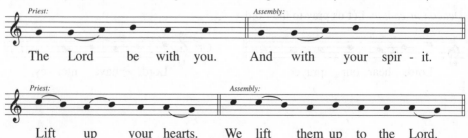

Priest: The Lord be with you. *Assembly:* And with your spir-it.

Priest: Lift up your hearts. *Assembly:* We lift them up to the Lord.

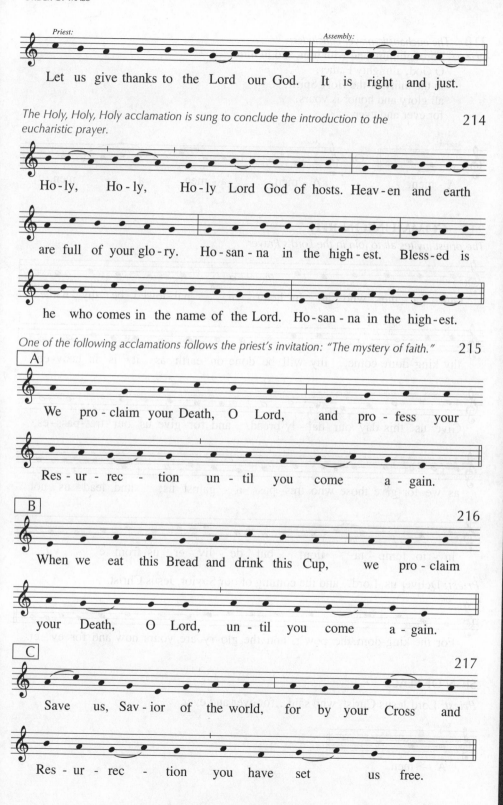

Priest: *Assembly:*

Let us give thanks to the Lord our God. It is right and just.

The Holy, Holy, Holy acclamation is sung to conclude the introduction to the eucharistic prayer.   **214**

Ho-ly, Ho-ly, Ho-ly Lord God of hosts. Heav-en and earth

are full of your glo-ry. Ho-san-na in the high-est. Bless-ed is

he who comes in the name of the Lord. Ho-san-na in the high-est.

One of the following acclamations follows the priest's invitation: "The mystery of faith."   **215**

A

We pro-claim your Death, O Lord, and pro-fess your

Res-ur-rec-tion un-til you come a-gain.

B   **216**

When we eat this Bread and drink this Cup, we pro-claim

your Death, O Lord, un-til you come a-gain.

C   **217**

Save us, Sav-ior of the world, for by your Cross and

Res-ur-rec-tion you have set us free.

218 *The eucharistic prayer concludes:*

Priest: Through him, and with him, and in him,
O God, almighty Father,
in the unity of the Holy Spirit,
all glory and honor is yours,
for ever and ever.

Assembly:
A - men.

Or:

Assembly:
A - men, a - men, a - men.

219 COMMUNION RITE

The priest invites all to join in the Lord's Prayer.

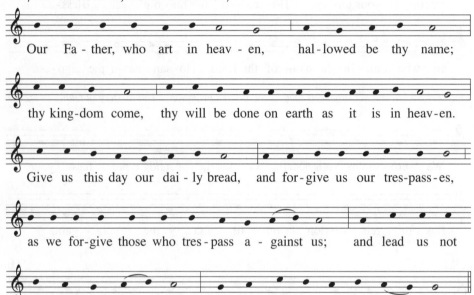

Our Fa - ther, who art in heav - en, hal - lowed be thy name;

thy king-dom come, thy will be done on earth as it is in heav-en.

Give us this day our dai - ly bread, and for-give us our tres-pass-es,

as we for-give those who tres - pass a - gainst us; and lead us not

in - to temp - ta - tion, but de - liv - er us from e - vil.

Priest: Deliver us, Lord…and the coming of our Savior, Jesus Christ.

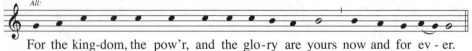

All:
For the king-dom, the pow'r, and the glo-ry are yours now and for ev - er.

SIGN OF PEACE

Priest: Lord Jesus Christ, who said…for ever and ever.

Assembly:
A - men.

Priest: Assembly:

The peace of the Lord be with you al-ways.   And with your spir - it.

Deacon or priest: Let us offer each other the sign of peace.

All exchange a sign of peace.

Then the eucharistic bread is solemnly broken and the consecrated bread and wine   220
are prepared for Holy Communion. The litany "Lamb of God" is sung during the
breaking of the bread.

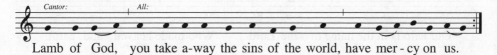

Cantor: All:

Lamb of God, you take a-way the sins of the world, have mer - cy on us.

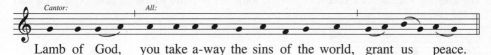

Cantor: All:

Lamb of God,   you take a-way the sins of the world, grant us   peace.

The priest then invites all to share in Holy Communion.   221

Priest: Behold the Lamb of God,
     behold him who takes away the sins of the world.
     Blessed are those called to the supper of the Lamb.

All:

Lord, I   am not worthy that you should enter un - der my roof,

but only say the word and my soul   shall be   healed.

Minister of communion: The Body (Blood) of Christ.
          Communicant: **Amen.**

While the priest is receiving the Body of Christ, the communion song or psalm begins. After
communion, a time of silence is observed or a song of thanksgiving is sung. The rite concludes
with the prayer after communion to which all respond: **Amen.**

CONCLUDING RITES   222
The liturgy of the eucharist ends very simply. There may be announcements of events and
concerns for the community, then the priest gives a blessing and the assembly is dismissed.

GREETING AND FINAL BLESSING

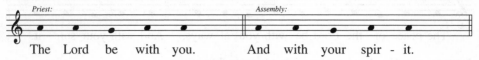

Priest: The Lord be with you. *Assembly:* And with your spir - it.

When a bishop blesses the people, he adds the following:

Bishop: Blessed be the name of the Lord. *Assembly:* Now and for ev - er.

Bishop: Our help is in the name of the Lord. *Assembly:* Who made heaven and earth.

The blessing may be in a simple or solemn form. All respond to the blessing or to each part of the blessing:

Assembly: A - men.

DISMISSAL

The deacon or priest then dismisses the assembly:

A Go forth, the Mass is ended.

B Go and announce the Gospel of the Lord.

C Go in peace, glorifying the Lord by your life.

Assembly: Thanks be to God.

D

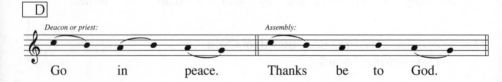

Deacon or priest: Go in peace. *Assembly:* Thanks be to God.

EASTER DISMISSAL

The deacon or priest then dismisses the assembly:

A Go forth, the Mass is ended, alleluia, alleluia.

B Go in peace, alleluia, alleluia.

Assembly: Thanks be to God, al - le - lú - ia, al-le - lú - ia.

Additional Chants

SIMPLE CHANTS

GREETING

223

Priest: In the name of the Father, and of the Son, and of the Holy Spirit.

A - men.

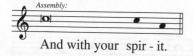

| A | *Priest:* | The grace of our Lord Jesus Christ,
and the love of God,
and the communion of the Holy Spirit
be with you all. |

| B | *Priest:* | Grace to you and peace from God our Father
and the Lord Jesus Christ. |

| C | *Priest:* | The Lord be with you. (*Bishop:* Peace be with you.) |

Assembly:

And with your spir - it.

PENITENTIAL ACT

224

B

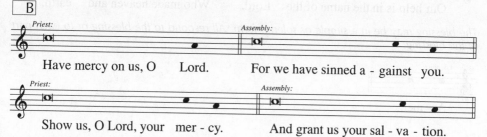

Priest:

Have mercy on us, O Lord.

Assembly:

For we have sinned a - gainst you.

Priest:

Show us, O Lord, your mer - cy.

Assembly:

And grant us your sal - va - tion.

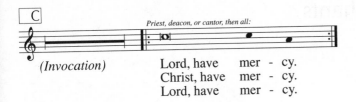

(Invocation)

Lord, have mer - cy.
Christ, have mer - cy.
Lord, have mer - cy.

Priest: May almighty God…everlasting life.

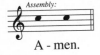

A - men.

225 GREETING AND FINAL BLESSING

The Lord be with you. And with your spir - it.

When a bishop blesses the people, he adds the following:

Blessed be the name of the Lord. Now and for ev - er.

Our help is in the name of the Lord. Who made heaven and earth.

The blessing may be in a simple or solemn form. All respond to the blessing or to each part of the blessing:

A - men.

CREDO I

I be-lieve in one God, the Fa-ther al-might-y, mak-er of heav-en and earth, of all things vis - i - ble and in - vis - i - ble. I be-lieve in one Lord Je - sus Christ, the Only Be - got-ten Son of God, born of the Father be - fore all a - ges. God from God, Light from Light, true God from true God, be - got-ten, not made, con - sub - stan - tial with the Fa - ther; through him all things were made. For us men and for our sal-va-tion he came down from heav-en, and by the Ho-ly Spir-it was in-car-nate of the Vir - gin Mar - y, and be - came man. For our sake he was cru - ci - fied un - der Pon-tius Pi - late, he suffered death and was bur-ied, and rose a-gain on the third day

in accordance with the Scrip-tures. He as-cend-ed in-to heav-en

and is seated at the right hand of the Fa-ther. He will come a-gain in glo-ry

to judge the living and the dead and his kingdom will have no end.

I be-lieve in the Ho-ly Spir-it, the Lord, the giv-er of life,

who pro-ceeds from the Father and the Son, who with the Fa-ther and the Son

is adored and glo-ri-fied, who has spoken through the proph-ets.

I be-lieve in one, ho-ly, ca-tho-lic and a-pos-tol-ic Church.

I con-fess one Bap-tism for the for-give-ness of sins

and I look for-ward to the res-ur-rec-tion of the dead

and the life of the world to come. A - men.

Setting One: Mass for a Servant Church

PENITENTIAL ACT 1

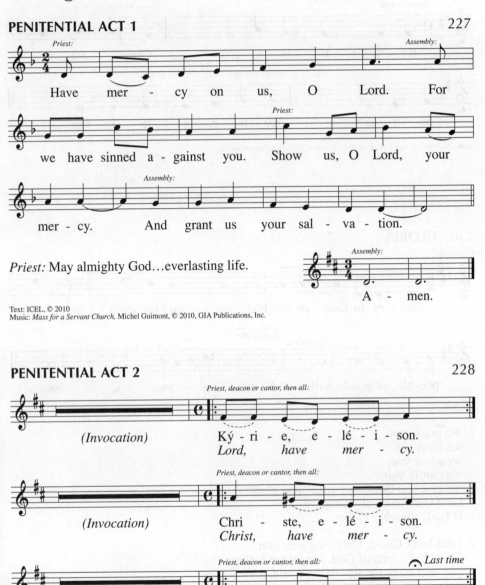

Priest:

Have mer - cy on us, O Lord. For

we have sinned a - gainst you. Show us, O Lord, your

mer - cy. And grant us your sal - va - tion.

Priest: May almighty God…everlasting life.

A - men.

Text: ICEL, © 2010
Music: *Mass for a Servant Church*, Michel Guimont, © 2010, GIA Publications, Inc.

PENITENTIAL ACT 2

Priest, deacon or cantor, then all:

(Invocation) Ký - ri - e, e - lé - i - son.
              Lord,   have   mer - cy.

Priest, deacon or cantor, then all:

(Invocation) Chri - ste, e - lé - i - son.
              Christ,   have   mer - cy.

Priest, deacon or cantor, then all: *Last time*

(Invocation) Ký - ri - e, e - lé - i - son.
              Lord,   have   mer - cy.

Priest: May almighty God…everlasting life.

A - men.

Music: *Mass for a Servant Church*, Michel Guimont, © 2010, GIA Publications, Inc.

229 KYRIE

Ký - ri - e, e - lé - i - son. Chri - ste, e -
lé - i - son. Ký - ri - e, e - lé - i - son.

Music: *Mass for a Servant Church*, Michel Guimont, © 2010, GIA Publications, Inc.

230 **GLORIA**

Refrain

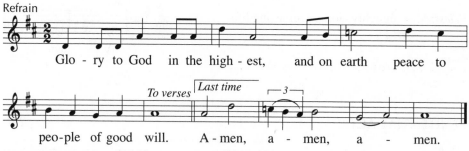

Glo - ry to God in the high - est, and on earth peace to
peo-ple of good will. *To verses* | *Last time* A - men, a - men, a - men.

Verses

1. We praise you,
   we bless you,
   we adore you,
   we glorify you,
   we give you thanks for your great glory,
   Lord God, heavenly King,
   O God, almighty Father.

2. Lord Jesus Christ, Only Begotten Son,
   Lord God, Lamb of God, Son of the Father,
   you take away the sins of the world,

have mer - cy on us, have mer - cy on us;
you take a - way the sins of the world, re - ceive our prayer, re -

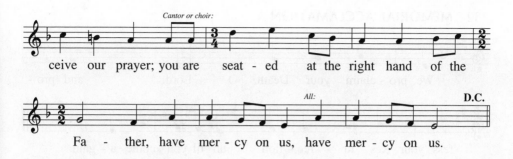

ceive our prayer; you are seat - ed at the right hand of the

Fa - ther, have mer - cy on us, have mer - cy on us.

3. For you alone are the Holy One,
   you alone are the Lord,
   you alone are the Most High,
   Jesus Christ,
   with the Holy Spirit,
   in the glory of God the Father.
   Amen.

Text: ICEL, © 2010
Music: *Mass for a Servant Church*, Michel Guimont, © 2010, GIA Publications, Inc.

HOLY, HOLY, HOLY 231

Ho - ly, Ho - ly, Ho - ly Lord God of hosts.

Heav'n and earth are full of your glo - ry. Ho -

san - na in the high - est. Bless - ed is he who

comes in the name of the Lord. Ho - san - na in the high - est.

Text: ICEL, © 2010
Music: *Mass for a Servant Church*, Michel Guimont, © 2010, GIA Publications, Inc.

232 MEMORIAL ACCLAMATION A

We pro-claim your Death, O Lord, and pro-fess your Res-ur-rec-tion un-til you come a-gain.

Text: ICEL, © 2010
Music: *Mass for a Servant Church,* Michel Guimont, © 2010, GIA Publications, Inc.

233 MEMORIAL ACCLAMATION B

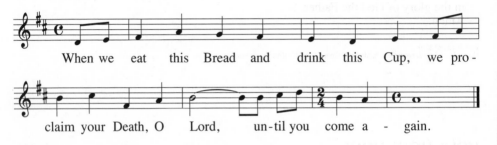

When we eat this Bread and drink this Cup, we pro-claim your Death, O Lord, un-til you come a-gain.

Text: ICEL, © 2010
Music: *Mass for a Servant Church,* Michel Guimont, © 2010, GIA Publications, Inc.

234 MEMORIAL ACCLAMATION C

Save us, Sav-ior of the world, for by your Cross and Res-ur-rec-tion you have set us free.

Text: ICEL, © 2010
Music: *Mass for a Servant Church,* Michel Guimont, © 2010, GIA Publications, Inc.

235 AMEN

A - men, a - men, a - men.

Music: *Mass for a Servant Church,* Michel Guimont, © 2010, GIA Publications, Inc.

LAMB OF GOD

Lamb of God, you take a-way the sins of the world, have mer-cy on us. Lamb of God, you take a-way the sins of the world, have mer-cy on us. Lamb of God, you take a-way the sins of the world, grant us peace.

Music: *Mass for a Servant Church,* Michel Guimont, © 2010, GIA Publications, Inc.

Setting Two: Missa Pacem

237 PENITENTIAL ACT

Priest, deacon or cantor, then all:

Lord,	have	mer	-	cy.
Christ,	have	mer	-	cy.
Lord,	have	mer	-	cy.

Music: *Missa Pacem*, L. Randolph Babin, © 2004, 2010, GIA Publications, Inc.

238 GLORIA

Refrain

Gló - ri - a! Gló - ri - a! Glo - ry to God in the high - est,

and on earth peace to peo - ple of good will.

Verses

1. We praise you,
   we bless you,
   we adore you,
   we glorify you,
   we give you thanks for your great glory,
   Lord God, heavenly King,
   O God, almighty Father.

2. Lord Jesus Christ, Only Begotten Son,
   Lord God, Lamb of God, Son of the Father,
   you take away the sins of the world,
   have mercy on us;
   you take away the sins of the world,
   receive our prayer;
   you are seated at the right hand of the Father,
   have mercy on us.

3. For you alone are the Holy One,
   you alone are the Lord,
   you alone are the Most High,
   Jesus Christ,
   with the Holy Spirit,
   in the glory of God the Father.
   Amen.

Text: ICEL, © 2010
Music: *Missa Pacem*, L. Randolph Babin, © 2004, 2010, GIA Publications, Inc.

GOSPEL ACCLAMATION

Al - le - lu - ia, al - le - lu - ia, al - le - lu - ia.

Music: *Missa Pacem*, L. Randolph Babin, © 2004, GIA Publications, Inc.

HOLY, HOLY, HOLY

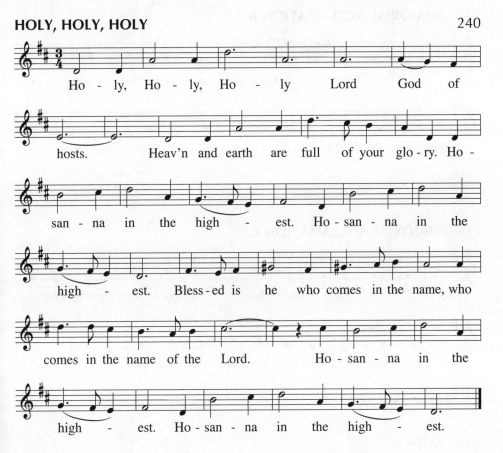

Ho - ly, Ho - ly, Ho - ly Lord God of hosts. Heav'n and earth are full of your glo - ry. Ho - san - na in the high - est. Ho - san - na in the high - est. Bless - ed is he who comes in the name, who comes in the name of the Lord. Ho - san - na in the high - est. Ho - san - na in the high - est.

Text: ICEL, © 2010
Music: *Missa Pacem*, L. Randolph Babin, © 2004, 2010, GIA Publications, Inc.

241 MEMORIAL ACCLAMATION A

We pro-claim your Death, O Lord, and pro-fess your Res-ur-rec-tion un-til you come a-gain.

Text: ICEL, © 2010
Music: *Missa Pacem*, L. Randolph Babin, © 2010, GIA Publications, Inc.

242 MEMORIAL ACCLAMATION B

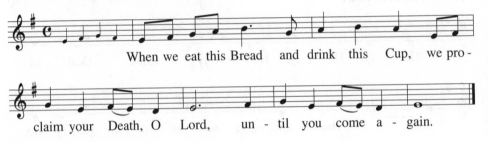

When we eat this Bread and drink this Cup, we pro-claim your Death, O Lord, un-til you come a-gain.

Text: ICEL, © 2010
Music: *Missa Pacem*, L. Randolph Babin, © 2010, GIA Publications, Inc.

243 MEMORIAL ACCLAMATION C

Save us, Sav-ior of the world, for by your Cross and Res-ur-rec-tion you have set us free.

Text: ICEL, © 2010
Music: *Missa Pacem*, L. Randolph Babin, © 2010, GIA Publications, Inc.

244 AMEN

A-men, a-men, a-men. A-men, a-men, a-men.

Music: *Missa Pacem*, L. Randolph Babin, © 2004, GIA Publications, Inc.

LAMB OF GOD

Cantor or choir: *All:*

Lamb of God, you take a - way the sins of the world, have mer - cy on us.

Repeat as needed

Last time   *Cantor or choir:*

us. Lamb of God, you take a - way the sins of the world, have mer - cy on us.

All:

Lamb of God, you take a - way the sins of the world, grant us peace.

Music: *Missa Pacem*, L. Randolph Babin, © 2004, GIA Publications, Inc.

Setting Three: Unity Mass

246 PENITENTIAL ACT

Priest: Have mer-cy on us, O Lord. *Assembly:* For we have sinned a-

gainst you. *Priest:* Show us, O Lord, your mer-cy.

Assembly: And grant us your sal - va - tion.

Priest: May almighty God...everlasting life.

Assembly: A - men.

Text: ICEL, © 2010
Music: *Unity Mass,* Norah Duncan IV, © 2010, GIA Publications, Inc.

247 KYRIE

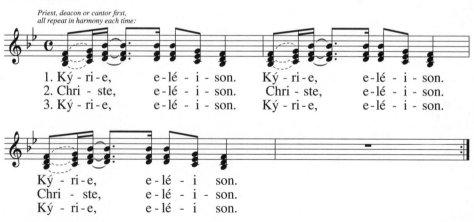

*Priest, deacon or cantor first,
all repeat in harmony each time:*

1. Ký - ri - e, e - lé - i - son. Ký - ri - e, e - lé - i - son.
2. Chri - ste, e - lé - i - son. Chri - ste, e - lé - i - son.
3. Ký - ri - e, e - lé - i - son. Ký - ri - e, e - lé - i - son.

Ký - ri - e, e - lé - i son.
Chri - ste, e - lé - i - son.
Ký - ri - e, e - lé - i son.

Music: *Unity Mass,* Norah Duncan IV, © 2010, GIA Publications, Inc.

GLORIA

248

Refrain

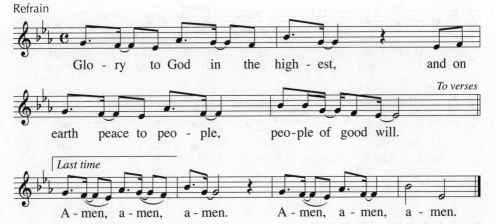

Glo - ry to God in the high - est, and on earth peace to peo - ple, peo-ple of good will.

To verses

Last time

A - men, a - men, a - men. A - men, a - men, a - men.

Verses

1. We praise you,
   we bless you,
   we adore you,
   we glorify you,
   we give you thanks for your great glory,
   Lord God, heavenly King,
   O God, almighty Father.

2. Lord Jesus Christ, Only Begotten Son,
   Lord God, Lamb of God, Son of the Father,
   you take away the sins of the world,
   have mercy on us;
   you take away the sins of the world,
   receive our prayer;
   you are seated at the right hand of the Father,
   have mercy on us.

3. For you alone are the Holy One,
   you alone are the Lord,
   you alone are the Most High,
   Jesus Christ,
   with the Holy Spirit,
   in the glory of God the Father.
   Amen.

Text: ICEL, © 2010
Music: *Unity Mass*, Norah Duncan IV, © 2010, GIA Publications, Inc.

249 GOSPEL ACCLAMATION

Al - le - lu - ia, al - le - lu - ia!
Lent: O   glo - ry to you,   O   Word   of   God,

Al - le - lu - ia, al - le - lu - ia!
Lord   Je - sus   Christ,   Lord   Je - sus   Christ.

Text: ICEL, © 1969
Music: *Unity Mass,* Norah Duncan IV, © 2010, GIA Publications, Inc.

250 HOLY, HOLY, HOLY

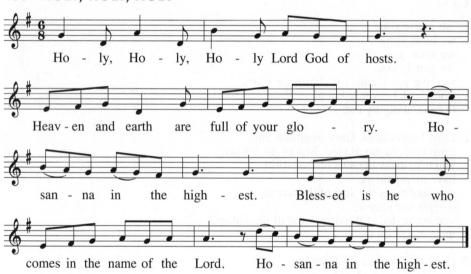

Ho - ly, Ho - ly, Ho - ly Lord God of hosts.

Heav - en and earth are full of your glo - ry. Ho -

san - na in the high - est. Bless-ed is he who

comes in the name of the Lord. Ho - san - na in the high - est.

Text: ICEL, © 2010
Music: *Unity Mass,* Norah Duncan IV, © 2010, GIA Publications, Inc.

251 MEMORIAL ACCLAMATION A

We pro - claim your Death, O Lord, and pro -

fess your Res - ur - rec - tion un - til you come a - gain.

Text: ICEL, © 2010
Music: *Unity Mass,* Norah Duncan IV, © 2010, GIA Publications, Inc.

MEMORIAL ACCLAMATION B 252

When we eat this Bread and drink this Cup, we proclaim your Death, O Lord, un - til you come a - gain.

Text: ICEL, © 2010
Music: *Unity Mass,* Norah Duncan IV, © 2010, GIA Publications, Inc.

MEMORIAL ACCLAMATION C 253

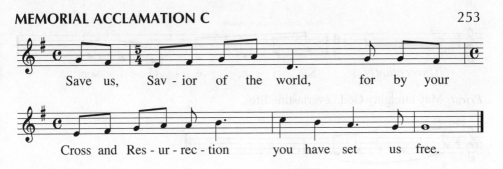

Save us, Sav - ior of the world, for by your
Cross and Res - ur - rec - tion you have set us free.

Text: ICEL, © 2010
Music: *Unity Mass,* Norah Duncan IV, © 2010, GIA Publications, Inc.

AMEN 254

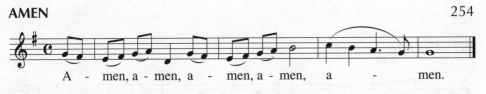

A - men, a - men, a - men, a - men, a - men.

Music: *Unity Mass,* Norah Duncan IV, © 2010, GIA Publications, Inc.

LAMB OF GOD 255

Lamb of God, you take a - way the sins of the world, have
mer - cy on us, have mer - cy on us. Lamb of God, you take a - way the
sins of the world, grant us peace, grant us peace.

Music: *Unity Mass,* Norah Duncan IV, © 2010, GIA Publications, Inc.

Setting Four: Storrington Mass

256 PENITENTIAL ACT

Priest, deacon or cantor, then all:

(Invocation)   Ký - ri - e,   e - lé - i - son.

Priest, deacon or cantor, then all:

(Invocation)   Chri - ste,   e - lé - i - son.

Priest, deacon or cantor, then all:

(Invocation)   Ký - ri - e,   e - lé - i - son.

Priest: May almighty God...everlasting life.

Assembly:

A - men.

Music: *Storrington Mass*, Marty Haugen, © 2010, GIA Publications, Inc.

257 GLORIA

Refrain

Glo - ry to God in the high-est,   and on earth peace to peo - ple

To verses   *Last time*

of good will.   will.   A - men, a - men, a - men.

Verses

1. We praise you,
   we bless you,
   we adore you,
   we glorify you,
   we give you thanks for your great glory,
   Lord God, heavenly King,
   O God, almighty Father.

2. Lord Jesus Christ, Only Begotten Son,
   Lord God, Lamb of God, Son of the Father,
   you take away the sins of the world,
   have mercy on us;
   you take away the sins of the world,
   receive our prayer;
   you are seated at the right hand of the Father,
   have mercy on us.

3. For you alone are the Holy One,
   you alone are the Lord,
   you alone are the Most High,
   Jesus Christ,
   with the Holy Spirit,
   in the glory of God the Father.
   Amen.

Text: ICEL, © 2010
Music: *Storrington Mass,* Marty Haugen, © 2010, GIA Publications, Inc.

GOSPEL ACCLAMATION 258

Al - le-lu-ia, al - le-lu-ia, al - le-lu - ia.

Al - le-lu-ia, al - le-lu-ia, al - le-lu - ia.

Music: *Storrington Mass,* Marty Haugen, © 2010, GIA Publications, Inc.

LENTEN GOSPEL ACCLAMATION 259

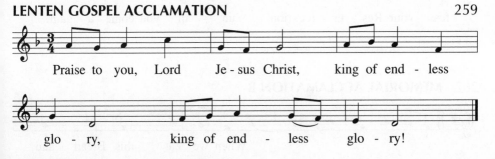

Praise to you, Lord Je - sus Christ, king of end - less

glo - ry, king of end - less glo - ry!

Text: ICEL, © 1969
Music: *Storrington Mass,* Marty Haugen, © 2010, GIA Publications, Inc.

260 HOLY, HOLY, HOLY

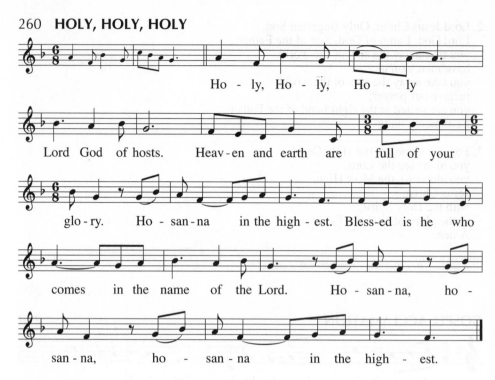

Ho - ly, Ho - ly, Ho - ly Lord God of hosts. Heav-en and earth are full of your glo - ry. Ho - san - na in the high - est. Bless-ed is he who comes in the name of the Lord. Ho - san - na, ho - san - na, ho - san - na in the high - est.

Text: ICEL, © 2010
Music: *Storrington Mass,* Marty Haugen, © 2010, GIA Publications, Inc.

261 MEMORIAL ACCLAMATION A

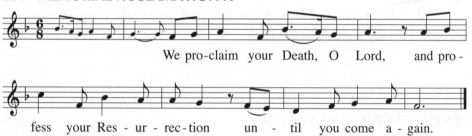

We pro-claim your Death, O Lord, and pro - fess your Res - ur - rec - tion un - til you come a - gain.

Text: ICEL, © 2010
Music: *Storrington Mass,* Marty Haugen, © 2010, GIA Publications, Inc.

262 MEMORIAL ACCLAMATION B

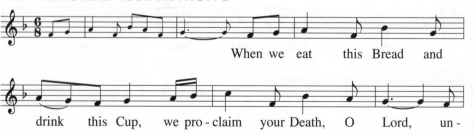

When we eat this Bread and drink this Cup, we pro - claim your Death, O Lord, un -

til you come a - gain, un - til you come a - gain.

Text: ICEL, © 2010
Music: *Storrington Mass*, Marty Haugen, © 2010, GIA Publications, Inc.

MEMORIAL ACCLAMATION C 263

Save us, Sav-ior of the world, for by your

Cross and Res - ur - rec - tion you have set us free.

Text: ICEL, © 2010
Music: *Storrington Mass*, Marty Haugen, © 2010, GIA Publications, Inc.

AMEN 264

A - men, a - men, a - men.

A - men, a - men, a - men.

Music: *Storrington Mass*, Marty Haugen, © 2010, GIA Publications, Inc.

LAMB OF GOD 265

Cantor: Assembly:

Lamb of God, you take a-way the sins of the world, have

To repeat | Last time Cantor: Assembly:

mer-cy on us. Lamb of God, you

take a-way the sins of the world, grant us peace, grant us peace.

Music: *Storrington Mass*, Marty Haugen, © 2010, GIA Publications, Inc.

Setting Five: Black Mountain Liturgy

266 KYRIE

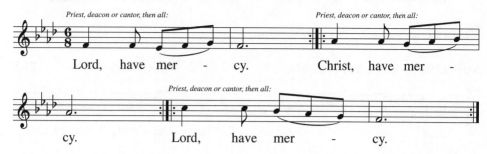

Priest, deacon or cantor, then all:

Lord, have mer - cy.

Priest, deacon or cantor, then all:

Christ, have mer - cy.

Priest, deacon or cantor, then all:

Lord, have mer - cy.

Music: *Black Mountain Liturgy,* Sally Ann Morris, © 2003, GIA Publications, Inc.

267 GLORIA

Refrain

Glo - ry to God in the high - est, and on earth peace to

peo - ple of good will.

To verses

1. We
2. ʾ
3. For

Verse 1

praise you, we bless you, we a - dore you, we

glo - ri - fy you, we give you thanks for your great glo - ry,

opt. **D.C.**

Lord God, heav - en - ly King, O God, al - might - y Fa - ther.

Verse 2

2. Lord Je - sus Christ, On - ly Be - got - ten Son, Lord

May be sung with or without refrains.

God, Lamb of God, Son of the Fa -
ther, you take a - way the sins of the world, have
mer - cy on us; you take a - way the
sins of the world, re - ceive our prayer;
you are seat - ed at the right hand of the Fa -

opt. **D.C.**

ther, have mer - cy on us. 3. For

Verse 3

you a - lone are the Ho - ly One, you a - lone are the
Lord, you a - lone are the Most High, Je - sus
Christ, with the Ho - ly Spir - it, in the

opt. **D.C.**

glo - ry of God the Fa - ther. A - men.

268 GOSPEL ACCLAMATION

Al - le - lu - ia, al - le - lu - ia.
Lent: Praise and hon-or to you, Lord Je - sus Christ!

Al - le - lu - ia, al - le - lu - ia.
Praise and hon-or to you, Lord Je - sus Christ!

Text: ICEL, © 1969
Music: *Black Mountain Liturgy,* Sally Ann Morris, © 2003, GIA Publications, Inc.

269 HOLY, HOLY, HOLY

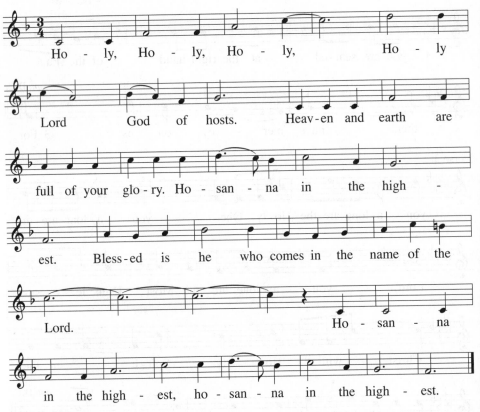

Ho - ly, Ho - ly, Ho - ly, Ho - ly

Lord God of hosts. Heav-en and earth are

full of your glo-ry. Ho - san - na in the high -

est. Bless-ed is he who comes in the name of the

Lord. Ho - san - na

in the high - est, ho - san - na in the high - est.

Text: ICEL, © 2010
Music: *Black Mountain Liturgy,* Sally Ann Morris, © 2003, 2010, GIA Publications, Inc.

MEMORIAL ACCLAMATION A 270

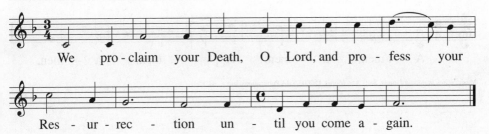

We pro-claim your Death, O Lord, and pro-fess your
Res-ur-rec-tion un-til you come a-gain.

Text: ICEL, © 2010
Music: *Black Mountain Liturgy*, Sally Ann Morris, © 2010, GIA Publications, Inc.

MEMORIAL ACCLAMATION B 271

When we eat this Bread and drink this Cup, we proclaim your Death, O Lord, un-til you come a-gain.

Text: ICEL, © 2010
Music: *Black Mountain Liturgy*, Sally Ann Morris, © 2010, GIA Publications, Inc.

MEMORIAL ACCLAMATION C 272

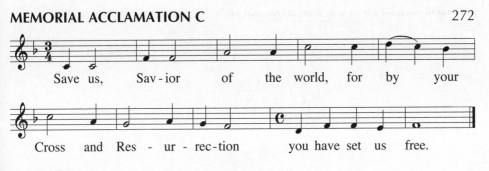

Save us, Sav-ior of the world, for by your
Cross and Res-ur-rec-tion you have set us free.

Text: ICEL, © 2010
Music: *Black Mountain Liturgy*, Sally Ann Morris, © 2010, GIA Publications, Inc.

273 AMEN

A - men, a - men. A - men, a - men.

Music: *Black Mountain Liturgy,* Sally Ann Morris, © 2003, GIA Publications, Inc.

274 LAMB OF GOD

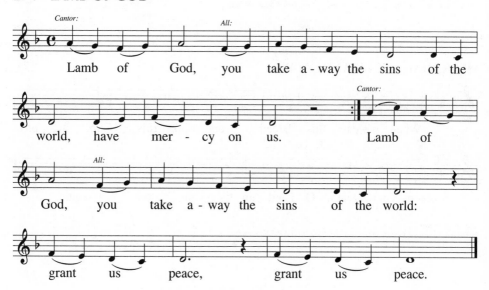

Lamb of God, you take a-way the sins of the world, have mer - cy on us. Lamb of God, you take a - way the sins of the world: grant us peace, grant us peace.

Music: *Black Mountain Liturgy,* Sally Ann Morris, © 2003, GIA Publications, Inc.

Setting Six: Misa Una Santa Fe / One Holy Faith Mass

PENITENTIAL ACT / ACTO PENITENCIAL

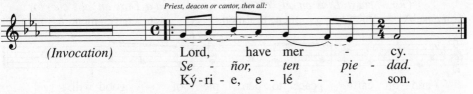

(Invocation)

Lord, have mer - cy.
Se - ñor, ten pie - dad.
Ký-ri - e, e - lé - i - son.

(Invocation)

Christ, have mer - cy.
Cris - to, ten pie - dad.
Chri - ste, e - lé - i - son.

(Invocation)

Lord, have mer - cy.
Se - ñor, ten pie - dad.
Ký-ri - e, e - lé - i - son.

Lord, have mer - cy, have mer - cy.
Se - ñor, ten pie - dad, ten pie-dad.
Ký-ri - e, e - lé - i - son, e - le - i - son.

Priest: May almighty God...everlasting life.
Dios todopoderoso...vida eterna.

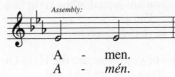

A - men.
A - mén.

Music: *Misa Una Santa Fe,* Ronald F. Krisman, © 2010, GIA Publications, Inc.

276 GLORIA

Refrain

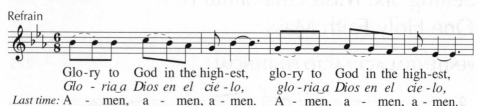

Glo-ry to God in the high-est, glo-ry to God in the high-est,
Glo - ria a Dios en el cie - lo, *glo - ria a Dios en el cie - lo,*
Last time: A - men, a - men, a - men. A - men, a - men, a - men.

and on earth peace to peo - ple of good will.
y en la tie-rra paz a los hom - bres que a-ma el Se - ñor.
A - men, a - men, a - men, a - men.

Verses

1. We praise you,
   we bless you,
   we adore you,
   we glorify you,
   we give you thanks for your great
      glory,
   Lord God, heavenly King,
   O God, almighty Father.

2. Lord Jesus Christ, Only Begotten Son,
   Lord God, Lamb of God, Son of the
      Father,
   you take away the sins of the world,
   have mercy on us;
   you take away the sins of the world,
   receive our prayer;
   you are seated at the right hand of the
      Father,
   have mercy on us.

3. For you alone are the Holy One,
   you alone are the Lord,
   you alone are the Most High,
   Jesus Christ,
   with the Holy Spirit,
   in the glory of God the Father.
   Amen.

1. *Por tu inmensa gloria*
   te alabamos,
   te bendecimos,
   te adoramos,
   te glorificamos,
   te damos gracias,
   Señor Dios, Rey celestial,
   Dios Padre todopoderoso.

2. *Señor, Hijo único, Jesucristo,*
   Señor Dios, Cordero de Dios, Hijo del
      Padre;
   tú que quitas el pecado del mundo,
   ten piedad de nosotros;
   tú que quitas el pecado del mundo,
   atiende nuestra súplica;
   tú que estás sentado a la derecha del
      Padre,
   ten piedad de nosotros,
   ten piedad de nosotros.

3. *Porque sólo tú eres Santo,*
   sólo tú Señor,
   sólo tú Altísimo,
   Jesucristo,
   con el Espíritu Santo
   en la gloria de Dios Padre.
   Amén.

Text: English, © 2010, ICEL
Music: *Misa Una Santa Fe*, Ronald F. Krisman, © 2010, GIA Publications, Inc.

GOSPEL ACCLAMATION / ACLAMACIÓN ANTES DEL EVANGELIO

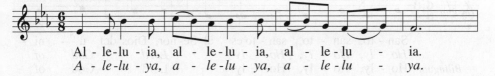

Al - le -lu - ia, al - le -lu - ia, al - le -lu - ia.
A - le -lu - ya, a - le -lu - ya, a - le -lu - ya.

Al - le -lu - ia, al - le -lu - ia, al - le -lu - ia.
A - le -lu - ya, a - le -lu - ya, a - le -lu - ya.

Music: *Misa Una Santa Fe,* Ronald F. Krisman, © 2010, GIA Publications, Inc.

LENTEN GOSPEL ACCLAMATION / ACLAMACIÓN ANTES DEL EVANGELIO DURANTE LA CUARESMA

Praise to you, Lord Je -sus Christ, king of end - less glo -ry.
A - la-ban - za a ti, oh Cris - to, rey de e-ter - na glo -ria.

Praise to you, Lord Je-sus Christ, king of end - less glo -ry.
A - la-ban - za a ti, oh Cris - to, rey de e-ter - na glo -ria.

*For a bilingual refrain, sing the italicized text.

Text: English, © 2010, ICEL
Music: *Misa Una Santa Fe,* Ronald F. Krisman, © 2010, GIA Publications, Inc.

PRAYER OF THE FAITHFUL / ORACIÓN DE LOS FIELES

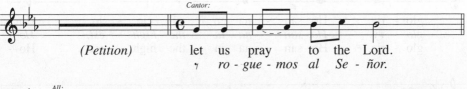

Cantor:

(Petition) let us pray to the Lord.
ro - gue - mos al Se - ñor.

All:

In your lov - ing - kind - ness, Lord, hear our prayer.
Ó - ye -nos en tu bon - dad, Dios del a - mor.
Bilingual: Ó - ye -nos en tu bon - dad. Lord, hear our prayer.

Music: *Misa Una Santa Fe,* Ronald F. Krisman, © 2010, GIA Publications, Inc.

280 SANTO, SANTO, SANTO / HOLY, HOLY, HOLY

San - to, san - to, san - to es el Se -ñor, Dios del u - ni -
Ho - ly, Ho - ly, Ho - ly Lord God of
Bilingual: Ho - ly, Ho - ly, Ho - ly Lord God of

ver - so. Lle - nos es - tán el cie - lo y la
hosts. *Heav - en and earth are full, are*
hosts. Heav - en and earth are full, are

tie - rra de tu glo - ria. San - to, san - to,
full of your glo - ry. *Ho - ly, Ho - ly,*
full of your glo - ry. San - to, san - to,

san - to es el Se - ñor, Dios del u - ni - ver - so.
Ho - ly Lord God of hosts.
san - to es el Se - ñor, Dios del u - ni - ver - so.

Lle - nos es - tán el cie - lo y la tie - rra de tu
Heav -en and earth are full, are full of your
Lle - nos es - tán el cie - lo y la tie - rra de tu

glo - ria. Ho - san - na en el cie - lo. Ho -
glo - ry. *Ho -san - na in the high - est.* *Ho -*
glo - ria. Ho - san - na in the high - est. Ho -

san - na en el cie - lo. Ho - san - na en el
san - na in the high - est. *Ho - san - na in the*
san - na in the high - est. Ho - san - na in the

cie - lo. Ho - san - na en el cie - lo.
high - est. Ho - san - na in the high - est.
high - est. Ho - san - na in the high - est.

Ben - di - to el que vie - ne en
⁊ Bless - ed is he who comes in the
Ben - di - to el que vie - ne en

nom - bre del Se - ñor. Ho - san - na en el
name of the Lord. Ho - san - na in the
nom - bre del Se - ñor. Ho - san - na en el

cie - lo. Ho - san - na en el cie - lo. Ho - san - na en el
high-est. Ho - san - na in the high - est. Ho - san - na in the
cie - lo. Ho - san - na en el cie - lo. Ho - san - na en el

cie - lo. Ho - san - na en el cie - lo.
high - est. Ho - san - na in the high - est.
cie - lo. Ho - san - na en el cie - lo.

Text: English, © 2010, ICEL
Music: *Misa Una Santa Fe,* Ronald F. Krisman, © 2010, GIA Publications, Inc.

281 **ACLAMACIÓN AL MEMORIAL A / MEMORIAL ACCLAMATION A**

A - nun - cia - mos tu muer - te, pro - cla -
We pro - claim your Death, O Lord, and pro -

ma - mos tu re - su - rrec - ción. ¡Ven, Se - ñor Je -
fess your Res - ur - rec - tion un - til you come a -

sús! ¡Ven, Se - ñor Je - sús!
gain, un - til you come a - gain.

Text: English, © 2010, ICEL
Music: *Misa Una Santa Fe*, Ronald F. Krisman, © 2010, GIA Publications, Inc.

282 **ACLAMACIÓN AL MEMORIAL B / MEMORIAL ACCLAMATION B**

Ca - da vez que co - me - mos de es - te pan
When we eat this Bread and drink this Cup,

y be - be - mos de es - te cá - liz, a - nun - cia - mos tu
we pro - claim your Death, O Lord, un - til you

muer - te, Se - ñor, has - ta que vuel - vas.
come a - gain, un - til you come a - gain.

Text: English, © 2010, ICEL
Music: *Misa Una Santa Fe*, Ronald F. Krisman, © 2010, GIA Publications, Inc.

ACLAMACIÓN AL MEMORIAL C / MEMORIAL ACCLAMATION C   283

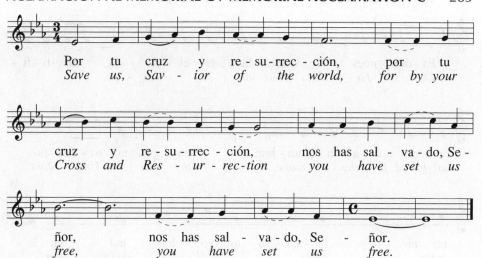

Por tu cruz y re-su-rrec-ción, por tu
Save us, Sav-ior of the world, for by your

cruz y re-su-rrec-ción, nos has sal-va-do, Se-
Cross and Res-ur-rec-tion you have set us

ñor, nos has sal-va-do, Se- ñor.
free, you have set us free.

Text: English, © 2010, ICEL
Music: *Misa Una Santa Fe,* Ronald F. Krisman, © 2010, GIA Publications, Inc.

AMÉN / AMEN   284

A - mén, a - mén.
A - men, a - men.

A - mén, a - mén.
A - men, a - men.

Music: *Misa Una Santa Fe,* Ronald F. Krisman, © 2010, GIA Publications, Inc.

285 EL PADRENUESTRO / THE LORD'S PRAYER

Pa - dre nues - tro, que_es - tás en el cie - lo, san - ti - fi -
Our *Fa* - *ther, who* *art* *in* *heav* - *en,*

ca - do se - a tu Nom - bre; ven - ga_a no - so - tros tu
hal - lowed be thy name; *thy* *king - dom*

rei - no; há - ga - se tu vo - lun - tad en la
come, *thy* *will be done on*

tie - rra co - mo_en el cie - lo. Da - nos hoy nues - tro
earth as it is in heav - en. *Give us this day our*

pan de ca - da dí - a; per - do - na nues - tras o - fen - sas,
dai - ly bread, and for - give us our tres - pass - es,

co - mo tam - bién no - so - tros per - do - na - mos a
as we for - give those who

los que nos o - fen - den; no nos de - jes ca - er en la
tres - pass a - gainst us; and lead us not in - to temp -

ten - ta - ción, y lí - bra - nos del mal.
ta - tion, but de - liv - er us from e - vil.

Priest: Líbranos de todos los males...nuestro Salvador, Jesucristo.
Deliver us, Lord...and the coming of our Savior, Jesus Christ.

Tu - yo es el rei - no, tu - yo el po - der y la
For the king - dom, the pow'r and the glo - ry are

glo - ria, por siem - pre, Se - ñor, la
yours now and for ev - er, are

glo - ria, por siem - pre, Se - ñor.
yours now and for ev - er.

Music: *Misa Una Santa Fe*, Ronald F. Krisman, © 2010, GIA Publications, Inc.

286 LAMB OF GOD / CORDERO DE DIOS

Cantor or assembly:

Lamb of God, you take a - way the
Cor - de - ro de Dios, que qui - tas el pe -

All:

sins of the world, have mer - cy, have
ca - do del mun - do, ten pie - dad,

mer - cy, have mer - cy on us.
ten pie - dad, ten pie - dad de no - so - tros.

Cantor or assembly:

Lamb of God, you take a - way the
Cor - de - ro de Dios, que qui - tas el pe -

All:

sins of the world, have mer - cy, have
ca - do del mun - do, ten pie - dad,

Repeat if desired

mer - cy, have mer - cy on us.
ten pie - dad, ten pie - dad de no - so - tros.

Cantor or assembly:

Lamb of God, you take a - way the sins of the
Cor - de - ro de Dios, que qui - tas el pe - ca - do del

All:

world, grant us, grant us, grant us peace.
mun - do, da - nos, da - nos, da - nos la paz.

Music: *Misa Una Santa Fe*, Ronald F. Krisman, © 2010, GIA Publications, Inc.

Setting Seven: Mass for the People of God

PENITENTIAL ACT

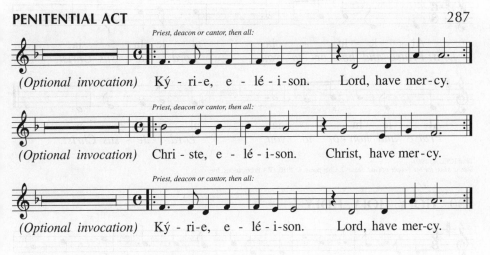

(Optional invocation) Ký - ri-e, e - lé - i-son. Lord, have mer-cy.

(Optional invocation) Chri - ste, e - lé - i-son. Christ, have mer-cy.

(Optional invocation) Ký - ri-e, e - lé - i-son. Lord, have mer-cy.

Music: *Mass for the People of God*, James J. Chepponis, © 2011, GIA Publications, Inc.

GLORIA

Refrain

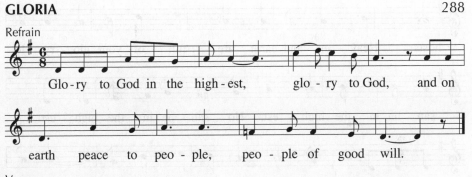

Glo-ry to God in the high-est, glo-ry to God, and on earth peace to peo-ple, peo-ple of good will.

Verses

1. We praise you,
   we bless you,
   we adore you,
   we glorify you,
   we give you thanks for your great glory,
   Lord God, heavenly King,
   O God, almighty Father.

2. Lord Jesus Christ, Only Begotten Son,
   Lord God, Lamb of God, Son of the Father,
   you take away the sins of the world,
   have mercy on us;
   you take away the sins of the world,
   receive our prayer;
   you are seated at the right hand of the Father,
   have mercy on us.

3. For you alone are the Holy One,
   you alone are the Lord,
   you alone are the Most High,
   Jesus Christ,
   with the Holy Spirit,
   in the glory of God the Father.
   Amen.

Text: ICEL, © 2010
Music: *Mass for the People of God*, James J. Chepponis, © 2011, GIA Publications, Inc.

289 GOSPEL ACCLAMATION

Al - le - lu - ia, al - le - lu - ia.
Lent: Praise and hon-or to you, *Lord Je - sus Christ.*

Al - le - lu - ia, al - le - lu - ia.
Praise and hon-or to you, *Lord Je - sus Christ.*

Text: ICEL, © 1969
Music: *Mass for the People of God,* James J. Chepponis, © 2010, GIA Publications, Inc.

290 HOLY, HOLY, HOLY

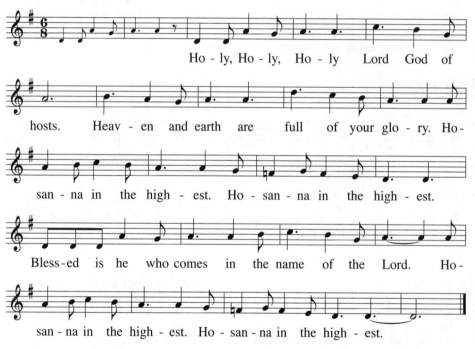

Ho - ly, Ho - ly, Ho - ly Lord God of

hosts. Heav - en and earth are full of your glo - ry. Ho-

san - na in the high - est. Ho - san - na in the high - est.

Bless-ed is he who comes in the name of the Lord. Ho-

san - na in the high - est. Ho - san - na in the high - est.

Text: ICEL, © 2010
Music: *Mass for the People of God,* James J. Chepponis, © 2011, GIA Publications, Inc.

291 MEMORIAL ACCLAMATION A

We pro-claim your Death, O Lord, and pro-

fess   your Res - ur - rec - tion   un - til   you come   a - gain.

Text: ICEL, © 2010
Music: *Mass for the People of God,* James J. Chepponis, © 2011, GIA Publications, Inc.

MEMORIAL ACCLAMATION B
292

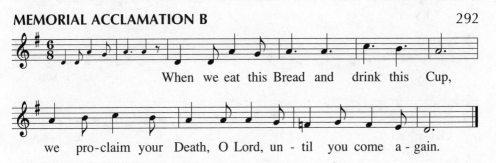

When we eat this Bread and   drink this   Cup,

we   pro-claim your Death, O Lord, un - til   you come   a - gain.

Text: ICEL, © 2010
Music: *Mass for the People of God,* James J. Chepponis, © 2011, GIA Publications, Inc.

MEMORIAL ACCLAMATION C
293

Save   us,   Sav - ior of   the   world,   for

by   your Cross   and   Res - ur - rec-tion   you have set   us free.

Text: ICEL, © 2010
Music: *Mass for the People of God,* James J. Chepponis, © 2011, GIA Publications, Inc.

AMEN
294

A - men,   a - men,   a - men,   a - men.

Music: *Mass for the People of God,* James J. Chepponis, © 2011, GIA Publications, Inc.

LAMB OF GOD
295

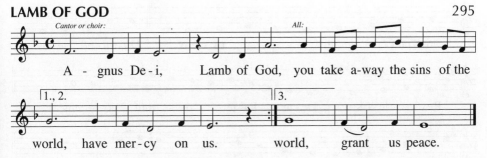

Cantor or choir: *All:*

A - gnus De - i,   Lamb of God, you take a-way the sins of the

1., 2.   **3.**

world,   have mer-cy   on us.   world,   grant   us peace.

Music: *Mass for the People of God,* James J. Chepponis, © 2011, GIA Publications, Inc.

Setting Eight: Cantus Missae

296 KYRIE

Kýri - e, * e - lé - i - son.

Chri - ste, e - lé - i - son.

Ký - ri - e, e - lé - i - son.

Ký - ri - e, * ** e - lé - i - son.

Music: Vatican Edition VIII; acc. by Richard Proulx, © 1995, GIA Publications, Inc.

297 GLORIA

Gló - ri - a in ex - cél - sis De - o. Et in ter - ra pax ho - mí - ni - bus

bo - nae vo - lun - tá - tis. Lau - dá - mus te.

Be - ne - dí - ci - mus te. A - do - rá - mus te.

Glo - ri - fi - cá - mus te. Grá - ti - as á - gi - mus ti - bi

pro - pter ma - gnam gló - ri - am tu - am. Dó - mi - ne De - us,

Rex cae - lé - stis, De - us Pa - ter o - mní - po - tens.

Dó - mi - ne Fi - li u - ni - gé - ni - te, Je - su Chri - ste.

Dó - mi - ne De - us, A - gnus De - i, Fí - li - us Pa - tris.

Qui tol - lis pec - cá - ta mun - di, mi - se - ré - re no - bis.

Qui tol - lis pec - cá - ta mun - di, sú - sci - pe de - pre - ca - ti - ó -

nem no - stram. Qui se - des ad déx - te - ram Pa - tris,

mi - se - ré - re no - bis. Quó - ni - am tu so - lus San - ctus.

Tu so - lus Dó - mi - nus. Tu so - lus Al - tís - si - mus,

Je - su Chri - ste. Cum San - cto Spí - ri - tu:

in gló - ri - a De - i Pa - tris. A - men.

Music: Vatican Edition VIII, acc. by Richard Proulx, © 1995, GIA Publications, Inc.

LITURGY OF THE WORD

FIRST READINGS

298

After the first reading:

Reader: Assembly:

Ver - bum Dó - mi - ni. De - o grá - ti - as.

After the second reading or if there is only one reading before the gospel:

Reader: Assembly:

Ver - bum Dó - mi - ni. De - o grá - ti - as.

299 GOSPEL

Before the gospel reading:

Deacon or priest: *Assembly:*

Dó - mi - nus vo - bís-cum.   Et cum spí - ri - tu tu - o.

Deacon or priest:

Lé - cti - o san - cti E - van - gé - li - i se - cún - dum

Assembly:

N...   Gló - ri - a ti - bi, Dó - mi - ne.

After the reading:

Deacon or priest: *Assembly:*

Ver-bum Dó - mi - ni.   Laus ti - bi, Chri - ste.

300 CREDO

Cre-do in u-num De - um,   Pa - trem o - mni-po - tén-tem, fa-

ctó-rem cae - li et ter-rae, vi - si - bí - li-um ó - mni-um

et in - vi - si - bí - li-um.   Et in u - num Dó - mi-num

Je - sum Chri-stum,   Fí - li - um De - i u - ni - gé - ni-tum.

Et ex Pa-tre na - tum an - te ó - mni - a saé - cu - la.

De - um de De - o,   lu - men de lú - mi - ne,   De - um ve - rum

qui ex Pa - tre Fi - li - ó - que pro - cé - dit.

Qui cum Pa - tre et Fí - li - o si - mul a - do - rá - tur et con-glo -

ri - fi - cá - tur: qui lo - cú - tus est per pro - phé-tas. Et u-nam,

san-ctam, ca - thó - li - cam et a - po - stó - li - cam Ec - clé - si - am.

Con-fí - te - or u-num ba - ptís - ma in re-mis-si - ó-nem pec-ca -

tó - rum. Et ex-spé - cto re - sur - re - cti - ó - nem

mor - tu - ó - rum. Et vi - tam ven - tú - ri saé - cu - li.

A - men.

Music: Vatican Edition III; acc. by Richard Proulx, © 1995, GIA Publications, Inc.

301 PRAYER OF THE FAITHFUL

Cantor: *All:*

(Petition) ex - au - dí - re di - gné-ris. Te ro - gá-mus, au - di nos.

LITURGY OF THE EUCHARIST

302 PREFACE DIALOGUE

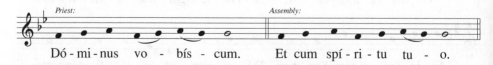

Priest: *Assembly:*

Dó - mi - nus vo - bís - cum. Et cum spí - ri - tu tu - o.

SANCTUS 303

Music: Vatican Edition VIII; acc. by Richard Proulx, © 1995, GIA Publications, Inc.

304 SANCTUS

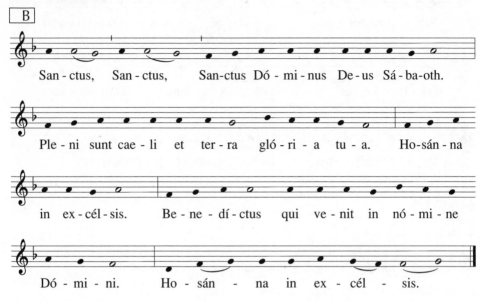

San - ctus, San - ctus, San-ctus Dó - mi - nus De - us Sá - ba-oth.

Ple - ni sunt cae - li et ter - ra gló - ri - a tu - a. Ho-sán - na

in ex - cél - sis. Be - ne - dí - ctus qui ve - nit in nó - mi - ne

Dó - mi - ni. Ho - sán - na in ex - cél - sis.

Music: Vatican Edition XVIII; acc. by Richard Proulx, © 1995, GIA Publications, Inc.

305 MEMORIAL ACCLAMATION

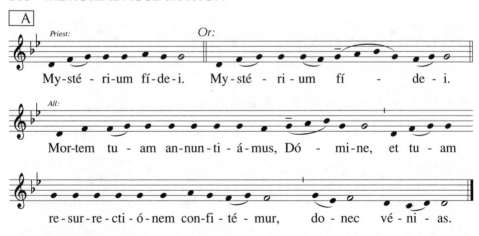

Priest: *Or:*

My - sté - ri-um fí-de-i. My - sté - ri - um fí - de - i.

All:

Mor-tem tu - am an-nun-ti - á-mus, Dó - mi-ne, et tu - am

re - sur-re - cti - ó - nem con-fi - té - mur, do - nec vé - ni - as.

Music: Vatican Edition; acc. by Richard Proulx, © 1995, GIA Publications, Inc.

306 MEMORIAL ACCLAMATION

Priest:

My - sté - ri-um fí - de - i.

Mor-tem tu - am an - nun - ti - á - mus, Dó-mi-ne, et tu-am re-sur-re - cti - ó - nem con - fi - té - mur, do - nec vé - ni - as.

Music: Vatican Edition; acc. by Richard Proulx, © 1995, GIA Publications, Inc.

AMEN 307

After the doxology:

Priest: ...per ó - mni - a saé - cu - la sae-cu - ló - rum. Assembly: A - men.

COMMUNION RITE

THE LORD'S PRAYER 308

Priest: Prae - cé - ptis sa - lu - tá - ri - bus mó - ni - ti, et di - ví - na in - sti - tu - ti - ó - ne for - má - ti, au - dé - mus dí - ce - re:

All: Pa - ter no - ster, qui es in cae - lis: san-cti - fi - cé - tur no - men tu - um; ad - vé - ni - at re - gnum tu-um; fi - at vo - lún-tas tu - a, si - cut in cae - lo, et in ter - ra.

Pa - nem no-strum co - ti - di - á - num da no - bis hó - di - e;

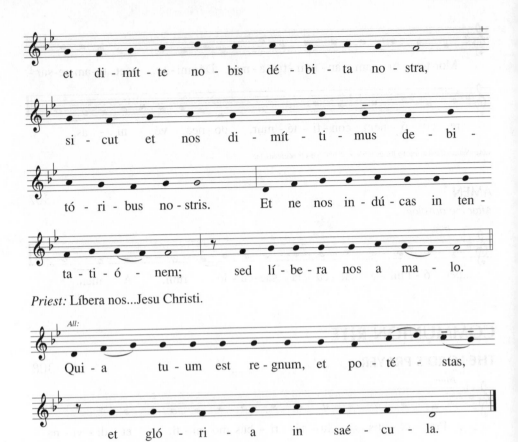

et di - mít - te no - bis dé - bi - ta no - stra,

si - cut et nos di - mít - ti - mus de - bi -

tó - ri - bus no - stris. Et ne nos in - dú - cas in ten -

ta - ti - ó - nem; sed lí - be - ra nos a ma - lo.

Priest: Líbera nos...Jesu Christi.

All:

Qui - a tu - um est re - gnum, et po - té - stas,

et gló - ri - a in saé - cu - la.

309 SIGN OF PEACE

Priest:

Qui vivis et regnas in saécula sae - cu - ló - rum.

Assembly:

A - men.

Priest:

Pax Dó - mi - ni sit sem - per

Assembly:

vo - bís - cum. Et cum spí - ri - tu tu - o.

AGNUS DEI

310

A - gnus De - i, ∗ qui tol - lis pec - cá -
ta mun - di: mi - se - ré - re no - bis.

A - gnus De - i, ∗ qui tol - lis pec - cá -
ta mun - di: mi - se - ré - re no - bis.

A - gnus De - i, ∗ qui tol - lis pec - cá -
ta mun - di: do - na no - bis pa - cem.

Music: Vatican Edition VIII; acc. by Richard Proulx, © 1995, GIA Publications, Inc.

AGNUS DEI

311

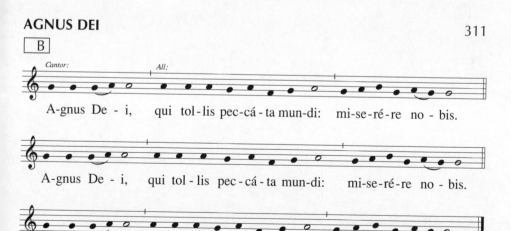

A-gnus De - i, qui tol-lis pec-cá-ta mun-di: mi-se-ré-re no - bis.

A-gnus De - i, qui tol-lis pec-cá-ta mun-di: mi-se-ré-re no - bis.

A-gnus De - i, qui tol-lis pec-cá-ta mun-di: do-na no-bis pa-cem.

Music: Vatican Edition XVIII; acc. by Richard Proulx, © 1995, GIA Publications, Inc.

CONCLUDING RITES

312 DISMISSAL

Deacon or priest, then all:

I - te, mis - sa est.
De - o grá - ti - as.

Music: Vatican Edition VIII; acc. by Richard Proulx, © 1995, GIA Publications, Inc.

Or:

Deacon or priest: *Assembly:*

I - te, mis - sa est.   De - o grá - ti - as.

For Easter Sunday and the octave of Easter:

Deacon or priest, then all:

I - te, mis - sa est, al - le - lú - ia, al - le - lú - ia.
De - o grá - ti - as, al - le - lú - ia, al - le - lú - ia.

Service Music

SPRINKLING SONG

Lord Je - sus, from your wound - ed side flowed streams of cleans - ing wa - ter. Al - le - lu - ia, al - le - lu - ia, al - le - lu - ia. The world was washed of all its sin, all life made new a - gain. Al - le - lu - ia, al - le - lu - ia, al - le - lu - ia.

Text: ICEL, © 1973
Music: *Festival Liturgy,* Richard Hillert, © 1983, GIA Publications, Inc.

SPRINKLING SONG

Refrain

Al - le - lu - ia, al - le - lu - ia, al - le - lu - ia.

Music: SURGIT IN HAEC DIES, 12th C., adapt. by Leo Nestor, © 2011, GIA Publications, Inc.

315 **SPRINKLING SONG**

Refrain

Springs of wa-ter, bless the Lord! Give him glo-ry and praise for ev-er!

Verses

Cantor:

1. O - ceans of earth, sing glo-ry to God! Praise to the one who
2. Riv - ers and lakes, sing glo-ry to God! Praise, all you ponds and
3. Brooks of the hills, sing glo-ry to God! Praise to the source of
4. Show - ers and springs, sing glo-ry to God! Praise, all you liv - ing

formed you! Sound from your depths a hymn that tells the
bogs! Rich with the life that God cre - ates, now
life! Danc - ing with joy from peak to val - ley,
wa - ters! Show - er the earth with life and good-ness,

won - ders God has done!
let your song be heard!
laugh-ing and clear your song! Oh Bless-ed be God for
show - er the grace of God!

All: D.C.

ev - er! Bless - ed be God for ev - er!

Text: Refrain trans. © 1973, ICEL; additional text by Marty Haugen, © 1994, GIA Publications, Inc.
Music: Marty Haugen, © 1994, GIA Publications, Inc.

SPRINKLING SONG

A - spér - ges me, Dó - mi - ne hys -
Cleanse me from sin, O Lord God, wash

só - po, et mun-dá - bor: la - vá - bis me,
me with hys - sop branch - es: cleanse me from guilt,

et su - per ni - vem de - al - bá - bor.
and I shall be clean as the new snow.

Mi - se - ré - re me - i, De - us, se - cún -
Have mer - cy on me, O my God, ac - cord -

D.C. *(ad lib.)*

dum magnam miseri - cór - di - am tu - am.
ing to your great com - pas - sion.

Gló - ri - a Patri, et Fílio, et Spi - rí - tu - i San - cto:
Glo - ry be to the Father
and to the Son, and to the Ho - ly Spir - it:

Si - cut erat in princípio, et nunc, et sem - per,
As it was in the beginning, is now and ev - er shall be,

D.C.

et in saécula sae - cu - ló - rum. A - men.
world with - out end. A - men.

Text: *Roman Missal*; Psalm 51:9, 1; trans. by Richard Proulx, © 1975, GIA Publications, Inc.
Music: Vatican Edition, Mode VII; adapt. by Richard Proulx, © 1975, GIA Publications, Inc.

317 KYRIE

Priest, deacon or cantor, then all:

Lord, have mer - cy. Christ, have mer - cy.

Priest, deacon or cantor, then all:

Lord, have mer - cy.

Music: *Litany of the Saints;* adapt. by Richard Proulx, © 1971, GIA Publications, Inc.

Or:

Priest, deacon or cantor, then all:

Ký - ri - e, e - lé - i - son. Chri - ste, e - lé - i - son.

Priest, deacon or cantor, then all:

Ký - ri - e, e - lé - i - son.

Music: *Litany of the Saints;* adapt. by Richard Proulx, © 1971, GIA Publications, Inc.

318 KYRIE

Priest, deacon or cantor, then all:

Ký - ri-e, e - lé-i-son. Ký - ri-e, e - lé-i-son.

Ký - ri-e, e - lé - i - son. son.

Priest, deacon or cantor, then all:

Cris-to, ten pie-dad, Cris-to, ten pie-dad, Cris-to, ten pie-dad de no-

so - tros. Cris-to, ten pie-dad, Cris-to, ten pie-dad,

Cris-to, ten pie-dad de no - so - tros. so - tros.

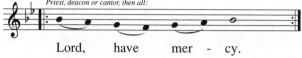

Priest, deacon or cantor, then all:

Lord, have mer-cy. Lord, have mer-cy.

Lord, have mer - cy.

Music: Norah Duncan IV, © 2011, GIA Publications, Inc.

KYRIE

319

Priest, deacon or cantor, then all:

Ký-ri-e, e - lé-i-son,

Ký-ri-e, e - lé-i-son, Ký-ri - e, e - lé-i-son.

1. 2. *Cantor or choir:*

Chri - ste, e - lé-i-son,

Chri - ste, e - lé-i-son, Chri - ste, e -

lé - i - son, e - lé-i - son.

All:

Ký-ri-e, e - lé-i-son, Ký-ri-e, e - lé-i-son, Ký-ri -

e, e - lé-i-son, e - lé-i - son.

Music: *Music for Celebration*, David Hurd, © 1979, GIA Publications, Inc.

320 GLORIA

Glo-ry to God in the high-est, and on earth peace to peo-ple of good will. We praise you, we bless you, we a-dore you, we glo-ri-fy you, we give you thanks for your great glo-ry, Lord God, heav'n-ly King, O God, al-might-y Fa-ther. Lord Je-sus Christ, On-ly Be-got-ten Son, Lord God, Lamb of God, Son of the Fa-ther, you take a-way the sins of the world, have mer-cy on us; you take a-way the sins of the world, re-ceive our prayer; you are seat-ed at the right hand of the Fa-ther, have mer-cy on us. For you a-lone are the Ho-ly One, you a-lone are the Lord,

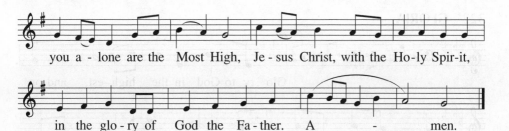

you a - lone are the Most High, Je - sus Christ, with the Ho - ly Spir - it,

in the glo - ry of God the Fa - ther. A - men.

Text: ICEL, © 2010
Music: *A New Mass for Congregations*, Carroll T. Andrews, revised by Ronald F. Krisman, © 1970, 2011, GIA Publications, Inc.

GLORIA 321

Refrain

Gló - ri - a! Gló - ri - a! Glo - ry to God in the high - est, and on

earth peace to peo - ple, to peo - ple of good will.

Verses

1. We praise you,
   we bless you,
   we adore you,
   we glorify you,
   we give you thanks for your great glory,
   Lord God, heavenly King,
   O God, almighty Father.

2. Lord Jesus Christ, Only Begotten Son,
   Lord God, Lamb of God, Son of the Father,
   you take away the sins of the world,
   have mercy on us;
   you take away the sins of the world,
   receive our prayer;
   you are seated at the right hand of the Father,
   have mercy on us.

3. For you alone are the Holy One,
   you alone are the Lord,
   you alone are the Most High,
   Jesus Christ,
   with the Holy Spirit,
   in the glory of God the Father.
   Amen.

Text: ICEL, © 2010
Music: *Jubilation Mass*, James J. Chepponis, © 1999, 2010, GIA Publications, Inc.

322 GLORIA

All:
Glo - ry to God in the high - est, and on earth peace to peo - ple of good will. We praise you, we bless you, we a - dore you, we glo - ri - fy you, we give you thanks for your great glo - ry, Lord God, heav - en - ly King, O God, al - might - y Fa - ther.

Choir (Cong. ad lib.):
Lord Je - sus Christ, On - ly Be - got - ten Son, Lord God, Lamb of God, Son of the Fa - ther, you take a - way the sins of the world, have mer - cy on us; you take a - way the sins of the world, re - ceive our prayer; you are seat - ed at the right hand of the Fa - ther, have mer - cy on us.

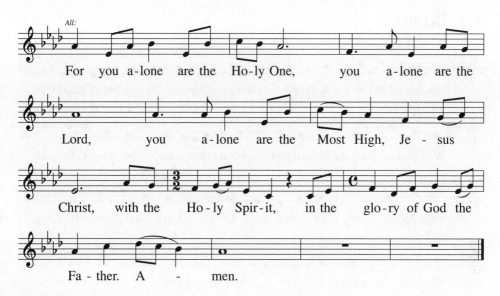

For you a-lone are the Ho-ly One, you a-lone are the Lord, you a-lone are the Most High, Je - sus Christ, with the Ho-ly Spir-it, in the glo-ry of God the Fa - ther. A - men.

Text: ICEL, © 2010
Music: *Holy Name of Jesus Gloria*, Norah Duncan IV, © 2011, GIA Publications, Inc.

GLORIA 323

Refrain

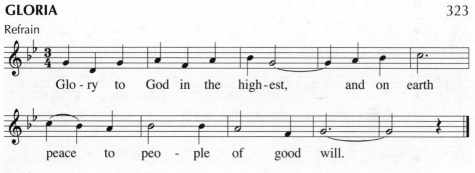

Glo - ry to God in the high-est, and on earth peace to peo - ple of good will.

Verses

1. We praise you,
   we bless you,
   we adore you,
   we glorify you,
   we give you thanks for your great glory,
   Lord God, heavenly King,
   O God, almighty Father.

2. Lord Jesus Christ, Only Begotten Son,
   Lord God, Lamb of God, Son of the
      Father,
   you take away the sins of the world,
   have mercy on us;

   you take away the sins of the world,
   receive our prayer;
   you are seated at the right hand of the
      Father,
   have mercy on us.

3. For you alone are the Holy One,
   you alone are the Lord,
   you alone are the Most High,
   Jesus Christ,
   with the Holy Spirit,
   in the glory of God the Father.
   Amen.

Text: ICEL, © 2010
Music: *Mass of Creation*, Marty Haugen, © 1984, 1985, 2010, GIA Publications, Inc.

324 GLORIA

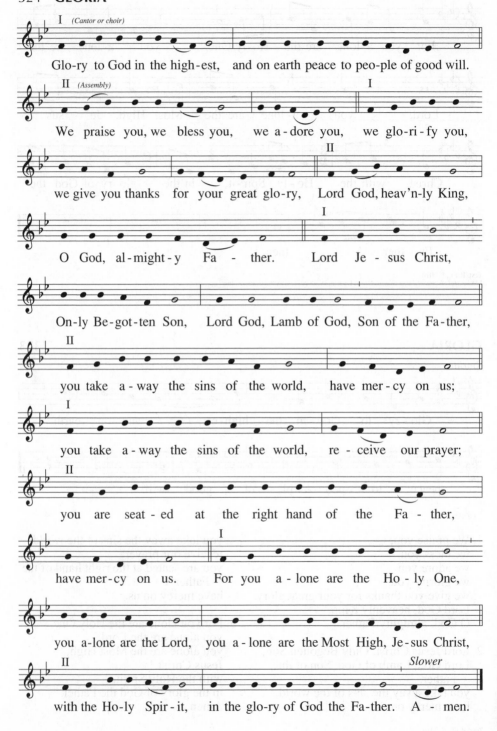

I *(Cantor or choir)*

Glo-ry to God in the high-est, and on earth peace to peo-ple of good will.

II *(Assembly)* I

We praise you, we bless you, we a-dore you, we glo-ri-fy you,

II

we give you thanks for your great glo-ry, Lord God, heav'n-ly King,

I

O God, al-might-y Fa - ther. Lord Je - sus Christ,

On-ly Be-got-ten Son, Lord God, Lamb of God, Son of the Fa-ther,

II

you take a-way the sins of the world, have mer-cy on us;

I

you take a-way the sins of the world, re - ceive our prayer;

II

you are seat-ed at the right hand of the Fa - ther,

I

have mer-cy on us. For you a - lone are the Ho - ly One,

you a-lone are the Lord, you a-lone are the Most High, Je-sus Christ,

II *Slower*

with the Ho-ly Spir-it, in the glo-ry of God the Fa-ther. A - men.

Text: ICEL, © 2010
Music: *Congregational Mass;* John Lee, revised by Ronald F. Krisman, © 1970, 2011, GIA Publications, Inc.

CHILDREN'S DISMISSAL FOR LITURGY OF THE WORD 325

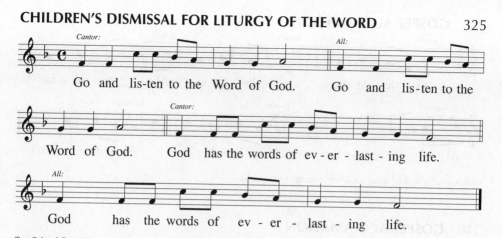

Cantor: Go and lis-ten to the Word of God. *All:* Go and lis-ten to the Word of God. *Cantor:* God has the words of ev-er-last-ing life. *All:* God has the words of ev-er-last-ing life.

Text: Robert J. Batastini
Music: Robert J. Batastini
© 2003, GIA Publications, Inc.

GOSPEL ACCLAMATION 326

Al-le-lu-ia, al-le-lu-ia, al-le-lu-ia.

Music: Chant Mode VI; acc. by Richard Proulx, © 1985, GIA Publications, Inc.

GOSPEL ACCLAMATION 327

Al-le-lu-ia! Al-le-lu-ia! Al-le-lu-ia! Al-le-lu-ia!

Music: Norah Duncan IV, © 1987, GIA Publications, Inc.

GOSPEL ACCLAMATION 328

Al-le-lu-ia, al-le-lu-ia, al-le-lu-ia.

Music: A. Gregory Murray, OSB, © 1958, The Grail, GIA Publications, Inc., agent

329 GOSPEL ACCLAMATION

Music: *Alleluia in C,* Howard Hughes, SM, © 1973, 1982, GIA Publications, Inc.

330 GOSPEL ACCLAMATION

Music: Alleluia 7; Jacques Berthier, © 1984, Les Presses de Taizé, GIA Publications, Inc., agent

331 GOSPEL ACCLAMATION

Music: O FILII ET FILIAE, Mode II; acc. by Richard Proulx, © 1975, GIA Publications, Inc.

332 GOSPEL ACCLAMATION

Music: Richard Proulx, © 1980, ICEL

GOSPEL ACCLAMATION 333

Al - le - lu - ia, al - le - lu - ia.

Al - le - lu - ia, al - le - lu - ia.

Music: Fintan O'Carroll, © 1985, GIA Publications, Inc.

GOSPEL ACCLAMATION 334

Al - le - lu - ia, al - le - lu - ia, al - le - lu - ia.
Lent: Glo - ry to you, Word of God, Lord Je - sus Christ.

Al - le - lu - ia, al - le - lu - ia, al - le - lu - ia.
Glo - ry to you, Word of God, Lord Je - sus Christ!

Text: ICEL, © 1969
Music: *Jubilation Mass,* James J. Chepponis, © 1999, GIA Publications, Inc.

GOSPEL ACCLAMATION 335

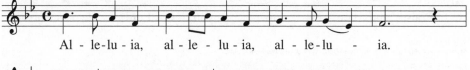

Al - le - lu - ia, al - le - lu - ia, al - le - lu - ia.

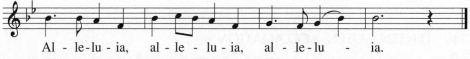

Al - le - lu - ia, al - le - lu - ia, al - le - lu - ia.

Music: *Festival Alleluia,* James J. Chepponis, © 1999, Morningstar Music Publishers

336 GOSPEL ACCLAMATION

Al - le - lu - ia, al - le - lu - ia, al - le -
lu - ia, al - le - lu - ia, al - le - lu - ia.

Music: Richard Proulx, © 1975, GIA Publications, Inc.

337 LENTEN GOSPEL ACCLAMATION

Praise to you, Lord Je - sus Christ, king of end - less glo - ry!

Text: ICEL, © 1969
Music: Frank Schoen, © 1970, GIA Publications, Inc.

338 LENTEN GOSPEL ACCLAMATION

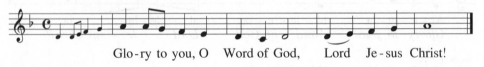

Glo - ry to you, O Word of God, Lord Je - sus Christ!

Text: ICEL, © 1969
Music: Richard Proulx, © 1975, GIA Publications, Inc.

339 LENTEN GOSPEL ACCLAMATION

Praise and hon - or to you, O Lord Je - sus Christ.

Text: ICEL, © 1969
Music: *Kyrie Orbis Factor*, acc. by David Hurd, © 1979, GIA Publications, Inc.

340 LENTEN GOSPEL ACCLAMATION

Glo - ry and praise to you, Lord Je - sus Christ!

Text: ICEL, © 1969
Music: David M. Young, © 1981, GIA Publications, Inc.

NICENE CREED

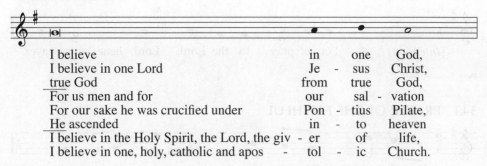

I believe in one God,
I believe in one Lord Je - sus Christ,
true God from true God,
For us men and for our sal - vation
For our sake he was crucified under Pon - tius Pilate,
He ascended in - to heaven
I believe in the Holy Spirit, the Lord, the giv - er of life,
I believe in one, holy, catholic and apos - tol - ic Church.

the Fa - ther al - mighty,
the Only Begotten Son of God,
begot - ten, not made,
he came down from heaven,
he suffered death and was buried,
and is seated at the right hand of the Father.
who proceeds from the Father and the Son,
I confess one Baptism for the forgive - ness of sins

maker of heav - en and earth,
born of the Father be - fore all ages.
consubstantial with the Father;
and by the Holy Spirit was incarnate of the Vir - gin Mary,
and rose again on the third day
He will come again in glory to judge the living and the dead
who with the Father and the Son is a - dored and glorified,
and I look forward to the resurrection of the dead

of all things visible and in - visible.
God from God, Light from Light,
through him all things were made.
and be - came man.
in accordance with the Scriptures.
and his kingdom will have no end.
who has spoken through the prophets.
and the life of the world to come. A - men.

Text: ICEL, © 2010
Music: *Jubilation Mass*, James J. Chepponis, © 1999, 2010, GIA Publications, Inc.

342 PRAYER OF THE FAITHFUL

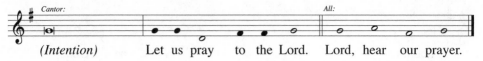

(Intention) Let us pray to the Lord. Lord, hear our prayer.

Music: Byzantine chant

343 PRAYER OF THE FAITHFUL

Ký - ri - e, Ký - ri - e, e - lé - i - son.

Music: Jacques Berthier, © 1980, Les Presses de Taizé, GIA Publications, Inc., agent

344 PRAYER OF THE FAITHFUL

Gra - cious Lord, hear us we pray.

Music: Ronald F. Krisman, © 1977, GIA Publications, Inc.

345 PRAYER OF THE FAITHFUL

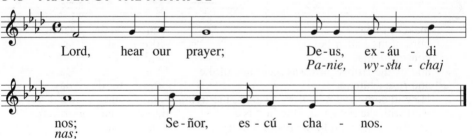

Lord, hear our prayer; De - us, ex - áu - di
Pa - nie, wy - słu - chaj

nos; Se - ñor, es - cú - cha - nos.
nas;

Music: Michael Hay, © 1994, World Library Publications

346 PRAYER OF THE FAITHFUL

God ev - er faith - ful, God ev - er mer - ci - ful,

God of your peo - ple, hear our prayer.

Text: Michael Joncas
Music: *Mass for John Carroll*, Michael Joncas
© 1990, GIA Publications, Inc.

HOLY, HOLY, HOLY–MISSA EMMANUEL 347

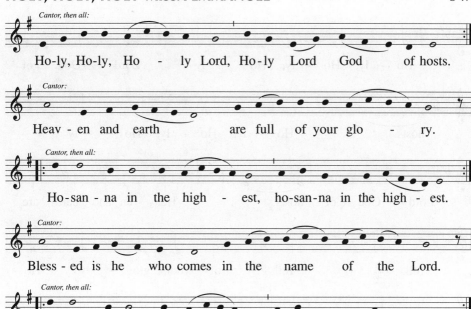

Cantor, then all:
Ho-ly, Ho-ly, Ho - ly Lord, Ho-ly Lord God of hosts.

Cantor:
Heav - en and earth are full of your glo - ry.

Cantor, then all:
Ho-san - na in the high - est, ho-san-na in the high - est.

Cantor:
Bless - ed is he who comes in the name of the Lord.

Cantor, then all:
Ho-san - na in the high - est, ho-san-na in the high - est.

Text: ICEL, © 2010
Music: *Missa Emmanuel,* Richard Proulx, © 1991, 2010, GIA Publications, Inc.

MEMORIAL ACCLAMATION A 348

Cantor, then all:
We pro - claim your Death, O Lord, and pro - fess your

Res - ur - rec - tion un - til you come a - gain.

Text: ICEL, © 2010
Music: *Missa Emmanuel,* adapt. by Robert J. Batastini, © 2011, GIA Publications, Inc.

AMEN 349

Cantor, then all:
A - men, a - men, a - men, a - men.

Music: *Missa Emmanuel,* Richard Proulx, © 1991, 2002, GIA Publications, Inc.

350 HOLY, HOLY, HOLY–DEUTSCHE MESSE

Ho - ly, Ho - ly, Ho - ly Lord God of hosts. Ho - ly, Ho - ly, Ho - ly Lord God of hosts. Heav - en and earth are full, full of your glo - ry. Ho - san - na in the high - est. Ho - san - na in the high - est. Bless - ed is he who comes in the name of the Lord. Ho - san - na in the high - est. Ho - san - na in the high - est.

Text: ICEL, © 2010
Music: *Deutsche Messe*, Franz Schubert, 1797–1828, adapt. by Richard Proulx, © 1985, 1989, 2010, GIA Publications, Inc.

MEMORIAL ACCLAMATION C 351

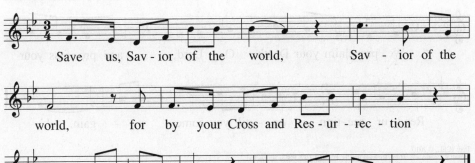

Save us, Sav-ior of the world, Sav-ior of the

world, for by your Cross and Res-ur-rec-tion

you have set us free, you have set us free.

Text: ICEL, © 2010
Music: *Deutsche Messe*, Franz Schubert, 1797–1828, adapt. by Richard Proulx, © 1985, 1989, 2010, GIA Publications, Inc.

AMEN 352

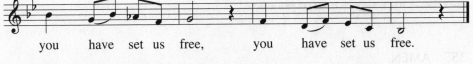

A - men, a - men, a - men, a - men, a - men.

Music: *Deutsche Messe*, Franz Schubert, 1797–1828, adapt. by Richard Proulx, © 1985, 1989, GIA Publications, Inc.

HOLY, HOLY, HOLY–A COMMUNITY MASS 353

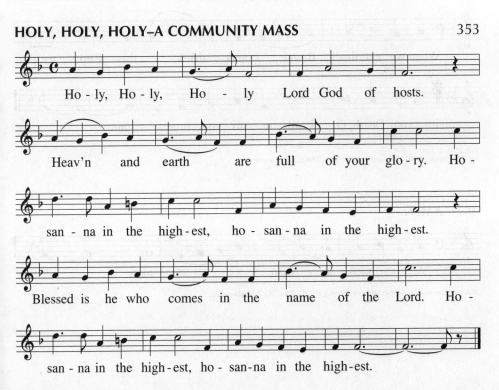

Ho-ly, Ho-ly, Ho - ly Lord God of hosts.

Heav'n and earth are full of your glo-ry. Ho-

san-na in the high-est, ho-san-na in the high-est.

Blessed is he who comes in the name of the Lord. Ho-

san-na in the high-est, ho-san-na in the high-est.

Text: ICEL, © 2010
Music: *A Community Mass*, Richard Proulx, © 1971, GIA Publications, Inc.

354 MEMORIAL ACCLAMATION A

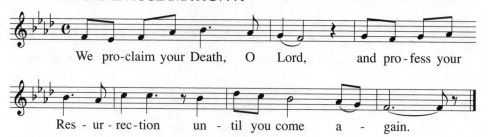

We pro-claim your Death,   O   Lord,   and pro-fess your
Res - ur - rec - tion   un - til you come   a - gain.

Text: ICEL, © 2010
Music: *A Community Mass*, Richard Proulx, © 2010, GIA Publications, Inc.

355 AMEN

A - men,   a - men,   a - men.

Music: *A Community Mass*, Richard Proulx, © 1971, 1977, GIA Publications, Inc.

356 MEMORIAL ACCLAMATION B

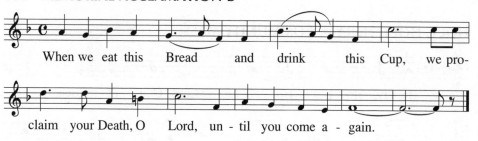

When we eat this   Bread   and   drink   this   Cup,   we proclaim your Death, O   Lord, un - til you come a - gain.

Text: ICEL, © 2010
Music: *A Community Mass*, Richard Proulx, © 1988, 2010, GIA Publications, Inc.

357 AMEN

A - men, a - men,   a - men.

Music: *A Community Mass*, Richard Proulx (adapt.), © 1971, 2011, GIA Publications, Inc.

HOLY, HOLY, HOLY–LAND OF REST 358

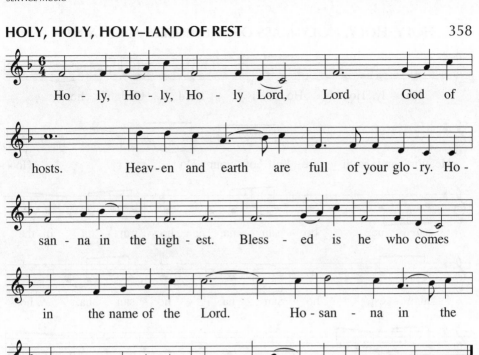

Ho - ly, Ho - ly, Ho - ly Lord, Lord God of
hosts. Heav-en and earth are full of your glo - ry. Ho -
san - na in the high - est. Bless - ed is he who comes
in the name of the Lord. Ho - san - na in the
high - est, ho - san - na in the high - est.

Text: ICEL, © 2010
Music: *Land of Rest*, adapt. by Marcia Pruner, © 1980, alt., Church Pension Fund; acc. by Richard Proulx, © 1986, 2011, GIA Publications, Inc.; choral arr. by Kelly Dobbs-Mickus, © 2004, GIA Publications, Inc.

MEMORIAL ACCLAMATION B 359

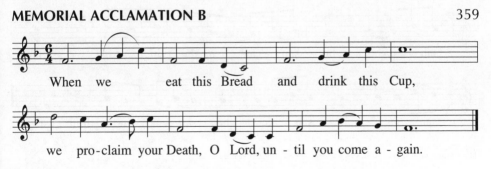

When we eat this Bread and drink this Cup,
we pro-claim your Death, O Lord, un - til you come a - gain.

Text: ICEL, © 2010
Music: *Land of Rest*, acc. by Richard Proulx, © 1986, GIA Publications, Inc.; choral arr. and adapt. by Kelly Dobbs-Mickus, © 2004, 2011, GIA Publications, Inc.

AMEN 360

A - men, a - men, a - men.

Music: *Land of Rest*, adapt. by Richard Proulx, © 1986, GIA Publications, Inc.; choral arr. by Kelly Dobbs-Mickus, © 2004, GIA Publications, Inc.

361 HOLY, HOLY, HOLY–MASS OF THE ANGELS AND SAINTS

Ho - ly, Ho - ly, Ho - ly Lord God of hosts.

Heav'n and earth are full of your glo - ry. Ho -

san - na, ho - san - na, ho - san - na in the

high - est, ho - san - na, ho - san - na, ho -

san - na in the high - est. Bless - ed is he who comes in the

name of the Lord. Ho - san - na, ho -

san - na, ho - san - na in the high - est, ho -

san - na, ho - san - na, ho - san - na in the high - est.

Text: ICEL, © 2010
Music: *Mass of the Angels and Saints*, Steven R. Janco, © 1996, 2010, GIA Publications, Inc.

362 MEMORIAL ACCLAMATION C

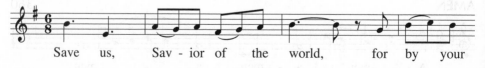

Save us, Sav - ior of the world, for by your

Cross and Res - ur - rec - tion you have set us free.

Text: ICEL, © 2010
Music: *Mass of the Angels and Saints,* Steven R. Janco, © 2010, GIA Publications, Inc.

AMEN 363

A - men, a - men, a - men.

A - men, a - men, a - men.

Music: *Mass of the Angels and Saints,* Steven R. Janco, © 1996, GIA Publications, Inc.

PREFACE DIALOGUE–MASS OF CREATION 364

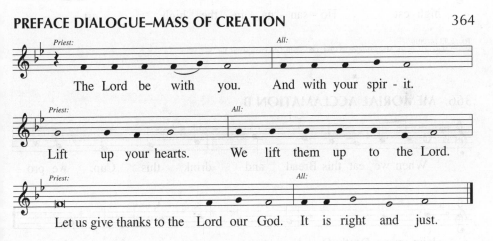

Priest: The Lord be with you. *All:* And with your spir - it.

Priest: Lift up your hearts. *All:* We lift them up to the Lord.

Priest: Let us give thanks to the Lord our God. *All:* It is right and just.

Text: ICEL, © 2010
Music: *Mass of Creation,* Marty Haugen, © 1984, 1985, 2010, GIA Publications, Inc.

365 HOLY, HOLY, HOLY

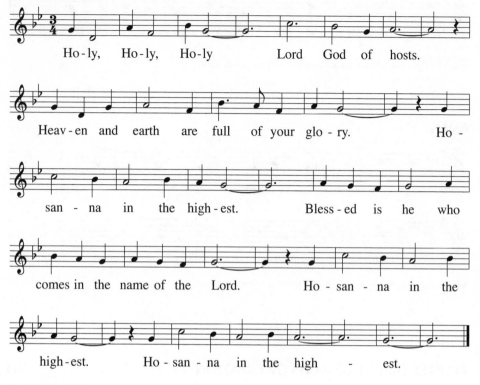

Ho-ly, Ho-ly, Ho-ly Lord God of hosts.

Heav-en and earth are full of your glo-ry. Ho -

san - na in the high - est. Bless - ed is he who

comes in the name of the Lord. Ho - san - na in the

high - est. Ho - san - na in the high - est.

Text: ICEL, © 2010
Music: *Mass of Creation*, Marty Haugen, © 1984, 1985, 2010, GIA Publications, Inc.

366 MEMORIAL ACCLAMATION B

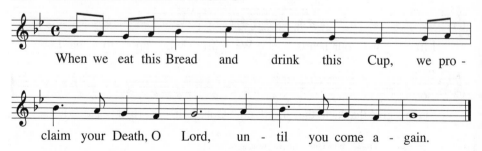

When we eat this Bread and drink this Cup, we pro -

claim your Death, O Lord, un - til you come a - gain.

Text: ICEL, © 2010
Music: *Mass of Creation*, Marty Haugen, © 2010, GIA Publications, Inc.

367 AMEN

A - men, a - men, a - men.

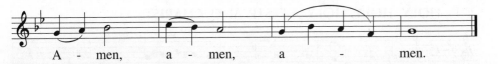

A - men, a - men, a - men.

Music: *Mass of Creation,* Marty Haugen, © 1984, 1985, GIA Publications, Inc.

HOLY, HOLY, HOLY–PEOPLE'S MASS 368

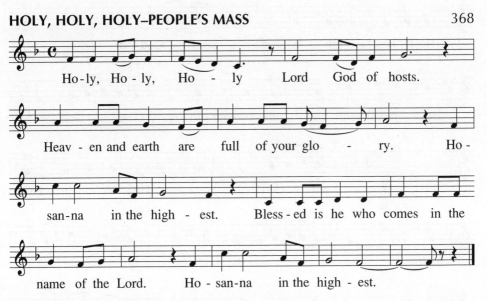

Ho - ly, Ho - ly, Ho - ly Lord God of hosts.

Heav - en and earth are full of your glo - ry. Ho -

san - na in the high - est. Bless - ed is he who comes in the

name of the Lord. Ho - san - na in the high - est.

Text: ICEL, © 2010
Music: *People's Mass,* Jan Vermulst; acc. by Richard Proulx, © 1970, 1987, 2010, World Library Publications

MEMORIAL ACCLAMATION B 369

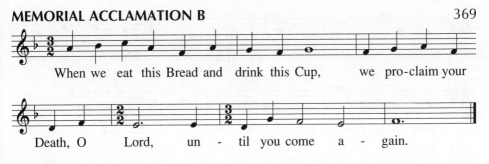

When we eat this Bread and drink this Cup, we pro-claim your

Death, O Lord, un - til you come a - gain.

Text: ICEL, © 2010
Music: *Danish Amen Mass,* David Kraehenbuehl; acc. by Charles G. Frischmann, © 1970, 1973, 2011, World Library Publications

AMEN 370

A - men, a - men, a - men.

Music: Danish Amen

371 HOLY, HOLY, HOLY–A FESTIVAL EUCHARIST

Cantor or choir:

Ho - ly, Ho - ly, Ho - ly Lord, Lord God of hosts.

All:

Ho - ly, Ho - ly, Ho - ly Lord, Lord God of hosts.

Cantor or choir:

Heav - en and earth are full of your glo - ry. Lord God of

hosts. *All:* Lord God of hosts. *Cantor or choir:* Ho - san - na in the

high - est, ho - san - na in the high - est, ho - san - na in the

high - est. *All:* Ho - san - na in the high - est, ho - san - na in the

high - est, ho - san - na in the high - est. *Cantor or choir:* Bless - ed is he who

comes in the name of the Lord. *All:* Ho - san - na in the

high - est, ho - san - na in the high - est, ho - san - na in the

high - est, ho - san - na in the high - est.

Text: ICEL, © 2010
Music: *A Festival Eucharist*, Richard Proulx, © 1975, 2011, GIA Publications, Inc.

MEMORIAL ACCLAMATION B 372

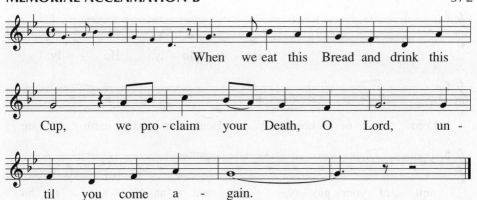

When we eat this Bread and drink this Cup, we pro-claim your Death, O Lord, un-til you come a - gain.

Text: ICEL, © 2010
Music: *A Festival Eucharist,* Richard Proulx, © 1975, 2011, GIA Publications, Inc.

AMEN 373

A - men, a - men, a - men, a - men.

Music: *A Festival Eucharist,* Richard Proulx, © 1975, GIA Publications, Inc.

374 HOLY, HOLY, HOLY–MASS FOR THE CITY

Ho - ly, Ho - ly, Ho - ly Lord God of hosts. Heav - en and earth are full of your glo - ry. Ho - san - na, ho - san - na, ho - san - na in the high - est. Bless - ed is he who comes in the name of the Lord. Ho - san - na, ho - san - na, ho - san - na in the high - est. Ho - san - na, ho - san - na, ho - san - na in the high - est.

Text: ICEL, © 2010
Music: *Mass for the City*, Richard Proulx, © 1991, 2010, GIA Publications, Inc.

375 MEMORIAL ACCLAMATION B

When we eat this Bread and drink this Cup, we pro- claim your Death, O Lord, un - til you come a - gain.

Text: ICEL, © 2010
Music: *Mass for the City*, Richard Proulx, © 1991, 2010, GIA Publications, Inc.

AMEN

A - men, a - men, a - men.

Music: *Mass for the City*, Richard Proulx, © 1995, GIA Publications, Inc.

HOLY, HOLY, HOLY–NEW MASS FOR JOHN CARROLL

Ho - ly, Ho - ly, Ho - ly Lord God of hosts.

Heav - en and earth, heav - en and earth are full of your

glo - ry. Ho - san - na, ho - san - na, ho - san - na in the

high - est. Ho - san - na, ho - san - na, ho -

san - na in the high - est. Bless - ed is he,

bless - ed is he who comes in the name of the Lord. Ho -

san - na, ho - san - na, ho - san - na in the high - est. Ho -

san - na, ho - san - na, ho - san - na in the high - est.

Text: ICEL, © 2010
Music: *New Mass for John Carroll*, Michael Joncas, © 2011, GIA Publications, Inc.

378 MEMORIAL ACCLAMATION A

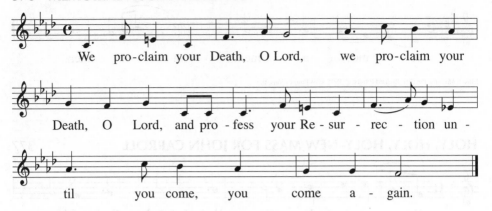

We pro-claim your Death, O Lord, we pro-claim your
Death, O Lord, and pro-fess your Re - sur - rec - tion un -
til you come, you come a - gain.

Text: ICEL, © 2010
Music: *New Mass for John Carroll*, Michael Joncas, © 2011, GIA Publications, Inc.

379 AMEN

A - men, a - men, a - men, a - men, a - men.
A - men, a - men, a - men, a - men, a - men.

Music: *New Mass for John Carroll*, Michael Joncas, © 2010, GIA Publications, Inc.

380 THE LORD'S PRAYER

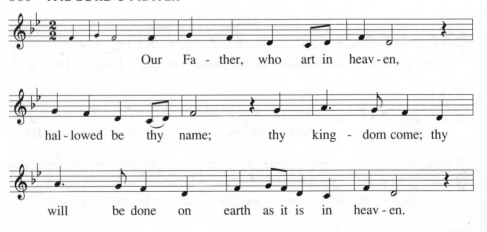

Our Fa - ther, who art in heav - en,
hal - lowed be thy name; thy king - dom come; thy
will be done on earth as it is in heav - en.

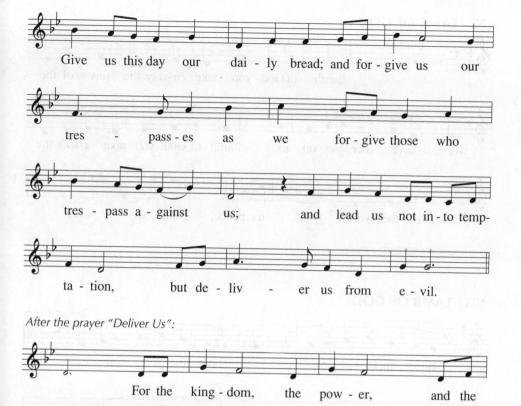

Give us this day our dai - ly bread; and for - give us our

tres - pass - es as we for - give those who

tres - pass a - gainst us; and lead us not in - to temp-

ta - tion, but de - liv - er us from e - vil.

After the prayer "Deliver Us":

For the king - dom, the pow - er, and the

glo - ry are yours now and for ev - er.

Music: *A Festival Eucharist,* Richard Proulx, © 1975, GIA Publications, Inc.

LAMB OF GOD

381

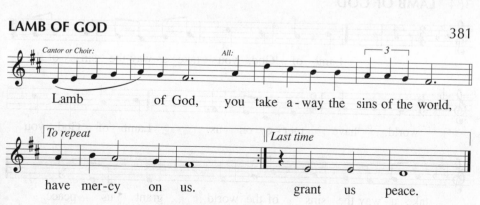

Cantor or Choir: *All:*   ⌐ 3 ⌐

Lamb of God, you take a - way the sins of the world,

|To repeat| |Last time|

have mer - cy on us. grant us peace.

Music: *Holy Cross Mass,* David Clark Isele, © 1979, GIA Publications, Inc.

382 LAMB OF GOD

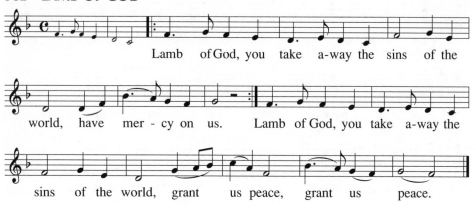

Lamb of God, you take a-way the sins of the world, have mer - cy on us. Lamb of God, you take a-way the sins of the world, grant us peace, grant us peace.

Music: Richard Proulx, © 1975, GIA Publications, Inc.

383 LAMB OF GOD

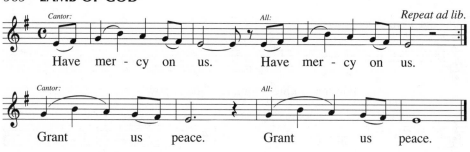

Cantor: Have mer - cy on us. All: Have mer - cy on us. Repeat ad lib.

Cantor: Grant us peace. All: Grant us peace.

Music: *Mass of the Angels and Saints*, Steven R. Janco, © 1996, GIA Publications, Inc.

384 LAMB OF GOD

Lamb of God, you take a - way the sins of the world, have mer - cy on us. Lamb of God, you take a - way the sins of the world, grant us peace.

Music: *A Community Mass*, Richard Proulx, © 1971, 1977, GIA Publications, Inc.

LAMB OF GOD

Cantor: A - gnus De - i, qui tol - lis pec - cá - ta mun - di, *All:* mi - se - ré - re no - bis, mi - se - ré - re no - bis. *Cantor:* Cor - de - ro de Dios, que qui - tas el pe - ca - do del mun-do, *All:* ten pie-dad de no - so-tros, ten pie-dad de no - so-tros. *Repeat ad lib. All:* Lamb of God, you take a-way the sins of the world, grant us peace, grant us peace.

Music: Norah Duncan IV, © 2011, GIA Publications, Inc.

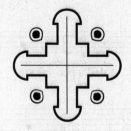

Hymns and Songs

O Come, O Come, Emmanuel 386

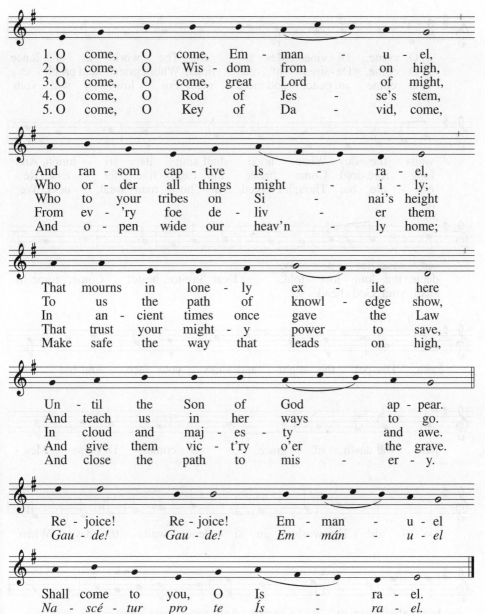

1. O come, O come, Emman - u - el,
2. O come, O Wis - dom from on high,
3. O come, O come, great Lord of might,
4. O come, O Rod of Jes - se's stem,
5. O come, O Key of Da - vid, come,

And ran - som cap - tive Is - ra - el,
Who or - der all things might - i - ly;
Who to your tribes on Si - nai's height
From ev - 'ry foe de - liv - er them
And o - pen wide our heav'n - ly home;

That mourns in lone - ly ex - ile here
To us the path of knowl - edge show,
In an - cient times once gave the Law
That trust your might - y power to save,
Make safe the way that leads on high,

Un - til the Son of God ap - pear.
And teach us in her ways to go.
In cloud and maj - es - ty and awe.
And give them vic - t'ry o'er the grave.
And close the path to mis - er - y.

Re - joice! Re - joice! Em - man - u - el
Gau - de! Gau - de! Em - mán - u - el

Shall come to you, O Is - ra - el.
Na - scé - tur pro te Ís - ra - el.

6. O come, O Dayspring from on high,
   And cheer us by your drawing nigh;
   Disperse the gloomy clouds of night,
   And death's dark shadow put to flight.

7. O come, Desire of nations, bind
   In one the hearts of humankind;
   O bid our sad divisions cease,
   And be for us our King of Peace.

Text: *Veni, veni Emmanuel*; Latin 9th C.; tr. by John M. Neale, 1818–1866, alt.
Tune: VENI EMMANUEL, LM with refrain; Mode I, 15th C. French; adapt. by Thomas Helmore, 1811–1890; acc. by Richard Proulx, 1937–2010,
© 1975, GIA Publications, Inc.

387 O Come, Divine Messiah!

1. O come, Di-vine Mes-si - ah! The world in si - lence
2. O come, De-sired of na - tions, Whom priest and proph - et
3. O come in peace and meek - ness, For low - ly will your

waits the day When hope shall sing its tri - umph, And
long fore-told. Come break the cap - tive fet - ters, Re -
cra - dle be: Though clothed in hu - man weak - ness We

sad - ness flee a - way.
deem the long - lost fold. Dear Sav-ior, haste! Come, come to
shall your God - head see.

earth. Dis-pel the night and show your face, And bid us

hail the dawn of grace. O come, Di - vine Mes -

si - ah! The world in si - lence waits the day When

hope shall sing its tri - umph, And sad - ness flee a - way.

Text: *Venez, divin Messie;* Abbé Simon-Joseph Pellegrin, 1663–1745; tr. by Mary of St. Philip, SND, 1825–1904, alt.
Tune: VENEZ, DIVIN MESSIE, 7 8 7 6 with refrain; French carol, 16th C.; harm. by Healey Willan, 1880–1968, © 1958, The Basilian Fathers, assigned to Ralph Jusko Publications, Inc.

Savior of the Nations, Come   388

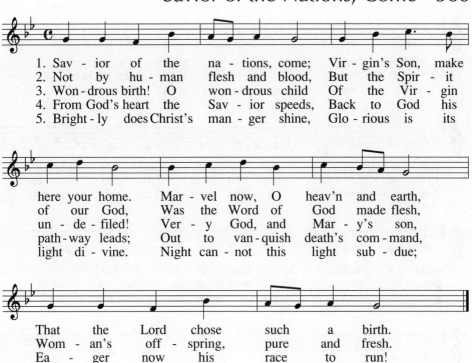

1. Sav - ior of the na - tions, come; Vir - gin's Son, make
2. Not by hu - man flesh and blood, But the Spir - it
3. Won - drous birth! O won - drous child Of the Vir - gin
4. From God's heart the Sav - ior speeds, Back to God his
5. Bright - ly does Christ's man - ger shine, Glo - rious is its

here your home. Mar - vel now, O heav'n and earth,
of our God, Was the Word of God made flesh,
un - de - filed! Ver - y God, and Mar - y's son,
path - way leads; Out to van - quish death's com - mand,
light di - vine. Night can - not this light sub - due;

That the Lord chose such a birth.
Wom - an's off - spring, pure and fresh.
Ea - ger now his race to run!
Back to reign at God's right hand.
Let our faith shine ev - er new.

Text: *Veni Redemptor gentium*; ascr. to St. Ambrose of Milan, 340–397; German tr. by Martin Luther, 1483–1546; English tr. sts. 1–3, 5 by
William M. Reynolds, 1812–1876, alt.; st. 4 by Martin L. Seltz, 1909–1967, alt., © 2006, Augsburg Fortress
Tune: NUN KOMM DER HEIDEN HEILAND, 77 77; *Geistliche Gesangbüchlein*, Wittenberg, 1524

Prepare the Way of the Lord   389

Canon

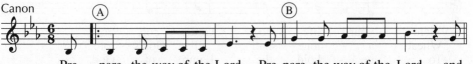

Pre - pare the way of the Lord. Pre-pare the way of the Lord, and

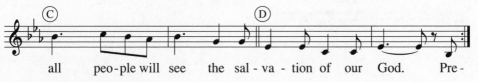

all peo-ple will see the sal - va - tion of our God. Pre-

Text: Luke 3:4, 6; Taizé Community, 1984
Tune: Jacques Berthier, 1923–1994
© 1984, Les Presses de Taizé, GIA Publications, Inc., agent

390 Wild and Lone the Prophet's Voice

1. Wild and lone the proph - et's voice
Ech - oes through the des - ert still, Call - ing us to
make a choice, Bid - ding us to do God's will:
"Turn from sin and be bap - tized; Cleanse your heart and
mind and soul. Quit - ting all the sins you prized,
Yield your life to God's con - trol."

2. "Bear the fruit re - pent - ance sows:
Lives of jus - tice, truth, and love. Trust no oth - er
claim than those; Set your heart on things a - bove.
Soon the Lord will come in pow'r, Burn - ing clean the
thresh - ing floor: Then will flames the chaff de - vour;
Wheat a - lone shall fill God's store."

3. With such preach - ing stark and bold
John pro - claimed sal - va - tion near, And his time - less
warn - ings hold Words of hope to all who hear.
So we dare to jour - ney on, Led by faith through
ways un - trod, Till we come at last like John
To be - hold the Lamb of God.

Text: Carl P. Daw, Jr. b.1944, © 1989, Hope Publishing Company
Tune: ABERYSTWYTH, 7 7 7 7 D; Joseph Parry, 1841–1903

City of God, Jerusalem 391

1. Cit-y of God, Je-ru-sa-lem, Where he has set his
2. Sing and be glad, Je-ru-sa-lem, For God does not for-
3. Sor-row no more, Je-ru-sa-lem, Dis-card your rags of
4. Look all a-round, Je-ru-sa-lem, Sur-vey from west to

love; Church of Christ that is one on earth With Je-
get; He who said he would come to save Nev-er
shame! Take your crown as a gift from God Who has
east; Sons and daugh-ters of God the king Are in-

ru-sa-lem a-bove: Here as we walk this
failed his peo-ple yet. Though we are tempt-ed
called you by his name. Put off your sin, and
vit-ed to his feast. Out of their ex-ile

chang-ing world Our joys are mixed with tears, But the
by de-spair And daunt-ed by de-feat, Our in-
wear the robe Of glo-ry in its place; You will
far a-way His scat-tered fam-'ly come, And the

day will be soon when the Sav-ior re-turns
vin-ci-ble Lord will be seen in his strength,
shine in his light, you will share in his joy,
streets will re-sound with the song of the saints

And his voice will ban-ish our fears.
And his tri-umph will be com-plete.
You will praise his won-der-ful grace.
When the Sav-ior wel-comes us home.

Text: Baruch 4–5; Christopher M. Idle, b.1938, © 1982, The Jubilate Group (admin. by Hope Publishing Company)
Tune: PURPOSE, 8 6 8 7 8 6 12 8; Martin Shaw, 1875–1958, © Oxford University Press

392 On Jordan's Bank

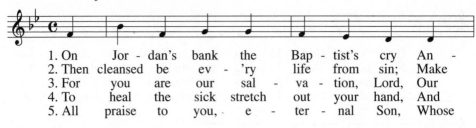

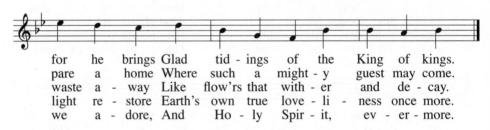

1. On Jordan's bank the Baptist's cry Announces that the Lord is nigh; Awake and hearken, for he brings Glad tidings of the King of kings.

2. Then cleansed be ev'ry life from sin; Make straight the way for God within, And let each heart prepare a home Where such a mighty guest may come.

3. For you are our salvation, Lord, Our refuge and our great reward; Without your grace we waste away Like flow'rs that with-er and decay.

4. To heal the sick stretch out your hand, And bid the fall-en sin-ner stand; Shine forth and let your light restore Earth's own true love-li-ness once more.

5. All praise to you, e-ter-nal Son, Whose advent has our free-dom won, Whom with the Fa-ther we a-dore, And Ho-ly Spir-it, ev-er-more.

Text: *Jordanis oras praevia*; Charles Coffin, 1676–1749; tr. by John Chandler, 1806–1876, alt.
Tune: WINCHESTER NEW, LM; adapt. from *Musikalisches Handbuch*, Hamburg, 1690

393 Awaken, Sleepers

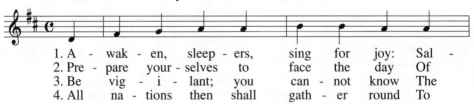

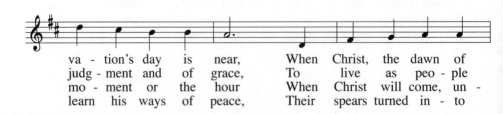

1. A-wak-en, sleep-ers, sing for joy: Sal-vation's day is near, When Christ, the dawn of

2. Pre-pare your-selves to face the day Of judg-ment and of grace, To live as peo-ple

3. Be vig-i-lant; you can-not know The mo-ment or the hour When Christ will come, un-

4. All na-tions then shall gath-er round To learn his ways of peace, Their spears turned in-to

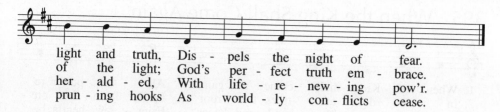

light and truth, Dis - pels the night of fear.
of the light; God's per - fect truth em - brace.
her - ald - ed, With life - re - new - ing pow'r.
prun - ing hooks As world - ly con - flicts cease.

Text: Michael Forster, b.1946, alt., © 1993, Kevin Mayhew, Ltd
Tune: TALLIS' ORDINAL, CM; Thomas Tallis, c. 1505–1585

Come, O Long-Expected Jesus 394

1. Come, O long - ex - pect - ed Je - sus, Born to set your
2. Born your peo - ple to de - liv - er, Born a child, and

peo - ple free; From our fears and sins re - lease us:
yet a king; Born to reign in us for - ev - er,

Christ, in you our rest shall be. Is - rael's strength and
Now your grac - ious king - dom bring. By your own e -

con - so - la - tion, Hope to all the earth im - part;
ter - nal Spir - it Rule in all our hearts a - lone;

Dear de - sire of ev - 'ry na - tion,
By your all - suf - fi - cient mer - it

En - ter ev - 'ry long - ing heart.
Raise us to your glo - rious throne.

Text: Haggai 2:7; Charles Wesley, 1707–1788, alt.
Tune: JEFFERSON, 8 7 8 7 D; William Walker's *Southern Harmony*, 1855; acc. by Theophane Hytrek, OSF, 1915–1992, © 1981, ICEL
Alternate tune: STUTTGART, 4 stanzas

395 When the King Shall Come Again

1. When the King shall come a-gain, All his pow'r re-
2. In the des-ert trees take root Fresh from his cre-
3. Strength-en fee-ble hands and knees, Faint-ing hearts, be
4. There God's high-way shall be seen Where no roar-ing

veal-ing, Splen-dor shall an-nounce his reign,
a-tion; Plants and flow'rs and sweet-est fruit
cheer-ful! God, who comes for such as these,
li-on, Noth-ing e-vil or un-clean,

Life and joy and heal-ing: Earth no
Join the cel-e-bra-tion; Riv-ers
Seeks and saves the fear-ful. Deaf ears
Walks the road to Zi-on. Ran-somed

long-er in de-cay, Hope no more frus-trat-ed;
spring up from the earth, Bar-ren lands a-dorn-ing;
hear the si-lent tongues Sing a-way their weep-ing;
peo-ple home-ward bound, All your prais-es voic-ing,

This is God's re-demp-tion day
Val-leys, this is your new birth,
Blind eyes see the life-less ones
See your Lord with glo-ry crowned,

Long-ing-ly a-wait-ed.
Moun-tains, greet the morn-ing!
Walk-ing, run-ning, leap-ing.
Share in his re-joic-ing!

Text: Isaiah 35; Christopher M. Idle, b.1938, alt., © 1982, The Jubilate Group (admin. by Hope Publishing Company)
Tune: GAUDEAMUS PARITER, 7 6 7 6 D; Johann Horn, c. 1495–1547

Though Famed in Israel's Royal History   396

1. Though famed in Is - rael's roy - al his - t'ry,
2. Who would ex - pect a hum - ble man - ger
3. All we re - call of gain or glo - ry
4. Kin - dle, O God, your gifts with - in us,

Beth - le - hem would that past ex - cel
To cra - dle such a ho - ly birth?
Can scarce pre - dict what still may be;
Stir up our faith, re - new our nerve.

When God re - vealed a great - er mys-t'ry,
How could flesh clothe the stars' ar - rang - er
God is the Au - thor of our sto - ry,
When tempt - ing pow - ers seek to win us,

The Word made flesh, Em - man - u - el:
Or sheathe the hands that formed the earth?
Whose will is sov - 'reign, bound - less, free:
Help us re - mem - ber whom we serve:

Through Mar - y born from Da - vid's line,
God's ways con - found the world - ly - wise,
Yet liv - ing in this time and place
Trans - form our lives and build in them

A Sav - ior hu - man and di - vine.
Dis - arm the sure with bright sur - prise.
We can be ves - sels of God's grace.
A new and will - ing Beth - le - hem.

Text: Carl P. Daw, Jr., b.1944, © 1998, Hope Publishing Company
Tune: WER NUR DEN LIEBEN GOTT, 9 8 9 8 88; Georg Neumark, 1621–1681

397 Like a Bird

1. Like a bird that spreads her wings to gath-er in her
2. From the ends of earth you call your sons and daugh-ters
3. For the na-tions you pre-pare and spread a splen-did

young, So you o-pen wide your arms to
home, Say-ing, "Gath-er now from far and
feast, Gath-er ev-'ry tribe and race, the

gath - er in your own. For our free re-sponse you
near, my peo-ple, come." For our sim-ple trust you
great - est to the least. For one fam-'ly, how you

wait, Ear - ly morn-ing, noon, and late.
yearn Till, at last in love, we turn.
long; 'Round your ta - ble, vast the throng.

Come and wake us, come and wake us, come and wake us to your

wel-come. Ma-ra-na - tha, come.

Text: Delores Dufner, OSB, b.1939
Tune: WAKE US, 13 13 77 with refrain; Michael Joncas, b.1951
© 2011, GIA Publications, Inc.

People, Look East 398

1. Peo - ple, look East. The time is near
2. Fur - rows, be glad. Though earth is bare,
3. Birds, though you long have ceased to build,
4. Stars, keep the watch. When night is dim,
5. An - gels an - nounce with shouts of mirth

Of the crown - ing of the year.
One more seed is plant - ed there.
Guard the nest that must be filled.
One more light the bowl shall brim,
Him who brings new life to earth.

Make your house fair as you are a - ble,
Give up your strength the seed to nour - ish,
E - ven the hour when wings are fro - zen
Shin - ing be - yond the frost - y weath - er,
Set ev - 'ry peak and val - ley hum - ming

Trim the hearth and set the ta - ble.
That in course the flow'r may flour - ish.
God for fledg - ing - time has cho - sen.
Bright as sun and moon to - geth - er.
With the word, the Lord is com - ing.

Peo - ple, look East and sing to - day—

Love, the Guest, is on the way.
Love, the Rose, is on the way.
Love, the Bird, is on the way.
Love, the Star, is on the way.
Love, the Lord, is on the way.

Text: Eleanor Farjeon, 1881–1965, © David Higham Assoc. Ltd.
Tune: BESANÇON, 87 98 87; French carol; harm. by Martin Shaw, 1875–1958, © Oxford University Press

399 Are You the Coming One

1. "Are you the com - ing one For whom the
2. "Are you the com - ing one For whom all
3. "Are you the com - ing one For whom the
4. "Are you the com - ing one For whom the_op -
5. "Are you the com - ing one For whom cre -

a - ges long?" "See, pris - 'ners break their
peo - ple yearn?" "The wan - d'rers lost in
suf - f'ring sigh?" "The lame, the sick, the
pressed still wait?" "The ty - rant's pride at
a - tion cries?" "The earth, de - filed, shall

cru - el chains And fill the night with song!"
a - lien ways Shall home, re - deemed, re - turn!"
deaf and blind— I an - swer when they cry!"
last shall fall; All crook - ed ways be straight!"
be re - stored And life from death a - rise!"

Text: Herman G. Stuempfle, Jr., 1923–2007, © 1993, GIA Publications, Inc.
Tune: ST. THOMAS (Williams), SM; Aaron Williams, 1731–1776; harm. by Lowell Mason, 1792–1872

400 A Morning Star Draws Near

1. A morn - ing star draws near the earth To
2. All you, bap - tized in cleans - ing streams, Re -
3. We shall not sow our fields in vain, Nor
4. On all the ho - ly mount of God, No
5. "Pre - pare a path - way for our God!" Pro -

hail the ris - ing dawn. "Pre - pare a path - way
pent and turn from sin. A Liv - ing Foun - tain -
tend, that oth - ers reap. Our vines shall bloom, Je -
e - vil shall de - stroy. Our mouths shall fill with
claims the ser - vant John. Our long - a - wait - ed

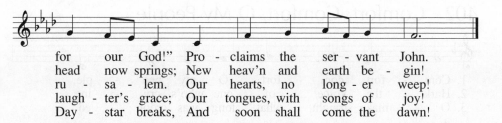

for	our	God!"	Pro -	claims	the	ser -	vant	John.
head	now	springs;	New	heav'n	and	earth	be -	gin!
ru -	sa -	lem.	Our	hearts,	no	long -	er	weep!
laugh -	ter's	grace;	Our	tongues,	with	songs	of	joy!
Day -	star	breaks,	And	soon	shall	come	the	dawn!

Text: Mary Louise Bringle, b.1953, © 2006, GIA Publications, Inc.
Tune: MORNING SONG, CM; Wyeth's *Repository of Sacred Music*, 1813; harm. by Richard Proulx, 1937–2010, © 1975, GIA Publications, Inc.

Come, Lord, and Tarry Not!   401

1. Come, Lord, and tar - ry not! Bring the long -
2. Come, for your saints still wait; Dai - ly as -
3. Come, for cre - a - tion groans With long - ing
4. Come, and make all things new; Build up this
5. Come, and be - gin your reign Of ev - er -

looked - for day! O why these years of wait - ing
cends their sigh; The Spir - it and the Bride say,
for your stay, Worn out with these long years of
ru - ined earth; Re - store our fad - ed par - a -
last - ing peace; Come, take the king - dom to your -

here, These a - ges of de - lay?
"Come!" Do you not hear the cry?
ill, These a - ges of de - cay.
dise, Cre - a - tion's sec - ond birth.
self, Great King of Right - eous - ness!

Text: Revelation 22:17, attr. to Horatius Bonar, alt., 1808–1889
Tune: ST. BRIDE, SM; Samuel Howard, 1710–1782

402 Comfort, Comfort, O My People

1. Com - fort, com - fort, O my peo - ple,
2. Hark, the voice of one who's cry - ing
3. O make straight what long was crook - ed,

Speak of peace, now says our God.
In the des - ert far and near,
Make the rough - er plac - es plain.

Com - fort those who sit in dark - ness,
Bid - ding all to full re - pent - ance
Let your hearts be true and hum - ble,

Mourn - ing un - der sor - rows' load.
Since the king - dom now is here.
As be - fits his ho - ly reign.

Speak un - to Je - ru - sa - lem
Oh, that warn - ing cry o - bey!
For the glo - ry of the Lord

Of the peace that waits for them.
Now pre - pare for God a way!
Now o'er earth is shed a - broad.

Tell of all the sins I cov - er,
Let the val - leys rise to meet him
And all flesh shall see the to - ken

And that war - fare now is o - ver.
And the hills bow down to greet him.
That his word is nev - er bro - ken.

Text: Isaiah 40:1–8; *Tröstet, tröstet, meine Lieben;* Johann Olearius, 1611–1684; tr. by Catherine Winkworth, 1827–1878, alt.
Tune: GENEVA 42, 8 7 8 7 77 88; *Genevan Psalter,* 1551; harm. adapt. from Claude Goudimel, 1505–1572

The King Shall Come When Morning Dawns 403

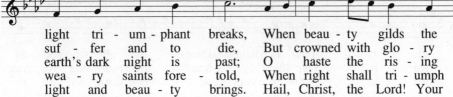

1. The King shall come when morn - ing dawns And
2. Not, as of old, a lit - tle child, To
3. The King shall come when morn - ing dawns And
4. And let the end - less bliss be - gin, By
5. The King shall come when morn - ing dawns And

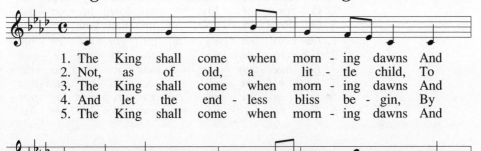

light tri - um - phant breaks, When beau - ty gilds the
suf - fer and to die, But crowned with glo - ry
earth's dark night is past; O haste the ris - ing
wea - ry saints fore - told, When right shall tri - umph
light and beau - ty brings. Hail, Christ, the Lord! Your

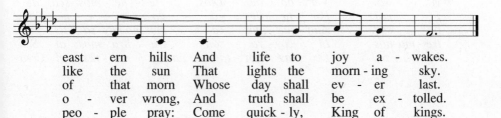

east - ern hills And life to joy a - wakes.
like the sun That lights the morn - ing sky.
of that morn Whose day shall ev - er last.
o - ver wrong, And truth shall be ex - tolled.
peo - ple pray: Come quick - ly, King of kings.

Text: John Brownlie, 1857–1925, alt.
Tune: MORNING SONG, CM; Wyeth's *Repository of Sacred Music*, 1813; arr. by Robert J. Batastini, b.1942, © 1994, GIA Publications, Inc.

404 My Soul in Stillness Waits / En el Silencio Te Aguardo

you;	Come,	light	the	hearts	of	all	in	dark	and
Word;	Come,	make	us	whole,	be	com - fort		to	our
you,	Our	hope	re - born		in	dy - ing		and	in
zón.	*Ven,*	*con*	*tu*	*luz,*	*a*	*los que_es - tán*			*en*
ti.	*Ven*	*y*	*res - táu - ra - nos,*		*sé*	*nues - tro*		*con -*	
ti.	*Y*	*por*	*tu*	*pas -*	*cua*	*da - nos la_es - pe -*			
ción.	*Dios*	*de*	*la*	*paz,*	*en - sé - ña - nos*			*tus*	
ñor.	*So - mos*		*el*	*pue -*	*blo que Dios*		*es - co -*		
dor.	*Es - tás*		*a -*	*quí,*	*Se - ñor de*		*las*	*es -*	

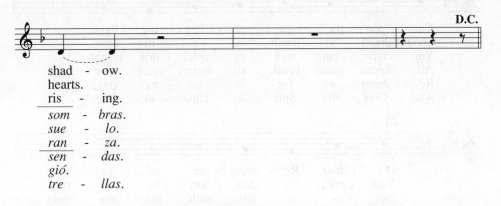

D.C.

shad -	ow.
hearts.	
ris -	ing.
som -	*bras.*
sue -	*lo.*
ran -	*za.*
sen -	*das.*
gió.	
tre -	*llas.*

4. O Key of Knowledge, guide us in our pilgrimage;
   we ever seek, yet unfulfilled remain;
   open to us the pathway of your peace.

5. Come, let us bow before the God who made us;
   let ev'ry heart be opened to the Lord,
   for we are all the people of his hand.

6. Here we shall meet the Maker of the heavens,
   Creator of the mountains and the seas,
   Lord of the stars, and present to us now.

Text: Psalm 95 and "O" Antiphons; Marty Haugen, b.1950; tr. by Ronald F. Krisman, b.1946
Tune: Marty Haugen, b.1950
© 1982, 2005, GIA Publications, Inc.

405 Creator of the Stars of Night

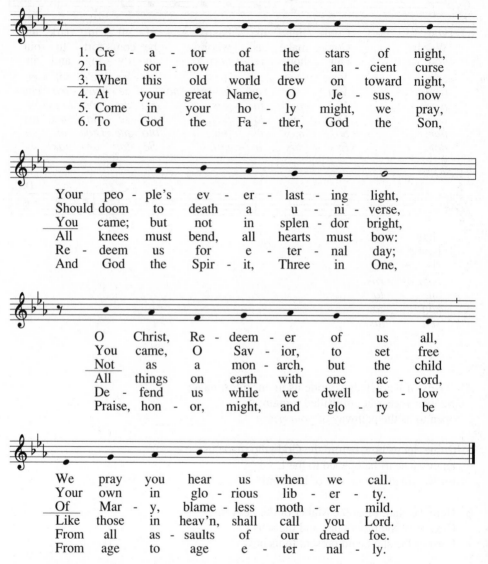

1. Cre - a - tor of the stars of night,
2. In sor - row that the an - cient curse
3. When this old world drew on toward night,
4. At your great Name, O Je - sus, now
5. Come in your ho - ly might, we pray,
6. To God the Fa - ther, God the Son,

Your peo - ple's ev - er - last - ing light,
Should doom to death a u - ni - verse,
You came; but not in splen - dor bright,
All knees must bend, all hearts must bow:
Re - deem us for e - ter - nal day;
And God the Spir - it, Three in One,

O Christ, Re - deem - er of us all,
You came, O Sav - ior, to set free
Not as a mon - arch, but the child
All things on earth with one ac - cord,
De - fend us while we dwell be - low
Praise, hon - or, might, and glo - ry be

We pray you hear us when we call.
Your own in glo - rious lib - er - ty.
Of Mar - y, blame - less moth - er mild.
Like those in heav'n, shall call you Lord.
From all as - saults of our dread foe.
From age to age e - ter - nal - ly.

Text: *Creator alme siderum*, Latin 9th. C., revised 1632; tr. *The Hymnal 1982*, alt., © 1985, The Church Pension Fund
Tune: CONDITOR ALME SIDERUM, LM; Mode IV, Sarum, 9th C.; acc. by Gerard Farrell, OSB, 1919–2009, © 1986, GIA Publications, Inc.

Awake! Awake, and Greet the New Morn 406

1. A - wake! A - wake, and greet the new morn, For
2. To us, to all in sor - row and fear, Em -
3. In dark - est night his com - ing shall be, When
4. Re - joice, re - joice, take heart in the night, Though

an - gels her - ald its dawn - ing. Sing out your joy, for
man - u - el comes a - sing - ing; His hum - ble song is
all the world is de - spair - ing, As morn - ing light so
dark the win - ter and cheer - less, The ris - ing sun shall

soon he is born, Be - hold the Child of our long - ing!
qui - et and near, Yet fills the earth with its ring - ing.
qui - et and free, So warm and gen - tle and car - ing.
crown you with light; Be strong and lov - ing and fear - less.

Come as a ba - by weak and poor, To bring all hearts to -
Mu - sic to heal the bro - ken soul And hymns of lov - ing -
Then shall the mute break forth in song, The lame shall leap in
Love be our song and love our prayer And love our end - less

geth - er, He o - pens wide the heav'n - ly door And
kind - ness, The thun - der of his an - thems roll To
won - der, The weak be raised a - bove the strong, And
sto - ry. May God fill ev - 'ry day we share And

lives now in - side us for ev - er.
shat - ter all ha - tred and blind - ness.
weap - ons be bro - ken a - sun - der.
bring us at last in - to glo - ry.

Text: Marty Haugen, b.1950
Tune: REJOICE, REJOICE, 9 8 9 8 8 7 8 9; Marty Haugen, b.1950
© 1983, GIA Publications, Inc.

407 Unexpected and Mysterious

1. Un - ex - pect - ed and mys - te - rious Is the
2. In a mo - men - tar - y meet - ing Of e -
3. We are called to pon - der mys - t'ry And a -

gen - tle word of grace. Ev - er - lov - ing and sus -
ter - ni - ty and time, Mar - y learned that she would
wait the com-ing Christ, To em - bod - y God's com -

tain - ing Is the peace of God's em - brace.
car - ry Both the mor - tal and di - vine.
pas - sion For each frag - ile hu - man life.

If we fal - ter in our cour - age And we
Then she learned of God's com - pas - sion, Of E -
God is with us in our long - ing To bring

doubt what we have known, God is faith - ful to con -
liz - a - beth's great joy, And she ran to greet the
heal - ing to the earth, While we watch with joy and

sole us As a moth - er tends her own.
wom - an Who would rec - og - nize her boy.
won - der For the prom - ised Sav - ior's birth.

Text: Jeannette M. Lindholm, b.1961, © 2002, admin. by Augsburg Fortress
Tune: DOMHNACH TRIONOIDE, 8 7 8 7 D; Gaelic melody; harm. by Richard Proulx, 1937–2010, © 1975, GIA Publications, Inc.

Alternate tune: PLEADING SAVIOR

Now the Heavens Start to Whisper 408

1. Now the heav-ens start to whis-per As the veil is
2. Heav-y clouds that block the moon-light Now be-gin to
3. Christ, e-ter-nal sun of jus-tice, Christ, the rose of

grow-ing thin. Earth from slum-ber wakes to lis-ten
drift a-way. Dia-mond bril-liance through the dark-ness
wis-dom's seed, Come to bless with fire and fra-grance

To the stir-ring, faint with-in: Seed of prom-ise,
Shines the hope of com-ing day. Christ, the morn-ing
Hours of yearn-ing, hurt, and need. In the lone-ly,

deep-ly plant-ed, Child to spring from Jes-se's stem!
star of splen-dor, Gleams with-in a world grown dim.
in the stran-ger, In the out-cast hid from view:

Like the soil be-neath the frost-line,
Heav-en's em-ber fans to full-ness;
Child who comes to grace the man-ger,

Hearts grow soft to wel-come him.
Hearts grow warm to wel-come him.
Teach our hearts to wel-come you.

Text: Mary Louise Bringle, b.1953, © 2006, GIA Publications, Inc.
Tune: SUO GAN, 8 7 8 7 D; Welsh melody; arr. by Nicholas Palmer, b.1963, © 2008, GIA Publications, Inc.

409 Sleepers, Wake!

1. "Sleep-ers, wake!" A voice a-stounds us, The
2. Zi - on hears the watch-men sing - ing; Her
3. Lamb of God, the heav'ns a - dore you; Let

shout of ram - part-guards sur - rounds us: "A -
heart with joy - ful hope is spring - ing, She
saints and an - gels sing be - fore you, As

wake, Je - ru - sa - lem, a - rise!" Mid - night's peace their
wakes and hur - ries through the night. Forth he comes, her
harps and cym - bals swell the sound. Twelve great pearls, the

cry has bro - ken, Their ur - gent sum - mons
Bride-groom glo - rious In strength of grace, in
cit - y's por - tals: Through them we stream to

clear - ly spo - ken: "The time has come, O maid - ens wise!
truth vic - to - rious: Her star is ris'n, her light grows bright.
join th' im-mor - tals As we with joy your throne sur - round.

Rise up, and give us light; The Bride - groom is in
Now come, most wor - thy Lord, God's Son, In - car - nate
No eye has known the sight, No ear heard such de -

sight. Al - le - lu - ia! Your lamps pre - pare And
Word, Al - le - lu - ia! We fol - low all And
light: Al - le - lu - ia! There - fore we sing To

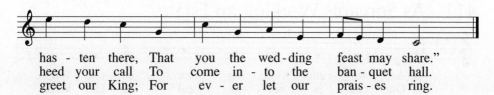

has - ten there, That you the wed - ding feast may share."
heed your call To come in - to the ban - quet hall.
greet our King; For ev - er let our prais - es ring.

Text: Philipp Nicolai, 1556–1608; tr. by Carl P. Daw, Jr., b.1944, © 1982, Hope Publishing Company
Tune: WACHET AUF, 89 8 89 8 66 4 88; Philipp Nicolai, 1556–1608; harm. by J. S. Bach, 1685–1750

Wait for the Lord   410

Ostinato Refrain

Wait for the Lord, whose day is near.
Spanish: Con - tem - pla - ré tu vi - da en mí.
Polish: Pan blis - ko jest, o - cze - kuj Go.
Italian: Cri - sto Ge - sù io spe - ro in Te.
Vietnamese: Hãy biết đợi Chúa Đây ngày gần rồi

Wait for the Lord: be strong, take heart!
Con - tem - pla - ré, Se - ñor, tu a - mor.
Pan blis - ko jest, w Nim ser - ca moc!
Sei tu Si - gnor la pa - ce del cuor.
Chờ mong Thiên Chúa: tâm trí kiên cường.

Text: Isaiah 40, Philippians 4, Matthew 6–7; Taizé Community, 1984
Tune: Jacques Berthier, 1923–1994
© 1984, Les Presses de Taizé, GIA Publications, Inc., agent

411 As Servants Working an Estate

1. As ser - vants work - ing an es - tate Whose own - er is a - way, And whose re - turn they all a - wait Though no one knows the day, So none of us can name the hour, The sea - son or the year When Christ with all of heav - en's pow'r Will sud - den - ly ap - pear.

2. Our task is not to cal - cu - late What an - gels do not know, But faith - ful - ly to watch and wait And Christ's com - pas - sion show. Not load - ing frag - ile hu - man schemes With hopes they can - not bear, We trust the prom - ise that re - deems The pres - ent from de - spair.

3. For Christ the Lord will sure - ly come, The king whom kings will fear, And with God's per - fect jus - tice plumb The jus - tice we do here, Re - veal - ing that the pres - ent age And ev - 'ry age that's past Are not the fi - nal mor - al gauge That judg - es us at last.

4. So guide, Lord Christ, our ev - 'ry choice That when our hearts shall hear Your step, your knock, your call - ing voice We will not hide in fear, But wel - come you from realms a - bove To your es - tate be - low, Where jus - tice, mer - cy, peace, and love A - bun - dant - ly will grow.

Text: Thomas H. Troeger, b.1945, © 1986, Oxford University Press
Tune: LLANGLOFFAN, CMD; Welsh melody

Maranatha, Lord Messiah   412

Verses

1. Gra - cious God of Wis - dom, who hear your peo - ple's
2. Might - y Voice on Si - nai, whom Mos - es heard in
3. Fra - grant Bud of Jes - se, whose bloom - ing kings re -
4. Da - vid's Key of Heav - en, re - lease us from our
5. Blaz - ing Sun of Jus - tice, the flame of east - ern
6. Sov - ereign of all na - tions, our cor - ner-stone of
7. Je - sus, be God with us, Em - man - u - el fore -

cry, Teach us ways of pru - dence, O
awe, Ad - o - nai, now lead us with
vere, Root your words with - in us, God's
sins. Freed from er - ror's pris - on, our
dawn, Scat - ter cling - ing shad - ows, that
trust, De - liv - er, in your mer - cy, your
told. Like a shep - herd feed us, in

Breath of God Most High.
ho - ly arm and law.
Word for all to hear.
life in you be - gins. Ma-ra-
gloom of death be gone.
crea - tures made from dust.
safe - ly gath - ered fold.

Refrain

na - tha, Lord Mes - si - ah, long a - wait - ed from a -

far. Come and make your home a - mong us. Let us

1.–6.   To verses   7.

see your birth - ing star.   star.

Text: Based on the "O" Antiphons; Kathy Powell, b.1942
Tune: BIRTHING STAR, 12 12 with refrain; Kathy Powell, b.1942
© 1999, GIA Publications, Inc.

413 Silent Night / Noche de Paz

1. Si - lent night, ho - ly night! All is calm,
2. Si - lent night, ho - ly night! Shep - herds quake
3. Si - lent night, ho - ly night! Son of God,

1. ¡No-che de paz, no - che de a - mor! To - do duer - me_en
2. ¡No-che de paz, no - che de a - mor! O - ye hu-mil - de_el
3. ¡No-che de paz, no - che de a - mor! Mi - ra qué gran

all is bright Round yon vir - gin
at the sight; Glo - ries stream from
love's pure light Ra - diant beams from

de - rre - dor, En - tre los as - tros que_es -
fiel pas - tor, Co - ros ce - les - tes que_a -
res - plan - dor Lu - ce_en el ros - tro del

moth - er and child. Ho - ly In - fant so
heav - en a - far; Heav'n - ly hosts sing
thy ho - ly face, With the dawn of re -

par - cen su luz, Be - lla_a-nun - cian - do_al ni -
nun - cian sa - lud, Gra - cias y glo - rias en
ni - ño Je - sús, En el pe - se - bre, del

ten - der and mild, Sleep in heav - en - ly
al - le - lu - ia! Christ, the Sav - ior, is
deem - ing grace, Je - sus, Lord, at thy

ñi - to Je - sús, Bri - lla la_es - tre - lla de
gran ple - ni - tud, Por nues - tro buen Re - den -
mun - do la luz, As - tro de_e - ter - no ful -

peace, Sleep in heav - en - ly peace.
born! Christ, the Sav - ior, is born!
birth, Je - sus, Lord, at thy birth.

paz, Bri - lla la_es - tre - lla de paz.
tor, Por nues - tro buen Re - den - tor.
gor, As - tro de_e - ter - no ful - gor.

Text: *Stille Nacht, heilige Nacht;* Joseph Mohr, 1792–1848; English tr. by John F. Young, 1820–1885; Spanish tr. by Federico Fliedner, 1845–1901
Tune: STILLE NACHT, 66 89 66; Franz X. Gruber, 1787–1863

Hark! The Herald Angels Sing 414

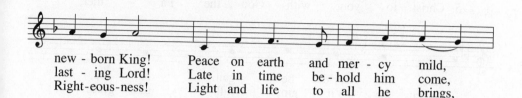

1. Hark! The her - ald an - gels sing, "Glo - ry to the
2. Christ, by high - est heav'n a - dored; Christ, the ev - er -
3. Hail the heav'n - born Prince of Peace! Hail the Sun of

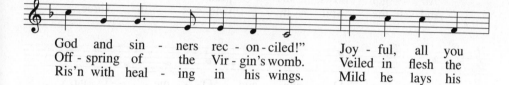

new - born King! Peace on earth and mer - cy mild,
last - ing Lord! Late in time be - hold him come,
Right-eous-ness! Light and life to all he brings,

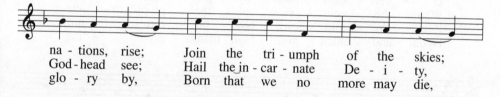

God and sin - ners rec - on-ciled!" Joy - ful, all you
Off - spring of the Vir - gin's womb. Veiled in flesh the
Ris'n with heal - ing in his wings. Mild he lays his

na - tions, rise; Join the tri - umph of the skies;
God - head see; Hail the in - car - nate De - i - ty,
glo - ry by, Born that we no more may die,

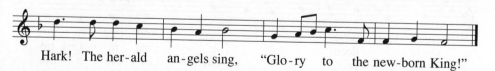

With the an-gel - ic host pro-claim, "Christ is born in Beth - le-hem!"
Pleased as man with us to dwell, Je - sus, our Em-man - u - el.
Born to raise each child of earth, Born to give us sec - ond birth.

Hark! The her-ald an-gels sing, "Glo-ry to the new-born King!"

Text: Charles Wesley, 1707–1788, alt.
Tune: MENDELSSOHN, 77 77 D with refrain; Felix Mendelssohn, 1809–1847

415 Of the Father's Love Begotten

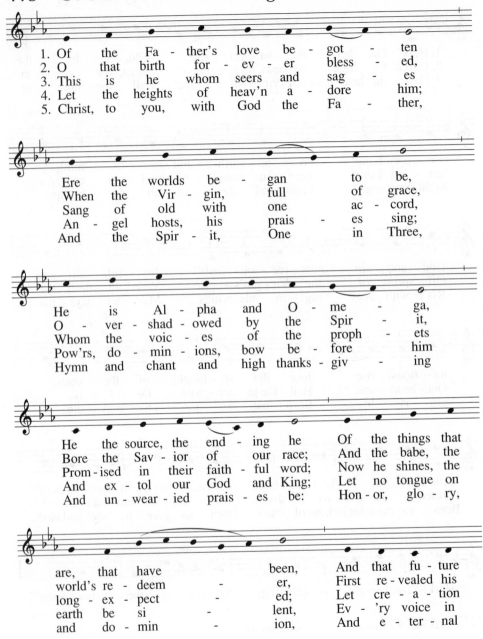

1. Of the Fa - ther's love be - got - ten
2. O that birth for - ev - er bless - ed,
3. This is he whom seers and sag - es
4. Let the heights of heav'n a - dore him;
5. Christ, to you, with God the Fa - ther,

Ere the worlds be - gan to be,
When the Vir - gin, full of grace,
Sang of old with one ac - cord,
An - gel hosts, his prais - es sing;
And the Spir - it, One in Three,

He is Al - pha and O - me - ga,
O - ver - shad - owed by the Spir - it,
Whom the voic - es of the proph - ets
Pow'rs, do - min - ions, bow be - fore him
Hymn and chant and high thanks - giv - ing

He the source, the end - ing he Of the things that
Bore the Sav - ior of our race; And the babe, the
Prom - ised in their faith - ful word; Now he shines, the
And ex - tol our God and King; Let no tongue on
And un - wear - ied prais - es be: Hon - or, glo - ry,

are, that have been, And that fu - ture
world's re - deem - er, First re - vealed his
long - ex - pect - ed; Let cre - a - tion
earth be si - lent, Ev - 'ry voice in
and do - min - ion, And e - ter - nal

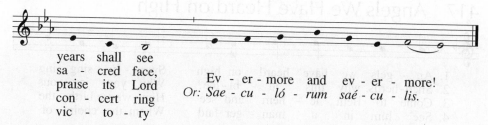

years shall see
sa - cred face,
praise its Lord
con - cert ring
vic - to - ry

Ev - er - more and ev - er - more!
Or: Sae - cu - ló - rum saé - cu - lis.

Text: *Corde natus ex Parentis;* Aurelius Prudentius, 348–413; tr. by John M. Neale, 1818–1866 and Henry W. Baker, 1821–1877, alt.
Tune: DIVINUM MYSTERIUM, 8 7 8 7 8 7 7; 12th C.; Mode V; acc. by Richard Proulx, 1937–2010, © 1985, GIA Publications, Inc.

Infant Holy, Infant Lowly 416

1. In - fant ho - ly, In - fant low - ly, For his bed a
2. Flocks were sleep - ing; Shep-herds, keep - ing Vig - il till the

cat - tle stall; Ox - en low - ing, Lit - tle know - ing
morn-ing new, Saw the glo - ry, Heard the sto - ry,

Christ the babe is Lord of all. Swift are wing - ing
Tid - ings of a gos - pel true. Thus re - joic - ing,

An - gels sing - ing, No - els ring - ing, Tid - ings bring - ing:
Free from sor - row, Prais-es voic - ing, Greet the mor - row:

Repeat ad lib.

Christ the babe is Lord of all!
Christ the babe was born for you!

Text: Polish carol; para. by Edith M. G. Reed, 1885–1933
Tune: W ŻŁOBIE LEŻY, 44 7 44 7 4444 7; Polish carol; harm. by A. E. Rusbridge, 1917–1969, © Bristol Churches Housing Assoc. Ltd.

417 Angels We Have Heard on High

1. An - gels we have heard on high Sweet - ly sing - ing
2. Shep - herds, why this ju - bi - lee? Why your joy - ous
3. Come to Beth - le - hem and see Him whose birth the
4. See him in a man - ger laid Whom the choirs of

o'er the plains, And the moun - tains in re - ply
strains pro - long? Say what may the tid - ings be
an - gels sing; Come, a - dore on bend - ed knee
an - gels praise; Mar - y, Jo - seph, lend your aid,

Ech - o back their joy - ous strains.
Which in - spire your heav'n - ly song.
Christ the Lord, the new - born King.
While our hearts in love we raise.

Gló - - - ri - a
in ex - cél - sis De - o. Gló - -
- - ri - a in ex - cél - sis De - o.

Text: *Les anges dans nos campagnes;* French carol, c. 18th C.; tr. from *Crown of Jesus Music,* London, 1862
Tune: GLORIA, 7 7 7 7 with refrain; French carol

You Came among Us at Christmas Time 418

Verses

1. Long a - go and far a - way Heav - en rang with
2. Born our hu - man, ho - ly kin, Child di - vine to
3. Christ is born to set us free; He is born our
4. Still he dwells a - mong us here In the poor and
5. Though as God he reigns on high, Ra - diant in his
6. Chris - tians all, re - joice and sing; Fes - tive bells, the

joy to - day; Je - sus in a man - ger lay In
us is giv'n; Prince of Peace and King of heav'n, The
Lord to be, God for all e - ter - ni - ty, The
home - less near Till at last he shall ap - pear, The
maj - es - ty, Christ, who loves hu - man - i - ty, Will
good news ring! 'Tis the birth - day of our King; Cre -

Beth - le - hem up - on a Christ - mas morn - ing.
Word of God is born for us of Mar - y.
Ho - ly One, a - dored by all for - ev - er.
Prince of Peace up - on the clouds of heav - en.
come to take us home with him in glo - ry.
ate for him with - in your hearts a dwell - ing.

Refrain

You came a - mong us at Christ - mas time, A Child both hu - man

and di - vine. Now you come to give your-self in Bread and Wine.

Je - sus, Je - sus, Still you come to love and save and free us.

Text: Delores Dufner, OSB, b.1939, © 2011, GIA Publications, Inc.
Tune: RESONET IN LAUDIBUS, 777 11 with refrain; German, 14th C.; harm. by Ralph Vaughan Williams, 1872–1958

419 It Came upon the Midnight Clear

1. It came up-on the mid-night clear, That
glo-rious song of old, From an-gels bend-ing
near the earth To touch their harps of gold: "Peace
on the earth, good will to all, From
heav'n's all-gra-cious King." The world in sol-emn
still-ness lay, To hear the an-gels sing.

2. Still through the clo-ven skies they come With
peace-ful wings un-furled, And still their heav'n-ly
mu-sic floats O'er all the wea-ry world. A-
bove its sad and low-ly plains They
bend on hov-'ring wing, And ev-er o'er its
Ba-bel sounds The bless-ed an-gels sing.

3. Yet with the woes of sin and strife The
world has suf-fered long; Be-neath the heav'n-ly
hymn have rolled Two thou-sand years of wrong; And
war-ring hu-man-kind hears not The
tid-ings which they bring; O hush the noise and
cease your strife And hear the an-gels sing.

4. For lo! The days are has-t'ning on, By
proph-ets seen of old, When with the ev-er-
cir-cling years Shall come the time fore-told, When
peace shall o-ver all the earth Its
an-cient splen-dors fling, And all the world give
back the song Which now the an-gels sing.

Text: Edmund H. Sears, 1810–1876, alt.
Tune: CAROL, CMD; Richard S. Willis, 1819–1900

God Rest You Merry, Gentlemen 420

1. God rest you mer - ry, gen - tle - men, Let noth - ing you dis-
2. In Beth - le - hem in Ju - dah This bless - ed babe was
3. From God our heav'n - ly Fa - ther A bless - ed an - gel
4. The shep - herds at those tid - ings Re - joic - ed much in
5. Now to the Lord sing prais - es, All you with - in this

may; Re - mem - ber Christ our Sav - ior Was
born, And laid with - in a man - ger Up -
came, And un - to cer - tain shep - herds Brought
mind, And left their flocks a - feed - ing In
place, And with true love and char - i - ty Each

born on Christ - mas day To save us all from
on this bless - ed morn, For which his moth - er
tid - ings of the same, How that in Beth - le -
tem - pest, storm, and wind, And went to Beth - le -
oth - er now em - brace; This ho - ly tide of

Sa - tan's pow'r When we were gone a - stray.
Mar - y Did noth - ing take in scorn.
hem was born The Son of God by name.
hem straight - way, This bless - ed babe to find.
Christ - mas All oth - ers shall re - place.

O tid - ings of com - fort and joy, com-fort and

joy; O tid - ings of com - fort and joy!

Text: English carol, 18th C.
Tune: GOD REST YOU MERRY, 8 6 8 6 8 6 with refrain; English carol, 18th C.; harm. by John Stainer, 1840–1901

421 Sing Alleluia

Verses

1. Dark is the night and deep are the shad-ows;
2. Who would be-lieve that here in a man-ger
3. Great is the joy of Mar - y, his moth-er.
4. Hope for the poor, re - lease for the cap - tive,

Qui - et the ba - by bathed in lan-tern light.
God comes a - mong us as a ti - ny child?
Great is the joy of Jo - seph by her side.
Love for the out - cast, light for wea - ry eyes;

Hushed are the sounds of cat - tle and shep - herds;
See in his eyes the glo - ry of heav - en;
Great is the joy of all those in dark - ness.
Word that brings life, em - brac - ing hu - man - i - ty,

Sweet is the mu - sic the an - gels bring this night.
Hear in his laugh-ter the joy of God on high.
Here lies the Sav - ior so soon to die and rise.
Je - sus, com-pan - ion, be born in - to our lives.

Refrain

Sing al - le - lu - ia, sing al - le - lu - ia.

Wel - come the Sav - ior, the prom-ise of new life.

Sing al - le - lu - ia, sing al - le - lu - ia.

All of cre - a - tion, sing this night.

Text: Francis Patrick O'Brien, b.1958
Tune: BRAINTREE, 10 10 10 11 with refrain; Francis Patrick O'Brien, b.1958
© 1996, GIA Publications, Inc.

Sing We Now of Christmas   422

1. Sing we now of Christ-mas, No-ël sing we here.
2. An-gels called to shep-herds, "Leave your flocks at rest.
3. In a stall they found him with his moth-er mild.
4. Wise men from the O-rient jour-neyed from a-far
5. Gold and myrrh they of-fered, gifts of great-est price.
6. Praise we now our Sav-ior on this ho-ly night.

Sing our grate-ful prais-es to the Child so dear.
Jour-ney forth to Beth-l'hem; find the In-fant blest."
Jo-seph, at the man-ger, watched the ho-ly Child.
Bear-ing cost-ly treas-ure, guid-ed by a star.
There was ne'er a sta-ble so like par-a-dise.
Let us gath-er 'round him, Christ, the Lord of light.

Sing we No-ël, the King is born, No-ël!

Sing we now of Christ-mas, sing we here No-ël!

Text: French carol; tr. anonymous; adaptation, hymnal version, © 2011, GIA Publications, Inc.
Tune: NOËL NOUVELET, 11 11 with refrain; French carol; harm. by Thomas Foster, b.1938, © 1986, GIA Publications, Inc.

Glória, Glória   423

Canon—4 voices

Gló-ri-a, gló-ri-a, in ex-cél-sis De-o!

Gló-ri-a, gló-ri-a, al-le-lú-ia, al-le-lú-ia!

Tune: Jacques Berthier, 1923–1994, © 1979, 1988, Les Presses de Taizé, GIA Publications, Inc., agent

424 Joy to the World / Al Mundo Paz

1. Joy   to the world,   the Lord is   come! Let
2. Joy   to the earth,   the Sav - ior reigns! Let
3. No   more let sin   and sor - row grow, Nor
4. He   rules the world with truth and grace, And

1. ¡Al   mun - do paz,   na - ció Je - sús, Na -
2. ¡Al   mun - do paz,   el Sal - va - dor En
3. ¡Al   mun - do Dios   go - ber - na - rá   Con

earth re - ceive her   king;   Let ev - 'ry
us   our songs em - ploy;   While fields and
thorns in - fest the ground;   He comes to
makes the na - tions prove   The glo - ries

ció   ya nues - tro Rey!   El co - ra -
tie - rra rei - na - rá!   Ya es fe -
gra - cia_y con po - der!   A las na -

heart pre - pare him   room   And heav'n and na - ture
floods, rocks, hills and   plains Re - peat the sound - ing
make his bless - ings flow   Far as the curse is
of   his right - eous - ness,   And won - ders of his

zón   ya tie - ne   luz,   Y   paz su san - ta
liz   el pe - ca - dor,   Je - sús per - dón le
cio - nes mos - tra - rá   Su_a - mor y su po -

sing,   And heav'n and na - ture sing,   And
joy,   Re - peat the sound - ing joy,   Re -
found, Far as the curse is found,   Far
love,   And won - ders of his love,   And

grey,   Y   paz su san - ta grey,   Y
da,   Je - sús per - dón le da,   Je -
der,   Su_a - mor y su po - der,   Su_a -

heav'n,   and   heav'n   and   na - ture   sing.
peat,   re - peat   the   sound - ing   joy.
as,   far   as   the   curse   is   found.
won - ders,   won -   ders   of   his   love.
paz,   *y*   *paz*   *su*   *san* - *ta*   *grey.*
sús,   *Je* - *sús*   *per* - *dón*   *le*   *da.*
mor,   *su_a* - *mor*   *y*   *su*   *po* - *der.*

Text: Psalm 98; Isaac Watts, 1674–1748; tr. anonymous
Tune: ANTIOCH, CM with repeat; arr. from George F. Handel, 1685–1759, in T. Hawkes' *Collection of Tunes*, 1833

Angels, from the Realms of Glory 425

1. An - gels,   from   the   realms   of   glo - ry,
2. Shep - herds,   in   the   field   a - bid - ing,
3. Sag - es,   leave   your   con -   tem - pla - tions,
4. Though an   in - fant   now   we   view   him,

Wing   your flight   o'er   all   the earth;   You   who   sang   cre -
Watch - ing   o'er   your   flocks by night,   God   on   earth   is
Bright - er   vi - sions   beam a - far;   Seek   the   great   De -
He   shall   fill   his   heav'n - ly throne,   Gath - er   all   the

a - tion's sto - ry,   Now   pro - claim   Mes - si - ah's birth:
now   re - sid - ing,   Yon - der shines   the   in - fant light.
sire   of   na - tions;   You   have   seen   his   morn - ing   star.
na - tions to him;   Ev - 'ry   knee   shall   then bow down.

Come   and wor - ship,   come   and wor - ship,

Wor - ship   Christ,   the   new - born   King.

Text: Sts. 1–3, James Montgomery, 1771–1854; st. 4, *Christmas Box,* 1825
Tune: REGENT SQUARE, 8 7 8 7 with refrain; Henry Smart, 1813–1879

426 O Come, All Ye Faithful / Venid, Fieles Todos / Adéste Fidéles

1. O come, all ye faith-ful, joy-ful and tri-um-phant, O
2. God of God, Light of Light,
1. *Ve - nid, fie-les to-dos, a Be-lén mar-che-mos De*
2. *El que_es Hi-jo_e-ter-no del e-ter-no Pa-dre, Y*
1. Ad - é - ste fi - dé - les, laé - ti, tri-um-phán - tes, Ve-
2. De - um de De - o, Lu - men de Lú - mi-ne

come ye, O come ye to Beth - le - hem;
Lo! He comes forth from the Vir - gin's womb.
go - zo triun - fan - tes, y lle - nos de_a-mor; Y_al
Dios ver - da - de - ro que_al mun - do cre - ó, Al
ní - te, ve - ní - te in Béth - le - hem.
Ge - stant pu - él - lae ví - sce - ra.

Come and be-hold him, born the King of an - gels;
Our ver - y God, be - got-ten not cre - a - ted,
Rey de los cie - los con - tem - plar po - dre - mos;
se - no vir - gí - neo vi - no de_u - na ma - dre;
Na - tum vi - dé - te, Re - gem an - ge - ló - rum.
De - um ve - rum, gé - ni-tum, non fa - ctum.

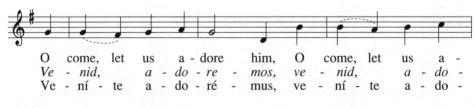

O come, let us a - dore him, O come, let us a -
Ve - nid, a - do - re - mos, ve - nid, a - do -
Ve - ní - te a - do - ré - mus, ve - ní - te a - do -

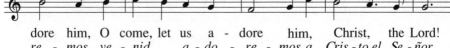

dore him, O come, let us a - dore him, Christ, the Lord!
re - mos, ve - nid, a - do - re - mos a Cris-to_el Se - ñor.
ré - mus, ve - ní - te a - do - ré - mus Dó - mi-num.

3. Sing, choirs of angels,
   sing in exultation,
   Sing, all ye citizens of heav'n above!
   Glory to God, all
   glory in the highest;

4. Yea, Lord, we greet thee,
   born this happy morning,
   Jesus, to thee be all glory giv'n;
   Word of the Father,
   now in flesh appearing;

3. Cantad jubilosas,
  célicas criaturas:
  Resuenen los cielos con vuestra canción;
  ¡Al Dios bondadoso,
  gloria en las alturas;

4. Jesús, celebramos
  tu bendito nombre
  Con himnos solemnes de grato loor;
  Por siglos eternos
  todo ser te adore;

3. Cantet nunc io,
  chorus angelórum,
  Cantet nunc aula caeléstium.
  Glória, glória in excélsis Deo.

4. Ergo qui natus
  Die hodiérna,
  Jesu tibi sit glória.
  Patris aetérnae verbum caro factum.

Text: *Adeste fideles;* John F. Wade, c.1711–1786; English tr. by Frederick Oakeley, 1802–1880, alt.; Spanish tr. by Juan Bautista Cabrera, 1837–1916
Tune: ADESTE FIDELES, Irregular with refrain; John F. Wade, c.1711–1786

Good Christian Friends, Rejoice   427

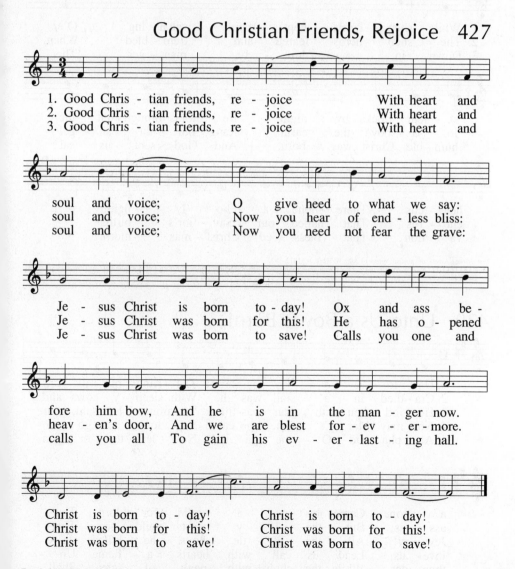

1. Good Chris - tian friends, re - joice   With heart and soul and voice; O give heed to what we say: Je - sus Christ is born to - day! Ox and ass be - fore him bow, And he is in the man - ger now. Christ is born to - day! Christ is born to - day!

2. Good Chris - tian friends, re - joice   With heart and soul and voice; Now you hear of end - less bliss: Je - sus Christ was born for this! He has o - pened heav - en's door, And we are blest for - ev - er - more. Christ was born for this! Christ was born for this!

3. Good Chris - tian friends, re - joice   With heart and soul and voice; Now you need not fear the grave: Je - sus Christ was born to save! Calls you one and calls you all To gain his ev - er - last - ing hall. Christ was born to save! Christ was born to save!

Text: *In dulci jubilo;* Latin and German, 14th C.; tr. by John M. Neal, 1818–1866
Tune: IN DULCI JUBILO, 66 77 78 55; 14th C. German melody; harm. by Robert L. Pearsall, 1795–1856

428 Go Tell It on the Mountain

Refrain

Go tell it on the moun-tain, O-ver the hills and ev - 'ry-where;

Go tell it on the moun - tain That Je - sus Christ is born!

Verses

1. While shep - herds kept their watch - ing O'er
2. The shep - herds feared and trem - bled When,
3. Down in a low - ly man - ger The

si - lent flocks by night, Be - hold, through - out the
lo, a - bove the earth Rang out the an - gel
hum - ble Christ was born, And God sent us sal -

D.C.

heav - ens There shone a ho - ly light.
cho - rus That hailed our Sav - ior's birth.
va - tion That bless - ed Christ - mas morn.

Text: African American spiritual; verses by John W. Work, Jr., 1872–1925
Tune: GO TELL IT ON THE MOUNTAIN, 7 6 7 6 with refrain; African American spiritual; harm. by Robert J. Batastini, b.1942, © 1995, GIA
  Publications, Inc.

429 Unto Us a Boy Is Born!

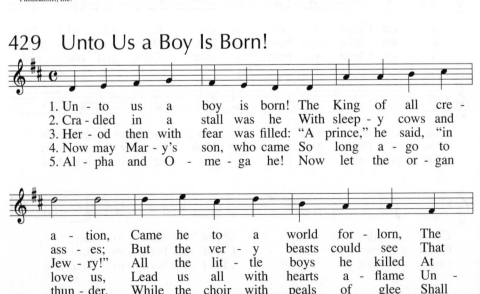

1. Un - to us a boy is born! The King of all cre -
2. Cra - dled in a stall was he With sleep - y cows and
3. Her - od then with fear was filled: "A prince," he said, "in
4. Now may Mar - y's son, who came So long a - go to
5. Al - pha and O - me - ga he! Now let the or - gan

a - tion, Came he to a world for - lorn, The
ass - es; But the ver - y beasts could see That
Jew - ry!" All the lit - tle boys he killed At
love us, Lead us all with hearts a - flame Un -
thun - der, While the choir with peals of glee Shall

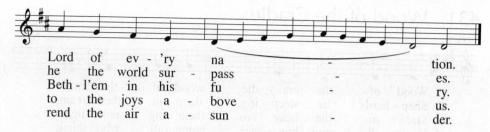

Lord of ev - 'ry na - - - - tion.
he the world sur - pass - - - es.
Beth - l'em in his fu - - - ry.
to the joys a - bove - - - us.
rend the air a - sun - - - der.

Text: *Puer nobis nascitur*; Latin, 15th C.; tr. by Percy Dearmer, 1867–1936, © 1928, Oxford University Press
Tune: PUER NOBIS NASCITUR, 7 7 7 7; *Piae Cantiones*, 1582; harm. by Geoffrey Shaw, 1879–1943, © A. R. Mowbray and Co. Ltd.

Love Has Come 430

1. Love has come, a light in the dark - ness! Love shines
2. Love is born! Come, share in the won - der. Love is
3. Love has come and nev - er will leave us! Love is

forth in the Beth - le - hem skies. See, all heav - en has
God now a - sleep in the hay. See the glow in the
life ev - er - last - ing and free. Love is Je - sus with -

come to pro - claim it. Hear how their song of joy a -
eyes of his moth - er. What is the name her heart is
in and a - mong us. Love is the peace our hearts are

ris - es: Love! Love! Born un - to you, a Sav - ior!
say - ing? Love! Love! Love is the name she whis - pers.
seek - ing. Love! Love! Love is the gift of Christ - mas.

Love! Love! Glo - ry to God on high!
Love! Love! Je - sus, Em - man - u - el!
Love! Love! Glo - ry to God on high!

Text: Ken Bible, b.1950, © 1996, LNWhymns.com. Admin. by Music Services
Tune: UN FLAMBEAU, 9 9 10 9 9 8; French carol; harm. by Ronald F. Krisman, b.1946, © 2011, GIA Publications, Inc.

431 Wood of the Cradle

Verses

1. Wood of the cra - dle, wood of the cross,
2. Shep - herds lie sleep - ing, deep in their dreams;
3. Star in the heav - ens bear - ing new light,
4. Come, all who hun - ger, come, all who thirst;

Bear - ing a life - time of joy and of loss,
An - gels a - wak - en them. "What could this mean?
Guid - ing the sag - es and a - ges this night:
Come, all who seek him, God's joy on the earth.

Who is your loved one? Who could he be,
Whom do you her - ald? Whom must we find? A
Where will you lead us? Where can he be, The
Find him a shel - ter, bright, safe, and warm;

Born in a man - ger to die on a tree?
child in a man - ger? Our God born in time?"
child born of mys - t'ry who died on a tree?
See in all peo - ple his love be - ing born.

Refrain

This, this is Je - sus the Lord, Here in the bod - y and

blood out-poured. Come, come, walk in his ways. Kneel at the

man - ger and rise from the grave.

Text: Francis Patrick O'Brien, b.1958
Tune: ABINGTON, 9 10 9 10 with refrain; Francis Patrick O'Brien, b.1958
© 2002, GIA Publications, Inc.

A Child Is Born in Bethlehem / 432
Puer Natus in Béthlehem

1. A child is born in Beth - le - hem, Al - le - lu - ia.
2. The Lord who reigns be - yond the skies, Al - le - lu - ia.
3. The ox and ass in neigh-b'ring stall, Al - le - lu - ia.
4. The shep - herds hear the an - gels sing, Al - le - lu - ia.

1. *Pu - er na - tus in Béth - le - hem, Al - le - lú - ia.*
2. *Hic ja - cet in prae - sé - pi - o, Al - le - lú - ia.*
3. *Co - gnó - vit bos et á - si - nus, Al - le - lú - ia.*
4. *Et Án - ge - lus pa - stó - ri - bus, Al - le - lú - ia.*

Ex - ult for joy, Je - ru - sa - lem, Al - le - lu - ia,
Now in a low - ly man - ger lies, Al - le - lu - ia,
Know that this child is Lord of all, Al - le - lu - ia,
"To - day is born your Lord and King," Al - le - lu - ia,

Un - de gau - det Je - rú - sa - lem, Al - le - lú - ia,
Qui re - gnat si - ne tér - mi - no, Al - le - lú - ia,
Quod pu - er e - rat Dó - mi - nus, Al - le - lú - ia,
Re - vé - lat quod sit Dó - mi - nus, Al - le - lú - ia,

al - le - lu - ia. Our joy - ful hearts we raise! Christ is born: O
al - le - lú - ia. In cor - dis jú - bi - lo, Chri-stum na - tum

come a - dore him And sing new hymns of praise.
a - do - ré - mus Cum no - vo cán - ti - co.

5. Of virgin-mother born this night, Alleluia.
   He is our God, the Light from Light, Alleluia, alleluia.

6. Our human race he enters in, Alleluia.
   But bears no single taint of sin, Alleluia, alleluia.

7. That we, from sin's allure set free, Alleluia.
   Like him, and so like God, may be, Alleluia, alleluia.

5. *De Matre natus Vírgine, Allelúia.*
   Qui lumen est de lúmine, Allelúia, allelúia.

6. *In carne nobis símilis, Allelúia.*
   Peccáto sed dissímilis, Allelúia, allelúia.

7. *Ut rédderet nos hómines, Allelúia.*
   Deo et sibi símiles, Allelúia, allelúia.

Text: *Puer natus in Bethlehem;* Latin 14th C.; tr. by Ronald F. Krisman, b.1946, © 2011, GIA Publications, Inc.
Tune: PUER NATUS, 88 with alleluias and refrain; Mode I; acc. by Richard Proulx, 1937–2010, © 1986, GIA Publications, Inc.

433 From Heaven Above

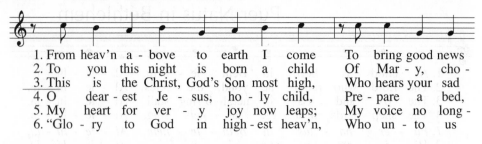

1. From heav'n a - bove   to   earth   I   come   To   bring good news
2. To   you   this night   is   born   a   child   Of   Mar - y,   cho -
3. This   is   the Christ, God's Son most high,   Who hears your   sad
4. O   dear - est   Je - sus,   ho - ly   child,   Pre - pare   a   bed,
5. My   heart for   ver - y   joy now   leaps;   My   voice no   long -
6. "Glo - ry   to   God   in   high - est heav'n,   Who un - to   us

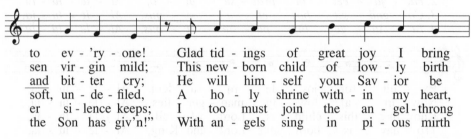

to   ev - 'ry - one!   Glad tid - ings   of   great   joy   I   bring
sen   vir - gin   mild;   This new - born child   of   low - ly   birth
and   bit - ter   cry;   He   will   him - self   your   Sav - ior   be
soft, un - de - filed,   A   ho - ly   shrine with - in   my   heart,
er   si - lence keeps;   I   too   must   join   the   an - gel - throng
the   Son   has   giv'n!"   With an - gels   sing   in   pi - ous mirth

To   all   the   world,   and   glad - ly   sing:
Shall be   the   joy   of   all   the   earth.
And from   all   sin   will   set   you   free.
That you   and   I   may   nev - er   part.
To   sing   this   sweet - est   cra - dle - song:
A   glad   new   year   to   all   the   earth!

Text: Luke 2:1–18; *Vom Himmel hoch da komm ich her*; Martin Luther, 1483–1546; tr. from *Lutheran Book of Worship*, 1978, alt., © Augsburg Fortress
Tune: VOM HIMMEL HOCH, LM; attr. to Martin Luther, 1483–1546; Schumann's *Geistliche Lieder*, 1539; harm. by Hans Leo Hassler, 1564–1612

434 Glory / Gloria

Glo - ry, glo - ry, glo - ry,   glo - ry be to God on   high,
Glo - ria, glo - ria, glo - ria   en   las al - tu - ras   a   Dios,

and   on   earth   peace to all peo - ple in whom God is well   pleased.
y en la tie - rra paz   a la gen - te   que a - ma el Se - ñor.

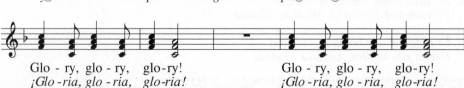

Glo - ry, glo - ry, glo - ry!   Glo - ry, glo - ry, glo - ry!
¡Glo - ria, glo - ria, glo - ria!   ¡Glo - ria, glo - ria, glo - ria!

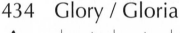

Glo - ry, glo - ry, glo - ry!
¡Glo - ria, glo - ria, glo - ria!

Text: Based on Luke 2:14; Pablo Sosa, b.1933
Tune: Pablo Sosa, b.1933
© 1989, GIA Publications, Inc.

O Little Town of Bethlehem   435

1. O lit - tle town of Beth - le - hem, How still we see thee
2. For Christ is born of Mar - y And, gath - ered all a -
3. How si - lent - ly, how si - lent - ly The won - drous gift is
4. O ho - ly Child of Beth - le - hem, De - scend to us, we

lie! A - bove thy deep and dream - less sleep The
bove While mor - tals sleep, the an - gels keep Their
giv'n! So God im - parts to hu - man hearts The
pray; Cast out our sin and en - ter in, Be

si - lent stars go by; Yet in the dark streets
watch of won - d'ring love. O morn - ing stars, to -
bless - ings of his heav'n. No ear may hear his
born in us to - day. We hear the Christ - mas

shin - eth The ev - er - last - ing Light. The hopes and
geth - er Pro - claim the ho - ly birth, And prais - es
com - ing, But in this world of sin, Where meek souls
an - gels The great glad tid - ings tell; O come to

fears of all the years Are met in thee to - night.
sing to God the King, And peace to all on earth!
will re - ceive him, still The dear Christ en - ters in.
us, a - bide with us, Our Lord Em - man - u - el!

Text: Phillips Brooks, 1835–1893
Tune: ST. LOUIS, 8 6 8 6 7 6 8 6; Lewis H. Redner, 1831–1908

436 Star-Child

Verses

1. Star - Child, earth - Child, Go - be-tween of God,
2. Street child, beat child, No place left to go,
3. Grown child, old child, Mem - 'ry full of years,
4. Spared child, spoiled child, Hav - ing, want - ing more,
5. Hope - for - peace Child, God's stu - pen - dous sign,

Love Child, Christ Child, Heav - en's light - ning rod:
Hurt child, used child No one wants to know:
Sad child, lost child, Sto - ry told in tears:
Wise child, faith child Know - ing joy in store:
Down - to - earth Child, Star of stars that shine:

Refrain

This year, this year let the day ar - rive when

Christ-mas comes for ev-'ry-one, ev - 'ry-one a - live.

Text: Shirley Erena Murray, b.1931, © 1994, Hope Publishing Company
Tune: NOAH'S SONG, 4 5 4 5 with refrain; Ronald F. Krisman, b.1946, © 2003, GIA Publications, Inc.

437 Away in a Manger

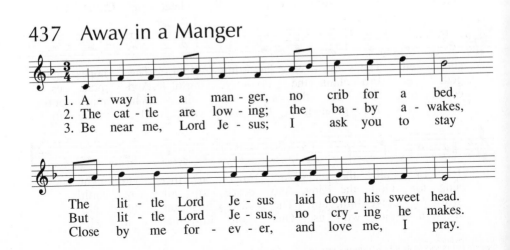

1. A - way in a man - ger, no crib for a bed,
2. The cat - tle are low - ing; the ba - by a - wakes,
3. Be near me, Lord Je - sus; I ask you to stay

The lit - tle Lord Je - sus laid down his sweet head.
But lit - tle Lord Je - sus, no cry - ing he makes.
Close by me for - ev - er, and love me, I pray.

The stars in the bright sky looked down where he lay,
I love you, Lord Je - sus! Look down from the sky
Bless all the dear chil - dren in your ten - der care,

The lit - tle Lord Je - sus, a - sleep on the hay.
And stay by my cra - dle till morn - ing is nigh.
And fit us for heav - en, to live with you there.

Text: St. 1, 2, anonymous; st. 3, John T. McFarland, 1851–1913
Tune: CRADLE SONG, 11 11 11 11; William J. Kirkpatrick, 1838–1921

Lo, How a Rose E'er Blooming 438

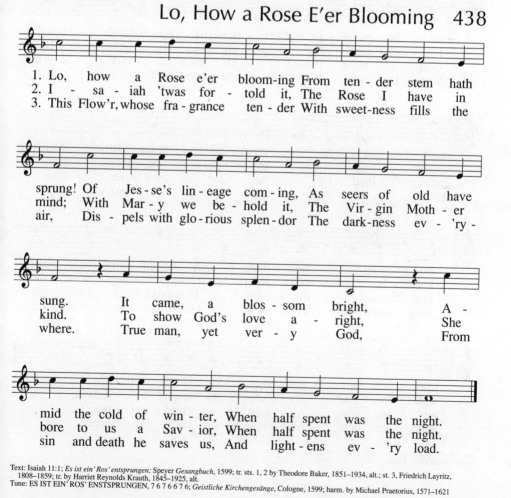

1. Lo, how a Rose e'er bloom-ing From ten - der stem hath
2. I - sa - iah 'twas for - told it, The Rose I have in
3. This Flow'r, whose fra - grance ten - der With sweet-ness fills the

sprung! Of Jes - se's lin - eage com - ing, As seers of old have
mind; With Mar - y we be - hold it, The Vir - gin Moth - er
air, Dis - pels with glo - rious splen - dor The dark-ness ev - 'ry -

sung. It came, a blos - som bright, A -
kind. To show God's love a - right, She
where. True man, yet ver - y God, From

mid the cold of win - ter, When half spent was the night.
bore to us a Sav - ior, When half spent was the night.
sin and death he saves us, And light - ens ev - 'ry load.

Text: Isaiah 11:1; *Es ist ein' Ros' entsprungen;* Speyer *Gesangbuch,* 1599; tr. sts. 1, 2 by Theodore Baker, 1851–1934, alt.; st. 3, Friedrich Layritz,
1808–1859; tr. by Harriet Reynolds Krauth, 1845–1925, alt.
Tune: ES IST EIN' ROS' ENSTSPRUNGEN, 7 6 7 6 6 7 6; *Geistliche Kirchengesänge,* Cologne, 1599; harm. by Michael Praetorius, 1571–1621

439 Come, Sing a Home and Family

1. Come, sing a home and fam - i - ly In
2. At Mar - y's ta - ble Je - sus learned To
3. By Jo - seph's side young Je - sus learned To
4. What - ev - er form our fam - 'ly takes, The

Naz - a - reth of old, Whose hum - ble grace a
bless, give thanks, and eat, To wel - come all as
work and read and pray, The law and love of
gos - pel way we seek: To feed the hun - gry,

no - ble place In Chris - tian life now holds: A
hon - ored guests By wash - ing wea - ry feet. Her
God a - bove Placed in his heart to stay. While
heal the sick, Lift up the poor and weak. In

maid - en's ho - ly, vi - brant faith, Which
sweep - ing floors and light - ing lamps, Her
cra - dled by the car - pen - ter, The
dai - ly life and sim - ple tasks Our

said, "Let it be done!" A dream - er who risked
knead - ing bread with leav'n, Her jour - neys to the
boy came to dis - cern That prod - i - gal, for -
song must nev - er cease Of dream - ing work - er,

life and limb Pro - tect - ing God's own Son.
well fore - told To Christ the reign of heav'n.
giv - ing arms A - wait a child's re - turn.
maid - en bold, And child of last - ing peace.

Text: Alan J. Hommerding, b.1956, © 1994, World Library Publications
Tune: CAROL, CMD; Richard S. Willis, 1819–1900

Once in Royal David's City 440

1. Once in roy - al Da - vid's cit - y Stood a
2. He came down to earth from heav - en Who is
3. And, through all his won - drous child - hood, He would
4. For he is our child - hood's pat - tern, Day by
5. And our eyes at last shall see him, Through his

low - ly cat - tle shed, Where a moth - er laid her
God and Lord of all, And his shel - ter was a
hon - or and o - bey, Love and watch the low - ly
day like us he grew; He was lit - tle, weak, and
own re - deem - ing love; For that child so dear and

ba - by In a man - ger for his bed.
sta - ble, And his cra - dle was a stall.
maid - en In whose gen - tle arms he lay.
help - less, Tears and smiles like us he knew.
gen - tle Is our Lord in heav'n a - bove.

Mar - y was that moth - er mild;
With the poor and meek and low - ly
Chris - tian chil - dren all should be
And he feels for all our sad - ness,
And he leads his chil - dren on

Je - sus Christ, her lit - tle child.
Lived on earth our Sav - ior ho - ly.
Kind, o - be - dient, good as he.
And he shares in all our glad - ness.
To the place where he is gone.

Text: Cecil F. Alexander, 1818–1895, alt.
Tune: IRBY, 8 7 8 7 77; Henry J. Gauntlett, 1805–1876; harm. by Arthur H. Mann, 1850–1929, © 1957, Novello & Company Limited

441 The First One to Know

1. The first one to know what the Word was to be
2. When Jo - seph held gen - tly the son of his wife,
3. By hear - ing the sto - ry and song of that night

Was Mar - y, who wel - comed the great mys - ter - y.
He felt the con - nec - tion of life touch - ing life.
May we, like the shep - herds, see Beth - le - hem's light:

Be - yond com - pre - hen - sion, she car - ried her son
He cra - dled a fu - ture that he could not see,
The Word that cre - at - ed came in - to its own,

And knew she ex - pect - ed the Sav - ior, the One.
The teach - er and guide that this in - fant would be.
And first, as a ba - by, the Sav - ior was known.

Text: Adam M. L. Tice, b.1979, © 2009, GIA Publications, Inc.
Tune: PADERBORN, 11 11 11 11; Paderborn *Gesangbuch*, 1765; harm. by Sydney H. Nicholson, 1875–1947

442 Our Savior's Infant Cries Were Heard

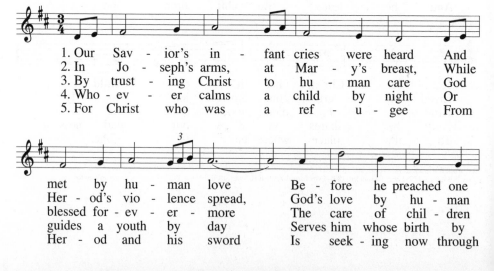

1. Our Sav - ior's in - fant cries were heard And
2. In Jo - seph's arms, at Mar - y's breast, While
3. By trust - ing Christ to hu - man care God
4. Who - ev - er calms a child by night Or
5. For Christ who was a ref - u - gee From

met by hu - man love Be - fore he preached one
Her - od's vio - lence spread, God's love by hu - man
blessed for - ev - er - more The care of chil - dren
guides a youth by day Serves him whose birth by
Her - od and his sword Is seek - ing now through

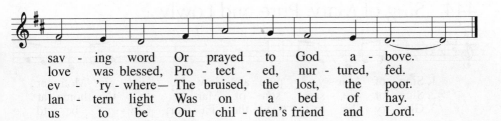

sav - ing word   Or prayed   to   God   a - bove.
love   was blessed, Pro - tect - ed, nur - tured, fed.
ev - 'ry - where— The bruised,   the   lost,   the   poor.
lan - tern light   Was   on   a   bed   of   hay.
us   to   be   Our   chil - dren's friend and   Lord.

Text: Thomas H. Troeger, b.1945, © 1986, Oxford University Press
Tune: ST. COLUMBA, CM; Irish melody

Within the Father's House 443

1. With - in   the   Fa - ther's   house   The
2. The   doc - tors   of   the   law   Gaze
3. Yet   not   to   them   is   giv'n   The
4. The   se - cret   of   the   Lord   Es -
5. Lord, en - ter   now   our   souls   And
6. Till   we   be - hold   your   face   And

Son   has   found   his   home,   And   to   his   tem - ple
on   the   won - drous child   And   mar - vel   at   his
might - y   truth   to   know,   To   lift   the   earth - ly
capes each   hu - man   eye,   And   faith - ful,   pon - d'ring
teach   us   by   your   grace   Each   dim   re - veal - ing
know,   as   we   are   known,   You,   Ho - ly   Spir - it,

sud - den - ly   The   Lord   of   life   has   come.
gra - cious words   Of   wis - dom   un - de - filed.
veil   which hides   In - car - nate   God   be - low.
hearts a - wait   The   full   e - piph - a - ny.
of   your - self   With   lov - ing   awe   to   trace,
Fa - ther, Son,   Co - e - qual   Three   in   One.

Text: James R. Woodford, 1820–1885, alt.
Tune: OPTATUS VOTIS OMNIUM, SM; anonymous; harm. by George R. Woodward, 1848–1934, alt.

444 Sing of Mary, Pure and Lowly

1. Sing of Mar - y, pure and low - ly, Vir - gin Moth - er
2. Sing of Je - sus, son of Mar - y, In the home at
3. Glo - ry be to God the Fa - ther; Glo - ry be to

un - de - filed. Sing of God's own Son most ho - ly,
Naz - a - reth. Toil and la - bor can - not wea - ry
God the Son; Glo - ry be to God the Spir - it;

Who be - came her lit - tle child. Fair - est Child of
Love en - dur - ing un - to death. Con - stant was the
Glo - ry to the Three in One. From the heart of

fair - est Moth - er, God the Lord who came to earth,
love he gave her, Though he went forth from her side,
bless - ed Mar - y, From all saints the song as - cends,

Word - made - flesh, our ver - y broth - er,
Forth to preach, and heal, and suf - fer,
And the Church the strain re - ech - oes

Takes our na - ture by his birth.
Till on Cal - va - ry he died.
Un - to earth's re - mot - est ends.

Text: Roland F. Palmer, 1891–1985, © Estate of Roland Palmer
Tune: PLEADING SAVIOR, 8 7 8 7 D; *Christian Lyre*, 1830; harm. by Richard Proulx, 1937–2010, © 1986, GIA Publications, Inc.

Virgin-Born, We Bow before You   445

1. Vir - gin - born, we bow be - fore you: Bless - ed was the
2. Bless - ed she by all cre - a - tion, Who brought forth the

womb that bore you; Mar - y, Moth - er meek and mild,
world's sal - va - tion. Bless - ed they who, ev - er blest,

Bless - ed was she in her Child. Bless - ed
Love you most and serve you best. Vir - gin -

was the breast that fed you; Bless - ed was the
born, we bow be - fore you; Bless - ed was the

hand that led you; Bless - ed was the moth - er's
womb that bore you; Mar - y, Moth - er meek and

eye, Watch - ing o'er your in - fan - cy.
mild, Bless - ed was she in her Child.

Text: Reginald Heber, 1783–1826, alt.
Tune: MON DIEU, PRÊTE-MOI L'OREILLE, 88 77 D; attr. to Louis Bourgeois, c.1510–1561; harm. by Claude Goudimel, 1505–1572, alt.

446 Gentle Mary Laid Her Child

1. Gen-tle Mar-y laid her child   Low-ly in a man-ger.
2. An-gels sang a-bout his birth;   Wise men sought and found him.
3. Gen-tle Mar-y laid her child   Low-ly in a man-ger.

There he lay, the un-de-filed,   To the world a stran-ger.
Heav-en's star shone bright-ly forth,   Glo-ry all a-round him.
He is still the un-de-filed,   But no more a stran-ger.

Such a babe in such a place,   "Can he be the Sav-ior?"
Shep-herds saw the won-drous sight,   Heard the an-gels sing-ing.
Son of God, of hum-ble birth,   Beau-ti-ful the sto-ry;

Ask the saved of all the race   Who have found his fa - vor.
All the plains were lit that night;   All the hills were ring - ing.
Praise his name in all the earth,   Hail the King of glo - ry!

Text: Joseph S. Cook, 1859–1933
Tune: TEMPUS ADEST FLORIDUM, 7 6 7 6 D; *Piae Cantiones*, 1582; arr. by Ernest C. MacMillan, 1893–1973

447 The God Whom Earth and Sea and Sky

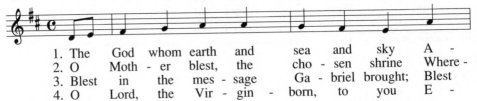

1. The God whom earth and   sea and sky   A -
2. O Moth-er blest, the   cho-sen shrine   Where -
3. Blest in the mes-sage   Ga-briel brought;   Blest
4. O Lord, the Vir-gin-born, to   you   E -

dore and praise and mag-ni-fy,   Whose might they claim, whose
in the ar-chi-tect di-vine,   Whose hand con-tains the
by the work the Spir-it wrought;   Most blest, to bring to
ter-nal praise and laud are due,   Whom with the Fa-ther

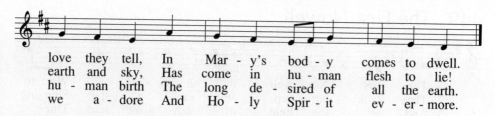

love	they	tell,	In	Mar - y's	bod - y	comes to dwell.
earth	and	sky,	Has	come in	hu - man	flesh to lie!
hu - man	birth	The	long	de - sired of	all the earth.
we	a - dore	And	Ho - ly	Spir - it	ev - er - more.

Text: *Quem terra, pontus, aethera*; Venantius Fortunatus, c.530–609; tr. by John M. Neale, 1818–1866, alt.
Tune: EISENACH, LM; Johann H. Schein, 1586–1630; harm. by J. S. Bach, 1685–1750

What Star Is This 448

1. What star is this, with beams so bright, More love - ly
2. 'Tis now ful - filled what God de - creed: "From Ja - cob
3. While out - ward signs the star dis - plays, An in - ward
4. O Je - sus, while the star of grace In - vites us
5. To God the Fa - ther, God the Son, And God the

than the noon - day light? 'Tis sent to an - nounce a
shall a star pro - ceed." And lo! The east - ern
light the Lord con - veys. It urg - es them, with
all to seek your face, Let not our sloth - ful
Spir - it, Three in One, May ev - 'ry tongue and

new - born king, Glad tid - ings of our God to bring.
sag - es stand To read in heav'n the Lord's com - mand.
force be - nign, To seek the Giv - er of the sign.
hearts re - fuse The guid - ance of your light to use.
na - tion raise An end - less song of thank - ful praise!

Text: *Quem stella sole pulchrior*, Charles Coffin, 1676–1749; tr. by John Chandler, 1806–1876, alt.
Tune: PUER NOBIS, LM; adapt. by Michael Praetorius, 1571–1621

449 The First Nowell

1. The first No-well the an-gel did say Was to
2. They look - ed up and saw a star Shin-ing
3. And by the light of that same star Three
4. This star drew nigh to the north - west, O'er
5. Then en - tered in those wise men three, Full
6. Then let us all with one ac - cord Sing

cer - tain poor shep-herds in fields as they lay; In
in the east be - yond them far; And
wise men came from coun - try far; To
Beth - le - hem it took its rest; And
rev - 'rent - ly up - on their knee, And
prais - es to our heav - 'nly Lord, Who

fields where they lay keep - ing their sheep, On a
to the earth it gave great light, And
seek for a king was their in - tent, And to
there it did both stop and stay Right
of - fered there in his pres - ence Their
made the heav'ns and earth of naught, And

cold win - ter's night that was so deep.
so it con - tin - ued both day and night.
fol - low the star where - ev - er it went.
o - ver the place where Je - sus lay.
gold and myrrh and frank - in - cense.
with his blood our life has bought.

No - well, No - well, No - well, No - well!

Born is the King of Is - ra - el.

Text: English carol, 17th C.
Tune: THE FIRST NOWELL, Irregular with refrain; English carol; harm. from *Christmas Carols New and Old*, 1871

As with Gladness Men of Old 450

1. As with glad - ness men of old Did the guid - ing
2. As with joy - ful steps they sped To that low - ly
3. As they of - fered gifts most rare At that man - ger
4. Ho - ly Je - sus, ev - 'ry day Keep us in the
5. In the heav'n - ly cit - y bright None shall need cre -

star be - hold; As with joy they hailed its light,
man - ger - bed, There to bend the knee be - fore
crude and bare; So may we this ho - ly day,
nar - row way; And when earth - ly things are past,
at - ed light; You, its light, its joy, its crown,

Lead - ing on - ward, beam - ing bright; So, most gra - cious
Him, whom heav'n and earth a - dore; So may we with
Drawn to you with - out de - lay, All our cost - liest
Bring our ran - somed souls at last Where they need no
You, its sun which goes not down; There for - ev - er

Lord, may we Ev - er - more your splen - dor see.
hur - ried pace Run to seek your throne of grace.
treas - ures bring, Christ, to you, our heav'n - ly King.
star to guide, Where no clouds your glo - ry hide.
may we sing Al - le - lu - ias to our King.

Text: William C. Dix, 1837–1898, alt.
Tune: DIX, 77 77 77; arr. from Conrad Kocher, 1786–1872, by William H. Monk, 1823–1889

451 Songs of Thankfulness and Praise

1. Songs of thank-ful - ness and praise, Je - sus, Lord, to
2. Man - i - fest at Jor - dan's stream, Proph-et, Priest, and
3. Man - i - fest in mak - ing whole Pal - sied limbs and
4. Grant us grace to see you, Lord, Pres - ent in your

you we raise, Man - i - fest - ed by the star
King su - preme; And at Ca - na, wed - ding guest,
faint - ing soul; Man - i - fest in val - iant fight,
ho - ly word. By that grace which you en - dow,

To the sag - es from a - far; Branch of roy - al
In your God - head man - i - fest; Man - i - fest in
Quell - ing all the dev - il's might; Man - i - fest in
Help us im - i - tate you now, That we, pure like

Da - vid's stem In your birth at Beth - le - hem;
pow'r di - vine, Chang - ing wa - ter in - to wine;
gra - cious will, Ev - er bring - ing good from ill;
you, may be At your great e - piph - a - ny;

An - thems be to you ad-dressed, God in flesh made man - i - fest.
An - thems be to you ad-dressed, God in flesh made man - i - fest.
An - thems be to you ad-dressed, God in flesh made man - i - fest.
And may praise you, ev - er blest, God in flesh made man - i - fest.

Text: Christopher Wordsworth, 1807–1885, alt.
Tune: SALZBURG, 77 77 D; Jakob Hintze, 1622–1702, harm. by J. S. Bach, 1685–1750

We Three Kings of Orient Are 452

1. We three kings of O - ri - ent are; Bear - ing
2. Born a King on Beth - le - hem's plain, Gold I
3. Frank - in - cense to of - fer have I; In - cense
4. Myrrh is mine: its bit - ter per - fume Breathes a
5. Glo - rious now be - hold him a - rise, King and

gifts, we trav - erse a - far Field and foun - tain,
bring to crown him a - gain; King for - ev - er,
owns a De - i - ty nigh; Prayer and prais - ing,
life of gath - er - ing gloom; Sor - rowing, sigh - ing,
God and Sac - ri - fice; "Al - le - lu - ia,

Moor and moun - tain, Fol - low - ing yon - der star.
Ceas - ing nev - er, O - ver us all to reign.
Glad - ly rais - ing, Wor - ship - ing God on high.
Bleed - ing, dy - ing, Sealed in the stone - cold tomb.
Al - le - lu - ia!" Sounds through the earth and skies.

O star of won - der, star of night, Star with

roy - al beau - ty bright, West - ward lead - ing,

still pro - ceed - ing, Guide us to the per - fect Light.

Text: Matthew 2:1–11; John H. Hopkins, Jr., 1820–1891, alt.
Tune: KINGS OF ORIENT, 88 44 6 with refrain; John H. Hopkins, Jr., 1820–1891

453 The People Who Walked in Darkness

Verses

1. The people who walked in darkness   A-waken to
2. For God has enlarged the nation,   And prospered the
3. The yoke of despair and bondage,   The chains and the
4. For us now a child is given,   For all the de-
5. How vast is our God's dominion!   How far truth and

see a great light. The people who dwelt in the land of the
fruit of its land. God's people are blest with the harvest of
slave-master's rod Are shattered and scattered like dust in a
spised and forlorn. The rule of compassion shall rest on his
mercy extend. The zeal of the Lord will accomplish its

shad-ow   Rise to a Star shining bright.
vic-t'ry,   Gift from a bountiful hand.
wind-storm   Loosed by the justice of God.
shoul-der.   God's own Messiah is born!
pur-pose: Justice shall reign without end.

Refrain

His name is

Won-der-ful, Coun-sel-or, Al-might-y God, Fa-ther for-ev-er,

Prince of Peace. Won-der-ful, Coun-sel-or, Al-might-y God,

To verses **D.C.**   *Last time*

Fa-ther for-ev-er, Prince of Peace.   Peace.

Text: Isaiah 9:1–6; Mary Louise Bringle, b.1953
Tune: ISAIAH 9, 8 8 12 7 with refrain; Sally Ann Morris, b.1952
© 2009, GIA Publications, Inc.

What Child Is This   454

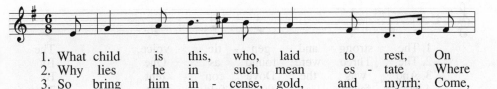

1. What child is this, who, laid to rest, On
2. Why lies he in such mean es - tate Where
3. So bring him in - cense, gold, and myrrh; Come,

Mar - y's lap is sleep - ing, Whom an - gels greet with
ox and ass are feed - ing? Good Chris - tian, fear; for
peas - ant, king, to own him. The King of kings sal -

an - thems sweet While shep - herds watch are keep - ing?
sin - ners here The si - lent Word is plead - ing.
va - tion brings; Let lov - ing hearts en - throne him.

This, this is Christ the King, Whom shep - herds guard and an-gels sing;

Haste, haste to bring him laud, The babe, the son of Mar - y.

Text: William C. Dix, 1837–1898
Tune: GREENSLEEVES, 8 7 8 7 with refrain; English melody, 16th C.; harm. by John Stainer, 1840–1901

455 The Strong and Gentle Voice

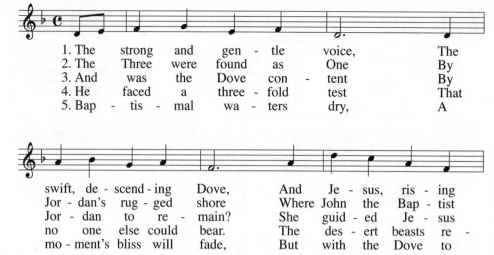

1. The strong and gen - tle voice, The
2. The Three were found as One By
3. And was the Dove con - tent By
4. He faced a three - fold test That
5. Bap - tis - mal wa - ters dry, A

swift, de - scend - ing Dove, And Je - sus, ris - ing
Jor - dan's rug - ged shore Where John the Bap - tist
Jor - dan to re - main? She guid - ed Je - sus
no one else could bear. The des - ert beasts re -
mo - ment's bliss will fade, But with the Dove to

from the stream, Met joy - ful - ly in love.
preached the way Of jus - tice for the poor.
on to know Temp - ta - tion, thirst, and pain.
mained with him And an - gels gave him care.
lead us on We need not be a - fraid.

Text: Adam M. L. Tice, b.1979, © 2009, GIA Publications, Inc.
Tune: NEW RESTORATION, SM; Sally Ann Morris, b.1952, © 1998, GIA Publications, Inc.

456 When Jesus Came to Jordan

1. When Je - sus came to Jor - dan To be bap-tized by John,
2. He came to share temp - ta - tion, Our ut - most woe and loss,
3. Come, Ho - ly Spir - it, aid us To keep the vows we make;

He did not come for par - don, But as the Sin - less One.
For us and our sal - va - tion To die up - on the cross.
This ver - y day in - vade us, And ev - 'ry bond - age break.

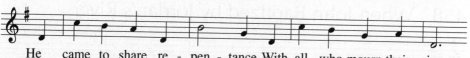

He came to share re - pen - tance With all who mourn their sins,
So when the Dove de - scend - ed On him, the Son of Man,
Come, give our lives di - rec - tion, The gift we cov - et most:

To speak the vi - tal sen - tence With which good news be - gins.
The hid - den years had end - ed, The age of grace be - gan.
To share the res - ur - rec - tion That leads to Pen - te - cost.

Text: Fred Pratt Green, 1903–2000
Tune: MERLE'S TUNE, 7 6 7 6 D; Hal H. Hopson, b.1933
© 1980, music, © 1983, Hope Publishing Company

To Jordan Jesus Humbly Came 457

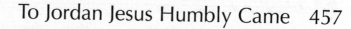

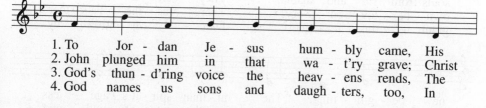

1. To Jor - dan Je - sus hum - bly came, His
2. John plunged him in that wa - t'ry grave; Christ
3. God's thun - d'ring voice the heav - ens rends, The
4. God names us sons and daugh - ters, too, In

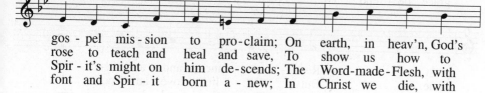

gos - pel mis - sion to pro-claim; On earth, in heav'n, God's
rose to teach and heal and save, To show us how to
Spir - it's might on him de-scends; The Word-made-Flesh, with
font and Spir - it born a - new; In Christ we die, with

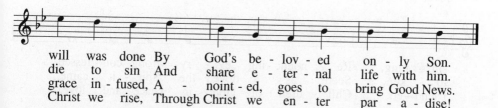

will was done By God's be - lov - ed on - ly Son.
die to sin And share e - ter - nal life with him.
grace in - fused, A - noint - ed, goes to bring Good News.
Christ we rise, Through Christ we en - ter par - a - dise!

Text: Alan J. Hommerding, b.1956, © 2004, World Library Publications
Tune: WINCHESTER NEW, LM; adapt. from *Musikalisches Handbuch*, Hamburg, 1690

458 When John Baptized by Jordan's River

1. When John bap-tized by Jor-dan's riv-er
2. There as the Lord, bap-tized and pray-ing,
3. O Son of Man, our na-ture shar-ing,

In faith and hope the peo-ple came, That John and
Rose from the stream, the sin-less one, A voice was
In whose o-be-dience all are blest, Sav-ior, our

Jor-dan might de-liv-er Their trou-bled
heard from heav-en say-ing, "This is my
sins and sor-rows bear-ing, Hear us and

souls from sin and shame. They came to seek a
own be-lov-ed Son." There as the Fa-ther's
grant us this re-quest: Dai-ly to grow, by

new be-gin-ning, The hu-man spir-it's age-less
word was spo-ken, Not in the pow'r of wind and
grace de-fend-ed, Filled with the Spir-it from a-

quest, Re-pen-tance, and an end of
flame, But of his love and peace the
bove; In Christ bap-tized, be-loved, be-

sin-ning, Re-nounc-ing ev-'ry wrong con-fessed.
to-ken, Seen as a dove, the Spir-it came.
friend-ed, Chil-dren of God in peace and love.

Text: Timothy Dudley-Smith, b.1926, © 1984, Hope Publishing Company
Tune: RENDEZ À DIEU, 9 8 9 8 D; *Genevan Psalter*, 1551; attr. to Louis Bourgeois, c.1510–1561

Jesus, Tempted in the Desert   459

1. Je - sus, tempt - ed in the des - ert,
2. Je - sus, tempt - ed at the tem - ple,
3. Je - sus, tempt - ed on the moun - tain
4. When we face temp - ta - tion's pow - er,

Lone - ly, hun - gry, filled with dread: "Use your pow'r," the
High a - bove its an - cient wall: "Throw your - self from
By the lure of vast do - main: "Fall be - fore me!
Lone - ly, strug - gling, filled with dread, Christ, who knew the

tempt - er tells him; "Turn these bar - ren rocks to bread!"
loft - y tur - ret; An - gels wait to break your fall!"
Be my ser - vant! Glo - ry, fame, you're sure to gain!"
tempt - er's ho - ur, Come and be our liv - ing bread.

"Not a - lone by bread," he an - swers,
Je - sus shuns such emp - ty mar - vels,
Je - sus sees the daz - zling vi - sion,
By your grace, pro - tect, pre - serve us

"Can the hu - man heart be filled.
Feats that fick - le crowds re - quest:
Turns his eyes an - oth - er way:
Lest we fall, your trust be - tray.

On - ly by the Word that calls us
"God, whose grace pro - tects, pre - serves us,
"God a - lone de - serves our hom - age!
Yours, a - bove all oth - er voic - es,

Is our deep - est hun - ger stilled!"
We must nev - er vain - ly test."
God a - lone will I o - bey!"
Be the Word we hear, o - bey.

Text: Matthew 4:1–11, Luke 4:1–13; Herman G. Stuempfle, Jr., 1923–2007, © 1993, GIA Publications, Inc.
Tune: EBENEZER, 8 7 8 7 D; Thomas J. Williams, 1869–1944

460 Restore Us, O God

Canon

Re - store us, O God; let your face shine,

let your face shine, that we may be saved.

we may be saved.

Repeat until completion of canon.

Text: Psalm 80:3, 7, 19
Tune: James E. Clemens, © 2008, James E. Clemens

461 Lord, Who throughout These Forty Days

1. Lord, who through - out these for - ty days For
2. As you with Sa - tan did con - tend And
3. As you did hun - ger and did thirst, So
4. And through these days of pen - i - tence, And
5. A - bide with us that, when this life Of

us did fast and pray, Teach us to o - ver -
did the vic - t'ry win, O give us strength in
teach us, gra - cious Lord, To die to self, and
through your Pas - sion - tide, For ev - er - more, in
suf - fer - ing is past, An East - er of un -

come our sins, And close by you to stay.
you to fight, In you to con - quer sin.
on - ly live By your most ho - ly word.
life and death, O Lord, with us a - bide.
end - ing joy We may at - tain at last!

Text: Claudia F. Hernaman, 1838–1898, alt.
Tune: ST. FLAVIAN, CM; John Day's *Psalter,* 1562; harm. based on the original *faux-bourdon* setting

Somebody's Knockin' at Your Door   462

Some-bod-y's knock-in' at your door. Some-bod-y's

knock-in' at your door. O sin-ner, why don't you

an-swer? Some-bod-y's knock-in' at your door.

Solo: / *All:*

1. Knocks like Je-sus,
2. Can't you hear him?
3. Je-sus calls you,
4. Can't you trust him?

Some-bod-y's knock-in' at your door.

Solo: / *All:*

Knocks like Je-sus,
Can't you hear him?
Je-sus calls you,
Can't you trust him?

Some-bod-y's knock-in' at your door.

O sin-ner, why don't you an-swer?

Some-bod-y's knock-in' at your door.

Text: African American spiritual
Tune: SOMEBODY'S KNOCKIN', Irregular; African American spiritual; harm. by Richard Proulx, 1937–2010, © 1986, GIA Publications, Inc.

463 From Ashes to the Living Font

1. From ash - es to the liv - ing font Your
2. Through fast - ing, prayer, and char - i - ty Your
3. *Insert appropriate stanza*
4. From ash - es to the liv - ing font Your

Church must jour - ney, Lord, Bap - tized in grace, in
voice speaks deep with - in, Re - turn - ing us to

Church must jour - ney still, Through cross and tomb to

grace re - newed By your most ho - ly word.
ways of truth And turn - ing us from sin.

East - er joy, In Spir - it - fire ful - filled.

Year A

Sundays I & II

3. From desert to the mountaintop
In Christ our way we see,
So, tempered by temptation's might
We might transfigured be.

Sunday III

3. For thirsting hearts let waters flow,
Our fainting souls revive;
And at the well your waters give
Our everlasting life.

Sunday IV

3. We sit beside the road and plead,
"Come, save us, David's son!"
Now with your vision heal our eyes,
The world's true Light alone.

Sunday V

3. Our graves split open, bring us back,
Your promise to proclaim;
To darkened tombs call out, "Arise!"
And glorify your name.

Year B

Sundays I & II

3. From desert to the mountaintop
In Christ our way we see,
So, tempered by temptation's might
We might transfigured be.

Sunday III

3. Come, purify our hearts and lives,
Cast out our sinful ways;
As temples of the Spirit, cleansed,
Restore us for your praise.

Sunday IV

3. The Son of Man is lifted up,
Our eyes behold the sign:
You are God's own beloved Son,
The source of life divine.

Sunday V

3. Unless, like grains of wheat, we fall
Upon the ground to die,
We cannot share the gift of life,
Raised up, like you, on high.

Year C
Sundays I & II
3. From desert to the mountaintop
   In Christ our way we see,
   So, tempered by temptation's might
   We might transfigured be.

Sunday III
3. You call us to be penitent,
   You tend us patiently,
   Preserving us from perishing,
   So fruitful we might be.

Sunday IV
3. When we repent, you run to us,
   Forgiving arms spread wide;
   You celebrate when we return,
   And come home to your side.

Sunday V
3. When we self-righteously condemn,
   You ask: "Who has no sin?"
   We hear you say "Go, sin no more."
   New life in you begins.

Text: Alan J. Hommerding, b.1956, © 1994, 2011, World Library Publications
Tune: ST. FLAVIAN, CM; John Day's *Psalter,* 1562

Crucem Tuam / O Lord, Your Cross   464

Ostinato Refrain

Cru - cem tu - am a - do - rá - mus Dó - mi - ne, re - sur - re - cti - ó - nem tu - am lau - dá - mus Dó - mi - ne. Lau - dá - mus et glo - ri - fi - cá - mus. Re - sur - re - cti - ó - nem tu - am lau - dá - mus Dó - mi - ne.

O Lord, your cross we a - dore and glo - ri - fy; for your ho - ly res - ur - rec - tion we praise you, Lord of life. We praise you and we glo - ri - fy you. For your ho - ly res - ur - rec - tion we praise you, Lord of life.

Text: Taizé Community, 1991
Tune: Jacques Berthier, 1923–1994
© 1991, Les Presses de Taizé, GIA Publications, Inc., agent

465 The Cross of Jesus

1. Come, O God, re - new your peo - ple,
2. Deep with - in cre - ate a new heart;
3. In the dark - ness that sur - rounds us
4. Call us forth to walk in jus - tice;

We who long to see your face.
Melt a - way the win - ter chill.
We have lost you from our sight.
Res - cue us from sin and grave.

Strength - en hearts that have grown fee - ble;
Help us now to make a new start;
E - ven though your love has found us,
Through the pow - er of your Spir - it,

Fill our lives with truth and grace.
Help us now to know your will.
We em - brace the powers of night.
Breathe in us the breath that saves.

On - ly you can win our free - dom;
Washed in wa - ters of for - give - ness,
Scat - ter now our deep - est dark - ness;
Strength - en us in our com - mun - ion,

On - ly you can bring us peace.
Cleansed in wa - ters of new birth,
Guide our hearts in - to the light.
One in Word and cup and bread.

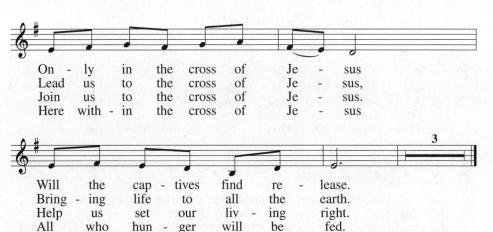

On - ly in the cross of Je - sus
Lead us to the cross of Je - sus,
Join us to the cross of Je - sus.
Here with - in the cross of Je - sus

3

Will the cap - tives find re - lease.
Bring - ing life to all the earth.
Help us set our liv - ing right.
All who hun - ger will be fed.

Text: Francis Patrick O'Brien, b.1958
Tune: TREMONT, 8 7 8 7 D; Francis Patrick O'Brien, b.1958
© 1996, GIA Publications, Inc.

Forty Days and Forty Nights   466

1. For - ty days and for - ty nights You were fast - ing
2. Shall not we your sor - row share And from world - ly
3. Then, if Sa - tan on us press, Flesh or spir - it
4. So shall we have peace di - vine; Ho - lier glad - ness
5. Keep, O keep us, Sav - ior dear, Ev - er con - stant

in the wild; For - ty days and for - ty nights
joys ab - stain, Fast - ing with un - ceas - ing prayer,
to as - sail, Vic - tor in the wil - der - ness,
ours shall be. 'Round us, too, shall an - gels shine,
by your side, That with you we may ap - pear

Tempt - ed, and yet un - de - filed.
Strong with you to suf - fer pain?
Grant we may not faint nor fail!
Such as served you faith - ful - ly.
At the e - ter - nal East - er - tide.

Text: George H. Smyttan, 1822–1870, alt.
Tune: HEINLEIN, 7 7 7 7; attr. to Martin Herbst, 1654–1681, *Nürnbergisches Gesangbuch,* 1676

467 The Glory of These Forty Days

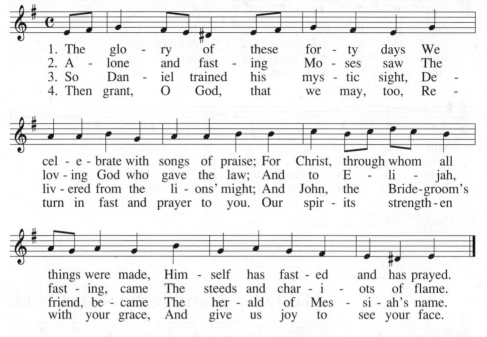

1. The glo - ry of these for - ty days We
2. A - lone and fast - ing Mo - ses saw The
3. So Dan - iel trained his mys - tic sight, De -
4. Then grant, O God, that we may, too, Re -

cel - e - brate with songs of praise; For Christ, through whom all
lov - ing God who gave the law; And to E - li - jah,
liv - ered from the li - ons' might; And John, the Bride-groom's
turn in fast and prayer to you. Our spir - its strength - en

things were made, Him - self has fast - ed and has prayed.
fast - ing, came The steeds and char - i - ots of flame.
friend, be - came The her - ald of Mes - si - ah's name.
with your grace, And give us joy to see your face.

Text: *Clarum decus jejunii*; ascr. to St. Gregory the Great, c.540–604; tr. by Maurice F. Bell, 1862–1947, alt.
Tune: ERHALT UNS HERR, LM; Klug's *Geistliche Lieder*, 1543; harm. by Ronald F. Krisman, b.1946, © 2011, GIA Publications, Inc.

468 Before the Fruit Is Ripened by the Sun

1. Be - fore the fruit is rip - ened by the sun,
2. Be - fore our East - er prais - es loud - ly ring,
3. Be - fore we gain the grace that comes through loss,

Be - fore the pet - als or the leaves un - coil,
Be - fore the mas - sive rock is rolled a - side,
Be - fore we live by more than bread and breath,

Be - fore the first fine silk - en root is spun,
Be - fore the fear of death has lost its sting,
Be - fore we lift in joy an emp - ty cross,

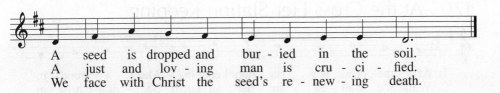

A   seed   is dropped and   bur - ied   in   the   soil.
A   just   and lov - ing   man   is cru - ci - fied.
We   face   with Christ the   seed's re - new - ing death.

Text: Thomas H. Troeger, b.1945, © 1986, Oxford University Press, Inc.
Tune: SURSUM CORDA, 10 10 10 10; Alfred M. Smith, 1879–1971, © Mrs. Alfred M. Smith

Parce Dómine / Spare Us, Gracious Lord   469

Par - ce Dó - mi - ne,   par - ce pó - pu - lo   tu - o:
Spare us, gra - cious Lord,   *spare your peo - ple, who   have   sinned:*

ne   in ae - tér - num   i - ra - scá - ris no - bis.
spare us, lest we face   your re - proach for - ev - er.

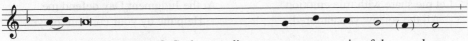

1. Have   mercy on me, O God, according to your mer - ci - ful   love;
2. Wash   me completely   from my   in - iq - ui - ty,
3. My   transgressions,   tru - ly   I   know   them;
4. A -   gainst you, you   a - lone, have I   sinned;
5. Cre - ate a   pure heart for me, O God;

D.C.

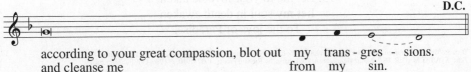

according to your great compassion, blot out my trans - gres - sions.
and cleanse me   from my   sin.
my sin is always   be - fore me.
what is evil in your sight   I   have   done.
renew a steadfast spirit   with - in   me.

Text: *Parce Domine*; Joel 2:17; tr. by Ronald F. Krisman, b.1946, © 2011, GIA Publications, Inc.; verses, Psalm 51:3–6, 12, *The Revised Grail Psalms*,
© 2010, Conception Abbey and The Grail, admin. by GIA Publications, Inc.
Tune: PARCE DOMINE; Mode I with Tonus Peregrinus; acc. by Robert LeBlanc, b.1948, © 1986, GIA Publications, Inc.

470 At the Cross Her Station Keeping

1. At the cross her sta - tion keep-ing, Mar - y stood in
2. While she wait - ed in her an-guish, See - ing Christ in
3. With what pain and des - o - la - tion, With what no - ble
4. Ev - er pa - tient in her yearn-ing, Though her tear - filled

sor - row, weep - ing, When her Son was cru - ci - fied.
tor - ment lan - guish, Bit - ter sor - row pierced her heart.
res - ig - na - tion, Mar - y watched her dy - ing Son.
eyes were burn - ing, Mar - y gazed up - on her Son.

5. Who, that sorrow contemplating,
   On that passion meditating,
   Would not share the Virgin's grief?

6. Christ she saw, for our salvation,
   Scourged with cruel acclamation,
   Bruised and beaten by the rod.

7. Christ she saw with life-blood failing,
   All her anguish unavailing,
   Saw him breathe his very last.

8. Mary, fount of love's devotion,
   Let me share with true emotion
   All the sorrow you endured.

9. Virgin, ever interceding,
   Hear me in my fervent pleading:
   Fire me with your love of Christ.

10. Mother, may this prayer be granted:
    That Christ's love may be implanted
    In the depths of my poor soul.

11. At the cross, your sorrow sharing,
    All your grief and torment bearing,
    Let me stand and mourn with you.

12. Fairest maid of all creation,
    Queen of hope and consolation,
    Let me feel your grief sublime.

13. Virgin, in your love befriend me,
    At the Judgment Day defend me.
    Help me by your constant prayer.

14. Savior, when my life shall leave me,
    Through your mother's prayers receive me
    With the fruits of victory.

15. Let me to your love be taken,
    Let my soul in death awaken
    To the joys of Paradise.

Text: *Stabat mater dolorosa;* Jacopone da Todi, 1230–1306; trans. by Anthony G. Petti, 1932–1985, © 1971, Faber Music, Ltd.
Tune: STABAT MATER, 88 7; Mainz *Gesangbuch,* 1661; harm. by Richard Proulx, 1937–2010, © 1986, GIA Publications, Inc.

O Sun of Justice 471

1. O Sun of jus - tice, Je - sus Christ, Dis - pel the
2. In this our "time ac - cept - a - ble" Touch ev - 'ry
3. The day, your day, in beau - ty dawns When in your
4. O lov - ing Trin - i - ty, our God, To you we

dark - ness of our hearts, Till your blest light makes
heart with sor - row, Lord, That, turned from sin, re -
light earth blooms a - new; Led back a - gain to
bow through end - less days, And in your grace new -

night - time flee And brings the joys your day im - parts.
newed by grace, We may press on toward love's re - ward.
life's true way, May we, for - giv'n, re - joice in you.
born we sing New hymns of grat - i - tude and praise.

Text: *Jam Christe sol justitiae;* Latin, 6th C.; tr. by Peter J. Scagnelli, b.1949, © 1982
Tune: JESU DULCIS MEMORIA, LM; Mode I; acc. by Richard Proulx, 1937–2010, © 1975, GIA Publications, Inc.

This Is the Time of Fulfillment 472

This is the time of ful - fill - ment! The

reign of God is at hand!

Text: Mark 1:15, James J. Chepponis, b.1956
Tune: James J. Chepponis, b.1956
© 1994, GIA Publications, Inc.

473 Hear Us, Almighty Lord / Atténde Dómine

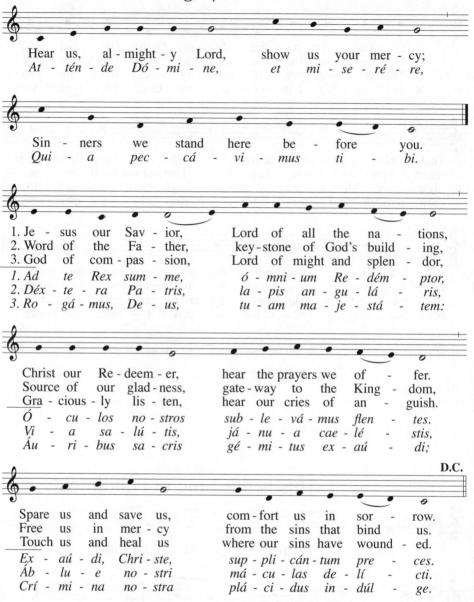

Hear us, al - might - y Lord, show us your mer - cy;
At - tén - de Dó - mi - ne, et mi - se - ré - re,

Sin - ners we stand here be - fore you.
Qui - a pec - cá - vi - mus ti - bi.

1. Je - sus our Sav - ior, Lord of all the na - tions,
2. Word of the Fa - ther, key - stone of God's build - ing,
3. God of com - pas - sion, Lord of might and splen - dor,
1. Ad te Rex sum - me, ó - mni - um Re - dém - ptor,
2. Déx - te - ra Pa - tris, la - pis an - gu - lá - ris,
3. Ro - gá - mus, De - us, tu - am ma - je - stá - tem:

Christ our Re - deem - er, hear the prayers we of - fer.
Source of our glad - ness, gate - way to the King - dom,
Gra - cious - ly lis - ten, hear our cries of an - guish.
Ó - cu - los no - stros sub - le - vá - mus flen - tes.
Vi - a sa - lú - tis, já - nu - a cae - lé - stis,
Áu - ri - bus sa - cris gé - mi - tus ex - aú - di;

D.C.

Spare us and save us, com - fort us in sor - row.
Free us in mer - cy from the sins that bind us.
Touch us and heal us where our sins have wound - ed.
Ex - aú - di, Chri - ste, sup - pli - cán - tum pre - ces.
Áb - lu - e no - stri má - cu - las de - lí - cti.
Crí - mi - na no - stra plá - ci - dus in - dúl - ge.

4. Humbly confessing that we have offended,
   Stripped of illusions, naked in our sorrow,
   Pardon, Lord Jesus, those your blood has ransomed.

5. Innocent captive, you were led to slaughter,
   Sentenced by sinners when they brought false witness.
   Keep from damnation those your death has rescued.

4. *Tibi fatémur, crímina admíssa,*
   Contríto corde pándimus occúlta;
   Tua, Redémptor, píetas ignóscat.

5. *Ínnocens captus, nec repúgnans ductus.*
   Téstibus falsis, pro ímpiis damnátus:
   Quos redemísti, tu consérva, Christe.

Text: *Attende Domine*, Latin, 10th C.; tr. by Ralph Wright, OSB, b.1938, © 1980, ICEL
Tune: ATTENDE DOMINE, 11 11 11 with refrain; Mode V; acc. by Richard Proulx, 1937–2010, © 1975, GIA Publications, Inc.

Again We Keep This Solemn Fast 474

1. A - gain we keep this sol - emn fast,
   A gift of faith from a - ges past,
   These for - ty days that, year by year,
   Bid con - trite hearts to Christ draw near.

2. The law and proph - ets from of old
   In fig - ured ways this Lent fore - told,
   Which Christ, all a - ges' Lord and Guide,
   In these last days has sanc - ti - fied.

3. More spar - ing, there - fore, let us make
   The words we speak, the food we take,
   Our sleep, our laugh - ter, ev - 'ry sense;
   Learn peace through ho - ly pen - i - tence.

4. Let us a - void each harm - ful way
   That lures the care - less mind a - stray;
   By watch - ful prayer our spir - its free
   From schem - ing of the En - e - my.

5. We pray, O bless - ed Three in One,
   Our God while end - less a - ges run,
   That this, our Lent of for - ty days,
   May bring us growth and give you praise.

Text: *Ex more docti mystico*; ascr. to St. Gregory the Great, c.540–604; tr. by Peter J. Scagnelli, b.1949, after John M. Neale, 1818–1866, © 1975, 2011
Tune: ERHALT UNS HERR, LM; Klug's *Geistliche Lieder*, 1543; harm. by J. S. Bach, 1685–1750

475 Return to God / Volvamos Hoy a Nuestro Dios

Refrain

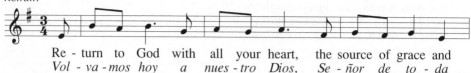

Re - turn to God with all your heart, the source of grace and
Vol - va - mos hoy a nues - tro Dios, Se - ñor de to - da

mer - cy; come seek the ten - der faith-ful-ness of God.
gra - cia, bus - can - do su per - dón y le - al - tad.

Verses

1. Now the time of grace has come,
   the day of salvation;
   come and learn now the way of our God.

1. *Día de la salvación,*
   y tiempo favorable;
   caminemos por las sendas de Dios.

2. I will take your heart of stone
   and place a heart within you,
   a heart of compassion and love.

2. *Quitaré tu corazón de piedra;*
   te daré un corazón
   de amor y compassión.

3. If you break the chains of oppression,
   if you set the pris'ner free;
   if you share your bread with the hungry,
   give protection to the lost;
   give a shelter to the homeless,
   clothe the naked in your midst,
   then your light shall break forth
   like the dawn.

3. *Si tú rompes vínculos injustos,*
   y a los presos das libertad;
   ofreciendo pan al hambriento,
   protección al extraviado;
   dando abrigo a quien está
      sin techo,
   y vestido al desnudo;
   surgirá tu luz como la aurora.

Text: Marty Haugen, b.1950; tr. by Ronald F. Krisman, b.1946
Tune: Marty Haugen, b.1950
© 1990, 1991, 2005, GIA Publications, Inc.

476 Restore in Us, O God

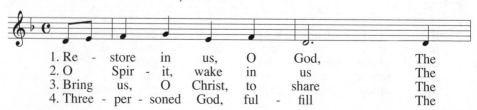

1. Re - store in us, O God, The
2. O Spir - it, wake in us The
3. Bring us, O Christ, to share The
4. Three - per - soned God, ful - fill The

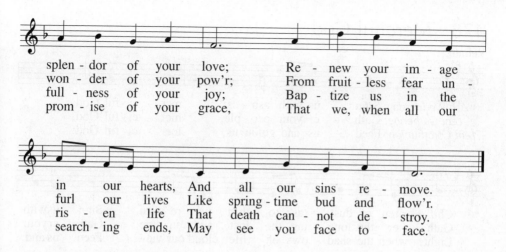

splen - dor of your love; Re - new your im - age
won - der of your pow'r; From fruit - less fear un -
full - ness of your joy; Bap - tize us in the
prom - ise of your grace, That we, when all our

in our hearts, And all our sins re - move.
furl our lives Like spring - time bud and flow'r.
ris - en life That death can - not de - stroy.
search - ing ends, May see you face to face.

Text: Carl P. Daw, Jr., b.1944, © 1989, Hope Publishing Company
Tune: NEW RESTORATION, SM; Sally Ann Morris, b.1952, © 1998, GIA Publications, Inc.

Once We Sang and Danced with Gladness 477

1. Once we sang and danced with glad - ness, Once de -
2. All the wil - lows bow in weep - ing, All the
3. God, who came to dwell a - mong us, God, who
4. Come, O Christ, a - mong these ash - es, Come to

light filled ev - 'ry breath; Now we sit a - mong the
riv - ers rage and moan, As cre - a - tion joins our
suf - fered our dis - grace, From your own heart, grieved and
wipe our tears a - way, Death de - stroy and sor - row

ash - es, All our dreams de - stroyed by death.
plead - ing: "God, do not leave us a - lone."
wound - ed, Come the rich - es of your grace.
ban - ish; Now and al - ways, come and stay.

Text: Susan Briehl, b.1952, © 2003, GIA Publications, Inc.
Tune: KAS DZIEDAJA, 8 7 8 7; Latvian melody; acc. by Robert J. Batastini, b.1942, © 1995, GIA Publications, Inc.

478 Merciful God

Refrain

Ash Wednesday: Sign us with ash - es, mer - ci - ful God,
Lent Gathering: Gath - er your peo - ple, mer - ci - ful God,
Lent Communion: Feed us and guide us, mer - ci - ful God:

Chil - dren of dust, as to dust we re - turn. Sign us with
Gath - er the long - ing, the lost, and un - sure. Gath - er your
Light, when the shad - ows of life cloud our view. Feed us and

ash - es, mer - ci - ful God; Mark us and make us your
peo - ple, mer - ci - ful God, Name us and claim us as
guide us, mer - ci - ful God, Peo - ple who hun - ger for

[To verses] [Last time]

own. own, mark us and make us your own.
yours. yours, name us and claim us as yours.
you. you, peo - ple who hun - ger for you.

Verses

1. Sure - ly, you a - lone can save us. You pay our price with
2. Sure - ly, you a - lone up - hold us. You give us strength for
3. Sure - ly, you a - lone can heal us. Yours is the will to
4. Sure - ly, you a - lone can free us. You break the bonds of
5. Sure - ly, you a - lone re - fine us. You give us grace for
6. Sure - ly, you a - lone re - deem us. You fill our dust with

pre - cious blood. Reach - ing through your great com -
all our needs. Shield - ing with a fa - ther's
make us whole. Sooth - ing with a moth - er's
guilt and sin. Brac - ing, till we walk up -
lives made new, Forg - ing, through your fire and
ho - ly breath. Burst - ing from the grave in

D.C.

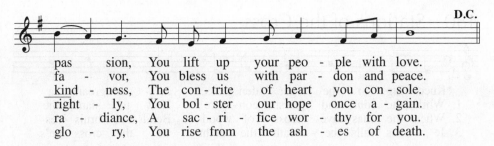

pas - sion, You lift up your peo - ple with love.
fa - vor, You bless us with par - don and peace.
kind - ness, The con - trite of heart you con - sole.
right - ly, You bol - ster our hope once a - gain.
ra - diance, A sac - ri - fice wor - thy for you.
glo - ry, You rise from the ash - es of death.

Text: Mary Louise Bringle, b.1953, © 2006, 2009, GIA Publications, Inc.
Tune: INDIGO, LM with refrain; Tony E. Alonso, b.1980, © 2009, GIA Publications, Inc.

As the Winter Days Grow Longer   479

1. As the win - ter days grow long - er, Draw - ing short the
2. As the vines burst in - to blos - som, Fra - grant in the
3. As we jour - ney through this sea - son, Pil - grims through a

hours of night; As our ea - ger ex - pec - ta - tion
morn - ing air, Lift - ing spir - its with their sweet-ness,
thirst - y land, Quench us with your liv - ing pres - ence;

Waits for East - er's dawn - ing light— Yearn - ing peo - ple,
Lur - ing hearts to thank - ful prayer— Lent - en peo - ple,
Guide us with your lov - ing hand. Wan - d'ring peo - ple,

here we gath - er, Turn - ing watch-ful eyes to you:
here we gath - er, Seek - ing lives re - freshed from sin.
here we gath - er, Called to rest a - long our way.

God who bless - es earth with spring - time,
God who bless - es earth with spring - time,
God who bless - es earth with spring - time,

Shine with - in our world a - new!
Bloom with - in our hearts a - gain!
Grant us Sab - bath joy this day!

Text: Mary Louise Bringle, b.1953, © 2006, GIA Publications, Inc.
Tune: SUO GAN, 8 7 8 7 D; Welsh melody; arr. by Nicholas Palmer, b.1963, © 2008, GIA Publications, Inc.

480 Stations of the Cross

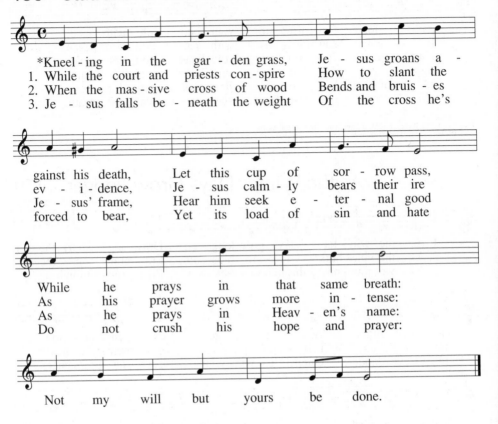

*Kneel-ing in the gar-den grass, Je-sus groans a-gainst his death, Let this cup of sor-row pass, While he prays in that same breath: Not my will but yours be done.

1. While the court and priests con-spire How to slant the ev-i-dence, Je-sus calm-ly bears their ire As his prayer grows more in-tense: Not my will but yours be done.

2. When the mas-sive cross of wood Bends and bruis-es Je-sus' frame, Hear him seek e-ter-nal good As he prays in Heav-en's name: Not my will but yours be done.

3. Je-sus falls be-neath the weight Of the cross he's forced to bear, Yet its load of sin and hate Do not crush his hope and prayer: Not my will but yours be done.

This stanza begins the devotions. Stanzas 1–14 accompany each station.

1. Jesus is condemned to death

2. Jesus carries his Cross

3. Jesus falls the first time

4. Jesus meets his afflicted mother
Jesus reads in Mary's eyes
all the sorrow mothers bear,
and he prays his friend supplies
grace to strengthen her own prayer:
 Not my will but yours be done.

5. Simon of Cyrene helps Jesus to carry his Cross
We with Simon of Cyrene
help the Savior bear the cross.
Step by step we slowly glean
what true faith and prayer will cost:
 Not my will but yours be done.

6. Veronica wipes the face of Jesus
Seek the courage and the grace
that Veronica displays
when she wipes the bleeding face
of the one who bravely prays:
    Not my will but yours be done.

7. Jesus falls the second time
Jesus trips and falls again
as he struggles through the street
where the mob's unceasing din
mocks the prayer his lips repeat:
    Not my will but yours be done.

8. Jesus meets the women of Jerusalem
Christ directs the women's tears
toward the coming judgment day
when God weighs our faithless years
with our willingness to pray:
    Not my will but yours be done.

9. Jesus falls a third time
Jesus stumbles one last time,
nearly broken by the load,
yet by prayer finds strength to climb
Calvary's final stretch of road:
    Not my will but yours be done.

10. Jesus is stripped of his clothes
Naked to the sun and clouds
and the jeers and gawking stare
of the soldiers and the crowds,
Christ continues with his prayer:
    Not my will but yours be done.

11. Jesus is nailed to the Cross
While the soldiers throw their dice,
they ignore their victim's groans,
lost to them the sacrifice
and the prayer that Jesus moans:
    Not my will but yours be done.

12. Jesus dies on the Cross
Jesus gives one loud last cry
at the moment of his death
while his prayer moves heaven's sky
with his final, parting breath:
    Not my will but yours be done.

**13. The body of Jesus is taken
    down from the Cross**
As they take the body down
and they wrap it in a sheet,
in their hearts they hear the sound
that his lips no more repeat:
    Not my will but yours be done.

14. Jesus is laid in the tomb
Quiet is the hollowed cave.
Peace and tears and grief descend.
Mourners offer at the grave
what they learned from Christ their
    friend:
    Not my will but yours be done.

Text: Thomas H. Troeger, b.1945, © 1994, Oxford University Press
Tune: VIA CRUCIS, 7 7 7 7 with refrain; William P. Rowan, b.1951, © 1995, GIA Publications, Inc.

481　Palm Sunday Processional

Cantor:

1. When they heard that Je - sus was com - ing,
2. Spread their cloaks and branch - es be - fore him,
3. Blest is he, like Da - vid be - fore him.
4. Guid - ing cloud and pil - lar of fire,
5. Vi - sion blest, and hope for the fu - ture,
6. Won - drous bread and stream in the des - ert,
7. Eye of God, who sees to the heart of us,
8. Ris - ing sun, the light of the world,
9. Friend in death, who weeps for our dy - ing,
10. Friend in death, who wakes us to new life,

Assembly:

Sing ho - san - na to the cho - sen one!

Cantor:

All the peo - ple went out to meet him.
Chil - dren sang, with palm branch-es wav - ing.
Blest is he, God's bless - ing up - on him.
Sa - tan's foe and friend of the sin - ner.
God's be - lov - ed, ra - diant with glo - ry.
Heav'n - ly food and God's liv - ing wa - ter.
Heal - ing touch and sight for our blind - ness.
Word of life, who gives us the Spir - it.
Friend in death, who rolls back the stone for us.
Friend in life: we sing glad ho - san - nas.

Assembly:

Sing ho - san - na to the cho - sen one!

Sing ho - san - na, sing ho - san - na,

sing ho - san - na to the cho - sen one!

Text: Rory Cooney, b.1952
Tune: Rory Cooney, b.1952
© 1999, GIA Publications, Inc.

No Tramp of Soldiers' Marching Feet   482

1. No tramp of sol - diers' march - ing feet With
2. And yet he comes. The chil - dren cheer; With
3. What fad - ing flow'rs his road a - dorn; The
4. Now he, who bore for mor - tals' sake The

ban - ners and with drums, No sound of mu - sic's
palms his path is strown. With ev - 'ry step the
palms, how soon laid down! No bloom or leaf but
cross and all its pains And chose a ser - vant's

mar - tial beat: "The King of glo - ry comes!" To
cross draws near: The King of glo - ry's throne. A -
on - ly thorn The King of glo - ry's crown. The
form to take, The King of glo - ry reigns. Ho -

greet what pomp of king - ly pride No
stride a colt he pass - es by As
sol - diers mock, the rab - ble cries, The
san - na to the Sav - ior's Name Till

bells in tri - umph ring, No cit - y gates swing
loud ho - san - nas ring, Or else the ver - y
streets with tu - mult ring, As Pi - late to the
heav - en's raf - ters ring, And all the ran - somed

o - pen wide: "Be - hold, be - hold your King!"
stones would cry: "Be - hold, be - hold your King!"
mob re - plies: "Be - hold, be - hold your King!"
host pro - claim: "Be - hold, be - hold your King!"

Text: Timothy Dudley-Smith, b.1926, © 1984, Hope Publishing Company
Tune: KINGSFOLD, CMD; English melody; harm. by Ralph Vaughan Williams, 1872–1958

483 All Glory, Laud, and Honor

Refrain

All glo - ry, laud, and hon - or To you, Re-deem-er, King!

To whom the lips of chil - dren Made sweet ho - san - nas ring.

Verses

1. You are the King of Is - ra - el And Da - vid's roy - al Son,
2. The com - pa - ny of an - gels Are prais - ing you on high;
3. The peo - ple of the He - brews With palms be - fore you went;
4. To you, be - fore your pas - sion, They sang their hymns of praise.
5. Their prais - es you ac - cept - ed; Ac - cept the prayers we bring,

D.C.

Now in the Lord's Name com - ing, Our King and Bless - ed One.
And we, with all cre - a - tion, In cho - rus make re - ply.
Our praise and prayers and an - thems Be - fore you we pre - sent.
To you, now high ex - alt - ed, Our mel - o - dy we raise.
Great source of love and good - ness, Our Sav - ior and our King.

Text: *Gloria, laus et honor;* Theodulph of Orléans, c.760–821; tr. by John M. Neale, 1818–1866, alt.
Tune: ST. THEODULPH, 7 6 7 6 with refrain; Melchior Teschner, 1584–1635

484 Stay with Me

Ostinato Refrain

Stay with me, re - main here with me, watch and
Spanish: Ve - la - ré con - ti - go, Se - ñor, mien - tras yo
German: Blei - bet hier und wa - chet mit mir, wa - chet und

pray, watch and pray.
vi - va, mien - tras yo vi - va.
be - tet, wa - chet und be - tet.

Text: Matthew 26:36–42; Taizé Community
Tune: Jacques Berthier, 1923–1994
© 1984, Les Presses de Taizé, GIA Publications, Inc., agent

So You Must Do 485

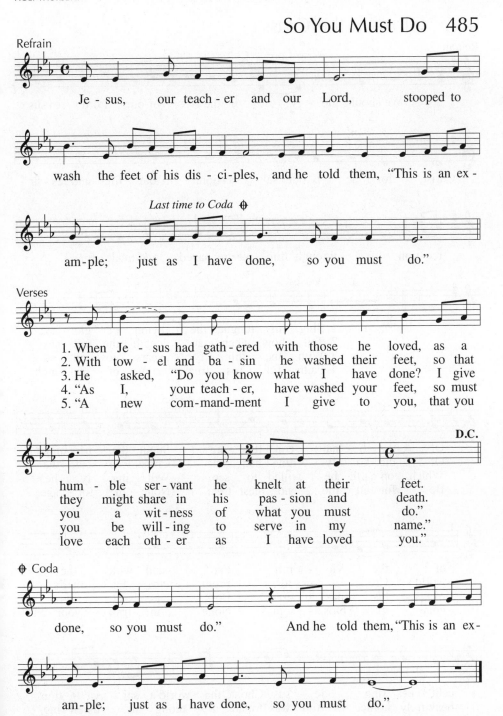

Refrain

Je - sus, our teach - er and our Lord, stooped to wash the feet of his dis - ci - ples, and he told them, "This is an ex - am - ple; just as I have done, so you must do."

Last time to Coda

Verses

1. When Je - sus had gath - ered with those he loved, as a hum - ble ser - vant he knelt at their feet.
2. With tow - el and ba - sin he washed their feet, so that they might share in his pas - sion and death.
3. He asked, "Do you know what I have done? I give you a wit - ness of what you must do."
4. "As I, your teach - er, have washed your feet, so must you be will - ing to serve in my name."
5. "A new com - mand - ment I give to you, that you love each oth - er as I have loved you."

D.C.

Coda

done, so you must do." And he told them, "This is an ex - am - ple; just as I have done, so you must do."

Text: John 13:1–15, adapt. by Marty Haugen, b.1950
Tune: Marty Haugen, b.1950
© 1998, GIA Publications, Inc.

486 Glory in the Cross

Refrain

We should glo - ry in the cross of our Lord Je - sus Christ, for he is our sal - va - tion, our life and res - ur - rec - tion; through him we are saved and made free.

4   Verses

1. Sing, my tongue, the hymn of glo - ry;
2. Tell how, when at length the full - ness
3. With the thir - ty years now end - ed,
4. Faith - ful Cross, true sign of tri - umph,

Of the fi - nal con - flict sing. Shout the tri - umph
Of the ho - ly time had come, Christ was sent, the
Which on earth he willed to see, Will - ing - ly he
Be for all the no - blest tree; None in fol - iage,

of the vic - tim; Far and wide the
world's Cre - a - tor, From the Fa - ther's
meets his pas - sion, Born to set his
none in blos - som, None in fruit your

ech - oes ring: Je - sus Christ, the world's sal - va - tion,
heav'n - ly home, And was found a - mong us dwell - ing,
peo - ple free; On the cross the Lamb is lift - ed,
peer may be; Sym - bol of the world's re - demp - tion,

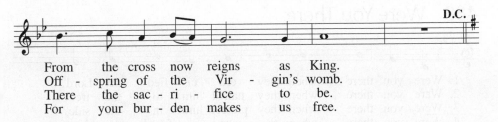

From   the cross   now   reigns   as   King.
Off - spring of   the   Vir - gin's womb.
There   the sac - ri - fice   to   be.
For   your bur - den makes   us   free.

Text: Refrain from *Rite of Holy Week*, © 1972, ICEL; verses by Venantius Fortunatus, c.530–609; verses 1–3 tr. by Steven R. Janco, b.1961, alt.,
     © 1997, GIA Publications, Inc.; verse 4 tr. by John M. Neale, 1818–1866, alt.
Tune: GLORY IN THE CROSS, 8 7 8 7 8 7 with refrain; Steven R. Janco, b.1961, © 1997, GIA Publications, Inc.

Jesu, Jesu, Fill Us with Your Love   487

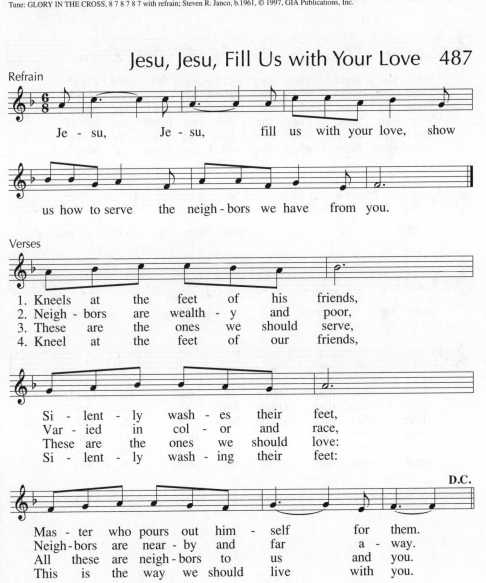

Refrain

Je - su,   Je - su,   fill us with your love,   show

us how to serve   the neigh - bors we have   from you.

Verses

1. Kneels   at   the   feet   of   his   friends,
2. Neigh - bors   are   wealth - y   and   poor,
3. These   are   the   ones   we   should   serve,
4. Kneel   at   the   feet   of   our   friends,

Si - lent - ly   wash - es   their   feet,
Var - ied   in   col - or   and   race,
These are   the   ones   we   should   love:
Si - lent - ly   wash - ing   their   feet:

Mas - ter who pours out him - self   for   them.
Neigh-bors are near - by and   far   a - way.
All   these are neigh - bors to   us   and   you.
This is   the way   we   should   live   with   you.

Text: Tom Colvin, 1925–2000, alt.
Tune: CHEREPONI, 7 7 9 with refrain; Ghanian folk song; adapt. by Tom Colvin, 1925–2000; acc. by Jane M. Marshall, b.1924
© 1969, and arr. © 1982, Hope Publishing Company

488 Were You There

1. Were you there when they cru - ci - fied my Lord?
2. Were you there when they nailed him to the tree?
3. Were you there when they pierced him in the side?
4. Were you there when the sun re - fused to shine?
5. Were you there when they laid him in the tomb?
6. Were you there when they rolled the stone a - way?

Were you there when they cru - ci - fied my Lord?
Were you there when they nailed him to the tree?
Were you there when they pierced him in the side?
Were you there when the sun re - fused to shine?
Were you there when they laid him in the tomb?
Were you there when they rolled the stone a - way?

Oh! Some - times it caus - es me to

trem - ble, trem - ble, trem - ble. Were you

there when they cru - ci - fied my Lord?
there when they nailed him to the tree?
there when they pierced him in the side?
there when the sun re - fused to shine?
there when they laid him in the tomb?
there when they rolled the stone a - way?

Text: African American spiritual
Tune: WERE YOU THERE, 10 10 with refrain; African American spiritual; harm. by C. Winfred Douglas, 1867–1944, © 1940, 1943, 1961,
The Church Pension Fund

O Sacred Head Surrounded / 489
Oh Rostro Ensangrentado

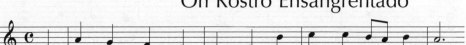

1. O Sa - cred Head, sur - round - ed By crown of pierc - ing thorn!
2. I see your strength and vig - or All fad - ing in the strife,
3. In this, your bit - ter pas - sion, Good Shep - herd, think of me

1. ¡Oh ros - tro_en - san - gren - ta - do, I - ma - gen del do - lor,
2. Cu - brió tu no - ble fren - te La pa - li - dez mor - tal,
3. Se - ñor, tú_has so - por - ta - do Lo que yo me - re - cí;

O bleed - ing Head, so wound - ed, Re - viled and put to scorn!
And death with cru - el rig - or, Be - reav - ing you of life;
With your most sweet com - pas - sion, Un - worth - y though I be:

Que su - fres re - sig - na - do La bur - la y_el fu - ror!
Cual ve - lo trans - pa - ren - te De tu su - frir, se - ñal.
La cul - pa que_has car - ga - do, Car - gar - la yo de - bí.

The pow'r of death comes o'er you, The glow of life de - cays,
O ag - o - ny and dy - ing! O love to sin - ners free!
Be - neath your cross a - bid - ing For ev - er would I rest,

So - por - tas la tor - tu - ra, La sa - ña, la mal - dad;
Ce - rró - se_a - que - lla bo - ca, La len - gua_en - mu - de - ció,
Mas mí - ra - me, con - fí - o En tu cruz y pa - sión.

Yet an - gel hosts a - dore you And trem - ble as they gaze.
Je - sus, all grace sup - ply - ing, O turn your face on me.
In your dear love con - fid - ing, And with your pres - ence blest.

En tan cruel a - mar - gu - ra, ¡Qué gran - de_es tu bon - dad!
La frí - a muer - te to - ca Al que la vi - da dio.
O - tór - ga - me, Dios mí - o, La gra - cia del per - dón.

Text: *Salve caput cruentatum*; ascr. to St. Bernard of Clairvaux, 1091–1153; English tr. by Henry W. Baker, 1821–1877; Spanish tr. by Federico Fliedner, 1845–1901
Tune: PASSION CHORALE, 7 6 7 6 D; Hans Leo Hassler, 1564–1612; harm. by J. S. Bach, 1685–1750

490 My Song Is Love Unknown

1. My song is love un - known, My Sav - ior's love to
2. He came from his blest throne Sal - va - tion to be -
3. Some - times they strew his way And his sweet prais - es
4. Why, what has my Lord done? What makes this rage and
5. They rise, and needs will have My dear Lord made a -
6. In life no house, no home My Lord on earth might
7. Here might I stay and sing No sto - ry so di -

me, Love to the love - less shown That they might
stow; But peo - ple scorned him; none The longed - for
sing, Re - sound - ing all the day Ho - san - nas
spite? He made the lame to run, He gave the
way; A mur - der - er they save, The Prince of
have; In death no friend - ly tomb But what a
vine! Nev - er was love, dear King, Nev - er was

love - ly be. Oh, who am I, That for my sake
Christ would know. But, O my friend, My friend in - deed,
to their King. Then "Cru - ci - fy!" Is all their breath,
blind their sight. Sweet in - jur - ies! Yet they at these
life they slay. Yet cheer-ful he To suf - f'ring goes
stran - ger gave. What may I say? Heav'n was his home;
grief like thine. This is my friend, In whose sweet praise

My Lord should take Frail flesh and die?
Who at my need His life did spend!
And for his death They thirst and cry.
Them - selves dis - please And 'gainst him rise.
That he his foes From thence might free.
But mine the tomb Where - in he lay.
I all my days Could glad - ly spend!

Text: Samuel Crossman, c.1624–1683, alt.
Tune: LOVE UNKNOWN, 6 6 6 6 4 44 4; John Ireland, 1879–1962, © John Ireland Trust

Sing, My Tongue, the Glorious Battle   491

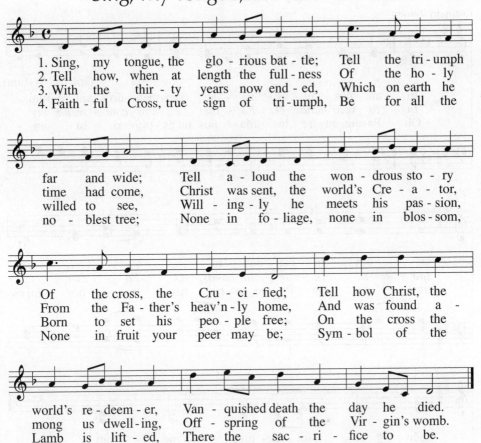

1. Sing, my tongue, the glo - rious bat - tle; Tell the tri - umph
2. Tell how, when at length the full - ness Of the ho - ly
3. With the thir - ty years now end - ed, Which on earth he
4. Faith - ful Cross, true sign of tri - umph, Be for all the

far and wide; Tell a - loud the won - drous sto - ry
time had come, Christ was sent, the world's Cre - a - tor,
willed to see, Will - ing - ly he meets his pas - sion,
no - blest tree; None in fo - liage, none in blos - som,

Of the cross, the Cru - ci - fied; Tell how Christ, the
From the Fa - ther's heav'n - ly home, And was found a -
Born to set his peo - ple free; On the cross the
None in fruit your peer may be; Sym - bol of the

world's re - deem - er, Van - quished death the day he died.
mong us dwell - ing, Off - spring of the Vir - gin's womb.
Lamb is lift - ed, There the sac - ri - fice to be.
world's re - demp - tion, For your bur - den makes us free.

Text: *Pange lingua gloriosi lauream certaminis*; Venantius Fortunatus, c.530–609; tr. by John M. Neale, 1818–1866, alt.
Tune: FORTUNATUS NEW, 8 7 8 7 8 7; Carl F. Schalk, b.1929, © 1967, Concordia Publishing House

Alternate tune: PICARDY

All You Who Pass This Way   492

Refrain

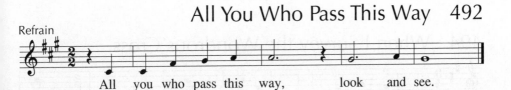

All you who pass this way, look and see.

Text: From the Passion Gospels; Taizé Community, 1984
Tune: Jacques Berthier, 1923–1994
© 1984, Les Presses de Taizé, GIA Publications, Inc., agent

493 In Manus Tuas, Pater

Ostinato Refrain

(spí - ri-tum)

In	ma - nus	tu - as,	Pa -	ter, com-mén - do	spí - ri-tum
In	*- to your hands,*	*O*	*Fa -*	*ther, I now com - mend*	*my*
Oh	Pa-dre, en - tre	tus	ma -	nos mi es-pí - ri - tu	en -

me	- um.	In ma - nus	tu - as,	Pa -	ter,	com-
spir	*- it.*	*In - to your hands,*	*O*	*Fa -*	*ther,*	*I*
tre	- go.	Oh Pa-dre, en - tre	tus	ma -	nos	mi es-

Last time

mén	- do	spí - ri - tum	me	- um.	In
now	*com - mend*	*my*	*spir*	*- it.*	*In -*
pí	- ri - tu	en -	tre	- go.	Oh

Last time

Text: Psalm 31:6, Luke 23:46; Taizé Community
Tune: Taizé Community
© 2007, 2011, Les Presses de Taizé, GIA Publications, Inc., agent

494 When I Survey the Wondrous Cross

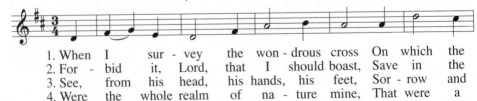

1. When	I	sur - vey	the won - drous cross	On which	the
2. For -	bid	it, Lord,	that I should boast,	Save in	the
3. See,	from	his head,	his hands, his feet,	Sor - row	and
4. Were	the	whole realm	of na - ture mine,	That were	a

Prince of glo - ry died, My rich - est gain I
death of Christ, my God; All the vain things that
love flow min - gled down; Did e'er such love and
pres - ent far too small: Love so a - maz - ing,

count but loss, And pour con - tempt on all my pride.
charm me most— I sac - ri - fice them to his blood.
sor - row meet, Or thorns com - pose so rich a crown?
so di - vine, De - mands my soul, my life, my all.

Text: Isaac Watts, 1674–1748
Tune: ROCKINGHAM, LM; adapt. by Edward Miller, 1735–1807

Now the Green Blade Rises 495

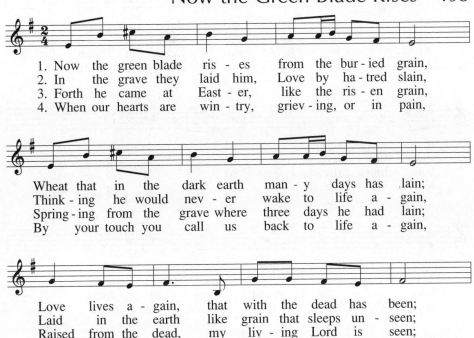

1. Now the green blade ris - es from the bur - ied grain,
2. In the grave they laid him, Love by ha - tred slain,
3. Forth he came at East - er, like the ris - en grain,
4. When our hearts are win - try, griev - ing, or in pain,

Wheat that in the dark earth man - y days has lain;
Think - ing he would nev - er wake to life a - gain,
Spring - ing from the grave where three days he had lain;
By your touch you call us back to life a - gain,

Love lives a - gain, that with the dead has been;
Laid in the earth like grain that sleeps un - seen;
Raised from the dead, my liv - ing Lord is seen;
Fields of our hearts that dead and bare have been;

Love is come a - gain, like wheat a - ris - ing green.

Text: John M. C. Crum, 1872–1958, *Oxford Book of Carols*, alt., © Oxford University Press
Tune: NOËL NOUVELET, 11 11 10 11; French carol; harm. by Thomas Foster, b.1938, © 1986, GIA Publications, Inc.

496 Christ the Lord Is Risen Today

1. Christ the Lord is ris'n to - day, Al - le - lu - ia! All on earth with an - gels say: Al - le - lu - ia! Raise your joys and tri - umphs high, Al - le - lu - ia! Sing, O heav'ns; and, earth, re - ply: Al - le - lu - ia!

2. Lives a - gain our glo - rious king, Al - le - lu - ia! Where, O death, is now your sting? Al - le - lu - ia! Once he died our souls to save, Al - le - lu - ia! Where your vic - to - ry, O grave?

3. Love's re - deem - ing work is done, Al - le - lu - ia! Fought the fight, the bat - tle won, Al - le - lu - ia! Death in vain for - bids him rise, Al - le - lu - ia! Christ has o - pened par - a - dise.

4. Soar we now where Christ has led, Al - le - lu - ia! Fol - l'wing our ex - alt - ed Head, Al - le - lu - ia! Made like him, like him we rise, Al - le - lu - ia! Ours the cross, the grave, the skies.

Al - le - lu - ia!

Text: Charles Wesley, 1707–1788, alt.
Tune: LLANFAIR, 77 77 with alleluias; Robert Williams, 1781–1821

If Christ Had Not Been Raised from Death   497

1. If Christ had not been raised from death Our
2. If Christ still lay with - in the tomb Then
3. If Christ had not been tru - ly raised His

faith would be in vain, Our preach - ing but a
death would be the end, And we should face our
Church would live a lie; His name should nev - er -

waste of breath, Our sin and guilt re - main.
fi - nal doom With nei - ther guide nor friend.
more be praised, His words de - serve to die.

But now the Lord is ris'n in - deed; He
But now the Sav - ior is raised up, So
But now our great Re - deem - er lives; Through

rules in earth and heav'n. His Gos - pel meets a
when a Chris - tian dies We mourn, yet look to
him we are re - stored. His word en - dures, his

world of need— In Christ we are for - giv'n.
God in hope— In Christ the saints a - rise!
Church re - vives— In Christ, our ris - en Lord.

Text: Christopher M. Idle, b. 1938, © 1985, The Jubilate Group (admin. by Hope Publishing Company)
Tune: IN NOMINE DEI, CMD; Sally Ann Morris, b.1952, © 2009, GIA Publications, Inc.

498 Christ Is Risen! Shout Hosanna!

1. Christ is ris - en! Shout ho - san - na! Cel - e - brate this
2. Christ is ris - en! Raise your spir - its From the cav - erns
3. Christ is ris - en! Earth and heav - en Nev - er - more shall

day of days! Christ is ris - en! Hush in won - der:
of de - spair. Walk with glad - ness in the morn - ing.
be the same. Break the bread of new cre - a - tion

All cre - a - tion is a - mazed. In the des - ert
See what love can do and dare. Drink the wine of
Where the world is still in pain. Tell its grim, de -

all - sur-round-ing, See, a spread-ing tree has grown. Bring a taste
res - ur - rec - tion, Not a ser - vant, but a friend. Joy and peace
mon - ic cho - rus: "Christ is ris - en! Get you gone!" Sing Ho - san -

Final ending

of love un - known.
shall nev - er end.
na ev - 'ry one!

Text: Brian Wren, b.1936, © 1986, Hope Publishing Company
Tune: HOSANNA, 8 7 8 7 D; David Haas, b.1957, © 1991, GIA Publications, Inc.

Day of Delight   499

Refrain

Day of de-light and beau-ty un-bound-ed, Tell the
news, the gos-pel spread! Day of all won-der,
day of all splen-dor, Praise Christ ris-en from the dead!

Verses

1. Sing of the sun, from dark-ness ap-pear-ing;
2. Sing now of mourn-ing turned in-to danc-ing;

Sing of the seed, from bar-ren earth green-ing;
Sing now the mys-t'ry, hope of our glo-ry;

Sing of cre-a-tion, al-le-lu-ia!
Sing with thanks-giv-ing, al-le-lu-ia!

Sing of the stream, from Je-sus' side flow-ing;
Sing now of fast-ing turned in-to feast-ing;

Sing of the saints, in wa-ter made ho-ly;
Sing the Lord's fa-vor last-ing for-ev-er;

D.C.

Sing of sal-va-tion, al-le-lu-ia!
Sing, all things liv-ing, al-le-lu-ia!

Text: Delores Dufner, OSB, b.1939, © 2011, GIA Publications, Inc.
Tune: IN DIR IST FREUDE, 10 10 9 D with refrain; Giovanni Giacomo Gastoldi, c.1554–1609

500 Goodness Is Stronger than Evil

Good-ness is strong-er than e - vil; love is strong-er than

hate; light is strong-er than dark - ness;

life is strong-er than death. Vic-t'ry is ours, vic-t'ry is

ours through him who loved us. Vic-t'ry is

ours, vic-t'ry is ours through him who loved us.

Text: Desmond Tutu, b.1931, ©; adapt. by John L. Bell, b.1949.
Tune: GOODNESS IS STRONGER, Irregular; John L. Bell, b.1949, © 1996, Iona Community, GIA Publications, Inc., agent

501 Be Joyful, Mary

1. Be joy - ful, Mar - y, heav'n - ly Queen,
2. The Son you bore by heav - en's grace, Be
3. The Lord has ris - en from the dead, *Gau -*
4. Now pray to God, O Vir - gin fair,

                Your grief is changed to joy se - rene,
joy - ful, Mar - y! Did by his death our guilt e - rase,
de, Ma - rí - a! He rose in glo - ry as he said,
                That he our souls to heav - en bear,

Al - le - lu - ia!
Al - le - lu - ia!   Re - joice, re - joice, O Mar - y!
Al - le - lu - ia!   *Lae - tá - re, O Ma - rí - a!*
Al - le - lu - ia!

Text: *Regina caeli jubila*; Latin, 17th C.; tr. anon. in *Psallite*, 1901
Tune: REGINA CAELI, 8 5 8 4 7; Leisentritt's *Gesangbuch*, 1584, alt.

This Joyful Eastertide 502

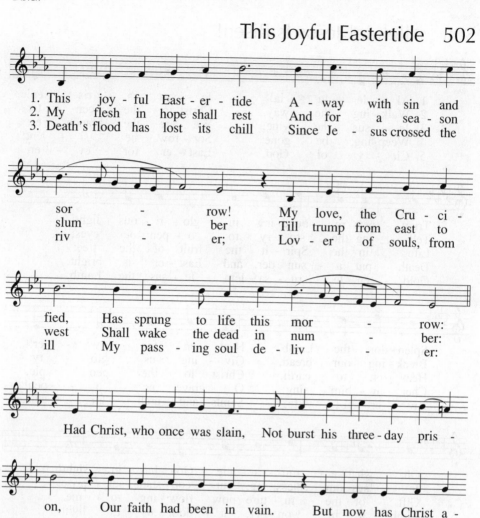

1. This joy - ful East - er - tide A - way with sin and
2. My flesh in hope shall rest And for a sea - son
3. Death's flood has lost its chill Since Je - sus crossed the

sor - row! My love, the Cru - ci -
slum - ber Till trump from east to
riv - er; Lov - er of souls, from

fied, Has sprung to life this mor - row:
west Shall wake the dead in num - ber:
ill My pass - ing soul de - liv - er:

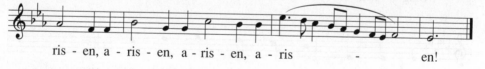

Had Christ, who once was slain, Not burst his three - day pris -

on, Our faith had been in vain. But now has Christ a -

ris - en, a - ris - en, a - ris - en, a - ris - en!

Text: George R. Woodward, 1848–1934
Tune: VRUECHTEN, 6 7 6 7 with refrain; Melody in Oudaen's *David's Psalmen*, 1685; harm. by Paul G. Bunjes, 1914–1998, © 1969,
    Concordia Publishing House

503 Alleluia! Jesus Is Risen!

1. Al - le - lu - ia! Je - sus is ris - en!
2. Walk - ing the way, Christ in the cen - ter
3. Je - sus the vine, We are the branch - es;
4. Weep - ing, be gone; Sor - row, be si - lent:
5. Cit - y of God, East - er for - ev - er,

Trum - pets re - sound - ing in glo - ri - ous light!
Tell - ing the sto - ry to o - pen our eyes;
Life in the Spir - it the fruit of the tree;
Death put a - sun - der, and East - er is bright.
Gold - en Je - ru - sa - lem, Je - sus the Lamb,

Splen - dor, the Lamb, Heav - en for - ev - er!
Break - ing our bread, Giv - ing us glo - ry:
Heav - en to earth, Christ to the peo - ple,
Cher - u - bim sing: O grave, be o - pen!
Riv - er of life, Saints and arch - an - gels,

Oh, what a mir - a - cle God has in sight!
Je - sus our bless - ing, our con - stant sur - prise.
Gift of the fu - ture now flow - ing to me.
Clothe us in won - der, a - dorn us in light.
Sing with cre - a - tion to God the I AM!

Je - sus is ris - en and we shall a - rise.

Give God the glo - ry! Al - le - lu - ia!

Text: Herbert F. Brokering, 1926–2009, © 1995, Augsburg Fortress
Tune: EARTH AND ALL STARS, 4 5 10 D with refrain; David N. Johnson, 1922–1987, © 1969, *Contemporary Worship 1*, admin. by Augsburg Fortress

Earth, Earth, Awake! 504

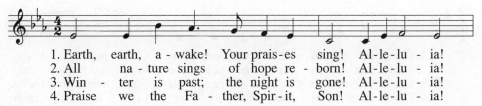

1. Earth, earth, a - wake! Your prais - es sing! Al - le - lu - ia!
2. All na - ture sings of hope re - born! Al - le - lu - ia!
3. Win - ter is past; the night is gone! Al - le - lu - ia!
4. Praise we the Fa - ther, Spir - it, Son! Al - le - lu - ia!

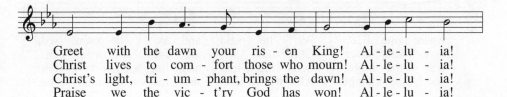

Greet with the dawn your ris - en King! Al - le - lu - ia!
Christ lives to com - fort those who mourn! Al - le - lu - ia!
Christ's light, tri - um - phant, brings the dawn! Al - le - lu - ia!
Praise we the vic - t'ry God has won! Al - le - lu - ia!

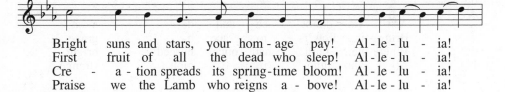

Bright suns and stars, your hom - age pay! Al - le - lu - ia!
First fruit of all the dead who sleep! Al - le - lu - ia!
Cre - a - tion spreads its spring - time bloom! Al - le - lu - ia!
Praise we the Lamb who reigns a - bove! Al - le - lu - ia!

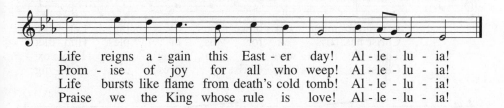

Life reigns a - gain this East - er day! Al - le - lu - ia!
Prom - ise of joy for all who weep! Al - le - lu - ia!
Life bursts like flame from death's cold tomb! Al - le - lu - ia!
Praise we the King whose rule is love! Al - le - lu - ia!

Text: Herman G. Stuempfle, Jr., 1923–2007
Tune: STUEMPFLE, LM with alleluias; Sally Ann Morris, b.1952
© 1996, GIA Publications, Inc.

505 Christ Has Risen

1. Christ has ris-en while earth slum-bers, Christ has ris-en
2. Christ has ris-en for the peo-ple Whom he died to
3. Christ has ris-en to com-pan-ion For-mer friends who
4. Christ has ris-en and for-ev-er Lives to chal-lenge

where hope died, As he said and as he prom-ised,
love and save; Christ has ris-en for the wom-en
fear the night, Sens-ing loss and lim-i-ta-tion
and to change All whose lives are messed or man-gled,

As we doubt-ed and de-nied.
Bring-ing flow'rs to grace his grave.
Where their faith had once burned bright.
All who find re-li-gion strange.

Let the moon em-brace the bless-ing; Let the
Christ has ris-en for dis-ci-ples, Hud-dled
They be-moan what is no long-er, They ex-
Christ is ris-en, Christ is pres-ent Mak-ing

sun sus-tain the cheer; Let the world con-firm the
in an up-stairs room. He whose word in-spired cre-
pect no hope-ful sign Till Christ ends their con-ver-
us what he has been: Ev-i-dence of trans-for-

ru-mor: Christ is ris-en, God is here!
a-tion Can't be si-lenced by the tomb.
sa-tion, Break-ing bread and shar-ing wine.
ma-tion In which God is known and seen.

Text: John L. Bell, b.1949, © 1988, Iona Community, GIA Publications, Inc., agent
Tune: ANITA, 8 7 8 7 D; Sally Ann Morris, b.1952, © 2001, GIA Publications, Inc.

Who Are You Who Walk in Sorrow 506

1. Who are you who walk in sorrow
2. Who is this who joins our journey,
3. Who are you? Our eyes are opened
4. Who are we who travel with you

Down Emmaus' barren road, Hearts dis-
Walking with us stride by stride? Unknown
In the breaking of the bread— Christ, the
On our way through life to death? Women,

traught and hope defeated, Bent beneath grief's
Stranger, can you fathom Depths of grief for
victim, now the victor Living, risen
men, the young, the aging, Wakened by the

crushing load? Nameless mourners, we will join you,
one who died? Then the wonder! When we told you
from the dead! Great Companion on our journey,
Spirit's breath! At the font you claim and name us,

We who also mourn our dead. We have stood by
How our dreams to dust had turned, Then you opened
Still surprise us with your grace! Make each day a
Born of water and the Word. At the table

graves unyielding, Eaten death's bare, bitter bread.
wide the Scriptures Till our hearts within us burned!
new Emmaus; On our hearts your image trace!
still you feed us, Host us as our Risen Lord!

Text: Herman G. Stuempfle, Jr., 1923–2007, © 2000, National Association of Pastoral Musicians, admin. by GIA Publications, Inc.
Tune: HOLY MANNA, 8 7 8 7 D; William Moore, fl.1830; acc. by Kelly Dobbs-Mickus, b.1966, © 2003, GIA Publications, Inc.

507 O Sons and Daughters

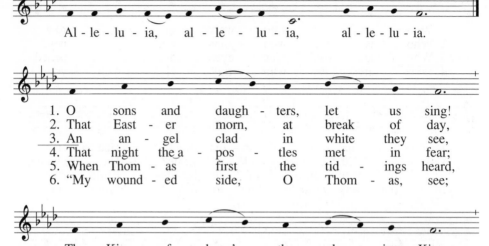

Al - le - lu - ia, al - le - lu - ia, al - le - lu - ia.

1. O   sons and   daugh - ters,   let   us   sing!
2. That   East - er   morn,   at   break   of   day,
3. An   an - gel   clad   in   white   they   see,
4. That   night the a - pos - tles   met   in   fear;
5. When Thom - as   first   the   tid - ings heard,
6. "My   wound - ed side,   O   Thom - as, see;

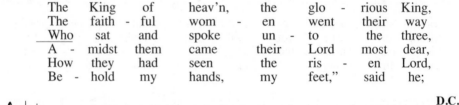

The   King   of   heav'n,   the   glo - rious King,
The   faith - ful   wom - en   went   their   way
Who   sat   and   spoke   un - to   the   three,
A - midst them   came   their   Lord   most dear,
How   they   had   seen   the   ris - en   Lord,
Be - hold my   hands,   my   feet,"   said   he;

D.C.

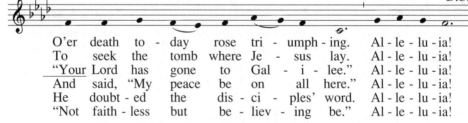

O'er   death to - day   rose   tri - umph - ing.   Al - le - lu - ia!
To   seek the   tomb   where Je - sus   lay.   Al - le - lu - ia!
"Your Lord has   gone   to   Gal - i - lee."   Al - le - lu - ia!
And   said, "My   peace   be   on   all   here."   Al - le - lu - ia!
He   doubt - ed   the   dis - ci - ples' word.   Al - le - lu - ia!
"Not faith - less but   be - liev - ing be."   Al - le - lu - ia!

7. No longer Thomas then denied;
   He saw the feet, the hands, the side;
   "You are my Lord and God," he cried. Alleluia!

8. How blest are they who have not seen,
   And yet whose faith has constant been,
   For they eternal life shall win. Alleluia!

9. On this most holy day of days,
   To God your hearts and voices raise,
   In laud and jubilee and praise. Alleluia!

Text: *O filii et filiae;* Jean Tisserand, d.1494; tr. by John M. Neale, 1818–1866, alt.
Tune: O FILII ET FILIAE, 888 with alleluia and refrain; Mode II, French carol, 15th C.; acc. by Richard Proulx, 1937–2010,
   © 1975, GIA Publications, Inc.

This Is a Day of New Beginnings   508

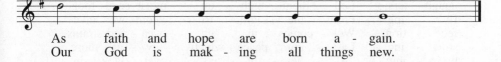

1. This is a day of new be - gin - nings,
2. Then let us, with the Spir - it's dar - ing,

Time to re - mem - ber, and move on,
Step from the past, and leave be - hind

Time to be - lieve what love is bring - ing,
Our dis - ap - point - ment, guilt, and griev - ing,

Lay - ing to rest the pain that's gone.
Seek - ing new paths, and sure to find.

For by the life and death of Je - sus,
Christ is a - live, and goes be - fore us

Love's might - y Spir - it, now as then,
To show and share what love can do.

Can make for us a world of dif - f'rence
This is a day of new be - gin - nings;

As faith and hope are born a - gain.
Our God is mak - ing all things new.

Text: Brian Wren, b.1936, © 1983, 1987, Hope Publishing Company. Communion stanza omitted with permission.
Tune: RENDEZ À DIEU, 9 8 9 8 D; *Genevan Psalter*, 1551; Louis Bourgeois, c.1510–1561

509 Come, You Faithful, Raise the Strain

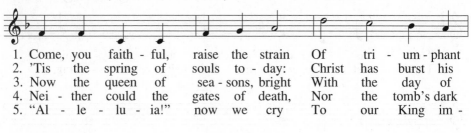

1. Come, you faith - ful, raise the strain Of tri - um - phant
2. 'Tis the spring of souls to - day: Christ has burst his
3. Now the queen of sea - sons, bright With the day of
4. Nei - ther could the gates of death, Nor the tomb's dark
5. "Al - le - lu - ia!" now we cry To our King im -

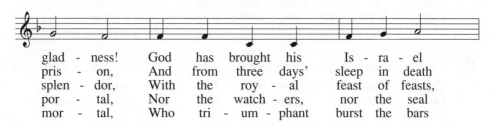

glad - ness! God has brought his Is - ra - el
pris - on, And from three days' sleep in death
splen - dor, With the roy - al feast of feasts,
por - tal, Nor the watch - ers, nor the seal
mor - tal, Who tri - um - phant burst the bars

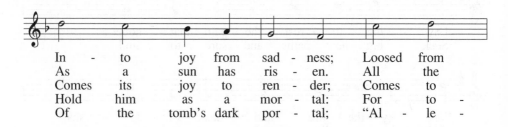

In - to joy from sad - ness; Loosed from
As a sun has ris - en. All the
Comes its joy to ren - der; Comes to
Hold him as a mor - tal: For to -
Of the tomb's dark por - tal; "Al - le -

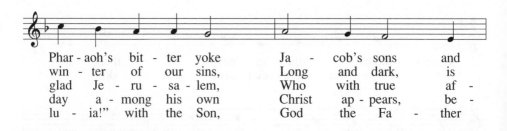

Phar - aoh's bit - ter yoke Ja - cob's sons and
win - ter of our sins, Long and dark, is
glad Je - ru - sa - lem, Who with true af -
day a - mong his own Christ ap - pears, be -
lu - ia!" with the Son, God the Fa - ther

daugh - ters; Led them with un - moist - ened foot
fly - ing From the Light, to whom we give
fec - tion Wel - comes in un - wea - ried strains
stow - ing Last - ing peace which ev - er - more
prais - ing; "Al - le - lu - ia!" yet a - gain

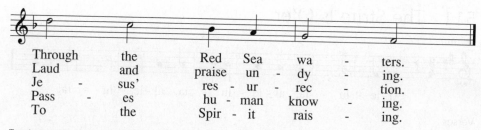

Through   the   Red   Sea   wa   -   ters.
Laud   and   praise   un   -   dy   -   ing.
Je - sus'   res - ur - rec   -   tion.
Pass - es   hu - man   know   -   ing.
To   the   Spir - it   rais   -   ing.

Text: Ασωμεν παντες λαοι; John of Damascus, c.675–c.749; tr. by John M. Neale, 1818–1886, alt.
Tune: GAUDEAMUS PARITER, 7 6 7 6 D; Johann Horn, c.1495–1547

Christ Is Alive! 510

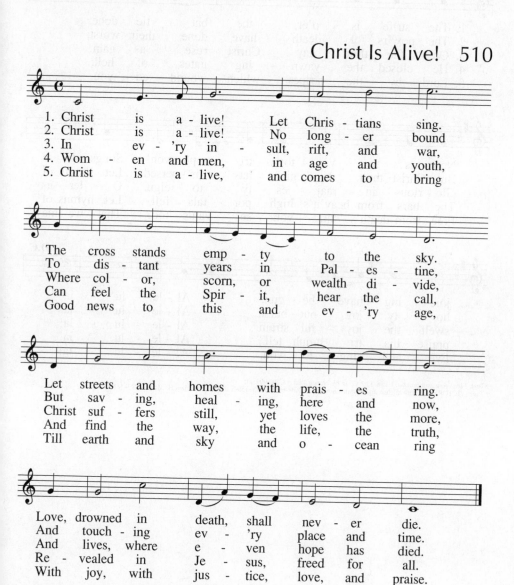

1. Christ   is   a - live!   Let   Chris - tians   sing.
2. Christ   is   a - live!   No   long - er   bound
3. In   ev - 'ry   in - sult,   rift,   and   war,
4. Wom - en   and   men,   in   age   and   youth,
5. Christ   is   a - live,   and   comes   to   bring

The   cross   stands   emp - ty   to   the   sky.
To   dis - tant   years   in   Pal - es - tine,
Where   col - or,   scorn,   or   wealth di - vide,
Can   feel   the   Spir - it,   hear   the   call,
Good   news   to   this   and   ev - 'ry   age,

Let   streets   and   homes   with   prais - es   ring.
But   sav - ing,   heal - ing,   here   and   now,
Christ   suf - fers   still,   yet   loves   the   more,
And   find   the   way,   the   life,   the   truth,
Till   earth   and   sky   and   o - cean   ring

Love,   drowned   in   death,   shall   nev - er   die.
And   touch - ing   ev - 'ry   place   and   time.
And   lives,   where   e - ven   hope   has   died.
Re - vealed   in   Je - sus,   freed   for   all.
With   joy,   with   jus - tice,   love,   and   praise.

Text: Romans 6:5–11; Brian Wren, b.1936, © 1975, 1995, Hope Publishing Company
Tune: TRURO, LM; Williams' *Psalmodia Evangelica*, 1789

511 The Strife Is O'er

Refrain

Al - le - lu - ia, al - le - lu - ia, al - le - lu - ia!

Verses

1. The strife is o'er, the bat - tle done;
2. The pow'rs of death have done their worst;
3. On the third day Christ rose a - gain,
4. He closed the yawn - ing gates of hell;
5. Lord, by the stripes which wound - ed you,

Now is the Vic - tor's tri - umph won! Songs of re -
But Christ their le - gions has dis - persed. Let shouts of
Glo - rious in maj - es - ty to reign. O let us
The bars from heav'n's high por - tals fell. Let hymns of
Free from death's sting your ser - vants too, That we may

D.C.

joic - ing have be - gun. Al - le - lu - ia!
ho - ly joy out - burst. Al - le - lu - ia!
swell the joy - ful strain. Al - le - lu - ia!
praise his tri - umph tell. Al - le - lu - ia!
live and sing to you. Al - le - lu - ia!

Text: *Finita jam sunt praelia;* Latin, 12th C.; tr. by Francis Pott, 1832–1909, alt.
Tune: VICTORY, 888 with alleluia and refrain; Giovanni da Palestrina, 1525–1594; adapt. by William H. Monk, 1823–1889

At the Lamb's High Feast We Sing 512

1. At the Lamb's high feast we sing Praise to our vic -
2. Where the Pas - chal blood is poured, Death's dark an - gel
3. Might - y vic - tim from on high, Hell's fierce pow'rs be -
4. East - er tri - umph, East - er joy, This a - lone can

to - rious King, Who has washed us in the tide
sheathes his sword; Is - rael's hosts tri - umph - ant go
neath you lie; You have con - quered in the fight,
sin de - stroy; From sin's pow'r, Lord, set us free,

Flow - ing from his pierc - ed side. Praise we him, whose
Through the wave that drowns the foe. Praise we Christ, whose
You have brought us life and light. Now no more can
New - born souls in you to be. Fa - ther, who the

love di - vine Gives his sa - cred Blood for wine,
blood was shed, Pas - chal vic - tim, Pas - chal bread;
death ap - pall, Now no more the grave en - thrall;
crown shall give, Sav - ior, by whose death we live,

Gives his Bod - y for the feast:
With sin - cer - i - ty and love
You have o - pened par - a - dise,
Spir - it, guide through all our days:

Christ the vic - tim, Christ the priest.
Eat we man - na from a - bove.
And in you your saints shall rise.
Three in One, your name we praise.

Text: *Ad regias agni dapes;* Latin, 4th C.; tr. by Robert Campbell, 1814–1868, alt.
Tune: SALZBURG, 77 77 D; Jakob Hintze, 1622–1702; harm. by J. S. Bach, 1685–1750

513 They Disbelieved for Joy

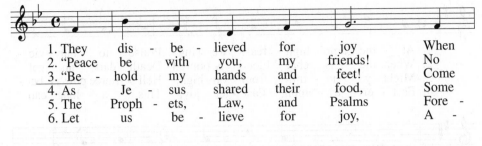

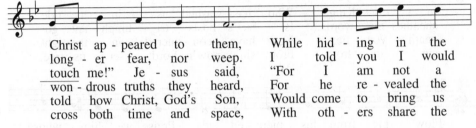

1. They dis - be - lieved for joy When
2. "Peace be with you, my friends! No
3. "Be - hold my hands and feet! Come
4. As Je - sus shared their food, Some
5. The Proph - ets, Law, and Psalms Fore -
6. Let us be - lieve for joy, A -

Christ ap - peared to them, While hid - ing in the
long - er fear, nor weep. I told you I would
touch me!" Je - sus said, "For I am not a
won - drous truths they heard, For he re - vealed the
told how Christ, God's Son, Would come to bring us
cross both time and space, With oth - ers share the

Up - per Room In old Je - ru - sa - lem.
come a - gain. My prom - is - es I keep.
phan - tom ghost. God raised me from the dead!"
hid - den plan That lay with - in God's Word.
back to God, Through love to make us one.
Word of God And wit - ness to God's grace.

Text: Rae E. Whitney, b.1927, © 2000, Selah Publishing Co., Inc.
Tune: FESTAL SONG, SM; William H. Walter, 1825–1893

514 That Easter Day with Joy Was Bright

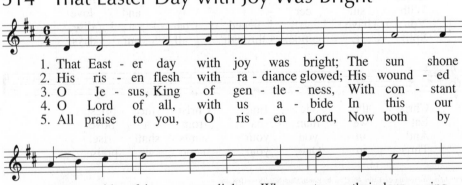

1. That East - er day with joy was bright; The sun shone
2. His ris - en flesh with ra - diance glowed; His wound - ed
3. O Je - sus, King of gen - tle - ness, With con - stant
4. O Lord of all, with us a - bide In this our
5. All praise to you, O ris - en Lord, Now both by

out with fair - er light When, to their long - ing
hands and feet he showed. Those scars their sol - emn
love our hearts pos - sess That we may give you
joy - ful East - er - tide; From ev - 'ry weap - on
heav'n and earth a - dored; To God the Fa - ther

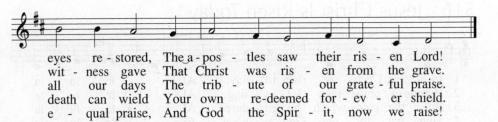

eyes re-stored, The a-pos-tles saw their ris-en Lord!
wit-ness gave That Christ was ris-en from the grave.
all our days The trib-ute of our grate-ful praise.
death can wield Your own re-deemed for-ev-er shield.
e-qual praise, And God the Spir-it, now we raise!

Text: *Claro paschali gaudio*; Latin 5th C.; tr. by John M. Neale, 1818–1866, alt.
Tune: PUER NOBIS, LM; adapt. by Michael Praetorius, 1571–1621

This Is the Feast of Victory   515

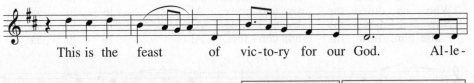

This is the feast of vic-to-ry for our God. Al-le-

lu - ia, al-le-lu-ia, al-le-lu - ia.   lu - ia.

To verses   *Last time*

1.   Wor-thy is Christ, the Lamb who was slain, whose
2. Pow - er, rich-es, wis-dom, and strength, and
3. Sing with all the peo-ple of God, and
4. Bless - ing, hon-or, glo-ry, and might be to
5. For the Lamb who was slain has be-

D.C.

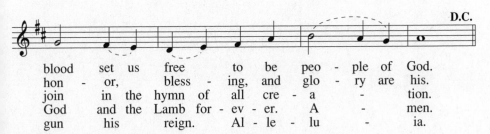

blood set us free to be peo-ple of God.
hon-or, bless-ing, and glo-ry are his.
join in the hymn of all cre-a - tion.
God and the Lamb for-ev-er. A - men.
gun his reign. Al-le-lu - ia.

Text: Based on Revelation 5, © 1978, *Lutheran Book of Worship*, admin. by Augsburg Fortress
Tune: FESTIVAL CANTICLE, Irregular with refrain; Richard Hillert, 1923–2010, © 1975, 1988, Richard Hillert

516 Jesus Christ Is Risen Today

1. Je - sus Christ is ris'n to - day, Al - le - lu - ia!
2. Hymns of praise then let us sing, Al - le - lu - ia!
3. But the pains which he en - dured, Al - le - lu - ia!
4. Sing we to our God a - bove, Al - le - lu - ia!

Our tri - um-phant ho - ly day, Al - le - lu - ia!
Un - to Christ, our heav'n-ly King, Al - le - lu - ia!
Our sal - va - tion have pro - cured; Al - le - lu - ia!
Praise e - ter - nal, as his love; Al - le - lu - ia!

Who did once up - on the cross, Al - le - lu - ia!
Who en - dured the cross and grave, Al - le - lu - ia!
Now a - bove the sky he's King, Al - le - lu - ia!
Praise him, now his might con - fess, Al - le - lu - ia!

Suf - fer to re - deem our loss. Al - le - lu - ia!
Sin - ners to re - deem and save. Al - le - lu - ia!
Where the an - gels ev - er sing. Al - le - lu - ia!
Fa - ther, Son, and Spir - it blest. Al - le - lu - ia!

Text: St. 1, *Surrexit Christus hodie*, Latin, 14th C.; para. in *Lyra Davidica*, 1708, alt.; st. 2, 3, *The Compleat Psalmodist*, c.1750, alt.; st. 4, Charles
Wesley, 1707–1788, alt.
Tune: EASTER HYMN, 77 77 with alleluias; *Lyra Davidica*, 1708

Rise to Sing! The Light Is Breaking   517

1. Rise to sing! The light is break-ing, Gleam-ing gift of
2. Love-ly shine the courts of heav-en; Morn-ing stars now
3. Hail the dawn of new cre-a-tion! Gone are suf-f'ring,

day be-gun. Hope now springs, like blos-soms wak-ing,
bright-ly burn. Christ a-ris-es like the leav-en,
grief, and sighs. Glo-rious now the con-sum-ma-tion.

O-p'ning to the ris-ing sun. Those who sow in
Fes-tal bread for hearts that yearn. Death is swal-lowed
Mu-sic soars to fill the skies: Or-gans pip-ing,

pain and sor-row With the dawn in joy shall reap.
up in vic-t'ry. Where is now your sting, O grave?
church bells chim-ing, On this day, all earth shall ring.

God, who gov-erns each to-mor-row,
Earth, a-wake to ra-diant mys-t'ry:
In the grace of God's good tim-ing,

Wipes all tears from those who weep.
Christ shall come a-gain to save!
With the saints, we rise to sing!

Text: Mary Louise Bringle, b.1953, © 2002, GIA Publications, Inc.
Tune: PETHEL, 8 7 8 7 D; William P. Rowan, b.1951, © 2001, William P. Rowan, admin. by GIA Publications, Inc.

518 Joyful Bells Ringing / Suenen Campanas

Verses

1. Joy - ful bells
2. Song - birds are
3. New life breaks
4. Death has been

1. *Sue - nen cam -*
2. *Can - ta el*
3. *La vi - da*
4. *Des - de hoy la*

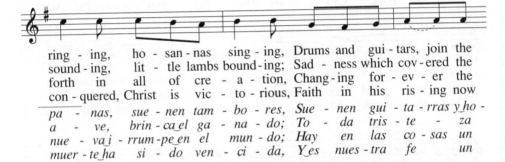

ring - ing, ho - san - nas sing - ing, Drums and gui - tars, join the
sound - ing, lit - tle lambs bound - ing; Sad - ness which cov - ered the
forth in all of cre - a - tion, Chang - ing for - ev - er the
con - quered, Christ is vic - to - rious, Faith in his ris - ing now

pa - nas, sue - nen tam - bo - res, Sue - nen gui - ta - rras y ho -
a - ve, brin - ca el ga - na - do; To - da tris - te - za
nue - va i - rrum - pe en el mun - do; Hay en las co - sas un
muer - te ha si - do ven - ci - da, Y es nues - tra fe un

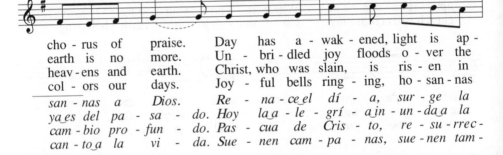

cho - rus of praise. Day has a - wak - ened, light is ap -
earth is no more. Un - bri - dled joy floods o - ver the
heav - ens and earth. Christ, who was slain, is ris - en in
col - ors our days. Joy - ful bells ring - ing, ho - san - nas

san - nas a Dios. Re - na - ce el dí - a, sur - ge la
ya es del pa - sa - do. Hoy la a - le - grí - a in - un - da a la
cam - bio pro - fun - do. Pas - cua de Cris - to, re - su - rrec -
can - to a la vi - da. Sue - nen cam - pa - nas, sue - nen tam -

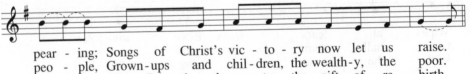

pear - ing; Songs of Christ's vic - to - ry now let us raise.
peo - ple, Grown - ups and chil - dren, the wealth - y, the poor.
glo - ry, Of - f'ring through wa - ter the gift of re - birth.
sing - ing, Drums and gui - tars, join the cho - rus of praise.

luz; Can - te - mos, her - ma - nos, un him - no a Je - sús.
gen - te, Del ni - ño al más gran - de, del ri - co al más po - bre.
ción, A - bre el pa - so a la vi - da de Dios.
bo - res, Sue - nen gui - ta - rras y ho - san - nas a Dios.

Refrain

Christ the Lord   is ris-en to-day!   Christ the Lord   is ris-en to-day!
¡Por - que Cris - to re - su - ci - tó!   ¡Por - que Cris - to re - su - ci - tó!

Al - le - lu - ia, al - le - lu - ia! Christ the Lord   is ris-en to-
¡A - le - lu - ya, a - le - lu - ya! ¡Por - que Cris - to re - su - ci -

| To repeat | Last time |

day!   day!
tó!   tó!

Text: Osvaldo Catena, SSS, 1920–1986, alt., © Editorial Bonum; tr. by Ronald F. Krisman, b.1946, © 2011, GIA Publications, Inc.
Tune: BERTOLINO, 10 10 10 10 with refrain; Miguel Bertolino, alt. with the permission of *Seminario Latinoamericano*; harm. by Ronald F. Krisman, b.1946, © 2011, GIA Publications, Inc.

Regína Caeli / Mary, Heaven's Queen   519

Re - gí - na   cae - li   lae - tá - re,   al - le - lú - ia:
Mar - y, heav - en's Queen,   sing for joy,   al - le - lu - ia:

Qui - a   quem me - ru - í - sti por - tá - re,   al - le - lú - ia:
The One   you mer - it - ed to bring to birth,   al - le - lu - ia:

Re - sur - réx - it,   sic - ut dix - it,   al - le - lú - ia:
Rose from the dead,   as   he   had said,   al - le - lu - ia:

O - ra pro no - bis De - um,   al - le - lú - ia.
In - ter - cede for   us   with God,   al - le - lu - ia.

Text: *Regina caeli laetare*, Latin 12th C.; tr. by Ronald F. Krisman, b.1946, © 2011, GIA Publications, Inc.
Tune: RÉGINA CAELI, Irregular; Mode VI; acc. by Ronald F. Krisman, b.1946, © 2011, GIA Publications, Inc.

520 Christ the Lord Is Risen Today

1. Christ the Lord is ris'n to - day;
2. For the sheep the Lamb has bled,
3. Christ, the Vic - tim un - de - filed,
4. Chris - tians, on this hap - py day
5. Christ, who once for sin - ners bled,
6. Hail, e - ter - nal Hope on high!

Chris - tians, haste your vows to pay;
Sin - less in the sin - ner's stead.
God and sin - ners rec - on - ciled,
Raise your hearts with joy and say:
Now the first - born from the dead,
Hail, O King of vic - to - ry!

Make your joy and prais - es known
Christ the Lord is ris'n on high;
When in fierce and blood - y strife
"Christ the Lord is ris'n on high;
Throned in end - less might and pow'r,
Hail, our Prince of life a - dored!

At the Pas - chal Vic - tim's throne.
Now he lives, no more to die.
Met to - geth - er death and life.
Now he lives, no more to die."
Lives and reigns for - ev - er - more.
Show us mer - cy, gra - cious Lord.

Al - le - lu - ia. Al - le - lu - ia, al -

le - lu - ia, al - le - lu - ia.

Text: *Victimae paschali laudes*; ascr. to Wipo of Burgundy, d.1048; tr. by Jane E. Leeson, 1809–1881, alt.
Tune: SURGIT IN HAEC DIES, 77 77 with alleluias; 12th C.; acc. by Richard Proulx, 1937–2010, © 1980, GIA Publications, Inc.

We Walk His Way / Ewe, Thina   521

Refrain

We walk his way.
E - we, thi - na.
We walk
E - we,

We walk his way.
E - we, thi - na.

We walk his way.
E - we, thi - na.

his way.
thi - na.

We walk
E - we,

We walk his way.
E - we, thi - na.

We walk his way.
E - we, thi - na.

We walk his way.
E - we, thi - na.

Verses

1. Unarmed, he faces forces of demons and death.

2. He breaks the bonds of hell, dying on the cross.

3. The tree of freedom blooms by his empty grave.

1. Sizowa nyathela amadimoni.

Text: South African; tr. by Anders Nyberg, b.1955, and Sven-Bernhard Fast
Tune: South African; arr. by Anders Nyberg, b.1955
© 1984, Utryck, Walton Music Corp., agent

522 Be Not Afraid

Ostinato Refrain

Be not a-fraid, sing out for joy! Christ is ris-en, al-le-
Czech: *Ne-boj-te se,* *ra-duj-te se!* *Kris-tus slav-ný ví-těz*
Polish: Nie bój-cie się, ra-duj-cie się! Chry-stus rze-czy-wi-ście
Croatian: *O-dag-naj strah* *i ra-duj se!* *Krist je do-is-ta us-*

lu - ia! Be not a-fraid, sing out for joy!
z hro-bu vstal. *Ne-boj-te se,* *ra-duj-te se!*
z gro-bu wstał. Nie bój-cie się, ra-duj-cie się!
krs-nu - o! *O-dag-naj strah* *i ra-duj se!*

Christ is ris-en, al-le-lu - ia!
Kris-tus slav-ný ví-těz z hro-bu vstal.
Chry-stus rze-czy-wi-ście z gro-bu wstał.
Krist je do-is-ta us-krs-nu - o!

Text: Taizé Community
Tune: Taizé Community
© 2007, Les Presses de Taizé, GIA Publications, Inc., agent

Christ the Lord Is Risen! 523

1. Christ the Lord is ris'n! Christ the Lord is ris'n!
2. He has con - quered death. He has con - quered death.
3. Sin has done its worst. Sin has done its worst.
4. He is King of kings. He is King of kings.
5. He is Lord of lords. He is Lord of lords.
6. All the world is his. All the world is his.
7. Come and wor - ship him. Come and wor - ship him.
8. Christ our Lord is ris'n! Christ our Lord is ris'n!
9. Hal - le - lu - jah! Hal - le - lu - jah!

Je - su. Christ the Lord is ris'n!
Je - su. He has con - quered death.
Je - su. Sin has done its worst.
Je - su. He is King of kings.
Je - su. He is Lord of lords.
Je - su. All the world is his.
Je - su. Come and wor - ship him.
Je - su. Christ our Lord is ris'n!
Je - su. Hal - le - lu - jah!

Christ the Lord is ris'n! Je - su.
He has con - quered death. Je - su.
Sin has done its worst. Je - su.
He is King of kings. Je - su.
He is Lord of lords. Je - su.
All the world is his. Je - su.
Come and wor - ship him. Je - su.
Christ our Lord is ris'n! Je - su.
Hal - le - lu - jah! Je - su.

ext: Tom Colvin, 1925–2000
ıne: GARU, 55 2 55 2, Ghanian folk song, adapt. by Tom Colvin, 1925–2000, arr. by Kevin R. Hackett, b.1956
1969, Hope Publishing Company

524 Hail Thee, Festival Day!

Verses 2, 4, 6

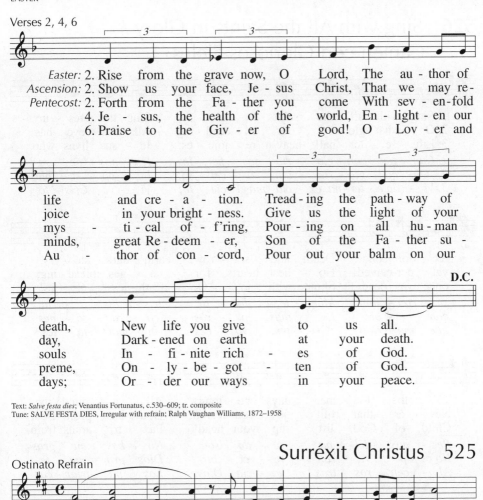

Easter: 2. Rise from the grave now, O Lord, The au - thor of
Ascension: 2. Show us your face, Je - sus Christ, That we may re-
Pentecost: 2. Forth from the Fa - ther you come With sev - en-fold
4. Je - sus, the health of the world, En - light - en our
6. Praise to the Giv - er of good! O Lov - er and

life and cre - a - tion. Tread - ing the path-way of
joice in your bright - ness. Give us the light of your
mys - ti - cal of - f'ring, Pour - ing on all hu - man
minds, great Re - deem - er, Son of the Fa - ther su-
Au - thor of con - cord, Pour out your balm on our

D.C.

death, New life you give to us all.
day, Dark - ened on earth at your death.
souls In - fi - nite rich - es of God.
preme, On - ly - be - got - ten of God.
days; Or - der our ways in your peace.

Text: *Salve festa dies*; Venantius Fortunatus, c.530–609; tr. composite
Tune: SALVE FESTA DIES, Irregular with refrain; Ralph Vaughan Williams, 1872–1958

Surréxit Christus   525

Ostinato Refrain

Sur - ré - xit Chri - stus, al - le - lú - ia!
The Lord is ris - en, *al - le - lu - ia!*
Lithuanian: Jau ke - les Kris - tus, a - le - liu - ja!

(hum)

Can - tá - te Dó - mi - no, al - le - lú - ia!
Sing out and praise the Lord, *al - le - lu - ia!*
Gie - do - kim Vieš - pa - čiui, a - le - liu - ja!

(hum)

Text: Daniel 3; Taizé Community, 1984
Tune: Jacques Berthier, 1923–1994
© 1984, Les Presses de Taizé, GIA Publications, Inc., agent

526 Sing with All the Saints in Glory / Canten con Gloriosos Fieles

1. Sing with all the saints in glo - ry, Sing the res - ur -
2. O what glo - ry, far ex - ceed - ing All that eye has
3. Life e - ter - nal! heav'n re - joic - es: Je - sus lives who

1. Can - ten con glo - rio - sos fie - les Him - nos de re -
2. ¡Oh! qué glo - ria tan ex - cel - sa, Im - po - si - ble
3. Vi - da_e - ter - na,_ex - cla - ma_el cie - lo; Vi - ve Cris - to

rec - tion song! Death and sor - row, earth's dark sto - ry,
yet per-ceived! Ho - liest hearts, for a - ges plead - ing,
once was dead. Shout with joy, O death - less voic - es!

su - rrec - ción. Muer - te_y due - lo, tris - te_his - to - ria,
con - ce - bir. Los más pu - ros co - ra - zo - nes
que mu - rió. ¡Gri - ten, vo - ces in - mor - ta - les!

To the for - mer days be - long. All a - round the
Nev - er that full joy con-ceived. God has prom - ised,
Child of God, lift up your head! Pa - tri - archs from

Pe - nas del pa - sa - do son. Nu - bes ne - gras
No_es - pe - ra - ron re - ci - bir. Dios pro - me - te,
Al - cen ros - tros ha - cia Dios. Los pa - triar - cas

clouds are break-ing, Soon the storms of time shall cease; In God's
Christ pre - pares it, There on high our wel-come waits. Ev - 'ry
dis - tant a - ges, Saints all long-ing for their heav'n, Proph-ets,

se di - si - pan, La tor - men - ta ce - sa ya. Des - per -
Cris - to_o - fre - ce El ban - que - te ce - les - tial. Pa - ra
del pa - sa - do, Los que_es-pe - ran ce - le - brar, To - dos

like - ness we a - wak-en, Know-ing ev - er - last-ing peace.
hum - ble spir - it shares it; Christ has passed the_e - ter - nal gates.
psalm-ists, seers, and sag - es, All a - wait the glo - ry giv'n.

tan - do en su_i - ma-gen, Dios la_e - ter - na paz nos da.
to - dos los hu - mil-des, Vi - da_en Cris - to_es e - ter - nal.
sa - bios y pro - fe - tas Glo - ria_an - he - lan sin ce - sar.

4. Life eternal! O what wonders
Crowd on faith; what joy unknown,
When, amid earth's closing thunders,
Saints shall stand before the throne!
Oh, to enter that bright portal,
See that glowing firmament,
Know, with you, O God immortal,
Jesus Christ whom you have sent!

4. ¡Vida_eterna! ¡Gozo_eterno!
Fieles cantan a_una voz.
Cesan truenos y nos vemos
Frente_al trono tuyo, Dios.
Y_al pasar por tus portales,
Brilla_el cielo con fulgor.
Celebramos tu venida
En tu Hijo_el Salvador.

Text: 1 Corinthians 15:20; William J. Irons, 1812–1883, alt.; tr. by Alberto Merubia, b.1919, © 2010, GIA Publications, Inc.
Tune: HYMN TO JOY, 8 7 8 7 D; arr. from Ludwig van Beethoven, 1770–1827, by Edward Hodges, 1796–1867

I Know That My Redeemer Lives! 527

1. I know that my Re - deem - er lives!
2. He lives to bless me with his love;
3. He lives and grants me dai - ly breath;
4. He lives, all glo - ry to his name;

What joy this blest as - sur - ance gives!
He lives to plead for me a - bove;
He lives, and I shall con - quer death;
He lives, my Sav - ior, still the same;

He lives, he lives who once was dead;
He lives my hun - gry soul to feed;
He lives my man - sion to pre - pare;
What joy this blest as - sur - ance gives:

He lives, my ev - er - last - ing Head!
He lives to help in time of need.
He lives to bring me safe - ly there.
I know that my Re - deem - er lives!

Text: Samuel Medley, 1738–1799
Tune: DUKE STREET, LM; John Hatton, c.1710–1793

528 Christ the Lord Is Risen Today

1. Christ the Lord is ris'n to - day;
2. Christ, the Vic - tim un - de - filed,
3. Say, O won-d'ring Mar - y, say
4. Christ, who once for sin - ners bled,

Chris-tians, haste your
God and sin - ners
What you saw a -
Now the first-born

vows to pay;
rec - on - ciled,
long your way.
from the dead,

Make your joy and
When in fierce and
"I be - held the
Throned in end - less

prais - es known
blood - y strife
glo - ry bright
might and pow'r,

At the Pas - chal Vic - tim's throne.
Met to - geth - er death and life.
Of the ris - en Lord of light,
Lives and reigns for - ev - er - more.

For the sheep the
Chris - tians, on this
Emp - ty tomb and
Hail, e - ter - nal

Lamb has bled, Sin - less in the
hap - py day Raise your hearts with
an - gels seen Where Christ's bod - y
Hope on high! Hail, O King of

sin-ner's stead. Christ the
joy and say: "Christ the
once had been. Christ my
vic - to - ry! Hail, our

Lord is ris'n on high; Now he lives, no more to die.
Lord is ris'n on high; Now he lives, no more to die."
hope, raised glo - rious - ly, Makes his way to Gal - i - lee."
Prince of life a - dored! Show us mer - cy, gra-cious Lord.

Text: *Victimae paschali laudes;* ascr. to Wipo of Burgundy, d.1048; tr. by Jane E. Leeson, 1809–1881, alt.
Tune: VICTIMAE PASCHALI, 77 77 D; Würth's *Katholisches Gesangbuch*, 1859; revised in *Catholic Youth's Hymn Book*, 1871

Hail the Day That Sees Him Rise 529

1. Hail the day that sees him rise, Al - le - lu - ia!
2. There the glo - rious tri - umph waits; Al - le - lu - ia!
3. High - est heav'n its Lord re - ceives, Al - le - lu - ia!
4. See, he lifts his hands a - bove; Al - le - lu - ia!
5. Christ, for us still in - ter - cede, Al - le - lu - ia!
6. There we shall with you re - main, Al - le - lu - ia!

To his throne a - bove the skies; Al - le - lu - ia!
Lift your heads, e - ter - nal gates; Al - le - lu - ia!
Yet he loves the earth he leaves; Al - le - lu - ia!
See, he shows the wounds of love; Al - le - lu - ia!
By your suf - f'ring for us plead; Al - le - lu - ia!
Part - ners of your end - less reign; Al - le - lu - ia!

Christ, the Lamb for sin - ners giv'n, Al - le - lu - ia!
Christ has con - quered death and sin; Al - le - lu - ia!
Though re - turn - ing to his throne, Al - le - lu - ia!
Hark, his gra - cious lips be - stow, Al - le - lu - ia!
Make us wor - thy of the place, Al - le - lu - ia!
There your face un - cloud-ed see, Al - le - lu - ia!

Now as - cends the high - est heav'n. Al - le - lu - ia!
Take the King of glo - ry in! Al - le - lu - ia!
Still he calls the world his own. Al - le - lu - ia!
Bless - ings on his Church be - low. Al - le - lu - ia!
Which you of - fer us by grace. Al - le - lu - ia!
Live with you e - ter - nal - ly. Al - le - lu - ia!

Text: Charles Wesley, 1707–1788, alt.; st. 5 from *The New Century Hymnal*, © 1992, The Pilgrim Press
Tune: LLANFAIR, 77 77 with alleluias; Robert Williams, 1781–1821

530   A Hymn of Glory Let Us Sing!

1. A hymn of glo - ry let us sing! New
2. The ho - ly ap - os - tol - ic band Up -
3. To whom the shin - ing an - gels cry, "Why
4. "You see him now, as - cend - ing high Up
5. O Lord, our home - ward path - way bend, That

songs through - out the world shall ring: Al - le - lu - ia! Al - le -
on the Mount of Ol - ives stand. Al - le - lu - ia! Al - le -
stand and gaze up - on the sky?" Al - le - lu - ia! Al - le -
to the por - tals of the sky." Al - le - lu - ia! Al - le -
our un - wea - ried hearts as - cend, Al - le - lu - ia! Al - le -

lu - ia! Christ, by a road be - fore un - trod, As -
lu - ia! And with his faith - ful fol - l'wers see Their
lu - ia! "This is the Sav - ior," thus they say. "This
lu - ia! "Here - af - ter Je - sus you shall see Re -
lu - ia! Where, seat - ed on your Fa - ther's throne, You

cends un - to the throne of God.
Lord as - cend in maj - es - ty.
is his glo - rious tri - umph day." Al - le - lu - ia! Al - le -
turn - ing in great maj - es - ty."
reign as King of kings a - lone.

lu - ia! Al - le - lu - ia! Al - le - lu - ia! Al - le - lu - ia!

Text: *Hymnum canamus gloriae;* Venerable Bede, 673–735; tr. by Benjamin Webb, 1819–1885, *The Hymnal Noted,* 1854, alt.
Tune: LASST UNS ERFREUEN, LM with alleluias; *Geistliche Kirchengesänge,* Cologne, 1623; harm. by Ralph Vaughan Williams, 1872–1958

Since Our Great High Priest, Christ Jesus   531

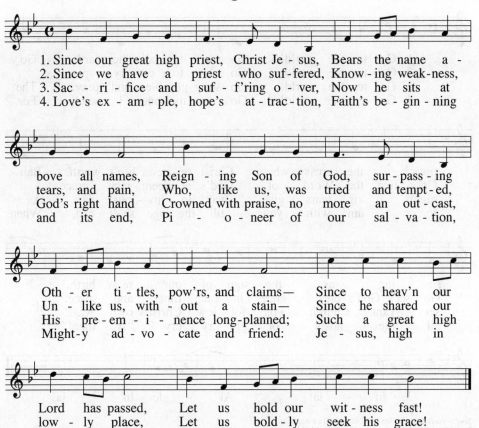

1. Since our great high priest, Christ Je - sus, Bears the name a -
2. Since we have a priest who suf-fered, Know - ing weak-ness,
3. Sac - ri - fice and suf - f'ring o - ver, Now he sits at
4. Love's ex - am - ple, hope's at - trac-tion, Faith's be - gin - ning

bove all names, Reign - ing Son of God, sur - pass - ing
tears, and pain, Who, like us, was tried and tempt - ed,
God's right hand Crowned with praise, no more an out - cast,
and its end, Pi - o - neer of our sal - va - tion,

Oth - er ti - tles, pow'rs, and claims— Since to heav'n our
Un - like us, with - out a stain— Since he shared our
His pre - em - i - nence long-planned; Such a great high
Might - y ad - vo - cate and friend: Je - sus, high in

Lord has passed, Let us hold our wit - ness fast!
low - ly place, Let us bold - ly seek his grace!
priest we have, Strong to help, su - preme to save!
glo - ry raised, Our as - cend - ed Lord be praised!

Text: Christopher M. Idle, b.1938, © 1973, The Jubilate Group (admin. by Hope Publishing Company)
Tune: ALL SAINTS, 8 7 8 7 77; *Geistreiches Gesangbuch*, Darmstadt, 1698; harm. by William H. Monk, 1823–1889, alt.

532 Go to the World!

1. Go to the world! Go in-to all the earth. Go
2. Go to the world! Go in-to ev-'ry place.
3. Go to the world! Go strug-gle, bless and pray. The
4. Go to the world! Go as the ones I send, For

preach the cross where Christ re-news life's worth, Bap-
Go live the Word of God's re-deem-ing grace.
nights of tears give way to joy-ous day. As
I am with you till the age shall end, When

tiz - ing as the sign of our re - birth.
Go seek God's pres - ence in each time and space.
ser - vant Church you fol-low Christ's own way. Al -
all the hosts of glo - ry cry "A - men!"

le - lu - ia! Al - le - lu - ia!

Text: Sylvia G. Dunstan, 1955–1993, © 1991, GIA Publications, Inc.
Tune: SINE NOMINE, 10 10 10 with alleluias; Ralph Vaughan Williams, 1872–1958

533 Fire of God, Undying Flame

1. Fire of God, un - dy - ing Flame,
2. Breath of God, that swept in pow'r
3. Strength of God, your might with - in
4. Truth of God, your pierc - ing rays
5. Love of God, your grace pro - found

Spir - it who in splen-dor came, Let your heat my
In the Pen - te - cos - tal hour, Ho - ly Breath, be
Con - quers sor - row, pain, and sin; For - ti - fy from
Pen - e - trate my se - cret ways. May the light that
Knows not ei - ther age or bound. Come, my heart's own

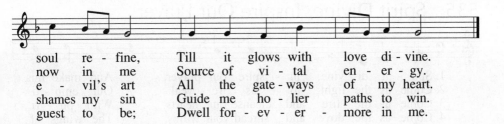

soul re - fine, Till it glows with love di - vine.
now in me Source of vi - tal en - er - gy.
e - vil's art All the gate - ways of my heart.
shames my sin Guide me ho - lier paths to win.
guest to be; Dwell for - ev - er - more in me.

Text: Albert F. Bayly, 1901–1984, alt., © 1988, Oxford University Press
Tune: NUN KOMM DER HEIDEN HEILAND, 77 77; *Geistliche Gesangbüchlein*, Wittenberg, 1524

Come Down, O Love Divine 534

1. Come down, O Love di - vine, Seek now this soul of
2. O let it free - ly burn, Till earth - ly pas - sions
3. And so the yearn - ing strong, With which the soul will

mine, And vis - it it with your own ar - dor glow - ing;
turn To dust and ash - es in its heat con - sum - ing;
long, Shall far out-pass the pow'r of hu - man tell - ing;

O Com-fort - er, draw near, With - in my heart ap -
And let your glo - rious light Shine ev - er on my
No soul can guess Love's grace Till it be - come the

pear, And kin - dle it, your ho - ly flame be - stow-ing.
sight, And clothe me round, the while my path il - lum - ing.
place Where - in the Ho - ly Spir - it makes a dwell-ing.

Text: *Discendi, Amor Santo*; Bianco da Siena, d.1434; tr. by Richard F. Littledale, 1833–1890, alt.
Tune: DOWN AMPNEY, 66 11 D; Ralph Vaughan Williams, 1872–1958

535 Spirit Divine, Inspire Our Prayer

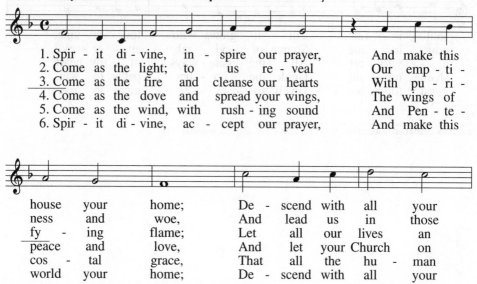

1. Spir - it di - vine, in - spire our prayer,   And make this
2. Come as the light; to us re - veal   Our emp - ti -
3. Come as the fire and cleanse our hearts   With pu - ri -
4. Come as the dove and spread your wings,   The wings of
5. Come as the wind, with rush - ing sound   And Pen - te -
6. Spir - it di - vine, ac - cept our prayer,   And make this

house your home;   De - scend with all your
ness and woe,   And lead us in those
fy - ing flame;   Let all our lives an
peace and love,   And let your Church on
cos - tal grace,   That all the hu - man
world your home;   De - scend with all your

gra - cious pow'r;   Come, Ho - ly Spir - it, come!
paths of life   Where all the right - eous go.
of - f'ring be   To our Re - deem - er's name.
earth be - come   Blest as the Church a - bove.
race may see   The glo - ry of your face.
gra - cious pow'r;   Come, Ho - ly Spir - it, come!

Text: Andrew Reed, 1788–1862, alt.
Tune: GRÄFENBERG, CM; Johann Crüger, 1598–1662

O Spirit All-Embracing 536

1. O Spir-it all-em-brac-ing and coun-sel-or all-wise,
2. O Beau-ty ev-er blaz-ing in flow-er, field, and face,
3. Come, pas-sion's pow-er ho-ly, your in-sight here im-part,

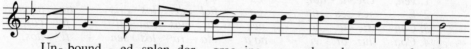

Un-bound-ed splen-dor grac-ing a shore-less sea of skies:
You show your-self a-maz-ing in un-ex-pect-ed place.
And give your ser-vants low-ly an un-der-stand-ing heart

Un-fail-ing is your treas-ure, un-fad-ing your re-ward;
We see you and re-mem-ber what once our dreams had been;
To know your care more clear-ly when faith and love are tried,

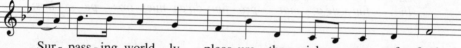

Sur-pass-ing world-ly pleas-ure, the rich-es you af-ford.
You fan the glow-ing em-ber and kin-dle hope with-in.
To seek you more sin-cere-ly when false i-deals have died:

Come, stream of end-less flow-ing, and res-cue us from death;
Come, fire of glo-ry gra-cious, bless all who trust in you;
For vi-sion we im-plore you, for wis-dom's pure de-light;

Come, wind of spring-time blow-ing, and warm us by your breath.
Un-dy-ing flame te-na-cious, burn in your Church a-new.
In prayer we come be-fore you to wait up-on your light.

Text: Delores Dufner, OSB, b.1939, © 1995, 2003, GIA Publications, Inc.
Tune: THAXTED, 13 13 13 13 13 13; Gustav Holst, 1874–1934

537 Come, Spirit Blest / Ven, Creador

1. Come, Spir-it Blest, Cre - a - tor God, de - scend-ing
2. You, Par - a - clete, our deep-est con - so - la - tion,
3. With sev-en gifts you bless and sanc - ti - fy us.
4. Send ho - ly light; il - lu - mi - nate our sen - ses.

1. Ven, Cre - a - dor, Es - pí - ri - tu di - vi - no,
2. E - res tes - ti - go fiel de los cris - tia - nos,
3. Con sie - te do - nes tú nos san - ti - fi - cas,
4. Con luz di - vi - na a - cla - ra los sen - ti - dos,

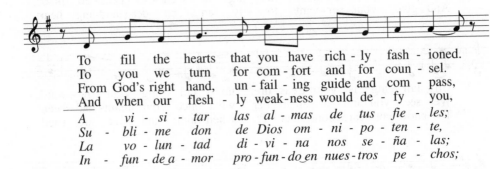

To fill the hearts that you have rich - ly fash - ioned.
To you we turn for com - fort and for coun - sel.
From God's right hand, un - fail - ing guide and com - pass,
And when our flesh - ly weak-ness would de - fy you,

A vi - si - tar las al - mas de tus fie - les;
Su - bli - me don de Dios om - ni - po - ten - te,
La vo - lun - tad di - vi - na nos se - ña - las;
In - fun - de a - mor pro - fun - do en nues-tros pe - chos;

Vis - it us with your grace and your com - pas - sion,
Sooth - ing oil, liv - ing fire, and brim - ming foun - tain,
You in - deed are the One the Fa - ther prom - ised.
Grant us cour - age that nev - er would de - ny you.

Y con - ce - de que nues - tros co - ra - zo - nes
Ca - ri - dad, fuen - te vi - va, e - ter - no fue - go,
Pro - me - ti - do del Pa - dre sem - pi - ter - no,
Con tu gra - cia in - fi - ni - ta for - ta - le - ce

That the song of our prais - es be un - end - ing.
In our hearts you give love its sure foun - da - tion.
With the fire of the Word, your tongues in - spire us.
With the strength of your love, breach our de - fens - es.

Se a - li - men - ten con dá - di - vas ce - les - tes.
Que das vi - da di - vi - na a nues - tras men - tes.
Nos o - fre - ces el don de la pa - la - bra.
La fla - que - za car - nal de nues - tros cuer - pos.

5. Draw errant feet away from sin's deception,
   And by your power, deliver us from evil.
   Banish far ev'ry foe and ev'ry peril.
   Let our lives know the peace of your protection.

6. Seal in our hearts the creed that we inherit:
   Through you we know the Father and his blessing,
   And Christ Jesus, his only Son confessing;
   We proclaim you their true and living Spirit.

7. Glory to God, the Father of all mercies;
   And to the Son, be endless glory given;
   To the Spirit, who reigns with them in heaven,
   Be all glory, forever and forever.

5. *Con tu poder, rechaza al enemigo,*
   Danos la paz que todos esperamos;
   Así guiando seguro nuestras vidas,
   Te pedimos nos libres del pecado.

6. *Haz que por ti, al Padre conozcamos,*
   Y al Verbo eterno, su Hijo Jesucristo;
   Y creamos en ti en todo tiempo,
   Tú que eres su Espíritu divino.

7. *Gloria sin fin al Padre y a su Hijo,*
   Que resurgió triunfante de la muerte,
   Y al Espíritu Santo, que los une
   Desde siempre, por siempre, y para siempre.

Text: Francisco Luis Bernárdez, 1900–1978, © Losada; tr. by Mary Louise Bringle, b.1953, © 2009, GIA Publications, Inc.
Tune: VEN CREADOR, 11 11 11 11; Ronald F. Krisman, b.1946, © 2009, GIA Publications, Inc.

Veni Sancte Spíritus   538

Ostinato Refrain

Text: *Come Holy Spirit;* Verses drawn from the Pentecost Sequence; Taizé Community, 1978
Tune: Jacques Berthier, 1923–1994
© 1979, Les Presses de Taizé, GIA Publications, Inc., agent

539 Laus Tibi Sancte Spíritus

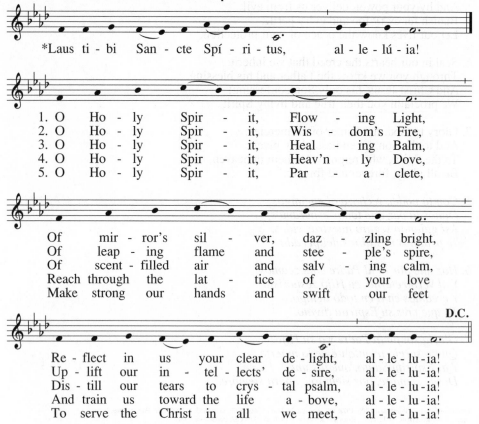

*Laus ti - bi San - cte Spí - ri - tus, al - le - lú - ia!

1. O Ho - ly Spir - it, Flow - ing Light,
2. O Ho - ly Spir - it, Wis - dom's Fire,
3. O Ho - ly Spir - it, Heal - ing Balm,
4. O Ho - ly Spir - it, Heav'n - ly Dove,
5. O Ho - ly Spir - it, Par - a - clete,

Of mir - ror's sil - ver, daz - zling bright,
Of leap - ing flame and stee - ple's spire,
Of scent - filled air and salv - ing calm,
Reach through the lat - tice of your love
Make strong our hands and swift our feet

Re - flect in us your clear de - light, al - le - lu -ia!
Up - lift our in - tel - lects' de - sire, al - le - lu -ia!
Dis - till our tears to crys - tal psalm, al - le - lu -ia!
And train us toward the life a - bove, al - le - lu -ia!
To serve the Christ in all we meet, al - le - lu -ia!

Praise to you, Holy Spirit, alleluia!

Text: Inspired by writings of Hildegard of Bingen, 1098–1179; Mary Louise Bringle, b.1953, © 2002, GIA Publications, Inc.
Tune: O FILII ET FILIAE, 888 with alleluia and refrain; Mode II, French carol, 15th C.; acc. by Richard Proulx, 1937–2010, © 1975, GIA Publications, Inc.

540 Holy Spirit, Come to Us

Ostinato Refrain

Ho - ly Spir-it, come to us, kin-dle in us the fire of your love.
Ven, Es - pí - ri - tu de Dios, y de tu a - mor en - cien - de la lla - ma.
Ve - ni San-cte Spí - ri - tus, tu - i a - mó - ris i - gnem ac - cén - de.

Ho - ly Spir - it, come to us, Ho - ly Spir - it, come to us.
Ven, Es - pí - ri - tu de_a - mor, ven, Es - pí - ri - tu de_a - mor.
Ve - ni San - cte Spí - ri - tus, ve - ni San - cte Spí - ri - tus

Text: John 13:35, 15:12–13, 1 John 3:16, 4:10, 16
Tune: Jacques Berthier, 1923–1994
© 1998, Les Presses de Taizé, GIA Publications, Inc., agent

Holy Spirit, Lord Divine 541

1. Ho - ly Spir - it, Lord di - vine, Come, from heights of
2. Of con - sol - ers, wis - est, best, And our soul's most
3. Light most bless - ed, shine with grace In our heart's most
4. Cleanse our soil - ed hearts of sin, Ar - id souls re -
5. On the faith - ful who are true And pro - fess their

heav'n and shine, Come with bless - ed ra - diance bright!
wel - come guest, Sweet re - fresh - ment, sweet re - pose.
se - cret place, Fill your faith - ful through and through.
fresh with - in, Wound - ed lives to health re - store.
faith in you, In your sev'n - fold gift de - scend!

Come, O Fa - ther of the poor, Come, whose treas - ured
In our la - bor rest most sweet, Pleas - ant cool - ness
Left with - out your pres - ence here, Life it - self would
Bend the stub - born heart and will, Melt the fro - zen,
Give us vir - tue's sure re - ward, Give us your sal -

gifts en - dure, Come, our heart's un - fail - ing light!
in the heat, Con - so - la - tion in our woes.
dis - ap - pear, Noth - ing thrives a - part from you!
warm the chill, Guide the way - ward home once more!
va - tion, Lord, Give us joys that nev - er end!

Text: *Veni Sancte Spiritus*, 13th. C.; tr. by Peter J. Scagnelli; b.1949, © 1983
Tune: WEBBE, 77 7 D; *An Essay on the Church Plain Chant*, 1782; adapt. by Samuel Webbe, 1740–1816, alt.; harm. from *Hymns Ancient and Modern*, 1916

542 Praise the Spirit in Creation

1. Praise the
2. Praise the
3. Praise the
4. Tell of
5. Pray we

Spir - it in cre - a - tion, Breath of God, life's or - i-
Spir - it, close com - pan - ion Of our in - most thoughts and
Spir - it, who en - light - ened Priests and proph - ets with the
how the as - cend - ed Je - sus Armed a peo - ple for his
then, O Lord the Spir - it, On our lives de - scend in

gin: Spir - it mov - ing on the wa - ters Quick-'ning
ways; Who, in show - ing us God's won - ders, Is him-
word; His the truth be - hind the wis - doms Which as
own; How a hun - dred men and wom - en Turned the
might; Let your flame break out with - in us, Fire our

worlds to life with - in, Source of breath to all things
self the pow'r to gaze; And God's will, to those who
yet know not our Lord; By whose love and pow'r, in
known world up - side down, To its dark and fur - thest
hearts and clear our sight, Till, white - hot in your pos-

breath - ing, Life in whom all lives be - gin.
lis - ten, By a still, small voice con - veys.
Je - sus, God him - self was seen and heard.
cor - ners By the wind of heav - en blown.
ses - sion, We, too, set the world a - light.

Text: Michael Hewlett, 1916–2010, alt., © 1975, Michael Hewlett/Oxford University Press
Tune: JULION, 8 7 8 7 8 7; David Hurd, b.1950, © 1983, GIA Publications, Inc.

Veni Creátor Spíritus   543

1. Ve - ni   Cre - á - tor   Spí - ri - tus,
2. Qui dí - ce - ris   Pa - rá - cli - tus,
3. Tu se - pti - fór - mis   mú - ne - re,
4. Ac - cén - de   lu - men   sén - si - bus,
5. Ho - stem   re - pél - las   lón - gi - us,
6. Per   te   sci - á - mus   da   Pa - trem,
7. De - o   Pa - tri   sit   gló - ri - a,

Men - tes   tu - ó - rum   ví - si - ta:
Al - tís - si - mi   do - num   De - i,
Dí - gi - tus   pa - tér - nae   déx - te - rae,
In - fún - de a - mó - rem   cór - di - bus,
Pa - cém - que   do - nes   pró - ti - nus:
No - scá - mus   at - que   Fí - li - um
Et   Fí - li - o,   qui a   mór - tu - is

Im - ple   su - pér - na   grá - ti - a
Fons vi - vus,   i - gnis,   cá - ri - tas,
Tu ri - te   pro - mís - sum Pa - tris,
In - fír - ma   no - stri   cór - po - ris
Du - ctó - re   sic   te   práe - vi - o,
Te - que u - tri - ús - que   Spí - ri - tum
Sur - ré - xit,   ac   Pa - rá - cli - to,

Quae   tu   cre - á - sti   pé - cto - ra.
Et   spi - ri - tá - lis   ún - cti - o.
Ser - mó - ne   di - tans   gút - tu - ra.
Vir - tú - te   fir - mans   pér - pe - ti.
Vi - té - mus   o - mne   nó - xi - um.
Cre - dá - mus   o - mni   tém - po - re.
In   sae - cu - ló - rum   saé - cu - la.   A - men.

Text: *Veni Creator Spiritus,* attr. to Rabanus Maurus, 776–856
Tune: VENI CREATOR SPIRITUS, LM; Mode VIII; acc. by Richard Proulx, 1937–2010, © 1975, GIA Publications, Inc.

English paraphrases are found at nos. 537, 544, and 546.

544 Come, Holy Ghost

1. Come, Ho - ly Ghost, Cre - a - tor blest, And in our
2. O Com - fort - er, to thee we cry, Thou heav'n - ly
3. O Ho - ly Ghost, through thee a - lone Know we the
4. Praise we the Lord, Fa - ther and Son, And Ho - ly

hearts take up thy rest; Come with thy grace
gift of God most high, Thou fount of life,
Fa - ther and the Son; Be this our firm
Spir - it with them one; And may the Son

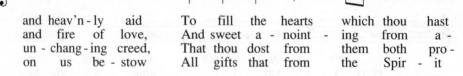

and heav'n - ly aid To fill the hearts which thou hast
and fire of love, And sweet a - noint - ing from a -
un - chang - ing creed, That thou dost from them both pro -
on us be - stow All gifts that from the Spir - it

made, To fill the hearts which thou hast made.
bove, And sweet a - noint - ing from a - bove.
ceed, That thou dost from them both pro - ceed.
flow, All gifts that from the Spir - it flow.

Text: *Veni Creator Spiritus;* attr. to Rabanus Maurus, 776–856; tr. by Edward Caswall, 1814–1878, alt.
Tune: LAMBILLOTTE, LM with repeat; Louis Lambillotte, SJ, 1796–1855; harm. by Richard Proulx, 1937–2010, © 1986, GIA Publications, Inc.

545 Living Spirit, Holy Fire

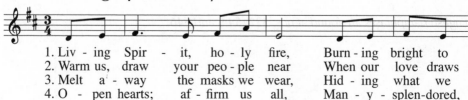

1. Liv - ing Spir - it, ho - ly fire, Burn - ing bright to
2. Warm us, draw your peo - ple near When our love draws
3. Melt a - way the masks we wear, Hid - ing what we
4. O - pen hearts; af - firm us all, Man - y - splen-dored,

light our way, Blaze a - mong us and in - spire
weak or cold. Free our fro - zen hearts from fear,
know and feel. Risk - ing growth, we want to share
one in you; We em - brace the work, the call:

Lives that praise you day by day.
That each sto - ry may be told.
Love in ac - tion, love that's real.
You are mak - ing all things new.

Text: Ruth Duck, b.1947, © 2005, GIA Publications, Inc.
Tune: HOLY FIRE, 7 7 7 7; Lori True, b.1961, © 2007, GIA Publications, Inc.

O Holy Spirit, by Whose Breath 546

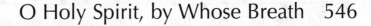

1. O Ho - ly Spir - it, by whose breath Life ris - es
2. You are the seek - er's sure re - source, Of burn - ing
3. In you God's en - er - gy is shown, To us your
4. Flood our dull sens - es with your light; In mu - tual
5. From in - ner strife grant us re - lease; Turn na - tions
6. Praise to the Fa - ther, Christ the Word, And to the

vi - brant out of death: Come to cre - ate, re -
love the liv - ing source, Pro - tec - tor in the
var - ied gifts make known. Teach us to speak, teach
love our hearts u - nite. Your pow'r the whole cre -
to the ways of peace. To full - er life your
Spir - it: God the Lord, To whom all hon - or,

new, in - spire; Come, kin - dle in our hearts your fire.
midst of strife, The giv - er and the Lord of life.
us to hear; Yours is the tongue and yours the ear.
a - tion fills; Con - firm our weak, un - cer - tain wills.
peo - ple bring That as one bod - y we may sing:
glo - ry be Both now and for e - ter - ni - ty.

Text: *Veni Creator Spiritus;* attr. to Rabanus Maurus, 776–865; tr. by John W. Grant, 1919–2006, © 1971
Tune: VENI CREATOR SPIRITUS, LM; Mode VIII; setting by Richard J. Wojcik, b.1923, © 1975, GIA Publications, Inc.

547 Spirit of God within Me

1. Spir - it of God with - in me, Pos-sess my hu - man
2. Spir - it of truth with - in me, Pos-sess my thought and
3. Spir - it of love with - in me, Pos-sess my hands and
4. Spir - it of life with - in me, Pos-sess this life of

frame; Fan the dull em - bers of my heart, Stir
mind; Light - en a - new the in - ward eye By
heart; Break through the bonds of self - con - cern That
mine; Come as the wind of heav-en's breath, Come

up the liv - ing flame. Strive till that im - age A - dam lost,
Sa - tan ren - dered blind. Shine on the words that wis-dom speaks,
seeks to stand a - part. Grant me the love that suf - fers long,
as the fire di - vine! Spir - it of Christ, the liv - ing Lord,

New mint - ed and re - stored, In shin - ing
And grant me pow'r to see The truth made
That hopes, be - lieves, and bears, The love ful -
Reign in this house of clay, Till from its

splen - dor bright-ly bears The like-ness of the Lord.
known to all in Christ, And in that truth be free.
filled in sac - ri - fice That cares as Je - sus cares.
dust with Christ I rise To ev - er - last - ing day.

Text: Timothy Dudley-Smith, b.1926, © 1968, Hope Publishing Company
Tune: WILLOW RIVER, 7 6 8 6 8 6 8 6; Michael Joncas, b.1951, © 1985, 1988, GIA Publications, Inc.

O Dawn of All Creation 548

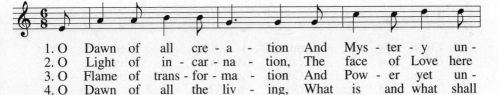

1. O Dawn of all cre - a - tion And Mys - ter - y un -
2. O Light of in - car - na - tion, The face of Love here
3. O Flame of trans - for - ma - tion And Pow - er yet un -
4. O Dawn of all the liv - ing, What is and what shall

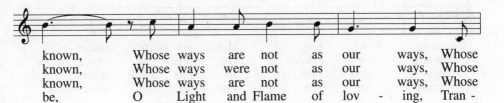

known, Whose ways are not as our ways, Whose
known, Whose ways were not as our ways, Whose
known, Whose ways are not as our ways, Whose
be, O Light and Flame of lov - ing, Tran -

thoughts are not our own: In grace you made and
thoughts were not our own: In fol - ly was your
thoughts are not our own: In per - il you are
scen - dent Mys - ter - y: You dwell where none can

blessed us; In mer - cy you for - gave; In ten - der - ness and
wis - dom; Your wealth, in pov - er - ty; A cross, your ex - al -
fear - less; In hu - man weak - ness, strong; In bond - age you are
fol - low, In worlds be - yond our own, Yet all who seek may

long - ing, In faith - ful - ness you save.
ta - tion; De - feat, your vic - to - ry.
free - dom; In griev - ing hearts, a song.
find you In flesh and blood and bone.

Text: Delores Dufner, OSB, b.1939, © 1999, 2003, GIA Publications, Inc.
Tune: ANDÚJAR, 7 6 7 6 D; David Hurd, b.1950, © 1984, GIA Publications, Inc.

549 Come Now, Almighty King

1. Come now, al - might - y King, Help us your
2. Come now, in - car - nate Word, Mer - ci - ful,
3. Come, ho - ly Com - fort - er, Your sa - cred
4. To the great One in Three, E - ter - nal

name to sing, Help us to praise.
might - y Lord, Our prayer at - tend.
wit - ness bear In this glad hour.
prais - es be For - ev - er - more!

Fa - ther all glo - ri - ous, Ev - er vic - to - ri - ous,
Come and your peo - ple bless, And give your word suc - cess,
Your grace to us im - part, Now rule in ev - 'ry heart,
Your sov - 'reign maj - es - ty May we in glo - ry see

Come and reign o - ver us, An - cient of Days.
Grant us your ho - li - ness, Sav - ior and Friend.
Nev - er from us de - part, Spir - it of pow'r.
And, to e - ter - ni - ty, Love and a - dore.

Text: Anon.; *Collection of Hymns for Social Worship*, 1757, alt.
Tune: ITALIAN HYMN, 66 4 666 4; Felice de Giardini, 1716–1796

550 How Wonderful the Three-in-One

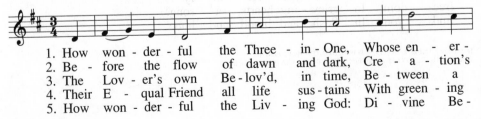

1. How won - der - ful the Three - in - One, Whose en - er -
2. Be - fore the flow of dawn and dark, Cre - a - tion's
3. The Lov - er's own Be - lov'd, in time, Be - tween a
4. Their E - qual Friend all life sus - tains With green - ing
5. How won - der - ful the Liv - ing God: Di - vine Be -

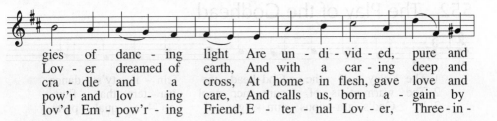

gies of danc - ing light Are un - di - vid - ed, pure and
Lov - er dreamed of earth, And with a car - ing deep and
cra - dle and a cross, At home in flesh, gave love and
pow'r and lov - ing care, And calls us, born a - gain by
lov'd Em - pow'r - ing Friend, E - ter - nal Lov - er, Three - in -

good, Com - mun - ing love in shared de - light.
wise, All things con - ceived and brought to birth.
life To heal our bro - ken - ness and loss.
grace, In Love's com - mun - ing life to share.
One, Our hope's be - gin - ning, way and end.

Text: Brian Wren, b.1936, © 1989, Hope Publishing Company
Tune: ROCKINGHAM, LM; adapted by Edward Miller, 1735–1807

O God, Almighty Father 551

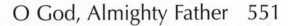

1. O God, al - might - y Fa - ther, Cre - a - tor of all things, The
2. O Je - sus, Word in - car - nate, Re - deem - er most a - dored, All
3. O God, the Ho - ly Spir - it, Who lives with - in our soul, Send

heav - ens stand in won - der, While earth your glo - ry sings.
glo - ry, praise, and hon - or Be yours, O sov - 'reign Lord.
forth your light and lead us To our e - ter - nal goal.

O most ho - ly Trin - i - ty, Un - di - vid - ed u - ni - ty,

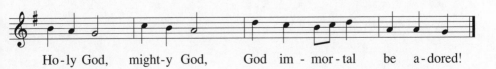

Ho - ly God, might - y God, God im - mor - tal be a - dored!

Text: *Gott Vater sei gepriesen*; anon; tr. by Irvin Udulutsch, OFM Cap., 1920–2010, alt. © 1959, 1977, Order of Saint Benedict, admin. Liturgical Press
Tune: GOTT VATER SEI GEPRIESEN, 7 6 7 6 with refrain; Limburg *Gesangbuch*, 1838; harm. by Healey Willan, 1880–1968, © 1958,
Ralph Jusko Publications, Inc.

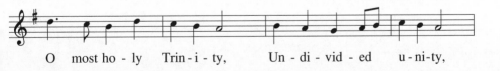

552 The Play of the Godhead

1. The play of the God-head, the Trin - i - ty's dance,
2. The warm mists of sum - mer, cool wa - ters that flow,
3. In God's gra - cious im - age of co - e - qual parts,

Em - brac - es the earth in a sa - cred ro - mance,
Turn crys - tal as ice when the win - try winds blow.
We gath - er as danc - ers, u - nit - ing our hearts.

With God the Cre - a - tor, and Christ the true Son,
The tap - root that nur - tures, the shoot grow - ing free,
Men, wom - en, and chil - dren, and all liv - ing things,

En - twined with the Spir - it, a web dai - ly spun
The life - giv - ing fruit, full and ripe on the tree:
We join in the round of bright na - ture that rings

In span - gles of mys - t'ry, the great Three in One.
More mys - tic and won - drous, the great One in Three.
With rap - ture and rhy - thm: Cre - a - tion now sings!

Text: Mary Louise Bringle, b.1953
Tune: BEDFORD PARK, 11 11 11 11 11 11; Robert J. Batastini, b.1942
© 2002, 2003, GIA Publications, Inc.

Holy, Holy, Holy! Lord God Almighty!   553

1. Ho - ly, Ho - ly, Ho - ly! Lord God Al - might - y! Ear - ly in the morn - ing our song shall rise to thee. Ho - ly, Ho - ly, Ho - ly, mer - ci - ful and might - y! God in three Per - sons, bless - ed Trin - i - ty.

2. Ho - ly, Ho - ly, Ho - ly! All the saints a - dore thee, Cast - ing down their gold - en crowns a - round the glass - y sea; Cher - u - bim and ser - a - phim fall - ing down be - fore thee, God ev - er - last - ing through e - ter - ni - ty.

3. Ho - ly, Ho - ly, Ho - ly! Though the dark - ness hide thee, Though the eye made blind by sin thy glo - ry may not see, On - ly thou art ho - ly; there is none be - side thee, Per - fect in pow'r, in love, and pu - ri - ty.

4. Ho - ly, Ho - ly, Ho - ly! Lord God Al - might - y! All thy works shall praise thy Name in earth and sky and sea. Ho - ly, Ho - ly, Ho - ly, mer - ci - ful and might - y! God in three Per - sons, bless - ed Trin - i - ty.

Text: Reginald Heber, 1783–1826, alt.
Tune: NICAEA, 11 12 12 10; John B. Dykes, 1823–1876

554　Come, Join the Dance of Trinity

1. Come, join the dance of Trin - i - ty, Be -
2. Come, see the face of Trin - i - ty, New -
3. Come, speak a - loud of Trin - i - ty, As
4. With - in the dance of Trin - i - ty, Be -

fore all worlds be - gun, The in - ter - weav - ing
born in Beth - le - hem; Then blood - ied by a
wind and tongues of flame Set peo - ple free at
fore all worlds be - gun, We sing the prais - es

of the Three, The Fa - ther, Spir - it, Son. The
crown of thorns Out - side Je - ru - sa - lem. The
Pen - te - cost To tell the Sav - ior's name. We
of the Three, The Fa - ther, Spir - it, Son. Let

u - ni - verse of space and time Did
dance of Trin - i - ty is meant For
know the yoke of sin and death, Our
voic - es rise and in - ter - weave, By

not a - rise by chance, But as the Three, in
hu - man flesh and bone; When fear con - fines the
necks have worn it smooth; Go tell the world of
love and hope set free, To shape in song this

love and hope, Made room with - in their dance.
dance in death, God rolls a - way the stone.
weight and woe That we are free to move!
joy, this life: The dance of Trin - i - ty.

Text: Richard Leach, b.1953, © 2001, Selah Publishing Co., Inc.
Tune: THE FLIGHT OF THE EARLS; CMD; Irish melody; harm. by Ronald F. Krisman, b.1946, © 2011, GIA Publications, Inc.

Father, Lord of All Creation 555

1. Fa - ther, Lord of all cre - a - tion,
2. Je - sus Christ, the Man for Oth - ers,
3. Ho - ly Spir - it, rush - ing, burn - ing

Ground of Be - ing, Life, and Love, Height and depth be -
We, your peo - ple, make our prayer: May our sis - ters
Wind and flame of Pen - te - cost, Fire our hearts a -

yond de - scrip - tion, On - ly life in you can prove:
and our broth - ers Know that we their bur - dens share.
fresh with yearn - ing To re - gain what we have lost.

You are mor - tal life's de - pen - dence;
Where your name binds us to - geth - er
May your love u - nite our ac - tion,

Thought, speech, sight are ours by grace. Yours is ev - 'ry
You, Lord Christ, will sure - ly be; Where no self - ish -
Nev - er - more to speak a - lone: God, in us a -

hour's ex - ist - ence, Sov - 'reign Lord of time and space.
ness can sev - er, There your love the world may see.
bol - ish fac - tion; God, through us your love make known.

Text: Stewart Cross, 1928–1989, ©, alt.
Tune: GENEVA, 8 7 8 7 D; George H. Day, 1883–1966, © 1942, The Church Pension Fund

556 Hidden Here before Me / Adóro Te Devóte

1. Hid - den here be - fore me, Lord, I wor-ship you,
2. See - ing, touch-ing, tast - ing: these are all de-ceived;
3. On - ly God was hid - den when you came to die;
4. I am not like Thom - as, who could see and touch;

1. A - dó - ro te de - vó - te, la - tens Dé - i - tas,
2. Vi - sus, ta - ctus, gu - stus in te fál - li - tur,
3. In cru - ce la - te - bat so - la Dé - i - tas,
4. Pla - gas, si - cut Tho - mas, non in - tú - e - or

Hid - den in these sym - bols, yet com - plete - ly true.
On - ly through the hear - ing can it be be - lieved.
Hu - man na - ture al - so here es - capes the eye.
Though your wounds are hid - den, I be - lieve as much.

Quae sub his fi - gú - ris ve - re lá - ti - tas:
Sed au - dí - tu so - lo tu - to cré - di - tur:
At hic la - tet si - mul et hu - má - ni - tas:
De - um ta - men me - um te con - fí - te - or:

Lord, my soul sur - ren - ders, long - ing to o - bey,
Noth - ing is more cer - tain: Christ has told me so;
Both are my pro - fes - sion, both are my be - lief;
Let me say so bold - ly, mean - ing what I say,

Ti - bi se cor me - um to - tum súb - ji - cit,
Cre - do quid-quid di - xit De - i Fí - li - us:
Am - bo ta - men cre - dens at - que cón - fi - tens
Fac me ti - bi sem - per ma - gis cré - de - re,

And in con - tem - pla - tion whol - ly faints a - way.
What the Truth has ut - tered, I be - lieve and know.
Bring me to your King - dom, like the dy - ing thief.
Lov - ing you and trust - ing, now and ev - 'ry day.

Qui - a te con - tém - plans to - tum dé - fi - cit.
Nil hoc ver - bo ve - ri - tá - tis vé - ri - us.
Pe - to quod pe - tí - vit la - tro paé - ni - tens.
In te spem ha - bé - re, te di - lí - ge - re.

5. Record of the Passion when the Lamb was slain,
   Living bread that brings us back to life again:
   Feed me with your presence, make me live on you;
   Let that lovely fragrance fill me through and through.

6. Once a nesting pelican gashed herself to blood
   For the preservation of her starving brood.
   Now heal me with your blood, take away my guilt:
   All the world is ransomed if one drop is spilt.

7. Jesus, for the present seen as through a mask,
   Give me what I thirst for, give me what I ask:
   Let me see your glory in a blaze of light,
   And instead of blindness give me, Lord, my sight.

5. *O memoriále mortis Dómini,*
   Panis vivus vitam praestans hómini,
   Praesta meae menti de te vívere,
   Et ti illi semper dulce sápere.

6. *Pie pellicáne, Jesu Dómine,*
   Me immúndum munda tuo sánguine,
   Cuius una stilla salvum fácere,
   Totum mundum quit ab omni scélere.

7. *Jesu, quem velátum nunc aspício,*
   Oro fiat illud quod tam sítio:
   Ut te reveláta cernens fácie,
   Visu sim beátus tuae glóriae.

Text: *Adoro te devote*, attr. to St. Thomas Aquinas, c.1225–1274; English tr. from *A Book of Prayers*, © 1982, ICEL
Tune: ADORO TE DEVOTE, 11 11 11 11; Mode V, *Processionale*, Paris, 1697; acc. by Richard Proulx, 1937–2010, © 1986, GIA Publications, Inc.

557 O Food of Exiles Lowly / O Esca Viatórum

1. O Food of ex - iles low - ly, O Bread of an - gels
2. O cleans-ing wa - ter, stream - ing From Je - sus' side, re -
3. O Lord, we kneel be - fore you And fer - vent - ly a -

1. O es - ca vi - a - tó - rum, O pa - nis an - ge -
2. O lym - pha, fons a - mó - ris, Qui pu - ro Sal - va -
3. O Je - su, tu - um vul - tum Quem có - li - mus oc -

ho - ly, O Man - na from on high! We
deem - ing All those of A - dam's race! O
dore you, Now veiled in heav - 'nly bread. Our

ló - rum, O man - na caé - li - tum! E -
tó - ris E cor - de pró - flu - is! Te
cúl - tum Sub pa - nis spé - ci - e. Fac

hun - ger for your bless - ing, All good in you pos -
quench-ing foun-tain flow - ing, Our ev - 'ry want be -
hope is in your prom - ise: To see you in your

su - ri - én - tes ci - ba, Dul - cé - di - ne non
si - ti - én - tes po - ta, Haec so - la no - stra
ut, re - mó - to ve - lo, Post lí - be - ra in

sess - ing; With fa - vor hear our hearts' out - cry.
stow - ing, O come and fill our souls with grace.
full - ness, The sa - cred bod - y's mys - tic Head.

pri - va, Cor - da quae - rén - ti - um.
vo - ta, His u - na súf - fi - cis.
cae - lo Cer - ná - mus fá - ci - e!

Text: *O esca viatorum;* Mainz *Gesangbuch,* 1661; tr. by M. Owen Lee, CSB, b.1930, *The New Saint Basil Hymnal,* © The Willis Music Co.
Tune: INNSBRUCK, 77 6 77 8; Heinrich Isaac, 1450–1517; harm. by J. S. Bach, 1685–1750

Tell the Gospel's Boundless Riches 558

1. Tell the gos - pel's bound - less rich - es, Plan of
2. See the love of God in Je - sus, Car - ing
3. Praise the heart of God in Je - sus, Self - less
4. Live the new com - mand - ment giv - en: "As I

God from a - ges past: Christ em - brac - es all cre -
for the poor op - pressed, Call - ing out to wea - ry
to his fi - nal breath, Giv - ing for our life his
did, so you must do: Wash the feet of one an -

a - tion With a love pro - found and vast.
pil - grims, "Come to me and find your rest."
bod - y, Lov - ing e - ven un - to death.
oth - er, Lov - ing all as I love you."

Know this love sur - pass - ing knowl - edge; Know its
See the love re - vealed by Je - sus, Who with
Praise the sa - cred heart of Je - sus, Ten - der
Live the love of Christ a - mong us, Feed - ing,

breadth and depth and height; Know the heart of God in
gen - tle, hum - ble heart Par - doned and be - friend - ed
love's most tell - ing sign, Heart of God's im - mense com -
heal - ing, set - ting free, Seek - ing out and bring - ing

Je - sus, Heart of mer - cy, warmth, and light.
sin - ners, Wel - comed lep - ers set a - part.
pas - sion, Heart both hu - man and di - vine.
oth - ers In - to love's com - mu - ni - ty.

Text: Delores Dufner, OSB, b.1939, © 2009, GIA Publications, Inc.
Tune: RUSTINGTON, 8 7 8 7 D; Charles H. H. Parry, 1848–1918

559 O Christ, Your Heart Compassionate

1. O Christ, your heart com - pas - sion - ate, Bore ev - 'ry hu - man pain. Its beat - ing was the pulse of God; Its breadth, God's vast do - main. The heart of God, the heart of Christ, Com - bined in per - fect rhyme To write God's love in hu - man deeds, E - ter - ni - ty in time.

2. As once you wel - comed those cast down And healed the sick, the blind, So may all bruised and bro - ken lives Through us your help still find. Lord, join our hearts with those who weep That none may weep a - lone, And help us bear an - oth - er's pain As though it were our own.

3. O Christ, cre - ate new hearts in us That beat in time with yours, That, joined by faith with your great heart, Be - come Love's o - pen doors. We are your bod - y, ris - en Christ; Our hearts, our hands, we yield That through our life may be re - vealed Your love may be re - vealed.

4. O Love that made the dis - tant stars Yet marks the spar - row's fall, Whose arms, stretched wide up - on a cross, Em - brace and bear us all: Come, make your Church a ser - vant Church That walks your ser - vant ways, That through our life and love rise up to you, A sac - ri - fice of praise!

Text: Herman G. Stuempfle, Jr., 1923–2007, © 2006, GIA Publications, Inc.
Tune: RESIGNATION, CMD; Funk's *Compilation of Genuine Church Music*, 1832; harm. by Richard Proulx, 1937–2010, © 1975, GIA Publications, Inc.

To Christ, the Prince of Peace   560

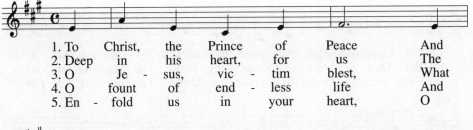

1. To Christ, the Prince of Peace   And
2. Deep in his heart, for us   The
3. O Je - sus, vic - tim blest,   What
4. O fount of end - less life   And
5. En - fold us in your heart,   O

Son of God most high,   The rul - er of the
wound of love he bore,   That love with which he
else but pur - est love   Could make your sa - cred
spring of wa - ter clear,   O heav'n - ly flame which
Je - sus, Sav - ior blest,   So shall we find your

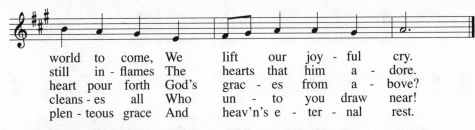

world to come, We   lift our joy - ful cry.
still in - flames The   hearts that him a - dore.
heart pour forth God's   grac - es from a - bove?
cleans - es all Who   un - to you draw near!
plen - teous grace And   heav'n's e - ter - nal rest.

Text: *Summi parentis filio*; Roman Breviary, 1736; tr. by Edward Caswall, 1814–1876, alt.
Tune: FESTAL SONG, SM; William H. Walter, 1825–1893

At the Name of Jesus   561

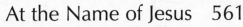

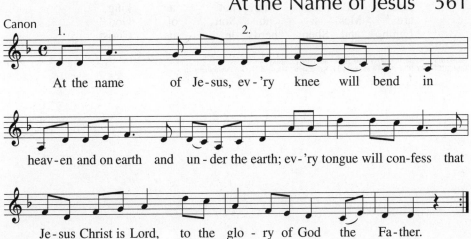

Canon

At the name   of Je-sus, ev-'ry knee will bend in

heav-en and on earth   and un - der the earth; ev-'ry tongue will con-fess that

Je - sus Christ is Lord,   to the glo - ry of God the Fa-ther.

Text: Philippians 2:10–11
Tune: James E. Clemens, © 2008, James E. Clemens

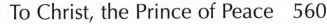

562 Let Kings and Prophets Yield Their Name

1. Let kings and proph-ets yield their name To Je-sus, true A-noint-ed One, For whom a na-tion looked in hope Yet failed to see that God had done A strange and un-ex-pect-ed thing: God sent a ser-vant, not a king.

2. But God re-veals to search-ing faith The truths that pi-ous dog-mas hide: When Je-sus asked the twelve his name, Blunt Pe-ter stepped forth and re-plied In words that seemed both right and odd: "You are Mes-si-ah, Son of God."

3. Give us, O God, the grace to know The lim-its of our cer-tain-ty: Help us, like Pe-ter, to de-clare The still-un-fold-ing mys-ter-y Of One who reigns though sac-ri-ficed, Our Lamb and Shep-herd, Je-sus Christ.

Text: Carl P. Daw, Jr., b.1944, © 1990, Hope Publishing Company
Tune: HICKORY HILL, 8 8 8 8 88; Ronald F. Krisman, b.1946, © 2011, GIA Publications, Inc.

Alternate tune: MELITA

At the Name of Jesus 563

1. At the Name of Je - sus Ev - 'ry knee shall bow, Ev - 'ry tongue con - fess him King of glo - ry now. It is God's good pleas - ure We should call him Lord, Who from the be - gin - ning Was the might - y Word.

2. At his voice cre - a - tion Sprang at once to sight, All the an - gel fac - es, All the hosts of light, Thrones and Dom - i - na - tions, Stars up - on their way, All the heav'n - ly or - ders In their great ar - ray.

3. Hum - bled for a sea - son, To re - ceive a Name From the lips of sin - ners Un - to whom he came, Faith - ful - ly he bore it Spot - less to the last; Brought it back vic - to - rious When from death he passed.

4. In your hearts en - throne him; There let him sub - due All that is not ho - ly, All that is not true. Crown him as your cap - tain In temp - ta - tion's hour; Let his will en - fold you In its light and pow'r.

5. Chris - tians, this Lord Je - sus Shall re - turn a - gain On the clouds of glo - ry, O'er the earth to reign. Love and faith - ful serv - ice We his peo - ple vow, And our hearts con - fess him King of glo - ry now.

Text: Philippians 2:5–7; Caroline M. Noel, 1817–1877, alt.
Tune: KING'S WESTON, 6 5 6 5 D; Ralph Vaughan Williams, 1872–1958, alt., © 1931, Oxford University Press

564 Rejoice, the Lord Is King!

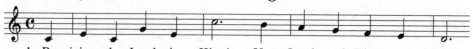

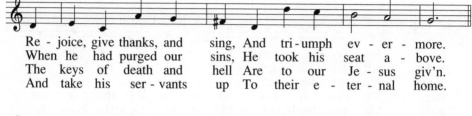

1. Re - joice, the Lord is King! Your Lord and King a - dore!
2. The Lord, our Sav - ior, reigns, The God of truth and love.
3. His king-dom can - not fail, He rules o'er earth and heav'n.
4. Re - joice in glo - rious hope! For Christ the Judge shall come

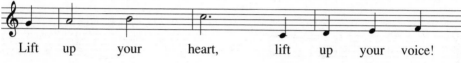

Re - joice, give thanks, and sing, And tri - umph ev - er - more.
When he had purged our sins, He took his seat a - bove.
The keys of death and hell Are to our Je - sus giv'n.
And take his ser - vants up To their e - ter - nal home.

Lift up your heart, lift up your voice!

Re - joice, a - gain I say, re - joice!

Text: Charles Wesley, 1707–1788, alt.
Tune: DARWALL'S 148TH, 6 6 6 6 with refrain; John Darwall, 1731–1789; harm. from *The Hymnal 1940*

565 The King of Glory

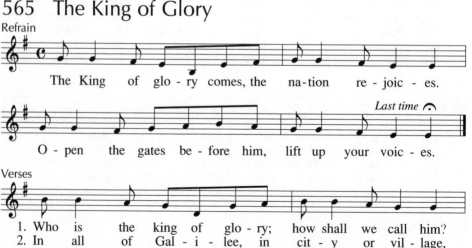

Refrain

The King of glo - ry comes, the na - tion re - joic - es.

Last time

O - pen the gates be - fore him, lift up your voic - es.

Verses

1. Who is the king of glo - ry; how shall we call him?
2. In all of Gal - i - lee, in cit - y or vil - lage,
3. Sing then of Da - vid's Son, our Sav - ior and broth - er;
4. He gave his life for us, the pledge of sal - va - tion,
5. He con - quered sin and death; he tru - ly has ris - en.

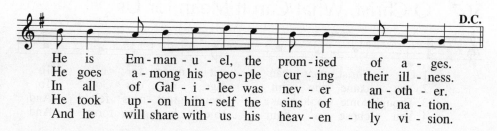

He is Em - man - u - el, the prom - ised of a - ges.
He goes a - mong his peo - ple cur - ing their ill - ness.
In all of Gal - i - lee was nev - er an - oth - er.
He took up - on him - self the sins of the na - tion.
And he will share with us his heav - en - ly vi - sion.

Text: Willard F. Jabusch, b.1930, © 1966, 1982, Willard F. Jabusch. Administered by OCP.
Tune: KING OF GLORY, 12 12 with refrain; Israeli; harm. by Richard Proulx, 1937–2010, © 1986, GIA Publications, Inc.

All Hail the Power of Jesus' Name! 566

1. All hail the pow'r of Je - sus' name! Let an - gels pros - trate
2. Crown him, you mar - tyrs of our God Who from his al - tar
3. O seed of Is - rael's cho - sen race Now ran - somed from the
4. Oh, that with yon - der sa - cred throng We at his feet may

fall. Bring forth the roy - al di - a - dem, And
call: Ex - tol the stem of Jes - se's rod, And
fall, Hail him who saves you by his grace, And
fall! We'll join the ev - er - last - ing song And

crown him Lord of all. Bring forth the roy - al
crown him Lord of all. Ex - tol the stem of
crown him Lord of all. Hail him who saves you
crown him Lord of all. We'll join the ev - er -

di - a - dem, And crown him Lord of all!
Jes - se's rod, And crown him Lord of all!
by his grace, And crown him Lord of all!
last - ing song And crown him Lord of all!

Text: Edward Perronet, 1726–1792; alt. by John Rippon, 1751–1836, alt.
Tune: CORONATION, 8 6 8 6 8 6; Oliver Holden, 1765–1844

567 O Christ, What Can It Mean for Us

1. O Christ, what can it mean for us To claim you as our king? What roy-al face have you re-vealed Whose praise the Church would sing? As-pir-ing not to glo-ry's height, To pow-er, wealth, and fame, You walked a dif-f'rent, low-ly way, An-oth-er's will your aim.

2. You came, the im-age of our God, To heal and to for-give, To shed your blood for sin-ners' sake That we might rise and live. To break the law of death you came, The law of love to bring: A dif-f'rent rule of right-eous-ness, A dif-f'rent kind of king.

3. Though some would make their great-ness felt And lord it o-ver all, You said the first must be the last And serv-ice be our call. O Christ, in work-place, church, and home, Let none to pow-er cling; For still, through us, you come to serve, A dif-f'rent kind of king.

4. You chose a hum-ble hu-man form And shunned the world's re-nown; You died for us up-on a cross With thorns your on-ly crown. But still, be-yond the span of years, Our glad ho-san-nas ring, For now at God's right hand you reign, A dif-f'rent kind of king!

Text: Delores Dufner, OSB, b.1939, © 2001, 2003, GIA Publications, Inc.
Tune: IN NOMINE DEI, CMD; Sally Ann Morris, b.1952, © 2009, GIA Publications, Inc.

Alternate tune: KINGSFOLD

Christ Is the King!   568

1. Christ   is   the   King!   O   friends,   re - joice;
2. O   mag - ni - fy   the   Lord,   and   raise
3. They   with   a   faith   for   ev - er   new
4. O   Chris - tian   wom - en,   Chris - tian   men,
5. Christ through   all   a - ges   is   the   same;

Broth - ers   and   sis - ters,   with   one   voice
An - thems   of   joy   and   ho - ly   praise
Fol - lowed   the   King,   and   round him   drew
All   the   world   o - ver,   seek   a - gain
Place   the   same   hope   in   his great   name;

Let   the   world   know   he   is   your   choice.
For   Christ's   brave   saints   of   an - cient   days.
Thou - sands   of   men   and   wom - en   true.
The   Way   dis - ci - ples   fol - lowed   then.
With   the   same   faith   his   word pro - claim.

Al - le - lu - ia,   al - le - lu - ia,   al - le - lu - ia.

6. Let Love's all reconciling might
Your scattered companies unite
In service to the Lord of light.
Alleluia, alleluia, alleluia.

7. So shall the Church at last be one;
So shall God's will on earth be done,
New lamps be lit, new tasks begun.
Alleluia, alleluia, alleluia.

Text: George K. A. Bell, 1883–1958, alt., © Oxford University Press
Tune: GELOBT SEI GOTT, 888 with alleluias; Melchior Vulpius, c.1570–1615

569 Jesus Shall Reign

1. Je - sus shall reign wher - e'er the sun
2. To him shall end - less prayer be made,
3. Peo - ple and realms of ev - 'ry tongue
4. Bless - ings a - bound wher - e'er he reigns:
5. Let ev - 'ry crea - ture rise and bring

Does its suc - ces - sive jour - neys run;
And prais - es throng to crown his head;
Dwell on his love with sweet - est song;
The pris - 'ners leap to lose their chains,
Bless - ing and hon - or to our King,

His king - dom stretch from shore to shore,
His name like sweet per - fume shall rise
And in - fant voic - es shall pro - claim
The wea - ry find e - ter - nal rest,
An - gels de - scend with songs a - gain,

Till moons shall wax and wane no more.
With ev - 'ry morn - ing sac - ri - fice.
Their ear - ly bless - ings on his name.
And all who suf - fer want are blest.
And earth re - peat the loud A - men.

Text: Isaac Watts, 1674–1748, alt.
Tune: DUKE STREET, LM; John Hatton, c.1710–1793

To Jesus Christ, Our Sovereign King   570

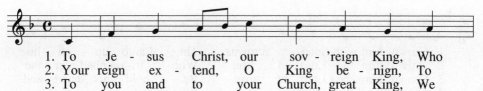

1. To Je - sus Christ, our sov - 'reign King, Who
2. Your reign ex - tend, O King be - nign, To
3. To you and to your Church, great King, We

is the world's sal - va - tion, All praise and hom - age
ev - 'ry land and na - tion; For in your king - dom,
pledge our hearts' ob - la - tion Un - til be - fore your

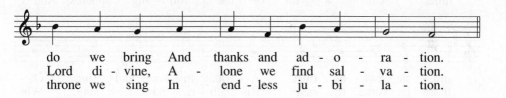

do we bring And thanks and ad - o - ra - tion.
Lord di - vine, A - lone we find sal - va - tion.
throne we sing In end - less ju - bi - la - tion.

Christ Je - sus, Vic - tor! Christ Je - sus, Rul - er!

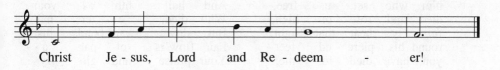

Christ Je - sus, Lord and Re - deem - er!

Text: Martin B. Hellriegel, 1890–1981, alt., © 1941, Irene C. Mueller
Tune: ICH GLAUB AN GOTT, 8 7 8 7 with refrain; Mainz *Gesangbuch*, 1870; harm. by Richard Proulx, 1937–2010, © 1986, GIA Publications, Inc.

571 Crown Him with Many Crowns

1. Crown him with man - y crowns, The Lamb up - on his
2. Crown him the Lord of life, Who tri - umphed o'er the
3. Crown him the Lord of love— Be - hold his hands and
4. Crown him the Lord of peace, Whose pow'r a scep - ter
5. Crown him the Lord of years, The mas - ter of all

throne. Hark! How the heav'n - ly an - them drowns All
grave, And rose vic - to - rious in the strife For
side, Rich wounds, yet vis - i - ble a - bove, In
sways From pole to pole, that wars may cease, Ab -
time, Cre - a - tor of the roll - ing spheres, And

mu - sic but its own. A - wake, my soul, and sing Of
those he came to save. His glo - ries now we sing, Who
beau - ty glo - ri - fied. No an - gel in the sky Can
sorbed by prayer and praise. His reign shall know no end, And
ris - en Lord sub - lime. All hail, Re - deem - er, hail! For

him who set us free, And hail him as your
died and rose on high, Who died, e - ter - nal
ful - ly bear that sight, But down - ward bends his
round his pierc - ed feet Fair flow'rs of par - a -
you have died for me; Your praise and glo - ry

heav'n - ly King Through all e - ter - ni - ty.
life to bring, And lives that death may die.
burn - ing eye At mys - ter - ies so bright.
dise ex - tend Their fra - grance ev - er sweet.
shall not fail Through - out e - ter - ni - ty.

Text: Revelation 19:12; st. 1, 3–5, Matthew Bridges, 1800–1894; st. 2, Godfrey Thring, 1823–1903
Tune: DIADEMATA, SMD; George J. Elvey, 1816–1893

I Sing the Mighty Power of God 572

1. I sing the might - y pow'r of God That
2. I sing the good - ness of the Lord That
3. There's not a plant or flow'r be - low But

made the moun-tains rise, That spread the flow - ing
filled the earth with food. God formed the crea - tures
makes your glo - ries known; And clouds a - rise and

seas a - broad, And built the loft - y skies. I
with a word And then pro-nounced them good. Lord,
tem - pests blow By or - der from your throne. Your

sing the wis - dom that or - dained The
how your won - ders are dis - played Wher -
crea - tures, count - less though they be, Are

sun to rule by day; The moon shines full at
e'er I turn my eye, If I sur - vey the
sub - ject to your care. There's not a place where

God's com - mand, And all the seas o - bey.
ground I tread, Or gaze up - on the sky!
we can flee, But you are pre - sent there.

Text: Isaac Watts, 1674–1748, alt.
Tune: MOZART, CMD; adapt. from Wolfgang A. Mozart, 1756–1791

573 Let All Creation Bless the Lord

1. Let all cre - a - tion bless the Lord, Till heav'n with
2. All liv - ing things up - on the earth, Green fer - tile
3. O men and wom - en ev - 'ry - where, Lift up a

praise is ring - ing. Sun, moon, and stars, peal out a
hills and moun - tains, Sing to the God who gave you
hymn of glo - ry. Let all who know God's stead - fast

chord, Stir up the an - gels' sing - ing. Sing, wind and
birth! Be joy-ful, springs and foun - tains! Lithe wa - ter -
care Tell out sal - va - tion's sto - ry. No tongue be

rain! Sing, snow and sleet! Make mu - sic, day, night, cold and
life, bright air - borne birds, Wild rov - ing beasts, tame flocks and
si - lent; sing your part, You hum - ble souls and meek of

heat: Ex - alt the God who made you.
herds: Ex - alt the God who made you.
heart: Ex - alt the God who made you.

Text: Based on Daniel 3:57–88, Carl P. Daw, Jr., b.1944, © 1989, Hope Publishing Company
Tune: LOBT GOTT DEN HERREN, 8 7 8 7 88 7; Melchior Vulpius, c.1570–1615, *Ein schön geistlich Gesangbuch*, 1609

All Things Bright and Beautiful   574

Refrain

All things bright and beau - ti - ful, All
crea - tures great and small, All things wise and
won - der - ful: The Lord God made them all.

Verses

1. Each lit - tle flow'r that o - pens, Each
2. The pur - ple - head - ed moun - tains, The
3. The cold wind in the win - ter, The
4. God gave us eyes to see them, And

lit - tle bird that sings, God made their glow - ing
riv - er run - ning by, The sun - set, and the
pleas-ant sum - mer sun, The ripe fruits in the
lips that we might tell How great is God Al -

D.C.

col - ors, God made their ti - ny wings.
morn - ing That bright - ens up the sky.
gar - den: God made them ev - 'ry one.
might - y, Who has made all things well.

Text: Cecil F. Alexander, 1818–1895, alt.
Tune: ROYAL OAK, 7 6 7 6 with refrain; English melody; adapt. by Martin Shaw, 1875–1958

575 Many and Great, O God

1. Man-y and great, O God, are your works,
2. Grant un-to us com-mun-ion with you,

Mak-er of earth and sky. Your hands have
O Star-a-bid-ing One. Come close to

set the heav-ens with stars; Your fin-gers spread the
us and stay by our side; With you are found the

moun-tains and plains. Lo, at your word the
true gifts that last. Bless us with life that

wa-ters were formed; Deep seas o-bey your voice.
nev-er shall end, E-ter-nal life with you.

Text: *Wakantanka tuku nitawa;* Dakota hymn; para. by Philip Frazier, 1892–1964
Tune: LACQUIPARLE, 9 6 9 9 9 6; *Dakota Odowan,* 1879; acc. by John L. Bell, b.1949, © 1993, Iona Community, GIA Publications, Inc., agent

Canticle of the Sun 576

Refrain

The heav-ens are tell-ing the glo-ry of God, and all cre-a-tion is shout-ing for joy. Come, dance in the for-est, come, play in the field, and sing, sing to the glo-ry of the Lord.

Verses

1. Praise for the sun, the bring-er of day, He car-ries the
2. Praise for the wind that blows through the trees, The seas' might-y
3. Praise for the rain that wa-ters our fields, And bless-es our
4. Praise for the fire who gives us his light, The warmth of the
5. Praise for the earth who makes life to grow, The crea-tures you
6. Praise for our death that makes our life real, The knowl-edge of

light of the Lord in his rays; The moon and the stars who
storms, ⁊ the gen-tl-est breeze; They blow where they will, they
crops ⁊ so all the earth yields; From death un-to life her
sun ⁊ to bright-en our night; He danc-es with joy, his
made ⁊ to let your life show; The flow-ers and trees that
loss ⁊ that helps us to feel; The gift of your-self, your

D.C.

light up the way Un-to your throne.
blow where they please To please the Lord.
mys-t'ry re-vealed Springs forth in joy.
spir-it so bright, He sings of you.
help us to know The heart of love.
pres-ence re-vealed To lead us home.

Text: *Altissimu, onnipotente bon Signore*; St. Francis of Assisi, 1181–1226; adapt. by Marty Haugen, b.1950
Tune: Marty Haugen, b.1950
© 1980, GIA Publications, Inc.

577 God of the Sparrow

1. God of the spar - row   God of the whale
2. God of the earth - quake God of the storm
3. God of the rain - bow   God of the cross
4. God of the hun - gry   God of the sick
5. God of the neigh - bor   God of the foe
6. God of the a - ges   God near at hand

God of the swirl - ing stars
God of the trum - pet blast
God of the emp - ty grave
God of the prod - i - gal
God of the prun - ing hook
God of the lov - ing heart

How does the crea - ture say   Awe
How does the crea - ture cry   Woe
How does the crea - ture say   Grace
How does the crea - ture say   Care
How does the crea - ture say   Love
How do your chil - dren say   Joy

1.–5.

How does the crea - ture say   Praise
How does the crea - ture cry   Save
How does the crea - ture say   Thanks
How does the crea - ture say   Life
How does the crea - ture say   Peace
How do your chil - dren say

6.

Home

Text: Jaroslav J. Vajda, 1919–2008, © 1983, Concordia Publishing House
Tune: ROEDER, 9 6 7 7; Carl F. Schalk, b.1929, © 1983, GIA Publications, Inc.

How Great Thou Art 578

1. O Lord my God, when I in awe-some
2. When through the woods and for-est glades I
3. And when I think that God, his Son not
4. When Christ shall come with shout of ac-cla-

won-der Con-sid-er all the works thy hands have
wan-der And hear the birds sing sweet-ly in the
spar-ing, Sent him to die, I scarce can take it
ma-tion And take me home, what joy shall fill my

made, I see the stars, I hear the roll-ing
trees, When I look down from loft-y moun-tain
in That on the cross, my bur-den glad-ly
heart! Then I shall bow in hum-ble ad-o-

thun-der, Thy pow'r through-out the u-ni-verse dis-played!
gran-deur And hear the brook and feel the gen-tle breeze,
bear-ing, He bled and died to take a-way my sin!
ra-tion And there pro-claim, "My God, how great thou art!"

Then sings my soul, my Sav-ior God, to thee: How great thou

art, how great thou art! Then sings my soul, my Sav-ior God, to

thee: How great thou art, how great thou art!

Text: Stuart K. Hine, 1899–1989
Tune: HOW GREAT THOU ART, 11 10 11 10 with refrain; Stuart K. Hine, 1899–1989
© 1949, 1953, Stuart K. Hine Trust. Print rights administered by Hope Publishing Company in the USA.

579 Go Down, Moses

1. When Is - rael was in E - gypt's land,
2. The Lord told Mo - ses what to do,
3. As Is - rael stood by the wa - ter side,
4. When they had reached the oth - er shore,
5. Oh, let us all from bon - dage flee,

Op - pressed so hard they
To lead the chil - dren of
At God's com - mand it
They sang the song of
And let us all in

Let my peo-ple go;

could not stand,
Is - rael through,
did di - vide,
tri - umph o'er,
Christ be free,

Let my peo - ple go.

Go down, Mo-ses, way down in E - gypt land,

Tell ol' Phar-aoh, let my peo-ple go.

Text: Exodus; African American spiritual
Tune: GO DOWN MOSES, Irregular with refrain; African American spiritual

O God, You Search Me 580

1. O God, you search me and you know me. All my
2. You know my rest-ing and my ris-ing. You dis-
3. Be - fore a word is on my tongue, Lord, You have
4. Al - though your Spir - it is up - on me, Still I
5. For you cre - at - ed me and shaped me, Gave me

thoughts lie o - pen to your gaze. When I
cern my pur - pose from a - far, And with
known its mean - ing through and through. You are
search for shel - ter from your light. There is
life with - in my moth - er's womb. For the

walk or lie down you are be - fore me: Ev - er the
love ev - er - last - ing you be - siege me: In ev - 'ry
with me be - yond my un - der - stand - ing: God of my
no - where on earth I can es - cape you: E - ven the
won - der of who I am, I praise you: Safe in your

mak - er and keep - er of my days.
mo - ment of life or death, you are.
pres - ent, my past and fu - ture, too.
dark - ness is ra - diant in your sight.
hands, all cre - a - tion is made new.

Text: Based on Psalm 139; Bernadette Farrell, b.1957
Tune: Bernadette Farrell, b.1957
© 1992, Bernadette Farrell. Published by OCP.

581 We Are Known and Not Unnumbered

1. We are known and not un-num - bered Like the
2. We are known and not for-got - ten Like a
3. We are known and not re - ject - ed Like a
4. We are known, re - mem-bered, cher - ished, When we

stars that fill the sky. Vast the cos - mic sweep be -
he - ro's fad - ed wreath. Time through end - less a - ges
beg - gar held at bay. Though we mar, dis - tort your
wan - der lost, a - lone. Though we break the bonds that

yond us, Faint the in - fant's new-born cry; Yet your
stretch - es, Brief our mo-ment's mor - tal breath; Yet your
im - age, Though we turn from you a - way, Still you
bind us, Still you name us as your own. We may

ear, O God, is lis - t'ning When the heart can scarce-ly sigh.
hand, O God, sup - ports us, Holds us both in life and death.
seek us out in mer - cy, Hear and an - swer when we pray.
fill this crowd-ed plan - et, Yet you love us each as one.

Text: Herman G. Stuempfle, Jr., 1923–2007, © 2006, GIA Publications, Inc.
Tune: LAUDA ANIMA, 8 7 8 7 8 7; John Goss, 1800–1880

582 When You, Lord, Walked

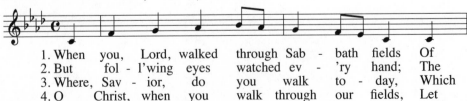

1. When you, Lord, walked through Sab - bath fields Of
2. But fol - l'wing eyes watched ev - 'ry hand; The
3. Where, Sav - ior, do you walk to - day, Which
4. O Christ, when you walk through our fields, Let

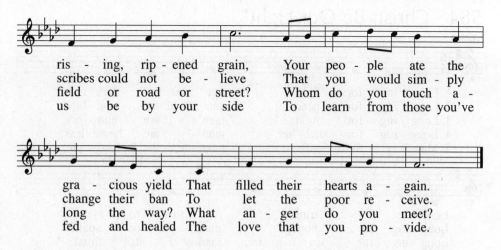

ris - ing, rip - ened grain, Your peo - ple ate the
scribes could not be - lieve That you would sim - ply
field or road or street? Whom do you touch a -
us be by your side To learn from those you've

gra - cious yield That filled their hearts a - gain.
change their ban To let the poor re - ceive.
long the way? What an - ger do you meet?
fed and healed The love that you pro - vide.

Text: Sylvia G. Dunstan, 1955–1993, © 1991, GIA Publications, Inc.
Tune: MORNING SONG, CM; Wyeth's *Repository of Sacred Music*, 1813; harm. by Richard Proulx, 1937–2010, © 1975, GIA Publications, Inc.

Arise, Your Light Has Come! 583

1. A - rise, your light has come! The
2. A - rise, your light has come! Fling
3. A - rise, your light has come! All
4. A - rise, your light has come! The

Spir - it's call o - bey; Show forth the glo - ry
wide the pris - on door; Pro - claim the cap - tive's
you in sor - row born, Bind up the bro - ken -
moun - tains burst in song! Rise up like ea - gles

of your God Which shines on you to - day.
lib - er - ty, Good tid - ings to the poor.
heart - ed ones And com - fort those who mourn.
on the wing; God's pow'r will make us strong.

Text: Ruth Duck, b.1947, alt., © 1992, GIA Publications, Inc.
Tune: FESTAL SONG, SM; William H. Walter, 1825–1893

584   Christ, Be Our Light!

Verses

1. Long-ing for light, we wait in dark-ness.
2. Long-ing for peace, our world is trou-bled.
3. Long-ing for food, man-y are hun-gry.
4. Long-ing for shel-ter, man-y are home-less.
5. Man-y the gifts, man-y the peo-ple,

Long-ing for truth, we turn to you.
Long-ing for hope, man-y de-spair.
Long-ing for wa-ter, man-y still thirst.
Long-ing for warmth, man-y are cold.
Man-y the hearts that yearn to be-long.

Make us your own, your ho-ly peo-ple,
Your word a-lone has pow'r to save us.
Make us your bread, bro-ken for oth-ers,
Make us your build-ing, shel-ter-ing oth-ers,
Let us be ser-vants to one an-oth-er,

Light for the world to see.
Make us your liv-ing voice.
Shared un-til all are fed.
Walls made of liv-ing stone.
Mak-ing your king-dom come.

Refrain

Christ, be our light! Shine in our hearts.

Shine through the dark-ness. Christ, be our light!

Shine in your Church gath-ered to-day.

Text: Bernadette Farrell, b.1957
Tune: CHRIST, BE OUR LIGHT, 9 8 9 6 with refrain; Bernadette Farrell, b.1957
© 1993, 2000, Bernadette Farrell. Published by OCP.

I Want to Walk as a Child of the Light 585

1. I want to walk as a child of the light.
2. I want to see the bright-ness of God.
3. I'm look-ing for the com-ing of Christ.

I want to fol - low Je - sus.
I want to look at Je - sus.
I want to be with Je - sus.

God set the stars to give light to the world. The
Clear sun of right-eous-ness shine on my path And
When we have run with pa-tience the race, We

star of my life is Je - sus.
show me the way to the Fa - ther.
shall know the joy of Je - sus.

In him there is no dark - ness at all. The

night and the day are both a - like. The

Lamb is the light of the cit - y of God.

Shine in my heart, Lord Je - sus.

Text: Ephesians 5:8–10, Revelation 21:23, John 12:46, 1 John 1:5, Hebrews 12:1; Kathleen Thomerson, b.1934
Tune: HOUSTON, 10 7 10 8 with refrain; Kathleen Thomerson, b.1934
© 1970, 1975, Celebration

586 We Are Marching / Siyahamba

We are march - ing* in the light of God, we are
Si - ya - hamb' e - ku-kha-nyen' kwen-khos', si - ya -

1.
march-ing in the light of God.
hamb' e - ku - kha-nyen' kwen-khos'.

2.
march - ing in the light of, the
hamb' e - ku-kha-nyen' kwen, kha -

God.
khos'.

God.
khos'.

We are march - ing,
Si - ya - ham - ba,

light of God. We are march-ing,
nyen' kwen - khos'. Si - ya - ham - ba,

march-ing, we are
ham - ba, si - ya -

Oo

march - ing, march-ing, we are march-ing in the light of God.
ham - ba, ham - ba, si - ya - hamb' e - ku-kha-nyen' kwen-khos'.

Alternate text: dancing, singing, praying

Text: South African
Tune: South African
© 1984, Utryck, Walton Music Corporation, agent

Lord Jesus Christ / Jésus le Christ   587

Ostinato Refrain

Lord Je - sus Christ, your light shines with - in us.
French: Jé - sus le Christ, lu - mière in - té - rieu - re,
Spanish: Cris - to Je - sús, oh fue - go que a-bra - sa,
Polish: Je - zu, Tyś jest świat - łoś - cią mej du - szy.

Let not my doubts nor my dark - ness speak to me.
ne lais - se pas mes té - nè - bres me par - ler.
que las ti - nie - blas en mí no ten - gan voz.
Niech ciem-ność ma nie prze - ma - wia do mnie już.

Lord Je - sus Christ, your light shines with - in us.
Jé - sus le Christ, lu - mière in - té - rieu - re,
Cris - to Je - sús, di - si - pa mis som - bras.
Je - zu, Tyś jest świat - łoś - cią mej du - szy.

Let my heart al - ways wel - come your love.
don - ne - moi d'ac-cueil - lir ton a - mour.
Y que en mí só - lo ha - ble tu A - mor.
Daj mi moc przy - jąć dziś mi - łość Twą.

Text: Psalm 139
Tune: Jacques Berthier, 1923–1994
© 1998, Les Presses de Taizé, GIA Publications, Inc., agent

588 Light Shone in Darkness

1. Light shone in dark-ness at the world's cre - a - tion,
2. Light shone in dark-ness at the new cre - a - tion;
3. Light shines in dark-ness till the full cre - a - tion;

Bath - ing in beau - ty na - ture's rev - e - la - tion.
Christ rose in glo - ry, won for us sal - va - tion.
Christ's Bod - y, groan-ing, suf - fers trib - u - la - tion,

All that has be - ing, cry in ad - o - ra - tion,
Sing, earth and heav - en, hymns of ju - bi - la - tion.
Longs for God's jus - tice, glob - al trans-for - ma - tion,

"Praise for the light. A - men!"
Praise for the light. A - men!
Prays for the light. A - men!

Text: Delores Dufner, OSB, b.1939, © 2001, 2003, GIA Publications, Inc.
Tune: MIGHTY SAVIOR, 11 11 11 6; David Hurd, b.1950, © 1985, GIA Publications, Inc.

589 O Radiant Christ, Incarnate Word

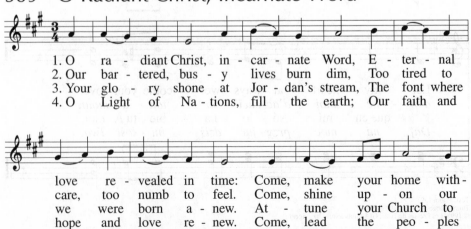

1. O ra - diant Christ, in - car - nate Word, E - ter - nal
2. Our bar - tered, bus - y lives burn dim, Too tired to
3. Your glo - ry shone at Jor - dan's stream, The font where
4. O Light of Na - tions, fill the earth; Our faith and

love re - vealed in time: Come, make your home with-
care, too numb to feel. Come, shine up - on our
we were born a - new. At - tune your Church to
hope and love re - new. Come, lead the peo - ples

in	our hearts,	That	we	may	dwell	in	light	sub -	lime.
shad - owed	world:	Your	ra -	diance	bathes	with	pow'r	to	heal.
know	you near;	Il -	lu -	mine	all	we	say	and	do.
to	your peace,	As	stars	once	led	the	way	to	you.

Text: Ruth Duck, b.1947, © 1992, GIA Publications, Inc.
Tune: WAREHAM, LM; William Knapp, 1698–1768

Word of God, Come Down on Earth 590

1. Word	of	God,	come	down on earth,	Liv -	ing	rain	from
2. Word	e -	ter -	nal,	throned on high,	Word	that	brought	to
3. Word	that	caused	blind	eyes to see,	Speak	and	heal	our
4. Word	that	speaks	God's	ten - der love,	One	with	God	be -

heav'n de - scend - ing;	Touch	our	hearts and	bring	to	birth
life cre - a - tion,	Word	that	came from	heav'n	to	die,
mor - tal blind - ness;	Deaf	we	are: our	heal - er	be;
yond all tell - ing,	Word	that	sends us	from	a - bove

Faith and hope and	love	un -	end - ing.	Word	al - might - y,
Cru - ci - fied for	our	sal -	va - tion,	Sav - ing Word,	the
Loose our tongues to	tell	your	kind - ness.	Be	our Word in
God the Spir - it,	with	us	dwell - ing,	Word	of truth, to

we re - vere you;	Word made flesh,	we	long	to	hear you.
world re - stor - ing,	Speak to	us,	your	love	out - pour - ing.
pit - y spo - ken,	Heal the world,	by	our	sin	bro - ken.
all truth lead us;	Word of life,	with	one	Bread	feed us.

Text: James Quinn, SJ, 1919–2010, © 1969. Used by permission of Selah Publishing Co., Inc.
Tune: LIEBSTER JESU, 7 8 7 8 88; Johann R. Ahle, 1625–1673; harm. by George H. Palmer, 1846–1926

591 Praise to You, O Christ, Our Savior

Refrain

Praise to you, O Christ, our Sav-ior, Word of the Fa-ther,

call-ing us to life; Son of God who

leads us to free-dom: glo-ry to you, Lord Je-sus Christ!

Verses

1. You are the Word who calls us out of dark-ness;
2. You are the one whom proph-ets hoped and longed for;
3. You are the Word who calls us to be ser-vants;
4. You are the Word who binds us and u-nites us;

You are the Word who leads us in-to light;
You are the one who speaks to us to-day;
You are the Word whose on-ly law is love;
You are the Word who calls us to be one;

You are the Word who brings us through the des-ert:
You are the one who leads us to our fu-ture:
You are the Word-made-flesh who lives a-mong us:
You are the Word who teach-es us for-give-ness:

D.C.

Glo-ry to you, Lord Je-sus Christ!
Glo-ry to you, Lord Je-sus Christ!
Glo-ry to you, Lord Je-sus Christ!
Glo-ry to you, Lord Je-sus Christ!

Text: Bernadette Farrell, b.1957
Tune: Bernadette Farrell, b.1957
© 1986, Bernadette Farrell. Published by OCP.

God Has Spoken by the Prophets   592

1. God has spo-ken by the proph-ets, Spo-ken
2. God has spo-ken by Christ Je-sus, Christ, the
3. God is speak-ing by the Spir-it, Speak-ing

his un-chang-ing word, Each from age to age pro-
ev-er-last-ing Son, Bright-ness of the Fa-ther's
to our hearts a-gain, In the age-less Word de-

claim-ing God, the one, the right-eous Lord.
glo-ry, With the Fa-ther ev-er one;
clar-ing God's own mes-sage, now as then.

In the world's de-spair and tur-moil, One firm
Spo-ken by the Word in-car-nate, God from
Through the rise and fall of na-tions One sure

an-chor holds us fast: God e-ter-nal reigns for-
God, be-fore time was; Light from Light, to earth de-
faith is hold-ing fast: God a-bides, his word un-

ev-er, God the first and God the last.
scend-ing, Christ re-veals our God to us.
chang-ing, God the first and God the last.

Text: George W. Briggs, 1875–1959, alt., © 1953, 1981, The Hymn Society (admin. by Hope Publishing Company)
Tune: RUSTINGTON, 8 7 8 7 D; Charles H. H. Parry, 1848–1918

Alternate tune: NETTLETON

593 This Is a Story Full of Love

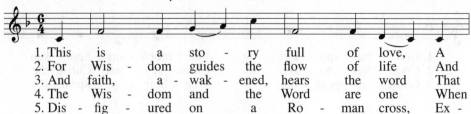

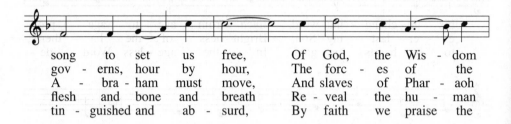

1. This is a sto - ry full of love, A
2. For Wis - dom guides the flow of life And
3. And faith, a - wak - ened, hears the word That
4. The Wis - dom and the Word are one When
5. Dis - fig - ured on a Ro - man cross, Ex -

song to set us free, Of God, the Wis - dom
gov - erns, hour by hour, The forc - es of the
A - bra - ham must move, And slaves of Phar - aoh
flesh and bone and breath Re - veal the hu - man
tin - guished and ab - surd, By faith we praise the

and the Word, The Key - stone and the Key.
u - ni - verse, The fra - grance of a flow'r.
take the road To free - dom, law, and love.
face of God, The child of Naz - a - reth.
pow'r of God, The Wis - dom and the Word.

6. Arising over earthly pow'rs,
   Our Savior has begun
   To catch them in a web of love
   And weave them into one.

7. Praise God, the Wisdom and the Word,
   Till all the world can see
   That Jesus is the First and Last,
   The Keystone and the Key.

Text: Brian Wren, b.1936, © 1986, Hope Publishing Company
Tune: LAND OF REST, CM; American melody; harm. by Annabel M. Buchanan, 1888–1983, © 1938 (Renewed) The H.W. Gray Company

594 A Year of God's Favor

1. A year of God's fa - vor Christ prom - ised, and more:
2. This word is ful - filled in be - liev - ers to - day,
3. Ful - filled in our liv - ing be God's word to - day,

Good news to the pris - 'ner, the weak, and the poor,
In wom - en and men who would fol - low Christ's way.
Ful - filled in our lov - ing, our work, and our play,

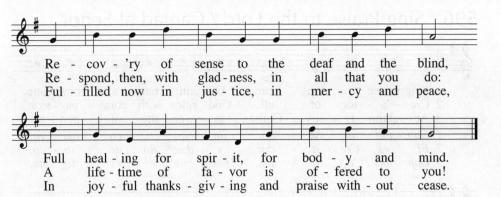

Re - cov - 'ry of sense to the deaf and the blind,
Re - spond, then, with glad - ness, in all that you do:
Ful - filled now in jus - tice, in mer - cy and peace,

Full heal - ing for spir - it, for bod - y and mind.
A life - time of fa - vor is of - fered to you!
In joy - ful thanks - giv - ing and praise with - out cease.

Text: Delores Dufner, OSB, b.1939, © 1995, 2003, GIA Publications, Inc.
Tune: ST. DENIO, 11 11 11 11; adapt. from a Welsh ballad in John Robert's *Hymns of the Sanctuary*, 1839

In This Place Your Word Is Planted   595

1. In this place your Word is plant - ed;
2. Let your plant - ing not be wast - ed,
3. Help us treas - ure Ho - ly Wis - dom,
4. Blest are they who, truth re - ceiv - ing,

On our path the seed is sown. To the Church your
Wilt - ed soon in ston - y field. Let our world - ly
Sa - vor ev - 'ry word you give. Help us cher - ish
Know its val - ue more than gold. Blest are they who,

Word is spo - ken; In our hearts a light has shone.
cares not choke it, Rob - bing you of right - ful yield.
Je - sus' gos - pel, Bread by which your peo - ple live.
per - se - ver - ing, Bear good fruit a hun - dred - fold.

Text: Delores Dufner, OSB, b.1939, © 2011, GIA Publications, Inc.
Tune: STUTTGART, 8 7 8 7; *Psalmodia Sacra*, 1715; harm. by Kenneth D. Smith, b.1928, © Christian Education

596 Sing Praise to the Lord / Cantad al Señor

1. Sing praise to the Lord, O sing out a new song.
2. Cre - a - tor of all, God rules with com - pas - sion.
3. Ac - claim Je - sus Christ as wor - thy of hon - or.

1. Can - tad al Se - ñor un cán - ti - co nue - vo.
2. Él es Cre - a - dor y due - ño de to - do.
3. Can - tad a Je - sús, por - que él es dig - no.

Sing praise to the Lord, O sing out a new song.
Cre - a - tor of all, God rules with com - pas - sion.
Ac - claim Je - sus Christ as wor - thy of hon - or.

Can - tad al Se - ñor un cán - ti - co nue - vo.
Él es Cre - a - dor y due - ño de to - do.
Can - tad a Je - sús, por - que él es dig - no.

Sing praise to the Lord, O sing out a new song.
Cre - a - tor of all, God rules with com - pas - sion.
Ac - claim Je - sus Christ as wor - thy of hon - or.

Can - tad al Se - ñor un cán - ti - co nue - vo.
Él es Cre - a - dor y due - ño de to - do.
Can - tad a Je - sús, por - que él es dig - no.

Sing praise to the Lord, sing praise to our God.
¡Can - tad al Se - ñor, can - tad al Se - ñor!

4. Give thanks to the Lord, who sends us the Spirit. . .
   Sing praise to the Lord, sing praise to our God.

5. Sing praise to the Lord, "Amen, Alleluia!". . .
   Sing praise to the Lord, sing praise to our God.

4. Es él quien nos da su Espíritu Santo. . .
   ¡Cantad al Señor, cantad al Señor!

5. Cantad al Señor: "¡Amén, aleluya!". . .
   ¡Cantad al Señor, cantad al Señor!

Text: Traditional Brazilian; Spanish tr. anonymous; English tr. by Ronald F. Krisman, b.1946, © 2005, GIA Publications, Inc.
Tune: CANTAI AO SENHOR, 11 11 11 10; traditional Brazilian; harm. by Ronald F. Krisman, b.1946, © 2005, GIA Publications, Inc.

Glory and Praise to Our God   597

Refrain

Glo - ry and praise to our God, who a - lone gives
light to our days. Man - y are the
bless-ings he bears to those who trust in his ways.

Verses 1–3

1. We, the daugh - ters and sons of him who built the
2. In his wis - dom he strength - ens us, like gold that's
3. Ev - 'ry mo - ment of ev - 'ry day our God is

val - leys and plains, Praise the won-ders our God has
test - ed in fire. Though the pow - er of sin pre -
wait - ing to save, Al - ways read - y to seek the

D.C.

done in ev - 'ry heart that sings.
vails, our God is there to save.
lost, to an - swer those who pray.

Verse 4

4. God has wa - tered our bar - ren land and spent his
mer - ci - ful rain. Now the riv - ers of life run

D.C.

full for an - y - one to drink.

Text: Psalm 65, 66; Dan Schutte, b.1947
Tune: Dan Schutte, b.1947; acc. by Theophane Hytrek, OSF, 1915–1992, alt.
© 1976, Daniel L. Schutte and OCP

598 Laudáte, Laudáte Dóminum

Refrain

Lau - dá - te, lau - dá - te Dó - mi - num, o - mnes
We praise you, we praise your ho - ly name, God of

gen - tes, lau - dá - te Dó - mi - num. Ex - sul - tá - te, ju - bi -
jus - tice, e - ter - nal - ly the same. May our liv - ing be thanks-

lá - te per an - nos Dó - mi - ni, o - mnes gen - tes. Lau -
giv - ing, re - joic-ing in your name now and al - ways. We

dá - te, lau - dá - te Dó - mi - num, o - mnes gen - tes, lau -
praise you, we praise your ho - ly name, God of jus - tice, e -

dá - te Dó - mi - num. Ex - sul - tá - te, ju - bi -
ter - nal - ly the same. May our liv - ing be thanks-

Last time

lá - te per an - nos Dó - mi - ni, o - mnes gen - tes.
giv - ing, re - joic-ing in your name now and al - ways.

Verses 1–3

1. In the faith of Christ we walk hand in hand,
2. In the name of Christ we will spread the seed;
3. In the pow'r of Christ we pro - claim one Lord.

1. Ca - mi - na - mos jun - tos en la fe de Cris - to.
2. Con los po - bres com - par - ti - mos luz de Cris - to,
3. Los bau - ti - za - dos en un so - lo Se - ñor,

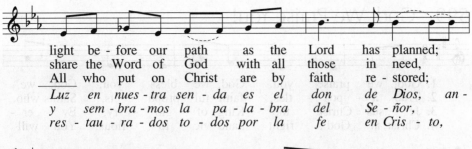

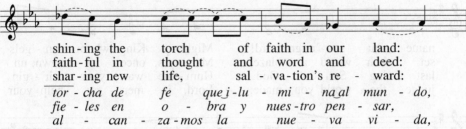

light be - fore our path as the Lord has planned;
share the Word of God with all those in need,
All who put on Christ are by faith re - stored;
Luz en nues - tra sen - da es el don de Dios, an -
y sem - bra - mos la pa - la - bra del Se - ñor,
res - tau - ra - dos to - dos por la fe en Cris - to,

shin - ing the torch of faith in our land:
faith - ful in thought and word and deed:
shar - ing new life, sal - va - tion's re - ward:
tor - cha de fe que i - lu - mi - na al mun - do,
fie - les en o - bra y nues - tro pen - sar,
al - can - za - mos la nue - va vi - da,

D.C.

in the name of Christ Je - sus.
en el nom - bre de Cris - to.

Verses 4–6

4. In the life of Christ, through the blood
  he shed,
we are justified, and by him are fed,
nourished by word and living bread:
in the name of Christ Jesus.

5. In the Church of God we are unified,
by the Spirit's pow'r we are sanctified,
temples of grace, where God may abide:
by the pow'r of the Spirit.

6. Praise to God the Father while ages run.
Praise to Christ the Savior, God's only Son,
praise to the Holy Spirit be sung:
omnes gentes, laudáte.

4. *Oigan al Señor y síganle,*
vengan a alabar y comer de él,
alimentados con pan de vida,
en el nombre de Cristo.

5. *En la Iglesia estamos unidos,*
santificados por el Espíritu,
morada de la gracia de Dios,
por el poder del Espíritu.

6. *Siempre bendito sea el Padre,*
siempre bendito sea el Hijo de Dios,
siempre bendito el Espíritu Santo,
omnes gentes, laudáte.

Ordination Verses

1. In the Church we answer the Savior's call,
  serving, as he showed us, both great and small,
  sharing the Lord's compassion for all:
  in the name of Christ Jesus.

2. In the name of Christ we baptize and teach,
  truth upon our lips in the way we preach,
  raising the cup of blessing for each:
  in the name of Christ Jesus.

Text: Christopher Walker, b.1947
Tune: Christopher Walker, b.1947
© 1997, Christopher Walker. Published by OCP.

599 God, We Praise You!

1. God, we praise you! God, we bless you! God, we
2. True a - pos - tles, faith - ful proph - ets, Saints who
3. Je - sus Christ, the King of glo - ry, Ev - er -
4. Christ, at God's right hand vic - to - rious, You will

name you sov-'reign Lord! Might-y King whom an - gels
set their world a - blaze, Mar - tyrs, once un - known, un -
last - ing Son of God, Hum - ble was your vir - gin
judge the world you made; Lord, in mer - cy help your

wor - ship, Fa - ther, by your Church a - dored: All cre -
heed - ed, Join one grow - ing song of praise, While your
moth - er, Hard the lone - ly path you trod: By your
ser - vants For whose free - dom you have paid: Raise us

a - tion shows your glo - ry, Heav'n and
Church on earth con - fess - es One ma -
cross is sin de - feat - ed, Hell con -
up from dust to glo - ry, Guard us

earth draw near your throne, Sing - ing "Ho - ly, ho - ly,
jes - tic Trin - i - ty: Fa - ther, Son, and Ho - ly
front - ed face to face, Heav - en o - pened to be -
from all sin to - day; King en-throned a - bove all

ho - ly, Lord of hosts, and God a - lone!"
Spir - it, God, our hope e - ter - nal - ly.
liev - ers, Sin - ners jus - ti - fied by grace.
prais - es, Save your peo - ple, God, we pray.

Text: Based on the *Te Deum*; Christopher M. Idle, b.1938, © 1982, The Jubilate Group (admin. by Hope Publishing Company)
Tune: NETTLETON, 8 7 8 7 D; Wyeth's *Repository of Sacred Music*, 1813

Sing a New Song 600

Refrain

Sing a new song un - to the Lord; let your song be
sung from moun - tains high. Sing a new song
un - to the Lord, sing-ing al - le - lu - ia.

Verses

1. Shout with glad - ness! Dance for joy! O come be -
2. Rise, O chil - dren, from your sleep; your Sav - ior
3. Glad my soul for I have seen the glo - ry

fore the Lord. And play for God on
now has come. He has turned your
of the Lord. The trum - pet sounds; the

D.C.

glad tam - bou - rines, and let your trum - pet sound.
sor - row to joy, and filled your soul with song.
dead shall be raised. I know my Sav - ior lives.

Text: Based on Psalm 98:1, 4–6; Dan Schutte, b.1947
Tune: Dan Schutte, b.1947
© 1972, OCP

601 The God of Abraham Praise

1. The God of A-br'ham praise, Who reigns en-throned a - bove,
2. He by him-self has sworn, I on his oath de - pend;
3. There dwells the Lord, our King, The Lord, our Right-eous-ness,
4. The God who reigns on high The great arch - an - gels sing,

An - cient of ev - er - last-ing days And God of love.
I shall, on ea - gle - wings up-borne, To heav'n as - cend.
Tri - umph-ant o'er the world and sin, The Prince of peace.
And "Ho - ly, ho - ly, ho - ly!" cry, "Al - might - y King!

To him up - lift your voice, At whose su - preme com - mand
I shall be-hold his face, I shall his pow'r a - dore,
On Zi-on's sa - cred height His king - dom still main - tains,
Who was and is the same, For all e - ter - ni - ty.

From earth we rise and seek the joys At his right hand.
And sing the won-ders of his grace For - ev - er - more.
And, glo - rious with his saints in light, For - ev - er reigns.
To you, Lord God, the great I AM, All glo - ry be!"

Text: *Yigdal Elohim Hai*; ascr. to Daniel ben Judah Dayyan, fl.1400; para. by Thomas Olivers, 1725–1799, alt.
Tune: LEONI, 6 6 8 4 D; from the *Yigdal*; adapt. by Meyer Lyon, c.1751–1797

602 Christ Is the World's Light

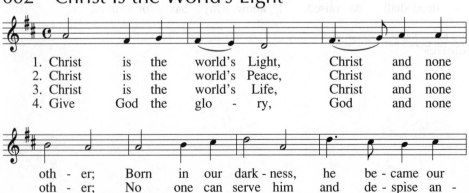

1. Christ is the world's Light, Christ and none
2. Christ is the world's Peace, Christ and none
3. Christ is the world's Life, Christ and none
4. Give God the glo - ry, God and none

oth - er; Born in our dark - ness, he be - came our
oth - er; No one can serve him and de - spise an -
oth - er; Sold once for sil - ver, mur - dered here, our
oth - er; Give God the glo - ry, Spir - it, Son, and

broth - er.   If   we have   seen him,   we   have seen the
oth - er.   Who   else   u - nites us,   one   in God the
broth - er—   He,   who re - deems us,   reigns   with God the
Fa - ther;   Give God the   glo - ry,   God - with - us,   our

Fa - ther: Glo - ry to God   on   high.
Fa - ther?   Glo - ry to God   on   high.
Fa - ther: Glo - ry to God   on   high.
broth - er: Glo - ry to God   on   high.

Text: Fred Pratt Green, 1903–2000, © 1969, Hope Publishing Company
Tune: CHRISTE SANCTORUM, 10 11 11 6; Paris *Antiphoner*, 1681

Bless the Lord   603

Ostinato Refrain

Bless the Lord, my soul,   and bless God's ho - ly   name.
Spanish: Ten - go sed   de ti,   oh fuen - te del a - mor.
Portuguese: Ben - diz o   Se - nhor,   lou - va o seu San - to   no - me.

Bless   the Lord,   my soul,   who leads me in - to life.
Ten - go sed   de ti: tu a - mor es   li - ber - tad.
Ben - diz o   Se - nhor,   que à vi - da nos con - duz.

Text: Psalm 103
Tune: Jacques Berthier, 1923–1994
© 1998, Les Presses de Taizé, GIA Publications, Inc., agent

604 Praise the Lord! You Heavens, Adore Him

1. Praise the Lord! You heav'ns, a - dore him;
2. Praise the Lord! For he is glo - rious;
3. Wor - ship, hon - or, glo - ry, bless - ing,

Praise him, an - gels in the height.
Nev - er shall his prom - ise fail.
Glad thanks - giv - ing, Lord, we bring:

Sun and moon, re - joice be - fore him;
God has made his saints vic - to - rious;
Young and old, your praise ex - press - ing

Praise him, all you stars of light.
Sin and death shall not pre - vail.
In the joy - ful hymns we sing.

Praise the Lord, for he has spo - ken;
Praise the God of our sal - va - tion!
All the saints in heav'n a - dore you;

Worlds his might - y voice o - beyed;
Hosts on high, his pow'r pro - claim.
We would bow be - fore your throne.

Laws which nev - er shall be bro - ken
Heav'n and earth and all cre - a - tion,
As your an - gels serve be - fore you,

For   their   guid - ance   he   has   made.
Praise   and   mag - ni - fy   his   name.
So   on   earth   your   will   be   done.

Text: Psalm 148; sts. 1, 2, *Foundling Hospital Collection*, 1796; st. 3, Edward Osler, 1798–1863, alt.
Tune: HYFRYDOL, 8 7 8 7 D; Rowland H. Prichard, 1811–1887

Shout for Joy, Loud and Long   605

1. Shout for joy, loud and long; God be praised
2. By God's word all was made, Heav'n and earth,
3. Yet our pride made us fall! So Christ came
4. Now has Christ tru - ly ris'n, And his Spir -

with a song! To the Lord we be - long,
light and shade, Na - ture's won - ders dis - played,
for us all, Not the right - eous to call,
it is giv'n To all those un - der heav'n

Chil - dren of the Fa - ther, God the great life - giv - er!
We to rule cre - a - tion From its first foun - da - tion.
By his cross and pas - sion Bring - ing us sal - va - tion!
Who will walk be - side him, Though they once de - nied him!

Shout for joy, joy, joy! Shout for joy, joy, joy!

God is love, God is light, God is ev - er - last - ing!

Text: David Mowbray, b.1938, alt., © 1982, Hope Publishing Company
Tune: PERSONENT HODIE, 666 66 with refrain; *Piae Cantiones*, 1582; harm. by Richard Proulx, 1937–2010, © 1978, GIA Publications, Inc.

606 New Songs of Celebration

1. New songs of cel-e-bra-tion ren-der To God who has great
2. Joy-ful-ly, heart-i-ly re-sound-ing, Let ev-'ry in-stru-
3. Riv-ers and seas and tor-rents roar-ing, Hon-or the Lord with

won-ders done; Love sits en-throned in age-less splen-dor;
ment and voice Peal out the praise of grace a-bound-ing,
wild ac-claim; Moun-tains and stones, look up a-dor-ing,

Come and a-dore the Might-y One. God has made known
Call-ing the whole world to re-joice. Trum-pets and or-
And find a voice to praise God's name. Right-eous, com-mand-

the great sal-va-tion Which all the saints with
gans, set in mo-tion Such sounds as make the
ing, ev-er glo-rious, Prais-es be sung that

joy con-fess. God has re-vealed to ev-'ry na-tion
heav-ens ring; All things that live in earth and o-cean,
nev-er cease: Just is our God, whose truth vic-to-rious

Truth and un-end-ing right-eous-ness.
Sound forth the song, your prais-es bring.
Es-tab-lish-es the world in peace.

Text: Psalm 98; Erik Routley, 1917–1982, © 1974, Hope Publishing Company
Tune: RENDEZ À DIEU, 9 8 9 8 D; *Genevan Psalter*, 1551; attr. to Louis Bourgeois, c.1510–1561

All Creatures of Our God and King   607

1. All crea-tures of our God and King, Lift
2. O rush-ing wind and breez-es soft, O
3. O flow-ing wa-ter, pure and clear, Make
4. Dear moth-er earth, who day by day Un -
5. And ev-'ry one of ten-der heart, For -

up your voice and with us sing: Al - le - lu - ia!
clouds that ride the winds a - loft, Sing your prais - es!
mu - sic for your Lord to hear. Sing your prais - es!
fold rich bless-ings on our way, Sing your prais - es!
giv - ing oth - ers, take your part, Sing your prais - es!

Al - le - lu - ia! O burn - ing sun with gold - en beam
Al - le - lu - ia! O ris - ing morn, in praise re - joice,
Al - le - lu - ia! O fire so mas - ter - ful and bright,
Al - le - lu - ia! The flow'rs and fruits that in you grow,
Al - le - lu - ia! All you who pain and sor - row bear,

And sil - ver moon with soft - er gleam,
O lights of eve - ning, find a voice.
Pro - vid - ing us with warmth and light,
Let them God's glo - ry al - so show.
Praise God and cast on him your care.

Sing your prais - es! Al - le - lu - ia! Al - le - lu - ia,

al - le - lu - ia, al - le - lu - ia!

6. And you, most kind and gentle death,
   Waiting to hush our final breath,
   Sing your praises! Alleluia!
   You lead to heav'n the child of God,
   Where Christ our Lord the way has trod.
   Sing your praises! Alleluia!
   Alleluia, alleluia, alleluia!

7. Let all things their Creator bless,
   And worship God in humbleness,
   Sing your praises! Alleluia!
   Praise God the Father, God the Son,
   And God the Spirit, Three in One!
   Sing your praises! Alleluia!
   Alleluia, alleluia, alleluia!

Text: *Altissimu, onnipotente bon Signore*; St. Francis of Assisi, 1182–1226; tr. by William H. Draper, 1855–1933, alt.
Tune: LASST UNS ERFREUEN, LM with alleluias; *Geistliche Kirchengesänge*, Cologne, 1623; harm. by Ralph Vaughan Williams, 1872–1958

608 When in Our Music God Is Glorified

1. When in our mu - sic God is glo - ri - fied,
2. How of - ten, mak - ing mu - sic, we have found
3. So has the Church, in lit - ur - gy and song,
4. And did not Je - sus sing a psalm that night
5. Let ev - 'ry in - stru-ment be tuned for praise!

And ad - o - ra - tion leaves no room for pride,
A new di - men - sion in the world of sound,
In faith and love, through cen - tu - ries of wrong,
When ut - most e - vil strove a - gainst the light?
Let all re - joice who have a voice to raise!

It is as though the whole cre - a - tion cried:
As wor - ship moved us to a more pro - found
Borne wit - ness to the truth in ev - 'ry tongue:
Then let us sing, for whom he won the fight:
And may God give us faith to sing al - ways:

Al - le - lu - ia!

Text: Fred Pratt Green, 1903–2000, © 1972, Hope Publishing Company
Tune: ENGELBERG, 10 10 10 with alleluia; Charles V. Stanford, 1852–1924

609 Adorámus Te Dómine

Ostinato Refrain

(hum)

A - do - rá - mus te Dó - mi - ne.
We a - dore you, Lord Je - sus Christ.

*Korean: 오 주를찬미하나이다.

Korean transliteration: O ju-leul chan-mi-ha-na-i-da.

Text: Taizé Community
Tune: Jacques Berthier, 1923–1994
© 1979, Les Presses de Taizé, GIA Publications, Inc., agent

Praise, My Soul, the King of Heaven   610

1. Praise, my soul, the King of heav - en; To his
2. Praise him for his grace and fa - vor To his
3. Fa - ther - like he tends and spares us; Well our
4. Frail as sum-mer's flow'r we flour - ish, Blows the
5. An - gels, help us to a - dore him; You be -

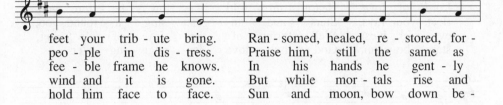

feet your trib - ute bring. Ran - somed, healed, re - stored, for -
peo - ple in dis - tress. Praise him, still the same as
fee - ble frame he knows. In his hands he gent - ly
wind and it is gone. But while mor - tals rise and
hold him face to face. Sun and moon, bow down be -

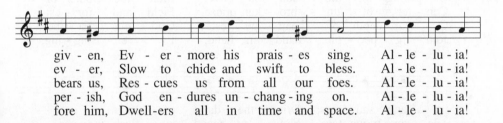

giv - en, Ev - er - more his prais - es sing. Al - le - lu - ia!
ev - er, Slow to chide and swift to bless. Al - le - lu - ia!
bears us, Res - cues us from all our foes. Al - le - lu - ia!
per - ish, God en - dures un - chang - ing on. Al - le - lu - ia!
fore him, Dwell-ers all in time and space. Al - le - lu - ia!

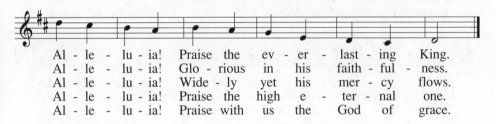

Al - le - lu - ia! Praise the ev - er - last - ing King.
Al - le - lu - ia! Glo - rious in his faith - ful - ness.
Al - le - lu - ia! Wide - ly yet his mer - cy flows.
Al - le - lu - ia! Praise the high e - ter - nal one.
Al - le - lu - ia! Praise with us the God of grace.

Text: Psalm 103; Henry F. Lyte, 1793–1847, alt.
Tune: LAUDA ANIMA, 8 7 8 7 8 7; John Goss, 1800–1880

611 Joyful, Joyful, We Adore You

1. Joy - ful, joy - ful, we a - dore you, God of glo - ry,
2. All your works with joy sur - round you, Earth and heav'n re -
3. You are giv - ing and for - giv - ing, Ev - er bless - ing,
4. Mor - tals, join the might - y cho - rus, Which the morn - ing

Lord of love; Hearts un - fold like flow'rs be - fore you,
flect your rays, Stars and an - gels sing a - round you,
ev - er blest, Well - spring of the joy of liv - ing,
stars be - gan; God's own love is reign - ing o'er us,

O - p'ning to the sun a - bove. Melt the clouds of
Cen - ter of un - bro - ken praise. Field and for - est,
O - cean - depth of hap - py rest! God our Fa - ther,
Join - ing peo - ple hand in hand. Ev - er sing - ing,

sin and sad - ness; Drive the dark of doubt a - way;
vale and moun - tain, Flow - 'ry mead - ow, flash - ing sea,
Christ our broth - er, Let your light up - on us shine;
march we on - ward, Vic - tors in the midst of strife;

Giv - er of im - mor - tal glad-ness, Fill us with the light of day!
Chant-ing bird, and flow-ing foun-tain, Sound their praise e - ter-nal-ly!
Teach us how to love each oth - er, Lift us to the joy di-vine.
Joy - ful mu - sic leads us sun-ward In the tri-umph-song of life.

Text: Henry van Dyke, 1852–1933, alt.
Tune: HYMN TO JOY, 8 7 8 7 D; arr. from Ludwig van Beethoven, 1770–1827, by Edward Hodges, 1796–1867

612 Sing Praise to the Lord!

1. Sing praise to the Lord! Praise God in the height!
2. Sing praise to the Lord! Praise God on the earth,
3. Sing praise to the Lord, all things that give sound,
4. Sing praise to the Lord! Thanks - giv - ing and song

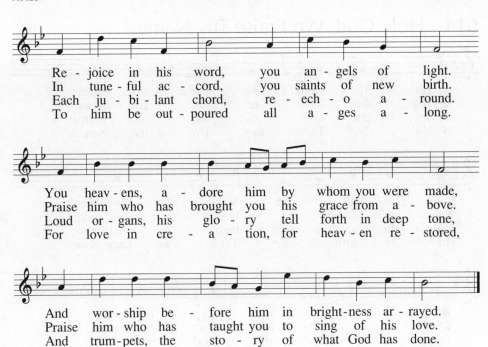

Re - joice in his word, you an - gels of light.
In tune - ful ac - cord, you saints of new birth.
Each ju - bi - lant chord, re - ech - o a - round.
To him be out - poured all a - ges a - long.

You heav - ens, a - dore him by whom you were made,
Praise him who has brought you his grace from a - bove.
Loud or - gans, his glo - ry tell forth in deep tone,
For love in cre - a - tion, for heav - en re - stored,

And wor - ship be - fore him in bright-ness ar - rayed.
Praise him who has taught you to sing of his love.
And trum-pets, the sto - ry of what God has done.
For grace of sal - va - tion, sing praise to the Lord!

Text: Psalm 150; Henry W. Baker, 1821–1877, alt.
Tune: LAUDATE DOMINUM, 10 10 11 11; Charles H. H. Parry, 1840–1918

Magníficat 613

Canon

Ⓐ
Ma - gní - fi - cat, ma - gní - fi - cat, Ⓑ Ma - gní - fi - cat á - ni - ma

Ⓒ
me - a Dó - mi - num. Ma - gní - fi - cat, ma - gní - fi - cat,

Ⓓ
Ma - gní - fi - cat á - ni - ma me - a!

Text: Luke 1:46, *My soul magnifies the Lord;* Taizé Community, 1978
Tune: Jacques Berthier, 1923–1994

614 Holy God, We Praise Thy Name

1. Ho - ly God, we praise thy name;
2. Hark! the loud ce - les - tial hymn
3. Lo, the ap - os - tol - ic train
4. Ho - ly Fa - ther, Ho - ly Son,

Lord of all, we bow be - fore thee!
An - gel choirs a - bove are rais - ing;
Joins, the sa - cred name to hal - low;
Ho - ly Spir - it, Three we name thee;

All on earth thy scep - ter claim,
Cher - u - bim and Ser - a - phim,
Proph - ets swell the loud re - frain,
While in es - sence on - ly One,

All in heav'n a - bove a - dore thee;
In un - ceas - ing cho - rus prais - ing,
And the white - robed mar - tyrs fol - low;
Un - di - vid - ed God we claim thee;

In - fi - nite thy vast do - main,
Fill the heav'ns with sweet ac - cord:
And from morn to set - ting sun,
And a - dor - ing bend the knee,

Repeat ad lib.

Ev - er - last - ing is thy reign.
"Ho - ly, ho - ly, ho - ly Lord!"
Through the Church the song goes on.
While we own the mys - ter - y.

Text: *Grosser Gott, wir loben dich;* ascr. to Ignaz Franz, 1719–1790; tr. by Clarence Walworth, 1820–1900, alt.
Tune: GROSSER GOTT, 7 8 7 8 77; *Katholisches Gesangbuch,* Vienna, c.1774

God, Whose Song Became Creation   615

1. God, whose song be - came cre - a - tion, Touch our lips with
2. Songs so new and yet so an - cient, Songs with no ge -
3. Sing - ers past and sing - ers pres - ent, Sing - ers that are

burn - ing coals. Free our hearts to sing your prais - es
og - ra - phy, Songs un-changed, yet ev - er chang-ing,
yet to be, Sing - ers share through time and dis - tance

While your mu - sic shapes our souls. We would sing with
Songs that set their sing - ers free; Sung on streets and
Your trans-form - ing mel - o - dy. Now we join that

oth - er na - tions, Sing with worlds as yet un - known,
sung in kitch - ens, Sung in church - es, sung in jails,
time - less cy - cle, As one cho - rus in your sight.

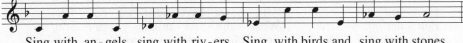

Sing with an - gels, sing with riv - ers, Sing with birds and sing with stones.
Sung in si - lence, sung in cha - os, Sung when-ev - er speak-ing fails.
Mak - er God, who gave us mu - sic, May our song be your de - light!

Text: Based on Psalm 96:1; Jacque B. Jones, b.1950, © 2011, GIA Publications, Inc.
Tune: GIFTS; 8 7 8 7 D; Hal H. Hopson, b.1933, © 2001, Hope Publishing Company

616 Praise to the Lord, the Almighty

1. Praise to the Lord, the Al-might-y, the King of cre-
2. Praise to the Lord, who o'er all things is won-drous-ly
3. Praise to the Lord, who will pros-per your work and de-
4. Praise to the Lord! O let all that is in me a-

a - tion! O my soul, praise him, for
reign - ing And, as on wings of an
fend you; Sure-ly his good - ness and
dore him! All that has life and breath,

he is your health and sal - va - tion!
ea - gle, up - lift-ing, sus - tain - ing.
mer - cy shall dai - ly at - tend you.
come now with prais-es be - fore him!

All you who hear, Now to his tem-ple draw near.
Have you not seen All you have need-ed has been
Pon - der a - new What the Al-might-y can do,
Let the "A - men" Sound from his peo-ple a - gain!

Praise him in glad ad - o - ra - tion!
Met by his gra - cious or - dain - ing?
Who with his love does be - friend you.
Glad - ly with praise we a - dore him!

Text: *Lobe den Herren, den mächtigen König*; Joachim Neander, 1650–1680; tr. by Catherine Winkworth, 1827–1878, alt.
Tune: LOBE DEN HERREN, 14 14 47 8; *Stralsund Gesangbuch*, 1665

Sing Praise to God Who Reigns Above 617

1. Sing praise to God who reigns a - bove, The
2. O God, what your great pow'r has made, In
3. We seek you, Lord, in our dis - tress; O
4. All who con - fess Christ's ho - ly name, Give

God of all cre - a - tion, The God of pow'r, the
mer - cy you are keep - ing; By morn - ing glow or
God, in mer - cy hear us. O Sav - ior, see our
God the praise and glo - ry! And all who know God's

God of love, The God of our sal - va - tion. With
eve - ning shade, Your eye is nev - er sleep - ing; In
help - less - ness And come with peace to cheer us. For
pow'r, pro - claim: Give God the praise and glo - ry! Cast

heal - ing balm our souls are filled; All our la - ments with
the do - min - ion of your might All things are just and
this we thank and praise you, Lord, Who are by one and
ev - 'ry i - dol from its throne; God is the Lord, and

peace are stilled. To God all praise and glo - ry!
good and right. To God all praise and glo - ry!
all a - dored. To God all praise and glo - ry!
God a - lone: To God all praise and glo - ry!

Text: *Sei Lob und Ehr' dem höchsten Gut*; Johann J. Schütz, 1640–1690; tr. by Frances E. Cox, 1812–1897, alt.
Tune: MIT FREUDEN ZART, 8 7 8 7 88 7; Bohemian Brethren's *Kirchengesänge*, 1566

618 Alabaré

Refrain

A - la - ba - ré, a - la - ba - ré, we
A - la - ba - ré, a - la - ba - ré, a -

sing the prais - es of our God. A - la - ba - ré, a - la - ba -
la - ba - ré a mi Se - ñor. A - la - ba - ré, a - la - ba -

ré, we sing the prais - es of our God.
ré, a - la - ba - ré a mi Se - ñor.

Verses

1. John had a vis - ion of those re - deemed by Je - sus, And
2. One in our prais - ing, with joy - ful hearts and voic - es, We
3. We are your chil - dren, O God, e - ter - nal Fa - ther. You
1. *Juan vio el nú - me - ro de los re - di - mi - dos, Y*
2. *To - dos u - ni - dos, a - le - gres can - ta - mos*
3. *So - mos tus hi - jos, Dios Pa - dre e - ter - no,*

all were prais - ing God with one ac - cord.
glo - ri - fy the Lord who reigns a - bove:
guide us and pro - tect us all our days.
to - dos a - la - ba - ban al Se - ñor.
Glo - ria y a - la - ban - zas al Se - ñor.
Tú nos has cre - a - do por a - mor.

Thou - sands were pray - ing, thou - sands were sing - ing, But
Praise to the Fa - ther, praise to Christ Je - sus, And
With all cre - a - tion, in ju - bi - la - tion, We
U - nos o - ra - ban, o - tros can - ta - ban, Y
¡Glo - ria al Pa - dre! ¡Glo - ria al Hi - jo! Y
Te a - do - ra - mos, te ben - de - ci - mos, Y

D.S.

all were joined in prais - es to the Lord.
praise to God the Spir - it, bond of love. A - la - ba -
hon - or you with songs of end - less praise.
to - dos a - la - ba - ban al Se - ñor.
¡Glo - ria al Es - pí - ri - tu de a - mor! A - la - ba -
to - dos can - ta - mos en tu ho - nor.

Text: Manuel José Alonso, José Pagán; tr. by Ronald F. Krisman, b.1946
Tune: Manuel José Alonso, José Pagán; acc. by Ronald F. Krisman, b.1946
© 1979, 2011, Manuel José Alonso and José Pagán. Published by OCP.

Jubiláte, Sérvite 619

Canon

Ju - bi - lá - te De - o o - mnis ter - ra.
Raise a song of glad-ness, peo - ples of the earth.
Al Se - ñor a - cla - ma, tie - rra en - te - ra.

Sér - vi - te Dó - mi - no in lae - tí - ti - a.
Christ has come, bring - ing peace, joy to ev - 'ry heart.
Sír - ve - lo, dán - do - le gra - cias por su a - mor.

Al - le - lú - ia, al - le - lú - ia, in lae - tí - ti - a!
Al - le - lu - ia, al - le - lu - ia, joy to ev - 'ry heart!
¡A - le - lu - ya, a - le - lu - ya, gra - cias por su a - mor!

Al - le - lú - ia, al - le - lú - ia, in lae - tí - ti - a!
Al - le - lu - ia, al - le - lu - ia, joy to ev - 'ry heart!
¡A - le - lu - ya, a - le - lu - ya, gra - cias por su a - mor!

Text: Psalm 100, *Rejoice in God, all the earth, Serve the Lord with gladness*; Taizé Community, 1978
Tune: Jacques Berthier, 1923–1994
© 1979, 2011, Les Presses de Taizé, GIA Publications, Inc., agent

620 Let All Mortal Flesh Keep Silence

1. Let all mor - tal flesh keep si - lence,
2. King of kings, yet born of Mar - y,
3. Rank on rank the host of heav - en
4. At his feet the six - winged ser - aph;

And with fear and trem - bling stand;
As of old on earth he stood,
Spreads its van - guard on the way;
Cher - u - bim with sleep - less eye

Pon - der noth - ing earth - ly - mind - ed,
Lord of lords in hu - man ves - ture,
As the Light of Light, de - scend - ing
Veil their fac - es to the Pres - ence,

For with bless - ing in his hand
In the Bod - y and the Blood
From the realms of end - less day,
As with cease - less voice they cry:

Christ our God, to earth de - scend -
He will give to all the faith -
Comes, the pow'rs of hell to van -
"Al - le - lu - ia, al - le - lu -

ing, Comes, our hom - age to de - mand.
ful His own self for heav'n - ly food.
quish, As the dark - ness clears a - way.
ia! Al - le - lu - ia, Lord Most High!"

Text: Liturgy of St. James, 5th C.; para. by Gerard Moultrie, 1829–1885, alt.
Tune: PICARDY, 8 7 8 7 8 7; French carol; harm. by Richard Proulx, 1937–2010, © 1986, GIA Publications, Inc.

Soli Deo Glória 621

1. O God of bless-ings, all praise to you!
2. All praise for proph-ets, through grace in-spired
3. All praise for mu-sic, deep gift pro-found,
4. All praise for Je-sus, best gift di-vine

Your love sur-rounds us our whole life through.
To preach and wit-ness with hearts on fire.
Through hands and voic-es in ho-ly sound:
Through word and wit-ness, in bread and wine;

You are the free-dom of those op-pressed;
Your Spir-it choos-es the weak and small
The psalms of Da-vid, and Mar-y's praise,
In-car-nate Love Song of bound-less grace,

You are the com-fort of all dis-tressed:
To sing the new reign where might-y fall;
In word-less splen-dor and lyr-ic phrase.
Priest, teach-er, proph-et in time and space,

Come now, O ho-ly and wel-come Guest:
With them may we live your Gos-pel call:
With all cre-a-tion one song we raise:
Your stead-fast kind-ness with hu-man face:

*So-li De-o gló-ri-a, So-li De-o gló-ri-a!

*Glory be to God alone.

Text: Marty Haugen, b.1950
Tune: SOLI DEO GLORIA, 99 999 77; Marty Haugen, b.1950
© 1999, GIA Publications, Inc.

622 Praise Our God and Savior

Ostinato Refrain

Praise our God and Sav - ior, O praise our
Polish: Wy - sła - wiaj - cie Pa - na, O Wy - sła -
Spanish: En - to - ne - mos him - nos, O al Se -
Italian: E - sul - ta - te in Di - o, O E - sul -

God and Sav - ior, O for God's love en -
wiaj - cie Pa - na, O Śpie - waj Pa - nu
ñor can - te - mos, O pue - blos to - dos,
ta - te in Di - o, O Can - ta la ter - ra al

Last time

dures for - ev - er, al - le - lu - ia, al - le - lu - ia! Praise our
ca - ła zie - mio, al - le - lu - ja, al - le - lu - ja! Wy - sła -
a - la - bad - le, ¡a - le - lu - ya, a - le - lu - ya! En - to -
suo Si - gno - re, al - le - lu - ia, al - le - lu - ia! E - sul -

Last time

Text: Psalm 136, Luke, 1:68–79; Taizé Community
Tune: Taizé Community
© 2007, 2011, Les Presses de Taizé, GIA Publications, Inc., agent

Heaven Is Singing for Joy / 623
El Cielo Canta Alegría

Verses

1. Heav - en is sing - ing for joy, al - le -
2. Heav - en is sing - ing for joy, al - le -
3. Heav - en is sing - ing for joy, al - le -

1. El cie - lo can - ta_a - le - grí - a, ¡a - le -
2. El cie - lo can - ta_a - le - grí - a, ¡a - le -
3. El cie - lo can - ta_a - le - grí - a, ¡a - le -

lu - ia, for in your life and in
lu - ia, for in your heart and in
lu - ia, for your life and

lu - ya! por - que_en tu vi - da_y la
lu - ya! por - que_a tu vi - da_y la
lu - ya! por - que tu vi - da_y la

mine is shin - ing the glo - ry of God.
mine a - bides the one love of our God.
mine u - nite in the love of our God.

mí - a bri - lla la glo - ria de Dios.
mí - a las u - ne_el a - mor de Dios.
mí - a pro - cla - ma - rán al Se - ñor.

Refrain

Al - le - lu - ia, al - le - lu - ia!
¡A - le - lu - ya, a - le - lu - ya!

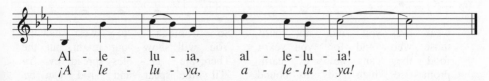

Al - le - lu - ia, al - le - lu - ia!
¡A - le - lu - ya, a - le - lu - ya!

Text: Pablo Sosa, b.1933
Tune: ALEGRÍA, Irregular with alleluias; Pablo Sosa, b.1933
© 1958, GIA Publications, Inc.

624 Canticle of the Turning

Verses

1. My soul cries out with a joy - ful shout that the
2. Though I am small, my God, my all, you
3. From the halls of power to the for - tress tower, not a
4. Though the na - tions rage from age to age, we re -

God of my heart is great, And my spir - it sings of the
work great things in me, And your mer - cy will last from the
stone will be left on stone. Let the king be - ware for your
mem - ber who holds us fast: God's mer - cy must de -

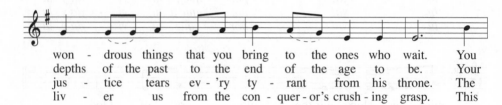

won - drous things that you bring to the ones who wait. You
depths of the past to the end of the age to be. Your
jus - tice tears ev - 'ry ty - rant from his throne. The
liv - er us from the con - quer - or's crush - ing grasp. This

fixed your sight on your ser - vant's plight, and my
ver - y name puts the proud to shame, and to
hun - gry poor shall weep no more, for the
sav - ing word that our fore - bears heard is the

weak - ness you did not spurn, So from east to west shall my
those who would for you yearn, You will show your might, put the
food they can nev - er earn; There are ta - bles spread, ev - 'ry
prom - ise which holds us bound, 'Til the spear and rod can be

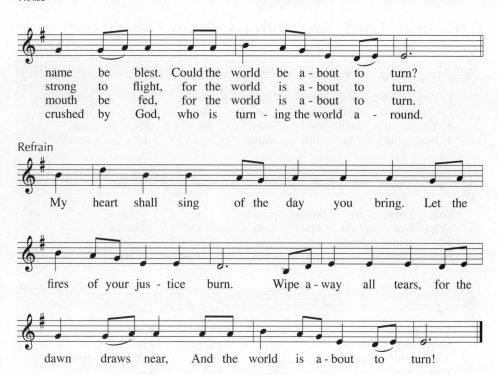

name	be	blest.	Could the	world	be	a - bout	to	turn?
strong	to	flight,	for the	world	is	a - bout	to	turn.
mouth	be	fed,	for the	world	is	a - bout	to	turn.
crushed	by	God,	who is	turn - ing the world	a -	round.

Refrain

My heart shall sing of the day you bring. Let the

fires of your jus - tice burn. Wipe a - way all tears, for the

dawn draws near, And the world is a - bout to turn!

Text: Luke 1:46–58; Rory Cooney, b.1952
Tune: STAR OF THE COUNTY DOWN, Irregular with refrain; Irish melody; arr. by Rory Cooney, b.1952
© 1990, GIA Publications, Inc.

Laudáte Dóminum 625

Ostinato Refrain

Lau - dá - te Dó - mi - num, lau - dá - te Dó - mi - num, o - mnes

gen - tes, al - le - lú - ia. al - le - lú - ia.

1. 2.

Text: Psalm 117, *Praise the Lord, all you peoples*; Taizé Community, 1980
Tune: Jacques Berthier, 1923–1994
© 1980, Les Presses de Taizé, GIA Publications, Inc., agent

626 You, Lord, Are Both Lamb and Shepherd

1. You, Lord, are both Lamb and Shep - herd.
2. Clothed in light up - on the moun - tain,
3. You, who walk each day be - side us,
4. Wor - thy is our earth - ly Je - sus!

You, Lord, are both prince and slave.
Stripped of might up - on the cross,
Sit in pow - er at God's side.
Wor - thy is our cos - mic Christ!

You, peace - mak - er and sword - bring - er
Shin - ing in e - ter - nal glo - ry,
You, who preach a way that's nar - row,
Wor - thy your de - feat and vic - t'ry.

Of the way you took and gave.
Beg - gar'd by a sol - dier's toss.
Have a love that reach - es wide.
Wor - thy still your peace and strife.

You, the ev - er - last - ing in - stant;
You, the ev - er - last - ing in - stant;
You, the ev - er - last - ing in - stant;
You, the ev - er - last - ing in - stant;

You, whom we both scorn and crave.
You, who are both gift and cost.
You, who are our pil - grim guide.
You, who are our death and life.

Text: *Christus Paradox*, Sylvia G. Dunstan, 1955–1993, © 1991, GIA Publications, Inc.
Tune: PICARDY, 8 7 8 7 8 7; French carol; harm. by Richard Proulx, 1937–2010, © 1986, GIA Publications, Inc.

O God beyond All Praising 627

1. O God be-yond all prais-ing, we wor-ship you to - day
*2. The flow'r of earth-ly splen-dor in time must sure-ly die,
3. Then hear, O gra-cious Sav - ior, ac - cept the love we bring,

And sing the love a - maz-ing that songs can-not re - pay;
Its frag - ile bloom sur - ren - der to you, the Lord most high;
That we who know your fa - vor may serve you as our King;

For we can on - ly won - der at ev - 'ry gift you send,
But hid - den from all na - ture the e - ter - nal seed is sown,
And wheth - er our to - mor-rows be filled with good or ill,

At bless-ings with - out num-ber and mer-cies with-out end.
Though small in mor - tal stat - ure to heav-en's gar - den grown.
We'll tri-umph through our sor-rows and rise to bless you still,

We lift our hearts be - fore you and wait up - on your word;
For Christ, the man from heav - en, from death has set us free,
To mar - vel at your beau - ty and glo - ry in your ways,

We hon - or and a - dore you, our great and might-y Lord.
And we through him are giv - en the fin - al vic - to - ry!
And make a joy - ful du - ty our sac - ri - fice of praise.

*May be omitted.

Text: Michael Perry, 1942–1996, © 1982, The Jubilate Group (admin. by Hope Publishing Company)
Tune: THAXTED, 13 13 13 13 13 13; Gustav Holst, 1874–1934

628 Come, Christians, Join to Sing

1. Come, Chris-tians, join to sing   Al - le - lu - ia!   A - men!
2. Come, lift your hearts on high: Al - le - lu - ia!   A - men!
3. Praise yet the Lord a - gain: Al - le - lu - ia!   A - men!

Loud praise to Christ our King,   Al - le - lu - ia!   A - men!
Let prais - es fill the sky: Al - le - lu - ia!   A - men!
Life shall not end the strain: Al - le - lu - ia!   A - men!

Let all, with heart and voice,   Be - fore his throne re-joice;
He is our guide and friend;   Our needs he will at-tend;
On heav-en's bliss - ful shore   His good-ness we'll a-dore,

Praise is his gra-cious choice.   Al - le - lu - ia!   A - men!
His love shall nev - er end.   Al - le - lu - ia!   A - men!
Sing - ing for - ev - er - more: Al - le - lu - ia!   A - men!

Text: Christian H. Bateman, 1813–1889
Tune: MADRID, 6 6 6 6 66 6 6; Spanish melody; arr. by Benjamin Carr, 1768–1831; harm. by David Evans, 1874–1948

629 Sing a New Song to the Lord

1. Sing a new song to the Lord,   He to whom won - ders be -
2. Now to the ends of the earth   See his sal - va - tion is
3. Sing a new song and re - joice,   Pub - lish his prais - es a -
4. Join with the hills and the sea   Thun-ders of praise to pro -

long;   Re - joice in his tri - umph and tell   of his
shown;   And still he re - mem-bers his mer - cy   and
broad;   Let voic - es in cho - rus,   with trum - pet   and
long;   In judg - ment and jus - tice   he comes   to the

pow'r,   O   sing   to the   Lord   a new song!
truth,   Un - chang - ing in   love   to his   own.
horn,   Re - sound   for the   joy   of the Lord!
earth,   O   sing   to the   Lord   a new song!

Text: Psalm 98; Timothy Dudley-Smith, b.1926, © 1973, Hope Publishing Company
Tune: CANTATE DOMINO (ONSLOW SQUARE), Irregular; David G. Wilson, b.1940, © 1973, The Jubilate Group
   (admin. by Hope Publishing Company)

Immortal, Invisible, God Only Wise 630

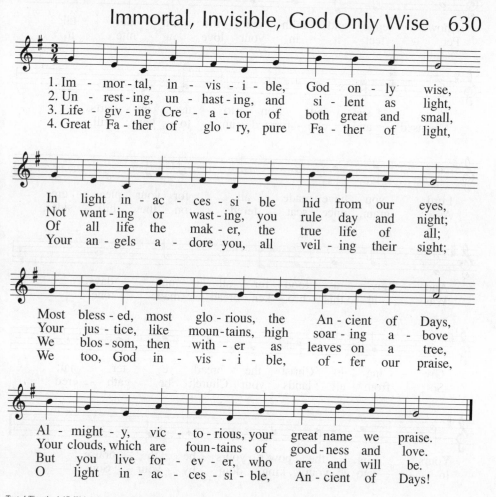

1. Im - mor - tal, in - vis - i - ble, God on - ly wise,
2. Un - rest - ing, un - hast - ing, and si - lent as light,
3. Life - giv - ing Cre - a - tor of both great and small,
4. Great Fa - ther of glo - ry, pure Fa - ther of light,

In light in - ac - ces - si - ble hid from our eyes,
Not want - ing or wast - ing, you rule day and night;
Of all life the mak - er, the true life of all;
Your an - gels a - dore you, all veil - ing their sight;

Most bless - ed, most glo - rious, the An - cient of Days,
Your jus - tice, like moun - tains, high soar - ing a - bove
We blos - som, then with - er as leaves on a tree,
We too, God in - vis - i - ble, of - fer our praise,

Al - might - y, vic - to - rious, your great name we praise.
Your clouds, which are foun - tains of good - ness and love.
But you live for - ev - er, who are and will be.
O light in - ac - ces - si - ble, An - cient of Days!

Text: 1 Timothy 1:17; Walter C. Smith, 1824–1908, alt.
Tune: ST. DENIO, 11 11 11 11; adapt. from a Welsh ballad in John Robert's *Hymns of the Sanctuary*, 1839

631 Father, We Thank You, Who Have Planted

1. Fa - ther, we thank you, who have plant - ed
2. Watch o'er your Church, O Lord, in mer - cy,

Your ho - ly name with - in our hearts.
Save it from e - vil, guard it still;

Knowl - edge and faith and life im - mor - tal
Per - fect it in your love, u - nite it,

Je - sus your Son to us im - parts.
Cleansed and con - formed un - to your will.

Lord, you have made all for your pleas - ure,
As grain, once scat - tered on the hill - sides,

And giv'n us food for all our days,
Was in this bro - ken bread made one,

Giv - ing in Christ the bread e - ter - nal;
So from all lands your Church be gath - ered

Yours is the pow'r, yours be the praise.
In - to your king - dom by your Son.

Text: From the *Didache*, c.110; tr. by F. Bland Tucker, 1895–1984, alt., © 1940, The Church Pension Fund
Tune: RENDEZ À DIEU, 9 8 9 8 D; *Genevan Psalter*, 1551; attr. to Louis Bourgeois, c.1510–1561

For the Beauty of the Earth   632

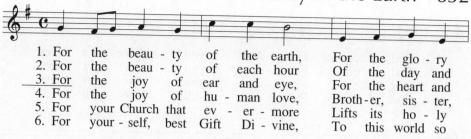

1. For the beau - ty of the earth, For the glo - ry
2. For the beau - ty of each hour Of the day and
3. For the joy of ear and eye, For the heart and
4. For the joy of hu - man love, Broth - er, sis - ter,
5. For your Church that ev - er - more Lifts its ho - ly
6. For your - self, best Gift Di - vine, To this world so

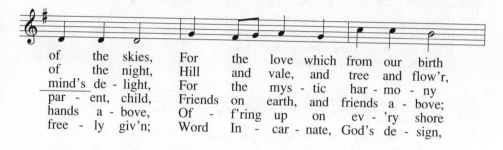

of the skies, For the love which from our birth
of the night, Hill and vale, and tree and flow'r,
mind's de - light, For the mys - tic har - mo - ny
par - ent, child, Friends on earth, and friends a - bove;
hands a - bove, Of - f'ring up on ev - 'ry shore
free - ly giv'n; Word In - car - nate, God's de - sign,

O - ver and a - round us lies:
Sun and moon, and stars of light:
Link - ing sense to sound and sight: Lord of all, to
For all gen - tle thoughts and mild:
Its pure sac - ri - fice of love:
Peace on earth and joy in heav'n:

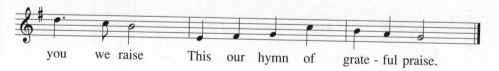

you we raise This our hymn of grate - ful praise.

Text: Folliot S. Pierpont, 1835–1917, alt.
Tune: DIX, 7 7 7 7 with refrain; arr. from Conrad Kocher, 1786–1872, by William H. Monk, 1823–1889

633 God, Our Father, You Have Granted

1. God, our Fa - ther, you have grant - ed
2. God, our Fa - ther, you have show - ered
3. God, our Fa - ther, you have kept us
4. God, our Fa - ther, still go with us

Gifts that deep - en with the years— Love that binds our
Bless-ings rich be - yond com - pare— Chil - dren, fam - 'ly,
When the road grew steep and long; Giv - en pa - tience
On the way be - yond our sight. Be our guide through

lives to - geth - er, Hearts made one through laugh - ter, tears.
friends sur-round-ing, Work to do and joys to share.
and en - dur - ance, Cheered the dark - est night with song.
all our jour - ney, Strength by day and star by night.

For your good - ness poured up - on us,
For your good - ness poured up - on us,
For your good - ness poured up - on us,
For your good - ness nev - er fail - ing,

Hear our prayer of thanks and praise!

Text: Herman G. Stuempfle, Jr., 1923–2007, © 2000, GIA Publications, Inc.
Tune: REGENT SQUARE, 8 7 8 7 8 7; Henry Smart, 1813–1879

634 We Praise You, O God

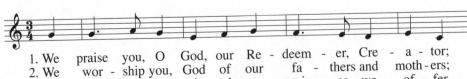

1. We praise you, O God, our Re - deem - er, Cre - a - tor;
2. We wor - ship you, God of our fa - thers and moth-ers;
3. With voic - es u - nit - ed our prais - es we of - fer

In grate - ful de - vo - tion our trib - ute we bring.
Through tri - al and tem - pest our guide you have been.
And glad - ly our songs of thanks - giv - ing we raise.

We lay it be - fore you; we kneel and a - dore you;
When per - ils o'er - take us, you nev - er for - sake us,
You, Lord, are be - side us, your strong arm to guide us.

We bless your ho - ly name; glad prais - es we sing.
And with your help, O Lord, our bat - tles we win.
To you, our great Re - deem - er, glo - ry and praise!

Text: Julia C. Cory, 1882–1963, alt.
Tune: KREMSER, 12 11 12 11; Valerius' *Nederlandtsch Gedenckclanck*, 1626; harm. by Edward Kremser, 1838–1914

Confitémini Dómino / 635
Come and Fill Our Hearts

Ostinato Refrain

Con - fi - té - mi - ni Dó - mi - no quó - ni - am
Come and fill our hearts with your peace. You a - lone, O Lord, are
Spanish: Llé - na - nos, Se - ñor, de tu paz. Por - que só - lo e - res
Lithuanian: Aš pa - si - ti - kiu Vieš - pa - čiu, nes Jis mums

bo - nus. Con - fi - té - mi - ni Dó - mi - no, Al - le - lú - ia!
ho - ly. Come and fill our hearts with your peace, Al - le - lu - ia!
san - to. Llé - na - nos, Se - ñor, de tu paz, ¡A - le - lu - ya!
ge - ras. Aš pa - si - ti - kiu Vieš - pa - čiu, A - le - liu - ja!

Text: Psalm 136, *Give thanks to the Lord for he is good;* Taizé Community, 1982
Tune: Jacques Berthier, 1923–1994
© 1982, 1991, 2011, Les Presses de Taizé, GIA Publications, Inc., agent

636 Let All Things Now Living

1. Let all things now liv-ing A song of thanks-giv-ing
2. God rules all the forc-es: The stars in their cours-es

To God the Cre - a - tor tri - um - phant - ly raise,
And sun in its or - bit o - be - dient - ly shine;

Who fash-ioned and made us, Pro - tect - ed and stayed us,
The hills and the moun-tains, The riv - ers and foun-tains,

And guides us with care to the end of our days.
The deeps of the o - cean pro - claim God di - vine.

God's ban - ners are o'er us, God's light goes be - fore us,
We too should be voic-ing Our love and re - joic-ing;

A pil - lar of fire shin - ing forth in the night,
With glad ad - o - ra - tion a song let us raise

Till shad - ows have van-ished And dark - ness is ban-ished,
Till all things now liv - ing U - nite in thanks-giv - ing:

As for - ward we trav - el from light in - to light.
"To God in the high - est, ho - san - na and praise!"

Text: Katherine K. Davis, 1892–1980, alt., © 1939, 1966, E. C. Schirmer Music Co.
Tune: ASH GROVE, 66 11 66 11 D; Welsh melody; harm. by Gerald H. Knight, 1908–1979, © The Royal School of Church Music

Now Thank We All Our God 637

1. Now thank we all our God With hearts and hands and
2. O may this boun-teous God Through all our life be
3. All praise and thanks to God The Fa-ther now be

voic - es, Who won-drous things has done, In
near us, With ev - er joy - ful hearts And
giv - en, The Son, and him who reigns With

whom his world re - joic - es; Who from our moth-ers'
bless - ed peace to cheer us; Pre - serve us in his
them in high-est heav - en— The one e - ter - nal

arms Has blessed us on our way With
grace, And guide us in dis - tress, And
God, Whom earth and heav'n a - dore— For

count-less gifts of love, And still is ours to - day.
free us from all harm Till heav - en we pos - sess.
thus it was, is now, And shall be ev - er - more.

Text: *Nun danket alle Gott;* Martin Rinkhart, 1586–1649; tr. by Catherine Winkworth, 1827–1878, alt.
Tune: NUN DANKET, 6 7 6 7 6 6 6 6; Johann Crüger, 1598–1662; harm. by A. Gregory Murray, OSB, 1905–1992

638 Sing a Happy Alleluia

1. Sing a hap - py al - le - lu - ia,
2. We're the proof of God's good hu - mor,
3. Sa - rah laughed at God's good tim - ing,
4. Ev - 'ry day sing al - le - lu - ia!

Sing it out with heart and style—
We're the twin - kle in God's eye,
Mar - y sang and Da - vid danced,
We are loved, though so ab - surd,

We're the ech - o of God's laugh - ter,
Made to shine, re - flect the glo - ry,
Je - sus smiled and hugged the chil - dren—
Hu - man, fool - ish, cho - sen peo - ple,

We're the im - age of God's smile.
Giv - en light and space to fly.
So is life for us en - hanced.
God still takes us at our word!

Al - le - lu - ia, all cre - a - tion, al - le -

lu - ia, ev - 'ry - one! Al-le - lu - ia, all cre - a - tion, al-le -

lu - ia, ev - 'ry - one!

Text: Shirley Erena Murray, b.1931, © 1992, Hope Publishing Company
Tune: ANITA, 8 7 8 7 with refrain; Sally Ann Morris, b.1952, © 2001, GIA Publications, Inc.

In the Lord I'll Be Ever Thankful 639

Ostinato Refrain

In the Lord I'll be ev - er thank-ful, in the Lord I will re-
Spanish: El Se - ñor es mi for - ta - le - za, el Se - ñor es mi can-
Portuguese: O Se - nhor é a mi-nha for - ça, ao Se - nhor o meu can-
Polish: Pan jest mo - cą swo-je-go lu - du. Pieś-nią mo - ją jest
Tagalog: Sa Di - yos mag-pa - pa - sa - la - mat sa kan-ya'y ma-ga-ka-

joice! Look to God, do not be a - fraid; lift up your
ción. Él nos da la sal - va - ción. En él con-
to. E - le é nos - so sal - va - dor. Ne - le eu con-
Pan. Mo - ja tar - cza i mo - ja moc, On jest mym
lak mas-dan siya at huwag man-gam - ba si - ya'y ka-

voic - es, the Lord is near; lift up your voic - es, the Lord is near.
fí - o, no te - me - ré. En él con - fí - o, no te - me - ré.
fi - o e na-da temo, ne - le eu con - fi - o e na - da temo.
Bo - giem, nie jes - tem sam. W Nim mo - ja si - ła, nie jes - tem sam.
pi - ling si - ya'y a - ma, si - ya'y ka - pi - ling si - ya'y a - ma.

640　Shepherd, Do You Tramp the Hills

1. "Shep - herd, do you tramp the hills, Track-ing down one
2. "Wom - an, do you scour the house Just to find one
3. "Fa - ther, does your heart still bleed For a child who
4. Shep - herd, search-er, par - ent's care— By what im - age

stray - ing sheep, Leav - ing nine - ty - nine be - hind
coin that's lost? Since you have the oth - er nine,
chose to roam— Reb - el, row - dy, far a - way,
can we name Spend - thrift love, im - pas-sioned grace,

With no guard the watch to keep?" "But that one I
Is it real - ly worth the cost?" "But that coin you
Spurn - ing love and scorn - ing home?" "But that rest - less,
In - can - des - cent as a flame? Christ, be - yond all

call by name; She will hear and know my voice.
count so small Has for me a spe - cial worth.
reck - less boy Nev - er can my love out - run!
words you spoke, Sto - ries that with won - der glow,

Night and day I'll search the land
When it's found, the sight will fill
When his foot - steps lead him back,
You have shown us on a cross

Till I find her and re - joice!"
All my house and heart with mirth!"
I'll re - joice to call him 'Son!'"
Love that will not let us go!

Text: Herman G. Stuempfle, Jr., 1923–2007, © 2000, GIA Publications, Inc.
Tune: ABERYSTWYTH, 7 7 7 7 D; Joseph Parry, 1841–1903

What Wondrous Love Is This   641

1. What won-drous love is this, O my soul, O my soul!
2. To God and to the Lamb I will sing, I will sing;
3. And when from death I'm free, I'll sing on, I'll sing on;

What won-drous love is this, O my soul!
To God and to the Lamb I will sing.
And when from death I'm free, I'll sing on.

What won-drous love is this that caused the Lord of bliss
To God and to the Lamb, who is the great I AM,
And when from death I'm free, I'll sing and joy-ful be,

To bear the dread-ful curse for my soul, for my soul;
While mil-lions join the theme, I will sing, I will sing;
And through e-ter-ni-ty I'll sing on, I'll sing on;

To bear the dread-ful curse for my soul!
While mil-lions join the theme, I will sing.
And through e-ter-ni-ty I'll sing on.

Text: Alexander Means, 1801–1883
Tune: WONDROUS LOVE, 12 9 12 12 9; *Southern Harmony*, 1835; harm. by Richard Proulx, 1937–2010, © 1975, GIA Publications, Inc.

642 Love Divine, All Loves Excelling

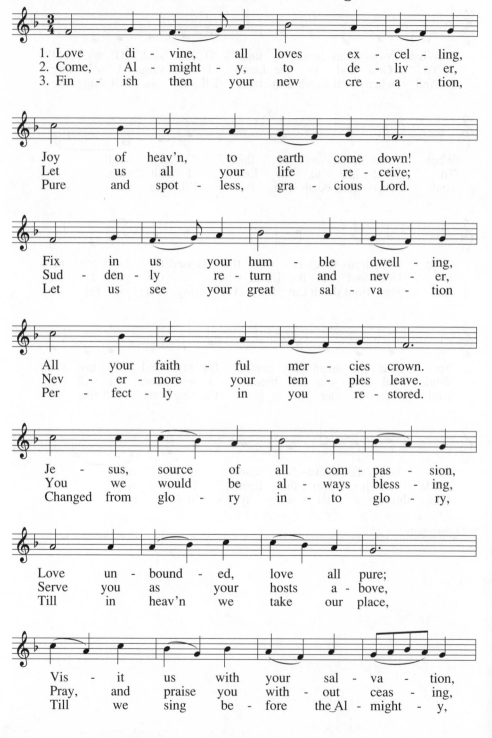

1. Love di - vine, all loves ex - cel - ling,
2. Come, Al - might - y, to de - liv - er,
3. Fin - ish then your new cre - a - tion,

Joy of heav'n, to earth come down!
Let us all your life re - ceive;
Pure and spot - less, gra - cious Lord.

Fix in us your hum - ble dwell - ing,
Sud - den - ly re - turn and nev - er,
Let us see your great sal - va - tion

All your faith - ful mer - cies crown.
Nev - er - more your tem - ples leave.
Per - fect - ly in you re - stored.

Je - sus, source of all com - pas - sion,
You we would be al - ways bless - ing,
Changed from glo - ry in - to glo - ry,

Love un - bound - ed, love all pure;
Serve you as your hosts a - bove,
Till in heav'n we take our place,

Vis - it us with your sal - va - tion,
Pray, and praise you with - out ceas - ing,
Till we sing be - fore the Al - might - y,

Let your love in us en - dure.
Glo - ry in your pre - cious love.
Lost in won - der, love, and praise.

Text: Charles Wesley, 1707–1788, alt.
Tune: HYFRYDOL, 8 7 8 7 D; Rowland H. Prichard, 1811–1887

Surely It Is God Who Saves Me 643

1. Sure - ly it is God who
2. Make God's deeds known to the

saves me; I shall trust and have no fear; For the
peo - ples: Tell out his ex - alt - ed Name. Praise the

Lord de - fends and shields me, And his sav - ing help is
Lord, who has done great things; All his works God's might pro -

near. So re - joice as you draw wa - ter From sal -
claim. Zi - on, lift your voice in sing - ing; For with

va - tion's heal - ing spring; In the day of your de -
you has come to dwell, In your ver - y midst, the

liv - 'rance Thank the Lord, his mer - cies sing.
great and Ho - ly One of Is - ra - el.

Text: Isaiah 12:1–6; Carl P. Daw, Jr., b.1944, © 1982, 1990, Hope Publishing Company
Tune: RAQUEL, 8 7 8 7 D; Skinner Chávez-Melo, 1944–1992, © 1987, Estate of Skinner Chávez-Melo

Alternate tune: PLEADING SAVIOR

644 The One Who Longs to Make Us Whole

1. The One who longs to make us whole Is
2. The One who saves us from our-selves Is
3. The One who un - der - stands our need Ac -

wait - ing to em - brace Our bro - ken lives so
wait - ing to re - lease Our hearts from chains of
cepts us as we are; And, like a loved one,

we can know The pow'r of heal - ing grace. God's
self - re-proach, Our fail - ure to find peace. When
wel - comes us When we have wan - dered far. God

love sur - rounds our suf - fer - ing, And
harm - ful hab - its leave us bruised, Dis -
nev - er says we come too late To

keeps us through the night. God helps us bear our
traught from in - ner pain, God comes to us through
be for - giv - en, free, But prom - is - es we

deep de - spair Till we see morn - ing light.
trust - ed friends, And helps us hope a - gain.
can be - come The self we're meant to be!

Text: Edith Sinclair Downing, b.1922, © 1998, Selah Publishing Co., Inc.
Tune: THE FLIGHT OF THE EARLS; CMD; Irish melody; harm. by Ronald F. Krisman, b.1946, © 2011, GIA Publications, Inc.

There's a Wideness in God's Mercy 645

1. There's a wide-ness in God's mer-cy Like the wide-ness
2. For the love of God is broad-er Than the meas-ures
3. Trou-bled souls, why will you scat-ter Like a crowd of

of the sea; There's a kind-ness in God's jus-tice
of the mind; And the heart of the E-ter-nal
fright-ened sheep? Fool-ish hearts, why will you wan-der

Which is more than lib-er-ty. There is plen-ti-
Is most won-der-ful-ly kind. If our love were
From a love so true and deep? There is wel-come

ful re-demp-tion In the blood that has been shed;
but more faith-ful, We should rest up-on God's word;
for the sin-ner, And more grac-es for the good;

There is joy for all the mem-bers
And our lives would be thanks-giv-ing
There is mer-cy with the Sav-ior,

In the sor-rows of the Head.
For the good-ness of our Lord.
There is heal-ing in his blood.

Text: Frederick W. Faber, 1814–1863, alt.
Tune: IN BABILONE, 8 7 8 7 D; *Oude en Nieuwe Hollantse Boerenlieties en Contredansen,* c.1710

646 There Is a Balm in Gilead

Refrain

There is a balm in Gil - e - ad To make the wound - ed whole; There is a balm in Gil - e - ad To heal the sin - sick soul.

Verses

1. Some - times I feel dis - cour - aged And think my work's in vain, But then the Ho - ly Spir - it Re - vives my soul a - gain.

2. Don't ev - er be dis - cour - aged, For Je - sus is your friend; And if you lack for knowl - edge, He'll ne'er re - fuse to lend.

3. If you can - not preach like Pe - ter, If you can - not pray like Paul, You can tell the love of Je - sus And say, "He died for all."

D.C.

Text: Jeremiah 8:22, African American spiritual
Tune: BALM IN GILEAD, Irregular with refrain; African American spiritual; acc. by Robert J. Batastini, b.1942, © 1987, GIA Publications, Inc.

When Jesus Passed through Jericho   647

1. When Je - sus passed through Jer - i - cho, The
2. He watched be - neath the sway - ing boughs The
3. The friend of sin - ners Je - sus was And

peo - ple crowd - ed round To see the one who
man from Gal - i - lee. And Je - sus saw his
is the same to - day. He nev - er sees a

healed the sick, By whom the lost were found.
lone - ly face And said, "Come, eat with me."
lone - ly face And looks the oth - er way.

Zac - chae - us, small and scorned by all, Thought
Zac - chae - us took the Lord straight home And,
In - stead, when bowed by guilt or grief We

he should al - so see The Mas - ter when he
while they shared a meal, Told Je - sus he would
seek the Lord to see. He sets be - fore us

came to town, And so he climbed a tree.
help the poor And nev - er cheat or steal.
bread and wine And says, "Come, eat with me."

Text: Herman G. Stuempfle, Jr., 1923–2007, © 1993, GIA Publications, Inc.
Tune: FOREST GREEN, CMD; English melody; harm. by Ralph Vaughan Williams, 1872–1958, alt.

648 What Love and Deep Devotion /
Porque de Tal Manera

Ostinato Refrain

What love and deep de - vo-tion God showed for the world,
Por - que de tal ma - ne - ra al mun - do a-mó Dios,

send-ing us the Son most ho - ly, Je - sus our Lord,
que le dio a su pro - pio Hi - jo, Cris - to Je - sús,

will-ing, too, that ev-'ry per-son be - liev - ing in him shall not
pa - ra que ca-da per - so - na que en él cre - e - rá, no se

per - ish, but have and cher - ish life ev - er - last-ing.
pier - da, si - no que ten - ga vi - da e - ter - na.

Text: Ronald F. Krisman, b.1946
Tune: Ronald F. Krisman, b.1946
© 2008, GIA Publications, Inc.

God the Sculptor of the Mountains 649

1. God the
2. God the
3. God the
4. God the

1. sculp - tor of the moun - tains, God the mill - er of the
2. nui - sance to the Phar - aoh, God the cleav - er of the
3. dress - er of the vine - yard, God the plant - er of the
4. un - ex - pect - ed in - fant, God the calm, de - ter - mined

1. sand, God the jew - 'ler of the heav - ens, God the
2. sea, God the pil - lar in the dark - ness, God the
3. wheat, God the reap - er of the har - vest, God the
4. youth, God the ta - ble - turn - ing proph - et, God the

1. pot - ter of the land: You are womb of all cre -
2. bea - con of the free: You are fount of all de -
3. source of all we eat: You are host at ev - 'ry
4. res - ur - rect - ed truth: You are pres - ent ev - 'ry

1. a - tion, We are form - less; shape us now.
2. liv - 'rance, We are sight - less; lead us now.
3. ta - ble, We are hun - gry; feed us now.
4. mo - ment, We are search - ing; meet us now.

Text: John Thornburg, b.1954, © 1993
Tune: JULION, 8 7 8 7 8 7; David Hurd, b.1950, © 1983, GIA Publications, Inc.

650 Amazing Grace!

1. A - maz - ing grace! how sweet the sound, That
2. 'Twas grace that taught my heart to fear, And
3. The Lord has prom - ised good to me, His
4. Through man - y dan - gers, toils, and snares, I
5. When we've been there ten thou - sand years, Bright

saved a wretch like me! I once was lost, but
grace my fears re - lieved; How pre - cious did that
word my hope se - cures; He will my shield and
have al - read - y come; 'Tis grace has brought me
shin - ing as the sun, We've no less days to

now am found; Was blind, but now I see.
grace ap - pear The hour I first be - lieved!
por - tion be As long as life en - dures.
safe thus far, And grace will lead me home.
sing God's praise Than when we'd first be - gun.

Text: St. 1–4, John Newton, 1725–1807; st. 5, attr. to John Rees, fl.1859
Tune: NEW BRITAIN, CM; *Virginia Harmony*, 1831; harm. by John Barnard, b.1948, © 1982, The Jubilate Group
   (admin. by Hope Publishing Company)

651 Keep in Mind

Refrain

Keep in mind that Je - sus Christ has died for

us and is ris - en from the dead. He is our sav - ing

Lord, he is joy for all a - ges.

Verse 1

1. If we die with the Lord, we shall live with the Lord.
   If we en - dure with the Lord, we shall reign with the Lord.

Verses 2, 3

2. In Christ all our sor - row, in Christ all our joy.
   In him hope of glo - ry, in him all our love.
3. In Christ our re - demp - tion, in Christ all our grace.
   In him our sal - va - tion, in him all our peace.

Text: 2 Timothy 2:8–12, Lucien Deiss, CSSp, 1921–2007
Tune: Lucien Deiss, CSSp, 1921–2007
© 1965, World Library Publications

Shall Tribulation or Distress   652

1. Shall trib - u - la - tion or dis - tress, Shall per - se -
2. Shall ill - ness, hun - ger, or de - spair, Shall lone - ly
3. No, nei - ther an - gel hosts nor thrones, Nor height nor

cu - tion, fire, or sword, Or an - y per - il of this
grief or anx-ious fears, Or deeds of ha - tred and dis -
depth of e - vil's reach, Nor pres-ent things, nor things to

world— Or e - ven death, Or e - ven death— Shall an - y
dain— Or e - ven death, Or e - ven death— Shall an - y
come— Not e - ven death, Not e - ven death— Not an - y

pow'r of earth or heav'n Di - vide us from your love, O Christ?
pow'r of earth or heav'n Di - vide us from your love, O Christ?
pow'r of earth or heav'n Can part us from your love, O Christ.

Text: Based on Romans 8:35, 38; Mary Louise Bringle, b.1953
Tune: ROMANS 8, 8 8 8 4 4 4 8 8; Sally Ann Morris, b.1952
© 2006, GIA Publications, Inc.

653 God Is Forgiveness

Ostinato Refrain

God is for-give-ness. Dare to for-give and God will be with you.
Polish: *Bóg jest mi - łoś - cią miej-cie od - wa - gę żyć dla mi - łoś - ci.*
Spanish: Dios es ter - nu - ra. Dios vi-ve en ti; a - tré - ve-te a a-mar.

God is for - give - ness. Love, and do not fear.
Bóg jest mi - łos - cią. Nie lę - kaj - cie się.
Dios es ter - nu - ra. No hay por - qué te - mer.

Text: Taizé Community
Tune: Taizé Community
© 2007, 2011, Les Presses de Taizé, GIA Publications, Inc., agent

654 When My Soul Is Sore and Troubled

1. When my soul is sore and trou - bled,
2. When my voice grows faint from cry - ing,
3. When my mus - cles burn from strain - ing,
4. When I know the Spir - it lis - tens,

When my mind is heav - y - bur - dened,
When my song is weak and bro - ken,
When my shoul - ders ache with sor - row,
When I know that Christ cries with me,

Then I cry, "My God, my God."
Then I cry, "My God, my God."
Then I cry, "My God, my God."
Then I sing, "My God, my God."

Text: Adam M. L. Tice, b.1979
Tune: PERILYPOS PSYCHE, 8 8 7; Ronald F. Krisman, b.1946
© 2009, GIA Publications, Inc.

Eternal Spirit of the Living Christ 655

1. E - ter - nal Spir - it of the liv - ing Christ,
2. Come, pray in me the prayer I need this day;
3. Come with the strength I lack, bring vi - sion clear

I know not how to ask or what to say;
Help me to see your pur - pose and your will,
Of hu - man need; oh, give me eyes to see

I on - ly know my need, as deep as life,
Where I have failed, what I have done a - miss;
Ful - fill - ment of my life in love out - poured:

And on - ly you can teach me how to pray.
Held in for - giv - ing love, let me be still.
My life in you, O Christ; your love in me.

Text: Frank von Christierson, 1900–1996, © 1974, The Hymn Society. Administered by Hope Publishing Company
Tune: SURSUM CORDA, 10 10 10 10; Alfred M. Smith, 1879–1971, © Mrs. Alfred M. Smith

656 Jesus, Come! For We Invite You

1. Je - sus, come! for we in - vite you,
2. Je - sus, come! trans-form our pleas - ures,
3. Je - sus, come! in new cre - a - tion,
4. Je - sus, come! sur - prise our dull - ness,

Guest and mas - ter, friend and Lord;
Guide us in - to paths un - known;
Heav'n brought near by pow'r di - vine;
Make us will - ing to re - ceive

Now, as once at Ca - na's wed - ding,
Bring your gifts, com - mand your ser - vants,
Give your un - ex - pect - ed glo - ry
More than we can yet i - mag - ine,

Speak, and let us hear your word:
Let us trust in you a - lone:
Chang - ing wa - ter in - to wine:
All the best you have to give:

Lead us through our need or doubt - ing,
Though your hand may work in se - cret,
Rouse the faith of your dis - ci - ples—
Let us find your hid - den rich - es,

Hope be born and joy re - stored.
All shall see what you have done.
Come, our first and great - est Sign!
Taste your love, be - lieve, and live!

Text: John 2; Christopher M. Idle, b.1938, © 1982, The Jubilate Group (admin. by Hope Publishing Company)
Tune: BEST GIFT, 8 7 8 7 8 7; Ronald F. Krisman, b.1946, © 1986, GIA Publications, Inc.

Lead Me, Guide Me 657

Refrain

Lead me, guide me, a-long the way, For if you

lead me, I can-not stray. Lord, let me walk each

day with thee. Lead me, O Lord, lead me.

Verses

1. I am weak and I need thy strength and pow'r To
2. Help me tread in the paths of right-eous-ness. Be my
3. I am lost if you take your hand from me, I am

help me o-ver my weak-est hour. Help me through the
aid when Sa-tan and sin op-press. I am put-ting
blind with-out thy Light to see. Lord, just al-ways

D.C.

dark-ness thy face to see. Lead me, O Lord, lead me.
all my trust in thee. Lead me, O Lord, lead me.
let me thy ser-vant be. Lead me, O Lord, lead me.

Text: Doris M. Akers, 1922–1995
Tune: LEAD ME, Irregular with refrain; Doris M. Akers, 1922–1995; harm. by Richard Smallwood, b.1948
© 1953, (renewed), arr. © 2011, Doris M. Akers, admin. by Chappell & Co., Inc.

658 Lord, Teach Us How to Pray

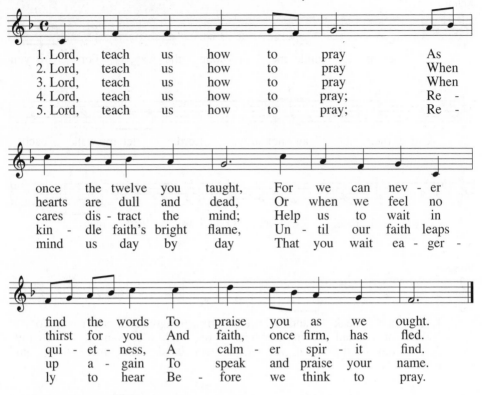

1. Lord, teach us how to pray As
2. Lord, teach us how to pray When
3. Lord, teach us how to pray When
4. Lord, teach us how to pray; Re -
5. Lord, teach us how to pray; Re -

once the twelve you taught, For we can nev - er
hearts are dull and dead, Or when we feel no
cares dis - tract the mind; Help us to wait in
kin - dle faith's bright flame, Un - til our faith leaps
mind us day by day That you wait ea - ger -

find the words To praise you as we ought.
thirst for you And faith, once firm, has fled.
qui - et - ness, A calm - er spir - it find.
up a - gain To speak and praise your name.
ly to hear Be - fore we think to pray.

Text: Herman G. Stuempfle, Jr., 1923–2007, © 2000, GIA Publications, Inc.
Tune: ST. THOMAS (Williams), SM; Aaron Williams, 1731–1776; harm. by Lowell Mason, 1792–1872

659 Jesus, Show Us How to Pray

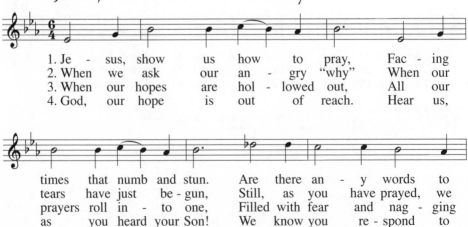

1. Je - sus, show us how to pray, Fac - ing
2. When we ask our an - gry "why" When our
3. When our hopes are hol - lowed out, All our
4. God, our hope is out of reach. Hear us,

times that numb and stun. Are there an - y words to
tears have just be - gun, Still, as you have prayed, we
prayers roll in - to one, Filled with fear and nag - ging
as you heard your Son! We know you re - spond to

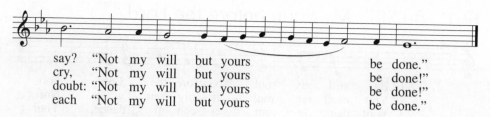

say? "Not my will but yours be done."
cry, "Not my will but yours be done!"
doubt: "Not my will but yours be done!"
each "Not my will but yours be done."

Text: Adam M. L. Tice, b.1979, © 2009, GIA Publications, Inc.
Tune: THE CALL, 7 7 7 7; Ralph Vaughan Williams, 1872–1958

As a Chalice Cast of Gold 660

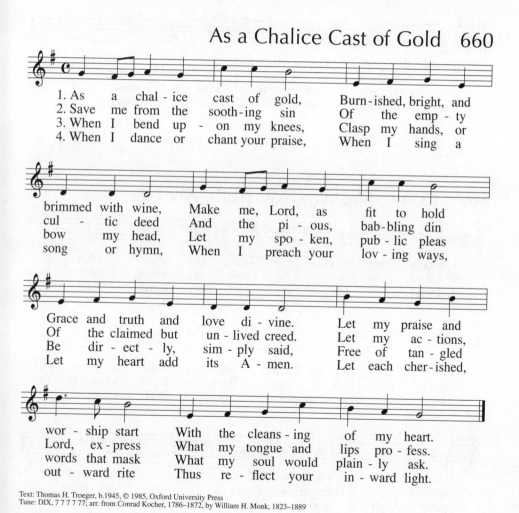

1. As a chal - ice cast of gold, Burn-ished, bright, and
2. Save me from the sooth-ing sin Of the emp - ty
3. When I bend up - on my knees, Clasp my hands, or
4. When I dance or chant your praise, When I sing a

brimmed with wine, Make me, Lord, as fit to hold
cul - tic deed And the pi - ous, bab-bling din
bow my head, Let my spo - ken, pub - lic pleas
song or hymn, When I preach your lov - ing ways,

Grace and truth and love di - vine. Let my praise and
Of the claimed but un - lived creed. Let my ac - tions,
Be dir - ect - ly, sim - ply said, Free of tan - gled
Let my heart add its A - men. Let each cher - ished,

wor - ship start With the cleans - ing of my heart.
Lord, ex - press What my tongue and lips pro - fess.
words that mask What my soul would plain - ly ask.
out - ward rite Thus re - flect your in - ward light.

Text: Thomas H. Troeger, b.1945, © 1985, Oxford University Press
Tune: DIX, 7 7 7 7 77; arr. from Conrad Kocher, 1786–1872, by William H. Monk, 1823–1889

661 Be Still, My Soul, before the Lord

1. Be still, my soul, be-fore the Lord, For God is al - ways near. Be - fore your mind is moved to pray, God lis - tens and will hear.
2. You need not mul - ti - ply your words Nor pray with prac - ticed art. Be - yond all speech, God un - der-stands The hun - ger of your heart.
3. Wait, then, in qui - et con - fi - dence, Your anx - ious thoughts at rest. God knows your needs be - fore you ask And works for what is best.
4. Be still, my soul, be-fore the Lord; On God in pa - tience wait. God's love, un - seen, sur - rounds your life; God's help will not be late.

Text: Herman G. Stuempfle, Jr., 1923–2007, © 2000, GIA Publications, Inc.
Tune: SHANTI, CM; Marty Haugen, b.1950; acc. by Randall Sensmeier, b.1948, © 1984, 2006, GIA Publications, Inc.

662 Come, My Way, My Truth, My Life

1. Come, my Way, my Truth, my Life: Such a way as gives us breath; Such a truth as ends all strife; Such a life as kill - eth death.
2. Come, my Light, my Feast, my Strength: Such a light as shows a feast; Such a feast as mends in length; Such a strength as makes his guest.
3. Come, my Joy, my Love, my Heart: Such a joy as none can move; Such a love as none can part; Such a heart as joys in love.

Text: George Herbert, 1593–1632
Tune: THE CALL, 7 7 7 7; Ralph Vaughan Williams, 1872–1958

Seek Ye First 663

1. Seek ye first the king-dom of God
2. Ask, and it shall be giv-en un-to you,
3. You do not live by bread a - lone,
4. Where two or three are gath-ered in my name,

and his right - eous - ness,
seek, and you shall find,
but by ev - 'ry word,
there am I in their midst;

and all these things shall be add - ed un-to you;
knock, and the door shall be o - pened un-to you;
that comes forth from the mouth of God;
and what-so - ev - er you ask I will do;

Al - le - lu, al - le - lu - ia.

2. *Optional Refrain, Descant, or Canon:*

Al - le - lu - ia, al - le - lu - ia,

al - le - lu - ia, al - le - lu, al-le-lu - ia.

May be sung as a two-voice canon.

Text: Matthew 6:33, 7:7; adapt. by Karen Lafferty, b.1948
Tune: SEEK YE FIRST, Irregular; Karen Lafferty, b.1948

664　We Cannot Measure How You Heal

1. We can-not meas-ure how you heal Or an-swer ev-'ry
2. The pain that will not go a-way, The guilt that clings from
3. So some have come who need your help, And some have come to

suf-f'rer's prayer, Yet we be-lieve your grace re-sponds
things long past, The fear of what the fu-ture holds,
make a-mends, As hands which shaped and saved the world

Where faith and doubt u-nite to care. Your hands, though
Are pres-ent as if meant to last. But pres-ent
Are pres-ent in the touch of friends. Lord, let your

blood-ied on the cross, Sur-vive to hold and
too is love which tends The hurt we nev-er
Spir-it meet us here To mend the bod-y,

heal and warn, To car-ry all through death to
hoped to find, The pri-vate ag-o-nies in-
mind, and soul, To dis-en-tan-gle peace from

life And cra-dle chil-dren yet un-born.
side, The mem-o-ries that haunt the mind.
pain, And make your bro-ken peo-ple whole.

Text: John L. Bell, b.1949, © 1989, Iona Community, GIA Publications, Inc., agent
Tune: RADIANT CITY, LMD; Thomas Pavlechko, b.1962, © 1994, Hope Publishing Company

Have Mercy, Lord 665

Ostinato Refrain

Have mer - cy, Lord, have mer - cy.

Have mer - cy, Lord, have mer - cy.

Verses*

1. Where are those who thirst for jus-tice? Where are those who yearn for peace?
2. Make us ones who thirst for jus-tice. Make us ones who work for peace.
3. Ho - ly Spir - it, come a - mong us, Mend our bro - ken hearts, we pray.
4. Free us from our nar - row vi - sion, Count-ing worth by what we own.
5. Break our chains of anx-ious cling-ing, Bound by fear and pride and greed.

Why must fear and ha - tred blind us? When will cap - tives find re - lease?
Help un - tie the fears that bind us. Grant our cap - tive hearts re - lease.
Mold us in - to true dis - ci - ples, Ones who fol - low Je - sus' way.
Help us not to serve two mas - ters, But to name you God a - lone.
Forge us in - to bold dis - ci - ples, Serv - ing you through those in need.

Verses may be sung concurrent with refrain, or in alternation with it.

Text: Mary Louise Bringle, b.1953, © 2004, 2009, GIA Publications, Inc.
Tune: THADDEUS, 8 7 8 7 with refrain; Sally Ann Morris, b.1952, © 2004, GIA Publications, Inc.

666 Silence! Frenzied, Unclean Spirit

1. "Si - lence! Fren - zied, un - clean spir - it,"
2. Lord, the de - mons still are thriv - ing
3. Si - lence, Lord, the un - clean spir - it,

Cried God's heal - ing, ho - ly One.
In the grey cells of the mind:
In our mind and in our heart.

"Cease your rant - ing! Flesh can't bear it.
Ty - rant voic - es shrill and driv - ing,
Speak your word that, when we hear it,

Flee as night be - fore the sun."
Twist - ed thoughts that grip and bind,
All our de - mons shall de - part.

At Christ's voice the de - mon trem - bled,
Doubts that stir the heart to pan - ic,
Clear our thought and calm our feel - ing,

From its vic - tim mad - ly rushed,
Fears dis - tort - ing rea - son's sight,
Still the frac - tured, war - ring soul.

While the crowd that was as - sem - bled
Guilt that makes our lov - ing fran - tic,
By the pow - er of your heal - ing

Stood in ³ won - der, stunned and hushed.
Dreams that cloud the soul with fright.
Make us faith - ful, true, and whole.

Text: Thomas H. Troeger, b.1945, © 1986, Oxford University Press
Tune: EBENEZER, 8 7 8 7 D; Thomas J. Williams, 1869–1944

O Lord, Hear My Prayer 667

Ostinato Refrain

O Lord, hear my prayer, O Lord, hear my prayer:
Se - ñor, ten pie - dad, Se - ñor, ten pie - dad:

when I call an - swer me. O Lord, hear my prayer, O
si te_in - vo - co, ó - ye - me. Se - ñor, ten pie - dad, Se -

Last time

Lord, hear my prayer. Come and lis - ten to me. O
ñor, ten pie - dad: Ven, y_es - cu - cha mi voz. Se -

Last time

Text: Psalm 102; Taizé Community, 1982
Tune: Jacques Berthier, 1923–1994
© 1982, 2011, Les Presses de Taizé, GIA Publications, Inc., agent

668 God Weeps with Us Who Weep and Mourn

1. God weeps with us who weep and mourn, God's
2. Through tears and sor - row, God, we share A
3. And yet, be - cause, like us, you weep, We

tears flow down with ours, And God's own heart is
sense of your vast grief; The weight of bear - ing
trust you will re - ceive And in your ten - der

bruised and worn From all the heav - y hours Of
ev - 'ry prayer For heal - ing and re - lief, The
heart will keep The ones for whom we grieve, While

watch - ing while the soul's bright fire Burned
bur - den of our ques - tions why, The
with your tears our hearts will taste The

low - er day by day, And pulse and breath and
doubts that they en - gage, And as our friends and
deep, dear core of things From which both life and

love's de - sire Dimmed down to ash and clay.
loved ones die, Our hope - less - ness and rage.
death are graced By love's re - new - ing springs.

Text: Thomas H. Troeger, b.1945, © 2002, Oxford University Press
Tune: MOSHIER, CMD; Sally Ann Morris, b.1952, © 1998, GIA Publications, Inc.

When Streets Resound with Cries of Grief   669

1. When streets re - sound   with cries of   grief   And   na - ture
2. When with one voice   the peo - ple   cry,   But   no   one
3. If   in   the com -   fort of our   ease   We   watch the
4. Where we re - spond   to Je - sus'   call   With works of

fills the world with   fear,   Will   cha - os crush   our   sure be -
hears the poor   and   meek,   Can   we be - lieve,   as   chil - dren
may - hem grow   and   kill,   Ig -   nor - ing des -   p'rate cries and
love and char - i -   ty,   Though all we build   may   fail   and

lief   That,   in   dis - as - ter, Christ   is   here?
die,   That God   is   strong when we   are   weak?
pleas,   How   can   we   claim to   do   God's will?
fall,   There God   is   still, and God   will   be.

Text: Adam M. L. Tice, b.1979, © 2009, 2011, GIA Publications, Inc.
Tune: MATNEY, LM; Sally Ann Morris, b.1952, © 1998, GIA Publications, Inc.

670 When Painful Memories Haunt Each Day

1. When pain - ful mem - 'ries haunt each day And
2. When dreams at last bring peace and rest, And

dreams dis - turb the night, When life is washed with
fear has lost con - trol, When, tried by strug - gle,

shades of gray And phan - toms fill our sight,
we are blessed With right - ful mind and soul,

Christ, stay be - side us and em - brace The
Stay close be - side us as be - fore, To

child who dwells with - in; Come, Heal - er, touch our
guide us all our days. Christ, take the lives that

lives with grace; Re - store our lives a - gain.
you re - store And fit them for your praise.

Text: Ruth Duck, b.1947, © 1996, The Pilgrim Press
Tune: MOSHIER, CMD; Sally Ann Morris, b.1952, © 1998, GIA Publications, Inc.

May the Lord, Mighty God 671

1., 3. May the Lord, might-y God, bless and
2. Lift your eyes and see God's face full of

keep you for-ev - er, grant you peace, per - fect
grace for-ev - er. May the Lord, might-y

peace, cour - age in ev - 'ry en-deav - or.
God, bless and keep you for-ev - er.

Text: Numbers 6:24–26; unknown
Tune: WEN-TI, Irregular; Chinese, Pao-chen Li; adapt. by I-to Loh, b.1936, © 1983, Abingdon Press; acc. by Ronald F. Krisman, b.1946, © 2011,
  GIA Publications, Inc.

May the Grace of Christ Our Savior 672

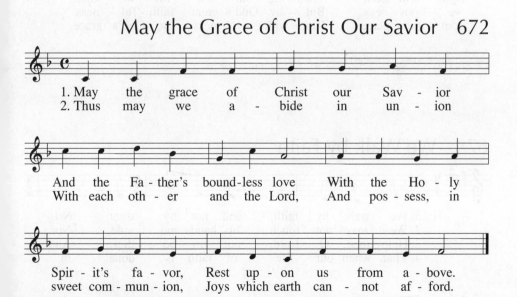

1. May the grace of Christ our Sav - ior
2. Thus may we a - bide in un - ion

And the Fa - ther's bound-less love With the Ho - ly
With each oth - er and the Lord, And pos - sess, in

Spir - it's fa - vor, Rest up - on us from a - bove.
sweet com - mun - ion, Joys which earth can - not af - ford.

Text: 2 Corinthians 13–14; John Newton, 1725–1807
Tune: STUTTGART, 8 7 8 7; *Psalmodia Sacra*, 1715; adapt. and harm. by William H. Havergal, 1793–1870, alt.

673 Faith Begins by Letting Go

1. Faith be - gins by let - ting go, Giv - ing up what
2. Faith en - dures by hold - ing on, Keep - ing mem - 'ry's
3. Faith ma - tures by reach - ing out, Stretch-ing minds, en -

had seemed sure, Tak - ing risks and press - ing on,
roots a - live So that hope may bear its fruit;
larg - ing hearts, Shar - ing strug - gles, liv - ing prayer,

Though the way feels less se - cure: Pil - grim - age both
Prom - ise - fed, our souls will thrive, Not through mer - it
Bind - ing up the bro - ken parts: Till we find the

right and odd, Trust - ing all our life to God.
we pos - sess But by God's great faith - ful - ness.
com - mon - place Ripe with wit - ness to God's grace.

Text: Carl P. Daw, Jr., b.1944, © 1996, Hope Publishing Company
Tune: DIX, 7 7 7 7 7 77; arr. from Conrad Kocher, 1786–1872, by William H. Monk, 1823–1889

674 We Walk by Faith

1., 5. We walk by faith, and not by sight; No
2. We may not touch his hands and side, Nor
3. Help then, O Lord, our un - be - lief; And
4. That, when our life of faith is done, In

gra - cious words we hear From him who spoke as
fol - low where he trod; But in his prom - ise
may our faith a - bound To call on you when
realms of clear - er light We may be - hold you

none e'er spoke; But we be - lieve him near.
we re - joice, And cry, "My Lord and God!"
you are near, And seek where you are found:
as you are, With full and end - less sight.

Text: Henry Alford, 1810–1871, alt.
Tune: SHANTI, CM; Marty Haugen, b.1950; acc. by Randall Sensmeier, b.1948, © 1984, 2006, GIA Publications, Inc.

He Comes to Us as One Unknown 675

1. He comes to us as one un - known, A
2. He comes when souls in si - lence lie And
3. He comes to us in sound of seas, The
4. He comes in love as once he came By
5. He comes in truth when faith is grown; Be -

breath un - seen, un - heard; As though with - in a
thoughts of day de - part; Half seen up - on the
o - cean's fume and foam; Yet small and still up -
flesh and blood and birth; To bear with - in our
lieved, o - beyed, a - dored: The Christ in all the

heart of stone, Or shriv - eled seed in dark - ness sown, A
in - ward eye, A fall - ing star a - cross the sky Of
on the breeze, A wind that stirs the tops of trees, A
mor - tal frame A life, a death, a sav - ing Name, For
scrip - tures shown, As yet un - seen, but not un - known, Our

pulse of be - ing stirred, A pulse of be - ing stirred.
night with - in the heart, Of night with - in the heart.
voice to call us home, A voice to call us home.
ev - 'ry child of earth, For ev - 'ry child of earth.
Sav - ior and our Lord, Our Sav - ior and our Lord.

Text: Timothy Dudley-Smith, b.1926, © 1984, Hope Publishing Company
Tune: REPTON, 8 6 88 66; Charles H. H. Parry, 1848–1918

676 A Living Faith

1. Faith of our fa - thers, liv - ing still
2. Faith of our moth - ers, dar - ing faith,
3. Faith of our sis - ters, broth - ers too,
4. Faith born of God, O call us yet;

In spite of dun - geon, fire, and sword;
Your work for Christ is love re - vealed,
Who still must bear op - pres - sion's might,
Bind us with all who fol - low you,

Oh, how our hearts beat high with joy
Spread-ing God's word from pole to pole,
Rais - ing on high, in pris - ons dark,
Shar - ing the strug - gle of your cross

When - e'er we hear that glo - rious word.
Mak - ing love known and free - dom real.
The cross of Christ still burn - ing bright.
Un - til the world is made a - new.

Faith of our fa - thers, ho - ly faith,
Faith of our moth - ers, ho - ly faith,
Faith for to - day, O liv - ing faith,
Faith born of God, O liv - ing faith,

We will be true to you till death.

Text: St. 1, Frederick W. Faber, 1814–1863, alt.; sts. 2–4, Joseph R. Alfred, b.1947, © 1981, alt.
Tune: ST. CATHERINE, 8 8 8 8 8 8; Henry F. Hemy, 1818–1888; adapt. by James G. Walton, 1821–1905

O God, Who Gives Us Life and Breath   677

1. O God, who gives us life and breath, Who shapes us in the womb, Who guards our lives from birth to death, Then leads us from the tomb: De- liver us from fears that kill The life we have from you. Help us to know your Spir-it still Is mak-ing all things new.

2. O God, who calls your peo-ple out, To ven-ture and to dare, To plumb the bleak a-byss of doubt And find you e-ven there: When we de-spair in wan-der-ing wastes of emp-ty lies, Re-fresh us with the liv-ing spring Of hope that nev-er dies.

3. O God of cov-e-nant and law, Re-vealed in cloud and flame, Your might-y deeds e-voke our awe; We dare not speak your name. Yet we by faith are drawn to you And will your peo-ple prove, As on our hearts you write a-new The cov-e-nant of love.

Text: Carl P. Daw, Jr., b.1944, © 1990, Hope Publishing Company
Tune: IN NOMINE DEI, CMD; Sally Ann Morris, b.1952, © 2009, GIA Publications, Inc.

678 Center of My Life

Refrain

O Lord, you are the cen-ter of my life:

I will al-ways praise you, I will al-ways serve you,

I will al-ways keep you in my sight.

Verses 1–3

1. Keep me safe, O God, I take ref-uge in you. I
2. I will bless the Lord who gives me coun-sel, who
3. And so my heart re-joic-es, my soul is glad;

say to the Lord, "You are my God. My
e - ven at night di-rects my heart. I
e - ven in safe-ty shall my bod-y rest. For

hap - pi - ness lies in you a - lone; my
keep the Lord ev - er in my sight: since
you will not leave my soul a-mong the dead, nor

D.C.

hap - pi - ness lies in you a - lone."
he is at my right hand, I shall stand firm.
let your be - lov - ed know de - cay.

Verse 4

4. You will show me the path of life, the

full - ness of joy in your pres - ence, at your right hand,

D.C.

at your right hand hap - pi - ness for ev - er.

Text: Psalm 16; verses trans. © 1963, The Grail, GIA Publications, Inc., agent; refrain, Paul Inwood, b.1947, © 1985, Paul Inwood
Tune: Paul Inwood, b.1947, © 1985, Paul Inwood
Published by OCP.

Show Me Your Hands, Your Feet, Your Side 679

1. Show me your hands, your feet, your side; I
2. "Fear not! Let peace be in your soul. Reach
3. Not e - ven East - er takes a - way The
4. So blessed are those who have not seen Yet

will not be de - ceived. Un - less I see, how
out and touch and know I died and yet I
marks that Je - sus bears. The Ris - en Christ still
cry, "My Lord and God!" Who touch earth's pain in

can I trust The news that I've re - ceived?
am a - live With wounds that ev - er show."
wears the wounds Of scourge and nail and spear.
Je - sus' name And tell good news a - broad.

Text: Sylvia G. Dunstan, 1955–1993, © 1991, GIA Publications, Inc.
Tune: LAND OF REST, CM; American melody; harm. by Annabel M. Buchanan, 1888–1983, © 1938 (Renewed) The H.W. Gray Company

680 Be Not Afraid

Verse 1

1. You shall cross the bar-ren des-ert, but you shall not die of thirst. You shall wan-der far in safe-ty though you do not know the way. You shall speak your words in for-eign lands and all will un-der-stand. You shall see the face of God and live.

Refrain

Be not a-fraid. I go be-fore you al-ways. Come, fol-low me, and I will give you rest.

Verse 2

2. If you pass through rag-ing wa-ters in the sea, you shall not drown. If you walk a-mid the burn-ing flames, you shall not be harmed. If you stand be-fore the

pow'r of hell and death is at your side,

D.S.

know that I am with you through it all.

Verse 3

3. Bless-ed are your poor, for the king-dom shall be

theirs. Blest are you that weep and mourn, for

one day you shall laugh. And if wick-ed tongues in -

sult and hate you all be-cause of me,

D.S.

bless-ed, bless-ed are you!

Text: Isaiah 43:2–3, Luke 6:20ff; Bob Dufford, SJ, b.1943
Tune: Bob Dufford, SJ, b.1943; acc. by Theophane Hytrek, OSF, 1915–1992
© 1975, 1978, Robert J. Dufford, SJ, and OCP

681 Good Shepherd, You Know Us

1. Good Shep-herd, you know us, you call us by name.
2. Good Shep-herd, you warn us of rob - bers and thieves,
3. Good Shep-herd, you lay down your life for the sheep.
4. At one with the Fa - ther, you made your - self known:

You lead us; we glad - ly ac - knowl-edge your claim.
The hire - ling, the wolf who de - stroys and de - ceives.
Your love is not fick - le, your gift is not cheap.
"I am the Good Shep - herd," at one with your own.

Your voice has com - pelled us; we come at your call.
All praise for your prom - ise on which we shall stand,
You spend your life free - ly, you take it a - gain.
You loved us be - fore we had heed - ed or heard;

And none you have cho - sen will fi - nal - ly fall.
That no one can snatch us from out of your hand.
You died, so we live; we are healed by your pain.
By grace we re - spond to your life - giv - ing word.

Text: Christopher M. Idle, b.1938, © 2001, 2002, 2005, The Jubilate Group (admin. by Hope Publishing Company)
Tune: ST. DENIO, 11 11 11 11; adapt. from a Welsh ballad in John Robert's *Hymns of the Sanctuary*, 1839

682 You Are the Way

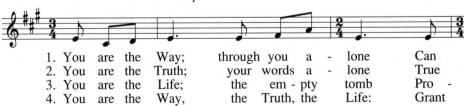

1. You are the Way; through you a - lone Can
2. You are the Truth; your words a - lone True
3. You are the Life; the em - pty tomb Pro -
4. You are the Way, the Truth, the Life: Grant

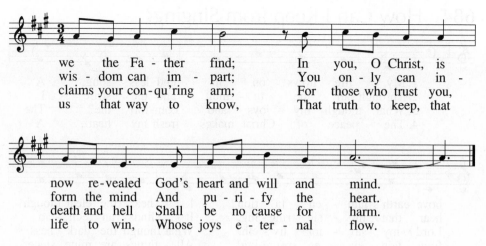

we   the Fa - ther   find;   In   you, O Christ, is
wis - dom can   im - part;   You   on - ly can   in -
claims your con-qu'ring arm;   For   those who trust you,
us   that way   to   know,   That truth to keep, that

now re-vealed God's heart and will   and   mind.
form the mind   And   pu - ri - fy   the   heart.
death and hell   Shall   be no cause for   harm.
life   to   win, Whose joys e - ter - nal   flow.

Text: George W. Doane, 1799–1859, alt.
Tune: SHANTI, CM; Marty Haugen, b.1950, © 1984, GIA Publications, Inc.

To Whom, Lord, Shall We Go? 683

1. To   whom, Lord,   shall   we   go?   Can
2. To   whom, Lord,   shall   we   go?   Though
3. To   whom, Lord,   shall   we   go?   Can
4. To   whom, Lord,   shall   we   go?   When
5. O   Christ, we   come   to   you,   God's

hun - g'ring hearts be   fed   And   sat - is - fied, ex -
far   from you   we   stray,   Will   search-ing   find   a
an - y   voice be   heard   That speaks a   prom-ise
dark-est   is   the   night,   Where can   we   turn to
own   be - lov - ed   Son.   Though we   should search till

cept   by   you,   The   true   and   liv - ing   Bread?
path more sure   Than   you,   the Truth, the   Way?
more se - cure   Than   yours, your - self   the   Word?
see   the   dawn   Ex -   cept   to   you,   the   Light?
time   shall end,   There   is   no   oth - er   one.

Text: John 6:56–69; Herman G. Stuempfle, Jr., 1923–2007, © 1997, GIA Publications, Inc.
Tune: FESTAL SONG, SM; William H. Walter, 1825–1893

684 How Can I Keep from Singing?

1. My life flows on in end-less song. A-
2. Through all the tu-mult and the strife I
3. What though my joys and com-fort die? The
4. The peace of Christ makes fresh my heart, A

bove earth's lam - en - ta - tion I hear the clear though
hear that mu - sic ring - ing. It finds an ech - o
Lord my sav - ior liv - eth. What though the dark - ness
foun - tain ev - er spring-ing! All things are mine since

far - off hymn That hails a new cre - a - tion.
in my soul. How can I keep from sing - ing?
gath - er round? Songs in the night he giv - eth.
I am his! How can I keep from sing - ing?

No storm can shake my in-most calm While to that Rock I'm

cling - ing. Since Christ is Lord of heav-en and earth,

How can I keep from sing - ing?

Text: Robert Lowry, 1826–1899, alt.
Tune: HOW CAN I KEEP FROM SINGING, 8 7 8 7 with refrain; Robert Lowry, 1826–1899; harm. by Robert J. Batastini, b.1942, © 1988, GIA
    Publications, Inc.

Nothing Is Impossible with God 685

Text: Based on Luke 1:26; James J. Chepponis, b.1956
Tune: ZUBIK, 12 15 15 with refrain; James J. Chepponis, b.1956
© 2001, GIA Publications, Inc.

686 Lord of All Hopefulness

1. Lord of all hope - ful - ness, Lord of all joy,
2. Lord of all ea - ger - ness, Lord of all faith,
3. Lord of all kind - li - ness, Lord of all grace,
4. Lord of all gen - tle - ness, Lord of all calm,

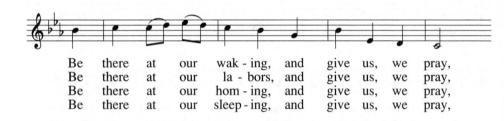

Whose trust, ev - er child - like, no cares could de - stroy,
Whose strong hands were skilled at the plane and the lathe,
Your hands swift to wel - come, your arms to em - brace,
Whose voice is con - tent - ment, whose pres - ence is balm,

Be there at our wak - ing, and give us, we pray,
Be there at our la - bors, and give us, we pray,
Be there at our hom - ing, and give us, we pray,
Be there at our sleep - ing, and give us, we pray,

Your bliss in our hearts, Lord, at the break of the day.
Your strength in our hearts, Lord, at the noon of the day.
Your love in our hearts, Lord, at the eve of the day.
Your peace in our hearts, Lord, at the end of the day.

Text: Jan Struther, 1901–1953, © 1931, Oxford University Press
Tune: SLANE, 10 11 11 12; Irish melody; harm. by Erik Routley, 1917–1982, © 1975, Hope Publishing Company

How Firm a Foundation   687

1. How firm a foun - da - tion, you saints of the Lord,
2. "Fear not, I am with you, O be not dis-mayed,
3. "When through the deep wa - ters I call you to go,
4. "The soul that on Je - sus still leans for re - pose,

Is laid for your faith in Christ Je - sus, the Word!
For I am your God, and will still give you aid;
The riv - ers of woe shall not you o - ver-flow;
I will not, I will not de - sert to its foes;

What more can God say than to you has been said,
I'll strength - en you, help you, and cause you to stand,
For I will be with you, your trou - bles to bless,
That soul, though all hell should en - deav - or to shake,

To you who for ref - uge to Je - sus have fled?
Up - held by my right - eous, om - nip - o - tent hand.
And sanc - ti - fy to you your deep - est dis - tress.
I'll nev - er, no nev - er, no nev - er for-sake!"

Text: 2 Peter 1:4; John Rippon's *A Selection of Hymns,* 1787, alt.
Tune: FOUNDATION, 11 11 11 11; Funk's *Compilation of Genuine Church Music,* 1832; harm. by Richard Proulx, 1937–2010, © 1975,
   GIA Publications, Inc.

688 A Mighty Fortress Is Our God

1. A might - y for - tress is our God,
2. No strength of ours can match his might!
3. Though hordes of dev - ils fill the land
4. God's Word for - ev - er shall a - bide,

A sword and shield vic - to - rious,   Who breaks the
We would be lost, re - ject - ed.   But now a
All threat-'ning to de - vour us,   We trem - ble
No thanks to foes, who fear it;   For God, our

cruel op - pres - sor's rod   And wins sal - va - tion
cham - pion comes to fight,   Whom God a - lone e -
not, un - moved we stand;   They can - not o - ver -
Lord, fights by our side   With weap - ons of the

glo - rious.   The old sa - tan - ic foe
lect - ed.   You ask who this may be?
pow'r us.   Let this world's ty - rant rage;
Spir - it.   Were they to take our house,

Has sworn to work us woe!   With craft and
The Lord of hosts is he!   Christ Je - sus,
In bat - tle we'll en - gage!   His might is
Goods, hon - or, child, or spouse,   Though life be

dread - ful might   He arms him - self to fight.
might - y Lord,   God's on - ly Son, a - dored.
doomed to fail;   God's judg - ment must pre - vail!
wrenched a - way,   They can - not win the day.

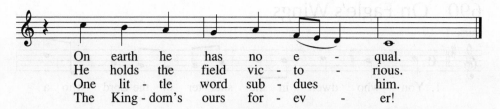

On earth he has no e - qual.
He holds the field vic - to - rious.
One lit - tle word sub - dues him.
The King - dom's ours for - ev - er!

Text: Psalm 46; *Ein' feste Burg ist unser Gott*; Martin Luther, 1483–1546; tr. © 1978, *Lutheran Book of Worship*, alt., admin. by Augsburg Fortress
Tune: EIN' FESTE BURG, 8 7 8 7 66 66 7; Martin Luther, 1483–1546; harm by J. S. Bach, 1685–1750

O God, Our Help in Ages Past 689

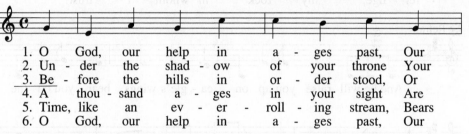

1. O God, our help in a - ges past, Our
2. Un - der the shad - ow of your throne Your
3. Be - fore the hills in or - der stood, Or
4. A thou - sand a - ges in your sight Are
5. Time, like an ev - er - roll - ing stream, Bears
6. O God, our help in a - ges past, Our

hope for years to come, Our shel - ter from the
saints have dwelt se - cure; Suf - fi - cient is your
earth re - ceived its frame, From ev - er - last - ing
like an eve - ning gone, Short as the watch that
all our years a - way; They fly for - got - ten,
hope for years to come, Still be our guard while

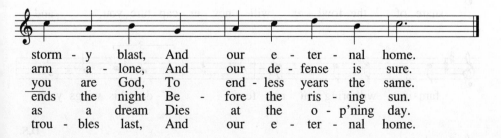

storm - y blast, And our e - ter - nal home.
arm a - lone, And our de - fense is sure.
you are God, To end - less years the same.
ends the night Be - fore the ris - ing sun.
as a dream Dies at the o - p'ning day.
trou - bles last, And our e - ter - nal home.

Text: Psalm 90; Isaac Watts, 1674–1748, alt.
Tune: ST. ANNE, CM; attr. to William Croft, 1678–1727; harm. composite from 18th C. versions

690 On Eagle's Wings

Verse 1

1. You who dwell in the shel-ter of the Lord, who a-bide in his shad-ow for life, say to the Lord: "My ref-uge, my rock in whom I trust!"

℁ Refrain

And he will raise you up on ea-gle's wings, bear you on the breath of dawn, make you to shine like the sun, and hold you in the palm of his hand.

Last time to Coda ✠   To verses

2. The

Verse 2

snare of the fowl-er will nev-er cap-ture you, and fam-ine will bring you no fear: un-der his wings your ref-uge, his faith-ful-ness your shield.

D.S.

Verse 3

3. You need not fear the ter - ror of the night, nor the ar - row that flies by day; though thou - sands fall a - bout you, near you it shall not come.

D.S.

Verse 4

4. For to his an - gels he's giv - en a com-mand to guard you in all of your ways; up - on their hands they will bear you up, lest you dash your foot a-gainst a stone.

D.S.

Coda

And hold you, hold you in the palm of his hand.

Text: Psalm 91; Michael Joncas, b.1951
Tune: Michael Joncas, b.1951
© 1979, OCP

691 The Lord Is My Savior

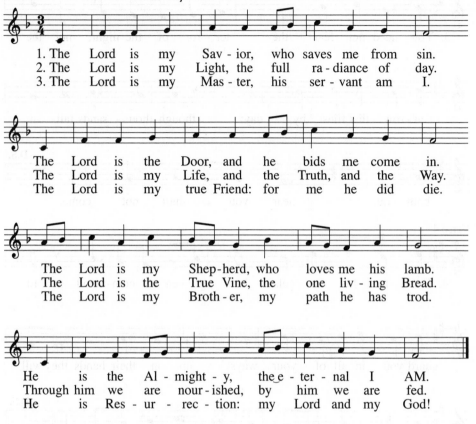

1. The Lord is my Sav-ior, who saves me from sin.
2. The Lord is my Light, the full ra-diance of day.
3. The Lord is my Mas-ter, his ser-vant am I.

The Lord is the Door, and he bids me come in.
The Lord is my Life, and the Truth, and the Way.
The Lord is my true Friend: for me he did die.

The Lord is my Shep-herd, who loves me his lamb.
The Lord is the True Vine, the one liv-ing Bread.
The Lord is my Broth-er, my path he has trod.

He is the Al-might-y, the e-ter-nal I AM.
Through him we are nour-ished, by him we are fed.
He is Res-ur-rec-tion: my Lord and my God!

Text: Rae E. Whitney, b.1927, © 1994, Selah Publishing Co., Inc.
Tune: PADERBORN, 11 11 11 11; Paderborn *Gesangbuch*, 1765; harm. by Sydney H. Nicholson, 1875–1947

692 The Storm Is Strong

1. The storm is strong; we face the wind. The
2. But you, O Christ, are with us here. We
3. Who can you be? What pow'r your say That

wa-ter ris-es; waves crash in. Where are we now? Where
turn to you in all our fear. The sin-gle word you
e-ven winds and sea o-bey? Re-move our fear of

will	we	be?	There	is	no	mer - cy	on	this	sea.
say	is	"peace,"	And	wind	and	waves and	storm	all	cease.
death	and	harm.	Give	us	your	faith and	still	our	storm.

Text: Sylvia G. Dunstan, 1955–1993, © 1991, GIA Publications, Inc.
Tune: ERHALT UNS HERR, LM; Klug's *Geistliche Lieder*, 1543; harm. by J. S. Bach, 1685–1750

Love One Another 693

Refrain

Love one an - oth - er, for love is of God.

Love one an - oth - er, for God is love.

Verses

1. God loved the world so much he sent us his only son,
   that all who believe in him might have eternal life.

2. Since God has given his love to us, therefore let us love one another.
   If we love one another, God will love us, and live in us in perfect love.

3. Ev'ryone who loves is begotten of God and knows him as the Father.
   But they who do not love do not know God, for God is love.

4. Let not your hearts be troubled, for love has no room for fear.
   In love all fear is forgotten, for God is here with us.

5. God is love, and they who abide in love,
   abide in God, and God in them.

Text: 1 John 4; James J. Chepponis, b. 1956
Tune: James J. Chepponis, b. 1956
© 1983, GIA Publications, Inc.

694 Where True Love and Charity Are Found / Ubi Cáritas

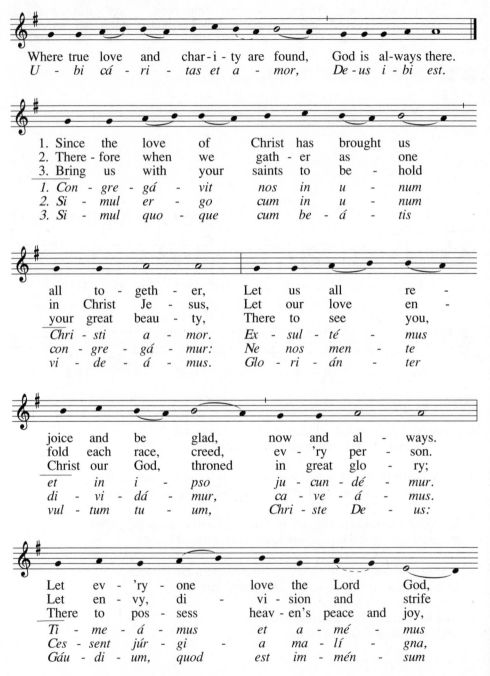

Where true love and char-i-ty are found, God is al-ways there.
U - bi cá - ri - tas et a - mor, De-us i - bi est.

1. Since the love of Christ has brought us
2. There - fore when we gath - er as one
3. Bring us with your saints to be - hold

1. Con - gre - gá - vit nos in u - num
2. Si - mul er - go cum in u - num
3. Si - mul quo - que cum be - á - tis

all to - geth - er, Let us all re -
in Christ Je - sus, Let our love en -
your great beau - ty, There to see you,

Chri - sti a - mor. Ex - sul - té - mus
con - gre - gá - mur: Ne nos men - te
vi - de - á - mus. Glo - ri - án - ter

joice and be glad, now and al - ways.
fold each race, creed, ev - 'ry per - son.
Christ our God, throned in great glo - ry;

et in i - pso ju - cun - dé - mur.
di - vi - dá - mur, ca - ve - á - mus.
vul - tum tu - um, Chri - ste De - us:

Let ev - 'ry - one love the Lord God,
Let en - vy, di - vi - sion and strife
There to pos - sess heav - en's peace and joy,

Ti - me - á - mus et a - mé - mus
Ces - sent júr - gi - a ma - lí - gna,
Gáu - di - um, quod est im - mén - sum

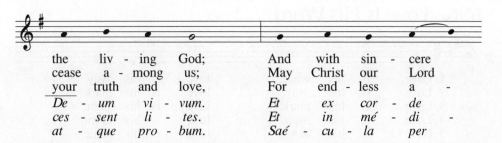

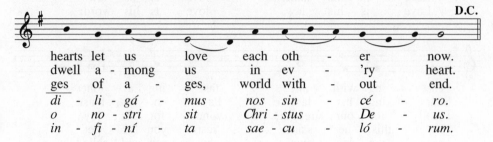

the liv - ing God; And with sin - cere
cease a - mong us; May Christ our Lord
your truth and love, For end - less a -
De - um vi - vum. Et ex cor - de
ces - sent li - tes. Et in mé - di -
at - que pro - bum. Saé - cu - la per

D.C.

hearts let us love each oth - er now.
dwell a - mong us in ev - 'ry heart.
ges of a - ges, world with - out end.
di - li - gá - mus nos sin - cé - ro.
o no - stri sit Chri - stus De - us.
in - fi - ní - ta sae - cu - ló - rum.

Text: *Ubi caritas et amor*, Latin, 9th C.; tr. by Richard Proulx, 1937–2010, © 1975, 1986, GIA Publications, Inc.
Tune: UBI CARITAS, 12 12 12 12 with refrain; Mode VI; acc. by Richard Proulx, 1937–2010, © 1986, GIA Publications, Inc.

Your Ways Are Not Our Own   695

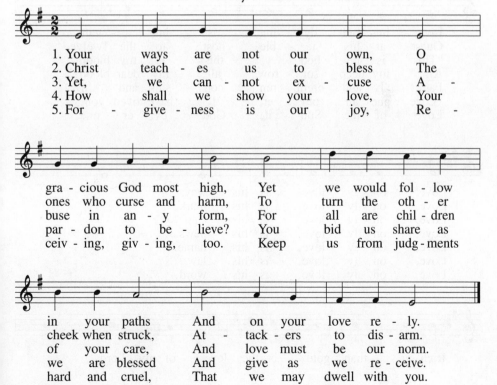

1. Your ways are not our own, O
2. Christ teach - es us to bless The
3. Yet, we can - not ex - cuse A -
4. How shall we show your love, Your
5. For - give - ness is our joy, Re -

gra - cious God most high, Yet we would fol - low
ones who curse and harm, To turn the oth - er
buse in an - y form, For all are chil - dren
par - don to be - lieve? You bid us share as
ceiv - ing, giv - ing, too. Keep us from judg - ments

in your paths And on your love re - ly.
cheek when struck, At - tack - ers to dis - arm.
of your care, And love must be our norm.
we are blessed And give as we re - ceive.
hard and cruel, That we may dwell with you.

Text: Lavon Bayler, b.1933, © 1988, The Pilgrim Press
Tune: SOUTHWELL, SM; William Daman, *The Psalmes of David*, 1579, alt.

696 Love Is His Word

1. Love is his word, love is his way.
2. Love is his way, love is his mark.
3. Love is his mark, love is his sign.
4. Love is his sign, love is his news.
5. Love is his news, love is his name.
6. Love is his name, love is his law.
7. Love is his law, love is his word:

Feast - ing with all, fast - ing a - lone,
Shar - ing his last Pass - o - ver feast.
Bread for our strength, wine for our joy.
"Do this," he said, "lest you for - get
We are his own, cho - sen and called,
Hear his com - mand, all who are his:
Love of the Lord, Fa - ther and Word.

Liv - ing and dy - ing, ris - ing a - gain.
Guest at his ta - ble, host to the Twelve.
"This is my bod - y, this is my blood."
All my deep sor - row, all my dear blood."
Fam - 'ly and breth - ren, cou - sins and kin.
"Love one an - oth - er, I have loved you."
Love of the Spir - it, God ev - er one.

Love, on - ly love, is his way.
Love, on - ly love, is his mark.
Love, on - ly love, is his sign.
Love, on - ly love, is his news.
Love, on - ly love, is his name.
Love, on - ly love, is his law.
Love, on - ly love, is his word.

Rich - er than gold is the love of my Lord,

Bet - ter than splen - dor and wealth.

Rich - er than gold is the love of my Lord,

Bet - ter than splen - dor and wealth.

Text: Luke Connaughton, 1917–1979, © 1970, Mayhew McCrimmon Ltd.
Tune: MELOS, 8 8 9 7 with refrain; Ronald F. Krisman, b.1946 © 2001, GIA Publications, Inc.

Lord of All Nations, Grant Me Grace 697

1. Lord of all na - tions, grant me grace To love all
2. Break down the walls that would di - vide Your chil - dren,
3. For - give me, Lord, where I have erred By love - less
4. Give me your cour - age, Lord, to speak When-ev - er
5. With your own love may I be filled, And by your

peo - ple, ev - 'ry race, To see each per - son as I
Lord, on ev - 'ry side. My neigh-bor's good let me pur -
act and thought-less word. Make me to see the wrong I
strong op - press the weak. Should I my - self as vic - tim
Ho - ly Spir - it willed, That all whose lives are touched by

ought, My kin - dred, whom your love has bought.
sue; Let Chris - tian love bind warm and true.
do Will cru - ci - fy my Lord a - new.
live, Re - mem - b'ring you, may I for - give.
mine May know your heal - ing touch di - vine.

Text: Philippians 2:1–18; Olive W. Spannaus, b.1916, © 1969, 1997, Concordia Publishing House
Tune: BEATUS VIR, LM; Slovak melody, 16th C.; harm. by Richard Hillert, 1923–2010, © 1969, Concordia Publishing House

698 No Greater Love

Refrain

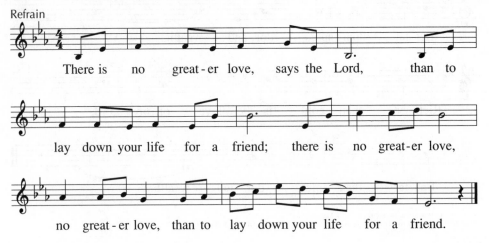

There is no great-er love, says the Lord, than to

lay down your life for a friend; there is no great-er love,

no great-er love, than to lay down your life for a friend.

Verses

1. As the Father has loved me, so I have loved you.
   Live on in my love.
   You will live in my love if you keep my commands,
   even as I have kept my Father's.

2. All this I tell you that my joy may be yours
   and your joy may be complete.
   Love one another as I have loved you:
   This is my command.

3. You are my friends if you keep my commands;
   no longer slaves but friends to me.
   All I heard from my Father,
   I have made known to you: Now I call you friends.

4. It was not you who chose me, it was I who chose you,
   chose you to go forth and bear fruit.
   Your fruit must endure, so you will receive
   all you ask the Father in my name.

Text: John 15:9–17; Michael Joncas, b.1951
Tune: Michael Joncas, b.1951
© 1988, GIA Publications, Inc.

699 Love Is the Law That Jesus Taught

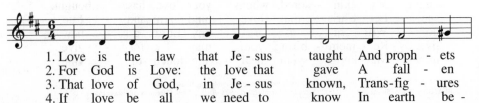

1. Love is the law that Je - sus taught And proph - ets
2. For God is Love: the love that gave A fall - en
3. That love of God, in Je - sus known, Trans-fig - ures
4. If love be all we need to know In earth be -

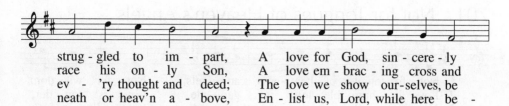

strug - gled to im - part, A love for God, sin - cere - ly
race his on - ly Son, A love em - brac - ing cross and
ev - 'ry thought and deed; The love we show our-selves, be
neath or heav'n a - bove, En - list us, Lord, while here be -

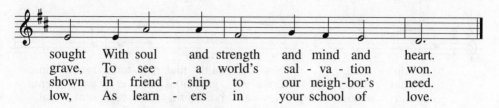

sought With soul and strength and mind and heart.
grave, To see a world's sal - va - tion won.
shown In friend - ship to our neigh-bor's need.
low, As learn - ers in your school of love.

Text: Timothy Dudley-Smith, b.1926, © 2010, Hope Publishing Company
Tune: BEATUS VIR, LM; Slovak melody, 16th C.; harm. by Richard Hillert, 1923–2010, © 1969, Concordia Publishing House

Where Charity and Love Prevail 700

1. Where char - i - ty and love pre - vail,
2. With grate - ful joy and ho - ly fear
3. For - give we now each oth - er's faults
4. Let strife a - mong us be un - known,
5. Let us re - call that in our midst
6. No race nor creed can love ex - clude

There God is ev - er found; Brought here to - geth - er
God's char - i - ty we learn; Let us with heart and
As we our faults con - fess; And let us love each
Let all con - ten - tion cease; Be God's the glo - ry
Dwells God's be - got - ten Son; As mem - bers of his
If hon - ored be God's name; Our fam - i - ly em -

by Christ's love, By love are we thus bound.
mind and soul Now love God in re - turn.
oth - er well In Chris - tian ho - li - ness.
that we seek, Be ours God's ho - ly peace.
bod - y joined, We are in Christ made one.
brac - es all Whose Fa - ther is the same.

Text: *Ubi caritas;* tr. by Omer Westendorf, 1916–1997
Tune: CHRISTIAN LOVE, CM; Paul Benoit, OSB, 1893–1979
© 1960, World Library Publications

701 Not for Tongues of Heaven's Angels

1. Not for tongues of heav-en's an - gels,
2. Love is hum-ble, love is gen - tle,
3. Nev - er jeal - ous, nev - er self - ish,
4. In the day this world is fad - ing

Not for wis-dom
Love is ten - der,
Love will not re -
Faith and hope will

to dis - cern,
true, and kind;
joice in wrong;
play their part;

Not for faith that mas-ters moun-tains,
Love is gra-cious, ev - er pa - tient,
Nev - er boast-ful nor re - sent - ful,
But when Christ is seen in glo - ry

For this bet - ter gift we yearn:
Gen - er - ous of heart and mind:
Love be - lieves and suf - fers long:
Love shall reign in ev - 'ry heart:

May love be ours, Lord;

may love be ours. May love be ours, O Lord.

Text: 1 Corinthians 13:1–13; Timothy Dudley-Smith, b.1926, © 1985, Hope Publishing Company
Tune: COMFORT, 8 7 8 7 with refrain; Michael Joncas, b.1951, © 1988, GIA Publications, Inc.

702 Ubi Cáritas

Refrain

U - bi cá - ri - tas et a - mor,
Where true char - i - ty and love a - bide,
Spanish: Don - de hay a - mor y ca - ri - dad,
Korean: 사 랑 의 나 눔 있 는 곳 에
Tagalog: Sa pag - ma - ma - hal na - ro - roon ang Diyos.

Korean transliteration: Sa-lang-ui na-num iss-neun gos-e.
Ha-neu-nim-kke-seo gye-si-do—da.

u - bi cá - ri - tas De - us i - bi est.
God is dwell-ing there; God is dwell-ing there.
don - de hay a - mor Dios a - llí es - tá.
하 느 님 께 서 계 시 도 다.
Sa pag - ma - ma - hal na - ro - roon ang Diyos.

Text: 1 Corinthians 13:2–8, 13; Taizé Community, 1978
Tune: Jacques Berthier, 1923–1994
© 1979, 2009, 2011, Les Presses de Taizé, GIA Publications, Inc., agent

Your Hand, Though Hidden, Guides Us   703

1. Your hand, though hid - den, guides us By ways un-seen, un-
2. Your hand, though hid - den, heals us As when, in Gal - i -
3. Your hand, though hid - den, holds us When all sup-port is

known, Through all our rest - less search - ing On
lee, You touched the bound, the bur - dened With
gone, When earth's best help is fu - tile And

paths we think our own. With si - lent step you
grace that set them free. Come now, O Lord, with
hu - man strength un - done. Then, though the night close

has - ten To meet us where we stray. Then
heal - ing For grief and pain and sin. Come,
round us And wind and wave as - sail, You

pa - tient-ly you lead us A - long our pil - grim way.
touch our lives with mer - cy And make us whole a - gain.
grasp us in the dark - ness With love that does not fail.

Text: Herman G. Stuempfle, Jr., 1923–2007, © 1997, GIA Publications, Inc.
Tune: KING'S LYNN, 7 6 7 6 D; English melody; harm. by Ralph Vaughan Williams, 1872–1958

Alternate tune: AURELIA

704 You Are Mine / Contigo Estoy

Verses

1. I will come to you in the si - lence,
2. I am hope for all who are hope - less,
3. I am strength for all the de - spair - ing,
4. am the Word that leads all to free - dom,

I

1. Te ha-bla - ré en la paz del si - len - cio,
2. es - pe - ran - za de quien an - he - la,
3. Soy la for - ta - le - za del dé - bil;
4. Soy pa - la - bra li - be - ra - do - ra,

la

la

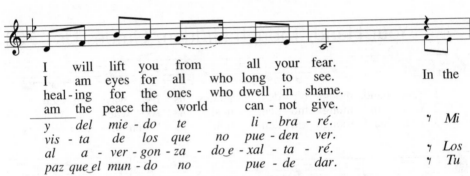

I will lift you from all your fear.
I am eyes for all who long to see.
heal - ing for the ones who dwell in shame.
am the peace the world can - not give.

In the

y del mie - do te li - bra - ré.
vis - ta de los que no pue - den ver.
al a - ver - gon - za - do e - xal - ta - ré.
paz que el mun - do no pue - de dar.

⅞ Mi

⅞ Los

⅞ Tu

You will hear my voice, I claim you as my choice,
shad - ows of the night, I will be your light,
All the blind will see, the lame will all run free,
I will call your name, em - brac - ing all your pain.

be

and

Stand

voz es - cu - cha - rás, y mí - o tú se - rás.
Con in - ten - si - dad bri - lla - ré en la os-cu - ri - dad.
cie - gos ve - rán, los li - sia - dos co - rre - rán.
nom - bre lla - ma - ré; tu llan - to to - ma - ré.

Mi

Le -

still and know I am here. *(To verse 2)*
come and rest in me. *(To refrain)*
all will know my name. *(To refrain)*
up, now walk, and live! *(To refrain)*

Jun - to a ti es - ta - ré. *(A la Estrofa 2)*
Tu des-can - so quie - ro ser. *(Al Estribillo)*
nom - bre re - ve - la - ré. *(Al Estribillo)*
ván - ta - te a ca - mi - nar. *(Al Estribillo)*

2. Soy

Refrain

Do not be a-fraid, I am with you. I have called you each by
A-quíes-toy con-ti-go, no te-mas. *Yo por nom-bre te lla-*

name. Come and fol-low me, I will bring you home; I
mé. Ven y sí-gue-me. Yo te lle-va-ré. Te

love you and you are mine. 4. I
a - mo y con-ti-go es - toy.

Text: David Haas, b.1957; tr. by Santiago Fernández, b.1971
Tune: David Haas, b.1957
© 1991, 2005, GIA Publications, Inc.

O Jesus, Joy of Loving Hearts 705

1. O   Je - sus, joy   of   lov - ing hearts, The fount of
2. For   you   our   rest - less spir - its yearn, Wher-e'er our
3. We   taste you, ev - er - liv - ing bread, And long to
4. O   Je - sus, ev - er with us stay! Make all   our

life   and   light   of   all,   From ev - 'ry bliss that
chang - ing lot   is   cast;   Glad, when your pres - ence
feast up - on   you still.   We   drink of   you,   the
mo - ments calm and bright! O   chase the night of

earth im - parts We turn, un - filled, to   hear your call.
we   dis - cern, Blest, when by faith we   hold you fast.
foun - tain-head, That you   our thirst - ing souls may fill.
sin   a - way!   Shed o'er the world your ho - ly light!

Text: *Jesu, dulcedo cordium;* attr. to St. Bernard of Clairvaux, 1091–1153; para. by Ray Palmer, 1808–1887, alt.
Tune: WAREHAM, LM; William Knapp, 1698–1768

706 O Christ, Who Shared Our Mortal Life

1. O Christ, who shared our mor - tal life And
2. & 3. *Insert appropriate stanzas*
4. Death's pow - er holds us still in thrall And

end - ed death's long reign, Who healed the sick and
bears us toward the tomb. Death's dark - 'ning cloud hangs

raised the dead, Who bore our grief and pain: We
like a pall That threat - ens earth with doom. But

know our years on earth are few, That
you have bro - ken death's em - brace And

death is al - ways near. Come now to us, O
torn a - way its sting. Re - store to life our

Lord of Life; Bring hope that con - quers fear!
mor - tal race And raise us, ris - en King!

Raising of Jairus' Daughter *(Matthew 9:18–26; Mark 5:21–43)*
2a. A ruler, proud but bent by grief,
    Fell down before your feet:
    "My little girl lies gravely ill,
    Come now and death defeat!"
    A multitude had gathered round
    To hear the truth you taught,
    But, leaving them, you turned to help
    A father sore distraught.

3a. You pressed through crowds to reach the child,
   Whose limbs with death grew cold.
   "She is not dead; she only sleeps!"
   The grieving folk you told.
   And then you took her hand and said,
   "My child, I bid you rise!"
   She rose, as those around you stood
   With wide and wond'ring eyes!

Raising of the Widow's Son *(Luke 7:11–17)*
2b. The ranks of death with trophy grim
   Through ancient streets once trod
   And suddenly confronted you,
   The mighty Son of God.
   A widow's tears evoked your word;
   You stopped the bearers' tread.
   "Weep not!" in pity then you spoke
   To her whose son was dead.

3b. The ranks of death, the Lord of Life,
   Stood face to face that hour:
   And you took up the age-old strife
   With words of awesome pow'r.
   "Young man, arise!" you ordered loud,
   And death defeated lay.
   The widow's son cast off his shroud
   And strode from death away.

Raising of Lazarus *(John 11:1–45)*
2c. Two weeping sisters, worn by grief
   And mired in deepest gloom,
   Stood watching where their brother lay
   Within a rock-sealed tomb.
   O Lord, you met them as they mourned,
   And wept compassion's tear.
   But Martha, sore with sorrow, said,
   "He'd lived had you been here!"

3c. "The resurrection and the life
   For all the world am I!
   And those who hear and trust my word
   Shall live, although they die!"
   The stone was rolled from Laz'rus' tomb;
   You called him forth by name;
   And waking, breathing once again,
   From death to life he came!

Text: Herman G. Stuempfle, Jr., 1923–2007, alt., © 1993, GIA Publications, Inc.
Tune: KINGSFOLD, CMD; English melody; harm. by Ralph Vaughan Williams, 1872–1958

707 I Heard the Voice of Jesus Say

1. I heard the voice of Je - sus say, "Come
2. I heard the voice of Je - sus say, "Be -
3. I heard the voice of Je - sus say, "I

un - to me and rest; Lay down, O wea - ry
hold, I free - ly give The liv - ing wa - ter;
am this dark world's light; Look un - to me, your

one, lay down Your head up - on my breast." I
thirst - y one, Stoop down and drink and live." I
morn shall rise, And all your day be bright." I

came to Je - sus as I was, So
came to Je - sus, and I drank Of
looked to Je - sus, and I found In

wea - ry, worn, and sad; I found in him a
that life - giv - ing stream; My thirst was quenched, my
him my star, my sun; And in that light of

rest - ing place, And he has made me glad.
soul re - vived, And now I live in him.
life I'll walk Till trav - 'ling days are done.

Text: Horatius Bonar, 1808–1889
Tune: KINGSFOLD, CMD; English melody; harm. by Ralph Vaughan Williams, 1872–1958

My Shepherd, You Supply My Need   708

1. My Shep - herd, you sup - ply my need; Most
2. When I walk through the shades of death, Your
3. The sure pro - vi - sions of my God At -

ho - ly is your name. In pas - tures green you
pres - ence is my stay. One word of your sup -
tend me all my days. O may your house be

make me feed Be - side the liv - ing stream. You
port - ing breath Drives all my fears a - way. Your
my a - bode And all my work be praise! There

bring my wan - d'ring spir - it back When I for -
hand, in sight of all my foes, Does still my
would I find a set - tled rest, While oth - ers

sake your ways, And lead me, for your
ta - ble spread. My cup with bless - ings
go and come; No more a stran - ger

mer - cy's sake, In paths of truth and grace.
o - ver - flows; Your oil a - noints my head.
or a guest, But like a child at home.

Text: Psalm 23; Isaac Watts, 1674–1748, alt.
Tune: RESIGNATION, CMD; Funk's *Compilation of Genuine Church Music*, 1832; harm. by John L. Bell, b.1949, © 1993, Iona Community,
   GIA Publications, Inc., agent

709 The Living God My Shepherd Is

1. The liv - ing God my shep-herd is, I know no
2. You lead me where cool wa - ters flow By rip - pling
3. I noth - ing fear; for you, O Lord, Are with me
4. And so through all the length of days, Your mer - cy

care or need. You guide me where rich pas - tures grow,
stream and rill, Where I may taste the springs of life,
night and day, In - tent, with shep-herd's staff and rod,
waits on me, At last with - in my Fa - ther's house

A - long the ver - dant mead, Where ev - 'ry day, By
My thirst-ing spir - it fill; You near me bide And
To guide me when I stray, And in the fold You
Your glo - ry I shall see; You ev - er - more Will

pleas - ant way, My hun-g'ring soul may feed.
home - ward guide My va - grant heart and will.
will up - hold My faint - ing heart al - ways.
I a - dore Through all e - ter - ni - ty.

Text: Psalm 23; J. Driscoll, SJ, 1946, © Peter Janson-Smith
Tune: BROTHER JAMES' AIR, 8 6 8 6 44 6; J. L. Macbeth Bain, c.1840–1925; harm. by Gordon P. Jacob, 1895–1984, © Campbell, Thompson and
    McLaughlin, Ltd.

With a Shepherd's Care   710

Refrain

With a shep-herd's care God leads us. With a fa-ther's strength God guides us. With a moth-er's love God nur-tures us and cra-dles us in gen-tle arms.

Verses

1. When we are lost and can-not find the way, God
2. When we are weak, and cares press all a-round, God
3. When we are scared and feel so all a-lone, God

cares for us and keeps us safe. For
strength-ens us to face each day. For
loves us and is by our side. For

God is our light and our faith - ful guide, who
God is our rock and our sav - ing help, who
God is our hope and our con - stant friend, who

D.C.

leads us with a shep - herd's care.
guides us with a fa - ther's strength.
nur - tures with a moth - er's love.

Text: James J. Chepponis, b.1956
Tune: SHEPHERD'S CARE, 10 8 10 8 with refrain; James J. Chepponis, b.1956
© 1992, GIA Publications, Inc.

711　O God, You Are My God Alone

1. O God, you are my God a-lone, Whom ea-ger-ly I seek, Though long-ing fills my soul with thirst And leaves my bod-y weak. Just like a dry and bar-ren land A-waits a fresh-'ning show'r, I long with-in your house to see Your glo-ry and your pow'r.

2. Your faith-ful love sur-pass-es life, E-vok-ing all my praise. Through ev-'ry day, to bless your name, My hands in joy I'll raise. My deep-est needs you sat-is-fy As with a sump-tuous feast. So, on my lips and in my heart, Your praise has nev-er ceased.

3. Through-out the night I lie in bed And call you, Lord, to mind; In dark-est hours I med-i-tate How God, my strength, is kind. Be-neath the shad-ow of your wing, I live and feel se-cure; And dai-ly as I fol-low close, Your right hand keeps me sure.

Text: Psalm 63; John L. Bell, b.1949, © 1993, Iona Community, GIA Publications, Inc., agent
Tune: RESIGNATION, CMD; Funk's *Compilation of Genuine Church Music*, 1832; harm. by Richard Proulx, 1937–2010, © 1975, GIA Publications, Inc.

The King of Love My Shepherd Is   712

1. The King of love my shep-herd is, Whose good-ness fails me nev-er; I noth-ing lack if I am his And he is mine for-ev-er.
2. Where streams of liv-ing wa-ter flow, My ran-somed soul he's lead-ing, And, where the ver-dant pas-tures grow, With food ce-les-tial feed-ing.
3. Con-fused and fool-ish oft I strayed, But yet in love he sought me, And on his shoul-der gent-ly laid, And home, re-joic-ing, brought me.
4. In death's dark vale I fear no ill With you, dear Lord, be-side me, Your rod and staff my com-fort still, Your cross be-fore to guide me.
5. You spread a ta-ble in my sight, Your sav-ing grace be-stow-ing; And, oh, what trans-port of de-light From your pure chal-ice flow-ing!
6. And so, through all the length of days Your good-ness fails me nev-er; Good Shep-herd, may I sing your praise With-in your house for-ev-er.

Text: Psalm 23; Henry W. Baker, 1821–1877, alt.
Tune: ST. COLUMBA, 8 7 8 7; Irish melody; harm. by A. Gregory Murray, OSB, 1905–1992, © Downside Abbey

713 Eye Has Not Seen

Refrain

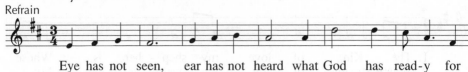

Eye has not seen, ear has not heard what God has read-y for

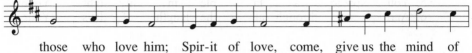

those who love him; Spir-it of love, come, give us the mind of

Je - sus, teach us the wis - dom of God.

Verses 1-3

1. When pain and sor - row weigh us down, be near to us, O
2. Our lives are but a sin - gle breath, we flow-er and we
3. To those who see with eyes of faith, the Lord is ev - er

Lord; for - give the weak - ness of our faith, and
fade, yet all our days are in your hands, so
near, re - flect-ed in the fac - es of

D.C.

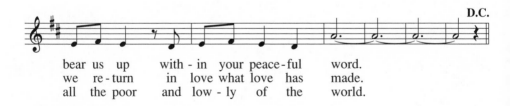

bear us up with - in your peace-ful word.
we re - turn in love what love has made.
all the poor and low - ly of the world.

Verse 4

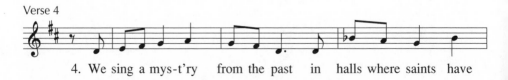

4. We sing a mys-t'ry from the past in halls where saints have

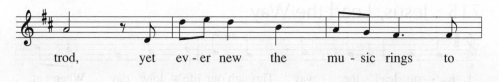

trod,   yet   ev-er new   the   mu-sic rings   to

D.C.

Je-sus, Liv-ing   Song   of   God.

Text: 1 Corinthians 2:9–10; Marty Haugen, b.1950
Tune: Marty Haugen, b.1950
© 1982, GIA Publications, Inc.

How Sweet the Name of Jesus Sounds   714

1. How   sweet   the   name   of   Je - sus   sounds   To
2. It   makes   the   wound - ed   spir - it   whole   And
3. Blest Name! The   rock   on   which   we   build,   Our
4. O   Je - sus,   shep - herd,   guard - ian,   friend,   Our

all   be - liev - ing   ears!   It   soothes our   sor - rows,
calms   the   heart   dis - tressed: 'Tis   man - na   for   the
shield   and   rest - ing   place,   Our   nev - er - fail - ing
proph - et,   priest,   and   king,   Our   Lord,   our   life,   our

heals   our   wounds, And   drives   a - way   our   fears.
hun - gry   soul, And   for   the   wea - ry,   rest.
store - house, filled With   count - less   gifts   of   grace!
way,   our   end,   Ac - cept   the   praise   we   bring.

Text: John Newton, 1725–1807, alt.
Tune: ST. PETER, CM; Alexander R. Reinagle, 1799–1877

715 Jesus, Lead the Way

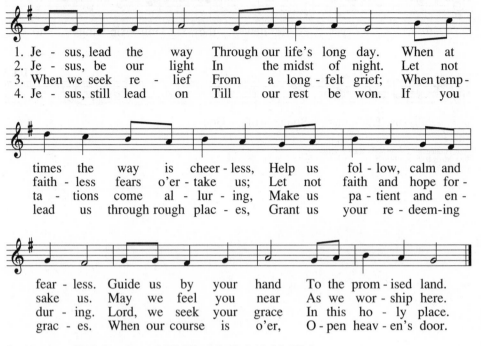

1. Je - sus, lead the way Through our life's long day. When at
2. Je - sus, be our light In the midst of night. Let not
3. When we seek re - lief From a long - felt grief; When temp -
4. Je - sus, still lead on Till our rest be won. If you

times the way is cheer - less, Help us fol - low, calm and
faith - less fears o'er - take us; Let not faith and hope for -
ta - tions come al - lur - ing, Make us pa - tient and en -
lead us through rough plac - es, Grant us your re - deem - ing

fear - less. Guide us by your hand To the prom - ised land.
sake us. May we feel you near As we wor - ship here.
dur - ing. Lord, we seek your grace In this ho - ly place.
grac - es. When our course is o'er, O - pen heav - en's door.

Text: *Jesu, geh voran;* Nicholas L. von Zinzendorf, 1700–1760; tr. by Jane Borthwick, 1813–1897, alt.
Tune: ROCHELLE, 55 88 55; Adam Drese, 1620–1701; harm. alt.

716 Come to Me

Ostinato Refrain

Come to me, come to me, weak and heav - y lad - en; lad - en;

trust in me, lean on me. I will give you rest. give you rest.

Text: Matthew 11:28; John L. Bell, b.1949
Tune: John L. Bell, b.1949
© 2008, Iona Community, GIA Publications, Inc., agent

Come to Me, O Weary Traveler 717

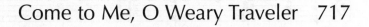

1. Come to me, O wea - ry trav - 'ler; Come to me with
2. Do not fear, my yoke is eas - y; Do not fear, my
3. Take my yoke and leave your trou - bles; Take my yoke and
4. Rest in me, O wea - ry trav - 'ler; Rest in me and

your dis - tress; Come to me, you heav - y bur-dened;
bur - den's light; Do not fear the path be - fore you;
come with me. Take my yoke, I am be - side you;
do not fear. Rest in me, my heart is gen - tle;

Come to me and find your rest.
Do not run from me in fright.
Take and learn hu - mil - i - ty.
Rest and cast a - way your care.

Text: Matthew 11:28–30; Sylvia G. Dunstan, 1955–1993, © 1991, GIA Publications, Inc.
Tune: DUNSTAN, 8 7 8 7; Bob Moore, b.1962, © 1993, GIA Publications, Inc.

Alternate tune: STUTTGART

718 Nada Te Turbe / Nothing Can Trouble

Ostinato Refrain

Na - da te tur - be, na - da te es-pan - te. Quien a Dios tie - ne
Noth-ing can trou-ble, noth-ing can fright-en. Those who seek God shall
Korean: 두 려 워 말 라 걱 정 을 말 라 주 님 계 시 니

na - da   le fal - ta.   So - lo Dios   bas - ta.
nev-er   go want - ing.   God a - lone   fills   us.
아 쉬   움 없   네   주 님 안   에   서

Korean transliteration: Du-lyeo-wo mal-la geog-jeong-eul mal-la
Ju-nim gye-si-ni a-swi-um eobs-ne.
Du-lyeo-wo mal-la geog-jeong-eul mal-la
Ju-nim an-e-seo.

Text: St. Teresa of Jesus; Taizé Community, 1986, 1991
Tune: Jacques Berthier, 1923–1994
© 1986, 1991, Les Presses de Taizé, GIA Publications, Inc., agent

719 If You Have Faith / Si Tienen Fe

Ostinato Refrain

If   you have faith   but the   size   of   a   mus-tard seed,
Si   tie - nen   fe   co-mo_un gra - no   de mos - ta - za,

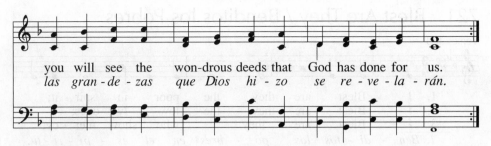

you will see the won-drous deeds that God has done for us.
las gran-de-zas que Dios hi-zo se re-ve-la-rán.

Text: Ronald F. Krisman, b.1946
Tune: Ronald F. Krisman, b.1946
© 2008, GIA Publications, Inc.

The Kingdom of God 720

1. The king-dom of God is jus-tice and joy;
2. The king-dom of God is mer-cy and grace;
3. The king-dom of God is chal-lenge and choice:
4. God's king-dom is come, the gift and the goal;

For Je-sus re-stores what sin would de-stroy.
The cap-tives are freed, the sin-ners find place,
Be-lieve the good news, re-pent and re-joice!
In Je-sus be-gun, in heav-en made whole.

God's pow-er and glo-ry in Je-sus we know;
The out-cast are wel-comed God's ban-quet to share;
God's love for us sin-ners brought Christ to his cross:
The heirs of the king-dom shall an-swer his call;

And here and here-af-ter the king-dom shall grow.
And hope is a-wak-ened in place of de-spair.
Our cri-sis of judg-ment for gain or for loss.
And all things cry "Glo-ry!" to God all in all.

Text: Bryn A. Rees, 1911–1983, © 1973, Alexander Scott
Tune: LAUDATE DOMINUM, 10 10 11 11; Charles H. H. Parry, 1848–1918

721 Blest Are They / Benditos los Pobres

Verses 1–3

1. Blest are they, the poor in spir - it;
2. Blest are they, the low - ly ones;
3. Blest are they who show mer - cy;

1. Ben - di - tos los po - bres en el es - pí - ri - tu,
2. Ben - di - tos son los pa - cien - tes,
3. Ben - di - tos son los com - pa - si - vos,

theirs is the king - dom of God.
they shall in - her - it the earth.
mer - cy shall be theirs.

su - yo es el rei - no de Dios. Di -
he - re - da - rán la tie - rra. Di -
ob - ten - drán pie - dad. Di -

Blest are they, full of sor - row;
Blest are they who hun - ger and thirst;
Blest are they, the pure of heart;

cho - sos son los que llo - ran,
cho - sos los que tie - nen sed y ham - bre,
cho - sos los lim - pios de co - ra - zón,

they shall be con - soled.
they shall have their fill.
they shall see God.

re - ci - bi - rán con - sue - lo.
por - que se - rán sa - cia - dos.
e - llos ve - rán a Dios.

Refrain

Re - joice and be glad! Bless-ed are
¡A - lé - gren-se y con - tén - ten - se! ¡Son los ben -

you, ho-ly are you! Re-joice and be glad!
di - tos de nues-tro Dios! ¡A - lé-gren-se y con -tén-ten-se!

Yours is the king-dom of God!
¡Su - yo_es el rei - no de Dios!

Verses 4, 5

4. Blest are they who seek peace;
5. Blest are you who suf - fer hate,
4. Ben - di - tos los que por la paz tra - ba-jan,
5. Ben - di - tos son los per - se - gui-dos,

they are the chil - dren of God.
all be - cause of me. Re -
e - llos son hi - jos de Dios. Di -
to - do por cau - sa mí - a. ¡A -

Blest are they who suf - fer in faith; the
joice and be glad, yours is the king - dom;
cho - sos los que por la fe su - fren,
lé - gren - se! Su re - com - pen - sa

To refrain

glo - ry of God is theirs.
shine for all to see.
su - ya_es la glo - ria de Dios.
gran-de_en el cie - lo se - rá.

Text: Matthew 5:3–12; David Haas, b.1957, tr. by Ronald F. Krisman, b.1946
Tune: David Haas, b.1957; vocal arr. by David Haas and Michael Joncas, b.1951
© 1985, 2005, GIA Publications, Inc.

722 The Reign of God

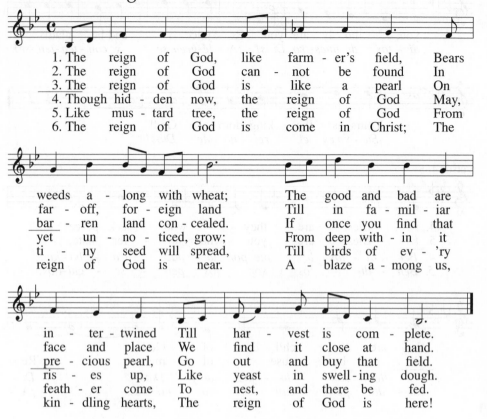

1. The reign of God, like farm - er's field, Bears
2. The reign of God can - not be found In
3. The reign of God is like a pearl On
4. Though hid - den now, the reign of God May,
5. Like mus - tard tree, the reign of God From
6. The reign of God is come in Christ; The

weeds a - long with wheat; The good and bad are
far - off, for - eign land Till in fa - mil - iar
bar - ren land con - cealed. If once you find that
yet un - no - ticed, grow; From deep with - in it
ti - ny seed will spread, Till birds of ev - 'ry
reign of God is near. A - blaze a - mong us,

in - ter - twined Till har - vest is com - plete.
face and place We find it close at hand.
pre - cious pearl, Go out and buy that field.
ris - es up, Like yeast in swell - ing dough.
feath - er come To nest, and there be fed.
kin - dling hearts, The reign of God is here!

Text: Matthew 13:24–33, 44–49, Mark 4:26–34; Delores Dufner, OSB, b.1939, © 1995, 2003, GIA Publications, Inc.
Tune: McKEE, CM; African American; adapt. by Harry T. Burleigh, 1866–1949

When Jesus Came Preaching 723
the Kingdom of God

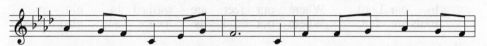

1. When Je - sus came preach-ing the King - dom of God With the
2. Since Je - sus came preach-ing the King - dom of God, What a
3. Still Je - sus comes preach-ing the King - dom of God In a

love that has pow'r to per-suade, The sick were made whole, both in
change in our lives he has made! How man - y have shared in the
world that is sick and a - fraid; His gos - pel has spread like the

bod - y and soul, And e - ven the de - mons o - beyed.
joy of their Lord, In self - giv - ing have loved and o - beyed!
leav - en in bread By the love that has a pow'r to per-suade.

But he need - ed a few he could trust to be true, To
But let none of us doubt what re - li - gion's a - bout, Or by
So let none of us swerve from our mis - sion to serve, That has

share in his work from the start: When Je - sus came preach-ing the
what it is shamed and be-trayed: Do just - ly, love mer - cy, walk
made us his Church from the start: May Je - sus, the Light of the

King - dom of God, God's gift to the hum - ble of heart.
hum - bly with God, Is the rule of life Je - sus o - beyed.
World, send us out In the strength of the hum - ble of heart.

Text: Fred Pratt Green, 1903–2000, © 1974, Hope Publishing Company
Tune: SAMANTHRA, Irregular; *Southern Harmony*, 1835; harm. by Austin C. Lovelace, 1919–2010, © 1986, GIA Publications, Inc.

724 Let Us Come Now to the Kingdom

1. Let us come now to the king-dom Where we're greet-ed
2. Let us come now to the king-dom Where all hun-gry

by our Lord, Where our feet are washed in glo-ry
souls are fed, Where our drink is peace and glad-ness

And our en-er-gies re-stored, Where the saints have
And God's right-eous-ness our bread, Where each stran-ger

come to join us From the west and from the east,
is our neigh-bor And each neigh-bor next of kin,

Where from north and south they've gath-ered
Where Christ waits for all God's chil-dren,

To help cel-e-brate the feast!
So the ban-quet can be-gin!

Text: Rae E. Whitney, b.1927, © 1994, Selah Publishing Co., Inc.
Tune: HOLY MANNA, 8 7 8 7 D; William Moore, fl.1830; harm. by Charles Anders, b.1929, © 1969, *Contemporary Worship I: Hymns*

We Will Walk with God / Sizohamba   725

We will walk with God, my broth-ers, we will walk with God.
We will walk with God, my sis-ters, we will walk with God.
Si - zo-ham-ba na - ye, wo wo wo, si - zo-ham-ba na - ye.

We will go re - joic-ing   till the king-dom has come.
Ngom-hla wen-ja - bu - la,   si - zo-ham-ba na - ye.

We will go re - joic-ing   till the king-dom has come.
Ngom-hla wen-ja - bu - la,   si - zo-ham-ba na - ye.

Text: Swaziland traditional; transcribed by Swedish Youth Exchange Project, ©; tr. by John L. Bell, b.1949, © 2002, Iona Community,
   GIA Publications, Inc., agent
Tune: Swaziland traditional; transcribed by Swedish Youth Exchange Project, ©

726 The Church of Christ Cannot Be Bound

1. The Church of Christ can-not be bound By
2. True faith will o-pen up the door And
3. True love will not sit i-dly by When
4. If what we have we free-ly share To
5. The Church of Christ can-not be bound By

walls of wood or stone. Where char-i-ty and
step in-to the street. True serv-ice will seek
jus-tice is de-nied. True mer-cy hears the
meet our neigh-bor's need, Then we ex-tend the
walls of wood or stone. Where char-i-ty and

love are found, There can the Church be known.
out the poor And ask to wash their feet.
home-less cry And wel-comes them in-side.
Spir-it's care Through ev-'ry self-less deed.
love are found, There can the Church be known.

Text: Adam M. L. Tice, b.1979, © 2005, GIA Publications, Inc.
Tune: McKEE, CM; African American; adapt. by Harry T. Burleigh, 1866–1949

Sing a New Church 727

1. Sum - moned by the God who made us Rich in
2. Ra - diant ris - en from the wa - ter, Robed in
3. Trust the good - ness of cre - a - tion; Trust the
4. Bring the hopes of ev - 'ry na - tion; Bring the
5. Draw to - geth - er at one ta - ble All the

our di - ver - si - ty, Gath-ered in the name of
ho - li - ness and light, Male and fe - male in God's
Spir - it strong with - in. Dare to dream the vi - sion
art of ev - 'ry race. Weave a song of peace and
hu - man fam - i - ly; Shape a cir - cle ev - er

Je - sus, Rich - er still in u - ni - ty:
im - age, Male and fe - male, God's de - light:
prom - ised, Sprung from seed of what has been.
jus - tice; Let it sound through time and space.
wid - er And a peo - ple ev - er free.

Let us bring the gifts that dif - fer And, in

splen - did, var - ied ways, Sing a new Church in - to

be - ing, One in faith and love and praise.

Text: Delores Dufner, OSB, b.1939, © 1991, Sisters of St. Benedict. Published by OCP.
Tune: NETTLETON, 8 7 8 7 with refrain, from Wyeth's *Repository of Sacred Music*, 1813

728 Where Christ Is, His Church Is There

1. Where Christ is, his Church is there. What a faith to
2. Where Christ is, his King-dom grows. His the truth that
3. Where Christ is, his Church is there. What a faith to

hold and share! Those who hold it must not part
o - ver-throws Ev - 'ry harsh and god - less creed
hold and share! Those who hold it must not part

Church and King-dom in their heart. They, their wor - ship
Born of fear or hate or greed. Some who nev - er
Church and King-dom in their heart. Taught by Christ, they

end - ed, know: In that world to which they go,
called him Lord Speak his rec - on - cil - ing word:
count as his All who share his sym - pa - thies:

Though no bells in - vite to prayer,
His all love that o - ver - flows.
Cer - tain, when his work is done,

Where Christ is, his Church is there.
Where Christ is, his King - dom grows.
Church and King - dom shall be one.

Text: Fred Pratt Green, 1903–2000, © 1971, Hope Publishing Company
Tune: SALZBURG, 77 77 D; Jakob Hintze, 1622–1702; harm. by J. S. Bach, 1685–1750

You Strode within the Temple, Lord 729

1. You strode with - in the Tem - ple, Lord, Where
2. The tem - ple of your bod - y, Lord, They
3. Make ev - 'ry heart your tem - ple, Lord, Each
4. Come, vis - it, Lord of right - eous - ness, The

mer - chants vied for gain, And cried, "Your wares cor -
crushed when you were slain; But af - ter three days'
life a ho - ly place. For - give the sins that
Church that bears your name. Drive out our fear and

rupt God's house, This place of prayer pro - fane!" With
sleep in death, God raised it up a - gain. And
flaw your plan, Your pa - tient work de - face. In
un - be - lief, The pride that is our shame. Re -

cord - ed whip and fier - y wrath You
now you have a dwell - ing place On
love that does not shrink from truth These
new the life we share, O Christ, In

put God's foes to flight. They could not bear the
earth, in all its lands. Your peo - ple are your
tem - ples pu - ri - fy. And then in mer - cy,
love and prayer and praise. Then send us forth, our

search - ing beam Of your un - shield - ed light.
tem - ple, Lord, A house not made with hands.
Lord, re - main; Your Spir - it's gifts sup - ply.
strength re - stored, To serve you all our days.

Text: Herman G. Stuempfle, Jr., 1923–2007, © 2000, GIA Publications, Inc.
Tune: KINGSFOLD, CMD; English melody; harm. by Ralph Vaughan Williams, 1872–1958

730 Christ, You Formed the Church, Your Body

1. Christ, you formed the Church, your Bod-y, By your ris-ing
2. One the Spir-it who dis-trib-utes Gifts in great di-
3. Give us pas-tors who will feed us With the Word that
4. Christ, your Spir-it's breath re-news us, Guides us on our

from the dead, Born a-new through Word and wa-ter,
ver-si-ty: Some to lead and some to fol-low,
sets us free. Send us then to love and la-bor,
pil-grim way. Strength, com-pas-sion, wis-dom, cour-age

We the mem-bers, you the Head. With your Word you
Each to serve you faith-ful-ly. All one bod-y,
Each day's life our lit-ur-gy. Help us, Christ, in
Are the gifts for which we pray. Grant that, as your

call and guide us; At your ta-ble we are fed!
man-y mem-bers, Help us live in u-ni-ty!
ev-'ry call-ing, Do your work of min-is-try!
saints be-fore us, We may serve in this new day!

Text: Herman G. Stuempfle, Jr., 1923–2007, © 2006, GIA Publications, Inc.
Tune: FORTUNATUS NEW, 8 7 8 7 8 7; Carl F. Schalk, b.1929, © 1967, Concordia Publishing House

731 One Is the Body

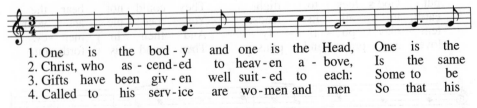

1. One is the bod-y and one is the Head, One is the
2. Christ, who as-cend-ed to heav-en a-bove, Is the same
3. Gifts have been giv-en well suit-ed to each: Some to be
4. Called to his serv-ice are wo-men and men So that his

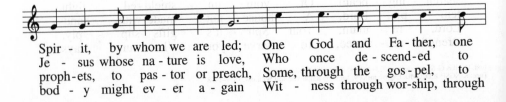

Spir-it, by whom we are led; One God and Fa-ther, one
Je-sus whose na-ture is love, Who once de-scend-ed to
proph-ets, to pas-tor or preach, Some, through the gos-pel, to
bod-y might ev-er a-gain Wit-ness through wor-ship, through

faith   and   one   call   for   all.
bring   to   this   earth   new   birth.
chal - lenge,   con - vert,   and   teach.
deed,   and   through word   to   Christ   our   Lord.

Text: John L. Bell, b.1949
Tune: PEACOCK, 10 10 12; John L. Bell, b.1949
© 1997, 2002, Iona Community, GIA Publications, Inc., agent

Christ Is Made the Sure Foundation   732

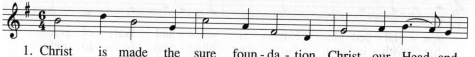

1. Christ   is   made   the   sure   foun - da - tion, Christ, our   Head and
2. To   this   tem - ple, where   we   call   you, Come, O   Lord   of
3. Here   be - stow   on   all   your   ser - vants What   they   ask   of
4. Praise   and   hon - or   to   the   Fa - ther, Praise   and   hon - or

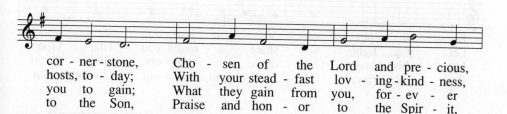

cor - ner - stone,   Cho - sen   of   the   Lord   and   pre - cious,
hosts, to - day;   With   your stead - fast   lov - ing - kind - ness,
you   to   gain;   What   they   gain   from   you,   for - ev - er
to   the   Son,   Praise   and   hon - or   to   the   Spir - it,

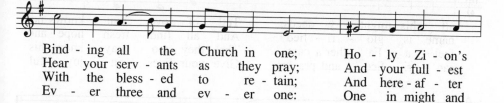

Bind - ing   all   the   Church in   one;   Ho - ly   Zi - on's
Hear   your   serv - ants   as   they   pray;   And   your   full - est
With   the   bless - ed   to   re - tain;   And   here - af - ter
Ev - er   three   and   ev - er   one: One   in   might and

help   for - ev - er   And   our   con - fi - dence   a - lone.
ben - e - dic - tion Shed   in   all   its   bright   ar - ray.
in   your   glo - ry   Ev - er - more   with   you   to   reign.
one   in   glo - ry   While   un - end - ing   a - ges   run!

Text: *Angularis fundamentum*; 11th C.; tr. by John M. Neale, 1818–1866, alt.
Tune: WESTMINSTER ABBEY, 8 7 8 7 8 7; adapt. from an anthem of Henry Purcell, 1659–1695, by Ernest Hawkins, 1807–1868

733 Church of God, Elect and Glorious

1. Church of God, e-lect and glo-rious, Ho-ly na-tion, cho-sen race; Called as God's own spe-cial peo-ple, Roy-al priests and heirs of grace: Know the pur-pose of your call-ing, Show to all his might-y deeds; Tell of love that knows no lim-its, Grace that meets all hu-man needs.

2. God has called you out of dark-ness In-to his most marv-'lous light, Brought his truth to life with-in you, Turned your blind-ness in-to sight. Let your light so shine a-round you That God's name is glo-ri-fied And all find fresh hope and pur-pose In Christ Je-sus cru-ci-fied.

3. Once you were an a-lien peo-ple, Strang-ers to God's heart of love; But he brought you home in mer-cy, Cit-i-zens of heav'n a-bove. Let his love flow out to oth-ers, Let them feel a Fa-ther's care, That they too may know his wel-come And his count-less bless-ings share.

4. Church of God, e-lect and ho-ly, Be the peo-ple he in-tends, Strong in faith and swift to an-swer Each com-mand your Mas-ter sends. Roy-al priests, ful-fill your call-ing Through your sac-ri-fice and prayer; Give your lives in joy-ful serv-ice; Sing his praise, his love de-clare.

Text: J. E. Seddon, © 1982, The Jubilate Group (admin. by Hope Publishing Company)
Tune: ABBOT'S LEIGH, 8 7 8 7 D; Cyril V. Taylor, 1907–1991, © 1942, ren. 1970, Hope Publishing Company

As a Fire Is Meant for Burning   734

1. As a fire is meant for burn - ing   With a
2. We are learn - ers; we are teach - ers;   We are
3. As a green bud in the spring - time   Is a

bright and warm-ing flame,   So the Church is meant for
pil - grims on the way.   We are seek - ers; we are
sign of life re - newed,   So may we be signs of

mis - sion, Giv - ing glo - ry   to God's name.
giv - ers; We are ves - sels   made of clay.
one - ness Mid earth's peo - ples,   man - y hued.

As we wit - ness to the gos - pel,   We would
By our gen - tle, lov - ing ac - tions,   We would
As a rain - bow lights the heav - ens   When a

build a bridge of care,   Join - ing hands a - cross the
show that Christ is light.   In a hum - ble, lis - t'ning
storm is past and gone,   May our lives re - flect the

na - tions, Find - ing neigh - bors ev - 'ry - where.
Spir - it, We would live to God's de - light.
ra - diance Of God's new and glor - ious dawn.

Text: Ruth Duck, b.1947, © 1992, GIA Publications, Inc.
Tune: BEACH SPRING, 8 7 8 7 D; *The Sacred Harp*, 1844; harm. by Ronald A. Nelson, b.1927, © 1978, *Lutheran Book of Worship*,
    admin. by Augsburg Fortress

735 Living Stones

1. Liv - ing stones, we raise a tem - ple Where the
2. Made of mar - ble, brick, or tim - ber, And the
3. Formed in faith, we join to - geth - er At the

Spir - it comes to dwell In each act of lov - ing
la - bor of our hands, May our build - ings house a
ta - ble of our Lord. When we share in cel - e -

serv - ice, In the gos - pel truth we tell. In the
peo - ple Who em - bod - y God's com - mands: In a
bra - tion, We de - part with strength re - stored: To cre -

plac - es where we wor - ship, Plain or
world where home - less mil - lions Live a -
ate a realm of jus - tice And the

lav - ish, large or small, As the Church of God in -
ban - doned on the street, May we of - fer warmth and
bless - ings of sha - lom, Where each heart be - comes an

car - nate, Christ is cor - ner - stone of all.
shel - ter And the bread of life to eat.
al - tar, And the world it - self, God's home.

Text: Mary Louise Bringle, b.1953, © 2006, GIA Publications, Inc.
Tune: NETTLETON, 8 7 8 7 D; from Wyeth's *Repository of Sacred Music*, 1813

The Church's One Foundation 736

1. The Chur-ch's one foun - da - tion Is Je - sus Christ, her
2. E - lect from ev - 'ry na - tion, Yet one o'er all the
3. Through toil and trib - u - la - tion And tu - mult of her
4. Yet she on earth has u - nion With God, the Three in

Lord; She is his new cre - a - tion By wa - ter
earth; Her char - ter of sal - va - tion: One Lord, one
war She waits the con - sum - ma - tion Of peace for -
One, And mys - tic sweet com - mun - ion With those whose

and the Word. From heav'n he came and sought her To
faith, one birth. One ho - ly name she bless - es, Par -
ev - er - more Till with the vi - sion glo - rious Her
rest is won. O bless - ed heav'n - ly cho - rus! Lord,

be his ho - ly bride; With his own blood he
takes one ho - ly food, And to one hope she
long - ing eyes are blessed, And the great Church vic -
save us by your grace That we, like saints be -

bought her, And for her life he died.
press - es With ev - 'ry grace en - dued.
to - rious Shall be the Church at rest.
fore us, May see you face to face.

Text: Samuel J. Stone, 1839–1900, alt.
Tune: AURELIA, 7 6 7 6 D; Samuel S. Wesley, 1810–1876

737 If Life Is Like a Wedding Feast

1. If   life   is   like   a   wed - ding   feast   And
2. If   life   is   like   a   wed - ding   feast   And
3. And   God   is   mak - ing   life   a   feast,   Em -

we   are   cast   as   guests,   Then   it   is   trag - ic
we   are   cast   as   hosts,   Then   it   is   lim - it -
brac - ing   us   as   guests   So   that   with   self - for -

not   to   know   The   life   God   man - i - fests.   Dis -
ing   to   list   The   ones   we   like   the   most   And
get - ting   grace   We   gath - er   and   are   blessed   To

tract - ed   by   ap - pear - anc - es,   Se - duced   by
leave   a - part,   out - side,   un - known,   Un - count - ed
taste   and   know   that   God   is   good   And   spreads   the

praise   or   place,   If   we   re - main   out -
oth - er   souls,   When   love   sug - gests   there
ta - ble   wide,   So   wide   we   know   to

side   our - selves   We   miss   this   mo - ment's   grace.
is   no   feast   Till   all   the   parts   are   whole.
say   with   God,   Come, all   my friends,   in - side.

Text: Michael Hudson, © 2004; admin. by Church Publishing Inc.
Tune: RESIGNATION, CMD; Funk's *Compilation of Genuine Church Music*, 1832; harm. by Richard Proulx, 1937–2010, © 1975, GIA Publications, Inc.

O Blessed Are the Poor in Spirit   738

1. O bless-ed are the poor in spirit;
3. O bless-ed are the meek;
5. O bless-ed are the merciful;
7. O bless-ed are the peacemakers;
9. O bless-ed are you when the world re-viles you and persecutes you;

1. for theirs is the kingdom of heav - en.
3. for they shall in - her - it the earth.
5. for they shall obtain mer - cy.
7. for they shall be called the chil - dren of God.
9. and utters all manner of evil against you falsely for my sake.

2. O bless-ed are those who mourn;
4. O bless-ed are those who hunger and thirst af - ter righteousness;
6. O bless-ed are the pure in heart;
8. O bless-ed are those who are perse - cut - ed for righteousness' sake;
10. Re - joice and be ex - ceedingly glad;

2. for they shall be com - fort - ed.
4. for they shall be sat - is - fied.
6. for they shall see God.
8. for theirs is the kingdom of heav - en.
10. for great is your reward in heav - en.

Text: Matthew 5:3–12; *The Beatitudes*
Tune: KONTAKION, Irregular; Russian Orthodox Liturgy, adapt. by Richard Proulx, 1937–2010, © 1985, GIA Publications, Inc.

739 My Elder Son, Go Work Today!

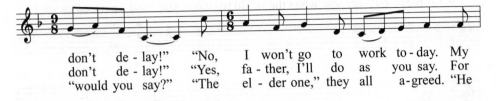

1. "My el - der son, go work to - day! The corn is ripe, so
2. "My sec - ond son, go work to - day! The corn is ripe, so
3. "Who did the fa - ther's will that day? Which son," said Je - sus,

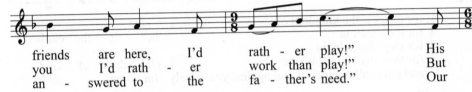

don't de - lay!" "No, I won't go to work to - day. My
don't de - lay!" "Yes, fa - ther, I'll do as you say. For
"would you say?" "The el - der one," they all a - greed. "He

friends are here, I'd rath - er play!" His
you I'd rath - er work than play!" But
an - swered to the fa - ther's need." Our

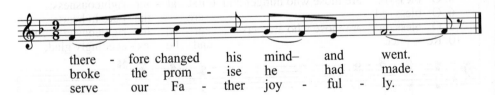

fa - ther's need made him re - pent. He
though he said he'd go, he stayed, And
minds can change; love sets us free To

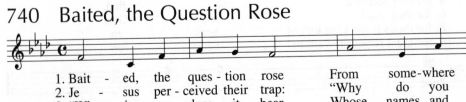

there - fore changed his mind— and went.
broke the prom - ise he had made.
serve our Fa - ther joy - ful - ly.

Text: Rae E. Whitney, b.1927, © 1995, Selah Publishing Co., Inc.
Tune: HICKORY HILL, 88 88 88; Ronald F. Krisman, b.1946, © 2011, GIA Publications, Inc.

Alternate tune: ST. CATHERINE

740 Baited, the Question Rose

1. Bait - ed, the ques - tion rose From some - where
2. Je - sus per - ceived their trap: "Why do you
3. "Whose im - age does it bear, Whose names and
4. "Give Cae - sar what is his; God, what is
5. May we dis - cern, O God, Your dai - ly
6. Help us fit trib - ute yield Through prayers and

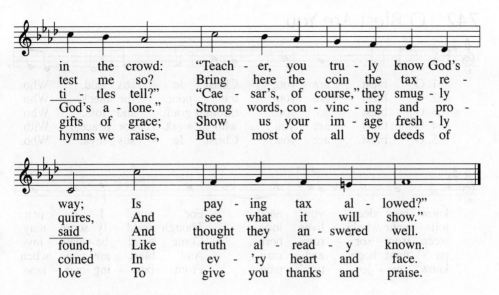

in the crowd:	"Teach - er, you tru - ly know God's
test me so?	Bring here the coin the tax re -
ti - tles tell?"	"Cae - sar's, of course," they smug - ly
God's a - lone."	Strong words, con - vinc - ing and pro -
gifts of grace;	Show us your im - age fresh - ly
hymns we raise,	But most of all by deeds of

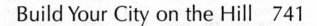

way;	Is pay - ing tax al - lowed?"
quires,	And see what it will show."
said	And thought they an - swered well.
found,	Like truth al - read - y known.
coined	In ev - 'ry heart and face.
love	To give you thanks and praise.

Text: Carl P. Daw, Jr., b.1944, © 1996, Hope Publishing Company
Tune: ST. BRIDE, SM; Samuel Howard, 1710–1782

Build Your City on the Hill   741

1. Build your cit - y	on the hill, For	it must not be
2. Set your lamp up - on	the stand; Do	not con - ceal its
3. Salt is found with - in	the earth, And	in the bread is
4. Lamp and cit - y,	salt and yeast Are	signs of grace and

hid - den!	As Christ's bod - y	liv - ing still,	Bear
glow - ing!	In the night the	wait - ing land	Re -
leav - en.	Bland and stale they	have no worth,	But
fa - vor.	As the peo - ple	of the Feast	We

wit - ness as you're bid	-	den.
joic - es with its show	-	ing.
fresh they lift to heav	-	en.
glo - ri - fy our Sav	-	ior.

Text: Matthew 5:13–16; Sylvia G. Dunstan, 1953–1993, © 1991, GIA Publications, Inc.
Tune: PUER NOBIS NASCITUR, 7 7 7 7; Piae Cantiones, 1582; harm. by Geoffrey Shaw, 1879–1943, © A. R. Mowbray and Co. Ltd.

742 O Blest Are You

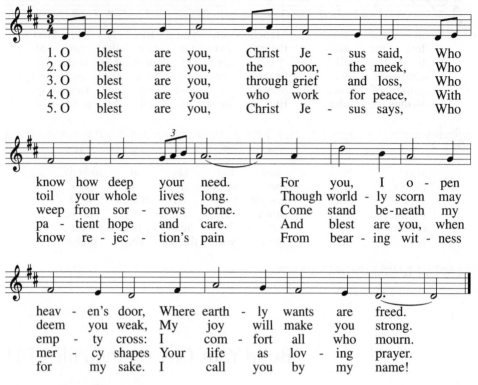

1. O blest   are you,   Christ Je - sus said,   Who
2. O blest   are you,   the   poor,   the meek,   Who
3. O blest   are you,   through grief and loss,   Who
4. O blest   are you   who   work   for peace,   With
5. O blest   are you,   Christ Je - sus says,   Who

know how deep   your   need.   For   you,   I   o - pen
toil   your whole   lives   long.   Though world - ly scorn may
weep from sor - rows   borne. Come stand be - neath my
pa - tient hope and   care.   And   blest are you,   when
know re - jec - tion's pain   From   bear - ing wit - ness

heav - en's door, Where earth - ly wants   are   freed.
deem   you weak, My   joy   will make   you   strong.
emp - ty cross: I   com - fort all   who   mourn.
mer - cy shapes Your life   as   lov - ing prayer.
for   my sake. I   call   you   by   my   name!

Text: Mary Louise Bringle, b.1953, © 2006, GIA Publications, Inc.
Tune: ST. COLUMBA, CM; Irish melody

743 To Love Just Those Who Love You

1. To   love just those who   love   you Is   rare - ly hard to   do,
2. To   laugh with those who   please you And share a sim - ple joy
3. Since Christ is Truth and Teach - er, The Day Star and the Day,

For   e - ven un - be - liev - ers Love those who love them   too.
Is   dif-f'rent from en - dur - ing The   peo - ple who an - noy.
The   Life and our Life - giv - er, Way - far - er and the Way,

But   you must love, said   Je - sus, Those you don't care a - bout,
And   those you hate, said   Je - sus, Or   wound you deep with - in,
If   you would come, said   Je - sus, And my com - pan - ion be,

And feed them if they're hun - gry, Though you then go with - out.
Are still your Fa - ther's chil - dren And must be claimed as kin.
In love and joy and suf - f'ring You'll walk God's path with me.

Text: Rae E. Whitney, b.1927, © 1992, Selah Publishing Co., Inc.
Tune: AURELIA, 7 6 7 6 D; Samuel S. Wesley, 1810–1876

What Is the World Like 744

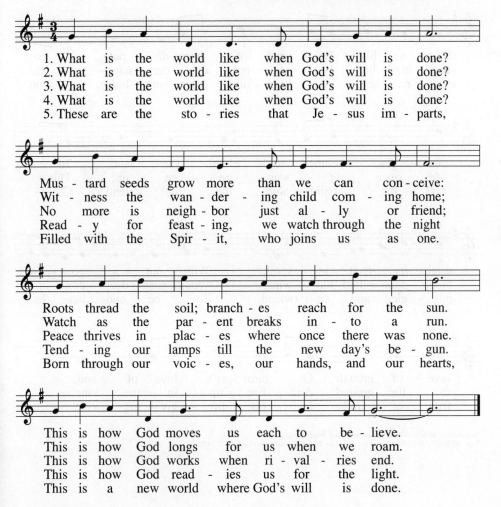

1. What is the world like when God's will is done?
2. What is the world like when God's will is done?
3. What is the world like when God's will is done?
4. What is the world like when God's will is done?
5. These are the sto - ries that Je - sus im - parts,

Mus - tard seeds grow more than we can con - ceive:
Wit - ness the wan - der - ing child com - ing home;
No more is neigh - bor just al - ly or friend;
Read - y for feast - ing, we watch through the night
Filled with the Spir - it, who joins us as one.

Roots thread the soil; branch - es reach for the sun.
Watch as the par - ent breaks in - to a run.
Peace thrives in plac - es where once there was none.
Tend - ing our lamps till the new day's be - gun.
Born through our voic - es, our hands, and our hearts,

This is how God moves us each to be - lieve.
This is how God longs for us when we roam.
This is how God works when ri - val - ries end.
This is how God read - ies us for the light.
This is a new world where God's will is done.

Text: Adam M. L. Tice, b.1979
Tune: NEW WORLD, 10 10 10 10; Sally Ann Morris, b.1952
© 2009, GIA Publications, Inc.

745 The Keeper of a Vineyard

1. The keep - er of a vine - yard dreamed Of
2. The keep - er had a child, first - born, Who
3. And then the plant, fresh charged, would be It -

vines a - live with fruit And tend - ed vine and
came to work the land. The mal - con - tents de -
self a vein of grace, A way the keep - er

dream a - like Down years of sharp dis - pute, As
sired his life But did not un - der - stand— This
might ex - tend A hope - ful, green em - brace, Con -

oth - ers came to claim the land, To
life, once it was giv - en up, This
nect - ing child and foe and friend, Co -

drink its fruit as spoil, With - out a grow - er's
blood, once spilled like wine, Would soak deep down in -
min - gled and en - twined, To be and bear the

love of growth Or farm - er's love of soil.
to the ground And rise up in the vine.
fruit of God In one life - giv - ing vine.

Text: Michael Hudson, © 2004; admin. by Church Publishing Inc.
Tune: KINGSFOLD, CMD; English melody; harm. by Ralph Vaughan Williams, 1872–1958

If Christ Is Charged with Madness   746

1. If Christ is charged with mad - ness, It's
2. Thus when Christ seized and plun - dered The
3. Christ spoke to all this rant - ing, A
4. De - spite his deft ex - plain - ing, Christ
5. Yet earth needs heav - en's mad - ness To

mad - ness that's di - vine, A vi - sion - ar - y
de - mons' dark do - main, His friends and foes both
viv - id, lu - cid word, A par - a - ble sup -
still ap - peared dis - traught To guard - i - ans main -
seize with grace and bind The guilt, the hurt, the

glad - ness This world can - not con - fine,
won - dered If he were not in - sane.
plant - ing The charg - es he had heard.
tain - ing Ac - cept - ed bounds of thought.
sad - ness, The fear and hate that blind.

The mad - ness of con - ceiv - ing What
They charged his soul was riv - en, His
"A house that is di - vid - ed, A
The force of faith in ac - tion Seems
In - trude, O Christ, im - pas - sioned With

no one else can see, Then act - ing and be -
heart and mind pos - sessed By forc - es he had
king - dom, soul, or land With rag - ing wars in -
mad - ness to each age And of - ten the re -
mad - ness that's di - vine Up - on the world we've

liev - ing So it will come to be.
driv - en From those who were dis - tressed.
side it Can - not sur - vive and stand."
ac - tion Is fear dis - guised as rage.
fash - ioned, And give it your de - sign.

Text: Thomas H. Troeger, b.1945, © 1986, Oxford University Press
Tune: KING'S LYNN, 7 6 7 6 D; English melody; harm. by Ralph Vaughan Williams, 1872–1958

Alternate tune: AURELIA

747 God, Your Knowing Eye Can See

1. God, your know - ing eye can see How we use the
2. Woe to us with earth - ly wealth, Wast - ing mon - ey,
3. Blest are those we see as poor, Meek and hun - gry,
4. Give us eyes to see the blest; Give us ears to

gifts you gave: Earth and all that it can be,
land, and food, Think-ing we de - serve our health
those who mourn. Blest are those whom we ig - nore,
hear their cry. Let us give the wea - ry rest;

Which we slash and burn and pave; And the peo - ple
More than those whom we ex - clude: Those who strug - gle
Those we mock, and those we scorn. Blest are we when
Let us com - fort those who die. Help us help each

you cre - ate Whom we per - se - cute and hate.
just to live; Those who need what we could give.
mak-ing peace, Caus - ing all our wars to cease.
oth - er live, Us - ing all the gifts you give.

Text: Adam M. L. Tice, b.1979, © 2009, GIA Publications, Inc.
Tune: CÂMARA, 7 7 7 7 77; Chris Ángel, b.1976, © 2009, GIA Publications, Inc.

Alternate tune: DIX

748 What Does the Lord Require

1. What does the Lord re - quire for praise and of - fer - ing?
2. Rul - ers of earth, give ear! Should you not jus - tice show?
3. Still down the a - ges ring the proph-et's stern com-mands.
4. How shall our life ful - fill God's law so hard and high?

What sac - ri - fice de - sire, or trib - ute bid you bring?
Will God your plead-ing hear, while crime and cruel - ty grow?
To mer-chant, work - er, king he brings God's high de - mands:
Let Christ en - due our will with grace to for - ti - fy.

Do just - ly; love mer - cy; walk hum - bly with your God.
Do just - ly; love mer - cy; walk hum - bly with your God.
Do just - ly; love mer - cy; walk hum - bly with your God.
Then just - ly, in mer - cy, we'll hum - bly walk with God.

Text: Micah 6:6–8; Albert F. Bayly, 1901–1984, alt., © 1988, Oxford University Press
Tune: SHARPTHORNE, 12 12 12; Erik Routley, 1917–1982, © 1969, Hope Publishing Company

God Made from One Blood 749

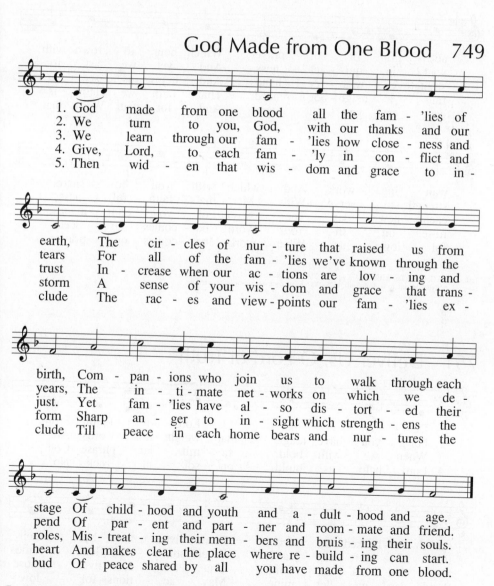

1. God made from one blood all the fam - 'lies of
2. We turn to you, God, with our thanks and our
3. We learn through our fam - 'lies how close - ness and
4. Give, Lord, to each fam - 'ly in con - flict and
5. Then wid - en that wis - dom and grace to in -

earth, The cir - cles of nur - ture that raised us from
tears For all of the fam - 'lies we've known through the
trust In - crease when our ac - tions are lov - ing and
storm A sense of your wis - dom and grace that trans -
clude The rac - es and view - points our fam - 'lies ex -

birth, Com - pan - ions who join us to walk through each
years, The in - ti - mate net - works on which we de -
just. Yet fam - 'lies have al - so dis - tort - ed their
form Sharp an - ger to in - sight which strength - ens the
clude Till peace in each home bears and nur - tures the

stage Of child - hood and youth and a - dult - hood and age.
pend Of par - ent and part - ner and room - mate and friend.
roles, Mis - treat - ing their mem - bers and bruis - ing their souls.
heart And makes clear the place where re - build - ing can start.
bud Of peace shared by all you have made from one blood.

Text: Thomas H. Troeger, b.1945, © 1986, Oxford University Press
Tune: FOUNDATION, 11 11 11 11; Funk's *Compilation of Genuine Church Music*, 1832; harm. by Richard Proulx, 1937–2010.
© 1975, GIA Publications, Inc.

750 Lord, Grant Us Grace to Know the Time

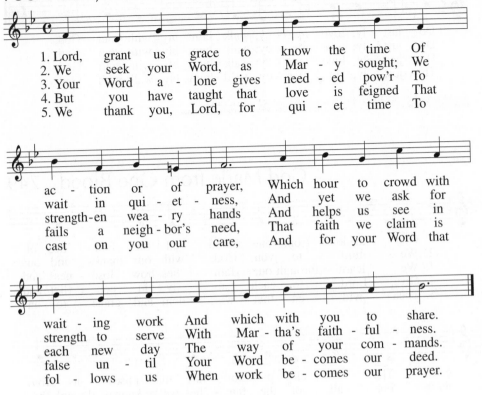

1. Lord, grant us grace to know the time Of
2. We seek your Word, as Mar-y sought; We
3. Your Word a-lone gives need-ed pow'r To
4. But you have taught that love is feigned That
5. We thank you, Lord, for qui-et time To

ac-tion or of prayer, Which hour to crowd with
wait in qui-et-ness, And yet we ask for
strength-en wea-ry hands And helps us see in
fails a neigh-bor's need, That faith we claim is
cast on you our care, And for your Word that

wait-ing work And which with you to share.
strength to serve With Mar-tha's faith-ful-ness.
each new day The way of your com-mands.
false un-til Your Word be-comes our deed.
fol-lows us When work be-comes our prayer.

Text: Herman G. Stuempfle, Jr.,1923–2007, © 1997, GIA Publications, Inc.
Tune: ST. ANNE, CM; attr. to William Croft, 1678–1727; harm. composite from 18th c. versions

751 Deliver Us, O Lord of Truth

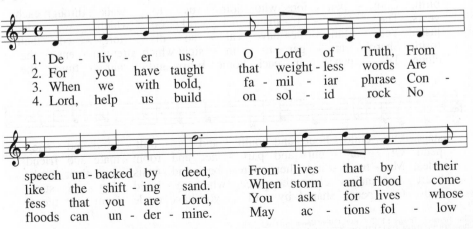

1. De-liv-er us, O Lord of Truth, From
2. For you have taught that weight-less words Are
3. When we with bold, fa-mil-iar phrase Con-
4. Lord, help us build on sol-id rock No

speech un-backed by deed, From lives that by their
like the shift-ing sand. When storm and flood come
fess that you are Lord, You ask for lives whose
floods can un-der-mine. May ac-tions fol-low

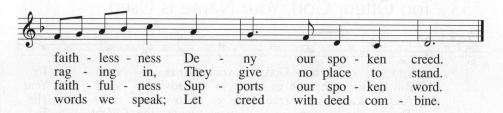

faith - less - ness De - ny our spo - ken creed.
rag - ing in, They give no place to stand.
faith - ful - ness Sup - ports our spo - ken word.
words we speak; Let creed with deed com - bine.

Text: Herman G. Stuempfle, Jr., 1923–2007, © 1997, GIA Publications, Inc.
Tune: DETROIT, CM; Supplement to *Kentucky Harmony*, 1820; harm. by Gerald H. Knight, 1908–1979, © The Royal School of Church Music

The Word of God   752

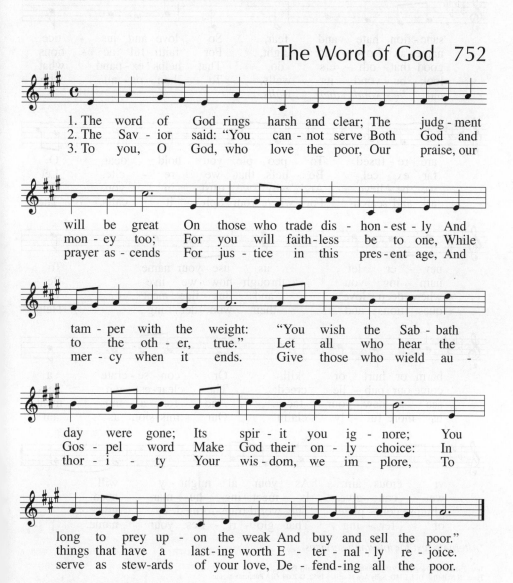

1. The word of God rings harsh and clear; The judg - ment
2. The Sav - ior said: "You can - not serve Both God and
3. To you, O God, who love the poor, Our praise, our

will be great On those who trade dis - hon - est - ly And
mon - ey too; For you will faith - less be to one, While
prayer as - cends For jus - tice in this pres - ent age, And

tam - per with the weight: "You wish the Sab - bath
to the oth - er, true." Let all who hear the
mer - cy when it ends. Give those who wield au -

day were gone; Its spir - it you ig - nore; You
Gos - pel word Make God their on - ly choice: In
thor - i - ty Your wis - dom, we im - plore, To

long to prey up - on the weak And buy and sell the poor."
things that have a last - ing worth E - ter - nal - ly re - joice.
serve as stew-ards of your love, De - fend - ing all the poor.

Text: Michael Forster, alt., © Kevin Mayhew Ltd.
Tune: ELLACOMBE, CMD; *Gesangbuch der Herzogl*, Wirtemberg, 1784

753 Too Often, God, Your Name Is Used

1. Too of - ten, God, your name is used To sanc - tion hate and fear, So love and jus - tice are re - fused To peo - ple you hold dear. O nev - er let us use your name To harm or hurt or kill, Or con - se - crate a vi - cious aim As your al - might - y will.

2. But move through us in deeds that spell Your name as Love and Light, For faith - ful ac - tions far ex - cel Be - liefs that we re - cite. Let nam - ing you through how we live Be - come our pub - lic creed: The clear - est wit - ness we can give Is meet - ing hu - man need.

3. And keep us read - y to re - ceive The good that oth - ers do, That helps ex - pand what we be - lieve And why we trust in you. For where deep love and jus - tice meet We see a - new your face And for a mo - ment glimpse com - plete The world trans - formed by grace.

4. That vi - sion o - pens wide the Church To look be - yond its walls, To hon - or all who ask and search For where your Spir - it calls. Their ques - tions and their won - der - ing Help us more ful - ly claim Our mis - sion as an of - fer - ing That glo - ri - fies your name.

4. *Thus syn - a - gogue and mosque and church Look out be - yond their walls,

*Alternate text for interfaith services.

Text: Thomas H. Troeger, b.1945, © 2009, Oxford University Press
Tune: IN NOMINE DEI, CMD; Sally Ann Morris, b.1952, © 2009, GIA Publications, Inc.

Alternate tune: KINGSFOLD

When We Are Living / Pues Si Vivimos 754

1. When we are liv - ing, we are in Christ
2. While we are liv - ing, we have fruit to
3. When sad or hurt - ing, when we feel a -
4. Through-out this wide world man - y peo - ple

1. *Pues si vi - vi - mos,* *pa - ra él vi -*
2. *En es - ta vi - da* *fru - tos hay que*
3. *En la tris - te - za* *y en el do -*
4. *En es - te mun - do* *por do - quier ha -*

Je - sus, And when we die,
bear. Good works of serv - ice:
lone, When glimps - ing beau - ty,
mourn, Seek-ing con - so - la - tion

vi - mos; *Y si mo - ri - mos,*
dar, *Y bue - nas o - bras*
lor, *En la be - lle - za*
brá *Gen - te que llo - ra*

we re - main in him. Both in our
these are ours to share. If we are
and when love is known: Both in our
for their sor - rows borne; And when we

pa - ra él mo - ri - mos. *Se - a que vi -*
he - mos de_o - fren - dar. *Se - a ya que*
y en el a - mor, *Se - a que su -*
y sin con - so - lar. *Se - a que_a - yu -*

liv - ing, and in our dy - ing,
giv - ing or are re - ceiv - ing,
suf - f'ring and our re - joic - ing,
help them or when we feed them,

va - mos *o que mu - ra - mos,*
de - mos *o que re - ci - ba - mos,*
fra - mos *o que go - ce - mos,*
de - mos *o que_a - li - men - te - mos,*

We are the Lord's, we be - long to him.
So - mos del Se - ñor, *so - mos del Se - ñor.*

Text: Verse 1, Romans 14:8; traditional Mexican; vss. 2–4, Roberto Escamilla, b.1931, © 1983, Abingdon Press; tr. by Ronald F. Krisman, b.1946,
© 2004, Abingdon Press
Tune: SOMOS DEL SEÑOR, Irregular; traditional Mexican; arr. by Ronald F. Krisman, b.1946, © 2004, GIA Publications, Inc.

755　Lord, Make Us Servants of Your Peace

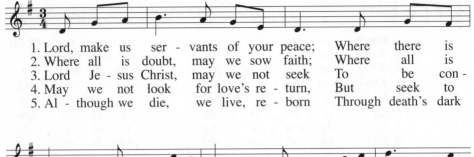

1. Lord, make us ser - vants of your peace; Where there is
2. Where all is doubt, may we sow faith; Where all is
3. Lord Je - sus Christ, may we not seek To be con -
4. May we not look for love's re - turn, But seek to
5. Al - though we die, we live, re - born Through death's dark

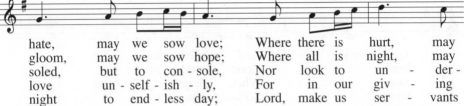

hate, may we sow love; Where there is hurt, may
gloom, may we sow hope; Where all is night, may
soled, but to con - sole, Nor look to un - der -
love un - self - ish - ly, For in our giv - ing
night to end - less day; Lord, make us ser - vants

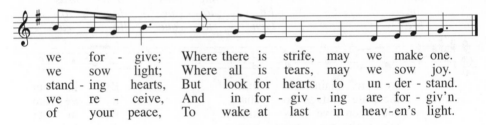

we for - give; Where there is strife, may we make one.
we sow light; Where all is tears, may we sow joy.
stand - ing hearts, But look for hearts to un - der - stand.
we re - ceive, And in for - giv - ing are for - giv'n.
of your peace, To wake at last in heav - en's light.

Text: Based on a prayer attrib. to St. Francis of Assisi; James Quinn, SJ, 1919–2010, © 1994, Used by permission of Selah Publishing Co., Inc.
Tune: O WALY WALY, LM; English melody; harm. by Martin West, b.1929, © 1983, Hope Publishing Comapny

756　The Virtue of Humility

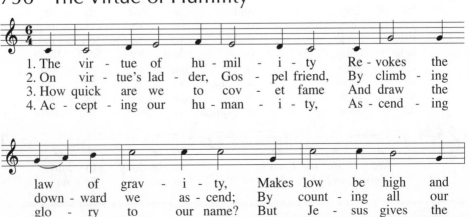

1. The vir - tue of hu - mil - i - ty Re - vokes the
2. On vir - tue's lad - der, Gos - pel friend, By climb - ing
3. How quick are we to cov - et fame And draw the
4. Ac - cept - ing our hu - man - i - ty, As - cend - ing

law of grav - i - ty, Makes low be high and
down - ward we as - cend; By count - ing all our
glo - ry to our name? But Je - sus gives the
by hu - mil - i - ty, From Je - sus let us

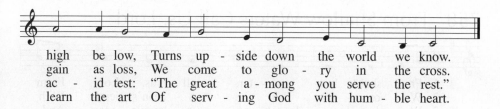

high be low, Turns up - side down the world we know.
gain as loss, We come to glo - ry in the cross.
ac - id test: "The great a - mong you serve the rest."
learn the art Of serv - ing God with hum - ble heart.

Text: Delores Dufner, OSB, b.1939, © 1995, 1996, GIA Publications, Inc.
Tune: PUER NOBIS, LM; adapt. by Michael Praetorius, 1571–1621

Two People Came to Church to Pray   757

1. Two peo - ple came to church to pray, As -
2. Two peo - ple came to church to pray, As -
3. Two peo - ple came to church to pray, And

sured that God would hear. The first had man - y
sured that God would hear. The sec - ond prayed a
God knew ev - 'ry thought; But one was jus - ti -

words to say, And spoke them, loud and clear: "I
dif - f'rent way, Both hum - ble and sin - cere: "O
fied that day, The oth - er one was not. When

thank you, God, and give you praise That
God, be mer - ci - ful to me! For -
what we pray be - comes a boast, We

I am blessed to be A mod - el of your
give your sin - ful child." By ut - ter - ing this
win no great re - ward; For what our God de -

ho - ly ways For all who care to see."
sim - ple plea, A soul was rec - on - ciled.
sires the most Is hum - ble hearts out - poured.

Text: Adam M. L. Tice, b.1979, © 2008, GIA Publications, Inc.
Tune: FOREST GREEN, CMD; English melody; harm. by Ralph Vaughan Williams, 1872–1958

758 From Shallow Waters Call Us, Lord

1. From shal - low wa - ters call us, Lord, From
2. We can - not fish the o - cean's depths With
3. We dare to launch on un - known seas And
4. For nei - ther fear nor scorn nor death Could

safe - ty near the shore, And bid us launch up -
nets shrunk small by fear. We need the gift of
cast our nets a - broad, For you have bid us
turn you back to land. You knew no storms could

on the depths Where faith is test - ed more. Let
great - er faith When we your sum - mons hear. And,
grasp by faith The prom - is - es of God. O
car - ry you Be - yond your Fa - ther's hand. Your

not past fail - ures hope de - stroy Nor
if we plead un - wor - thi - ness For
Christ, you crossed the same wide seas You
cross seemed but a frag - ile craft Up -

cau - tion par - a - lyze, But help us fol - low
what your call de - mands, Then may we trust you'll
send us now to sail; Be pres - ent when we
on an an - gry sea, Till Eas - ter dawn brought

where you lead And wait for Love's sur - prise.
cleanse and calm Our soiled, un - stead - y hands.
reach the depths With strength that does not fail!
light and peace Through Love that sets us free!

Text: Herman G. Stuempfle, Jr., 1923–2007, © 2006, GIA Publications, Inc.
Tune: KINGSFOLD, CMD; English melody; harm. by Ralph Vaughan Williams, 1872–1958

Unless a Grain of Wheat 759

Refrain

Un - less a grain of wheat shall fall up -
on the ground and die, it re - mains but a
sin - gle grain with no life.

Verses

1. ⁂ If we have died with him, then we shall
2. If an - y - one serves me, then they must
3. ⁂ ⁂ Make your home in me as I make
4. ⁂ If you re - main in me and my word
5. ⁂ ⁂ Those who love me are loved by my
6. ⁂ ⁂ Peace I leave with you, my peace I

live with him; if we hold firm, we shall
fol - low me; where - ev - er I am, my
mine in you; those who re - main in me
lives in you, then you will be my dis -
Fa - ther; we shall be with them and
give to you; peace which the world can - not

D.C.

reign with him.
ser - vants will be.
bear much fruit.
ci - ples.
dwell in them.
give is my gift.

Text: John 12:24; Bernadette Farrell, b.1957
Tune: Bernadette Farrell, b.1957
© 1983, Bernadette Farrell. Published by OCP.

760 Lord, When You Came / Pescador de Hombres

Verses

1. Lord, when you came to the sea - shore
2. Lord, you knew what my boat car - ried:
3. Lord, have you need of my la - bor,
4. Lord, send me where you would have me,

1. Tú has ve - ni - do_a la_o - ri - lla,
2. Tú sa - bes bien lo que ten - go;
3. Tú ne - ce - si - tas mis ma - nos,
4. Tú, pes - ca - dor de_o - tros la - gos,

You weren't seek - ing the wise or the wealth - y,
Nei - ther mon - ey nor weap - ons for fight - ing,
Hands for serv - ice, a heart made for lov - ing,
To a vil - lage, or heart of the cit - y;

No_has bus - ca - do ni_a sa - bios, ni_a ri - cos;
En mi bar - ca no_hay o - ro ni_es - pa - das,
Mi can - san - cio que_a o - tros des - can - se,
an - sia_e - ter - na de al - mas que_es-pe - ran,

But on - ly ask - ing that I might fol - low.
But nets for fish - ing, my dai - ly la - bor.
My arms for lift - ing the poor and bro - ken?
I will re-mem - ber that you are with me.

Tan só - lo quie - res que yo te si - ga.
Tan só - lo re - des y mi tra - ba - jo.
A - mor que quie - ra se - guir a - man - do.
A - mi - go bue - no, que_a - sí me lla - mas.

Refrain

O Lord, in my eyes you were gaz - ing,
Se - ñor, me_has mi - ra - do_a los o - jos,

Kind-ly smil - ing, my name you were
son - ri - en - do has di - cho mi

say - ing; All I treas - ured,
nom - bre; En la a - re - na

I have left on the sand there; Close to
he de - ja - do mi bar - ca; Jun - to a

you, I will find oth - er seas.
ti bus - ca - ré o - tro mar.

Text: *Pescador de Hombres,* Cesáreo Gabaráin, 1936–1991, © 1979, published by OCP; tr. by Willard F. Jabusch, b.1930, © 1982, administered by OCP
Tune: PESCADOR DE HOMBRES, 8 10 10 with refrain; Cesáreo Gabaráin, 1936–1991, © 1979, published by OCP; acc. by Diana Kodner, b.1957

Take Up Your Cross 761

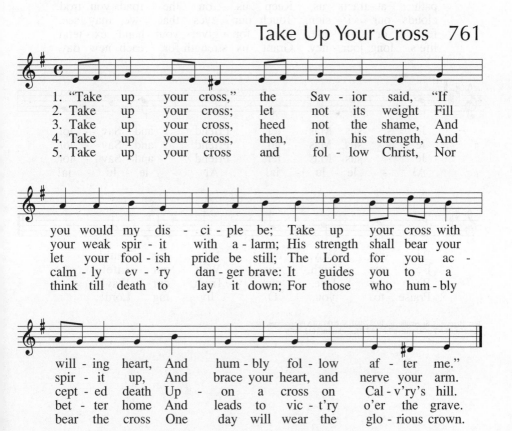

1. "Take up your cross," the Sav - ior said, "If
2. Take up your cross; let not its weight Fill
3. Take up your cross, heed not the shame, And
4. Take up your cross, then, in his strength, And
5. Take up your cross and fol - low Christ, Nor

you would my dis - ci - ple be; Take up your cross with
your weak spir - it with a - larm; His strength shall bear your
let your fool - ish pride be still; The Lord for you ac -
calm - ly ev - 'ry dan - ger brave: It guides you to a
think till death to lay it down; For those who hum - bly

will - ing heart, And hum - bly fol - low af - ter me."
spir - it up, And brace your heart, and nerve your arm.
cept - ed death Up - on a cross on Cal - v'ry's hill.
bet - ter home And leads to vic - t'ry o'er the grave.
bear the cross One day will wear the glo - rious crown.

Text: Charles W. Everest, 1814–1877, alt.
Tune: ERHALT UNS HERR, LM; Klug's *Geistliche Lieder,* 1543; harm. by J. S. Bach, 1685–1750

762 Christ, the Way We're Called to Follow

1. Christ, the Way we're called to fol - low,
2. Christ, the Truth be - yond all knowl - edge,
3. Christ, the Life so full, so lov - ing,
4. Christ, our Mas - ter, Friend, and Sav - ior,

Christ, the Way that leads to God, When some oth - er
Christ, the Truth that sets us free, When con - fu - sion
Christ, the Life that nev - er ends, When we fail or
Christ, the Life, the Truth, the Way, Guide us through our

path at - tracts us, Keep us on the road you trod.
clouds our vi - sion, Touch our eyes that we may see.
fear or stum - ble, Lord, for - give; your hand ex - tend.
life's long jour - ney, Grant us strength for each new day.

Je - sus, Mas - ter, Friend and Sav - ior,
Je - sus, Mas - ter, Friend and Sav - ior,
Je - sus, Mas - ter, Friend and Sav - ior,
Al - le - lu - ia! Al - le - lu - ia!

Be our Way, our Life, our Truth!
Be our Truth, our Way, our Life!
Be our Life, our Truth, our Way!
Praise to you, O liv - ing Lord!

Text: Herman G. Stuempfle, Jr., 1923–2007, © 2006, GIA Publications, Inc.
Tune: REGENT SQUARE, 8 7 8 7 8 7; Henry Smart, 1813–1879

We Have Been Told 763

Refrain

We have been told, we've seen his face and
heard his voice a - live in our hearts:
"Live in my love with all your heart;
as the Fa - ther has loved me, so I have loved
you."

Verse 1

1. "I am the vine, you are the branch - es, and
all who live in me will bear great fruit."

D.C.

Verses 2, 3

2. "You are my friends, if you keep my com - mands;
3. "No great - er love is there than this: to

no long - er slaves, I call you friends."
lay down one's life for a friend."

D.C.

Text: David Haas, b.1957.
Tune: David Haas, b.1957; vocal arr. by David Haas, Marty Haugen, b.1950

764 Now We Remain

Refrain

We hold the death of the Lord deep in our hearts. Liv-ing, now we re-main with Je - sus, the Christ.

Verses

1. Once we were peo - ple a - fraid, lost in the night. Then by your cross we were saved— Dead be - came liv - ing, Life from your giv - ing.
2. Some-thing which we have known, some-thing we've touched, What we have seen with our eyes; This we have heard: Life - giv - ing Word.
3. He chose to give of him - self, be - came our bread: Bro - ken, that we might live— Love be - yond love, Pain for our pain.
4. We are the pres - ence of God; this is our call: Now to be - come bread and wine— Food for the hun - gry, Life for the wea - ry.

For to live with the

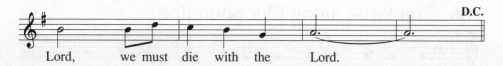

Lord, we must die with the Lord.

Text: Corinthians, 1 John, 2 Timothy; David Haas, b.1957
Tune: David Haas, b.1957
© 1983, GIA Publications, Inc.

The Baptist Bore Witness 765

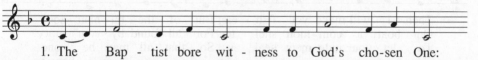

1. The Bap - tist bore wit - ness to God's cho-sen One:
2. This Christ now in - vites us, the Church here to - day,
3. Be - liev - ers, called forth to make peace and u - nite,

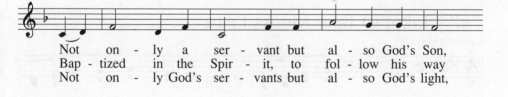

Not on - ly a ser - vant but al - so God's Son,
Bap - tized in the Spir - it, to fol - low his way
Not on - ly God's ser - vants but al - so God's light,

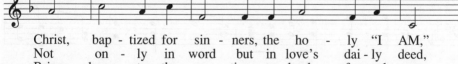

Christ, bap - tized for sin - ners, the ho - ly "I AM,"
Not on - ly in word but in love's dai - ly deed,
Bring hope to the na - tions, to lands far and near,

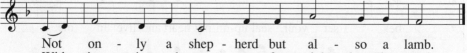

Not on - ly a shep - herd but al - so a lamb.
With jus - tice and mer - cy for neigh - bors in need.
Pro - claim - ing sal - va - tion: "The king - dom is here!"

Text: Delores Dufner, OSB, b.1939, © 2011, GIA Publications, Inc.
Tune: FOUNDATION, 11 11 11 11; Funk's *Compilation of Genuine Church Music*, 1832; harm. by Richard Proulx, 1937–2010, © 1975,
  GIA Publications, Inc.

766 You Walk along Our Shoreline

1. You walk a - long our shore-line, Where land meets un - known sea.
2. You call us, Christ, to gath - er The peo - ple of the earth.
3. We cast our net, O Je - sus; We cry the king-dom's name;

We hear your voice of pow - er, "Now come and fol - low me.
We can - not fish for on - ly Those lives we think have worth.
We work for love and jus - tice; We learn to hope through pain.

And if you still will fol - low Through storm and wave and shoal,
We spread your net of gos - pel A - cross the wa - ter's face,
You call us, Lord, to gath - er God's daugh-ters and God's sons,

Then I will make you fish - ers, But of the hu - man soul."
Our boat a com - mon shel - ter For all found by your grace.
To let your judg-ment heal us So that all may be one.

Text: Sylvia G. Dunstan, 1955–1993, © 1991, GIA Publications, Inc.
Tune: AURELIA, 7 6 7 6 D; Samuel S. Wesley, 1810–1876

767 Take, O Take Me As I Am

Ostinato Refrain

Take, O take me as I am; sum - mon out what I shall

be; set your seal up-on my heart and live in me.

Text: John L. Bell, b.1949
Tune: John L. Bell, b.1949
© 1995, Iona Community, GIA Publications, Inc., agent

O Christ, Who Called the Twelve 768

1. O Christ, who called the Twelve To rise and fol-low you, For-sak-ing old, fa-mil-iar ways For ven-tures bold and new: Grant us to hear your call To risk se-cu-ri-ty And, bound in heart and will to you, Find per-fect lib-er-ty.

2. O Christ, who taught the Twelve The truth for a-ges sealed, Whose words and works a-wak-ened faith, The ways of God re-vealed: In-struct us now, we pray, By your em-pow'r-ing Word. True teach-er, be for all who seek Their light, their life, their Lord.

3. O Christ, who led the Twelve A-mong the des-o-late And broke as bread of life for all Your love com-pas-sion-ate: Lead us a-long the ways Where hope has near-ly died And help us climb the lone-ly hills Where love is cru-ci-fied.

4. O Christ, who sent the Twelve On roads they'd nev-er trod To serve, to suf-fer, teach, pro-claim The near-er reign of God: Send us on ways where faith Tran-scends ti-mid-i-ty, Where love in-forms and hope sus-tains Both life and min-is-try.

5. O Christ, the a-pos-tles' Lord, The mar-tyrs' strength and song, The cru-ci-fied and ris-en king To whom the saints be-long: Though gen-er-a-tions pass, Our trib-ute still we bring, Our hymns a sac-ri-fice of praise, Our lives an of-fer-ing.

Text: Herman G. Stuempfle, Jr., 1923–2007, © 1993, GIA Publications, Inc.
Tune: TERRA BEATA, SMD; English melody; adapt. by Franklin L. Sheppard, 1852–1930

769 Not Alone, but Two by Two

1. Not a - lone, but two by two, Je - sus sent dis -
2. Have we still such dar - ing hearts? Can we claim their
3. Ho - ly Spir - it, breathe through us With your u - ni -

ci - ples out: Yoked to share their grow - ing faith,
faith and nerve? Do we tru - ly love the world
fy - ing might; Kin - dle cleans - ing, melt - ing flames

Spurred by cour - age, slowed by doubt. Tak - ing but a
Je - sus calls for us to serve? Can we plant a -
Till our frac - tured wills u - nite. Bind our hearts in

walk - ing stick, Mon - ey - less and san - dal - shod,
gain the seed Sown in mu - tual min - is - try,
mu - tual love, Par - a - dox that sets self free;

Forth they went to preach and heal,
Pat - terned on a life of faith
Let our com - mon wit - ness show

Trust - ing all their needs to God.
Root - ed in com - mu - ni - ty?
God's shared life in Trin - i - ty.

Text: Carl P. Daw, Jr., b.1944, © 1994, Hope Publishing Company
Tune: ABERYSTWYTH, 7 7 7 7 D; Joseph Parry, 1841–1903

Fishermen Are Sailing Homeward   770

1. Fish - er - men are sail - ing home - ward In the dawn's un -
2. Ris - en Je - sus, still you meet us When our la - bor
3. Stum - bl'ing Pe - ter, who de - nied him, Meets his Lord up -
4. Ris - en Je - sus, in your mer - cy, Still you call us

cer - tain light. Nets are emp - ty, hearts dis - cour - aged
seems in vain. Still your call con - tests our fail - ures:
on the shore. "Do you love me," Je - sus asks him,
each by name, In bap - tis - mal wa - ters wash us,

From a long and fu - tile night.
"Cast your emp - ty nets a - gain!"
"You whose heart with shame is sore?"
Cleans - ing us from sin and shame.

Char - coal glows a - long the shore - line
Grant us strength to do your bid - ding,
Pe - ter pledg - es his de - vo - tion,
Still you sum - mon us to serve you,

Where a Stran - ger's form is seen. Through the morn - ing
Faith to fol - low where you lead. Then a - wake our
Vows his love is strong and deep; Then the Lord of
Ves - sels made of com - mon clay. Shape us till we

mist he calls them: "Cast your emp - ty nets a - gain."
hearts to won - der When your gifts our hopes ex - ceed!
Love re - stores him: "Be my shep - herd; feed my sheep!"
bear your im - age In the tasks of each new day!

Text: Herman G. Stuempfle, Jr., 1923–2007, © 2006, GIA Publications, Inc.
Tune: HYMN TO JOY, 8 7 8 7 D; arr. from Ludwig van Beethoven, 1770–1827, by Edward Hodges, 1796–1867

771 Who Follows Jesus?

1. Who fol - lows Je - sus? Who will hear his teach-ing?
2. We are ap - point-ed, we who need his heal - ing.
3. Freed by this call - ing, this is our thanks-giv - ing:
4. Christ con - quered dy - ing, and his liv - ing frees us

Is it the per - fect that the Word is reach-ing?
We need the mes - sage which he is re - veal - ing.
We sing the mys - t'ry— Christ, who died, is liv - ing!
If we will choose him, go - ing where he leads us.

Is it the health - y that he has a - noint-ed?
Though far from per - fect, we are called by Je - sus.
There, in the cav - ern where our God was ly - ing,
Christ is the vic - t'ry! Threats of death are hol - low.

Who is ap - point - ed?
His call - ing frees us.
Christ con - quered dy - ing.
So we will fol - low.

Text: Adam M. L. Tice, b.1979, © 2009, GIA Publications, Inc.
Tune: MIGHTY SAVIOR, 11 11 11 5; David Hurd, b.1950, © 1985, GIA Publications, Inc.

Called to Labor in God's Vineyard 772

1. Called to la-bor in God's vine-yard, Ea-ger to ac-
2. Called to la-bor in God's vine-yard, Not a-lone, but
3. Called to la-bor in God's vine-yard, Help us, Lord, in

cept the task, Us-ing ev-'ry skill and tal-ent,
joined as one, Shar-ing com-mon goals and val-ues,
all we do. As the vines are heav-y-lad-en,

Do-ing all that God would ask, May we give our-
Striv-ing till the task is done, May we work with
Send more work-ers called by you. May our work bear

selves com-plete-ly To the work that is at hand,
one an-oth-er In a just and hon-est way,
fruit e-ter-nal And our fer-vor nev-er cease,

Of-fer-ing our will-ing serv-ice
Wheth-er hired at dawn or sun-set,
Till at last, the har-vest gath-ered,

As the stew-ards of the land.
Not ex-pect-ing great-er pay.
We may rest and know your peace.

Text: James J. Chepponis, b.1956, © 2011, GIA Publications, Inc.
Tune: IN BABILONE, 8 7 8 7 D; *Oude en Nieuwe Hollantse Boerenlieties en Contredansen,* c.1710

773 The Summons

1. Will you come and fol - low me If I but call your name? Will you go where you don't know And nev - er be the same? Will you let my love be shown, Will you let my name be known, Will you let my life be grown In you and you in me?

2. Will you leave your - self be - hind If I but call your name? Will you care for cruel and kind And nev - er be the same? Will you risk the hos - tile stare Should your life at - tract or scare? Will you let me an - swer prayer In you and you in me?

3. Will you let the blind - ed see If I but call your name? Will you set the pris - 'ners free And nev - er be the same? Will you kiss the lep - er clean, And do such as this un - seen, Will you ad - mit to what I mean In you and you in me?

4. Will you love the "you" you hide If I but call your name? Will you quell the fear in - side And nev - er be the same? Will you use the faith you've found To re - shape the world a - round, Through my sight and touch and sound In you and you in me?

5. Lord, your sum - mons ech - oes true When you but call my name. Let me turn and fol - low you And nev - er be the same. In your com - pa - ny I'll go Where your love and foot - steps show. Thus I'll move and live and grow In you and you in me.

Text: John L. Bell, b.1949, © 1987, Iona Community, GIA Publications, Inc., agent
Tune: KELVINGROVE, 7 6 7 6 777 6; Scottish melody; arr. by John L. Bell, b.1949, © 1987, Iona Community, GIA Publications, Inc., agent

Two Fishermen 774

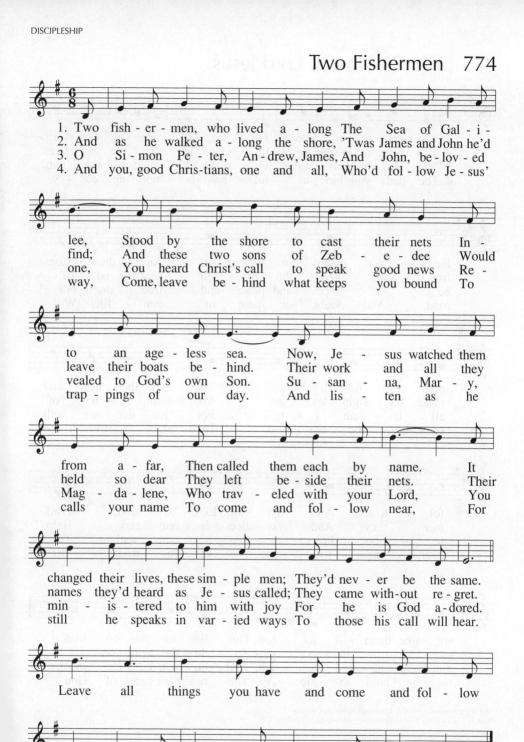

1. Two fish-er-men, who lived a-long The Sea of Gal-i-
2. And as he walked a-long the shore, 'Twas James and John he'd
3. O Si-mon Pe-ter, An-drew, James, And John, be-lov-ed
4. And you, good Chris-tians, one and all, Who'd fol-low Je-sus'

lee, Stood by the shore to cast their nets In-
find; And these two sons of Zeb-e-dee Would
one, You heard Christ's call to speak good news Re-
way, Come, leave be-hind what keeps you bound To

to an age-less sea. Now, Je-sus watched them
leave their boats be-hind. Their work and all they
vealed to God's own Son. Su-san-na, Mar-y,
trap-pings of our day. And lis-ten as he

from a-far, Then called them each by name. It
held so dear They left be-side their nets. Their
Mag-da-lene, Who trav-eled with your Lord, You
calls your name To come and fol-low near, For

changed their lives, these sim-ple men; They'd nev-er be the same.
names they'd heard as Je-sus called; They came with-out re-gret.
min-is-tered to him with joy For he is God a-dored.
still he speaks in var-ied ways To those his call will hear.

Leave all things you have and come and fol-low

me, and come and fol-low me.

775 You Call to Us, Lord Jesus

1. You call to us, Lord Je - sus, As once in Gal - i -
2. You came to preach de - liv - 'rance, To set the cap - tives
3. You sum - mon us to vi - sions Of what this world can
4. The path you bid us fol - low Is not an eas - y

lee You called to James and An - drew, "Come
free, To heal the bro - ken - heart - ed, To
be, Of hope and peace and free - dom For
road, And doubt or pain or con - flict Will

now and fol - low me." They left their nets and
make the sight - less see. Your min - is - try of
all hu - man - i - ty. For jus - tice we will
some - times be our load. Lord, grant us strength and

fol - lowed, And did not look be - hind; Lord,
mer - cy And jus - tice is our task; Help
la - bor For ev - 'ry hu - man soul Till
cour - age To walk the way you trod, Till

we like them will fol - low, Our life in you to find.
us like true dis - ci - ples To do the work you ask.
greed and ha - tred van - ish, And hu - man-kind is whole.
we be - hold in glo - ry The ra - diant face of God.

Text: Joy F. Patterson, b.1931, © 1994, Hope Publishing Company
Tune: ELLACOMBE, 7 6 7 6 D; *Gesangbuch der Herzogl,* Wirtemberg, 1784

The Love of the Lord 776

1. All that I count - ed as gain
2. Rich - es and hon - ors will fade,
3. Sil - ver and gold have I none,
4. Faith is the wealth I pos - sess

Now I con - sid - er as loss,
Earth - ly de - light dis - ap - pear,
No land to count as my home, Yet
Find - ing its source in my God:

Emp - ty and worth - less to me In the
Fade like the grass of the field In the
wealth be - yond meas - ure I own In the
Faith in the prom - ise of Christ Is my

1., 3.
light of the love of the Lord.
light of the love of the Lord.

2., 4.
light of the love of the Lord.
life and my love of the Lord.

What more could bring us hope than to know the pow'r of his

life? What more could bring us peace than to

share in his suf-f'ring and death? What more could be our

fi - nal wish than to live in the love of the Lord?

Text: Philippians 3:8–14; Michael Joncas, b.1951
Tune: CARITAS DOMINI, 7 7 7 9 D with refrain; Michael Joncas, b.1951
© 1988, GIA Publications, Inc.

777 I Danced in the Morning

1. I danced in the morn-ing when the world was be-gun, And I
2. I danced for the scribe and the phar - i - see, But
3. I danced on the Sab-bath and I cured the lame: The
4. I danced on a Fri - day when the sky turned black; It's
5. They cut me down and I leapt up high;

danced in the moon and the stars and the sun, And I
they would not dance, and they would-n't fol - low me; I
ho - ly peo - ple said it was a shame. They
hard to dance with the dev - il on your back. They
I am the life that - 'll nev - er, nev - er die; I'll

came down from heav - en and I danced on the earth; At
danced for the fish - er - men, for James and John; They
whipped and they stripped and they hung me high, And
bur - ied my bod - y and they thought I'd gone; But
live in you if you'll live in me:

Beth - le - hem I had my birth.
came with me and the dance went on.
left me there on a Cross to die.
I am the dance and I still go on.
I am the Lord of the Dance, said he.

Dance, then, wher - ev - er you may be; I am the

Lord of the Dance, said he, And I'll lead you all, wher-

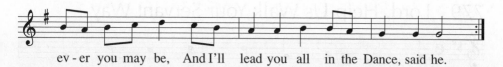

ev - er you may be, And I'll lead you all in the Dance, said he.

Text: Sydney Carter, 1915–2004, © 1963, Stainer & Bell, Ltd., London, England. (Admin. by Hope Publishing Company)
Tune: LORD OF THE DANCE, Irregular with refrain; adapted from a traditional Shaker melody by Sydney Carter, 1915–2004, © 1963,
Stainer & Bell, Ltd., London, England. (Admin. by Hope Publishing Company)

For God Risk Everything! 778

1. For God risk ev - 'ry - thing! Since ev - 'ry - thing we
2. How shriv - eled, Lord, the soul That grips what it re -
3. From hearts that hide and hoard The treas - ures that you

own, Our laugh - ter, tears, the songs we sing, Our
ceives And dares not free its anx - ious hold But
send Free us, till we by faith, O Lord, Shall

breath, our flesh and bone, Are no more ours to
fool - ish - ly be - lieves That you are too se -
act as you in - tend, Till we risk all for

keep Than wind that rush - es by Or dreams that flick - er
vere To par - don an - y loss, For - get - ting how your
you, Risk ev - 'ry - thing you give, And risk - ing, learn what

in our sleep Or clouds that fade to sky.
son made clear For - give - ness on the cross.
Je - sus knew: By risk - ing all, we live.

Text: Thomas H. Troeger, b.1945, © 2002, Oxford University Press
Tune: TERRA BEATA, SMD; English melody; adapt. by Franklin L. Sheppard, 1852–1930

779 Lord, Help Us Walk Your Servant Way

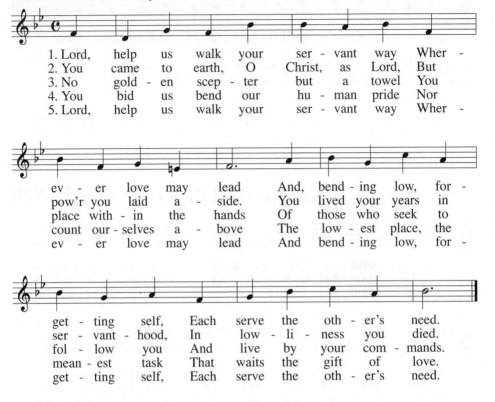

1. Lord, help us walk your ser - vant way Wher -
2. You came to earth, O Christ, as Lord, But
3. No gold - en scep - ter but a towel You
4. You bid us bend our hu - man pride Nor
5. Lord, help us walk your ser - vant way Wher -

ev - er love may lead And, bend - ing low, for -
pow'r you laid a - side. You lived your years in
place with - in the hands Of those who seek to
count our - selves a - bove The low - est place, the
ev - er love may lead And bend - ing low, for -

get - ting self, Each serve the oth - er's need.
ser - vant - hood, In low - li - ness you died.
fol - low you And live by your com - mands.
mean - est task That waits the gift of love.
get - ting self, Each serve the oth - er's need.

Text: Herman G. Stuempfle, Jr., 1923–2007, © 1997, GIA Publications, Inc.
Tune: ST. ANNE, CM; attr. to William Croft, 1678–1727; harm. composite from 18th c. versions

780 Lord, Whose Love in Humble Service

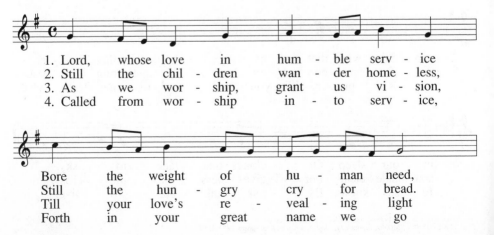

1. Lord, whose love in hum - ble serv - ice
2. Still the chil - dren wan - der home - less,
3. As we wor - ship, grant us vi - sion,
4. Called from wor - ship in - to serv - ice,

Bore the weight of hu - man need,
Still the hun - gry cry for bread.
Till your love's re - veal - ing light
Forth in your great name we go

Who up - on the cross, for - sak - en,
Still the cap - tives long for free - dom,
In its height and depth and great - ness
To the child, the youth, the a - ged,

Of - fered mer - cy's per - fect deed:
Still in grief we mourn our dead.
Dawns up - on our hu - man sight,
Love in liv - ing deeds to show.

We, your ser - vants, bring the wor - ship
As you, Lord, in deep com - pas - sion,
Mak - ing known the needs and bur - dens
Hope and health, good - will and com - fort,

Not of voice a - lone, but heart,
Healed the sick and freed the soul,
Your com - pas - sion bids us bear,
Coun - sel, aid, and peace we give

Con - se - crat - ing to your pur - pose
Use the love your Spir - it kin - dles
Stir - ring us to faith - ful serv - ice,
That your chil - dren, Lord, in free - dom,

Ev - 'ry gift that you im - part.
Still to save and make us whole.
Your a - bun - dant life to share.
May your mer - cy know, and live.

Text: Albert F. Bayly, 1901–1984, alt., © 1988, Oxford University Press
Tune: IN BABILONE, 8 7 8 7 D; *Oude en Nieuwe Hollantse Boerenlieties en Contredansen*, c.1710

781 God Has Chosen Me

Verses

1. God has cho-sen me, God has cho-sen me To
2. God has cho-sen me, God has cho-sen me To
3. God is call-ing me, God is call-ing me In

bring good news to the poor. God has cho-sen me,
set a-light a new fire. God has cho-sen me,
all whose cry is un-heard. God is call-ing me,

God has cho-sen me To bring new sight to those
God has cho-sen me To bring to birth a new
God is call-ing me To raise up the voice with no

search-ing for light: God has cho-sen me, cho-sen me:
king-dom on earth: God has cho-sen me, cho-sen me:
pow-er or choice: God is call-ing me, call-ing me:

Refrain

And to tell the world that God's king-dom is near, To re-

move op-pres-sion and break down fear, Yes, God's time is near,

God's time is near, God's time is near, God's time is near.

Text: Bernadette Farrell, b.1957
Tune: Bernadette Farrell, b.1957
© 1990, Bernadette Farrell. Published by OCP.

God the Spirit, Guide and Guardian   782

1. God the Spir - it, guide and guard - ian, Wind-sped
2. Christ our Sav - ior, Sov - 'reign, Shep - herd, Word-made-
3. Great Cre - a - tor, Life - be - stow - er, Truth be -
4. Tri - une God, mys - te - rious Be - ing, Un - di -

flame and hov - 'ring dove, Breath of life and voice of
flesh, Love cru - ci - fied, Teach-er, heal - er, suf - f'ring
yond all thought's re - call, Fount of wis - dom, womb of
vid - ed and di - verse, Deep-er than our minds can

proph - ets, Sign of bless - ing, pow'r of love:
Ser - vant, Friend of sin - ners, foe of pride:
mer - cy, Giv - ing and for - giv - ing all:
fath - om, Great - er than our creeds re - hearse:

Give to those who lead your peo - ple Fresh a -
In your tend - ing may your ser - vants Learn and
As you know our strength and weak - ness, So may
Help us in our var - ied call - ings Your full

noint - ing of your grace; Send them forth as bold a -
live a shep - herd's care; Grant them cour - age and com -
those the Church ex - alts O - ver - see her life stead -
im - age to pro - claim, That our min - is - tries u -

pos - tles To your Church in ev - 'ry place.
pas - sion Shown through word and deed and prayer.
fast - ly Yet not o - ver - look her faults.
nit - ing May give glo - ry to your Name.

Text: Carl P. Daw, Jr., b.1944, © 1989, Hope Publishing Company
Tune: SHALLOWFORD, 8 7 8 7 D; Sally Ann Morris, b.1952, © 1998, GIA Publications, Inc.

Alternate tune: HYMN TO JOY

783 Here I Am, Lord

Verses

1. I, the Lord of sea and sky, I have heard my
2. I, the Lord of snow and rain, I have borne my
3. I, the Lord of wind and flame, I will tend the

peo - ple cry. All who dwell in dark and sin
peo - ple's pain. I have wept for love of them.
poor and lame. I will set a feast for them.

My hand will save. I, who made the
They turn a - way. I will break their
My hand will save. Fin - est bread I

stars of night, I will make their dark - ness bright.
hearts of stone, Give them hearts for love a - lone.
will pro - vide Till their hearts be sat - is - fied.

Who will bear my light to them? Whom shall I send?
I will speak my word to them. Whom shall I send?
I will give my life to them. Whom shall I send?

Refrain

Here I am, Lord. Is it I, Lord? I have heard you

call - ing in the night. I will go, Lord, if you

lead me. I will hold your peo - ple in my heart.

Text: Isaiah 6; Dan Schutte, b.1947
Tune: HERE I AM, LORD, 77 7 4 D with refrain; Dan Schutte, b.1947; arr. by Michael Pope, SJ, and John Weissrock
© 1981, OCP

You Are Called to Tell the Story 784

1. You are called to tell the sto - ry, Pass - ing words of
2. You are called to teach the rhy - thm Of the dance that
3. You are called to set the ta - ble, Bless - ing bread as
4. May the One whose love is broad - er Than the meas - ure

life a - long, Then to blend your voice with oth - ers
nev - er ends, Then to move with - in the cir - cle,
Je - sus blessed, Then to come with thirst and hun - ger,
of all space Give us words to sing the sto - ry,

As you sing the sa - cred song. Christ be known in
Hand in hand with strang - ers, friends. Christ be known in
Need - ing care like all the rest. Christ be known in
Move a - mong us in this place. Christ be known in

all our sing - ing, Fill - ing all with songs of
all our danc - ing, Touch - ing all with hands of
all our shar - ing, Feed - ing all with signs of
all our liv - ing, Fill - ing all with gifts of

love, Fill - ing all with songs of love.
love, Touch - ing all with hands of love.
love, Feed - ing all with signs of love.
love, Fill - ing all with gifts of love.

Text: Ruth Duck, b.1947, © 1992, GIA Publications, Inc.
Tune: CWM RHONDDA, 8 7 8 7 8 77; John Hughes, 1873–1932

785 The Church of Christ, in Every Age

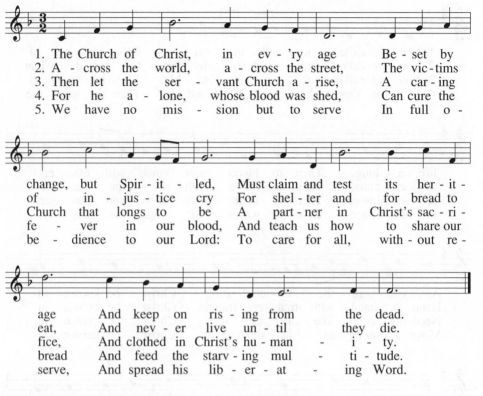

1. The Church of Christ, in ev-'ry age Be-set by
2. A-cross the world, a-cross the street, The vic-tims
3. Then let the ser-vant Church a-rise, A car-ing
4. For he a-lone, whose blood was shed, Can cure the
5. We have no mis-sion but to serve In full o-

change, but Spir-it-led, Must claim and test its her-it-
of in-jus-tice cry For shel-ter and for bread to
Church that longs to be A part-ner in Christ's sac-ri-
fe-ver in our blood, And teach us how to share our
be-dience to our Lord: To care for all, with-out re-

age And keep on ris-ing from the dead.
eat, And nev-er live un-til they die.
fice, And clothed in Christ's hu-man-i-ty.
bread And feed the starv-ing mul-ti-tude.
serve, And spread his lib-er-at-ing Word.

Text: Fred Pratt Green, 1903–2000, © 1971, Hope Publishing Company
Tune: DUNEDIN, LM; Vernon Griffiths, 1894–1985, © 1971, Faber Music Ltd.

786 God Sends Us Forth

1. God sends us forth to love and serve,
2. Nour-ished by Christ, our Word and Bread,
3. Called to the ones the world ig-nores—
4. So, with the cross to lead the way,

Make known God's name and live God's word,
Burn-ing with love and Spir-it-led,
Hun-gry and thirst-y, weak and poor—
Let us go forth in peace to-day,

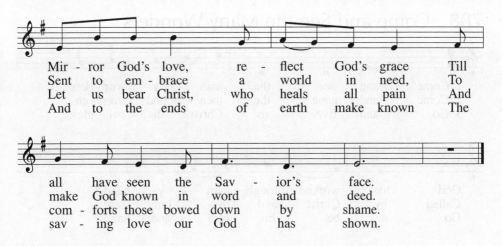

Mir - ror God's love, re - flect God's grace Till
Sent to em - brace a world in need, To
Let us bear Christ, who heals all pain And
And to the ends of earth make known The

all have seen the Sav - ior's face.
make God known in word and deed.
com - forts those bowed down by shame.
sav - ing love our God has shown.

Text: Tony E. Alonso, b.1980
Tune: GAILHAC, LM; Tony E. Alonso, b.1980
© 2009, GIA Publications, Inc.

The Spirit Sends Us Forth to Serve   787

1. The Spir - it sends us forth to serve; We
2. We go to com - fort those who mourn And
3. We go to be the hands of Christ, To
4. Then let us go to serve in peace, The

go in Je - sus' name To bring glad tid - ings
set the bur - dened free; Where hope is dim, to
scat - ter joy like seed And, all our days, to
gos - pel to pro - claim. God's Spir - it has em -

to the poor, God's fa - vor to pro - claim.
share a dream And help the blind to see.
cher - ish life, To do the lov - ing deed.
pow - ered us; We go in Je - sus' name.

Text: Delores Dufner, OSB, b.1939, © 1993, Sisters of St. Benedict. Published by OCP.
Tune: AZMON, CM; Carl G. Gläser, 1784–1829; harm. by Lowell Mason, 1792–1872

788 Come and See the Many Wonders

1. Come and see the man - y won - ders
2. Come and name the men and wom - en
3. Go and live as Christ's dis - ci - ples.

God has worked through man - y hands.
Called by Christ and by him sent.
Go and be his face and hands,

Come and count the man - y bless-ings,
They pro - claimed the King - dom's com - ing
And pro - claim by word and ac - tion

Wo - ven from so man - y strands.
In his Word and Sac - ra - ment.
That God's love is Christ's com - mand.

We have seen the face of Je - sus,
Sing of found - ers and of build - ers,
Raise a song of glad thanks - giv - ing;

Who has dwelt a - mong us here:
Pas - tors, teach - ers, ser - vants all,
Let it ring that all may hear:

Christ, the source of all our bless-ings,
Who by lives of faith and serv - ice
Praise the Fa - ther, Son, and Spir - it,

Bless - ings grow - ing year by year.
Have ful - filled their Sav - ior's call.
Source of bless - ings year by year.

Text: Harry Hagan, OSB, © 2010, Saint Meinrad's Abbey
Tune: ABBOT'S LEIGH, 8 7 8 7 D; Cyril V. Taylor, 1907–1991, © 1942, 1970, Hope Publishing Company

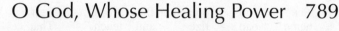

O God, Whose Healing Power 789

1. O God, whose heal - ing pow - er Is pres - ent ev - 'ry-
2. O Christ, who came a - mong us To heal the sick, the
3. O Spir - it, ho - ly, heal-ing, De-scend to us to-

where, Per - vad - ing all cre - a - tion With your e - ter - nal
blind, To bless the poor and bur-dened, The bro - ken heart to
day. Re - store to all cre - a - tion The peace for which we

care: Look now in your com - pas - sion Up -
bind: Send us where they are wait - ing For
pray. Re - deem us from the pow - ers That

on this world of pain And lives now bound and
hands to help and heal And, through the gifts we
rav - age and de - stroy Till earth and all its

bro - ken Make free and whole a - gain.
of - fer, Your grace a - gain re - veal.
peo - ple Shall greet the dawn with joy.

Text: Herman G. Stuempfle, Jr., 1923–2007
Tune: HEALING WORDS, 7 6 7 6 D; Randall Sensmeier, b.1948
© 1997, GIA Publications, Inc.

790 Lord, You Give the Great Commission

1. Lord, you give the great com - mis - sion: "Heal the sick and preach the word." Lest the Church ne - glect its mis - sion And the Gos - pel go un - heard, Help us wit - ness to your pur - pose With re - newed in - teg - ri - ty;

2. Lord, you call us to your serv - ice: "In my name bap - tize and teach." That the world may trust your prom - ise, Life a - bun - dant meant for each, Give us all new fer - vor, draw us Clos - er in com - mun - i - ty;

3. Lord, you make the com - mon ho - ly: "This my bod - y, this my blood." Let us all, for earth's true glo - ry, Dai - ly lift life heav - en - ward, Ask - ing that the world a - round us Share your chil - dren's lib - er - ty;

4. Lord, you show us love's true meas - ure: "Fa - ther, what they do, for - give." Yet we hoard as pri - vate treas - ure All that you so free - ly give. May your care and mer - cy lead us To a just so - ci - e - ty;

5. Lord, you bless with words as - sur - ing: "I am with you to the end." Faith and hope and love re - stor - ing, May we serve as you in - tend, And, a - mid the cares that claim us, Hold in mind e - ter - ni - ty;

With the Spir - it's gifts em - pow'r us For the work of min - is - try.

Text: Jeffery Rowthorn, b.1934, © 1978, Hope Publishing Company
Tune: ABBOT'S LEIGH, 8 7 8 7 D; Cyril V. Taylor, 1907–1991, © 1942, ren. 1970, Hope Publishing Company

Alternate tune: HYFRYDOL

God, Bless Your Church with Strength! 791

1. God, bless your Church with strength! Wher - ev - er we may be, Build up your ser - vants as we work In com - mon min - is - try. Urge us from fledg - ling faith To ven - ture and to soar, Through o - pen skies to sing the praise Of Christ, whom we a - dore.

2. God, bless your Church with life! May all our branch - es thrive, Un - blem - ished, whole - some, bear - ing fruit, A - bun - dant - ly a - live. From you, one Ho - ly Vine, In free - dom may we grow. Sus - tain us in our mis - sion, Lord, Your love and peace to show.

3. God, bless your Church with hope! De - spite cha - ot - ic days May we in dark - ness shine, to light A path - way through life's maze. May jus - tice be our aim And kind - ness ours to share; And let us walk in hum - ble - ness, As - sured our God is there.

Text: John A. Dalles, b.1954, © 2000, GIA Publications, Inc.
Tune: DIADEMATA, SMD; George J. Elvey, 1816–1893

792 Go Make of All Disciples

1. "Go make of all dis - ci - ples." We hear the call, O
2. "Go make of all dis - ci - ples," Bap - tiz - ing in the
3. "Go make of all dis - ci - ples." We at your feet would
4. "Go make of all dis - ci - ples." We wel-come your com -

Lord,   That comes from you, our Fa - ther, In
name   Of Fa - ther, Son, and Spir - it— From
stay   Un - til each life's vo - ca - tion Shows
mand.   "Lo, I am with you al - ways." We

your e - ter - nal Word.   In - spire our ways of
age to age the same.   We call each new dis -
forth your ho - ly way.   We cul - ti - vate the
take your guid - ing hand.   The task looms large be -

learn - ing Through earn - est, fer - vent prayer, And
ci - ple To fol - low you, O Lord, Re -
na - ture God plants in ev - 'ry heart, Re -
fore us— We fol - low with - out fear. In

let our dai - ly liv - ing Re - veal you ev - 'ry - where.
deem - ing soul and bod - y By wa - ter and the Word.
veal - ing in our wit - ness The Mas - ter Teach-er's art.
heav'n and earth your pow - er Shall bring God's king - dom here.

Text: Matthew 28:19–20; Leon M. Adkins, 1896–1986, alt. © 1964, Abingdon Press
Tune: ELLACOMBE, 7 6 7 6 D; *Gesangbuch der Herzogl*, Wirtemberg, 1784

See My Hands and Feet 793

1. Touch that soothes and heals the hurt - ing,
2. Feed the hun - gry, clothe the na - ked,
3. Love and serve with - out dis - tinc - tion
4. Hands that beck - on lit - tle chil - dren,

Hands that break a loaf of bread; Steps that walk be -
Vis - it ones in need of care, Give the home-less
All earth's peo - ple, first and least. Know with - in each
Bind a wound, pre - pare a meal, Feet that rush to

side the wea - ry, Bear - ing bur - dens in their stead:
warmth and shel - ter: Christ will find a wel-come there.
act of kind - ness Hope and whole - ness are in-creased.
share good tid - ings, Christ a - ris - en, still re - veal.

See my hands and feet, said Je - sus,

Love a - ris - en from the grave. Be my hands and

feet, said Je - sus, Live as ones I died to save.

Text: Mary Louise Bringle, b.1953, © 2002, GIA Publications, Inc.
Tune: GENEVA, 8 7 8 7 with refrain; George H. Day, 1883–1966, © 1942, The Church Pension Fund

794 To Be Your Presence

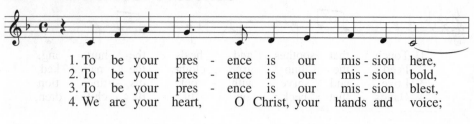

1. To be your pres - ence is our mis - sion here,
2. To be your pres - ence is our mis - sion bold,
3. To be your pres - ence is our mis - sion blest,
4. We are your heart, O Christ, your hands and voice;

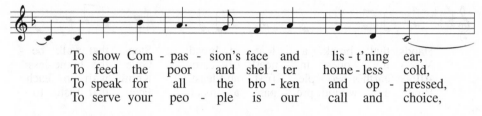

To show Com - pas - sion's face and lis - t'ning ear,
To feed the poor and shel - ter home - less cold,
To speak for all the bro - ken and op - pressed,
To serve your peo - ple is our call and choice,

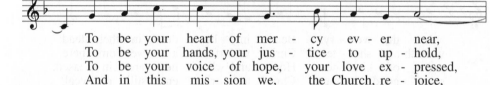

To be your heart of mer - cy ev - er near,
To be your hands, your jus - tice to up - hold,
To be your voice of hope, your love ex - pressed,
And in this mis - sion we, the Church, re - joice,

al - le - lu - ia!
*(1.) your heart of mer - cy, Christ!
(2.) your hands of jus - tice, Christ!
(3.) your voice of hope, O Christ!
(4.) to be your pres - ence here!

*During Lent

Text: Delores Dufner, OSB, b.1939, © 2000, 2003, GIA Publications, Inc.
Tune: ENGELBERG, 10 10 10 with alleluia; Charles V. Stanford, 1852–1924

795 The Thirsty Cry for Water, Lord

1. The thirst - y cry for wa - ter, Lord; The hun - gry plead for
2. The cup of wa - ter poured in love The pangs of thirst will
3. But help us al - so hear the cry Of hun - g'ring, thirst - ing
4. And come to us, O ris - en Christ, Our rest - less souls re -

bread. And man-y long to rise a-gain Where hope, cast
still. The bread of earth you bid us share, The fam-ished
hearts For liv-ing wa-ter, bread of life Your grace a-
lieve; And sat-is-fy our starv-ing hearts That we may

down, lies dead, Where hope, cast down, lies dead.
child can fill, The fam-ished child can fill.
lone im-parts, Your grace a-lone im-parts.
rise and live, That we may rise and live.

Text: Herman G. Stuempfle, Jr., 1923–2007, © 1997, GIA Publications, Inc.
Tune: WIDOW'S GOLD, 8 6 8 66; Randall Sensmeier, b.1948, © 2001, 2011, GIA Publications, Inc.

As the Birds of the Air   796

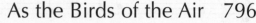

1. As the birds of the air Trust in God for their
2. What we need, Je-sus knows: Things to eat, shel-ter,
3. E-ven still, there re-main Peo-ple lost in their
4. And yet, God has sup-plied E-nough goods to di-

care With-out fear, for they know they will feed,
clothes, Hu-man touch, fear-less love, and good friends.
pain: Need-ing food, dry with thirst, all a-lone.
vide If we turn from our fear, hate, and greed.

So in faith we should trust, Know-ing God will be just,
When he walked here on earth And took part in our birth,
And does God just ig-nore All the grief of the poor?
We can an-swer a prayer With our love, grace, and care,

And pro-vide us with all that we need.
He re-lied on the gifts that God sends.
Who will hear when we weep, wail, or groan?
And through us God can meet ev-'ry need.

Text: Adam M. L. Tice, b.1979, © 2009, GIA Publications, Inc.
Tune: MIDDLEBURY, 66 9 66 9, Southern Harmony, 1835; harm. by Jack W. Burnam, b.1946, © 1984

797 God, Whose Purpose Is to Kindle

1. God, whose pur - pose is to kin - dle,
2. God, who still a sword de - liv - ers
3. God, who in your ho - ly gos - pel

Now ig - nite us with your fire.
Rath - er than a plac - id peace,
Wills that all should tru - ly live,

While the earth a - waits your burn - ing,
With your sharp - ened Word dis - turb us,
Make us sense our share of fail - ure,

With your pas - sion us in - spire.
From com - pla - cen - cy re - lease!
Our tran - quil - i - ty for - give.

O - ver - come our sin - ful calm - ness,
Save us now from sat - is - fac - tion,
Teach us cour - age as we strug - gle

Stir us with your sav - ing name.
When we pri - vate - ly are free,
In all lib - er - at - ing strife.

Bap - tize with your fier - y Spir - it,
Yet are un - dis - turbed in spir - it
Lift the small - ness of our vi - sion

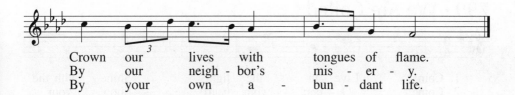

Crown our lives with tongues of flame.
By our neigh - bor's mis - er - y.
By your own a - bun - dant life.

Text: David E. Trueblood, 1900–1994, alt., © 1967, David Elton Trueblood
Tune: EBENEZER, 8 7 8 7 D; Thomas J. Williams, 1869–1944

For the Healing of the Nations   798

1. For the heal - ing of the na - tions, Lord, we pray with
2. Lead your peo - ple in - to free - dom, From de - spair your
3. All that kills a - bun - dant liv - ing, Let it from the
4. You, cre - a - tor God, have writ - ten Your great name on

one ac - cord; For a just and e - qual shar - ing
world re - lease That, re-deemed from war and ha - tred,
earth be banned: Pride of sta - tus, race, or school - ing,
hu - man - kind; For our grow - ing in your like - ness

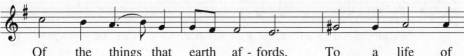

Of the things that earth af - fords. To a life of
All may come and go in peace. Show us how, through
Dog - mas that ob - scure your plan. In our com - mon
Bring the life of Christ to mind, That by our re -

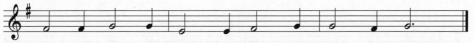

love in ac - tion Help us rise and pledge our word.
care and good - ness, Fear will die and hope in - crease.
quest for jus - tice May we hal - low life's brief span.
sponse and serv - ice Earth its des - ti - ny may find.

Text: Fred Kaan, 1929–2009, alt., © 1968, Hope Publishing Company
Tune: WESTMINSTER ABBEY, 8 7 8 7 8 7; adapt. from an anthem of Henry Purcell, 1659–1695, by Ernest Hawkins, 1807–1868

799 We Are Called

1. Come! Live in the light! Shine with the
2. Come! O-pen your heart! Show your
3. Sing! Sing a new song! Sing of that

joy and the love of the Lord! We are called
mer-cy to all those in fear! We are called
great day when all will be one! God will reign,

to be light for the king-dom, to
to be hope for the hope-less so all
and we'll walk with each oth-er as

live in the free-dom of the cit-y of God!
ha-tred and blind-ness will be no more!
sis-ters and broth-ers u-nit-ed in love!

We are called to act with jus-tice, we are called to

love ten-der-ly, we are called to serve one an-oth-er,

to walk hum-bly with God!

Text: Micah 6:8; David Haas, b.1957
Tune: David Haas, b.1957
© 1988, GIA Publications, Inc.

Jesus, Our Divine Companion 800

1. Je - sus, our di - vine com-pan - ion, By your low - ly
2. All who tread the path of la - bor Fol - low where your
3. Ev - 'ry task, how - ev - er sim - ple, Fills the soul with

hu - man birth You have come to join all work - ers,
feet have trod; All who work with - out com-plain - ing
grace a - new; Ev - 'ry act of hu - man kind - ness

Bur - den-bear - ers of the earth. As the car - pen -
Do the ho - ly will of God. You, the peace sur -
Done in love is done to you. Je - sus, our di -

ter of Naz - 'reth, Toil - ing for your dai - ly food,
pas - sing knowl-edge, Dwell with us in dai - ly strife;
vine com-pan - ion, Help us all to do our best;

By your pa - tience and your cour - age,
You, the Bread of heav - en, bro - ken
Bless us in our dai - ly la - bor,

You have taught us work is good.
In the sac - ra - ment of life.
Lead us to the Sab - bath rest.

Text: Henry van Dyke, 1852–1933, alt.
Tune: PLEADING SAVIOR, 8 7 8 7 D; *Christian Lyre*, 1830; harm. by Richard Proulx, 1937–2010, © 1986, GIA Publications, Inc.

801   Lift Every Voice and Sing

1. Lift ev - 'ry voice and sing, Till earth and heav - en
2. Ston - y the road we trod, Bit - ter the chas - t'ning
3. God of our wea - ry years, God of our si - lent

ring, Ring with the har - mo - nies of lib - er -
rod, Felt in the days when hope un - born had
tears, Thou who hast brought us thus far on the

ty; Let our re - joic - ing rise High as the lis - t'ning
died; Yet with a stead - y beat, Have not our wea - ry
way; Thou who hast by thy might Led us in - to the

skies, Let it re-sound loud as the roll - ing sea.
feet Come to the place for which our peo - ple sighed?
light, Keep us for - ev - er in the path, we pray.

Sing a song full of the faith that the dark past has
We have come o - ver a way that with tears has been
Lest our feet stray from the plac - es, our God, where we

taught us; Sing a song full of the
wa - tered; We have come, tread - ing our
met thee; Lest our hearts, drunk with the

hope that the pres - ent has brought us; Fac - ing the
path through the blood of the slaugh - tered; Out from the
wine of the world, we for - get thee; Shad - owed be -

ris - ing sun Of our new day be - gun,
gloom - y past, Till now we stand at last
neath thy hand, May we for - ev - er stand,

Let us march on till vic - to - ry is won.
Where the bright gleam of our bright star is cast.
True to our God, true to our na - tive land.

Text: James W. Johnson, 1871–1938
Tune: ANTHEM, 66 10 66 10 14 14 66 10; J. Rosamund Johnson, 1873–1954

We Cannot Own the Sunlit Sky   802

1. We can - not own the sun - lit sky, The
2. When bod - ies shiv - er in the night And,
3. God calls hu - man - i - ty to join As

moon, the wild - flow'rs grow - ing, For we are part of
wea - ry, wait for morn - ing, When chil - dren have no
part - ners in cre - at - ing A fu - ture free from

all that is With - in life's riv - er flow - ing.
bread but tears, And war - horns sound their warn - ing,
want or fear, Life's good - ness cel - e - brat - ing.

With o - pen hands re - ceive and share The
God calls hu - man - i - ty to wake, To
That new world beck - ons from a - far, In -

gifts of God's cre - a - tion, That all may have a -
join in com - mon la - bor, That all may have a -
vites our shared en - deav-or, That all may have a -

bun - dant life In ev - 'ry earth - ly na - tion.
bun - dant life In one-ness with their neigh-bor.
bun - dant life And peace en - dure for - ev - er.

Text: Ruth Duck, b.1947, © 1992, GIA Publications, Inc.
Tune: HOW CAN I KEEP FROM SINGING, 8 7 8 7 D; Robert Lowry, 1826–1899; harm. by Robert J. Batastini, b.1942, © 1988, GIA
  Publications, Inc.

803 If You Believe and I Believe

If you be-lieve and I be-lieve and we to-geth-er pray,

The Ho-ly Spir-it must come down and set God's peo-ple free,

And set God's peo-ple free, and set God's peo-ple free;

The Ho-ly Spir-it must come down and set God's peo-ple free.

Text: Zimbabwean traditional
Tune: Zimbabwean traditional; adapt. of English traditional; as taught by Tarasai; arr. by John L. Bell, b.1949, © 1991, Iona Community, GIA Publications, Inc., agent

804 We Sing Your Praise, O Christ

1. We sing your praise, O Christ, With
2. When eyes are fixed a - bove Where
3. We fall up - on our knees And
4. Let praise we of - fer you Be

hearts ex - alt - ed high. For - give us when we
you in glo - ry reign, Lord, low - er them to
fold our hands in prayer. Lord, o - pen them that
ech - oed in our deeds. Let love of you be

fail to hear Our neigh - bor's an - guished cry.
earth a - gain To see a world in pain.
grace re - ceived Be grace we glad - ly share.
man - i - fest In serv - ing oth - ers' needs.

Text: Herman G. Stuempfle, Jr., 1923–2007, © 1997, GIA Publications, Inc.
Tune: SOUTHWELL, SM; William Daman, The Psalmes of David, 1579, alt.

God, Whose Giving Knows No Ending   805

1. God, whose giv - ing knows no end - ing, From your
2. Skills and time are ours for press - ing Toward the
3. Treas - ure, too, you have en - trust - ed, Gain through

rich and end - less store: Na - ture's won - der, Je - sus'
goals of Christ, your Son: All at peace in health and
pow'rs your grace con - ferred; Ours to use for home and

wis - dom, Cost - ly cross, grave's shat - tered door,
free - dom, Rac - es joined, the Church made one.
kin - dred, And to spread the gos - pel word.

Gift - ed by you, we turn to you, Of - f'ring
Now di - rect our dai - ly la - bor, Lest we
O - pen wide our hands in shar - ing, As we

up our - selves in praise; Thank - ful song shall rise for -
strive for self a - lone; Born with tal - ents, make us
heed Christ's age - less call, Heal - ing, teach - ing, and re -

ev - er, Gra - cious do - nor of our days.
ser - vants Fit to an - swer at your throne.
claim - ing, Serv - ing you by lov - ing all.

Text: Robert L. Edwards, 1915–2006, © 1961, The Hymn Society (admin. by Hope Publishing Company)
Tune: RUSTINGTON, 8 7 8 7 D; Charles H. H. Parry, 1848–1918

Alternate tune: IN BABILONE

806 Come to Us, Creative Spirit

1. Come to us, cre-a-tive Spir-it; In our Fa-ther's
2. Po-et, paint-er, mu-sic mak-er, All your treas-ures
3. Word from God, e-ter-nal spring-ing, Fill our minds, we
4. In all plac-es and for ev-er Glo-ry be ex-

house Ev-'ry hu- man tal-ent hal-low,
bring; Crafts-man, ac- tor, grace-ful danc-er,
pray; And in all ar-tis-tic vi-sion
pressed To the Son, with God the Fa-ther

Hid-den skills a-rouse That, with-in your earth-ly
Make your of-fer-ing. Join your hands in cel-e-
Give in-teg-ri-ty. May the flame with-in us
And the Spir-it blessed. In our wor-ship and our

tem-ple, Wise and sim-ple May re-joice.
bra-tion; Let cre-a-tion Shout and sing!
burn-ing Kin-dle yearn-ing Day by day.
liv-ing Keep us striv-ing For the best.

Text: David Mowbray, b.1938, © 1979, Stainer & Bell, Ltd., London, England (admin. by Hope Publishing Company)
Tune: CASTLEWOOD, 8 5 8 5 84 3; Richard Proulx, 1937–2010, © 1986, GIA Publications, Inc.

807 Lord, Whose Then Shall They Be

1. Lord, whose then shall they be, These
2. We trust earth's tran-sient gifts To
3. But noth-ing born of earth Un-
4. O Christ, who of-fered all, Teach
5. Help us to hold in trust The

treas-ured goods we store? Shall all the wealth we
feed and sat-is-fy, To form a rock on
shak-en can a-bide. Like sand it soon is
us the truth a-gain: That on-ly what we
treas-ured goods we store And share them where you

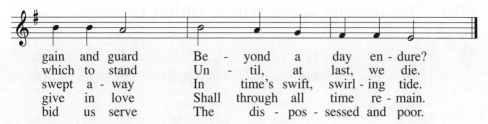

gain and guard   Be - yond a   day en - dure?
which to stand   Un - til, at   last, we die.
swept a - way   In   time's swift, swirl - ing tide.
give in love   Shall through all   time re - main.
bid us serve   The   dis - pos - sessed and poor.

Text: Herman G. Stuempfle, Jr., 1923–2007, © 1997, GIA Publications, Inc.
Tune: SOUTHWELL, SM; William Daman, *The Psalmes of David*, 1579, alt.

Touch the Earth Lightly   808

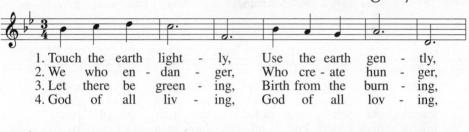

1. Touch the earth light - ly,   Use the earth gen - tly,
2. We who en - dan - ger,   Who cre - ate hun - ger,
3. Let there be green - ing,   Birth from the burn - ing,
4. God of all liv - ing,   God of all lov - ing,

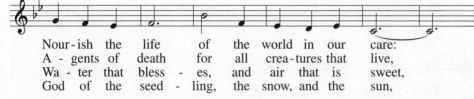

Nour-ish the life   of   the world in our   care:
A - gents of death   for   all crea-tures that live,
Wa - ter that bless - es,   and   air that is   sweet,
God of the seed - ling,   the snow, and the   sun,

Gift of great won - der,   Ours to sur - ren - der,
We who would fos - ter   Clouds of dis - as - ter—
Health in God's gar - den,   Hope in God's chil - dren,
Teach us, de - flect us,   Christ re - con - nect us,

1.–3.   4.

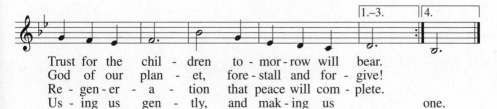

Trust for the chil - dren   to - mor - row will bear.
God of our plan - et,   fore - stall and for - give!
Re - gen - er - a - tion   that peace will com - plete.
Us - ing us gen - tly,   and mak - ing us   one.

Text: Shirley Erena Murray, b.1931
Tune: TENDERNESS, 55 10 D; Colin Gibson, b.1933
© 1992, Hope Publishing Company

809 The Temple Rang with Golden Coins

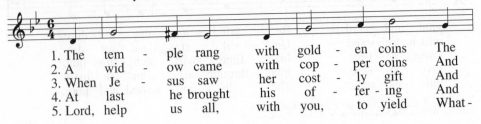

1. The tem - ple rang with gold - en coins The
2. A wid - ow came with cop - per coins And
3. When Je - sus saw her cost - ly gift And
4. At last he brought his of - fer - ing And
5. Lord, help us all, with you, to yield What -

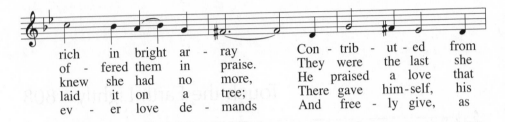

rich in bright ar - ray Con - trib - ut - ed from
of - fered them in praise. They were the last she
knew she had no more, He praised a love that
laid it on a tree; There gave him - self, his
ev - er love de - mands And free - ly give, as

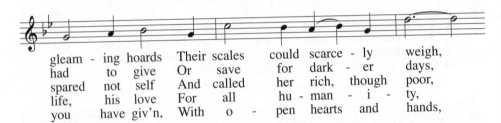

gleam - ing hoards Their scales could scarce - ly weigh,
had to give Or save for dark - er days,
spared not self And called her rich, though poor,
life, his love For all hu - man - i - ty,
you have giv'n, With o - pen hearts and hands,

Their scales could scarce - ly weigh.
Or save for dark - er days.
And called her rich, though poor.
For all hu - man - i - ty.
With o - pen hearts and hands.

Text: Mark 12:41–44, Herman G. Stuempfle, Jr., 1923–2007, © 1993, GIA Publications, Inc.
Tune: WIDOW'S GOLD, 8 6 8 66; Randall Sensmeier, b.1948, © 2001, GIA Publications, Inc.

Alternate tune: CHRISTIAN LOVE
*Omit when singing this text to a CM tune.

With Gifts That Differ by Your Grace   810

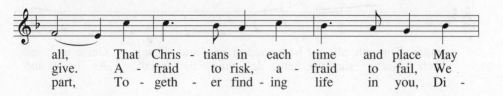

1. With gifts that dif - fer by your grace Your Spir - it fits us
2. And yet, be - cause our faith is frail, We bur - y gifts you
3. Come, Spir - it, build your Church a - new, That all may do their

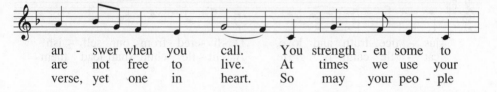

all, That Chris - tians in each time and place May
give. A - fraid to risk, a - fraid to fail, We
part, To - geth - er find - ing life in you, Di -

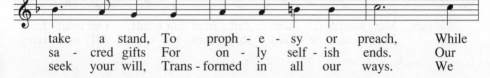

an - swer when you call. You strength - en some to
are not free to live. At times we use your
verse, yet one in heart. So may your peo - ple

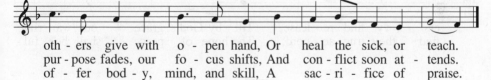

take a stand, To proph - e - sy or preach, While
sa - cred gifts For on - ly self - ish ends. Our
seek your will, Trans - formed in all our ways. We

oth - ers give with o - pen hand, Or heal the sick, or teach.
pur - pose fades, our fo - cus shifts, And con - flict soon at - tends.
of - fer bod - y, mind, and skill, A sac - ri - fice of praise.

Text: Ruth Duck, b.1947, © 1996, The Pilgrim Press
Tune: MOZART, CMD; adapt. from Wolfgang A. Mozart, 1756–1791

811 O Day of Peace

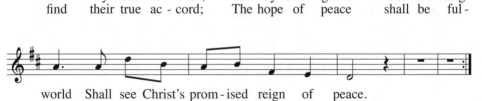

1. O day of peace that dim - ly
2. Then shall the wolf dwell with the

shines Through all our hopes and prayers and dreams, Guide us to
lamb Nor shall the fierce de - vour the small; As beasts and

jus - tice, truth and love, De - liv - ered from our self - ish
cat - tle calm - ly graze, A lit - tle child shall lead them

schemes. May swords of hate fall from our hands, Our hearts from
all. Then en - e - mies shall learn to love, All crea - tures

en - vy find re - lease, Till by God's grace our war - ring
find their true ac - cord; The hope of peace shall be ful -

world Shall see Christ's prom - ised reign of peace.
filled, For all the earth shall know the Lord.

Text: Carl P. Daw, Jr., b.1944, © 1982, Hope Publishing Company
Tune: JERUSALEM, LMD; Charles H. H. Parry, 1848–1918; harm. by Richard Proulx, 1937–2010, © 1986, GIA Publications, Inc.

O God of Every Nation 812

1. O God of ev - 'ry na - tion, Of
2. From search for wealth and pow - er And
3. Lord, strength - en those who la - bor That
4. Keep bright in us the vi - sion Of

ev - 'ry race and land, Re - deem the whole cre -
scorn of truth and right, From trust in bombs that
all may find re - lease From fear of rat - tling
days when wars shall cease, When ha - tred and di -

a - tion With your al - might - y hand. Where
show - er De - struc - tion through the night, From
sa - ber, From dread of war's in - crease. When
vi - sion Give way to love and peace, Till

hate and fear di - vide us And
pride of race and sta - tion And
hope and cour - age fal - ter, Lord,
dawns the morn - ing glo - rious When

bit - ter threats are hurled, In love and mer - cy
blind - ness to your way, De - liv - er ev - 'ry
let your voice be heard; With faith that none can
truth and jus - tice reign, And Christ shall rule vic -

guide us And heal our strife - torn world.
na - tion, E - ter - nal God, we pray.
al - ter, Your ser - vants un - der - gird.
to - rious O'er all the world's do - main.

Text: William W. Reid, Jr., b.1923, alt., © 1958, 1986, The Hymn Society (admin. by Hope Publishing Company)
Tune: PASSION CHORALE, 7 6 7 6 D; Hans Leo Hassler, 1564–1612; harm. by J. S. Bach, 1685–1750

813 O God of Love, O King of Peace

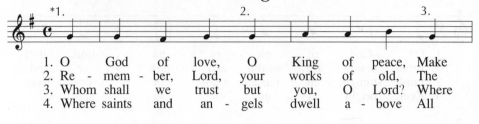

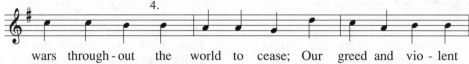

1. O God of love, O King of peace, Make
2. Re - mem - ber, Lord, your works of old, The
3. Whom shall we trust but you, O Lord? Where
4. Where saints and an - gels dwell a - bove All

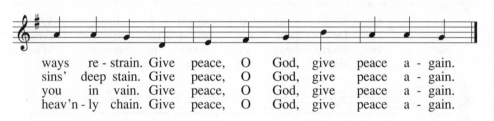

wars through - out the world to cease; Our greed and vio - lent
won - ders that your peo - ple told; Re - mem - ber not our
rest but on your faith - ful word? None ev - er called on
hearts are joined in ho - ly love; Oh, bind us in that

ways re - strain. Give peace, O God, give peace a - gain.
sins' deep stain. Give peace, O God, give peace a - gain.
you in vain. Give peace, O God, give peace a - gain.
heav'n - ly chain. Give peace, O God, give peace a - gain.

May be sung as a two- or four-voice canon.

Text: Henry W. Baker, 1821–1877, alt.
Tune: TALLIS' CANON, LM; Thomas Tallis, c.1505–1585

814 Peace I Leave You

Peace I leave you, my peace I give. Let your
German: Frie - den, Frie - den hin - ter - las - se ich euch. Mei - nen
Polish: Po - kój, po - kój, po - kój mój da - ję wam. Nie lę -
Spanish: Paz les de - jo, mi paz yo les doy. Que no

hearts be free from fear. My peace I give to you.
Frie - den ge - be ich euch. Eu - er Herz ver - za - ge nicht.
kaj - cie się, mó - wi Pan. Po - kój mój zo - sta - wiam wam.
te - ma el co - ra - zón. Mi paz, mi paz les doy.

Text: Taizé Community
Tune: Taizé Community
© 2007, 2011, Les Presses de Taizé, GIA Publications, Inc., agent

Everything That Has Voice   815

1. Ev - 'ry - thing   that has voice,   Sing for peace,
2. All the world   longs for peace,   Cries for peace,
3. Ev - 'ry - one   who has breath,   You and I,

Speak for peace;   Giv - en chance, giv - en choice,   Work for
Dies for peace;   Let the chil - dren ev - 'ry place   Sleep in
Pass - ers - by,   Ev - 'ry ten - ant of the earth,   Plant for

peace,   Write for peace,   Res - o - nat - ing ev - 'ry -
peace,   Grow in peace,   Home and coun - try safe to
peace,   Gath - er peace;   Cul - ti - vate a neigh - bor -

where,   Ech - o - ing our com - mon care: Ev - 'ry -
be   Where the spir - it ris - es free: All the
hood   Cher - ish - ing our neigh - bors' good: Ev - 'ry -

thing   that has voice,   Sing for peace!
world   longs for peace,   Cries for peace.
one   who has breath,   Live in peace!

Text: Shirley Erena Murray, b.1931, © 2004, Hope Publishing Company
Tune: SING FOR PEACE, 6 33 6 33 77 6 3; Marty Haugen, b.1950, © 2005, GIA Publications, Inc.

816 Oh, Look and Wonder / Miren Qué Bueno

Refrain

Oh, look and won - der how good it is!
¡Mir - en qué bue - no, qué bue - no es!

Verses

1. How good it is when broth - ers dwell in
2. How good it is when sis - ters dwell in
3. How good it is when all earth's peo - ple
1. ¡Mi - ren qué bue - no_es cuan - do los her -
2. ¡Mi - ren qué bue - no_es cuan - do las her -
3. ¡Mi - ren qué bue - no_es cuan - do nos reu -

peace with one an - oth - er: it is like pre - cious
peace with one an - oth - er: fresh like the morn - ing
dwell in peace to - geth - er: there is where God will
ma - nos es - tán jun - tos! Es co - mo_a - cei - te
ma - nas es - tán jun - tas! Se pa - re - ce_al ro -
ni - mos to - dos jun - tos! Por - que_el Se - ñor ahí

D.C.

oil when run - ning fresh on Aa - ron's beard.
dew that falls on Zi - on's ho - ly hill.
pour the bless - ing, life for - ev - er - more.
bue - no de - rra - ma - do so - bre_Aa - rón.
cí - o so - bre los mon - tes de Sión.
man - da vi - da_e - ter - na_y ben - di - ción.

Text: Psalm 133; Pablo D. Sosa, b.1933
Tune: Pablo D. Sosa, b.1933

Jesus Promises Communion   817

1. Je - sus prom - is - es com - mun - ion So that
2. Ho - ly Spir - it, come de - light us With a
3. God, we of - fer our thanks-giv - ing For the

we might live as one, Blessed with - in the great re -
taste of heav - en's peace; In this Eu - cha - rist u -
gift of com - mon creed; And the Gos - pel way of

un - ion In the bod - y of God's Son. Taste and
nite us As our lone - ly hun - gers cease. Bring to -
liv - ing Form-ing faith in word and deed. For we

see with one an - oth - er Bread of
geth - er all who wan - der From the
share this ho - ly vi - sion Where your

life and cup of joy; We are called to love each
feast you con - se - crate, And re - store that grace we
Church can sing "A - men": Christ, who died and now is

oth - er, Build-ing up what sins de - stroy.
squan - der With di - vi - sions we cre - ate.
ris - en, Lives in us and comes a - gain.

Text: Adam M. L. Tice, b.1979, © 2009, GIA Publications, Inc.
Tune: NETTLETON, 8 7 8 7 D; Wyeth's *Repository of Sacred Music,* 1813

818 Help Us Accept Each Other

1. Help us ac-cept each oth - er As Christ ac-cept-ed us;
2. Teach us, O Lord, your les - sons, As in our dai-ly life
3. Let your ac - cep-tance change us So that we may be moved
4. Lord, for to-day's en - coun - ters With all who are in need,

Teach us as sis - ter, broth - er, Each per - son to em - brace.
We strug-gle to be hu - man And search for hope and faith.
In liv - ing sit - u - a - tions To do the truth in love;
Who hun-ger for ac - cep-tance, For jus - tice, and for bread,

Be pres - ent, Lord, a - mong us, And bring us to be - lieve:
Teach us to care for peo - ple, For all, not just for some;
To prac-tice your ac - cep-tance Un - til we know by heart
We need new eyes for see - ing, New hands for hold-ing on:

We are our-selves ac - cept - ed And meant to love and live.
To love them as we find them, Or as they may be - come.
The ta - ble of for - give - ness And laugh-ter's heal-ing art.
Re - new us with your Spir - it; Lord, free us, make us one!

Text: Romans 15:7; Fred Kaan, 1929–2009, © 1975, Hope Publishing Company
Tune: AURELIA, 7 6 7 6 D; Samuel Sebastian Wesley, 1810–1876

819 How Good and Pleasant, Lord, It Is

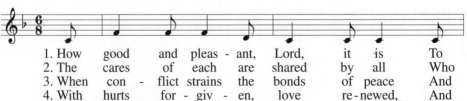

1. How good and pleas - ant, Lord, it is To
2. The cares of each are shared by all Who
3. When con - flict strains the bonds of peace And
4. With hurts for - giv - en, love re-newed, And

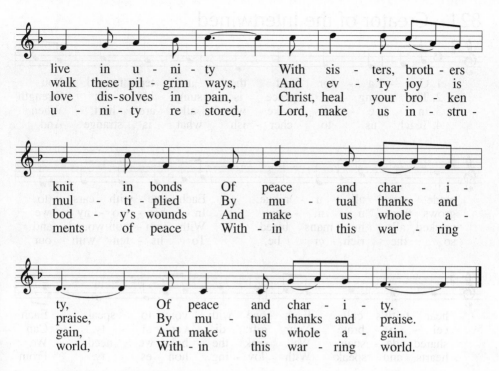

live   in   u - ni - ty   With   sis - ters,   broth - ers
walk   these   pil - grim   ways,   And   ev - 'ry   joy   is
love   dis-solves   in   pain,   Christ, heal   your   bro - ken
u   -   ni - ty   re - stored,   Lord,   make   us   in - stru -

knit   in   bonds   Of   peace   and   char - i -
mul - ti - plied   By   mu - tual   thanks   and
bod - y's   wounds   And   make   us   whole   a -
ments   of   peace   With - in   this   war - ring

ty,   Of   peace   and   char - i - ty.
praise,   By   mu - tual   thanks   and   praise.
gain,   And   make   us   whole   a - gain.
world,   With - in   this   war - ring   world.

Text: Herman G. Stuempfle, Jr., 1923–2007, © 2006, GIA Publications, Inc.
Tune: DOVE OF PEACE, 8 6 8 66; American melody; harm. by Charles H. Webb, b.1933, © 1989, The United Methodist Publishing House

Peace with the Father   820

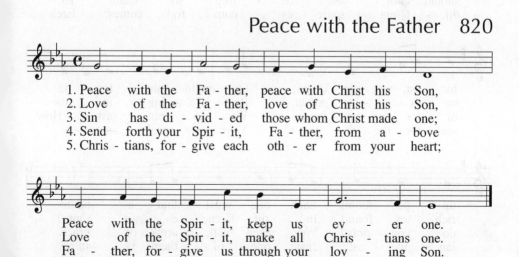

1. Peace   with   the   Fa - ther,   peace   with   Christ   his   Son,
2. Love   of   the   Fa - ther,   love   of   Christ   his   Son,
3. Sin   has   di - vid - ed   those whom Christ made   one;
4. Send   forth   your   Spir - it,   Fa - ther,   from   a - bove
5. Chris - tians,   for - give   each   oth - er   from   your   heart;

Peace   with   the   Spir - it,   keep   us   ev - er   one.
Love   of   the   Spir - it,   make   all   Chris - tians   one.
Fa - ther,   for - give   us through your   lov - ing   Son.
On   us,   your   chil - dren,   one   with   Christ   in   love.
Christ   be   a - mong   us,   nev - er - more   to   part.

Text: James Quinn, SJ, 1919–2010, © 1969. Used by permission of Selah Publishing, Inc.
Tune: COENA DOMINI, 10 10; Arthur S. Sullivan, 1842–1900

821 Creator of the Intertwined

1. Cre - a - tor of the in - ter - twined, You
2. The song of peace is sung by all; Strength
3. In e - vil's wake we all are hurt; When
4. Teach us to cher - ish what is strange And

made us all u - nique: Each one with ears to
grows from u - ni - ty. In har - mo - ny we
pricked, all hu - mans bleed. With com - mon wounds and
so the rich - er be, To lis - ten with our

hear faith's call, Each one with voice to speak. Each
cel - e - brate Your gift: di - ver - si - ty. Can
shared de - spair, We seek the balm we need. We
hearts, and speak With lov - ing hon - es - ty. From

wor - ships where the call is heard: In
we not sing each oth - er's songs, Speak
should not ask be - fore we reach To
dif - f'rent sourc - es com - fort comes; Each

for - est, tem - ple, dome, On moun - tain top, in
un - fa - mil - iar prayer, Re - joic - ing in the
of - fer our em - brace. We do not ask, "How
seeks for the di - vine. Your voice speaks man - y

up - per room; Each one must find a home.
rich - es found In dif - f'renc - es we share?
do you pray?" We reach with arms of grace.
lan - guag - es; Just one of them is mine.

Text: Jacque B. Jones, b.1950, © 2004, 2011, GIA Publications, Inc. and National Association of Congregational Christian Churches
Tune: KINGSFOLD, CMD; English melody; harm. by Ralph Vaughan Williams, 1872–1958

We Are Many Parts / Muchos Miembros Hay   822

Refrain

We are man-y parts, we are all one bod-y,
Mu-chos miem-bros hay, en un so-lo cuer-po;

and the gifts we have we are giv-en to share.
nues-tros do-nes son pa-ra dar y ser-vir.

May the Spir-it of love make us one in-deed;
Que el Es-pí-ri-tu de Dios nos u-na en su a-mor;

one, the love that we share, one, our hope in de-
com-par-tien-do el do-lor, com-ba-tien-do el te-

Last time

spair, one, the cross that we bear.
mor, com-pla-cien-do al Se-ñor.

Verses

1. God of all, we look to you, We would be your
2. So my pain is pain for you, In your joy is
3. All you seek-ers, great and small, Seek the great-est
1. *Oh Se-ñor, que-re-mos ser Ser-vi-do-res*
2. *Mi do-lor te due-le a ti; Si te go-zas,*
3. *Quie-nes bus-can de ver-dad Su ma-yor fe-*

D.C.

ser-vants true, Let us be your love to all the world.
my joy, too; All is brought to-geth-er in the Lord.
gift of all; If you love, then you will know the Lord.
por do-quier; Y a la hu-ma-ni-dad lle-var tu a-mor.
soy fe-liz; To-do se u-ne en tor-no al Se-ñor.
li-ci-dad: A-men y co-no-ce-rán a Dios.

Text: 1 Corinthians 12, 13; Marty Haugen, b.1950; tr. by Santiago Fernández, b.1971
Tune: Marty Haugen, b.1950
© 1980, 1986, 2005, GIA Publications, Inc.

823 I Am the Vine

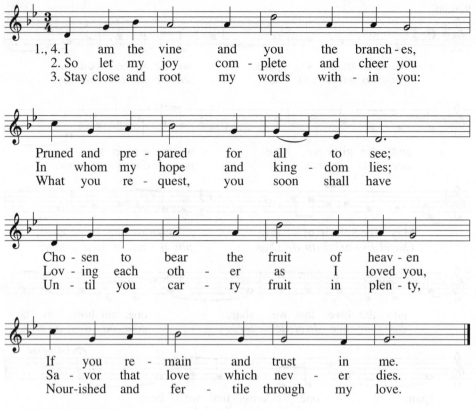

1., 4. I am the vine and you the branch-es,
2. So let my joy com - plete and cheer you
3. Stay close and root my words with - in you:

Pruned and pre - pared for all to see;
In whom my hope and king - dom lies;
What you re - quest, you soon shall have

Cho - sen to bear the fruit of heav - en
Lov - ing each oth - er as I loved you,
Un - til you car - ry fruit in plen - ty,

If you re - main and trust in me.
Sa - vor that love which nev - er dies.
Nour-ished and fer - tile through my love.

Text: John 15:5; John L. Bell, b.1949
Tune: VINE AND BRANCHES, 9 8 9 8; John L. Bell, b.1949
© 1995, Iona Community, GIA Publications, Inc., agent

824 In Christ There Is No East or West

1. In Christ there is no east or west, In
2. In him shall true hearts ev - 'ry - where Their
3. Join hands, dis - ci - ples in the faith, What-
4. In Christ now meet both east and west, In

him no south or north, But one great fam - 'ly
high com - mun - ion find; His serv - ice is the
e'er your race may be! Who serve each oth - er
him meet south and north; All Christ - ly souls are

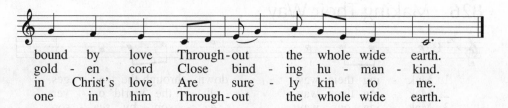

bound   by   love   Through-out   the   whole   wide   earth.
gold - en   cord   Close   bind - ing   hu - man - kind.
in   Christ's   love   Are   sure - ly   kin   to   me.
one   in   him   Through-out   the   whole   wide   earth.

Text: Galatians 3:23; William A. Dunkerley, 1852–1941, alt.
Tune: McKEE, CM; African American; adapt. by Harry T. Burleigh, 1866–1949

On This Day, the First of Days   825

1. On   this   day,   the   first   of   days,
2. On   this   day   the e - ter - nal   Son
3. Word - made - flesh,   all   prais - es   be!
4. Ho - ly   Spir - it,   you   im - part
5. God,   the   bless - ed   Three   in   One,

God   the   Fa - ther's   name   we   praise,   Who,   cre - a - tion's
O - ver   death   his   tri - umph   won;   On   this   day   the
You   from   sin   have   set   us   free;   And   with   you   we
Gifts   of   love   to   ev - 'ry   heart;   Give   us   light   and
May   your   ho - ly   will   be   done;   In   your   word   our

Lord   and   spring,   Did   the   world   from   dark-ness   bring.
Spir - it   came   With   its   gifts   of   liv - ing   flame.
die   and   rise   Un - to   God   in   sac - ri - fice.
grace,   we   pray;   Fill   our   hearts   this   ho - ly   day.
souls   are   free,   As   we   praise   the   Trin - i - ty.

Text: *Die parente temporum;* Le Mans *Breviary,* 1748; tr. by Henry W. Baker, 1821–1877, alt.
Tune: LÜBECK, 77 77; *Geistreiches Gesangbuch,* 1704, Johann Freylinghausen

826 Making Their Way

1. Mak - ing their way down through the a - ges,
2. Mak - ing their way all the world o - ver,
3. Mak - ing our way sea - son by sea - son,

Sin - ners and saints have heard God's call: Wealth-y and poor,
Chris-tians as - sem - ble on this day, Hear - ing the Word,
Pil - grims, we jour - ney till life's end, Trav - el-ing light,

pow - er-ful, low - ly, Je - sus' dis - ci - ples, one and all.
shar - ing the Ban-quet, Learn-ing to walk in Je - sus' way.
shar - ing the rich - es, Car - ing for stran - ger as for friend,

Gath - ered for wor - ship, of - fer-ing thanks, The great - est
Mem - bers of Christ, u - nit - ed in love, They seek our
Till in the joy of long - ing ful-filled, To - geth - er

with the least Have come to share this feast.
God to know, And so to - geth - er grow.
we will come To our e - ter - nal home.

Text: Delores Dufner, OSB, b.1939, © 2011, GIA Publications, Inc.
Tune: KOMT NU MET ZANG, 9 8 9 8 9 66; Valerius' *Nederlandtsch Gedenckclanck*, 1626; acc. by Adriaan Engels, 1906–2003, © OCP

827 Prepare a Room for Me

May be sung in alternating stanzas by cantor and assembly.

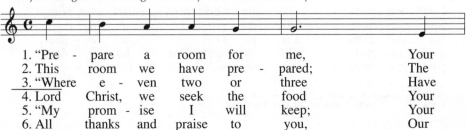

1. "Pre - pare a room for me, Your
2. This room we have pre - pared; The
3. "Where e - ven two or three Have
4. Lord Christ, we seek the food Your
5. "My prom - ise I will keep; Your
6. All thanks and praise to you, Our

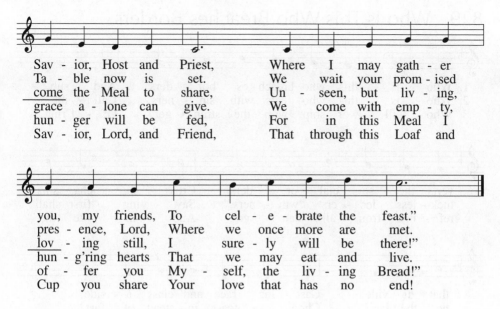

Sav -	ior,	Host	and	Priest,	Where	I	may	gath -	er
Ta -	ble	now	is	set.	We	wait	your	prom -	ised
come	the	Meal	to	share,	Un -	seen,	but	liv -	ing,
grace	a -	lone	can	give.	We	come	with	emp -	ty,
hun -	ger	will	be	fed,	For	in	this	Meal	I
Sav -	ior,	Lord,	and	Friend,	That	through	this	Loaf	and

you,	my	friends,	To	cel -	e -	brate	the	feast."
pres -	ence,	Lord,	Where	we	once	more	are	met.
lov -	ing	still,	I	sure -	ly	will	be	there!"
hun -	g'ring	hearts	That	we	may	eat	and	live.
of -	fer	you	My -	self,	the	liv -	ing	Bread!"
Cup	you	share	Your	love	that	has	no	end!

Text: Herman G. Stuempfle, Jr., 1923–2007, © 2000, GIA Publications, Inc.
Tune: OPTATUS VOTIS OMNIUM, SM; anonymous; harm. by George R. Woodward, 1848–1934, alt.

Uyai Mose / Come All You People 828

Ostinato Refrain

U - ya - i mo - se,   ti - na - ma - te Mwa - ri,
Come all   you peo - ple,   come and   praise your Mak - er,

U - ya - i mo - se,   ti - na - ma - te Mwa - ri,
Come all   you peo - ple,   come and   praise your Mak - er,

U - ya - i mo - se,   ti - na - ma - te Mwa - ri,
Come all   you peo - ple,   come and   praise your Mak - er,

U - ya - i   mo - se   zvi - no.
Come now   and   wor - ship   the   Lord.

Text: Alexander Gondo, b.1936
Tune: Alexander Gondo, b.1936; arr. by John L. Bell, b.1949, © 1994, Iona Community, GIA Publications, Inc., agent

829 Who Is This Who Breaches Borders

1. Who is this who breach-es bor - ders And sub -
2. Who is this who eats with sin - ners, Call - ing
3. Who will wor - ship with the stran - ger, Of - f'ring

verts the so - cial or - ders, Cross - ing cha - sms
luck - less los - ers "win - ners," Say - ing "first shall
ref - uge from all dan - ger, And in - vite the

that di - vide, Cast - ing race and class a - side?
be the last," Choos - ing feast in - stead of fast?
last and least To the full - ness of God's feast?

This is Je - sus with the bro - ken, Liv - ing
This is Je - sus, God's a - noint - ed, Who pro -
This is Je - sus' bod - y, liv - ing In the

out what he has spo - ken: "Blest are those who
claims the time ap - point - ed For the pris - on -
sim - ple act of giv - ing And the love that

suf - fer hate; Woe to those the world calls great."
er's re - lease, And the ju - bi - lee of peace.
we ex - tend As a foe be - comes our friend.

Text: Adam M. L. Tice, b.1979, © 2009, GIA Publications, Inc.
Tune: MON DIEU, PRÊTE-MOI L'OREILLE, 88 77 D; attr. to Louis Bourgeois, c.1510–1561; harm. by Claude Goudimel, 1505–1572, alt.

Lord Christ, the People Flocked to You 830

1. Lord Christ, the peo - ple flocked to you Like
2. To - day, O Christ, we come to you With
3. Lord Christ, Good Shep - herd of the flock, Your

sheep with - out a guide, And you, with words that
hun - gers un - ful - filled: Our grief, our guilt, our
Church with shep - herds bless: True ser - vants who will

glowed with grace, The truth of God sup - plied. And,
needs and cares, Our rest - less - ness un - stilled. To -
preach your Word With grace and faith - ful - ness. And

when the eve - ning sun had set Up - on those
day we seek the Word of truth That you a -
when they place in wait - ing hands The blessed and

hun - gry folk, You fed them in that
lone sup - ply. To - day we bring the
bro - ken bread, Be pres - ent, Lord, that

des - ert place With bread you blessed and broke.
gift of bread For you to mul - ti - ply.
in this place Your peo - ple may be fed.

Text: Herman G. Stuempfle, Jr., 1923–2007, © 2006, GIA Publications, Inc.
Tune: RESIGNATION, CMD; Funk's *Compilation of Genuine Church Music*, 1832; harm. by Richard Proulx, 1937–2010, © 1975, GIA Publications, Inc.

831 As We Gather at Your Table

1. As we gath - er at your ta - ble,
2. Turn our wor - ship in - to wit - ness
3. Gra - cious Spir - it, help us sum - mon

As we lis - ten to your word,
In the sac - ra - ment of life;
Oth - er guests to share that feast

Help us know, O God, your pres - ence;
Send us forth to love and serve you,
Where tri - um - phant Love will wel - come

Let our hearts and minds be stirred. Nour - ish us with
Bring - ing peace where there is strife. Give us, Christ, your
Those who had been last and least. There no more will

sa - cred sto - ry Till we claim it as our own;
great com - pas - sion To for - give as you for - gave;
en - vy blind us Nor will pride our peace de - stroy,

Teach us through this ho - ly ban - quet
May we still be - hold your im - age
As we join with saints and an - gels

How to make Love's vic - t'ry known.
In the world you died to save.
To re - peat the sound - ing joy.

Text: Carl P. Daw, Jr., b.1944, © 1989, Hope Publishing Company
Tune: HOLY MANNA, 8 7 8 7 D; William Moore, fl.1830; acc. by Kelly Dobbs-Mickus, b.1966, © 2003, GIA Publications, Inc.

We Come with Joy in Jesus Christ 832

1. We come with joy in Je - sus Christ, Who
2. A lit - tle bread is all we have, So
3. Like rip - ples in a pool, our gifts, How -

knows our hu - man need, Who, moved with pit - y
mea - ger our sup - ply; A lit - tle time, a
ev - er small they are, Will reach and heal a

for the poor, Would ev - 'ry hun - ger feed.
lit - tle love Can hard - ly sat - is - fy.
need - y world, Will com - fort near and far.

He blessed the fish and bar - ley loaves Till
But let us bring the best we have, De -
For Christ will bless our bit of bread, The

food was mul - ti - plied; His boun - ty o - ver -
spite our pov - er - ty, And of - fer all our
loaves our hands pro - vide, Till emp - ty bas - kets

flowed their want And all were sat - is - fied.
gifts to Christ, Im - per - fect though they be.
o - ver - flow And all are sat - is - fied.

Text: Delores Dufner, OSB, b.1939, alt., © 1994, GIA Publications, Inc.
Tune: ELLACOMBE, CMD; *Gesangbuch der Herzogl*, Wirtemberg, 1784

833 All Are Welcome

1. Let us build a house where love can dwell And
2. Let us build a house where proph - ets speak, And
3. Let us build a house where love is found In
4. Let us build a house where hands will reach Be -
5. Let us build a house where all are named, Their

all can safe - ly live, A place where saints and
words are strong and true, Where all God's chil - dren
wa - ter, wine and wheat: A ban - quet hall on
yond the wood and stone To heal and strength - en,
songs and vi - sions heard And loved and treas - ured,

chil - dren tell How hearts learn to for -
dare to seek To dream God's reign a -
ho - ly ground, Where peace and jus - tice
serve and teach, And live the Word they've
taught and claimed As words with - in the

give. Built of hopes and dreams and vi - sions, Rock of
new. Here the cross shall stand as wit - ness And as
meet. Here the love of God, through Je - sus, Is re -
known. Here the out - cast and the stran - ger Bear the
Word. Built of tears and cries and laugh - ter, Prayers of

faith and vault of grace; Here the
sym - bol of God's grace; Here as
vealed in time and space; As we
im - age of God's face; Let us
faith and songs of grace, Let this

love of Christ shall end di - vi - sions:
one we claim the faith of Je - sus:
share in Christ the feast that frees us:
bring an end to fear and dan - ger:
house pro - claim from floor to raft - er:

All are wel-come, all are wel-come, all are wel-come in this place.

Text: Marty Haugen, b.1950
Tune: TWO OAKS, 9 6 8 6 8 7 10 with refrain; Marty Haugen, b.1950
© 1994, GIA Publications, Inc.

O Christ, within These Walls 834

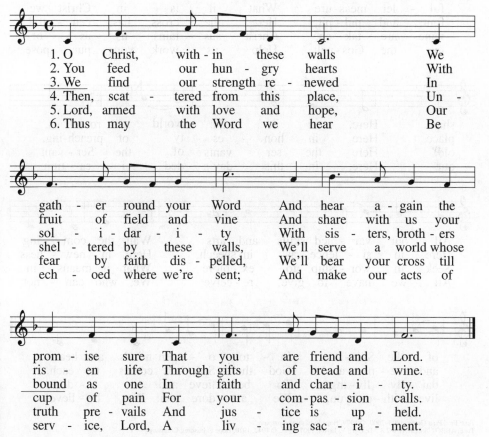

1. O Christ, with-in these walls We
2. You feed our hun-gry hearts With
3. We find our strength re-newed In
4. Then, scat-tered from this place, Un-
5. Lord, armed with love and hope, Our
6. Thus may the Word we hear Be

gath-er round your Word And hear a-gain the
fruit of field and vine And share with us your
sol-i-dar-i-ty With sis-ters, broth-ers
shel-tered by these walls, We'll serve a world whose
fear by faith dis-pelled, We'll bear your cross till
ech-oed where we're sent; And make our acts of

prom-ise sure That you are friend and Lord.
ris-en life Through gifts of bread and wine.
bound as one In faith and char-i-ty.
cup of pain For your com-pas-sion calls.
truth pre-vails And jus-tice is up-held.
serv-ice, Lord, A liv-ing sac-ra-ment.

Text: Herman G. Stuempfle, Jr., 1923–2007, © 1997, GIA Publications, Inc.
Tune: LIVING BREAD, SM; Randall Sensmeier, b.1948, © 2001, GIA Publications, Inc.

835 God Is Here! As We His People

1. God is here! As we his peo-ple Meet to of-fer praise and prayer, May we find in ful-ler meas-ure What it is in Christ we share. Here, as in the world a-round us, All our var-ied skills and arts Wait the com-ing of the Spir-it In-to o-pen minds and hearts.

2. Here are sym-bols to re-mind us Of our life-long need of grace; Here are ta-ble, font, and pul-pit; Here in hon-es-ty of preach-ing, Here in si-lence, as in speech, Here, in new-ness and re-new-al, God the Spir-it comes to each.

3. Here our chil-dren find a wel-come In the Shep-herd's flock and fold; Here, as bread and wine are tak-en, Christ sus-tains us as of old. Here the ser-vants of the Ser-vant Seek in wor-ship to ex-plore What it means in dai-ly liv-ing To be-lieve and to a-dore.

4. Lord of all, of Church and king-dom, In an age of change and doubt, Keep us faith-ful to the Gos-pel; Help us work your pur-pose out. Here, in this day's ded-i-ca-tion, All we have to give, re-ceive; We, who can-not live with-out you, We a-dore you! We be-lieve!

Text: Fred Pratt Green, 1903–2000, © 1979, Hope Publishing Company
Tune: ABBOT'S LEIGH, 8 7 8 7 D; Cyril V. Taylor, 1907–1991, © 1942, 1970, Hope Publishing Company

Gather Us In 836

1. Here in this place new light is stream - ing,
2. We are the young— our lives are a mys - t'ry,
3. Here we will take the wine and the wa - ter,

Now is the dark - ness van - ished a - way,
We are the old— who yearn for your face,
Here we will take the bread of new birth,

See in this space our fears and our dream - ings,
We have been sung through - out all of his - t'ry,
Here you shall call your sons and your daugh - ters,

Brought here to you in the light of this day.
Called to be light to the whole hu - man race.
Call us a - new to be salt for the earth.

Gath - er us in— the lost and for - sak - en, Gath - er us in— the
Gath - er us in— the rich and the haugh - ty, Gath - er us in— the
Give us to drink the wine of com - pas - sion, Give us to eat the

blind and the lame; Call to us now, and we shall a - wak - en,
proud and the strong; Give us a heart so meek and so low - ly,
bread that is you; Nour - ish us well, and teach us to fash - ion

We shall a - rise at the sound of our name.
Give us the cour - age to en - ter the song.
Lives that are ho - ly and hearts that are true.

Text: Marty Haugen, b.1950
Tune: GATHER US IN, 10 9 10 10 D; Marty Haugen, b.1950
© 1982, GIA Publications, Inc.

837 All People That on Earth Do Dwell

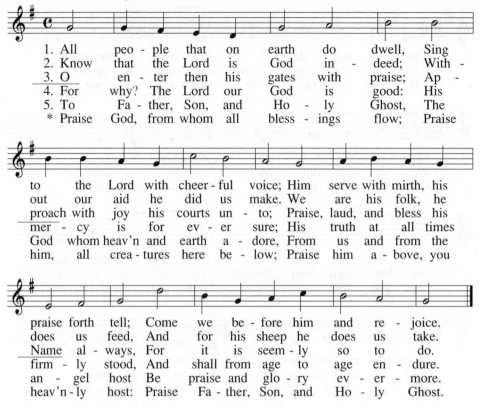

1. All peo-ple that on earth do dwell, Sing
2. Know that the Lord is God in-deed; With-
3. O en-ter then his gates with praise; Ap-
4. For why? The Lord our God is good: His
5. To Fa-ther, Son, and Ho-ly Ghost, The
* Praise God, from whom all bless-ings flow; Praise

to the Lord with cheer-ful voice; Him serve with mirth, his
out our aid he did us make. We are his folk, he
proach with joy his courts un-to; Praise, laud, and bless his
mer-cy is for ev-er sure; His truth at all times
God whom heav'n and earth a-dore, From us and from the
him, all crea-tures here be-low; Praise him a-bove, you

praise forth tell; Come we be-fore him and re-joice.
does us feed, And for his sheep he does us take.
Name al-ways, For it is seem-ly so to do.
firm-ly stood, And shall from age to age en-dure.
an-gel host Be praise and glo-ry ev-er-more.
heav'n-ly host: Praise Fa-ther, Son, and Ho-ly Ghost.

May be sung alone or as an alternate to stanza 5.

Text: Psalm 100; William Kethe, d. c.1593; Doxology, Thomas Ken, 1637–1711
Tune: OLD HUNDREDTH, LM; Louis Bourgeois, c.1510–1561

838 They Came, a Milling Crowd

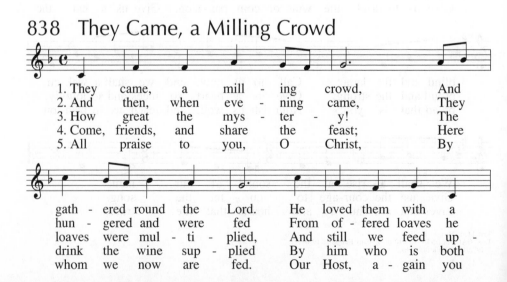

1. They came, a mill-ing crowd, And
2. And then, when eve-ning came, They
3. How great the mys-ter-y! The
4. Come, friends, and share the feast; Here
5. All praise to you, O Christ, By

gath-ered round the Lord. He loved them with a
hun-gered and were fed From of-fered loaves he
loaves were mul-ti-plied, And still we feed up-
drink the wine sup-plied By him who is both
whom we now are fed. Our Host, a-gain you

shep - herd's heart And fed them with his Word.
blessed and broke And made their liv - ing bread.
on the crumbs And still are sat - is - fied!
guest and host; For us, the cru - ci - fied.
share with us Your - self, the liv - ing bread.

Text: Herman G. Stuempfle, Jr., 1923–2007, © 1993, GIA Publications, Inc.
Tune: ST. THOMAS (Williams), SM; Aaron Williams, 1731–1776; harm. by Lowell Mason, 1792–1872

Only-Begotten, Word of God Eternal 839

1. On - ly - be - got - ten, Word of God e -
2. Ho - ly this dwell - ing where the Lord is
3. Lord, we be - seech you, as we throng your
4. God in three Per - sons, Fa - ther ev - er -

ter - nal, Lord of cre - a - tion, mer - ci - ful and
pres - ent; This is none oth - er than the gate of
tem - ple, By your past bless - ings, by your pres - ent
last - ing, Son co - e - ter - nal, ev - er bless - ed

might - y, Hear us, your ser - vants, when our tune - ful
heav - en; Stran - gers and pil - grims, seek - ing homes e -
boun - ty, Smile on your chil - dren, and with ten - der
Spir - it, Yours be the glo - ry, praise and ad - o -

voic - es Rise to your pres - ence.
ter - nal, Pass through its por - tals.
mer - cy Hear our pe - ti - tions.
ra - tion, Now and for - ev - er.

Text: *Christe cunctorum dominator alme*; Latin, 9th C.; tr. by Maxwell J. Blacker, 1822–1888, alt.
Tune: ISTE CONFESSOR, 11 11 11 5; Poitiers *Antiphoner*, 1746; harm. by Carl F. Schalk, b.1929, © 1969, Concordia Publishing House

840 Risen Lord, We Gather Round You

1. Ris - en Lord, we gath - er round you,
2. Sis - ters, broth - ers, stand be - side us,
*3. By the Loaf and Cup you of - fer,
4. "Go where lives are bruised and bro - ken;

Drawn by words for - ev - er new: "Come, my peo - ple,
Called from ev - 'ry land and race. One the Bread of
Strength - en us to fol - low you. By your Bod - y,
Go where chil - dren waste and blight. Go a - mong the

all are wel - come; Share the feast pre - pared for you!"
Life that feeds us, One the Cup of brim - ming grace.
ris - en, giv - en, Heal us, Christ, and make us new.
lost, for - got - ten; Be for them my heal - ing Light.

Emp - ty hands and hearts that hun - ger,
Form us, Lord, a sin - gle bod - y,
Help us hear your ur - gent sum - mons,
Take the Bread of Life I give you;

Christ, we bring to you to - day. Here you feed us
Free from en - mi - ty and strife. Je - sus, by your
Cut - ting through our fear of loss: "Go, my peo - ple!
Share it with a world in pain. Go, my peo - ple!

with your Bod - y, Gift of love for which we pray.
res - ur - rec - tion, Fill us with the Spir - it's life.
Be my ser - vants! Bear with me the wait - ing cross!"
I am with you Till on earth my love shall reign!"

*Stanza 3 may be replaced by an appropriate stanza taken from the following page.

Alternate Stanza 3 for various occasions:

Feasts of the Blessed Virgin Mary
3. God, you made your servant Mary
   Chosen vessel of your Word,
   Bearer of the Christ among us,
   Mother of our Risen Lord!
   We would also be your servants,
   Human vessels that you claim.
   May we be Christ's present bearers;
   Help us magnify your name!

Sacraments of Initiation
3. Christ, our Shepherd, still you lead us
   Where baptismal waters flow.
   There by grace you bless and claim us;
   There the Spirit's gifts bestow.
   Through your Church you call and
        feed us
   With the Bread by which we live.
   Grant that, as your chosen people,
   We may bread to others give.

Evening Mass of the Lord's Supper
3. With your friends this night you gathered,
   Gave them bread you blessed to eat.
   Though their Lord, you moved among them
   Washing weary, dusty feet.
   Jesus, by your great example,
   Teach our hearts humility.
   Help us take the towel and basin,
   Serve in selfless charity.

Ordination
3. Loaves you blessed along the lakeside
   By your grace were multiplied.
   When disciples took and shared them,
   Hungry folk were satisfied.
   Christ, you still ordain your servants
   For the Breaking of the Bread.
   Through these empty hands we offer,
   Let your Church again be fed.

Chrism Mass
3. Risen Lord, we bring before you
   Precious oil for you to bless.
   May it bear your living presence,
   Oil of gladness, sign of grace.
   Heal the sick, restore the fallen,
   Show the poor compassion's face.
   Let it be your benediction,
   Binding all in love's embrace.

Text: Herman G. Stuempfle, Jr., 1923–2007, alt.
Tune: GREENSBURG, 8 7 8 7 D; Bob Moore, b.1962
© 2002, GIA Publications, Inc.

841 I Rejoiced When I Heard Them Say

1. I re - joiced when I heard them
2. Strong - ly built is Je - ru - sa -
3. Pray for peace in Je - ru - sa -
4. For the love of my fam - i - ly and

say: "Let us go to the house of the
lem, There the tribes of the Lord go
lem, May they pros - per who love you
friends And the sake of the house of the

Lord." Our feet are stand - ing with - in your
up, Seek - ing their jus - tice and bring - ing
well; E - ter - nal peace be with - in your
Lord, I ev - er pray for your health and

gates, O Je - ru - sa - lem.
thanks, O Je - ru - sa - lem.
walls, O Je - ru - sa - lem.
peace, O Je - ru - sa - lem.

I re - joiced when I heard them say:

"Let us go to the house of the Lord!"

I re - joiced when I heard them say:

"Let us go to the house of the Lord!"

Text: Psalm 122; Richard Proulx, 1937–2010
Tune: MA YEDIDUT, Irregular with refrain; Hasidic melody, arr. by Richard Proulx, 1937–2010
© 1993, GIA Publications, Inc.

Diverse in Culture, Nation, Race 842

1. Di - verse in cul - ture, na - tion, race, We
2. God, let us be a bridge of care Con -
3. When cha - sms wid - en, storms a - rise, O
4. God, let us be a ta - ble spread With

come to - geth - er by your grace. God, let us be a
nect - ing peo - ple ev - 'ry - where. Help us con - front all
Ho - ly Spir - it, make us wise. Let our re - solve, like
gifts of love and bro - ken bread, Where all find wel - come,

meet - ing ground Where hope and heal - ing love are found.
fear and hate And lust for pow'r that sep - a - rate.
steel, be strong To stand with those who suf - fer wrong.
grace at - tends, And en - e - mies a - rise as friends.

*May be sung as a two- or four-voice canon.

Text: Ruth Duck, b.1947, © 1992, GIA Publications, Inc.
Tune: TALLIS' CANON, LM; Thomas Tallis, c.1505–1585

Jesus Christ, Yesterday, Today, and Forever / 843
Jesucristo Ayer

Ostinato Refrain

Je - sus Christ, Je - sus Christ,
Je - su - cris - to a - yer, Je - su - cris - to hoy,

yes - ter - day, to - day, and for - ev - er.
siem - pre se - rá el Se - ñor.

Text: Suzanne Toolan, RSM, b.1927; Spanish tr. by Ronald F. Krisman, b.1946
Tune: Suzanne Toolan, RSM, b.1927
© 1988, 2004, GIA Publications, Inc.

844 All Who Hunger, Gather Gladly

1. All who hun - ger, gath - er glad - ly;
2. All who hun - ger, nev - er stran - gers,
3. All who hun - ger, sing to - geth - er;

Ho - ly man - na is our bread. Come from wil - der -
Seek - er, be a wel - come guest. Come from rest - less -
Je - sus Christ is liv - ing bread. Come from lone - li -

ness and wan - d'ring. Here, in truth, we will be fed.
ness and roam - ing. Here, in joy, we keep the feast.
ness and long - ing. Here, in peace, we have been led.

You that yearn for days of full - ness,
We that once were lost and scat - tered
Blest are those who from this ta - ble

All a - round us is our food. Taste and see the
In com - mun - ion's love have stood. Taste and see the
Live their days in grat - i - tude. Taste and see the

grace e - ter - nal. Taste and see that God is good.
grace e - ter - nal. Taste and see that God is good.
grace e - ter - nal. Taste and see that God is good.

Text: Sylvia G. Dunstan, 1955–1993, © 1991, GIA Publications, Inc.
Tune: HOLY MANNA, 8 7 8 7 D; William Moore, fl.1830

How Shocking Were the People   845

1. How shock-ing were the peo - ple Who gath-ered there to
2. The pi - ous scorned their com - p'ny And count-ed them im -
3. O Christ, we gath - er round you As did those folk of
4. All praise to you for mer - cy That cov - ers sin and

eat: The tax col - lect - ors, har - lots, And out - casts
pure. They would not risk con - ta - gion By en - t'ring
old. We come, our lives un - wor - thy, Our hearts es -
shame; For love that sees our se - crets, Yet calls us

from the street! And Je - sus sat a - mong them, A
such a door! When Je - sus heard their grum - bling, He
tranged and cold. And still you stand a - mong us, A
each by name; For bread and wine that feed us; For

guest, and yet their Host, His arms out-stretched, em -
spoke while at the meal, "The sick, and not the
guest, and yet our Host, And wel-come to the
words of peace that heal; For shar - ing still with

brac - ing The lone - ly and the lost.
health - y, Are those I've come to heal!"
Ta - ble The lone - ly and the lost.
sin - ners This ho - ly, joy - ous meal!

Text: Matthew 9:9–13, 15–23; Mark 2:13–22; Herman G. Stuempfle, Jr., 1923–2007, © 2000, GIA Publications, Inc.
Tune: LLANGLOFFAN, 7 6 7 6 D; Welsh melody

846 To You, O God, We Sing / Cantemos al Señor

Verses

1. To you, O God, we sing A hymn of ju - bi -
2. To you, O God, we sing A hymn of praise and
1. *Can - te - mos al Se - ñor Un him - no de_a - le -*
2. *Can - te - mos al Se - ñor Un him - no de_a - la -*

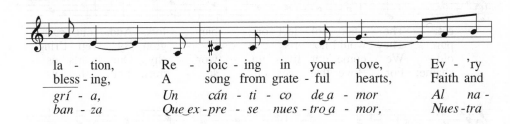

la - tion, Re - joic - ing in your love, Ev - 'ry
bless - ing, A song from grate - ful hearts, Faith and
grí - a, Un cán - ti - co de_a - mor Al na -
ban - za Que_ex-pre - se nues-tro_a - mor, Nues-tra

day a new cre - a - tion. You made the earth and
hope and love ex - press - ing. Cre - a - tion, with one
cer el nue - vo dí - a. Él hi - zo_el cie - lo_el
fe,_y nues-tra_es - pe - ran - za. To - da la cre - a -

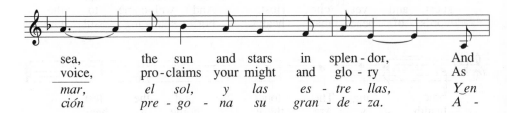

sea, the sun and stars in splen - dor, And
voice, pro - claims your might and glo - ry As
mar, el sol, y las es - tre - llas, Y_en
ción pre - go - na su gran - de - za. A -

saw that they were good, full of beau - ty and of won - der.
peo - ple ev - 'ry - where tell a - gain sal - va - tion's sto - ry.
e - llos vio bon - dad, pues sus o - bras e - ran be - llas.
sí nues-tro can - tar va_a-nun-cian - do su be - lle - za.

Refrain

Al - le - lu - ia! Al - le - lu - ia! To
¡A - le - lu - ya! ¡A - le - lu - ya! Can-

1., 3.   2.   D.C.

you, O God, we sing Al - le - lu - ia! ia!
te - mos al Se - ñor ¡A - le - lu - ya! ya!

4.

ia! To you, O God, we sing Al - le - lu - ia!
ya! Can - te - mos al Se - ñor ¡A - le - lu - ya!

Text: Based on Psalm 19; Carlos Rosas, b.1939; tr. by Ronald F. Krisman, b.1946
Tune: ROSAS, 6 7 6 8 D with refrain; Carlos Rosas, b.1939; acc. by Ronald F. Krisman, b.1946
© 1976, 2011, OCP

Morning Has Broken   847

1. Morn-ing has bro - ken Like the first morn - ing, Black-bird has
2. Sweet the rain's new fall Sun - lit from heav - en, Like the first
3. Mine is the sun - light! Mine is the morn - ing Born of the

spo - ken Like the first bird. Praise for the sing - ing! Praise for the
dew - fall On the first grass. Praise for the sweet - ness Of the wet
one light E - den saw play! Praise with e - la - tion, Praise ev - 'ry

morn - ing! Praise for them, spring - ing Fresh from the Word!
gar - den, Sprung in com - plete - ness Where his feet pass.
morn - ing, God's re - cre - a - tion Of the new day!

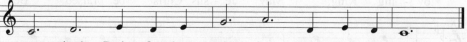

Text: Eleanor Farjeon, 1881-1965, *The Children's Bells,* © David Higham Assoc., Ltd.
Tune: BUNESSAN, 5 5 5 4 D; Gaelic melody; acc. by Marty Haugen, b.1950, © 1987, GIA Publications, Inc.

848 The Earth Is Turning toward the Sun

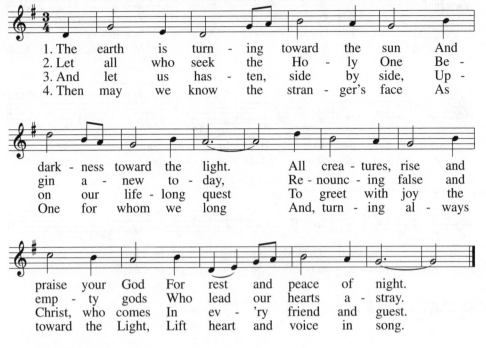

1. The earth is turn - ing toward the sun And
2. Let all who seek the Ho - ly One Be -
3. And let us has - ten, side by side, Up -
4. Then may we know the stran - ger's face As

dark - ness toward the light. All crea - tures, rise and
gin a - new to - day, Re - nounc - ing false and
on our life - long quest To greet with joy the
One for whom we long And, turn - ing al - ways

praise your God For rest and peace of night.
emp - ty gods Who lead our hearts a - stray.
Christ, who comes In ev - 'ry friend and guest.
toward the Light, Lift heart and voice in song.

Text: Delores Dufner, OSB, b.1939, © 2011, GIA Publications, Inc.
Tune: MARTYRDOM, CM; Hugh Wilson, 1764–1824

849 When Morning Gilds the Sky

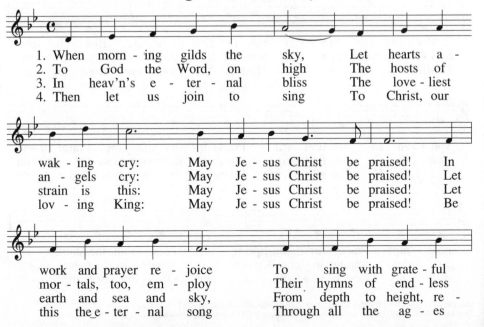

1. When morn - ing gilds the sky, Let hearts a -
2. To God the Word, on high The hosts of
3. In heav'n's e - ter - nal bliss The love - liest
4. Then let us join to sing To Christ, our

wak - ing cry: May Je - sus Christ be praised! In
an - gels cry: May Je - sus Christ be praised! Let
strain is this: May Je - sus Christ be praised! Let
lov - ing King: May Je - sus Christ be praised! Be

work and prayer re - joice To sing with grate - ful
mor - tals, too, em - ploy Their hymns of end - less
earth and sea and sky, From depth to height, re -
this the e - ter - nal song Through all the ag - es

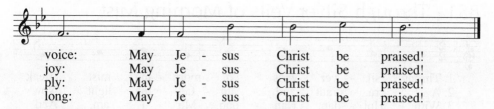

voice:	May	Je - sus	Christ	be	praised!
joy:	May	Je - sus	Christ	be	praised!
ply:	May	Je - sus	Christ	be	praised!
long:	May	Je - sus	Christ	be	praised!

Text: *Wach ich früh Morgens auf; Katholisches Gesangbuch*, Würzburg, 1828; tr. by Edward Caswall, 1814–1878, alt.
Tune: LAUDES DOMINI, 66 6 D; Joseph Barnby, 1838–1896

This Day God Gives Me 850

1. This day God gives me Strength of high heav - en,
2. This day God sends me Strength as my guard - ian,
3. God's way is my way, God's shield is round me,
4. Ris - ing I thank you, Might - y and strong One,

Sun and moon shin - ing, Flame in my hearth,
Might to up - hold me, Wis - dom as guide.
God's host de - fends me, Sav - ing from ill.
King of cre - a - tion, Giv - er of rest,

Flash - ing of light - ning, Wind in its swift - ness,
Your eyes are watch - ful, Your ears are lis - t'ning,
An - gels of heav - en, Drive from me al - ways
Firm - ly con - fess - ing God in three Per - sons,

Depths of the o - cean, Firm - ness of earth.
Your lips are speak - ing, Friend at my side.
All that would harm me; Stand by me still.
One - ness of God - head, Trin - i - ty blest.

Text: Ascribed to St. Patrick; James Quinn, SJ, 1919–2010, © 1969. Used by permission of Selah Publishing Co., Inc.
Tune: RAABE, 5 5 5 4 D; Carl F. Schalk, b.1929; © 2003, GIA Publications, Inc.

851 Through Silver Veils of Morning Mist

1. Through sil - ver veils of morn - ing mist Break
2. A ra - diant and un - fad - ing light Now
3. With Hul - dah, Han - nah, Mir - i - am, And

rays of gold - en sun. In am - e - thyst and
shines be - fore our eyes, Il - lu - min - ing all
wom - en - folk un - named, We cher - ish our in -

ru - by skies, A new day has be - gun. More
minds that seek With truth to make us wise. God's
her - i - tance Of proph - e - cy pro - claimed: The

treas - ured yet than sil - ver, gold, Or an - y pre - cious
Wis - dom calls us to the feast Of wine and liv - ing
need - y shall be lift - ed up; The weak shall be made

gem, God's Wis - dom breaks up - on the earth And
bread, Where fruits of grace and peace a - bound And
strong. And Wis - dom's flow - 'ring Tree of Life Shall

wakes our morn - ing hymn.
hun - gry hearts are fed.
blos - som in our song.

Text: Mary Louise Bringle, b.1953, © 2002, GIA Publications, Inc.
Tune: LUCY, CMD; Sally Ann Morris, b.1952, © 2009, GIA Publications, Inc.

Day Is Done 852

1. Day is done, but Love un-fail-ing Dwells ev - er
2. Dark de-scends, but Light un-end-ing Shines through our
3. Eyes will close, but you un-sleep-ing Watch by our

here; Shad - ows fall, but hope, pre - vail - ing,
night; You are with us, ev - er lend - ing
side; Death may come, in Love's safe-keep - ing

Calms ev - 'ry fear. God, our Mak - er, none for - sak - ing,
New strength to sight. One in love, your truth con-fess-ing,
Still we a - bide. God of love, all e - vil quell-ing,

Take our hearts, of Love's own mak - ing; Watch our sleep-ing,
One in hope of heav - en's bless-ing, May we see, in
Sin for - giv - ing, fear dis-pel - ling, Stay with us, our

guard our wak - ing, Be al - ways near.
love's pos - sess - ing, Love's end - less light!
hearts in - dwell - ing, This e - ven - tide.

Text: James Quinn, SJ, 1919–2010, © 1969. Used by permission of Selah Publishing Co., Inc.
Tune: AR HYD Y NOS, 8 4 8 4 888 4; Welsh melody

853 The Day You Gave Us, Lord, Is Ended

1. The day you gave us, Lord, is end - ed;
2. We thank you that your Church, un - sleep-ing
3. A - cross each con - ti - nent and is - land,
4. The sun, which bids us rest, is wak - ing
5. So be it, Lord! Your throne shall nev - er,

The dark - ness falls at your be - hest.
While earth rolls on - ward in - to light,
As dawn leads on an - oth - er day,
Your chil - dren un - der west - ern skies,
Like earth's proud em - pires, pass a - way;

To you our morn - ing hymns as - cend-ed;
Through all the world its watch is keep-ing,
The voice of prayer is nev - er si - lent,
And hour by hour, as day is break-ing,
Your king - dom stands, and grows for - ev - er

Your praise shall sanc - ti - fy our rest.
And nev - er rests by day or night.
Nor dies the strain of praise a - way.
Fresh hymns of thank - ful praise a - rise.
Un - til there dawns your glo - rious day.

Text: John Ellerton, 1826–1893, alt.
Tune: ST. CLEMENT, 9 8 9 8; Clement C. Scholefield, 1839–1904

God of Day and God of Darkness 854

1. God of day and God of dark - ness, Now we
2. Still the na - tions curse the dark - ness, Still the
3. You shall be the path that guides us, You the
4. Praise to you in day and dark - ness, You our

stand be - fore the night; As the shad - ows stretch and
rich op - press the poor; Still the earth is bruised and
light that in us burns; Shin - ing deep with - in all
source and you our end; Praise to you who love and

deep - en, Come and make our dark - ness bright. All cre -
bro - ken By the ones who still want more. Come and
peo - ple, Yours the love that we must learn. For our
nur - ture As a fa - ther, moth - er, friend. Grant us

a - tion still is groan - ing For the dawn - ing of your
wake us from our sleep - ing, So our hearts can - not ig -
hearts shall wan - der rest - less 'Til they safe to you re -
all a peace-ful rest - ing, Let each mind and bod - y

might, When the Sun of peace and jus - tice
nore All your peo - ple lost and bro - ken,
turn; Find - ing you in one an - oth - er,
mend, So we rise re - freshed to - mor - row,

Fills the earth with ra - diant light.
All your chil - dren at our door.
We shall all your face dis - cern.
Hearts re - newed to king - dom tend.

Text: Marty Haugen, b.1950, © 1985, 1994, GIA Publications, Inc.
Tune: BEACH SPRING, 8 7 8 7 D; The Sacred Harp, 1844; harm. by Marty Haugen, b.1950, © 1985, GIA Publications, Inc.

855 Christ, Mighty Savior

1. Christ, might - y   Sav - ior,   Light   of   all   cre -
2. Now   comes   the   day's end   as   the   sun   is
3. There - fore   we   come now   eve - ning   rites   to
4. Give   heed,   we   pray you,   to   our   sup - pli -
5. Though   bod - ies   slum - ber,   hearts   shall   keep their

a - tion,   You   make   the   day - time
set - ting: Mir - ror   of   day - break,
of - fer,   Joy - ful - ly   chant - ing
ca - tion: That   you   may   grant   us
vig - il,   For   ev - er   rest - ing

ra - diant with the   sun - light,   And   to   the
pledge   of   res - ur - rec - tion;   While   in   the
ho - ly hymns to   praise you,   With   all   cre -
par - don   for   of - fens - es,   Strength for   our
in   the peace of   Je - sus,   In   light   or

night give   glit - ter - ing   a - dorn - ment,
heav - ens   choirs   of   stars ap - pear - ing
a - tion   join - ing hearts and   voic - es,
weak hearts,   rest   for   ach - ing   bod - ies,
dark - ness   wor - ship - ing   our   Sav - ior

Stars   in   the   heav - ens.
Hal - low   the   night - fall.
Sing - ing   your   glo - ry.
Sooth - ing   the   wea - ry.
Now   and   for - ev - er.

Text: *Christe, lux mundi*; Mozarabic Rite, 10th C.; tr. by Alan G. McDougall, 1895–1964, rev. by Anne K. LeCroy, b.1930, and others, © 1982,
The United Methodist Publishing House (admin. by The Copyright Company)
Tune: MIGHTY SAVIOR, 11 11 11 5; David Hurd, b.1950, © 1985, GIA Publications, Inc.

Praise and Thanksgiving / Te Damos Gracias   856

1. Praise and thanks - giv - ing, Fa - ther, we of - fer,
2. Lord, bless the la - bor We bring to serve you,
3. Fa - ther, pro - vid - ing Food for your chil - dren,
4. Then will your bless - ing Reach ev - 'ry peo - ple,

1. *¡Te da - mos gra - cias Por cuan - to_has he - cho,*
2. *¡Ben - di - ce,_oh Cris - to, Lo que tra - e - mos;*
3. *¡Oh, Pa - ra - cle - to Que_a - quí_en la tie - rra*
4. *Y_a - sí que_al - can - ce Tu_a - mor a to - dos,*

For all things liv - ing You have made good:
That with our neigh - bor We may be fed.
By your wise guid - ing Teach us to share
Free - ly con - fess - ing Your gra - cious hand.

Oh Pa - dre_e - ter - no, En tu bon - dad:
Díg - na - te_a to - dos A - li - men - tar!
A to - dos cui - das Con tu bon - dad:
Y tus pie - da - des Ben - de - ci - rán.

Har - vest of sown fields, Fruits of the or - chard,
Sow - ing or till - ing, We would work with you,
One with an - oth - er, So that, re - joic - ing
Where you are reign - ing No one will hun - ger,

Nues - tras co - se - chas, Fru - tos del cam - po
Ben - di - ce_a cuan - tos Jun - to con - ti - go
Que_u - nos y o - tros, Jun - tos o - bre - mos
Ba - jo tu rei - no Na - die ca - re - ce:

Hay from the mown fields, Blos - som and wood.
Har - vest - ing, mill - ing, For dai - ly bread.
With us, all oth - ers May know your care.
Your love sus - tain - ing, Fruit - ful the land.

Con que co - ro - nas Nues - tra_he - re - dad!
El pan pro - cu - ran Mul - ti - pli - car.
Co - mo_ins - tru - men - tos De tu pie - dad!
Tu_a - mor fe - cun - do Nos brin - da pan.

Text: Albert F. Bayly, 1901–1984, © 1988, Oxford University Press; tr. by Dimas Planas-Belfort, 1934–1992, alt., © 1989, Editorial Avance Luterano
Tune: BUNESSAN, 5 5 5 4 D; Gaelic melody; harm. by Robert J. Batastini, b.1942, © 1999, GIA Publications, Inc.

857 For the Fruits of All Creation

1. For the fruits of all cre - a - tion, Thanks be to
2. In the just re - ward of la - bor, God's will is
3. For the har - vests of the Spir - it, Thanks be to

God. For the gifts to ev - 'ry na - tion,
done. In the help we give our neigh - bor,
God. For the good we all in - her - it,

Thanks be to God. For the plow - ing, sow - ing, reap - ing,
God's will is done. In our world-wide task of car - ing
Thanks be to God. For the won - ders that a - stound us,

Si - lent growth while we are sleep - ing, Fu - ture needs in
For the hun - gry and de - spair - ing, In the har - vests
For the truths that still con-found us, Most of all, that

earth's safe keep - ing, Thanks be to God.
we are shar - ing, God's will is done.
love has found us, Thanks be to God.

Text: Fred Pratt Green, 1903–2000, © 1970, Hope Publishing Company
Tune: AR HYD Y NOS, 8 4 8 4 888 4; Welsh melody

Come, You Thankful People, Come 858

1. Come, you thank - ful peo - ple, come; Raise the song of
2. All the world is God's own field, Fruit un - to his
3. For the Lord our God shall come And shall take his
4. E - ven so, Lord, quick - ly come To your fi - nal

har - vest home. All is safe - ly gath - ered in
praise to yield; Wheat and tares to - geth - er sown,
har - vest home; From his field shall in that day
har - vest home. Gath - er all your peo - ple in,

Ere the win - ter storms be - gin. God, our Mak - er,
Un - to joy or sor - row grown. First the blade, and
All of - fens - es purge a - way, Giv - ing an - gels
Free from sor - row, free from sin, There, for ev - er

does pro - vide For our wants to be sup - plied.
then the ear, Then the full corn shall ap - pear.
charge at last In the fire the tares to cast,
pu - ri - fied, In your pres - ence to a - bide.

Come to God's own tem - ple, come.
Lord of har - vest, grant that we
But the fruit - ful ears to store
Come with all your an - gels, come!

Raise the song of har - vest home.
Whole - some grain and pure may be.
In God's gar - ner ev - er - more.
Raise the glo - rious har - vest home.

Text: Henry Alford, 1810–1871, alt.
Tune: ST. GEORGE'S WINDSOR, 77 77 D; George J. Elvey, 1816–1893

859 God, Whose Farm Is All Creation

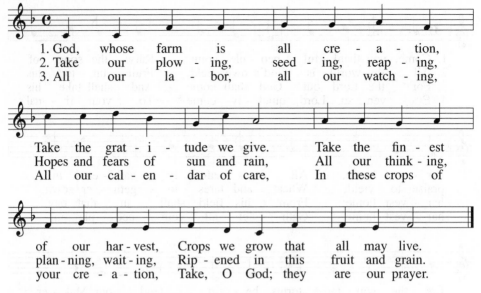

1. God, whose farm is all cre - a - tion,
Take the grat - i - tude we give. Take the fin - est
of our har - vest, Crops we grow that all may live.

2. Take our plow - ing, seed - ing, reap - ing,
Hopes and fears of sun and rain, All our think - ing,
plan - ning, wait - ing, Rip - ened in this fruit and grain.

3. All our la - bor, all our watch - ing,
All our cal - en - dar of care, In these crops of
your cre - a - tion, Take, O God; they are our prayer.

Text: John Arlott, 1914–1991, © Oxford University Press
Tune: STUTTGART, 8 7 8 7; *Psalmodia Sacra*, 1715; harm. by Kenneth D. Smith, b.1928, © Christian Education

860 Christ Is Surely Coming

1. Christ is sure - ly com - ing Bring - ing his re - ward,
Al - pha and O - me - ga, First and Last and Lord:
Root and stem of Da - vid, Bril - liant Morn - ing Star:
Meet your Judge and Sav - ior, Na - tions near and far!

2. See the ho - ly cit - y! There they en - ter in,
All by Christ made ho - ly, Washed from ev - 'ry sin:
Thirst - y ones, de - sir - ing All he loves to give,
Come for liv - ing wa - ter, Free - ly drink, and live!

3. Grace be with God's peo - ple! Praise his ho - ly name!
Fa - ther, Son, and Spir - it, Ev - er - more the same.
Hear the cer - tain prom - ise From the e - ter - nal home:
"Sure - ly I come quick - ly!" Come, Lord Je - sus, come!

Text: Christopher M. Idle, b.1938, © 1975, The Jubilate Group (admin. by Hope Publishing Company)
Tune: KING'S WESTON, 6 5 6 5 D; Ralph Vaughan Williams, 1872–1958, alt., © 1931, Oxford University Press

Soon and Very Soon   861

1. Soon and ver - y soon   we are goin'   to see   the King,
2. No   more cry - in' there,   we are goin'   to see   the King,
3. No   more dy - in' there,   we are goin'   to see   the King,
4. Soon and ver - y soon   we are goin'   to see   the King,

Soon and ver - y soon   we are goin'   to see   the King,
No   more cry - in' there,   we are goin'   to see   the King,
No   more dy - in' there,   we are goin'   to see   the King,
Soon and ver - y soon   we are goin'   to see   the King,

Soon and ver - y soon   we are goin'   to see   the King.
No   more cry - in' there,   we are goin'   to see   the King.
No   more dy - in' there,   we are goin'   to see   the King.   Hal - le -
Soon and ver - y soon   we are goin'   to see   the King.

1., 2.

lu - jah,   hal - le - lu - jah,   we're goin'   to see   the King!

3., 4.

Hal - le - lu - jah,   hal - le - lu -

jah, hal - le - lu - jah, hal - le - lu - jah.

Text: Andraé Crouch, b.1942
Tune: SOON AND VERY SOON, 12 12 12 14; Andraé Crouch, b.1942
© 1976, Crouch Music/Bud John Songs, admin. at EMICMGPublishing.com

862 God Is Working His Purpose Out

1. God is work - ing his pur - pose out As
2. From ut - most east to ut - most west, Wher -
3. March we forth in the strength of God, With the
4. All we can do is worth - less toil Un -

year suc - ceeds to year. God is work - ing his
ev - er foot has trod, By the mouth of man - y
ban - ner of Christ un - furled, That the light of the glo - rious
less God bless-es the deed. Vain - ly we hope for the

pur - pose out, And the time is draw - ing near.
mes - sen - gers Goes forth the voice of God:
gos - pel of truth May shine through - out the world.
har - vest - tide Till God gives life to the seed. Yet

Near - er and near - er draws the time, The
"Give ear to me, you con - ti - nents, You
Fight we the fight with sor - row and sin To
near - er and near - er draws the time, The

time that shall sure - ly be, When the earth shall be filled with the
isles, give ear to me, That the earth may be filled with the
set their cap-tives free, That the earth may be filled with the
time that shall sure - ly be, When the earth shall be filled with the

1.–3. | 4.

glo - ry of God As the wa - ters cov-er the sea.
glo - ry of God As the wa - ters cov-er the sea."
glo - ry of God As the wa - ters cov-er the sea.
glo - ry of God As the wa - ters cov-er the sea.

Text: Habakkuk 1:14; Arthur C. Ainger, 1841–1919, alt.
Tune: PURPOSE, Irregular; Martin Shaw, 1875–1958, © Oxford University Press

When the Lord in Glory Comes   863

1. When the Lord in glo - ry comes Not the trum - pets, not the drums, Not the an - them, not the psalm, Not the thun - der, not the calm, Not the time, But his voice when he ap - pears Shall be mu - sic to my ears; But his voice when he ap - pears Shall be mu - sic to my ears.

2. When the shout the heav - ens raise, Not the cho - rus, not the praise, Not the si - lenc - es sub - lime, Not the sounds of space and

When the Lord is seen a - gain Not the glo - ries of his reign, Not the light - nings through the storm, Not the ra - diance of his form, Not his gems, But his face up - on my sight Shall be dark - ness in - to light; But his face up - on my sight Shall be dark - ness in - to light.

pomp and pow'r a - lone, Not the splen - dors of his throne, Not his robe and di - a - dems, Not the gold and not the

3. When the Lord to hu - man eyes Shall be - stride our nar - row skies, Not the child of hum - ble birth, Not the car - pen - ter of earth, Not the grave, He it is to whom I fall, Je - sus Christ, my All in all; He it is to whom I fall, Je - sus Christ, my All in all.

man by all de - nied, Not the vic - tim cru - ci - fied, But the God who died to save, But the vic - tor of the

Text: Timothy Dudley-Smith, b.1926, © 1967, Hope Publishing Company
Tune: ST. JOHN'S, 77 77 77 D; Bob Moore, b.1962, © 1993, GIA Publications, Inc.

864 Mine Eyes Have Seen the Glory

1. Mine eyes have seen the glo - ry of the
2. I have seen him in the watch - fires of a
3. He has sound - ed forth the trum - pet that shall
4. In the beau - ty of the lil - ies Christ was

com - ing of the Lord; He is tram - pling out the
hun - dred cir - cling camps; They have build - ed him an
nev - er call re - treat; He is sift - ing out all
born a - cross the sea, With a glo - ry in his

vin - tage where the grapes of wrath are stored; He has
al - tar in the eve - ning dews and damps. I can
hu - man hearts be - fore his judg - ment seat. O be
bos - om that trans - fig - ures you and me. As he

loosed the fate - ful light - ning of his ter - ri - ble swift sword:
read the right - eous sen - tence by the dim and flar - ing lamps;
swift, my soul, to an - swer him; be ju - bi - lant, my feet!
died to make us ho - ly, let us live to make all free

His truth is march - ing on.
His day is march - ing on.
Our God is march - ing on.
While God is march - ing on.

Glo - ry, glo - ry! Hal - le - lu - jah! Glo - ry,

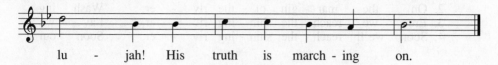

glo - ry! Hal - le - lu - jah! Glo - ry, glo - ry! Hal - le -

lu - jah! His truth is march - ing on.

Text: Julia W. Howe, 1819–1910, alt.
Tune: BATTLE HYMN OF THE REPUBLIC, 15 15 15 6 with refrain; attr. to William Steffe, d.1911

From the Father's Throne on High 865

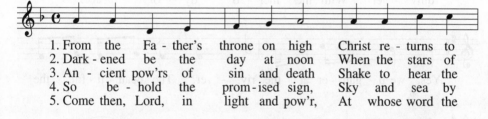

1. From the Fa - ther's throne on high Christ re - turns to
2. Dark - ened be the day at noon When the stars of
3. An - cient pow'rs of sin and death Shake to hear the
4. So be - hold the prom - ised sign, Sky and sea by
5. Come then, Lord, in light and pow'r, At whose word the

rule and reign. Child of earth, he came to die;
heav - en fall: Earth and sky and sun and moon,
trum - pet blown; From the winds' re - mot - est breath
tu - mult riv'n, And the King of kings di - vine
worlds be - gan. In the un - ex - pect - ed hour

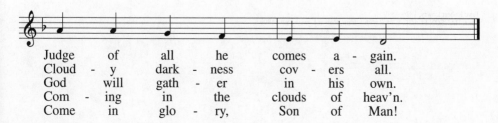

Judge of all he comes a - gain.
Cloud - y dark - ness cov - ers all.
God will gath - er in his own.
Com - ing in the clouds of heav'n.
Come in glo - ry, Son of Man!

Text: Timothy Dudley-Smith, b.1926, © 1987, Hope Publishing Company
Tune: HEINLEIN, 7 7 7 7; attr. to Martin Herbst, 1654–1681, *Nürnbergisches Gesangbuch*, 1676

866 Shall We Gather at the River

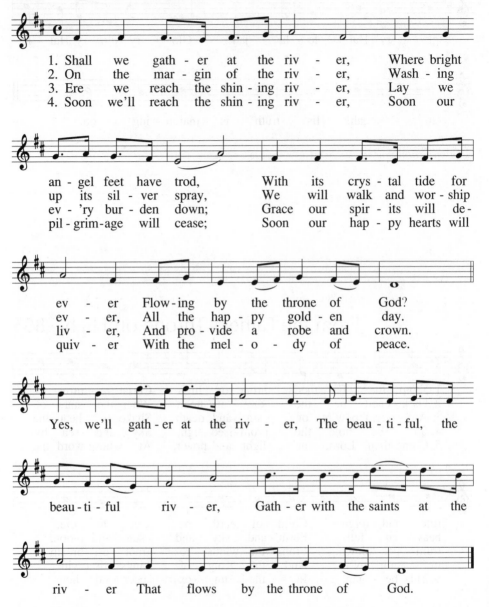

1. Shall we gath - er at the riv - er, Where bright
2. On the mar - gin of the riv - er, Wash - ing
3. Ere we reach the shin - ing riv - er, Lay we
4. Soon we'll reach the shin - ing riv - er, Soon our

an - gel feet have trod, With its crys - tal tide for
up its sil - ver spray, We will walk and wor - ship
ev - 'ry bur - den down; Grace our spir - its will de-
pil - grim-age will cease; Soon our hap - py hearts will

ev - er Flow-ing by the throne of God?
ev - er, All the hap - py gold - en day.
liv - er, And pro - vide a robe and crown.
quiv - er With the mel - o - dy of peace.

Yes, we'll gath - er at the riv - er, The beau - ti - ful, the

beau - ti - ful riv - er, Gath - er with the saints at the

riv - er That flows by the throne of God.

Text: Robert Lowry, 1826–1899
Tune: HANSON PLACE, 8 7 8 7 with refrain; Robert Lowry, 1826–1899

Jerusalem, My Happy Home   867

1. Je - ru - sa - lem, my hap - py home, When
2. Your saints are crowned with glo - ry great; They
3. There Da - vid stands with harp in hand As
4. Our La - dy sings Ma - gni - fi - cat With
5. There Mag - da - lene has left her tears, And
6. Je - ru - sa - lem, Je - ru - sa - lem, God

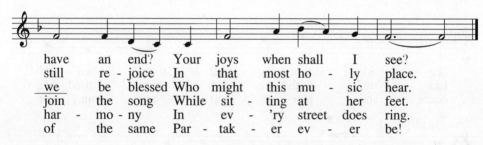

shall I with you be? When shall my sor - rows
see God face to face; They tri - umph still, they
mas - ter of the choir: Ten thou - sand times would
tune sur - pass - ing sweet; And all the vir - gins
cheer - ful - ly does sing With bless - ed saints, whose
grant that I may see Your end - less joy, and

have an end? Your joys when shall I see?
still re - joice In that most ho - ly place.
we be blessed Who might this mu - sic hear.
join the song While sit - ting at her feet.
har - mo - ny In ev - 'ry street does ring.
of the same Par - tak - er ev - er be!

Text: F.B.P., 16th C., alt.
Tune: LAND OF REST, CM; American melody; harm. by Richard Proulx, 1937–2010, © 1975, GIA Publications, Inc.

868 Martha, Mary, Waiting, Weeping

1. Mar - tha, Mar - y, wait - ing, weep - ing, Bowed be -
2. Je - sus spoke to Mar - tha's griev - ing, "Res - ur -
3. Je - sus, res - ur - rect - ed, giv - ing Life to

neath the weight of gloom, Kept their watch where Laz - 'rus,
rec - tion, Life, am I! All who hear my Word, be -
all you name your own: Help us know in hours of

sleep - ing, Lay with - in a rock - sealed tomb. Je - sus,
liev - ing, Live with me, al - though they die." Then to
griev - ing We have not been left a - lone. Come, when

late in com - ing, met them, Shed with
Laz - 'rus' tomb he led them, Called their
doubt and fear as - sail us; Join our

them com - pas - sion's tear. Mar - tha, sore with sor - row,
broth - er forth by name. Liv - ing, lov - ing, hope ex -
jour - ney toward the grave. There your mer - cy will not

charged him, "He'd have lived had you been here!"
ceed - ing, Freed from death, to Christ he came.
fail us; There you speak with pow'r to save.

Text: Herman G. Stuempfle, Jr., 1923–2007, © 1997, GIA Publications, Inc.
Tune: BEACH SPRING, 8 7 8 7 D; *The Sacred Harp*, 1844; harm. by Ronald A. Nelson, b.1927, © 1978, *Lutheran Book of Worship*,
admin. by Augsburg Fortress

Jesus, Remember Me 869

Ostinato Refrain

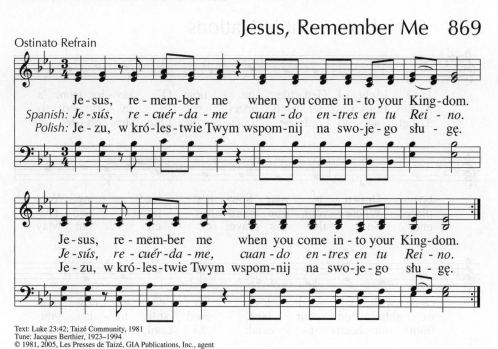

Je-sus, re-mem-ber me when you come in-to your King-dom.
Spanish: Je-sús, re-cuér-da-me cuan-do en-tres en tu Rei-no.
Polish: Je-zu, w kró-les-twie Twym wspom-nij na swo-je-go słu-gę.

Je-sus, re-mem-ber me when you come in-to your King-dom.
Je-sús, re-cuér-da-me, cuan-do en-tres en tu Rei-no.
Je-zu, w kró-les-twie Twym wspom-nij na swo-je-go słu-gę.

Text: Luke 23:42; Taizé Community, 1981
Tune: Jacques Berthier, 1923–1994
© 1981, 2005, Les Presses de Taizé, GIA Publications, Inc., agent

Long-Awaited Holy One 870

1. Long - a - wait - ed Ho - ly One, Sim - eon hailed you
2. Light of all the na - tions, shine! Show, to those who
3. Ra - diance of God's ho - ly face, Shine your love in

as God's Son. An - na wel-comed you with praise,
wait, a sign: God on earth, our host and guest,
ev - 'ry place. Splen-dor of God's glo - ry bright,

Glad ful - fill - ment of her days.
In our flesh made man - i - fest.
Lead us to e - ter - nal light!

Text: Delores Dufner, OSB, b.1939, © 1984, 1992, 2003, 2011, GIA Publications, Inc.
Tune: NUN KOMM DER HEIDEN HEILAND, 77 77; *Geistliche Gesangbüchlein*, Wittenberg, 1524

871 O Light of Gentile Nations

1. O Light of Gen-tile na - tions, O Sav-ior from a -
2. Yes, Lord, your ser-vants meet you In ev - 'ry ho - ly
3. Let us, O Lord, be faith - ful Like Sim-eon to the

bove, Drawn by your Spir - it's lead - ing, We
place Where your true word has prom - ised That
end, So that his prayer ex - ult - ant May

come with joy and love To en - ter now your
we should see your face. And still to - day you
from our hearts as - cend: "O Lord, now let your

tem - ple And wait with watch - ful mind, As
grant us, Who gath - er round you here, In
ser - vant De - part in peace, I pray, Since

Sim - eon once had wait - ed His Sav - ior God to find.
arms of faith to bear you, As did that a - ged seer.
I have seen my Sav - ior, Have here be - held his day."

Text: Johann Franck, 1618–1677; tr. by Catherine Winkworth, 1827–1878, alt.
Tune: LLANGLOFFAN, 7 6 7 6 D; Welsh melody

Now Let Your Servant Go in Peace 872

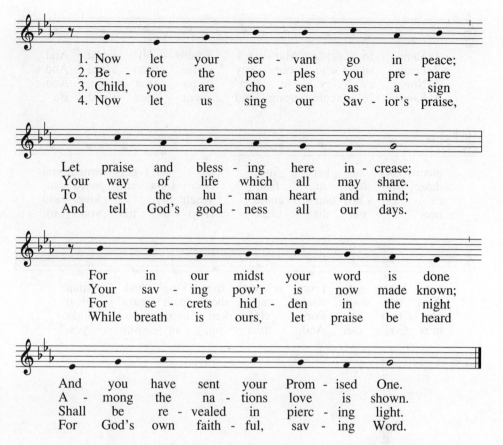

1. Now let your ser - vant go in peace;
2. Be - fore the peo - ples you pre - pare
3. Child, you are cho - sen as a sign
4. Now let us sing our Sav - ior's praise,

Let praise and bless - ing here in - crease;
Your way of life which all may share.
To test the hu - man heart and mind;
And tell God's good - ness all our days.

For in our midst your word is done
Your sav - ing pow'r is now made known;
For se - crets hid - den in the night
While breath is ours, let praise be heard

And you have sent your Prom - ised One.
A - mong the na - tions love is shown.
Shall be re - vealed in pierc - ing light.
For God's own faith - ful, sav - ing Word.

Text: *Nunc dimittis,* Luke 2:29–35; Ruth Duck, b.1947, © 1992, GIA Publications, Inc.
Tune: CONDITOR ALME SIDERUM, LM; Mode IV, Sarum, 9th C.; acc. by Gerard Farrell, OSB, 1919–2009, © 1986, GIA Publications, Inc.

873 Saint Joseph, Mary's Faithful Spouse

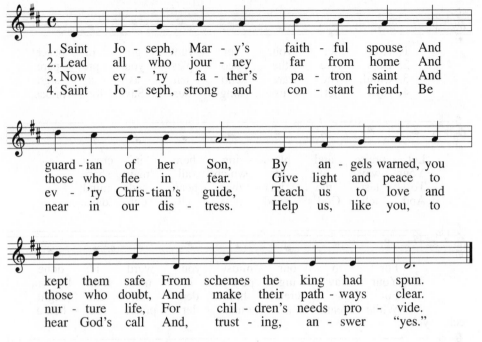

1. Saint Jo - seph, Mar - y's faith - ful spouse And
2. Lead all who jour - ney far from home And
3. Now ev - 'ry fa - ther's pa - tron saint And
4. Saint Jo - seph, strong and con - stant friend, Be

guard - ian of her Son, By an - gels warned, you
those who flee in fear. Give light and peace to
ev - 'ry Chris - tian's guide, Teach us to love and
near in our dis - tress. Help us, like you, to

kept them safe From schemes the king had spun.
those who doubt, And make their path - ways clear.
nur - ture life, For chil - dren's needs pro - vide.
hear God's call And, trust - ing, an - swer "yes."

Text: Delores Dufner, OSB, b.1939, © 2011, GIA Publications, Inc.
Tune: TALLIS' ORDINAL, CM; Thomas Tallis, c.1505–1585

874 Come Now and Praise the Humble Saint

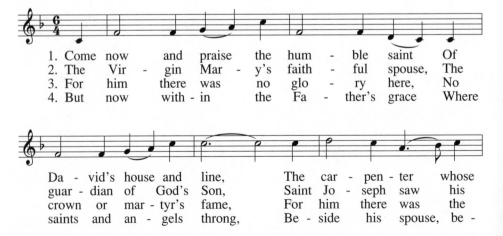

1. Come now and praise the hum - ble saint Of
2. The Vir - gin Mar - y's faith - ful spouse, The
3. For him there was no glo - ry here, No
4. But now with - in the Fa - ther's grace Where

Da - vid's house and line, The car - pen - ter whose
guar - dian of God's Son, Saint Jo - seph saw his
crown or mar - tyr's fame, For him there was the
saints and an - gels throng, Be - side his spouse, be -

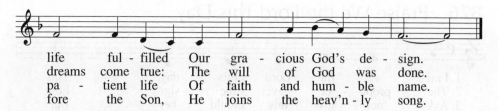

life   ful - filled   Our   gra - cious God's   de -   sign.
dreams   come   true: The   will   of   God   was   done.
pa -   tient   life   Of   faith   and   hum - ble   name.
fore   the   Son,   He   joins   the   heav'n - ly   song.

Text: Sts. 1, 3–4, George W. Williams, b.1922, alt., © 1979, The Hymn Society (admin. by Hope Publishing Company); st. 2, Ronald F. Krisman, b.1946, © 2011, GIA Publications, Inc.
Tune: LAND OF REST, CM; American melody; harm. by Richard Proulx, 1937–2010, © 1975, GIA Publications, Inc.

The Angel Gabriel from Heaven Came   875

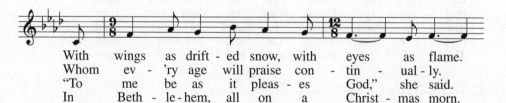

1. The   an - gel   Ga - bri - el   from   heav - en   came,
2. "How blest   a - mong   all wom - en   you   shall   be,
3. Then   gen - tle Mar - y   meek - ly   bowed   her   head.
4. Of   her,   Em - man - u - el,   the   Christ,   was   born

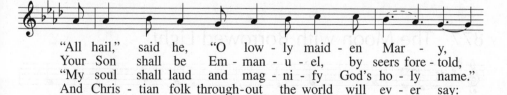

With   wings   as drift - ed snow,   with   eyes   as   flame.
Whom   ev - 'ry   age   will praise con - tin - ual - ly.
"To   me   be   as   it pleas - es   God,"   she said.
In   Beth - le - hem,   all   on   a   Christ - mas morn.

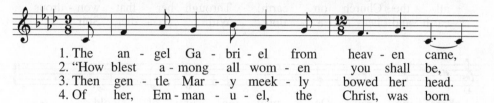

"All hail,"   said he,   "O low - ly maid - en   Mar - y,
Your Son   shall be   Em - man - u - el,   by seers fore - told,
"My soul   shall laud and mag - ni - fy God's ho - ly name."
And Chris - tian folk through-out the world will ev - er say:

Most high - ly fa - vored la - dy."   Gló -   ri - a!
Most high - ly fa - vored la - dy."   Gló -   ri - a!
Most high - ly fa - vored la - dy,   Gló -   ri - a!
"Most high - ly fa - vored la - dy."   Gló -   ri - a!

Text: Basque carol; para. by Sabine Baring-Gould, 1834–1924, alt.
Tune: GABRIEL'S MESSAGE, 10 10 12 10; Basque carol; harm. by Charles E. Pettman, 1865–1943

876 Praise We the Lord This Day

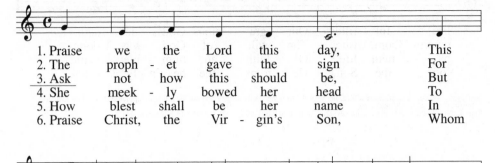

1. Praise we the Lord this day, This
2. The proph - et gave the sign For
3. Ask not how this should be, But
4. She meek - ly bowed her head To
5. How blest shall be her name In
6. Praise Christ, the Vir - gin's Son, Whom

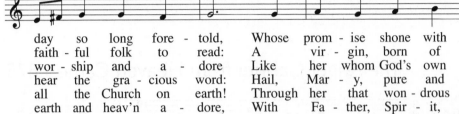

day so long fore - told, Whose prom - ise shone with
faith - ful folk to read: A vir - gin, born of
wor - ship and a - dore Like her whom God's own
hear the gra - cious word: Hail, Mar - y, pure and
all the Church on earth! Through her that won - drous
earth and heav'n a - dore, With Fa - ther, Spir - it,

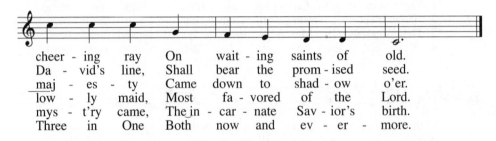

cheer - ing ray On wait - ing saints of old.
Da - vid's line, Shall bear the prom - ised seed.
maj - es - ty Came down to shad - ow o'er.
low - ly maid, Most fa - vored of the Lord.
mys - t'ry came, The in - car - nate Sav - ior's birth.
Three in One Both now and ev - er - more.

Text: Matthew 1:23; *Hymns for the Festivals and Saints' Days*, 1846, alt.
Tune: SWABIA, SM; Johann M. Speiss, 1715–1772; adapt. by William H. Havergal, 1793–1870

877 The Moon with Borrowed Light

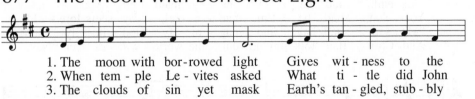

1. The moon with bor - rowed light Gives wit - ness to the
2. When tem - ple Le - vites asked What ti - tle did John
3. The clouds of sin yet mask Earth's tan - gled, stub - bly

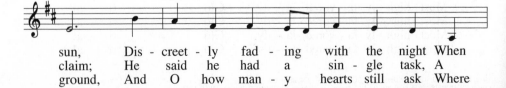

sun, Dis - creet - ly fad - ing with the night When
claim; He said he had a sin - gle task, A
ground, And O how man - y hearts still ask Where

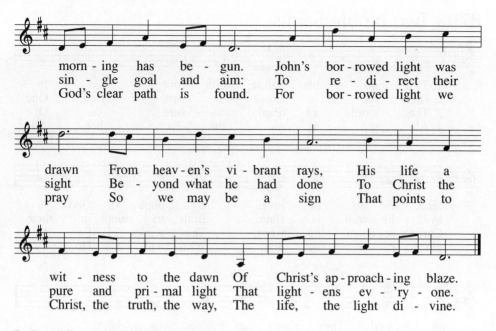

morn - ing has be - gun. John's bor - rowed light was
sin - gle goal and aim: To re - di - rect their
God's clear path is found. For bor - rowed light we

drawn From heav - en's vi - brant rays, His life a
sight Be - yond what he had done To Christ the
pray So we may be a sign That points to

wit - ness to the dawn Of Christ's ap - proach - ing blaze.
pure and pri - mal light That light - ens ev - 'ry - one.
Christ, the truth, the way, The life, the light di - vine.

Text: Thomas H. Troeger, b.1945, © 1986, Oxford University Press
Tune: TERRA BEATA, SMD; English melody; adapt. by Franklin L. Sheppard, 1852–1930

The Great Forerunner of the Morn 878

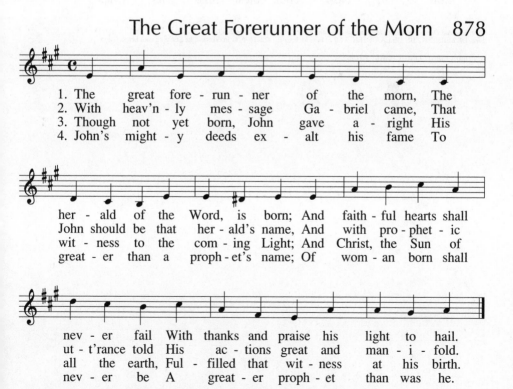

1. The great fore - run - ner of the morn, The
2. With heav'n - ly mes - sage Ga - briel came, That
3. Though not yet born, John gave a - right His
4. John's might - y deeds ex - alt his fame To

her - ald of the Word, is born; And faith - ful hearts shall
John should be that her - ald's name, And with pro - phet - ic
wit - ness to the com - ing Light; And Christ, the Sun of
great - er than a proph - et's name; Of wom - an born shall

nev - er fail With thanks and praise his light to hail.
ut - t'rance told His ac - tions great and man - i - fold.
all the earth, Ful - filled that wit - ness at his birth.
nev - er be A great - er proph - et than was he.

Text: *Praecursor altus luminis*; Venerable Bede, 673–735; tr. by John M. Neale, 1818–1866, alt.
Tune: WINCHESTER NEW, LM; adapt. from *Musikalisches Handbuch*, Hamburg, 1690

879 Two Noble Saints

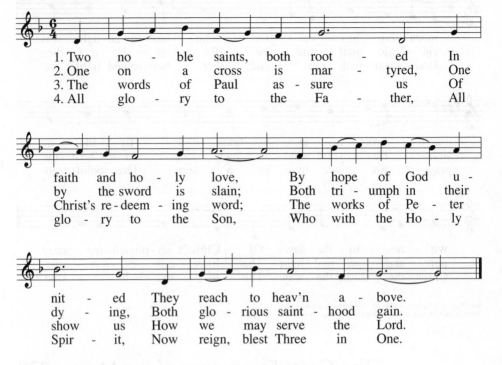

1. Two no - ble saints, both root - ed In
2. One on a cross is mar - tyred, One
3. The words of Paul as - sure us Of
4. All glo - ry to the Fa - ther, All

faith and ho - ly love, By hope of God u -
by the sword is slain; Both tri - umph in their
Christ's re - deem - ing word; The works of Pe - ter
glo - ry to the Son, Who with the Ho - ly

nit - ed They reach to heav'n a - bove.
dy - ing, Both glo - rious saint - hood gain.
show us How we may serve the Lord.
Spir - it, Now reign, blest Three in One.

Text: Based on *Decora lux aeternitatis auream*, by Anne K. LeCroy, b.1930, © 1982, alt.
Tune: DE EERSTEN ZIJN DE LAATSTEN, 7 6 7 6; Frits Mehrtens, 1922–1975, © Interkerkelijke Stichting voor het Kerklied

Alternate tune: ELLACOMBE, *2 stanzas*

Transform Us   880

1. Trans - form us as you, trans - fig - ured,
2. Trans - form us as you, trans - fig - ured,
3. Trans - form us as you, trans - fig - ured,

Stood a - part on Ta - bor's height.
Once spoke with those ho - ly ones.
Would not stay with - in a shrine.

Lead us up our sa - cred moun - tains,
We, sur - round - ed by the wit - ness
Keep us from our great temp - ta - tion—

Search us with re - veal - ing light.
Of those saints whose work is done,
Time and truth we quick - ly bind.

Lift us from where we have fall - en,
Live in this world as your Bod - y,
Lead us down those dai - ly path - ways

Full of ques - tions, filled with fright.
Cho - sen daugh - ters, cho - sen sons.
Where our love is not con - fined.

Text: Sylvia G. Dunstan, 1955–1993, © 1993, GIA Publications, Inc.
Tune: PICARDY, 8 7 8 7 8 7; French carol; harm. by Richard Proulx, 1937–2010, © 1986, GIA Publications, Inc.

881 How Good, Lord, to Be Here!

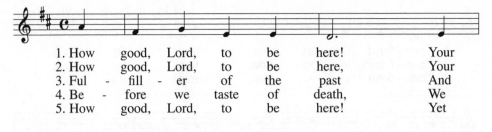

1. How good, Lord, to be here! Your
2. How good, Lord, to be here, Your
3. Ful - fill - er of the past And
4. Be - fore we taste of death, We
5. How good, Lord, to be here! Yet

glo - ry fills the night; Your face and gar - ments,
beau - ty to be - hold Where Mo - ses and E -
hope of things to be, We hail your bod - y
see your king - dom come; We long to hold the
we may not re - main; But since you bid us

like the sun, Shine with un - bor - rowed light.
li - jah stand, Your mes - sen - gers of old.
glo - ri - fied And our re - demp - tion see.
vi - sion bright And make this hill our home.
leave the mount, Come with us to the plain.

Text: Luke 9:32–33; Joseph A. Robinson, 1858–1933, alt.
Tune: SWABIA, SM; Johann M. Speiss, 1715–1772; adapt. by William H. Havergal, 1793–1870

882 Salve Regína / Hail, Queen of Heaven

Sal - ve Re - gí - na, ma - ter mi - se - ri - cór - di - ae:
Hail, Queen of Heav - en, hail, our Moth - er com - pas - sion - ate,

Vi - ta, dul - cé - do et spes no - stra sal - ve.
True life and com - fort and our hope, we greet you!

Ad te cla - má - mus, éx - su - les fí - li - i He - vae.
To you we ex - iles, chil-dren of Eve, raise our voic - es.

Ad te sus - pi - rá - mus, ge - mén - tes et flen - tes
We send up sighs to you, as mourn-ing and weep-ing,

in hac la - cri - má - rum val - le. E - ia er - go,
we pass through this vale of sor - row. Then turn to us,

ad - vo - cá - ta no - stra, il - los tu - os
O most gra - cious Wom - an, those eyes of yours,

mi - se - ri - cór - des ó - cu - los ad nos con - vér - te.
so full of love and ten - der-ness, so full of pit - y.

Et Je - sum, be - ne - dí - ctum fru - ctum ven - tris tu - i,
And grant us af - ter these, our days of lone - ly ex - ile,

no - bis post hoc ex - sí - li - um o - stén - de.
the sight of your blest Son and Lord, Christ Je - sus.

O cle - mens, O pi - a,
O gen - tle, O lov - ing,

O dul - cis Vir - go Ma - rí - a.
O ho - ly, sweet Vir - gin Mar - y.

Text: *Salve Regina, mater misericordiae,* c.1080, tr. by John C. Selner, SS, 1904–1992, © 1954, GIA Publications, Inc.
Tune: SALVE REGINA, Irregular; Mode V; acc. by Gerard Farrell, OSB, 1919–2009, alt., © 1986, GIA Publications, Inc.

883 Hail, Holy Queen Enthroned Above

1. Hail, ho - ly Queen en - throned a - bove, O Ma - rí - a. Hail,
2. The cause of joy to all be - low, O Ma - rí - a. The
3. O gen - tle, lov - ing, ho - ly one, O Ma - rí - a. The

Queen of mer - cy and of love, O Ma - rí - a.
spring through which all grac - es flow, O Ma - rí - a.
God of light be - came your Son, O Ma - rí - a.

Tri - umph, all ye Cher - u - bim; Sing with us, ye
An - gels, all your prais - es bring; Earth and heav - en,
Tri - umph, all ye Cher - u - bim; Sing with us, ye

Ser - a - phim. Heav'n and earth re - sound the hymn:
with us sing; All cre - a - tion ech - o - ing:
Ser - a - phim. Heav'n and earth re - sound the hymn:

Sal - ve, Sal - ve, Sal - ve Re - gí - na.

Text: *Salve Regina, mater misericordiae*; c.1080; tr. *Roman Hymnal*, 1884; st. 2–3, adapt. by M. Owen Lee, CSB, b.1930
Tune: SALVE REGINA COELITUM, 8 4 8 4 777 4 5; *Choralmelodien zum Heiligen Gesänge*, 1808; harm. by Healey Willan, 1880–1968,
© Willis Music Co.

We Glory in the Cross   884

1. We glo-ry in the cross, In Christ, the cru-ci-fied.
2. The arms of Je-sus' cross En-com-pass all the earth;
3. The fol-ly of the cross Is wis-dom to the wise;
4. The beau-ty of the cross Is love re-vealed in death;

In him we die to sin and self And in God's
In this em-brace we find our peace And in this
For all who choose to die with Christ, With Christ will
With grate-ful lips we sing our praise, With mind and

grace a-bide. We glo-ry in the cross, In
death, new birth. We glo-ry in the cross, Sal-
al-so rise. The mys-t'ry of God's plan Un-
heart and breath. In joy we jour-ney on, In

Christ, the ris-en Lord. In him we know the
va-tion's shape and sign, The pledge of ev-er-
folds on Je-sus' cross: The bless-ings of a-
hope of fu-ture bright; Christ Je-sus walks the

Spir-it's life And pow'r of Gos-pel word.
last-ing life, The span of God's de-sign.
bun-dant life Are won by pain and loss.
way with us Through dark-ness in-to light.

Text: Delores Dufner, OSB, b.1939, © 2002, 2003, GIA Publications, Inc.
Tune: MORGANSGATE, SMD; Ronald F. Krisman, b.1946, © 2011, GIA Publications, Inc.

885 Lift High the Cross / Alcen la Cruz

Refrain

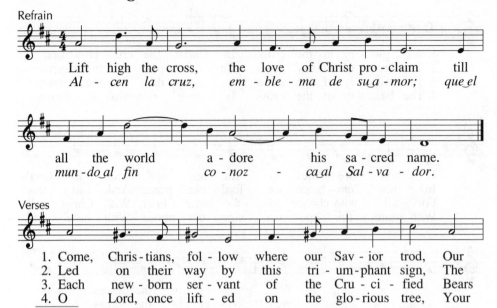

Lift high the cross, the love of Christ pro-claim till
Al - cen la cruz, em - ble - ma de su_a-mor; que_el

all the world a - dore his sa - cred name.
mun -do_al fin co - noz - ca_al Sal - va - dor.

Verses

1. Come, Chris-tians, fol - low where our Sav - ior trod, Our
2. Led on their way by this tri - um-phant sign, The
3. Each new - born ser - vant of the Cru - ci - fied Bears
4. O Lord, once lift - ed on the glo - rious tree, Your

1. *Va - mos, cris - tia - nos, tras nues -tro Se - ñor; El*
2. *Ba - jo_es - te sig - no de su gran po - der El*
3. *Ca - da cre - yen - te del que_en cruz mu - rió En*
4. *Cuan - do te_al - za - ron glo - rio-so_en la cruz, A -*

D.C.

King vic - to - rious, Christ, the Son of God.
hosts of God in con - quering ranks com - bine.
on the brow the seal of him who died.
death has bought us life e - ter - nal - ly.

rey vic-to - rio - so, Cris - to,_Hi - jo de Dios.
pue - blo de Dios a - van - za sin te - mer.
su fren-te lle - va_el sig - no_en que ven - ció.
llí pro-me - tis - te lle -var - nos a la luz.

5. So shall our song of triumph ever be: 5. *Himnos de gloria_alcemos sin cesar;*
   Praise to the Crucified for victory!   *Al rey vencedor que en cruz supo triunfar.*

Text: 1 Corinthians 1:18; George W. Kitchin, 1827–1912, and Michael R. Newbolt, 1874–1956, alt.; tr. by Dimas Planas-Belfort, 1934–1992, and Ángel Mattos, alt.
Tune: CRUCIFER, 10 10 with refrain; Sydney H. Nicholson, 1875–1947
© 1974, 1997, Hope Publishing Company

Ye Watchers and Ye Holy Ones 886

1. Ye watch-ers and ye ho-ly ones, Bright ser-aphs, cher-u-bim, and thrones, Raise the glad strain: "Al-le-lu-ia!" Cry out, do-min-ions, prince-doms, pow'rs, Vir-tues, arch-an-gels, an-gels' choirs: "Al-le-lu-ia! Al-le-lu-ia!" Al-le-lu-ia, al-le-lu-ia, al-le-lu-ia!

2. O high-er than the cher-u-bim, More glo-rious than the ser-a-phim, Lead their prais-es: "Al-le-lu-ia!" O bear-er of the e-ter-nal Word, Most gra-cious, mag-ni-fy the Lord: "Al-le-lu-ia! Al-le-lu-ia!"

3. Re-spond, ye souls in end-less rest, Ye pa-tri-archs and proph-ets blest: "Al-le-lu-ia, Al-le-lu-ia!" Ye ho-ly twelve, ye mar-tyrs strong, All saints tri-um-phant, raise the song: "Al-le-lu-ia!"

4. O friends, in glad-ness let us sing, Su-per-nal an-thems ech-o-ing: "Al-le-lu-ia, Al-le-lu-ia!" To God the Fa-ther, God the Son, And God the Spir-it, Three in One: "Al-le-lu-ia!"

Text: John A. Riley, 1858–1945
Tune: LASST UNS ERFREUEN, LM with alleluias; *Geistliche Kirchengesänge*, Cologne, 1623; harm. by Ralph Vaughan Williams, 1872–1958

887 As Stars Adorn the Night-Veiled Sky

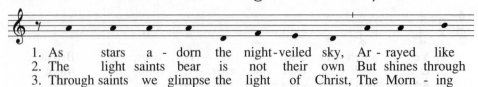

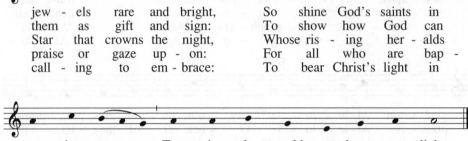

1. As stars a - dorn the night-veiled sky, Ar - rayed like
2. The light saints bear is not their own But shines through
3. Through saints we glimpse the light of Christ, The Morn - ing
4. That light is ours to claim and share, Not mere - ly
5. The saints in - spire and chal - lenge us Our ho - ly

jew - els rare and bright, So shine God's saints in
them as gift and sign: To show how God can
Star that crowns the night, Whose ris - ing her - alds
praise or gaze up - on: For all who are bap -
call - ing to em - brace: To bear Christ's light in

ev - 'ry age To give the world new hope, new light.
use and bless Frail hu - man means for ends di - vine.
God's new day, The prom - ised dawn of life and light.
tized be - come Light-bear - ers through the Ris - en One.
our own day, To be the ves - sels of God's grace.

Text: Carl P. Daw, Jr., b.1944, © 1997, Hope Publishing Company
Tune: JESU DULCIS MEMORIA, LM; Mode I; acc. by Richard Proulx, 1937–2010, © 1975, GIA Publications, Inc.

888 Who Are These, Like Stars Appearing?

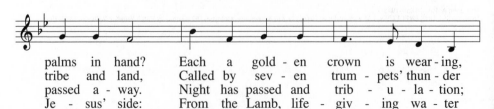

1. Who are these, like stars ap - pear-ing? Who are these with
2. Throngs in white be - yond all num-bers, Called from ev - 'ry
3. Death shall no more be their por - tion; For - mer things have
4. Ho - ly cit - y, bright as crys - tal, Sav - ing stream from

palms in hand? Each a gold - en crown is wear-ing,
tribe and land, Called by sev - en trum - pets' thun - der
passed a - way. Night has passed and trib - u - la - tion;
Je - sus' side: From the Lamb, life - giv - ing wa - ter

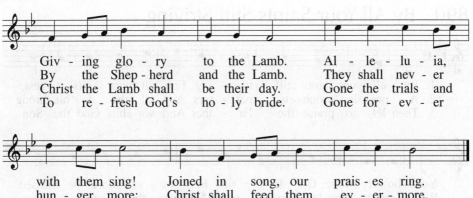

Giv - ing glo - ry to the Lamb. Al - le - lu - ia,
By the Shep - herd and the Lamb. They shall nev - er
Christ the Lamb shall be their day. Gone the trials and
To re - fresh God's ho - ly bride. Gone for - ev - er

with them sing! Joined in song, our prais - es ring.
hun - ger more; Christ shall feed them ev - er - more.
gone the fears; Christ has wiped a - way all tears.
dark of night; Christ shall be your last - ing light!

Text: Delores Dufner, OSB, b.1939, © 2011, GIA Publications, Inc.
Tune: ALL SAINTS, 8 7 8 7 77; *Geistreiches Gesangbuch*, Darmstadt, 1698; harm. by William H. Monk, 1823–1889, alt.

Sing Praise to God for Friends 889

1. Sing praise to God for friends who bring Our
2. We may not see their fold - ed hands Nor
3. And so those clouds of wit - ness - es Whose
4. Sing praise for that great com - pa - ny Of

needs to Christ the Lord, Who pray that he will
know what prayers they raise, But Christ will al - ways
race has now been run Still lift their prayers by
all who in - ter - cede, Who by the hid - den

bend to us And speak his heal - ing Word.
hear the voice That for an - oth - er prays.
day and night For us be - fore God's throne.
hand of prayer Sup - port us in our need.

Text: Herman G. Stuempfle, Jr., 1923–2007, © 1997, GIA Publications, Inc.
Tune: AZMON, CM; Carl G. Gläser, 1784–1829; harm. by Lowell Mason, 1792–1872

890 By All Your Saints Still Striving

1. By all your saints still striv - ing, For all your saints at rest,
*2. A - pos - tles, proph - ets, mar - tyrs, And all the no - ble throng
3. Then let us praise the Fa - ther And wor - ship God the Son

Your ho - ly Name, O Je - sus, For - ev - er - more be blessed.
Who wear the spot-less rai - ment And raise the cease-less song:
And sing to God the Spir - it, E - ter - nal Three in One,

You rose, our King vic - to - rious, That they might wear the crown
For them and those whose wit - ness Is on - ly known to you,
Till all the ran - somed num - ber Who stand be - fore the throne

And share the light of glo - ry Re - flect - ed from your throne.
By walk-ing in their foot - steps We give you praise a - new.
As - cribe all pow'r and glo - ry And praise to God a - lone.

Stanza 2 may be replaced by an appropriate stanza taken from the following.

January 25: Conversion of Paul
Praise for the light from heaven,
Praise for the voice of awe,
Praise for the glorious vision
The persecutor saw.
O Lord, for Paul's conversion
We bless your Name today.
Come shine within our darkness
And guide us in the Way.

February 22: Chair of Peter
We praise you, Lord, for Peter,
So eager and so bold,
Thrice falling, yet repentant,
Thrice charged to feed your fold.
Lord, make your pastors faithful
To guard your flock from harm,
And hold them, when they waver,
With your almighty arm.

March 19: Joseph, Husband of Mary
All praise, O God, for Joseph,
The guardian of your Son,
Who saved him from King Herod
When safety there was none.
He taught the trade of builder,
When they to Naz'reth came,
And Joseph's love made "Father"
To be, for Christ, God's name.

March 25: Annunciation of Our Lord
We sing with joy of Mary,
Whose heart with awe was stirred
When, youthful and astonished,
She heard the angel's word.
Yet she her voice upraises
To magnify God's Name,
As once for our salvation
Your mother she became.

April 25: Mark

For Mark, O Lord, we praise you,
The weak by grace made strong;
His witness in his gospel
Becomes victorious song.
May we, in all our weakness,
Receive your pow'r divine,
And all, as fruitful branches,
Grow strong in you, the Vine.

May 3: Philip and James

We praise you, Lord, for Philip,
Blest guide to Greek and Jew,
And for young James, the faithful
Who heard and followed you.
O grant us grace to know you,
The Way, the Truth, the Life,
And wrestle with temptation
Till victors in the strife.

May 14: Matthias

For one in place of Judas,
The apostles sought God's choice;
The lot fell to Matthias,
For whom we now rejoice.
May we, as true apostles,
Your holy Church defend,
And not betray our calling,
But serve you to the end.

June 11: Barnabas

For Barnabas we praise you,
Appointed by your call,
Who, filled with faith and Spirit,
Proclaimed your word with Paul.
Give us your grace, O Savior,
That we become the same:
Companions in your mission,
Who bear the Christian name.

June 24: Birth of John the Baptist

All praise for John the Baptist,
Forerunner of the Word,
Our true Elijah, making
A highway for the Lord.
The last and greatest prophet,
He saw the dawning ray
Of light that grows in splendor
Until the perfect day.

June 29: Peter and Paul

We praise you for Saint Peter,
We praise you for Saint Paul.
They taught both Jew and Gentile
That Christ is all in all.
To cross and sword they yielded
And saw your kingdom come:
O God, your two apostles
Won life through martyrdom.

July 3: Thomas

All praise, O Lord, for Thomas,
Whose short-lived doubtings prove
Your perfect two-fold nature,
The depth of your true love.
May all who live with questions
Have faith in you restored.
Grant us the grace to know you,
Made flesh, yet God and Lord.

July 22: Mary Magdalene

For Magdalene we praise you,
Steadfast at cross and tomb.
Your "Mary!" in the garden
Dispelled her tears and gloom.
Apostle to the apostles,
She ran to spread the word;
Send us to shout the good news
That we have seen the Lord.

July 25: James

For James, O Lord, we praise you,
Who fell to Herod's sword.
He drank your cup of suff'ring
And thus fulfilled your word.
Lord, curb our vain impatience
For glory and for fame;
Equip us for such suff'rings
As glorify your Name.

August 24: Bartholomew

We praise you for Nathanael,
Surnamed Bartholomew.
We know not his achievements
But know that he was true;
For he at the Ascension
Was an apostle still.
May we discern your presence
And seek, like him, your will.

September 21: Matthew

We praise you, Lord, for Matthew,
Whose gospel words declare
That, worldly gain forsaking,
Your path of life we share.
From greed and love of money
O raise our eyes anew,
That we, whate'er our calling,
May rise and follow you.

October 18: Luke

For Luke, belov'd physician,
All praise, whose gospel shows
The healer of the nations,
The one who shares our woes.
Your wine and oil, O Savior,
Upon our spirits pour,
And with true balm of Gilead
Anoint us evermore.

October 28: Simon and Jude

Praise, Lord, for your apostles,
Saint Simon and Saint Jude.
One love, one hope impelled them
To tread the way, renewed.
May we with zeal as earnest
The faith of Christ maintain,
Be bound in love together,
And life eternal gain.

November 30: Andrew

All praise, O Lord, for Andrew,
The first to follow you;
He witnessed to his brother,
"This is Messiah true."
You called him from his fishing
Upon Lake Galilee;
He rose to meet your challenge,
"Leave all and follow me."

December 26: Stephen

All praise, O Lord, for Stephen
Who, martyred, saw you stand
To help in time of torment,
To plead at God's right hand.
Like you, our suff'ring Savior,
His enemies he blessed,
With "Lord, receive my spirit,"
His faith, in death, confessed.

December 27: John

For John, belov'd disciple,
Exiled to Patmos' shore,
And for his faithful record,
We praise you evermore.
Praise for the mystic vision
His words to us unfold.
Instill in us his longing,
Your glory to behold.

December 28: Holy Innocents

We praise you for the infants,
Whom your mysterious love
Called early from life's conflicts
To share your peace above.
O Rachel, cease your weeping;
They rest from earthly cares.
Lord, grant us crowns as brilliant
And lives as pure as theirs.

Text: Based on Horatio Nelson, 1823–1913, by Jerry D. Godwin, b.1944, © 1985, The Church Pension Fund; stanzas for Barnabas and Mary Magdalene, © 2006, Augsburg Fortress
Tune: ST. THEODULPH, 7 6 7 6 D; Melchior Teschner, 1584–1635

For All the Saints   891

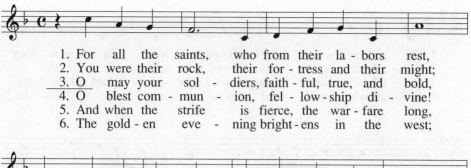

1. For all the saints, who from their la - bors rest,
2. You were their rock, their for - tress and their might;
3. O may your sol - diers, faith - ful, true, and bold,
4. O blest com - mun - ion, fel - low - ship di - vine!
5. And when the strife is fierce, the war - fare long,
6. The gold - en eve - ning bright - ens in the west;

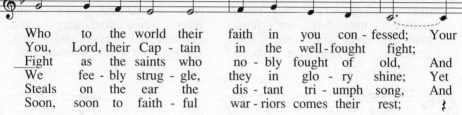

Who to the world their faith in you con - fessed; Your
You, Lord, their Cap - tain in the well - fought fight;
Fight as the saints who no - bly fought of old, And
We fee - bly strug - gle, they in glo - ry shine; Yet
Steals on the ear the dis - tant tri - umph song, And
Soon, soon to faith - ful war - riors comes their rest;

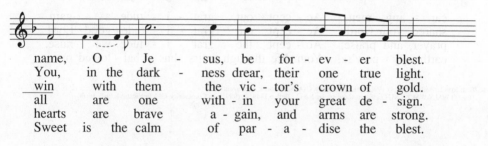

name, O Je - sus, be for - ev - er blest.
You, in the dark - ness drear, their one true light.
win with them the vic - tor's crown of gold.
all are one with - in your great de - sign.
hearts are brave a - gain, and arms are strong.
Sweet is the calm of par - a - dise the blest.

Al - le - lu - ia! Al - le - lu - ia!

7. But then there breaks a yet more glorious day;
   The saints triumphant rise in bright array;
   The King of glory passes on his way.
   Alleluia! Alleluia!

8. From earth's wide bounds, from ocean's farthest coast,
   Through gates of pearl streams in the countless host,
   Singing to Father, Son, and Holy Ghost:
   Alleluia! Alleluia!

Text: William W. How, 1823–1897, alt.
Tune: SINE NOMINE, 10 10 10 with alleluias; Ralph Vaughan Williams, 1872–1958

892 For All the Saints Who've Shown Your Love

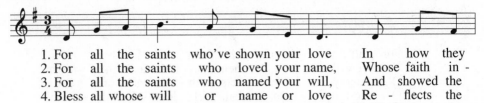

1. For all the saints who've shown your love In how they
2. For all the saints who loved your name, Whose faith in -
3. For all the saints who named your will, And showed the
4. Bless all whose will or name or love Re - flects the

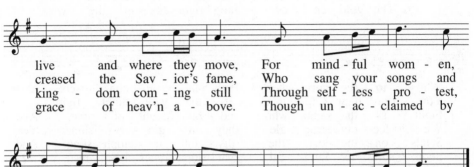

live and where they move, For mind - ful wom - en,
creased the Sav - ior's fame, Who sang your songs and
king - dom com - ing still Through self - less pro - test,
grace of heav'n a - bove. Though un - ac - claimed by

car - ing men, Ac - cept our grat - i - tude a - gain.
shared your word, Ac - cept our grat - i - tude, good Lord.
prayer, and praise, Ac - cept the grat - i - tude we raise.
earth - ly pow'rs, Your life through theirs has hal - lowed ours.

Text: John L. Bell, b.1949, © 1996, Iona Community, GIA Publications, Inc., agent
Tune: O WALY WALY, LM; English melody; arr. by John L. Bell, b.1949, © 1989, Iona Community, GIA Publications, Inc., agent

893 Immaculate Mary

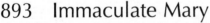

1. Im - mac - u - late Mar - y, your prais - es we sing;
2. Pre - des - tined for Christ by e - ter - nal de - cree,
3. To you by an an - gel, the Lord God made known
4. Most blest of all wom - en, you heard and be - lieved;
5. The an - gels re - joiced when you brought forth God's Son;

You reign now in splen - dor with Je - sus our King.
God willed you both vir - gin and moth - er to be.
The grace of the Spir - it, the gift of the Son.
Most blest is the fruit of your womb then con - ceived.
Your joy is the joy of all a - ges to come.

A - ve, a - ve, a - ve, Ma - rí - a.

A - ve, a - ve, Ma - rí - a.

6. Your child is the Savior, all hope lies in him:
   He gives us new life and redeems us from sin.

7. In glory for ever now close to your Son,
   All ages will praise you for all God has done.

Text: St. 1, Jeremiah Cummings, 1814–1866, alt.; sts. 2–7, Brian Foley, 1919–2000, © 1971, Faber Music Ltd.
Tune: LOURDES HYMN, 11 11 with refrain; French melody, Grenoble, 1882

How Blessed Is This Place 894

1. How bless - ed is this place, O Lord, Where you are
2. Here let your sa - cred fire of old De - scend to
3. Here let your wea - ry one find rest, The trou - bled
4. Here your an - gel - ic spir - its send Their sol - emn

wor - shiped and a - dored; In faith we here an
kin - dle spir - its cold; And may our prayers, when
heart, your com - fort blest, The guilt - y one, a
praise with ours to blend, And grant the vi - sion,

al - tar raise To your great glo - ry, God of praise.
here we bend, Like in - cense sweet to you as - cend.
sure re - treat, The sin - ner, par - don at your feet.
in - ly giv'n, Of this your house, the gate of heav'n.

Text: Ernest E. Ryden, 1886–1981, alt., sts. 1–3, © Lutheran Church in America; st. 4, © 1958, Service Book and Hymnal
Tune: ROCKINGHAM, LM; adapted by Edward Miller, 1735–1807

895 For Builders Bold

1. For build - ers bold whose vi - sion pure Saw
2. As here they raised a soar - ing spire Which
3. Here saints new - born you gen - er - ate Through
4. We come, O Lord, in - her - i - tors From

more than brick or stone, Who laid in hope foun -
thrusts toward worlds a - bove, So may our prayers, like
wa - ter and the Word; Through loaf and cup com -
those whose work is done. Lord, make us now con -

da - tions sure With Christ the cor - ner - stone; For
tongues of fire, Leap kin - dled by your love. And
mu - ni - cate The gift of Christ the Lord. We
trib - u - tors To years be - yond our own. Let

those who hon - ored your com - mands And
let your liv - ing Word de - scend As
gath - er, Christ's own fam - i - ly; Christ's
faith's en - kin - dled flame not fail; Let

trust - ed your strong Word, Who of - fered faith - ful
seed on wait - ing hearts And, fruit - ful there, its
meal of love we share. Come, help us live in
love's best gifts in - crease. Let hope in Christ's sure

hearts and hands, We give you thanks, O Lord.
grace ex - tend To earth's most dis - tant parts.
u - ni - ty, Each oth - er's bur - dens bear.
Word pre - vail Till earth and time shall cease.

Text: Herman G. Stuempfle, Jr., 1923–2007, © 1993, GIA Publications, Inc.
Tune: FOREST GREEN, CMD; English melody; harm. by Ralph Vaughan Williams, 1872–1958, alt.

Sing We of the Blessed Mother   896

1. Sing we of the Bless-ed Moth-er, Who re-ceived the
2. Sing we, too, of Mar-y's sor-rows, Of the sword that
3. Sing a-gain the joys of Mar-y When she saw the
4. Sing the great-est joy of Mar-y When on earth her

an-gel's word And, o-be-dient to the sum-mons,
pierced her through, When be-neath the cross of Je-sus
ris-en Lord, And in prayer with Christ's a-pos-tles
work was done, And the Lord of all cre-a-tion

Bore in love the in-fant Lord. Sing we of the
She his weight of suf-f'ring knew, Looked up-on her
Wait-ed on his prom-ised word. From on high the
Brought her to his heav'n-ly home. Vir-gin Moth-er,

joys of Mar-y, At whose breast that child was fed,
Son and Sav-ior Reign-ing from the aw-ful tree,
blaz-ing glo-ry Of the Spir-it's pres-ence came:
Mar-y bless-ed, Raised on high and crowned with grace,

Who is Son of God e-ter-nal
Saw the price of our re-demp-tion
Heav'n-ly breath of God's own be-ing
May your Son, the world's re-deem-er,

And the ev-er-last-ing Bread.
Paid to set the sin-ner free.
To-kened in the wind and flame.
Grant us all to see his face.

Text: George B. Timms, 1910–1997, © 1975, Oxford University Press
Tune: ALLE TAGE SING UND SAGE, 8 7 8 7 D; Trier *Gesangbuch*, 1695

897 Mary, First among Believers

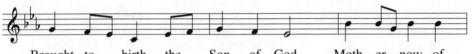

1. Mar - y, first a - mong be - liev - ers, Trust - ing in the
*2. Mar - y, first a - mong the ex - iles, Seek - ing ref - uge
3. Mar - y, first a - mong dis - ci - ples, Lis - t'ning, learn - ing
*4. Mar - y, first a - mong the suf - f'ring, Stand - ing bowed be -
5. Mar - y, first a - mong the bless - ed, Robed in heav - en's

an - gel's word, You con - sent - ed and, con - ceiv - ing,
in the night, You left home with spouse and In - fant,
from your Son, You held dear his words and ac - tions,
neath the cross, You knew all the pain and an - guish
beau - ty bright, You re - joice with saints and an - gels

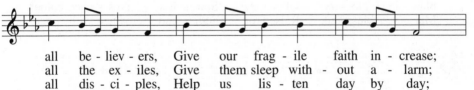

Brought to birth the Son of God. Moth - er now of
Flee - ing Her - od's sword in fright. Moth - er now of
Pon - d'ring each, for - get - ting none. Moth - er now of
Of op - pres - sion, grief, and loss. Moth - er now of
In your Son's re - splen - dent light. Moth - er now of

all be - liev - ers, Give our frag - ile faith in - crease;
all the ex - iles, Give them sleep with - out a - larm;
all dis - ci - ples, Help us lis - ten day by day;
all the suf - f'ring, May we show Com - pas - sion's face;
all the bless - ed, Make your pil - grim peo - ple strong;

May we, trust - ing in God's prom - ise,
Give them cloth - ing, food, and shel - ter;
O - pen to the Spir - it's prompt - ing,
May the vic - tims of in - jus - tice
Keep us faith - ful till we join you,

*Stanzas 2 and 4 may be omitted.

Doubts and use - less fears re - lease.
Keep them safe and free from harm.
Help us fol - low Je - sus' way.
Know, through us, God's love and grace.
Prais - ing God in end - less song.

Text: Delores Dufner, OSB, b.1939, © 2011, GIA Publications, Inc.
Tune: PLEADING SAVIOR, 8 7 8 7 D; *Christian Lyre*, 1830; harm. by Richard Proulx, 1937–2010, © 1986, GIA Publications, Inc.

When, to Mary, the Word 898

1. When, to Mar - y, the Word From the throne of the
2. At the sound of her voice Did her cous - in re -
3. Like our Moth - er, we should Give our neigh - bor our
4. And as John sure - ly knew, Al - though hid - den from

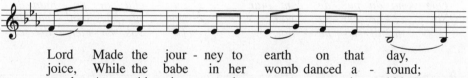

Lord Made the jour - ney to earth on that day,
joice, While the babe in her womb danced a - round;
good, As with - in us the se - cret is hid;
view, That the Lord was in - deed with them there,

Mar - y turned not with - in But, with haste, to her kin;
For when Je - sus, the Lamb, Spoke his si - lent "I AM,"
For, in truth, then will show For all oth - ers to know
So may we with de - light Take with - in our own sight

She set out for a land far a - way.
Proph - et's ears filled with joy at the sound.
All the won - ders that God for us did.
Je - sus, liv - ing in souls ev - 'ry - where.

Text: Patricia Blaze Clark, 1938–2009, © 1998, GIA Publications, Inc.
Tune: MIDDLEBURY, 66 9 66 9, *Southern Harmony*, 1835; harm. by Jack W. Burnam, b.1946, © 1984

899 Come As We Journey along Our Way / Santa María del Camino

Verses

1. Trav - 'ling on life's dai - ly jour - ney,
2. Though some will tell us, dis - cour - aged,
3. While peo - ple aim - less - ly wan - der,
4. Though man - y steps on the jour - ney

1. Mien - tras re - co - rres la vi - da
2. Aun - que te di - gan al - gu - nos
3. Si por el mun - do los hom - bres
4. Aun - que pa - rez - can tus pa - sos

We nev - er walk a - lone. Mar - y, our Moth - er, is
"Noth - ing can ev - er change," Fight for a new world of
Mar - y is at their side. She lends her hand to her
Seem to be made in vain, Still we are forg - ing a

Tú nun - ca so - lo es - tás; Con - ti - go por el ca -
Que na - da pue - de cam - biar, Lu - cha por un mun - do
Sin co - no - cer - se van, No nie - gues nun - ca tu
I - nú - til ca - mi - nar, Tú vas ha - cien - do ca -

with us, Shar - ing our pil - grim road.
jus - tice; Fight till the truth is gained.
chil - dren, Those who in love a - bide.
path - way Oth - ers will walk one day.

mi - no San - ta Ma - rí - a va.
nue - vo, Lu - cha por la ver - dad.
ma - no Al que con - ti - go es - tá.
mi - nos, O - tros los se - gui - rán.

Refrain

Come as we jour - ney a - long our way, San - ta Ma - rí - a, come.
Ven con no - so - tros al ca - mi - nar; San - ta Ma - rí - a, ven.

Come as we jour - ney a - long our way,
Ven con no - so - tros al ca - mi - nar;

San - ta Ma - rí - a,   come.
San - ta Ma - rí - a,   ven.

Text: Juan A. Espinosa, b.1940; tr. by Mary Louise Bringle, b.1953
Tune: Juan A. Espinosa, b.1940; arr. by John Schiavone, b.1947
© 1973, 2011, Juan A. Espinosa. Published by OCP.

Stainless the Maiden / Serdeczna Matko   900

1. Stain - less the Maid - en   whom he chose for   moth - er;
2. Lan - tern in   dark - ness,   when the sick are   sigh - ing,
3. Je - sus has con - quered;   to his side he   raised her;
1. *Ser - de-czna Ma - tko,   O - pie - kun - ko   lu - dzi,*
2. *Do   ko - góż ma - my,   wzdy - chać nę - dzne dzia - tki?*
3. *Za - słu - ży - li - śmy,   to praw - da, przez zło - ści,*

Nine   months she   wait - ed,   bear - ing Christ, our   broth - er;
Thresh - old   of   bright - ness,   com - fort for the   dy - ing,
Queen   of   the   an - gels,   ev - 'ry saint has praised her.
Niech   Cię płacz   sie - rot   do li - to - ści   wzbu - dzi!
Tyl - ko   do   Cie - bie,   u - ko - cha - nej   Ma - tki:
By   nas Bóg   ka - rał   ró - zgą su - ro - wo - ści

Think   of   her   glad - ness   when at   last she   saw   him:
High   she   is   hold - ing   for   a   world a - dor - ing,
Yet,   in   her   splen - dor,   Mar - y   goes on   draw - ing
Wy - gnań - cy   E - wy,   do Cie - bie wo - ła - my:
U   któ - rej   Ser - ce   o - twar - te ka - żde - mu,
Lecz   kie - dy   Oj - ciec   ro - zgnie - wa - ny   sie - cze,

Repeat ad lib.

God   in   a   man - ger,   Beth - le - hem   a   heav - en!
Hope   of   the   na - tions,   Je - sus Christ, our   broth - er.
Sin - ners and ex - iles   to their prom - ised   glo - ry.
Zli - tuj się, zli - tuj,   niech się nie tu - ła - my!
A   o - so - bli - wie   nę - dzą stra - pio - ne - mu!
Szczę - śli - wy kto   się   do Ma - tki   u - cie - cze.

Text: Polish traditional; English paraphrase by Willard F. Jabusch, b.1930, © 1976, 1977
Tune: SERDECZNA MATKO, 11 11 D; Polish traditional; adapt. by Kelly Dobbs-Mickus, b.1966, from an arr. by Richard Proulx, 1937–2010.
© 2011, GIA Publications, Inc.

901 As a Star on Cloudless Evenings / Como Estrella en Claro Cielo

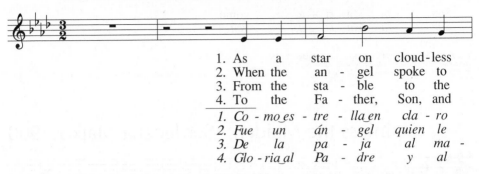

1. As a star on cloud-less
2. When the an - gel spoke to
3. From the sta - ble to the
4. To the Fa - ther, Son, and

1. Co - mo_es - tre - lla_en cla - ro
2. Fue un án - gel quien le
3. De la pa - ja al ma -
4. Glo - ria_al Pa - dre y al

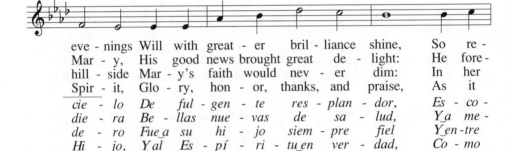

eve - nings Will with great - er bril - liance shine, So re -
Mar - y, His good news brought great de - light: He fore -
hill - side Mar - y's faith would nev - er dim: In her
Spir - it, Glo - ry, hon - or, thanks, and praise, As it

cie - lo De ful - gen - te res - plan - dor, Es - co -
die - ra Be - llas nue - vas de sa - lud, Ya me -
de - ro Fue_a su hi - jo siem - pre fiel Y_en-tre
Hi - jo, Y_al Es - pí - ri - tu_en ver - dad, Co - mo

splen - dent was the maid - en Cho - sen for the Lord's de -
told the Light's ap - pear - ance When but half - spent was the
tears and in her laugh - ter She had pledged her life to
was in the be - gin - ning And shall be for end - less

gi - da fue Ma - rí - a Por de - sig - nio del Se -
dia - dos de_u - na no - che Dios al mun - do_en - vió la
lá - gri - mas y ri - sas Con - sa - gró su vi - da_a
e - ra al prin - ci - pio, Es a - ho - ra y se -

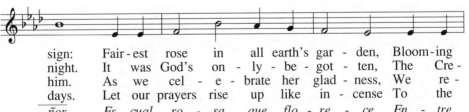

sign: Fair - est rose in all earth's gar - den, Bloom-ing
night. It was God's on - ly - be - got - ten, The Cre -
him. As we cel - e - brate her glad - ness, We re -
days. Let our prayers rise up like in - cense To the

ñor. Es cual ro - sa que flo - re - ce En - tre
luz. Es su fru - to en - gen - dra - do, Del Crea -
él. Hoy ce - le - bro su_a - le - grí - a, Hoy ce -
rá. Mi_a - la - ban - za_a Dios se_e - le - va Co - mo_in-

on a thorn - y vine, Vir - gin moth - er, pure of
a - tor's gift su - preme: Je - sus Christ, the Word in -
call her deep - est pain, Ten - der and un - self - ish
tri - une God a - dored, Join - ing with the song of
car - dos de un jar - dín; *Es don - ce - lla, vir - gen*
dor su - pre - mo don; *Es Je - sús, Ver - bo En - car -*
le - bro su do - lor, *Ma - dre tier - na y ab - ne -*
cien - so en el al - tar; *Yo tam - bién, co - mo Ma -*

spir - it, Sprung from Da - vid's roy - al line.
car - nate, Sent to com - fort and re - deem.
moth - er Of the world's most pre - cious Gain.
Mar - y As we mag - ni - fy the Lord.
pu - ra, Del li - na - je de Da - vid.
na - do, Del hu - ma - no, re - den - ción.
ga - da Del ben - di - to Sal - va - dor.
rí - a, Can - to mi Ma - gní - fi - cat.

Text: Skinner Chávez-Melo, 1944–1992, © 1987, Estate of Skinner Chávez-Melo; tr. by Ronald F. Krisman, b.1946, © 2005, GIA Publications, Inc.
Tune: RAQUEL, 8 7 8 7 D; Skinner Chávez-Melo, 1944-1992, © 1987, Estate of Skinner Chávez-Melo

Ave María 902

A - ve Ma - rí - a, grá - ti - a ple - na,

Dó - mi - nus te - cum, be - ne - dí - cta tu in mu - li - é -

ri - bus, et be - ne - dí - ctus fru - ctus ven - tris tu - i, Je - sus.

San - cta Ma - rí - a, Ma - ter De - i, o - ra pro no - bis pec - ca -

tó - ri - bus, nunc et in ho - ra mor - tis no - strae. A - men.

Text: *Hail, Mary, full of grace,* Luke 1:29; Latin, 13th C.
Tune: AVE MARIA, Irregular; Mode I; acc. by Robert LeBlanc, b.1948, © 1986, GIA Publications, Inc.

903 O Sanctíssima / O Most Holy One

1. O san - ctís - si - ma, O pi - ís - si - ma,
2. Tu so - lá - ti - um Et re - fú - gi - um,
3. Ec - ce dé - bi - les, Per - quam flé - bi - les,
4. Vir - go ré - spi - ce, Ma - ter, á - spi - ce,

1. *O most ho - ly one, O most low - ly one,*
2. *Com - fort in our tears, Ref - uge in our fears,*
3. *See us pow - er - less. In our hope - less - ness*
4. *Maid - en, look on us, Moth - er, care for us.*

Dul - cis vir - go Ma - rí - a!
Vir - go ma - ter Ma - rí - a!
Sal - va nos, O Ma - rí - a!
Au - di nos, O Ma - rí - a!

Praise to you, vir - gin Mar - y!
Vir - gin moth - er, sweet Mar - y!
Save us! Aid us, O Mar - y!
Hear our plead - ing, O Mar - y!

Ma - ter a - má - ta, In - te - me - rá - ta,
Quid - quid o - ptá - mus, Per te spe - rá - mus,
Tol - le lan - guó - res, Sa - na do - ló - res,
Tu me - di - cí - nam, Por - tas di - ví - nam;

Kind, lov - ing Moth - er, Graced like no oth - er,
What - e'er our souls need Grant us, as we plead:
Come, take our sad - ness; Fill us with glad - ness.
You bring us heal - ing, God's love re - veal - ing.

O - ra, o - ra pro no - bis.
O - ra, o - ra pro no - bis.
O - ra, o - ra pro no - bis.
O - ra, o - ra pro no - bis.

Pray, O pray for us, Mar - y!
Pray, O pray for us, Mar - y!
Pray, O pray for us, Mar - y!
Pray, O pray for us, Mar - y!

Text: St. 1, *Stimmen der Völker in Liedern,* 1807; st. 2, *Arundel Hymnal,* 1902; tr. Neil Borgstrom, b.1953, © 1994, 2011, GIA Publications, Inc.
Tune: O DU FRÖLICHE, 55 7 55 7; Tattersall's *Improved Psalmody,* 1794

All Who Put Their Faith in Jesus   904

1. All who
2. Bless-ed
3. There-fore
4. Praise, O

put their faith in Je - sus, Sing the won - ders that were
were the cho-sen peo-ple Out of whom the Lord did
let all faith-ful peo-ple Sing the hon - or of her
Mar - y, praise the Fa - ther, Praise your Sav - ior and your

done When the love of God the Fa - ther O - ver
come; Bless-ed was the land of prom - ise Fash-ioned
name; Let the Church, in her fore - shad - owed, Part in
Son; Praise the ev - er - last-ing Spir - it, Who has

sin the vic - t'ry won, When God made the Vir - gin
for his earth-ly home; Far more bless - ed was the
her thanks-giv-ing claim; What Christ's moth - er sang in
made you ark and throne; O - ver all the earth ex -

Mar - y Moth - er of his on - ly Son.
moth - er, She who bore him in her womb.
glad - ness Let Christ's peo - ple sing the same.
alt - ed, Hum - bly praise the Three in One.

Text: Vincent S. S. Coles, 1845–1929, alt.
Tune: JULION, 8 7 8 7 8 7; David Hurd, b.1950, © 1983, GIA Publications, Inc.

905 Let All on Earth Their Voices Raise

1. Let all on earth their voic - es raise,
2. Lord, at your word they bore the light
3. Lord, by your will to them was giv'n
4. Lord, in your might they spoke the word
5. And when the thrones are set on high

Re - sound - ing heav'n's tri - um - phant praise
Of gos - pel truth o'er dark - est night.
To bind and loose in earth and heav'n.
Which cured di - sease and health re - stored.
And judg - ment's awe - some hour draws nigh,

To God, who gave the a - pos - tles grace
To us that heav'n - ly light im - part;
Our chains un - bind, our sins un - do,
To us its heal - ing pow'r pro - long;
Then, Lord, with them pro - nounce us blest,

To run on earth their glo - rious race.
Make glad our eyes and cheer our heart.
And in our hearts your grace re - new.
Sup - port the weak, con - firm the strong.
And take us to your end - less rest.

Text: *Exsultet coelum laudibus*; Latin, 11th C.; tr. by Richard Mant, 1776–1848, alt.
Tune: TRURO, LM; Williams' *Psalmodia Evangelica*, 1789

Blessed Feasts of Blessed Martyrs   906

1. Bless-ed feasts of bless-ed mar-tyrs, Ho-ly wom-en,
2. Faith pre-vail-ing, hope un-fail-ing, Lov-ing Christ with
3. There-fore, you co-heirs of glo-ry, All who dwell with

ho-ly men, With the mem-'ry of their wit-ness
sin-gle heart, Thus they, glo-rious and vic-to-rious,
Christ on high, Join to ours your sup-pli-ca-tion

Greet we your re-turn a-gain. Wor-thy deeds are
Brave-ly bore the mar-tyr's part, By con-tempt of
When be-fore him we draw nigh, Pray-ing that, this

theirs, and won-ders, Wor-thy of the name they bore;
ev-'ry an-guish, By un-yield-ing bat-tle done;
life com-plet-ed, All its fleet-ing mo-ments past,

We, our joy-ful prais-es sing-ing,
Vic-tors at the last, they tri-umph,
By his grace we may be wor-thy

Hon-or them for-ev-er-more.
With the host of an-gels one.
Of e-ter-nal bliss at last.

Text: *O beata beatorum*, Latin, 12th. C.; tr. John M. Neale, 1818–1866, alt.
Tune: IN BABILONE, 8 7 8 7 D; *Oude en Nieuwe Hollantse Boerenlieties en Contredansen*, c.1710

907 Around the Throne a Glorious Band

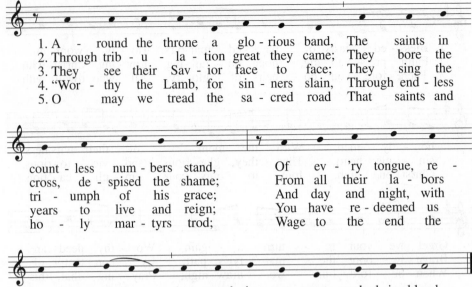

1. A - round the throne a glo - rious band, The saints in
2. Through trib - u - la - tion great they came; They bore the
3. They see their Sav - ior face to face; They sing the
4. "Wor - thy the Lamb, for sin - ners slain, Through end - less
5. O may we tread the sa - cred road That saints and

count - less num - bers stand,   Of ev - 'ry tongue, re -
cross, de - spised the shame;   From all their la - bors
tri - umph of his grace;   And day and night, with
years to live and reign;   You have re - deemed us
ho - ly mar - tyrs trod;   Wage to the end the

deemed to God,   Ar - rayed in gar - ments washed in blood.
now they rest   In God's e - ter - nal glo - ry blest.
cease - less praise, To him their loud ho - san - nas raise:
by your blood,   And made us kings and priests to God."
glo - rious strife, And win, like them, the crown of life!

Text: Rowland Hill, 1744–1833, alt.
Tune: JESU DULCIS MEMORIA, LM; Mode I; acc. by Richard Proulx, 1937–2010, © 1975, GIA Publications, Inc.

908 For All the Faithful Women

1. For all the faith - ful wom - en Who served in
2. *Insert appropriate stanza*
3. O God, for saints and ser - vants, Those named and
4. All praise to God the Fa - ther! All praise to

days of old,   To you shall thanks be giv - en; To
those un - known, In whom through all the a - ges Your
God the Son!   All praise to God the Spir - it, Who

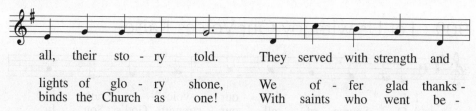

all, their sto - ry told. They served with strength and
lights of glo - ry shone, We of - fer glad thanks -
binds the Church as one! With saints who went be -

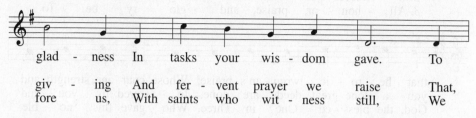

glad - ness In tasks your wis - dom gave. To
giv - ing And fer - vent prayer we raise That,
fore us, With saints who wit - ness still, We

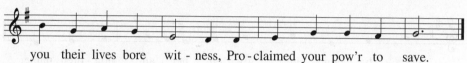

you their lives bore wit - ness, Pro - claimed your pow'r to save.
faith - ful in your serv - ice, Our lives may sing your praise.
sing glad Al - le - lu - ias And strive to do your will.

2a. Miriam *(Exodus 15:19–21)*
We praise your name for Miriam,
Who sang triumphantly
While Pharaoh's vaunted army
Lay drowned beneath the sea.
As Israel marched to freedom,
Their chains of bondage gone,
So may we reach the kingdom
Your mighty arm has won.

2c. Martha and Mary *(Luke 10:38–42)*
We sing of busy Martha,
Who toiled with pot and pan
While Mary sat in silence
To hear the Word again.
Christ, keep our hearts attentive
To truth that you declare,
And strengthen us for service
When work becomes our prayer.

2b. Hannah *(1 Samuel 1:1 – 2:10)*
To Hannah, praying childless
Before your throne of grace,
You gave a son and called him
To serve before your face.
Grant us her perseverance;
Lord, teach us how to pray
And trust in your deliv'rance
When darkness hides our way.

2d. Mary, Mother of the Lord *(Luke 1:26–38)*
We honor faithful Mary,
Fair maiden, full of grace.
She bore the Christ, our brother,
Who saved our human race.
May we, with her, surrender
Ourselves to your command
And lay upon your altar
Our gifts of heart and hand.

2e. Mary Magdalene *(John 20:1–18)*
We sing your praise for Mary,
Who came at Easter dawn
To look for Jesus' body
But found her Lord was gone.
As joyfully she saw him
In resurrection light,
May we by faith behold him,
The Day who ends our night!

Text: Herman G. Stuempfle, Jr., 1923-2007, © 1993, GIA Publications, Inc.
Tune: MERLE'S TUNE, 7 6 7 6 D; Hal H. Hopson, b.1933, © 1983, Hope Publishing Company

Alternate tune: ST. THEODULPH

909 Let Us with Joy Our Voices Raise

1. Let us with joy our voic - es raise In that he - ro - ic wom - an's praise, Whose cour - age, strength, and ho - ly fame Have giv - en her an hon - ored name.

2. O Source of all our strength, God's Son, In you a - lone great deeds are done. In - spired by you, and through her prayer, May we bear wit - ness ev - 'ry - where.

3. All hon - or, praise, and glo - ry be To God, the bless - ed One in Three, Who gave this no - ble wom - an grace, A life of vir - tue to em - brace.

Text: *Fortem virili pectore;* Silvio Antoniano, 1540–1603; tr. and st. 3 by Roger Nachtwey, b.1930, alt., © 1965, FEL Publications, Ltd.
Tune: EISENACH, LM; Johann H. Schein, 1586–1630; harm. by J. S. Bach, 1685–1750

910 This Is the Feast Day of the Lord's True Witness

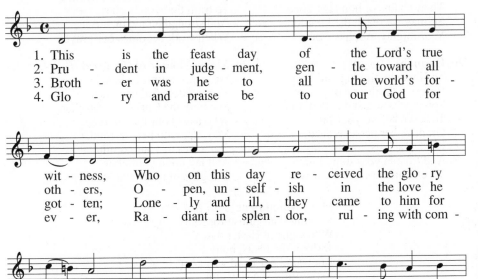

1. This is the feast day of the Lord's true wit - ness, Who on this day re - ceived the glo - ry due him. Let all cre - a - tion cel - e - brate his

2. Pru - dent in judg - ment, gen - tle toward all oth - ers, O - pen, un - self - ish in the love he of - fered. All of his days the gos - pel was his

3. Broth - er was he to all the world's for - got - ten; Lone - ly and ill, they came to him for heal - ing. God gave him pow - er, gifts for our sal -

4. Glo - ry and praise be to our God for ev - er, Ra - diant in splen - dor, rul - ing with com - pass - ion, Guid - ing cre - a - tion on - ward to ful -

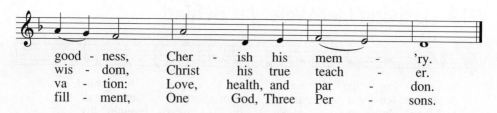

good - ness,   Cher - ish his mem - 'ry.
wis - dom,   Christ his true teach - er.
va - tion: Love, health, and par - don.
fill - ment,   One God, Three Per - sons.

Text: *Iste confessor Domini, colentes*; Latin, 8th C.; tr. by Peter J. Scagnelli, b.1949, © 1976
Tune: ISTE CONFESSOR, 11 11 11 5; Poitiers *Antiphoner*, 1746; harm. by Carl F. Schalk, b.1929, © 1969, Concordia Publishing House

Jesus, at the Jordan Baptized 911

1. Je - sus, at the Jor - dan bap-tized By your proph - et -
2. Break - ing not the bruised and bat-tered, Quench-ing not the
3. Saints, through-out the ag - es bap-tized, Born of Spir - it,
4. Chris - tian, at the foun - tain bap-tized, Mem - ber of God's

cous - in John, Spir - it-blest for works of jus - tice,
ti - ny flame, Free - ing pris - 'ners from con - fine - ment,
born to light, Liv - ing now with Christ, who called you,
house - hold here, For the deeds of mer - cy mis - sioned,

Fa - vored ser - vant, cho - sen one: Al - le - lu - ia,
Heal - ing deaf and blind and lame: Al - le - lu - ia,
Let us share your glo - ry bright. Al - le - lu - ia,
Show the world a love sin - cere. Al - le - lu - ia,

al - le - lu - ia, You are God's be - lov - ed Son!
al - le - lu - ia, Light of Na - tions is your name!
al - le - lu - ia, Fam - 'ly ho - ly, God's de - light!
al - le - lu - ia, Son be - lov - ed, daugh - ter dear!

Text: Delores Dufner, OSB, b.1939, © 2011, GIA Publications, Inc.
Tune: FORTUNATUS NEW, 8 7 8 7 8 7; Carl F. Schalk, b.1929, © 1967, Concordia Publishing House

912 Leaving Her Water Jar Behind

1. Leav - ing her wa - ter jar be - hind,
2. "Come, see a man who told me all
3. When Je - sus spoke, his words brought life,
4. By all the wells of our own day,

The wom - an ran from Ja - cob's well;
That I have ev - er claimed or done!
Like wa - ter poured on shriv - eled seed:
This Je - sus waits to meet us still,

Her dai - ly chores had fled her mind,
Such wis - dom from his lips did fall!
His truth as pierc - ing as a knife,
Where our pre - tens - es fall a - way

For she had won - drous news to tell:
Could this be God's A - noint - ed One?"
His grace yet great - er than their need.
When we ask him our lives to fill.

For - sak - ing what had drawn her first,
Her neigh - bors heard, then with her ran
So they pre - vailed on him to stay
Come with your thirst - y heart and mind;

She quenched in - stead a deep - er thirst.
To meet this wise and ho - ly man.
And teach them more an - oth - er day.
You too may leave your jar be - hind.

Text: Carl P. Daw, Jr., b.1944, © 2005, Hope Publishing Company
Tune: ST. CATHERINE, 8 8 8 8 8 8; Henry F. Hemy, 1818–1888; adapt. by James G. Walton, 1821–1905

God, Who at the Font Once Named Us   913

1. God, who at the font once named us
2. God, who in the wa - ter washed us,
3. God, with Christ's own cross you marked us,
4. God, whose flam - ing, whirl - wind Spir - it
5. Fa - ther, Son and Ho - ly Spir - it,

Sons and daugh - ters, born of grace, Bathed us
Cleans - ing us from sin's deep stain, Raised us
Made us yours e - ter - nal - ly. By that
Touched your peo - ple while they prayed, Kin - dle
Hear the grate - ful hymns we raise! You have

in bap - tis - mal wa - ters, Bound our lives in
up, a new cre - a - tion, Freed, for - giv - en,
sign you chose and claimed us For Christ's work of
faith and love a - mong us; Make our wit - ness
blessed, up - held and led us From the font through

love's em - brace: Make us one in Christ's vast fam - 'ly
whole a - gain: Fill us with your gra - cious Spir - it;
min - is - try. When he calls us, where he leads us,
un - a - fraid, Serv - ing all with Christ's com - pas - sion,
all our days. Yours the hon - or, yours the glo - ry,

Drawn from ev - 'ry land and race.
Let Christ's life with - in us reign!
Help us fol - low faith - ful - ly.
Seek - ing jus - tice, long de - layed.
Tri - une God, to you be praise!

Text: Herman G. Stuempfle, Jr., 1923–2007, © 1999, World Library Publications
Tune: REGENT SQUARE, 8 7 8 7 8 7; Henry Smart, 1813–1879

914   O Breathe on Me, O Breath of God

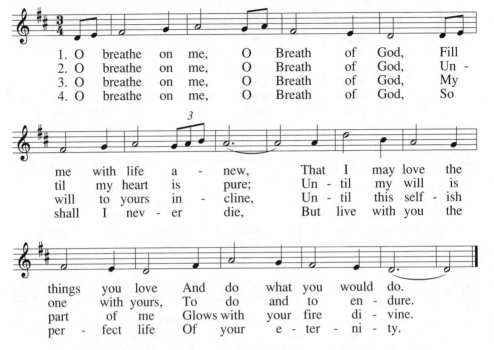

1. O breathe on me, O Breath of God, Fill me with life a - new, That I may love the things you love And do what you would do.
2. O breathe on me, O Breath of God, Un - til my heart is pure; Un - til my will is one with yours, To do and to en - dure.
3. O breathe on me, O Breath of God, My will to yours in - cline, Un - til this self - ish part of me Glows with your fire di - vine.
4. O breathe on me, O Breath of God, So shall I nev - er die, But live with you the per - fect life Of your e - ter - ni - ty.

Text: Edwin Hatch, 1835–1889
Tune: ST. COLUMBA, CM; Irish melody; harm. by A. Gregory Murray, OSB, 1905–1992, © Downside Abbey

915   Awake, O Sleeper, Rise from Death

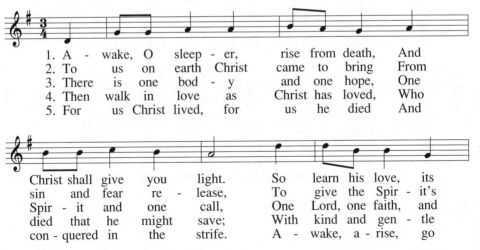

1. A - wake, O sleep - er, rise from death, And Christ shall give you light.
2. To us on earth Christ came to bring From sin and fear re - lease,
3. There is one bod - y and one hope, One Spir - it and one call,
4. Then walk in love as Christ has loved, Who died that he might save;
5. For us Christ lived, for us he died And con - quered in the strife.

So learn his love, its
To give the Spir - it's
One Lord, one faith, and
With kind and gen - tle
A - wake, a - rise, go

length and	breadth,	Its	full - ness,	depth,	and	height.
u -	ni - ty,	The	ver - y	bond	of	peace.
one	bap - tism,	One	Fa - ther	of	us	all.
hearts	for - give	As	God in	Christ	for -	gave.
forth in	faith,	And	Christ shall	give	you	life.

Text: Ephesians 3–5; F. Bland Tucker, 1895–1984, © 1980, Augsburg Fortress
Tune: AZMON, CM; Carl G. Gläser, 1784–1829; harm. by Lowell Mason, 1792–1872

This Is Our Faith   916

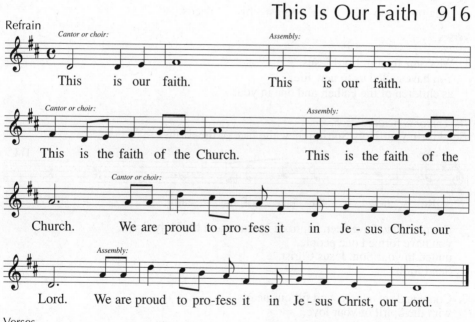

Verses

1. Great is the mystery we profess!
   Christ, revealed in the flesh;
   Christ, made just in the Spirit;
   Christ, seen by the angels.

2. Great is the mystery we profess!
   Christ, proclaimed among the nations;
   Believed throughout the world;
   Christ, exalted in glory.

Text: Refrain from *Rite of Baptism for Children*, © 1969, ICEL; verses based on 1 Timothy 3:16; Lucien Deiss, alt., © 1965, 1966, 1968, 1973,
World Library Publications
Tune: Charles Gardner, b.1947, © 2004, World Library Publications

917 Blessed Be God, Who Chose You in Christ

Refrain

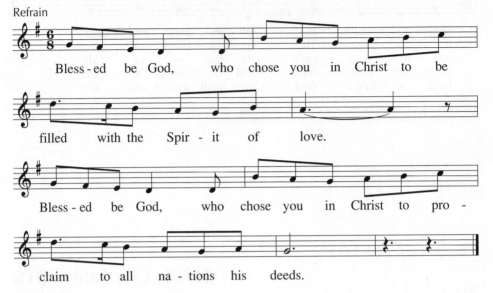

Bless-ed be God, who chose you in Christ to be filled with the Spir-it of love. Bless-ed be God, who chose you in Christ to pro-claim to all na-tions his deeds.

Verses

1. We come to you, Lord Jesus.
   You have called us to new life,
   as children of the Father, and one in you.

The cantor concludes each verse:
Send forth your Holy Spirit, renew the face of the earth.

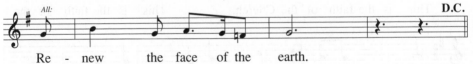

Re - new the face of the earth.

2. From all who have been baptized in water and the Holy Spirit,
   you have formed one people,
   united in your Son, Jesus Christ.
   Send forth...

3. Come and set us free, and fill our hearts
   with the Spirit of your love,
   that we may live in your peace.
   Send forth...

4. You call those who have been baptized
   to announce the Good News of Jesus Christ
   to people ev'rywhere.
   Send forth...

Text: Adapted from the *Rite of Baptism*, James J. Chepponis, b.1956
Tune: James J. Chepponis, b.1956
© 1982, GIA Publications, Inc.

We Praise You, Lord, for Jesus Christ   918

1. We praise you, Lord, for Je - sus Christ, Who
2. We praise you that this child now shares The
3. We praise you, Lord, that now this child Is
4. We praise you, Lord, for Je - sus Christ, Who

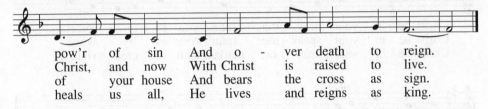

died and rose a - gain, Who lives to break the
free - dom Christ can give, Has died to sin with
graft - ed to the vine, Is made a mem - ber
loves this child we bring: He frees, for - gives, and

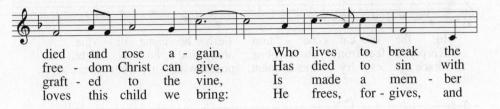

pow'r of sin And o - ver death to reign.
Christ, and now With Christ is raised to live.
of your house And bears the cross as sign.
heals us all, He lives and reigns as king.

Text: Judith Beatrice O'Neill, 1930–2006, © 1970
Tune: NEW BRITAIN, CM; *Virginia Harmony*, 1831; harm. by John Barnard, b.1948, © 1982, The Jubilate Group (admin. by Hope Publishing Company)

Baptized in Water   919

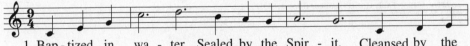
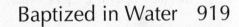

1. Bap - tized in wa - ter, Sealed by the Spir - it, Cleansed by the
2. Bap - tized in wa - ter, Sealed by the Spir - it, Dead in the
3. Bap - tized in wa - ter, Sealed by the Spir - it, Marked with the

blood of Christ our King: Heirs of sal - va - tion, Trust - ing his
tomb with Christ our King: One with his ris - ing, Freed and for -
sign of Christ our King: Born of one Fa - ther, We are his

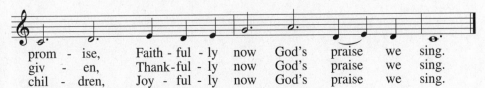

prom - ise, Faith - ful - ly now God's praise we sing.
giv - en, Thank - ful - ly now God's praise we sing.
chil - dren, Joy - ful - ly now God's praise we sing.

Text: Michael Saward, b.1932, © 1982, The Jubilate Group (admin. by Hope Publishing Company)
Tune: BUNESSAN, 5 5 8 D; Gaelic melody; acc. A. Gregory Murray, OSB, 1905–1992, © Downside Abbey

920 Christ Be in Your Senses

1. Christ be in your sens - es, marked with sa - cred sign.
2. Christ be in your vi - sion, guard you day and night;
3. Christ be in your breath-ing, con - stant - ly im - part

In the In - car - na - tion flesh be - came di - vine.
Keep your feet from stum - bling, shine God's ho - ly light.
Grace to ev - 'ry move-ment, peace with - in your heart.

Christ be in your hear - ing, tune you to re - joice;
Christ be in your speak - ing, train your ev - 'ry word.
Christ be in your sens - es, marked with sa - cred sign.

In each shout or whis - per, hear God's call - ing voice.
In your dai - ly wit - ness let God's truth be heard.
In the Spir - it's pres - ence, flesh be - comes di - vine.

Text: Mary Louise Bringle, b.1953
Tune: APPALACHIAN FALL, 11 11 11 11; William P. Rowan, b.1951
© 2002, GIA Publications, Inc.

There Is One Lord 921

Ostinato Refrain

There is one Lord, one faith, one bap-tis-m,
Hay un Se-ñor, u-na fe, un bau-tis-mo,

There is one God who is Fa-ther of all.
Un so-lo Dios, quien es Pa-dre de to-dos.

Text: Ephesians 4, Taizé Community, 1984
Tune: Jacques Berthier, 1923–1994
© 1984, 2007, Les Presses de Taizé, GIA Publications, Inc., agent

Crashing Waters at Creation 922

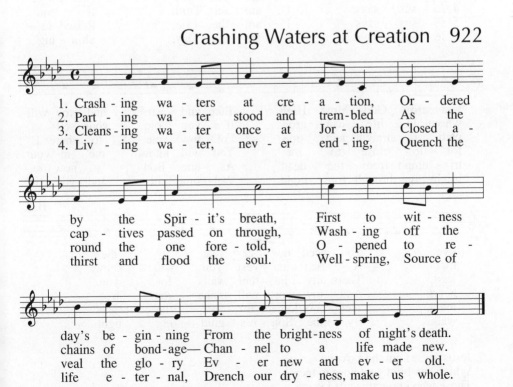

1. Crash - ing wa - ters at cre - a - tion, Or - dered
2. Part - ing wa - ter stood and trem - bled As the
3. Cleans - ing wa - ter once at Jor - dan Closed a -
4. Liv - ing wa - ter, nev - er end - ing, Quench the

by the Spir - it's breath, First to wit - ness
cap - tives passed on through, Wash - ing off the
round the one fore - told, O - pened to re -
thirst and flood the soul. Well - spring, Source of

day's be - gin - ning From the bright-ness of night's death.
chains of bond-age— Chan - nel to a life made new.
veal the glo - ry Ev - er new and ev - er old.
life e - ter - nal, Drench our dry - ness, make us whole.

Text: Sylvia G. Dunstan, 1955–1993, © 1991, GIA Publications, Inc.
Tune: RESTORATION, 8 7 8 7; *Southern Harmony*, 1835; harm. by George E. Mims, b.1938, © 1979, George E. Mims

923 I Receive the Living God

Refrain

I re-ceive the liv-ing God, And my heart is full of joy. I re-ceive the liv-ing God, And my heart is full of joy.

Verses

1. Je - sus says: I am the Bread Sent to
2. Je - sus says: I am the Vine, Far from
3. Je - sus says: I am the Way, And my
4. Je - sus says: I am the Truth. If you
5. Je - sus says: I am the Life, Raised in
6. Je - sus says: I am the Day, Shin - ing

1. you from God Most High. Take and eat, and you will
2. whom no life can grow. If you join your-self to
3. path is straight and true. Fol - low me to where I
4. fol - low close to me, You will know me in your
5. tri - umph from the dead. As one Bod - y now re -
6. bright - ly through your night. Wel - come me, and you will

D.C.

1. live; You need nev - er fear to die.
2. me, A rich har - vest you will know.
3. lead; There my Fa - ther waits for you.
4. heart, And my word will make you free.
5. main, Mem - bers joined to me, the Head.
6. walk By the Spir - it's guid - ing light.

7. Jesus says: I am the Love
   Which can bind you close to me.
   Those who know this gift I bring
   Will find true community.

8. Jesus says: I am the Peace
Which the world cannot bestow.
Learn to love and live in me,
And in you my Reign will grow.

9. Jesus says: I am the Lamb,
And my death set sinners free.
Those who drink the cup I drink
Must take up this work with me.

Text: Vss. 1–3, 5–9, Bernard Geoffroy, b.1946; tr. by Ronald F. Krisman, b.1946, © 2011, GIA Publications, Inc.; vs. 4, anonymous
Tune: LIVING GOD, 7 7 7 7 with refrain; Dom Clément Jacob, OSB, 1906–1977, adapt.; harm. by Richard Proulx, 1937–2010, © 1986,
    GIA Publications, Inc.

Bread of Life, Cup of Blessing 924

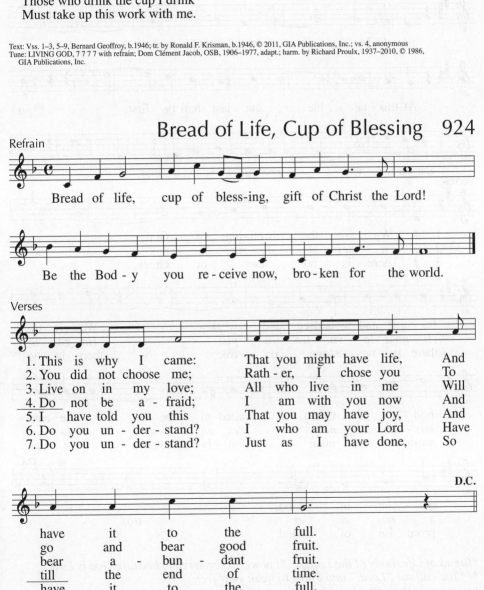

Refrain

Bread of life, cup of bless-ing, gift of Christ the Lord!

Be the Bod-y you re-ceive now, bro-ken for the world.

Verses

1. This	is	why	I	came:	That you	might have	life,	And
2. You	did	not choose	me;		Rath-er,	I	chose you	To
3. Live	on	in	my	love;	All who	live	in me	Will
4. Do	not	be	a-fraid;		I	am with	you now	And
5. I	have told	you	this		That you	may	have joy,	And
6. Do	you	un-der-stand?			I	who	am your Lord	Have
7. Do	you	un-der-stand?			Just as	I	have done,	So

D.C.

have	it	to	the	full.
go	and	bear	good	fruit.
bear	a-bun-dant			fruit.
till	the	end	of	time.
have	it	to	the	full.
knelt	and	washed	your	feet.
al-so		you	must	do.

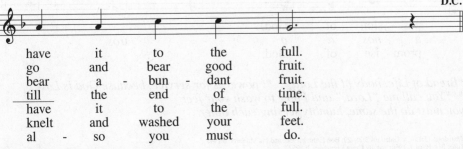

Text: Delores Dufner, OSB, b.1939
Tune: BREAD BROKEN, 5 5 6 with refrain; Michel Guimont, b.1950
© 2008, GIA Publications, Inc.

925   Pan de Vida

Refrain

*Pan de Vi - da, cuer-po del Se - ñor,

cup of bless - ing, blood of Christ the Lord.

At this ta - ble the last shall be first, **po-

Verses

der es ser - vir, por-que Dios es a - mor.

1. ♩ We are the dwell-ing of God, We are the
***2. Us - te - des me lla - man "Se - ñor," me in-
3. ♩ There is no Jew or Greek, there is no

fra - gile and wound-ed and weak.
cli - no_a la - var - les los pies.
there is no slave or free;

bod - y of Christ, called to be the com -
mis - mo, hu - mil - des, sir - vién - do - se
wom-an or man; on - ly heirs of the

D.C.

pas - sion of God.
u - nos a o - tros.
prom - ise of God.

*Bread of Life, body of the Lord,   **power is for service, because God is Love.
***You call me "Lord," and I bow to wash your feet:
you must do the same, humbly serving each other.

Text: John 13:13–14, Galatians 3:28–29; Bob Hurd, b.1950, and Pia Moriarty, b.1948
Tune: Bob Hurd, b.1950; acc. by Craig Kingsbury, b.1952
© 1988, Bob Hurd and Pia Moriarty. Published by OCP.

I Come with Joy   926

1. I come with joy, a child of God, For-
2. I come with Chris-tians far and near To
3. As Christ breaks bread, and bids us share, Each
4. The Spir-it of the ris-en Christ, Un-
5. To-geth-er met, to-geth-er bound By

giv-en, loved, and free, The life of Je-sus
find, as all are fed, The new com-mu-ni-
proud di-vi-sion ends. The love that made us,
seen, but ev-er near, Is in such friend-ship
all that God has done, We'll go with joy, to

to re-call, In love laid down for
ty of love In Christ's com-mun-ion
makes us one, And stran-gers now are
bet-ter known, A-live a-mong us
give the world The love that makes us

me, In love laid down for me.
bread, In Christ's com-mun-ion bread.
friends, And stran-gers now are friends.
here, A-live a-mong us here.
one, The love that makes us one.

Text: Brian Wren, b.1936, © 1971, 1995, Hope Publishing Company
Tune: DOVE OF PEACE, 8 6 8 66; American melody; harm. by Charles H. Webb, b.1933, © 1989, The United Methodist Publishing House

927 Amen to the Body of Christ

Refrain

A - men to the Bod - y of Christ we re - ceive, bread for the full - ness of life. A - men to the Bod - y of Christ we be - come, bread for the life of the world.

Verses

1. Je - sus said, "I was hun - gry and you gave me
2. Je - sus said, "I was home - less and you took me
3. Je - sus said, "I was sick and you vis - it - ed
4. Je - sus said, "You are blest who have cared for the
5. At the judg - ment one day, may we hear Je - sus

food; I was thirst - y and you gave me drink.
in; I was na - ked, and you shared your cloak.
me, In dis - tress and you came to my help.
weak, Who have wel - comed the stran - ger as guest.
say, "Come, re - ceive now the joy of your God.

What you do for my loved ones, My poor and my least
What you do for my loved ones, My poor and my least
What you do for my loved ones, My poor and my least
What you do for my loved ones, My poor and my least
What you did for my loved ones, My poor and my least

D.C.

ones, That you do al - so for me."
ones, That you do al - so for me."
ones, That you do al - so for me."
ones, That you do al - so for me."
ones, That you did al - so for me."

Text: Delores Dufner, OSB, b.1939
Tune: AMEN, 12 9 7 6 7 with refrain; Michel Guimont, b.1950
© 2008, GIA Publications, Inc.

Come to the Banquet 928

Refrain

Come to the ban - quet, come to the feast. Eat the Bread of

life! Share in the sing - ing, share in the joy.

To verses | *Last time*

Drink the Cup of love! love! Share the joy!

Verses

1. Draw near and take the Bod - y of the
2. Our great Re - deem - er, God's e - ter - nal
3. Let us ap - proach with faith - ful hearts sin -
4. With heav'n - ly bread Christ makes the hun - gry

Lord, And drink with faith the Blood for you out - poured.
Son, Has by his cross and blood the vic - t'ry won.
cere And claim the prom - ise of sal - va - tion here.
whole; His liv - ing wa - ter fills the thirst - ing soul.

Saved by his Bod - y, hal - lowed by his Blood, With
He spent his life for great - est and for least. Praise
Christ rules our hearts, and all his saints de - fends; He
Be - fore your pres - ence, Lord, all peo - ple bow. In

D.C.

souls re - freshed we give our thanks to God.
Christ, the Pas - chal Vic - tim, Christ the Priest.
gives be - liev - ers life that nev - er ends.
this your feast of love be with us now.

Text: *Sancti, venite, corpus sumite,* 7th C., tr. John M. Neale, 1818–1866, alt.; refrain, James J. Chepponis, b.1956, © 2000, GIA Publications, Inc.
Tune: ST. MALACHY, 10 10 10 10 with refrain; James J. Chepponis, b.1956, © 2000, GIA Publications, Inc.

929 Ave Verum

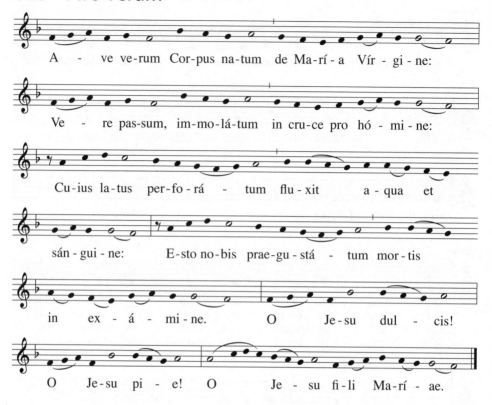

A - ve ve-rum Cor-pus na-tum de Ma-rí - a Vír - gi - ne:

Ve - re pas-sum, im-mo-lá-tum in cru-ce pro hó - mi - ne:

Cu-ius la-tus per-fo-rá - tum flu - xit a - qua et

sán - gui - ne: E-sto no-bis prae-gu-stá - tum mor-tis

in ex - á - mi - ne. O Je-su dul - cis!

O Je-su pi - e! O Je - su fi-li Ma-rí - ae.

Translation: Hail, true Body, born of the Virgin Mary,
the very Body which suffered and was sacrificed
on the cross for humankind,
and whose pierced side overflowed with water and blood:
In the agony of death be for us a foretaste of heaven,
O kind and loving Jesus, son of Mary.

Text: *Ave verum*, ascr. to Innocent VI, d.1362
Tune: AVE VERUM, Irregular; Mode VI; acc. by Ronald F. Krisman, b.1946, © 2011, GIA Publications, Inc.

930 In Memory of You

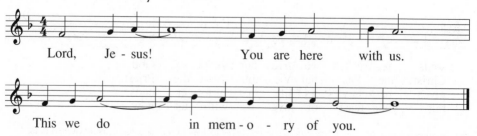

Lord, Je - sus! You are here with us.

This we do in mem-o - ry of you.

Text: Alexander Peloquin, 1918–1997
Tune: Alexander Peloquin, 1918–1997
© 1976, GIA Publications, Inc.

One Bread, One Body 931

Refrain

One bread, one bod-y, one Lord of all,

one cup of bless-ing which we bless. And

we, though man-y, through-out the earth,

we are one bod-y in this one Lord.

Verses

1. Gen-tile or Jew,   Ser-vant or free,
2. Man-y the gifts,   Man-y the works,
3. Grain for the fields,   Scat-tered and grown,

D.C.

Wom-an or man   no more.
One in the Lord   of all.
Gath-ered to one   for all.

Text: 1 Corinthians 10:16–17, 12:4, 12–13, 20; Galatians 3:28; Ephesians 4:46; the *Didache* 9; John Foley, SJ, b.1939
Tune: ONE BREAD, ONE BODY, 4 4 6 with refrain; John Foley, SJ, b.1939
© 1978, John B. Foley, SJ, and OCP

932 As the Bread of Life Is Broken

Refrain

As the bread of life is bro-ken, the cup of love out-poured,

We are one in Christ, our Sav-ior, and sent to serve the Lord.

Verses

1. We, the man - y who are gath - ered, are u-
2. In the word of God pro - claimed here the good
3. In the bread of life here giv - en, we be -
4. Sent as bless - ing for God's peo - ple, to go

nit - ed now as one. In this joy - ful cel - e -
news of truth is heard. In the tell - ing of the
come what we re - ceive. In the cup of love here
forth in love and peace, In our wit - ness to God's

bra - tion, we re - call what God has done.
sto - ries, we are o - pen to God's word.
of - fered, we af - firm what we be - lieve.
king - dom, may our char - i - ty in - crease.

Text: James J. Chepponis, b.1956, © 2002, Birnamwood Publications, a div. of MorningStar Music Publishers, Inc.
Tune: THAXTED, 14 14 15 15; Gustav Holst, 1874–1934

Jesus, Ever-Flowing Fountain 933

Refrain

Je-sus, ev-er-flow-ing foun-tain, Give us wa-ter from your well.

In the gra-cious gift you of - fer There is joy no tongue can tell.

Verses

1. Come to me, all pil - grims thirst - y; Drink the
2. Come to me, all trav - 'lers wea - ry; Come that
3. Come to me, be - liev - ers bur - dened; Find re -
4. Come to me, re - pen - tant sin - ners; Leave be -
5. Come to me, dis - tressed and need - y; I will
6. Come to me, a - ban - doned, or - phaned; Lone - ly

wa - ter I will give. If you knew what gift I
I may give you rest. Drink the cup of life I
fresh-ment in this place. Come, re - ceive the gift I
hind your guilt and shame. If you knew di - vine com -
be your trust - ed friend. Seek the gift of life I
ways no long - er roam. Come, ac - cept the gift I

D.C.

of - fer, You would come to me and live.
of - fer; At this ta - ble be my guest.
of - fer; Turn to me and seek my face.
pas - sion, You would turn and call my name.
of - fer; Come, your o - pen hands ex - tend.
of - fer; Come and make in me your home.

Text: Delores Dufner, OSB, b.1939
Tune: GRACIOUS GIFT, 8 7 8 7 with refrain; Michel Guimont, b.1950
© 2008, GIA Publications, Inc.

934 Amén. El Cuerpo de Cristo

Refrain

A - mén. El Cuer - po de Cris - to. A - mén. La

San-gre del Se - ñor. *Eat-ing your Bod-y,* *drink-ing your Blood, we be-*

come what we re-ceive. A - mén. A - mén.

Verses

1. A - mén. *We re - mem - ber your dy - ing*
2. A - mén. *Now we of - fer the sac - ri -*
3. A - mén. *Lord, you make us one bod - y*
4. A - mén. *We find you when we serve the*
5. A - mén. *We look for - ward to your re -*

and your ris - ing. A - mén. Y con - ti - go, Se -
fice you gave us. A - mén. Te o-fre - ce - mos, Se -
and one spir - it. A - mén. En tu cuer - po, Se -
poor and low - ly. A - mén. A ti mis - mo ser -
turn in glo - ry. A - mén. Es - pe - ra - mos el

D.C.

ñor, re - su - ci - ta - mos. A - mén.
ñor, to - do lo que so - mos. A - mén.
ñor, un pue - blo san - to. A - mén.
vi - mos en los po - bres. A - mén.
día de tu ve - ni - da. A - mén.

Text: John Schiavone, b.1947
Tune: John Schiavone, b.1947
© 1995, John Schiavone. Published by OCP.

Draw Near   935

Refrain

Draw near, draw near! Take the Bod-y
of your Lord. Draw near, draw near!
Drink the Blood for you out-poured.

Verses

1. Draw near and take the Bod-y of the Lord,
2. Christ, our Re-deem - er, God's e - ter - nal Son,
3. Let us ap-proach with faith - ful hearts sin - cere
4. With heav'n-ly bread Christ makes the hun-gry whole;

And drink with faith the Blood for you out-poured.
Has by his cross and blood the vic - t'ry won.
And claim the prom - ise of sal - va - tion here.
His liv-ing wa - ter fills the thirst - ing soul.

Saved by his Bod - y and his ho - ly Blood, With
He spent his life for great-est and for least. Praise
Christ rules our hearts, and all his saints de - fends; He
Al - pha - O - me - ga, un - to whom shall bow All

D.C.

souls re - freshed we give our thanks to God.
Christ the Pas - chal Vic - tim, Christ the Priest.
gives be - liev - ers life that nev - er ends.
na - tions of the earth, be with us now.

Text: *Sancti, venite, Christi corpus sumite*, 7th C.; tr. by John M. Neale, 1818–1866, alt.
Tune: NEALE, 10 10 10 10 with refrain; Steven R. Janco, b.1961, © 1992, World Library Publications

936 Where Two or Three Are Gathered

Refrain

Here in the Bread that is bro - ken, here in the Cup that is poured, here in the Word that is spo - ken: Je - sus Christ is Lord! Here where the poor find their treas - ure, here where the great-est are least, come find a love be-yond meas - ure in this heav'n - ly feast.

Verses

1. Where two or three are gath-ered, Gath-ered in my name, I come with words of com - fort
2. Where two or three are gath-ered, I am there as well, In - vit - ing my dis - ci - ples
3. Where two or three are gath-ered, I am there with you. I lead you in - to free - dom,
4. Where two or three are gath-ered, Gath-ered in my name, I wash your feet in serv - ice.
5. Where two or three are gath-ered, I am there as well. The bless - ings of the king - dom
6. Where two or three are gath-ered, I am there with you. My gifts of peace and mer - cy

D.C.

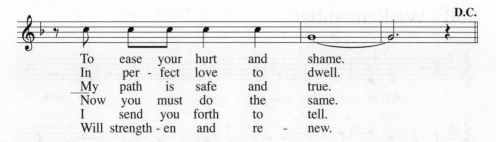

To ease your hurt and shame.
In per-fect love to dwell.
My path is safe and true.
Now you must do the same.
I send you forth to tell.
Will strength-en and re-new.

Text: Liam Lawton, b.1959
Tune: HEAVENLY FEAST, 7 5 7 5 with refrain; Liam Lawton, b.1959; arr. by Paul A. Tate, b.1968
© 2009, Sumerset Recordings and GIA Publications, Inc.

Draw Us in the Spirit's Tether 937

1. Draw us in the Spir-it's teth-er, For when
2. As dis-ci-ples used to gath-er In the
3. All our meals and all our liv-ing Make as

hum-bly in your name Two or
name of Christ to sup, Then with
sac-ra-ments of you, That by

three are met to-geth-er, You are in the
thanks to God the Fa-ther Break the bread and
car-ing, help-ing, giv-ing, We may be dis-

midst of them. Al-le-lu-ia! Al-le-lu-ia!
bless the cup. Al-le-lu-ia! Al-le-lu-ia!
ci-ples true. Al-le-lu-ia! Al-le-lu-ia!

Touch we now your gar-ment's hem.
So now bind our friend-ship up.
We will serve with faith a-new.

Text: Percy Dearmer, 1867–1936, alt., © 1931, Oxford University Press
Tune: UNION SEMINARY, 8 7 8 7 44 7; Harold Friedell, 1905–1958, © 1957, The H. W. Gray Co., Inc.; harm. by Jet Turner, 1928–1984,
      © Chalice Press

938 We Remember

Refrain

We re-mem-ber how you loved us to your death,
and still we cel-e-brate, for you are with us here;
and we be-lieve that we will see you when you come
in your glo-ry, Lord. We re-mem-ber, we
cel-e-brate, we be-lieve.

Verses

1. Here, a mil-lion wound-ed souls Are
2. Now we re-cre-ate your love, We
3. Christ, the Fa-ther's great "A-men" To
4. See the face of Christ re-vealed In

yearn-ing just to touch you and be healed;
bring the bread and wine to share a meal:
all the hopes and dreams of ev-'ry heart,
ev-'ry per-son stand-ing by your side:

D.C.

Gath-er all your peo-ple, and hold them to your heart.
Sign of grace and mer-cy, the pres-ence of the Lord.
Peace be-yond all tell-ing, and free-dom from all fear.
Gifts to one an-oth-er, and tem-ples of your love.

Text: Marty Haugen, b.1950
Tune: WE REMEMBER, 7 10 12 with refrain; Marty Haugen, b.1950
© 1980, GIA Publications, Inc.

You Satisfy the Hungry Heart 939

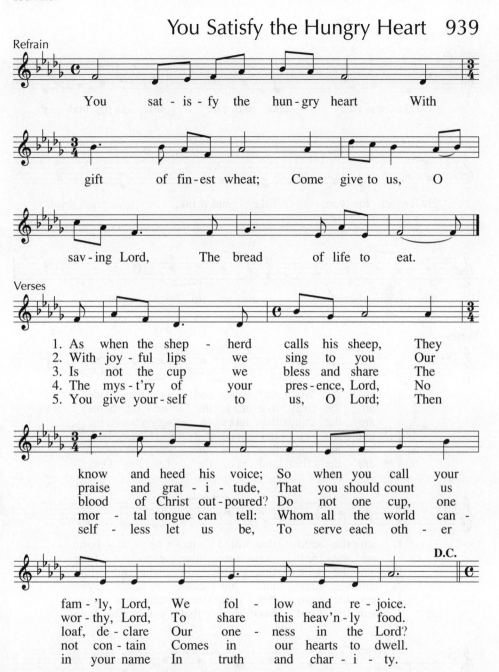

Refrain

You sat-is-fy the hun-gry heart With gift of fin-est wheat; Come give to us, O sav-ing Lord, The bread of life to eat.

Verses

1. As when the shep - herd calls his sheep, They
2. With joy - ful lips we sing to you Our
3. Is not the cup we bless and share The
4. The mys - t'ry of your pres - ence, Lord, No
5. You give your - self to us, O Lord; Then

know and heed his voice; So when you call your
praise and grat - i - tude, That you should count us
blood of Christ out - poured? Do not one cup, one
mor - tal tongue can tell: Whom all the world can -
self - less let us be, To serve each oth - er

D.C.

fam - 'ly, Lord, We fol - low and re - joice.
wor - thy, Lord, To share this heav'n - ly food.
loaf, de - clare Our one - ness in the Lord?
not con - tain Comes in our hearts to dwell.
in your name In truth and char - i - ty.

Text: Omer Westendorf, 1916–1997
Tune: BICENTENNIAL, CM with refrain; Robert E. Kreutz, 1922–1996
© 1977, Archdiocese of Philadelphia. Published by International Liturgy Publications

940 Take and Eat

Refrain

Take and eat; take and eat: this is my bod - y giv-en up for you. Take and drink; take and drink: this is my blood giv - en up for you.

Verses

1. I am the Word that spoke and light was made;
2. I am the way that leads the ex - ile home;
3. I am the Lamb that takes a - way your sin;
4. I am the cor - ner - stone that God has laid;
5. I am the light that came in - to the world;
6. I am the first and last, the Liv - ing One;

I am the seed that died to be re - born;
I am the truth that sets the cap - tive free;
I am the gate that guards you night and day;
A cho - sen stone and pre - cious in his eyes;
I am the light that dark - ness can - not hide;
I am the Lord who died that you might live;

I am the bread that comes from heav'n a - bove;
I am the life that rais - es up the dead;
You are my flock: you know the shep-herd's voice;
You are God's dwell - ing place, on me you rest;
I am the morn - ing star that nev - er sets;
I am the bride-groom, this my wed - ding song;

D.C.

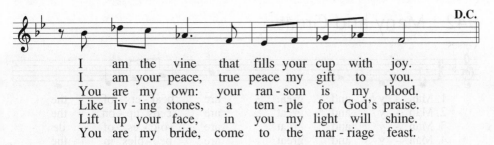

I am the vine that fills your cup with joy.
I am your peace, true peace my gift to you.
You are my own: your ran - som is my blood.
Like liv - ing stones, a tem - ple for God's praise.
Lift up your face, in you my light will shine.
You are my bride, come to the mar - riage feast.

Text: Verse text, James Quinn, SJ, 1919–2010, © 1989. Used by permission of Selah Publishing Co., Inc.; refrain text, Michael Joncas, b.1951,
© 1989, GIA Publications, Inc.
Tune: CORPUS DOMINI, 10 10 10 10 with refrain; Michael Joncas, b.1951, © 1989, GIA Publications, Inc.

Shepherd of Souls 941

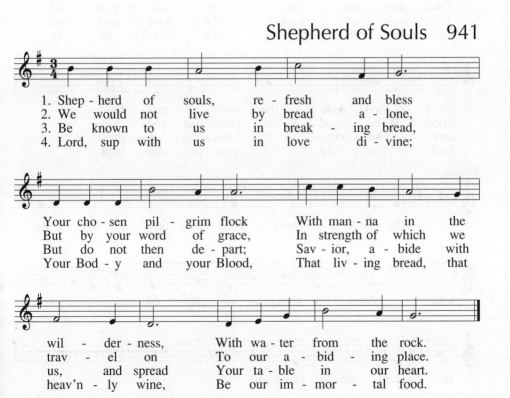

1. Shep - herd of souls, re - fresh and bless
2. We would not live by bread a - lone,
3. Be known to us in break - ing bread,
4. Lord, sup with us in love di - vine;

Your cho - sen pil - grim flock With man - na in the
But by your word of grace, In strength of which we
But do not then de - part; Sav - ior, a - bide with
Your Bod - y and your Blood, That liv - ing bread, that

wil - der - ness, With wa - ter from the rock.
trav - el on, To our a - bid - ing place.
us, and spread Your ta - ble in our heart.
heav'n - ly wine, Be our im - mor - tal food.

Text: James Montgomery, 1771–1854, alt.
Tune: ST. AGNES, CM; John B. Dykes, 1823–1876; harm. by Richard Proulx, 1937–2010, © 1986, GIA Publications, Inc.

942 Many and Great

Verses

1. Man - y and great are bear - ers of the
2. Man - y and great are seeds up - on the
3. Man - y and great are voic - es of de -
4. Man - y and great are peb - bles in the

Word: The Christ speaks; the heart seeks.
field: The hand sows; the seeds grow.
spair: The rain falls; the voice calls.
sand: The sun glows; the wind blows.

Gath - ered as one, we lis - ten to the
Take now and eat the cov - e - nant ful -
Take now and drink the wine of hope and
Take now and spread the Word to ev - 'ry

Word And share the meal of new birth.
filled, The bread of prom - ise and life.
care; Our cup of bless - ing we share.
land, The Word of good - ness and hope.

Refrain

The wheat grows from spring - time to fall; the

wine flows; in Christ we re - call the shar - ing of our

lives with one and all.

Text: Ricky Manalo, CSP, b.1965
Tune: Ricky Manalo, CSP, b.1965
© 1995, Ricky Manalo, CSP. Published by OCP.

Eat This Bread 943

Refrain

Eat this bread, drink this cup,
Co - man de es - te pan, be - ban de es - te cá - liz,

come to him and nev - er be hun - gry.
ven - gan, y no ten - drán ham - bre.

Eat this bread, drink this cup,
Co - man de es - te pan, be - ban de es - te cá - liz,

trust in him and you will not thirst.
cre - an, y no ten - drán sed.

Text: John 6; adapt. by Robert J. Batastini, b.1942, and the Taizé Community
Tune: Jacques Berthier, 1923–1994
© 1984, 2005, Les Presses de Taizé, GIA Publications, Inc., agent

944　In the Breaking of the Bread

Refrain

In the break-ing of the bread We have come to know the Lord,

And in drink-ing from the cup We have shared the life of God.

Verses for Easter Season

1. As we walk the dust-y road　Shar-ing
2. As we gath-er on this day,　As we
3. Like dis-ci-ples long a-go　On a
4. At the ban-quet Je-sus blessed　We re-
5. Let us, as we walk the road,　Meet the

all our doubts and fears, Some-one joins us on the
hear the sto-ries told, In the sto-ry of the
path by faith be-gun, In the joy of East-er
mem-ber and give praise For the gra-cious love of
stran-ger as a friend; Let us, with the Ris-en

D.C.

way, Gives us hope in place of tears.
cross Our life's mean-ing will un-fold.
light We will meet the Ris-en One.
God O-ver-flow-ing all our days.
Christ, Trav-el till our jour-ney's end.

Verses for Ordinary Time

1. As we gather on this day,
   As we hear the stories told,
   In the Word of God proclaimed
   Life's true meaning will unfold.

2. As we share the holy meal
   And remember Christ the Lord,
   As we eat and drink in faith,
   Bonds of love will be restored.

3. With the riches of this feast
   Hungry hearts are satisfied,
   As with joyful lips we sing,
   Praising Jesus glorified.

4. Many grains become one loaf;
   Many grapes become the wine:
   Thus let us one body be,
   Who at this one table dine.

5. At the banquet Jesus blessed
   We remember and give praise
   For the gracious love of God
   Overflowing all our days.

Text: Delores Dufner, OSB, b.1939
Tune: BREAKING BREAD, 7 7 7 7 with refrain; Michel Guimont, b.1950
© 2008, GIA Publications, Inc.

Taste and See   945

Refrain

Taste and see, taste and see the good-ness of the Lord. O taste and see, taste and see the good-ness of the Lord, of the Lord.

Verses

1. I will bless the Lord at all times.
2. Glo-ri-fy the Lord with me.
3. Wor-ship the Lord, all you peo-ple.

Praise shall al-ways be on my lips;
To-geth-er let us all praise God's name.
You'll want for noth-ing if you ask.

my soul shall glo-ry in the Lord
I called the Lord who an-swered me;
Taste and see that the Lord is good;

for God has been so good to me.
from all my trou-bles I was set free.
in God we need put all our trust.

Text: Psalm 34; James E. Moore, Jr., b.1951
Tune: James E. Moore, Jr., b.1951
© 1983, GIA Publications, Inc.

946 Come, Join the Feasting /
Vengan Todos al Banquete

Refrain

"Come," you bid us, "join the feast - ing   At this   ban - quet,
"Ven - gan to - dos al   ban - que - te,"   *Nos in - vi - tas*

rich - ly spread,   Where your thirst   is   quenched in
hoy,   Se - ñor.   *Por - que no hay   ni   sed   ni*

full - ness,   And your hun - gry   hearts are   fed."
ham - bre   A   la fies - ta   de tu_a - mor.

Verses

1. Je - sus Christ,   you now in - vite us   To   com -
2. We   re - spond,   O Lord, with long - ing   To   your
3. For your gifts   so free - ly giv - en,   What is

1. *Je - su - cris - to,   nos con - vi - das   A   tu*
2. *A   tu   dul - ce   lla - ma - mien - to   A - cu -*
3. *Res - pon - dien - do_a tan - tos do - nes,   ¿Qué po -*

mun - ion   in   this   place,   With   the bread   of   life you
kind and   gen - tle   call.   May   the faith   and love you
ours in   turn   to   give   But   our hearts, our   ver - y

san - ta   co - mu - nión,   O - fre - cien - do_el pan de
di - mos,   oh   Se - ñor.   ¡Que_en tu   co - mu - nión, au -
de - mos   o - fre - cer?   To - ma   nues - tros   co - ra -

D.C.

of - fer,   And the   chal - ice   of   your   grace.
nour - ish   Grow to   be   our   all   in   all!
be - ing,   Ev - 'ry   mo - ment that we   live?

vi - da   Y   la   co - pa   del   per - dón.
men - to   Ha - llen nues - tra   fe   y_a - mor!
zo - nes,   Nues - tras   al - mas,   nues - tro   ser.

4. To your table, now, rejoicing
   In the love that makes us one,
   Joined in pardon and redemption,
   Christ our Lord, to you we come!

5. As we share this meal, we promise
   In your holy love to stay;
   And to live as your disciples,
   Faithful till our dying day.

4. *Hoy venimos a tu mesa*
   En amor y santa unión
   Celebrando jubilosos
   Tu perdón y redención.

5. *En tu mesa prometemos*
   En tu santo amor vivir;
   Y que fieles te seremos,
   Buen Jesús, hasta el morir.

Text: Spanish refrain by Ronald F. Krisman, b.1946; vss. by Juan Bautista Cabrera, 1837–1916; tr. by Mary Louise Bringle, b.1953;
   Spanish refrain and tr., © 2007, GIA Publications, Inc.
Tune: CABRERA, 8 7 8 7 with refrain; Ronald F. Krisman, b.1946, © 2007, GIA Publications, Inc.

Draw Near and Take the Body of the Lord   947

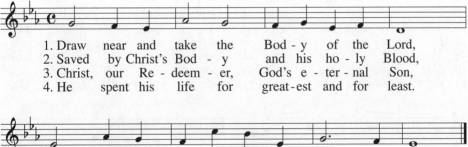

1. Draw near and take the Body of the Lord,
2. Saved by Christ's Body and his holy Blood,
3. Christ, our Redeemer, God's eternal Son,
4. He spent his life for greatest and for least.

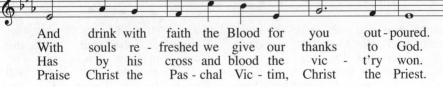

And drink with faith the Blood for you out-poured.
With souls refreshed we give our thanks to God.
Has by his cross and blood the vic-t'ry won.
Praise Christ the Pas-chal Vic-tim, Christ the Priest.

5. Let us approach with faithful hearts sincere
   And claim the promise of salvation here.

6. Christ rules our hearts, and all his saints defends;
   He gives believers life that never ends.

7. With heav'nly bread Christ makes the hungry whole;
   His living water fills the thirsting soul.

8. Alpha-Omega, unto whom shall bow
   All nations of the earth, be with us now.

Text: *Sancti, venite, Christe corpus sumite*; Latin, 7th C.; tr. by John M. Neale, 1818–1866, alt.
Tune: COENA DOMINI, 10 10; Arthur S. Sullivan, 1842–1900

948 Bread of Life from Heaven / Pan de Vida Eterna

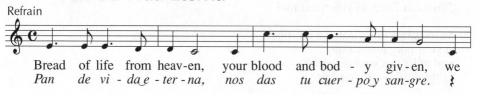

Refrain

Bread   of life from heav-en,   your blood   and bod - y giv-en,   we
Pan   *de vi - da̱e̱ - ter - na,*   *nos das*   *tu cuer - po̱y san-gre.*

eat   this bread and drink this cup un - til you come a - gain.
Has - ta que vuel - vas tú, Se - ñor, co - me - mos en tu̱a̱-mor.

Verses

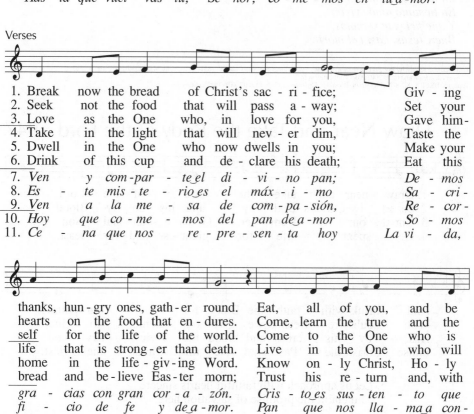

1. Break   now the bread   of Christ's sac - ri - fice;   Giv - ing
2. Seek   not the food   that will pass a - way;   Set your
3. Love   as the One   who, in love for you,   Gave him-
4. Take   in the light   that will nev - er dim,   Taste the
5. Dwell   in the One   who now dwells in you;   Make your
6. Drink   of this cup   and de - clare his death;   Eat this
7. *Ven*   *y com-par - te̱el di - vi - no pan;*   *De - mos*
8. *Es - te mis - te - rio̱es el máx - i - mo*   *Sa - cri-*
9. *Ven*   *a la me - sa de com - pa - sión,*   *Re - cor-*
10. *Hoy*   *que co - me - mos del pan de̱a̱-mor*   *So - mos*
11. *Ce - na que nos   re - pre - sen - ta hoy*   *La vi - da,*

thanks, hun - gry ones, gath - er round.   Eat,   all of you,   and be
hearts   on the food that en - dures.   Come, learn the true   and the
self   for the life of the world.   Come to the One   who is
life   that is strong - er than death.   Live in the One   who will
home   in the life - giv-ing Word.   Know on - ly Christ,   Ho - ly
bread   and be - lieve Eas - ter morn;   Trust his re - turn   and, with
gra - cias con gran cor - a - zón.   *Cris - to̱es sus - ten - to que*
fi - cio de fe y de̱a̱-mor.   *Pan que nos lla - ma̱a̱ con-*
de - mos a Cris - to Je - sús.   *Él nos da vi - da con*
u - no en Cris - to Je - sús.   *Ce - na que̱es fuen - te de̱in-*
muer - te, y re - su -rrec - ción   *De Je - su - cris - to, que̱es*

D.C.

sat - is - fied;	In	Christ's	pres - ence	the	loaves	will	a - bound.
liv - ing Way,	That	the	full - ness	of	life	may	be yours.
food for you,	That	your	hun - ger	and	thirst	be	no more.
come and then	Raise	you	up	at	the	last	with the blest.
One of God,	And	be - lieve	in	the	truth	you have heard.
ev - 'ry breath,	Praise	the	One	in	whom you	are	re - born.
u - ni - rá	A	los	miem - bros	de	ca - da	na - ción.
me - mo - rar	Ya	se - guir	a	Je - sús	Sal - va - dor.
ple - ni - tud;	Nos	pro - te - ge	y	nos	guí - a en su luz.
spi - ra - ción	Pa - ra	ser	en	el	mun - do la luz.
nues - tro Dios	Quien nos	lla - ma	y	nos	da	sal - va - ción.

Text: Based on John 6; adapt. by Susan R. Briehl, b.1952; Spanish by Jaime Cortez, b.1963
Tune: ARGENTINE SANTO, 9 9 9 9 with refrain; Argentine melody; adapt. and verses by Marty Haugen, b.1950
© 2001, GIA Publications, Inc.

This Is the Body of Christ   949

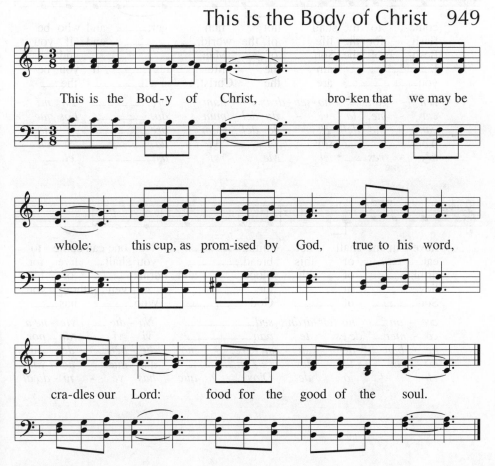

This is the Bod-y of Christ, bro-ken that we may be

whole; this cup, as prom-ised by God, true to his word,

cra-dles our Lord: food for the good of the soul.

Text: John L. Bell, b.1949
Tune: John L. Bell, b.1949
© 1998, Iona Community, GIA Publications, Inc., agent

950 I Am the Bread of Life / Yo Soy el Pan de Vida

Verses

1.___ I am the Bread of life. You who
2. The bread that___ I will give is my
3. Un - less___ you___ eat of the
4.___ I am the Res - ur - rec - tion,___
5.___ Yes, Lord,___ we be - lieve that___

1.___ Yo soy el Pan de Vi - da. A mí
2. El pan que___ yo da - ré es mi
3.___ Si us - te - des no co - men la___
4. Yo soy la___ Re - su - rrec - ción,___
5.___ Sí, Se - ñor, cre - e - mos que___

come to me shall not hun - ger;___ and who be -
flesh for the life of the world,___ and if you
flesh of the Son of Man___ and___
I___ am the life.___ If you be -
you___ are the Christ,___ the___

ven - gan:___ no ten -drán ham - bre.___ En mí
car - ne, la vi - da del mun - do.___ Los que
car - ne del Hi - jo del Hom - bre,___ y no
Yo___ soy la Vi - da.___ Si en
tú e - res___ el Me - sí - as,___ el___

lieve in me shall not thirst.___ No one can come to
eat___ of this bread,___ you shall___ live for
drink___ of his blood,- and drink___ of his
lieve___ in___ me,___ e - ven___ though you
Son___ of___ God,___ Who___ has___

cre - an:___ no ten-drán sed.___ Na - die___ vie - ne a
co - men de es - te pan___ vi - vi - rán por
be - ben___ de su san-gre, no be - ben___ de su
mí us - te - des cre - en,___ aun-que___ ha - yan
Hi - jo de Dios,- que has ve - ni - do al

me   un - less   the   Fa - ther   beck - ons.
ev - er,_____   you   shall   live   for   ev - er.
blood,   you   shall   not have life   with - in   you.
die,_____   you   shall   live   for   ev - er.
come ____   in - to____   the____   world.____
mí   *si mi Pa - dre*   *no   lo_a - tra - e.*
siem - pre,_____   vi - vi - rán   por   siem - pre.
san - gre,   no po -drán   te - ner   mi   vi - da.
muer - to,_____   vi - vi - rán   por   siem - pre.
mun - do_____   pa - ra   re - di - mir - nos.

Refrain

And I will   raise   you   up,   and I will
Yo los re - su   -   ci -ta - ré,   Yo los re -

raise   you   up,   and I will raise   you
su   -   ci - ta - ré,   Yo los re - su   -   ci - ta -

up   on   the   last   day.
ré   en   el   dí - a   fi - nal.

Text: John 6 and 11; Suzanne Toolan, RSM, b.1927; tr. anon., rev. by Ronald F. Krisman, b.1946
Tune: BREAD OF LIFE, Irregular with refrain; Suzanne Toolan, RSM, b.1927
© 1966, 1970, 1986, 1993, 2005, GIA Publications, Inc.

951 All Who Hunger

Verses

1. All who hun-ger, gath - er glad - ly; Ho - ly man - na
2. All who hun-ger, nev - er stran-gers; Seek-er, be a
3. All who hun-ger, sing to-geth - er; Je - sus Christ is

is our bread. Come from wil - der-ness and wan-d'ring.
wel - come guest. Come from rest - less-ness and roam - ing.
liv - ing bread. Come from lone - li - ness and long - ing.

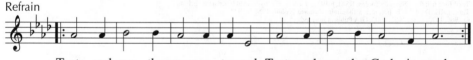

Here, in truth, we will be fed. You that yearn for
Here, in joy, we keep the feast. We that once were
Here, in peace, we have been led. Blest are those who

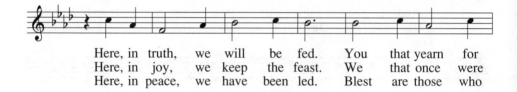

days of full-ness, All a - round us is our food.
lost and scat-tered In com - mun-ion's love have stood.
from this ta - ble Live their days in grat - i - tude.

Refrain

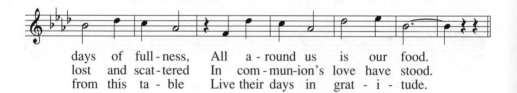

Taste and see the grace e - ter-nal. Taste and see that God is good.

Text: Sylvia G. Dunstan, 1955–1993, © 1991, GIA Publications, Inc.
Tune: GRACE ETERNAL, 8 7 8 7 8 7 with refrain; Bob Moore, b.1962, © 1993, GIA Publications, Inc.

Taste and See   952

Refrain

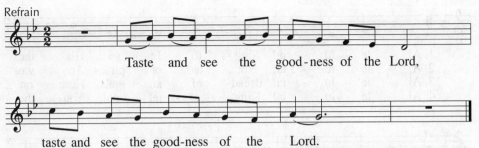

Taste and see the good-ness of the Lord,

taste and see the good-ness of the Lord.

Verses

1. I will bless the LORD at all times;
   praise of him is always in my mouth.
   In the LORD my soul shall make its boast;
   the humble shall hear and be glad.

2. Glorify the LORD with me;
   together let us praise his name.
   I sought the LORD, and he answered me,
   from all my terrors he set me free.

3. Look toward him and be radiant;
   let your faces not be abashed.
   This lowly one called; the LORD heard,
   and rescued him from all his distress.

4. Fear the LORD, you his holy ones.
   They lack nothing, those who fear him.
   The rich suffer want and go hungry,
   but those who seek the LORD lack no blessing.

5. Come, children, and hear me,
   that I may teach you the fear of the LORD.
   The LORD is close to the brokenhearted;
   those whose spirit is crushed he will save.

Text: Psalm 34:2–3, 4–5, 6–7, 8–9, *The Revised Grail Psalms*, © 2010, Conception Abbey and The Grail, admin. by GIA Publications, Inc.; refrain, *Lectionary for Mass*, © 1969, 1981, 1997, ICEL
Tune: Brian Luckner, b.1959, © 2002, GIA Publications, Inc.

953 Alleluia! Sing to Jesus!

1. Al - le - lu - ia! Sing to Je - sus! His the
2. Al - le - lu - ia! Not as or - phans Are we
3. Al - le - lu - ia! Bread of an - gels, Here on
4. Al - le - lu - ia! King e - ter - nal, You the

scep - ter, his the throne. Al - le - lu - ia! His the
left in sor - row now; Al - le - lu - ia! He is
earth our food, our stay! Al - le - lu - ia! Here the
Lord of lords we own; Al - le - lu - ia! Born of

tri - umph, His the vic - to - ry a - lone.
near us; Faith be - lieves, nor ques - tions how.
sin - ful Flee to you from day to day.
Mar - y, Earth your foot - stool, heav'n your throne.

Hark! The songs of peace - ful Zi - on Thun - der
Though the cloud from sight re - ceived him When the
In - ter - ces - sor, friend of sin - ners, Earth's re -
You with - in the veil have en - tered, Robed in

like a might - y flood: "Je - sus out of ev - 'ry
for - ty days were o'er, Shall our hearts for - get his
deem - er, plead for me, Where the songs of all the
flesh, our great high priest; Here on earth both priest and

na - tion Has re - deemed us by his blood."
prom - ise: "I am with you ev - er - more"?
sin - less Sweep a - cross the crys - tal sea.
vic - tim In the eu - cha - ris - tic feast.

Text: Revelation 5:9; William C. Dix, 1837–1898
Tune: HYFRYDOL, 8 7 8 7 D; Rowland H. Prichard, 1811–1887

Lord, Who at Your First Eucharist   954

1. Lord, who at your first Eu - cha - rist did pray
2. For all your Church, O Lord, we in - ter - cede;
3. We pray for those who wan - der from your fold;
4. So, Lord, at length when sac - ra - ments shall cease,

That all your Church might be for - ev - er one,
O make our lack of char - i - ty to cease.
O bring them back, Good Shep - herd of the sheep,
May we be one with all your Church a - bove,

Help us at ev - 'ry Eu - cha - rist to say
Draw us the near - er each to each, we plead,
Back to the faith which saints be - lieved of old,
One with your saints in one un - bro - ken peace,

With long - ing heart and soul, "Your will be done."
By draw - ing all to you, O Prince of Peace.
Back to the Church which still that faith does keep.
One with your saints in one un - bound - ed love.

Thus may we all one Bread, one Bod - y be,
Thus may we all one Bread, one Bod - y be,
Thus may we all one Bread, one Bod - y be,
More bless - ed still, in peace and love to be

Through this blest Sac - ra - ment of U - ni - ty.
Through this blest Sac - ra - ment of U - ni - ty.
Through this blest Sac - ra - ment of U - ni - ty.
One with the Trin - i - ty in u - ni - ty.

Text: William H. Turton, 1859–1938, alt.
Tune: UNDE ET MEMORES, 10 10 10 10 10 10; William H. Monk, 1823–1889, alt.

955 To the Wedding Feast

Verses

1. To the wed - ding feast God calls us; Come, re-
2. Come, you poor who have no mon - ey; Choose a
3. Here the or - phan finds a fam - 'ly; Here the
4. Hap - py all who are in - vit - ed To the
5. Nour - ished at this fes - tive ta - ble, Let us

joic - ing to be fed! Let the thirst - y drink this
meal to sat - is - fy. At this ban - quet God will
home - less find a place; Here each guest is warm - ly
Lamb's own wed - ding feast! All shall gath - er at one
each to love at - tend Till we know God's life a -

chal - ice; Let the hun - gry eat this bread.
feed us, Wipe the tear from ev - 'ry eye.
wel - comed By a gra - cious host's em - brace.
ta - ble, From the great - est to the least.
bun - dant: Feast for - ev - er, jour - ney's end.

Refrain

All is read - y; Christ in - vites us: At this

ta - ble let us dine. God has made a ban - quet

read - y: Rich - est food and fin - est wine!

Life-Giving Bread, Saving Cup   956

Refrain

Life - giv-ing Bread, sav - ing Cup, we of - fer in thanks-
giv-ing, O God. Life - giv-ing Bread,
sav - ing Cup, we of - fer as a sign of our love.

Verses

1. For bread that is bro - ken, we give thanks;   For
2. We thank you, O Fa - ther, for your name,   Which
3. Cre - a - tor of all, we of - fer thanks;   You
4. Re - mem - ber your Church, which sings your praise;   Per -

wine that is poured, we give praise.   For
you give to dwell in our hearts.   You
give us a share in your life.   You
fect it in truth and in love.   And

life and for knowl-edge of the king - dom: All
bring us to - geth - er as one fam - 'ly: All
strength - en our bod - y and our spir - it: All
gath - er your peo - ple all to - geth - er   To

D.C.

praise to you un - til the end of time!
praise to you un - til the end of time!
praise to you un - til the end of time!
praise you un - til the end of time!

Text: Adapted from the *Didache*, 2nd C.; James J. Chepponis, b.1956
Tune: LIFE-GIVING BREAD, 9 8 10 10 with refrain; James J. Chepponis, b.1956
© 1987, GIA Publications, Inc.

957 Grant to Us, O Lord

Refrain

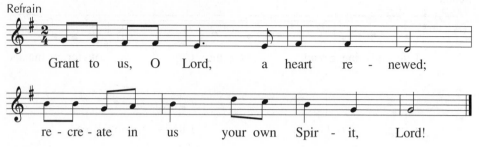

Grant to us, O Lord, a heart re - newed;

re - cre - ate in us your own Spir - it, Lord!

Verses

1. Behold, the days are coming, says the Lord our God,
   when I will make a new covenant with the house of Israel.

2. Deep within their being I will implant my law;
   I will write it in their hearts.

3. I will be their God, and they shall be my people.

4. And for all their faults I will grant forgiveness;
   nevermore will I remember their sins.

Text: Jeremiah 31:31–34
Tune: Lucien Deiss, CSSp, 1921–2007
© 1965, 1966, 1968, 1973, World Library Publications

958 A Woman Knelt Where Jesus Sat to Eat

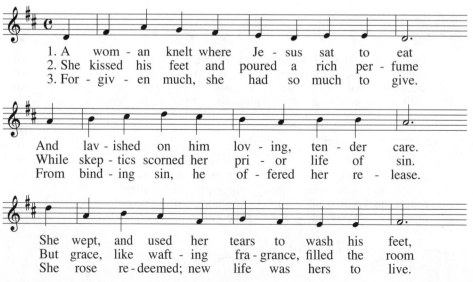

1. A wom - an knelt where Je - sus sat to eat
2. She kissed his feet and poured a rich per - fume
3. For - giv - en much, she had so much to give.

And lav - ished on him lov - ing, ten - der care.
While skep - tics scorned her pri - or life of sin.
From bind - ing sin, he of - fered her re - lease.

She wept, and used her tears to wash his feet,
But grace, like waft - ing fra - grance, filled the room
She rose re - deemed; new life was hers to live.

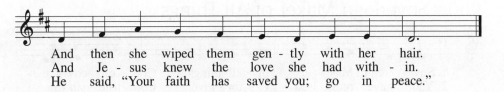

And then she wiped them gen - tly with her hair.
And Je - sus knew the love she had with - in.
He said, "Your faith has saved you; go in peace."

Text: Luke 7:36–50; Adam M. L. Tice, b.1979, © 2010, GIA Publications, Inc.
Tune: SURSUM CORDA, 10 10 10 10; Alfred M. Smith, 1879–1971, © Mrs. Alfred M. Smith

If I Have Been the Source of Pain / 959
Si Fui Motivo de Dolor

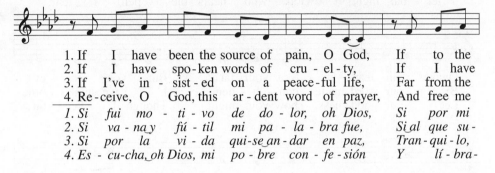

1. If I have been the source of pain, O God, If to the
2. If I have spo-ken words of cru - el - ty, If I have
3. If I've in - sist - ed on a peace-ful life, Far from the
4. Re - ceive, O God, this ar - dent word of prayer, And free me

1. Si fui mo - ti - vo de do - lor, oh Dios, Si por mi
2. Si va - na y fú - til mi pa - la - bra fue, Si al que su-
3. Si por la vi - da qui-se an-dar en paz, Tran - qui - lo,
4. Es - cu-cha, oh Dios, mi po - bre con - fe - sión Y lí - bra-

weak I have re - fused my strength, If, in re -
left some suf - f'ring un - re - lieved, Con - demn not
strug - gles that the gos - pel brings, When you pre -
from temp - ta - tion's sub - tle snare; With ten - der

cau - sa el dé - bil tro - pe - zó, Si en tus ca -
frí - a en su do - lor de - jé, No me con -
li - bre y sin lu - char por ti, Cuan-do an - he -
me de ten - ta - ción su - til; Pre - ser - va

bel - lion, I have strayed a - way, For - give me, God.
my in - sen - si - tiv - i - ty. For - give me, God.
fer to guide me to the strife, For - give me, God.
pa - tience, lead me to your care. A - men, a - men.

mi - nos yo no qui - se an-dar, ¡Per - dón, oh Dios!
de - nes, tú, por mi mal - dad. ¡Per - dón, oh Dios!
la - bas ver - me en la lid, ¡Per - dón, oh Dios!
siem-pre mi al-ma en tu re - dil. A - mén, a - mén.

Text: Sara Menéndez de Hall, alt., based on a text by C. Maude Battersby; tr. by Janet W. May, © 1992, The Pilgrim Press
Tune: CAMACUÁ, 10 10 10 4; Pablo D. Sosa, b.1933, © 1988, GIA Publications, Inc.

960 Sovereign Maker of All Things

1. Sov - 'reign Mak - er of all things, God of cov - e -
2. You have prom - ised to for - give Con - trite sin - ners
3. Let me not be lost in sin, Ban - ished to e -

nant and grace, Ev - 'ry crea - ture knows your pow'r,
who re - pent; So I come with hum - bled heart,
ter - nal night; God who hears the pen - i - tent,

Quakes with fear be - fore your face. But your mer - cy
By your word made con - fi - dent. I have sinned, Lord,
Let your good - ness show your might. Though I be un -

far ex - ceeds What our minds can com - pre - hend;
I have sinned: Well I know my wick - ed - ness.
wor - thy, Lord, Your great mer - cy will I claim,

Deep com - pas - sion stays your hand,
Yet I make this prayer to you:
Till I join the hosts a - bove

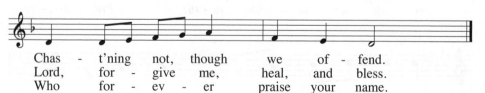

Chas - t'ning not, though we of - fend.
Lord, for - give me, heal, and bless.
Who for - ev - er praise your name.

Text: Carl P. Daw, Jr., b.1944, © 1990, Hope Publishing Company
Tune: ABERYSTWYTH, 7 7 7 7 D; Joseph Parry, 1841–1903

The Scheming Elders Challenged Christ   961

1. The schem-ing el-ders chal-lenged Christ: "What
2. With-out re-ply the Lord bent down, And,
3. "Where have they gone?" the teach-er asked; "Ac-
4. We do not know what Je-sus wrote In

do you have to say? We caught her in a-
reach-ing out his hand, In si-lence he be-
cus-ers, I see none." "You looked a-way," the
dust up-on the ground: A si-lent an-swer

dul-ter-y. We'll stone her here to-day. Come,
gan to trace Up-on the shift-ing sand. Then,
wom-an said; "They left us one by one." "Does
to the shouts Of those who gath-ered round. But

teach-er, speak! Why hes-i-tate? We
stand-ing, said, "Let an-y-one Who
no one here con-demn you now?" She
we re-mem-ber what he said: He

know what Mo-ses said. The law is clear, her
has no sin or blame Step for-ward now and
an-swered, "No one, sir." "Then go in peace and
chal-lenged us to dare To look with-in be-

guilt is known, And she will soon be dead."
be the first To stone her in her shame."
sin no more," Was his com-mand to her.
fore we judge, And find com-pas-sion there.

Text: John 8:2–11; Jacque B. Jones, b.1950, © 2011, GIA Publications, Inc.
Tune: LLANGLOFFAN, CMD; Welsh melody

962 Come, You Sinners, Poor and Needy

1. Come, you sin - ners, poor and need - y,
2. Come, you thirst - y, come, and wel - come,
3. Come, you wea - ry, heav - y lad - en,

Weak and wound - ed, sick and sore, Je - sus, Son of
God's free boun - ty glo - ri - fy: True be - lief and
Lost and ru - ined by the fall; If you tar - ry

God, will save you, Full of pit - y, love, and pow'r.
true re - pen - tance, Ev - 'ry grace that brings you nigh.
till you're bet - ter, You will nev - er come at all.

I will a - rise and go to Je - sus, He will em - brace me

in his arms; In the arms of my dear

Sav - ior, Oh, there are ten thou - sand charms.

Text: Verses, Joseph Hart, 1712–1768, *Hymns Composed on Various Subjects*, 1759, alt.; refrain anonymous
Tune: RESTORATION, 8 7 8 7 with refrain; *Southern Harmony*, 1835; harm. by George E. Mims, b.1938, © 1979, George E. Mims

Our Father, We Have Wandered   963

1. Our Fa - ther, we have wan - dered And
2. And now at length dis - cern - ing The
3. O Lord of all the liv - ing, Both

hid - den from your face; In fool - ish - ness have
e - vil that we do, Be - hold us, Lord, re -
ban - ished and re - stored, Com - pas - sion - ate, for -

squan - dered Your leg - a - cy of grace. But
turn - ing With hope and trust to you. In
giv - ing, And ev - er - car - ing Lord, Grant

now, in ex - ile dwell - ing, We
haste you come to meet us And
now that our trans - gress - ing, Our

rise with fear and shame, As, dis - tant but com -
home re - joic - ing bring, In glad - ness there to
faith - less - ness may cease. Stretch out your hand in

pell - ing, We hear you call our name.
greet us, With calf and robe and ring.
bless - ing, In par - don, and in peace.

Text: Kevin Nichols, 1929–2006, © 1980, ICEL
Tune: PASSION CHORALE, 7 6 7 6 D; Hans Leo Hassler, 1564–1612; harm. by J. S. Bach, 1685–1750

964 Yes, I Shall Arise

Refrain

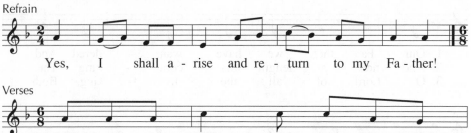

Yes, I shall a - rise and re - turn to my Fa - ther!

Verses

1. To you, O Lord, I lift up my
2. Look down on me, have mer - cy, O
3. My heart and soul shall yearn for your
4. Do not with - hold your good - ness from
5. To you I pray; have pit - y on

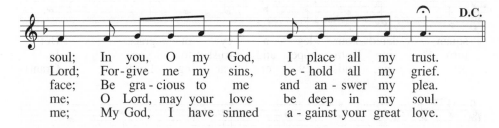

D.C.

soul; In you, O my God, I place all my trust.
Lord; For - give me my sins, be - hold all my grief.
face; Be gra - cious to me and an - swer my plea.
me; O Lord, may your love be deep in my soul.
me; My God, I have sinned a - gainst your great love.

6. Mercy I cry, O Lord, wash me clean;
   And cleaner than snow my spirit shall be.

7. Give me again the joy of your help;
   Now open my lips, your praise I will sing.

8. Happy are they, forgiven by God;
   Their sins blotted out, their guilt is no more.

9. You are my joy, my refuge and strength;
   Let all upright hearts give praise to the Lord.

10. My soul will sing, my heart will rejoice;
    The blessings of God will fill all my days.

Text: Psalm 51; Lucien Deiss, CSSp, 1921–2007
Tune: PRODIGAL, 9 10 with refrain; Lucien Deiss, CSSp, 1921–2007
© 1965, 1966, 1973, World Library Publications

Healer of Our Every Ill 965

Refrain

Heal-er of our ev-'ry ill, Light of each to-mor-row,

Give us peace be-yond our fear And hope be-yond our sor - row.

Verses

1. You who know our fears and sad - ness,
2. In the pain and joy, be - hold - ing
3. Give us strength to love each oth - er,
4. You who know each thought and feel - ing,

Grace us with your peace and glad - ness.
How your grace is still un - fold - ing,
Ev - 'ry sis - ter, ev - 'ry broth - er.
Teach us all your way of heal - ing.

D.C.

Spir - it of all com - fort, fill our hearts.
Give us all your vi - sion, God of love.
Spir - it of all kind - ness, be our guide.
Spir - it of com - pas - sion, fill each heart.

Text: Marty Haugen, b.1950
Tune: HEALER OF OUR EVERY ILL, 88 9 with refrain; Marty Haugen, b.1950
© 1987, GIA Publications, Inc.

966 Have Mercy, Lord, on Us

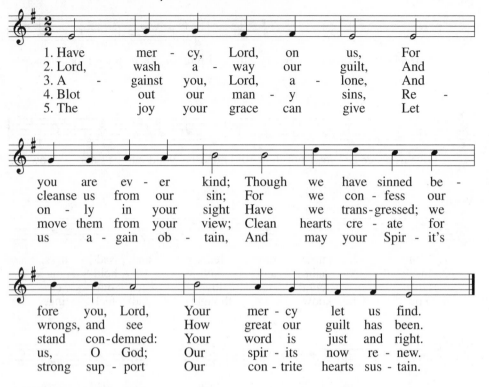

1. Have mer - cy, Lord, on us, For you are ev - er kind; Though we have sinned be - fore you, Lord, Your mer - cy let us find.
2. Lord, wash a - way our guilt, And cleanse us from our sin; For we con - fess our wrongs, and see How great our guilt has been.
3. A - gainst you, Lord, a - lone, And on - ly in your sight Have we trans-gressed; we stand con-demned: Your word is just and right.
4. Blot out our man - y sins, Re - move them from your view; Clean hearts cre - ate for us, O God; Our spir - its now re - new.
5. The joy your grace can give Let us a - gain ob - tain, And may your Spir - it's strong sup - port Our con - trite hearts sus - tain.

Text: Psalm 51; Nahum Tate, 1652–1715, and Nicholas Brady, 1659–1726, alt.
Tune: SOUTHWELL, SM; William Daman, *The Psalmes of David*, 1579, alt.

967 Forgive Our Sins

1. "For - give our sins as we for - give," You taught us, Lord, to pray; But you a - lone can
2. How can your par - don reach and bless The un - for - giv - ing heart That broods on wrongs and
3. In blaz - ing light your cross re - veals The truth we dim - ly knew: How small are oth - ers'
4. Lord, cleanse the depths with - in our souls And bid re - sent - ment cease. Then, by your mer - cy

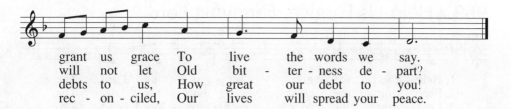

grant us grace To live the words we say.
will not let Old bit - ter - ness de - part?
debts to us, How great our debt to you!
rec - on - ciled, Our lives will spread your peace.

Text: Rosamond E. Herklots, 1905–1987, alt., © Oxford University Press
Tune: DETROIT, CM; Supplement to *Kentucky Harmony*, 1820; harm. by Gerald H. Knight, 1908–1979, © The Royal School of Church Music

The Master Came to Bring Good News   968

1. The Mas - ter came to bring good news, The
2. The Law's ful - filled through Je - sus Christ, The
3. To seek the sin - ners Je - sus came, To
4. For - give us, Lord, as we for - give And

news of love and free - dom, To heal the sick and
man who lived for oth - ers. The law of Christ is:
live a - mong the friend - less, To show them love that
seek to help each oth - er. For - give us, Lord, and

seek the poor, To build the peace - ful king - dom.
Serve in love Our sis - ters and our broth - ers.
they might share The king - dom that is end - less.
we shall live To pray and work to - geth - er.

Fa - ther, for - give us! Through Je - sus hear us!

As we for - give one an - oth - er!

Text: Ralph Finn, b.1941, © 1965, GIA Publications, Inc.
Tune: ICH GLAUB AN GOTT, 8 7 8 7 with refrain; Mainz *Gesangbuch*, 1870; harm. by Richard Proulx, 1937–2010, © 1986, GIA Publications, Inc.

969　Help Us Forgive, Forgiving Lord

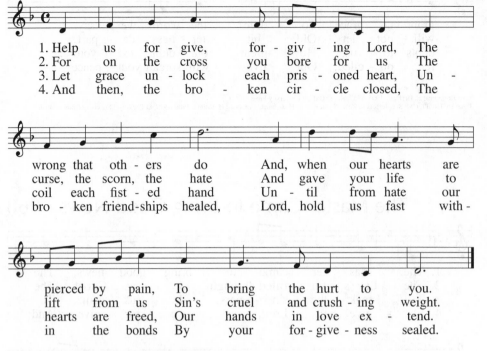

1. Help us for - give, for - giv - ing Lord, The
2. For on the cross you bore for us The
3. Let grace un - lock each pris - oned heart, Un -
4. And then, the bro - ken cir - cle closed, The

wrong that oth - ers do And, when our hearts are
curse, the scorn, the hate And gave your life to
coil each fist - ed hand Un - til from hate our
bro - ken friend-ships healed, Lord, hold us fast with -

pierced by pain, To bring the hurt to you.
lift from us Sin's cruel and crush - ing weight.
hearts are freed, Our hands in love ex - tend.
in the bonds By your for - give - ness sealed.

Text: Herman G. Stuempfle, Jr., 1923–2007, © 1997, GIA Publications, Inc.
Tune: DETROIT, CM; Supplement to *Kentucky Harmony*, 1820; harm. by Gerald H. Knight, 1908–1979, © The Royal School of Church Music

970　Out of the Depths

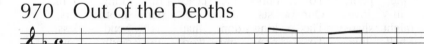

1. Out of the depths, O God, we call to you.
2. Out of the depths of fear, O God, we speak.
3. God of the lov - ing heart, we praise your name.

Wounds of the past re - main, af - fect - ing all we do.
Break - ing the si - lenc - es, the sear - ing truth we seek.
Dance through our lives and loves; a - noint with Spir - it flame.

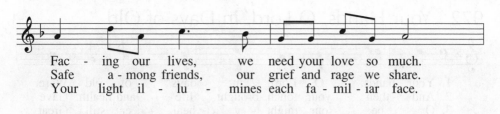

Fac - ing our lives, we need your love so much.
Safe a - mong friends, our grief and rage we share.
Your light il - lu - mines each fa - mil - iar face.

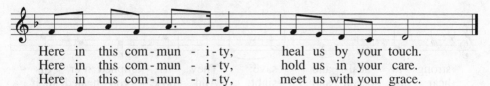

Here in this com - mun - i - ty, heal us by your touch.
Here in this com - mun - i - ty, hold us in your care.
Here in this com - mun - i - ty, meet us with your grace.

Text: Psalm 130:1; Ruth Duck, b.1947, © 1992, GIA Publications, Inc.
Tune: FENNVILLE, 10 12 10 12; Robert J. Batastini, b.1942, © 1994, GIA Publications, Inc.

In All Our Grief 971

1. In all our grief and fear we turn to you.
2. Help us to put a - side the an - gry word,
3. You did not e - ven spare your on - ly Son.
4. God, when we suf - fer all that we can bear,

O God, you know all that we think or do,
The clench - ing fist, the wish and will to hurt.
He lived our griefs and bore all e - vil done,
Then let us know that you in truth are near

You know the pain we put each oth - er through.
Teach us the way in which love best is served.
But through his cross, re - demp - tion has been won.
And will not leave us lost in all our fear.

Lord, have mer - cy. Christ, have mer - cy. Lord, grant us peace.

Text: Sylvia G. Dunstan, 1955–1993, © 1991, GIA Publications, Inc.
Tune: FREDERICKTOWN, 10 10 10 with refrain; Charles R. Anders, b.1929, © 1978, *Lutheran Book of Worship*, admin. by Augsburg Fortress

972 Your Hands, O Lord, in Days of Old

1. Your hands, O Lord, in days of old Were
strong to heal and save; They tri-umphed o'er disease and death, O'er dark-ness and the grave. To
you they came, the blind, the mute, The
pal-sied, and the lame, The lep-er set a-
part and shunned, The sick, and those in shame.

2. And then your touch brought life and health, Gave
hear-ing, speech, and sight; And those you healed, their
strength re-stored, Ac-claimed you Lord of light. And
so, O Lord, be near to bless, The
might-y now as then, In ev-'ry street, in
ev-'ry home, In ev-'ry trou-bled friend.

3. O be our might-y heal-er still, Great
Lord of life and death; Re-store and strength-en,
soothe and bless, With your al-might-y breath. On
hands that work and eyes that see, Your
heal-ing wis-dom pour, That whole and sick, and
weak and strong, May praise you ev-er-more.

Text: Matthew 14:35–36; Edward H. Plumptre, 1821–1891, alt., © 1986, GIA Publications, Inc.
Tune: MOZART, CMD; adapt. from Wolfgang A. Mozart, 1756–1791

When Memory Fades 973

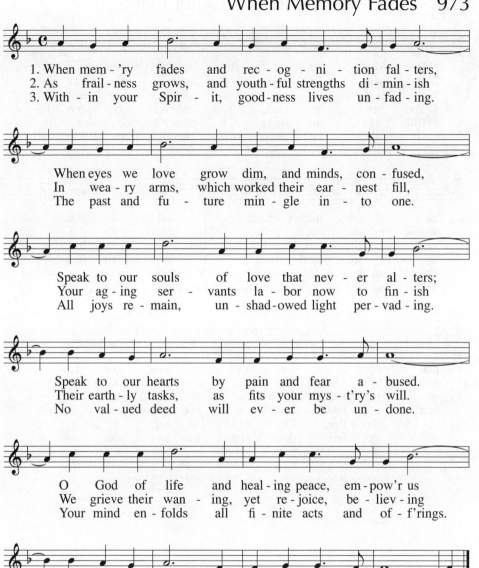

1. When mem - 'ry   fades   and   rec - og - ni - tion fal - ters,
2. As   frail - ness   grows,   and youth - ful strengths di - min - ish
3. With - in   your   Spir - it,   good - ness lives   un - fad - ing.

When eyes we   love   grow dim, and minds, con - fused,
In   wea - ry   arms,   which worked their ear - nest   fill,
The   past and   fu -   ture min - gle   in - to   one.

Speak to   our   souls   of   love that nev - er   al - ters;
Your ag - ing   ser - vants la - bor now   to   fin - ish
All   joys re - main,   un - shad - owed light per - vad - ing.

Speak to   our hearts   by   pain and fear   a - bused.
Their earth - ly tasks,   as   fits your mys - t'ry's   will.
No   val - ued deed   will   ev - er   be   un - done.

O   God   of   life   and heal - ing peace, em - pow'r us
We   grieve their wan - ing, yet   re - joice, be - liev - ing
Your mind en - folds   all   fi - nite acts   and of - f'rings.

With pa - tient cour - age, by your grace   in - fused.
Your arms, un - wea - ried, shall up - hold   us   still.
Held   in your heart,   our death - less life   is   won!

Text: Mary Louise Bringle, b.1953, © 2002, GIA Publications, Inc.
Tune: FINLANDIA, 11 10 11 10 11 10; Jean Sibelius, 1865–1957

974 Here, Master, in This Quiet Place

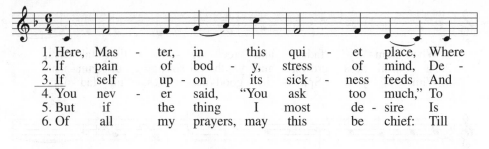

1. Here, Mas - ter, in this qui - et place, Where
2. If pain of bod - y, stress of mind, De -
3. If self up - on its sick - ness feeds And
4. You nev - er said, "You ask too much," To
5. But if the thing I most de - sire Is
6. Of all my prayers, may this be chief: Till

an - y - one may kneel, I al - so come to
stroys my in - ward peace, In prayer for oth - ers
turns my life to gall, Let me not brood up -
an - y trou - bled soul. I long to feel your
not your way for me, May faith, when test - ed
faith is ful - ly grown, Lord, dis - be - lieve my

ask for grace, Be - liev - ing you can heal.
may I find The se - cret of re - lease.
on my needs, But sim - ply tell you all.
heal - ing touch— Will you not make me whole?
in the fire, Prove its in - teg - ri - ty.
un - be - lief, And claim me as your own.

Text: Fred Pratt Green, 1903–2000, © 1974, Hope Publishing Company
Tune: LAND OF REST, CM; American melody; harm. by Richard Proulx, 1937–2010, © 1975, GIA Publications, Inc.

975 Banned and Banished by Their Neighbors

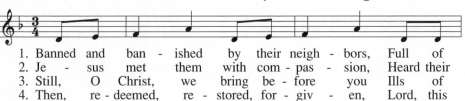

1. Banned and ban - ished by their neigh - bors, Full of
2. Je - sus met them with com - pas - sion, Heard their
3. Still, O Christ, we bring be - fore you Ills of
4. Then, re - deemed, re - stored, for - giv - en, Lord, this

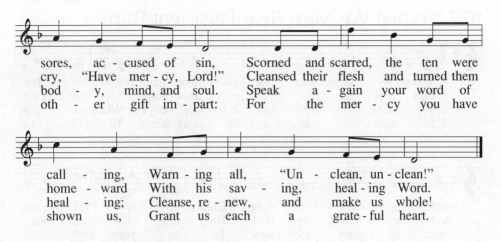

sores,   ac - cused of sin,"   Scorned and scarred,   the   ten   were
cry,   "Have   mer - cy,   Lord!"   Cleansed their flesh   and   turned them
bod - y,   mind, and soul.   Speak   a - gain   your word   of
oth - er   gift im - part: For   the   mer - cy   you   have

call - ing,   Warn - ing   all,   "Un - clean, un - clean!"
home - ward   With   his   sav - ing,   heal - ing   Word.
heal - ing;   Cleanse, re - new,   and   make us   whole!
shown   us,   Grant us   each   a   grate - ful   heart.

Text: Herman G. Stuempfle, Jr., 1923–2007, © 1997, GIA Publications, Inc.
Tune: KAS DZIEDAJA, 8 7 8 7; Latvian melody; acc. by Ronald F. Krisman, b.1946, © 2011, GIA Publications, Inc.

He Healed the Darkness of My Mind 976

1. He healed the dark - ness of my mind   The day he
2. Let oth - ers call   my faith a   lie   Or try to
3. Ask me not how!   But I know who   Has o - pened

gave   my sight to   me.   It was not   sin   that
stir   up doubt in   me.   Look at me   now!   None
up   new worlds to   me.   This Je - sus   does   what

made   me blind;   It was no   sin - ner made me   see.
can   de - ny   I once was blind, and   now I   see!
none   can do;   I once was blind, and   now I   see!

Text: John 9; Fred Pratt Green, 1903–2000, © 1982, Hope Publishing Company
Tune: O WALY WALY, LM; English melody; arr. by John L. Bell, b.1949, © 1989, Iona Community, GIA Publications, Inc., agent

977 When We Must Bear Persistent Pain

1. When we must bear per - sis - tent pain And suf - fer
2. Sup - port us as we learn new ways To care for
3. We thank you for the bet - ter days When we may
4. In ease or pain, in life and death, To you our

with no cure in sight, Come, Ho - ly Pres - ence,
bod - ies new - ly frail. Help us en - dure, and
smile to greet the sun, To do your work with
fra - gile lives be - long, And so we trust you

breathe your peace With gifts of warmth and heal - ing light.
live and love. Hear our com - plaint when pa - tience fails.
clear - ing mind, And bless your name when day is done.
in all things. You are our hope, our health, our song.

Text: Ruth Duck, b.1947, © 2005, GIA Publications, Inc.
Tune: PROSPECT, LM; *Southern Harmony*; harm. by David N. Johnson, 1922–1987, © 1978, *Lutheran Book of Worship*, admin. by Augsburg Fortress

978 O Christ, the Healer

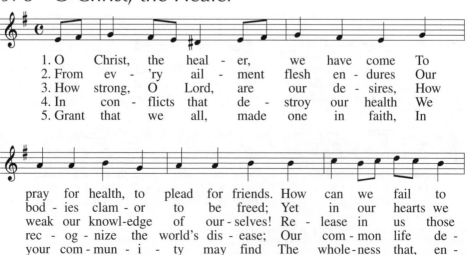

1. O Christ, the heal - er, we have come To
2. From ev - 'ry ail - ment flesh en - dures Our
3. How strong, O Lord, are our de - sires, How
4. In con - flicts that de - stroy our health We
5. Grant that we all, made one in faith, In

pray for health, to plead for friends. How can we fail to
bod - ies clam - or to be freed; Yet in our hearts we
weak our knowl-edge of our - selves! Re - lease in us those
rec - og - nize the world's dis - ease; Our com - mon life de -
your com - mun - i - ty may find The whole-ness that, en -

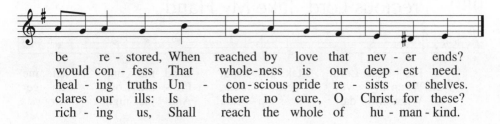

be re - stored, When reached by love that nev - er ends?
would con - fess That whole-ness is our deep - est need.
heal - ing truths Un - con - scious pride re - sists or shelves.
clares our ills: Is there no cure, O Christ, for these?
rich - ing us, Shall reach the whole of hu - man - kind.

Text: Fred Pratt Green, 1903–2000, © 1969, Hope Publishing Company
Tune: ERHALT UNS HERR, LM; Klug's *Geistliche Lieder*, 1543; harm. by Ronald F. Krisman, b.1946, © 2011, GIA Publications, Inc.

A Blind Man Sat beside the Road 979

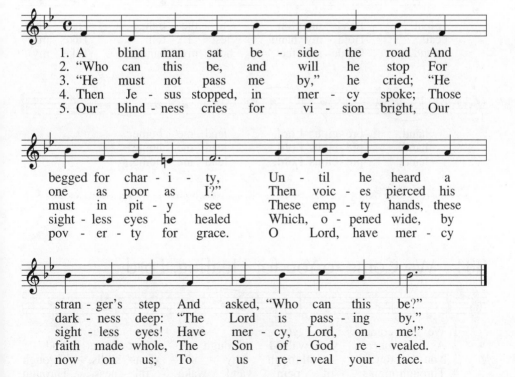

1. A blind man sat be - side the road And
2. "Who can this be, and will he stop For
3. "He must not pass me by," he cried; "He
4. Then Je - sus stopped, in mer - cy spoke; Those
5. Our blind - ness cries for vi - sion bright, Our

begged for char - i - ty, Un - til he heard a
one as poor as I?" Then voic - es pierced his
must in pit - y see These emp - ty hands, these
sight - less eyes he healed Which, o - pened wide, by
pov - er - ty for grace. O Lord, have mer - cy

stran - ger's step And asked, "Who can this be?"
dark - ness deep: "The Lord is pass - ing by."
sight - less eyes! Have mer - cy, Lord, on me!"
faith made whole, The Son of God re - vealed.
now on us; To us re - veal your face.

Text: Herman G. Stuempfle, Jr., 1923–2007, © 1993, GIA Publications, Inc.
Tune: ST. ANNE, CM; attr. to William Croft, 1678–1727; harm. composite from 18th C. versions

980 Precious Lord, Take My Hand

1. Pre - cious Lord, take my hand, Lead me on, let me
2. When my way grows drear, Pre - cious Lord, lin - ger
3. When the dark - ness ap-pears And the night draws

stand, I am tired, I am weak, I am
near, When my life is al - most
near, And the day is past and

worn. Through the storm, through the
gone, Hear my cry, hear my
gone, At the riv - er I

night, Lead me on to the light. Take my
call, Hold my hand lest I fall. Take my
stand, Guide my feet, hold my hand. Take my

hand, pre - cious Lord, lead me home.
hand, pre - cious Lord, lead me home.
hand, pre - cious Lord, lead me home.

Text: Thomas A. Dorsey, 1899–1993
Tune: PRECIOUS LORD, 66 9 D; George N. Allen, 1812–1877; adapt. by Thomas A. Dorsey, 1899–1993; arr. by Kelly Dobbs-Mickus, b.1966
© 1938, (renewed), arr. © 1994, Warner-Tamerlane Publishing Corp.

981 We Come to You for Healing, Lord

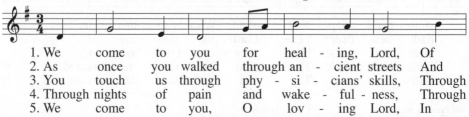

1. We come to you for heal - ing, Lord, Of
2. As once you walked through an - cient streets And
3. You touch us through phy - si - cians' skills, Through
4. Through nights of pain and wake - ful - ness, Through
5. We come to you, O lov - ing Lord, In

bod - y, mind, and soul, And pray that by your
reached toward those in pain, We know you come a -
nurs - es' gifts of care, And through the love of
days when strength runs low, Grant us your gift of
our dis - tress and pain, In trust that through our

Spir - it's touch We may a - gain be whole.
mong us still With pow'r to heal a - gain.
faith - ful friends Who lift our lives in prayer.
pa - tience, Lord, Your calm - ing peace to know.
nights and days Your grace will heal, sus - tain.

Text: Herman G. Stuempfle, Jr., 1923–2007, © 2006, GIA Publications, Inc.
Tune: MARTYRDOM, CM; Hugh Wilson, 1764–1824

When Love Is Found 982

1. When love is found and hope comes home, Sing and be
2. When love has flow'red in trust and care, Build both each
3. When love is tried as loved ones change, Hold still to
4. When love is torn, and trust be - trayed, Pray strength to
5. Praise God for love, praise God for life, In age or

glad that two are one. When love ex - plodes and
day, that love may dare To reach be - yond home's
hope, though all seems strange, Till ease re - turns and
love till tor - ments fade, Till lov - ers keep no
youth, in calm or strife. Lift up your hearts! Let

fills the sky, Praise God, and share our Mak - er's joy.
warmth and light, To serve and strive for truth and right.
love grows wise Through lis - t'ning ears and o - pened eyes.
score of wrong But hear through pain love's East - er song.
love be fed Through death and life in bro - ken bread.

Text: Brian Wren, b.1936, © 1983, Hope Publishing Company
Tune: O WALY WALY, LM; English melody; harm. by Martin West, b.1929, © 1983, Hope Publishing Company

983 God of Love, Embrace Your People

1. God of love, em - brace your peo - ple. Gath - ered in your
2. Christ our light, shine forth in splen - dor; Lead these two in
3. God the Spir - it, grant them bless - ings Day by day and

name, we pray: Bless this cou - ple, who in glad - ness
days a - head. In their joys and in their sor - rows
year by year. Help them grow in love to - geth - er,

Pledge their vows of love to - day. You cre - at - ed
By your Word may they be fed. Through the love of
Con - fi - dent that you are near. In the chal - lenge

man and wom - an In your im - age, to be one.
friends and fam - 'ly Let them know your love out-poured;
of to - mor - row Guide them ev - er in your ways.

May your love be al - ways pres - ent
In the Church, where all find wel - come,
May their prom - ise last for - ev - er,

In the un - ion here be - gun.
May they serve you, gra - cious Lord.
Love en - dur - ing all their days.

Text: James J. Chepponis, b.1956, © 2011, GIA Publications, Inc.
Tune: HYMN TO JOY, 8 7 8 7 D; arr. from Ludwig van Beethoven, 1770–1827, by Edward Hodges, 1796–1867

God, in the Planning 984

1. God, in the plan - ning and pur - pose of life,
2. Je - sus was found, at a sim - i - lar feast,
3. There - fore we pray that his spir - it pre - side
4. Praise then the Mak - er, the Spir - it, the Son,

Hal - lowed the un - ion of hus - band and wife:
Tak - ing the roles of both wait - er and priest,
O - ver the wed - ding of bride - groom and bride,
Source of the love through which two are made one.

This we em - bod - y where love is dis - played,
Turn - ing cre - at - ed things in - to di - vine,
Help - ing them share what is ten - der and true,
God's is the glo - ry, the good - ness, and grace

Rings are pre - sent - ed and prom - is - es made.
Tears in - to laugh - ter and wa - ter to wine.
Light - ing with love all they dream of and do.
Seen in this mar - riage and known in this place.

Text: John L. Bell, b.1949, © 1989, Iona Community, GIA Publications, Inc., agent
Tune: SLANE, 10 10 10 10; Irish melody; harm. by Erik Routley, 1917–1982, © 1975, Hope Publishing Company

985 Love Has Brought Us Here Together

1. Love has brought us here together:
2. Love is gen - tle, love is pa - tient,
3. Love does not re - joice at e - vil;

Love of fam - 'ly, love of friends;
Soft in words and kind in deeds.
Love re - joic - es in the right.

Love, our vow till death should part us;
Love is strong and nev - er pom - pous;
Keen in giv - ing and for - giv - ing,

Love, God's gift, that nev - er ends.
Love puts first the oth - er's needs.
Spread - ing love is love's de - light.

From our birth, through - out our life - time,
Not quick - tem - pered or re - sent - ful,
When two peo - ple pledge their un - ion,

Love's in - sis - tence calls our name.
Prone to take of - fense or brood,
All who wit - ness are re - newed,

Floods of wa - ters can - not drown it
Love ex - cels in grace and mer - cy,
Feast - ing at love's earth - ly ban - quet,

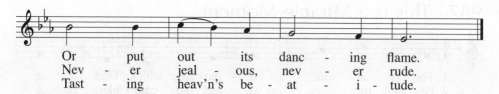

Or   put   out   its   danc - ing   flame.
Nev - er   jeal - ous,   nev - er   rude.
Tast - ing   heav'n's   be - at - i - tude.

Text: Mary Louise Bringle, b.1953, © 2010, GIA Publications, Inc.
Tune: HYFRYDOL, 8 7 8 7 D; Rowland H. Prichard, 1811–1887

Let's Praise the Creator   986

1. Let's praise the Cre - a - tor, who gave us each oth - er
2. The love that we wish them, the love that we pray for
3. In vows that are hon - ored, in kiss - ing and bless - ing

In friend - ship and kin - ship to cel - e - brate life.
Is strong - er than storms and more gen - tle than breath,
May hap - pi - ness shine like the gold of a ring.

Let's sing our de - light in this man and this wom - an,
En - dures ev - 'ry trou - ble, is self - less and faith - ful,
In pas - sion - ate joy and com - pas - sion - ate car - ing

The prom - ise of joy as a hus - band and wife.
More pre - cious than life and more last - ing than death.
May theirs be the gifts that true lov - ing can bring.

Text: Shirley Erena Murray, b.1931, © 1992, Hope Publishing Company
Tune: KREMSER, 12 11 12 11; Valerius' *Nederlandtsch Gedenckclanck*, 1626; harm. by Edward Kremser, 1838–1914

987 This Is a Miracle-Moment

1. This is a mir - a - cle - mo-ment which God is re -
2. Few are the days when we feel so com - plete-ly as -
3. Now, as the wit - ness-es gath-ered at this cel - e -
4. "Vast is the o - cean of choic-es and hopes that are

veal - ing. Now is the time for the
tound - ed: Lost in our joy, by our
bra - tion, We praise the One who, in
swell - ing. Love is the boat for the

vows the Cre - a - tor is seal - ing.
loved ones so ful - ly sur - round - ed.
Christ, is this coup - le's foun - da - tion.
jour - ney, so deep and com - pel - ling.

This is the place. Here is the foun - tain of grace,
This is the day When, in God's sin - gu - lar way,
To them we say, On this un - par - al - leled day,
Put out to sea! See how sub - lime God can be!

Source of all mer - cy and heal - ing.
Love is com - plete - ly un - bound - ed.
"Hear our sin - cere ex - hor - ta - tion:
Rest in God's ho - ly in - dwell - ing."

Text: John Thornburg, b.1954, © 2010, GIA Publications, Inc.
Tune: LOBE DEN HERREN, 14 14 47 8; *Stralsund Gesangbuch*, 1665

Dwellers in the Holy City   988

1. Dwell - ers   in   the   ho - ly   cit - y,
2. Fam - 'ly   born   to   God's own   house - hold,
3. Sing - ers   in   the   choir   of   heav - en,
4. Saints a - round   the   ban - quet   gath - ered,

O - pen   wide   the   gold - en   door;   May   our
Bring   our   faith - ful   friend with - in,   Free   of
Let   your   prayer like   in - cense   rise;   Let   our
Claim her/him   now   as   next   of   kin;   Lead   her/him

friend   from   this   world   sum - moned Know God's   pres - ence
suf - f'ring,   pain   and   sor - row,   Free   of   weak - ness,
friend,   in   song,   now   join   you,   Prais - ing   God   in
to   the   fam - 'ly   ta - ble;   Let   the   feast   of

ev - er - more.   Saints   and   an - gels,   make her/him
free   of   sin.   May   her/his   pass - ing   lead   to
par - a - dise.   And   may   we,   re - joic - ing,
joy   be - gin.   Friends   at   God's own   ta - ble

wel - come,   Glad   at   home   for   ev - er - more.
glo - ry,   Vic - t'ry   o - ver   death   and   sin.
join   you,   Prais - ers   all   in   par - a - dise.
seat - ed,   Let   the   feast - ing   now   be - gin!

Text: Delores Dufner, OSB, b.1939, © 2011, GIA Publications, Inc.
Tune: LAUDA ANIMA, 8 7 8 7 8 7; John Goss, 1800–1880

989 Rest in Peace, Earth's Journey Ended

1. Rest in peace, earth's jour - ney end - ed, You whom Christ re -
2. Hap - py soul, to Christ u - nit - ed, Calm - er now and
3. May we meet, dear Lord, in heav - en, Each for - giv - ing,

deemed, de - fend - ed: To the place where saints are one,
clear - er - sight - ed: Your new jour - ney now be - gins,
each for - giv - en, Each more gift - ed to pur - sue

Safe - ly brought by him a - lone. May he grant us
Freed from earth's be - set - ting sins. Press - ing on - ward
All you have for us to do. By your Spir - it's

like pro - tec - tion. Rest in peace, rest in peace,
to per - fec - tion, Hap - py soul, hap - py soul,
sure di - rec - tion May we meet, may we meet,

Rest in peace, earth's jour - ney end - ed.
Hap - py soul, to Christ u - nit - ed.
May we meet, dear Lord, in heav - en.

Text: Fred Pratt Green, 1903–2000, © 1982, Hope Publishing Company
Music: MOEHR, 88 77 8 6 8; Russell Schulz-Widmar, b.1944, © 1987, GIA Publications, Inc.

Saints of God   990

Refrain

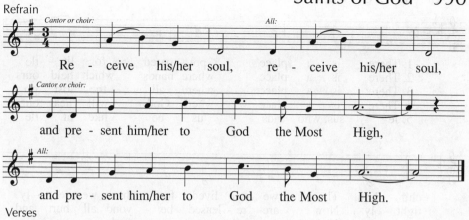

Re - ceive his/her soul, re - ceive his/her soul,

and pre - sent him/her to God the Most High,

and pre - sent him/her to God the Most High.

Verses

1. Saints of God, come to his/her aid!
   Hasten to meet him/her, angels of the Lord!

2. May Christ, who called you, take you to himself;
   may angels lead you to the bosom of Abraham.

3. Eternal rest grant unto him/her, O Lord,
   and let perpetual light shine upon him/her.

Text: *Order of Christian Funerals,* © 1985, ICEL
Music: Steven R. Janco, b.1961, © 1990, GIA Publications, Inc.

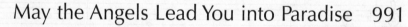

May the Angels Lead You into Paradise   991

Cantor, then all:

May the an - gels lead you in - to par - a - dise;

may the mar - tyrs come to wel - come you and

take you to the ho - ly cit - y, the

new and e - ter - nal Je - ru - sa - lem.

Text: *In paradisum; Rite of Funerals,* © 1970, ICEL
Tune: Howard Hughes, SM, b.1930, © 1977, ICEL

992 There Is a Place

1. There is a place pre - pared for lit - tle
2. There is a place where hands which held ours
3. There is a place where all the lost po -
4. There is a place where God will hear our
5. Je - sus, who bids us be like lit - tle

chil - dren, Those we once lived for, those we deep - ly
tight - ly Now are re - leased be - yond all hurt and
ten - tial Yields its full prom - ise, finds its true in -
ques - tions, Suf - fer our an - ger, share our speech-less
chil - dren, Shields those our arms are yearn-ing to em -

mourn, Those who from play, from learn - ing and from
fear, Healed by that love which al - so feels our
tent; Si - lenced no more, young voic - es ech - o
grief, Gen - tly re - pair the in - no-cence of
brace. God will en - sure that all are re - u -

laugh - ter, Cruel - ly were torn.
sor - row Tear af - ter tear.
free - ly As they were meant.
lov - ing And of be - lief.
nit - ed; There is a place.

Text: John L. Bell, b.1949
Tune: DUNBLANE PRIMARY, 11 10 11 4; John L. Bell, b.1949
© 1996, Iona Community, GIA Publications, Inc., agent

O Lord, You Died That All Might Live   993

1. O Lord, you died that all might live And
2. Lord, bless our friend who died in you. As
3. In green and pleas - ant pas - tures feed The
4. Per - fect us, Lord of pow'r and might, That,

rise to see the per - fect day. The
you have giv - en him/her re - lease, So
sheep that you have sum - moned hence; And
with our friend, we all may come To

full - ness of your mer - cy give To
raise him/her up, your ser - vant true, And
by the still, cool wa - ters lead Your
dwell with - in your cit - y bright, Je -

this our friend for whom we pray.
give him/her ev - er - last - ing peace.
flock in lov - ing prov - i - dence.
ru - sa - lem, our heav'n - ly home.

O Lamb of God, Re - deem - er blest, Grant

him/her e - ter - nal light and rest.

Text: Richard F. Littledale, 1833–1890, alt.
Tune: MELITA, LM with refrain; John B. Dykes, 1823–1876

994 I Know That My Redeemer Lives

Cantor:
I know that my Re-deem-er lives, and on the last day

I shall rise a-gain; in my bod-y I shall look on God, my

All:
Sav - ior, in my bod-y I shall look on God, my

Cantor:
Sav - ior. I my-self shall see him; my own eyes will

gaze on him, my own eyes will gaze on him; in my

All:
bod-y I shall look on God, my Sav - ior, in my bod-y I shall

Cantor:
look on God, my Sav - ior. This is the hope I

cher - ish, this is the hope I cher-ish in my heart;

in my bod - y I shall look on God, my Sav - ior,

All:
in my bod - y I shall look on God, my Sav - ior.

Text: *Rite of Funerals,* © 1970, ICEL
Tune: Howard Hughes, SM, b.1930, © 1977, ICEL

God of Our Fathers 995

1. God of our fa - thers, whose al - might - y hand
2. Your love di - vine has led us in the past,
3. From war's a - larms, from dead - ly pes - ti - lence,
4. Re - fresh your peo - ple on their toil - some way,

Leads forth in beau - ty all the star - ry band
In this free land by you our lot is cast;
Be your strong arm our ev - er sure de - fense;
Lead us from night to nev - er - end - ing day;

Of shin - ing worlds in splen - dor through the skies,
Be our strong rul - er, guar - dian, guide, and stay,
Your true re - li - gion in our hearts in - crease,
Fill all our lives with heav'n - born love and grace,

Our grate - ful songs be - fore your throne a - rise.
Your word our law, your paths our cho - sen way.
Your boun - teous good - ness nour - ish us in peace.
Un - til at last, we meet be - fore your face.

Text: Daniel C. Roberts, 1841–1907
Tune: NATIONAL HYMN, 10 10 10 10; George W. Warren, 1828–1902

996 America the Beautiful

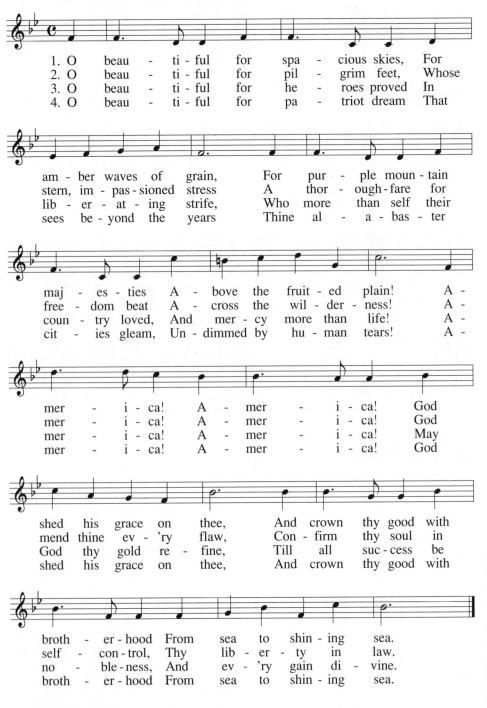

1. O beau - ti - ful for spa - cious skies, For
2. O beau - ti - ful for pil - grim feet, Whose
3. O beau - ti - ful for he - roes proved In
4. O beau - ti - ful for pa - triot dream That

am - ber waves of grain, For pur - ple moun - tain
stern, im - pas - sioned stress A thor - ough - fare for
lib - er - at - ing strife, Who more than self their
sees be - yond the years Thine al - a - bas - ter

maj - es - ties A - bove the fruit - ed plain! A -
free - dom beat A - cross the wil - der - ness! A -
coun - try loved, And mer - cy more than life! A -
cit - ies gleam, Un - dimmed by hu - man tears! A -

mer - i - ca! A - mer - i - ca! God
mer - i - ca! A - mer - i - ca! God
mer - i - ca! A - mer - i - ca! May
mer - i - ca! A - mer - i - ca! God

shed his grace on thee, And crown thy good with
mend thine ev - 'ry flaw, Con - firm thy soul in
God thy gold re - fine, Till all suc - cess be
shed his grace on thee, And crown thy good with

broth - er - hood From sea to shin - ing sea.
self - con - trol, Thy lib - er - ty in law.
no - ble - ness, And ev - 'ry gain di - vine.
broth - er - hood From sea to shin - ing sea.

Text: Katherine L. Bates, 1859–1929
Tune: MATERNA, CMD; Samuel A. Ward, 1848–1903

This Is My Song 997

1. This is my song, O God of all the na - tions,
2. My coun-try's skies are blu - er than the o - cean,
3. This is my prayer, O Lord of all earth's king - doms:

A song of peace for lands a - far and mine.
And sun - light beams on clo - ver - leaf and pine.
Your king-dom come; on earth your will be done.

This is my home, the coun - try where my heart is;
But oth - er lands have sun - light too, and clo - ver,
Let Christ be lift - ed up till all shall serve him,

Here are my hopes, my dreams, my ho - ly shrine.
And skies are ev - 'ry - where as blue as mine.
And hearts u - nit - ed learn to live as one.

But oth - er hearts in oth - er lands are beat - ing
So hear my song, O God of all the na - tions,
So hear my prayer, O God of all the na - tions.

With hopes and dreams as true and high as mine.
A song of peace for their land and for mine.
My - self I give you; let your will be done.

Text: St. 1, 2, Lloyd Stone, 1912–1993; st. 3, Georgia Harkness, 1891–1974, © 1964, Lorenz Publishing Co.
Tune: FINLANDIA, 11 10 11 10 11 10; Jean Sibelius, 1865–1957

998 My Country, 'Tis of Thee

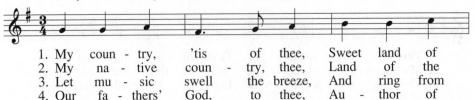

1. My coun - try, 'tis of thee, Sweet land of
2. My na - tive coun - try, thee, Land of the
3. Let mu - sic swell the breeze, And ring from
4. Our fa - thers' God, to thee, Au - thor of

lib - er - ty, Of thee I sing; Land where my
no - ble, free; Thy name I love; I love thy
all the trees Sweet free - dom's song; Let mor - tal
lib - er - ty, To thee we sing; Long may our

fa - thers died, Land of the pil - grim's pride,
rocks and rills, Thy woods and tem - pled hills;
tongues a - wake; Let all that breathe par - take;
land be bright With free - dom's ho - ly light;

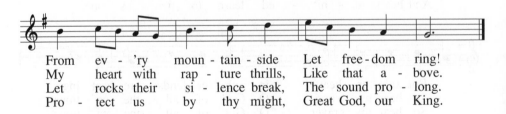

From ev - 'ry moun - tain - side Let free - dom ring!
My heart with rap - ture thrills, Like that a - bove.
Let rocks their si - lence break, The sound pro - long.
Pro - tect us by thy might, Great God, our King.

Text: Samuel F. Smith, 1808–1895
Tune: AMERICA, 66 4 666 4; *Thesaurus Musicus*, 1744

Greet Now the Swiftly Changing Year   999

1. Greet now the swift - ly chang - ing year With
2. When Je - sus came to wage sin's war, The
3. His love a - bun - dant far ex - ceeds The
4. With such a Lord to lead our way In
5. "All glo - ry be to God on high, And
6. God, Fa - ther, Son, and Spir - it, hear: To

joy and pen - i - tence sin - cere. Re - joice, re - joice, with
Name of names for us he bore. Re - joice, re - joice, with
vol - ume of a whole year's needs. Re - joice, re - joice, with
haz - ard or pros - per - i - ty, What need we fear in
peace on earth!" the an - gels cry. Re - joice, re - joice, with
all our pleas in - cline your ear; Up - on our lives rich

thanks em - brace An - oth - er year of grace.
thanks em - brace An - oth - er year of grace.
thanks em - brace An - oth - er year of grace.
earth or space In this new year of grace?
thanks em - brace An - oth - er year of grace.
bless - ing trace In this new year of grace.

Text: Slovak, 17th C.; tr. by Jaroslav J. Vajda, 1919–2008, alt., © 1969, Concordia Publishing House
Tune: SIXTH NIGHT, 88 86; Alfred V. Fedak, b.1953, © 1989, Selah Publishing Co.

Lectionary

1000 Advent / Christmas

In various ways and various places the Church has marked the days around the winter solstice (or the summer solstice in the southern hemisphere) in late December and early January. Customs, traditions, and rituals from the world's cultures have quite naturally found a home around the many-faceted celebration of the Word-made-flesh, the manifestation of God-with-us.

The present Roman calendar observes the season of Advent for three to four weeks prior to December 25. This season has a two-fold focus: the second coming of Jesus Christ at the end of human history and the historical incarnation of Jesus two thousand years ago.

Advent is filled with beautiful scripture readings, songs, prayers and gestures. These abound with images of God's promise and human longing, the beauty present in both darkness and light, the earth's sorrows and its fullness, and the goodness and mystery of time.

At Christmas this spirit blossoms in acclamation: the stories of nativity and epiphany, of Mary and of the Innocents, of Jesus baptized and of water become wine. Until well into January the songs and sights and smells of Christmas surround the Church not with sentimental fantasies but with everyday faith in a gracious God. The festivals of the Christmas season bear their own reflection of what is proclaimed on every Sunday of the year and in every baptism: our lives are caught up now in Jesus who was born of the virgin Mary, who suffered, died and has been raised.

The lectionary of Advent/Christmas is the foundation of these winter days. These scripture readings, proclaimed and pondered year after year, turn the Christian and the Church toward that peace and glory we name but do not yet know.

1001 FIRST SUNDAY OF ADVENT / A

READING I   *Isaiah 2:1–5 / 1*

This is what Isaiah, son of Amoz,
saw concerning Judah and Jerusalem.
    In days to come,
the mountain of the LORD's house
    shall be established as the highest
mountain
    and raised above the hills.
All nations shall stream toward it;
    many peoples shall come and say:

"Come, let us climb the LORD's mountain,
to the house of the God of Jacob,
that he may instruct us in his ways,
and we may walk in his paths."
For from Zion shall go forth instruction,
and the word of the LORD from
Jerusalem.
He shall judge between the nations,
and impose terms on many peoples.

They shall beat their swords into
plowshares
and their spears into pruning hooks;
one nation shall not raise the sword
against another,
nor shall they train for war again.
O house of Jacob, come,
let us walk in the light of the Lord!

RESPONSORIAL PSALM   *Psalm 122:1–2, 3–4ab, 4cd–5, 6–7, 8–9*

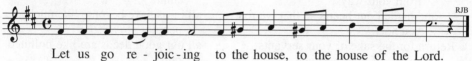

Let us go re - joic - ing to the house, to the house of the Lord.

I rejoiced when they said to me,
"Let us go to the house of the
LORD."
And now our feet are standing
within your gates, O Jerusalem. ℞.

Jerusalem is built as a city
bonded as one together.
It is there that the tribes go up,
the tribes of the LORD. ℞.

For Israel's witness it is
to praise the name of the LORD.
There were set the thrones for judgment,

the thrones of the house of David. ℞.

For the peace of Jerusalem pray,
"May they prosper, those who love
you."
May peace abide in your walls,
and security be in your towers. ℞.

For the sake of my family and friends,
let me say, "Peace upon you."
For the sake of the house of the LORD,
our God,
I will seek good things for you. ℞.

READING II   *Romans 13:11–14*

Brothers and sisters: You know the time; it is the hour now for you to awake from
sleep. For our salvation is nearer now than when we first believed; the night is
advanced, the day is at hand. Let us then throw off the works of darkness and put on
the armor of light; let us conduct ourselves properly as in the day, not in orgies and
drunkenness, not in promiscuity and lust, not in rivalry and jealousy. But put on the
Lord Jesus Christ, and make no provision for the desires of the flesh.

GOSPEL   *Matthew 24:37–44*

Jesus said to his disciples: "As it was in the days of Noah, so it will be at the coming
of the Son of Man. In those days before the flood, they were eating and drinking, mar-
rying and giving in marriage, up to the day that Noah entered the ark. They did not
know until the flood came and carried them all away. So will it be also at the coming
of the Son of Man. Two men will be out in the field; one will be taken, and one will
be left. Two women will be grinding at the mill; one will be taken, and one will be
left. Therefore, stay awake! For you do not know on which day your Lord will come.
Be sure of this: if the master of the house had known the hour of night when the thief

was coming, he would have stayed awake and not let his house be broken into. So too, you also must be prepared, for at an hour you do not expect, the Son of Man will come."

1002 FIRST SUNDAY OF ADVENT / B

READING I   *Isaiah 63:16b–17, 19b; 64:2–7 / 2*

You, LORD, are our father,
    our redeemer you are named forever.
Why do you let us wander, O LORD,
      from your ways,
    and harden our hearts so that we fear
      you not?
Return for the sake of your servants,
    the tribes of your heritage.
Oh, that you would rend the heavens
      and come down,
    with the mountains quaking before
      you,
while you wrought awesome deeds we
      could not hope for,
    such as they had not heard of from
      of old.
No ear has ever heard, no eye ever seen,
      any God but you
    doing such deeds for those who
      wait for him.
Would that you might meet us doing
      right,

that we were mindful of you in our
      ways!
Behold, you are angry, and we are
      sinful;
    all of us have become like unclean
      people,
    all our good deeds are like polluted
      rags;
we have all withered like leaves,
    and our guilt carries us away like
      the wind.
There is none who calls upon your
      name,
    who rouses himself to cling to you;
for you have hidden your face from us
    and have delivered us up to our
      guilt.
Yet, O LORD, you are our father;
    we are the clay and you the potter:
    we are all the work of your hands.

RESPONSORIAL PSALM   *Psalm 80:2ac and 3b, 15–16, 18–19*

HH, adapt.

Lord, make us turn to you; let us see your face and we shall be saved.

O shepherd of Israel, hear us,
    enthroned on the cherubim, shine
      forth.
    Rouse up your might and come
      to save us. ℟.

God of hosts, turn again, we implore;
    look down from heaven and see.
Visit this vine and protect it,
    the vine your right hand has planted,
    the son of man you have claimed
      for yourself. ℟.

May your hand be on the man at your
    right hand,
  the son of man you have confirmed
    as your own.

And we shall never forsake you again;
    give us life that we may call upon
    your name. ℞.

READING II
1 Corinthians 1:3–9

Brothers and sisters: Grace to you and peace from God our Father and the Lord Jesus
Christ.

I give thanks to my God always on your account for the grace of God bestowed
on you in Christ Jesus, that in him you were enriched in every way, with all discourse
and all knowledge, as the testimony to Christ was confirmed among you, so that you
are not lacking in any spiritual gift as you wait for the revelation of our Lord Jesus
Christ. He will keep you firm to the end, irreproachable on the day of our Lord Jesus
Christ. God is faithful, and by him you were called to fellowship with his Son, Jesus
Christ our Lord.

GOSPEL
Mark 13:33–37

Jesus said to his disciples: "Be watchful! Be alert! You do not know when the time
will come. It is like a man traveling abroad. He leaves home and places his servants
in charge, each with his own work, and orders the gatekeeper to be on the watch.
Watch, therefore; you do not know when the lord of the house is coming, whether in
the evening, or at midnight, or at cockcrow, or in the morning. May he not come suddenly and find you sleeping. What I say to you, I say to all: 'Watch!'"

FIRST SUNDAY OF ADVENT / C
1003

READING I
Jeremiah 33:14–16 / 3

The days are coming, says the LORD,
  when I will fulfill the promise
    I made to the house of Israel and
      Judah.
In those days, in that time,
  I will raise up for David a just shoot;

he shall do what is right and just in
  the land.
In those days Judah shall be safe
  and Jerusalem shall dwell secure;
  this is what they shall call her:
  "The LORD our justice."

RESPONSORIAL PSALM
Psalm 25:4–5, 8–9, 10 and 14

To you, O Lord, I lift my soul.

O LORD, make me know your ways.
  Teach me your paths.
Guide me in your truth, and teach me;
  for you are the God of my salvation.
I have hoped in you all day long. ℞.

Good and upright is the LORD;
  he shows the way to sinners.
He guides the humble in right judgment;
  to the humble he teaches his way. ℞.

All the LORD's paths are mercy
and faithfulness,
for those who keep his covenant
and commands.

The LORD's secret is for those
who fear him;
to them he reveals his covenant. ℟.

READING II
1 Thessalonians 3:12—4:2

Brothers and sisters: May the Lord make you increase and abound in love for one another and for all, just as we have for you, so as to strengthen your hearts, to be blameless in holiness before our God and Father at the coming of our Lord Jesus with all his holy ones. Amen.

Finally, brothers and sisters, we earnestly ask and exhort you in the Lord Jesus that, as you received from us how you should conduct yourselves to please God—and as you are conducting yourselves—you do so even more. For you know what instructions we gave you through the Lord Jesus.

GOSPEL
Luke 21:25–28, 34–36

Jesus said to his disciples: "There will be signs in the sun, the moon, and the stars, and on earth nations will be in dismay, perplexed by the roaring of the sea and the waves. People will die of fright in anticipation of what is coming upon the world, for the powers of the heavens will be shaken. And then they will see the Son of Man coming in a cloud with power and great glory. But when these signs begin to happen, stand erect and raise your heads because your redemption is at hand.

"Beware that your hearts do not become drowsy from carousing and drunkenness and the anxieties of daily life, and that day catch you by surprise like a trap. For that day will assault everyone who lives on the face of the earth. Be vigilant at all times and pray that you have the strength to escape the tribulations that are imminent and to stand before the Son of Man."

1004   SECOND SUNDAY OF ADVENT / A

READING I
Isaiah 11:1–10 / 4

On that day, a shoot shall sprout from
the stump of Jesse,
and from his roots a bud shall
blossom.
The spirit of the Lord shall rest upon him:
a spirit of wisdom and of
understanding,
a spirit of counsel and of strength,
a spirit of knowledge and of fear of
the LORD,
and his delight shall be the fear of
the LORD.
Not by appearance shall he judge,
nor by hearsay shall he decide,
but he shall judge the poor with justice,

and decide aright for the land's
afflicted.
He shall strike the ruthless with the rod
of his mouth,
and with the breath of his lips he
shall slay the wicked.
Justice shall be the band around his waist,
and faithfulness a belt upon his hips.
Then the wolf shall be a guest of the
lamb,
and the leopard shall lie down with
the kid;
the calf and the young lion shall browse
together,
with a little child to guide them.

The cow and the bear shall be neighbors,
  together their young shall rest;
  the lion shall eat hay like the ox.
The baby shall play by the cobra's den,
  and the child lay his hand on the
    adder's lair.
There shall be no harm or ruin on all my
  holy mountain;

for the earth shall be filled with
  knowledge of the LORD,
  as water covers the sea.
On that day, the root of Jesse,
  set up as a signal for the nations,
  the Gentiles shall seek out,
  for his dwelling shall be glorious.

RESPONSORIAL PSALM   *Psalm 72:1–2, 7–8, 12–13, 17*

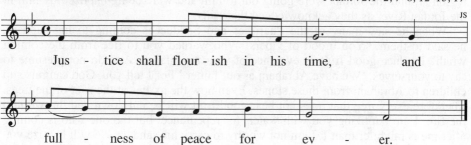

Jus - tice shall flour - ish in his time, and

full - ness of peace for ev - er.

O God, give your judgment to the king,
  to a king's son your justice,
that he may judge your people in justice,
  and your poor in right judgment. ℟.

In his days shall justice flourish,
  and great peace till the moon is no
    more.
He shall rule from sea to sea,
  from the River to the bounds
    of the earth. ℟.

For he shall save the needy when
    they cry,
  the poor, and those who are helpless.

He will have pity on the weak and
    the needy,
  and save the lives of the needy. ℟.

May his name endure forever,
  his name continue like the sun.
Every tribe shall be blest in him,
  all nations shall call him blessed. ℟.

READING II   *Romans 15:4–9*

Brothers and sisters: Whatever was written previously was written for our instruction, that by endurance and by the encouragement of the Scriptures we might have hope. May the God of endurance and encouragement grant you to think in harmony with one another, in keeping with Christ Jesus, that with one accord you may with one voice glorify the God and Father of our Lord Jesus Christ.

Welcome one another, then, as Christ welcomed you, for the glory of God. For I say that Christ became a minister of the circumcised to show God's truthfulness, to confirm the promises to the patriarchs, but so that the Gentiles might glorify God for his mercy. As it is written:

Therefore, I will praise you among the Gentiles
  and sing praises to your name.

GOSPEL *Matthew 3:1–12*

John the Baptist appeared, preaching in the desert of Judea and saying, "Repent, for the kingdom of heaven is at hand!" It was of him that the prophet Isaiah had spoken when he said:

A *voice of one crying out in the desert,*
Prepare the way of the Lord,
make straight his paths.

John wore clothing made of camel's hair and had a leather belt around his waist. His food was locusts and wild honey. At that time Jerusalem, all Judea, and the whole region around the Jordan were going out to him and were being baptized by him in the Jordan River as they acknowledged their sins.

When he saw many of the Pharisees and Sadducees coming to his baptism, he said to them, "You brood of vipers! Who warned you to flee from the coming wrath? Produce good fruit as evidence of your repentance. And do not presume to say to yourselves, 'We have Abraham as our father.' For I tell you, God can raise up children to Abraham from these stones. Even now the ax lies at the root of the trees. Therefore every tree that does not bear good fruit will be cut down and thrown into the fire. I am baptizing you with water, for repentance, but the one who is coming after me is mightier than I. I am not worthy to carry his sandals. He will baptize you with the Holy Spirit and fire. His winnowing fan is in his hand. He will clear his threshing floor and gather his wheat into his barn, but the chaff he will burn with unquenchable fire."

1005 SECOND SUNDAY OF ADVENT / B

READING I *Isaiah 40:1–5, 9–11 / 5*

Comfort, give comfort to my people,
    says your God.
Speak tenderly to Jerusalem, and
        proclaim to her
        that her service is at an end,
    her guilt is expiated;
indeed, she has received from the hand
        of the LORD
    double for all her sins.

A voice cries out:
In the desert prepare the way of
    the LORD!
    Make straight in the wasteland a
        highway for our God!
Every valley shall be filled in,
    every mountain and hill shall be
        made low;
    the rugged land shall be made a plain,
        the rough country, a broad valley.
Then the glory of the LORD shall be
    revealed,

and all people shall see it together;
    for the mouth of the LORD has
        spoken.

Go up on to a high mountain,
    Zion, herald of glad tidings;
cry out at the top of your voice,
    Jerusalem, herald of good news!
Fear not to cry out
    and say to the cities of Judah:
    Here is your God!
Here comes with power
    the Lord GOD,
    who rules by his strong arm;
here is his reward with him,
    his recompense before him.
Like a shepherd he feeds his flock;
    in his arms he gathers the lambs,
carrying them in his bosom,
    and leading the ewes with care.

RESPONSORIAL PSALM   *Psalm 85:9ab and 10, 11–12, 13–14*

Lord, let us see your kind-ness, and grant us your sal - va-tion.

I will hear what the LORD God speaks;
he speaks of peace for his people
and his faithful.
His salvation is near for those who fear him,
and his glory will dwell in our land. ℟.

Merciful love and faithfulness have met;
justice and peace have kissed.

Faithfulness shall spring from the earth,
and justice look down from
heaven. ℟.

Also the LORD will bestow his bounty,
and our earth shall yield its increase.
Justice will march before him,
and guide his steps on the way. ℟.

READING II   *2 Peter 3:8–14*

Do not ignore this one fact, beloved, that with the Lord one day is like a thousand
years and a thousand years like one day. The Lord does not delay his promise, as some
regard "delay," but he is patient with you, not wishing that any should perish but that
all should come to repentance. But the day of the Lord will come like a thief, and then
the heavens will pass away with a mighty roar and the elements will be dissolved by
fire, and the earth and everything done on it will be found out.

Since everything is to be dissolved in this way, what sort of persons ought you
to be, conducting yourselves in holiness and devotion, waiting for and hastening the
coming of the day of God, because of which the heavens will be dissolved in flames
and the elements melted by fire. But according to his promise we await new heavens
and a new earth in which righteousness dwells. Therefore, beloved, since you await
these things, be eager to be found without spot or blemish before him, at peace.

GOSPEL   *Mark 1:1–8*

The beginning of the gospel of Jesus Christ the Son of God.

As it is written in Isaiah the prophet:
Behold, I am sending my messenger ahead of you;
he will prepare your way.
A voice of one crying out in the desert:
"Prepare the way of the Lord,
make straight his paths."

John the Baptist appeared in the desert proclaiming a baptism of repentance for the
forgiveness of sins. People of the whole Judean countryside and all the inhabitants of
Jerusalem were going out to him and were being baptized by him in the Jordan River
as they acknowledged their sins. John was clothed in camel's hair, with a leather belt
around his waist. He fed on locusts and wild honey. And this is what he proclaimed:
"One mightier than I is coming after me. I am not worthy to stoop and loosen the
thongs of his sandals. I have baptized you with water; he will baptize you with the
Holy Spirit."

1006 SECOND SUNDAY OF ADVENT / C

READING I

Baruch 5:1–9 / 6

Jerusalem, take off your robe of
    mourning and misery;
    put on the splendor of glory from
      God forever:
wrapped in the cloak of justice from
    God,
    bear on your head the mitre
    that displays the glory of the eternal
      name.
For God will show all the earth your
    splendor:
    you will be named by God forever
    the peace of justice, the glory of
      God's worship.

Up, Jerusalem! stand upon the heights;
    look to the east and see your
      children
gathered from the east and the west
    at the word of the Holy One,
    rejoicing that they are remembered
      by God.

Led away on foot by their enemies they
    left you:
    but God will bring them back to you
    borne aloft in glory as on royal
      thrones.
For God has commanded
    that every lofty mountain be made
      low,
and that the age-old depths and gorges
    be filled to level ground,
    that Israel may advance secure in
      the glory of God.
The forests and every fragrant kind of
    tree
    have overshadowed Israel at God's
      command;
for God is leading Israel in joy
    by the light of his glory,
    with his mercy and justice for
      company.

RESPONSORIAL PSALM

Psalm 126:1–2ab, 2cd–3, 4–5, 6

The Lord has done great things for us;
we are filled with joy, we are filled with joy.

When the LORD brought back the
    exiles of Sion,
    we thought we were dreaming.
Then was our mouth filled with
    laughter;
    on our tongues, songs of joy. ℟.

Then the nations themselves said,
    "What great deeds the LORD
      worked for them!"
What great deeds the LORD worked
    for us!
    Indeed, we were glad. ℟.

Bring back our exiles, O LORD,
    as streams in the south.
Those who are sowing in tears
    will sing when they reap. ℟.

They go out, they go out, full of tears,
    bearing seed for the sowing;
they come back, they come back with
    a song,
    bearing their sheaves. ℟.

READING II

Philippians 1:4–6, 8–11

Brothers and sisters: I pray always with joy in my every prayer for all of you, because of your partnership for the gospel from the first day until now. I am confident of this, that the one who began a good work in you will continue to complete it until the day of Christ Jesus. God is my witness, how I long for all of you with the affection of Christ Jesus. And this is my prayer: that your love may increase ever more and more in knowledge and every kind of perception, to discern what is of value, so that you may be pure and blameless for the day of Christ, filled with the fruit of righteousness that comes through Jesus Christ for the glory and praise of God.

GOSPEL

Luke 3:1–6

In the fifteenth year of the reign of Tiberius Caesar, when Pontius Pilate was governor of Judea, and Herod was tetrarch of Galilee, and his brother Philip tetrarch of the region of Ituraea and Trachonitis, and Lysanias was tetrarch of Abilene, during the high priesthood of Annas and Caiaphas, the word of God came to John the son of Zechariah in the desert. John went throughout the whole region of the Jordan, proclaiming a baptism of repentance for the forgiveness of sins, as it is written in the book of the words of the prophet Isaiah:

A voice of one crying out in the desert:
"Prepare the way of the Lord,
make straight his paths.
Every valley shall be filled
and every mountain and hill shall be made low.
The winding roads shall be made straight,
and the rough ways made smooth,
and all flesh shall see the salvation of God."

THIRD SUNDAY OF ADVENT / A   1007

READING I

Isaiah 35:1–6a, 10 / 7

The desert and the parched land will
    exult;
  the steppe will rejoice and bloom.
They will bloom with abundant flowers,
  and rejoice with joyful song.
The glory of Lebanon will be given to
  them,
  the splendor of Carmel and Sharon;
they will see the glory of the LORD,
  the splendor of our God.
Strengthen the hands that are feeble,
  make firm the knees that are weak,
say to those whose hearts are frightened:
  Be strong, fear not!
Here is your God,

he comes with vindication;
with divine recompense
  he comes to save you.
Then will the eyes of the blind be
  opened,
  the ears of the deaf be cleared;
then will the lame leap like a stag,
  then the tongue of the mute will sing.

Those whom the LORD has ransomed
  will return
  and enter Zion singing,
  crowned with everlasting joy;
they will meet with joy and gladness,
  sorrow and mourning will flee.

RESPONSORIAL PSALM   *Psalm 146:6c–7, 8–9a, 9bc–10*

Or: Alleluia.

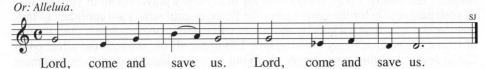

Lord, come and save us. Lord, come and save us.

It is the LORD who preserves fidelity
forever,
who does justice to those who are
oppressed.
It is he who gives bread to the hungry,
the LORD who sets prisoners free. ℟.

The LORD who opens the eyes of the blind,
the LORD who raises up those who
are bowed down.

It is the LORD who loves the just,
the LORD who protects the
stranger. ℟.

The LORD upholds the orphan and
the widow,
but thwarts the path of the wicked.
The LORD will reign forever,
the God of Sion from age to age. ℟.

READING II   *James 5:7–10*

Be patient, brothers and sisters, until the coming of the Lord. See how the farmer waits for the precious fruit of the earth, being patient with it until it receives the early and the late rains. You too must be patient. Make your hearts firm, because the coming of the Lord is at hand. Do not complain, brothers and sisters, about one another, that you may not be judged. Behold, the Judge is standing before the gates. Take as an example of hardship and patience, brothers and sisters, the prophets who spoke in the name of the Lord.

GOSPEL   *Matthew 11:2–11*

When John the Baptist heard in prison of the works of the Christ, he sent his disciples to Jesus with this question, "Are you the one who is to come, or should we look for another?" Jesus said to them in reply, "Go and tell John what you hear and see: the blind regain their sight, the lame walk, lepers are cleansed, the deaf hear, the dead are raised, and the poor have the good news proclaimed to them. And blessed is the one who takes no offense at me."

As they were going off, Jesus began to speak to the crowds about John, "What did you go out to the desert to see? A reed swayed by the wind? Then what did you go out to see? Someone dressed in fine clothing? Those who wear fine clothing are in royal palaces. Then why did you go out? To see a prophet? Yes, I tell you, and more than a prophet. This is the one about whom it is written:

Behold, I am sending my messenger ahead of you;
he will prepare your way before you.

Amen, I say to you, among those born of women there has been none greater than John the Baptist; yet the least in the kingdom of heaven is greater than he."

THIRD SUNDAY OF ADVENT / B — 1008

READING I — *Isaiah 61:1–2a, 10–11 / 8*

The spirit of the Lord GOD is upon me,
  because the LORD has anointed me;
he has sent me to bring glad tidings to
    the poor,
  to heal the brokenhearted,
to proclaim liberty to the captives
  and release to the prisoners,
to announce a year of favor from the LORD
  and a day of vindication by our God.

I rejoice heartily in the LORD,
  in my God is the joy of my soul;
for he has clothed me with a robe of
  salvation
and wrapped me in a mantle of
  justice,
like a bridegroom adorned with a
  diadem,
like a bride bedecked with her
  jewels.
As the earth brings forth its plants,
  and a garden makes its growth
    spring up,
so will the Lord GOD make justice and
  praise
  spring up before all the nations.

RESPONSORIAL PSALM — *Luke 1:46–48, 49–50, 53–54*

RJB

My soul re-joic-es, my soul re-joic-es in my God.

My soul glorifies the Lord,
  my spirit rejoices in God, my savior.
He looks on his servant in her
    nothingness;
  henceforth all ages will call me
    blessed. ℟.

The Almighty works marvels for me.
  Holy his name!

His mercy is from age to age,
  on those who fear him. ℟.

He fills the starving with good things,
  sends the rich away empty.
He protects Israel his servant,
  remembering his mercy. ℟.

READING II — *1 Thessalonians 5:16–24*

Brothers and sisters: Rejoice always. Pray without ceasing. In all circumstances give thanks, for this is the will of God for you in Christ Jesus. Do not quench the Spirit. Do not despise prophetic utterances. Test everything; retain what is good. Refrain from every kind of evil.

  May the God of peace make you perfectly holy and may you entirely, spirit, soul, and body, be preserved blameless for the coming of our Lord Jesus Christ. The one who calls you is faithful, and he will also accomplish it.

GOSPEL — *John 1:6–8, 19–28*

A man named John was sent from God. He came for testimony, to testify to the light, so that all might believe through him. He was not the light, but came to testify to the light.

  And this is the testimony of John. When the Jews from Jerusalem sent priests and Levites to him to ask him, "Who are you?" he admitted and did not deny it, but admitted, "I am not the Christ." So they asked him, "What are you then? Are you

Elijah?" And he said, "I am not." "Are you the Prophet?" He answered, "No." So they said to him, "Who are you, so we can give an answer to those who sent us? What do you have to say for yourself?" He said:

"I am *the voice of one crying out in the desert,*
make straight the way of the Lord,

as Isaiah the prophet said." Some Pharisees were also sent. They asked him, "Why then do you baptize if you are not the Christ or Elijah or the Prophet?" John answered them, "I baptize with water; but there is one among you whom you do not recognize, the one who is coming after me, whose sandal strap I am not worthy to untie." This happened in Bethany across the Jordan, where John was baptizing.

1009   THIRD SUNDAY OF ADVENT / C

READING I   *Zephaniah 3:14–18a / 9*

Shout for joy, O daughter Zion!
Sing joyfully, O Israel!
Be glad and exult with all your heart,
O daughter Jerusalem!
The LORD has removed the judgment
against you
he has turned away your enemies;
the King of Israel, the LORD, is in your
midst,
you have no further misfortune to
fear.

On that day, it shall be said to
Jerusalem:
Fear not, O Zion, be not
discouraged!
The LORD, your God, is in your midst,
a mighty savior;
he will rejoice over you with gladness,
and renew you in his love,
he will sing joyfully because of you,
as one sings at festivals.

RESPONSORIAL PSALM   *Isaiah 12:2–3, 4bcd, 5–6*

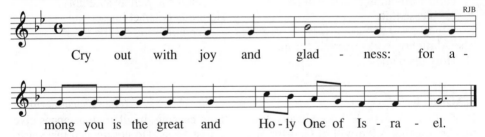

Cry out with joy and glad - ness: for a -
mong you is the great and Ho - ly One of Is - ra - el.

Truly, God is my salvation,
I trust, I shall not fear.
For the Lord is my strength, my song,
he became my savior.
With joy you will draw water
from the wells of salvation. ℟.

Give thanks to the Lord,
give praise to his name!
Make his mighty deeds

known to the peoples!
Declare the greatness of his name.
Sing a psalm to the Lord! ℟.

For he has done glorious deeds,
make them known to all the earth!
People of Zion,
sing and shout for joy
for great in your midst
is the Holy One of Israel. ℟.

READING II   *Philippians 4:4–7*

Brothers and sisters: Rejoice in the Lord always. I shall say it again: rejoice! Your kindness should be known to all. The Lord is near. Have no anxiety at all, but in everything, by prayer and petition, with thanksgiving, make your requests known to God. Then the peace of God that surpasses all understanding will guard your hearts and minds in Christ Jesus.

GOSPEL   *Luke 3:10–18*

The crowds asked John the Baptist, "What should we do?" He said to them in reply, "Whoever has two cloaks should share with the person who has none. And whoever has food should do likewise." Even tax collectors came to be baptized and they said to him, "Teacher, what should we do?" He answered them, "Stop collecting more than what is prescribed." Soldiers also asked him, "And what is it that we should do?" He told them, "Do not practice extortion, do not falsely accuse anyone, and be satisfied with your wages."

Now the people were filled with expectation, and all were asking in their hearts whether John might be the Christ. John answered them all, saying, "I am baptizing you with water, but one mightier than I is coming. I am not worthy to loosen the thongs of his sandals. He will baptize you with the Holy Spirit and fire. His winnowing fan is in his hand to clear his threshing floor and to gather the wheat into his barn, but the chaff he will burn with unquenchable fire." Exhorting them in many other ways, he preached good news to the people.

FOURTH SUNDAY OF ADVENT / A   1010

READING I   *Isaiah 7:10–14 / 10*

The Lord spoke to Ahaz, saying: Ask for a sign from the Lord, your God; let it be deep as the netherworld, or high as the sky! But Ahaz answered, "I will not ask! I will not tempt the Lord!" Then Isaiah said: Listen, O house of David! Is it not enough for you to weary people, must you also weary my God? Therefore the Lord himself will give you this sign: the virgin shall conceive, and bear a son, and shall name him Emmanuel.

RESPONSORIAL PSALM   *Psalm 24:1–2, 3–4ab, 5–6*

Let the Lord en-ter; he is king of glo-ry.

The Lord's is the earth and its fullness,
    the world, and those who dwell in it.
It is he who set it on the seas;
    on the rivers he made it firm. ℟.

Who shall climb the mountain of the
        Lord?
    Who shall stand in his holy place?
The clean of hands and pure of heart,

whose soul is not set on vain
    things. ℟.

Blessings from the Lord shall he receive,
    and right reward from the God who
        saves him.
Such are the people who seek him,
    who seek the face of the God of
        Jacob. ℟.

READING II   *Romans 1:1–7*

Paul, a slave of Christ Jesus, called to be an apostle and set apart for the gospel of God, which he promised previously through his prophets in the holy Scriptures, the gospel about his Son, descended from David according to the flesh, but established as Son of God in power according to the Spirit of holiness through resurrection from the dead, Jesus Christ our Lord. Through him we have received the grace of apostleship, to bring about the obedience of faith, for the sake of his name, among all the Gentiles, among whom are you also, who are called to belong to Jesus Christ; to all the beloved of God in Rome, called to be holy. Grace to you and peace from God our Father and the Lord Jesus Christ.

GOSPEL   *Matthew 1:18–24*

This is how the birth of Jesus Christ came about. When his mother Mary was betrothed to Joseph, but before they lived together, she was found with child through the Holy Spirit. Joseph her husband, since he was a righteous man, yet unwilling to expose her to shame, decided to divorce her quietly. Such was his intention when, behold, the angel of the Lord appeared to him in a dream and said, "Joseph, son of David, do not be afraid to take Mary your wife into your home. For it is through the Holy Spirit that this child has been conceived in her. She will bear a son and you are to name him Jesus, because he will save his people from their sins." All this took place to fulfill what the Lord had said through the prophet:

Behold, the virgin shall conceive and bear a son,
and they shall name him Emmanuel,

which means "God is with us." When Joseph awoke, he did as the angel of the Lord had commanded him and took his wife into his home.

1011   FOURTH SUNDAY OF ADVENT / B

READING I   *2 Samuel 7:1–5, 8b–12, 14a, 16 / 11*

When King David was settled in his palace, and the LORD had given him rest from his enemies on every side, he said to Nathan the prophet, "Here I am living in a house of cedar, while the ark of God dwells in a tent!" Nathan answered the king, "Go, do whatever you have in mind, for the LORD is with you." But that night the LORD spoke to Nathan and said: "Go, tell my servant David, 'Thus says the LORD: Should you build me a house to dwell in?'

"'It was I who took you from the pasture and from the care of the flock to be commander of my people Israel. I have been with you wherever you went, and I have destroyed all your enemies before you. And I will make you famous like the great ones of the earth. I will fix a place for my people Israel; I will plant them so that they may dwell in their place without further disturbance. Neither shall the wicked continue to afflict them as they did of old, since the time I first appointed judges over my people Israel. I will give you rest from all your enemies. The LORD also reveals to you that he will establish a house for you. And when your time comes and you rest with your ancestors, I will raise up your heir after you, sprung from your loins, and I will make his kingdom firm. I will be a father to him, and he shall be a son to me. Your house and your kingdom shall endure forever before me; your throne shall stand firm forever.'"

RESPONSORIAL PSALM *Psalm 89:2–3, 4–5, 27 and 29*

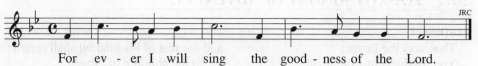

For ev - er I will sing the good - ness of the Lord.

I will sing forever of your mercies,
  O LORD;
  through all ages my mouth will
    proclaim your fidelity.
I have declared your mercy is
    established forever;
  your fidelity stands firm as the
    heavens. ℟.

"With my chosen one I have made a
    covenant;
  I have sworn to David my servant:

I will establish your descendants
    forever,
  and set up your throne through all
    ages." ℟.

"He will call out to me, 'You are my
    father,
  my God, the rock of my salvation.'
I will keep my faithful love for him
    always;
  with him my covenant shall last." ℟.

READING II *Romans 16:25–27*

Brothers and sisters: To him who can strengthen you, according to my gospel and the proclamation of Jesus Christ, according to the revelation of the mystery kept secret for long ages but now manifested through the prophetic writings and, according to the command of the eternal God, made known to all nations to bring about the obedience of faith, to the only wise God, through Jesus Christ be glory forever and ever. Amen.

GOSPEL *Luke 1:26–38*

The angel Gabriel was sent from God to a town of Galilee called Nazareth, to a virgin betrothed to a man named Joseph, of the house of David, and the virgin's name was Mary. And coming to her, he said, "Hail, full of grace! The Lord is with you." But she was greatly troubled at what was said and pondered what sort of greeting this might be. Then the angel said to her, "Do not be afraid, Mary, for you have found favor with God.

"Behold, you will conceive in your womb and bear a son, and you shall name him Jesus. He will be great and will be called Son of the Most High, and the Lord God will give him the throne of David his father, and he will rule over the house of Jacob forever, and of his kingdom there will be no end." But Mary said to the angel, "How can this be, since I have no relations with a man?" And the angel said to her in reply, "The Holy Spirit will come upon you, and the power of the Most High will overshadow you. Therefore the child to be born will be called holy, the Son of God. And behold, Elizabeth, your relative, has also conceived a son in her old age, and this is the sixth month for her who was called barren; for nothing will be impossible for God." Mary said, "Behold, I am the handmaid of the Lord. May it be done to me according to your word." Then the angel departed from her.

1012 FOURTH SUNDAY OF ADVENT / C

READING I   *Micah 5:1–4a / 12*

Thus says the LORD:
You, Bethlehem-Ephrathah
    too small to be among the clans of
        Judah,
from you shall come forth for me
    one who is to be ruler in Israel;
whose origin is from of old,
    from ancient times.
Therefore the Lord will give them up,
    until the time
    when she who is to give birth has
        borne,

and the rest of his kindred shall return
    to the children of Israel.
He shall stand firm and shepherd his
        flock
    by the strength of the LORD,
    in the majestic name of the LORD,
        his God;
and they shall remain, for now his
        greatness
    shall reach to the ends of the earth;
he shall be peace.

RESPONSORIAL PSALM   *Psalm 80:2ac and 3b, 15–16, 18–19*

HH, adapt.

Lord, make us turn to you; let us see your face and we shall be saved.

O shepherd of Israel, hear us,
    enthroned on the cherubim, shine
        forth.
    Rouse up your might and come to
        save us. ℟.

God of hosts, turn again, we implore;
    look down from heaven and see.
Visit this vine and protect it,
    the vine your right hand has planted,
    the son of man you have claimed
        for yourself. ℟.

May your hand be on the man at your
    right hand,
    the son of man you have confirmed
    as your own.
And we shall never forsake you again;
    give us life that we may call upon
    your name. ℟.

READING II   *Hebrews 10:5–10*

Brothers and sisters: When Christ came into the world, he said:
    "Sacrifice and offering you did not desire,
        but a body you prepared for me;
    in holocausts and sin offerings you took no delight.
    Then I said, 'As is written of me in the scroll,
    behold, I come to do your will, O God.'"

First he says, "Sacrifices and offerings, holocausts and sin offerings, you neither desired nor delighted in." These are offered according to the law. Then he says, "Behold, I come to do your will." He takes away the first to establish the second. By this "will," we have been consecrated through the offering of the body of Jesus Christ once for all.

GOSPEL *Luke 1:39–45*

Mary set out and traveled to the hill country in haste to a town of Judah, where she entered the house of Zechariah and greeted Elizabeth. When Elizabeth heard Mary's greeting, the infant leaped in her womb, and Elizabeth, filled with the Holy Spirit, cried out in a loud voice and said, "Blessed are you among women, and blessed is the fruit of your womb. And how does this happen to me, that the mother of my Lord should come to me? For at the moment the sound of your greeting reached my ears, the infant in my womb leaped for joy. Blessed are you who believed that what was spoken to you by the Lord would be fulfilled."

DECEMBER 25: CHRISTMAS—VIGIL MASS / ABC 1013

READING I *Isaiah 62:1–5 / 13*

For Zion's sake I will not be silent,
    for Jerusalem's sake I will not be
      quiet,
until her vindication shines forth like
    the dawn
    and her victory like a burning torch.

Nations shall behold your vindication,
    and all the kings your glory;
you shall be called by a new name
    pronounced by the mouth of the
    LORD.
You shall be a glorious crown in the

hand of the LORD,
    a royal diadem held by your God.
No more shall people call you
    "Forsaken,"
    or your land "Desolate,"
but you shall be called "My Delight,"
    and your land "Espoused."
For the LORD delights in you
    and makes your land his spouse.
As a young man marries a virgin,
    your Builder shall marry you;
and as a bridegroom rejoices in his bride
    so shall your God rejoice in you.

RESPONSORIAL PSALM *Psalm 89:4–5, 16–17, 27 and 29*

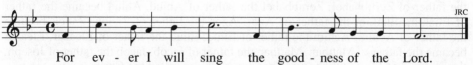

For ev-er I will sing the good-ness of the Lord.

"With my chosen one I have made a
    covenant;
    I have sworn to David my servant:
I will establish your descendants forever,
    and set up your throne through all
      ages." ℟.

How blessed the people who know your

praise,
    who walk, O LORD, in the light of
    your face,
who find their joy every day in your
    name,
who make your justice their joyful
    acclaim. ℟.

"He will call out to me, 'You are my father,   always;
   my God, the rock of my salvation.'   with him my covenant shall last." ℟.
I will keep my faithful love for him

READING II   *Acts 13:16–17, 22–25*

When Paul reached Antioch in Pisidia and entered the synagogue, he stood up, motioned with his hand, and said, "Fellow Israelites and you others who are God-fearing, listen. The God of this people Israel chose our ancestors and exalted the people during their sojourn in the land of Egypt. With uplifted arm he led them out of it. Then he removed Saul and raised up David as king; of him he testified, 'I have found David, son of Jesse, a man after my own heart; he will carry out my every wish.' From this man's descendants God, according to his promise, has brought to Israel a savior, Jesus. John heralded his coming by proclaiming a baptism of repentance to all the people of Israel; and as John was completing his course, he would say, 'What do you suppose that I am? I am not he. Behold, one is coming after me; I am not worthy to unfasten the sandals of his feet.'"

GOSPEL   *Matthew 1:1–25 or 1:18–25*
For short form read only the part in brackets.

The book of the genealogy of Jesus Christ, the son of David, the son of Abraham.

Abraham became the father of Isaac, Isaac the father of Jacob, Jacob the father of Judah and his brothers. Judah became the father of Perez and Zerah, whose mother was Tamar. Perez became the father of Hezron, Hezron the father of Ram, Ram the father of Amminadab. Amminadab became the father of Nahshon, Nahshon the father of Salmon, Salmon the father of Boaz, whose mother was Rahab. Boaz became the father of Obed, whose mother was Ruth. Obed became the father of Jesse, Jesse the father of David the king.

David became the father of Solomon, whose mother had been the wife of Uriah. Solomon became the father of Rehoboam, Rehoboam the father of Abijah, Abijah the father of Asaph. Asaph became the father of Jehoshaphat, Jehoshaphat the father of Joram, Joram the father of Uzziah. Uzziah became the father of Jotham, Jotham the father of Ahaz, Ahaz the father of Hezekiah. Hezekiah became the father of Manasseh, Manasseh the father of Amos, Amos the father of Josiah. Josiah became the father of Jechoniah and his brothers at the time of the Babylonian exile.

After the Babylonian exile, Jechoniah became the father of Shealtiel, Shealtiel the father of Zerubbabel, Zerubbabel the father of Abiud. Abiud became the father of Eliakim, Eliakim the father of Azor, Azor the father of Zadok. Zadok became the father of Achim, Achim the father of Eliud, Eliud the father of Eleazar. Eleazar became the father of Matthan, Matthan the father of Jacob, Jacob the father of Joseph, the husband of Mary. Of her was born Jesus who is called the Christ.

Thus the total number of generations from Abraham to David is fourteen generations; from David to the Babylonian exile, fourteen generations; from the Babylonian exile to the Christ, fourteen generations.

Now [this is how the birth of Jesus Christ came about. When his mother Mary was betrothed to Joseph, but before they lived together, she was found with child through the Holy Spirit. Joseph her husband, since he was a righteous man, yet unwilling to expose her to shame, decided to divorce her quietly. Such was his intention when, behold, the angel of the Lord appeared to him in a dream and said, "Joseph, son of David, do not be afraid to take Mary your wife into your home. For it is through the

Holy Spirit that this child has been conceived in her. She will bear a son and you are to name him Jesus, because he will save his people from their sins." All this took place to fulfill what the Lord had said through the prophet:

Behold, the virgin shall conceive and bear a son,
and they shall name him Emmanuel,

which means "God is with us." When Joseph awoke, he did as the angel of the Lord had commanded him and took his wife into his home. He had no relations with her until she bore a son, and he named him Jesus.]

DEC. 25: CHRISTMAS—MASS DURING THE NIGHT / ABC   1014

READING I   *Isaiah 9:1–6 / 14*

The people who walked in darkness
   have seen a great light;
   upon those who dwelt in the land of
      gloom
   a light has shone.
You have brought them abundant joy
   and great rejoicing,
   as they rejoice before you as at the
      harvest,
   as people make merry when
      dividing spoils.
For the yoke that burdened them,
   the pole on their shoulder,
and the rod of their taskmaster
   you have smashed, as on the day of
      Midian.
For every boot that tramped in battle,

every cloak rolled in blood,
   will be burned as fuel for flames.
For a child is born to us, a son is given
   us;
   upon his shoulder dominion rests
They name him Wonder-Counselor,
   God-Hero,
   Father-Forever, Prince of Peace.
His dominion is vast
   and forever peaceful,
from David's throne, and over his
   kingdom,
   which he confirms and sustains
by judgment and justice,
   both now and forever.
The zeal of the LORD of hosts will do
   this!

RESPONSORIAL PSALM   *Psalm 96:1–2a, 2b–3, 11–12, 13*

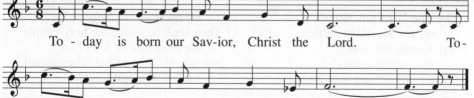

To-day is born our Sav-ior, Christ the Lord. Today is born our Sav-ior, Christ the Lord.

O sing a new song to the LORD;
   sing to the LORD, all the earth.
   O sing to the LORD; bless his name. ℟.

Proclaim his salvation day by day.
   Tell among the nations his glory,
   and his wonders among all the
      peoples. ℟.

Let the heavens rejoice and earth be
   glad;
   let the sea and all within it thunder
      praise.
Let the land and all it bears rejoice.
Then will all the trees of the wood
   shout for joy. ℟.

At the presence of the LORD, for he comes,
    he comes to judge the earth.
He will judge the world with justice;

he will govern the peoples with his
    truth. ℟.

READING II *Titus 2:11–14*

Beloved: The grace of God has appeared, saving all and training us to reject godless ways and worldly desires and to live temperately, justly, and devoutly in this age, as we await the blessed hope, the appearance of the glory of our great God and savior Jesus Christ, who gave himself for us to deliver us from all lawlessness and to cleanse for himself a people as his own, eager to do what is good.

GOSPEL *Luke 2:1–14*

In those days a decree went out from Caesar Augustus that the whole world should be enrolled. This was the first enrollment, when Quirinius was governor of Syria. So all went to be enrolled, each to his own town. And Joseph too went up from Galilee from the town of Nazareth to Judea, to the city of David that is called Bethlehem, because he was of the house and family of David, to be enrolled with Mary, his betrothed, who was with child. While they were there, the time came for her to have her child, and she gave birth to her firstborn son. She wrapped him in swaddling clothes and laid him in a manger, because there was no room for them in the inn.

Now there were shepherds in that region living in the fields and keeping the night watch over their flock. The angel of the Lord appeared to them and the glory of the Lord shone around them, and they were struck with great fear. The angel said to them, "Do not be afraid; for behold, I proclaim to you good news of great joy that will be for all the people. For today in the city of David a savior has been born for you who is Christ and Lord. And this will be a sign for you: you will find an infant wrapped in swaddling clothes and lying in a manger." And suddenly there was a multitude of the heavenly host with the angel, praising God and saying:

    "Glory to God in the highest
        and on earth peace to those on whom his favor rests."

1015   DEC. 25: CHRISTMAS—MASS AT DAWN / ABC

READING I *Isaiah 62:11–12 / 15*

See, the LORD proclaims
    to the ends of the earth:
say to daughter Zion,
    your savior comes!
Here is his reward with him,

his recompense before him.
They shall be called the holy people,
    the redeemed of the LORD,
and you shall be called "Frequented,"
    a city that is not forsaken.

RESPONSORIAL PSALM *Psalm 97:1 and 6, 11–12*

JRC

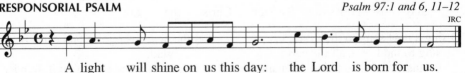

A light will shine on us this day: the Lord is born for us.

The LORD is king, let earth rejoice;
    let the many islands be glad.
The skies proclaim his justice;
    all peoples see his glory. ℟.

Light shines forth for the just one,
    and joy for the upright of heart.
Rejoice in the LORD, you just;
    to the memory of his holiness give
        thanks. ℟.

READING II
Titus 3:4–7

Beloved:

When the kindness and generous love
of God our savior appeared,
not because of any righteous deeds
we had done
but because of his mercy,
he saved us through the bath of
rebirth

and renewal by the Holy Spirit,
whom he richly poured out on us
through Jesus Christ our savior,
so that we might be justified by his
grace
and become heirs in hope of
eternal life.

GOSPEL
Luke 2:15–20

When the angels went away from them to heaven, the shepherds said to one another, "Let us go, then, to Bethlehem to see this thing that has taken place, which the Lord has made known to us." So they went in haste and found Mary and Joseph, and the infant lying in the manger. When they saw this, they made known the message that had been told them about this child. All who heard it were amazed by what had been told them by the shepherds. And Mary kept all these things, reflecting on them in her heart. Then the shepherds returned, glorifying and praising God for all they had heard and seen, just as it had been told to them.

DEC. 25: CHRISTMAS—MASS DURING THE DAY / ABC   1016

READING I
Isaiah 52:7–10 / 16

How beautiful upon the mountains
are the feet of him who brings
glad tidings,
announcing peace, bearing good news,
announcing salvation, and saying
to Zion,
"Your God is King!"

Hark! Your sentinels raise a cry,
together they shout for joy,

for they see directly, before their eyes,
the Lord restoring Zion.
Break out together in song,
O ruins of Jerusalem!
For the Lord comforts his people,
he redeems Jerusalem.
The Lord has bared his holy arm
in the sight of all the nations;
all the ends of the earth will behold
the salvation of our God.

RESPONSORIAL PSALM
Psalm 98:1, 2–3ab, 3cd–4, 5–6

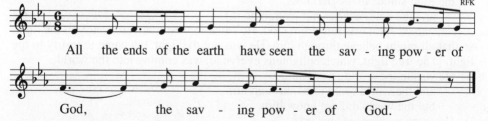

All the ends of the earth have seen the sav - ing pow - er of God, the sav - ing pow - er of God.

O sing a new song to the Lord,
for he has worked wonders.
His right hand and his holy arm
have brought salvation. ℟.

The Lord has made known his
salvation,
has shown his deliverance to the
nations.
He has remembered his merciful love
and his truth for the house of
Israel. ℟.

All the ends of the earth have seen
the salvation of our God.
Shout to the LORD, all the earth;
break forth into joyous song,
and sing out your praise. ℟.

Sing psalms to the LORD with the harp,
with the harp and the sound of song.
With trumpets and the sound of the
horn,
raise a shout before the King,
the LORD. ℟.

READING II
Hebrews 1:1–6

Brothers and sisters: In times past, God spoke in partial and various ways to our ancestors through the prophets; in these last days, he has spoken to us through the Son, whom he made heir of all things and through whom he created the universe,
who is the refulgence of his glory, the very imprint of his being,
and who sustains all things by his mighty word.
When he had accomplished purification from sins,
he took his seat at the right hand of the Majesty on high,
as far superior to the angels
as the name he has inherited is more excellent than theirs.

For to which of the angels did God ever say:
You are my son; this day I have begotten you?
Or again:
I will be a father to him, and he shall be a son to me?
And again, when he leads the firstborn into the world, he says:
Let all the angels of God worship him.

GOSPEL
John 1:1–18 or 1:1–5, 9–14

For short form read only the parts in brackets.

[In the beginning was the Word,
and the Word was with God,
and the Word was God.
He was in the beginning with God.
All things came to be through him,
and without him nothing came to be.
What came to be through him was life,
and this life was the light of the human race;
the light shines in the darkness,
and the darkness has not overcome it.]
A man named John was sent from God. He came for testimony, to testify to the light, so that all might believe through him. He was not the light, but came to testify to the light. [The true light, which enlightens everyone, was coming into the world.
He was in the world,
and the world came to be through him,
but the world did not know him.
He came to what was his own,
but his own people did not accept him.

But to those who did accept him he gave power to become children of God, to those who believe in his name, who were born not by natural generation nor by human choice nor by a man's decision but of God.

And the Word became flesh
    and made his dwelling among us,
    and we saw his glory,
    the glory as of the Father's only Son,
    full of grace and truth.]
John testified to him and cried out, saying, "This was he of whom I said, 'The one who is coming after me ranks ahead of me because he existed before me.'" From his fullness we have all received, grace in place of grace, because while the law was given through Moses, grace and truth came through Jesus Christ. No one has ever seen God. The only Son, God, who is at the Father's side, has revealed him.

HOLY FAMILY OF JESUS, MARY AND JOSEPH / ABC   1017

READING I   *Sirach 3:2–6, 12–14 / 17*

God sets a father in honor over his
    children;
    a mother's authority he confirms
    over her sons.
Whoever honors his father atones
    for sins,
    and preserves himself from them.
When he prays, he is heard;
    he stores up riches who reveres
    his mother.
Whoever honors his father is
    gladdened by children,
    and, when he prays, is heard.
Whoever reveres his father will live a
long life;
    he who obeys his father brings
    comfort to his mother.

My son, take care of your father when
    he is old;
    grieve him not as long as he lives.
Even if his mind fail, be considerate of
    him;
    revile him not all the days of his life;
kindness to a father will not be forgotten,
    firmly planted against the debt of
    your sins
    —a house raised in justice to you.

RESPONSORIAL PSALM   *Psalm 128:1–2, 3, 4–5*

O bless-ed are those who fear the Lord and walk in his ways.

Blessed are all who fear the LORD,
    and walk in his ways!
By the labor of your hands you shall eat.
    You will be blessed and prosper. ℟.

Your wife like a fruitful vine
    in the heart of your house;
your children like shoots of the olive
    around your table. ℟.

Indeed thus shall be blessed
    the man who fears the LORD.
May the LORD bless you from Sion.
May you see Jerusalem prosper
    all the days of your life! ℟.

READING II   *Colossians 3:12–21 or 3:12–17*

For short form read only the part in brackets.

[Brothers and sisters: Put on, as God's chosen ones, holy and beloved, heartfelt compassion, kindness, humility, gentleness, and patience, bearing with one another and forgiving one another, if one has a grievance against another; as the Lord has forgiven you, so must you also do. And over all these put on love, that is, the bond of perfection. And let the peace of Christ control your hearts, the peace into which you were also called in one body. And be thankful. Let the word of Christ dwell in you richly, as in all wisdom you teach and admonish one another, singing psalms, hymns, and spiritual songs with gratitude in your hearts to God. And whatever you do, in word or in deed, do everything in the name of the Lord Jesus, giving thanks to God the Father through him.]

Wives, be subordinate to your husbands, as is proper in the Lord. Husbands, love your wives, and avoid any bitterness toward them. Children, obey your parents in everything, for this is pleasing to the Lord. Fathers, do not provoke your children, so they may not become discouraged.

GOSPEL / A   *Matthew 2:13–15, 19–23*

When the magi had departed, behold, the angel of the Lord appeared to Joseph in a dream and said, "Rise, take the child and his mother, flee to Egypt, and stay there until I tell you. Herod is going to search for the child to destroy him." Joseph rose and took the child and his mother by night and departed for Egypt. He stayed there until the death of Herod, that what the Lord had said through the prophet might be fulfilled, *Out of Egypt I called my son.*

When Herod had died, behold, the angel of the Lord appeared in a dream to Joseph in Egypt and said, "Rise, take the child and his mother and go to the land of Israel, for those who sought the child's life are dead." He rose, took the child and his mother, and went to the land of Israel. But when he heard that Archelaus was ruling over Judea in place of his father Herod, he was afraid to go back there. And because he had been warned in a dream, he departed for the region of Galilee. He went and dwelt in a town called Nazareth, so that what had been spoken through the prophets might be fulfilled, *He shall be called a Nazorean.*

GOSPEL / B   *Luke 2:22–40 or 2:22, 39–40*

For short form read only the parts in brackets.

[When the days were completed for their purification according to the law of Moses, they took him up to Jerusalem to present him to the Lord,] just as it is written in the law of the Lord, *Every male that opens the womb shall be consecrated to the Lord,* and to offer the sacrifice of *a pair of turtledoves or two young pigeons,* in accordance with the dictate in the law of the Lord.

Now there was a man in Jerusalem whose name was Simeon. This man was righteous and devout, awaiting the consolation of Israel, and the Holy Spirit was upon him. It had been revealed to him by the Holy Spirit that he should not see death before he had seen the Christ of the Lord. He came in the Spirit into the temple; and when the parents brought in the child Jesus to perform the custom of the law in regard to him, he took him into his arms and blessed God, saying:

"Now, Master, you may let your servant go

in peace, according to your word,
for my eyes have seen your salvation,
    which you prepared in sight of all the peoples,
a light for revelation to the Gentiles,
    and glory for your people Israel."

The child's father and mother were amazed at what was said about him; and Simeon blessed them and said to Mary his mother, "Behold, this child is destined for the fall and rise of many in Israel, and to be a sign that will be contradicted—and you yourself a sword will pierce—so that the thoughts of many hearts may be revealed." There was also a prophetess, Anna, the daughter of Phanuel, of the tribe of Asher. She was advanced in years, having lived seven years with her husband after her marriage, and then as a widow until she was eighty-four. She never left the temple, but worshiped night and day with fasting and prayer. And coming forward at that very time, she gave thanks to God and spoke about the child to all who were awaiting the redemption of Jerusalem.

[When they had fulfilled all the prescriptions of the law of the Lord, they returned to Galilee, to their own town of Nazareth. The child grew and became strong, filled with wisdom; and the favor of God was upon him.]

GOSPEL / C   *Luke 2:41–52*

Each year Jesus' parents went to Jerusalem for the feast of Passover, and when he was twelve years old, they went up according to festival custom. After they had completed its days, as they were returning, the boy Jesus remained behind in Jerusalem, but his parents did not know it. Thinking that he was in the caravan, they journeyed for a day and looked for him among their relatives and acquaintances, but not finding him, they returned to Jerusalem to look for him. After three days they found him in the temple, sitting in the midst of the teachers, listening to them and asking them questions, and all who heard him were astounded at his understanding and his answers. When his parents saw him, they were astonished, and his mother said to him, "Son, why have you done this to us? Your father and I have been looking for you with great anxiety." And he said to them, "Why were you looking for me? Did you not know that I must be in my Father's house?" But they did not understand what he said to them. He went down with them and came to Nazareth, and was obedient to them; and his mother kept all these things in her heart. And Jesus advanced in wisdom and age and favor before God and man.

IN YEAR B, THESE READINGS MAY BE USED   1018

READING I   *Genesis 15:1–6; 21:1–3*

The word of the LORD came to Abram in a vision, saying:
    "Fear not, Abram!
        I am your shield;
        I will make your reward very great."
But Abram said, "O Lord GOD, what good will your gifts be, if I keep on being child-less and have as my heir the steward of my house, Eliezer?" Abram continued, "See, you have given me no offspring, and so one of my servants will be my heir." Then the word of the LORD came to him: "No, that one shall not be your heir; your own issue shall be your heir." The Lord took Abram outside and said, "Look up at the sky and

count the stars, if you can. Just so," he added, "shall your descendants be." Abram put his faith in the LORD, who credited it to him as an act of righteousness.

The LORD took note of Sarah as he had said he would; he did for her as he had promised. Sarah became pregnant and bore Abraham a son in his old age, at the set time that God had stated. Abraham gave the name Isaac to this son of his whom Sarah bore him.

RESPONSORIAL PSALM *Psalm 105:1–2, 3–4, 6–7, 8–9*

The Lord re-mem-bers his cov-e-nant for ev - er.

Give thanks to the LORD; proclaim his
    name.
  Make known his deeds among the
    peoples.
O sing to him, sing his praise;
  tell all his wonderful works! ℟.

Glory in his holy name;
  let the hearts that seek the LORD
    rejoice.
Turn to the LORD and his strength;
  constantly seek his face. ℟.

O children of Abraham, his servant,
  O descendants of the Jacob he chose,
he, the LORD, is our God;
  his judgments are in all the earth. ℟.

He remembers his covenant forever:
  the promise he ordained for a
    thousand generations,
the covenant he made with Abraham,
  the oath he swore to Isaac. ℟.

READING II *Hebrews 11:8, 11–12, 17–19*

Brothers and sisters: By faith Abraham obeyed when he was called to go out to a place that he was to receive as an inheritance; he went out, not knowing where he was to go. By faith he received power to generate, even though he was past the normal age—and Sarah herself was sterile—for he thought that the one who had made the promise was trustworthy. So it was that there came forth from one man, himself as good as dead, descendants as numerous as the stars in the sky and as countless as the sands on the seashore.

By faith Abraham, when put to the test, offered up Isaac, and he who had received the promises was ready to offer his only son, of whom it was said, "Through Isaac descendants shall bear your name." He reasoned that God was able to raise even from the dead, and he received Isaac back as a symbol.

1019 IN YEAR C, THESE READINGS MAY BE USED

READING I *1 Samuel 1:20–22, 24–28*

In those days Hannah conceived, and at the end of her term bore a son whom she called Samuel, since she had asked the LORD for him. The next time her husband Elkanah was going up with the rest of his household to offer the customary sacrifice to the LORD and to fulfill his vows, Hannah did not go, explaining to her husband, "Once the child is weaned, I will take him to appear before the LORD and to remain there forever; I will offer him as a perpetual nazirite."

Once Samuel was weaned, Hannah brought him up with her, along with a three-year-old bull, an ephah of flour, and a skin of wine, and presented him at the temple of the Lord in Shiloh. After the boy's father had sacrificed the young bull, Hannah, his mother, approached Eli and said: "Pardon, my lord! As you live, my lord, I am the woman who stood near you here, praying to the Lord. I prayed for this child, and the Lord granted my request. Now I, in turn, give him to the Lord; as long as he lives, he shall be dedicated to the Lord." Hannah left Samuel there.

RESPONSORIAL PSALM   *Psalm 84:2–3, 5–6, 9–10*

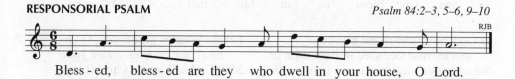

Bless - ed,   bless - ed are they   who dwell in your house, O Lord.

How lovely is your dwelling place,
  O Lord of hosts.
My soul is longing and yearning
  for the courts of the Lord.
My heart and my flesh cry out
  to the living God. ℟.

Blessed are they who dwell in your house,
  forever singing your praise.

Blessed the people whose strength is in
  you,
  whose heart is set on pilgrim
  ways. ℟.

O Lord God of hosts, hear my prayer;
  give ear, O God of Jacob.
Turn your eyes, O God, our shield;
  look on the face of your anointed. ℟.

READING II   *1 John 3:1–2, 21–24*

Beloved: See what love the Father has bestowed on us that we may be called the children of God. And so we are. The reason the world does not know us is that it did not know him. Beloved, we are God's children now; what we shall be has not yet been revealed. We do know that when it is revealed we shall be like him, for we shall see him as he is.

Beloved, if our hearts do not condemn us, we have confidence in God and receive from him whatever we ask, because we keep his commandments and do what pleases him. And his commandment is this: we should believe in the name of his Son, Jesus Christ, and love one another just as he commanded us. Those who keep his commandments remain in him, and he in them, and the way we know that he remains in us is from the Spirit he gave us.

JAN. 1: SOLEMNITY OF MARY, HOLY MOTHER OF GOD / ABC 1020

READING I   *Numbers 6:22–27 / 18*

The Lord said to Moses: "Speak to Aaron and his sons and tell them: This is how you shall bless the Israelites. Say to them:
  The Lord bless you and keep you!
  The Lord let his face shine upon you, and be gracious to you!
  The Lord look upon you kindly and give you peace!
So shall they invoke my name upon the Israelites, and I will bless them."

RESPONSORIAL PSALM *Psalm 67:2–3, 5, 6 and 8*

May God bless us in his mer - cy,
may God bless us in his mer - cy.

O God, be gracious and bless us
and let your face shed its light upon us.
So will your ways be known upon earth
and all nations learn your salvation. ℟.

Let the nations be glad and shout for joy,
with uprightness you rule the
peoples;
you guide the nations on earth. ℟.

Let the peoples praise you, O God;
let all the peoples praise you.
May God still give us his blessing
that all the ends of the earth may
revere him. ℟.

READING II *Galatians 4:4–7*
Brothers and sisters: When the fullness of time had come, God sent his Son, born of a woman, born under the law, to ransom those under the law, so that we might receive adoption as sons. As proof that you are sons, God sent the Spirit of his Son into our hearts, crying out, "Abba, Father!" So you are no longer a slave but a son, and if a son then also an heir, through God.

GOSPEL *Luke 2:16–21*
The shepherds went in haste to Bethlehem and found Mary and Joseph, and the infant lying in the manger. When they saw this, they made known the message that had been told them about this child. All who heard it were amazed by what had been told them by the shepherds. And Mary kept all these things, reflecting on them in her heart. Then the shepherds returned, glorifying and praising God for all they had heard and seen, just as it had been told to them.

When eight days were completed for his circumcision, he was named Jesus, the name given him by the angel before he was conceived in the womb.

1021 EPIPHANY OF THE LORD / ABC

READING I *Isaiah 60:1–6 / 20*
Rise up in splendor, Jerusalem! Your
light has come,
the glory of the Lord shines upon
you.
See, darkness covers the earth,
and thick clouds cover the peoples;

but upon you the LORD shines,
and over you appears his glory.
Nations shall walk by your light,
and kings by your shining radiance.
Raise your eyes and look about;
they all gather and come to you:

your sons come from afar,
and your daughters in the arms of
their nurses.

Then you shall be radiant at what
you see,
your heart shall throb and overflow,
for the riches of the sea shall be
emptied out before you,

the wealth of nations shall be
brought to you.
Caravans of camels shall fill you,
dromedaries from Midian and Ephah;
all from Sheba shall come
bearing gold and frankincense,
and proclaiming the praises of the
LORD.

RESPONSORIAL PSALM   *Psalm 72:1–2, 7–8, 10–11, 12–13*

Lord, ev - 'ry na - tion on earth will a - dore you.

O God, give your judgment to the king,
to a king's son your justice,
that he may judge your people in justice,
and your poor in right judgment. ℟.

In his days shall justice flourish,
and great peace till the moon is no
more.
He shall rule from sea to sea,
from the River to the bounds of the
earth. ℟.

The kings of Tarshish and the islands
shall pay him tribute.
The kings of Sheba and Seba
shall bring him gifts.
Before him all kings shall fall prostrate,
all nations shall serve him. ℟.

For he shall save the needy when they
cry,
the poor, and those who are helpless.
He will have pity on the weak and the
needy,
and save the lives of the needy. ℟.

READING II   *Ephesians 3:2–3a, 5–6*

Brothers and sisters: You have heard of the stewardship of God's grace that was given
to me for your benefit, namely, that the mystery was made known to me by revelation.
It was not made known to people in other generations as it has now been revealed
to his holy apostles and prophets by the Spirit: that the Gentiles are coheirs, members
of the same body, and copartners in the promise in Christ Jesus through the gospel.

GOSPEL   *Matthew 2:1–12*

When Jesus was born in Bethlehem of Judea, in the days of King Herod, behold, magi
from the east arrived in Jerusalem, saying, "Where is the newborn king of the Jews?
We saw his star at its rising and have come to do him homage." When King Herod
heard this, he was greatly troubled, and all Jerusalem with him. Assembling all the
chief priests and the scribes of the people, he inquired of them where the Christ was
to be born. They said to him, "In Bethlehem of Judea, for thus it has been written
through the prophet:

And you, Bethlehem, land of Judah,
are by no means least among the rulers of Judah;
since from you shall come a ruler,
who is to shepherd my people Israel."

Then Herod called the magi secretly and ascertained from them the time of the star's appearance. He sent them to Bethlehem and said, "Go and search diligently for the child. When you have found him, bring me word, that I too may go and do him homage." After their audience with the king they set out. And behold, the star that they had seen at its rising preceded them, until it came and stopped over the place where the child was. They were overjoyed at seeing the star, and on entering the house they saw the child with Mary his mother. They prostrated themselves and did him homage. Then they opened their treasures and offered him gifts of gold, frankincense, and myrrh. And having been warned in a dream not to return to Herod, they departed for their country by another way.

1022 BAPTISM OF THE LORD / ABC

READING I   *Isaiah 42:1–4, 6–7 / 21*

Thus says the LORD:
Here is my servant whom I uphold,
   my chosen one with whom I am
      pleased,
upon whom I have put my spirit;
   he shall bring forth justice to the
      nations,
not crying out, not shouting,
   not making his voice heard in the
      street.
A bruised reed he shall not break,
   and a smoldering wick he shall not
      quench,
until he establishes justice on the earth;

the coastlands will wait for his
   teaching.

I, the LORD, have called you for the
   victory of justice,
I have grasped you by the hand;
I formed you, and set you
   as a covenant of the people,
   a light for the nations,
to open the eyes of the blind,
   to bring out prisoners from
      confinement,
   and from the dungeon, those who
      live in darkness.

RESPONSORIAL PSALM   *Psalm 29:1a and 2, 3ac–4, 3b and 9b–10*

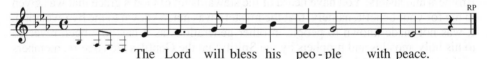

The Lord will bless his peo-ple with peace.

Ascribe to the LORD, you heavenly powers,
   ascribe to the LORD glory and strength.
Ascribe to the LORD the glory of his name;
   bow down before the LORD, majestic
      in holiness. ℟.

The voice of the LORD upon the waters,
   the LORD on the immensity of waters;
the voice of the LORD full of power;

the voice of the LORD full of
   splendor. ℟.

The God of glory thunders;
   in his temple they all cry, "Glory!"
The LORD sat enthroned above the
   flood;
   the LORD sits as king forever. ℟.

READING II   *Acts 10:34–38*

Peter proceeded to speak to those gathered in the house of Cornelius, saying: "In truth, I see that God shows no partiality. Rather, in every nation whoever fears him and acts uprightly is acceptable to him. You know the word that he sent to the Israelites as he proclaimed peace through Jesus Christ, who is Lord of all, what has happened all over Judea, beginning in Galilee after the baptism that John preached, how God anointed Jesus of Nazareth with the Holy Spirit and power. He went about doing good and healing all those oppressed by the devil, for God was with him."

GOSPEL / A
Matthew 3:13–17

Jesus came from Galilee to John at the Jordan to be baptized by him. John tried to prevent him, saying, "I need to be baptized by you, and yet you are coming to me?" Jesus said to him in reply, "Allow it now, for thus it is fitting for us to fulfill all righteousness." Then he allowed him. After Jesus was baptized, he came up from the water and behold, the heavens were opened for him, and he saw the Spirit of God descending like a dove and coming upon him. And a voice came from the heavens, saying, "This is my beloved Son, with whom I am well pleased."

GOSPEL / B
Mark 1:7–11

This is what he proclaimed:

"One mightier than I is coming after me. I am not worthy to stoop and loosen the thongs of his sandals. I have baptized you with water; he will baptize you with the Holy Spirit."

It happened in those days that Jesus came from Nazareth of Galilee and was baptized in the Jordan by John. On coming up out of the water he saw the heavens being torn open and the Spirit, like a dove, descending upon him. And a voice came from the heavens, "You are my beloved Son; with you I am well pleased."

GOSPEL / C
Luke 3:15–16, 21–22

The people were filled with expectation, and all were asking in their hearts whether John might be the Christ. John answered them all, saying, "I am baptizing you with water, but one mightier than I is coming. I am not worthy to loosen the thongs of his sandals. He will baptize you with the Holy Spirit and fire."

After all the people had been baptized and Jesus also had been baptized and was praying, heaven was opened and the Holy Spirit descended upon him in bodily form like a dove. And a voice came from heaven, "You are my beloved Son; with you I am well pleased."

IN YEAR B, THESE READINGS MAY BE USED   1023

READING I
Isaiah 55:1–11

Thus says the LORD:
All you who are thirsty,
  come to the water!
You who have no money,
  come, receive grain and eat;
come, without paying and without cost,
  drink wine and milk!
Why spend your money for what is
  not bread,

your wages for what fails to satisfy?
Heed me, and you shall eat well,
  you shall delight in rich fare.
Come to me heedfully,
  listen, that you may have life.
I will renew with you the everlasting
  covenant,
  the benefits assured to David.

As I made him a witness to the peoples,
    a leader and commander of nations,
so shall you summon a nation you
    knew not,
        and nations that knew you not
        shall run to you,
because of the LORD, your God
        the Holy One of Israel, who has
        glorified you.

Seek the LORD while he may be found,
    call him while he is near.
Let the scoundrel forsake his way,
    and the wicked man his thoughts;
let him turn to the LORD for mercy;
    to our God, who is generous in
        forgiving.
For my thoughts are not your thoughts,
    nor are your ways my ways, says
        the LORD.

As high as the heavens are above the
    earth
so high are my ways above your
    ways
and my thoughts above your
    thoughts.

For just as from the heavens
    the rain and snow come down
and do not return there
    till they have watered the earth,
    making it fertile and fruitful,
giving seed to the one who sows
    and bread to the one who eats,
so shall my word be
    that goes forth from my mouth;
my word shall not return to me void,
    but shall do my will,
    achieving the end for which I sent it.

RESPONSORIAL PSALM

Isaiah 12:2–3, 4bcd, 5–6

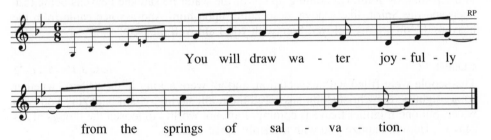

You will draw wa - ter joy - ful - ly from the springs of sal - va - tion.

Truly, God is my salvation,
    I trust, I shall not fear.
For the Lord is my strength, my song,
    he became my savior.
With joy you will draw water
    from the wells of salvation. ℟.

Give thanks to the Lord,
    give praise to his name!
Make his mighty deeds

known to the peoples!
Declare the greatness of his name.
    Sing a psalm to the Lord! ℟.

For he has done glorious deeds,
    make them known to all the earth!
People of Zion,
    sing and shout for joy
for great in your midst
    is the Holy One of Israel. ℟.

READING II

1 John 5:1–9

Beloved: Everyone who believes that Jesus is the Christ is begotten by God, and everyone who loves the Father loves also the one begotten by him. In this way we know
that we love the children of God when we love God and obey his commandments. For
the love of God is this, that we keep his commandments. And his commandments are

not burdensome, for whoever is begotten by God conquers the world. And the victory that conquers the world is our faith. Who indeed is the victor over the world but the one who believes that Jesus is the Son of God?

This is the one who came through water and blood, Jesus Christ, not by water alone, but by water and blood. The Spirit is the one who testifies, and the Spirit is truth. So there are three that testify, the Spirit, the water, and the blood, and the three are of one accord. If we accept human testimony, the testimony of God is surely greater. Now the testimony of God is this, that he has testified on behalf of his Son.

IN YEAR C, THESE READINGS MAY BE USED 1024

READING I   *Isaiah 40:1–5, 9–11*

Comfort, give comfort to my people,
  says your God.
Speak tenderly to Jerusalem, and
    proclaim to her
  that her service is at an end,
  her guilt is expiated;
indeed, she has received from the hand
    of the LORD
  double for all her sins.

A voice cries out:
In the desert prepare the way of the
    LORD!
  Make straight in the wasteland a
    highway for our God!
Every valley shall be filled in,
  every mountain and hill shall be
    made low;
  the rugged land shall be made a plain,
  the rough country, a broad valley.
Then the glory of the LORD shall be

revealed
  and all people shall see it together;
  for the mouth of the LORD has
    spoken.

Go up onto a high mountain,
  Zion, herald of glad tidings;
cry out at the top of your voice,
  Jerusalem, herald of good news!
Fear not to cry out
  and say to the cities of Judah:
  Here is your God!
Here comes with power
  the Lord GOD,
  who rules by a strong arm;
here is his reward with him,
  his recompense before him.
Like a shepherd he feeds his flock;
  in his arms he gathers the lambs,
carrying them in his bosom,
  and leading the ewes with care.

RESPONSORIAL PSALM   *Psalm 104:1b–2, 3–4, 24–25, 27–28, 29–30*

O bless the Lord, bless the Lord, my soul, O my soul.

O LORD my God, how great you are,
  clothed in majesty and honor,
wrapped in light as with a robe!
  You stretch out the heavens like a
    tent. ℟.

On the waters you establish your
    dwelling.
  You make the clouds your chariot;
  you ride on the wings of the wind.
You make the winds your messengers,
  flame and fire your servants. ℟.

How many are your works, O LORD!
In wisdom you have made them all.
The earth is full of your creatures.
Vast and wide is the span of the sea,
with its creeping things past counting,
living things great and small. ℟.

All of these look to you
to give them their food in due season.
You give it, they gather it up;
you open wide your hand, they are
well filled. ℟.

You take away their breath, they die,
returning to the dust from which
they came.
You send forth your spirit, and they
are created,
and you renew the face of the
earth. ℟.

READING II   *Titus 2:11–14; 3:4–7*

Beloved: The grace of God has appeared, saving all and training us to reject godless ways and worldly desires and to live temperately, justly, and devoutly in this age, as we await the blessed hope, the appearance of the glory of our great God and savior Jesus Christ, who gave himself for us to deliver us from all lawlessness and to cleanse for himself a people as his own, eager to do what is good.

When the kindness and generous love
of God our savior appeared,
not because of any righteous deeds we had done
but because of his mercy,
He saved us through the bath of rebirth
and renewal by the Holy Spirit,
whom he richly poured out on us
through Jesus Christ our savior,
so that we might be justified by his grace
and become heirs in hope of eternal life.

Lent / Easter

On a Wednesday in February or early March the Church enters into prayer and fasting and almsgiving, attending with great seriousness to its calling. Forty days later on a Thursday evening, that season of Lent ends. From Holy Thursday night until Easter Sunday afternoon, the Church keeps the Paschal Triduum, the "Easter Three Days." Good Friday and Holy Saturday find Christians fasting, keeping vigil, remembering the passion, death and resurrection of the Lord until, at the great Vigil liturgy, the Church celebrates this paschal mystery in baptism, confirmation and eucharist. Then, for the fifty days of Eastertime the Church again sings the alleluia and rejoices to bring God's peace to the world.

The origins of Lent are bound up with the final stages in the initiation of those seeking to be baptized. After months or years of learning gradually the Christian way of life, the catechumens were called to spend the last weeks before baptism in fasting and prayer. The whole Church stayed by the catechumens in these days. The lenten season was also kept intensely by those doing penance for their sins. Today both catechumens and penitents keep Lent with the whole Church. Lent's scriptures, prayers and rites give clarity and strength to the life-long struggle against evil. That struggle is waged with many forms of prayer and fasting and practices of charity.

The origins of the fifty days of Eastertime are even more ancient. This is the springtime rejoicing of people who know their dependence on fields and flocks. It is the rejoicing of Israel remembering the exodus from slavery to freedom. It became the rejoicing of the Church in the resurrection of Jesus and the presence of that risen life in the newly baptized. The Eastertime lectionary is filled with a lively peace and the quiet exuberance of those who believe that evil is not finally triumphant. When the fifty days conclude at Pentecost the Church knows again how disturbing, how restless, how strong is the Spirit given by Christ.

1026 ASH WEDNESDAY

READING I

Joel 2:12–18 / 219

Even now, says the LORD,
 return to me with your whole heart,
 with fasting, and weeping, and
  mourning;
Rend your hearts, not your garments,
 and return to the LORD, your God.
For gracious and merciful is he,
 slow to anger, rich in kindness,
 and relenting in punishment.
Perhaps he will again relent
 and leave behind him a blessing,
Offerings and libations,
 for the LORD, your God.

Blow the trumpet in Zion!
 proclaim a fast,
 call an assembly;
Gather the people,
 notify the congregation;

Assemble the elders,
 gather the children
 and the infants at the breast;
Let the bridegroom quit his room,
 and the bride her chamber.
Between the porch and the altar
 let the priests, the ministers of the
  LORD, weep,
And say, "Spare, O LORD, your people,
 and make not your heritage a
  reproach,
 with the nations ruling over them!
Why should they say among the
  peoples,
 'Where is their God?'"

Then the LORD was stirred to concern
 for his land
and took pity on his people.

RESPONSORIAL PSALM

Psalm 51:3–4, 5–6a, 12–13, 14 and 17

Be mer - ci - ful, O Lord, for we have sinned.

Have mercy on me, O God,
 according to your merciful love;
according to your great compassion,
 blot out my transgressions.
Wash me completely from my iniquity,
 and cleanse me from my sin. ℟.

My transgressions, truly I know them;
 my sin is always before me.
Against you, you alone, have I sinned;
 what is evil in your sight I have
  done. ℟.

Create a pure heart for me, O God;
 renew a steadfast spirit within me.
Do not cast me away from your presence;
 take not your holy spirit from me. ℟.

Restore in me the joy of your salvation;
 sustain in me a willing spirit.
O Lord, open my lips
 and my mouth shall proclaim your
  praise. ℟.

READING II

2 Corinthians 5:20—6:2

Brothers and sisters: We are ambassadors for Christ, as if God were appealing through
us. We implore you on behalf of Christ, be reconciled to God. For our sake he made
him to be sin who did not know sin, so that we might become the righteousness of
God in him.

Working together, then, we appeal to you not to receive the grace of God in vain. For he says:

> In an acceptable time I heard you,
>> and on the day of salvation I helped you.

Behold, now is a very acceptable time; behold, now is the day of salvation.

GOSPEL

Matthew 6:1–6, 16–18

Jesus said to his disciples: "Take care not to perform righteous deeds in order that people may see them; otherwise, you will have no recompense from your heavenly Father. When you give alms, do not blow a trumpet before you, as the hypocrites do in the synagogues and in the streets to win the praise of others. Amen, I say to you, they have received their reward. But when you give alms, do not let your left hand know what your right is doing, so that your almsgiving may be secret. And your Father who sees in secret will repay you.

"When you pray, do not be like the hypocrites, who love to stand and pray in the synagogues and on street corners so that others may see them. Amen, I say to you, they have received their reward. But when you pray, go to your inner room, close the door, and pray to your Father in secret. And your Father who sees in secret will repay you.

"When you fast, do not look gloomy like the hypocrites. They neglect their appearance, so that they may appear to others to be fasting. Amen, I say to you, they have received their reward. But when you fast, anoint your head and wash your face, so that you may not appear to be fasting, except to your Father who is hidden. And your Father who sees what is hidden will repay you."

FIRST SUNDAY OF LENT / A

READING I

Genesis 2:7–9; 3:1–7 / 22

The LORD God formed man out of the clay of the ground and blew into his nostrils the breath of life, and so man became a living being.

Then the LORD God planted a garden in Eden, in the east, and placed there the man whom he had formed. Out of the ground the LORD God made various trees grow that were delightful to look at and good for food, with the tree of life in the middle of the garden and the tree of the knowledge of good and evil.

Now the serpent was the most cunning of all the animals that the LORD God had made. The serpent asked the woman, "Did God really tell you not to eat from any of the trees in the garden?" The woman answered the serpent: "We may eat of the fruit of the trees in the garden; it is only about the fruit of the tree in the middle of the garden that God said, 'You shall not eat it or even touch it, lest you die.'" But the serpent said to the woman: "You certainly will not die! No, God knows well that the moment you eat of it your eyes will be opened and you will be like gods who know what is good and what is evil." The woman saw that the tree was good for food, pleasing to the eyes, and desirable for gaining wisdom. So she took some of its fruit and ate it; and she also gave some to her husband, who was with her, and he ate it. Then the eyes of both of them were opened, and they realized that they were naked; so they sewed fig leaves together and made loincloths for themselves.

RESPONSORIAL PSALM　　　　　　　　　　　*Psalm 51:3–4, 5–6a, 12–13, 14 and 17*

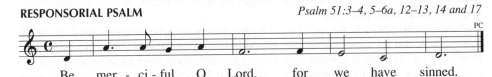

Have mercy on me, O God,
　　according to your merciful love;
according to your great compassion,
　　blot out my transgressions.
Wash me completely from my iniquity,
　　and cleanse me from my sin. ℟.

My transgressions, truly I know them;
　　my sin is always before me.
Against you, you alone, have I sinned;
　　what is evil in your sight I have
　　　　done. ℟.

Create a pure heart for me, O God;
　　renew a steadfast spirit within me.
Do not cast me away from your presence;
　　take not your holy spirit from me. ℟.

Restore in me the joy of your salvation;
　　sustain in me a willing spirit.
O Lord, open my lips
　　and my mouth shall proclaim your
　　　　praise. ℟.

READING II　　　　　　　　　　　*Romans 5:12–19 or 5:12, 17–19*
For short form read only the parts in brackets.

[Brothers and sisters: Through one man sin entered the world, and through sin, death, and thus death came to all men, inasmuch as all sinned—] for up to the time of the law, sin was in the world, though sin is not accounted when there is no law. But death reigned from Adam to Moses, even over those who did not sin after the pattern of the trespass of Adam, who is the type of the one who was to come.

　　But the gift is not like the transgression. For if by the transgression of the one, the many died, how much more did the grace of God and the gracious gift of the one man Jesus Christ overflow for the many. And the gift is not like the result of the one who sinned. For after one sin there was the judgment that brought condemnation; but the gift, after many transgressions, brought acquittal. [For if, by the transgression of the one, death came to reign through that one, how much more will those who receive the abundance of grace and of the gift of justification come to reign in life through the one Jesus Christ. In conclusion, just as through one transgression condemnation came upon all, so, through one righteous act, acquittal and life came to all. For just as through the disobedience of the one man the many were made sinners, so, through the obedience of the one, the many will be made righteous.]

GOSPEL

Matthew 4:1–11

At that time Jesus was led by the Spirit into the desert to be tempted by the devil. He fasted for forty days and forty nights, and afterwards he was hungry. The tempter approached and said to him, "If you are the Son of God, command that these stones become loaves of bread."
He said in reply, "It is written:

One does not live on bread alone,
but on every word that comes forth
from the mouth of God."

Then the devil took him to the holy city, and made him stand on the parapet of the temple, and said to him, "If you are the Son of God, throw yourself down. For it is written:

He will command his angels concerning you
and with their hands they will support you,
lest you dash your foot against a stone."

Jesus answered him, "Again it is written, *You shall not put the Lord, your God, to the test."* Then the devil took him up to a very high mountain, and showed him all the kingdoms of the world in their magnificence, and he said to him, "All these I shall give to you, if you will prostrate yourself and worship me." At this, Jesus said to him, "Get away, Satan! It is written:

The Lord, your God, shall you worship
and him alone shall you serve."

Then the devil left him and, behold, angels came and ministered to him.

RITE OF ELECTION

At the beginning of Lent, it is the responsibility of the bishop to call those who are judged ready to prepare for the sacraments of initiation at Easter. The bishop is to consult first with the pastors, catechists and others. The rite may take place at the cathedral. If the rite takes place in the parish church, the bishop may designate the pastor to act in his place.

This rite is also called the "Enrollment of Names." Each candidate now gives his/her name, or writes it down. When all have been enrolled, the bishop says: "You have been chosen to be initiated into the sacred mysteries at the Easter Vigil." He then speaks to them and to their sponsors about their lenten preparation for baptism.

The faithful join in prayers of intercession for the elect, as the catechumens are now called. If the eucharist is to be celebrated, the elect are first dismissed.

FIRST SUNDAY OF LENT / B

1028

READING I

Genesis 9:8–15 / 23

God said to Noah and to his sons with him: "See, I am now establishing my covenant with you and your descendants after you and with every living creature that was with you: all the birds, and the various tame and wild animals that were with you and came out of the ark. I will establish my covenant with you, that never again shall all bodily creatures be destroyed by the waters of a flood; there shall not be another flood to devastate the earth." God added: "This is the sign that I am giving for all ages to come, of the covenant between me and you and every living creature with you: I set my bow in the clouds to serve as a sign of the covenant between me and the earth. When I bring clouds over the earth, and the bow appears in the clouds, I will recall the covenant I have made between me and you and all living beings, so that the waters shall never again become a flood to destroy all mortal beings."

RESPONSORIAL PSALM *Psalm 25:4–5ab, 6 and 7bc, 8–9*

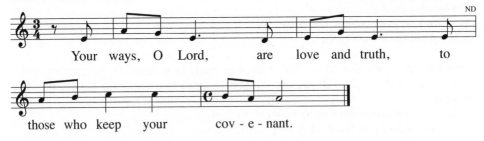

O LORD, make me know your ways.
 Teach me your paths.
Guide me in your truth, and teach me;
 for you are the God of my
  salvation. ℟.

Remember your compassion, O LORD,
 and your merciful love,
 for they are from of old.
In your merciful love remember me,

because of your goodness,
 O LORD. ℟.

Good and upright is the LORD;
 he shows the way to sinners.
He guides the humble in right
  judgment;
 to the humble he teaches his
  way. ℟.

READING II *1 Peter 3:18–22*

Beloved: Christ suffered for sins once, the righteous for the sake of the unrighteous, that he might lead you to God. Put to death in the flesh, he was brought to life in the Spirit. In it he also went to preach to the spirits in prison, who had once been disobedient while God patiently waited in the days of Noah during the building of the ark, in which a few persons, eight in all, were saved through water. This prefigured baptism, which saves you now. It is not a removal of dirt from the body but an appeal to God for a clear conscience, through the resurrection of Jesus Christ, who has gone into heaven and is at the right hand of God, with angels, authorities, and powers subject to him.

GOSPEL *Mark 1:12–15*

The Spirit drove Jesus out into the desert, and he remained in the desert for forty days, tempted by Satan. He was among wild beasts, and the angels ministered to him.
 After John had been arrested, Jesus came to Galilee proclaiming the gospel of God: "This is the time of fulfillment. The kingdom of God is at hand. Repent, and believe in the gospel."

RITE OF ELECTION

See no. 1027

FIRST SUNDAY OF LENT / C   1029

READING I

Deuteronomy 26:4–10 / 24

Moses spoke to the people, saying: "The priest shall receive the basket from you and shall set it in front of the altar of the LORD, your God. Then you shall declare before the LORD, your God, 'My father was a wandering Aramean who went down to Egypt with a small household and lived there as an alien. But there he became a nation great, strong, and numerous. When the Egyptians maltreated and oppressed us, imposing hard labor upon us, we cried to the LORD, the God of our fathers, and he heard our cry and saw our affliction, our toil, and our oppression. He brought us out of Egypt with his strong hand and outstretched arm, with terrifying power, with signs and wonders; and bringing us into this country, he gave us this land flowing with milk and honey. Therefore, I have now brought you the firstfruits of the products of the soil which you, O LORD, have given me.' And having set them before the Lord, your God, you shall bow down in his presence."

RESPONSORIAL PSALM

Psalm 91:1–2, 10–11, 12–13, 14–15

Be with me, Lord, when I am in trou - ble.

He who dwells in the shelter of the
Most High,
and abides in the shade of the
Almighty,
says to the LORD, "My refuge,
my stronghold, my God in whom I
trust!" ℟.

Upon you no evil shall fall,
no plague approach your tent.
For you has he commanded his angels
to keep you in all your ways. ℟.

They shall bear you upon their hands,
lest you strike your foot against a
stone.
On the lion and the viper you will tread,
and trample the young lion and the
serpent. ℟.

Since he clings to me in love, I will
free him,
protect him, for he knows my name.
When he calls on me, I will answer
him;
I will be with him in distress;
I will deliver him, and give him
glory. ℟.

READING II

Romans 10:8–13

Brothers and sisters: What does Scripture say?
The word is near you,
in your mouth and in your heart
—that is, the word of faith that we preach—, for, if you confess with your mouth that

Jesus is Lord and believe in your heart that God raised him from the dead, you will be saved. For one believes with the heart and so is justified, and one confesses with the mouth and so is saved. For the Scripture says, *No one who believes in him will be put to shame.* For there is no distinction between Jew and Greek; the same Lord is Lord of all, enriching all who call upon him. For "everyone who calls on the name of the Lord will be saved."

GOSPEL   *Luke 4:1–13*

Filled with the Holy Spirit, Jesus returned from the Jordan and was led by the Spirit into the desert for forty days, to be tempted by the devil. He ate nothing during those days, and when they were over he was hungry. The devil said to him, "If you are the Son of God, command this stone to become bread." Jesus answered him, "It is written, *One does not live on bread alone.*" Then he took him up and showed him all the kingdoms of the world in a single instant. The devil said to him, "I shall give to you all this power and glory; for it has been handed over to me, and I may give it to whomever I wish. All this will be yours, if you worship me." Jesus said to him in reply, "It is written:

> *You shall worship the Lord, your God,*
> *and him alone shall you serve.*"

Then he led him to Jerusalem, made him stand on the parapet of the temple, and said to him, "If you are the Son of God, throw yourself down from here, for it is written:

> *He will command his angels concerning you, to guard you,*

and:

> *With their hands they will support you,*
> *lest you dash your foot against a stone.*"

Jesus said to him in reply, "It also says, *You shall not put the Lord, your God, to the test.*" When the devil had finished every temptation, he departed from him for a time.

RITE OF ELECTION
See no. 1027

1030   SECOND SUNDAY OF LENT / A

READING I   *Genesis 12:1–4a / 25*

The LORD said to Abram: "Go forth from the land of your kinsfolk and from your father's house to a land that I will show you.

> "I will make of you a great nation,
> and I will bless you;
> I will make your name great,
> so that you will be a blessing.
> I will bless those who bless you
> and curse those who curse you.
> All the communities of the earth
> shall find blessing in you."

Abram went as the LORD directed him.

RESPONSORIAL PSALM   *Psalm 33:4–5, 18–19, 20 and 22*

Lord, let your mer-cy be on us,   as we place our trust in   you.

The word of the LORD is faithful,
   and all his works to be trusted.
The LORD loves justice and right,
   and his merciful love fills the earth. ℟.

Yes, the LORD's eyes are on those who
    fear him,
   who hope in his merciful love,

to rescue their souls from death,
   to keep them alive in famine. ℟.

Our soul is waiting for the LORD.
   He is our help and our shield.
May your merciful love be upon us,
   as we hope in you, O LORD. ℟.

READING II   *2 Timothy 1:8b–10*

Beloved: Bear your share of hardship for the gospel with the strength that comes from God.

He saved us and called us to a holy life, not according to our works but according to his own design and the grace bestowed on us in Christ Jesus before time began, but now made manifest through the appearance of our savior Christ Jesus, who destroyed death and brought life and immortality to light through the gospel.

GOSPEL   *Matthew 17:1–9*

Jesus took Peter, James, and John his brother, and led them up a high mountain by themselves. And he was transfigured before them; his face shone like the sun and his clothes became white as light. And behold, Moses and Elijah appeared to them, conversing with him. Then Peter said to Jesus in reply, "Lord, it is good that we are here. If you wish, I will make three tents here, one for you, one for Moses, and one for Elijah." While he was still speaking, behold, a bright cloud cast a shadow over them, then from the cloud came a voice that said, "This is my beloved Son, with whom I am well pleased; listen to him." When the disciples heard this, they fell prostrate and were very much afraid. But Jesus came and touched them, saying, "Rise, and do not be afraid." And when the disciples raised their eyes, they saw no one else but Jesus alone.

As they were coming down from the mountain, Jesus charged them, "Do not tell the vision to anyone until the Son of Man has been raised from the dead."

SECOND SUNDAY OF LENT / B   1031

READING I   *Genesis 22:1–2, 9a, 10–13, 15–18 / 26*

God put Abraham to the test. He called to him, "Abraham!" "Here I am!" he replied. Then God said: "Take your son Isaac, your only one, whom you love, and go to the land of Moriah. There you shall offer him up as a holocaust on a height that I will point out to you."

When they came to the place of which God had told him, Abraham built an altar there and arranged the wood on it. Then he reached out and took the knife to slaughter his son. But the LORD's messenger called to him from heaven, "Abraham, Abraham!" "Here I am!" he answered. "Do not lay your hand on the boy," said the messenger. "Do not do the least thing to him. I know now how devoted you are to God, since you did not withhold from me your own beloved son." As Abraham looked about, he spied a ram caught by its horns in the thicket. So he went and took the ram and offered it up as a holocaust in place of his son.

Again the LORD's messenger called to Abraham from heaven and said: "I swear by myself, declares the LORD, that because you acted as you did in not withholding from me your beloved son, I will bless you abundantly and make your descendants as countless as the stars of the sky and the sands of the seashore; your descendants shall take possession of the gates of their enemies, and in your descendants all the nations of the earth shall find blessing—all this because you obeyed my command."

RESPONSORIAL PSALM *Psalm 116:10 and 15, 16–17, 18–19*

I will walk be - fore the Lord, in the land of the liv - ing.

I trusted, even when I said,
  "I am sorely afflicted."
How precious in the eyes of the LORD
  is the death of his faithful. ℟.

Your servant, LORD, your servant am I,
  the son of your handmaid;
  you have loosened my bonds.

A thanksgiving sacrifice I make;
  I will call on the name of the
  LORD. ℟.

My vows to the LORD I will fulfill
  before all his people,
in the courts of the house of the LORD,
  in your midst, O Jerusalem. ℟.

READING II *Romans 8:31b–34*

Brothers and sisters: If God is for us, who can be against us? He who did not spare his own Son but handed him over for us all, how will he not also give us everything else along with him?

Who will bring a charge against God's chosen ones? It is God who acquits us, who will condemn? Christ Jesus it is who died—or, rather, was raised—who also is at the right hand of God, who indeed intercedes for us.

GOSPEL *Mark 9:2–10*

Jesus took Peter, James, and John and led them up a high mountain apart by themselves. And he was transfigured before them, and his clothes became dazzling white, such as no fuller on earth could bleach them. Then Elijah appeared to them along with Moses, and they were conversing with Jesus. Then Peter said to Jesus in reply, "Rabbi, it is good that we are here! Let us make three tents: one for you, one for Moses, and one for Elijah." He hardly knew what to say, they were so terrified. Then a cloud came, casting a shadow over them; from the cloud came a voice, "This is my beloved Son. Listen to him." Suddenly, looking around, they no longer saw anyone but Jesus alone with them.

As they were coming down from the mountain, he charged them not to relate what they had seen to anyone, except when the Son of Man had risen from the dead. So they kept the matter to themselves, questioning what rising from the dead meant.

SECOND SUNDAY OF LENT / C 1032

READING I *Genesis 15:5–12, 17–18 / 27*

The Lord God took Abram outside and said, "Look up at the sky and count the stars, if you can. Just so," he added, "shall your descendants be." Abram put his faith in the LORD, who credited it to him as an act of righteousness.

He then said to him, "I am the LORD who brought you from Ur of the Chaldeans to give you this land as a possession." "O Lord GOD," he asked, "how am I to know that I shall possess it?" He answered him, "Bring me a three-year-old heifer, a three-year-old she-goat, a three-year-old ram, a turtledove, and a young pigeon." Abram brought him all these, split them in two, and placed each half opposite the other; but the birds he did not cut up. Birds of prey swooped down on the carcasses, but Abram stayed with them. As the sun was about to set, a trance fell upon Abram, and a deep, terrifying darkness enveloped him.

When the sun had set and it was dark, there appeared a smoking fire pot and a flaming torch, which passed between those pieces. It was on that occasion that the LORD made a covenant with Abram, saying: "To your descendants I give this land, from the Wadi of Egypt to the Great River, the Euphrates."

RESPONSORIAL PSALM *Psalm 27:1, 7–8, 9abc, 13–14*

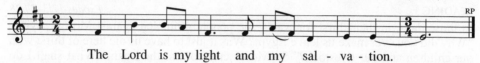

The Lord is my light and my sal - va - tion.

The LORD is my light and my salvation;
  whom shall I fear?
The LORD is the stronghold of my life;
  whom should I dread? ℟.

O LORD, hear my voice when I call;
  have mercy and answer me.
Of you my heart has spoken, "Seek his
  face."
It is your face, O LORD, that I seek. ℟.

Hide not your face from me.
Dismiss not your servant in anger;
  you have been my help.
Do not abandon or forsake me. ℟.

I believe I shall see the LORD's goodness
  in the land of the living.
Wait for the LORD; be strong;
  be stouthearted, and wait for the
  LORD! ℟.

READING II *Philippians 3:17—4:1 or 3:20—4:1*
For short form read only the parts in brackets. The word in parantheses is omitted in the long form.

Join with others in being imitators of me, [brothers and sisters,] and observe those who thus conduct themselves according to the model you have in us. For many, as I have often told you and now tell you even in tears, conduct themselves as enemies of the cross of Christ. Their end is destruction. Their God is their stomach; their glory is in their "shame." Their minds are occupied with earthly things. But [our citizenship is in heaven, and from it we also await a savior, the Lord Jesus Christ. He will change our lowly body to conform with his glorified body by the power that enables him also to bring all things into subjection to himself.

Therefore, my brothers and sisters, whom I love and long for, my joy and crown, in this way stand firm in the Lord, [(beloved.)]

GOSPEL   *Luke 9:28b–36*

Jesus took Peter, John, and James and went up the mountain to pray. While he was praying his face changed in appearance and his clothing became dazzling white. And behold, two men were conversing with him, Moses and Elijah, who appeared in glory and spoke of his exodus that he was going to accomplish in Jerusalem. Peter and his companions had been overcome by sleep, but becoming fully awake, they saw his glory and the two men standing with him. As they were about to part from him, Peter said to Jesus, "Master, it is good that we are here; let us make three tents, one for you, one for Moses, and one for Elijah." But he did not know what he was saying. While he was still speaking, a cloud came and cast a shadow over them, and they became frightened when they entered the cloud. Then from the cloud came a voice that said, "This is my chosen Son; listen to him." After the voice had spoken, Jesus was found alone. They fell silent and did not at that time tell anyone what they had seen.

1033   THIRD SUNDAY OF LENT / A

READING I   *Exodus 17:3–7 / 28*

In those days, in their thirst for water, the people grumbled against Moses, saying, "Why did you ever make us leave Egypt? Was it just to have us die here of thirst with our children and our livestock?" So Moses cried out to the LORD, "What shall I do with this people? A little more and they will stone me!" The LORD answered Moses, "Go over there in front of the people, along with some of the elders of Israel, holding in your hand, as you go, the staff with which you struck the river. I will be standing there in front of you on the rock in Horeb. Strike the rock, and the water will flow from it for the people to drink." This Moses did, in the presence of the elders of Israel. The place was called Massah and Meribah, because the Israelites quarreled there and tested the LORD, saying, "Is the LORD in our midst or not?"

RESPONSORIAL PSALM   *Psalm 95:1–2, 6–7c, 7d–9*

If to - day you hear his voice, hard - en not your hearts.

Come, let us ring out our joy to the LORD;
  hail the rock who saves us.
Let us come into his presence, giving
      thanks;
  let us hail him with a song of praise. ℟.

O come; let us bow and bend low.
  Let us kneel before the God who
      made us,
for he is our God and we

the people who belong to his pasture,
  the flock that is led by his hand. ℟.

O that today you would listen to his
  voice!
  "Harden not your hearts as at Meribah,
  as on that day at Massah in the desert
when your forebears put me to the test;
  when they tried me, though they saw
      my work." ℟.

READING II   *Romans 5:1–2, 5–8*

Brothers and sisters: Since we have been justified by faith, we have peace with God through our Lord Jesus Christ, through whom we have gained access by faith to this grace in which we stand, and we boast in hope of the glory of God.

And hope does not disappoint, because the love of God has been poured out into our hearts through the Holy Spirit who has been given to us. For Christ, while we were still helpless, died at the appointed time for the ungodly. Indeed, only with difficulty does one die for a just person, though perhaps for a good person one might even find courage to die. But God proves his love for us in that while we were still sinners Christ died for us.

GOSPEL   *John 4:5–42 or 4:5–15, 19b–26, 39a, 40–42*
For short form read only the parts in brackets.

[Jesus came to a town of Samaria called Sychar, near the plot of land that Jacob had given to his son Joseph. Jacob's well was there. Jesus, tired from his journey, sat down there at the well. It was about noon.

A woman of Samaria came to draw water. Jesus said to her, "Give me a drink." His disciples had gone into the town to buy food. The Samaritan woman said to him, "How can you, a Jew, ask me, a Samaritan woman, for a drink?" —For Jews use nothing in common with Samaritans.— Jesus answered and said to her, "If you knew the gift of God and who is saying to you, 'Give me a drink,' you would have asked him and he would have given you living water." The woman said to him, "Sir, you do not even have a bucket and the cistern is deep; where then can you get this living water? Are you greater than our father Jacob, who gave us this cistern and drank from it himself with his children and his flocks?" Jesus answered and said to her, "Everyone who drinks this water will be thirsty again; but whoever drinks the water I shall give will never thirst; the water I shall give will become in him a spring of water welling up to eternal life." The woman said to him, "Sir, give me this water, so that I may not be thirsty or have to keep coming here to draw water."]

Jesus said to her, "Go call your husband and come back." The woman answered and said to him, "I do not have a husband." Jesus answered her, "You are right in saying, 'I do not have a husband.' For you have had five husbands, and the one you have now is not your husband. What you have said is true." The woman said to him, "Sir, [I can see that you are a prophet. Our ancestors worshiped on this mountain; but you people say that the place to worship is in Jerusalem." Jesus said to her, "Believe me, woman, the hour is coming when you will worship the Father neither on this mountain nor in Jerusalem. You people worship what you do not understand; we worship what we understand, because salvation is from the Jews. But the hour is coming, and is now here, when true worshipers will worship the Father in Spirit and truth; and indeed the Father seeks such people to worship him. God is Spirit, and those who worship him must worship in Spirit and truth." The woman said to him, "I know that the Messiah is coming, the one called the Christ; when he comes, he will tell us everything." Jesus said to her, "I am he, the one speaking with you."]

At that moment his disciples returned, and were amazed that he was talking with a woman, but still no one said, "What are you looking for?" or "Why are you talking with her?" The woman left her water jar and went into the town and said to the people, "Come see a man who told me everything I have done. Could he possibly be the Christ?" They went out of the town and came to him. Meanwhile, the disciples urged him, "Rabbi, eat." But he said to them, "I have food to eat of which you do not know." So the disciples said to one another, "Could someone have brought him something to eat?" Jesus said to them, "My food is to do the will of the one who sent me and to finish his work. Do you not say, 'In four months the harvest will be here'? I tell you, look up and see the fields ripe for the harvest. The reaper is already receiving payment and gathering crops for eternal life, so that the sower and reaper can rejoice together. For here the saying is verified that 'One sows and another reaps.' I sent you to reap what you have not worked for; others have done the work, and you are sharing the fruits of their work."

[Many of the Samaritans of that town began to believe in him] because of the word of the woman who testified, "He told me everything I have done." [When the Samaritans came to him, they invited him to stay with them; and he stayed there two days. Many more began to believe in him because of his word, and they said to the woman, "We no longer believe because of your word; for we have heard for ourselves, and we know that this is truly the savior of the world."]

FIRST SCRUTINY

During Lent, the elect (those catechumens who have been called to prepare for baptism at Easter) are called to come before the community for exorcisms and prayers. This takes place after the liturgy of the word on the Third, Fourth, and Fifth Sundays of Lent. These rites are intended to purify the hearts and minds of the elect, to strengthen them against temptation, to help them progress in the love of God.

The presider asks the assembly to pray in silence for the elect, then to join in intercessions for them. The presider lays hands on each of the elect and prays that the elect be delivered from the power of evil and become witnesses to the gospel. A song or psalm may be sung, then the elect are dismissed as usual and the faithful continue with the liturgy of the eucharist.

1034 THIRD SUNDAY OF LENT / B

READING I   *Exodus 20:1–17 or 20:1–3, 7–8, 12–17 / 29*

For short form read only the parts in brackets.

[In those days, God delivered all these commandments: "I, the LORD, am your God, who brought you out of the land of Egypt, that place of slavery. You shall not have other gods besides me.] You shall not carve idols for yourselves in the shape of anything in the sky above or on the earth below or in the waters beneath the earth; you shall not bow down before them or worship them. For I, the LORD, your God, am a jealous God, inflicting punishment for their fathers' wickedness on the children of those who hate me, down to the third and fourth generation; but bestowing mercy down to the thousandth generation on the children of those who love me and keep my commandments.

["You shall not take the name of the LORD, your God, in vain. For the LORD will not leave unpunished the one who takes his name in vain.

"Remember to keep holy the sabbath day.] Six days you may labor and do all your work, but the seventh day is the sabbath of the LORD, your God. No work may be done then either by you, or your son or daughter, or your male or female slave, or your beast, or by the alien who lives with you. In six days the LORD made the heavens and the earth, the sea and all that is in them; but on the seventh day he rested. That is why the LORD has blessed the sabbath day and made it holy.

["Honor your father and your mother, that you may have a long life in the land which the LORD, your God, is giving you.

You shall not kill.

You shall not commit adultery.

You shall not steal.

You shall not bear false witness against your neighbor.

You shall not covet your neighbor's house. You shall not covet your neighbor's wife, nor his male or female slave, nor his ox or ass, nor anything else that belongs to him."]

RESPONSORIAL PSALM   *Psalm 19:8, 9, 10, 11*

Lord, you have the words of ev-er-last-ing life.

The law of the LORD is perfect;
  it revives the soul.
The decrees of the LORD are steadfast;
  they give wisdom to the simple. ℟.

The fear of the LORD is pure,
  abiding forever.
The judgments of the LORD are true;
  they are, all of them, just. ℟.

The precepts of the LORD are right;
  they gladden the heart.
The command of the LORD is clear;
  it gives light to the eyes. ℟.

They are more to be desired than gold,
  than quantities of gold.
And sweeter are they than honey,
  than honey flowing from the
  comb. ℟.

READING II   *1 Corinthians 1:22–25*

Brothers and sisters: Jews demand signs and Greeks look for wisdom, but we proclaim Christ crucified, a stumbling block to Jews and foolishness to Gentiles, but to those who are called, Jews and Greeks alike, Christ the power of God and the wisdom of God. For the foolishness of God is wiser than human wisdom, and the weakness of God is stronger than human strength.

GOSPEL   *John 2:13–25*

Since the Passover of the Jews was near, Jesus went up to Jerusalem. He found in the temple area those who sold oxen, sheep, and doves, as well as the money changers seated there. He made a whip out of cords and drove them all out of the temple area, with the sheep and oxen, and spilled the coins of the money changers and overturned their tables, and to those who sold doves he said, "Take these out of here, and stop making my Father's house a marketplace." His disciples recalled the words of Scripture, *Zeal for your house will consume me*. At this the Jews answered and said to him, "What sign can you show us for doing this?" Jesus answered and said to them, "Destroy this temple and in three days I will raise it up." The Jews said, "This temple has been under construction for forty-six years, and you will raise it up in three days?" But he was speaking about the temple of his body. Therefore, when he was raised from the dead, his disciples remembered that he had said this, and they came to believe the Scripture and the word Jesus had spoken.

While he was in Jerusalem for the feast of Passover, many began to believe in his name when they saw the signs he was doing. But Jesus would not trust himself to them because he knew them all, and did not need anyone to testify about human nature. He himself understood it well.

FIRST SCRUTINY

See no. 1033

1035 THIRD SUNDAY OF LENT / C

READING I   *Exodus 3:1–8a, 13–15 / 30*

Moses was tending the flock of his father-in-law Jethro, the priest of Midian. Leading the flock across the desert, he came to Horeb, the mountain of God. There an angel of the LORD appeared to Moses in fire flaming out of a bush. As he looked on, he was surprised to see that the bush, though on fire, was not consumed. So Moses decided, "I must go over to look at this remarkable sight, and see why the bush is not burned."

When the LORD saw him coming over to look at it more closely, God called out to him from the bush, "Moses! Moses!" He answered, "Here I am." God said, "Come no nearer! Remove the sandals from your feet, for the place where you stand is holy ground. I am the God of your fathers," he continued, "the God of Abraham, the God of Isaac, the God of Jacob." Moses hid his face, for he was afraid to look at God. But the LORD said, "I have witnessed the affliction of my people in Egypt and have heard their cry of complaint against their slave drivers, so I know well what they are suffering. Therefore I have come down to rescue them from the hands of the Egyptians and lead them out of that land into a good and spacious land, a land flowing with milk and honey."

Moses said to God, "But when I go to the Israelites and say to them, 'The God of your fathers has sent me to you,' if they ask me, 'What is his name?' what am I to tell them?" God replied, "I am who am." Then he added, "This is what you shall tell the Israelites: I AM sent me to you."

God spoke further to Moses, "Thus shall you say to the Israelites: The LORD, the God of your fathers, the God of Abraham, the God of Isaac, the God of Jacob, has sent me to you.

"This is my name forever;
    thus am I to be remembered through all generations."

RESPONSORIAL PSALM   *Psalm 103:1–2, 3–4, 6–7, 8 and 11*

The Lord is kind and mer-ci-ful.

Bless the LORD, O my soul,
    and all within me, his holy name.
Bless the LORD, O my soul,
    and never forget all his benefits. ℟.

It is the Lord who forgives all your sins,
    who heals every one of your ills,
who redeems your life from the grave,
    who crowns you with mercy and
        compassion. ℟.

The LORD does just deeds,
gives full justice to all who are
oppressed.
He made known his ways to Moses,
and his deeds to the children of
Israel. ℟.

The LORD is compassionate and
gracious,
slow to anger and rich in mercy.
For as the heavens are high above the
earth,
so strong his mercy for those who
fear him. ℟.

READING II *1 Corinthians 10:1–6, 10–12*

I do not want you to be unaware, brothers and sisters, that our ancestors were all under the cloud and all passed through the sea, and all of them were baptized into Moses in the cloud and in the sea. All ate the same spiritual food, and all drank the same spiritual drink, for they drank from a spiritual rock that followed them, and the rock was the Christ. Yet God was not pleased with most of them, for they were struck down in the desert.

These things happened as examples for us, so that we might not desire evil things, as they did. Do not grumble as some of them did, and suffered death by the destroyer. These things happened to them as an example, and they have been written down as a warning to us, upon whom the end of the ages has come. Therefore, whoever thinks he is standing secure should take care not to fall.

GOSPEL *Luke 13:1–9*

Some people told Jesus about the Galileans whose blood Pilate had mingled with the blood of their sacrifices. Jesus said to them in reply, "Do you think that because these Galileans suffered in this way they were greater sinners than all other Galileans? By no means! But I tell you, if you do not repent, you will all perish as they did! Or those eighteen people who were killed when the tower at Siloam fell on them—do you think they were more guilty than everyone else who lived in Jerusalem? By no means! But I tell you, if you do not repent, you will all perish as they did!"

And he told them this parable: "There once was a person who had a fig tree planted in his orchard, and when he came in search of fruit on it but found none, he said to the gardener, 'For three years now I have come in search of fruit on this fig tree but have found none. So cut it down. Why should it exhaust the soil?' He said to him in reply, 'Sir, leave it for this year also, and I shall cultivate the ground around it and fertilize it; it may bear fruit in the future. If not you can cut it down.'"

FIRST SCRUTINY
See no. 1033

FOURTH SUNDAY OF LENT / A 1036

READING I *1 Samuel 16:1b, 6–7, 10–13a / 31*

The LORD said to Samuel: "Fill your horn with oil, and be on your way. I am sending you to Jesse of Bethlehem, for I have chosen my king from among his sons."

As Jesse and his sons came to the sacrifice, Samuel looked at Eliab and thought, "Surely the LORD's anointed is here before him." But the LORD said to Samuel: "Do not judge from his appearance or from his lofty stature, because I have rejected him. Not as man sees does God see, because man sees the appearance but the LORD looks into the heart." In the same way Jesse presented seven sons before Samuel, but Samuel said to Jesse, "The Lord has not chosen any one of these." Then Samuel asked Jesse, "Are these all the sons you have?" Jesse replied, "There is still the youngest, who is tending the sheep." Samuel said to Jesse, "Send for him; we will not begin the sacrificial banquet until he arrives here." Jesse sent and had the young man brought to them. He was ruddy, a youth handsome to behold and making a splendid appearance. The Lord said, "There—anoint him, for this is the one!" Then Samuel, with the horn of oil in hand, anointed David in the presence of his brothers; and from that day on, the spirit of the Lord rushed upon David.

RESPONSORIAL PSALM   *Psalm 23:1–3a, 3b–4, 5, 6*

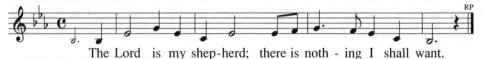

The Lord is my shep-herd; there is noth - ing I shall want.

The Lord is my shepherd;
 there is nothing I shall want.
Fresh and green are the pastures
 where he gives me repose.
Near restful waters he leads me;
 he revives my soul. ℟.

He guides me along the right path,
 for the sake of his name.
Though I should walk in the valley of
  the shadow of death,
 no evil would I fear, for you are
  with me.

Your crook and your staff will give
 me comfort. ℟.

You have prepared a table before me
 in the sight of my foes.
My head you have anointed with oil;
 my cup is overflowing. ℟.

Surely goodness and mercy shall
  follow me
 all the days of my life.
In the Lord's own house shall I dwell
 for length of days unending. ℟.

READING II   *Ephesians 5:8–14*
Brothers and sisters: You were once darkness, but now you are light in the Lord. Live as children of light, for light produces every kind of goodness and righteousness and truth. Try to learn what is pleasing to the Lord. Take no part in the fruitless works of darkness; rather expose them, for it is shameful even to mention the things done by them in secret; but everything exposed by the light becomes visible, for everything that becomes visible is light. Therefore, it says:
 "Awake, O sleeper,
 and arise from the dead,
 and Christ will give you light."

GOSPEL   *John 9:1–41 or 9:1, 6–9, 13–17, 34–38*
For short form read only the parts in brackets.

[As Jesus passed by he saw a man blind from birth.] His disciples asked him, "Rabbi, who sinned, this man or his parents, that he was born blind?" Jesus answered, "Neither he nor his parents sinned; it is so that the works of God might be made visible through him. We have to do the works of the one who sent me while it is day. Night is coming when no one can work. While I am in the world, I am the light of the world." When he had said this, [he spat on the ground and made clay with the saliva, and smeared the clay on his eyes, and said to him, "Go wash in the Pool of Siloam" —which means Sent—. So he went and washed, and came back able to see.

His neighbors and those who had seen him earlier as a beggar said, "Isn't this the one who used to sit and beg?" Some said, "It is," but others said, "No, he just looks like him." He said, "I am."] So they said to him, "How were your eyes opened?" He replied, "The man called Jesus made clay and anointed my eyes and told me, 'Go to Siloam and wash.' So I went there and washed and was able to see." And they said to him, "Where is he?" He said, "I don't know."

[They brought the one who was once blind to the Pharisees. Now Jesus had made clay and opened his eyes on a sabbath. So then the Pharisees also asked him how he was able to see. He said to them, "He put clay on my eyes, and I washed, and now I can see." So some of the Pharisees said, "This man is not from God, because he does not keep the sabbath." But others said, "How can a sinful man do such signs?" And there was a division among them. So they said to the blind man again, "What do you have to say about him, since he opened your eyes?" He said, "He is a prophet."]

Now the Jews did not believe that he had been blind and gained his sight until they summoned the parents of the one who had gained his sight. They asked them, "Is this your son, who you say was born blind? How does he now see?" His parents answered and said, "We know that this is our son and that he was born blind. We do not know how he sees now, nor do we know who opened his eyes. Ask him, he is of age; he can speak for himself." His parents said this because they were afraid of the Jews, for the Jews had already agreed that if anyone acknowledged him as the Christ, he would be expelled from the synagogue. For this reason his parents said, "He is of age; question him."

So a second time they called the man who had been blind and said to him, "Give God the praise! We know that this man is a sinner." He replied, "If he is a sinner, I do not know. One thing I do know is that I was blind and now I see." So they said to him, "What did he do to you? How did he open your eyes?" He answered them, "I told you already and you did not listen. Why do you want to hear it again? Do you want to become his disciples, too?" They ridiculed him and said, "You are that man's disciple; we are disciples of Moses! We know that God spoke to Moses, but we do not know where this one is from." The man answered and said to them, "This is what is so amazing, that you do not know where he is from, yet he opened my eyes. We know that God does not listen to sinners, but if one is devout and does his will, he listens to him. It is unheard of that anyone ever opened the eyes of a person born blind. If this man were not from God, he would not be able to do anything." [They answered and said to him, "You were born totally in sin, and are you trying to teach us?" Then they threw him out.

When Jesus heard that they had thrown him out, he found him and said, "Do you believe in the Son of Man?" He answered and said, "Who is he, sir, that I may believe in him?" Jesus said to him, "You have seen him, the one speaking with you is he." He said, "I do believe, Lord," and he worshiped him.] Then Jesus said, "I came into this world for judgment, so that those who do not see might see, and those who do see might become blind."

Some of the Pharisees who were with him heard this and said to him, "Surely we are not also blind, are we?" Jesus said to them, "If you were blind, you would have no sin; but now you are saying, 'We see,' so your sin remains.

SECOND SCRUTINY

During Lent, the elect (those catechumens who have been called to prepare for baptism at Easter) are called to come before the community for exorcisms and prayers. This takes place after the liturgy of the word on the Third, Fourth, and Fifth Sundays of Lent. These rites are intended to purify the hearts and minds of the elect, to strengthen them against temptation, to help them progress in the love of God.

The presider asks the assembly to pray in silence for the elect, then to join in intercessions for them. The presider lays hands on each of the elect and prays that the elect be delivered from the power of evil and become witnesses to the gospel. A song or psalm may be sung, then the elect are dismissed as usual and the faithful continue with the liturgy of the eucharist.

1037 FOURTH SUNDAY OF LENT / B

READING I   *2 Chronicles 36:14–16, 19–23 / 32*

In those days, all the princes of Judah, the priests, and the people added infidelity to infidelity, practicing all the abominations of the nations and polluting the LORD's temple which he had consecrated in Jerusalem.

Early and often did the LORD, the God of their fathers, send his messengers to them, for he had compassion on his people and his dwelling place. But they mocked the messengers of God, despised his warnings, and scoffed at his prophets, until the anger of the LORD against his people was so inflamed that there was no remedy. Their enemies burnt the house of God, tore down the walls of Jerusalem, set all its palaces afire, and destroyed all its precious objects. Those who escaped the sword were carried captive to Babylon, where they became servants of the king of the Chaldeans and his sons until the kingdom of the Persians came to power. All this was to fulfill the word of the LORD spoken by Jeremiah: "Until the land has retrieved its lost sabbaths, during all the time it lies waste it shall have rest while seventy years are fulfilled."

In the first year of Cyrus, king of Persia, in order to fulfill the word of the LORD spoken by Jeremiah, the LORD inspired King Cyrus of Persia to issue this proclamation throughout his kingdom, both by word of mouth and in writing: "Thus says Cyrus, king of Persia: All the kingdoms of the earth the LORD, the God of heaven, has given to me, and he has also charged me to build him a house in Jerusalem, which is in Judah. Whoever, therefore, among you belongs to any part of his people, let him go up, and may his God be with him!"

RESPONSORIAL PSALM   *Psalm 137:1–2, 3, 4–5, 6*

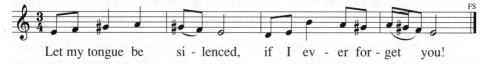

Let my tongue be si - lenced, if I ev - er for - get you!

By the rivers of Babylon
    there we sat and wept,
    remembering Sion;
on the poplars that grew there
    we hung up our harps. ℟.
	For it was there that they asked us,
	    our captors, for songs,
	    our oppressors, for joy.
	"Sing to us," they said,
	    "one of Sion's songs." ℟.

O how could we sing
the song of the LORD
on foreign soil?
If I forget you, Jerusalem,
let my right hand wither! ℟.

O let my tongue
cleave to my palate
if I remember you not,
if I prize not Jerusalem
as the first of my joys! ℟.

READING II
Ephesians 2:4–10

Brothers and sisters: God, who is rich in mercy, because of the great love he had for us, even when we were dead in our transgressions, brought us to life with Christ —by grace you have been saved—, raised us up with him, and seated us with him in the heavens in Christ Jesus, that in the ages to come he might show the immeasurable riches of his grace in his kindness to us in Christ Jesus. For by grace you have been saved through faith, and this is not from you; it is the gift of God; it is not from works, so no one may boast. For we are his handiwork, created in Christ Jesus for the good works that God has prepared in advance, that we should live in them.

GOSPEL
John 3:14–21

Jesus said to Nicodemus: "Just as Moses lifted up the serpent in the desert, so must the Son of Man be lifted up, so that everyone who believes in him may have eternal life."

For God so loved the world that he gave his only Son, so that everyone who believes in him might not perish but might have eternal life. For God did not send his Son into the world to condemn the world, but that the world might be saved through him. Whoever believes in him will not be condemned, but whoever does not believe has already been condemned, because he has not believed in the name of the only Son of God. And this is the verdict, that the light came into the world, but people preferred darkness to light, because their works were evil. For everyone who does wicked things hates the light and does not come toward the light, so that his works might not be exposed. But whoever lives the truth comes to the light, so that his works may be clearly seen as done in God.

SECOND SCRUTINY
See no. 1036

FOURTH SUNDAY OF LENT / C 1038

READING I
Joshua 5:9a, 10–12 / 33

The LORD said to Joshua, "Today I have removed the reproach of Egypt from you."

While the Israelites were encamped at Gilgal on the plains of Jericho, they celebrated the Passover on the evening of the fourteenth of the month. On the day after the Passover, they ate of the produce of the land in the form of unleavened cakes and parched grain. On that same day after the Passover, on which they ate of the produce of the land, the manna ceased. No longer was there manna for the Israelites, who that year ate of the yield of the land of Canaan.

RESPONSORIAL PSALM   *Psalm 34:2–3, 4–5, 6–7*

Taste and see the good - ness of the Lord.

I will bless the LORD at all times;
  praise of him is always in my mouth.
In the LORD my soul shall make its boast;
  the humble shall hear and be glad. ℟.

Glorify the LORD with me;
  together let us praise his name.
I sought the LORD, and he answered me;

from all my terrors he set me free. ℟.

Look toward him and be radiant;
  let your faces not be abashed.
This lowly one called; the LORD heard,
  and rescued him from all his
  distress. ℟.

READING II   *2 Corinthians 5:17–21*

Brothers and sisters: Whoever is in Christ is a new creation: the old things have passed away; behold, new things have come. And all this is from God, who has reconciled us to himself through Christ and given us the ministry of reconciliation, namely, God was reconciling the world to himself in Christ, not counting their trespasses against them and entrusting to us the message of reconciliation. So we are ambassadors for Christ, as if God were appealing through us. We implore you on behalf of Christ, be reconciled to God. For our sake he made him to be sin who did not know sin, so that we might become the righteousness of God in him.

GOSPEL   *Luke 15:1–3, 11–32*

Tax collectors and sinners were all drawing near to listen to Jesus, but the Pharisees and scribes began to complain, saying, "This man welcomes sinners and eats with them." So to them Jesus addressed this parable: "A man had two sons, and the younger son said to his father, 'Father give me the share of your estate that should come to me.' So the father divided the property between them. After a few days, the younger son collected all his belongings and set off to a distant country where he squandered his inheritance on a life of dissipation. When he had freely spent everything, a severe famine struck that country, and he found himself in dire need. So he hired himself out to one of the local citizens who sent him to his farm to tend the swine. And he longed to eat his fill of the pods on which the swine fed, but nobody gave him any. Coming to his senses he thought, 'How many of my father's hired workers have more than enough food to eat, but here am I, dying from hunger. I shall get up and go to my father and I shall say to him, "Father, I have sinned against heaven and against you. I no longer deserve to be called your son; treat me as you would treat one of your hired workers."' So he got up and went back to his father. While he was still a long way off, his father caught sight of him, and was filled with compassion. He ran to his son, embraced him and kissed him. His son said to him, 'Father, I have sinned against heaven and against you; I no longer deserve to be called your son.' But his father ordered his servants, 'Quickly bring the finest robe and put it on him; put a ring on his finger and sandals on his feet. Take the fattened calf and slaughter it. Then let us celebrate with a feast, because this son of mine was dead, and has come to life again; he was lost, and has been found.' Then the celebration began. Now the older son had been out in the field and, on his way back, as he neared the house, he heard the sound of music and dancing. He called one of the servants and asked what this might mean. The servant said to him, 'Your brother has returned and your father has slaughtered the fattened calf because he has him back safe and sound.' He became angry, and when he refused to enter the house, his father came out and pleaded with him. He said to his father in reply, 'Look, all these years I served you and not once did I disobey your orders; yet you never gave me even a young goat to feast on with my friends. But when your son returns who swallowed up your property with prostitutes, for him you slaughter the fattened calf.' He said to him, 'My son, you are here with me always; everything I have is yours. But now we must celebrate and rejoice, because your brother was dead and has come to life again; he was lost and has been found.'"

SECOND SCRUTINY

See no. 1036

FIFTH SUNDAY OF LENT / A   1039

READING I   *Ezekiel 37:12–14 / 34*

Thus says the Lord GOD: O my people, I will open your graves and have you rise from them, and bring you back to the land of Israel. Then you shall know that I am the LORD, when I open your graves and have you rise from them, O my people! I will put my spirit in you that you may live, and I will settle you upon your land; thus you shall know that I am the LORD. I have promised, and I will do it, says the LORD.

RESPONSORIAL PSALM   *Psalm 130:1–2, 3–4, 5–6ab and 7a, 7b–8*

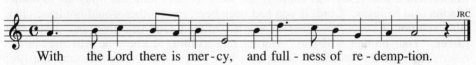

With the Lord there is mer-cy, and full-ness of re-demp-tion.

Out of the depths I cry to you, O LORD;
　Lord, hear my voice!
O let your ears be attentive
　to the sound of my pleadings. ℟.

If you, O LORD, should mark iniquities,
　Lord, who could stand?
But with you is found forgiveness,
　that you may be revered. ℟.

I long for you, O LORD,
　my soul longs for his word.
My soul hopes in the Lord
　more than watchmen for daybreak.
Let Israel hope for the LORD. ℟.

For with the LORD there is mercy,
　in him is plentiful redemption.
It is he who will redeem Israel
　from all its iniquities. ℟.

READING II   *Romans 8:8–11*

Brothers and sisters: Those who are in the flesh cannot please God. But you are not in the flesh; on the contrary, you are in the spirit, if only the Spirit of God dwells in you. Whoever does not have the Spirit of Christ does not belong to him. But if Christ is in you, although the body is dead because of sin, the spirit is alive because of righteousness. If the Spirit of the one who raised Jesus from the dead dwells in you, the one who raised Christ from the dead will give life to your mortal bodies also, through his Spirit dwelling in you.

GOSPEL   *John 11:1–45 or 11:3–7, 17, 20–27, 33b–45*

For short form read only the parts in brackets. The words in parantheses are omitted in the long form.

Now a man was ill, Lazarus from Bethany, the village of Mary and her sister Martha. Mary was the one who had anointed the Lord with perfumed oil and dried his feet with her hair; it was her brother Lazarus who was ill. So [the sisters (of Lazarus) sent word to Jesus saying, "Master, the one you love is ill." When Jesus heard this he said, "This illness is not to end in death, but is for the glory of God, that the Son of God may be glorified through it." Now Jesus loved Martha and her sister and Lazarus. So when he heard that he was ill, he remained for two days in the place where he was. Then after this he said to his disciples, "Let us go back to Judea."] The disciples said to him, "Rabbi, the Jews were just trying to stone you, and you want to go back there?" Jesus answered, "Are there not twelve hours in a day? If one walks during the day, he does not stumble, because he sees the light of this world. But if one walks at night, he stumbles, because the light is not in him." He said this, and then told them, "Our friend Lazarus is asleep, but I am going to awaken him." So the disciples said to him, "Master, if he is asleep, he will be saved." But Jesus was talking about his death, while they thought that he meant ordinary sleep. So then Jesus said to them clearly, "Lazarus has died. And I am glad for you that I was not there, that you may believe. Let us go to him." So Thomas, called Didymus, said to his fellow disciples, "Let us also go to die with him."

[When Jesus arrived, he found that Lazarus had already been in the tomb for four days.] Now Bethany was near Jerusalem, only about two miles away. And many of the Jews had come to Martha and Mary to comfort them about their brother. [When Martha heard that Jesus was coming, she went to meet him; but Mary sat at home. Martha said to Jesus, "Lord, if you had been here, my brother would not have died. But even now I know that whatever you ask of God, God will give you." Jesus said to her, "Your brother will rise." Martha said to him, "I know he will rise, in the resurrection on the last day." Jesus told her, "I am the resurrection and the life; whoever believes in me, even if he dies, will live, and everyone who lives and believes in me will never die. Do you believe this?" She said to him, "Yes, Lord. I have come to believe that you are the Christ, the Son of God, the one who is coming into the world."]

When she had said this, she went and called her sister Mary secretly, saying, "The teacher is here and is asking for you." As soon as she heard this, she rose quickly and went to him. For Jesus had not yet come into the village, but was still where Martha had met him. So when the Jews who were with her in the house comforting her saw Mary get up quickly and go out, they followed her, presuming that she was going to the tomb to weep there. When Mary came to where Jesus was and saw him, she fell at his feet and said to him, "Lord, if you had been here, my brother would not have died." When Jesus saw her weeping and the Jews who had come with her weeping, [he became perturbed and deeply troubled, and said, "Where have you laid him?" They said to him, "Sir, come and see." And Jesus wept. So the Jews said, "See how he loved him." But some of them said, "Could not the one who opened the eyes of the blind man have done something so that this man would not have died?"

So Jesus, perturbed again, came to the tomb. It was a cave, and a stone lay across it. Jesus said, "Take away the stone." Martha, the dead man's sister, said to him, "Lord, by now there will be a stench; he has been dead for four days." Jesus said to her, "Did I not tell you that if you believe you will see the glory of God?" So they took away the stone. And Jesus raised his eyes and said, "Father, I thank you for hearing me. I know that you always hear me; but because of the crowd here I have said this, that they may believe that you sent me." And when he had said this, he cried out in a loud voice, "Lazarus, come out!" The dead man came out, tied hand and foot with burial bands, and his face was wrapped in a cloth. So Jesus said to them, "Untie him and let him go."

Now many of the Jews who had come to Mary and seen what he had done began to believe in him.]

THIRD SCRUTINY

During Lent, the elect (those catechumens who have been called to prepare for baptism at Easter) are called to come before the community for exorcisms and prayers. This takes place after the liturgy of the word on the Third, Fourth, and Fifth Sundays of Lent. These rites are intended to purify the hearts and minds of the elect, to strengthen them against temptation, to help them progress in the love of God.

The presider asks the assembly to pray in silence for the elect, then to join in intercessions for them. The presider lays hands on each of the elect and prays that the elect be delivered from the power of evil and become witnesses to the gospel. A song or psalm may be sung, then the elect are dismissed as usual and the faithful continue with the liturgy of the eucharist.

FIFTH SUNDAY OF LENT / B   1040

READING I   *Jeremiah 31:31–34 / 35*

The days are coming, says the LORD, when I will make a new covenant with the house of Israel and the house of Judah. It will not be like the covenant I made with their fathers the day I took them by the hand to lead them forth from the land of Egypt; for they broke my covenant, and I had to show myself their master, says the LORD. But this is the covenant that I will make with the house of Israel after those days, says the LORD. I will place my law within them and write it upon their hearts; I will be their God, and they shall be my people. No longer will they have need to teach their friends and relatives how to know the LORD. All, from least to greatest, shall know me, says the LORD, for I will forgive their evildoing and remember their sin no more.

RESPONSORIAL PSALM   *Psalm 51:3–4, 12–13, 14–15*

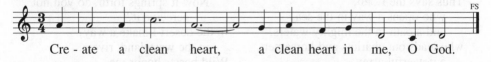

Cre - ate a clean heart, a clean heart in me, O God.

Have mercy on me, O God,
according to your merciful love;
according to your great compassion,
blot out my transgressions.
Wash me completely from my iniquity,
and cleanse me from my sin. ℟.

Create a pure heart for me, O God;
renew a steadfast spirit within me.

Do not cast me away from your
presence;
take not your holy spirit from me. ℟.

Restore in me the joy of your salvation;
sustain in me a willing spirit.
I will teach transgressors your ways,
that sinners may return to you. ℟.

READING II   *Hebrews 5:7–9*

In the days when Christ Jesus was in the flesh, he offered prayers and supplications with loud cries and tears to the one who was able to save him from death, and he was heard because of his reverence. Son though he was, he learned obedience from what he suffered; and when he was made perfect, he became the source of eternal salvation for all who obey him.

GOSPEL   *John 12:20–33*

Some Greeks who had come to worship at the Passover Feast came to Philip, who was from Bethsaida in Galilee, and asked him, "Sir, we would like to see Jesus." Philip went and told Andrew; then Andrew and Philip went and told Jesus. Jesus answered them, "The hour has come for the Son of Man to be glorified. Amen, amen, I say to you, unless a grain of wheat falls to the ground and dies, it remains just a grain of wheat; but if it dies, it produces much fruit. Whoever loves his life loses it, and whoever hates his life in this world will preserve it for eternal life. Whoever serves me must follow me, and where I am, there also will my servant be. The Father will honor whoever serves me.

"I am troubled now. Yet what should I say? 'Father, save me from this hour'? But it was for this purpose that I came to this hour. Father, glorify your name." Then a voice came from heaven, "I have glorified it and will glorify it again." The crowd there heard it and said it was thunder; but others said, "An angel has spoken to him." Jesus answered and said, "This voice did not come for my sake but for yours. Now is the time of judgment on this world; now the ruler of this world will be driven out. And when I am lifted up from the earth, I will draw everyone to myself." He said this indicating the kind of death he would die.

THIRD SCRUTINY
See no. 1039

1041 FIFTH SUNDAY OF LENT / C

READING I   *Isaiah 43:16–21 / 36*

Thus says the LORD,
  who opens a way in the sea
  and a path in the mighty waters,
who leads out chariots and horsemen,
  a powerful army,
till they lie prostrate together, never to
    rise,
  snuffed out and quenched like a wick.
Remember not the events of the past,
  the things of long ago consider not;
see, I am doing something new!

Now it springs forth, do you not
  perceive it?
In the desert I make a way,
  in the wasteland, rivers.
Wild beasts honor me,
  jackals and ostriches,
for I put water in the desert
  and rivers in the wasteland
  for my chosen people to drink,
the people whom I formed for myself,
  that they might announce my praise.

RESPONSORIAL PSALM   *Psalm 126:1–2ab, 2cd–3, 4–5, 6*

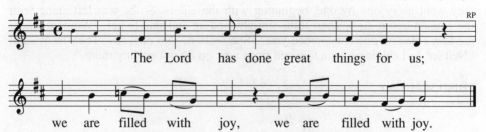

The Lord has done great things for us; we are filled with joy, we are filled with joy.

When the LORD brought back the exiles
    of Sion,
  we thought we were dreaming.
Then was our mouth filled with laughter;
  on our tongues, songs of joy. ℟.

Then the nations themselves said,
    "What great deeds
  the LORD worked for them!"
What great deeds the LORD worked for us!
  Indeed, we were glad. ℟.

Bring back our exiles, O LORD,
  as streams in the south.
Those who are sowing in tears
  will sing when they reap. ℟.

They go out, they go out, full of tears,
  bearing seed for the sowing;
they come back, they come back with
  a song,
bearing their sheaves. ℟.

READING II   *Philippians 3:8–14*

Brothers and sisters: I consider everything as a loss because of the supreme good of knowing Christ Jesus my Lord. For his sake I have accepted the loss of all things and I consider them so much rubbish, that I may gain Christ and be found in him, not having any righteousness of my own based on the law but that which comes through faith in Christ, the righteousness from God, depending on faith to know him and the power of his resurrection and the sharing of his sufferings by being conformed to his death, if somehow I may attain the resurrection from the dead.

It is not that I have already taken hold of it or have already attained perfect maturity, but I continue my pursuit in hope that I may possess it, since I have indeed been taken possession of by Christ Jesus. Brothers and sisters, I for my part do not consider myself to have taken possession. Just one thing: forgetting what lies behind but straining forward to what lies ahead, I continue my pursuit toward the goal, the prize of God's upward calling, in Christ Jesus.

GOSPEL   *John 8:1–11*

Jesus went to the Mount of Olives. But early in the morning he arrived again in the temple area, and all the people started coming to him, and he sat down and taught them. Then the scribes and the Pharisees brought a woman who had been caught in adultery and made her stand in the middle. They said to him, "Teacher, this woman was caught in the very act of committing adultery. Now in the law, Moses commanded us to stone such women. So what do you say?" They said this to test him, so that they could have some charge to bring against him. Jesus bent down and began to write on the ground with his finger. But when they continued asking him, he straightened up and said to them, "Let the one among you who is without sin be the first to throw a stone at her." Again he bent down and wrote on the ground. And in response, they went away one by one, beginning with the elders. So he was left alone with the woman before him. Then Jesus straightened up and said to her, "Woman, where are they? Has no one condemned you?" She replied, "No one, sir." Then Jesus said, "Neither do I condemn you. Go, and from now on do not sin any more."

THIRD SCRUTINY
See no. 1039

1042 PALM SUNDAY OF THE PASSION OF THE LORD

Passion or Palm Sunday is the last Sunday in Lent. Its closeness to the end of Lent has given this liturgy two distinct features: the procession with palms and the gospel reading of the Lord's passion. The blessing and carrying of palms celebrates Jesus' entrance into Jerusalem to accomplish his paschal mystery. The reading of the passion comes as a conclusion to all the gospel readings of the lenten Sundays: these scriptures yearly prepare catechumens and the faithful to approach the celebration of Christ's death and resurrection. That celebration takes place most especially in the sacraments of initiation at the Easter Vigil.

COMMEMORATION OF THE LORD'S ENTRANCE INTO JERUSALEM

This rite may be very simple or may involve the entire assembly in a procession with the blessing of palms and the gospel reading of Jesus' entrance into Jerusalem. Depending on the local Church, then, some of the following hymns, psalms and readings will be used.

1043 OPENING ANTIPHON

The following or another appropriate acclamation may be sung.

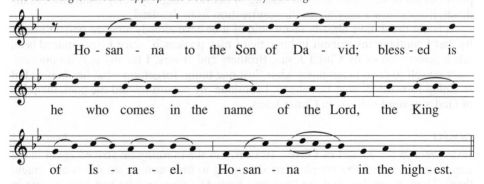

Ho-san-na to the Son of Da-vid; bless-ed is he who comes in the name of the Lord, the King of Is-ra-el. Ho-san-na in the high-est.

Text: ICEL, © 2010
Music: ICEL, © 2010; acc. by Richard Proulx, © 1985, 2011, GIA Publications, Inc.

1044 BLESSING OF BRANCHES

All hold branches as these are blessed. The branches may be of palm or from a tree that is native to the area. The green or flowering branches signify the victory of life.

GOSPEL / A

Matthew 21:1–11 / 37 1045

When Jesus and the disciples drew near Jerusalem and came to Bethphage on the Mount of Olives, Jesus sent two disciples, saying to them, "Go into the village opposite you, and immediately you will find an ass tethered, and a colt with her. Untie them and bring them here to me. And if anyone should say anything to you, reply, 'The master has need of them.' Then he will send them at once." This happened so that what had been spoken through the prophet might be fulfilled:

Say to daughter Zion,
"Behold, your king comes to you,
   meek and riding on an ass,
   and on a colt, the foal of a beast of burden."

The disicples went and did as Jesus had ordered them. They brought the ass and the colt and laid their cloaks over them, and he sat upon them. The very large crowd spread their cloaks on the road, while others cut branches from the trees and strewed them on the road. The crowds preceding him and those following kept crying out and saying:

"Hosanna to the Son of David;
   blessed is he who comes in the name of the Lord;
hosanna in the highest."

And when he entered Jerusalem the whole city was shaken and asked, "Who is this?" And the crowds replied, "This is Jesus the prophet, from Nazareth in Galilee."

GOSPEL / B

Mark 11:1–10 1046

When Jesus and his disciples drew near to Jerusalem, to Bethphage and Bethany at the Mount of Olives, he sent two of his disciples and said to them, "Go into the village opposite you, and immediately on entering it, you will find a colt tethered on which no one has ever sat. Untie it and bring it here. If anyone should say to you, 'Why are you doing this?' reply, 'The Master has need of it and will send it back here at once.'" So they went off and found a colt tethered at a gate outside on the street, and they untied it. Some of the bystanders said to them, "What are you doing, untying the colt?" They answered them just as Jesus had told them to, and they permitted them to do it. So they brought the colt to Jesus and put their cloaks over it. And he sat on it. Many people spread their cloaks on the road, and others spread leafy branches that they had cut from the fields. Those preceding him as well as those following kept crying out:

"Hosanna!
   Blessed is he who comes in the name of the Lord!
   Blessed is the kingdom of our father David that is to come!
Hosanna in the highest!"

Or:

GOSPEL / B

John 12:12–16

When the great crowd that had come to the feast heard that Jesus was coming to Jerusalem, they took palm branches and went out to meet him, and cried out:

"Hosanna!
"Blessed is he who comes in the name of the Lord,
   the king of Israel."

Jesus found an ass and sat upon it, as is written:

Fear no more, O daughter Zion;
see, your king comes, seated upon an ass's colt.
His disciples did not understand this at first, but when Jesus had been glorified they remembered that these things were written about him and that they had done this for him.

1047 GOSPEL / C

Luke 19:28–40

Jesus proceeded on his journey up to Jerusalem. As he drew near to Bethphage and Bethany at the place called the Mount of Olives, he sent two of his disciples. He said, "Go into the village opposite you, and as you enter it you will find a colt tethered on which no one has ever sat. Untie it and bring it here. And if anyone should ask you, 'Why are you untying it?' you will answer, 'The Master has need of it.'" So those who had been sent went off and found everything just as he had told them. And as they were untying the colt, its owners said to them, "Why are you untying this colt?" They answered, "The Master has need of it." So they brought it to Jesus, threw their cloaks over the colt, and helped Jesus to mount. As he rode along, the people were spreading their cloaks on the road; and now as he was approaching the slope of the Mount of Olives, the whole multitude of his disciples began to praise God aloud with joy for all the mighty deeds they had seen. They proclaimed:

"Blessed is the king who comes
in the name of the Lord.
Peace in heaven
and glory in the highest."

Some of the Pharisees in the crowd said to him, "Teacher, rebuke your disciples." He said in reply, "I tell you, if they keep silent, the stones will cry out!"

1048 PROCESSION

All join in the procession or at least in the song. Such a movement of people expresses the experience of Lent: the Church has been called to move on, to go ever further toward the paschal mystery of death and resurrection. The following or another appropriate hymn or song may be sung.

This dialogue may be used:

Priest, deacon, or other minister: Let us go forth in peace.

In the name of Christ.   A - men.

All   glo - ry,   laud,   and   hon - or   To

you, Re - deem - er,   King!   To   whom   the   lips   of

chil - dren Made sweet ho - san - nas ring.

1. You are the King of Is - ra - el And
2. The com - pa - ny of an - gels Are
3. The peo - ple of the He - brews With
4. To you, be - fore your pas - sion, They
5. Their prais - es you ac - cept - ed; Ac -

Da - vid's roy - al Son, Now in the Lord's Name
prais - ing you on high; And we, with all cre -
palms be - fore you went; Our praise and prayers and
sang their hymns of praise. To you, now high ex -
cept the prayers we bring, Great source of love and

D.C.

com - ing, Our King and Bless - ed One.
a - tion In cho - rus make re - ply.
an - thems Be - fore you we pre - sent.
alt - ed, Our mel - o - dy we raise.
good - ness, Our Sav - ior and our King.

Text: *Gloria, laus et honor*; Theodulph of Orléans, c.760–821; tr. by John M. Neale, 1818–1866, alt.
Tune: GLORIA, LAUS ET HONOR, 7 6 7 6 with refrain; Mode 1; acc. by Richard Proulx, 1937–2010, © 1983, GIA Publications, Inc.

The commemoration of the Lord's entrance into Jerusalem, whether this is done in a simple or solemn manner, concludes with the opening prayer of the Mass.

LITURGY OF THE WORD / ABC   1049

READING I   *Isaiah 50:4–7 / 38*

The Lord GOD has given me
   a well-trained tongue,
that I might know how to speak to the
   weary
   a word that will rouse them.
Morning after morning
   he opens my ear that I may hear;
and I have not rebelled,
   have not turned back.
I gave my back to those who beat me,

my cheeks to those who plucked my
   beard;
my face I did not shield
   from buffets and spitting.

The Lord GOD is my help,
   therefore I am not disgraced;
I have set my face like flint,
   knowing that I shall not be put to
   shame.

RESPONSORIAL PSALM *Psalm 22:8–9, 17–18a, 19–20, 23–24*

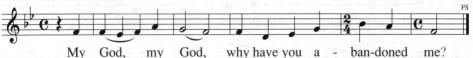

My God, my God, why have you a - ban-doned me?

All who see me deride me;
　they curl their lips, they toss their
　　heads:
"He trusted in the LORD, let him save him;
　let him release him, for in him he
　　delights." ℟.

For dogs have surrounded me;
　a band of the wicked besets me.
They tear holes in my hands and my feet;
　I can count every one of my bones. ℟.

They divide my clothing among them,
　they cast lots for my robe.
But you, O LORD, do not stay afar off;
　my strength, make haste to help me! ℟.

I will tell of your name to my kin,
　and praise you in the midst of the
　　assembly;
"You who fear the LORD, give him praise;
　all descendants of Jacob, give him
　　glory;
　revere him, all you descendants of
　　Israel." ℟.

READING II *Philippians 2:6–11*

Christ Jesus, though he was in the form
　of God,
　did not regard equality with God
　something to be grasped.
Rather, he emptied himself,
　taking the form of a slave,
　coming in human likeness;
　and found human in appearance,
　he humbled himself,
　becoming obedient to the point of
　　death,

even death on a cross.
Because of this, God greatly exalted him
　and bestowed on him the name
　which is above every name,
　that at the name of Jesus
　every knee should bend,
　of those in heaven and on earth and
　　under the earth,
　and every tongue confess that
　Jesus Christ is Lord,
　to the glory of God the Father.

1050　**GOSPEL / A** *Matthew 26:14 – 27:66 or 27:11–54*

For short form read only the part in brackets.

One of the Twelve, who was called Judas Iscariot, went to the chief priests and said, "What are you willing to give me if I hand him over to you?" They paid him thirty pieces of silver, and from that time on he looked for an opportunity to hand him over.

On the first day of the Feast of Unleavened Bread, the disciples approached Jesus and said, "Where do you want us to prepare for you to eat the Passover?" He said, "Go into the city to a certain man and tell him, 'The teacher says, "My appointed time draws near; in your house I shall celebrate the Passover with my disciples."'" The disciples then did as Jesus had ordered, and prepared the Passover.

When it was evening, he reclined at table with the Twelve. And while they were eating, he said, "Amen, I say to you, one of you will betray me." Deeply distressed at this, they began to say to him one after another, "Surely it is not I, Lord?" He said in reply, "He who has dipped his hand into the dish with me is the one who will betray me. The Son of Man indeed goes, as it is written of him, but woe to that man by whom the Son of Man is betrayed. It would be better for that man if he had never been born." Then Judas, his betrayer, said in reply, "Surely it is not I, Rabbi?" He answered, "You have said so."

While they were eating, Jesus took bread, said the blessing, broke it, and giving it to his disciples said, "Take and eat; this is my body." Then he took a cup, gave thanks, and gave it to them, saying, "Drink from it, all of you, for this is my blood of the covenant, which will be shed on behalf of many for the forgiveness of sins. I tell you, from now on I shall not drink this fruit of the vine until the day when I drink it with you new in the kingdom of my Father." Then, after singing a hymn, they went out to the Mount of Olives.

Then Jesus said to them, "This night all of you will have your faith in me shaken, for it is written:

I will strike the shepherd,
*   and the sheep of the flock will be dispersed;*

but after I have been raised up, I shall go before you to Galilee." Peter said to him in reply, "Though all may have their faith in you shaken, mine will never be." Jesus said to him, "Amen, I say to you, this very night before the cock crows, you will deny me three times." Peter said to him, "Even though I should have to die with you, I will not deny you." And all the disciples spoke likewise.

Then Jesus came with them to a place called Gethsemane, and he said to his disciples, "Sit here while I go over there and pray." He took along Peter and the two sons of Zebedee, and began to feel sorrow and distress. Then he said to them, "My soul is sorrowful even to death. Remain here and keep watch with me." He advanced a little and fell prostrate in prayer, saying, "My Father, if it is possible, let this cup pass from me; yet, not as I will, but as you will." When he returned to his disciples he found them asleep. He said to Peter, "So you could not keep watch with me for one hour? Watch and pray that you may not undergo the test. The spirit is willing, but the flesh is weak." Withdrawing a second time, he prayed again, "My Father, if it is not possible that this cup pass without my drinking it, your will be done!" Then he returned once more and found them asleep, for they could not keep their eyes open. He left them and withdrew again and prayed a third time, saying the same thing again. Then he returned to his disciples and said to them, "Are you still sleeping and taking your rest? Behold, the hour is at hand when the Son of Man is to be handed over to sinners. Get up, let us go. Look, my betrayer is at hand."

While he was still speaking, Judas, one of the Twelve, arrived, accompanied by a large crowd, with swords and clubs, who had come from the chief priests and the elders of the people. His betrayer had arranged a sign with them, saying, "The man I shall kiss is the one; arrest him." Immediately he went over to Jesus and said, "Hail, Rabbi!" and he kissed him. Jesus answered him, "Friend, do what you have come for." Then stepping forward they laid hands on Jesus and arrested him. And behold, one of those who accompanied Jesus put his hand to his sword, drew it, and struck the high priest's servant, cutting off his ear. Then Jesus said to him, "Put your sword back into its sheath, for all who take the sword will perish by the sword. Do you think that I cannot call upon my Father and he will not provide me at this moment with more than twelve legions of angels? But then how would the Scriptures be fulfilled which say that it must come to pass in this way?" At that hour Jesus said to the crowds, "Have you come out as against a robber, with swords and clubs to seize me? Day after day I sat teaching in the temple area, yet you did not arrest me. But all this has come to pass that the writings of the prophets may be fulfilled." Then all the disciples left him and fled.

Those who had arrested Jesus led him away to Caiaphas the high priest, where the scribes and the elders were assembled. Peter was following him at a distance as far as the high priest's courtyard, and going inside he sat down with the servants to see the outcome. The chief priests and the entire Sanhedrin kept trying to obtain false testimony against Jesus in order to put him to death, but they found none, though many false witnesses came forward. Finally two came forward who stated, "This man said, 'I can destroy the temple of God and within three days rebuild it.'" The high priest rose and addressed him, "Have you no answer? What are these men testifying against you?" But Jesus was silent. Then the high priest said to him, "I order you to tell us under oath before the living God whether you are the Christ, the Son of God." Jesus said to him in reply, "You have said so. But I tell you:

From now on you will see 'the Son of Man
    seated at the right hand of the Power'
    and 'coming on the clouds of heaven.'"

Then the high priest tore his robes and said, "He has blasphemed! What further need have we of witnesses? You have now heard the blasphemy; what is your opinion?" They said in reply, "He deserves to die!" Then they spat in his face and struck him, while some slapped him, saying, "Prophesy for us, Christ: who is it that struck you?"

Now Peter was sitting outside in the courtyard. One of the maids came over to him and said, "You too were with Jesus the Galilean." But he denied it in front of everyone, saying, "I do not know what you are talking about!" As he went out to the gate, another girl saw him and said to those who were there, "This man was with Jesus the Nazorean." Again he denied it with an oath, "I do not know the man!" A little later the bystanders came over and said to Peter, "Surely you too are one of them; even your speech gives you away." At that he began to curse and to swear, "I do not know the man." And immediately a cock crowed. Then Peter remembered the word that Jesus had spoken: "Before the cock crows you will deny me three times." He went out and began to weep bitterly.

When it was morning, all the chief priests and the elders of the people took counsel against Jesus to put him to death. They bound him, led him away, and handed him over to Pilate, the governor.

Then Judas, his betrayer, seeing that Jesus had been condemned, deeply regretted what he had done. He returned the thirty pieces of silver to the chief priests and elders, saying, "I have sinned in betraying innocent blood." They said, "What is that to us? Look to it yourself." Flinging the money into the temple, he departed and went off and hanged himself. The chief priests gathered up the money, but said, "It is not lawful to deposit this in the temple treasury, for it is the price of blood." After consultation, they used it to buy the potter's field as a burial place for foreigners. That is why that field even today is called the Field of Blood. Then was fulfilled what had been said through Jeremiah the prophet, *And they took the thirty pieces of silver, the value of a man with a price on his head, a price set by some of the Israelites, and they paid it out for the potter's field just as the Lord had commanded me.*

Now [Jesus stood before the governor, and he questioned him, "Are you the king of the Jews?" Jesus said, "You say so." And when he was accused by the chief priests and elders, he made no answer. Then Pilate said to him, "Do you not hear how many things they are testifying against you?" But he did not answer him one word, so that the governor was greatly amazed.

Now on the occasion of the feast the governor was accustomed to release to the crowd one prisoner whom they wished. And at that time they had a notorious prisoner called Barabbas. So when they had assembled, Pilate said to them, "Which one do you want me to release to you, Barabbas, or Jesus called Christ?" For he knew that it was out of envy that they had handed him over. While he was still seated on the bench, his wife sent him a message, "Have nothing to do with that righteous man. I suffered much in a dream today because of him." The chief priests and the elders persuaded the crowds to ask for Barabbas but to destroy Jesus. The governor said to them in reply, "Which of the two do you want me to release to you?" They answered, "Barabbas!" Pilate said to them, "Then what shall I do with Jesus called Christ?" They all said, "Let him be crucified!" But he said, "Why? What evil has he done?" They only shouted the louder, "Let him be crucified!" When Pilate saw that he was not succeeding at all, but that a riot was breaking out instead, he took water and washed his hands in the sight of the crowd, saying, "I am innocent of this man's blood. Look to it yourselves." And the whole people said in reply, "His blood be upon us and upon our children." Then he released Barabbas to them, but after he had Jesus scourged, he handed him over to be crucified.

Then the soldiers of the governor took Jesus inside the praetorium and gathered the whole cohort around him. They stripped off his clothes and threw a scarlet military cloak about him. Weaving a crown out of thorns, they placed it on his head, and a reed in his right hand. And kneeling before him, they mocked him, saying, "Hail, King of the Jews!" They spat upon him and took the reed and kept striking him on the head. And when they had mocked him, they stripped him of the cloak, dressed him in his own clothes, and led him off to crucify him.

As they were going out, they met a Cyrenian named Simon; this man they pressed into service to carry his cross.

And when they came to a place called Golgotha—which means Place of the Skull—, they gave Jesus wine to drink mixed with gall. But when he had tasted it, he refused to drink. After they had crucified him, they divided his garments by casting lots; then they sat down and kept watch over him there. And they placed over his head the written charge against him: This is Jesus, the King of the Jews. Two revolutionaries were crucified with him, one on his right and the other on his left. Those passing by reviled him, shaking their heads and saying, "You who would destroy the temple and rebuild it in three days, save yourself, if you are the Son of God, and come down from the cross!" Likewise the chief priests with the scribes and elders mocked him and said, "He saved others; he cannot save himself. So he is the king of Israel! Let him come down from the cross now, and we will believe in him. He trusted in God; let him deliver him now if he wants him. For he said, 'I am the Son of God.'" The revolutionaries who were crucified with him also kept abusing him in the same way.

From noon onward, darkness came over the whole land until three in the afternoon. And about three o'clock Jesus cried out in a loud voice, "*Eli, Eli, lema sabachthani?*" which means, "My God, my God, why have you forsaken me?" Some of the bystanders who heard it said, "This one is calling for Elijah." Immediately one of them ran to get a sponge; he soaked it in wine, and putting it on a reed, gave it to him to drink. But the rest said, "Wait, let us see if Elijah comes to save him." But Jesus cried out again in a loud voice, and gave up his spirit.

Here all kneel and pause for a short time.

And behold, the veil of the sanctuary was torn in two from top to bottom. The earth quaked, rocks were split, tombs were opened, and the bodies of many saints who had fallen asleep were raised. And coming forth from their tombs after his resurrection, they entered the holy city and appeared to many. The centurion and the men with him who were keeping watch over Jesus feared greatly when they saw the earthquake and all that was happening, and they said, "Truly, this was the Son of God!"] There were many women there, looking on from a distance, who had followed Jesus from Galilee, ministering to him. Among them were Mary Magdalene and Mary the mother of James and Joseph, and the mother of the sons of Zebedee.

When it was evening, there came a rich man from Arimathea named Joseph, who was himself a disciple of Jesus. He went to Pilate and asked for the body of Jesus; then Pilate ordered it to be handed over. Taking the body, Joseph wrapped it in clean linen and laid it in his new tomb that he had hewn in the rock. Then he rolled a huge stone across the entrance to the tomb and departed. But Mary Magdalene and the other Mary remained sitting there, facing the tomb.

The next day, the one following the day of preparation, the chief priests and the Pharisees gathered before Pilate and said, "Sir, we remember that this impostor while still alive said, 'After three days I will be raised up.' Give orders, then, that the grave be secured until the third day, lest his disciples come and steal him and say to the people, 'He has been raised from the dead.' This last imposture would be worse than the first." Pilate said to them, "The guard is yours; go, secure it as best you can." So they went and secured the tomb by fixing a seal to the stone and setting the guard.

1051   GOSPEL / B

Mark 14:1—15:47 or 15:1–39

For short form read only the part in brackets.

The Passover and the Feast of Unleavened Bread were to take place in two days' time. So the chief priests and the scribes were seeking a way to arrest him by treachery and put him to death. They said, "Not during the festival, for fear that there may be a riot among the people."

When he was in Bethany reclining at table in the house of Simon the leper, a woman came with an alabaster jar of perfumed oil, costly genuine spikenard. She broke the alabaster jar and poured it on his head. There were some who were indignant. "Why has there been this waste of perfumed oil? It could have been sold for more than three hundred days' wages and the money given to the poor." They were infuriated with her. Jesus said, "Let her alone. Why do you make trouble for her? She has done a good thing for me. The poor you will always have with you, and whenever you wish you can do good to them, but you will not always have me. She has done what she could. She has anticipated anointing my body for burial. Amen, I say to you, wherever the gospel is proclaimed to the whole world, what she has done will be told in memory of her."

Then Judas Iscariot, one of the Twelve, went off to the chief priests to hand him over to them. When they heard him they were pleased and promised to pay him money. Then he looked for an opportunity to hand him over.

On the first day of the Feast of Unleavened Bread, when they sacrificed the Passover lamb, his disciples said to him, "Where do you want us to go and prepare for you to eat the Passover?" He sent two of his disciples and said to them, "Go into the city and a man will meet you, carrying a jar of water. Follow him. Wherever he enters, say to the master of the house, 'The Teacher says, "Where is my guest room where I may eat the Passover with my disciples?"' Then he will show you a large upper room furnished and ready. Make the preparations for us there." The disciples then went off, entered the city, and found it just as he had told them; and they prepared the Passover.

When it was evening, he came with the Twelve. And as they reclined at table and were eating, Jesus said, "Amen, I say to you, one of you will betray me, one who is eating with me." They began to be distressed and to say to him, one by one, "Surely it is not I?" He said to them, "One of the Twelve, the one who dips with me into the dish. For the Son of Man indeed goes, as it is written of him, but woe to that man by whom the Son of Man is betrayed. It would be better for that man if he had never been born."

While they were eating, he took bread, said the blessing, broke it, and gave it to them, and said, "Take it; this is my body." Then he took a cup, gave thanks, and gave it to them, and they all drank from it. He said to them, "This is my blood of the covenant, which will be shed for many. Amen, I say to you, I shall not drink again the fruit of the vine until the day when I drink it new in the kingdom of God." Then, after singing a hymn, they went out to the Mount of Olives.

Then Jesus said to them, "All of you will have your faith shaken, for it is written:

I will strike the shepherd,
and the sheep will be dispersed.

But after I have been raised up, I shall go before you to Galilee." Peter said to him, "Even though all should have their faith shaken, mine will not be." Then Jesus said to him, "Amen, I say to you, this very night before the cock crows twice you will deny me three times." But he vehemently replied, "Even though I should have to die with you, I will not deny you." And they all spoke similarly.

Then they came to a place named Gethsemane, and he said to his disciples, "Sit here while I pray." He took with him Peter, James, and John, and began to be troubled and distressed. Then he said to them, "My soul is sorrowful even to death. Remain here and keep watch." He advanced a little and fell to the ground and prayed that if it were possible the hour might pass by him; he said, "Abba, Father, all things are possible to you. Take this cup away from me, but not what I will but what you will." When he returned he found them asleep. He said to Peter, "Simon, are you asleep? Could you not keep watch for one hour? Watch and pray that you may not undergo the test. The spirit is willing but the flesh is weak." Withdrawing again, he prayed, saying the same thing. Then he returned once more and found them asleep, for they could not keep their eyes open and did not know what to answer him. He returned a third time and said to them, "Are you still sleeping and taking your rest? It is enough. The hour has come. Behold, the Son of Man is to be handed over to sinners. Get up, let us go. See, my betrayer is at hand."

Then, while he was still speaking, Judas, one of the Twelve, arrived, accompanied by a crowd with swords and clubs who had come from the chief priests, the scribes, and the elders. His betrayer had arranged a signal with them, saying, "The man I shall kiss is the one; arrest him and lead him away securely." He came and immediately went over to him and said, "Rabbi." And he kissed him. At this they laid hands on him and arrested him. One of the bystanders drew his sword, struck the high priest's servant, and cut off his ear. Jesus said to them in reply, "Have you come out as against a robber, with swords and clubs, to seize me? Day after day I was with you teaching in the temple area, yet you did not arrest me; but that the Scriptures may be fulfilled." And they all left him and fled. Now a young man followed him wearing nothing but a linen cloth about his body. They seized him, but he left the cloth behind and ran off naked.

They led Jesus away to the high priest, and all the chief priests and the elders and the scribes came together. Peter followed him at a distance into the high priest's courtyard and was seated with the guards, warming himself at the fire. The chief priests and the entire Sanhedrin kept trying to obtain testimony against Jesus in order to put him to death, but they found none. Many gave false witness against him, but their testimony did not agree. Some took the stand and testified falsely against him, alleging, "We heard him say, 'I will destroy this temple made with hands and within three days I will build another not made with hands.'" Even so their testimony did not agree. The high priest rose before the assembly and questioned Jesus, saying, "Have you no answer? What are these men testifying against you?" But he was silent and answered nothing. Again the high priest asked him and said to him, "Are you the Christ, the son of the Blessed One?" Then Jesus answered, "I am;

> and 'you will see the Son of Man
> seated at the right hand of the Power
> and coming with the clouds of heaven.'"

At that the high priest tore his garments and said, "What further need have we of witnesses? You have heard the blasphemy. What do you think?" They all condemned him as deserving to die. Some began to spit on him. They blindfolded him and struck him and said to him, "Prophesy!" And the guards greeted him with blows.

While Peter was below in the courtyard, one of the high priest's maids came along. Seeing Peter warming himself, she looked intently at him and said, "You too were with the Nazarene, Jesus." But he denied it saying, "I neither know nor understand what you are talking about." So he went out into the outer court. Then the cock crowed. The maid saw him and began again to say to the bystanders, "This man is one of them." Once again he denied it. A little later the bystanders said to Peter once more, "Surely you are one of them; for you too are a Galilean." He began to curse and to swear, "I do not know this man about whom you are talking." And immediately a cock crowed a second time. Then Peter remembered the word that Jesus had said to him, "Before the cock crows twice you will deny me three times." He broke down and wept.

[As soon as morning came, the chief priests with the elders and the scribes, that is, the whole Sanhedrin held a council. They bound Jesus, led him away, and handed him over to Pilate. Pilate questioned him, "Are you the king of the Jews?" He said to him in reply, "You say so." The chief priests accused him of many things. Again Pilate questioned him, "Have you no answer? See how many things they accuse you of." Jesus gave him no further answer, so that Pilate was amazed.

Now on the occasion of the feast he used to release to them one prisoner whom they requested. A man called Barabbas was then in prison along with the rebels who had committed murder in a rebellion. The crowd came forward and began to ask him to do for them as he was accustomed. Pilate answered, "Do you want me to release to you the king of the Jews?" For he knew that it was out of envy that the chief priests had handed him over. But the chief priests stirred up the crowd to have him release Barabbas for them instead. Pilate again said to them in reply, "Then what do you want me to do with the man you call the king of the Jews?" They shouted again, "Crucify him." Pilate said to them, "Why? What evil has he done?" They only shouted the louder, "Crucify him." So Pilate, wishing to satisfy the crowd, released Barabbas to them and, after he had Jesus scourged, handed him over to be crucified.

The soldiers led him away inside the palace, that is, the praetorium, and assembled the whole cohort. They clothed him in purple and, weaving a crown of thorns, placed it on him. They began to salute him with, "Hail, King of the Jews!" and kept striking his head with a reed and spitting upon him. They knelt before him in homage. And when they had mocked him, they stripped him of the purple cloak, dressed him in his own clothes, and led him out to crucify him.

They pressed into service a passer-by, Simon, a Cyrenian, who was coming in from the country, the father of Alexander and Rufus, to carry his cross.

They brought him to the place of Golgotha —which is translated Place of the Skull—. They gave him wine drugged with myrrh, but he did not take it. Then they crucified him and divided his garments by casting lots for them to see what each should take. It was nine o'clock in the morning when they crucified him. The inscription of the charge against him read, "The King of the Jews." With him they crucified two revolutionaries, one on his right and one on his left. Those passing by reviled him, shaking their heads and saying, "Aha! You who would destroy the temple and rebuild it in three days, save yourself by coming down from the cross." Likewise the chief priests, with the scribes, mocked him among themselves and said, "He saved others; he cannot save himself. Let the Christ, the King of Israel, come down now from the cross that we may see and believe." Those who were crucified with him also kept abusing him.

At noon darkness came over the whole land until three in the afternoon. And at three o'clock Jesus cried out in a loud voice, *"Eloi, Eloi, lema sabachthani?"* which is translated, "My God, my God, why have you forsaken me?" Some of the bystanders who heard it said, "Look, he is calling Elijah." One of them ran, soaked a sponge with wine, put it on a reed and gave it to him to drink saying, "Wait, let us see if Elijah comes to take him down." Jesus gave a loud cry and breathed his last.

Here all kneel and pause for a short time.

The veil of the sanctuary was torn in two from top to bottom. When the centurion who stood facing him saw how he breathed his last he said, "Truly this man was the Son of God!"] There were also women looking on from a distance. Among them were Mary Magdalene, Mary the mother of the younger James and of Joses, and Salome. These women had followed him when he was in Galilee and ministered to him. There were also many other women who had come up with him to Jerusalem.

When it was already evening, since it was the day of preparation, the day before the sabbath, Joseph of Arimathea, a distinguished member of the council, who was himself awaiting the kingdom of God, came and courageously went to Pilate and asked for the body of Jesus. Pilate was amazed that he was already dead. He summoned the centurion and asked him if Jesus had already died. And when he learned of it from the centurion, he gave the body to Joseph. Having bought a linen cloth, he took him down, wrapped him in the linen cloth, and laid him in a tomb that had been hewn out of the rock. Then he rolled a stone against the entrance to the tomb. Mary Magdalene and Mary the mother of Joses watched where he was laid.

GOSPEL / C *Luke 22:14–23:56 or 23:1–49* 1052

For short form read only the part in brackets.

When the hour came, Jesus took his place at table with the apostles. He said to them, "I have eagerly desired to eat this Passover with you before I suffer, for, I tell you, I shall not eat it again until there is fulfillment in the kingdom of God." Then he took a cup, gave thanks, and said, "Take this and share it among yourselves; for I tell you that from this time on I shall not drink of the fruit of the vine until the kingdom of God comes." Then he took the bread, said the blessing, broke it, and gave it to them, saying, "This is my body, which will be given for you; do this in memory of me." And likewise the cup after they had eaten, saying, "This cup is the new covenant in my blood, which will be shed for you.

"And yet behold, the hand of the one who is to betray me is with me on the table; for the Son of Man indeed goes as it has been determined; but woe to that man by whom he is betrayed." And they began to debate among themselves who among them would do such a deed.

Then an argument broke out among them about which of them should be regarded as the greatest. He said to them, "The kings of the Gentiles lord it over them and those in authority over them are addressed as 'Benefactors'; but among you it shall not be so. Rather, let the greatest among you be as the youngest, and the leader as the servant. For who is greater: the one seated at table or the one who serves? Is it not the one seated at table? I am among you as the one who serves. It is you who have stood by me in my trials; and I confer a kingdom on you, just as my Father has conferred one on me, that you may eat and drink at my table in my kingdom; and you will sit on thrones judging the twelve tribes of Israel.

"Simon, Simon, behold Satan has demanded to sift all of you like wheat, but I have prayed that your own faith may not fail; and once you have turned back, you must strengthen your brothers." He said to him, "Lord, I am prepared to go to prison and to die with you." But he replied, "I tell you, Peter, before the cock crows this day, you will deny three times that you know me."

He said to them, "When I sent you forth without a money bag or a sack or sandals, were you in need of anything?" "No, nothing," they replied. He said to them, "But now one who has a money bag should take it, and likewise a sack, and one who does not have a sword should sell his cloak and buy one. For I tell you that this Scripture must be fulfilled in me, namely, *He was counted among the wicked*; and indeed what is written about me is coming to fulfillment." Then they said, "Lord, look, there are two swords here." But he replied, "It is enough!"

Then going out, he went, as was his custom, to the Mount of Olives, and the disciples followed him. When he arrived at the place he said to them, "Pray that you may not undergo the test." After withdrawing about a stone's throw from them and kneeling, he prayed, saying, "Father, if you are willing, take this cup away from me; still, not my will but yours be done." And to strengthen him an angel from heaven appeared to him. He was in such agony and he prayed so fervently that his sweat became like drops of blood falling on the ground. When he rose from prayer and returned to his disciples, he found them sleeping from grief. He said to them, "Why are you sleeping? Get up and pray that you may not undergo the test."

While he was still speaking, a crowd approached and in front was one of the Twelve, a man named Judas. He went up to Jesus to kiss him. Jesus said to him, "Judas, are you betraying the Son of Man with a kiss?" His disciples realized what was about to happen, and they asked, "Lord, shall we strike with a sword?" And one of them struck the high priest's servant and cut off his right ear. But Jesus said in reply, "Stop, no more of this!" Then he touched the servant's ear and healed him. And Jesus said to the chief priests and temple guards and elders who had come for him, "Have you come out as against a robber, with swords and clubs? Day after day I was with you in the temple area, and you did not seize me; but this is your hour, the time for the power of darkness."

After arresting him they led him away and took him into the house of the high priest; Peter was following at a distance. They lit a fire in the middle of the courtyard and sat around it, and Peter sat down with them. When a maid saw him seated in the light, she looked intently at him and said, "This man too was with him." But he denied it saying, "Woman, I do not know him." A short while later someone else saw him and said, "You too are one of them"; but Peter answered, "My friend, I am not." About an hour later, still another insisted, "Assuredly, this man too was with him, for he also is a Galilean." But Peter said, "My friend, I do not know what you are talking about." Just as he was saying this, the cock crowed, and the Lord turned and looked at Peter; and Peter remembered the word of the Lord, how he had said to him, "Before the cock crows today, you will deny me three times." He went out and began to weep bitterly. The men who held Jesus in custody were ridiculing and beating him. They blindfolded him and questioned him, saying, "Prophesy! Who is it that struck you?" And they reviled him in saying many other things against him.

When day came the council of elders of the people met, both chief priests and scribes, and they brought him before their Sanhedrin. They said, "If you are the Christ, tell us," but he replied to them, "If I tell you, you will not believe, and if I question, you will not respond. But from this time on the Son of Man will be seated at the right hand of the power of God." They all asked, "Are you then the Son of God?" He replied to them, "You say that I am." Then they said, "What further need have we for testimony? We have heard it from his own mouth."

[*Short form begins:* The elders of the people, chief priests and scribes, arose and brought Jesus before Pilate.] Then the whole assembly of them arose and brought him before Pilate. [They brought charges against him, saying, "We found this man misleading our people; he opposes the payment of taxes to Caesar and maintains that he is the Christ, a king." Pilate asked him, "Are you the king of the Jews?" He said to him in reply, "You say so." Pilate then addressed the chief priests and the crowds, "I find this man not guilty." But they were adamant and said, "He is inciting the people with his teaching throughout all Judea, from Galilee where he began even to here."

On hearing this Pilate asked if the man was a Galilean; and upon learning that he was under Herod's jurisdiction, he sent him to Herod who was in Jerusalem at that time. Herod was very glad to see Jesus; he had been wanting to see him for a long time, for he had heard about him and had been hoping to see him perform some sign. He questioned him at length, but he gave him no answer. The chief priests and scribes, meanwhile, stood by accusing him harshly. Herod and his soldiers treated him contemptuously and mocked him, and after clothing him in resplendent garb, he sent him back to Pilate. Herod and Pilate became friends that very day, even though they had been enemies formerly. Pilate then summoned the chief priests, the rulers, and the people and said to them, "You brought this man to me and accused him of inciting the people to revolt. I have conducted my investigation in your presence and have not found this man guilty of the charges you have brought against him, nor did Herod, for he sent him back to us. So no capital crime has been committed by him. Therefore I shall have him flogged and then release him."

But all together they shouted out, "Away with this man! Release Barabbas to us." —Now Barabbas had been imprisoned for a rebellion that had taken place in the city and for murder.— Again Pilate addressed them, still wishing to release Jesus, but they continued their shouting, "Crucify him! Crucify him!" Pilate addressed them a third time, "What evil has this man done? I found him guilty of no capital crime. Therefore I shall have him flogged and then release him." With loud shouts, however, they persisted in calling for his crucifixion, and their voices prevailed. The verdict of Pilate was that their demand should be granted. So he released the man who had been imprisoned for rebellion and murder, for whom they asked, and he handed Jesus over to them to deal with as they wished.

As they led him away they took hold of a certain Simon, a Cyrenian, who was coming in from the country; and after laying the cross on him, they made him carry it behind Jesus. A large crowd of people followed Jesus, including many women who mourned and lamented him. Jesus turned to them and said, "Daughters of Jerusalem, do not weep for me; weep instead for yourselves and for your children for indeed, the days are coming when people will say, 'Blessed are the barren, the wombs that never bore and the breasts that never nursed.' At that time people will say to the mountains, 'Fall upon us!' and to the hills, 'Cover us!' for if these things are done when the wood is green what will happen when it is dry?" Now two others, both criminals, were led away with him to be executed.

When they came to the place called the Skull, they crucified him and the criminals there, one on his right, the other on his left. Then Jesus said, "Father, forgive them, they know not what they do." They divided his garments by casting lots. The people stood by and watched; the rulers, meanwhile, sneered at him and said, "He saved others, let him save himself if he is the chosen one, the Christ of God." Even the soldiers jeered at him. As they approached to offer him wine they called out, "If you are King of the Jews, save yourself." Above him there was an inscription that read, "This is the King of the Jews."

Now one of the criminals hanging there reviled Jesus, saying, "Are you not the Christ? Save yourself and us." The other, however, rebuking him, said in reply, "Have you no fear of God, for you are subject to the same condemnation? And indeed, we have been condemned justly, for the sentence we received corresponds to our crimes, but this man has done nothing criminal." Then he said, "Jesus, remember me when you come into your kingdom." He replied to him, "Amen, I say to you, today you will be with me in Paradise."

It was now about noon and darkness came over the whole land until three in the afternoon because of an eclipse of the sun. Then the veil of the temple was torn down the middle. Jesus cried out in a loud voice, "Father, into your hands I commend my spirit"; and when he had said this he breathed his last.

Here all kneel and pause for a short time.

The centurion who witnessed what had happened glorified God and said, "This man was innocent beyond doubt." When all the people who had gathered for this spectacle saw what had happened, they returned home beating their breasts; but all his acquaintances stood at a distance, including the women who had followed him from Galilee and saw these events.]

Now there was a virtuous and righteous man named Joseph who, though he was a member of the council, had not consented to their plan of action. He came from the Jewish town of Arimathea and was awaiting the kingdom of God. He went to Pilate and asked for the body of Jesus. After he had taken the body down, he wrapped it in a linen cloth and laid him in a rock-hewn tomb in which no one had yet been buried. It was the day of preparation, and the sabbath was about to begin. The women who had come from Galilee with him followed behind, and when they had seen the tomb and the way in which his body was laid in it, they returned and prepared spices and perfumed oils. Then they rested on the sabbath according to the commandment.

"The Easter Triduum of the passion and resurrection of Christ is...the culmination of the entire liturgical year. What Sunday is to the week, the solemnity of Easter is to the liturgical year" (General Norms for the Liturgical Year, #18).

Lent ends quietly on Thursday afternoon. The Church enters the Triduum ("three days"). On Thursday night the Church begins a time of prayer and fasting, a time of keeping watch, that lasts into the great Vigil between Saturday and Sunday. The Church emphasizes that the fasting of Good Friday and, if possible, Holy Saturday is integral to the keeping of these days and the preparation for the sacraments of initiation celebrated at the Vigil. On Thursday night and on Friday afternoon or evening the Church gathers to pray and to remember the many facets of the single mystery.

THURSDAY OF THE LORD'S SUPPER: EVENING MASS 1054

On Thursday night Lent has ended and the Church, at this Mass of the Lord's Supper, enters into the Paschal Triduum. From the very first moment the all-embracing experience of these three days is proclaimed: "We should glory in the Cross of our Lord Jesus Christ, in whom is our salvation, life and resurrection, through whom we are saved and delivered." This is the whole of the great Triduum. On Thursday night, the liturgy draws us toward this through Scripture, through the mandatum or washing of feet, which is the direct expression of our service to one another and the world, and through the eucharistic banquet itself.

LITURGY OF THE WORD / ABC

READING I   *Exodus 12:1–8, 11–14 / 39*

The LORD said to Moses and Aaron in the land of Egypt, "This month shall stand at the head of your calendar; you shall reckon it the first month of the year. Tell the whole community of Israel: On the tenth of this month every one of your families must procure for itself a lamb, one apiece for each household. If a family is too small for a whole lamb, it shall join the nearest household in procuring one and shall share in the lamb in proportion to the number of persons who partake of it. The lamb must be a year-old male and without blemish. You may take it from either the sheep or the goats. You shall keep it until the fourteenth day of this month, and then, with the whole assembly of Israel present, it shall be slaughtered during the evening twilight. They shall take some of its blood and apply it to the two doorposts and the lintel of every house in which they partake of the lamb. That same night they shall eat its roasted flesh with unleavened bread and bitter herbs.

"This is how you are to eat it: with your loins girt, sandals on your feet and your staff in hand, you shall eat like those who are in flight. It is the Passover of the LORD. For on this same night I will go through Egypt, striking down every firstborn of the land, both man and beast, and executing judgment on all the gods of Egypt—I, the LORD! But the blood will mark the houses where you are. Seeing the blood, I will pass over you; thus, when I strike the land of Egypt, no destructive blow will come upon you.

"This day shall be a memorial feast for you, which all your generations shall celebrate with pilgrimage to the LORD, as a perpetual institution."

RESPONSORIAL PSALM *Psalm 116:12–13, 15 and 16bc, 17–18*

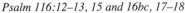

Our bless-ing cup is a com-mun-ion with the Blood of Christ.

How can I repay the LORD
  for all his goodness to me?
The cup of salvation I will raise;
  I will call on the name of the LORD. ℟.

How precious in the eyes of the LORD
  is the death of his faithful.
Your servant am I, the son of your

handmaid;
you have loosened my bonds. ℟.

A thanksgiving sacrifice I make;
  I will call on the name of the LORD.
My vows to the LORD I will fulfill
  before all his people. ℟.

READING II *1 Corinthians 11:23–26*

Brothers and sisters: I received from the Lord what I also handed on to you, that the Lord Jesus, on the night he was handed over, took bread, and, after he had given thanks, broke it and said, "This is my body that is for you. Do this in remembrance of me." In the same way also the cup, after supper, saying, "This cup is the new covenant in my blood. Do this, as often as you drink it, in remembrance of me." For as often as you eat this bread and drink the cup, you proclaim the death of the Lord until he comes.

GOSPEL *John 13:1–15*

Before the feast of Passover, Jesus knew that his hour had come to pass from this world to the Father. He loved his own in the world and he loved them to the end. The devil had already induced Judas, son of Simon the Iscariot, to hand him over. So, during supper, fully aware that the Father had put everything into his power and that he had come from God and was returning to God, he rose from supper and took off his outer garments. He took a towel and tied it around his waist. Then he poured water into a basin and began to wash the disciples' feet and dry them with the towel around his waist. He came to Simon Peter, who said to him, "Master, are you going to wash my feet?" Jesus answered and said to him, "What I am doing, you do not understand now, but you will understand later." Peter said to him, "You will never wash my feet." Jesus answered him, "Unless I wash you, you will have no inheritance with me." Simon Peter said to him, "Master, then not only my feet, but my hands and head as well." Jesus said to him, "Whoever has bathed has no need except to have his feet washed, for he is clean all over; so you are clean, but not all." For he knew who would betray him; for this reason, he said, "Not all of you are clean."

So when he had washed their feet and put his garments back on and reclined at table again, he said to them, "Do you realize what I have done for you? You call me 'teacher' and 'master,' and rightly so, for indeed I am. If I, therefore, the master and teacher, have washed your feet, you ought to wash one another's feet. I have given you a model to follow, so that as I have done for you, you should also do."

WASHING OF FEET

1055

The homily is followed by the washing of feet, the mandatum (from the Latin word for "command": "A new commandment I give to you..."). This is a simple gesture of humble service: the priest, assisted by other ministers, washes the feet of various members of the assembly. Such a gesture, with the song which accompanies it, speaks directly of the way of life Christians seek. The following or another appropriate hymn or song may be sung.

Man - dá - tum no - vum do vo - bis, di - cit Dó - mi - nus, di - cit Dó - mi - nus.

Text: *I give you a new commandment*; Taizé Community, 1979
Tune: Jacques Berthier, 1923–1994
© 1979, Les Presses de Taizé, GIA Publications, Inc., agent

The Mass continues with the Prayer of the Faithful.

1056 TRANSFER OF THE MOST BLESSED SACRAMENT

When the communion rite is concluded, the eucharistic bread that remains is solemnly carried from the altar to a specially prepared place of repose. The following hymn accompanies the procession.

1. Hail our Sav - ior's glo - rious Bod - y, Which his Vir - gin
2. To the Vir - gin, for our heal - ing, His own Son the
3. On that pas - chal eve - ning see him With the cho - sen
4. By his word the Word al - might - y Makes of bread his
5. Come, a - dore this won - drous pres - ence; Bow to Christ, the
6. Glo - ry be to God the Fa - ther, Praise to his co -

1. Pan - ge lin - gua glo - ri - ó - si, Cór - po - ris my -
2. No - bis da - tus, no - bis na - tus Ex in - tá - cta
3. In su - pré - mae no - cte coe - nae, Re - cúm - bens cum
4. Ver - bum ca - ro, pa - nem ve - rum Ver - bo car - nem
5. Tan - tum er - go Sa - cra - mén - tum Ve - ne - ré - mur
6. Ge - ni - tó - ri, Ge - ni - tó - que Laus et ju - bi -

Moth - er bore; Hail the Blood which, shed for sin - ners,
Fa - ther sends; From the Fa - ther's love pro - ceed - ing
twelve re - cline, To the old law still o - be - dient
flesh in - deed; Wine be - comes his ver - y life-blood;
source of grace! Here is kept the an - cient prom - ise
e - qual Son, Ad - o - ra - tion to the Spir - it,

sté - ri - um San - gui - nís - que pre - ti - ó - si,
Vír - gi - ne, Et in mun - do con - ver - sá - tus,
frá - tri - bus, Ob - ser - vá - ta le - ge ple - ne
éf - fi - cit: Fit - que san - guis Chri - sti me - rum,
cér - nu - i: Et an - tí - quum do - cu - mén - tum
lá - ti - o, Sa - lus, ho - nor, vir - tus quo - que

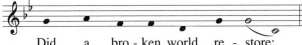

Did a bro - ken world re - store; Hail the sac - ra -
Sow - er, seed and word de - scends; Won - drous life of
In its feast of love di - vine; Love di - vine, the
Faith God's liv - ing Word must heed! Faith a - lone may
Of God's earth - ly dwell - ing place. Sight is blind be -
Bond of love, in God - head one. Blest be God by

Quem in mun - di pré - ti - um Fru - ctus ven - tris
Spar - so ver - bi sé - mi - ne, Su - i mo - ras
Ci - bis in le - gá - li - bus, Ci - bum tur - bae
Et si sen - sus dé - fi - cit, Ad fir - mán - dum
No - vo ce - dat rí - tu - i; Prae - stet fi - des
Sit et be - ne - dí - cti - o: Pro - ce - dén - ti

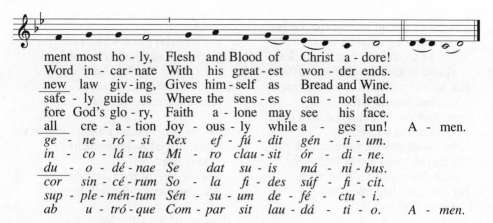

ment	most	ho - ly,	Flesh	and	Blood	of	Christ	a - dore!	
Word	in - car - nate		With	his	great - est		won - der	ends.	
new	law	giv - ing,	Gives	him - self	as		Bread	and Wine.	
safe - ly	guide	us	Where	the	sens - es		can - not	lead.	
fore	God's	glo - ry,	Faith	a - lone	may	see	his	face.	
all	cre - a - tion	Joy - ous - ly	while a - ges	run!	A - men.
ge - ne - ró - si	Rex	ef - fú - dit	gén - ti - um.
in - co - lá - tus	Mi - ro	clau - sit	ór - di - ne.
du - o - dé - nae	Se	dat	su - is	má - ni - bus.
cor	sin - cé - rum	So - la	fi - des	súf - fi - cit.
sup - ple - mén - tum	Sén - su - um	de - fé - ctu - i.
ab	u - tró - que	Com - par	sit	lau - dá - ti - o.	A - men.

Text: *Pange lingua*, Thomas Aquinas, 1227–1274; tr. by James Quinn, SJ, 1919–2010, © 1969. Used by permission of Selah Publishing, Inc.
Tune: PANGE LINGUA GLORIOSI, 8 7 8 7; Mode III; acc. by Eugene Lapierre, 1899–1970, © 1964, GIA Publications, Inc.

The liturgy has no concluding rite, no dismissal. Rather, the Church continues to watch and pray throughout the Triduum.

GOOD FRIDAY: CELEBRATION OF THE PASSION OF THE LORD 1057

In Good Friday's liturgy of the word and adoration of the cross there is great solemnity as the Church ponders the "mystery of faith": the passion, death and resurrection of our Lord Jesus Christ. Fasting and praying during these days, the catechumens and the baptized assemble on Good Friday in the afternoon or evening for the Passion liturgy, which begins in silence.

LITURGY OF THE WORD / ABC

READING I   *Isaiah 52:13–53:12 / 40*

See, my servant shall prosper,
    he shall be raised high and greatly
        exalted.
Even as many were amazed at him—
    so marred was his look beyond
        human semblance
    and his appearance beyond that of
        the sons of man—
so shall he startle many nations,
    because of him kings shall stand
        speechless;
for those who have not been told shall
    see,
those who have not heard shall
    ponder it.

Who would believe what we have heard?

To whom has the arm of the LORD
    been revealed?
He grew up like a sapling before him,
    like a shoot from the parched earth;
there was in him no stately bearing to
    make us look at him,
    nor appearance that would attract us
        to him.
He was spurned and avoided by people,
    a man of suffering, accustomed to
        infirmity,
one of those from whom people hide
    their faces,
    spurned, and we held him in no
        esteem.

Yet it was our infirmities that he bore,
    our sufferings that he endured,
while we thought of him as stricken,
    as one smitten by God and afflicted.
But he was pierced for our offenses,
    crushed for our sins;
upon him was the chastisement that
        makes us whole,
    by his stripes we were healed.
We had all gone astray like sheep,
    each following his own way;
but the LORD laid upon him
    the guilt of us all.

Though he was harshly treated, he
        submitted
    and opened not his mouth;
like a lamb led to the slaughter
    or a sheep before the shearers,
    he was silent and opened not his mouth.
Oppressed and condemned, he was
        taken away,
    and who would have thought any
        more of his destiny?
When he was cut off from the land of
        the living,
    and smitten for the sin of his people,
a grave was assigned him among the

wicked
    and a burial place with evildoers,
though he had done no wrong
    nor spoken any falsehood.
But the LORD was pleased
    to crush him in infirmity.

If he gives his life as an offering for sin,
    he shall see his descendants in a
        long life,
    and the will of the LORD shall be
        accomplished through him.

Because of his affliction
    he shall see the light
        in fullness of days;
through his suffering, my servant shall
        justify many,
    and their guilt he shall bear.
Therefore I will give him his portion
        among the great,
    and he shall divide the spoils with
        the mighty,
because he surrendered himself to death
    and was counted among the wicked;
and he shall take away the sins of many,
    and win pardon for their offenses.

RESPONSORIAL PSALM   *Psalm 31:2 and 6, 12–13, 15–16, 17 and 25*

Fa - ther, in - to your hands   I com-mend my spir-it,   my spir-it.

In you, O LORD, I take refuge.
    Let me never be put to shame.
    In your justice, set me free.
Into your hands I commend my spirit.
    You will redeem me, O LORD,
        O faithful God. ℟.

Because of all my foes
    I have become a reproach,
an object of scorn to my neighbors
    and of fear to my friends.
Those who see me in the street
    flee from me.
I am forgotten, like someone dead,

and have become like a broken
    vessel. ℟.

But as for me, I trust in you, O LORD;
    I say, "You are my God.
My lot is in your hands, deliver me
    from the hands of my enemies
    and those who pursue me. ℟.

"Let your face shine on your servant.
    Save me in your merciful love."
Be strong, let your heart take courage,
    all who hope in the LORD. ℟.

READING II

Hebrews 4:14–16; 5:7–9

Brothers and sisters: Since we have a great high priest who has passed through the heavens, Jesus, the Son of God, let us hold fast to our confession. For we do not have a high priest who is unable to sympathize with our weaknesses, but one who has similarly been tested in every way, yet without sin. So let us confidently approach the throne of grace to receive mercy and to find grace for timely help.

In the days when Christ was in the flesh, he offered prayers and supplications with loud cries and tears to the one who was able to save him from death, and he was heard because of his reverence. Son though he was, he learned obedience from what he suffered; and when he was made perfect, he became the source of eternal salvation for all who obey him.

GOSPEL

John 18:1–19:42

Jesus went out with his disciples across the Kidron valley to where there was a garden, into which he and his disciples entered. Judas his betrayer also knew the place, because Jesus had often met there with his disciples. So Judas got a band of soldiers and guards from the chief priests and the Pharisees and went there with lanterns, torches, and weapons. Jesus, knowing everything that was going to happen to him, went out and said to them, "Whom are you looking for?" They answered him, "Jesus the Nazorean." He said to them, "I AM." Judas his betrayer was also with them. When he said to them, "I AM," they turned away and fell to the ground. So he again asked them, "Whom are you looking for?" They said, "Jesus the Nazorean." Jesus answered, "I told you that I AM. So if you are looking for me, let these men go." This was to fulfill what he had said, "I have not lost any of those you gave me." Then Simon Peter, who had a sword, drew it, struck the high priest's slave, and cut off his right ear. The slave's name was Malchus. Jesus said to Peter, "Put your sword into its scabbard. Shall I not drink the cup that the Father gave me?"

So the band of soldiers, the tribune, and the Jewish guards seized Jesus, bound him, and brought him to Annas first. He was the father-in-law of Caiaphas, who was high priest that year. It was Caiaphas who had counseled the Jews that it was better that one man should die rather than the people.

Simon Peter and another disciple followed Jesus. Now the other disciple was known to the high priest, and he entered the courtyard of the high priest with Jesus. But Peter stood at the gate outside. So the other disciple, the acquaintance of the high priest, went out and spoke to the gatekeeper and brought Peter in. Then the maid who was the gatekeeper said to Peter, "You are not one of this man's disciples, are you?" He said, "I am not." Now the slaves and the guards were standing around a charcoal fire that they had made, because it was cold, and were warming themselves. Peter was also standing there keeping warm.

The high priest questioned Jesus about his disciples and about his doctrine. Jesus answered him, "I have spoken publicly to the world. I have always taught in a synagogue or in the temple area where all the Jews gather, and in secret I have said nothing. Why ask me? Ask those who heard me what I said to them. They know what I said." When he had said this, one of the temple guards standing there struck Jesus and said, "Is this the way you answer the high priest?" Jesus answered him, "If I have spoken wrongly, testify to the wrong; but if I have spoken rightly, why do you strike me?" Then Annas sent him bound to Caiaphas the high priest.

Now Simon Peter was standing there keeping warm. And they said to him, "You are not one of his disciples, are you?" He denied it and said, "I am not." One of the slaves of the high priest, a relative of the one whose ear Peter had cut off, said,

"Didn't I see you in the garden with him?" Again Peter denied it. And immediately the cock crowed.

Then they brought Jesus from Caiaphas to the praetorium. It was morning. And they themselves did not enter the praetorium, in order not to be defiled so that they could eat the Passover. So Pilate came out to them and said, "What charge do you bring against this man?" They answered and said to him, "If he were not a criminal, we would not have handed him over to you." At this, Pilate said to them, "Take him yourselves, and judge him according to your law." The Jews answered him, "We do not have the right to execute anyone," in order that the word of Jesus might be fulfilled that he said indicating the kind of death he would die. So Pilate went back into the praetorium and summoned Jesus and said to him, "Are you the King of the Jews?" Jesus answered, "Do you say this on your own or have others told you about me?" Pilate answered, "I am not a Jew, am I? Your own nation and the chief priests handed you over to me. What have you done?" Jesus answered, "My kingdom does not belong to this world. If my kingdom did belong to this world, my attendants would be fighting to keep me from being handed over to the Jews. But as it is, my kingdom is not here." So Pilate said to him, "Then you are a king?" Jesus answered, "You say I am a king. For this I was born and for this I came into the world, to testify to the truth. Everyone who belongs to the truth listens to my voice." Pilate said to him, "What is truth?"

When he had said this, he again went out to the Jews and said to them, "I find no guilt in him. But you have a custom that I release one prisoner to you at Passover. Do you want me to release to you the King of the Jews?" They cried out again, "Not this one but Barabbas!" Now Barabbas was a revolutionary.

Then Pilate took Jesus and had him scourged. And the soldiers wove a crown out of thorns and placed it on his head, and clothed him in a purple cloak, and they came to him and said, "Hail, King of the Jews!" And they struck him repeatedly. Once more Pilate went out and said to them, "Look, I am bringing him out to you, so that you may know that I find no guilt in him." So Jesus came out, wearing the crown of thorns and the purple cloak. And he said to them, "Behold, the man!" When the chief priests and the guards saw him they cried out, "Crucify him, crucify him!" Pilate said to them, "Take him yourselves and crucify him. I find no guilt in him." The Jews answered, "We have a law, and according to that law he ought to die, because he made himself the Son of God." Now when Pilate heard this statement, he became even more afraid, and went back into the praetorium and said to Jesus, "Where are you from?" Jesus did not answer him. So Pilate said to him, "Do you not speak to me? Do you not know that I have power to release you and I have power to crucify you?" Jesus answered him, "You would have no power over me if it had not been given to you from above. For this reason the one who handed me over to you has the greater sin." Consequently, Pilate tried to release him; but the Jews cried out, "If you release him, you are not a Friend of Caesar. Everyone who makes himself a king opposes Caesar."

When Pilate heard these words he brought Jesus out and seated him on the judge's bench in the place called Stone Pavement, in Hebrew, Gabbatha. It was preparation day for Passover, and it was about noon. And he said to the Jews, "Behold, your king!" They cried out, "Take him away, take him away! Crucify him!" Pilate said to them, "Shall I crucify your king?" The chief priests answered, "We have no king but Caesar." Then he handed him over to them to be crucified.

So they took Jesus, and, carrying the cross himself, he went out to what is called the Place of the Skull, in Hebrew, Golgotha. There they crucified him, and with him two others, one on either side, with Jesus in the middle. Pilate also had an inscription written and put on the cross. It read, "Jesus the Nazorean, the King of the Jews." Now many of the Jews read this inscription, because the place where Jesus was crucified was near the city; and it was written in Hebrew, Latin, and Greek. So the chief priests of the Jews said to Pilate, "Do not write 'The King of the Jews,' but that he said, 'I am the King of the Jews'." Pilate answered, "What I have written, I have written."

When the soldiers had crucified Jesus, they took his clothes and divided them into four shares, a share for each soldier. They also took his tunic, but the tunic was seamless, woven in one piece from the top down. So they said to one another, "Let's not tear it, but cast lots for it to see whose it will be," in order that the passage of Scripture might be fulfilled that says:

They divided my garments among them,
    and for my vesture they cast lots.

This is what the soldiers did. Standing by the cross of Jesus were his mother and his mother's sister, Mary the wife of Clopas, and Mary of Magdala. When Jesus saw his mother and the disciple there whom he loved he said to his mother, "Woman, behold, your son." Then he said to the disciple, "Behold, your mother." And from that hour the disciple took her into his home.

After this, aware that everything was now finished, in order that the Scripture might be fulfilled, Jesus said, "I thirst." There was a vessel filled with common wine. So they put a sponge soaked in wine on a sprig of hyssop and put it up to his mouth. When Jesus had taken the wine, he said, "It is finished." And bowing his head, he handed over the spirit.

Here all kneel and pause for a short time.

Now since it was preparation day, in order that the bodies might not remain on the cross on the sabbath, for the sabbath day of that week was a solemn one, the Jews asked Pilate that their legs be broken and that they be taken down. So the soldiers came and broke the legs of the first and then of the other one who was crucified with Jesus. But when they came to Jesus and saw that he was already dead, they did not break his legs, but one soldier thrust his lance into his side, and immediately blood and water flowed out. An eyewitness has testified, and his testimony is true; he knows that he is speaking the truth, so that you also may come to believe. For this happened so that the Scripture passage might be fulfilled:

Not a bone of it will be broken.

And again another passage says:

They will look upon him whom they have pierced.

After this, Joseph of Arimathea, secretly a disciple of Jesus for fear of the Jews, asked Pilate if he could remove the body of Jesus. And Pilate permitted it. So he came and took his body. Nicodemus, the one who had first come to him at night, also came bringing a mixture of myrrh and aloes weighing about one hundred pounds. They took the body of Jesus and bound it with burial cloths along with the spices, according to the Jewish burial custom. Now in the place where he had been crucified there was a garden, and in the garden a new tomb, in which no one had yet been buried. So they laid Jesus there because of the Jewish preparation day; for the tomb was close by.

SOLEMN INTERCESSIONS

As at Sunday liturgy, the word service concludes with prayers of intercession. Today these prayers take a more solemn form as the Church lifts up to God its own needs and those of the world.

1058   ADORATION OF THE HOLY CROSS

An ancient liturgical text reads: "See here the true and most revered Tree. Hasten to kiss it and to cry out with faith: You are our help, most revered Cross." For many centuries the Church has solemnly venerated the relic or image of the cross on Good Friday. It is not present as a picture of suffering only but as a symbol of Christ's passover, where "dying he destroyed our death and rising restored our life." It is the glorious, the life-giving cross that the faithful venerate with song, prayer, kneeling and a kiss.

As the cross is shown to the assembly, the following is sung.

Priest or deacon: **Behold the wood of the Cross,
on which hung the salvation of the world.**

As the assembly comes forward to venerate the cross, the following or other hymns and songs may be sung.

Text: *We adore you, Lord;* Taizé Community, 1979
Tune: Jacques Berthier, 1923–1994
© 1979, Les Presses de Taizé, GIA Publications, Inc., agent

1059   HOLY COMMUNION

This liturgy concludes with a simple communion rite. All recite the Lord's Prayer and receive Holy Communion. There is no concluding rite or dismissal for the Church continues to be at prayer throughout the Triduum.

1060   HOLY SATURDAY

The Church continues to fast and pray and to make ready for this night's great Vigil. Saturday is a day of great quiet and reflection. Catechumens, sponsors and some of the faithful may assemble during the day for prayer, the recitation of the Creed, and for the rite of Ephphetha (opening of ears and mouth).

1061   EASTER VIGIL IN THE HOLY NIGHT

The long preparation of the catechumens, the lenten disciplines and fast of the faithful, the vigiling and fasting and prayer that have gone on since Thursday night—all culminate in the great liturgy of this night. On this night the Church assembles to spend much time listening to Scripture, praying psalms, acclaiming the death and resurrection of the Lord. Only then are the catechumens called forward and prayed over, challenged to renounce evil and affirm their faith in God, led to the font and baptized in the blessed water. The newly baptized are then anointed with chrism and the entire assembly joins in intercession and finally in the Eucharist.

LUCERNARIUM

BLESSING OF THE FIRE AND PREPARATION OF THE PASCHAL CANDLE

The night vigil begins with the kindling of new fire and the lighting of the paschal candle.

PROCESSION

The ministers and assembly go in procession to the place where Scripture will be read. The following is sung during the procession.

The Light of Christ. Thanks be to God.

EASTER PROCLAMATION: THE EXSULTET

In this ancient text the Church gives thanks and praise to God for all that is recalled this night: Adam's fall, the deliverance from Egypt, the passover of Christ, the wedding of earth and heaven, our reconciliation.

LITURGY OF THE WORD / ABC

At the Vigil, the liturgy of the word is an extended time of readings, silence and the singing of psalms. On this night when the faithful know the death and resurrection of the Lord in baptism and eucharist, the Church needs first to hear these scripture readings, which are the foundation of our life together: the creation story, Abraham and Isaac, the dividing of the sea, the poetry of Isaiah and Baruch and Ezekiel, the proclamation of Paul to the Romans and the gospel account of Jesus' resurrection.

READING I

For short form read only the parts in brackets.

Genesis 1:1–2:2 or 1:1, 26–31a / 41 1062

[In the beginning, when God created the heavens and the earth,] the earth was a formless wasteland, and darkness covered the abyss, while a mighty wind swept over the waters.

Then God said, "Let there be light," and there was light. God saw how good the light was. God then separated the light from the darkness. God called the light "day," and the darkness he called "night." Thus evening came, and morning followed—the first day.

Then God said, "Let there be a dome in the middle of the waters, to separate one body of water from the other." And so it happened: God made the dome, and it separated the water above the dome from the water below it. God called the dome "the sky." Evening came, and morning followed—the second day.

Then God said, "Let the water under the sky be gathered into a single basin, so that the dry land may appear." And so it happened: the water under the sky was gathered into its basin, and the dry land appeared. God called the dry land "the earth," and the basin of the water he called "the sea." God saw how good it was. Then God said, "Let the earth bring forth vegetation: every kind of plant that bears seed and every kind of fruit tree on earth that bears fruit with its seed in it." And so it happened: the earth brought forth every kind of plant that bears seed and every kind of fruit tree on earth that bears fruit with its seed in it. God saw how good it was. Evening came, and morning followed—the third day.

Then God said: "Let there be lights in the dome of the sky, to separate day from night. Let them mark the fixed times, the days and the years, and serve as luminaries in the dome of the sky, to shed light upon the earth." And so it happened: God made the two great lights, the greater one to govern the day, and the lesser one to govern the night; and he made the stars. God set them in the dome of the sky, to shed light upon the earth, to govern the day and the night, and to separate the light from the darkness. God saw how good it was. Evening came, and morning followed—the fourth day.

Then God said, "Let the water teem with an abundance of living creatures, and on the earth let birds fly beneath the dome of the sky." And so it happened: God created the great sea monsters and all kinds of swimming creatures with which the water teems, and all kinds of winged birds. God saw how good it was, and God blessed them, saying, "Be fertile, multiply, and fill the water of the seas; and let the birds multiply on the earth." Evening came, and morning followed—the fifth day.

Then God said, "Let the earth bring forth all kinds of living creatures: cattle, creeping things, and wild animals of all kinds." And so it happened: God made all kinds of wild animals, all kinds of cattle, and all kinds of creeping things of the earth. God saw how good it was. Then [God said: "Let us make man in our image, after our likeness. Let them have dominion over the fish of the sea, the birds of the air, and the cattle, and over all the wild animals and all the creatures that crawl on the ground."

God created man in his image;
in the image of God he created him;
male and female he created them.

God blessed them, saying: "Be fertile and multiply; fill the earth and subdue it. Have dominion over the fish of the sea, the birds of the air, and all the living things that move on the earth." God also said: "See, I give you every seed-bearing plant all over the earth and every tree that has seed-bearing fruit on it to be your food; and to all the animals of the land, all the birds of the air, and all the living creatures that crawl on the ground, I give all the green plants for food." And so it happened. God looked at everything he had made, and he found it very good.] Evening came, and morning followed—the sixth day.

Thus the heavens and the earth and all their array were completed. Since on the seventh day God was finished with the work he had been doing, he rested on the seventh day from all the work he had undertaken.

RESPONSORIAL PSALM   *1. Psalm 104:1–2a, 5–6, 10 and 12, 13–14, 24 and 35c*

RP

Lord, send out your Spir-it, and re-new the face of the earth.

Bless the LORD, O my soul!
O LORD my God, how great you are,
clothed in majesty and honor,
wrapped in light as with a robe! ℟.

You set the earth on its foundation,
immovable from age to age.
You wrapped it with the depths like a cloak;
the waters stood higher than the mountains. ℟.

You make springs gush forth in the
valleys;
they flow in between the hills.
There the birds of heaven build their
nests;
from the branches they sing their
song. ℟.

From your dwelling you water the hills;
by your works the earth has its fill.

You make the grass grow for the cattle
and plants to serve mankind's need,
that he may bring forth bread from
the earth. ℟.

How many are your works, O LORD!
In wisdom you have made them all.
The earth is full of your creatures.
Bless the LORD, O my soul. ℟.

Or:

RESPONSORIAL PSALM   *2. Psalm 33:4–5, 6–7, 12–13, 20 and 22*

The earth is full of the good-ness, the good-ness of the Lord.

The word of the LORD is faithful,
and all his works to be trusted.
The LORD loves justice and right,
and his merciful love fills the earth. ℟.

By the word of the LORD the heavens
were made,
by the breath of his mouth all their
host.
As in a flask, he collects the waves of
the ocean;
he stores up the depths of the sea. ℟.

Blessed the nation whose God is the
LORD,
the people he has chosen as his
heritage.
From the heavens the Lord looks forth;
he sees all the children of men. ℟.

Our soul is waiting for the LORD.
He is our help and our shield.
May your merciful love be upon us,
as we hope in you, O LORD. ℟.

READING II   *Genesis 22:1–18 or 22:1–2, 9a, 10–13, 15–18* 1063
For short form read only the parts in brackets.

[God put Abraham to the test. He called to him, "Abraham!" "Here I am," he replied.
Then God said: "Take your son Isaac, your only one, whom you love, and go to the
land of Moriah. There you shall offer him up as a holocaust on a height that I will
point out to you."] Early the next morning Abraham saddled his donkey, took with
him his son Isaac and two of his servants as well, and with the wood that he had cut
for the holocaust, set out for the place of which God had told him.

On the third day Abraham got sight of the place from afar. Then he said to his
servants: "Both of you stay here with the donkey, while the boy and I go on over
yonder. We will worship and then come back to you." Thereupon Abraham took the
wood for the holocaust and laid it on his son Isaac's shoulders, while he himself carried the fire and the knife. As the two walked on together, Isaac spoke to his father
Abraham: "Father!" Isaac said. "Yes, son," he replied. Isaac continued, "Here are the
fire and the wood, but where is the sheep for the holocaust?" "Son," Abraham answered,
"God himself will provide the sheep for the holocaust." Then the two continued going
forward.

[When they came to the place of which God had told him, Abraham built an altar there and arranged the wood on it.] Next he tied up his son Isaac, and put him on top of the wood on the altar. [Then he reached out and took the knife to slaughter his son. But the LORD's messenger called to him from heaven, "Abraham, Abraham!" "Here I am," he answered. "Do not lay your hand on the boy," said the messenger. "Do not do the least thing to him. I know now how devoted you are to God, since you did not withhold from me your own beloved son." As Abraham looked about, he spied a ram caught by its horns in the thicket. So he went and took the ram and offered it up as a holocaust in place of his son.] Abraham named the site Yahweh-yireh; hence people now say, "On the mountain the LORD will see."

[Again the LORD's messenger called to Abraham from heaven and said: "I swear by myself, declares the LORD, that because you acted as you did in not withholding from me your beloved son, I will bless you abundantly and make your descendants as countless as the stars of the sky and the sands of the seashore; your descendants shall take possession of the gates of their enemies, and in your descendants all the nations of the earth shall find blessing—all this because you obeyed my command."]

RESPONSORIAL PSALM   *Psalm 16:5 and 8, 9–10, 11*

JS

You are my in-her-i-tance, O Lord, O Lord.

O LORD, it is you who are my portion
  and cup;
  you yourself who secure my lot.
I keep the LORD before me always;
  with him at my right hand, I shall
    not be moved. ℟.

And so, my heart rejoices, my soul is
  glad;
  even my flesh shall rest in hope.

For you will not abandon my soul to
  hell,
  nor let your holy one see
    corruption. ℟.

You will show me the path of life,
  the fullness of joy in your presence,
  at your right hand, bliss forever. ℟.

1064   **READING III**   *Exodus 14:15—15:1*

The LORD said to Moses, "Why are you crying out to me? Tell the Israelites to go forward. And you, lift up your staff and, with hand outstretched over the sea, split the sea in two, that the Israelites may pass through it on dry land. But I will make the Egyptians so obstinate that they will go in after them. Then I will receive glory through Pharaoh and all his army, his chariots and charioteers. The Egyptians shall know that I am the LORD, when I receive glory through Pharaoh and his chariots and charioteers."

The angel of God, who had been leading Israel's camp, now moved and went around behind them. The column of cloud also, leaving the front, took up its place behind them, so that it came between the camp of the Egyptians and that of Israel. But the cloud now became dark, and thus the night passed without the rival camps coming any closer together all night long. Then Moses stretched out his hand over the sea, and the LORD swept the sea with a strong east wind throughout the night and so turned it into dry land. When the water was thus divided, the Israelites marched into the midst of the sea on dry land, with the water like a wall to their right and to their left.

The Egyptians followed in pursuit; all Pharaoh's horses and chariots and charioteers went after them right into the midst of the sea. In the night watch just before dawn the LORD cast through the column of the fiery cloud upon the Egyptian force a glance that threw it into a panic; and he so clogged their chariot wheels that they could hardly drive. With that the Egyptians sounded the retreat before Israel, because the LORD was fighting for them against the Egyptians.

Then the LORD told Moses, "Stretch out your hand over the sea, that the water may flow back upon the Egyptians, upon their chariots and their charioteers." So Moses stretched out his hand over the sea, and at dawn the sea flowed back to its normal depth. The Egyptians were fleeing head on toward the sea, when the LORD hurled them into its midst. As the water flowed back, it covered the chariots and the charioteers of Pharaoh's whole army which had followed the Israelites into the sea. Not a single one of them escaped. But the Israelites had marched on dry land through the midst of the sea, with the water like a wall to their right and to their left. Thus the LORD saved Israel on that day from the power of the Egyptians. When Israel saw the Egyptians lying dead on the seashore and beheld the great power that the LORD had shown against the Egyptians, they feared the LORD and believed in him and in his servant Moses.

Then Moses and the Israelites sang this song to the LORD:

I will sing to the LORD, for he is gloriously triumphant;
horse and chariot he has cast into the sea.

RESPONSORIAL PSALM   *Exodus 15:1–2, 3–4, 5–6, 17–18*

RJB

Let us sing to the Lord, let us sing to the Lord; he has cov-ered him-self in glo-ry.

I will sing to the Lord; glorious his
   triumph!
Horse and rider he has thrown into
   the sea!
The Lord is my strength, my song,
   my salvation.
This is my God and I extol him,
   my father's God and I give him
   praise. ℟.

The LORD is a warrior! The LORD is his
   name.
The chariots of Pharaoh he hurled into

the sea,
the flower of his army is drowned
   in the sea. ℟.

The deeps hide them; they sank like a
   stone.
Your right hand, Lord, glorious in its
   power,
your right hand, Lord, has
   shattered the enemy. ℟.

The people you have redeemed pass by.
You will lead them and plant them on
    your mountain,
the place, O Lord, where you have
    made your home,

the sanctuary, Lord, which your
    hands have made.
The Lord will reign for ever and
    ever! ℟.

1065   READING IV

Isaiah 54:5–14

The One who has become your
    husband is your Maker;
    his name is the Lord of hosts;
your redeemer is the Holy One of Israel,
    called God of all the earth.
The Lord calls you back,
    like a wife forsaken and grieved
      in spirit,
    a wife married in youth and then
      cast off,
    says your God.
For a brief moment I abandoned you,
    but with great tenderness I will
      take you back.
In an outburst of wrath, for a moment
    I hid my face from you;
but with enduring love I take pity on you,
    says the Lord, your redeemer.
This is for me like the days of Noah,
    when I swore that the waters of Noah
      should never again deluge the earth;
so I have sworn not to be angry with you,

or to rebuke you.
Though the mountains leave their place
    and the hills be shaken,
my love shall never leave you
    nor my covenant of peace be shaken,
    says the Lord, who has mercy on
      you.
O afflicted one, storm-battered and
    unconsoled,
    I lay your pavements in carnelians,
    and your foundations in sapphires;
I will make your battlements of rubies,
    your gates of carbuncles,
    and all your walls of precious stones.
All your children shall be taught by the
    Lord,
    and great shall be the peace of your
    children.
In justice shall you be established,
    far from the fear of oppression,
    where destruction cannot come near
    you.

RESPONSORIAL PSALM

Psalm 30:2 and 4, 5–6, 11 and 12a and 13b

JRC

I will praise you, Lord, for you have res-cued me.

I will extol you, Lord, for you have
    raised me up,
    and have not let my enemies rejoice
      over me.
O Lord, you have lifted up my soul
    from the grave,
    restored me to life from those who
      sink into the pit. ℟.

Sing psalms to the Lord, you faithful
    ones;
    give thanks to his holy name.

His anger lasts a moment; his favor
    all through life.
    At night come tears, but dawn
      brings joy. ℟.

Hear, O Lord, and have mercy on me;
    be my helper, O Lord.
You have changed my mourning into
    dancing.
    O Lord my God, I will thank you
      forever. ℟.

READING V

Thus says the LORD:
All you who are thirsty,
    come to the water!
You who have no money,
    come, receive grain and eat;
come, without paying and without
    cost,
    drink wine and milk!
Why spend your money for what is
    not bread,
    your wages for what fails to
    satisfy?
Heed me, and you shall eat well,
    you shall delight in rich fare.
Come to me heedfully,
    listen, that you may have life.
I will renew with you the everlasting
    covenant,
    the benefits assured to David.
As I made him a witness to the peoples,
    a leader and commander of nations,
so shall you summon a nation you
    knew not,
    and nations that knew you not
    shall run to you,
because of the LORD, your God,
    the Holy One of Israel, who has
    glorified you.

Seek the LORD while he may be found,

call him while he is near.
Let the scoundrel forsake his way,
    and the wicked man his thoughts;
let him turn to the LORD for mercy;
    to our God, who is generous in
    forgiving.
For my thoughts are not your thoughts,
    nor are your ways my ways, says the
    LORD.
As high as the heavens are above the
    earth,
    so high are my ways above your
    ways
    and my thoughts above your
    thoughts.

For just as from the heavens
    the rain and snow come down
and do not return there
    till they have watered the earth,
    making it fertile and fruitful,
giving seed to the one who sows
    and bread to the one who eats,
so shall my word be
    that goes forth from my mouth;
my word shall not return to me void,
    but shall do my will,
    achieving the end for which I sent it.

RESPONSORIAL PSALM

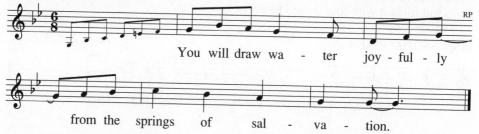

You will draw wa - ter joy - ful - ly
from the springs of sal - va - tion.

Truly, God is my salvation,
    I trust, I shall not fear.
For the Lord is my strength, my song,
    he became my savior.
With joy you will draw water
    from the wells of salvation. ℟.

Give thanks to the Lord,
    give praise to his name!
Make his mighty deeds
    known to the peoples!
Declare the greatness of his name.
    Sing a psalm to the Lord! ℟.

For he has done glorious deeds,
    make them known to all the earth!
People of Zion,

sing and shout for joy,
for great in your midst
    is the Holy One of Israel. ℟.

1067   READING VI

Baruch 3:9–15, 32—4:4

Hear, O Israel, the commandments of
    life:
    listen, and know prudence!
How is it, Israel,
    that you are in the land of your foes,
    grown old in a foreign land,
defiled with the dead,
    accounted with those destined for
    the netherworld?
You have forsaken the fountain of
    wisdom!
    Had you walked in the way of God,
    you would have dwelt in enduring
    peace.
Learn where prudence is,
    where strength, where understanding;
that you may know also
    where are length of days, and life,
    where light of the eyes, and peace.
Who has found the place of wisdom,
    who has entered into her treasuries?

The One who knows all things knows
    her;
    he has probed her by his
    knowledge—
the One who established the earth for
    all time,
    and filled it with four-footed beasts;

he who dismisses the light, and it
    departs,
    calls it, and it obeys him trembling;
before whom the stars at their posts
    shine and rejoice;
when he calls them, they answer, "Here
    we are!"
    shining with joy for their Maker.
Such is our God;
    no other is to be compared to him:
he has traced out the whole way of
    understanding,
    and has given her to Jacob, his
    servant,
    to Israel, his beloved son.

Since then she has appeared on earth,
    and moved among people.
She is the book of the precepts of God,
    the law that endures forever;
all who cling to her will live,
    but those will die who forsake her.
Turn, O Jacob, and receive her:
    walk by her light toward splendor.
Give not your glory to another,
    your privileges to an alien race.
Blessed are we, O Israel;
    for what pleases God is known to
    us!

RESPONSORIAL PSALM

Psalm 19:8, 9, 10, 11

RP

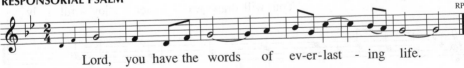

Lord, you have the words of ev-er-last-ing life.

The law of the LORD is perfect;
    it revives the soul.
The decrees of the LORD are steadfast;
    they give wisdom to the simple. ℟.

The precepts of the LORD are right;
    they gladden the heart.
The command of the LORD is clear;
    it gives light to the eyes. ℟.

The fear of the LORD is pure,
abiding forever.
The judgments of the LORD are true;
they are, all of them, just. ℟.

They are more to be desired than gold,
than quantities of gold.
And sweeter are they than honey,
than honey flowing from the comb. ℟.

READING VII
Ezekiel 36:16–17a, 18–28 1068

The word of the LORD came to me, saying: Son of man, when the house of Israel lived in their land, they defiled it by their conduct and deeds. Therefore I poured out my fury upon them because of the blood that they poured out on the ground, and because they defiled it with idols. I scattered them among the nations, dispersing them over foreign lands; according to their conduct and deeds I judged them. But when they came among the nations wherever they came, they served to profane my holy name, because it was said of them: "These are the people of the LORD, yet they had to leave their land." So I have relented because of my holy name which the house of Israel profaned among the nations where they came. Therefore say to the house of Israel: Thus says the Lord GOD: Not for your sakes do I act, house of Israel, but for the sake of my holy name, which you profaned among the nations to which you came. I will prove the holiness of my great name, profaned among the nations, in whose midst you have profaned it. Thus the nations shall know that I am the LORD, says the Lord GOD, when in their sight I prove my holiness through you. For I will take you away from among the nations, gather you from all the foreign lands, and bring you back to your own land. I will sprinkle clean water upon you to cleanse you from all your impurities, and from all your idols I will cleanse you. I will give you a new heart and place a new spirit within you, taking from your bodies your stony hearts and giving you natural hearts. I will put my spirit within you and make you live by my statutes, careful to observe my decrees. You shall live in the land I gave your fathers; you shall be my people, and I will be your God.

RESPONSORIAL PSALM
1. Psalm 42:3, 5bcd; 43:3, 4

RP

Like a deer that longs for run-ning streams, my soul longs for you, my God.

My soul is thirsting for God,
the living God;
when can I enter and appear
before the face of God? ℟.

For I would go to the place
of your wondrous tent,
all the way to the house of God,
amid cries of gladness and thanksgiving,
the throng keeping joyful festival. ℟.

O send forth your light and your truth;
they will guide me on.
They will bring me to your holy
mountain,
to the place where you dwell. ℟.

And I will come to the altar of God,
to God, my joy and gladness.
To you will I give thanks on the harp,
O God, my God. ℟.

Or: *2. Isaiah 12:2–3, 4bcd, 5–6*

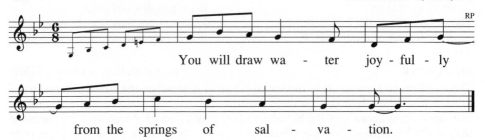

You will draw wa - ter joy - ful - ly

from the springs of sal - va - tion.

Truly, God is my salvation,
  I trust, I shall not fear.
For the Lord is my strength, my song,
  he became my savior.
With joy you will draw water
  from the wells of salvation. ℟.

Give thanks to the Lord,
  give praise to his name!
Make his mighty deeds

known to the peoples!
Declare the greatness of his name.
  Sing a psalm to the Lord! ℟.

For he has done glorious deeds,
  make them known to all the earth!
People of Zion,
  sing and shout for joy,
for great in your midst
  is the Holy One of Israel. ℟.

Or: *3. Psalm 51:12–13, 14–15, 18–19*

Cre - ate a clean heart, a clean heart in me, O God.

Create a pure heart for me, O God;
  renew a steadfast spirit within me.
Do not cast me away from your
      presence;
  take not your holy spirit from me. ℟.

Restore in me the joy of your salvation;
  sustain in me a willing spirit.
I will teach transgressors your ways,

that sinners may return to you. ℟.

For in sacrifice you take no delight;
  burnt offering from me would not
      please you.
My sacrifice to God, a broken spirit:
  a broken and humbled heart,
  O God, you will not spurn. ℟.

GLORIA

PRAYER

1069 EPISTLE   *Romans 6:3–11*

Brothers and sisters: Are you unaware that we who were baptized into Christ Jesus
were baptized into his death? We were indeed buried with him through baptism into
death, so that, just as Christ was raised from the dead by the glory of the Father, we
too might live in newness of life.

  For if we have grown into union with him through a death like his, we shall also
be united with him in the resurrection. We know that our old self was crucified with

him, so that our sinful body might be done away with, that we might no longer be in slavery to sin. For a dead person has been absolved from sin. If, then, we have died with Christ, we believe that we shall also live with him. We know that Christ, raised from the dead, dies no more; death no longer has power over him. As to his death, he died to sin once and for all; as to his life, he lives for God. Consequently, you too must think of yourselves as being dead to sin and living for God in Christ Jesus.

RESPONSORIAL PSALM

Psalm 118:1–2, 16–17, 22–23

Chant Mode VIII

Al - le - lu - ia.

Give praise to the LORD, for he is good;
  his mercy endures forever.
Let the house of Israel say,
  "His mercy endures forever." ℟.

"The LORD's right hand has done mighty
  deeds;
  his right hand is exalted."

I shall not die, I shall live
  and recount the deeds of the
  LORD. ℟.

The stone that the builders rejected
  has become the cornerstone.
By the LORD has this been done,
  a marvel in our eyes. ℟.

GOSPEL / A

Matthew 28:1–10

After the sabbath, as the first day of the week was dawning, Mary Magdalene and the other Mary came to see the tomb. And behold, there was a great earthquake; for an angel of the Lord descended from heaven, approached, rolled back the stone, and sat upon it. His appearance was like lightning and his clothing was white as snow. The guards were shaken with fear of him and became like dead men. Then the angel said to the women in reply, "Do not be afraid! I know that you are seeking Jesus the crucified. He is not here, for he has been raised just as he said. Come and see the place where he lay. Then go quickly and tell his disciples, 'He has been raised from the dead, and he is going before you to Galilee; there you will see him.' Behold, I have told you." Then they went away quickly from the tomb, fearful yet overjoyed, and ran to announce this to his disciples. And behold, Jesus met them on their way and greeted them. They approached, embraced his feet, and did him homage. Then Jesus said to them, "Do not be afraid. Go tell my brothers to go to Galilee, and there they will see me."

GOSPEL / B

Mark 16:1–7

When the sabbath was over, Mary Magdalene, Mary, the mother of James, and Salome bought spices so that they might go and anoint him. Very early when the sun had risen, on the first day of the week, they came to the tomb. They were saying to one another, "Who will roll back the stone for us from the entrance to the tomb?" When they looked up, they saw that the stone had been rolled back; it was very large. On entering the tomb they saw a young man sitting on the right side, clothed in a white robe, and they were utterly amazed. He said to them, "Do not be amazed! You seek Jesus of Nazareth, the crucified. He has been raised; he is not here. Behold the place where they laid him. But go and tell his disciples and Peter, 'He is going before you to Galilee; there you will see him, as he told you.'"

GOSPEL / C *Luke 24:1–12*

At daybreak on the first day of the week the women who had come from Galilee with Jesus took the spices they had prepared and went to the tomb. They found the stone rolled away from the tomb; but when they entered, they did not find the body of the Lord Jesus. While they were puzzling over this, behold, two men in dazzling garments appeared to them. They were terrified and bowed their faces to the ground. They said to them, "Why do you seek the living one among the dead? He is not here, but he has been raised. Remember what he said to you while he was still in Galilee, that the Son of Man must be handed over to sinners and be crucified, and rise on the third day." And they remembered his words. Then they returned from the tomb and announced all these things to the eleven and to all the others. The women were Mary Magdalene, Joanna, and Mary the mother of James; the others who accompanied them also told this to the apostles, but their story seemed like nonsense and they did not believe them. But Peter got up and ran to the tomb, bent down, and saw the burial cloths alone; then he went home amazed at what had happened.

1070 BAPTISMAL LITURGY

After the homily the catechumens are called forward. The assembly chants the litany of the saints, invoking the holy women and men of all centuries. Patron saints of the Church and of the catechumens and the faithful may be included in the litany.

Cantor:
Lord, have mer - cy.
Christ, have mer - cy.
Lord, have mer - cy.

Assembly:
Lord, have mer - cy.
Christ, have mer - cy.
Lord, have mer - cy.

Cantor:		Assembly:
Holy Mary, Mother of	God,	pray for us.
Saint	Mich - ael,	pray for us.
Holy Angels of	God,	pray for us.
Saint John the	Bap - tist,	pray for us.
Saint	Jo - seph,	pray for us.
Saint Peter and Saint	Paul,	pray for us.
Saint	An - drew,	pray for us.
Saint	John,	pray for us.
Saint Mary	Mag - dalene,	pray for us.
Saint	Ste - phen,	pray for us.
Saint Ignatius of	An - tioch,	pray for us.
Saint	Law - rence,	pray for us.
Saint Perpetua and Saint Fe -	lic - ity,	pray for us.
Saint	Ag - nes,	pray for us.
Saint	Gre - gory,	pray for us.
Saint Au -	gus - tine,	pray for us.
Saint Atha -	na - sius,	pray for us.
Saint	Ba - sil,	pray for us.
Saint	Mar - tin,	pray for us.
Saint	Ben - edict,	pray for us.
Saint Francis and Saint	Dom - inic,	pray for us.
Saint Francis	Xa - vier,	pray for us.
Saint John Vi -	an - ney,	pray for us.
Saint Catherine of Si -	e - na,	pray for us.
Saint Teresa of	Je - sus,	pray for us.
All holy men and women, Saints of	God,	pray for us.

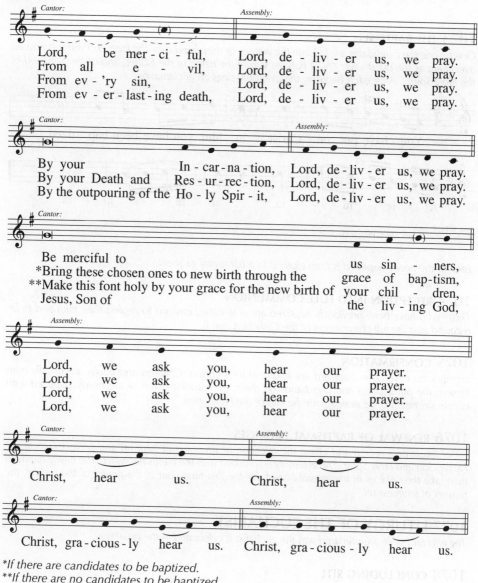

Cantor:
Assembly:

Lord,   be mer - ci - ful,   Lord, de - liv - er us, we pray.
From all   e - vil,   Lord, de - liv - er us, we pray.
From ev - 'ry sin,   Lord, de - liv - er us, we pray.
From ev - er - last - ing death,   Lord, de - liv - er us, we pray.

Cantor:
Assembly:

By your   In - car - na - tion,   Lord, de - liv - er us, we pray.
By your Death and   Res - ur - rec - tion,   Lord, de - liv - er us, we pray.
By the outpouring of the Ho - ly Spir - it,   Lord, de - liv - er us, we pray.

Cantor:

Be merciful to   us sin - ners,
*Bring these chosen ones to new birth through the   grace of bap-tism,
**Make this font holy by your grace for the new birth of your chil - dren,
Jesus, Son of   the liv - ing God,

Assembly:

Lord, we ask you, hear our prayer.
Lord, we ask you, hear our prayer.
Lord, we ask you, hear our prayer.
Lord, we ask you, hear our prayer.

Cantor:
Assembly:

Christ, hear us.   Christ, hear us.

Cantor:
Assembly:

Christ, gra - cious - ly hear us.   Christ, gra - cious - ly hear us.

*If there are candidates to be baptized.
**If there are no candidates to be baptized.

Text: *Litany of the Saints, Roman Missal*
Music: *Litany of the Saints, Roman Missal*
© 2010, ICEL

BLESSING OF WATER   1071

The priest gives thanks and praise to God over the waters of baptism. This acclamation is sung by all.

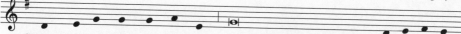

Springs of wa - ter, bless the Lord; praise and exalt him above all for ev - er.

Text: Refrain trans. © 1973, ICEL
Music: Marty Haugen, © 1994, GIA Publications, Inc.

RENUNCIATION OF SIN AND PROFESSION OF FAITH   1072

Each candidate for baptism is asked to reject sin and the ways of evil and to testify to faith in Father, Son and Holy Spirit.

1073 THE BAPTISMS

One by one the candidates are led into the waters, or they bend over the font, and water is poured over them as the priest says: "N., I baptize you in the name of the Father, and of the Son, and of the Holy Spirit." After each baptism, the assembly sings an acclamation.

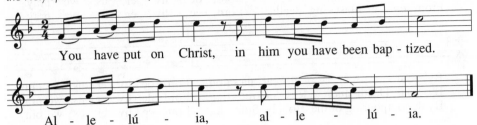

You have put on Christ, in him you have been bap - tized.

Al - le - lú - ia, al - le - lú - ia.

Text: ICEL, © 1969
Music: Howard Hughes, SM, © 1977, ICEL

Each of the newly baptized is then clothed in a baptismal garment.

1074 RECEPTION INTO FULL COMMUNION

Those who have been previously baptized are now called forward to profess their faith and to be received into the full communion of the Catholic Church.

1075 CONFIRMATION

Infants who have been baptized are anointed with chrism. Children and adults are usually confirmed: the priest prays and lays hands on them, then anoints each of the newly baptized with chrism saying: "N., be sealed with the Gift of the Holy Spirit."

1076 RENEWAL OF BAPTISMAL PROMISES

All of the faithful repeat and affirm the rejection of sin made at baptism and profess faith in the Father, Son and Holy Spirit. The assembly is sprinkled with the baptismal water. The newly baptized then take their places in the assembly and, for the first time, join in the prayer of the faithful, the prayers of intercession.

1077 LITURGY OF THE EUCHARIST

The gifts and table are prepared and the eucharist is celebrated in the usual way.

1078 CONCLUDING RITE

The dismissal is sung with "alleluia," and all respond.

Assembly:

Thanks be to God, al - le - lú - ia, al - le - lú - ia.

EASTER SUNDAY / ABC

READING I

Acts 10:34a, 37–43 / 42

Peter proceeded to speak and said: "You know what has happened all over Judea, beginning in Galilee after the baptism that John preached, how God anointed Jesus of Nazareth with the Holy Spirit and power. He went about doing good and healing all those oppressed by the devil, for God was with him. We are witnesses of all that he did both in the country of the Jews and in Jerusalem. They put him to death by hanging him on a tree. This man God raised on the third day and granted that he be visible, not to all the people, but to us, the witnesses chosen by God in advance, who ate and drank with him after he rose from the dead. He commissioned us to preach to the people and testify that he is the one appointed by God as judge of the living and the dead. To him all the prophets bear witness, that everyone who believes in him will receive forgiveness of sins through his name."

RESPONSORIAL PSALM

Psalm 118:1–2, 16–17, 22–23

Or: Alleluia.

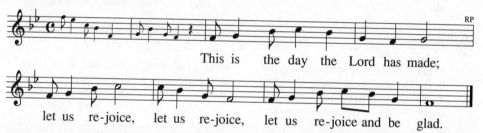

This is the day the Lord has made; let us re-joice, let us re-joice, let us re-joice and be glad.

Give praise to the LORD, for he is good;
  his mercy endures forever.
Let the house of Israel say,
  "His mercy endures forever." ℟.

"The LORD's right hand has done mighty deeds;
  his right hand is exalted."

I shall not die, I shall live
  and recount the deeds of the LORD. ℟.

The stone that the builders rejected
  has become the cornerstone.
By the LORD has this been done,
  a marvel in our eyes. ℟.

READING II

Colossians 3:1–4

Brothers and sisters: If then you were raised with Christ, seek what is above, where Christ is seated at the right hand of God. Think of what is above, not of what is on earth. For you have died, and your life is hidden with Christ in God. When Christ your life appears, then you too will appear with him in glory.

Or:

READING II

1 Corinthians 5:6b-8

Brothers and sisters: Do you not know that a little yeast leavens all the dough? Clear out the old yeast, so that you may become a fresh batch of dough, inasmuch as you are unleavened. For our paschal lamb, Christ, has been sacrificed. Therefore, let us celebrate the feast, not with the old yeast, the yeast of malice and wickedness, but with the unleavened bread of sincerity and truth.

1080 SEQUENCE

1. Chris-tians, praise the Pas-chal Vic-tim! Of-fer thank-ful sac-ri-fice!
1. Ví - cti - mae Pa-schá-li lau-des ím-mo-lent Chri-sti-á-ni.

2. Christ the Lamb has saved the sheep, Christ the just one paid the
3. Death and life fought bit-ter-ly for this won-drous vic-to-
2. A - gnus re - dé - mit o - ves: Chri-stus ín - no-cens Pa-
3. Mors et vi - ta du - él - lo con - fli - xé - re mi-rán-

price, re-con-cil-ing sin-ners to the Fa-ther.
ry; the Lord of life who died reigns glo-ri-fied!
tri re - con - ci - li - á - vit pec - ca - tó-res.
do: dux vi - tae mór - tu - us, re - gnat vi-vus.

4. O Mar-y, come and say what you saw at break of day.
6. Bright an-gels tes-ti-fied, shroud and grave clothes side by side!
4. Dic no - bis Ma - rí - a, quid vi - dí - sti in vi - a?
6. An - gé - li - cos te - stes, su - dá - ri - um, et ve-stes.

5. "The emp-ty tomb of my liv-ing Lord!
7. "Yes, Christ my hope rose glo-ri-ous-ly.
5. Se - púl - crum Chri - sti vi - vén - tis,
7. Sur - ré - xit Chri - stus spes me - a:

I saw Christ Je-sus ri-sen and a-dored!
He goes be-fore you in-to Gal-i-lee."
et gló - ri - am vi - di re - sur-gén - tis:
prae - cé - det su - os in Ga - li - láe - am.

8. Share the good news, sing joy-ful-ly: His death is vic-to-ry!
8. Sci - mus Chri - stum sur - re - xís - se a mór-tu - is ve-re:

Lord Je-sus, Vic-tor King, Show us mer-cy. A - men. Al-le-lú - ia.
tu no - bis vi-ctor Rex, mi - se - ré - re.

Text: *Víctimae pascháli laudes*, ascr. to Wipo of Burgundy, d.1048; tr. by Peter J. Scagnelli, b.1949, © 1983
Tune: VICTIMAE PASCHALI LAUDES, Irregular; Mode I; acc. by Richard Proulx, 1937–2010, © 1975, GIA Publications, Inc.

An alternate setting is found at no. 528.

At an afternoon or evening Mass, another Gospel may be read (see Lectionary for Mass).

GOSPEL

John 20:1–9

On the first day of the week, Mary of Magdala came to the tomb early in the morning, while it was still dark, and saw the stone removed from the tomb. So she ran and went to Simon Peter and to the other disciple whom Jesus loved, and told them, "They have taken the Lord from the tomb, and we don't know where they put him." So Peter and the other disciple went out and came to the tomb. They both ran, but the other disciple ran faster than Peter and arrived at the tomb first; he bent down and saw the burial cloths there, but did not go in. When Simon Peter arrived after him, he went into the tomb and saw the burial cloths there, and the cloth that had covered his head, not with the burial cloths but rolled up in a separate place. Then the other disciple also went in, the one who had arrived at the tomb first, and he saw and believed. For they did not yet understand the Scripture that he had to rise from the dead.

The rite of renewal of baptismal promises may take place after the homily, in which case the creed is omitted.

SECOND SUNDAY OF EASTER / ABC

1081

READING I / A

Acts 2:42–47 / 43

They devoted themselves to the teaching of the apostles and to the communal life, to the breaking of bread and to the prayers. Awe came upon everyone, and many wonders and signs were done through the apostles. All who believed were together and had all things in common; they would sell their property and possessions and divide them among all according to each one's need. Every day they devoted themselves to meeting together in the temple area and to breaking bread in their homes. They ate their meals with exultation and sincerity of heart, praising God and enjoying favor with all the people. And every day the Lord added to their number those who were being saved.

READING I / B

Acts 4:32–35 / 44

The community of believers was of one heart and mind, and no one claimed that any of his possessions was his own, but they had everything in common. With great power the apostles bore witness to the resurrection of the Lord Jesus, and great favor was accorded them all. There was no needy person among them, for those who owned property or houses would sell them, bring the proceeds of the sale, and put them at the feet of the apostles, and they were distributed to each according to need.

READING I / C

Acts 5:12–16 / 45

Many signs and wonders were done among the people at the hands of the apostles. They were all together in Solomon's portico. None of the others dared to join them, but the people esteemed them. Yet more than ever, believers in the Lord, great numbers of men and women, were added to them. Thus they even carried the sick out into the streets and laid them on cots and mats so that when Peter came by, at least his shadow might fall on one or another of them. A large number of people from the towns in the vicinity of Jerusalem also gathered, bringing the sick and those disturbed by unclean spirits, and they were all cured.

RESPONSORIAL PSALM *Psalm 118:2–4, 13–15, 22–24*

Or: Alleluia.

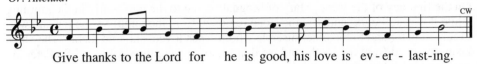

Give thanks to the Lord for he is good, his love is ev - er - last-ing.

Let the house of Israel say,
  "His mercy endures forever."
Let the house of Aaron say,
  "His mercy endures forever."
Let those who fear the LORD say,
  "His mercy endures forever." ℟.

I was thrust down, thrust down and falling,
  but the LORD was my helper.
The LORD is my strength and my song;

he was my savior.
There are shouts of joy and salvation
  in the tents of the just. ℟.

The stone that the builders rejected
  has become the cornerstone.
By the LORD has this been done,
  a marvel in our eyes.
This is the day the LORD has made;
  let us rejoice in it and be glad. ℟.

READING II / A *1 Peter 1:3–9*

Blessed be the God and Father of our Lord Jesus Christ, who in his great mercy gave us a new birth to a living hope through the resurrection of Jesus Christ from the dead, to an inheritance that is imperishable, undefiled, and unfading, kept in heaven for you who by the power of God are safeguarded through faith, to a salvation that is ready to be revealed in the final time. In this you rejoice, although now for a little while you may have to suffer through various trials, so that the genuineness of your faith, more precious than gold that is perishable even though tested by fire, may prove to be for praise, glory, and honor at the revelation of Jesus Christ. Although you have not seen him you love him; even though you do not see him now yet believe in him, you rejoice with an indescribable and glorious joy, as you attain the goal of your faith, the salvation of your souls.

READING II / B *1 John 5:1–6*

Beloved: Everyone who believes that Jesus is the Christ is begotten by God, and everyone who loves the Father loves also the one begotten by him. In this way we know that we love the children of God when we love God and obey his command-ments. For the love of God is this, that we keep his commandments. And his com-mandments are not burdensome, for whoever is begotten by God conquers the world. And the victory that conquers the world is our faith. Who indeed is the victor over the world but the one who believes that Jesus is the Son of God?

This is the one who came through water and blood, Jesus Christ, not by water alone, but by water and blood. The Spirit is the one that testifies, and the Spirit is truth.

READING II / C *Revelation 1:9–11a, 12–13, 17–19*

I, John, your brother, who share with you the distress, the kingdom, and the endur-ance we have in Jesus, found myself on the island called Patmos because I proclaimed God's word and gave testimony to Jesus. I was caught up in spirit on the Lord's day and heard behind me a voice as loud as a trumpet, which said, "Write on a scroll what you see." Then I turned to see whose voice it was that spoke to me, and when I turned, I saw seven gold lampstands and in the midst of the lampstands one like a son of man, wearing an ankle-length robe, with a gold sash around his chest.

When I caught sight of him, I fell down at his feet as though dead. He touched me with his right hand and said, "Do not be afraid. I am the first and the last, the one who lives. Once I was dead, but now I am alive forever and ever. I hold the keys to death and the netherworld. Write down, therefore, what you have seen, and what is happening, and what will happen afterwards."

GOSPEL *John 20:19–31*

On the evening of that first day of the week, when the doors were locked, where the disciples were, for fear of the Jews, Jesus came and stood in their midst and said to them, "Peace be with you." When he had said this, he showed them his hands and his side. The disciples rejoiced when they saw the Lord. Jesus said to them again, "Peace be with you. As the Father has sent me, so I send you." And when he had said this, he breathed on them and said to them, "Receive the Holy Spirit. Whose sins you forgive are forgiven them, and whose sins you retain are retained."

Thomas, called Didymus, one of the Twelve, was not with them when Jesus came. So the other disciples said to him, "We have seen the Lord." But he said to them, "Unless I see the mark of the nails in his hands and put my finger into the nailmarks and put my hand into his side, I will not believe."

Now a week later his disciples were again inside and Thomas was with them. Jesus came, although the doors were locked, and stood in their midst and said, "Peace be with you." Then he said to Thomas, "Put your finger here and see my hands, and bring your hand and put it into my side, and do not be unbelieving, but believe." Thomas answered and said to him, "My Lord and my God!" Jesus said to him, "Have you come to believe because you have seen me? Blessed are those who have not seen and have believed."

Now, Jesus did many other signs in the presence of his disciples that are not written in this book. But these are written that you may come to believe that Jesus is the Christ, the Son of God, and that through this belief you may have life in his name.

THIRD SUNDAY OF EASTER / A   1082

READING I *Acts 2:14, 22–33 / 46*

Then Peter stood up with the Eleven, raised his voice, and proclaimed: "You who are Jews, indeed all of you staying in Jerusalem. Let this be known to you, and listen to my words. You who are Israelites, hear these words. Jesus the Nazarene was a man commended to you by God with mighty deeds, wonders, and signs, which God worked through him in your midst, as you yourselves know. This man, delivered up by the set plan and foreknowledge of God, you killed, using lawless men to crucify him. But God raised him up, releasing him from the throes of death, because it was impossible for him to be held by it. For David says of him:

I saw the Lord ever before me,
  with him at my right hand I shall not be disturbed.
Therefore my heart has been glad and my tongue has exulted;
  my flesh, too, will dwell in hope,
because you will not abandon my soul to the netherworld,
  nor will you suffer your holy one to see corruption.
You have made known to me the paths of life;
  you will fill me with joy in your presence.

"My brothers, one can confidently say to you about the patriarch David that he died and was buried, and his tomb is in our midst to this day. But since he was a prophet and knew that God had sworn an oath to him that he would set one of his descendants upon his throne, he foresaw and spoke of the resurrection of the Christ, that neither was he abandoned to the netherworld nor did his flesh see corruption. God raised this Jesus; of this we are all witnesses. Exalted at the right hand of God, he received the promise of the Holy Spirit from the Father and poured him forth, as you see and hear."

RESPONSORIAL PSALM

Psalm 16:1–2a and 5, 7–8, 9–10, 11

Or: Alleluia.

Lord, you will show us the path of life.

Preserve me, O God, for in you I take
  refuge.
I say to the LORD, "You are my Lord."
O LORD, it is you who are my portion
  and cup;
you yourself who secure my lot. ℟.

I will bless the LORD who gives me
  counsel,
who even at night directs my heart.
I keep the LORD before me always;
  with him at my right hand, I shall
  not be moved. ℟.

And so, my heart rejoices, my soul is
  glad;
even my flesh shall rest in hope.
For you will not abandon my soul to
  hell,
nor let your holy one see
  corruption. ℟.

You will show me the path of life,
  the fullness of joy in your presence,
  at your right hand, bliss forever. ℟.

READING II

1 Peter 1:17–21

Beloved: If you invoke as Father him who judges impartially according to each one's works, conduct yourselves with reverence during the time of your sojourning, realizing that you were ransomed from your futile conduct, handed on by your ancestors, not with perishable things like silver or gold but with the precious blood of Christ as of a spotless unblemished lamb.

He was known before the foundation of the world but revealed in the final time for you, who through him believe in God who raised him from the dead and gave him glory, so that your faith and hope are in God.

GOSPEL

Luke 24:13–35

That very day, the first day of the week, two of Jesus' disciples were going to a village seven miles from Jerusalem called Emmaus, and they were conversing about all the things that had occurred. And it happened that while they were conversing and debating, Jesus himself drew near and walked with them, but their eyes were prevented from recognizing him. He asked them, "What are you discussing as you walk along?" They stopped, looking downcast. One of them, named Cleopas, said to him in reply, "Are you the only visitor to Jerusalem who does not know of the things that have taken place there in these days?" And he replied to them, "What sort of things?" They said to him, "The things that happened to Jesus the Nazarene, who was a prophet mighty in deed and word before God and all the people, how our chief priests and rulers both handed him over to a sentence of death and crucified him. But we were hoping that he would be the one to redeem Israel; and besides all this, it is now the third day since this took place. Some women from our group, however, have astounded us: they were at the tomb early in the morning and did not find his body; they came back and reported that they had indeed seen a vision of angels who announced that he was alive. Then some of those with us went to the tomb and found things just as the women had described, but him they did not see." And he said to them, "Oh, how foolish you are! How slow of heart to believe all that the prophets spoke! Was it not necessary that the Christ should suffer these things and enter into his glory?" Then beginning with Moses and all the prophets, he interpreted to them what referred to him in all the Scriptures. As they approached the village to which they were going, he gave the impression that he was going on farther. But they urged him, "Stay with us, for it is nearly evening and the day is almost over." So he went in to stay with them. And it happened that, while he was with them at table, he took bread, said the blessing, broke it, and gave it to them. With that their eyes were opened and they recognized him, but he vanished from their sight. Then they said to each other, "Were not our hearts burning within us while he spoke to us on the way and opened the Scriptures to us?" So they set out at once and returned to Jerusalem where they found gathered together the eleven and those with them who were saying, "The Lord has truly been raised and has appeared to Simon!" Then the two recounted what had taken place on the way and how he was made known to them in the breaking of bread.

THIRD SUNDAY OF EASTER / B

1083

READING I

Acts 3:13–15, 17–19 / 47

Peter said to the people: "The God of Abraham, the God of Isaac, and the God of Jacob, the God of our fathers, has glorified his servant Jesus, whom you handed over and denied in Pilate's presence when he had decided to release him. You denied the Holy and Righteous One and asked that a murderer be released to you. The author of life you put to death, but God raised him from the dead; of this we are witnesses. Now I know, brothers, that you acted out of ignorance, just as your leaders did; but God has thus brought to fulfillment what he had announced beforehand through the mouth of all the prophets, that his Christ would suffer. Repent, therefore, and be converted, that your sins may be wiped away."

RESPONSORIAL PSALM   *Psalm 4:2, 4, 7b–8a, 9*

Or: Alleluia.

Lord, let your face shine on us, your face shine on us.

I called, the God of justice gave me
    answer;
    from anguish you released me,
    have mercy and hear me! ℟.

Know that the LORD works wonders for
    his faithful one;
    the LORD will hear me whenever I
    call him. ℟.

Lift up the light of your face on us,
    O LORD.
You have put into my heart a
    greater joy. ℟.

In peace I will lie down and fall asleep,
    for you alone, O LORD, make me
    dwell in safety. ℟.

READING II   *1 John 2:1–5a*

My children, I am writing this to you so that you may not commit sin. But if anyone
does sin, we have an Advocate with the Father, Jesus Christ the righteous one. He is
expiation for our sins, and not for our sins only but for those of the whole world. The
way we may be sure that we know him is to keep his commandments. Those who
say, "I know him," but do not keep his commandments are liars, and the truth is not
in them. But whoever keeps his word, the love of God is truly perfected in him.

GOSPEL   *Luke 24:35–48*

The two disciples recounted what had taken place on the way, and how Jesus was
made known to them in the breaking of bread.
    While they were still speaking about this, he stood in their midst and said to them,
"Peace be with you." But they were startled and terrified and thought that they were
seeing a ghost. Then he said to them, "Why are you troubled? And why do questions
arise in your hearts? Look at my hands and my feet, that it is I myself. Touch me and
see, because a ghost does not have flesh and bones as you can see I have." And as he
said this, he showed them his hands and his feet. While they were still incredulous
for joy and were amazed, he asked them, "Have you anything here to eat?" They gave
him a piece of baked fish; he took it and ate it in front of them.
    He said to them, "These are my words that I spoke to you while I was still with
you, that everything written about me in the law of Moses and in the prophets and
psalms must be fulfilled." Then he opened their minds to understand the Scriptures.
And he said to them, "Thus it is written that the Christ would suffer and rise from
the dead on the third day and that repentance, for the forgiveness of sins, would be
preached in his name to all the nations, beginning from Jerusalem. You are witnesses
of these things."

1084 THIRD SUNDAY OF EASTER / C

READING I   *Acts 5:27–32, 40b–41 / 48*

When the captain and the court officers had brought the apostles in and made them
stand before the Sanhedrin, the high priest questioned them, "We gave you strict

orders, did we not, to stop teaching in that name? Yet you have filled Jerusalem with your teaching and want to bring this man's blood upon us." But Peter and the apostles said in reply, "We must obey God rather than men. The God of our ancestors raised Jesus, though you had him killed by hanging him on a tree. God exalted him at his right hand as leader and savior to grant Israel repentance and forgiveness of sins. We are witnesses of these things, as is the Holy Spirit whom God has given to those who obey him."

The Sanhedrin ordered the apostles to stop speaking in the name of Jesus, and dismissed them. So they left the presence of the Sanhedrin, rejoicing that they had been found worthy to suffer dishonor for the sake of the name.

RESPONSORIAL PSALM
Psalm 30:2 and 4, 5–6, 11 and 12a and 13b

Or: Alleluia.

I will praise you, Lord, for you have res-cued me.

I will extol you, LORD, for you have
  raised me up,
 and have not let my enemies rejoice
  over me.
O LORD, you have lifted up my soul
  from the grave,
 restored me to life from those who
  sink into the pit. ℟.

Sing psalms to the LORD, you faithful
  ones;
 give thanks to his holy name.

His anger lasts a moment; his favor all
  through life.
 At night come tears, but dawn
  brings joy. ℟.

Hear, O LORD, and have mercy on me;
  be my helper, O LORD.
You have changed my mourning into
  dancing.
 O LORD my God, I will thank you
  forever. ℟.

READING II
Revelation 5:11–14

I, John, looked and heard the voices of many angels who surrounded the throne and the living creatures and the elders. They were countless in number, and they cried out in a loud voice:
  "Worthy is the Lamb that was slain
    to receive power and riches, wisdom and strength,
    honor and glory and blessing."
Then I heard every creature in heaven and on earth and under the earth and in the sea, everything in the universe, cry out:
  "To the one who sits on the throne and to the Lamb
    be blessing and honor, glory and might,
    forever and ever."
The four living creatures answered, "Amen," and the elders fell down and worshiped.

GOSPEL
John 21:1–19 or 21:1–14

For short form read only the part in brackets.

[At that time, Jesus revealed himself again to his disciples at the Sea of Tiberias. He revealed himself in this way. Together were Simon Peter, Thomas called Didymus,

Nathanael from Cana in Galilee, Zebedee's sons, and two others of his disciples. Simon Peter said to them, "I am going fishing." They said to him, "We also will come with you." So they went out and got into the boat, but that night they caught nothing. When it was already dawn, Jesus was standing on the shore; but the disciples did not realize that it was Jesus. Jesus said to them, "Children, have you caught anything to eat?" They answered him, "No." So he said to them, "Cast the net over the right side of the boat and you will find something." So they cast it, and were not able to pull it in because of the number of fish. So the disciple whom Jesus loved said to Peter, "It is the Lord." When Simon Peter heard that it was the Lord, he tucked in his garment, for he was lightly clad, and jumped into the sea. The other disciples came in the boat, for they were not far from shore, only about a hundred yards, dragging the net with the fish. When they climbed out on shore, they saw a charcoal fire with fish on it and bread. Jesus said to them, "Bring some of the fish you just caught." So Simon Peter went over and dragged the net ashore full of one hundred fifty-three large fish. Even though there were so many, the net was not torn. Jesus said to them, "Come, have breakfast." And none of the disciples dared to ask him, "Who are you?" because they realized it was the Lord. Jesus came over and took the bread and gave it to them, and in like manner the fish. This was now the third time Jesus was revealed to his disciples after being raised from the dead.]

When they had finished breakfast, Jesus said to Simon Peter, "Simon, son of John, do you love me more than these?" Simon Peter answered him, "Yes, Lord, you know that I love you." Jesus said to him, "Feed my lambs." He then said to Simon Peter a second time, "Simon, son of John, do you love me?" Simon Peter answered him, "Yes, Lord, you know that I love you." Jesus said to him, "Tend my sheep." Jesus said to him the third time, "Simon, son of John, do you love me?" Peter was distressed that Jesus had said to him a third time, "Do you love me?" and he said to him, "Lord, you know every-thing; you know that I love you." Jesus said to him, "Feed my sheep. Amen, amen, I say to you, when you were younger, you used to dress yourself and go where you wanted; but when you grow old, you will stretch out your hands, and someone else will dress you and lead you where you do not want to go." He said this signifying by what kind of death he would glorify God. And when he had said this, he said to him, "Follow me."

1085 FOURTH SUNDAY OF EASTER / A

READING I   *Acts 2:14a, 36–41 / 49*

Then Peter stood up with the Eleven, raised his voice, and proclaimed: "Let the whole house of Israel know for certain that God has made both Lord and Christ, this Jesus whom you crucified."

Now when they heard this, they were cut to the heart, and they asked Peter and the other apostles, "What are we to do, my brothers?" Peter said to them, "Repent and be baptized, every one of you, in the name of Jesus Christ for the forgiveness of your sins; and you will receive the gift of the Holy Spirit. For the promise is made to you and to your children and to all those far off, whomever the Lord our God will call." He testified with many other arguments, and was exhorting them, "Save yourselves from this corrupt generation." Those who accepted his message were baptized, and about three thousand persons were added that day.

RESPONSORIAL PSALM

Psalm 23:1–3a, 3b–4, 5, 6

Or: Alleluia.

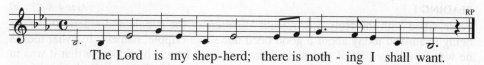

The Lord is my shep-herd; there is noth - ing I shall want.

The LORD is my shepherd;
there is nothing I shall want.
Fresh and green are the pastures
where he gives me repose.
Near restful waters he leads me;
he revives my soul. ℟.

He guides me along the right path,
for the sake of his name.
Though I should walk in the valley of
the shadow of death,
no evil would I fear, for you are
with me.

Your crook and your staff will give
me comfort. ℟.

You have prepared a table before me
in the sight of my foes.
My head you have anointed with oil;
my cup is overflowing. ℟.

Surely goodness and mercy shall
follow me
all the days of my life.
In the LORD's own house shall I dwell
for length of days unending. ℟.

READING II

1 Peter 2:20b–25

Beloved: If you are patient when you suffer for doing what is good, this is a grace before God. For to this you have been called, because Christ also suffered for you, leaving you an example that you should follow in his footsteps.

He committed no sin, and no deceit was found in his mouth.

When he was insulted, he returned no insult; when he suffered, he did not threaten; instead, he handed himself over to the one who judges justly. He himself bore our sins in his body upon the cross, so that, free from sin, we might live for righteousness. By his wounds you have been healed. For you had gone astray like sheep, but you have now returned to the shepherd and guardian of your souls.

GOSPEL

John 10:1–10

Jesus said: "Amen, amen, I say to you, whoever does not enter a sheepfold through the gate but climbs over elsewhere is a thief and a robber. But whoever enters through the gate is the shepherd of the sheep. The gatekeeper opens it for him, and the sheep hear his voice, as the shepherd calls his own sheep by name and leads them out. When he has driven out all his own, he walks ahead of them, and the sheep follow him, because they recognize his voice. But they will not follow a stranger; they will run away from him, because they do not recognize the voice of strangers." Although Jesus used this figure of speech, the Pharisees did not realize what he was trying to tell them.

So Jesus said again, "Amen, amen, I say to you, I am the gate for the sheep. All who came before me are thieves and robbers, but the sheep did not listen to them. I am the gate. Whoever enters through me will be saved, and will come in and go out and find pasture. A thief comes only to steal and slaughter and destroy; I came so that they might have life and have it more abundantly."

1086 **FOURTH SUNDAY OF EASTER / B**

READING I *Acts 4:8–12 / 50*

Peter, filled with the Holy Spirit, said: "Leaders of the people and elders: If we are being examined today about a good deed done to a cripple, namely, by what means he was saved, then all of you and all the people of Israel should know that it was in the name of Jesus Christ the Nazorean whom you crucified, whom God raised from the dead; in his name this man stands before you healed. He is *the stone rejected by you, the builders, which has become the cornerstone.* There is no salvation through anyone else, nor is there any other name under heaven given to the human race by which we are to be saved."

RESPONSORIAL PSALM *Psalm 118:1 and 8–9, 21–23, 26 and 21 and 29*

Or: Alleluia.

The stone re-ject-ed by the build-ers has be-come the cor-ner-stone.

Give praise to the LORD, for he is good;
   his mercy endures forever.
It is better to take refuge in the LORD
   than to trust in man;
it is better to take refuge in the LORD
   than to trust in princes. ℟.

I will thank you, for you have
   answered,
   and you are my savior.
The stone that the builders rejected
   has become the cornerstone.

By the LORD has this been done,
   a marvel in our eyes. ℟.

Blest is he who comes in the name of
   the LORD.
   We bless you from the house of the
   LORD.
I will thank you, for you have answered,
   and you are my savior.
Give praise to the LORD, for he is good;
   his mercy endures forever. ℟.

READING II *1 John 3:1–2*

Beloved: See what love the Father has bestowed on us that we may be called the children of God. Yet so we are. The reason the world does not know us is that it did not know him. Beloved, we are God's children now; what we shall be has not yet been revealed. We do know that when it is revealed we shall be like him, for we shall see him as he is.

GOSPEL *John 10:11–18*

Jesus said: "I am the good shepherd. A good shepherd lays down his life for the sheep. A hired man, who is not a shepherd and whose sheep are not his own, sees a wolf coming and leaves the sheep and runs away, and the wolf catches and scatters them. This is because he works for pay and has no concern for the sheep. I am the good shepherd, and I know mine and mine know me, just as the Father knows me and I know the Father; and I will lay down my life for the sheep. I have other sheep that do not belong to this fold. These also I must lead, and they will hear my voice, and there will be one flock, one shepherd. This is why the Father loves me, because I lay down my life in order to take it up again. No one takes it from me, but I lay it down on my own. I have power to lay it down, and power to take it up again. This command I have received from my Father."

FOURTH SUNDAY OF EASTER / C 1087

READING I
Acts 13:14, 43–52 / 51

Paul and Barnabas continued on from Perga and reached Antioch in Pisidia. On the sabbath they entered the synagogue and took their seats. Many Jews and worshipers who were converts to Judaism followed Paul and Barnabas, who spoke to them and urged them to remain faithful to the grace of God.

On the following sabbath almost the whole city gathered to hear the word of the Lord. When the Jews saw the crowds, they were filled with jealousy and with violent abuse contradicted what Paul said. Both Paul and Barnabas spoke out boldly and said, "It was necessary that the word of God be spoken to you first, but since you reject it and condemn yourselves as unworthy of eternal life, we now turn to the Gentiles. For so the Lord has commanded us, *I have made you a light to the Gentiles, that you may be an instrument of salvation to the ends of the earth."*

The Gentiles were delighted when they heard this and glorified the word of the Lord. All who were destined for eternal life came to believe, and the word of the Lord continued to spread through the whole region. The Jews, however, incited the women of prominence who were worshipers and the leading men of the city, stirred up a persecution against Paul and Barnabas, and expelled them from their territory. So they shook the dust from their feet in protest against them, and went to Iconium. The disciples were filled with joy and the Holy Spirit.

RESPONSORIAL PSALM
Psalm 100:1–2, 3, 5

Or: Alleluia.

We are his peo-ple: the sheep of his flock.

Cry out with joy to the LORD, all the earth.
Serve the LORD with gladness.
Come before him, singing for joy. ℟.

Know that he, the LORD, is God.
He made us; we belong to him.

We are his people, the sheep of his flock. ℟.

Indeed, how good is the LORD,
eternal his merciful love.
He is faithful from age to age. ℟.

READING II
Revelation 7:9, 14b–17

I, John, had a vision of a great multitude, which no one could count, from every nation, race, people, and tongue. They stood before the throne and before the Lamb, wearing white robes and holding palm branches in their hands.

Then one of the elders said to me, "These are the ones who have survived the time of great distress; they have washed their robes and made them white in the blood of the Lamb.

"For this reason they stand before God's throne
    and worship him day and night in his temple.
The one who sits on the throne will shelter them.
They will not hunger or thirst anymore,
    nor will the sun or any heat strike them.
For the Lamb who is in the center of the throne
    will shepherd them
    and lead them to springs of life-giving water,
    and God will wipe away every tear from their eyes."

GOSPEL *John 10:27–30*

Jesus said: "My sheep hear my voice; I know them, and they follow me. I give them eternal life, and they shall never perish. No one can take them out of my hand. My Father, who has given them to me, is greater than all, and no one can take them out of the Father's hand. The Father and I are one."

1088   **FIFTH SUNDAY OF EASTER / A**

READING I *Acts 6:1–7 / 52*

As the number of disciples continued to grow, the Hellenists complained against the Hebrews because their widows were being neglected in the daily distribution. So the Twelve called together the community of the disciples and said, "It is not right for us to neglect the word of God to serve at table. Brothers, select from among you seven reputable men, filled with the Spirit and wisdom, whom we shall appoint to this task, whereas we shall devote ourselves to prayer and to the ministry of the word." The proposal was acceptable to the whole community, so they chose Stephen, a man filled with faith and the Holy Spirit, also Philip, Prochorus, Nicanor, Timon, Parmenas, and Nicholas of Antioch, a convert to Judaism. They presented these men to the apostles who prayed and laid hands on them. The word of God continued to spread, and the number of the disciples in Jerusalem increased greatly; even a large group of priests were becoming obedient to the faith.

RESPONSORIAL PSALM *Psalm 33:1–2, 4–5, 18–19*

Or: Alleluia.

Lord, let your mer-cy be on us, as we place our trust in you.

Ring out your joy to the LORD, O you just;
    for praise is fitting for the upright.
Give thanks to the LORD upon the harp;
    with a ten-stringed lute sing him
      songs. ℟.

For the word of the LORD is faithful,
    and all his works to be trusted.
The LORD loves justice and right,

and his merciful love fills the
    earth. ℟.

Yes, the LORD's eyes are on those who
    fear him,
    who hope in his merciful love,
to rescue their souls from death,
    to keep them alive in famine. ℟.

READING II

1 Peter 2:4–9

Beloved: Come to him, a living stone, rejected by human beings but chosen and precious in the sight of God, and, like living stones, let yourselves be built into a spiritual house to be a holy priesthood to offer spiritual sacrifices acceptable to God through Jesus Christ. For it says in Scripture:

Behold, I am laying a stone in Zion,
a cornerstone, chosen and precious,
and whoever believes in it shall not be put to shame.

Therefore, its value is for you who have faith, but for those without faith:

The stone that the builders rejected
has become the cornerstone,

and

A stone that will make people stumble,
and a rock that will make them fall.

They stumble by disobeying the word, as is their destiny.

You are "a chosen race, a royal priesthood, a holy nation, a people of his own, so that you may announce the praises" of him who called you out of darkness into his wonderful light.

GOSPEL

John 14:1–12

Jesus said to his disciples: "Do not let your hearts be troubled. You have faith in God; have faith also in me. In my Father's house there are many dwelling places. If there were not, would I have told you that I am going to prepare a place for you? And if I go and prepare a place for you, I will come back again and take you to myself, so that where I am you also may be. Where I am going you know the way." Thomas said to him, "Master, we do not know where you are going; how can we know the way?" Jesus said to him, "I am the way and the truth and the life. No one comes to the Father except through me. If you know me, then you will also know my Father. From now on you do know him and have seen him." Philip said to him, "Master, show us the Father, and that will be enough for us." Jesus said to him, "Have I been with you for so long a time and you still do not know me, Philip? Whoever has seen me has seen the Father. How can you say, 'Show us the Father'? Do you not believe that I am in the Father and the Father is in me? The words that I speak to you I do not speak on my own. The Father who dwells in me is doing his works. Believe me that I am in the Father and the Father is in me, or else, believe because of the works themselves. Amen, amen, I say to you, whoever believes in me will do the works that I do, and will do greater ones than these, because I am going to the Father."

FIFTH SUNDAY OF EASTER / B

1089

READING I

Acts 9:26–31 / 53

When Saul arrived in Jerusalem he tried to join the disciples, but they were all afraid of him, not believing that he was a disciple. Then Barnabas took charge of him and brought him to the apostles, and he reported to them how he had seen the Lord, and that he had spoken to him, and how in Damascus he had spoken out boldly in the name of Jesus. He moved about freely with them in Jerusalem, and spoke out boldly in the name of the Lord. He also spoke and debated with the Hellenists, but they tried to kill him. And when the brothers learned of this, they took him down to Caesarea and sent him on his way to Tarsus.

The church throughout all Judea, Galilee, and Samaria was at peace. It was being built up and walked in the fear of the Lord, and with the consolation of the Holy Spirit it grew in numbers.

RESPONSORIAL PSALM   *Psalm 22:26b–27, 28 and 30, 31–32*

Or: Alleluia.

I will praise you, Lord, in the as-sem-bly of your peo-ple.

My vows I will pay before those who
    fear him.
    The poor shall eat and shall have
      their fill.
They shall praise the LORD, those who
    seek him.
    May their hearts live on forever and
      ever! ℟.

All the earth shall remember and return
    to the LORD,
    all families of the nations worship
      before him.

They shall worship him, all the mighty
    of the earth;
    before him shall bow all who go
      down to the dust. ℟.

And my soul shall live for him, my
    descendants serve him.
    They shall tell of the LORD to
      generations yet to come,
declare his saving justice to peoples
    yet unborn:
    "These are the things the LORD
      has done." ℟.

READING II   *1 John 3:18–24*

Children, let us love not in word or speech but in deed and truth.

Now this is how we shall know that we belong to the truth and reassure our hearts before him in whatever our hearts condemn, for God is greater than our hearts and knows everything. Beloved, if our hearts do not condemn us, we have confidence in God and receive from him whatever we ask, because we keep his commandments and do what pleases him. And his commandment is this: we should believe in the name of his Son, Jesus Christ, and love one another just as he commanded us. Those who keep his commandments remain in him, and he in them, and the way we know that he remains in us is from the Spirit he gave us.

GOSPEL   *John 15:1–8*

Jesus said to his disciples: "I am the true vine, and my Father is the vine grower. He takes away every branch in me that does not bear fruit, and every one that does he prunes so that it bears more fruit. You are already pruned because of the word that I spoke to you. Remain in me, as I remain in you. Just as a branch cannot bear fruit on its own unless it remains on the vine, so neither can you unless you remain in me. I am the vine, you are the branches. Whoever remains in me and I in him will bear much fruit, because without me you can do nothing. Anyone who does not remain in me will be thrown out like a branch and wither; people will gather them and throw them into a fire and they will be burned. If you remain in me and my words remain in you, ask for whatever you want and it will be done for you. By this is my Father glorified, that you bear much fruit and become my disciples."

FIFTH SUNDAY OF EASTER / C

READING I

Acts 14:21–27 / 54

After Paul and Barnabas had proclaimed the good news to that city and made a consider-able number of disciples, they returned to Lystra and to Iconium and to Antioch. They strengthened the spirits of the disciples and exhorted them to persevere in the faith, say-ing, "It is necessary for us to undergo many hardships to enter the kingdom of God." They appointed elders for them in each church and, with prayer and fasting, com-mended them to the Lord in whom they had put their faith. Then they traveled through Pisidia and reached Pamphylia. After proclaiming the word at Perga they went down to Attalia. From there they sailed to Antioch, where they had been commended to the grace of God for the work they had now accomplished. And when they arrived, they called the church together and reported what God had done with them and how he had opened the door of faith to the Gentiles.

RESPONSORIAL PSALM

Psalm 145:8–9, 10–11, 12–13ab

Or: Alleluia.

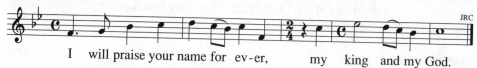

I will praise your name for ev-er, my king and my God.

The LORD is kind and full of compassion,
    slow to anger, abounding in mercy.
How good is the LORD to all,
    compassionate to all his creatures. ℟.

All your works shall thank you, O LORD,
    and all your faithful ones bless you.
They shall speak of the glory of your
    reign,

    and declare your mighty deeds. ℟.

To make known your might to the
    children of men,
and the glorious splendor of your
    reign.
Your kingdom is an everlasting kingdom;
    your rule endures for all
    generations. ℟.

READING II

Revelation 21:1–5a

Then I, John, saw a new heaven and a new earth. The former heaven and the former earth had passed away, and the sea was no more. I also saw the holy city, a new Jerusalem, coming down out of heaven from God, prepared as a bride adorned for her husband. I heard a loud voice from the throne saying, "Behold, God's dwelling is with the human race. He will dwell with them and they will be his people and God himself will always be with them as their God. He will wipe every tear from their eyes, and there shall be no more death or mourning, wailing or pain, for the old order has passed away."

    The One who sat on the throne said, "Behold, I make all things new."

GOSPEL

John 13:31–33a, 34–35

When Judas had left them, Jesus said, "Now is the Son of Man glorified, and God is glorified in him. If God is glorified in him, God will also glorify him in himself, and God will glorify him at once. My children, I will be with you only a little while longer.

I give you a new commandment: love one another. As I have loved you, so you also should love one another. This is how all will know that you are my disciples, if you have love for one another."

1091   SIXTH SUNDAY OF EASTER / A

READING I   *Acts 8:5–8, 14–17 / 55*

Philip went down to the city of Samaria and proclaimed the Christ to them. With one accord, the crowds paid attention to what was said by Philip when they heard it and saw the signs he was doing. For unclean spirits, crying out in a loud voice, came out of many possessed people, and many paralyzed or crippled people were cured. There was great joy in that city.

Now when the apostles in Jerusalem heard that Samaria had accepted the word of God, they sent them Peter and John, who went down and prayed for them, that they might receive the Holy Spirit, for it had not yet fallen upon any of them; they had only been baptized in the name of the Lord Jesus. Then they laid hands on them and they received the Holy Spirit.

RESPONSORIAL PSALM   *Psalm 66:1–3a, 4–5, 6–7a, 16 and 20*

Or: Alleluia.

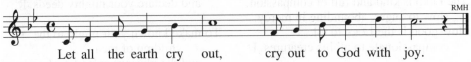

Let all the earth cry out, cry out to God with joy.

Cry out with joy to God, all the earth;
   O sing to the glory of his name.
O render him glorious praise.
   Say to God, "How awesome your
   deeds! ℟.

"Before you all the earth shall bow down,
   shall sing to you, sing to your name!"
Come and see the works of God:
   awesome his deeds among the
   children of men. ℟.

He turned the sea into dry land;
   they passed through the river on foot.
Let our joy, then, be in him;
   he rules forever by his might. ℟.

Come and hear, all who fear God;
   I will tell what he did for my soul.
Blest be God, who did not reject my
   prayer,
   nor withhold from me his merciful
   love. ℟.

READING II   *1 Peter 3:15–18*

Beloved: Sanctify Christ as Lord in your hearts. Always be ready to give an explanation to anyone who asks you for a reason for your hope, but do it with gentleness and reverence, keeping your conscience clear, so that, when you are maligned, those who defame your good conduct in Christ may themselves be put to shame. For it is better to suffer for doing good, if that be the will of God, than for doing evil. For Christ also suffered for sins once, the righteous for the sake of the unrighteous, that he might lead you to God. Put to death in the flesh, he was brought to life in the Spirit.

GOSPEL

John 14:15–21

Jesus said to his disciples: "If you love me, you will keep my commandments. And I will ask the Father, and he will give you another Advocate to be with you always, the Spirit of truth, whom the world cannot accept, because it neither sees nor knows him. But you know him, because he remains with you, and will be in you. I will not leave you orphans; I will come to you. In a little while the world will no longer see me, but you will see me, because I live and you will live. On that day you will realize that I am in my Father and you are in me and I in you. Whoever has my commandments and observes them is the one who loves me. And whoever loves me will be loved by my Father, and I will love him and reveal myself to him."

SIXTH SUNDAY OF EASTER / B
1092

READING I

Acts 10:25–26, 34–35, 44–48 / 56

When Peter entered, Cornelius met him and, falling at his feet, paid him homage. Peter, however, raised him up, saying, "Get up. I myself am also a human being."

Then Peter proceeded to speak and said, "In truth, I see that God shows no partiality. Rather, in every nation whoever fears him and acts uprightly is acceptable to him."

While Peter was still speaking these things, the Holy Spirit fell upon all who were listening to the word. The circumcised believers who had accompanied Peter were astounded that the gift of the Holy Spirit should have been poured out on the Gentiles also, for they could hear them speaking in tongues and glorifying God. Then Peter responded, "Can anyone withhold the water for baptizing these people, who have received the Holy Spirit even as we have?" He ordered them to be baptized in the name of Jesus Christ.

RESPONSORIAL PSALM

Psalm 98:1, 2–3ab, 3cd–4

Or: Alleluia.

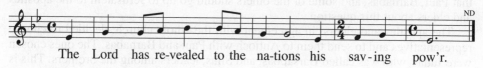

The Lord has re-vealed to the na-tions his sav-ing pow'r.

O sing a new song to the LORD,
for he has worked wonders.
His right hand and his holy arm
have brought salvation. ℟.

The LORD has made known his salvation,
has shown his deliverance to the
nations.
He has remembered his merciful love

and his truth for the house of
Israel. ℟.

All the ends of the earth have seen
the salvation of our God.
Shout to the LORD, all the earth;
break forth into joyous song,
and sing out your praise. ℟.

READING II   *1 John 4:7–10*

Beloved, let us love one another, because love is of God; everyone who loves is begotten by God and knows God. Whoever is without love does not know God, for God is love. In this way the love of God was revealed to us: God sent his only Son into the world so that we might have life through him. In this is love: not that we have loved God, but that he loved us and sent his Son as expiation for our sins.

GOSPEL   *John 15:9–17*

Jesus said to his disciples: "As the Father loves me, so I also love you. Remain in my love. If you keep my commandments, you will remain in my love, just as I have kept my Father's commandments and remain in his love.

"I have told you this so that my joy may be in you and your joy might be complete. This is my commandment: love one another as I love you. No one has greater love than this, to lay down one's life for one's friends. You are my friends if you do what I command you. I no longer call you slaves, because a slave does not know what his master is doing. I have called you friends, because I have told you everything I have heard from my Father. It was not you who chose me, but I who chose you and appointed you to go and bear fruit that will remain, so that whatever you ask the Father in my name he may give you. This I command you: love one another."

1093 SIXTH SUNDAY OF EASTER / C

READING I   *Acts 15:1–2, 22–29 / 57*

Some who had come down from Judea were instructing the brothers, "Unless you are circumcised according to the Mosaic practice, you cannot be saved." Because there arose no little dissension and debate by Paul and Barnabas with them, it was decided that Paul, Barnabas, and some of the others should go up to Jerusalem to the apostles and elders about this question.

The apostles and elders, in agreement with the whole church, decided to choose representatives and to send them to Antioch with Paul and Barnabas. The ones chosen were Judas, who was called Barsabbas, and Silas, leaders among the brothers. This is the letter delivered by them:

"The apostles and the elders, your brothers, to the brothers in Antioch, Syria, and Cilicia of Gentile origin: greetings. Since we have heard that some of our number who went out without any mandate from us have upset you with their teachings and disturbed your peace of mind, we have with one accord decided to choose representatives and to send them to you along with our beloved Barnabas and Paul, who have dedicated their lives to the name of our Lord Jesus Christ. So we are sending Judas and Silas who will also convey this same message by word of mouth: 'It is the decision of the Holy Spirit and of us not to place on you any burden beyond these necessities, namely, to abstain from meat sacrificed to idols, from blood, from meats of strangled animals, and from unlawful marriage. If you keep free of these, you will be doing what is right. Farewell.'"

RESPONSORIAL PSALM

Psalm 67:2–3, 5, 6 and 8

Or: Alleluia.

O God, O God, let all the na-tions praise you!

O God, be gracious and bless us
  and let your face shed its light
    upon us.
So will your ways be known upon earth
  and all nations learn your
    salvation. ℟.

Let the nations be glad and shout for joy,
  with uprightness you rule the

peoples;
  you guide the nations on earth. ℟.

Let the peoples praise you, O God;
  let all the peoples praise you.
May God still give us his blessing
  that all the ends of the earth may
    revere him. ℟.

READING II

Revelation 21:10–14, 22–23

The angel took me in spirit to a great, high mountain and showed me the holy city Jerusalem coming down out of heaven from God. It gleamed with the splendor of God. Its radiance was like that of a precious stone, like jasper, clear as crystal. It had a massive, high wall, with twelve gates where twelve angels were stationed and on which names were inscribed, the names of the twelve tribes of the Israelites. There were three gates facing east, three north, three south, and three west. The wall of the city had twelve courses of stones as its foundation, on which were inscribed the twelve names of the twelve apostles of the Lamb.

I saw no temple in the city for its temple is the Lord God almighty and the Lamb. The city had no need of sun or moon to shine on it, for the glory of God gave it light, and its lamp was the Lamb.

GOSPEL

John 14:23–29

Jesus said to his disciples: "Whoever loves me will keep my word, and my Father will love him, and we will come to him and make our dwelling with him. Whoever does not love me does not keep my words; yet the word you hear is not mine but that of the Father who sent me.

"I have told you this while I am with you. The Advocate, the Holy Spirit, whom the Father will send in my name, will teach you everything and remind you of all that I told you. Peace I leave with you; my peace I give to you. Not as the world gives do I give it to you. Do not let your hearts be troubled or afraid. You heard me tell you, 'I am going away and I will come back to you.' If you loved me, you would rejoice that I am going to the Father; for the Father is greater than I. And now I have told you this before it happens, so that when it happens you may believe."

1094 ASCENSION OF THE LORD / ABC

READING I *Acts 1:1–11 / 58*

In the first book, Theophilus, I dealt with all that Jesus did and taught until the day he was taken up, after giving instructions through the Holy Spirit to the apostles whom he had chosen. He presented himself alive to them by many proofs after he had suffered, appearing to them during forty days and speaking about the kingdom of God. While meeting with them, he enjoined them not to depart from Jerusalem, but to wait for "the promise of the Father about which you have heard me speak; for John baptized with water, but in a few days you will be baptized with the Holy Spirit."

When they had gathered together they asked him, "Lord, are you at this time going to restore the kingdom to Israel?" He answered them, "It is not for you to know the times or seasons that the Father has established by his own authority. But you will receive power when the Holy Spirit comes upon you, and you will be my witnesses in Jerusalem, throughout Judea and Samaria, and to the ends of the earth." When he had said this, as they were looking on, he was lifted up, and a cloud took him from their sight. While they were looking intently at the sky as he was going, suddenly two men dressed in white garments stood beside them. They said, "Men of Galilee, why are you standing there looking at the sky? This Jesus who has been taken up from you into heaven will return in the same way as you have seen him going into heaven."

RESPONSORIAL PSALM *Psalm 47:2–3, 6–7, 8–9*

Or: Alleluia.

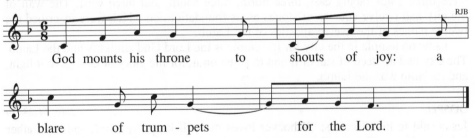

God mounts his throne to shouts of joy: a blare of trum - pets for the Lord.

All peoples, clap your hands.
　Cry to God with shouts of joy!
For the LORD, the Most High, is
　　awesome,
　the great king over all the earth. ℟.

God goes up with shouts of joy.
　The LORD goes up with trumpet blast.

Sing praise for God; sing praise!
　Sing praise to our king; sing
　praise! ℟.

God is king of all the earth.
　Sing praise with all your skill.
God reigns over the nations.
　God sits upon his holy throne. ℟.

READING II *Ephesians 1:17–23*

Brothers and sisters: May the God of our Lord Jesus Christ, the Father of glory, give you a Spirit of wisdom and revelation resulting in knowledge of him. May the eyes of your hearts be enlightened, that you may know what is the hope that belongs to his call, what are the riches of glory in his inheritance among the holy ones, and what is the surpassing greatness of his power for us who believe, in accord with the exercise of his great might, which he worked in Christ, raising him from the dead and seating him at his right hand in the heavens, far above every principality, authority, power, and dominion, and every name that is named not only in this age but also in the one to come. And he put all things beneath his feet and gave him as head over all things to the church, which is his body, the fullness of the one who fills all things in every way.

Or:

READING II / B   *Ephesians 4:1–13 or 4:1–7, 11–13*
For short form read only the parts in brackets.

[Brothers and sisters, I, a prisoner for the Lord, urge you to live in a manner worthy of the call you have received, with all humility and gentleness, with patience, bearing with one another through love, striving to preserve the unity of the spirit through the bond of peace: one body and one Spirit, as you were also called to the one hope of your call; one Lord, one faith, one baptism; one God and Father of all, who is over all and through all and in all.

But grace was given to each of us according to the measure of Christ's gift.] Therefore, it says:

He ascended on high and took prisoners captive;
he gave gifts to men.

What does "he ascended" mean except that he also descended into the lower regions of the earth? The one who descended is also the one who ascended far above all the heavens, that he might fill all things.

[And he gave some as apostles, others as prophets, others as evangelists, others as pastors and teachers, to equip the holy ones for the work of ministry, for building up the body of Christ, until we all attain to the unity of faith and knowledge of the Son of God, to mature manhood, to the extent of the full stature of Christ.]

Or:

READING II / C   *Hebrews 9:24–28; 10:19–23*
Christ did not enter into a sanctuary made by hands, a copy of the true one, but heaven itself, that he might now appear before God on our behalf. Not that he might offer himself repeatedly, as the high priest enters each year into the sanctuary with blood that is not his own; if that were so, he would have had to suffer repeatedly from the foundation of the world. But now once for all he has appeared at the end of the ages to take away sin by his sacrifice. Just as it is appointed that men and women die once, and after this the judgment, so also Christ, offered once to take away the sins of many, will appear a second time, not to take away sin but to bring salvation to those who eagerly await him.

Therefore, brothers and sisters, since through the blood of Jesus we have confidence of entrance into the sanctuary by the new and living way he opened for us through the veil, that is, his flesh, and since we have "a great priest over the house of God," let us approach with a sincere heart and in absolute trust, with our hearts sprinkled clean from an evil conscience and our bodies washed in pure water. Let us hold unwaveringly to our confession that gives us hope, for he who made the promise is trustworthy.

GOSPEL / A   *Matthew 28:16–20*

The eleven disciples went to Galilee, to the mountain to which Jesus had ordered them. When they saw him, they worshiped, but they doubted. Then Jesus approached and said to them, "All power in heaven and on earth has been given to me. Go, therefore, and make disciples of all nations, baptizing them in the name of the Father, and of the Son, and of the Holy Spirit, teaching them to observe all that I have commanded you. And behold, I am with you always, until the end of the age."

GOSPEL / B   *Mark 16:15–20*

Jesus said to his disciples: "Go into the whole world and proclaim the gospel to every creature. Whoever believes and is baptized will be saved; whoever does not believe will be condemned. These signs will accompany those who believe: in my name they will drive out demons, they will speak new languages. They will pick up serpents with their hands, and if they drink any deadly thing, it will not harm them. They will lay hands on the sick, and they will recover."

So then the Lord Jesus, after he spoke to them, was taken up into heaven and took his seat at the right hand of God. But they went forth and preached everywhere, while the Lord worked with them and confirmed the word through accompanying signs.

GOSPEL / C   *Luke 24:46–53*

Jesus said to his disciples: "Thus it is written that the Christ would suffer and rise from the dead on the third day and that repentance, for the forgiveness of sins, would be preached in his name to all the nations, beginning from Jerusalem. You are witnesses of these things. And behold I am sending the promise of my Father upon you; but stay in the city until you are clothed with power from on high."

Then he led them out as far as Bethany, raised his hands, and blessed them. As he blessed them he parted from them and was taken up to heaven. They did him homage and then returned to Jerusalem with great joy, and they were continually in the temple praising God.

1095   SEVENTH SUNDAY OF EASTER / A

READING I   *Acts 1:12–14 / 59*

After Jesus had been taken up to heaven the apostles returned to Jerusalem from the mount called Olivet, which is near Jerusalem, a sabbath day's journey away.

When they entered the city they went to the upper room where they were staying, Peter and John and James and Andrew, Philip and Thomas, Bartholomew and Matthew, James son of Alphaeus, Simon the Zealot, and Judas son of James. All these devoted themselves with one accord to prayer, together with some women, and Mary the mother of Jesus, and his brothers.

RESPONSORIAL PSALM

Psalm 27:1, 4, 7–8a

Or: Alleluia.

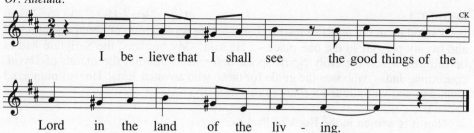

I be-lieve that I shall see the good things of the Lord in the land of the liv - ing.

The LORD is my light and my salvation;
  whom shall I fear?
The LORD is the stronghold of my life;
  whom should I dread? ℟.

There is one thing I ask of the LORD,
  only this do I seek:
to live in the house of the LORD

all the days of my life,
to gaze on the beauty of the LORD,
  to inquire at his temple. ℟.

O LORD, hear my voice when I call;
  have mercy and answer me.
Of you my heart has spoken,
  "Seek his face." ℟.

READING II

1 Peter 4:13–16

Beloved: Rejoice to the extent that you share in the sufferings of Christ, so that when his glory is revealed you may also rejoice exultantly. If you are insulted for the name of Christ, blessed are you, for the Spirit of glory and of God rests upon you. But let no one among you be made to suffer as a murderer, a thief, an evildoer, or as an intriguer. But whoever is made to suffer as a Christian should not be ashamed but glorify God because of the name.

GOSPEL

John 17:1–11a

Jesus raised his eyes to heaven and said, "Father, the hour has come. Give glory to your son, so that your son may glorify you, just as you gave him authority over all people, so that your son may give eternal life to all you gave him. Now this is eternal life, that they should know you, the only true God, and the one whom you sent, Jesus Christ. I glorified you on earth by accomplishing the work that you gave me to do. Now glorify me, Father, with you, with the glory that I had with you before the world began.

"I revealed your name to those whom you gave me out of the world. They belonged to you, and you gave them to me, and they have kept your word. Now they know that everything you gave me is from you, because the words you gave to me I have given to them, and they accepted them and truly understood that I came from you, and they have believed that you sent me. I pray for them. I do not pray for the world but for the ones you have given me, because they are yours, and everything of mine is yours and everything of yours is mine, and I have been glorified in them. And now I will no longer be in the world, but they are in the world, while I am coming to you."

1096   SEVENTH SUNDAY OF EASTER / B

READING I   *Acts 1:15–17, 20a, 20c–26 / 60*

Peter stood up in the midst of the brothers —there was a group of about one hundred and twenty persons in the one place—. He said, "My brothers, the Scripture had to be fulfilled which the Holy Spirit spoke beforehand through the mouth of David, concerning Judas, who was the guide for those who arrested Jesus. He was numbered among us and was allotted a share in this ministry.

"For it is written in the Book of Psalms:
May another take his office.

"Therefore, it is necessary that one of the men who accompanied us the whole time the Lord Jesus came and went among us, beginning from the baptism of John until the day on which he was taken up from us, become with us a witness to his resurrection." So they proposed two, Judas called Barsabbas, who was also known as Justus, and Matthias. Then they prayed, "You, Lord, who know the hearts of all, show which one of these two you have chosen to take the place in this apostolic ministry from which Judas turned away to go to his own place." Then they gave lots to them, and the lot fell upon Matthias, and he was counted with the eleven apostles.

RESPONSORIAL PSALM   *Psalm 103:1–2, 11–12, 19–20ab*

Or: Alleluia.

The Lord has set his throne in heav - en.

Bless the LORD, O my soul,
  and all within me, his holy name.
Bless the LORD, O my soul,
  and never forget all his benefits. ℟.

For as the heavens are high above the
    earth,
  so strong his mercy for those who
    fear him.

As far as the east is from the west,
  so far from us does he remove our
    transgressions. ℟.

The LORD has fixed his throne in heaven,
  and his kingdom is ruling over all.
Bless the LORD, all you his angels,
  mighty in power, fulfilling his
    word. ℟.

READING II   *1 John 4:11–16*

Beloved, if God so loved us, we also must love one another. No one has ever seen God. Yet, if we love one another, God remains in us, and his love is brought to perfection in us.

This is how we know that we remain in him and he in us, that he has given us of his Spirit. Moreover, we have seen and testify that the Father sent his Son as savior of the world. Whoever acknowledges that Jesus is the Son of God, God remains in him and he in God. We have come to know and to believe in the love God has for us.

God is love, and whoever remains in love remains in God and God in him.

GOSPEL *John 17:11b–19*

Lifting up his eyes to heaven, Jesus prayed saying: "Holy Father, keep them in your name that you have given me, so that they may be one just as we are one. When I was with them I protected them in your name that you gave me, and I guarded them, and none of them was lost except the son of destruction, in order that the Scripture might be fulfilled. But now I am coming to you. I speak this in the world so that they may share my joy completely. I gave them your word, and the world hated them, because they do not belong to the world any more than I belong to the world. I do not ask that you take them out of the world but that you keep them from the evil one. They do not belong to the world any more than I belong to the world. Consecrate them in the truth. Your word is truth. As you sent me into the world, so I sent them into the world. And I consecrate myself for them, so that they also may be consecrated in truth."

SEVENTH SUNDAY OF EASTER / C 1097

READING I *Acts 7:55–60 / 61*

Stephen, filled with the Holy Spirit, looked up intently to heaven and saw the glory of God and Jesus standing at the right hand of God, and Stephen said, "Behold, I see the heavens opened and the Son of Man standing at the right hand of God." But they cried out in a loud voice, covered their ears, and rushed upon him together. They threw him out of the city, and began to stone him. The witnesses laid down their cloaks at the feet of a young man named Saul. As they were stoning Stephen, he called out, "Lord Jesus, receive my spirit." Then he fell to his knees and cried out in a loud voice, "Lord, do not hold this sin against them"; and when he said this, he fell asleep.

RESPONSORIAL PSALM *Psalm 97:1 and 2b, 6 and 7c, 9*

Or: Alleluia.

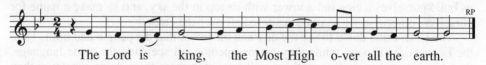

The Lord is king, the Most High o-ver all the earth.

The LORD is king, let earth rejoice;
 let the many islands be glad.
 Justice and right are the foundation
  of his throne. ℟.

The skies proclaim his justice;

all peoples see his glory.
 All you angels, worship him. ℟.

For you indeed are the LORD,
 most high above all the earth,
 exalted far above all gods. ℟.

READING II *Revelation 22:12–14, 16–17, 20*

I, John, heard a voice saying to me: "Behold, I am coming soon. I bring with me the recompense I will give to each according to his deeds. I am the Alpha and the Omega, the first and the last, the beginning and the end."

Blessed are they who wash their robes so as to have the right to the tree of life and enter the city through its gates.

"I, Jesus, sent my angel to give you this testimony for the churches. I am the root and offspring of David, the bright morning star."

The Spirit and the bride say, "Come." Let the hearer say, "Come." Let the one who thirsts come forward, and the one who wants it receive the gift of life-giving water.

The one who gives this testimony says, "Yes, I am coming soon." Amen! Come, Lord Jesus!

GOSPEL   *John 17:20–26*

Lifting up his eyes to heaven, Jesus prayed saying: "Holy Father, I pray not only for them, but also for those who will believe in me through their word, so that they may all be one, as you, Father, are in me and I in you, that they also may be in us, that the world may believe that you sent me. And I have given them the glory you gave me, so that they may be one, as we are one, I in them and you in me, that they may be brought to perfection as one, that the world may know that you sent me, and that you loved them even as you loved me. Father, they are your gift to me. I wish that where I am they also may be with me, that they may see my glory that you gave me, because you loved me before the foundation of the world. Righteous Father, the world also does not know you, but I know you, and they know that you sent me. I made known to them your name and I will make it known, that the love with which you loved me may be in them and I in them."

1098   PENTECOST SUNDAY—VIGIL MASS / ABC

READING I   *Genesis 11:1–9 / 62*

The whole world spoke the same language, using the same words. While the people were migrating in the east, they came upon a valley in the land of Shinar and settled there. They said to one another, "Come, let us mold bricks and harden them with fire." They used bricks for stone, and bitumen for mortar. Then they said, "Come, let us build ourselves a city and a tower with its top in the sky, and so make a name for ourselves; otherwise we shall be scattered all over the earth."

The LORD came down to see the city and the tower that the people had built. Then the LORD said: "If now, while they are one people, all speaking the same language, they have started to do this, nothing will later stop them from doing whatever they presume to do. Let us then go down there and confuse their language, so that one will not understand what another says." Thus the LORD scattered them from there all over the earth, and they stopped building the city. That is why it was called Babel, because there the LORD confused the speech of all the world. It was from that place that he scattered them all over the earth.

Or:

READING I   *Exodus 19:3–8a, 16–20b*

Moses went up the mountain to God. Then the LORD called to him and said, "Thus shall you say to the house of Jacob; tell the Israelites: You have seen for yourselves how I treated the Egyptians and how I bore you up on eagle wings and brought you here to myself. Therefore, if you hearken to my voice and keep my covenant, you shall be my special possession, dearer to me than all other people, though all the earth is mine. You shall be to me a kingdom of priests, a holy nation. That is what you must tell the Israelites." So Moses went and summoned the elders of the people. When he set before them all that the LORD had ordered him to tell them, the people all answered together, "Everything the LORD has said, we will do."

On the morning of the third day there were peals of thunder and lightning, and a heavy cloud over the mountain, and a very loud trumpet blast, so that all the people in the camp trembled. But Moses led the people out of the camp to meet God, and they stationed themselves at the foot of the mountain. Mount Sinai was all wrapped in smoke, for the LORD came down upon it in fire. The smoke rose from it as though from a furnace, and the whole mountain trembled violently. The trumpet blast grew louder and louder, while Moses was speaking, and God answering him with thunder.

When the LORD came down to the top of Mount Sinai, he summoned Moses to the top of the mountain.

Or:

READING I   *Ezekiel 37:1–14*

The hand of the LORD came upon me, and he led me out in the spirit of the LORD and set me in the center of the plain, which was now filled with bones. He made me walk among the bones in every direction so that I saw how many they were on the surface of the plain. How dry they were! He asked me: Son of man, can these bones come to life? I answered, "Lord GOD, you alone know that." Then he said to me: Prophesy over these bones, and say to them: Dry bones, hear the word of the LORD! Thus says the Lord GOD to these bones: See! I will bring spirit into you, that you may come to life. I will put sinews upon you, make flesh grow over you, cover you with skin, and put spirit in you so that you may come to life and know that I am the LORD. I, Ezekiel, prophesied as I had been told, and even as I was prophesying I heard a noise; it was a rattling as the bones came together, bone joining bone. I saw the sinews and the flesh come upon them, and the skin cover them, but there was no spirit in them. Then the LORD said to me: Prophesy to the spirit, prophesy, son of man, and say to the spirit: Thus says the Lord GOD: From the four winds come, O spirit, and breathe into these slain that they may come to life. I prophesied as he told me, and the spirit came into them; they came alive and stood upright, a vast army. Then he said to me: Son of man, these bones are the whole house of Israel. They have been saying, "Our bones are dried up, our hope is lost, and we are cut off." Therefore, prophesy and say to them: Thus says the Lord GOD: O my people, I will open your graves and have you rise from them, and bring you back to the land of Israel. Then you shall know that I am the LORD, when I open your graves and have you rise from them, O my people! I will put my spirit in you that you may live, and I will settle you upon your land; thus you shall know that I am the LORD. I have promised, and I will do it, says the LORD.

Or:

READING I   *Joel 3:1–5*

Thus says the LORD:
I will pour out my spirit upon all flesh.
Your sons and daughters shall prophesy,
    your old men shall dream dreams,
    your young men shall see visions;
even upon the servants and the
    handmaids,
    in those days, I will pour out my
    spirit.
And I will work wonders in the
    heavens and on the earth,
    blood, fire, and columns of smoke;

the sun will be turned to darkness,
    and the moon to blood,
at the coming of the day of the LORD,
    the great and terrible day.
Then everyone shall be rescued
    who calls on the name of the LORD;
for on Mount Zion there shall be a
    remnant,
    as the LORD has said,
and in Jerusalem survivors
    whom the LORD shall call.

RESPONSORIAL PSALM   *Psalm 104:1–2a, 24 and 35c, 27–28, 29bc–30*

Or: Alleluia.

Lord, send out your Spir-it,   and re-new the face of the earth.

Bless the LORD, O my soul!
  O LORD my God, how great you are,
clothed in majesty and honor,
  wrapped in light as with a robe! ℟.

How many are your works, O LORD!
  In wisdom you have made them all.
The earth is full of your creatures.
  Bless the LORD, O my soul.
    Alleluia! ℟.

All of these look to you

to give them their food in due season.
You give it, they gather it up;
  you open wide your hand, they are
  well filled. ℟.

You take away their breath, they die,
  returning to the dust from which they
  came.
You send forth your spirit, and they are
  created,
  and you renew the face of the earth. ℟.

READING II   *Romans 8:22–27*
Brothers and sisters: We know that all creation is groaning in labor pains even until now; and not only that, but we ourselves, who have the firstfruits of the Spirit, we also groan within ourselves as we wait for adoption, the redemption of our bodies. For in hope we were saved. Now hope that sees is not hope. For who hopes for what one sees? But if we hope for what we do not see, we wait with endurance.

In the same way, the Spirit too comes to the aid of our weakness; for we do not know how to pray as we ought, but the Spirit himself intercedes with inexpressible groanings. And the one who searches hearts knows what is the intention of the Spirit, because he intercedes for the holy ones according to God's will.

GOSPEL   *John 7:37–39*
On the last and greatest day of the feast, Jesus stood up and exclaimed, "Let anyone who thirsts come to me and drink. As Scripture says:
  Rivers of living water will flow from within him who believes in me."
He said this in reference to the Spirit that those who came to believe in him were to receive. There was, of course, no Spirit yet, because Jesus had not yet been glorified.

1099 PENTECOST SUNDAY—MASS DURING THE DAY / ABC

READING I   *Acts 2:1–11 / 63*
When the time for Pentecost was fulfilled, they were all in one place together. And suddenly there came from the sky a noise like a strong driving wind, and it filled the entire house in which they were. Then there appeared to them tongues as of fire, which parted and came to rest on each one of them. And they were all filled with the Holy Spirit and began to speak in different tongues, as the Spirit enabled them to proclaim.

Now there were devout Jews from every nation under heaven staying in Jerusalem. At this sound, they gathered in a large crowd, but they were confused because each one heard them speaking in his own language. They were astounded, and in amazement they asked, "Are not all these people who are speaking Galileans? Then how does each of us hear them in his native language? We are Parthians, Medes, and Elamites, inhabitants of Mesopotamia, Judea and Cappadocia, Pontus and Asia, Phrygia and Pamphylia, Egypt and the districts of Libya near Cyrene, as well as travelers from Rome, both Jews and converts to Judaism, Cretans and Arabs, yet we hear them speaking in our own tongues of the mighty acts of God."

RESPONSORIAL PSALM　　　　　　　　　　　　*Psalm 104:1ab and 24ac, 29bc–30, 31 and 34*

Or: Alleluia.

Lord, send out your Spir-it, and re-new the face of the earth.

Bless the LORD, O my soul!
　O LORD my God, how great you are.
How many are your works, O LORD!
　The earth is full of your creatures. ℟.

You take away their breath, they die,
　returning to the dust from which
　　they came.
You send forth your spirit, and they are

created,
and you renew the face of the
　earth. ℟.

May the glory of the LORD last forever!
　May the LORD rejoice in his works!
May my thoughts be pleasing to him.
　I will rejoice in the LORD. ℟.

READING II / ABC　　　　　　　　　　　　　　*1 Corinthians 12:3b–7, 12–13*

Brothers and sisters: No one can say, "Jesus is Lord," except by the Holy Spirit.

There are different kinds of spiritual gifts but the same Spirit; there are different forms of service but the same Lord; there are different workings but the same God who produces all of them in everyone. To each individual the manifestation of the Spirit is given for some benefit.

As a body is one though it has many parts, and all the parts of the body, though many, are one body, so also Christ. For in one Spirit we were all baptized into one body, whether Jews or Greeks, slaves or free persons, and we were all given to drink of one Spirit.

Or:

READING II / B　　　　　　　　　　　　　　　*Galatians 5:16–25*

Brothers and sisters, live by the Spirit and you will certainly not gratify the desire of the flesh. For the flesh has desires against the Spirit, and the Spirit against the flesh; these are opposed to each other, so that you may not do what you want. But if you are guided by the Spirit, you are not under the law. Now the works of the flesh are obvious: immorality, impurity, lust, idolatry, sorcery, hatreds, rivalry, jealousy, outbursts of fury, acts of selfishness, dissensions, factions, occasions of envy, drinking bouts, orgies, and the like. I warn you, as I warned you before, that those who do such things will not inherit the kingdom of God. In contrast, the fruit of the Spirit is love, joy, peace, patience, kindness, generosity, faithfulness, gentleness, self-control. Against such there is no law. Now those who belong to Christ Jesus have crucified their flesh with its passions and desires. If we live in the Spirit, let us also follow the Spirit.

Or:

READING II / C   *Romans 8:8–17*

Brothers and sisters: Those who are in the flesh cannot please God. But you are not in the flesh; on the contrary, you are in the spirit, if only the Spirit of God dwells in you. Whoever does not have the Spirit of Christ does not belong to him. But if Christ is in you, although the body is dead because of sin, the spirit is alive because of righteousness. If the Spirit of the one who raised Jesus from the dead dwells in you, the one who raised Christ from the dead will give life to your mortal bodies also, through his Spirit that dwells in you. Consequently, brothers and sisters, we are not debtors to the flesh, to live according to the flesh. For if you live according to the flesh, you will die, but if by the Spirit you put to death the deeds of the body, you will live.

For those who are led by the Spirit of God are sons of God. For you did not receive a spirit of slavery to fall back into fear, but you received a Spirit of adoption, through whom we cry, "Abba, Father!" The Spirit himself bears witness with our spirit that we are children of God, and if children, then heirs, heirs of God and joint heirs with Christ, if only we suffer with him so that we may also be glorified with him.

1100   SEQUENCE

1. Ho - ly Spir - it, Lord di - vine, Come, from heights of
2. Come, O Fa - ther of the poor, Come, whose treas - ured
1. Ve - ni San - cte Spí - ri - tus, Et e - mít - te
2. Ve - ni pa - ter páu - pe - rum, Ve - ni da - tor

heav'n and shine, Come with bless - ed ra - diance bright!
gifts en - dure, Come, our heart's un - fail - ing light!
caé - li - tus Lu - cis tu - ae rá - di - um.
mú - ne - rum, Ve - ni lu - men cór - di - um.

3. Of con - sol - ers, wis - est, best, And our soul's most
4. In our la - bor rest most sweet, Pleas - ant cool - ness
3. Con - so - lá - tor ó - pti - me, Dul - cis ho - spes
4. In la - bó - re ré - qui - es, In ae - stu tem -

wel - come guest, Sweet re - fresh - ment, sweet re - pose.
in the heat, Con - so - la - tion in our woes.
á - ni - mae, Dul - ce re - fri - gé - ri - um.
pé - ri - es, In fle - tu so - lá - ti - um.

5. Light most bless - ed, shine with grace In our heart's most
6. Left with - out your pres - ence here, Life it - self would
5. *O lux be - a - tís - si - ma, Re - ple cor - dis*
6. *Si - ne tu - o nú - mi - ne, Ni - hil est in*

se - cret place, Fill your faith - ful through and through.
dis - ap - pear, Noth - ing thrives a - part from you!
ín - ti - ma Tu - ó - rum fi - dé - li - um.
hó - mi - ne, Ni - hil est in - nó - xi - um.

7. Cleanse our soil - ed hearts of sin, Ar - id souls re -
8. Bend the stub - born heart and will, Melt the fro - zen,
7. *La - va quod est sór - di - dum, Ri - ga quod est*
8. *Fle - cte quod est rí - gi - dum, Fo - ve quod est*

fresh with - in, Wound - ed lives to health re - store.
warm the chill, Guide the way - ward home once more!
á - ri - dum, Sa - na quod est sáu - ci - um.
frí - gi - dum, Re - ge quod est dé - vi - um.

9. On the faith - ful who are true And pro - fess their
10. Give us vir - tue's sure re - ward, Give us your sal -
9. *Da tu - is fi - dé - li - bus, In te con - fi -*
10. *Da vir - tú - tis mé - ri - tum, Da sa - lú - tis*

faith in you, In your sev'n - fold gift de - scend!
va - tion, Lord, Give us joys that nev - er end!
dén - ti - bus, Sa - crum se - pte - ná - ri - um.
é - xi - tum, Da per - én - ne gáu - di - um.

A - men. Al - le - lú - ia.

Text: *Veni Sancte Spiritus*; attr. to Stephen Langston, ca. 1150–1228, et al.; tr. by Peter J. Scagnelli, b.1949, after Edward Caswall, 1814–1878, © 1983
Tune: VENI SANCTE SPIRITUS, 7 7 7; Dublin *Troper*, ca. 1360; Mode I; acc. by Adriaan Engels, 1906–2003, © Interkerkelijke Stichting voor het
Kerklied Den Haag

An alternate setting is found at no. 541.

GOSPEL / ABC   *John 20:19–23*

On the evening of that first day of the week, when the doors were locked, where the disciples were, for fear of the Jews, Jesus came and stood in their midst and said to them, "Peace be with you." When he had said this, he showed them his hands and his side. The disciples rejoiced when they saw the Lord. Jesus said to them again, "Peace be with you. As the Father has sent me, so I send you." And when he had said this, he breathed on them and said to them, "Receive the Holy Spirit. Whose sins you forgive are forgiven them, and whose sins you retain are retained."

Or:

GOSPEL / B   *John 15:26–27; 16:12–15*

Jesus said to his disciples: "When the Advocate comes whom I will send you from the Father, the Spirit of truth that proceeds from the Father, he will testify to me. And you also testify, because you have been with me from the beginning.

"I have much more to tell you, but you cannot bear it now. But when he comes, the Spirit of truth, he will guide you to all truth. He will not speak on his own, but he will speak what he hears, and will declare to you the things that are coming. He will glorify me, because he will take from what is mine and declare it to you. Everything that the Father has is mine; for this reason I told you that he will take from what is mine and declare it to you."

Or:

GOSPEL / C   *John 14:15–16, 23b–26*

Jesus said to his disciples: "If you love me, you will keep my commandments. And I will ask the Father, and he will give you another Advocate to be with you always.

"Whoever loves me will keep my word, and my Father will love him, and we will come to him and make our dwelling with him. Those who do not love me do not keep my words; yet the word you hear is not mine but that of the Father who sent me.

"I have told you this while I am with you. The Advocate, the Holy Spirit whom the Father will send in my name, will teach you everything and remind you of all that I told you."

Ordinary Time

When the Church assembles, time is always given to the reading of Scripture. This is the book the Church esteems: the Law and the prophets, the books of wisdom and psalms, the letters and writings of Paul and of the other apostles, the gospels themselves. Throughout the history of the Church the readings from Scripture have been arranged so that the various Sundays have their assigned texts. This book of assigned scripture readings is the lectionary. In the present Roman lectionary the readings are ordered according to a cycle of three years.

Most of each year is called "Ordinary Time" or "Sundays of the Year." These are the weeks between the Christmas season and Lent, and the long period between Pentecost (the conclusion of the Easter season) and Advent (usually the first Sunday in December). On the Sundays of Ordinary Time, the lectionary has us read through the letters of the New Testament and the gospels. In the first year of the cycle, the gospel of Matthew is read from beginning to end; in the second year, Mark; in the third, Luke. Likewise, each Sunday finds the Church picking up the reading of one of the letters of the New Testament roughly where the previous week's reading concluded. At present, the first reading at Sunday Mass in Ordinary Time is chosen from the Hebrew Scriptures; these texts show the richness and the continuity of faith.

Sunday by Sunday, year after year, the Church reads through its book in the weeks of Ordinary Time. Each Christian, each local Church, each generation listens and so finds its own life in God's word.

The Church assembles around Scripture and around the Lord's table on Sunday. This day is called by Christians the Lord's Day. Whether the Church is in Ordinary Time or in the seasons of Advent/Christmas or Lent/Easter, the Lord's Day is kept holy; it is the original feast day. The rhythm of the weekdays and the Sunday is the basic rhythm of life in Christian churches. The practices with which a Church keeps the Lord's Day vary, but always and everywhere Christians assemble on this day so that the Church may listen to God's word. Through the days of the week, the Sunday's scripture readings are to be for reflection and nourishment as they are repeated and pondered in the households of the assembly.

1102 MOST HOLY TRINITY / A

READING I   *Exodus 34:4b–6, 8–9 / 164*

Early in the morning Moses went up Mount Sinai as the LORD had commanded him, taking along the two stone tablets.

Having come down in a cloud, the LORD stood with Moses there and proclaimed his name, "LORD." Thus the LORD passed before him and cried out, "The LORD, the LORD, a merciful and gracious God, slow to anger and rich in kindness and fidelity." Moses at once bowed down to the ground in worship. Then he said, "If I find favor with you, O LORD, do come along in our company. This is indeed a stiff-necked people; yet pardon our wickedness and sins, and receive us as your own."

RESPONSORIAL PSALM   *Daniel 3:52, 53, 54, 55*

Cantor or choir:

You are blest, Lord God of our fa - thers.
Blest be your glo - ri - ous ho - ly name.
You are blest in the tem - ple of your glo - ry.
You are blest on the throne of your king - dom.
You are blest who gaze in - to the depths.
You are blest who sit a - bove the cher - u - bim.
You are blest in the firm - a - ment of heav - en.

Assembly:

To you glo - ry and praise for ev - er - more.

READING II   *2 Corinthians 13:11–13*

Brothers and sisters, rejoice. Mend your ways, encourage one another, agree with one another, live in peace, and the God of love and peace will be with you. Greet one another with a holy kiss. All the holy ones greet you.

The grace of the Lord Jesus Christ and the love of God and the fellowship of the Holy Spirit be with all of you.

GOSPEL   *John 3:16–18*

God so loved the world that he gave his only Son, so that everyone who believes in him might not perish but might have eternal life. For God did not send his Son into the world to condemn the world, but that the world might be saved through him. Whoever believes in him will not be condemned, but whoever does not believe has already been condemned, because he has not believed in the name of the only Son of God.

MOST HOLY TRINITY / B   1103

READING I   *Deuteronomy 4:32–34, 39–40 / 165*

Moses said to the people: "Ask now of the days of old, before your time, ever since God created man upon the earth; ask from one end of the sky to the other: Did anything so great ever happen before? Was it ever heard of? Did a people ever hear the voice of God speaking from the midst of fire, as you did, and live? Or did any god venture to go and take a nation for himself from the midst of another nation, by testings, by signs and wonders, by war, with strong hand and outstretched arm, and by great terrors, all of which the LORD, your God, did for you in Egypt before your very eyes? This is why you must now know, and fix in your heart, that the LORD is God in the heavens above and on earth below, and that there is no other. You must keep his statutes and commandments that I enjoin on you today, that you and your children after you may prosper, and that you may have long life on the land which the LORD, your God, is giving you forever."

RESPONSORIAL PSALM   *Psalm 33:4–5, 6 and 9, 18–19, 20 and 22*

Bless-ed the peo-ple the Lord has cho-sen to be his own.

The word of the LORD is faithful,
    and all his works to be trusted.
The LORD loves justice and right,
    and his merciful love fills the earth. ℟.

By the word of the LORD the
        heavens were made,
    by the breath of his mouth
        all their host.
He spoke, and it came to be.
    He commanded; it stood in place. ℟.

Yes, the LORD's eyes are on those who
        fear him,
    who hope in his merciful love,
    to rescue their souls from death,
        to keep them alive in famine. ℟.

Our soul is waiting for the LORD.
    He is our help and our shield.
May your merciful love be upon us,
    as we hope in you, O LORD. ℟.

READING II   *Romans 8:14–17*

Brothers and sisters: Those who are led by the Spirit of God are sons of God. For you did not receive a spirit of slavery to fall back into fear, but you received a Spirit of adoption, through whom we cry, "Abba, Father!" The Spirit himself bears witness with our spirit that we are children of God, and if children, then heirs, heirs of God and joint heirs with Christ, if only we suffer with him so that we may also be glorified with him.

GOSPEL   *Matthew 28:16–20*

The eleven disciples went to Galilee, to the mountain to which Jesus had ordered them. When they all saw him, they worshiped, but they doubted. Then Jesus approached and said to them, "All power in heaven and on earth has been given to me. Go, therefore, and make disciples of all nations, baptizing them in the name of the Father, and of the Son, and of the Holy Spirit, teaching them to observe all that I have commanded you. And behold, I am with you always, until the end of the age."

1104 MOST HOLY TRINITY / C

READING I   *Proverbs 8:22–31 / 166*

Thus says the wisdom of God:
"The LORD possessed me, the
   beginning of his ways,
  the forerunner of his prodigies of
   long ago;
from of old I was poured forth,
  at the first, before the earth.
When there were no depths I was
  brought forth,
  when there were no fountains or
   springs of water;
before the mountains were settled
   into place,
  before the hills, I was brought forth;
while as yet the earth and fields were
   not made,
  nor the first clods of the world.

"When the Lord established the heavens
   I was there,
  when he marked out the vault over
   the face of the deep;
when he made firm the skies above,
  when he fixed fast the foundations
   of the earth;
when he set for the sea its limit,
  so that the waters should not
   transgress his command;
then was I beside him as his craftsman,
  and I was his delight day by day,
playing before him all the while,
  playing on the surface of his earth;
  and I found delight in the human
   race."

RESPONSORIAL PSALM   *Psalm 8:4–5, 6–7, 8–9*

JRC

O Lord, our God, how won-der-ful your name in all the earth!

When I see the heavens, the work of
   your fingers,
  the moon and the stars which you
   arranged,
what is man that you should keep him
   in mind,
  the son of man that you care for
   him? ℟.

Yet you have made him little lower
   than the angels;

  with glory and honor you crowned
   him,
gave him power over the works of your
   hands:
  you put all things under his feet. ℟.

All of them, sheep and oxen,
  yes, even the cattle of the fields,
birds of the air, and fish of the sea
  that make their way through the
   waters. ℟.

READING II   *Romans 5:1–5*

Brothers and sisters: Therefore, since we have been justified by faith, we have peace
with God through our Lord Jesus Christ, through whom we have gained access by
faith to this grace in which we stand, and we boast in hope of the glory of God. Not
only that, but we even boast of our afflictions, knowing that affliction produces endurance, and endurance, proven character, and proven character, hope, and hope does not
disappoint, because the love of God has been poured out into our hearts through the
Holy Spirit that has been given to us.

GOSPEL

John 16:12–15

Jesus said to his disciples: "I have much more to tell you, but you cannot bear it now. But when he comes, the Spirit of truth, he will guide you to all truth. He will not speak on his own, but he will speak what he hears, and will declare to you the things that are coming. He will glorify me, because he will take from what is mine and declare it to you. Everything that the Father has is mine; for this reason I told you that he will take from what is mine and declare it to you."

MOST HOLY BODY AND BLOOD OF CHRIST / A — 1105

READING I

Deuteronomy 8:2–3, 14b–16a / 167

Moses said to the people: "Remember how for forty years now the LORD, your God, has directed all your journeying in the desert, so as to test you by affliction and find out whether or not it was your intention to keep his commandments. He therefore let you be afflicted with hunger, and then fed you with manna, a food unknown to you and your fathers, in order to show you that not by bread alone does one live, but by every word that comes forth from the mouth of the LORD.

"Do not forget the LORD, your God, who brought you out of the land of Egypt, that place of slavery; who guided you through the vast and terrible desert with its saraph serpents and scorpions, its parched and waterless ground; who brought forth water for you from the flinty rock and fed you in the desert with manna, a food unknown to your fathers."

RESPONSORIAL PSALM

Psalm 147:12–13, 14–15, 19–20

Or: Alleluia.

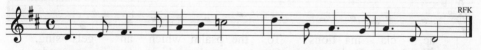

Praise the Lord, Je - ru - sa - lem.   Praise the Lord, Je - ru - sa - lem.

O Jerusalem, glorify the LORD!
  O Sion, praise your God!
He has strengthened the bars of your
    gates;
  he has blessed your children within
    you. ℟.

He established peace on your borders;
  he gives you your fill of finest wheat.

He sends out his word to the earth,
  and swiftly runs his command. ℟.

He reveals his word to Jacob;
  to Israel, his decrees and judgments.
He has not dealt thus with other nations;
  he has not taught them his
    judgments. ℟.

READING II

1 Corinthians 10:16–17

Brothers and sisters: The cup of blessing that we bless, is it not a participation in the blood of Christ? The bread that we break, is it not a participation in the body of Christ? Because the loaf of bread is one, we, though many, are one body, for we all partake of the one loaf.

1106 SEQUENCE (Optional)

1. Praise, O Zi - on, voic - es rais - ing, Glo - ri - fy your
2. Here re - call - ing Christ's own Pas - sion Come, dis - ci - ples,
3. Christ, the Pas - chal lamb o - be - dient, Gave him - self as
4. As we keep this won - drous mys - t'ry, Heart and mind in
5. Though a mul - ti - tude re - ceives him, Christ, in man - y

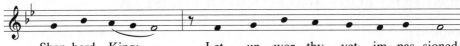

Shep - herd - King; Let un - wor - thy yet im - pas - sioned
as his friends; Bless - ing, break - ing, pour - ing, shar - ing—
God had planned; Now re - plac - ing for - mer of - f'rings,
faith com - bine. Here we eat the bread, his Bod - y,
parts, is one; Shared a - like by saints and sin - ners,

Thank - ful hymns of hom - age ring! Join your hum - ble
By these ac - tions, Christ still sends To the world his
In self - giv - ing, here he stands, Prays a - gain in
Drink his pre - cious Blood in wine; This, the death - less
He re - mains God's on - ly Son. This, the choice and

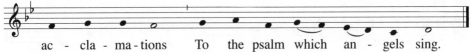

ac - cla - ma - tions To the psalm which an - gels sing.
Blood and Bod - y, Cov - e - nant which nev - er ends.
con - se - cra - tion; "Eat and drink!" his great com - mand.
Vic - tim's ta - ble Set in sac - ra - ment - al sign.
gift of heav - en: Sav - ing grace with - held from none.

6. Though the bread has now been broken,
Though the wine has now been poured,
Christ, here present in these symbols,
Still is whole, and truly Lord.
Through one meal one Church is
    nourished,
Leading to one life restored.

7. Bread of Angels! for God's children
Pilgrims' strength along the way;
God provides in love, as always,
Holy manna ev'ry day.
Christ, as Isaac on the altar,
Still our debt to God will pay.

8. Living bread, Good Shepherd, feed us,
Endless mercy offering;
With your hallowed saints unite us,
To your heav'nly banquet bring;
There will we, forever feasting,
"Amen! Alleluia!" sing!

Text: *Lauda Sion Salvatorem*, St. Thomas Aquinas, 1225–1274; tr. by Alan J. Hommerding, b.1956, © 2000, World Library Publications
Tune: PANGE LINGUA GLORIOSI, 8 7 8 7 8 7; Mode III; acc. by Eugene Lapierre, 1899–1970, © 1964, GIA Publications, Inc.

GOSPEL *John 6:51–58*

Jesus said to the Jewish crowds: "I am the living bread that came down from heaven; whoever eats this bread will live forever; and the bread that I will give is my flesh for the life of the world."

The Jews quarreled among themselves, saying, "How can this man give us his flesh to eat?" Jesus said to them, "Amen, amen, I say to you, unless you eat the flesh of the Son of Man and drink his blood, you do not have life within you. Whoever eats my flesh and drinks my blood has eternal life, and I will raise him on the last day. For my flesh is true food, and my blood is true drink. Whoever eats my flesh and drinks my blood remains in me and I in him. Just as the living Father sent me and I have life because of the Father, so also the one who feeds on me will have life because of me. This is the bread that came down from heaven. Unlike your ancestors who ate and still died, whoever eats this bread will live forever."

MOST HOLY BODY AND BLOOD OF CHRIST / B 1107

READING I *Exodus 24:3–8 / 168*

When Moses came to the people and related all the words and ordinances of the LORD, they all answered with one voice, "We will do everything that the LORD has told us." Moses then wrote down all the words of the LORD and, rising early the next day, he erected at the foot of the mountain an altar and twelve pillars for the twelve tribes of Israel. Then, having sent certain young men of the Israelites to offer holocausts and sacrifice young bulls as peace offerings to the LORD, Moses took half of the blood and put it in large bowls; the other half he splashed on the altar. Taking the book of the covenant, he read it aloud to the people, who answered, "All that the LORD has said, we will heed and do." Then he took the blood and sprinkled it on the people, saying, "This is the blood of the covenant that the LORD has made with you in accordance with all these words of his."

RESPONSORIAL PSALM *Psalm 116:12–13, 15 and 16bc, 17–18*

Or: Alleluia.

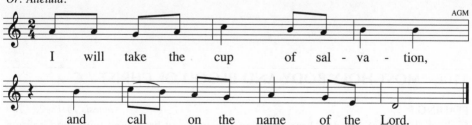

I will take the cup of sal - va - tion, and call on the name of the Lord.

How can I repay the LORD
for all his goodness to me?
The cup of salvation I will raise;
I will call on the name of the
LORD. ℟.

How precious in the eyes of the LORD
is the death of his faithful.
Your servant am I,

the son of your handmaid;
you have loosened my bonds. ℟.

A thanksgiving sacrifice I make;
I will call on the name of the
LORD.
My vows to the LORD I will fulfill
before all his people. ℟.

READING II   *Hebrews 9:11–15*

Brothers and sisters: When Christ came as high priest of the good things that have come to be, passing through the greater and more perfect tabernacle not made by hands, that is, not belonging to this creation, he entered once for all into the sanctuary, not with the blood of goats and calves but with his own blood, thus obtaining eternal redemption. For if the blood of goats and bulls and the sprinkling of a heifer's ashes can sanctify those who are defiled so that their flesh is cleansed, how much more will the blood of Christ, who through the eternal Spirit offered himself unblemished to God, cleanse our consciences from dead works to worship the living God.

For this reason he is mediator of a new covenant: since a death has taken place for deliverance from transgressions under the first covenant, those who are called may receive the promised eternal inheritance.

SEQUENCE   *See no. 1106*

GOSPEL   *Mark 14:12–16, 22–26*

On the first day of the Feast of Unleavened Bread, when they sacrificed the Passover lamb, Jesus' disciples said to him, "Where do you want us to go and prepare for you to eat the Passover?" He sent two of his disciples and said to them, "Go into the city and a man will meet you, carrying a jar of water. Follow him. Wherever he enters, say to the master of the house, 'The Teacher says, "Where is my guest room where I may eat the Passover with my disciples?"'" Then he will show you a large upper room furnished and ready. Make the preparations for us there." The disciples then went off, entered the city, and found it just as he had told them; and they prepared the Passover.

While they were eating, he took bread, said the blessing, broke it, gave it to them, and said, "Take it; this is my body." Then he took a cup, gave thanks, and gave it to them, and they all drank from it. He said to them, "This is my blood of the covenant, which will be shed for many. Amen, I say to you, I shall not drink again the fruit of the vine until the day when I drink it new in the kingdom of God." Then, after singing a hymn, they went out to the Mount of Olives.

1108   MOST HOLY BODY AND BLOOD OF CHRIST / C

READING I   *Genesis 14:18–20 / 169*

In those days, Melchizedek, king of Salem, brought out bread and wine, and being a priest of God Most High, he blessed Abram with these words:
    "Blessed be Abram by God Most High,
        the creator of heaven and earth;
    and blessed be God Most High,
        who delivered your foes into your hand."
Then Abram gave him a tenth of everything.

RESPONSORIAL PSALM   *Psalm 110:1, 2, 3, 4*

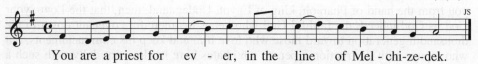

You are a priest for ev - er, in the line of Mel - chi-ze-dek.

The LORD's revelation to my lord:
"Sit at my right hand,
until I make your foes your
footstool." ℟.

on the day of your power.
In holy splendor, from the womb before
the dawn,
I have begotten you. ℟.

The LORD will send from Sion
your scepter of power:
rule in the midst of your foes. ℟.

With you is princely rule

The LORD has sworn an oath he will
not change:
"You are a priest forever,
in the line of Melchizedek." ℟.

READING II   *1 Corinthians 11:23–26*

Brothers and sisters: I received from the Lord what I also handed on to you, that the Lord Jesus, on the night he was handed over, took bread, and, after he had given thanks, broke it and said, "This is my body that is for you. Do this in remembrance of me." In the same way also the cup, after supper, saying, "This cup is the new covenant in my blood. Do this, as often as you drink it, in remembrance of me." For as often as you eat this bread and drink the cup, you proclaim the death of the Lord until he comes.

SEQUENCE *See no. 1106*

GOSPEL   *Luke 9:11b–17*

Jesus spoke to the crowds about the kingdom of God, and he healed those who needed to be cured. As the day was drawing to a close, the Twelve approached him and said, "Dismiss the crowd so that they can go to the surrounding villages and farms and find lodging and provisions; for we are in a deserted place here." He said to them, "Give them some food yourselves." They replied, "Five loaves and two fish are all we have, unless we ourselves go and buy food for all these people." Now the men there numbered about five thousand. Then he said to his disciples, "Have them sit down in groups of about fifty." They did so and made them all sit down. Then taking the five loaves and the two fish, and looking up to heaven, he said the blessing over them, broke them, and gave them to the disciples to set before the crowd. They all ate and were satisfied. And when the leftover fragments were picked up, they filled twelve wicker baskets.

MOST SACRED HEART OF JESUS / A   1109

READING I   *Deuteronomy 7:6–11 / 170*

Moses said to the people: "You are a people sacred to the LORD, your God; he has chosen you from all the nations on the face of the earth to be a people peculiarly his own. It was not because you are the largest of all nations that the LORD set his heart on you and chose you, for you are really the smallest of all nations. It was because the LORD loved you and because of his fidelity to the oath he had sworn to your fathers, that he brought you out with his strong hand from the place of slavery, and ransomed you from the hand of Pharaoh, king of Egypt. Understand, then, that the LORD, your God, is God indeed, the faithful God who keeps his merciful covenant down to the thousandth generation toward those who love him and keep his commandments, but who repays with destruction a person who hates him; he does not dally with such a one, but makes them personally pay for it. You shall therefore carefully observe the commandments, the statutes and the decrees that I enjoin on you today."

RESPONSORIAL PSALM   *Psalm 103:1–2, 3–4, 6–7, 8 and 10*

Bless the LORD, O my soul,
    and all within me, his holy name.
Bless the LORD, O my soul,
    and never forget all his benefits. ℟.

It is the Lord who forgives all your sins,
    who heals every one of your ills,
who redeems your life from the grave,
    who crowns you with mercy and
        compassion. ℟.

The LORD does just deeds,

gives full justice to all who are
    oppressed.
He made known his ways to Moses,
    and his deeds to the children of
        Israel. ℟.

The LORD is compassionate and gracious,
    slow to anger and rich in mercy.
He does not treat us according to our
    sins,
nor repay us according to our
    faults. ℟.

READING II   *1 John 4:7–16*

Beloved, let us love one another, because love is of God; everyone who loves is begotten by God and knows God. Whoever is without love does not know God, for God is love. In this way the love of God was revealed to us: God sent his only Son into the world so that we might have life through him. In this is love: not that we have loved God, but that he loved us and sent his Son as expiation for our sins. Beloved, if God so loved us, we also must love one another. No one has ever seen God. Yet, if we love one another, God remains in us, and his love is brought to perfection in us.

This is how we know that we remain in him and he in us, that he has given us of his Spirit. Moreover, we have seen and testify that the Father sent his Son as savior of the world. Whoever acknowledges that Jesus is the Son of God, God remains in him and he in God. We have come to know and to believe in the love God has for us.

God is love, and whoever remains in love remains in God and God in him.

GOSPEL   *Matthew 11:25–30*

At that time Jesus exclaimed: "I give praise to you, Father, Lord of heaven and earth, for although you have hidden these things from the wise and the learned you have revealed them to little ones. Yes, Father, such has been your gracious will. All things have been handed over to me by my Father. No one knows the Son except the Father, and no one knows the Father except the Son and anyone to whom the Son wishes to reveal him.

"Come to me, all you who labor and are burdened, and I will give you rest. Take my yoke upon you and learn from me, for I am meek and humble of heart; and you will find rest for yourselves. For my yoke is easy, and my burden light."

MOST SACRED HEART OF JESUS / B   1110

READING I
Hosea 11:1, 3–4, 8c–9 / 171

Thus says the LORD:
When Israel was a child I loved him,
   out of Egypt I called my son.
Yet it was I who taught Ephraim to
   walk,
   who took them in my arms;
I drew them with human cords,
   with bands of love;
I fostered them like one
   who raises an infant to his cheeks;
Yet, though I stooped to feed my child,

they did not know that I was their
   healer.

My heart is overwhelmed,
   my pity is stirred.
I will not give vent to my blazing anger,
   I will not destroy Ephraim again;
For I am God and not a man,
   the Holy One present among you;
   I will not let the flames consume you.

RESPONSORIAL PSALM
Isaiah 12:2–3, 4bcd, 5–6

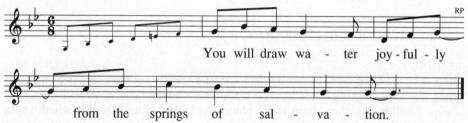

You will draw water joyfully from the springs of salvation.

Truly, God is my salvation,
   I trust, I shall not fear.
For the Lord is my strength, my song,
   he became my savior.
With joy you will draw water
   from the wells of salvation. ℟.

Give thanks to the Lord,
   give praise to his name!
Make his mighty deeds

known to the peoples!
Declare the greatness of his name.
   Sing a psalm to the Lord! ℟.

For he has done glorious deeds,
   make them known to all the earth!
People of Zion,
   sing and shout for joy,
for great in your midst
   is the Holy One of Israel. ℟.

READING II
Ephesians 3:8–12, 14–19

Brothers and sisters: To me, the very least of all the holy ones, this grace was given, to preach to the Gentiles the inscrutable riches of Christ, and to bring to light for all what is the plan of the mystery hidden from ages past in God who created all things, so that the manifold wisdom of God might now be made known through the church to the principalities and authorities in the heavens. This was according to the eternal purpose that he accomplished in Christ Jesus our Lord, in whom we have boldness of speech and confidence of access through faith in him.

For this reason I kneel before the Father, from whom every family in heaven and on earth is named, that he may grant you in accord with the riches of his glory to be strengthened with power through his Spirit in the inner self, and that Christ may dwell in your hearts through faith; that you, rooted and grounded in love, may have strength to comprehend with all the holy ones what is the breadth and length and height and depth, and to know the love of Christ which surpasses knowledge, so that you may be filled with all the fullness of God.

GOSPEL *John 19:31–37*

Since it was preparation day, in order that the bodies might not remain on the cross on the sabbath, for the sabbath day of that week was a solemn one, the Jews asked Pilate that their legs be broken and they be taken down. So the soldiers came and broke the legs of the first and then of the other one who was crucified with Jesus. But when they came to Jesus and saw that he was already dead, they did not break his legs, but one soldier thrust his lance into his side, and immediately blood and water flowed out. An eyewitness has testified, and his testimony is true; he knows that he is speaking the truth, so that you also may come to believe. For this happened so that the Scripture passage might be fulfilled:

Not a bone of it will be broken.

And again another passage says:

They will look upon him whom they have pierced.

1111 MOST SACRED HEART OF JESUS / C

READING I *Ezekiel 34:11–16 / 172*

Thus says the Lord God: I myself will look after and tend my sheep. As a shepherd tends his flock when he finds himself among his scattered sheep, so will I tend my sheep. I will rescue them from every place where they were scattered when it was cloudy and dark. I will lead them out from among the peoples and gather them from the foreign lands; I will bring them back to their own country and pasture them upon the mountains of Israel in the land's ravines and all its inhabited places. In good pastures will I pasture them, and on the mountain heights of Israel shall be their grazing ground. There they shall lie down on good grazing ground, and in rich pastures shall they be pastured on the mountains of Israel. I myself will pasture my sheep; I myself will give them rest, says the Lord God. The lost I will seek out, the strayed I will bring back, the injured I will bind up, the sick I will heal, but the sleek and the strong I will destroy, shepherding them rightly.

RESPONSORIAL PSALM *Psalm 23:1–3a, 3b–4, 5, 6*

RP

The Lord is my shep-herd; there is noth-ing I shall want.

The LORD is my shepherd;
   there is nothing I shall want.
Fresh and green are the pastures

where he gives me repose.
Near restful waters he leads me;
he revives my soul. ℟.

He guides me along the right path,
for the sake of his name.
Though I should walk in the valley of
the shadow of death,
no evil would I fear, for you are
with me.
Your crook and your staff will give
me comfort. ℟.

You have prepared a table before me
in the sight of my foes.

My head you have anointed with oil;
my cup is overflowing. ℟.

Surely goodness and mercy shall follow
me
all the days of my life.
In the LORD's own house shall I dwell
for length of days unending. ℟.

READING II *Romans 5:5b–11*

Brothers and sisters: The love of God has been poured out into our hearts through the
Holy Spirit that has been given to us. For Christ, while we were still helpless, died
at the appointed time for the ungodly. Indeed, only with difficulty does one die for a
just person, though perhaps for a good person one might even find courage to die. But
God proves his love for us in that while we were still sinners Christ died for us. How
much more then, since we are now justified by his blood, will we be saved through
him from the wrath. Indeed, if, while we were enemies, we were reconciled to God
through the death of his Son, how much more, once reconciled, will we be saved
by his life. Not only that, but we also boast of God through our Lord Jesus Christ,
through whom we have now received reconciliation.

GOSPEL *Luke 15:3–7*

Jesus addressed this parable to the Pharisees and scribes: "What man among you
having a hundred sheep and losing one of them would not leave the ninety-nine in
the desert and go after the lost one until he finds it? And when he does find it, he
sets it on his shoulders with great joy and, upon his arrival home, he calls together
his friends and neighbors and says to them, 'Rejoice with me because I have found
my lost sheep.' I tell you, in just the same way there will be more joy in heaven over
one sinner who repents than over ninety-nine righteous people who have no need of
repentance."

SECOND SUNDAY IN ORDINARY TIME / A 1112

READING I *Isaiah 49:3, 5–6 / 64*

The LORD said to me: You are my
servant,
Israel, through whom I show my
glory.
Now the LORD has spoken
who formed me as his servant
from the womb,
that Jacob may be brought back to him
and Israel gathered to him;
and I am made glorious in the sight

of the LORD,
and my God is now my strength!
It is too little, the LORD says, for you to
be my servant,
to raise up the tribes of Jacob,
and restore the survivors of Israel;
I will make you a light to the nations,
that my salvation may reach to the
ends of the earth.

RESPONSORIAL PSALM　　　　　　　　　　*Psalm 40:2 and 4ab, 7–8a, 8b–9, 10*

Here am I, Lord; I come to do your will.

I waited, I waited for the LORD,
　　and he stooped down to me; he
　　　　heard my cry.
He put a new song into my mouth,
　　praise of our God. ℟.

You delight not in sacrifice and
　　　　offerings,
　　but in an open ear.
You do not ask for holocaust and victim.
　　Then I said, "See, I have come." ℟.

In the scroll of the book it stands
　　written of me:
　　"I delight to do your will, O my
　　　　God;
　　your instruction lies deep within
　　　　me." ℟.

Your justice I have proclaimed
　　in the great assembly.
My lips I have not sealed;
　　you know it, O LORD. ℟.

READING II　　　　　　　　　　*1 Corinthians 1:1–3*

Paul, called to be an apostle of Christ Jesus by the will of God, and Sosthenes our brother, to the church of God that is in Corinth, to you who have been sanctified in Christ Jesus, called to be holy, with all those everywhere who call upon the name of our Lord Jesus Christ, their Lord and ours. Grace to you and peace from God our Father and the Lord Jesus Christ.

GOSPEL　　　　　　　　　　*John 1:29–34*

John the Baptist saw Jesus coming toward him and said, "Behold, the Lamb of God, who takes away the sin of the world. He is the one of whom I said, 'A man is coming after me who ranks ahead of me because he existed before me.' I did not know him, but the reason why I came baptizing with water was that he might be made known to Israel." John testified further, saying, "I saw the Spirit come down like a dove from heaven and remain upon him. I did not know him, but the one who sent me to baptize with water told me, 'On whomever you see the Spirit come down and remain, he is the one who will baptize with the Holy Spirit.' Now I have seen and testified that he is the Son of God."

1113　SECOND SUNDAY IN ORDINARY TIME / B

READING I　　　　　　　　　　*1 Samuel 3:3b–10, 19 / 65*

Samuel was sleeping in the temple of the LORD where the ark of God was. The LORD called to Samuel, who answered, "Here I am." Samuel ran to Eli and said, "Here I am. You called me." "I did not call you," Eli said. "Go back to sleep." So he went back to sleep. Again the LORD called Samuel, who rose and went to Eli. "Here I am," he said. "You called me." But Eli answered, "I did not call you, my son. Go back to sleep."

At that time Samuel was not familiar with the LORD, because the LORD had not revealed anything to him as yet. The LORD called Samuel again, for the third time.

Getting up and going to Eli, he said, "Here I am. You called me." Then Eli understood that the LORD was calling the youth. So he said to Samuel, "Go to sleep, and if you are called, reply, 'Speak, LORD, for your servant is listening.'" When Samuel went to sleep in his place, the LORD came and revealed his presence, calling out as before, "Samuel, Samuel!" Samuel answered, "Speak, for your servant is listening."

Samuel grew up, and the LORD was with him, not permitting any word of his to be without effect.

RESPONSORIAL PSALM   *Psalm 40:2 and 4ab, 7–8a, 8b–9, 10*

Here am I, Lord; I come to do your will.

I waited, I waited for the LORD,
  and he stooped down to me;
    he heard my cry.
He put a new song into my mouth,
  praise of our God. ℟.

You delight not in sacrifice and offerings,
  but in an open ear.
You do not ask for holocaust and
    victim.
  Then I said, "See, I have come." ℟.

In the scroll of the book it stands written
  of me:
  "I delight to do your will, O my God;
  your instruction lies deep within
  me." ℟.

Your justice I have proclaimed
  in the great assembly.
My lips I have not sealed;
  you know it, O LORD. ℟.

READING II   *1 Corinthians 6:13c–15a, 17–20*
Brothers and sisters: The body is not for immorality, but for the Lord, and the Lord is for the body; God raised the Lord and will also raise us by his power.

Do you not know that your bodies are members of Christ? But whoever is joined to the Lord becomes one Spirit with him. Avoid immorality. Every other sin a person commits is outside the body, but the immoral person sins against his own body. Do you not know that your body is a temple of the Holy Spirit within you, whom you have from God, and that you are not your own? For you have been purchased at a price. Therefore glorify God in your body.

GOSPEL   *John 1:35–42*
John was standing with two of his disciples, and as he watched Jesus walk by, he said, "Behold, the Lamb of God." The two disciples heard what he said and followed Jesus. Jesus turned and saw them following him and said to them, "What are you looking for?" They said to him, "Rabbi" —which translated means Teacher—, "where are you staying?" He said to them, "Come, and you will see." So they went and saw where Jesus was staying, and they stayed with him that day. It was about four in the afternoon. Andrew, the brother of Simon Peter, was one of the two who heard John and followed Jesus. He first found his own brother Simon and told him, "We have found the Messiah" —which is translated Christ. Then he brought him to Jesus. Jesus looked at him and said, "You are Simon the son of John; you will be called Cephas" —which is translated Peter.

1114 SECOND SUNDAY IN ORDINARY TIME / C

READING I   *Isaiah 62:1–5 / 66*

For Zion's sake I will not be silent,
    for Jerusalem's sake I will not be
       quiet,
until her vindication shines forth like
      the dawn
    and her victory like a burning torch.

Nations shall behold your vindication,
    and all the kings your glory;
you shall be called by a new name
    pronounced by the mouth of the
       LORD.
You shall be a glorious crown in the
hand of the LORD,
    a royal diadem held by your God.
No more shall people call you
    "Forsaken,"
    or your land "Desolate,"
but you shall be called "My Delight,"
    and your land "Espoused."
For the LORD delights in you
    and makes your land his spouse.
As a young man marries a virgin,
    your Builder shall marry you;
and as a bridegroom rejoices in his bride
    so shall your God rejoice in you.

RESPONSORIAL PSALM   *Psalm 96:1–2a, 2b–3, 7–8a, 9–10a and c*

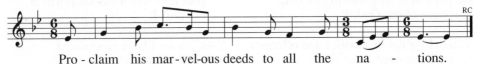

Pro - claim his mar - vel - ous deeds to all the na - tions.

O sing a new song to the LORD;
    sing to the LORD, all the earth.
    O sing to the LORD; bless his name. ℟.

Proclaim his salvation day by day.
    Tell among the nations his glory,
    and his wonders among all the
      peoples. ℟.

Give the LORD, you families of peoples,
give the LORD glory and power;
    give the LORD the glory of his
    name. ℟.

Worship the LORD in holy splendor.
    O tremble before him, all the earth.
Say to the nations, "The LORD is king."
    He will judge the peoples in
      fairness. ℟.

READING II   *1 Corinthians 12:4–11*

Brothers and sisters: There are different kinds of spiritual gifts but the same Spirit; there
are different forms of service but the same Lord; there are different workings but the
same God who produces all of them in everyone. To each individual the manifestation
of the Spirit is given for some benefit. To one is given through the Spirit the expression of wisdom; to another, the expression of knowledge according to the same Spirit;
to another, faith by the same Spirit; to another, gifts of healing by the one Spirit; to
another, mighty deeds; to another, prophecy; to another, discernment of spirits; to
another, varieties of tongues; to another, interpretation of tongues. But one and the same
Spirit produces all of these, distributing them individually to each person as he wishes.

GOSPEL   *John 2:1–11*

There was a wedding at Cana in Galilee, and the mother of Jesus was there. Jesus and
his disciples were also invited to the wedding. When the wine ran short, the mother
of Jesus said to him, "They have no wine." And Jesus said to her, "Woman, how does

your concern affect me? My hour has not yet come." His mother said to the servers, "Do whatever he tells you." Now there were six stone water jars there for Jewish ceremonial washings, each holding twenty to thirty gallons. Jesus told them, "Fill the jars with water." So they filled them to the brim. Then he told them, "Draw some out now and take it to the headwaiter." So they took it. And when the headwaiter tasted the water that had become wine, without knowing where it came from —although the servers who had drawn the water knew—, the headwaiter called the bridegroom and said to him, "Everyone serves good wine first, and then when people have drunk freely, an inferior one; but you have kept the good wine until now." Jesus did this as the beginning of his signs at Cana in Galilee and so revealed his glory, and his disciples began to believe in him.

THIRD SUNDAY IN ORDINARY TIME / A

1115

READING I

Isaiah 8:23 – 9:3 / 67

First the Lord degraded the land of Zebulun and the land of Naphtali; but in the end he has glorified the seaward road, the land west of the Jordan, the District of the Gentiles.

> Anguish has taken wing, dispelled is darkness:
>> for there is no gloom where but now there was distress.
> The people who walked in darkness
>> have seen a great light;
> upon those who dwelt in the land of gloom
>> a light has shone.
> You have brought them abundant joy
>> and great rejoicing,
> as they rejoice before you as at the harvest,
>> as people make merry when dividing spoils.
> For the yoke that burdened them,
>> the pole on their shoulder,
> and the rod of their taskmaster
>> you have smashed, as on the day of Midian.

RESPONSORIAL PSALM

Psalm 27:1, 4, 13–14

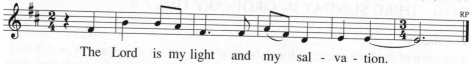

The Lord is my light and my sal-va-tion.

The LORD is my light and my salvation;
  whom shall I fear?
The LORD is the stronghold of my life;
  whom should I dread? ℞.

There is one thing I ask of the LORD,
  only this do I seek:
to live in the house of the LORD
  all the days of my life,

to gaze on the beauty of the LORD,
  to inquire at his temple. ℞.

I believe I shall see the LORD's goodness
  in the land of the living.
Wait for the LORD; be strong;
  be stouthearted, and wait for the
  LORD! ℞.

READING II   *1 Corinthians 1:10–13, 17*

I urge you, brothers and sisters, in the name of our Lord Jesus Christ, that all of you agree in what you say, and that there be no divisions among you, but that you be united in the same mind and in the same purpose. For it has been reported to me about you, my brothers and sisters, by Chloe's people, that there are rivalries among you. I mean that each of you is saying, "I belong to Paul," or "I belong to Apollos," or "I belong to Cephas," or "I belong to Christ." Is Christ divided? Was Paul crucified for you? Or were you baptized in the name of Paul? For Christ did not send me to baptize but to preach the gospel, and not with the wisdom of human eloquence, so that the cross of Christ might not be emptied of its meaning.

GOSPEL   *Matthew 4:12–23 or 4:12–17*

For short form read only the part in brackets.

[When Jesus heard that John had been arrested, he withdrew to Galilee. He left Nazareth and went to live in Capernaum by the sea, in the region of Zebulun and Naphtali, that what had been said through Isaiah the prophet might be fulfilled:

Land of Zebulun and land of Naphtali,
the way to the sea, beyond the Jordan,
Galilee of the Gentiles,
the people who sit in darkness have seen a great light,
on those dwelling in a land overshadowed by death
light has arisen.

From that time on, Jesus began to preach and say, "Repent, for the kingdom of heaven is at hand."]

As he was walking by the Sea of Galilee, he saw two brothers, Simon who is called Peter, and his brother Andrew, casting a net into the sea; they were fishermen. He said to them, "Come after me, and I will make you fishers of men." At once they left their nets and followed him. He walked along from there and saw two other brothers, James, the son of Zebedee, and his brother John. They were in a boat, with their father Zebedee, mending their nets. He called them, and immediately they left their boat and their father and followed him. He went around all of Galilee, teaching in their synagogues, proclaiming the gospel of the kingdom, and curing every disease and illness among the people.

1116 THIRD SUNDAY IN ORDINARY TIME / B

READING I   *Jonah 3:1–5, 10 / 68*

The word of the LORD came to Jonah, saying: "Set out for the great city of Nineveh, and announce to it the message that I will tell you." So Jonah made ready and went to Nineveh, according to the LORD's bidding. Now Nineveh was an enormously large city; it took three days to go through it. Jonah began his journey through the city, and had gone but a single day's walk announcing, "Forty days more and Nineveh shall be destroyed," when the people of Nineveh believed God; they proclaimed a fast and all of them, great and small, put on sackcloth.

When God saw by their actions how they turned from their evil way, he repented of the evil that he had threatened to do to them; he did not carry it out.

RESPONSORIAL PSALM *Psalm 25:4–5ab, 6 and 7bc, 8–9*

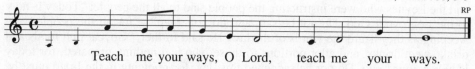

Teach me your ways, O Lord, teach me your ways.

O LORD, make me know your ways.
  Teach me your paths.
Guide me in your truth, and teach me;
  for you are the God of my salvation. ℟.

Remember your compassion, O LORD,
  and your merciful love,
  for they are from of old.

In your merciful love remember me,
  because of your goodness, O
  LORD. ℟.

Good and upright is the LORD;
  he shows the way to sinners.
He guides the humble in right judgment;
  to the humble he teaches his way. ℟.

READING II *1 Corinthians 7:29–31*

I tell you, brothers and sisters, the time is running out. From now on, let those having wives act as not having them, those weeping as not weeping, those rejoicing as not rejoicing, those buying as not owning, those using the world as not using it fully. For the world in its present form is passing away.

GOSPEL *Mark 1:14–20*

After John had been arrested, Jesus came to Galilee proclaiming the gospel of God: "This is the time of fulfillment. The kingdom of God is at hand. Repent, and believe in the gospel."

As he passed by the Sea of Galilee, he saw Simon and his brother Andrew casting their nets into the sea; they were fishermen. Jesus said to them, "Come after me, and I will make you fishers of men." Then they abandoned their nets and followed him. He walked along a little farther and saw James, the son of Zebedee, and his brother John. They too were in a boat mending their nets. Then he called them. So they left their father Zebedee in the boat along with the hired men and followed him.

THIRD SUNDAY IN ORDINARY TIME / C 1117

READING I *Nehemiah 8:2–4a, 5–6, 8–10 / 69*

Ezra the priest brought the law before the assembly, which consisted of men, women, and those children old enough to understand. Standing at one end of the open place that was before the Water Gate, he read out of the book from daybreak till midday, in the presence of the men, the women, and those children old enough to understand; and all the people listened attentively to the book of the law. Ezra the scribe stood on a wooden platform that had been made for the occasion. He opened the scroll so that all the people might see it —for he was standing higher up than any of the people—; and, as he opened it, all the people rose. Ezra blessed the LORD, the great God, and all the people, their hands raised high, answered, "Amen, amen!" Then they bowed down and prostrated themselves before the LORD, their faces to the ground. Ezra read plainly from the book of the law of God, interpreting it so that all could understand what was read. Then Nehemiah, that is, His Excellency, and Ezra the priest-scribe and the Levites who were instructing the people said to all the people: "Today is holy to the Lord your God. Do not be sad, and do not weep"— for all the people were weeping as they heard the words of the law. He said further: "Go, eat rich foods and drink sweet drinks, and allot portions to those who had nothing prepared; for today is holy to our Lord. Do not be saddened this day, for rejoicing in the Lord must be your strength!"

RESPONSORIAL PSALM *Psalm 19:8, 9, 10, 15*

JJC

Your words, Lord, are Spir-it and life, Spir-it and life.

The law of the Lord is perfect;
  it revives the soul.
The decrees of the Lord are steadfast;
  they give wisdom to the simple. ℟.

The precepts of the Lord are right;
  they gladden the heart.
The command of the Lord is clear;
  it gives light to the eyes. ℟.

The fear of the Lord is pure,
  abiding forever.
The judgments of the Lord are true;
  they are, all of them, just. ℟.

May the spoken words of my mouth,
  the thoughts of my heart,
win favor in your sight, O Lord,
  my rock and my redeemer! ℟.

READING II *1 Corinthians 12:12–30 or 12:12–14, 27*
For short form read only the parts in brackets.

[Brothers and sisters: As a body is one though it has many parts, and all the parts of the body, though many, are one body, so also Christ. For in one Spirit we were all baptized into one body, whether Jews or Greeks, slaves or free persons, and we were all given to drink of one Spirit.

Now the body is not a single part, but many.] If a foot should say, "Because I am not a hand I do not belong to the body," it does not for this reason belong any less to the body. Or if an ear should say, "Because I am not an eye I do not belong to the body," it does not for this reason belong any less to the body. If the whole body were an eye, where would the hearing be? If the whole body were hearing, where would the sense of smell be? But as it is, God placed the parts, each one of them, in the body as he intended. If they were all one part, where would the body be? But as it is, there are many parts, yet one body. The eye cannot say to the hand, "I do not need you," nor again the head to the feet, "I do not need you." Indeed, the parts of the body that seem to be weaker are all the more necessary, and those parts of the body that we consider less honorable we surround with greater honor, and our less presentable parts are treated with greater propriety, whereas our more presentable parts do not need this. But God has so constructed the body as to give greater honor to a part that is without it, so that there may be no division in the body, but that the parts may have the same concern for one another. If one part suffers, all the parts suffer with it; if one part is honored, all the parts share its joy.

Now [you are Christ's body, and individually parts of it.] Some people God has designated in the church to be, first, apostles; second, prophets; third, teachers; then, mighty deeds; then gifts of healing, assistance, administration, and varieties of tongues. Are all apostles? Are all prophets? Are all teachers? Do all work mighty deeds? Do all have gifts of healing? Do all speak in tongues? Do all interpret?

GOSPEL   *Luke 1:1–4; 4:14–21*

Since many have undertaken to compile a narrative of the events that have been fulfilled among us, just as those who were eyewitnesses from the beginning and ministers of the word have handed them down to us, I too have decided, after investigating everything accurately anew, to write it down in an orderly sequence for you, most excellent Theophilus, so that you may realize the certainty of the teachings you have received.

Jesus returned to Galilee in the power of the Spirit, and news of him spread throughout the whole region. He taught in their synagogues and was praised by all.

He came to Nazareth, where he had grown up, and went according to his custom into the synagogue on the sabbath day. He stood up to read and was handed a scroll of the prophet Isaiah. He unrolled the scroll and found the passage where it was written:

The Spirit of the Lord is upon me,
because he has anointed me
to bring glad tidings to the poor.
He has sent me to proclaim liberty to captives
and recovery of sight to the blind,
to let the oppressed go free,
and to proclaim a year acceptable to the Lord.

Rolling up the scroll, he handed it back to the attendant and sat down, and the eyes of all in the synagogue looked intently at him. He said to them, "Today this Scripture passage is fulfilled in your hearing."

FOURTH SUNDAY IN ORDINARY TIME / A   1118

READING I   *Zephaniah 2:3; 3:12–13 / 70*

Seek the LORD, all you humble of the
  earth,
 who have observed his law;
seek justice, seek humility;
 perhaps you may be sheltered
 on the day of the LORD's anger.

But I will leave as a remnant in your
  midst
 a people humble and lowly,

who shall take refuge in the name of the
  LORD:
 the remnant of Israel.
They shall do no wrong
 and speak no lies;
nor shall there be found in their mouths
 a deceitful tongue;
they shall pasture and couch their flocks
 with none to disturb them.

RESPONSORIAL PSALM *Psalm 146:6c–7, 8–9a, 9bc–10*

Or: Alleluia.

Bless - ed are the poor in spir - it;
the king - dom of heav - en is theirs!

It is the LORD who preserves fidelity forever,
who does justice to those who are oppressed.
It is he who gives bread to the hungry,
the LORD who sets prisoners free. ℟.

The LORD who opens the eyes of the blind,
the LORD who raises up those who are bowed down.

It is the LORD who loves the just,
the LORD who protects the stranger. ℟.

The LORD upholds the orphan and the widow,
but thwarts the path of the wicked.
The LORD will reign forever,
the God of Sion from age to age.
Alleluia. ℟.

READING II *1 Corinthians 1:26–31*

Consider your own calling, brothers and sisters. Not many of you were wise by human standards, not many were powerful, not many were of noble birth. Rather, God chose the foolish of the world to shame the wise, and God chose the weak of the world to shame the strong, and God chose the lowly and despised of the world, those who count for nothing, to reduce to nothing those who are something, so that no human being might boast before God. It is due to him that you are in Christ Jesus, who became for us wisdom from God, as well as righteousness, sanctification, and redemption, so that, as it is written, "Whoever boasts, should boast in the Lord."

GOSPEL *Matthew 5:1–12a*

When Jesus saw the crowds, he went up the mountain, and after he had sat down, his disciples came to him. He began to teach them, saying:
    "Blessed are the poor in spirit,
        for theirs is the kingdom of heaven.
    Blessed are they who mourn,
        for they will be comforted.
    Blessed are the meek,
        for they will inherit the land.
    Blessed are they who hunger and thirst for righteousness,
        for they will be satisfied.
    Blessed are the merciful,
        for they will be shown mercy.

Blessed are the clean of heart,
for they will see God.
Blessed are the peacemakers,
for they will be called children of God.
Blessed are they who are persecuted for the sake of righteousness,
for theirs is the kingdom of heaven.
Blessed are you when they insult you and persecute you and utter every kind of evil
against you falsely because of me. Rejoice and be glad, for your reward will be great
in heaven."

FOURTH SUNDAY IN ORDINARY TIME / B   1119

READING I   *Deuteronomy 18:15–20 / 71*

Moses spoke to all the people, saying: "A prophet like me will the LORD, your God,
raise up for you from among your own kin; to him you shall listen. This is exactly
what you requested of the LORD, your God, at Horeb on the day of the assembly, when
you said, 'Let us not again hear the voice of the LORD, our God, nor see this great
fire any more, lest we die.' And the LORD said to me, 'This was well said. I will raise
up for them a prophet like you from among their kin, and will put my words into his
mouth; he shall tell them all that I command him. Whoever will not listen to my words
which he speaks in my name, I myself will make him answer for it. But if a prophet
presumes to speak in my name an oracle that I have not commanded him to speak, or
speaks in the name of other gods, he shall die.'"

RESPONSORIAL PSALM   *Psalm 95:1–2, 6–7c, 7d–9*

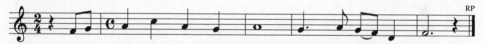

If to-day you hear his voice, hard-en not your hearts.

Come, let us ring out our joy to the
LORD;
hail the rock who saves us.
Let us come into his presence, giving
thanks;
let us hail him with a song of
praise. ℟.

O come; let us bow and bend low.
Let us kneel before the God who
made us,
for he is our God and we
the people who belong to his

pasture,
the flock that is led by his hand. ℟.

O that today you would listen to his
voice!
"Harden not your hearts as at
Meribah,
as on that day at Massah in the
desert
when your forebears put me to the test;
when they tried me, though they
saw my work." ℟.

READING II   *1 Corinthians 7:32–35*

Brothers and sisters: I should like you to be free of anxieties. An unmarried man is anxious about the things of the Lord, how he may please the Lord. But a married man is anxious about the things of the world, how he may please his wife, and he is divided. An unmarried woman or a virgin is anxious about the things of the Lord, so that she may be holy in both body and spirit. A married woman, on the other hand, is anxious about the things of the world, how she may please her husband. I am telling you this for your own benefit, not to impose a restraint upon you, but for the sake of propriety and adherence to the Lord without distraction.

GOSPEL   *Mark 1:21–28*

Then they came to Capernaum, and on the sabbath Jesus entered the synagogue and taught. The people were astonished at his teaching, for he taught them as one having authority and not as the scribes. In their synagogue was a man with an unclean spirit; he cried out, "What have you to do with us, Jesus of Nazareth? Have you come to destroy us? I know who you are—the Holy One of God!" Jesus rebuked him and said, "Quiet! Come out of him!" The unclean spirit convulsed him and with a loud cry came out of him. All were amazed and asked one another, "What is this? A new teaching with authority. He commands even the unclean spirits and they obey him." His fame spread everywhere throughout the whole region of Galilee.

1120   FOURTH SUNDAY IN ORDINARY TIME / C

READING I   *Jeremiah 1:4–5, 17–19 / 72*

The word of the LORD came to me, saying:
 Before I formed you in the womb I
  knew you,
  before you were born I dedicated
   you,
  a prophet to the nations I
   appointed you.

 But do you gird your loins;
  stand up and tell them
  all that I command you.
 Be not crushed on their account,
  as though I would leave you

  crushed before them;
 for it is I this day
  who have made you a fortified
   city,
 a pillar of iron, a wall of brass,
  against the whole land:
 against Judah's kings and princes,
  against its priests and people.
 They will fight against you but not
   prevail over you,
  for I am with you to deliver you,
   says the LORD.

RESPONSORIAL PSALM *Psalm 71:1–2, 3–4a, 5–6ab, 15ab and 17*

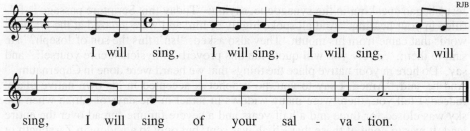

I will sing, I will sing, I will sing, I will sing, I will sing of your sal - va - tion.

In you, O LORD, I take refuge;
  let me never be put to shame.
In your justice, rescue me, free me;
  incline your ear to me and save
  me. ℟.

Be my rock, my constant refuge,
  a mighty stronghold to save me,
for you are my rock, my stronghold.
  My God, free me from the hand of
  the wicked. ℟.

It is you, O Lord, who are my hope,
  my trust, O LORD, from my youth.
On you I have leaned from my birth;
  from my mother's womb, you have
  been my help. ℟.

My mouth will tell of your justice,
  and all the day long of your
  salvation.
O God, you have taught me from my
  youth,
  and I proclaim your wonders
  still. ℟.

READING II *1 Corinthians 12:31 — 13:13 or 13:4–13*
For short form read only the parts in brackets.

[Brothers and sisters:] Strive eagerly for the greatest spiritual gifts. But I shall show you a still more excellent way.

If I speak in human and angelic tongues, but do not have love, I am a resounding gong or a clashing cymbal. And if I have the gift of prophecy, and comprehend all mysteries and all knowledge; if I have all faith so as to move mountains, but do not have love, I am nothing. If I give away everything I own, and if I hand my body over so that I may boast, but do not have love, I gain nothing.

[Love is patient, love is kind. It is not jealous, it is not pompous, it is not inflated, it is not rude, it does not seek its own interests, it is not quick-tempered, it does not brood over injury, it does not rejoice over wrongdoing but rejoices with the truth. It bears all things, believes all things, hopes all things, endures all things.

Love never fails. If there are prophecies, they will be brought to nothing; if tongues, they will cease; if knowledge, it will be brought to nothing. For we know partially and we prophesy partially, but when the perfect comes, the partial will pass away. When I was a child, I used to talk as a child, think as a child, reason as a child; when I became a man, I put aside childish things. At present we see indistinctly, as in a mirror, but then face to face. At present I know partially; then I shall know fully, as I am fully known. So faith, hope, love remain, these three; but the greatest of these is love.]

GOSPEL   *Luke 4:21–30*

Jesus began speaking in the synagogue, saying: "Today this Scripture passage is fulfilled in your hearing." And all spoke highly of him and were amazed at the gracious words that came from his mouth. They also asked, "Isn't this the son of Joseph?" He said to them, "Surely you will quote me this proverb, 'Physician, cure yourself,' and say, 'Do here in your native place the things that we heard were done in Capernaum.'" And he said, "Amen, I say to you, no prophet is accepted in his own native place. Indeed, I tell you, there were many widows in Israel in the days of Elijah when the sky was closed for three and a half years and a severe famine spread over the entire land. It was to none of these that Elijah was sent, but only to a widow in Zarephath in the land of Sidon. Again, there were many lepers in Israel during the time of Elisha the prophet; yet not one of them was cleansed, but only Naaman the Syrian." When the people in the synagogue heard this, they were all filled with fury. They rose up, drove him out of the town, and led him to the brow of the hill on which their town had been built, to hurl him down headlong. But Jesus passed through the midst of them and went away.

1121   FIFTH SUNDAY IN ORDINARY TIME / A

READING I   *Isaiah 58:7–10 / 73*

Thus says the LORD:
    Share your bread with the hungry,
        shelter the oppressed and the homeless;
    clothe the naked when you see them,
        and do not turn your back on your own.
    Then your light shall break forth like the dawn,
        and your wound shall quickly be healed;
    your vindication shall go before you,
        and the glory of the LORD shall be your rear guard.
    Then you shall call, and the LORD will answer,
        you shall cry for help, and he will say: Here I am!
    If you remove from your midst
        oppression, false accusation and malicious speech;
    if you bestow your bread on the hungry
        and satisfy the afflicted;
    then light shall rise for you in the darkness,
        and the gloom shall become for you like midday.

RESPONSORIAL PSALM

Psalm 112:4–5, 6–7, 8a and 9

Or: Alleluia.

The just man is a light in dark-ness to the up - right.

A light rises in the darkness for the
    upright;
  he is generous, merciful, and just.
It goes well for the man who deals
    generously and lends,
  who conducts his affairs with
    justice. ℟.

He will never be moved;
  forever shall the just be
    remembered.

He has no fear of evil news;
  with a firm heart, he trusts in the
    LORD. ℟.

With a steadfast heart he will not fear.
  Openhanded, he gives to the poor;
his justice stands firm forever.
  His might shall be exalted in
    glory. ℟.

READING II

1 Corinthians 2:1–5

When I came to you, brothers and sisters, proclaiming the mystery of God, I did not come with sublimity of words or of wisdom. For I resolved to know nothing while I was with you except Jesus Christ, and him crucified. I came to you in weakness and fear and much trembling, and my message and my proclamation were not with persuasive words of wisdom, but with a demonstration of Spirit and power, so that your faith might rest not on human wisdom but on the power of God.

GOSPEL

Matthew 5:13–16

Jesus said to his disciples: "You are the salt of the earth. But if salt loses its taste, with what can it be seasoned? It is no longer good for anything but to be thrown out and trampled underfoot. You are the light of the world. A city set on a mountain cannot be hidden. Nor do they light a lamp and then put it under a bushel basket; it is set on a lamp stand, where it gives light to all in the house. Just so, your light must shine before others, that they may see your good deeds and glorify your heavenly Father."

1122   FIFTH SUNDAY IN ORDINARY TIME / B

READING I   *Job 7:1–4, 6–7 / 74*

Job spoke, saying:
  Is not man's life on earth a drudgery?
    Are not his days those of hirelings?
  He is a slave who longs for the shade,
    a hireling who waits for his wages.
  So I have been assigned months of
    misery,
    and troubled nights have been
    allotted to me.

If in bed I say, "When shall I arise?"
  then the night drags on;
  I am filled with restlessness until the
    dawn.
My days are swifter than a weaver's
    shuttle;
  they come to an end without hope.
Remember that my life is like the wind;
  I shall not see happiness again.

RESPONSORIAL PSALM   *Psalm 147:1–2, 3–4, 5–6*

Or: Alleluia.

Praise the Lord, praise the Lord, who heals the   bro-ken - heart-ed.

How good to sing psalms to our God;
  how pleasant to chant fitting praise!
The LORD builds up Jerusalem
  and brings back Israel's exiles; ℟.

He heals the brokenhearted;
  he binds up all their wounds.

He counts out the number of the stars;
  he calls each one by its name. ℟.

Our Lord is great and almighty;
  his wisdom can never be measured.
The LORD lifts up the lowly;
  he casts down the wicked to the
    ground. ℟.

READING II   *1 Corinthians 9:16–19, 22–23*

Brothers and sisters: If I preach the gospel, this is no reason for me to boast, for an
obligation has been imposed on me, and woe to me if I do not preach it! If I do so
willingly, I have a recompense, but if unwillingly, then I have been entrusted with a
stewardship. What then is my recompense? That, when I preach, I offer the gospel
free of charge so as not to make full use of my right in the gospel.

   Although I am free in regard to all, I have made myself a slave to all so as to win
over as many as possible. To the weak I became weak, to win over the weak. I have
become all things to all, to save at least some. All this I do for the sake of the gospel,
so that I too may have a share in it.

GOSPEL   *Mark 1:29–39*

On leaving the synagogue Jesus entered the house of Simon and Andrew with James
and John. Simon's mother-in-law lay sick with a fever. They immediately told him
about her. He approached, grasped her hand, and helped her up. Then the fever left
her and she waited on them.

   When it was evening, after sunset, they brought to him all who were ill or possessed by demons. The whole town was gathered at the door. He cured many who
were sick with various diseases, and he drove out many demons, not permitting them
to speak because they knew him.

Rising very early before dawn, he left and went off to a deserted place, where he prayed. Simon and those who were with him pursued him and on finding him said, "Everyone is looking for you." He told them, "Let us go on to the nearby villages that I may preach there also. For this purpose have I come." So he went into their synagogues, preaching and driving out demons throughout the whole of Galilee.

FIFTH SUNDAY IN ORDINARY TIME / C   1123

READING I   *Isaiah 6:1–2a, 3–8 / 75*

In the year King Uzziah died, I saw the Lord seated on a high and lofty throne, with the train of his garment filling the temple. Seraphim were stationed above.

They cried one to the other, "Holy, holy, holy is the LORD of hosts! All the earth is filled with his glory!" At the sound of that cry, the frame of the door shook and the house was filled with smoke.

Then I said, "Woe is me, I am doomed! For I am a man of unclean lips, living among a people of unclean lips; yet my eyes have seen the King, the LORD of hosts!" Then one of the seraphim flew to me, holding an ember that he had taken with tongs from the altar.

He touched my mouth with it, and said, "See, now that this has touched your lips, your wickedness is removed, your sin purged."

Then I heard the voice of the Lord saying, "Whom shall I send? Who will go for us?" "Here I am," I said; "send me!"

RESPONSORIAL PSALM   *Psalm 138:1–2a, 2b–3, 4–5, 7c–8*

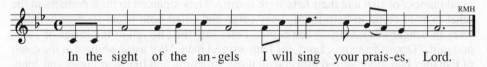

In the sight of the an-gels I will sing your prais-es, Lord.

I thank you, LORD, with all my heart;
    you have heard the words of my
      mouth.
In the presence of the angels I praise you.
    I bow down toward your holy
      temple. ℟.

I give thanks to your name
    for your merciful love and your
      faithfulness.
You have exalted your name over all.
On the day I called, you answered me;
    you increased the strength of my
      soul. ℟.

All earth's kings shall thank you,
    O LORD,
    when they hear the words of your
      mouth.
They shall sing of the ways of the LORD,
    "How great is the glory of the
      LORD!" ℟.

With your right hand you save me;
    the LORD will accomplish this for
      me.
O LORD, your merciful love is eternal;
    discard not the work of your
      hands. ℟.

READING II   *1 Corinthians 15:1–11 or 15:3–8, 11*

For short form read only the parts in brackets.

I am reminding you, [brothers and sisters,] of the gospel I preached to you, which you indeed received and in which you also stand. Through it you are also being saved, if you hold fast to the word I preached to you, unless you believed in vain. For [I handed on to you as of first importance what I also received: that Christ died for our sins in accordance with the Scriptures; that he was buried; that he was raised on the third day in accordance with the Scriptures; that he appeared to Cephas, then to the Twelve. After that, he appeared to more than five hundred brothers at once, most of whom are still living, though some have fallen asleep. After that he appeared to James, then to all the apostles. Last of all, as to one born abnormally, he appeared to me.] For I am the least of the apostles, not fit to be called an apostle, because I persecuted the church of God. But by the grace of God I am what I am, and his grace to me has not been ineffective. Indeed, I have toiled harder than all of them; not I, however, but the grace of God that is with me. [Therefore, whether it be I or they, so we preach and so you believed.]

GOSPEL   *Luke 5:1–11*

While the crowd was pressing in on Jesus and listening to the word of God, he was standing by the Lake of Gennesaret. He saw two boats there alongside the lake; the fishermen had disembarked and were washing their nets. Getting into one of the boats, the one belonging to Simon, he asked him to put out a short distance from the shore. Then he sat down and taught the crowds from the boat. After he had finished speaking, he said to Simon, "Put out into deep water and lower your nets for a catch." Simon said in reply, "Master, we have worked hard all night and have caught nothing, but at your command I will lower the nets." When they had done this, they caught a great number of fish and their nets were tearing. They signaled to their partners in the other boat to come to help them. They came and filled both boats so that the boats were in danger of sinking. When Simon Peter saw this, he fell at the knees of Jesus and said, "Depart from me, Lord, for I am a sinful man." For astonishment at the catch of fish they had made seized him and all those with him, and likewise James and John, the sons of Zebedee, who were partners of Simon. Jesus said to Simon, "Do not be afraid; from now on you will be catching men." When they brought their boats to the shore, they left everything and followed him.

SIXTH SUNDAY IN ORDINARY TIME / A 1124

READING I *Sirach 15:15–20 / 76*

If you choose you can keep the
commandments, they will save
you;
if you trust in God, you too shall live;
he has set before you fire and water;
to whichever you choose, stretch
forth your hand.
Before man are life and death, good
and evil,
whichever he chooses shall be given
him.
Immense is the wisdom of the Lord;
he is mighty in power, and all-seeing.
The eyes of God are on those who fear
him;
he understands man's every deed.
No one does he command to act unjustly,
to none does he give license to sin.

RESPONSORIAL PSALM *Psalm 119:1–2, 4–5, 17–18, 33–34*

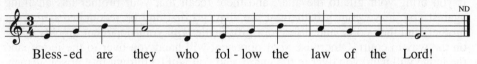

Bless-ed are they who fol-low the law of the Lord!

Blessed are those whose way is
blameless,
who walk in the law of the LORD!
Blessed are those who keep his decrees!
With all their hearts they seek him. ℟.

You have laid down your precepts
to be carefully kept.
May my ways be firm
in keeping your statutes. ℟.

Deal bountifully with your servant,
that I may live and keep your word.
Open my eyes, that I may see
the wonders of your law. ℟.

LORD, teach me the way of your
statutes,
and I will keep them to the end.
Grant me insight that I may keep your
law,
and observe it wholeheartedly. ℟.

READING II *1 Corinthians 2:6–10*

Brothers and sisters: We speak a wisdom to those who are mature, not a wisdom of
this age, nor of the rulers of this age who are passing away. Rather, we speak God's
wisdom, mysterious, hidden, which God predetermined before the ages for our glory,
and which none of the rulers of this age knew; for, if they had known it, they would
not have crucified the Lord of glory. But as it is written:

What eye has not seen, and ear has not heard,
and what has not entered the human heart,
what God has prepared for those who love him,

this God has revealed to us through the Spirit.
For the Spirit scrutinizes everything, even the depths of God.

GOSPEL *Matthew 5:17–37 or 5:20–22a, 27–28, 33–34a, 37*

For short form read only the parts in brackets.

[Jesus said to his disciples:] "Do not think that I have come to abolish the law or the prophets. I have come not to abolish but to fulfill. Amen, I say to you, until heaven and earth pass away, not the smallest letter or the smallest part of a letter will pass from the law, until all things have taken place. Therefore, whoever breaks one of the least of these commandments and teaches others to do so will be called least in the kingdom of heaven. But whoever obeys and teaches these commandments will be called greatest in the kingdom of heaven. [I tell you, unless your righteousness surpasses that of the scribes and Pharisees, you will not enter the kingdom of heaven.

"You have heard that it was said to your ancestors *You shall not kill; and whoever kills will be liable to judgment.* But I say to you, whoever is angry with brother will be liable to judgment;] and whoever says to brother, 'Raqa,' will be answerable to the Sanhedrin; and whoever says, 'You fool,' will be liable to fiery Gehenna. Therefore, if you bring your gift to the altar, and there recall that your brother has anything against you, leave your gift there at the altar, go first and be reconciled with your brother, and then come and offer your gift. Settle with your opponent quickly while on the way to court. Otherwise your opponent will hand you over to the judge, and the judge will hand you over to the guard, and you will be thrown into prison. Amen, I say to you, you will not be released until you have paid the last penny.

["You have heard that it was said, *You shall not commit adultery.* But I say to you, everyone who looks at a woman with lust has already committed adultery with her in his heart.] If your right eye causes you to sin, tear it out and throw it away. It is better for you to lose one of your members than to have your whole body thrown into Gehenna. And if your right hand causes you to sin, cut it off and throw it away. It is better for you to lose one of your members than to have your whole body go into Gehenna.

"It was also said, *Whoever divorces his wife must give her a bill of divorce.* But I say to you, whoever divorces his wife —unless the marriage is unlawful— causes her to commit adultery, and whoever marries a divorced woman commits adultery.

["Again you have heard that it was said to your ancestors, *Do not take a false oath, but make good to the Lord all that you vow.* But I say to you, do not swear at all;] not by heaven, for it is God's throne; nor by the earth, for it is his footstool; nor by Jerusalem, for it is the city of the great King. Do not swear by your head, for you cannot make a single hair white or black. [Let your 'Yes' mean 'Yes,' and your 'No' mean 'No.' Anything more is from the evil one."]

1125 SIXTH SUNDAY IN ORDINARY TIME / B

READING I *Leviticus 13:1–2, 44–46 / 77*

The Lord said to Moses and Aaron, "If someone has on his skin a scab or pustule or blotch which appears to be the sore of leprosy, he shall be brought to Aaron, the priest, or to one of the priests among his descendants. If the man is leprous and unclean, the priest shall declare him unclean by reason of the sore on his head.

"The one who bears the sore of leprosy shall keep his garments rent and his head bare, and shall muffle his beard; he shall cry out, 'Unclean, unclean!' As long as the sore is on him he shall declare himself unclean, since he is in fact unclean. He shall dwell apart, making his abode outside the camp."

RESPONSORIAL PSALM　　　　　　　　　　　　　*Psalm 32:1–2, 5, 11*

I turn to you, O Lord, in time of trou - ble,
and you fill me with the joy of sal - va - tion.

Blessed is he whose transgression is
　　forgiven,
　whose sin is remitted.
Blessed the man to whom the Lord
　　imputes no guilt,
　in whose spirit is no guile. ℟.

To you I have acknowledged my sin;
　my guilt I did not hide.

I said, "I will confess my transgression
　　to the Lord."
And you have forgiven the guilt of
　my sin. ℟.

Rejoice in the Lord; exult, you just!
　Ring out your joy, all you upright of
　heart! ℟.

READING II　　　　　　　　　　　　　　*1 Corinthians 10:31—11:1*

Brothers and sisters, Whether you eat or drink, or whatever you do, do everything for the glory of God. Avoid giving offense, whether to the Jews or Greeks or the church of God, just as I try to please everyone in every way, not seeking my own benefit but that of the many, that they may be saved. Be imitators of me, as I am of Christ.

GOSPEL　　　　　　　　　　　　　　　　　*Mark 1:40–45*

A leper came to Jesus and kneeling down begged him and said, "If you wish, you can make me clean." Moved with pity, he stretched out his hand, touched him, and said to him, "I do will it. Be made clean." The leprosy left him immediately, and he was made clean. Then, warning him sternly, he dismissed him at once.

　　He said to him, "See that you tell no one anything, but go, show yourself to the priest and offer for your cleansing what Moses prescribed; that will be proof for them."

　　The man went away and began to publicize the whole matter. He spread the report abroad so that it was impossible for Jesus to enter a town openly. He remained outside in deserted places, and people kept coming to him from everywhere.

SIXTH SUNDAY IN ORDINARY TIME / C　　　1126

READING I　　　　　　　　　　　　　　*Jeremiah 17:5–8 / 78*

Thus says the Lord:
　Cursed is the one who trusts in
　　human beings,
　who seeks his strength in flesh,
　whose heart turns away from the
　　Lord.

He is like a barren bush in the desert
　that enjoys no change of season,
　but stands in a lava waste,
　a salt and empty earth.
Blessed is the one who trusts in the
　　Lord.

whose hope is the LORD.
He is like a tree planted beside the
waters
that stretches out its roots to the
stream:

it fears not the heat when it comes;
its leaves stay green;
in the year of drought it shows no
distress,
but still bears fruit.

RESPONSORIAL PSALM

Psalm 1:1–2, 3, 4 and 6

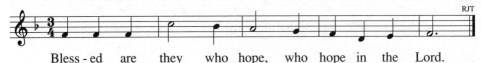

Bless-ed are they who hope, who hope in the Lord.

Blessed indeed is the man
who follows not the counsel of the
wicked,
nor stands in the path with sinners,
nor abides in the company of scorners,
but whose delight is the law of the LORD,
and who ponders his law day and
night. ℟.

He is like a tree that is planted
beside the flowing waters,

that yields its fruit in due season,
and whose leaves shall never fade;
and all that he does shall prosper. ℟.

Not so are the wicked, not so!
For they, like winnowed chaff,
shall be driven away by the wind;
for the LORD knows the way of the just,
but the way of the wicked will
perish. ℟.

READING II

1 Corinthians 15:12, 16–20

Brothers and sisters: If Christ is preached as raised from the dead, how can some among you say there is no resurrection of the dead? If the dead are not raised, neither has Christ been raised, and if Christ has not been raised, your faith is vain; you are still in your sins. Then those who have fallen asleep in Christ have perished. If for this life only we have hoped in Christ, we are the most pitiable people of all.

But now Christ has been raised from the dead, the firstfruits of those who have fallen asleep.

GOSPEL

Luke 6:17, 20–26

Jesus came down with the Twelve and stood on a stretch of level ground with a great crowd of his disciples and a large number of the people from all Judea and Jerusalem and the coastal region of Tyre and Sidon. And raising his eyes toward his disciples he said:
"Blessed are you who are poor,
for the kingdom of God is yours.
Blessed are you who are now hungry,
for you will be satisfied.
Blessed are you who are now weeping,
for you will laugh.
Blessed are you when people hate you,
and when they exclude and insult you,
and denounce your name as evil
on account of the Son of Man.

Rejoice and leap for joy on that day! Behold, your reward will be great in heaven. For their ancestors treated the prophets in the same way.

But woe to you who are rich,
    for you have received your consolation.
Woe to you who are filled now,
    for you will be hungry.
Woe to you who laugh now,
    for you will grieve and weep.
Woe to you when all speak well of you,
    for their ancestors treated the false
        prophets in this way."

SEVENTH SUNDAY IN ORDINARY TIME / A   1127

READING I
Leviticus 19:1–2, 17–18 / 79

The LORD said to Moses, "Speak to the whole Israelite community and tell them: Be holy, for I, the LORD, your God, am holy.

"You shall not bear hatred for your brother or sister in your heart. Though you may have to reprove your fellow citizen, do not incur sin because of him. Take no revenge and cherish no grudge against any of your people. You shall love your neighbor as yourself. I am the LORD."

RESPONSORIAL PSALM
Psalm 103:1–2, 3–4, 8 and 10, 12–13

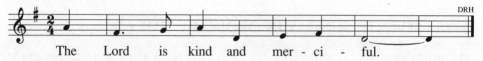

The Lord is kind and mer - ci - ful.

Bless the LORD, O my soul,
    and all within me, his holy name.
Bless the LORD, O my soul,
    and never forget all his benefits. ℟.

It is the Lord who forgives all your sins,
    who heals every one of your ills,
who redeems your life from the grave,
    who crowns you with mercy and
        compassion. ℟.

The LORD is compassionate and gracious,
    slow to anger and rich in mercy.

He does not treat us according to our
    sins,
    nor repay us according to our
    faults. ℟.

As far as the east is from the west,
    so far from us does he remove our
    transgressions.
As a father has compassion on his
    children,
    the LORD's compassion is on those
    who fear him. ℟.

READING II
1 Corinthians 3:16–23

Brothers and sisters: Do you not know that you are the temple of God, and that the Spirit of God dwells in you? If anyone destroys God's temple, God will destroy that person; for the temple of God, which you are, is holy.

Let no one deceive himself. If any one among you considers himself wise in this age, let him become a fool, so as to become wise. For the wisdom of this world is foolishness in the eyes of God, for it is written:

God catches the wise in their own ruses,
and again:
> *The Lord knows the thoughts of the wise,*
> *that they are vain.*

So let no one boast about human beings, for everything belongs to you, Paul or Apollos or Cephas, or the world or life or death, or the present or the future: all belong to you, and you to Christ, and Christ to God.

GOSPEL

Matthew 5:38–48

Jesus said to his disciples: "You have heard that it was said, *An eye for an eye and a tooth for a tooth*. But I say to you, offer no resistance to one who is evil. When someone strikes you on your right cheek, turn the other one as well. If anyone wants to go to law with you over your tunic, hand over your cloak as well. Should anyone press you into service for one mile, go for two miles. Give to the one who asks of you, and do not turn your back on one who wants to borrow.

"You have heard that it was said, *You shall love your neighbor and hate your enemy*. But I say to you, love your enemies and pray for those who persecute you, that you may be children of your heavenly Father, for he makes his sun rise on the bad and the good, and causes rain to fall on the just and the unjust. For if you love those who love you, what recompense will you have? Do not the tax collectors do the same? And if you greet your brothers only, what is unusual about that? Do not the pagans do the same? So be perfect, just as your heavenly Father is perfect."

1128 SEVENTH SUNDAY IN ORDINARY TIME / B

READING I

Isaiah 43:18–19, 21–22, 24b–25 / 80

Thus says the LORD:
Remember not the events of the past,
    the things of long ago consider not;
see, I am doing something new!
    Now it springs forth, do you not
        perceive it?
In the desert I make a way,
    in the wasteland, rivers.
The people I formed for myself,
that they might announce my praise.
Yet you did not call upon me, O Jacob,
    for you grew weary of me, O Israel.
You burdened me with your sins,
    and wearied me with your crimes.
It is I, I, who wipe out,
    for my own sake, your offenses;
    your sins I remember no more.

RESPONSORIAL PSALM

Psalm 41:2–3, 4–5, 13–14

Lord, heal my soul, for I have sinned a-gainst you.

Blessed is he who has concern for the
    poor.
In time of trouble, the LORD will
    rescue him.

The LORD will guard him, give him life,
    and make him blessed in the land,
    not give him up to the will of his
    foes. ℟.

The LORD will help him on his bed of pain;
you will bring him back from sickness to health.
As for me, I said, "LORD, have mercy on me;
heal my soul, for I have sinned

In my integrity you have upheld me,
and have set me in your presence forever.
Blest be the LORD, the God of Israel,
from age to age. Amen. Amen. ℟.

READING II   *2 Corinthians 1:18–22*

Brothers and sisters: As God is faithful, our word to you is not "yes" and "no." For the Son of God, Jesus Christ, who was proclaimed to you by us, Silvanus and Timothy and me, was not "yes" and "no," but "yes" has been in him. For however many are the promises of God, their Yes is in him; therefore, the Amen from us also goes through him to God for glory. But the one who gives us security with you in Christ and who anointed us is God; he has also put his seal upon us and given the Spirit in our hearts as a first installment.

GOSPEL   *Mark 2:1–12*

When Jesus returned to Capernaum after some days, it became known that he was at home. Many gathered together so that there was no longer room for them, not even around the door, and he preached the word to them. They came bringing to him a paralytic carried by four men. Unable to get near Jesus because of the crowd, they opened up the roof above him. After they had broken through, they let down the mat on which the paralytic was lying. When Jesus saw their faith, he said to the paralytic, "Child, your sins are forgiven." Now some of the scribes were sitting there asking themselves, "Why does this man speak that way? He is blaspheming. Who but God alone can forgive sins?" Jesus immediately knew in his mind what they were thinking to themselves, so he said, "Why are you thinking such things in your hearts? Which is easier, to say to the paralytic, 'Your sins are forgiven,' or to say, 'Rise, pick up your mat and walk?' But that you may know that the Son of Man has authority to forgive sins on earth" —he said to the paralytic, "I say to you, rise, pick up your mat, and go home." He rose, picked up his mat at once, and went away in the sight of everyone. They were all astounded and glorified God, saying, "We have never seen anything like this."

SEVENTH SUNDAY IN ORDINARY TIME / C   1129

READING I   *1 Samuel 26:2, 7–9, 12–13, 22–23 / 81*

In those days, Saul went down to the desert of Ziph with three thousand picked men of Israel, to search for David in the desert of Ziph. So David and Abishai went among Saul's soldiers by night and found Saul lying asleep within the barricade, with his spear thrust into the ground at his head and Abner and his men sleeping around him.

Abishai whispered to David: "God has delivered your enemy into your grasp this day. Let me nail him to the ground with one thrust of the spear; I will not need a second thrust!" But David said to Abishai, "Do not harm him, for who can lay hands on the LORD's anointed and remain unpunished?" So David took the spear and the water jug from their place at Saul's head, and they got away without anyone's seeing or knowing or awakening. All remained asleep, because the LORD had put them into a deep slumber.

Going across to an opposite slope, David stood on a remote hilltop at a great distance from Abner, son of Ner, and the troops. He said: "Here is the king's spear. Let an attendant come over to get it. The LORD will reward each man for his justice and faithfulness. Today, though the LORD delivered you into my grasp, I would not harm the LORD's anointed."

RESPONSORIAL PSALM   *Psalm 103:1–2, 3–4, 8 and 10, 12–13*

The Lord is kind and mer - ci - ful.

Bless the LORD, O my soul,
  and all within me, his holy name.
Bless the LORD, O my soul,
  and never forget all his benefits. ℟.

It is the Lord who forgives all your sins,
  who heals every one of your ills,
who redeems your life from the grave,
  who crowns you with mercy and
    compassion. ℟.

The LORD is compassionate and
    gracious,
  slow to anger and rich in mercy.

He does not treat us according to our
    sins,
  nor repay us according to our
    faults. ℟.

As far as the east is from the west,
  so far from us does he remove our
    transgressions.
As a father has compassion on his
    children,
  the LORD's compassion is on those
    who fear him. ℟.

READING II   *1 Corinthians 15:45–49*

Brothers and sisters: It is written, *The first man, Adam, became a living being,* the last Adam a life-giving spirit. But the spiritual was not first; rather the natural and then the spiritual. The first man was from the earth, earthly; the second man, from heaven. As was the earthly one, so also are the earthly, and as is the heavenly one, so also are the heavenly. Just as we have borne the image of the earthly one, we shall also bear the image of the heavenly one.

GOSPEL   *Luke 6:27–38*

Jesus said to his disciples: "To you who hear I say, love your enemies, do good to those who hate you, bless those who curse you, pray for those who mistreat you. To the person who strikes you on one cheek, offer the other one as well, and from the person who takes your cloak, do not withhold even your tunic. Give to everyone who asks of you, and from the one who takes what is yours do not demand it back. Do to others as you would have them do to you. For if you love those who love you, what credit is that to you? Even sinners love those who love them. And if you do good to those who do good to you, what credit is that to you? Even sinners do the same. If you lend money to those from whom you expect repayment, what credit is that to you? Even sinners lend to sinners, and get back the same amount. But rather, love your enemies and do good to them, and lend expecting nothing back; then your reward will be great and you will be children of the Most High, for he himself is kind to the ungrateful and the wicked. Be merciful, just as your Father is merciful.

"Stop judging and you will not be judged. Stop condemning and you will not be condemned. Forgive and you will be forgiven. Give, and gifts will be given to you; a good measure, packed together, shaken down, and overflowing, will be poured into your lap. For the measure with which you measure will in return be measured out to you."

EIGHTH SUNDAY IN ORDINARY TIME / A 1130

READING I *Isaiah 49:14–15 / 82*

Zion said, "The LORD has
 forsaken me;
 my LORD has forgotten me."
Can a mother forget her infant,
 be without tenderness for the child

of her womb?
Even should she forget,
 I will never forget you.

RESPONSORIAL PSALM *Psalm 62:2–3, 6–7, 8–9ab*

RJB

Rest in God a - lone, rest in God a - lone, my soul, my soul.

In God alone is my soul at rest;
 my salvation comes from him.
He alone is my rock, my salvation,
 my fortress; never shall I falter. ℟.

In God alone be at rest, my soul,
 for my hope is from him.
He alone is my rock, my salvation,

my fortress; never shall I falter. ℟.

In God is my salvation and glory,
 my rock of strength;
 in God is my refuge.
Trust him at all times, O people.
 Pour out your hearts before him. ℟.

READING II *1 Corinthians 4:1–5*

Brothers and sisters: Thus should one regard us: as servants of Christ and stewards of the mysteries of God. Now it is of course required of stewards that they be found trustworthy. It does not concern me in the least that I be judged by you or any human tribunal; I do not even pass judgment on myself; I am not conscious of anything against me, but I do not thereby stand acquitted; the one who judges me is the Lord. Therefore do not make any judgment before the appointed time, until the Lord comes, for he will bring to light what is hidden in darkness and will manifest the motives of our hearts, and then everyone will receive praise from God.

GOSPEL *Matthew 6:24–34*

Jesus said to his disciples: "No one can serve two masters. He will either hate one and love the other, or be devoted to one and despise the other. You cannot serve God and mammon.

"Therefore I tell you, do not worry about your life, what you will eat or drink, or about your body, what you will wear. Is not life more than food and the body more than clothing? Look at the birds in the sky; they do not sow or reap, they gather nothing into barns, yet your heavenly Father feeds them. Are not you more important than they? Can any of you by worrying add a single moment to your life-span? Why are you anxious about clothes? Learn from the way the wild flowers grow. They do not work or spin. But I tell you that not even Solomon in all his splendor was clothed like one of them. If God so clothes the grass of the field, which grows today and is thrown into the oven tomorrow, will he not much more provide for you, O you of little faith? So do not worry and say, 'What are we to eat?' or 'What are we to drink?' or 'What are we to wear?' All these things the pagans seek. Your heavenly Father knows that you need them all. But seek first the kingdom of God and his righteousness, and all these things will be given you besides. Do not worry about tomorrow; tomorrow will take care of itself. Sufficient for a day is its own evil."

1131   EIGHTH SUNDAY IN ORDINARY TIME / B

READING I   *Hosea 2:16b, 17b, 21–22 / 83*

Thus says the LORD:
I will lead her into the desert
 and speak to her heart.
She shall respond there as in the days
  of her youth,
 when she came up from the land
  of Egypt.

I will espouse you to me forever:
 I will espouse you in right and in
  justice,
 in love and in mercy;
I will espouse you in fidelity,
 and you shall know the LORD.

RESPONSORIAL PSALM   *Psalm 103:1–2, 3–4, 8 and 10, 12–13*

The Lord is kind and mer - ci - ful.

Bless the LORD, O my soul,
 and all within me, his holy name.
Bless the LORD, O my soul,
 and never forget all his benefits. ℟.

It is the Lord who forgives all your sins,
 who heals every one of your ills,
who redeems your life from the grave,
 who crowns you with mercy and
  compassion. ℟.

The LORD is compassionate and
  gracious,
 slow to anger and rich in mercy.

He does not treat us according to our
 sins,
 nor repay us according to our
 faults. ℟.

As far as the east is from the west,
 so far from us does he remove our
 transgressions.
As a father has compassion on his
 children,
 the LORD's compassion is on those
 who fear him. ℟.

READING II　　　　　　　　　　　　　　　　　　　*2 Corinthians 3:1b–6*

Brothers and sisters: Do we need, as some do, letters of recommendation to you or from you? You are our letter, written on our hearts, known and read by all, shown to be a letter of Christ ministered by us, written not in ink but by the Spirit of the living God, not on tablets of stone but on tablets that are hearts of flesh.

Such confidence we have through Christ toward God. Not that of ourselves we are qualified to take credit for anything as coming from us; rather, our qualification comes from God, who has indeed qualified us as ministers of a new covenant, not of letter but of spirit; for the letter brings death, but the Spirit gives life.

GOSPEL　　　　　　　　　　　　　　　　　　　　　*Mark 2:18–22*

The disciples of John and of the Pharisees were accustomed to fast. People came to him and objected, "Why do the disciples of John and the disciples of the Pharisees fast, but your disciples do not fast?" Jesus answered them, "Can the wedding guests fast while the bridegroom is with them? As long as they have the bridegroom with them they cannot fast. But the days will come when the bridegroom is taken away from them, and then they will fast on that day. No one sews a piece of unshrunken cloth on an old cloak. If he does, its fullness pulls away, the new from the old, and the tear gets worse. Likewise, no one pours new wine into old wineskins. Otherwise, the wine will burst the skins, and both the wine and the skins are ruined. Rather, new wine is poured into fresh wineskins."

EIGHTH SUNDAY IN ORDINARY TIME / C　　　　　1132

READING I　　　　　　　　　　　　　　　　　　　*Sirach 27:4–7 / 84*

When a sieve is shaken, the husks　　　　　The fruit of a tree shows the care it has
　　appear;　　　　　　　　　　　　　　　　had;
　so do one's faults when one speaks.　　　　so too does one's speech disclose the
As the test of what the potter molds is　　　　bent of one's mind.
　in the furnace,　　　　　　　　　　　　Praise no one before he speaks,
　so in tribulation is the test of the just.　　　for it is then that people are tested.

RESPONSORIAL PSALM　　　　　　　　　　　*Psalm 92:2–3, 13–14, 15–16*

Lord, it is good to give thanks to you.

It is good to give thanks to the LORD,　　　Planted in the house of the LORD,
　to make music to your name,　　　　　　they will flourish in the courts of
　　O Most High,　　　　　　　　　　　　our God. ℟.
to proclaim your loving mercy in the
　　morning,　　　　　　　　　　　　　Still bearing fruit when they are old,
　and your truth in the watches of　　　　　still full of sap, still green,
　　the night. ℟.　　　　　　　　　　　to proclaim that the LORD is upright.
　　　　　　　　　　　　　　　　　　　In him, my rock, there is no
The just will flourish like the palm tree,　　　wrong. ℟.
　and grow like a Lebanon cedar.

READING II   *1 Corinthians 15:54–58*

Brothers and sisters: When this which is corruptible clothes itself with incorruptibility and this which is mortal clothes itself with immortality, then the word that is written shall come about:

Death is swallowed up in victory.
Where, O death, is your victory?
Where, O death, is your sting?

The sting of death is sin, and the power of sin is the law. But thanks be to God who gives us the victory through our Lord Jesus Christ.

Therefore, my beloved brothers and sisters, be firm, steadfast, always fully devoted to the work of the Lord, knowing that in the Lord your labor is not in vain.

GOSPEL   *Luke 6:39–45*

Jesus told his disciples a parable, "Can a blind person guide a blind person? Will not both fall into a pit? No disciple is superior to the teacher; but when fully trained, every disciple will be like his teacher. Why do you notice the splinter in your brother's eye, but do not perceive the wooden beam in your own? How can you say to your brother, 'Brother, let me remove that splinter in your eye,' when you do not even notice the wooden beam in your own eye? You hypocrite! Remove the wooden beam from your eye first; then you will see clearly to remove the splinter in your brother's eye.

"A good tree does not bear rotten fruit, nor does a rotten tree bear good fruit. For every tree is known by its own fruit. For people do not pick figs from thornbushes, nor do they gather grapes from brambles. A good person out of the store of goodness in his heart produces good, but an evil person out of a store of evil produces evil; for from the fullness of the heart the mouth speaks."

1133   NINTH SUNDAY IN ORDINARY TIME / A

READING I   *Deuteronomy 11:18, 26–28, 32 / 85*

Moses told the people, "Take these words of mine into your heart and soul. Bind them at your wrist as a sign, and let them be a pendant on your forehead.

"I set before you here, this day, a blessing and a curse: a blessing for obeying the commandments of the LORD, your God, which I enjoin on you today; a curse if you do not obey the commandments of the LORD, your God, but turn aside from the way I ordain for you today, to follow other gods, whom you have not known. Be careful to observe all the statutes and decrees that I set before you today."

RESPONSORIAL PSALM   *Psalm 31:2–3a, 3bc–4, 17 and 25*

Lord,   Lord,   be   my   rock   of   safe - ty.

In you, O LORD, I take refuge.
   Let me never be put to shame.
In your justice, set me free;
   incline your ear to me, and speedily
     rescue me. ℟.

Be a rock of refuge for me,
   a mighty stronghold to save me.
For you are my rock, my stronghold!
   Lead me, guide me, for the sake of
     your name. ℟.

Let your face shine on your servant.
  Save me in your merciful love.

Be strong, let your heart take courage,
  all who hope in the LORD. ℟.

READING II   *Romans 3:21–25, 28*

Brothers and sisters, Now the righteousness of God has been manifested apart from the law, though testified to by the law and the prophets, the righteousness of God through faith in Jesus Christ for all who believe. For there is no distinction; all have sinned and are deprived of the glory of God. They are justified freely by his grace through the redemption in Christ Jesus, whom God set forth as an expiation, through faith, by his blood. For we consider that a person is justified by faith apart from works of the law.

GOSPEL   *Matthew 7:21–27*

Jesus said to his disciples: "Not everyone who says to me, 'Lord, Lord,' will enter the kingdom of heaven, but only the one who does the will of my Father in heaven. Many will say to me on that day, 'Lord, Lord, did we not prophesy in your name? Did we not drive out demons in your name? Did we not do mighty deeds in your name?' Then I will declare to them solemnly, 'I never knew you. Depart from me, you evildoers.'

"Everyone who listens to these words of mine and acts on them will be like a wise man who built his house on rock. The rain fell, the floods came, and the winds blew and buffeted the house. But it did not collapse; it had been set solidly on rock. And everyone who listens to these words of mine but does not act on them will be like a fool who built his house on sand. The rain fell, the floods came, and the winds blew and buffeted the house. And it collapsed and was completely ruined."

NINTH SUNDAY IN ORDINARY TIME / B   1134

READING I   *Deuteronomy 5:12–15 / 86*

Thus says the LORD: "Take care to keep holy the sabbath day as the LORD, your God, commanded you. Six days you may labor and do all your work; but the seventh day is the sabbath of the LORD, your God. No work may be done then, whether by you, or your son or daughter, or your male or female slave, or your ox or ass or any of your beasts, or the alien who lives with you. Your male and female slave should rest as you do. For remember that you too were once a slave in Egypt, and the LORD, your God, brought you from there with his strong hand and outstretched arm. That is why the LORD, your God, has commanded you to observe the sabbath day."

RESPONSORIAL PSALM   *Psalm 81:3–4, 5–6ab, 6c–8a, 10–11b*

Sing with joy to God!   Sing to God our help!

Raise a song and sound the timbrel,
  the sweet-sounding harp and the lute;
blow the trumpet at the new moon,
  when the moon is full, on our
    feast. ℟.

For this is a statute in Israel,
  a command of the God of Jacob.
He made it a decree for Joseph,
  when he went out from the land of
    Egypt. ℟.

A voice I did not know said to me:
"I freed your shoulder from the
  burden;
your hands were freed from the
  builder's basket.
  You called in distress and I
  delivered you." ℟.

"Let there be no strange god among
  you,
  nor shall you worship a foreign god.
I am the LORD your God,
  who brought you up from the land
  of Egypt." ℟.

READING II   *2 Corinthians 4:6–11*

Brothers and sisters: God who said, *Let light shine out of darkness,* has shone in our hearts to bring to light the knowledge of the glory of God on the face of Jesus Christ. But we hold this treasure in earthen vessels, that the surpassing power may be of God and not from us. We are afflicted in every way, but not constrained; perplexed, but not driven to despair; persecuted, but not abandoned; struck down, but not destroyed; always carrying about in the body the dying of Jesus, so that the life of Jesus may also be manifested in our body. For we who live are constantly being given up to death for the sake of Jesus, so that the life of Jesus may be manifested in our mortal flesh.

GOSPEL   *Mark 2:23–3:6 or 2:23–28*
For short form read only the part in brackets.

[As Jesus was passing through a field of grain on the sabbath, his disciples began to make a path while picking the heads of grain. At this the Pharisees said to him, "Look, why are they doing what is unlawful on the sabbath?" He said to them, "Have you never read what David did when he was in need and he and his companions were hungry? How he went into the house of God when Abiathar was high priest and ate the bread of offering that only the priests could lawfully eat, and shared it with his companions?" Then he said to them, "The sabbath was made for man, not man for the sabbath. That is why the Son of Man is lord even of the sabbath."]

Again he entered the synagogue. There was a man there who had a withered hand. They watched him closely to see if he would cure him on the sabbath so that they might accuse him. He said to the man with the withered hand, "Come up here before us." Then he said to them, "Is it lawful to do good on the sabbath rather than to do evil, to save life rather than to destroy it?" But they remained silent. Looking around at them with anger and grieved at their hardness of heart, he said to the man, "Stretch out your hand." He stretched it out and his hand was restored. The Pharisees went out and immediately took counsel with the Herodians against him to put him to death.

1135 NINTH SUNDAY IN ORDINARY TIME / C

READING I   *1 Kings 8:41–43 / 87*

In those days, Solomon prayed in the temple, saying, "To the foreigner, who is not of your people Israel, but comes from a distant land to honor you —since they will learn of your great name and your mighty hand and your outstretched arm—, when he comes and prays toward this temple, listen from your heavenly dwelling. Do all that foreigner asks of you, that all the peoples of the earth may know your name, may fear you as do your people Israel, and may acknowledge that this temple which I have built is dedicated to your honor."

RESPONSORIAL PSALM

Psalm 117:1, 2

Or: Alleluia.

Go out to all the world, and tell the Good News.

O praise the LORD, all you nations;
acclaim him, all you peoples! ℟.

For his merciful love has prevailed
over us;
and the LORD's faithfulness endures
forever. ℟.

READING II

Galatians 1:1–2, 6–10

Paul, an apostle not from human beings nor through a human being but through Jesus Christ and God the Father who raised him from the dead, and all the brothers who are with me, to the churches of Galatia.

I am amazed that you are so quickly forsaking the one who called you by the grace of Christ for a different gospel —not that there is another—. But there are some who are disturbing you and wish to pervert the gospel of Christ. But even if we or an angel from heaven should preach to you a gospel other than the one that we preached to you, let that one be accursed! As we have said before, and now I say again, if anyone preaches to you a gospel other than what you have received, let that one be accursed!

Am I now currying favor with humans or with God? Or am I seeking to please people? If I were still trying to please people, I would not be a slave of Christ.

GOSPEL

Luke 7:1–10

When Jesus had finished all his words to the people, he entered Capernaum. A centurion there had a slave who was ill and about to die, and he was valuable to him. When he heard about Jesus, he sent elders of the Jews to him, asking him to come and save the life of his slave. They approached Jesus and strongly urged him to come, saying, "He deserves to have you do this for him, for he loves our nation and built the synagogue for us." And Jesus went with them, but when he was only a short distance from the house, the centurion sent friends to tell him, "Lord, do not trouble yourself, for I am not worthy to have you enter under my roof. Therefore, I did not consider myself worthy to come to you; but say the word and let my servant be healed. For I too am a person subject to authority, with soldiers subject to me. And I say to one, 'Go,' and he goes; and to another, 'Come here,' and he comes; and to my slave, 'Do this,' and he does it." When Jesus heard this he was amazed at him and, turning, said to the crowd following him, "I tell you, not even in Israel have I found such faith." When the messengers returned to the house, they found the slave in good health.

TENTH SUNDAY IN ORDINARY TIME / A   1136

READING I

Hosea 6:3–6 / 88

In their affliction, people will say:
"Let us know, let us strive to know
the LORD;
as certain as the dawn is his coming,

and his judgment shines forth like
the light of day!
He will come to us like the rain,
like spring rain that waters the earth."

What can I do with you, Ephraim?
What can I do with you, Judah?
Your piety is like a morning cloud,
like the dew that early passes away.
For this reason I smote them through
the prophets,

I slew them by the words of my
mouth;
for it is love that I desire, not sacrifice,
and knowledge of God rather than
holocausts.

RESPONSORIAL PSALM

Psalm 50:1 and 8, 12–13, 14–15

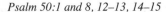

To the up-right I will show the sav-ing pow'r of God.

The God of gods, the Lord,
has spoken and summoned the earth,
from the rising of the sun to its
setting.
"I do not rebuke you for your sacrifices;
your offerings are always before
me." ℟.

"Were I hungry, I would not tell you,
for the world and its fullness is mine.

Do I eat the flesh of bulls,
or drink the blood of goats?" ℟.

"Give your praise as a sacrifice to God,
and fulfill your vows to the
Most High.
Then call on me in the day of distress.
I will deliver you and you shall
honor me." ℟.

READING II

Romans 4:18–25

Brothers and sisters: Abraham believed, hoping against hope, that he would become "the father of many nations," according to what was said, "Thus shall your descendants be." He did not weaken in faith when he considered his own body as already dead —for he was almost a hundred years old— and the dead womb of Sarah. He did not doubt God's promise in unbelief; rather, he was strengthened by faith and gave glory to God and was fully convinced that what he had promised he was also able to do. That is why *it was credited to him as righteousness.* But it was not for him alone that it was written that *it was credited to him;* it was also for us, to whom it will be credited, who believe in the one who raised Jesus our Lord from the dead, who was handed over for our transgressions and was raised for our justification.

GOSPEL

Matthew 9:9–13

As Jesus passed on from there, he saw a man named Matthew sitting at the customs post. He said to him, "Follow me." And he got up and followed him. While he was at table in his house, many tax collectors and sinners came and sat with Jesus and his disciples. The Pharisees saw this and said to his disciples, "Why does your teacher eat with tax collectors and sinners?" He heard this and said, "Those who are well do not need a physician, but the sick do. Go and learn the meaning of the words, 'I desire mercy, not sacrifice.' I did not come to call the righteous but sinners."

TENTH SUNDAY IN ORDINARY TIME / B

READING I
Genesis 3:9–15 / 89

After the man, Adam, had eaten of the tree, the LORD God called to the man and asked him, "Where are you?" He answered, "I heard you in the garden; but I was afraid, because I was naked, so I hid myself." Then he asked, "Who told you that you were naked? You have eaten, then, from the tree of which I had forbidden you to eat!" The man replied, "The woman whom you put here with me — she gave me fruit from the tree, and so I ate it." The LORD God then asked the woman, "Why did you do such a thing?" The woman answered, "The serpent tricked me into it, so I ate it."

Then the LORD God said to the serpent:
"Because you have done this, you shall be banned from
 all the animals
 and from all the wild creatures;
on your belly shall you crawl,
 and dirt shall you eat
 all the days of your life.
I will put enmity between you and the woman,
 and between your offspring and hers;
he will strike at your head,
 while you strike at his heel."

RESPONSORIAL PSALM
Psalm 130:1–2, 3–4, 5–6ab and 7a, 7b–8

JRC

With the Lord there is mer-cy, and full - ness of re - demp-tion.

Out of the depths I cry to you, O LORD;
 Lord, hear my voice!
O let your ears be attentive
 to the sound of my pleadings. ℟.

If you, O LORD, should mark iniquities,
 Lord, who could stand?
But with you is found forgiveness,
 that you may be revered. ℟.

I long for you, O LORD,
 my soul longs for his word.
My soul hopes in the Lord
 more than watchmen for daybreak. ℟.

Let Israel hope for the LORD.
For with the LORD there is mercy,
 in him is plentiful redemption.
It is he who will redeem Israel
 from all its iniquities. ℟.

READING II
2 Corinthians 4:13–5:1

Brothers and sisters: Since we have the same spirit of faith, according to what is written, *I believed, therefore I spoke,* we too believe and therefore we speak, knowing that the one who raised the Lord Jesus will raise us also with Jesus and place us with you in his presence. Everything indeed is for you, so that the grace bestowed in abundance on more and more people may cause the thanksgiving to overflow for the glory of God. Therefore, we are not discouraged; rather, although our outer self is wasting away, our inner self is being renewed day by day. For this momentary light affliction is producing for us an eternal weight of glory beyond all comparison, as we look not to what is seen but to what is unseen; for what is seen is transitory, but what is unseen is eternal. For we know that if our earthly dwelling, a tent, should be destroyed, we have a building from God, a dwelling not made with hands, eternal in heaven.

GOSPEL *Mark 3:20–35*

Jesus came home with his disciples. Again the crowd gathered, making it impossible for them even to eat. When his relatives heard of this they set out to seize him, for they said, "He is out of his mind." The scribes who had come from Jerusalem said, "He is possessed by Beelzebul," and "By the prince of demons he drives out demons."

Summoning them, he began to speak to them in parables, "How can Satan drive out Satan? If a kingdom is divided against itself, that kingdom cannot stand. And if a house is divided against itself, that house will not be able to stand. And if Satan has risen up against himself and is divided, he cannot stand; that is the end of him. But no one can enter a strong man's house to plunder his property unless he first ties up the strong man. Then he can plunder the house. Amen, I say to you, all sins and all blasphemies that people utter will be forgiven them. But whoever blasphemes against the Holy Spirit will never have forgiveness, but is guilty of an everlasting sin." For they had said, "He has an unclean spirit."

His mother and his brothers arrived. Standing outside they sent word to him and called him. A crowd seated around him told him, "Your mother and your brothers and your sisters are outside asking for you." But he said to them in reply, "Who are my mother and my brothers?" And looking around at those seated in the circle he said, "Here are my mother and my brothers. For whoever does the will of God is my brother and sister and mother."

1138 TENTH SUNDAY IN ORDINARY TIME / C

READING I *1 Kings 17:17–24 / 90*

Elijah went to Zarephath of Sidon to the house of a widow. The son of the mistress of the house fell sick, and his sickness grew more severe until he stopped breathing. So she said to Elijah, "Why have you done this to me, O man of God? Have you come to me to call attention to my guilt and to kill my son?" Elijah said to her, "Give me your son." Taking him from her lap, he carried the son to the upper room where he was staying, and put him on his bed. Elijah called out to the Lord: "O Lord, my God, will you afflict even the widow with whom I am staying by killing her son?" Then he stretched himself out upon the child three times and called out to the Lord: "O Lord, my God, let the life breath return to the body of this child." The Lord heard the prayer of Elijah; the life breath returned to the child's body and he revived. Taking the child, Elijah brought him down into the house from the upper room and gave him to his mother. Elijah said to her, "See! Your son is alive." The woman replied to Elijah, "Now indeed I know that you are a man of God. The word of the Lord comes truly from your mouth."

RESPONSORIAL PSALM   *Psalm 30:2 and 4, 5–6, 11 and 12a and 13b*

I will praise you, Lord,   for you have res - cued me.

I will extol you, LORD, for you have
    raised me up,
    and have not let my enemies rejoice
    over me.
O LORD, you have lifted up my soul
    from the grave,
    restored me to life from those who
    sink into the pit. ℟.

Sing psalms to the LORD, you faithful
    ones;
    give thanks to his holy name.

His anger lasts a moment; his favor all
    through life.
At night come tears, but dawn
    brings joy. ℟.

Hear, O LORD, and have mercy on me;
    be my helper, O LORD.
You have changed my mourning into
    dancing.
O LORD my God, I will thank you
    forever. ℟.

READING II   *Galatians 1:11–19*

I want you to know, brothers and sisters, that the gospel preached by me is not of
human origin. For I did not receive it from a human being, nor was I taught it, but it
came through a revelation of Jesus Christ.

    For you heard of my former way of life in Judaism, how I persecuted the church
of God beyond measure and tried to destroy it, and progressed in Judaism beyond
many of my contemporaries among my race, since I was even more a zealot for my
ancestral traditions. But when God, who from my mother's womb had set me apart
and called me through his grace, was pleased to reveal his Son to me, so that I might
proclaim him to the Gentiles, I did not immediately consult flesh and blood, nor did I
go up to Jerusalem to those who were apostles before me; rather, I went into Arabia
and then returned to Damascus.

    Then after three years I went up to Jerusalem to confer with Cephas and remained
with him for fifteen days. But I did not see any other of the apostles, only James the
brother of the Lord.

GOSPEL   *Luke 7:11–17*

Jesus journeyed to a city called Nain, and his disciples and a large crowd accompanied him. As he drew near to the gate of the city, a man who had died was being
carried out, the only son of his mother, and she was a widow. A large crowd from the
city was with her. When the Lord saw her, he was moved with pity for her and said
to her, "Do not weep." He stepped forward and touched the coffin; at this the bearers
halted, and he said, "Young man, I tell you, arise!" The dead man sat up and began
to speak, and Jesus gave him to his mother. Fear seized them all, and they glorified
God, exclaiming, "A great prophet has arisen in our midst," and "God has visited his
people." This report about him spread through the whole of Judea and in all the surrounding region.

1139 ELEVENTH SUNDAY IN ORDINARY TIME / A

READING I *Exodus 19:2–6a / 91*

In those days, the Israelites came to the desert of Sinai and pitched camp. While Israel was encamped here in front of the mountain, Moses went up the mountain to God. Then the LORD called to him and said, "Thus shall you say to the house of Jacob; tell the Israelites: You have seen for yourselves how I treated the Egyptians and how I bore you up on eagle wings and brought you here to myself. Therefore, if you hearken to my voice and keep my covenant, you shall be my special possession, dearer to me than all other people, though all the earth is mine. You shall be to me a kingdom of priests, a holy nation."

RESPONSORIAL PSALM *Psalm 100:1–2, 3, 5*

We are his peo - ple: the sheep of his flock.

Cry out with joy to the LORD, all the earth.
  Serve the LORD with gladness.
  Come before him, singing for joy. ℟.

Know that he, the LORD, is God.
  He made us; we belong to him.

We are his people, the sheep of his flock. ℟.

Indeed, how good is the LORD,
  eternal his merciful love.
He is faithful from age to age. ℟.

READING II *Romans 5:6–11*

Brothers and sisters: Christ, while we were still helpless, yet died at the appointed time for the ungodly. Indeed, only with difficulty does one die for a just person, though perhaps for a good person one might even find courage to die. But God proves his love for us in that while we were still sinners Christ died for us. How much more then, since we are now justified by his blood, will we be saved through him from the wrath. Indeed, if, while we were enemies, we were reconciled to God through the death of his Son, how much more, once reconciled, will we be saved by his life. Not only that, but we also boast of God through our Lord Jesus Christ, through whom we have now received reconciliation.

GOSPEL *Matthew 9:36—10:8*

At the sight of the crowds, Jesus' heart was moved with pity for them because they were troubled and abandoned, like sheep without a shepherd. Then he said to his disciples, "The harvest is abundant but the laborers are few; so ask the master of the harvest to send out laborers for his harvest."

Then he summoned his twelve disciples and gave them authority over unclean spirits to drive them out and to cure every disease and every illness. The names of the twelve apostles are these: first, Simon called Peter, and his brother Andrew; James, the son of Zebedee, and his brother John; Philip and Bartholomew, Thomas and Matthew the tax collector; James, the son of Alphaeus, and Thaddeus; Simon from Cana, and Judas Iscariot who betrayed him.

Jesus sent out these twelve after instructing them thus, "Do not go into pagan territory or enter a Samaritan town. Go rather to the lost sheep of the house of Israel. As you go, make this proclamation: 'The kingdom of heaven is at hand.' Cure the sick, raise the dead, cleanse lepers, drive out demons. Without cost you have received; without cost you are to give."

ELEVENTH SUNDAY IN ORDINARY TIME / B 1140

READING I

Ezekiel 17:22–24 / 92

Thus says the Lord GOD:

I, too, will take from the crest of the
    cedar,
    from its topmost branches tear
      off a tender shoot,
and plant it on a high and lofty
    mountain;
    on the mountain heights of Israel
      I will plant it.
It shall put forth branches and bear
    fruit,
    and become a majestic cedar.
Birds of every kind shall dwell

beneath it,
    every winged thing in the shade
      of its boughs.
And all the trees of the field shall
    know
    that I, the Lord,
bring low the high tree,
    lift high the lowly tree,
wither up the green tree,
    and make the withered tree
      bloom.
As I, the LORD, have spoken, so will I do.

RESPONSORIAL PSALM

Psalm 92:2–3, 13–14, 15–16

Lord, it is good to give thanks to you.

It is good to give thanks to the LORD,
    to make music to your name,
      O Most High,
to proclaim your loving mercy in the
    morning,
    and your truth in the watches of the
      night. ℟.

The just will flourish like the palm tree,
    and grow like a Lebanon cedar.

Planted in the house of the LORD,
    they will flourish in the courts of
      our God. ℟.

Still bearing fruit when they are old,
    still full of sap, still green,
to proclaim that the LORD is upright.
    In him, my rock, there is no
      wrong. ℟.

READING II

2 Corinthians 5:6–10

Brothers and sisters: We are always courageous, although we know that while we are at home in the body we are away from the Lord, for we walk by faith, not by sight. Yet we are courageous, and we would rather leave the body and go home to the Lord. Therefore, we aspire to please him, whether we are at home or away. For we must all appear before the judgment seat of Christ, so that each may receive recompense, according to what he did in the body, whether good or evil.

GOSPEL *Mark 4:26–34*

Jesus said to the crowds: "This is how it is with the kingdom of God; it is as if a man were to scatter seed on the land and would sleep and rise night and day and through it all the seed would sprout and grow, he knows not how. Of its own accord the land yields fruit, first the blade, then the ear, then the full grain in the ear. And when the grain is ripe, he wields the sickle at once, for the harvest has come."

He said, "To what shall we compare the kingdom of God, or what parable can we use for it? It is like a mustard seed that, when it is sown in the ground, is the smallest of all the seeds on the earth. But once it is sown, it springs up and becomes the largest of plants and puts forth large branches, so that the birds of the sky can dwell in its shade." With many such parables he spoke the word to them as they were able to understand it. Without parables he did not speak to them, but to his own disciples he explained everything in private.

1141 ELEVENTH SUNDAY IN ORDINARY TIME / C

READING I *2 Samuel 12:7–10, 13 / 93*

Nathan said to David: "Thus says the LORD God of Israel: 'I anointed you king of Israel. I rescued you from the hand of Saul. I gave you your lord's house and your lord's wives for your own. I gave you the house of Israel and of Judah. And if this were not enough, I could count up for you still more. Why have you spurned the Lord and done evil in his sight? You have cut down Uriah the Hittite with the sword; you took his wife as your own, and him you killed with the sword of the Ammonites. Now, therefore, the sword shall never depart from your house, because you have despised me and have taken the wife of Uriah to be your wife.'" Then David said to Nathan, "I have sinned against the LORD." Nathan answered David: "The LORD on his part has forgiven your sin: you shall not die."

RESPONSORIAL PSALM *Psalm 32:1–2, 5, 7, 11*

JRC

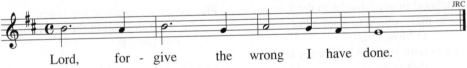

Lord, for - give the wrong I have done.

Blessed is he whose transgression is
　forgiven,
　　whose sin is remitted.
Blessed the man to whom the LORD
　　imputes no guilt,
　in whose spirit is no guile. ℟.

To you I have acknowledged my sin;
　my guilt I did not hide.
I said, "I will confess my transgression
　to the LORD."

And you have forgiven the guilt of
　my sin. ℟.

You are a hiding place for me;
　you keep me safe from distress;
　you surround me with cries of
　　deliverance. ℟.

Rejoice in the LORD; exult, you just!
　Ring out your joy, all you upright of
　heart! ℟.

READING II

Galatians 2:16, 19–21

Brothers and sisters: We who know that a person is not justified by works of the law but through faith in Jesus Christ, even we have believed in Christ Jesus that we may be justified by faith in Christ and not by works of the law, because by works of the law no one will be justified. For through the law I died to the law, that I might live for God. I have been crucified with Christ; yet I live, no longer I, but Christ lives in me; insofar as I now live in the flesh, I live by faith in the Son of God who has loved me and given himself up for me. I do not nullify the grace of God; for if justification comes through the law, then Christ died for nothing.

GOSPEL

Luke 7:36–8:3 or 7:36–50

For short form read only the part in brackets.

[A Pharisee invited Jesus to dine with him, and he entered the Pharisee's house and reclined at table. Now there was a sinful woman in the city who learned that he was at table in the house of the Pharisee. Bringing an alabaster flask of ointment, she stood behind him at his feet weeping and began to bathe his feet with her tears. Then she wiped them with her hair, kissed them, and anointed them with the ointment. When the Pharisee who had invited him saw this he said to himself, "If this man were a prophet, he would know who and what sort of woman this is who is touching him, that she is a sinner." Jesus said to him in reply, "Simon, I have something to say to you." "Tell me, teacher," he said. "Two people were in debt to a certain creditor; one owed five hundred days' wages and the other owed fifty. Since they were unable to repay the debt, he forgave it for both. Which of them will love him more?" Simon said in reply, "The one, I suppose, whose larger debt was forgiven." He said to him, "You have judged rightly."

Then he turned to the woman and said to Simon, "Do you see this woman? When I entered your house, you did not give me water for my feet, but she has bathed them with her tears and wiped them with her hair. You did not give me a kiss, but she has not ceased kissing my feet since the time I entered. You did not anoint my head with oil, but she anointed my feet with ointment. So I tell you, her many sins have been forgiven because she has shown great love. But the one to whom little is forgiven, loves little." He said to her, "Your sins are forgiven." The others at table said to themselves, "Who is this who even forgives sins?" But he said to the woman, "Your faith has saved you; go in peace."]

Afterward he journeyed from one town and village to another, preaching and proclaiming the good news of the kingdom of God. Accompanying him were the Twelve and some women who had been cured of evil spirits and infirmities, Mary, called Magdalene, from whom seven demons had gone out, Joanna, the wife of Herod's steward Chuza, Susanna, and many others who provided for them out of their resources.

TWELFTH SUNDAY IN ORDINARY TIME / A   1142

READING I

Jeremiah 20:10–13 / 94

Jeremiah said:
  "I hear the whisperings of many:
    'Terror on every side!
    Denounce! let us denounce him!'

All those who were my friends
  are on the watch for any misstep
  of mine.

'Perhaps he will be trapped; then we
can prevail,
and take our vengeance on him.'
But the LORD is with me, like a
mighty champion:
my persecutors will stumble,
they will not triumph.
In their failure they will be put to
utter shame,
to lasting, unforgettable confusion.

O LORD of hosts, you who test the just,
who probe mind and heart,
let me witness the vengeance you
take on them,
for to you I have entrusted my
cause.
Sing to the LORD,
praise the LORD,
for he has rescued the life of the poor
from the power of the wicked!"

RESPONSORIAL PSALM

Psalm 69:8–10, 14 and 17, 33–35

CAP

Lord, in your great love, an - swer me.

It is for you that I suffer taunts,
that shame has covered my face.
To my own kin I have become an
outcast,
a stranger to the children of my
mother.
Zeal for your house consumes me,
and taunts against you fall on me. ℟.

But I pray to you, O LORD,
for a time of your favor.
In your great mercy, answer me, O God,
with your salvation that never fails.
LORD, answer, for your mercy is kind;

in your great compassion, turn
toward me. ℟.

The poor when they see it will be glad,
and God-seeking hearts will revive;
for the LORD listens to the needy,
and does not spurn his own in their
chains.
Let the heavens and the earth give him
praise,
the seas and everything that moves
in them. ℟.

READING II

Romans 5:12–15

Brothers and sisters: Through one man sin entered the world, and through sin, death, and thus death came to all men, inasmuch as all sinned— for up to the time of the law, sin was in the world, though sin is not accounted when there is no law. But death reigned from Adam to Moses, even over those who did not sin after the pattern of the trespass of Adam, who is the type of the one who was to come.

But the gift is not like the transgression. For if by the transgression of the one the many died, how much more did the grace of God and the gracious gift of the one man Jesus Christ overflow for the many.

GOSPEL

Matthew 10:26–33

Jesus said to the Twelve: "Fear no one. Nothing is concealed that will not be revealed, nor secret that will not be known. What I say to you in the darkness, speak in the light; what you hear whispered, proclaim on the housetops. And do not be afraid of those who kill the body but cannot kill the soul; rather, be afraid of the one who can destroy both soul and body in Gehenna. Are not two sparrows sold for a small coin?

Yet not one of them falls to the ground without your Father's knowledge. Even all the hairs of your head are counted. So do not be afraid; you are worth more than many sparrows. Everyone who acknowledges me before others I will acknowledge before my heavenly Father. But whoever denies me before others, I will deny before my heavenly Father."

TWELFTH SUNDAY IN ORDINARY TIME / B 1143

READING I
Job 38:1, 8–11 / 95

The Lord addressed Job out of the storm and said:
> Who shut within doors the sea,
>   when it burst forth from the womb;
> when I made the clouds its garment
>   and thick darkness its swaddling
>   bands?

> When I set limits for it
>   and fastened the bar of its door,
> and said: Thus far shall you come but
>   no farther,
> and here shall your proud waves be
>   stilled!

RESPONSORIAL PSALM
Psalm 107:23–24, 25–26, 28–29, 30–31

Or: Alleluia.

Give thanks to the Lord, his love is ev-er-last-ing.

Some went down to the sea in ships,
    to trade on the mighty waters.
These have seen the deeds of the LORD,
    the wonders he does in the deep. ℟.

For he spoke and raised up the
        storm-wind,
    tossing high the waves of the sea
that surged to heaven and dropped to
        the depths.
    Their souls melted away in their
        distress. ℟.

Then they cried to the LORD in their
        need,
    and he rescued them from their
        distress.
He stilled the storm to a whisper,
    and the waves of the sea were
        hushed. ℟.

They rejoiced because of the calm,
    and he led them to the haven they
        desired.
Let them thank the LORD for his mercy,
    his wonders for the children of
        men. ℟.

READING II
2 Corinthians 5:14–17

Brothers and sisters: The love of Christ impels us, once we have come to the conviction that one died for all; therefore, all have died. He indeed died for all, so that those who live might no longer live for themselves but for him who for their sake died and was raised.

Consequently, from now on we regard no one according to the flesh; even if we once knew Christ according to the flesh, yet now we know him so no longer. So whoever is in Christ is a new creation: the old things have passed away; behold, new things have come.

GOSPEL *Mark 4:35–41*

On that day, as evening drew on, Jesus said to his disciples: "Let us cross to the other side." Leaving the crowd, they took Jesus with them in the boat just as he was. And other boats were with him. A violent squall came up and waves were breaking over the boat, so that it was already filling up. Jesus was in the stern, asleep on a cushion. They woke him and said to him, "Teacher, do you not care that we are perishing?" He woke up, rebuked the wind, and said to the sea, "Quiet! Be still!" The wind ceased and there was great calm. Then he asked them, "Why are you terrified? Do you not yet have faith?" They were filled with great awe and said to one another, "Who then is this whom even wind and sea obey?"

1144 TWELFTH SUNDAY IN ORDINARY TIME / C

READING I *Zechariah 12:10–11; 13:1 / 96*

Thus says the LORD: I will pour out on the house of David and on the inhabitants of Jerusalem a spirit of grace and petition; and they shall look on him whom they have pierced, and they shall mourn for him as one mourns for an only son, and they shall grieve over him as one grieves over a firstborn.

On that day the mourning in Jerusalem shall be as great as the mourning of Hadadrimmon in the plain of Megiddo.

On that day there shall be open to the house of David and to the inhabitants of Jerusalem, a fountain to purify from sin and uncleanness.

RESPONSORIAL PSALM *Psalm 63:2, 3–4, 5–6, 8–9*

My soul is thirst-ing for you, O Lord, thirst-ing for you my God.

O God, you are my God; at dawn
    I seek you;
    for you my soul is thirsting.
For you my flesh is pining,
    like a dry, weary land without
        water. ℟.

I have come before you in the sanctuary,
    to behold your strength and your
        glory.
Your loving mercy is better than life;
    my lips will speak your praise. ℟.

I will bless you all my life;
    in your name I will lift up my hands.
My soul shall be filled as with a
        banquet;
    with joyful lips, my mouth shall
        praise you. ℟.

For you have been my strength;
    in the shadow of your wings I
        rejoice.
My soul clings fast to you;
    your right hand upholds me. ℟.

READING II
Galatians 3:26–29

Brothers and sisters: Through faith you are all children of God in Christ Jesus. For all of you who were baptized into Christ have clothed yourselves with Christ. There is neither Jew nor Greek, there is neither slave nor free person, there is not male and female; for you are all one in Christ Jesus. And if you belong to Christ, then you are Abraham's descendant, heirs according to the promise.

GOSPEL
Luke 9:18–24

Once when Jesus was praying in solitude, and the disciples were with him, he asked them, "Who do the crowds say that I am?" They said in reply, "John the Baptist; others, Elijah; still others, 'One of the ancient prophets has arisen.'" Then he said to them, "But who do you say that I am?" Peter said in reply, "The Christ of God." He rebuked them and directed them not to tell this to anyone.

He said, "The Son of Man must suffer greatly and be rejected by the elders, the chief priests, and the scribes, and be killed and on the third day be raised." Then he said to all, "If anyone wishes to come after me, he must deny himself and take up his cross daily and follow me. For whoever wishes to save his life will lose it, but whoever loses his life for my sake will save it."

THIRTEENTH SUNDAY IN ORDINARY TIME / A 1145

READING I
2 Kings 4:8–11, 14–16a / 97

One day Elisha came to Shunem, where there was a woman of influence, who urged him to dine with her. Afterward, whenever he passed by, he used to stop there to dine. So she said to her husband, "I know that Elisha is a holy man of God. Since he visits us often, let us arrange a little room on the roof and furnish it for him with a bed, table, chair, and lamp, so that when he comes to us he can stay there." Sometime later Elisha arrived and stayed in the room overnight.

Later Elisha asked, "Can something be done for her?" His servant Gehazi answered, "Yes! She has no son, and her husband is getting on in years." Elisha said, "Call her." When the woman had been called and stood at the door, Elisha promised, "This time next year you will be fondling a baby son."

RESPONSORIAL PSALM
Psalm 89:2–3, 16–17, 18–19

For ev‐er I will sing the good‐ness of the Lord.

I will sing forever of your mercies,
O LORD;
    through all ages my mouth will
    proclaim your fidelity.
I have declared your mercy is
    established forever;
    your fidelity stands firm as the
    heavens. ℟.

How blessed the people who know your
praise,
    who walk, O LORD, in the light of
    your face,
who find their joy every day in your
    name,
    who make your justice their joyful
    acclaim. ℟.

For you are the glory of their strength;
>   by your favor it is that our might is
>   exalted.

Behold, the LORD is our shield;
>   he is the Holy One of Israel, our
>   king. ℟.

READING II
Romans 6:3–4, 8–11

Brothers and sisters: Are you unaware that we who were baptized into Christ Jesus were baptized into his death? We were indeed buried with him through baptism into death, so that, just as Christ was raised from the dead by the glory of the Father, we too might live in newness of life.

If, then, we have died with Christ, we believe that we shall also live with him. We know that Christ, raised from the dead, dies no more; death no longer has power over him. As to his death, he died to sin once and for all; as to his life, he lives for God. Consequently, you too must think of yourselves as dead to sin and living for God in Christ Jesus.

GOSPEL
Matthew 10:37–42

Jesus said to his apostles: "Whoever loves father or mother more than me is not worthy of me, and whoever loves son or daughter more than me is not worthy of me; and whoever does not take up his cross and follow after me is not worthy of me. Whoever finds his life will lose it, and whoever loses his life for my sake will find it.

"Whoever receives you receives me, and whoever receives me receives the one who sent me. Whoever receives a prophet because he is a prophet will receive a prophet's reward, and whoever receives a righteous man because he is a righteous man will receive a righteous man's reward. And whoever gives only a cup of cold water to one of these little ones to drink because the little one is a disciple— amen, I say to you, he will surely not lose his reward."

1146 THIRTEENTH SUNDAY IN ORDINARY TIME / B

READING I
Wisdom 1:13–15; 2:23–24 / 98

God did not make death,
>   nor does he rejoice in the
>   destruction of the living.
For he fashioned all things that they
>   might have being;
>   and the creatures of the world are
>   wholesome,
and there is not a destructive drug
>   among them
>   nor any domain of the netherworld

on earth,
>   for justice is undying.
For God formed man to be imperishable;
>   the image of his own nature he
>   made him.
But by the envy of the devil, death
>   entered the world,
>   and they who belong to his
>   company experience it.

RESPONSORIAL PSALM
Psalm 30:2 and 4, 5–6, 11 and 12a and 13b

JRC

I will praise you, Lord, for you have res-cued me.

I will extol you, LORD, for you have
    raised me up,
and have not let my enemies rejoice
    over me.
O LORD, you have lifted up my soul
    from the grave,
restored me to life from those who
    sink into the pit. ℟.

Sing psalms to the LORD, you faithful
    ones;
give thanks to his holy name.

His anger lasts a moment; his favor all
    through life.
At night come tears, but dawn brings
    joy. ℟.

Hear, O LORD, and have mercy on me;
    be my helper, O LORD.
You have changed my mourning into
    dancing.
O LORD my God, I will thank you
    forever. ℟.

READING II

2 Corinthians 8:7, 9, 13–15

Brothers and sisters: As you excel in every respect, in faith, discourse, knowledge, all earnestness, and in the love we have for you, may you excel in this gracious act also.

For you know the gracious act of our Lord Jesus Christ, that though he was rich, for your sake he became poor, so that by his poverty you might become rich. Not that others should have relief while you are burdened, but that as a matter of equality your abundance at the present time should supply their needs, so that their abundance may also supply your needs, that there may be equality. As it is written:
> *Whoever had much did not have more,*
> *and whoever had little did not have less.*

GOSPEL

Mark 5:21–43 or 5:21–24, 35b–43

For short form read only the parts in brackets.

[When Jesus had crossed again in the boat to the other side, a large crowd gathered around him, and he stayed close to the sea. One of the synagogue officials, named Jairus, came forward. Seeing him he fell at his feet and pleaded earnestly with him, saying, "My daughter is at the point of death. Please, come lay your hands on her that she may get well and live." He went off with him, and a large crowd followed him and pressed upon him.]

There was a woman afflicted with hemorrhages for twelve years. She had suffered greatly at the hands of many doctors and had spent all that she had. Yet she was not helped but only grew worse. She had heard about Jesus and came up behind him in the crowd and touched his cloak. She said, "If I but touch his clothes, I shall be cured." Immediately her flow of blood dried up. She felt in her body that she was healed of her affliction. Jesus, aware at once that power had gone out from him, turned around in the crowd and asked, "Who has touched my clothes?" But his disciples said to Jesus, "You see how the crowd is pressing upon you, and yet you ask, 'Who touched me?'" And he looked around to see who had done it. The woman, realizing what had happened to her, approached in fear and trembling. She fell down before Jesus and told him the whole truth. He said to her, "Daughter, your faith has saved you. Go in peace and be cured of your affliction."

[While he was still speaking, people from the synagogue official's house arrived and said, "Your daughter has died; why trouble the teacher any longer?" Disregarding the message that was reported, Jesus said to the synagogue official, "Do not be afraid; just have faith." He did not allow anyone to accompany him inside except Peter,

James, and John, the brother of James. When they arrived at the house of the synagogue official, he caught sight of a commotion, people weeping and wailing loudly. So he went in and said to them, "Why this commotion and weeping? The child is not dead but asleep." And they ridiculed him. Then he put them all out. He took along the child's father and mother and those who were with him and entered the room where the child was. He took the child by the hand and said to her, *"Talitha koum,"* which means, "Little girl, I say to you, arise!" The girl, a child of twelve, arose immediately and walked around. At that they were utterly astounded. He gave strict orders that no one should know this and said that she should be given something to eat.]

1147 THIRTEENTH SUNDAY IN ORDINARY TIME / C

READING I   *1 Kings 19:16b, 19–21 / 99*

The LORD said to Elijah: "You shall anoint Elisha, son of Shaphat of Abel-Meholah, as prophet to succeed you."

Elijah set out and came upon Elisha, son of Shaphat, as he was plowing with twelve yoke of oxen; he was following the twelfth. Elijah went over to him and threw his cloak over him. Elisha left the oxen, ran after Elijah, and said, "Please, let me kiss my father and mother goodbye, and I will follow you." Elijah answered, "Go back! Have I done anything to you?" Elisha left him and, taking the yoke of oxen, slaughtered them; he used the plowing equipment for fuel to boil their flesh, and gave it to his people to eat. Then Elisha left and followed Elijah as his attendant.

RESPONSORIAL PSALM   *Psalm 16:1–2a and 5, 7–8, 9–10, 11*

You are my in - her - i - tance, O Lord, O Lord.

Preserve me, O God, for in you I take refuge.
　I say to the LORD, "You are my Lord."
O LORD, it is you who are my portion and cup;
　you yourself who secure my lot. ℟.

I will bless the LORD who gives me counsel,
　who even at night directs my heart.
I keep the LORD before me always;
　with him at my right hand,
　　I shall not be moved. ℟.

And so, my heart rejoices, my soul is glad;
　even my flesh shall rest in hope.
For you will not abandon my soul to hell,
　nor let your holy one see corruption. ℟.

You will show me the path of life,
　the fullness of joy in your presence,
　at your right hand, bliss forever. ℟.

READING II   *Galatians 5:1, 13–18*

Brothers and sisters: For freedom Christ set us free; so stand firm and do not submit again to the yoke of slavery.

For you were called for freedom, brothers and sisters. But do not use this freedom as an opportunity for the flesh; rather, serve one another through love. For the whole law is fulfilled in one statement, namely, *You shall love your neighbor as yourself.* But if you go on biting and devouring one another, beware that you are not consumed by one another.

I say, then: live by the Spirit and you will certainly not gratify the desire of the flesh. For the flesh has desires against the Spirit, and the Spirit against the flesh; these are opposed to each other, so that you may not do what you want. But if you are guided by the Spirit, you are not under the law.

GOSPEL
Luke 9:51–62

When the days for Jesus' being taken up were fulfilled, he resolutely determined to journey to Jerusalem, and he sent messengers ahead of him. On the way they entered a Samaritan village to prepare for his reception there, but they would not welcome him because the destination of his journey was Jerusalem. When the disciples James and John saw this they asked, "Lord, do you want us to call down fire from heaven to consume them?" Jesus turned and rebuked them, and they journeyed to another village.

As they were proceeding on their journey someone said to him, "I will follow you wherever you go." Jesus answered him, "Foxes have dens and birds of the sky have nests, but the Son of Man has nowhere to rest his head."

And to another he said, "Follow me." But he replied, "Lord, let me go first and bury my father." But he answered him, "Let the dead bury their dead. But you, go and proclaim the kingdom of God." And another said, "I will follow you, Lord, but first let me say farewell to my family at home." To him Jesus said, "No one who sets a hand to the plow and looks to what was left behind is fit for the kingdom of God."

FOURTEENTH SUNDAY IN ORDINARY TIME / A — 1148

READING I
Zechariah 9:9–10 / 100

Thus says the LORD:
Rejoice heartily, O daughter Zion,
  shout for joy, O daughter Jerusalem!
See, your king shall come to you;
  a just savior is he,
meek, and riding on an ass,
  on a colt, the foal of an ass.
He shall banish the chariot from Ephraim,

and the horse from Jerusalem;
the warrior's bow shall be banished,
  and he shall proclaim peace to the
    nations.
His dominion shall be from sea to sea,
  and from the River to the ends of
    the earth.

RESPONSORIAL PSALM
Psalm 145:1–2, 8–9, 10–11, 13cd–14

Or: Alleluia.

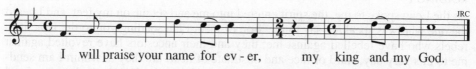

I will praise your name for ev-er, my king and my God.

I will extol you, my God and king,
  and bless your name forever and
  ever.

I will bless you day after day,
  and praise your name forever and
  ever. ℟.

The LORD is kind and full of compassion,
  slow to anger, abounding in mercy.
How good is the LORD to all,
  compassionate to all his creatures. ℟.

All your works shall thank you,
    O LORD,
  and all your faithful ones bless you.

They shall speak of the glory of your
    reign,
  and declare your mighty deeds. ℟.

The LORD is faithful in all his words,
  and holy in all his deeds.
The LORD supports all who fall,
  and raises up all who are bowed
    down. ℟.

READING II   *Romans 8:9, 11–13*

Brothers and sisters: You are not in the flesh; on the contrary, you are in the spirit, if only the Spirit of God dwells in you. Whoever does not have the Spirit of Christ does not belong to him. If the Spirit of the one who raised Jesus from the dead dwells in you, the one who raised Christ from the dead will give life to your mortal bodies also, through his Spirit that dwells in you. Consequently, brothers and sisters, we are not debtors to the flesh, to live according to the flesh. For if you live according to the flesh, you will die, but if by the Spirit you put to death the deeds of the body, you will live.

GOSPEL   *Matthew 11:25–30*

At that time Jesus exclaimed: "I give praise to you, Father, Lord of heaven and earth, for although you have hidden these things from the wise and the learned you have revealed them to little ones. Yes, Father, such has been your gracious will. All things have been handed over to me by my Father. No one knows the Son except the Father, and no one knows the Father except the Son and anyone to whom the Son wishes to reveal him."

"Come to me, all you who labor and are burdened, and I will give you rest. Take my yoke upon you and learn from me, for I am meek and humble of heart; and you will find rest for yourselves. For my yoke is easy, and my burden light."

1149   FOURTEENTH SUNDAY IN ORDINARY TIME / B

READING I   *Ezekiel 2:2–5 / 101*

As the LORD spoke to me, the spirit entered into me and set me on my feet, and I heard the one who was speaking say to me: Son of man, I am sending you to the Israelites, rebels who have rebelled against me; they and their ancestors have revolted against me to this very day. Hard of face and obstinate of heart are they to whom I am sending you. But you shall say to them: Thus says the LORD God! And whether they heed or resist —for they are a rebellious house— they shall know that a prophet has been among them.

RESPONSORIAL PSALM *Psalm 123:1–2a, 2bcd, 3–4*

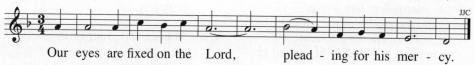

Our eyes are fixed on the Lord, plead - ing for his mer - cy.

To you have I lifted up my eyes,
  you who dwell in the heavens.
Behold, like the eyes of slaves
  on the hand of their lords. ℟.

Like the eyes of a servant
  on the hand of her mistress,
so our eyes are on the LORD our God,

till he show us his mercy. ℟.

Have mercy on us, LORD, have mercy.
  We are filled with contempt.
Indeed, all too full is our soul
  with the scorn of the arrogant,
  the disdain of the proud. ℟.

READING II *2 Corinthians 12:7–10*

Brothers and sisters: That I, Paul, might not become too elated, because of the abundance of the revelations, a thorn in the flesh was given to me, an angel of Satan, to beat me, to keep me from being too elated. Three times I begged the Lord about this, that it might leave me, but he said to me, "My grace is sufficient for you, for power is made perfect in weakness." I will rather boast most gladly of my weaknesses, in order that the power of Christ may dwell with me. Therefore, I am content with weaknesses, insults, hardships, persecutions, and constraints, for the sake of Christ; for when I am weak, then I am strong.

GOSPEL *Mark 6:1–6*

Jesus departed from there and came to his native place, accompanied by his disciples. When the sabbath came he began to teach in the synagogue, and many who heard him were astonished. They said, "Where did this man get all this? What kind of wisdom has been given him? What mighty deeds are wrought by his hands! Is he not the carpenter, the son of Mary, and the brother of James and Joses and Judas and Simon? And are not his sisters here with us?" And they took offense at him. Jesus said to them, "A prophet is not without honor except in his native place and among his own kin and in his own house." So he was not able to perform any mighty deed there, apart from curing a few sick people by laying his hands on them. He was amazed at their lack of faith.

FOURTEENTH SUNDAY IN ORDINARY TIME / C   1150

READING I *Isaiah 66:10–14c / 102*

Thus says the LORD:
Rejoice with Jerusalem and be glad
    because of her,
  all you who love her;
exult, exult with her,
  all you who were mourning over her!

Oh, that you may suck fully
  of the milk of her comfort,
that you may nurse with delight
  at her abundant breasts!
For thus says the LORD:

Lo, I will spread prosperity over
Jerusalem like a river,
and the wealth of the nations like
an overflowing torrent.
As nurslings, you shall be carried in
her arms,
and fondled in her lap;
as a mother comforts her child,
so will I comfort you;

in Jerusalem you shall find your
comfort.

When you see this, your heart shall
rejoice
and your bodies flourish like the
grass;
the LORD's power shall be known to
his servants.

RESPONSORIAL PSALM *Psalm 66:1–3a, 4–5, 6–7a, 16 and 20*

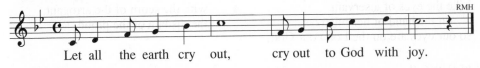

Let all the earth cry out, cry out to God with joy.

Cry out with joy to God, all the earth;
O sing to the glory of his name.
O render him glorious praise.
Say to God, "How awesome your
deeds! ℟.

"Before you all the earth shall bow down,
shall sing to you, sing to your name!"
Come and see the works of God:
awesome his deeds among the
children of men. ℟.

He turned the sea into dry land;
they passed through the river on
foot.
Let our joy, then, be in him;
he rules forever by his might. ℟.

Come and hear, all who fear God;
I will tell what he did for my soul.
Blest be God, who did not reject my
prayer,
nor withhold from me his merciful
love. ℟.

READING II *Galatians 6:14–18*

Brothers and sisters: May I never boast except in the cross of our Lord Jesus Christ, through which the world has been crucified to me, and I to the world. For neither does circumcision mean anything, nor does uncircumcision, but only a new creation. Peace and mercy be to all who follow this rule and to the Israel of God.

From now on, let no one make troubles for me; for I bear the marks of Jesus on my body.

The grace of our Lord Jesus Christ be with your spirit, brothers and sisters. Amen.

GOSPEL *Luke 10:1–12, 17–20 or 10:1–9*

For short form read only the part in brackets.

[At that time the Lord appointed seventy-two others whom he sent ahead of him in pairs to every town and place he intended to visit. He said to them, "The harvest is abundant but the laborers are few; so ask the master of the harvest to send out laborers for his harvest. Go on your way; behold, I am sending you like lambs among wolves. Carry no money bag, no sack, no sandals; and greet no one along the way. Into whatever house you enter, first say, 'Peace to this household.' If a peaceful person lives there, your peace will rest on him; but if not, it will return to you. Stay in the same house and eat and drink what is offered to you, for the laborer deserves his payment. Do not move about from one house to another. Whatever town you enter and they welcome you, eat what is set before you, cure the sick in it and say to them, 'The kingdom of God is at hand for you.'] Whatever town you enter and they do not receive you, go out into the streets and say, 'The dust of your town that clings to our feet, even that we shake off against you.' Yet know this: the kingdom of God is at hand. I tell you, it will be more tolerable for Sodom on that day than for that town."

The seventy-two returned rejoicing, and said, "Lord, even the demons are subject to us because of your name." Jesus said, "I have observed Satan fall like lightning from the sky. Behold, I have given you the power to 'tread upon serpents' and scorpions and upon the full force of the enemy and nothing will harm you. Nevertheless, do not rejoice because the spirits are subject to you, but rejoice because your names are written in heaven."

FIFTEENTH SUNDAY IN ORDINARY TIME / A   1151

READING I

Isaiah 55:10–11 / 103

Thus says the LORD:
Just as from the heavens
  the rain and snow come down
and do not return there
  till they have watered the earth,
    making it fertile and fruitful,
giving seed to the one who sows

and bread to the one who eats,
so shall my word be
  that goes forth from my mouth;
my word shall not return to me void,
  but shall do my will,
achieving the end for which I sent it.

RESPONSORIAL PSALM

Psalm 65:10abcd, 10e–11, 12–13, 14

The seed that falls on good ground will yield a fruit-ful har-vest.

You visit the earth, give it water;
  you fill it with riches.
God's ever-flowing river brims over
  to prepare the grain. ℟.

And thus you provide for the earth:
  you drench its furrows;
you level it, soften it with showers;
  you bless its growth. ℟.

You crown the year with your bounty.
  Abundance flows in your pathways;
in pastures of the desert it flows.
  The hills are girded with joy. ℟.

The meadows clothed with flocks.
  The valleys are decked with wheat.
They shout for joy; yes, they
  sing! ℟.

READING II   *Romans 8:18–23*

Brothers and sisters: I consider that the sufferings of this present time are as nothing compared with the glory to be revealed for us. For creation awaits with eager expectation the revelation of the children of God; for creation was made subject to futility, not of its own accord but because of the one who subjected it, in hope that creation itself would be set free from slavery to corruption and share in the glorious freedom of the children of God. We know that all creation is groaning in labor pains even until now; and not only that, but we ourselves, who have the firstfruits of the Spirit, we also groan within ourselves as we wait for adoption, the redemption of our bodies.

GOSPEL   *Matthew 13:1–23 or 13:1–9*

For short form read only the part in brackets.

[On that day, Jesus went out of the house and sat down by the sea. Such large crowds gathered around him that he got into a boat and sat down, and the whole crowd stood along the shore. And he spoke to them at length in parables, saying: "A sower went out to sow. And as he sowed, some seed fell on the path, and birds came and ate it up. Some fell on rocky ground, where it had little soil. It sprang up at once because the soil was not deep, and when the sun rose it was scorched, and it withered for lack of roots. Some seed fell among thorns, and the thorns grew up and choked it. But some seed fell on rich soil, and produced fruit, a hundred or sixty or thirtyfold. Whoever has ears ought to hear."]

The disciples approached him and said, "Why do you speak to them in parables?" He said to them in reply, "Because knowledge of the mysteries of the kingdom of heaven has been granted to you, but to them it has not been granted. To anyone who has, more will be given and he will grow rich; from anyone who has not, even what he has will be taken away. This is why I speak to them in parables, because *they look but do not see and hear but do not listen or understand.* Isaiah's prophecy is fulfilled in them, which says:

You shall indeed hear but not understand,
   you shall indeed look but never see.
Gross is the heart of this people,
   they will hardly hear with their ears,
   they have closed their eyes,
   lest they see with their eyes
   and hear with their ears
and understand with their hearts and be converted,
   and I heal them.

"But blessed are your eyes, because they see, and your ears, because they hear. Amen, I say to you, many prophets and righteous people longed to see what you see but did not see it, and to hear what you hear but did not hear it.

"Hear then the parable of the sower. The seed sown on the path is the one who hears the word of the kingdom without understanding it, and the evil one comes and steals away what was sown in his heart. The seed sown on rocky ground is the one who hears the word and receives it at once with joy. But he has no root and lasts only for a time. When some tribulation or persecution comes because of the word, he immediately falls away. The seed sown among thorns is the one who hears the word, but then worldly anxiety and the lure of riches choke the word and it bears no fruit. But the seed sown on rich soil is the one who hears the word and understands it, who indeed bears fruit and yields a hundred or sixty or thirtyfold."

FIFTEENTH SUNDAY IN ORDINARY TIME / B   1152

READING I   *Amos 7:12–15 / 104*

Amaziah, priest of Bethel, said to Amos, "Off with you, visionary, flee to the land of Judah! There earn your bread by prophesying, but never again prophesy in Bethel; for it is the king's sanctuary and a royal temple." Amos answered Amaziah, "I was no prophet, nor have I belonged to a company of prophets; I was a shepherd and a dresser of sycamores. The LORD took me from following the flock, and said to me, Go, prophesy to my people Israel."

RESPONSORIAL PSALM   *Psalm 85:9ab and 10, 11–12, 13–14*

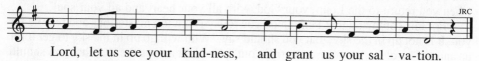

Lord, let us see your kind-ness,   and grant us your sal - va-tion.

I will hear what the LORD God speaks;
  he speaks of peace for his people
    and his faithful.
His salvation is near for those who fear
    him,
  and his glory will dwell in our land. ℟.

Merciful love and faithfulness have met;
  justice and peace have kissed.

Faithfulness shall spring from the earth,
  and justice look down from
    heaven. ℟.

Also the LORD will bestow his bounty,
  and our earth shall yield its increase.
Justice will march before him,
  and guide his steps on the way. ℟.

READING II   *Ephesians 1:3–14 or 1:3–10*
For short form read only the part in brackets.

[Blessed be the God and Father of our Lord Jesus Christ, who has blessed us in Christ with every spiritual blessing in the heavens, as he chose us in him, before the foundation of the world, to be holy and without blemish before him. In love he destined us for adoption to himself through Jesus Christ, in accord with the favor of his will, for the praise of the glory of his grace that he granted us in the beloved. In him we have redemption by his blood, the forgiveness of transgressions, in accord with the riches of his grace that he lavished upon us. In all wisdom and insight, he has made known to us the mystery of his will in accord with his favor that he set forth in him as a plan for the fullness of times, to sum up all things in Christ, in heaven and on earth.]

In him we were also chosen, destined in accord with the purpose of the One who accomplishes all things according to the intention of his will, so that we might exist for the praise of his glory, we who first hoped in Christ. In him you also, who have heard the word of truth, the gospel of your salvation, and have believed in him, were sealed with the promised holy Spirit, which is the first installment of our inheritance toward redemption as God's possession, to the praise of his glory.

GOSPEL   *Mark 6:7–13*

Jesus summoned the Twelve and began to send them out two by two and gave them authority over unclean spirits. He instructed them to take nothing for the journey but a walking stick—no food, no sack, no money in their belts. They were, however, to wear sandals but not a second tunic. He said to them, "Wherever you enter a house, stay there until you leave. Whatever place does not welcome you or listen to you, leave there and shake the dust off your feet in testimony against them." So they went off and preached repentance. The Twelve drove out many demons, and they anointed with oil many who were sick and cured them.

1153 FIFTEENTH SUNDAY IN ORDINARY TIME / C

READING I   *Deuteronomy 30:10–14 / 105*

Moses said to the people: "If only you would heed the voice of the LORD, your God, and keep his commandments and statutes that are written in this book of the law, when you return to the LORD, your God, with all your heart and all your soul.

"For this command that I enjoin on you today is not too mysterious and remote for you. It is not up in the sky, that you should say, 'Who will go up in the sky to get it for us and tell us of it, that we may carry it out?' Nor is it across the sea, that you should say, 'Who will cross the sea to get it for us and tell us of it, that we may carry it out?' No, it is something very near to you, already in your mouths and in your hearts; you have only to carry it out."

RESPONSORIAL PSALM   *Psalm 69:14 and 17, 30–31, 33–34, 36ab and 37*

JRC

Turn to the Lord in your need, and you will live.

I pray to you, O LORD,
   for a time of your favor.
In your great mercy, answer me, O God,
   with your salvation that never fails.
LORD, answer, for your mercy is kind;
   in your great compassion, turn
      toward me. ℟.

As for me in my poverty and pain,
   let your salvation, O God, raise me up.
Then I will praise God's name with a
      song;
   I will glorify him with thanksgiving. ℟.

The poor when they see it will be glad,
   and God-seeking hearts will revive;
for the LORD listens to the needy,
   and does not spurn his own in their
      chains. ℟.

For God will bring salvation to Sion,
   and rebuild the cities of Judah.
The children of his servants shall
      inherit it;
   those who love his name shall dwell
      there. ℟.

Or:

RESPONSORIAL PSALM   *Psalm 19:8, 9, 10, 11*

JJC

Your words, Lord, are Spir-it and life, Spir-it and life.

The law of the LORD is perfect;
   it revives the soul.

The decrees of the LORD are steadfast;
   they give wisdom to the simple. ℟.

The precepts of the LORD are right;
  they gladden the heart.
The command of the LORD is clear;
  it gives light to the eyes. ℟.

The fear of the LORD is pure,
  abiding forever.
The judgments of the LORD are true;

they are, all of them, just. ℟.

They are more to be desired than gold,
  than quantities of gold.
And sweeter are they than honey,
  than honey flowing from the
  comb. ℟.

READING II

Colossians 1:15–20

Christ Jesus is the image of the
  invisible God,
  the firstborn of all creation.
For in him were created all things in
  heaven and on earth,
  the visible and the invisible,
  whether thrones or dominions or
  principalities or powers;
  all things were created through him
  and for him.
He is before all things,
  and in him all things hold together.
He is the head of the body, the church.

He is the beginning, the firstborn from
  the dead,
  that in all things he himself might
  be preeminent.
For in him all the fullness was pleased to
  dwell,
  and through him to reconcile all
  things for him,
  making peace by the blood of his
  cross
  through him, whether those on earth
  or those in heaven.

GOSPEL

Luke 10:25–37

There was a scholar of the law who stood up to test him and said, "Teacher, what must I do to inherit eternal life?" Jesus said to him, "What is written in the law? How do you read it?" He said in reply, *"You shall love the Lord, your God, with all your heart, with all your being, with all your strength, and with all your mind, and your neighbor as yourself."* He replied to him, "You have answered correctly; do this and you will live."

But because he wished to justify himself, he said to Jesus, "And who is my neighbor?" Jesus replied, "A man fell victim to robbers as he went down from Jerusalem to Jericho. They stripped and beat him and went off leaving him half-dead. A priest happened to be going down that road, but when he saw him, he passed by on the opposite side. Likewise a Levite came to the place, and when he saw him, he passed by on the opposite side. But a Samaritan traveler who came upon him was moved with compassion at the sight. He approached the victim, poured oil and wine over his wounds and bandaged them. Then he lifted him up on his own animal, took him to an inn, and cared for him. The next day he took out two silver coins and gave them to the innkeeper with the instruction, 'Take care of him. If you spend more than what I have given you, I shall repay you on my way back.' Which of these three, in your opinion, was neighbor to the robbers' victim?" He answered, "The one who treated him with mercy." Jesus said to him, "Go and do likewise."

1154 SIXTEENTH SUNDAY IN ORDINARY TIME / A

READING I *Wisdom 12:13, 16–19 / 106*

There is no god besides you who have the care of all,
 that you need show you have not unjustly condemned.
For your might is the source of justice;
 your mastery over all things makes you lenient to all.
For you show your might when the perfection of your power is disbelieved;
 and in those who know you, you rebuke temerity.
But though you are master of might, you judge with clemency,
 and with much lenience you govern us;
 for power, whenever you will, attends you.
And you taught your people, by these deeds,
 that those who are just must be kind;
and you gave your children good ground for hope
 that you would permit repentance for their sins.

RESPONSORIAL PSALM *Psalm 86:5–6, 9–10, 15–16*

Lord, you are good and for - giv - ing.

O Lord, you are good and forgiving,
 full of mercy to all who call to you.
Give ear, O LORD, to my prayer,
 and attend to my voice in
  supplication. ℟.

All the nations you have made shall
  come;
 they will bow down before you,
  O Lord,
 and glorify your name,

for you are great and do marvelous
  deeds,
 you who alone are God. ℟.

But you, O God, are compassionate and
  gracious,
 slow to anger, O Lord,
abundant in mercy and fidelity;
 turn and take pity on me.
O give your strength to your servant. ℟.

READING II *Romans 8:26–27*

Brothers and sisters: The Spirit comes to the aid of our weakness; for we do not know how to pray as we ought, but the Spirit himself intercedes with inexpressible groanings. And the one who searches hearts knows what is the intention of the Spirit, because he intercedes for the holy ones according to God's will.

GOSPEL *Matthew 13:24–43 or 13:24–30*

For short form read only the part in brackets.

[Jesus proposed another parable to the crowds, saying: "The kingdom of heaven may be likened to a man who sowed good seed in his field. While everyone was asleep his enemy came and sowed weeds all through the wheat, and then went off. When the crop grew and bore fruit, the weeds appeared as well. The slaves of the householder came to him and said, 'Master, did you not sow good seed in your field? Where have the weeds come from?' He answered, 'An enemy has done this.' His slaves said to him, 'Do you want us to go and pull them up?' He replied, 'No, if you pull up the weeds you might uproot the wheat along with them. Let them grow together until harvest; then at harvest time I will say to the harvesters, "First collect the weeds and tie them in bundles for burning; but gather the wheat into my barn."'"]

He proposed another parable to them. "The kingdom of heaven is like a mustard seed that a person took and sowed in a field. It is the smallest of all the seeds, yet when full-grown it is the largest of plants. It becomes a large bush, and the 'birds of the sky come and dwell in its branches.'"

He spoke to them another parable. "The kingdom of heaven is like yeast that a woman took and mixed with three measures of wheat flour until the whole batch was leavened."

All these things Jesus spoke to the crowds in parables. He spoke to them only in parables, to fulfill what had been said through the prophet:

I will open my mouth in parables,
I will announce what has lain hidden from the foundation of the world.

Then, dismissing the crowds, he went into the house. His disciples approached him and said, "Explain to us the parable of the weeds in the field." He said in reply, "He who sows good seed is the Son of Man, the field is the world, the good seed the children of the kingdom. The weeds are the children of the evil one, and the enemy who sows them is the devil. The harvest is the end of the age, and the harvesters are angels. Just as weeds are collected and burned up with fire, so will it be at the end of the age. The Son of Man will send his angels, and they will collect out of his kingdom all who cause others to sin and all evildoers. They will throw them into the fiery furnace, where there will be wailing and grinding of teeth. Then the righteous will shine like the sun in the kingdom of their Father. Whoever has ears ought to hear."

SIXTEENTH SUNDAY IN ORDINARY TIME / B   1155

READING I   *Jeremiah 23:1–6 / 107*

Woe to the shepherds who mislead and scatter the flock of my pasture, says the LORD. Therefore, thus says the LORD, the God of Israel, against the shepherds who shepherd my people: You have scattered my sheep and driven them away. You have not cared for them, but I will take care to punish your evil deeds. I myself will gather the remnant of my flock from all the lands to which I have driven them and bring them back to their meadow; there they shall increase and multiply. I will appoint shepherds for them who will shepherd them so that they need no longer fear and tremble; and none shall be missing, says the LORD.

Behold, the days are coming, says the LORD,
when I will raise up a righteous shoot to David;
as king he shall reign and govern wisely,
he shall do what is just and right in the land.
In his days Judah shall be saved,
Israel shall dwell in security.
This is the name they give him:
"The LORD our justice."

RESPONSORIAL PSALM *Psalm 23:1–3a, 3b–4, 5, 6*

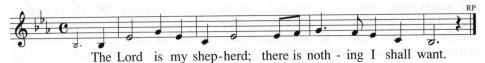

The Lord is my shep-herd; there is noth - ing I shall want.

The LORD is my shepherd;
there is nothing I shall want.
Fresh and green are the pastures
where he gives me repose.
Near restful waters he leads me;
he revives my soul. ℟.

He guides me along the right path,
for the sake of his name.
Though I should walk in the valley of
the shadow of death,
no evil would I fear, for you are
with me.

Your crook and your staff will give
me comfort. ℟.

You have prepared a table before me
in the sight of my foes.
My head you have anointed with oil;
my cup is overflowing. ℟.

Surely goodness and mercy shall
follow me
all the days of my life.
In the LORD's own house shall I dwell
for length of days unending. ℟.

READING II *Ephesians 2:13–18*

Brothers and sisters: In Christ Jesus you who once were far off have become near by the blood of Christ.

For he is our peace, he who made both one and broke down the dividing wall of enmity, through his flesh, abolishing the law with its commandments and legal claims, that he might create in himself one new person in place of the two, thus establishing peace, and might reconcile both with God, in one body, through the cross, putting that enmity to death by it. He came and preached peace to you who were far off and peace to those who were near, for through him we both have access in one Spirit to the Father.

GOSPEL *Mark 6:30–34*

The apostles gathered together with Jesus and reported all they had done and taught. He said to them, "Come away by yourselves to a deserted place and rest a while." People were coming and going in great numbers, and they had no opportunity even to eat. So they went off in the boat by themselves to a deserted place. People saw them leaving and many came to know about it. They hastened there on foot from all the towns and arrived at the place before them.

When he disembarked and saw the vast crowd, his heart was moved with pity for them, for they were like sheep without a shepherd; and he began to teach them many things.

1156 SIXTEENTH SUNDAY IN ORDINARY TIME / C

READING I *Genesis 18:1–10a / 108*

The LORD appeared to Abraham by the terebinth of Mamre, as he sat in the entrance of his tent, while the day was growing hot. Looking up, Abraham saw three men standing nearby. When he saw them, he ran from the entrance of the tent to greet them; and bowing to the ground, he said: "Sir, if I may ask you this favor, please do not go on past your servant. Let some water be brought, that you may bathe your feet, and then rest yourselves under the tree. Now that you have come this close to your servant, let me bring you a little food, that you may refresh yourselves; and afterward you may go on your way." The men replied, "Very well, do as you have said."

Abraham hastened into the tent and told Sarah, "Quick, three measures of fine flour! Knead it and make rolls." He ran to the herd, picked out a tender, choice steer, and gave it to a servant, who quickly prepared it. Then Abraham got some curds and milk, as well as the steer that had been prepared, and set these before the three men; and he waited on them under the tree while they ate.

They asked Abraham, "Where is your wife Sarah?" He replied, "There in the tent." One of them said, "I will surely return to you about this time next year, and Sarah will then have a son."

RESPONSORIAL PSALM   *Psalm 15:2–3a, 3bc–4ab, 5*

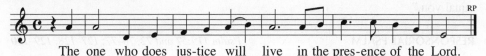

The one who does jus-tice will   live   in the pres-ence of the Lord.

Whoever walks without fault;
  who does what is just,
and speaks the truth from his heart;
  whoever does not slander with his
    tongue. ℟.

Who does no wrong to a neighbor,
  who casts no slur on a friend,
who looks with scorn on the wicked,

but honors those who fear the
  LORD. ℟.

Who lends no money at interest,
  and accepts no bribes against the
    innocent.
Such a one shall never be shaken. ℟.

READING II   *Colossians 1:24–28*

Brothers and sisters: Now I rejoice in my sufferings for your sake, and in my flesh I am filling up what is lacking in the afflictions of Christ on behalf of his body, which is the church, of which I am a minister in accordance with God's stewardship given to me to bring to completion for you the word of God, the mystery hidden from ages and from generations past. But now it has been manifested to his holy ones, to whom God chose to make known the riches of the glory of this mystery among the Gentiles; it is Christ in you, the hope for glory. It is he whom we proclaim, admonishing everyone and teaching everyone with all wisdom, that we may present everyone perfect in Christ.

GOSPEL   *Luke 10:38–42*

Jesus entered a village where a woman whose name was Martha welcomed him. She had a sister named Mary who sat beside the Lord at his feet listening to him speak. Martha, burdened with much serving, came to him and said, "Lord, do you not care that my sister has left me by myself to do the serving? Tell her to help me." The Lord said to her in reply, "Martha, Martha, you are anxious and worried about many things. There is need of only one thing. Mary has chosen the better part and it will not be taken from her."

1157 SEVENTEENTH SUNDAY IN ORDINARY TIME / A

READING I   *1 Kings 3:5, 7–12 / 109*

The LORD appeared to Solomon in a dream at night. God said, "Ask something of me and I will give it to you." Solomon answered: "O LORD, my God, you have made me, your servant, king to succeed my father David; but I am a mere youth, not knowing at all how to act. I serve you in the midst of the people whom you have chosen, a people so vast that it cannot be numbered or counted. Give your servant, therefore, an understanding heart to judge your people and to distinguish right from wrong. For who is able to govern this vast people of yours?"

The LORD was pleased that Solomon made this request. So God said to him: "Because you have asked for this— not for a long life for yourself, nor for riches, nor for the life of your enemies, but for understanding so that you may know what is right— I do as you requested. I give you a heart so wise and understanding that there has never been anyone like you up to now, and after you there will come no one to equal you."

RESPONSORIAL PSALM   *Psalm 119:57 and 72, 76–77, 127–128, 129–130*

Lord, I love your com-mands.

I have said, "O LORD, my portion
  is to obey your words."
The law from your mouth means more
    to me
  than large quantities of silver and
    gold. ℟.

Let your merciful love console me
  by your promise to your servant.
Show me compassion, that I may live,
  for your law is my delight. ℟.

That is why I love your commands
  more than finest gold,
why I rule my life by your precepts,
  and hate false ways. ℟.

Your decrees are wonderful indeed;
  therefore my soul obeys them.
The unfolding of your word gives light,
  and understanding to the simple. ℟.

READING II   *Romans 8:28–30*

Brothers and sisters: We know that all things work for good for those who love God, who are called according to his purpose. For those he foreknew he also predestined to be conformed to the image of his Son, so that he might be the firstborn among many brothers and sisters. And those he predestined he also called; and those he called he also justified; and those he justified he also glorified.

GOSPEL   *Matthew 13:44–52 or 13:44–46*
For short form read only the part in brackets.

[Jesus said to his disciples: "The kingdom of heaven is like a treasure buried in a field, which a person finds and hides again, and out of joy goes and sells all that he has and buys that field. Again, the kingdom of heaven is like a merchant searching for fine pearls. When he finds a pearl of great price, he goes and sells all that he has and buys it.] Again, the kingdom of heaven is like a net thrown into the sea, which collects fish of every kind. When it is full they haul it ashore and sit down to put what is good into buckets. What is bad they throw away. Thus it will be at the end of the age. The angels will go out and separate the wicked from the righteous and throw them into the fiery furnace, where there will be wailing and grinding of teeth.

"Do you understand all these things?" They answered, "Yes." And he replied, "Then every scribe who has been instructed in the kingdom of heaven is like the head of a household who brings from his storeroom both the new and the old."

SEVENTEENTH SUNDAY IN ORDINARY TIME / B 1158

READING I
2 Kings 4:42–44 / 110

A man came from Baal-shalishah bringing to Elisha, the man of God, twenty barley loaves made from the firstfruits, and fresh grain in the ear. Elisha said, "Give it to the people to eat." But his servant objected, "How can I set this before a hundred people?" Elisha insisted, "Give it to the people to eat. For thus says the LORD, 'They shall eat and there shall be some left over.'" And when they had eaten, there was some left over, as the LORD had said.

RESPONSORIAL PSALM
Psalm 145:10–11, 15–16, 17–18

The hand of the Lord feeds us; he an-swers all our needs.

All your works shall thank you,
    O LORD,
and all your faithful ones bless you.
They shall speak of the glory of your
    reign,
and declare your mighty deeds. ℟.

The eyes of all look to you,
    and you give them their food in
      due season.

You open your hand and satisfy
    the desire of every living thing. ℟.

The LORD is just in all his ways,
    and holy in all his deeds.
The LORD is close to all who call him,
    who call on him in truth. ℟.

READING II
Ephesians 4:1–6

Brothers and sisters: I, a prisoner for the Lord, urge you to live in a manner worthy of the call you have received, with all humility and gentleness, with patience, bearing with one another through love, striving to preserve the unity of the spirit through the bond of peace: one body and one Spirit, as you were also called to the one hope of your call; one Lord, one faith, one baptism; one God and Father of all, who is over all and through all and in all.

GOSPEL *John 6:1–15*

Jesus went across the Sea of Galilee. A large crowd followed him, because they saw the signs he was performing on the sick. Jesus went up on the mountain, and there he sat down with his disciples. The Jewish feast of Passover was near. When Jesus raised his eyes and saw that a large crowd was coming to him, he said to Philip, "Where can we buy enough food for them to eat?" He said this to test him, because he himself knew what he was going to do. Philip answered him, "Two hundred days' wages worth of food would not be enough for each of them to have a little." One of his disciples, Andrew, the brother of Simon Peter, said to him, "There is a boy here who has five barley loaves and two fish; but what good are these for so many?" Jesus said, "Have the people recline." Now there was a great deal of grass in that place. So the men reclined, about five thousand in number. Then Jesus took the loaves, gave thanks, and distributed them to those who were reclining, and also as much of the fish as they wanted. When they had had their fill, he said to his disciples, "Gather the fragments left over, so that nothing will be wasted." So they collected them, and filled twelve wicker baskets with fragments from the five barley loaves that had been more than they could eat. When the people saw the sign he had done, they said, "This is truly the Prophet, the one who is to come into the world." Since Jesus knew that they were going to come and carry him off to make him king, he withdrew again to the mountain alone.

1159 SEVENTEENTH SUNDAY IN ORDINARY TIME / C

READING I *Genesis 18:20–32 / 111*

In those days, the LORD said: "The outcry against Sodom and Gomorrah is so great, and their sin so grave, that I must go down and see whether or not their actions fully correspond to the cry against them that comes to me. I mean to find out."

While Abraham's visitors walked on farther toward Sodom, the LORD remained standing before Abraham. Then Abraham drew nearer and said: "Will you sweep away the innocent with the guilty? Suppose there were fifty innocent people in the city; would you wipe out the place, rather than spare it for the sake of the fifty innocent people within it? Far be it from you to do such a thing, to make the innocent die with the guilty so that the innocent and the guilty would be treated alike! Should not the judge of all the world act with justice?" The LORD replied, "If I find fifty innocent people in the city of Sodom, I will spare the whole place for their sake." Abraham spoke up again: "See how I am presuming to speak to my Lord, though I am but dust and ashes! What if there are five less than fifty innocent people? Will you destroy the whole city because of those five?" He answered, "I will not destroy it, if I find forty-five there." But Abraham persisted, saying "What if only forty are found there?" He replied, "I will forbear doing it for the sake of the forty." Then Abraham said, "Let not my Lord grow impatient if I go on. What if only thirty are found there?" He replied, "I will forbear doing it if I can find but thirty there." Still Abraham went on, "Since I have thus dared to speak to my Lord, what if there are no more than twenty?" The LORD answered, "I will not destroy it, for the sake of the twenty." But he still persisted: "Please, let not my Lord grow angry if I speak up this last time. What if there are at least ten there?" He replied, "For the sake of those ten, I will not destroy it."

RESPONSORIAL PSALM *Psalm 138:1–2a, 2bcd–3, 6–7ab, 7c–8*

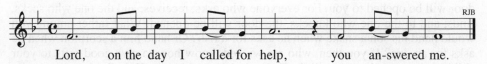

Lord, on the day I called for help, you an-swered me.

I thank you, LORD, with all my heart;
　　you have heard the words of my
　　　　mouth.
In the presence of the angels I praise you.
　　I bow down toward your holy
　　　　temple. ℟.

I give thanks to your name
　　for your merciful love and your
　　　　faithfulness.
You have exalted your name over all.
On the day I called, you answered me;
　　you increased the strength of my
　　　　soul. ℟.

The LORD is high, yet he looks on the
　　lowly,
and the haughty he knows from afar.
You give me life though I walk amid
　　affliction;
　　you stretch out your hand against
　　　　the anger of my foes. ℟.

With your right hand you save me;
　　the LORD will accomplish this for
　　　　me.
O LORD, your merciful love is eternal;
　　discard not the work of your
　　　　hands. ℟.

READING II *Colossians 2:12–14*

Brothers and sisters: You were buried with him in baptism, in which you were also raised with him through faith in the power of God, who raised him from the dead. And even when you were dead in transgressions and the uncircumcision of your flesh, he brought you to life along with him, having forgiven us all our transgressions; obliterating the bond against us, with its legal claims, which was opposed to us, he also removed it from our midst, nailing it to the cross.

GOSPEL *Luke 11:1–13*

Jesus was praying in a certain place, and when he had finished, one of his disciples said to him, "Lord, teach us to pray just as John taught his disciples." He said to them, "When you pray, say:

Father, hallowed be your name,
　　your kingdom come.
Give us each day our daily bread
and forgive us our sins
　　for we ourselves forgive everyone in debt to us,
　　and do not subject us to the final test."

And he said to them, "Suppose one of you has a friend to whom he goes at midnight and says, 'Friend, lend me three loaves of bread, for a friend of mine has arrived at my house from a journey and I have nothing to offer him,' and he says in reply from within, 'Do not bother me; the door has already been locked and my children and I are already in bed. I cannot get up to give you anything.' I tell you, if he does not get up to give the visitor the loaves because of their friendship, he will get up to give him whatever he needs because of his persistence.

"And I tell you, ask and you will receive; seek and you will find; knock and the door will be opened to you. For everyone who asks, receives; and the one who seeks, finds; and to the one who knocks, the door will be opened. What father among you would hand his son a snake when he asks for a fish? Or hand him a scorpion when he asks for an egg? If you then, who are wicked, know how to give good gifts to your children, how much more will the Father in heaven give the Holy Spirit to those who ask him?"

1160 EIGHTEENTH SUNDAY IN ORDINARY TIME / A

READING I
Isaiah 55:1–3 / 112

Thus says the LORD:
All you who are thirsty,
  come to the water!
You who have no money,
  come, receive grain and eat;
Come, without paying and without cost,
  drink wine and milk!
Why spend your money for what is
  not bread;

your wages for what fails to satisfy?
Heed me, and you shall eat well,
  you shall delight in rich fare.
Come to me heedfully,
  listen, that you may have life.
I will renew with you the everlasting
  covenant,
  the benefits assured to David.

RESPONSORIAL PSALM
Psalm 145:8–9, 15–16, 17–18

The hand of the Lord feeds us; he an-swers all our needs.

The LORD is kind and full of compassion,
  slow to anger, abounding in mercy.
How good is the LORD to all,
  compassionate to all his creatures. ℟.

The eyes of all look to you,
  and you give them their food in due
  season.

You open your hand and satisfy
  the desire of every living thing. ℟.

The LORD is just in all his ways,
  and holy in all his deeds.
The LORD is close to all who call him,
  who call on him in truth. ℟.

READING II
Romans 8:35, 37–39

Brothers and sisters: What will separate us from the love of Christ? Will anguish, or distress, or persecution, or famine, or nakedness, or peril, or the sword? No, in all these things we conquer overwhelmingly through him who loved us. For I am convinced that neither death, nor life, nor angels, nor principalities, nor present things, nor future things, nor powers, nor height, nor depth, nor any other creature will be able to separate us from the love of God in Christ Jesus our Lord.

GOSPEL
Matthew 14:13–21

When Jesus heard of the death of John the Baptist, he withdrew in a boat to a deserted place by himself. The crowds heard of this and followed him on foot from their towns. When he disembarked and saw the vast crowd, his heart was moved with pity for them, and he cured their sick. When it was evening, the disciples approached him and said, "This is a deserted place and it is already late; dismiss the crowds so that they can go to the villages and buy food for themselves." Jesus said to them, "There is no need for them to go away; give them some food yourselves." But they said to him, "Five loaves and two fish are all we have here." Then he said, "Bring them here to me," and he ordered the crowds to sit down on the grass. Taking the five loaves and the two fish, and looking up to heaven, he said the blessing, broke the loaves, and gave them to the disciples, who in turn gave them to the crowds. They all ate and were satisfied, and they picked up the fragments left over— twelve wicker baskets full. Those who ate were about five thousand men, not counting women and children.

EIGHTEENTH SUNDAY IN ORDINARY TIME / B 1161

READING I *Exodus 16:2–4, 12–15 / 113*

The whole Israelite community grumbled against Moses and Aaron. The Israelites said to them, "Would that we had died at the LORD's hand in the land of Egypt, as we sat by our fleshpots and ate our fill of bread! But you had to lead us into this desert to make the whole community die of famine!"

Then the LORD said to Moses, "I will now rain down bread from heaven for you. Each day the people are to go out and gather their daily portion; thus will I test them, to see whether they follow my instructions or not.

"I have heard the grumbling of the Israelites. Tell them: In the evening twilight you shall eat flesh, and in the morning you shall have your fill of bread, so that you may know that I, the LORD am your God."

In the evening quail came up and covered the camp. In the morning a dew lay all about the camp, and when the dew evaporated, there on the surface of the desert were fine flakes like hoarfrost on the ground. On seeing it, the Israelites asked one another, "What is this?" for they did not know what it was. But Moses told them, "This is the bread that the LORD has given you to eat."

RESPONSORIAL PSALM *Psalm 78:3 and 4bc, 23–24, 25 and 54*

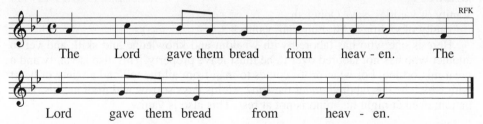

RFK

The Lord gave them bread from heav-en. The Lord gave them bread from heav-en.

The things we have heard and
   understood,
   the things our fathers have told us,
   we will tell to the next generation:
The glories of the Lord and his might,
   and the marvelous deeds he has
   done. R̰.

He commanded the clouds above,

and opened the gates of heaven.
He rained down manna to eat,
   and gave them bread from heaven. R̰.

Man ate the bread of angels.
   He sent them abundance of food.
So he brought them to his holy land,
   to the mountain his right hand
   had won. R̰.

READING II *Ephesians 4:17, 20–24*

Brothers and sisters: I declare and testify in the Lord that you must no longer live as the Gentiles do, in the futility of their minds; that is not how you learned Christ, assuming that you have heard of him and were taught in him, as truth is in Jesus, that you should put away the old self of your former way of life, corrupted through deceitful desires, and be renewed in the spirit of your minds, and put on the new self, created in God's way in righteousness and holiness of truth.

GOSPEL *John 6:24–35*

When the crowd saw that neither Jesus nor his disciples were there, they themselves got into boats and came to Capernaum looking for Jesus. And when they found him across the sea they said to him, "Rabbi, when did you get here?" Jesus answered them and said, "Amen, amen, I say to you, you are looking for me not because you saw signs but because you ate the loaves and were filled. Do not work for food that perishes but for the food that endures for eternal life, which the Son of Man will give you. For on him the Father, God, has set his seal." So they said to him, "What can we do to accomplish the works of God?" Jesus answered and said to them, "This is the work of God, that you believe in the one he sent." So they said to him, "What sign can you do, that we may see and believe in you? What can you do? Our ancestors ate manna in the desert, as it is written:

He gave them bread from heaven to eat."

So Jesus said to them, "Amen, amen, I say to you, it was not Moses who gave the bread from heaven; my Father gives you the true bread from heaven. For the bread of God is that which comes down from heaven and gives life to the world."

So they said to him, "Sir, give us this bread always." Jesus said to them, "I am the bread of life; whoever comes to me will never hunger, and whoever believes in me will never thirst."

1162 EIGHTEENTH SUNDAY IN ORDINARY TIME / C

READING I *Ecclesiastes 1:2; 2:21–23 / 114*

Vanity of vanities, says Qoheleth,

vanity of vanities! All things are vanity!

Here is one who has labored with wisdom and knowledge and skill, and yet to another who has not labored over it, he must leave property. This also is vanity and a great misfortune. For what profit comes to man from all the toil and anxiety of heart with which he has labored under the sun? All his days sorrow and grief are his occupation; even at night his mind is not at rest. This also is vanity.

RESPONSORIAL PSALM *Psalm 90:3–4, 5–6, 12–13, 14 and 17*

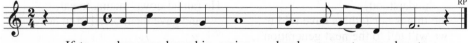

If to - day you hear his voice, hard - en not your hearts.

You turn man back to dust,
and say, "Return, O children of men."
To your eyes a thousand years

are like yesterday, come and gone,
or like a watch in the night. ℟.

You sweep them away like a dream,
 like grass which is fresh in the
  morning.
In the morning it sprouts and is fresh;
 by evening it withers and fades. ℟.

Then teach us to number our days,
 that we may gain wisdom of heart.
Turn back, O LORD! How long?

Show pity to your servants. ℟.

At dawn, fill us with your merciful love;
 we shall exult and rejoice all our days.
Let the favor of the Lord our God be
  upon us;
 give success to the work of our hands.
O give success to the work of our
  hands. ℟.

READING II   *Colossians 3:1–5, 9–11*

Brothers and sisters: If you were raised with Christ, seek what is above, where Christ
is seated at the right hand of God. Think of what is above, not of what is on earth.
For you have died, and your life is hidden with Christ in God. When Christ your life
appears, then you too will appear with him in glory.

Put to death, then, the parts of you that are earthly: immorality, impurity, passion,
evil desire, and the greed that is idolatry. Stop lying to one another, since you have
taken off the old self with its practices and have put on the new self, which is being
renewed, for knowledge, in the image of its creator. Here there is not Greek and Jew,
circumcision and uncircumcision, barbarian, Scythian, slave, free; but Christ is all
and in all.

GOSPEL   *Luke 12:13–21*

Someone in the crowd said to Jesus, "Teacher, tell my brother to share the inheritance
with me." He replied to him, "Friend, who appointed me as your judge and arbitra-
tor?" Then he said to the crowd, "Take care to guard against all greed, for though one
may be rich, one's life does not consist of possessions."

Then he told them a parable. "There was a rich man whose land produced a
bountiful harvest. He asked himself, 'What shall I do, for I do not have space to store
my harvest?' And he said, 'This is what I shall do: I shall tear down my barns and
build larger ones. There I shall store all my grain and other goods and I shall say to
myself, "Now as for you, you have so many good things stored up for many years,
rest, eat, drink, be merry!"' But God said to him, 'You fool, this night your life will
be demanded of you; and the things you have prepared, to whom will they belong?'
Thus will it be for all who store up treasure for themselves but are not rich in what
matters to God."

NINETEENTH SUNDAY IN ORDINARY TIME / A   1163

READING I   *1 Kings 19:9a, 11–13a / 115*

At the mountain of God, Horeb, Elijah came to a cave where he took shelter. Then
the LORD said to him, "Go outside and stand on the mountain before the LORD; the
LORD will be passing by." A strong and heavy wind was rending the mountains and
crushing rocks before the LORD— but the LORD was not in the wind. After the wind
there was an earthquake— but the LORD was not in the earthquake. After the earthquake there was fire— but the LORD was not in the fire. After the fire there was a tiny
whispering sound. When he heard this, Elijah hid his face in his cloak and went and
stood at the entrance of the cave.

RESPONSORIAL PSALM   *Psalm 85:9ab–10, 11–12, 13–14*

Lord, let us see your kind-ness, and grant us your sal - va-tion.

I will hear what the LORD God speaks;
   he speaks of peace for his people
      and his faithful.
His salvation is near for those who fear
      him,
   and his glory will dwell in our land. ℟.

Merciful love and faithfulness have met;
   justice and peace have kissed.

Faithfulness shall spring from the earth,
   and justice look down from
      heaven. ℟.

Also the LORD will bestow his bounty,
   and our earth shall yield its increase.
Justice will march before him,
   and guide his steps on the way. ℟.

READING II   *Romans 9:1–5*

Brothers and sisters: I speak the truth in Christ, I do not lie; my conscience joins with the Holy Spirit in bearing me witness that I have great sorrow and constant anguish in my heart. For I could wish that I myself were accursed and cut off from Christ for the sake of my own people, my kindred according to the flesh. They are Israelites; theirs the adoption, the glory, the covenants, the giving of the law, the worship, and the promises; theirs the patriarchs, and from them, according to the flesh, is the Christ, who is over all, God blessed forever. Amen.

GOSPEL   *Matthew 14:22–33*

After he had fed the people, Jesus made the disciples get into a boat and precede him to the other side, while he dismissed the crowds. After doing so, he went up on the mountain by himself to pray. When it was evening he was there alone. Meanwhile the boat, already a few miles offshore, was being tossed about by the waves, for the wind was against it. During the fourth watch of the night, he came toward them walking on the sea. When the disciples saw him walking on the sea they were terrified. "It is a ghost," they said, and they cried out in fear. At once Jesus spoke to them, "Take courage, it is I; do not be afraid." Peter said to him in reply, "Lord, if it is you, command me to come to you on the water." He said, "Come." Peter got out of the boat and began to walk on the water toward Jesus. But when he saw how strong the wind was he became frightened; and, beginning to sink, he cried out, "Lord, save me!" Immediately Jesus stretched out his hand and caught Peter, and said to him, "O you of little faith, why did you doubt?" After they got into the boat, the wind died down. Those who were in the boat did him homage, saying, "Truly, you are the Son of God."

1164   NINETEENTH SUNDAY IN ORDINARY TIME / B

READING I   *1 Kings 19:4–8 / 116*

Elijah went a day's journey into the desert, until he came to a broom tree and sat beneath it. He prayed for death, saying: "This is enough, O LORD! Take my life, for I am no better than my fathers." He lay down and fell asleep under the broom tree, but then an angel touched him and ordered him to get up and eat. Elijah looked and there at his head was a hearth cake and a jug of water. After he ate and drank, he lay down again, but the angel of the LORD came back a second time, touched him, and ordered, "Get up and eat, else the journey will be too long for you!" He got up, ate, and drank; then strengthened by that food, he walked forty days and forty nights to the mountain of God, Horeb.

RESPONSORIAL PSALM
Psalm 34:2–3, 4–5, 6–7, 8–9

Taste and see the good - ness of the Lord.

I will bless the LORD at all times;
  praise of him is always in my mouth.
In the LORD my soul shall make its boast;
  the humble shall hear and be glad. ℟.

Glorify the LORD with me;
  together let us praise his name.
I sought the LORD, and he answered me;
  from all my terrors he set me free. ℟.

Look toward him and be radiant;
  let your faces not be abashed.

This lowly one called; the LORD heard,
  and rescued him from all his
  distress. ℟.

The angel of the LORD is encamped
  around those who fear him,
  to rescue them.
Taste and see that the LORD is good.
  Blessed the man who seeks refuge
  in him. ℟.

READING II
Ephesians 4:30—5:2

Brothers and sisters: Do not grieve the Holy Spirit of God, with which you were sealed for the day of redemption. All bitterness, fury, anger, shouting, and reviling must be removed from you, along with all malice. And be kind to one another, compassionate, forgiving one another as God has forgiven you in Christ.

So be imitators of God, as beloved children, and live in love, as Christ loved us and handed himself over for us as a sacrificial offering to God for a fragrant aroma.

GOSPEL
John 6:41–51

The Jews murmured about Jesus because he said, "I am the bread that came down from heaven," and they said, "Is this not Jesus, the son of Joseph? Do we not know his father and mother? Then how can he say, 'I have come down from heaven'?" Jesus answered and said to them, "Stop murmuring among yourselves. No one can come to me unless the Father who sent me draw him, and I will raise him on the last day. It is written in the prophets:

They shall all be taught by God.

Everyone who listens to my Father and learns from him comes to me. Not that anyone has seen the Father except the one who is from God; he has seen the Father. Amen, amen, I say to you, whoever believes has eternal life. I am the bread of life. Your ancestors ate the manna in the desert, but they died; this is the bread that comes down from heaven so that one may eat it and not die. I am the living bread that came down from heaven; whoever eats this bread will live forever; and the bread that I will give is my flesh for the life of the world."

1165 NINETEENTH SUNDAY IN ORDINARY TIME / C

READING I   *Wisdom 18:6–9 / 117*

The night of the passover was known beforehand to our fathers,
    that, with sure knowledge of the oaths in which they put their faith,
    they might have courage.
Your people awaited the salvation of the just
    and the destruction of their foes.
For when you punished our adversaries,
    in this you glorified us whom you had summoned.
For in secret the holy children of the good were offering sacrifice
    and putting into effect with one accord the divine institution.

RESPONSORIAL PSALM   *Psalm 33:1 and 12, 18–19, 20 and 22*

Bless-ed   the peo-ple   the Lord has   cho-sen   to   be his own.

Ring out your joy to the LORD, O you
        just;
    for praise is fitting for the upright.
Blessed the nation whose God is
        the LORD,
    the people he has chosen as his
        heritage. ℟.

Yes, the LORD's eyes are on those
        who fear him,

who hope in his merciful love,
to rescue their souls from death,
    to keep them alive in famine. ℟.

Our soul is waiting for the LORD.
    He is our help and our shield.
May your merciful love be upon us,
    as we hope in you, O LORD. ℟.

READING II   *Hebrews 11:1–2, 8–19 or 11:1–2, 8–12*
For short form read only the part in brackets.

[Brothers and sisters: Faith is the realization of what is hoped for and evidence of things not seen. Because of it the ancients were well attested.

By faith Abraham obeyed when he was called to go out to a place that he was to receive as an inheritance; he went out, not knowing where he was to go. By faith he sojourned in the promised land as in a foreign country, dwelling in tents with Isaac and Jacob, heirs of the same promise; for he was looking forward to the city with foundations, whose architect and maker is God. By faith he received power to generate, even though he was past the normal age —and Sarah herself was sterile— for he thought that the one who had made the promise was trustworthy. So it was that there came forth from one man, himself as good as dead, descendants as numerous as the stars in the sky and as countless as the sands on the seashore.]

All these died in faith. They did not receive what had been promised but saw it and greeted it from afar and acknowledged themselves to be strangers and aliens on earth, for those who speak thus show that they are seeking a homeland. If they had been thinking of the land from which they had come, they would have had opportunity to return. But now they desire a better homeland, a heavenly one. Therefore, God is not ashamed to be called their God, for he has prepared a city for them.

By faith Abraham, when put to the test, offered up Isaac, and he who had received the promises was ready to offer his only son, of whom it was said, "Through Isaac descendants shall bear your name." He reasoned that God was able to raise even from the dead, and he received Isaac back as a symbol.

GOSPEL   *Luke 12:32–48 or 12:35–40*
For short form read only the parts in brackets.

[Jesus said to his disciples:] "Do not be afraid any longer, little flock, for your Father is pleased to give you the kingdom. Sell your belongings and give alms. Provide money bags for yourselves that do not wear out, an inexhaustible treasure in heaven that no thief can reach nor moth destroy. For where your treasure is, there also will your heart be.

["Gird your loins and light your lamps and be like servants who await their master's return from a wedding, ready to open immediately when he comes and knocks. Blessed are those servants whom the master finds vigilant on his arrival. Amen, I say to you, he will gird himself, have them recline at table, and proceed to wait on them. And should he come in the second or third watch and find them prepared in this way, blessed are those servants. Be sure of this: if the master of the house had known the hour when the thief was coming, he would not have let his house be broken into. You also must be prepared, for at an hour you do not expect, the Son of Man will come."]

Then Peter said, "Lord, is this parable meant for us or for everyone?" And the Lord replied, "Who, then, is the faithful and prudent steward whom the master will put in charge of his servants to distribute the food allowance at the proper time? Blessed is that servant whom his master on arrival finds doing so. Truly, I say to you, the master will put the servant in charge of all his property. But if that servant says to himself, 'My master is delayed in coming,' and begins to beat the menservants and the maidservants, to eat and drink and get drunk, then that servant's master will come on an unexpected day and at an unknown hour and will punish the servant severely and assign him a place with the unfaithful. That servant who knew his master's will but did not make preparations nor act in accord with his will shall be beaten severely; and the servant who was ignorant of his master's will but acted in a way deserving of a severe beating shall be beaten only lightly. Much will be required of the person entrusted with much, and still more will be demanded of the person entrusted with more."

TWENTIETH SUNDAY IN ORDINARY TIME / A   1166

READING I   *Isaiah 56:1, 6–7 / 118*

Thus says the LORD:
Observe what is right, do what is just;
   for my salvation is about to come,
   my justice, about to be revealed.

The foreigners who join themselves to
   the LORD,

ministering to him,
loving the name of the LORD,
   and becoming his servants—
all who keep the sabbath free from
   profanation
   and hold to my covenant,
them I will bring to my holy mountain

and make joyful in my house of
prayer;
their burnt offerings and sacrifices

will be acceptable on my altar,
for my house shall be called
a house of prayer for all peoples.

RESPONSORIAL PSALM *Psalm 67:2–3, 5, 6 and 8*

O God, O God, let all the na-tions praise you!

O God, be gracious and bless us
and let your face shed its light upon us.
So will your ways be known upon earth
and all nations learn your salvation. ℟.

Let the nations be glad and shout for joy,
with uprightness you rule the peoples;

you guide the nations on earth. ℟.

Let the peoples praise you, O God;
let all the peoples praise you.
May God still give us his blessing
that all the ends of the earth may
revere him. ℟.

READING II *Romans 11:13–15, 29–32*

Brothers and sisters: I am speaking to you Gentiles. Inasmuch as I am the apostle to
the Gentiles, I glory in my ministry in order to make my race jealous and thus save
some of them. For if their rejection is the reconciliation of the world, what will their
acceptance be but life from the dead?

For the gifts and the call of God are irrevocable. Just as you once disobeyed God
but have now received mercy because of their disobedience, so they have now disobeyed in order that, by virtue of the mercy shown to you, they too may now receive
mercy. For God delivered all to disobedience, that he might have mercy upon all.

GOSPEL *Matthew 15:21–28*

At that time, Jesus withdrew to the region of Tyre and Sidon. And behold, a Canaanite
woman of that district came and called out, "Have pity on me, Lord, Son of David!
My daughter is tormented by a demon." But Jesus did not say a word in answer to her.
Jesus' disciples came and asked him, "Send her away, for she keeps calling out after
us." He said in reply, "I was sent only to the lost sheep of the house of Israel." But the
woman came and did Jesus homage, saying, "Lord, help me." He said in reply, "It is
not right to take the food of the children and throw it to the dogs." She said, "Please,
Lord, for even the dogs eat the scraps that fall from the table of their masters." Then
Jesus said to her in reply, "O woman, great is your faith! Let it be done for you as you
wish." And the woman's daughter was healed from that hour.

1167 TWENTIETH SUNDAY IN ORDINARY TIME / B

READING I *Proverbs 9:1–6 / 119*

Wisdom has built her house,
she has set up her seven columns;
she has dressed her meat, mixed her wine,
yes, she has spread her table.

She has sent out her maidens; she calls
from the heights out over the city:
"Let whoever is simple turn in here;

to the one who lacks understanding,
she says,
Come, eat of my food,
and drink of the wine I have mixed!

Forsake foolishness that you may live;
advance in the way of
understanding."

RESPONSORIAL PSALM *Psalm 34:2–3, 4–5, 6–7*

Taste and see the good-ness of the Lord.

I will bless the LORD at all times;
praise of him is always in my mouth.
In the LORD my soul shall make its boast;
the humble shall hear and be glad. ℟.

Glorify the LORD with me;
together let us praise his name.
I sought the LORD, and he answered me;

from all my terrors he set me free. ℟.

Look toward him and be radiant;
let your faces not be abashed.
This lowly one called; the LORD heard,
and rescued him from all his
distress. ℟.

READING II *Ephesians 5:15–20*

Brothers and sisters: Watch carefully how you live, not as foolish persons but as wise, making the most of the opportunity, because the days are evil. Therefore, do not continue in ignorance, but try to understand what is the will of the Lord. And do not get drunk on wine, in which lies debauchery, but be filled with the Spirit, addressing one another in psalms and hymns and spiritual songs, singing and playing to the Lord in your hearts, giving thanks always and for everything in the name of our Lord Jesus Christ to God the Father.

GOSPEL *John 6:51–58*

Jesus said to the crowds: "I am the living bread that came down from heaven; whoever eats this bread will live forever; and the bread that I will give is my flesh for the life of the world."

The Jews quarreled among themselves, saying, "How can this man give us his flesh to eat?" Jesus said to them, "Amen, amen, I say to you, unless you eat the flesh of the Son of Man and drink his blood, you do not have life within you. Whoever eats my flesh and drinks my blood has eternal life, and I will raise him on the last day. For my flesh is true food, and my blood is true drink. Whoever eats my flesh and drinks my blood remains in me and I in him. Just as the living Father sent me and I have life because of the Father, so also the one who feeds on me will have life because of me. This is the bread that came down from heaven. Unlike your ancestors who ate and still died, whoever eats this bread will live forever."

TWENTIETH SUNDAY IN ORDINARY TIME / C 1168

READING I *Jeremiah 38:4–6, 8–10 / 120*

In those days, the princes said to the king: "Jeremiah ought to be put to death; he is demoralizing the soldiers who are left in this city, and all the people, by speaking such

things to them; he is not interested in the welfare of our people, but in their ruin."
King Zedekiah answered: "He is in your power"; for the king could do nothing with
them. And so they took Jeremiah and threw him into the cistern of Prince Malchiah,
which was in the quarters of the guard, letting him down with ropes. There was no
water in the cistern, only mud, and Jeremiah sank into the mud.

Ebed-melech, a court official, went there from the palace and said to him: "My
lord king, these men have been at fault in all they have done to the prophet Jeremiah,
casting him into the cistern. He will die of famine on the spot, for there is no more
food in the city." Then the king ordered Ebed-melech the Cushite to take three men
along with him, and draw the prophet Jeremiah out of the cistern before he should die.

RESPONSORIAL PSALM
Psalm 40:2, 3, 4, 18

RJB

Lord, come to my aid!

I waited, I waited for the LORD,
    and he stooped down to me;
he heard my cry. ℟.

He drew me from the deadly pit,
    from the miry clay.
He set my feet upon a rock,
    made my footsteps firm. ℟.

He put a new song into my mouth,
    praise of our God.
Many shall see and fear
    and shall trust in the LORD. ℟.

Wretched and poor though I am,
    the Lord is mindful of me.
You are my rescuer, my help;
    O my God, do not delay. ℟.

READING II
Hebrews 12:1–4

Brothers and sisters: Since we are surrounded by so great a cloud of witnesses, let us
rid ourselves of every burden and sin that clings to us and persevere in running the
race that lies before us while keeping our eyes fixed on Jesus, the leader and perfecter
of faith. For the sake of the joy that lay before him he endured the cross, despising
its shame, and has taken his seat at the right of the throne of God. Consider how he
endured such opposition from sinners, in order that you may not grow weary and lose
heart. In your struggle against sin you have not yet resisted to the point of shedding
blood.

GOSPEL
Luke 12:49–53

Jesus said to his disciples: "I have come to set the earth on fire, and how I wish it were
already blazing! There is a baptism with which I must be baptized, and how great is
my anguish until it is accomplished! Do you think that I have come to establish peace
on the earth? No, I tell you, but rather division. From now on a household of five will
be divided, three against two and two against three; a father will be divided against
his son and a son against his father, a mother against her daughter and a daughter
against her mother, a mother-in-law against her daughter-in-law and a daughter-in-
law against her mother-in-law."

TWENTY-FIRST SUNDAY IN ORDINARY TIME / A   1169

READING I
Isaiah 22:19–23 / 121

Thus says the LORD to Shebna, master of the palace:
"I will thrust you from your office
  and pull you down from your station.
On that day I will summon my servant
  Eliakim, son of Hilkiah;
I will clothe him with your robe,
  and gird him with your sash,
  and give over to him your authority.

He shall be a father to the inhabitants of Jerusalem,
  and to the house of Judah.
I will place the key of the House of David on Eliakim's shoulder;
  when he opens, no one shall shut,
  when he shuts, no one shall open.
I will fix him like a peg in a sure spot,
  to be a place of honor for his family."

RESPONSORIAL PSALM
Psalm 138:1–2a, 2bc and 3, 6 and 8bc

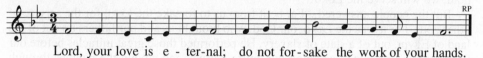

Lord, your love is e-ter-nal; do not for-sake the work of your hands.

I thank you, LORD, with all my heart;
  you have heard the words of my mouth.
In the presence of the angels I praise you.
  I bow down toward your holy temple. ℟.

I give thanks to your name
  for your merciful love and your faithfulness.

On the day I called, you answered me;
  you increased the strength of my soul. ℟.

The LORD is high, yet he looks on the lowly,
  and the haughty he knows from afar.
O LORD, your merciful love is eternal;
  discard not the work of your hands. ℟.

READING II
Romans 11:33–36

Oh, the depth of the riches and wisdom and knowledge of God! How inscrutable are his judgments and how unsearchable his ways!
> *For who has known the mind of the Lord*
> *or who has been his counselor?*
> *Or who has given the Lord anything*
> *that he may be repaid?*

For from him and through him and for him are all things. To him be glory forever. Amen.

GOSPEL
Matthew 16:13–20

Jesus went into the region of Caesarea Philippi and he asked his disciples, "Who do people say that the Son of Man is?" They replied, "Some say John the Baptist, others Elijah, still others Jeremiah or one of the prophets." He said to them, "But who do you say that I am?" Simon Peter said in reply, "You are the Christ, the Son of the living God." Jesus said to him in reply, "Blessed are you, Simon son of Jonah. For flesh and blood has not revealed this to you, but my heavenly Father. And so I say to you, you are Peter, and upon this rock I will build my church, and the gates of the netherworld shall not prevail against it. I will give you the keys to the kingdom of heaven. Whatever you bind on earth shall be bound in heaven; and whatever you loose on earth shall be loosed in heaven." Then he strictly ordered his disciples to tell no one that he was the Christ.

1170 TWENTY-FIRST SUNDAY IN ORDINARY TIME / B

READING I   *Joshua 24:1–2a, 15–17, 18b / 122*

Joshua gathered together all the tribes of Israel at Shechem, summoning their elders, their leaders, their judges, and their officers. When they stood in ranks before God, Joshua addressed all the people: "If it does not please you to serve the LORD, decide today whom you will serve, the gods your fathers served beyond the River or the gods of the Amorites in whose country you are now dwelling. As for me and my household, we will serve the LORD."

But the people answered, "Far be it from us to forsake the LORD for the service of other gods. For it was the LORD, our God, who brought us and our fathers up out of the land of Egypt, out of a state of slavery. He performed those great miracles before our very eyes and protected us along our entire journey and among the peoples through whom we passed. Therefore we also will serve the LORD, for he is our God."

RESPONSORIAL PSALM   *Psalm 34:2–3, 16–17, 18–19, 20–21*

Taste and see the good-ness of the Lord.

I will bless the LORD at all times;
   praise of him is always in my mouth.
In the LORD my soul shall make its boast;
   the humble shall hear and be glad. ℟.

The LORD turns his eyes to the just,
   and his ears are open to their cry.
The LORD turns his face against the
      wicked
   to destroy their remembrance from
      the earth. ℟.

When the just cry out, the LORD hears,

and rescues them in all their distress.
The LORD is close to the
      brokenhearted;
   those whose spirit is crushed he will
      save. ℟.

Many are the trials of the just man,
   but from them all the LORD will
      rescue him.
He will keep guard over all his bones;
   not one of his bones shall be
      broken. ℟.

READING II   *Ephesians 5:21–32 or 5:2a, 25–32*
For long form, omit the phrase in double brackets; for short form read only the parts in brackets.

[Brothers and sisters:] [[Live in love, as Christ loved us.]] Be subordinate to one another out of reverence for Christ. Wives should be subordinate to their husbands as to the Lord. For the husband is head of his wife just as Christ is head of the church, he himself the savior of the body. As the church is subordinate to Christ, so wives should be subordinate to their husbands in everything. [Husbands, love your wives, even as Christ loved the church and handed himself over for her to sanctify her, cleansing her by the bath of water with the word, that he might present to himself the church in splendor, without spot or wrinkle or any such thing, that she might be holy and without blemish. So also husbands should love their wives as their own bodies. He who loves his wife loves himself. For no one hates his own flesh but rather nourishes and cherishes it, even as Christ does the church, because we are members of his body.

For this reason a man shall leave his father and his mother
and be joined to his wife,
and the two shall become one flesh.

This is a great mystery, but I speak in reference to Christ and the church.]

GOSPEL *John 6:60–69*

Many of Jesus' disciples who were listening said, "This saying is hard; who can accept it?" Since Jesus knew that his disciples were murmuring about this, he said to them, "Does this shock you? What if you were to see the Son of Man ascending to where he was before? It is the spirit that gives life, while the flesh is of no avail. The words I have spoken to you are Spirit and life. But there are some of you who do not believe." Jesus knew from the beginning the ones who would not believe and the one who would betray him. And he said, "For this reason I have told you that no one can come to me unless it is granted him by my Father."

As a result of this, many of his disciples returned to their former way of life and no longer accompanied him. Jesus then said to the Twelve, "Do you also want to leave?" Simon Peter answered him, "Master, to whom shall we go? You have the words of eternal life. We have come to believe and are convinced that you are the Holy One of God."

TWENTY-FIRST SUNDAY IN ORDINARY TIME / C — 1171

READING I *Isaiah 66:18–21 / 123*

Thus says the LORD: I know their works and their thoughts, and I come to gather nations of every language; they shall come and see my glory. I will set a sign among them; from them I will send fugitives to the nations: to Tarshish, Put and Lud, Mosoch, Tubal and Javan, to the distant coastlands that have never heard of my fame, or seen my glory; and they shall proclaim my glory among the nations. They shall bring all your brothers and sisters from all the nations as an offering to the LORD, on horses and in chariots, in carts, upon mules and dromedaries, to Jerusalem, my holy mountain, says the LORD, just as the Israelites bring their offering to the house of the LORD in clean vessels. Some of these I will take as priests and Levites, says the LORD.

RESPONSORIAL PSALM *Psalm 117:1, 2*

Or: Alleluia.

Go out to all the world, and tell the Good News.

O praise the LORD, all you nations;
acclaim him, all you peoples! ℟.

For his merciful love has prevailed
over us;
and the LORD's faithfulness
endures forever. ℟.

READING II *Hebrews 12:5–7, 11–13*

Brothers and sisters, You have forgotten the exhortation addressed to you as children:
"My son, do not disdain the discipline of the Lord
or lose heart when reproved by him;
for whom the Lord loves, he disciplines;
he scourges every son he acknowledges."
Endure your trials as "discipline"; God treats you as sons. For what "son" is there whom his father does not discipline? At the time, all discipline seems a cause not for joy but for pain, yet later it brings the peaceful fruit of righteousness to those who are trained by it.

So strengthen your drooping hands and your weak knees. Make straight paths for your feet, that what is lame may not be disjointed but healed.

GOSPEL *Luke 13:22–30*

Jesus passed through towns and villages, teaching as he went and making his way to Jerusalem. Someone asked him, "Lord, will only a few people be saved?" He answered them, "Strive to enter through the narrow gate, for many, I tell you, will attempt to enter but will not be strong enough. After the master of the house has arisen and locked the door, then will you stand outside knocking and saying, 'Lord, open the door for us.' He will say to you in reply, 'I do not know where you are from.' And you will say, 'We ate and drank in your company and you taught in our streets.' Then he will say to you, 'I do not know where you are from. Depart from me, all you evildoers!' And there will be wailing and grinding of teeth when you see Abraham, Isaac, and Jacob and all the prophets in the kingdom of God and you yourselves cast out. And people will come from the east and the west and from the north and the south and will recline at table in the kingdom of God. For behold, some are last who will be first, and some are first who will be last."

1172   TWENTY-SECOND SUNDAY IN ORDINARY TIME / A

READING I *Jeremiah 20:7–9 / 124*

You duped me, O LORD, and I let
myself be duped;
you were too strong for me, and you
triumphed.
All the day I am an object of laughter;
everyone mocks me.

Whenever I speak, I must cry out,
violence and outrage is my message;
the word of the LORD has brought me

derision and reproach all the day.

I say to myself, I will not mention him,
I will speak in his name no more.
But then it becomes like fire burning in
my heart,
imprisoned in my bones;
I grow weary holding it in, I cannot
endure it.

RESPONSORIAL PSALM   *Psalm 63:2, 3–4, 5–6, 8–9*

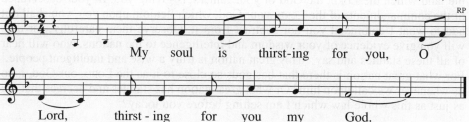

My soul is thirst-ing for you, O Lord, thirst-ing for you my God.

O God, you are my God; at dawn I
    seek you;
    for you my soul is thirsting.
For you my flesh is pining,
    like a dry, weary land without
    water. ℟.

I have come before you in the sanctuary,
    to behold your strength and your
    glory.
Your loving mercy is better than life;
    my lips will speak your praise. ℟.

I will bless you all my life;
    in your name I will lift up my hands.
My soul shall be filled as with a
    banquet;
    with joyful lips, my mouth shall
    praise you. ℟.

For you have been my strength;
    in the shadow of your wings I
    rejoice.
My soul clings fast to you;
    your right hand upholds me. ℟.

READING II   *Romans 12:1–2*

I urge you, brothers and sisters, by the mercies of God, to offer your bodies as a living sacrifice, holy and pleasing to God, your spiritual worship. Do not conform yourselves to this age but be transformed by the renewal of your mind, that you may discern what is the will of God, what is good and pleasing and perfect.

GOSPEL   *Matthew 16:21–27*

Jesus began to show his disciples that he must go to Jerusalem and suffer greatly from the elders, the chief priests, and the scribes, and be killed and on the third day be raised. Then Peter took Jesus aside and began to rebuke him, "God forbid, Lord! No such thing shall ever happen to you." He turned and said to Peter, "Get behind me, Satan! You are an obstacle to me. You are thinking not as God does, but as human beings do."

Then Jesus said to his disciples, "Whoever wishes to come after me must deny himself, take up his cross, and follow me. For whoever wishes to save his life will lose it, but whoever loses his life for my sake will find it. What profit would there be for one to gain the whole world and forfeit his life? Or what can one give in exchange for his life? For the Son of Man will come with his angels in his Father's glory, and then he will repay all according to his conduct."

TWENTY-SECOND SUNDAY IN ORDINARY TIME / B   1173

READING I   *Deuteronomy 4:1–2, 6–8 / 125*

Moses said to the people: "Now, Israel, hear the statutes and decrees which I am teaching you to observe, that you may live, and may enter in and take possession of the land which the LORD, the God of your fathers, is giving you. In your observance of the commandments of the LORD, your God, which I enjoin upon you, you shall not add to what I command you nor subtract from it. Observe them carefully, for thus will you give evidence of your wisdom and intelligence to the nations, who will hear of all these statutes and say, 'This great nation is truly a wise and intelligent people.' For what great nation is there that has gods so close to it as the LORD, our God, is to us whenever we call upon him? Or what great nation has statutes and decrees that are as just as this whole law which I am setting before you today?"

RESPONSORIAL PSALM   *Psalm 15:2–3a, 3bc–4ab, 5*

The one who does jus-tice will live in the pres-ence of the Lord.

Whoever walks without fault;
  who does what is just,
and speaks the truth from his heart;
  whoever does not slander with his
    tongue. ℟.

Who does no wrong to a neighbor,
  who casts no slur on a friend,
who looks with scorn on the wicked,

but honors those who fear the
  LORD. ℟.

Who lends no money at interest,
  and accepts no bribes against the
    innocent.
Such a one shall never be shaken. ℟.

READING II   *James 1:17–18, 21b–22, 27*
Dearest brothers and sisters: All good giving and every perfect gift is from above, coming down from the Father of lights, with whom there is no alteration or shadow caused by change. He willed to give us birth by the word of truth that we may be a kind of firstfruits of his creatures.

Humbly welcome the word that has been planted in you and is able to save your souls.

Be doers of the word and not hearers only, deluding yourselves.

Religion that is pure and undefiled before God and the Father is this: to care for orphans and widows in their affliction and to keep oneself unstained by the world.

GOSPEL   *Mark 7:1–8, 14–15, 21–23*
When the Pharisees with some scribes who had come from Jerusalem gathered around Jesus, they observed that some of his disciples ate their meals with unclean, that is, unwashed, hands. —For the Pharisees and, in fact, all Jews, do not eat without carefully washing their hands, keeping the tradition of the elders. And on coming from the marketplace they do not eat without purifying themselves. And there are many other things that they have traditionally observed, the purification of cups and jugs and kettles and beds.— So the Pharisees and scribes questioned him, "Why do your disciples not follow the tradition of the elders but instead eat a meal with unclean hands?" He responded, "Well did Isaiah prophesy about you hypocrites, as it is written:

This people honors me with their lips,
  but their hearts are far from me;

in vain do they worship me,
   teaching as doctrines human precepts.
You disregard God's commandment but cling to human tradition."

He summoned the crowd again and said to them, "Hear me, all of you, and understand. Nothing that enters one from outside can defile that person; but the things that come out from within are what defile.

"From within people, from their hearts, come evil thoughts, unchastity, theft, murder, adultery, greed, malice, deceit, licentiousness, envy, blasphemy, arrogance, folly. All these evils come from within and they defile."

TWENTY-SECOND SUNDAY IN ORDINARY TIME / C   1174

READING I   *Sirach 3:17–18, 20, 28–29 / 126*

My child, conduct your affairs with
   humility,
  and you will be loved more than a
   giver of gifts.
Humble yourself the more, the greater
   you are,
  and you will find favor with God.
What is too sublime for you, seek not,

into things beyond your strength
  search not.
The mind of a sage appreciates proverbs,
  and an attentive ear is the joy of the
  wise.
Water quenches a flaming fire,
  and alms atone for sins.

RESPONSORIAL PSALM   *Psalm 68:4–5ac, 6–7ab, 10–11*

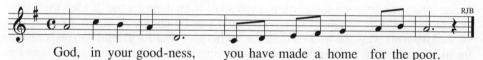

God, in your good-ness, you have made a home for the poor.

The just shall rejoice at the presence
  of God;
  they shall exult with glad rejoicing.
O sing to God; make music to his name.
  The LORD is his name. ℟.

Father of orphans, defender of widows:
  such is God in his holy place.
God gives the desolate a home to dwell in;
  he leads the prisoners forth into

prosperity. ℟.

You poured down, O God, a generous
  rain;
  when your people languished, you
  restored their inheritance.
It was there that your flock began to
  dwell.
In your goodness, O God, you
  provided for the poor. ℟.

READING II   *Hebrews 12:18–19, 22–24a*

Brothers and sisters: You have not approached that which could be touched and a blazing fire and gloomy darkness and storm and a trumpet blast and a voice speaking words such that those who heard begged that no message be further addressed to them. No, you have approached Mount Zion and the city of the living God, the heavenly Jerusalem, and countless angels in festal gathering, and the assembly of the firstborn enrolled in heaven, and God the judge of all, and the spirits of the just made perfect, and Jesus, the mediator of a new covenant, and the sprinkled blood that speaks more eloquently than that of Abel.

GOSPEL *Luke 14:1, 7–14*

On a sabbath Jesus went to dine at the home of one of the leading Pharisees, and the people there were observing him carefully.

He told a parable to those who had been invited, noticing how they were choosing the places of honor at the table. "When you are invited by someone to a wedding banquet, do not recline at table in the place of honor. A more distinguished guest than you may have been invited by him, and the host who invited both of you may approach you and say, 'Give your place to this man,' and then you would proceed with embarrassment to take the lowest place. Rather, when you are invited, go and take the lowest place so that when the host comes to you he may say, 'My friend, move up to a higher position.' Then you will enjoy the esteem of your companions at the table. For everyone who exalts himself will be humbled, but the one who humbles himself will be exalted." Then he said to the host who invited him, "When you hold a lunch or a dinner, do not invite your friends or your brothers or your relatives or your wealthy neighbors, in case they may invite you back and you have repayment. Rather, when you hold a banquet, invite the poor, the crippled, the lame, the blind; blessed indeed will you be because of their inability to repay you. For you will be repaid at the resurrection of the righteous."

1175 TWENTY-THIRD SUNDAY IN ORDINARY TIME / A

READING I *Ezekiel 33:7–9 / 127*

Thus says the LORD: You, son of man, I have appointed watchman for the house of Israel; when you hear me say anything, you shall warn them for me. If I tell the wicked, "O wicked one, you shall surely die," and you do not speak out to dissuade the wicked from his way, the wicked shall die for his guilt, but I will hold you responsible for his death. But if you warn the wicked, trying to turn him from his way, and he refuses to turn from his way, he shall die for his guilt, but you shall save yourself.

RESPONSORIAL PSALM *Psalm 95:1–2, 6–7c, 7d–9*

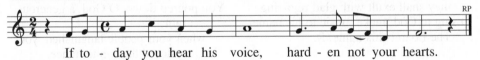

If to - day you hear his voice, hard - en not your hearts.

Come, let us ring out our joy to the LORD;
  hail the rock who saves us.
Let us come into his presence, giving
    thanks;
  let us hail him with a song of praise. ℟.

O come; let us bow and bend low.
  Let us kneel before the God who
    made us,
for he is our God and we
  the people who belong to his pasture,

the flock that is led by his hand. ℟.

O that today you would listen to his
    voice!
"Harden not your hearts as at
    Meribah,
  as on that day at Massah in the
    desert
when your forebears put me to the test;
  when they tried me, though they saw
    my work." ℟.

READING II

Romans 13:8–10

Brothers and sisters: Owe nothing to anyone, except to love one another; for the one who loves another has fulfilled the law. The commandments, "You shall not commit adultery; you shall not kill; you shall not steal; you shall not covet," and whatever other commandment there may be, are summed up in this saying, namely, "You shall love your neighbor as yourself." Love does no evil to the neighbor; hence, love is the fulfillment of the law.

GOSPEL

Matthew 18:15–20

Jesus said to his disciples: "If your brother sins against you, go and tell him his fault between you and him alone. If he listens to you, you have won over your brother. If he does not listen, take one or two others along with you, so that 'every fact may be established on the testimony of two or three witnesses.' If he refuses to listen to them, tell the church. If he refuses to listen even to the church, then treat him as you would a Gentile or a tax collector. Amen, I say to you, whatever you bind on earth shall be bound in heaven, and whatever you loose on earth shall be loosed in heaven. Again, amen, I say to you, if two of you agree on earth about anything for which they are to pray, it shall be granted to them by my heavenly Father. For where two or three are gathered together in my name, there am I in the midst of them."

TWENTY-THIRD SUNDAY IN ORDINARY TIME / B   1176

READING I

Isaiah 35:4–7a / 128

Thus says the LORD:
  Say to those whose hearts are
      frightened:
    Be strong, fear not!
  Here is your God,
      he comes with vindication;
  with divine recompense
      he comes to save you.
  Then will the eyes of the blind be
      opened,

the ears of the deaf be cleared;
then will the lame leap like a stag,
  then the tongue of the mute will
      sing.
Streams will burst forth in the desert,
  and rivers in the steppe.
The burning sands will become
      pools,
  and the thirsty ground, springs of
      water.

RESPONSORIAL PSALM

Psalm 146:6c–7, 8–9a, 9bc–10

Or: Alleluia.

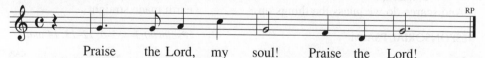

Praise the Lord, my soul! Praise the Lord!

It is the LORD who preserves fidelity
      forever,
  who does justice to those who are
      oppressed.
It is he who gives bread to the hungry,
  the LORD who sets prisoners free. ℟.

The LORD who opens the eyes of the
      blind,
  the LORD who raises up those who

are bowed down.
It is the LORD who loves the just,
  the LORD who protects the stranger. ℟.

The LORD upholds the orphan and the
      widow,
  but thwarts the path of the wicked.
The LORD will reign forever,
  the God of Sion from age to age.
      Alleluia. ℟.

READING II   *James 2:1–5*

My brothers and sisters, show no partiality as you adhere to the faith in our glorious Lord Jesus Christ. For if a man with gold rings and fine clothes comes into your assembly, and a poor person in shabby clothes also comes in, and you pay attention to the one wearing the fine clothes and say, "Sit here, please," while you say to the poor one, "Stand there," or "Sit at my feet," have you not made distinctions among yourselves and become judges with evil designs?

Listen, my beloved brothers and sisters. Did not God choose those who are poor in the world to be rich in faith and heirs of the kingdom that he promised to those who love him?

GOSPEL   *Mark 7:31–37*

Again Jesus left the district of Tyre and went by way of Sidon to the Sea of Galilee, into the district of the Decapolis. And people brought to him a deaf man who had a speech impediment and begged him to lay his hand on him. He took him off by himself away from the crowd. He put his finger into the man's ears and, spitting, touched his tongue; then he looked up to heaven and groaned, and said to him, "*Ephphatha!*" —that is, "Be opened!"— And immediately the man's ears were opened, his speech impediment was removed, and he spoke plainly. He ordered them not to tell anyone. But the more he ordered them not to, the more they proclaimed it. They were exceedingly astonished and they said, "He has done all things well. He makes the deaf hear and the mute speak."

1177 TWENTY-THIRD SUNDAY IN ORDINARY TIME / C

READING I   *Wisdom 9:13–18b / 129*

Who can know God's counsel,
   or who can conceive what the
     LORD intends?
For the deliberations of mortals are timid,
   and unsure are our plans.
For the corruptible body burdens the soul
   and the earthen shelter weighs
     down the mind that has many
      concerns.
And scarce do we guess the things on
earth,
and what is within our grasp we
   find with difficulty;
but when things are in heaven, who
   can search them out?
Or who ever knew your counsel, except
   you had given wisdom
and sent your holy spirit from on high?
And thus were the paths of those on
   earth made straight.

RESPONSORIAL PSALM   *Psalm 90:3–4, 5–6, 12–13, 14 and 17*

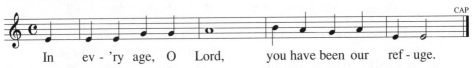

In ev-'ry age, O Lord, you have been our ref-uge.

You turn man back to dust,
   and say, "Return, O children of men."
To your eyes a thousand years
   are like yesterday, come and gone,
   or like a watch in the night. ℟.

You sweep them away like a dream,
   like grass which is fresh in the
    morning.
In the morning it sprouts and is fresh;
   by evening it withers and fades. ℟.

Then teach us to number our days,
  that we may gain wisdom of heart.
Turn back, O LORD! How long?
  Show pity to your servants. ℟.

At dawn, fill us with your merciful love;
  we shall exult and rejoice all our days.

Let the favor of the Lord our God be
  upon us;
give success to the work of our
  hands.
O give success to the work of our
  hands. ℟.

READING II
Philemon 9–10, 12–17

I, Paul, an old man, and now also a prisoner for Christ Jesus, urge you on behalf of my child Onesimus, whose father I have become in my imprisonment; I am sending him, that is, my own heart, back to you. I should have liked to retain him for myself, so that he might serve me on your behalf in my imprisonment for the gospel, but I did not want to do anything without your consent, so that the good you do might not be forced but voluntary. Perhaps this is why he was away from you for a while, that you might have him back forever, no longer as a slave but more than a slave, a brother, beloved especially to me, but even more so to you, as a man and in the Lord. So if you regard me as a partner, welcome him as you would me.

GOSPEL
Luke 14:25–33

Great crowds were traveling with Jesus, and he turned and addressed them, "If anyone comes to me without hating his father and mother, wife and children, brothers and sisters, and even his own life, he cannot be my disciple. Whoever does not carry his own cross and come after me cannot be my disciple. Which of you wishing to construct a tower does not first sit down and calculate the cost to see if there is enough for its completion? Otherwise, after laying the foundation and finding himself unable to finish the work the onlookers should laugh at him and say, 'This one began to build but did not have the resources to finish.' Or what king marching into battle would not first sit down and decide whether with ten thousand troops he can successfully oppose another king advancing upon him with twenty thousand troops? But if not, while he is still far away, he will send a delegation to ask for peace terms. In the same way, anyone of you who does not renounce all his possessions cannot be my disciple."

TWENTY-FOURTH SUNDAY IN ORDINARY TIME / A 1178

READING I
Sirach 27:30—28:7 / 130

Wrath and anger are hateful things,
  yet the sinner hugs them tight.
The vengeful will suffer the LORD's
    vengeance,
  for he remembers their sins in detail.
Forgive your neighbor's injustice;
  then when you pray, your own sins
    will be forgiven.
Could anyone nourish anger against
    another
  and expect healing from the LORD?
Could anyone refuse mercy to another

like himself,
  can he seek pardon for his own sins?
If one who is but flesh cherishes wrath,
  who will forgive his sins?
Remember your last days, set enmity
    aside;
  remember death and decay, and cease
    from sin!
Think of the commandments, hate not
    your neighbor;
  remember the Most High's covenant,
    and overlook faults.

RESPONSORIAL PSALM   *Psalm 103:1–2, 3–4, 9–10, 11–12*

The Lord is kind and mer-ci-ful, slow to an-ger, and rich in com - pas-sion.

Bless the LORD, O my soul,
    and all within me, his holy name.
Bless the LORD, O my soul,
    and never forget all his benefits. ℟.

It is the Lord who forgives all your sins,
    who heals every one of your ills,
who redeems your life from the grave,
    who crowns you with mercy and
        compassion. ℟.

He will not always find fault;
    nor persist in his anger forever.

He does not treat us according to our
    sins,
nor repay us according to our
    faults. ℟.

For as the heavens are high above the
    earth,
    so strong his mercy for those who
        fear him.
As far as the east is from the west,
    so far from us does he remove our
        transgressions. ℟.

READING II   *Romans 14:7–9*

Brothers and sisters: None of us lives for oneself, and no one dies for oneself. For if we live, we live for the Lord, and if we die, we die for the Lord; so then, whether we live or die, we are the Lord's. For this is why Christ died and came to life, that he might be Lord of both the dead and the living.

GOSPEL   *Matthew 18:21–35*

Peter approached Jesus and asked him, "Lord, if my brother sins against me, how often must I forgive? As many as seven times?" Jesus answered, "I say to you, not seven times but seventy-seven times. That is why the kingdom of heaven may be likened to a king who decided to settle accounts with his servants. When he began the accounting, a debtor was brought before him who owed him a huge amount. Since he had no way of paying it back, his master ordered him to be sold, along with his wife, his children, and all his property, in payment of the debt. At that, the servant fell down, did him homage, and said, 'Be patient with me, and I will pay you back in full.' Moved with compassion the master of that servant let him go and forgave him the loan. When that servant had left, he found one of his fellow servants who owed him a much smaller amount. He seized him and started to choke him, demanding, 'Pay back what you owe.' Falling to his knees, his fellow servant begged him, 'Be patient with me, and I will pay you back.' But he refused. Instead, he had the fellow servant put in prison until he paid back the debt. Now when his fellow servants saw what had happened, they were deeply disturbed, and went to their master and reported the whole affair. His master summoned him and said to him, 'You wicked servant! I forgave you your entire debt because you begged me to. Should you not have had pity on your fellow servant, as I had pity on you?' Then in anger his master handed him over to the torturers until he should pay back the whole debt. So will my heavenly Father do to you, unless each of you forgives your brother from your heart."

TWENTY-FOURTH SUNDAY IN ORDINARY TIME / B   1179

READING I
Isaiah 50:5–9a / 131

The Lord GOD opens my ear that I
    may hear;
and I have not rebelled,
    have not turned back.
I gave my back to those who beat me,
    my cheeks to those who plucked my
      beard;
my face I did not shield
    from buffets and spitting.

The Lord GOD is my help,

therefore I am not disgraced;
I have set my face like flint,
    knowing that I shall not be put to
      shame.
He is near who upholds my right;
    if anyone wishes to oppose me,
    let us appear together.
Who disputes my right?
    Let that man confront me.
See, the Lord GOD is my help;
    who will prove me wrong?

RESPONSORIAL PSALM
Psalm 116:1–2, 3–4, 5–6, 8–9

Or: Alleluia.

I will walk be-fore the Lord in the land of the liv-ing.

I love the LORD, for he has heard
    my voice, my appeal;
for he has turned his ear to me
    whenever I call. ℟.

They surrounded me, the snares of death;
    the anguish of the grave has found me;
    anguish and sorrow I found.
I called on the name of the LORD:
    "Deliver my soul, O LORD!" ℟.

How gracious is the LORD, and just;
    our God has compassion.
The LORD protects the simple;
    I was brought low, and he saved
      me. ℟.

He has kept my soul from death,
    my eyes from tears, and my feet
      from stumbling.
I will walk in the presence of the LORD
    in the land of the living. ℟.

READING II
James 2:14–18

What good is it, my brothers and sisters, if someone says he has faith but does not have works? Can that faith save him? If a brother or sister has nothing to wear and has no food for the day, and one of you says to them, "Go in peace, keep warm, and eat well," but you do not give them the necessities of the body, what good is it? So also faith of itself, if it does not have works, is dead.

Indeed someone might say, "You have faith and I have works." Demonstrate your faith to me without works, and I will demonstrate my faith to you from my works.

GOSPEL *Mark 8:27–35*

Jesus and his disciples set out for the villages of Caesarea Philippi. Along the way he asked his disciples, "Who do people say that I am?" They said in reply, "John the Baptist, others Elijah, still others one of the prophets." And he asked them, "But who do you say that I am?" Peter said to him in reply, "You are the Christ." Then he warned them not to tell anyone about him.

He began to teach them that the Son of Man must suffer greatly and be rejected by the elders, the chief priests, and the scribes, and be killed, and rise after three days. He spoke this openly. Then Peter took him aside and began to rebuke him. At this he turned around and, looking at his disciples, rebuked Peter and said, "Get behind me, Satan. You are thinking not as God does, but as human beings do."

He summoned the crowd with his disciples and said to them, "Whoever wishes to come after me must deny himself, take up his cross, and follow me. For whoever wishes to save his life will lose it, but whoever loses his life for my sake and that of the gospel will save it."

1180 TWENTY-FOURTH SUNDAY IN ORDINARY TIME / C

READING I *Exodus 32:7–11, 13–14 / 132*

The Lord said to Moses, "Go down at once to your people, whom you brought out of the land of Egypt, for they have become depraved. They have soon turned aside from the way I pointed out to them, making for themselves a molten calf and worshiping it, sacrificing to it and crying out, 'This is your God, O Israel, who brought you out of the land of Egypt!' I see how stiff-necked this people is," continued the Lord to Moses. "Let me alone, then, that my wrath may blaze up against them to consume them. Then I will make of you a great nation."

But Moses implored the Lord, his God, saying, "Why, O Lord, should your wrath blaze up against your own people, whom you brought out of the land of Egypt with such great power and with so strong a hand? Remember your servants Abraham, Isaac, and Israel, and how you swore to them by your own self, saying, 'I will make your descendants as numerous as the stars in the sky; and all this land that I promised, I will give your descendants as their perpetual heritage.'" So the Lord relented in the punishment he had threatened to inflict on his people.

RESPONSORIAL PSALM *Psalm 51:3–4, 12–13, 17 and 19*

I will rise and go to my fa - ther.

Have mercy on me, O God,
　according to your merciful love;
according to your great compassion,
　blot out my transgressions.
Wash me completely from my iniquity,
　and cleanse me from my sin. ℟.

Create a pure heart for me, O God;
　renew a steadfast spirit within me.
Do not cast me away from your
　presence;
　take not your holy spirit from me. ℟.

O Lord, open my lips
and my mouth shall proclaim your
praise.

My sacrifice to God, a broken spirit:
a broken and humbled heart,
O God, you will not spurn. ℟.

READING II
1 Timothy 1:12–17

Beloved: I am grateful to him who has strengthened me, Christ Jesus our Lord, because he considered me trustworthy in appointing me to the ministry. I was once a blasphemer and a persecutor and arrogant, but I have been mercifully treated because I acted out of ignorance in my unbelief. Indeed, the grace of our Lord has been abundant, along with the faith and love that are in Christ Jesus. This saying is trustworthy and deserves full acceptance: Christ Jesus came into the world to save sinners. Of these I am the foremost. But for that reason I was mercifully treated, so that in me, as the foremost, Christ Jesus might display all his patience as an example for those who would come to believe in him for everlasting life. To the king of ages, incorruptible, invisible, the only God, honor and glory forever and ever. Amen.

GOSPEL
Luke 15:1–32 or 15:1–10

For short form read only the part in brackets.

[Tax collectors and sinners were all drawing near to listen to Jesus, but the Pharisees and scribes began to complain, saying, "This man welcomes sinners and eats with them." So to them he addressed this parable. "What man among you having a hundred sheep and losing one of them would not leave the ninety-nine in the desert and go after the lost one until he finds it? And when he does find it, he sets it on his shoulders with great joy and, upon his arrival home, he calls together his friends and neighbors and says to them, 'Rejoice with me because I have found my lost sheep.' I tell you, in just the same way there will be more joy in heaven over one sinner who repents than over ninety-nine righteous people who have no need of repentance.

"Or what woman having ten coins and losing one would not light a lamp and sweep the house, searching carefully until she finds it? And when she does find it, she calls together her friends and neighbors and says to them, 'Rejoice with me because I have found the coin that I lost.' In just the same way, I tell you, there will be rejoicing among the angels of God over one sinner who repents."]

Then he said, "A man had two sons, and the younger son said to his father, 'Father give me the share of your estate that should come to me.' So the father divided the property between them. After a few days, the younger son collected all his belongings and set off to a distant country where he squandered his inheritance on a life of dissipation. When he had freely spent everything, a severe famine struck that country, and he found himself in dire need. So he hired himself out to one of the local citizens who sent him to his farm to tend the swine. And he longed to eat his fill of the pods on which the swine fed, but nobody gave him any. Coming to his senses he thought, 'How many of my father's hired workers have more than enough food to eat, but here am I, dying from hunger. I shall get up and go to my father and I shall say to him, "Father, I have sinned against heaven and against you. I no longer deserve to be called your son; treat me as you would treat one of your hired workers."' So he got up and went back to his father. While he was still a long way off, his father caught sight of him, and was filled with compassion. He ran to his son, embraced him and kissed him. His son said to him, 'Father, I have sinned against heaven and against you; I no longer deserve to be called your son.' But his father ordered his servants, 'Quickly bring the finest robe and put it on him; put a ring on his finger and sandals on his feet. Take the fattened calf and slaughter it. Then let us celebrate with a feast, because this son of mine was dead, and has come to life again; he was lost, and has been found.' Then the celebration began. Now the older son had been out in the field and, on his way back, as he neared the house, he heard the sound of music and dancing. He called one of the servants and asked what this might mean. The servant said to him, 'Your brother has returned and your father has slaughtered the fattened calf because he has him back safe and sound.' He became angry, and when he refused to enter the house, his father came out and pleaded with him. He said to his father in reply, 'Look, all these years I served you and not once did I disobey your orders; yet you never gave me even a young goat to feast on with my friends. But when your son returns, who swallowed up your property with prostitutes, for him you slaughter the fattened calf.' He said to him, 'My son, you are here with me always; everything I have is yours. But now we must celebrate and rejoice, because your brother was dead and has come to life again; he was lost and has been found.'"

1181 TWENTY-FIFTH SUNDAY IN ORDINARY TIME / A

READING I
Isaiah 55:6–9 / 133

Seek the LORD while he may be found,
 call him while he is near.
Let the scoundrel forsake his way,
 and the wicked his thoughts;
let him turn to the LORD for mercy;
 to our God, who is generous in
 forgiving.
For my thoughts are not your thoughts,

nor are your ways my ways, says the
 LORD.
As high as the heavens are above the
 earth,
so high are my ways above your
 ways
and my thoughts above your
 thoughts.

RESPONSORIAL PSALM
Psalm 145:2–3, 8–9, 17–18

JS

The Lord is near to all who call up-on him.

I will bless you day after day,
 and praise your name forever and
 ever.
The LORD is great and highly to be
 praised;
 his greatness cannot be measured. ℟.

The LORD is kind and full of compassion,
 slow to anger, abounding in mercy.

How good is the LORD to all,
 compassionate to all his creatures. ℟.

The LORD is just in all his ways,
 and holy in all his deeds.
The LORD is close to all who call him,
 who call on him in truth. ℟.

READING II
Philippians 1:20c-24, 27a

Brothers and sisters: Christ will be magnified in my body, whether by life or by death. For to me life is Christ, and death is gain. If I go on living in the flesh, that means fruitful labor for me. And I do not know which I shall choose. I am caught between the two. I long to depart this life and be with Christ, for that is far better. Yet that I remain in the flesh is more necessary for your benefit.

Only, conduct yourselves in a way worthy of the gospel of Christ.

GOSPEL

Matthew 20:1–16a

Jesus told his disciples this parable: "The kingdom of heaven is like a landowner who went out at dawn to hire laborers for his vineyard. After agreeing with them for the usual daily wage, he sent them into his vineyard. Going out about nine o'clock, the landowner saw others standing idle in the marketplace, and he said to them, 'You too go into my vineyard, and I will give you what is just.' So they went off. And he went out again around noon, and around three o'clock, and did likewise. Going out about five o'clock, the landowner found others standing around, and said to them, 'Why do you stand here idle all day?' They answered, 'Because no one has hired us.' He said to them, 'You too go into my vineyard.' When it was evening the owner of the vineyard said to his foreman, 'Summon the laborers and give them their pay, beginning with the last and ending with the first.' When those who had started about five o'clock came, each received the usual daily wage. So when the first came, they thought that they would receive more, but each of them also got the usual wage. And on receiving it they grumbled against the landowner, saying, 'These last ones worked only one hour, and you have made them equal to us, who bore the day's burden and the heat.' He said to one of them in reply, 'My friend, I am not cheating you. Did you not agree with me for the usual daily wage? Take what is yours and go. What if I wish to give this last one the same as you? Or am I not free to do as I wish with my own money? Are you envious because I am generous?' Thus, the last will be first, and the first will be last."

TWENTY-FIFTH SUNDAY IN ORDINARY TIME / B   1182

READING I

Wisdom 2:12, 17–20 / 134

The wicked say:
> Let us beset the just one, because he is obnoxious to us;
>> he sets himself against our doings,
> reproaches us for transgressions of the law
>> and charges us with violations of our training.
> Let us see whether his words be true;
>> let us find out what will happen to him.
> For if the just one be the son of God, God will defend him
>> and deliver him from the hand of his foes.
> With revilement and torture let us put the just one to the test
>> that we may have proof of his gentleness
>> and try his patience.
> Let us condemn him to a shameful death;
>> for according to his own words, God will take care of him.

RESPONSORIAL PSALM *Psalm 54:3–4, 5, 6 and 8*

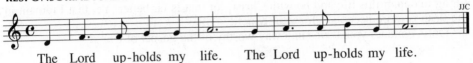

The Lord up-holds my life. The Lord up-holds my life.

O God, save me by your name;
  by your power, defend my cause.
O God, hear my prayer;
  give ear to the words of my mouth. ℟.

For the proud have risen against me,
  and the ruthless seek my life.
  They have no regard for God. ℟.

See, I have God for my help.
  The Lord sustains my soul.
I will sacrifice to you with willing
  heart,
  and praise your name, for it is
  good. ℟.

READING II *James 3:16—4:3*

Beloved: Where jealousy and selfish ambition exist, there is disorder and every foul practice. But the wisdom from above is first of all pure, then peaceable, gentle, compliant, full of mercy and good fruits, without inconstancy or insincerity. And the fruit of righteousness is sown in peace for those who cultivate peace.

Where do the wars and where do the conflicts among you come from? Is it not from your passions that make war within your members? You covet but do not possess. You kill and envy but you cannot obtain; you fight and wage war. You do not possess because you do not ask. You ask but do not receive, because you ask wrongly, to spend it on your passions.

GOSPEL *Mark 9:30–37*

Jesus and his disciples left from there and began a journey through Galilee, but he did not wish anyone to know about it. He was teaching his disciples and telling them, "The Son of Man is to be handed over to men and they will kill him, and three days after his death the Son of Man will rise." But they did not understand the saying, and they were afraid to question him.

They came to Capernaum and, once inside the house, he began to ask them, "What were you arguing about on the way?" But they remained silent. They had been discussing among themselves on the way who was the greatest. Then he sat down, called the Twelve, and said to them, "If anyone wishes to be first, he shall be the last of all and the servant of all." Taking a child, he placed it in the their midst, and putting his arms around it, he said to them, "Whoever receives one child such as this in my name, receives me; and whoever receives me, receives not me but the One who sent me."

1183 TWENTY-FIFTH SUNDAY IN ORDINARY TIME / C

READING I *Amos 8:4–7 / 135*

Hear this, you who trample upon the
  needy
  and destroy the poor of the land!
"When will the new moon be over,"
  you ask,

"that we may sell our grain,
  and the sabbath, that we may display
  the wheat?
We will diminish the ephah,
  add to the shekel,

and fix our scales for cheating!
We will buy the lowly for silver,
   and the poor for a pair of sandals;
   even the refuse of the wheat we will
      sell!"

The LORD has sworn by the pride of
   Jacob:
Never will I forget a thing they
   have done!

RESPONSORIAL PSALM

Psalm 113:1–2, 4–6, 7–8

Or: Alleluia.

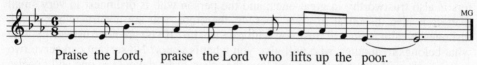

Praise the Lord,   praise the Lord who lifts up the poor.

Praise, O servants of the LORD,
   praise the name of the LORD!
May the name of the LORD be blest
   both now and forevermore! ℟.

High above all nations is the LORD,
   above the heavens his glory.
Who is like the LORD, our God,
   who dwells on high,

who lowers himself to look down
   upon heaven and earth? ℟.

From the dust he lifts up the lowly,
   from the ash heap he raises the
      poor,
to set them in the company of princes,
   yes, with the princes of his
      people. ℟.

READING II

1 Timothy 2:1–8

Beloved: First of all, I ask that supplications, prayers, petitions, and thanksgivings be offered for everyone, for kings and for all in authority, that we may lead a quiet and tranquil life in all devotion and dignity. This is good and pleasing to God our savior, who wills everyone to be saved and to come to knowledge of the truth.
   For there is one God.
   There is also one mediator between God and men,
   the man Christ Jesus,
   who gave himself as ransom for all.
This was the testimony at the proper time. For this I was appointed preacher and apostle —I am speaking the truth, I am not lying—, teacher of the Gentiles in faith and truth.
   It is my wish, then, that in every place the men should pray, lifting up holy hands, without anger or argument.

GOSPEL

Luke 16:1–13 or 16:10–13

For short form read only the parts in brackets.

[Jesus said to his disciples,] "A rich man had a steward who was reported to him for squandering his property. He summoned him and said, 'What is this I hear about you? Prepare a full account of your stewardship, because you can no longer be my steward.' The steward said to himself, 'What shall I do, now that my master is taking the position of steward away from me? I am not strong enough to dig and I am ashamed to beg. I know what I shall do so that, when I am removed from the stewardship, they may welcome me into their homes.' He called in his master's debtors one by one. To the first he said, 'How much do you owe my master?' He replied, 'One hundred measures of olive oil.' He said to him, 'Here is your promissory note. Sit down and quickly write one for fifty.' Then to another the steward said, 'And you, how much do you owe?' He replied, 'One hundred kors of wheat.' The steward said to him, 'Here is your promissory note; write one for eighty.' And the master commended that dishonest steward for acting prudently. "For the children of this world are more prudent in dealing with their own generation than are the children of light. I tell you, make friends for yourselves with dishonest wealth, so that when it fails, you will be welcomed into eternal dwellings. [The person who is trustworthy in very small matters is also trustworthy in great ones; and the person who is dishonest in very small matters is also dishonest in great ones. If, therefore, you are not trustworthy with dishonest wealth, who will trust you with true wealth? If you are not trustworthy with what belongs to another, who will give you what is yours? No servant can serve two masters. He will either hate one and love the other, or be devoted to one and despise the other. You cannot serve both God and mammon."]

1184   TWENTY-SIXTH SUNDAY IN ORDINARY TIME / A

READING I   *Ezekiel 18:25–28 / 136*

Thus says the Lord: You say, "The Lord's way is not fair!" Hear now, house of Israel: Is it my way that is unfair, or rather, are not your ways unfair? When someone virtuous turns away from virtue to commit iniquity, and dies, it is because of the iniquity he committed that he must die. But if he turns from the wickedness he has committed, and does what is right and just, he shall preserve his life; since he has turned away from all the sins that he has committed, he shall surely live, he shall not die.

RESPONSORIAL PSALM   *Psalm 25:4–5, 6–7, 8–9*

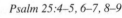
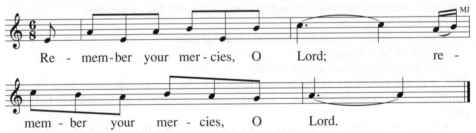

Re - mem-ber your mer - cies, O Lord; re - mem - ber your mer - cies, O Lord.

O Lord, make me know your ways.
  Teach me your paths.
Guide me in your truth, and teach me;
  for you are the God of my salvation. ℟.

Remember your compassion, O Lord,
  and your merciful love,
  for they are from of old.
Do not remember the sins of my youth,
  nor my transgressions.

In your merciful love remember me,
  because of your goodness,
  O Lord. ℟.

Good and upright is the Lord;
  he shows the way to sinners.
He guides the humble in right judgment;
  to the humble he teaches his
  way. ℟.

READING II   *Philippians 2:1–11 or 2:1–5*
For short form read only the part in brackets.

[Brothers and sisters: If there is any encouragement in Christ, any solace in love, any participation in the Spirit, any compassion and mercy, complete my joy by being of the same mind, with the same love, united in heart, thinking one thing. Do nothing out of selfishness or out of vainglory; rather, humbly regard others as more important than yourselves, each looking out not for his own interests, but also for those of others.
        Have in you the same attitude that is also in Christ Jesus,]
            Who, though he was in the form of God,
                did not regard equality with God
                something to be grasped.
            Rather, he emptied himself,
                taking the form of a slave,
                coming in human likeness;
                and found human in appearance,
                he humbled himself,
                becoming obedient to the point of death,
                even death on a cross.
            Because of this, God greatly exalted him
                and bestowed on him the name
                which is above every name,
                that at the name of Jesus
                every knee should bend,
                of those in heaven and on earth and under the earth,
                and every tongue confess that
                Jesus Christ is Lord,
                to the glory of God the Father.

GOSPEL   *Matthew 21:28–32*
Jesus said to the chief priests and elders of the people: "What is your opinion? A man had two sons. He came to the first and said, 'Son, go out and work in the vineyard today.' He said in reply, 'I will not,' but afterwards changed his mind and went. The man came to the other son and gave the same order. He said in reply, 'Yes, sir,' but did not go. Which of the two did his father's will?" They answered, "The first." Jesus said to them, "Amen, I say to you, tax collectors and prostitutes are entering the kingdom of God before you. When John came to you in the way of righteousness, you did not believe him; but tax collectors and prostitutes did. Yet even when you saw that, you did not later change your minds and believe him."

TWENTY-SIXTH SUNDAY IN ORDINARY TIME / B   1185

READING I   *Numbers 11:25–29 / 137*
The LORD came down in the cloud and spoke to Moses. Taking some of the spirit that was on Moses, the LORD bestowed it on the seventy elders; and as the spirit came to rest on them, they prophesied.
    Now two men, one named Eldad and the other Medad, were not in the gathering but had been left in the camp. They too had been on the list, but had not gone out to the tent; yet the spirit came to rest on them also, and they prophesied in the camp.

So, when a young man quickly told Moses, "Eldad and Medad are prophesying in the camp," Joshua, son of Nun, who from his youth had been Moses' aide, said, "Moses, my lord, stop them." But Moses answered him, "Are you jealous for my sake? Would that all the people of the LORD were prophets! Would that the LORD might bestow his spirit on them all!"

RESPONSORIAL PSALM

Psalm 19:8, 10, 12–13, 14

The pre-cepts of the Lord give joy to the heart.

The law of the LORD is perfect;
  it revives the soul.
The decrees of the LORD are steadfast;
  they give wisdom to the simple. ℟.

The fear of the LORD is pure,
  abiding forever.
The judgments of the LORD are true;
  they are, all of them, just. ℟.

So in them your servant finds
  instruction;
  great reward is in their keeping.
But who can detect their own errors?
  From hidden faults acquit me. ℟.

From presumption restrain your servant;
  may it not rule me.
Then shall I be blameless,
  clean from grave sin. ℟.

READING II

James 5:1–6

Come now, you rich, weep and wail over your impending miseries. Your wealth has rotted away, your clothes have become moth-eaten, your gold and silver have corroded, and that corrosion will be a testimony against you; it will devour your flesh like a fire. You have stored up treasure for the last days. Behold, the wages you withheld from the workers who harvested your fields are crying aloud; and the cries of the harvesters have reached the ears of the Lord of hosts. You have lived on earth in luxury and pleasure; you have fattened your hearts for the day of slaughter. You have condemned; you have murdered the righteous one; he offers you no resistance.

GOSPEL

Mark 9:38–43, 45, 47–48

At that time, John said to Jesus, "Teacher, we saw someone driving out demons in your name, and we tried to prevent him because he does not follow us." Jesus replied, "Do not prevent him. There is no one who performs a mighty deed in my name who can at the same time speak ill of me. For whoever is not against us is for us. Anyone who gives you a cup of water to drink because you belong to Christ, amen, I say to you, will surely not lose his reward.

"Whoever causes one of these little ones who believe in me to sin, it would be better for him if a great millstone were put around his neck and he were thrown into the sea. If your hand causes you to sin, cut it off. It is better for you to enter into life maimed than with two hands to go into Gehenna, into the unquenchable fire. And if your foot causes you to sin, cut if off. It is better for you to enter into life crippled than with two feet to be thrown into Gehenna. And if your eye causes you to sin, pluck it out. Better for you to enter into the kingdom of God with one eye than with two eyes to be thrown into Gehenna, where 'their worm does not die, and the fire is not quenched.'"

TWENTY-SIXTH SUNDAY IN ORDINARY TIME / C 1186

READING I

Amos 6:1a, 4–7 / 138

Thus says the LORD the God of hosts:
Woe to the complacent in Zion!
Lying upon beds of ivory,
    stretched comfortably on their
      couches,
they eat lambs taken from the flock,
    and calves from the stall!
Improvising to the music of the harp,
    like David, they devise their own
      accompaniment.

They drink wine from bowls
    and anoint themselves with the best
      oils;
yet they are not made ill by the
      collapse of Joseph!
Therefore, now they shall be the first to
    go into exile,
and their wanton revelry shall be
    done away with.

RESPONSORIAL PSALM

Psalm 146:6c–7, 8–9a, 9bc–10

Or: Alleluia.

Praise the Lord, my soul! Praise the Lord!

It is the LORD who preserves
    fidelity forever,
  who does justice to those who are
    oppressed.
It is he who gives bread to the hungry,
  the LORD who sets prisoners free. ℟.

The LORD who opens the eyes of the blind,
  the LORD who raises up those who
    are bowed down.

It is the LORD who loves the just,
  the LORD who protects the
    stranger. ℟.

The LORD upholds the orphan and the
  widow,
  but thwarts the path of the wicked.
The LORD will reign forever,
  the God of Sion from age to age.
  Alleluia. ℟.

READING II

1 Timothy 6:11–16

But you, man of God, pursue righteousness, devotion, faith, love, patience, and gentleness. Compete well for the faith. Lay hold of eternal life, to which you were called when you made the noble confession in the presence of many witnesses. I charge you before God, who gives life to all things, and before Christ Jesus, who gave testimony under Pontius Pilate for the noble confession, to keep the commandment without stain or reproach until the appearance of our Lord Jesus Christ that the blessed and only ruler will make manifest at the proper time, the King of kings and Lord of lords, who alone has immortality, who dwells in unapproachable light, and whom no human being has seen or can see. To him be honor and eternal power. Amen.

GOSPEL

Luke 16:19–31

Jesus said to the Pharisees: "There was a rich man who dressed in purple garments and fine linen and dined sumptuously each day. And lying at his door was a poor man named Lazarus, covered with sores, who would gladly have eaten his fill of the scraps that fell from the rich man's table. Dogs even used to come and lick his sores. When the poor man died, he was carried away by angels to the bosom of Abraham. The rich man also died and was buried, and from the netherworld, where he was in torment, he raised his eyes and saw Abraham far off and Lazarus at his side. And he cried out, 'Father Abraham, have pity on me. Send Lazarus to dip the tip of his finger in water and cool my tongue, for I am suffering torment in these flames.' Abraham replied, 'My child, remember that you received what was good during your lifetime while Lazarus likewise received what was bad; but now he is comforted here, whereas you are tormented. Moreover, between us and you a great chasm is established to prevent anyone from crossing who might wish to go from our side to yours or from your side to ours.' He said, 'Then I beg you, father, send him to my father's house, for I have five brothers, so that he may warn them, lest they too come to this place of torment.' But Abraham replied, 'They have Moses and the prophets. Let them listen to them.' He said, 'Oh no, father Abraham, but if someone from the dead goes to them, they will repent.' Then Abraham said, 'If they will not listen to Moses and the prophets, neither will they be persuaded if someone should rise from the dead.'"

1187　TWENTY-SEVENTH SUNDAY IN ORDINARY TIME / A

READING I　　　　　　　　　　　　　　　　　　*Isaiah 5:1–7 / 139*

Let me now sing of my friend,
　my friend's song concerning his
　　vineyard.
My friend had a vineyard
　on a fertile hillside;
he spaded it, cleared it of stones,
　and planted the choicest vines;
within it he built a watchtower,
　and hewed out a wine press.
Then he looked for the crop of grapes,
　but what it yielded was wild grapes.

Now, inhabitants of Jerusalem and
　people of Judah,
　judge between me and my vineyard:
What more was there to do for my
　vineyard
　that I had not done?
Why, when I looked for the crop of grapes,

did it bring forth wild grapes?
Now, I will let you know
　what I mean to do with my vineyard:
take away its hedge, give it to grazing,
　break through its wall, let it be
　　trampled!
Yes, I will make it a ruin:
　it shall not be pruned or hoed,
　but overgrown with thorns and
　　briers;
I will command the clouds
　not to send rain upon it.
The vineyard of the LORD of hosts is the
　house of Israel,
　and the people of Judah are his
　cherished plant;
he looked for judgment, but see,
　bloodshed!
for justice, but hark, the outcry!

RESPONSORIAL PSALM　　　　　　　　*Psalm 80:9 and 12, 13–14, 15–16, 19–20*

RJB

The vine-yard　　of the Lord　　is the house of Is - ra - el.

You brought a vine out of Egypt;
　you drove out the nations and
　　planted it.
It stretched out its branches to the sea;
　to the River it stretched out its
　　shoots. ℟.

Then why have you broken down its
　walls?
　It is plucked by all who pass by the
　way.
It is ravaged by the boar of the forest,
　devoured by the beasts of the field. ℟.

God of hosts, turn again, we implore;
　look down from heaven and see.
Visit this vine and protect it,
　the vine your right hand has planted,
　the son of man you have claimed
　　for yourself. ℟.

And we shall never forsake you again;
　give us life that we may call upon
　your name.
O Lᴏʀᴅ God of hosts, bring us back;
　let your face shine forth, and we
　shall be saved. ℟.

READING II   *Philippians 4:6–9*

Brothers and sisters: Have no anxiety at all, but in everything, by prayer and petition, with thanksgiving, make your requests known to God. Then the peace of God that surpasses all understanding will guard your hearts and minds in Christ Jesus.

Finally, brothers and sisters, whatever is true, whatever is honorable, whatever is just, whatever is pure, whatever is lovely, whatever is gracious, if there is any excellence and if there is anything worthy of praise, think about these things. Keep on doing what you have learned and received and heard and seen in me. Then the God of peace will be with you.

GOSPEL   *Matthew 21:33–43*

Jesus said to the chief priests and the elders of the people: "Hear another parable. There was a landowner who planted a vineyard, put a hedge around it, dug a wine press in it, and built a tower. Then he leased it to tenants and went on a journey. When vintage time drew near, he sent his servants to the tenants to obtain his produce. But the tenants seized the servants and one they beat, another they killed, and a third they stoned. Again he sent other servants, more numerous than the first ones, but they treated them in the same way. Finally, he sent his son to them, thinking, 'They will respect my son.' But when the tenants saw the son, they said to one another, 'This is the heir. Come, let us kill him and acquire his inheritance.' They seized him, threw him out of the vineyard, and killed him. What will the owner of the vineyard do to those tenants when he comes?" They answered him, "He will put those wretched men to a wretched death and lease his vineyard to other tenants who will give him the produce at the proper times." Jesus said to them, "Did you never read in the Scriptures:

The stone that the builders rejected
　　has become the cornerstone;
by the Lord has this been done,
　　and it is wonderful in our eyes?

Therefore, I say to you, the kingdom of God will be taken away from you and given to a people that will produce its fruit."

TWENTY-SEVENTH SUNDAY IN ORDINARY TIME / B   1188

READING I   *Genesis 2:18–24 / 140*

The Lᴏʀᴅ God said: "It is not good for the man to be alone. I will make a suitable partner for him." So the Lᴏʀᴅ God formed out of the ground various wild animals and various birds of the air, and he brought them to the man to see what he would call them; whatever the man called each of them would be its name. The man gave names to all the cattle, all the birds of the air, and all wild animals; but none proved to be the suitable partner for the man.

So the LORD God cast a deep sleep on the man, and while he was asleep, he took out one of his ribs and closed up its place with flesh. The LORD God then built up into a woman the rib that he had taken from the man. When he brought her to the man, the man said:

"This one, at last, is bone of my bones
and flesh of my flesh;
this one shall be called 'woman,'
for out of 'her man' this one has been taken."

That is why a man leaves his father and mother and clings to his wife, and the two of them become one flesh.

RESPONSORIAL PSALM
Psalm 128:1–2, 3, 4–5, 6

May the Lord bless and pro-tect us all the days of our life.

Blessed are all who fear the LORD,
and walk in his ways!
By the labor of your hands you shall eat.
You will be blessed and prosper. ℟.

Your wife like a fruitful vine
in the heart of your house;
your children like shoots of the olive
around your table. ℟.

Indeed thus shall be blessed
the man who fears the LORD.
May the LORD bless you from Sion.
May you see Jerusalem prosper
all the days of your life! ℟.

May you see your children's children.
On Israel, peace! ℟.

READING II
Hebrews 2:9–11

Brothers and sisters: He "for a little while" was made "lower than the angels," that by the grace of God he might taste death for everyone.

For it was fitting that he, for whom and through whom all things exist, in bringing many children to glory, should make the leader to their salvation perfect through suffering. He who consecrates and those who are being consecrated all have one origin. Therefore, he is not ashamed to call them "brothers."

GOSPEL
Mark 10:2–16 or 10:2–12

For short form read only the part in brackets.

[The Pharisees approached Jesus and asked, "Is it lawful for a husband to divorce his wife?" They were testing him. He said to them in reply, "What did Moses command you?" They replied, "Moses permitted a husband to write a bill of divorce and dismiss her." But Jesus told them, "Because of the hardness of your hearts he wrote you this commandment. But from the beginning of creation, *God made them male and female. For this reason a man shall leave his father and mother and be joined to his wife, and the two shall become one flesh.* So they are no longer two but one flesh. Therefore what God has joined together, no human being must separate." In the house the disciples again questioned Jesus about this. He said to them, "Whoever divorces his wife and marries another commits adultery against her; and if she divorces her husband and marries another, she commits adultery."]

And people were bringing children to him that he might touch them, but the disciples rebuked them. When Jesus saw this he became indignant and said to them, "Let the children come to me; do not prevent them, for the kingdom of God belongs to such as these. Amen, I say to you, whoever does not accept the kingdom of God like a child will not enter it." Then he embraced them and blessed them, placing his hands on them.

TWENTY-SEVENTH SUNDAY IN ORDINARY TIME / C   1189

READING I   *Habakkuk 1:2–3; 2:2–4 / 141*

How long, O Lᴏʀᴅ? I cry for help
  but you do not listen!
I cry out to you, "Violence!"
  but you do not intervene.
Why do you let me see ruin;
  why must I look at misery?
Destruction and violence are before me;
  there is strife, and clamorous discord.
Then the Lᴏʀᴅ answered me and said:
  Write down the vision clearly upon
the tablets,
  so that one can read it readily.
For the vision still has its time,
  presses on to fulfillment, and will
    not disappoint;
if it delays, wait for it,
  it will surely come, it will not be late.
The rash one has no integrity;
  but the just one, because of his faith,
    shall live.

RESPONSORIAL PSALM   *Psalm 95:1–2, 6–7c, 7d–9*

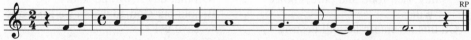

If to - day you hear his voice,   hard - en not your hearts.

Come, let us ring out our joy to the
    Lᴏʀᴅ;
  hail the rock who saves us.
Let us come into his presence, giving
    thanks;
  let us hail him with a song of
    praise. ℟.

O come; let us bow and bend low.
  Let us kneel before the God who
    made us,
for he is our God and we
  the people who belong to his
pasture,
  the flock that is led by his hand. ℟.

O that today you would listen to his
    voice!
  "Harden not your hearts as at
    Meribah,
  as on that day at Massah in the
    desert
when your forebears put me to the test;
  when they tried me, though they
    saw my work." ℟.

READING II   *2 Timothy 1:6–8, 13–14*

Beloved: I remind you to stir into flame the gift of God that you have through the imposition of my hands. For God did not give us a spirit of cowardice but rather of power and love and self-control. So do not be ashamed of your testimony to our Lord, nor of me, a prisoner for his sake; but bear your share of hardship for the gospel with the strength that comes from God.

Take as your norm the sound words that you heard from me, in the faith and love that are in Christ Jesus. Guard this rich trust with the help of the Holy Spirit that dwells within us.

GOSPEL   *Luke 17:5–10*

The apostles said to the Lord, "Increase our faith." The Lord replied, "If you have faith the size of a mustard seed, you would say to this mulberry tree, 'Be uprooted and planted in the sea,' and it would obey you.

"Who among you would say to your servant who has just come in from plowing or tending sheep in the field, 'Come here immediately and take your place at table'? Would he not rather say to him, 'Prepare something for me to eat. Put on your apron and wait on me while I eat and drink. You may eat and drink when I am finished'? Is he grateful to that servant because he did what was commanded? So should it be with you. When you have done all you have been commanded, say, 'We are unprofitable servants; we have done what we were obliged to do.'"

1190   TWENTY-EIGHTH SUNDAY IN ORDINARY TIME / A

READING I   *Isaiah 25:6–10a / 142*

On this mountain the Lord of hosts
  will provide for all peoples
a feast of rich food and choice wines,
  juicy, rich food and pure, choice
    wines.
On this mountain he will destroy
  the veil that veils all peoples,
the web that is woven over all nations;
  he will destroy death forever.
The Lord God will wipe away
  the tears from every face;
the reproach of his people he will
remove
from the whole earth; for the Lord
  has spoken.
On that day it will be said:
"Behold our God, to whom we looked to
  save us!
This is the Lord for whom we
  looked;
let us rejoice and be glad that he has
  saved us!"
For the hand of the Lord will rest on
  this mountain.

RESPONSORIAL PSALM   *Psalm 23:1–3a, 3b–4, 5, 6*

I shall live in the house of the Lord   all the   days of my life.

The Lord is my shepherd;
  there is nothing I shall want.
Fresh and green are the pastures

where he gives me repose.
Near restful waters he leads me;
  he revives my soul. ℟.

He guides me along the right path,
for the sake of his name.
Though I should walk in the valley of
the shadow of death,
no evil would I fear, for you are
with me.
Your crook and your staff will give
me comfort. ℟.

in the sight of my foes.
My head you have anointed with oil;
my cup is overflowing. ℟.
Surely goodness and mercy shall
follow me
all the days of my life.
In the LORD's own house shall I dwell
for length of days unending. ℟.

You have prepared a table before me

READING II
Philippians 4:12–14, 19–20

Brothers and sisters: I know how to live in humble circumstances; I know also how to live with abundance. In every circumstance and in all things I have learned the secret of being well fed and of going hungry, of living in abundance and of being in need. I can do all things in him who strengthens me. Still, it was kind of you to share in my distress.

My God will fully supply whatever you need, in accord with his glorious riches in Christ Jesus. To our God and Father, glory forever and ever. Amen.

GOSPEL
Matthew 22:1–14 or 22:1–10

For short form read only the part in brackets.

[Jesus again in reply spoke to the chief priests and elders of the people in parables, saying, "The kingdom of heaven may be likened to a king who gave a wedding feast for his son. He dispatched his servants to summon the invited guests to the feast, but they refused to come. A second time he sent other servants, saying, 'Tell those invited: "Behold, I have prepared my banquet, my calves and fattened cattle are killed, and everything is ready; come to the feast."' Some ignored the invitation and went away, one to his farm, another to his business. The rest laid hold of his servants, mistreated them, and killed them. The king was enraged and sent his troops, destroyed those murderers, and burned their city. Then he said to his servants, 'The feast is ready, but those who were invited were not worthy to come. Go out, therefore, into the main roads and invite to the feast whomever you find.' The servants went out into the streets and gathered all they found, bad and good alike, and the hall was filled with guests.] But when the king came in to meet the guests, he saw a man there not dressed in a wedding garment. The king said to him, 'My friend, how is it that you came in here without a wedding garment?' But he was reduced to silence. Then the king said to his attendants, 'Bind his hands and feet, and cast him into the darkness outside, where there will be wailing and grinding of teeth.' Many are invited, but few are chosen."

TWENTY-EIGHTH SUNDAY IN ORDINARY TIME / B   1191

READING I
Wisdom 7:7–11 / 143

I prayed, and prudence was given me;
I pleaded, and the spirit of wisdom came to me.
I preferred her to scepter and throne,

and deemed riches nothing in comparison with her,
nor did I liken any priceless gem to her;
because all gold, in view of her, is a little sand,
and before her, silver is to be accounted mire.
Beyond health and comeliness I loved her,
and I chose to have her rather than the light,
because the splendor of her never yields to sleep.
Yet all good things together came to me in her company,
and countless riches at her hands.

RESPONSORIAL PSALM

Psalm 90:12–13, 14–15, 16–17

RJB

Fill us with your love, O Lord, and we will sing for joy!

Teach us to number our days,
that we may gain wisdom of heart.
Turn back, O Lᴏʀᴅ! How long?
Show pity to your servants. ℟.

At dawn, fill us with your merciful love;
we shall exult and rejoice all our days.
Give us joy for the days of our affliction,
for the years when we looked upon
evil. ℟.

Let your deed be seen by your servants,
and your glorious power by their
children.
Let the favor of the Lord our God be
upon us;
give success to the work of our
hands.
O give success to the work of our
hands. ℟.

READING II

Hebrews 4:12–13

Brothers and sisters: Indeed the word of God is living and effective, sharper than any two-edged sword, penetrating even between soul and spirit, joints and marrow, and able to discern reflections and thoughts of the heart. No creature is concealed from him, but everything is naked and exposed to the eyes of him to whom we must render an account.

GOSPEL

Mark 10:17–30 or 10:17–27

For short form read only the part in brackets.

[As Jesus was setting out on a journey, a man ran up, knelt down before him, and asked him, "Good teacher, what must I do to inherit eternal life?" Jesus answered him, "Why do you call me good? No one is good but God alone. You know the commandments: *You shall not kill; you shall not commit adultery; you shall not steal; you shall not bear false witness; you shall not defraud; honor your father and your mother.*" He replied and said to him, "Teacher, all of these I have observed from my youth." Jesus, looking at him, loved him and said to him, "You are lacking in one thing. Go, sell what you have, and give to the poor and you will have treasure in heaven; then come, follow me." At that statement his face fell, and he went away sad, for he had many possessions.

Jesus looked around and said to his disciples, "How hard it is for those who have wealth to enter the kingdom of God!" The disciples were amazed at his words. So Jesus again said to them in reply, "Children, how hard it is to enter the kingdom of God! It is easier for a camel to pass through the eye of a needle than for one who is rich to enter the kingdom of God." They were exceedingly astonished and said among themselves, "Then who can be saved?" Jesus looked at them and said, "For human beings it is impossible, but not for God. All things are possible for God."] Peter began to say to him, "We have given up everything and followed you." Jesus said, "Amen, I say to you, there is no one who has given up house or brothers or sisters or mother or father or children or lands for my sake and for the sake of the gospel who will not receive a hundred times more now in this present age: houses and brothers and sisters and mothers and children and lands, with persecutions, and eternal life in the age to come."

TWENTY-EIGHTH SUNDAY IN ORDINARY TIME / C   1192

READING I   *2 Kings 5:14–17 / 144*

Naaman went down and plunged into the Jordan seven times at the word of Elisha, the man of God. His flesh became again like the flesh of a little child, and he was clean of his leprosy.

Naaman returned with his whole retinue to the man of God. On his arrival he stood before Elisha and said, "Now I know that there is no God in all the earth, except in Israel. Please accept a gift from your servant."

Elisha replied, "As the LORD lives whom I serve, I will not take it;" and despite Naaman's urging, he still refused. Naaman said: "If you will not accept, please let me, your servant, have two mule-loads of earth, for I will no longer offer holocaust or sacrifice to any other god except to the LORD."

RESPONSORIAL PSALM   *Psalm 98:1, 2–3ab, 3cd–4*

The Lord has re-vealed to the na-tions his sav-ing pow'r.

O sing a new song to the LORD,
   for he has worked wonders.
His right hand and his holy arm
   have brought salvation. ℟.

The LORD has made known his salvation,
   has shown his deliverance to the
      nations.
He has remembered his merciful love

and his truth for the house of
   Israel. ℟.

All the ends of the earth have seen
   the salvation of our God.
Shout to the LORD, all the earth;
   break forth into joyous song,
   and sing out your praise. ℟.

READING II   *2 Timothy 2:8–13*

Beloved: Remember Jesus Christ, raised from the dead, a descendant of David: such is my gospel, for which I am suffering, even to the point of chains, like a criminal. But the word of God is not chained. Therefore, I bear with everything for the sake of

those who are chosen, so that they too may obtain the salvation that is in Christ Jesus, together with eternal glory. This saying is trustworthy:
>If we have died with him
>>we shall also live with him;
>if we persevere
>>we shall also reign with him.
>But if we deny him
>>he will deny us.
>If we are unfaithful
>>he remains faithful,
>>for he cannot deny himself.

GOSPEL

Luke 17:11–19

As Jesus continued his journey to Jerusalem, he traveled through Samaria and Galilee. As he was entering a village, ten lepers met him. They stood at a distance from him and raised their voices, saying, "Jesus, Master! Have pity on us!" And when he saw them, he said, "Go show yourselves to the priests." As they were going they were cleansed. And one of them, realizing he had been healed, returned, glorifying God in a loud voice; and he fell at the feet of Jesus and thanked him. He was a Samaritan. Jesus said in reply, "Ten were cleansed, were they not? Where are the other nine? Has none but this foreigner returned to give thanks to God?" Then he said to him, "Stand up and go; your faith has saved you."

1193 TWENTY-NINTH SUNDAY IN ORDINARY TIME / A

READING I

Isaiah 45:1, 4–6 / 145

Thus says the LORD to his anointed,
>Cyrus,
>>whose right hand I grasp,
subduing nations before him,
>>and making kings run in his service,
opening doors before him
>>and leaving the gates unbarred:
For the sake of Jacob, my servant,
>>of Israel, my chosen one,
I have called you by your name,
>>giving you a title, though you

knew me not.
I am the LORD and there is no other,
>>there is no God besides me.
It is I who arm you, though you know
>>me not,
so that toward the rising and the
>>setting of the sun
people may know that there is none
>>besides me.
I am the LORD, there is no other.

RESPONSORIAL PSALM

Psalm 96:1 and 3, 4–5, 7–8, 9–10a and c

Give the Lord glo-ry, glo-ry and hon - or.

O sing a new song to the LORD;
>sing to the LORD, all the earth.
Tell among the nations his glory,

and his wonders among all the
>peoples. ℟.

For the LORD is great and highly to be
praised,
to be feared above all gods.
For the gods of the nations are naught.
It was the LORD who made the
heavens. ℟.

Give the LORD, you families of peoples,
give the LORD glory and power;

give the LORD the glory of his name.
Bring an offering and enter his
courts. ℟.

Worship the LORD in holy splendor.
O tremble before him, all the earth.
Say to the nations, "The LORD is king."
He will judge the peoples in
fairness. ℟.

READING II *1 Thessalonians 1:1–5b*

Paul, Silvanus, and Timothy to the church of the Thessalonians in God the Father and
the Lord Jesus Christ: grace to you and peace. We give thanks to God always for all
of you, remembering you in our prayers, unceasingly calling to mind your work of
faith and labor of love and endurance in hope of our Lord Jesus Christ, before our
God and Father, knowing, brothers and sisters loved by God, how you were chosen.
For our gospel did not come to you in word alone, but also in power and in the Holy
Spirit and with much conviction.

GOSPEL *Matthew 22:15–21*

The Pharisees went off and plotted how they might entrap Jesus in speech. They sent
their disciples to him, with the Herodians, saying, "Teacher, we know that you are a
truthful man and that you teach the way of God in accordance with the truth. And you
are not concerned with anyone's opinion, for you do not regard a person's status. Tell
us, then, what is your opinion: Is it lawful to pay the census tax to Caesar or not?"
Knowing their malice, Jesus said, "Why are you testing me, you hypocrites? Show
me the coin that pays the census tax." Then they handed him the Roman coin. He said
to them, "Whose image is this and whose inscription?" They replied, "Caesar's." At
that he said to them, "Then repay to Caesar what belongs to Caesar and to God what
belongs to God."

TWENTY-NINTH SUNDAY IN ORDINARY TIME / B   1194

READING I *Isaiah 53:10–11 / 146*

The LORD was pleased
to crush him in infirmity.

If he gives his life as an offering
for sin,
he shall see his descendants in a
long life,
and the will of the LORD shall be

accomplished through him.

Because of his affliction
he shall see the light in fullness
of days;
through his suffering, my servant shall
justify many,
and their guilt he shall bear.

RESPONSORIAL PSALM *Psalm 33:4–5, 18–19, 20 and 22*

Lord, let your mer-cy be on us, as we place our trust in you.

The word of the LORD is faithful,
and all his works to be trusted.
The LORD loves justice and right,
and his merciful love fills the earth. ℟.

Yes, the LORD's eyes are on those who
fear him,
who hope in his merciful love,

to rescue their souls from death,
to keep them alive in famine. ℟.

Our soul is waiting for the LORD.
He is our help and our shield.
May your merciful love be upon us,
as we hope in you, O LORD. ℟.

READING II *Hebrews 4:14–16*

Brothers and sisters: Since we have a great high priest who has passed through the heavens, Jesus, the Son of God, let us hold fast to our confession. For we do not have a high priest who is unable to sympathize with our weaknesses, but one who has similarly been tested in every way, yet without sin. So let us confidently approach the throne of grace to receive mercy and to find grace for timely help.

GOSPEL *Mark 10:35–45 or 10:42–45*
For short form read only the part in brackets.

James and John, the sons of Zebedee, came to Jesus and said to him, "Teacher, we want you to do for us whatever we ask of you." He replied, "What do you wish me to do for you?" They answered him, "Grant that in your glory we may sit one at your right and the other at your left." Jesus said to them, "You do not know what you are asking. Can you drink the cup that I drink or be baptized with the baptism with which I am baptized?" They said to him, "We can." Jesus said to them, "The cup that I drink, you will drink, and with the baptism with which I am baptized, you will be baptized; but to sit at my right or at my left is not mine to give but is for those for whom it has been prepared." When the ten heard this, they became indignant at James and John. [Jesus summoned them and said to them, "You know that those who are recognized as rulers over the Gentiles lord it over them, and their great ones make their authority over them felt. But it shall not be so among you. Rather, whoever wishes to be great among you will be your servant; whoever wishes to be first among you will be the slave of all. For the Son of Man did not come to be served but to serve and to give his life as a ransom for many."]

1195 TWENTY-NINTH SUNDAY IN ORDINARY TIME / C

READING I *Exodus 17:8–13 / 147*

In those days, Amalek came and waged war against Israel. Moses, therefore, said to Joshua, "Pick out certain men, and tomorrow go out and engage Amalek in battle. I will be standing on top of the hill with the staff of God in my hand." So Joshua did as Moses told him: he engaged Amalek in battle after Moses had climbed to the top of the hill with Aaron and Hur. As long as Moses kept his hands raised up, Israel had the better of the fight, but when he let his hands rest, Amalek had the better of the fight. Moses' hands, however, grew tired; so they put a rock in place for him to sit on. Meanwhile Aaron and Hur supported his hands, one on one side and one on the other, so that his hands remained steady till sunset. And Joshua mowed down Amalek and his people with the edge of the sword.

RESPONSORIAL PSALM   *Psalm 121:1–2, 3–4, 5–6, 7–8*

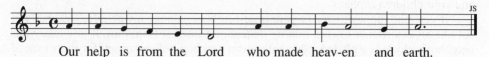

Our help is from the Lord who made heav-en and earth.

I lift up my eyes to the mountains;
    from where shall come my help?
My help shall come from the LORD,
    who made heaven and earth. ℟.

He will keep your foot from stumbling.
    Your guard will never slumber.
No, he sleeps not nor slumbers,
    Israel's guard. ℟.

The LORD your guard, the LORD

your shade
    at your right hand.
By day the sun shall not smite you,
    nor the moon in the night. ℟.

The LORD will guard you from evil;
    he will guard your soul.
The LORD will guard your going and
    coming,
both now and forever. ℟.

READING II   *2 Timothy 3:14—4:2*
Beloved: Remain faithful to what you have learned and believed, because you know from whom you learned it, and that from infancy you have known the sacred Scriptures, which are capable of giving you wisdom for salvation through faith in Christ Jesus. All Scripture is inspired by God and is useful for teaching, for refutation, for correction, and for training in righteousness, so that one who belongs to God may be competent, equipped for every good work.

I charge you in the presence of God and of Christ Jesus, who will judge the living and the dead, and by his appearing and his kingly power: proclaim the word; be persistent whether it is convenient or inconvenient; convince, reprimand, encourage through all patience and teaching.

GOSPEL   *Luke 18:1–8*
Jesus told his disciples a parable about the necessity for them to pray always without becoming weary. He said, "There was a judge in a certain town who neither feared God nor respected any human being. And a widow in that town used to come to him and say, 'Render a just decision for me against my adversary.' For a long time the judge was unwilling, but eventually he thought, 'While it is true that I neither fear God nor respect any human being, because this widow keeps bothering me I shall deliver a just decision for her lest she finally come and strike me.'" The Lord said, "Pay attention to what the dishonest judge says. Will not God then secure the rights of his chosen ones who call out to him day and night? Will he be slow to answer them? I tell you, he will see to it that justice is done for them speedily. But when the Son of Man comes, will he find faith on earth?"

1196 THIRTIETH SUNDAY IN ORDINARY TIME / A

READING I   *Exodus 22:20–26 / 148*

Thus says the LORD: "You shall not molest or oppress an alien, for you were once aliens yourselves in the land of Egypt. You shall not wrong any widow or orphan. If ever you wrong them and they cry out to me, I will surely hear their cry. My wrath will flare up, and I will kill you with the sword; then your own wives will be widows, and your children orphans.

"If you lend money to one of your poor neighbors among my people, you shall not act like an extortioner toward him by demanding interest from him. If you take your neighbor's cloak as a pledge, you shall return it to him before sunset; for this cloak of his is the only covering he has for his body. What else has he to sleep in? If he cries out to me, I will hear him; for I am compassionate."

RESPONSORIAL PSALM   *Psalm 18:2–3a, 3bc–4, 47 and 51ab*

I love you, LORD, my strength;
  O LORD, my rock, my fortress,
    my savior. ℟.

My God, my rock where I take refuge;
  my shield, my saving strength, my
    stronghold.
I cry out, "Praised be the LORD!"
  and see, I am saved from my foes. ℟.

The LORD lives, and blest be my Rock!
  May the God of my salvation be
    exalted.
The LORD gives great victories to his
    king,
  and shows merciful love for his
    anointed. ℟.

READING II   *1 Thessalonians 1:5c-10*

Brothers and sisters: You know what sort of people we were among you for your sake. And you became imitators of us and of the Lord, receiving the word in great affliction, with joy from the Holy Spirit, so that you became a model for all the believers in Macedonia and in Achaia. For from you the word of the Lord has sounded forth not only in Macedonia and in Achaia, but in every place your faith in God has gone forth, so that we have no need to say anything. For they themselves openly declare about us what sort of reception we had among you, and how you turned to God from idols to serve the living and true God and to await his Son from heaven, whom he raised from the dead, Jesus, who delivers us from the coming wrath.

GOSPEL   *Matthew 22:34-40*

When the Pharisees heard that Jesus had silenced the Sadducees, they gathered together, and one of them, a scholar of the law, tested him by asking, "Teacher, which commandment in the law is the greatest?" He said to him, "You shall love the Lord, your God, with all your heart, with all your soul, and with all your mind. This is the greatest and the first commandment. The second is like it: You shall love your neighbor as yourself. The whole law and the prophets depend on these two commandments."

THIRTIETH SUNDAY IN ORDINARY TIME / B   1197

READING I

Jeremiah 31:7–9 / 149

Thus says the LORD:
Shout with joy for Jacob,
    exult at the head of the nations;
    proclaim your praise and say:
The LORD has delivered his people,
    the remnant of Israel.
Behold, I will bring them back
    from the land of the north;
I will gather them from the ends of the
    world,
    with the blind and the lame in their
    midst,

the mothers and those with child;
    they shall return as an immense
    throng.
They departed in tears,
    but I will console them and guide
    them;
I will lead them to brooks of water,
    on a level road, so that none shall
    stumble.
For I am a father to Israel,
    Ephraim is my first-born.

RESPONSORIAL PSALM

Psalm 126:1–2ab, 2cd–3, 4–5, 6

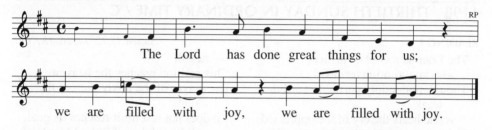

The Lord has done great things for us; we are filled with joy, we are filled with joy.

When the LORD brought back the
        exiles of Sion,
    we thought we were dreaming.
Then was our mouth filled with laughter;
    on our tongues, songs of joy. ℟.

Then the nations themselves said,
        "What great deeds
    the LORD worked for them!"
What great deeds the LORD worked for us!
    Indeed, we were glad. ℟.

Bring back our exiles, O LORD,
    as streams in the south.
Those who are sowing in tears
    will sing when they reap. ℟.

They go out, they go out, full of tears,
    bearing seed for the sowing;
they come back, they come back with
        a song,
    bearing their sheaves. ℟.

READING II

Hebrews 5:1–6

Brothers and sisters: Every high priest is taken from among men and made their representative before God, to offer gifts and sacrifices for sins. He is able to deal patiently with the ignorant and erring, for he himself is beset by weakness and so, for this reason, must make sin offerings for himself as well as for the people. No one takes this honor upon himself but only when called by God, just as Aaron was. In the same way, it was not Christ who glorified himself in becoming high priest, but rather the one who said to him:
    You are my son:
        this day I have begotten you;

just as he says in another place:
You are a priest forever
according to the order of Melchizedek.

GOSPEL   *Mark 10:46–52*

As Jesus was leaving Jericho with his disciples and a sizable crowd, Bartimaeus, a blind man, the son of Timaeus, sat by the roadside begging. On hearing that it was Jesus of Nazareth, he began to cry out and say, "Jesus, son of David, have pity on me." And many rebuked him, telling him to be silent. But he kept calling out all the more, "Son of David, have pity on me." Jesus stopped and said, "Call him." So they called the blind man, saying to him, "Take courage; get up, Jesus is calling you." He threw aside his cloak, sprang up, and came to Jesus. Jesus said to him in reply, "What do you want me to do for you?" The blind man replied to him, "Master, I want to see." Jesus told him, "Go your way; your faith has saved you." Immediately he received his sight and followed him on the way.

1198   THIRTIETH SUNDAY IN ORDINARY TIME / C

READING I   *Sirach 35:12–14, 16–18 / 150*

The LORD is a God of justice,
  who knows no favorites.
Though not unduly partial toward the
  weak,
  yet he hears the cry of the oppressed.
The Lord is not deaf to the wail of the
  orphan,
  nor to the widow when she pours out
  her complaint.
The one who serves God willingly is
heard;
  his petition reaches the heavens.
The prayer of the lowly pierces the
  clouds;
  it does not rest till it reaches its goal,
nor will it withdraw till the Most High
  responds,
  judges justly and affirms the right,
and the Lord will not delay.

RESPONSORIAL PSALM   *Psalm 34:2–3, 17–18, 19 and 23*

The Lord hears the cry of the poor.

I will bless the LORD at all times;
  praise of him is always in my mouth.
In the LORD my soul shall make its boast;
  the humble shall hear and be glad. ℟.

The LORD turns his face against the
  wicked
  to destroy their remembrance from
  the earth.
When the just cry out, the LORD hears,

and rescues them in all their
  distress. ℟.

The LORD is close to the brokenhearted;
  those whose spirit is crushed he will
  save.
The LORD ransoms the souls of his
  servants.
  All who trust in him shall not be
  condemned. ℟.

READING II   *2 Timothy 4:6–8, 16–18*

Beloved: I am already being poured out like a libation, and the time of my departure is at hand. I have competed well; I have finished the race; I have kept the faith. From now on the crown of righteousness awaits me, which the Lord, the just judge, will award to me on that day, and not only to me, but to all who have longed for his appearance.

At my first defense no one appeared on my behalf, but everyone deserted me. May it not be held against them! But the Lord stood by me and gave me strength, so that through me the proclamation might be completed and all the Gentiles might hear it. And I was rescued from the lion's mouth. The Lord will rescue me from every evil threat and will bring me safe to his heavenly kingdom. To him be glory forever and ever. Amen.

GOSPEL   *Luke 18:9–14*

Jesus addressed this parable to those who were convinced of their own righteousness and despised everyone else. "Two people went up to the temple area to pray; one was a Pharisee and the other was a tax collector. The Pharisee took up his position and spoke this prayer to himself, 'O God, I thank you that I am not like the rest of humanity — greedy, dishonest, adulterous — or even like this tax collector. I fast twice a week, and I pay tithes on my whole income.' But the tax collector stood off at a distance and would not even raise his eyes to heaven but beat his breast and prayed, 'O God, be merciful to me a sinner.' I tell you, the latter went home justified, not the former; for whoever exalts himself will be humbled, and the one who humbles himself will be exalted."

THIRTY-FIRST SUNDAY IN ORDINARY TIME / A   1199

READING I   *Malachi 1:14b–2:2b, 8–10 / 151*

A great King am I, says the LORD
   of hosts,
and my name will be feared
   among the nations.
And now, O priests, this
   commandment is for you:
  If you do not listen,
if you do not lay it to heart,
   to give glory to my name, says
   the LORD of hosts,
I will send a curse upon you
   and of your blessing I will make
   a curse.
You have turned aside from the way,

and have caused many to falter by
   your instruction;
you have made void the covenant of
   Levi,
  says the LORD of hosts.
I, therefore, have made you contemptible
   and base before all the people,
since you do not keep my ways,
  but show partiality in your decisions.
Have we not all the one father?
  Has not the one God created us?
Why then do we break faith with one
   another,
  violating the covenant of our fathers?

RESPONSORIAL PSALM *Psalm 131:1, 2, 3*

RJB

In you, Lord, in you, Lord, in you, Lord, I have found my peace.

O Lord, my heart is not proud,
 nor haughty my eyes.
I have not gone after things too great,
 nor marvels beyond me. ℟.

Truly, I have set my soul
 in tranquility and silence.

As a weaned child on its mother,
 as a weaned child is my soul within
 me. ℟.

O Israel, wait for the Lord,
 both now and forever. ℟.

READING II *1 Thessalonians 2:7b–9, 13*

Brothers and sisters: We were gentle among you, as a nursing mother cares for her children. With such affection for you, we were determined to share with you not only the gospel of God, but our very selves as well, so dearly beloved had you become to us. You recall, brothers and sisters, our toil and drudgery. Working night and day in order not to burden any of you, we proclaimed to you the gospel of God.

And for this reason we too give thanks to God unceasingly, that, in receiving the word of God from hearing us, you received not a human word but, as it truly is, the word of God, which is now at work in you who believe.

GOSPEL *Matthew 23:1–12*

Jesus spoke to the crowds and to his disciples, saying, "The scribes and the Pharisees have taken their seat on the chair of Moses. Therefore, do and observe all things whatsoever they tell you, but do not follow their example. For they preach but they do not practice. They tie up heavy burdens hard to carry and lay them on people's shoulders, but they will not lift a finger to move them. All their works are performed to be seen. They widen their phylacteries and lengthen their tassels. They love places of honor at banquets, seats of honor in synagogues, greetings in marketplaces, and the salutation 'Rabbi.' As for you, do not be called 'Rabbi.' You have but one teacher, and you are all brothers. Call no one on earth your father; you have but one Father in heaven. Do not be called 'Master'; you have but one master, the Christ. The greatest among you must be your servant. Whoever exalts himself will be humbled; but whoever humbles himself will be exalted."

1200 THIRTY-FIRST SUNDAY IN ORDINARY TIME / B

READING I *Deuteronomy 6:2–6 / 152*

Moses spoke to the people, saying: "Fear the Lord, your God, and keep, throughout the days of your lives, all his statutes and commandments which I enjoin on you, and thus have long life. Hear then, Israel, and be careful to observe them, that you may grow and prosper the more, in keeping with the promise of the LORD, the God of your fathers, to give you a land flowing with milk and honey.

"Hear, O Israel! The LORD is our God, the LORD alone! Therefore, you shall love the LORD, your God, with all your heart, and with all your soul, and with all your strength. Take to heart these words which I enjoin on you today."

RESPONSORIAL PSALM
Psalm 18:2–3a, 3bc–4, 47 and 51ab

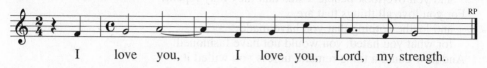

I love you, I love you, Lord, my strength.

I love you, LORD, my strength;
  O LORD, my rock, my fortress,
    my savior. ℟.

My God, my rock where I take refuge;
  my shield, my saving strength, my
    stronghold.
I cry out, "Praised be the LORD!"
  and see, I am saved from my foes. ℟.

The LORD lives, and blest be my Rock!
  May the God of my salvation be
    exalted.
The LORD gives great victories to his
  king,
  and shows merciful love for his
    anointed. ℟.

READING II
Hebrews 7:23–28

Brothers and sisters: The levitical priests were many because they were prevented by death from remaining in office, but Jesus, because he remains forever, has a priesthood that does not pass away. Therefore, he is always able to save those who approach God through him, since he lives forever to make intercession for them.

It was fitting that we should have such a high priest: holy, innocent, undefiled, separated from sinners, higher than the heavens. He has no need, as did the high priests, to offer sacrifice day after day, first for his own sins and then for those of the people; he did that once for all when he offered himself. For the law appoints men subject to weakness to be high priests, but the word of the oath, which was taken after the law, appoints a son, who has been made perfect forever.

GOSPEL
Mark 12:28b–34

One of the scribes came to Jesus and asked him, "Which is the first of all the commandments?" Jesus replied, "The first is this: *Hear, O Israel! The Lord our God is Lord alone! You shall love the Lord your God with all your heart, with all your soul, with all your mind, and with all your strength.* The second is this: *You shall love your neighbor as yourself.* There is no other commandment greater than these." The scribe said to him, "Well said, teacher. You are right in saying, 'He is One and there is no other than he.' And 'to love him with all your heart, with all your understanding, with all your strength, and to love your neighbor as yourself' is worth more than all burnt offerings and sacrifices." And when Jesus saw that he answered with understanding, he said to him, "You are not far from the kingdom of God." And no one dared to ask him any more questions.

1201 THIRTY-FIRST SUNDAY IN ORDINARY TIME / C

READING I *Wisdom 11:22−12:2 / 153*

Before the LORD the whole universe is as a grain
     from a balance
   or a drop of morning dew come down upon the earth.
But you have mercy on all, because you can do all things;
   and you overlook people's sins that they may repent.
For you love all things that are
   and loathe nothing that you have made;
   for what you hated, you would not have fashioned.
And how could a thing remain, unless you willed it;
   or be preserved, had it not been called forth by you?
But you spare all things, because they are yours,
   O LORD and lover of souls,
   for your imperishable spirit is in all things!
Therefore you rebuke offenders little by little,
   warn them and remind them of the sins
      they are committing,
   that they may abandon their wickedness
      and believe in you, O LORD!

RESPONSORIAL PSALM *Psalm 145:1−2, 8−9, 10−11, 13cd−14*

I will praise your name for ev-er, my king and my God.

I will extol you, my God and king,
   and bless your name forever and
      ever.
I will bless you day after day,
   and praise your name forever and
      ever. ℟.

The LORD is kind and full of
      compassion,
   slow to anger, abounding in mercy.
How good is the LORD to all,
   compassionate to all his creatures. ℟.

All your works shall thank you, O
      LORD,
   and all your faithful ones bless you.
They shall speak of the glory of your
      reign,
   and declare your mighty deeds. ℟.

The LORD is faithful in all his words,
   and holy in all his deeds.
The LORD supports all who fall,
   and raises up all who are bowed
      down. ℟.

READING II *2 Thessalonians 1:11−2:2*

Brothers and sisters: We always pray for you, that our God may make you worthy of his calling and powerfully bring to fulfillment every good purpose and every effort of faith, that the name of our Lord Jesus may be glorified in you, and you in him, in accord with the grace of our God and Lord Jesus Christ.

   We ask you, brothers and sisters, with regard to the coming of our Lord Jesus Christ and our assembling with him, not to be shaken out of your minds suddenly, or to be alarmed either by a "spirit," or by an oral statement, or by a letter allegedly from us to the effect that the day of the Lord is at hand.

GOSPEL *Luke 19:1–10*

At that time, Jesus came to Jericho and intended to pass through the town. Now a man there named Zacchaeus, who was a chief tax collector and also a wealthy man, was seeking to see who Jesus was; but he could not see him because of the crowd, for he was short in stature. So he ran ahead and climbed a sycamore tree in order to see Jesus, who was about to pass that way. When he reached the place, Jesus looked up and said, "Zacchaeus, come down quickly, for today I must stay at your house." And he came down quickly and received him with joy. When they all saw this, they began to grumble, saying, "He has gone to stay at the house of a sinner." But Zacchaeus stood there and said to the Lord, "Behold, half of my possessions, Lord, I shall give to the poor, and if I have extorted anything from anyone I shall repay it four times over." And Jesus said to him, "Today salvation has come to this house because this man too is a descendant of Abraham. For the Son of Man has come to seek and to save what was lost."

THIRTY-SECOND SUNDAY IN ORDINARY TIME / A   1202

READING I *Wisdom 6:12–16 / 154*

Resplendent and unfading is wisdom,
and she is readily perceived by
those who love her,
and found by those who seek her.
She hastens to make herself known
in anticipation of their desire;
whoever watches for her at dawn
shall not be disappointed,
for he shall find her sitting by his
gate.

For taking thought of wisdom is the
perfection of prudence,
and whoever for her sake keeps vigil
shall quickly be free from care;
because she makes her own rounds,
seeking those worthy of her,
and graciously appears to them in
the ways,
and meets them with all solicitude.

RESPONSORIAL PSALM *Psalm 63:2, 3–4, 5–6, 7–8*

My soul is thirst-ing for you, O Lord, thirst-ing for you my God.

O God, you are my God; at dawn I seek
you;
for you my soul is thirsting.
For you my flesh is pining,
like a dry, weary land without
water. ℟.

I have come before you in the sanctuary,
to behold your strength and your
glory.
Your loving mercy is better than life;
my lips will speak your praise. ℟.

I will bless you all my life;
in your name I will lift up my hands.
My soul shall be filled as with a
banquet;
with joyful lips, my mouth shall
praise you. ℟.

When I remember you upon my bed,
I muse on you through the watches
of the night.
For you have been my strength;
in the shadow of your wings I
rejoice. ℟.

READING II   *1 Thessalonians 4:13–18 or 4:13–14*

For short form read only the part in brackets.

[We do not want you to be unaware, brothers and sisters, about those who have fallen
asleep, so that you may not grieve like the rest, who have no hope. For if we believe
that Jesus died and rose, so too will God, through Jesus, bring with him those who
have fallen asleep.] Indeed, we tell you this, on the word of the Lord, that we who
are alive, who are left until the coming of the Lord, will surely not precede those who
have fallen asleep. For the Lord himself, with a word of command, with the voice
of an archangel and with the trumpet of God, will come down from heaven, and the
dead in Christ will rise first. Then we who are alive, who are left, will be caught up
together with them in the clouds to meet the Lord in the air. Thus we shall always be
with the Lord. Therefore, console one another with these words.

GOSPEL   *Matthew 25:1–13*

Jesus told his disciples this parable: "The kingdom of heaven will be like ten virgins
who took their lamps and went out to meet the bridegroom. Five of them were foolish
and five were wise. The foolish ones, when taking their lamps, brought no oil with
them, but the wise brought flasks of oil with their lamps. Since the bridegroom was
long delayed, they all became drowsy and fell asleep. At midnight, there was a cry,
'Behold, the bridegroom! Come out to meet him!' Then all those virgins got up and
trimmed their lamps. The foolish ones said to the wise, 'Give us some of your oil, for
our lamps are going out.' But the wise ones replied, 'No, for there may not be enough
for us and you. Go instead to the merchants and buy some for yourselves.' While they
went off to buy it, the bridegroom came and those who were ready went into the wedding feast with him. Then the door was locked. Afterwards the other virgins came and
said, 'Lord, Lord, open the door for us!' But he said in reply, 'Amen, I say to you, I do
not know you.' Therefore, stay awake, for you know neither the day nor the hour."

1203   THIRTY-SECOND SUNDAY IN ORDINARY TIME / B

READING I   *1 Kings 17:10–16 / 155*

In those days, Elijah the prophet went to Zarephath. As he arrived at the entrance of
the city, a widow was gathering sticks there; he called out to her, "Please bring me a
small cupful of water to drink." She left to get it, and he called out after her, "Please
bring along a bit of bread." She answered, "As the LORD, your God, lives, I have nothing baked; there is only a handful of flour in my jar and a little oil in my jug. Just now
I was collecting a couple of sticks, to go in and prepare something for myself and my
son; when we have eaten it, we shall die." Elijah said to her, "Do not be afraid. Go and
do as you propose. But first make me a little cake and bring it to me. Then you can
prepare something for yourself and your son. For the LORD, the God of Israel, says,

'The jar of flour shall not go empty, nor the jug of oil run dry, until the day when the LORD sends rain upon the earth.'" She left and did as Elijah had said. She was able to eat for a year, and he and her son as well; the jar of flour did not go empty, nor the jug of oil run dry, as the LORD had foretold through Elijah.

RESPONSORIAL PSALM

Psalm 146:6c–7, 8–9a, 9bc–10

Or: Alleluia.

Praise the Lord, my soul! Praise the Lord!

It is the LORD who preserves
    fidelity forever,
who does justice to those who are
    oppressed.
It is he who gives bread to the hungry,
    the LORD who sets prisoners free. ℟.

The LORD who opens the eyes of the blind,
    the LORD who raises up those who
    are bowed down.

It is the LORD who loves the just,
    the LORD who protects the
    stranger. ℟.

The LORD upholds the orphan and the
    widow,
but thwarts the path of the wicked.
The LORD will reign forever,
    the God of Sion from age to age.
    Alleluia. ℟.

READING II

Hebrews 9:24–28

Christ did not enter into a sanctuary made by hands, a copy of the true one, but heaven itself, that he might now appear before God on our behalf. Not that he might offer himself repeatedly, as the high priest enters each year into the sanctuary with blood that is not his own; if that were so, he would have had to suffer repeatedly from the foundation of the world. But now once for all he has appeared at the end of the ages to take away sin by his sacrifice. Just as it is appointed that human beings die once, and after this the judgment, so also Christ, offered once to take away the sins of many, will appear a second time, not to take away sin but to bring salvation to those who eagerly await him.

GOSPEL

Mark 12:38–44 or 12:41–44

For short form read only the parts in brackets. The word in parantheses is omitted in the long form.

In the course of his teaching Jesus said to the crowds, "Beware of the scribes, who like to go around in long robes and accept greetings in the marketplaces, seats of honor in synagogues, and places of honor at banquets. They devour the houses of widows and, as a pretext recite lengthy prayers. They will receive a very severe condemnation."

He [(Jesus) sat down opposite the treasury and observed how the crowd put money into the treasury. Many rich people put in large sums. A poor widow also came and put in two small coins worth a few cents. Calling his disciples to himself, he said to them, "Amen, I say to you, this poor widow put in more than all the other contributors to the treasury. For they have all contributed from their surplus wealth, but she, from her poverty, has contributed all she had, her whole livelihood."]

1204 THIRTY-SECOND SUNDAY IN ORDINARY TIME / C

READING I *2 Maccabees 7:1–2, 9–14 / 156*

It happened that seven brothers with their mother were arrested and tortured with whips and scourges by the king, to force them to eat pork in violation of God's law. One of the brothers, speaking for the others, said: "What do you expect to achieve by questioning us? We are ready to die rather than transgress the laws of our ancestors."

At the point of death he said: "You accursed fiend, you are depriving us of this present life, but the King of the world will raise us up to live again forever. It is for his laws that we are dying."

After him the third suffered their cruel sport. He put out his tongue at once when told to do so, and bravely held out his hands, as he spoke these noble words: "It was from Heaven that I received these; for the sake of his laws I disdain them; from him I hope to receive them again." Even the king and his attendants marveled at the young man's courage, because he regarded his sufferings as nothing.

After he had died, they tortured and maltreated the fourth brother in the same way. When he was near death, he said, "It is my choice to die at the hands of men with the hope God gives of being raised up by him; but for you, there will be no resurrection to life."

RESPONSORIAL PSALM *Psalm 17:1, 5–6, 8 and 15*

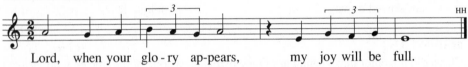

Lord, when your glo-ry ap-pears, my joy will be full.

O LORD, hear a cause that is just,
  pay heed to my cry.
Turn your ear to my prayer:
  no deceit is on my lips. ℞.

I kept my steps firmly in your paths.
  My feet have never faltered.
To you I call; for you will surely heed
    me, O God.
  Turn your ear to me; hear my
    words. ℞.

Guard me as the apple of your eye.
  Hide me in the shadow of your
    wings.
As for me, in justice I shall behold your
    face;
  when I awake I shall be filled with
    the vision of your presence. ℞.

READING II *2 Thessalonians 2:16—3:5*

Brothers and sisters: May our Lord Jesus Christ himself and God our Father, who has loved us and given us everlasting encouragement and good hope through his grace, encourage your hearts and strengthen them in every good deed and word.

Finally, brothers and sisters, pray for us, so that the word of the Lord may speed forward and be glorified, as it did among you, and that we may be delivered from perverse and wicked people, for not all have faith. But the Lord is faithful; he will strengthen you and guard you from the evil one. We are confident of you in the Lord that what we instruct you, you are doing and will continue to do. May the Lord direct your hearts to the love of God and to the endurance of Christ.

GOSPEL *Luke 20:27–38 or 20:27, 34–38*

For short form read only the parts in brackets.

[Some Sadducees, those who deny that there is a resurrection, came forward] and put this question to Jesus, saying, "Teacher, Moses wrote for us, *If someone's brother dies leaving a wife but no child, his brother must take the wife and raise up descendants for his brother.* Now there were seven brothers; the first married a woman but died childless. Then the second and the third married her, and likewise all the seven died childless. Finally the woman also died. Now at the resurrection whose wife will that woman be? For all seven had been married to her." [Jesus said to them, "The children of this age marry and remarry; but those who are deemed worthy to attain to the coming age and to the resurrection of the dead neither marry nor are given in marriage. They can no longer die, for they are like angels; and they are the children of God because they are the ones who will rise. That the dead will rise even Moses made known in the passage about the bush, when he called out 'Lord,' the God of Abraham, the God of Isaac, and the God of Jacob; and he is not God of the dead, but of the living, for to him all are alive."]

THIRTY-THIRD SUNDAY IN ORDINARY TIME / A 1205

READING I *Proverbs 31:10–13, 19–20, 30–31 / 157*

When one finds a worthy wife,
  her value is far beyond pearls.
Her husband, entrusting his heart to her,
  has an unfailing prize.
She brings him good, and not evil,
  all the days of her life.
She obtains wool and flax
  and works with loving hands.
She puts her hands to the distaff,
  and her fingers ply the spindle.
She reaches out her hands to the poor,
  and extends her arms to the needy.
Charm is deceptive and beauty fleeting;
  the woman who fears the LORD is to
  be praised.
Give her a reward for her labors,
  and let her works praise her at the
  city gates.

RESPONSORIAL PSALM *Psalm 128:1–2, 3, 4–5*

RFK

Bless-ed are those who fear the Lord.

Blessed are all who fear the LORD,
  and walk in his ways!
By the labor of your hands you shall eat.
  You will be blessed and prosper. ℟.

Your wife like a fruitful vine
  in the heart of your house;
your children like shoots of the olive
  around your table. ℟.

Indeed thus shall be blessed
  the man who fears the LORD.
May the LORD bless you from Sion.
  May you see Jerusalem prosper
  all the days of your life! ℟.

READING II   *1 Thessalonians 5:1–6*

Concerning times and seasons, brothers and sisters, you have no need for anything to be written to you. For you yourselves know very well that the day of the Lord will come like a thief at night. When people are saying, "Peace and security," then sudden disaster comes upon them, like labor pains upon a pregnant woman, and they will not escape.

But you, brothers and sisters, are not in darkness, for that day to overtake you like a thief. For all of you are children of the light and children of the day. We are not of the night or of darkness. Therefore, let us not sleep as the rest do, but let us stay alert and sober.

GOSPEL   *Matthew 25:14–30 or 25:14–15, 19–21*
For short form read only the parts in brackets.

[Jesus told his disciples this parable: "A man going on a journey called in his servants and entrusted his possessions to them. To one he gave five talents; to another, two; to a third, one—to each according to his ability. Then he went away.] Immediately the one who received five talents went and traded with them, and made another five. Likewise, the one who received two made another two. But the man who received one went off and dug a hole in the ground and buried his master's money.

["After a long time the master of those servants came back and settled accounts with them. The one who had received five talents came forward bringing the additional five. He said, 'Master, you gave me five talents. See, I have made five more.' His master said to him, 'Well done, my good and faithful servant. Since you were faithful in small matters, I will give you great responsibilities. Come, share your master's joy.'] Then the one who had received two talents also came forward and said, 'Master, you gave me two talents. See, I have made two more.' His master said to him, 'Well done, my good and faithful servant. Since you were faithful in small matters, I will give you great responsibilities. Come, share your master's joy.' Then the one who had received the one talent came forward and said, 'Master, I knew you were a demanding person, harvesting where you did not plant and gathering where you did not scatter; so out of fear I went off and buried your talent in the ground. Here it is back.' His master said to him in reply, 'You wicked, lazy servant! So you knew that I harvest where I did not plant and gather where I did not scatter? Should you not then have put my money in the bank so that I could have got it back with interest on my return? Now then! Take the talent from him and give it to the one with ten. For to everyone who has, more will be given and he will grow rich; but from the one who has not, even what he has will be taken away. And throw this useless servant into the darkness outside, where there will be wailing and grinding of teeth.'"

1206 THIRTY-THIRD SUNDAY IN ORDINARY TIME / B

READING I   *Daniel 12:1–3 / 158*

In those days, I Daniel,
   heard this word of the Lord:
"At that time there shall arise
   Michael, the great prince,
   guardian of your people;

it shall be a time unsurpassed in distress
   since nations began until that time.
At that time your people shall escape,
   everyone who is found written in the
   book.

"Many of those who sleep in the dust of
the earth shall awake;
some shall live forever,
others shall be an everlasting horror
and disgrace.

"But the wise shall shine brightly
like the splendor of the firmament,
and those who lead the many to justice
shall be like the stars forever."

RESPONSORIAL PSALM

Psalm 16:5 and 8, 9–10, 11

You are my in-her-i-tance, O Lord, O Lord.

O LORD, it is you who are my portion
and cup;
you yourself who secure my lot.
I keep the LORD before me always;
with him at my right hand, I shall
not be moved. ℟.

And so, my heart rejoices, my soul is
glad;
even my flesh shall rest in hope.

For you will not abandon my soul to
hell,
nor let your holy one see
corruption. ℟.

You will show me the path of life,
the fullness of joy in your presence,
at your right hand, bliss forever. ℟.

READING II

Hebrews 10:11–14, 18

Brothers and sisters: Every priest stands daily at his ministry, offering frequently those same sacrifices that can never take away sins. But this one offered one sacrifice for sins, and took his seat forever at the right hand of God; now he waits until his enemies are made his footstool. For by one offering he has made perfect forever those who are being consecrated.

Where there is forgiveness of these, there is no longer offering for sin.

GOSPEL

Mark 13:24–32

Jesus said to his disciples: "In those days after that tribulation
the sun will be darkened,
and the moon will not give its light,
and the stars will be falling from the sky,
and the powers in the heavens will be shaken.

"And then they will see 'the Son of Man coming in the clouds' with great power and glory, and then he will send out the angels and gather his elect from the four winds, from the end of the earth to the end of the sky.

"Learn a lesson from the fig tree. When its branch becomes tender and sprouts leaves, you know that summer is near. In the same way, when you see these things happening, know that he is near, at the gates. Amen, I say to you, this generation will not pass away until all these things have taken place. Heaven and earth will pass away, but my words will not pass away.

"But of that day or hour, no one knows, neither the angels in heaven, nor the Son, but only the Father."

1207 THIRTY-THIRD SUNDAY IN ORDINARY TIME / C

READING I *Malachi 3:19–20a / 159*

Lo, the day is coming, blazing like an oven,
when all the proud and all evildoers will be stubble,
and the day that is coming will set them on fire,
leaving them neither root nor branch, says the LORD of hosts.
But for you who fear my name, there will arise
the sun of justice with its healing rays.

RESPONSORIAL PSALM *Psalm 98:5–6, 7–9a, 9bc*

RC

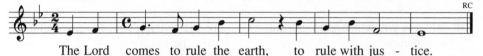

The Lord   comes   to rule the   earth,   to   rule with jus - tice.

Sing psalms to the LORD with the harp,
with the harp and the sound of song.
With trumpets and the sound of the horn,
raise a shout before the King,
the LORD. ℟.

Let the sea and all within it thunder;
the world, and those who dwell in it.

Let the rivers clap their hands,
and the hills ring out their joy
at the presence of the LORD, for he comes. ℟.

He comes to judge the earth.
He will judge the world with justice,
and the peoples with fairness. ℟.

READING II *2 Thessalonians 3:7–12*

Brothers and sisters: You know how one must imitate us. For we did not act in a disorderly way among you, nor did we eat food received free from anyone. On the contrary, in toil and drudgery, night and day we worked, so as not to burden any of you. Not that we do not have the right. Rather, we wanted to present ourselves as a model for you, so that you might imitate us. In fact, when we were with you, we instructed you that if anyone was unwilling to work, neither should that one eat. We hear that some are conducting themselves among you in a disorderly way, by not keeping busy but minding the business of others. Such people we instruct and urge in the Lord Jesus Christ to work quietly and to eat their own food.

GOSPEL *Luke 21:5–19*

While some people were speaking about how the temple was adorned with costly stones and votive offerings, Jesus said, "All that you see here—the days will come when there will not be left a stone upon another stone that will not be thrown down."

Then they asked him, "Teacher, when will this happen? And what sign will there be when all these things are about to happen?" He answered, "See that you not be deceived, for many will come in my name, saying, 'I am he,' and 'The time has come.' Do not follow them! When you hear of wars and insurrections, do not be terrified; for such things must happen first, but it will not immediately be the end." Then he said to them, "Nation will rise against nation, and kingdom against kingdom. There will be powerful earthquakes, famines, and plagues from place to place; and awesome sights and mighty signs will come from the sky.

"Before all this happens, however, they will seize and persecute you, they will hand you over to the synagogues and to prisons, and they will have you led before kings and governors because of my name. It will lead to your giving testimony. Remember, you are not to prepare your defense beforehand, for I myself shall give you a wisdom in speaking that all your adversaries will be powerless to resist or refute. You will even be handed over by parents, brothers, relatives, and friends, and they will put some of you to death. You will be hated by all because of my name, but not a hair on your head will be destroyed. By your perseverance you will secure your lives."

OUR LORD JESUS CHRIST, KING OF THE UNIVERSE / A   1208

READING I   *Ezekiel 34:11–12, 15–17 / 160*

Thus says the Lord GOD: I myself will look after and tend my sheep. As a shepherd tends his flock when he finds himself among his scattered sheep, so will I tend my sheep. I will rescue them from every place where they were scattered when it was cloudy and dark. I myself will pasture my sheep; I myself will give them rest, says the Lord GOD. The lost I will seek out, the strayed I will bring back, the injured I will bind up, the sick I will heal, but the sleek and the strong I will destroy, shepherding them rightly.

As for you, my sheep, says the Lord GOD, I will judge between one sheep and another, between rams and goats.

RESPONSORIAL PSALM   *Psalm 23:1–2a, 2b–3, 5–6*

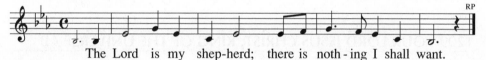

The Lord is my shep-herd; there is noth-ing I shall want.

The LORD is my shepherd;
    there is nothing I shall want.
Fresh and green are the pastures
    where he gives me repose. ℟.

Near restful waters he leads me;
    he revives my soul.
He guides me along the right path,
    for the sake of his name. ℟.

You have prepared a table before me
    in the sight of my foes.
My head you have anointed with oil;
    my cup is overflowing. ℟.

Surely goodness and mercy shall
    follow me
    all the days of my life.
In the LORD's own house shall I dwell
    for length of days unending. ℟.

READING II   *1 Corinthians 15:20–26, 28*

Brothers and sisters: Christ has been raised from the dead, the firstfruits of those who have fallen asleep. For since death came through man, the resurrection of the dead came also through man. For just as in Adam all die, so too in Christ shall all be brought to life, but each one in proper order: Christ the firstfruits; then, at his coming, those who belong to Christ; then comes the end, when he hands over the kingdom to his God and Father, when he has destroyed every sovereignty and every authority and power. For he must reign until he has put all his enemies under his feet. The last enemy to be destroyed is death. When everything is subjected to him, then the Son himself will also be subjected to the one who subjected everything to him, so that God may be all in all.

GOSPEL   *Matthew 25:31–46*

Jesus said to his disciples: "When the Son of Man comes in his glory, and all the angels with him, he will sit upon his glorious throne, and all the nations will be assembled before him. And he will separate them one from another, as a shepherd separates the sheep from the goats. He will place the sheep on his right and the goats on his left. Then the king will say to those on his right, 'Come, you who are blessed by my Father. Inherit the kingdom prepared for you from the foundation of the world. For I was hungry and you gave me food, I was thirsty and you gave me drink, a stranger and you welcomed me, naked and you clothed me, ill and you cared for me, in prison and you visited me.' Then the righteous will answer him and say, 'Lord, when did we see you hungry and feed you, or thirsty and give you drink? When did we see you a stranger and welcome you, or naked and clothe you? When did we see you ill or in prison, and visit you?' And the king will say to them in reply, 'Amen, I say to you, whatever you did for one of the least brothers of mine, you did for me.' Then he will say to those on his left, 'Depart from me, you accursed, into the eternal fire prepared for the devil and his angels. For I was hungry and you gave me no food, I was thirsty and you gave me no drink, a stranger and you gave me no welcome, naked and you gave me no clothing, ill and in prison, and you did not care for me.' Then they will answer and say, 'Lord, when did we see you hungry or thirsty or a stranger or naked or ill or in prison, and not minister to your needs?' He will answer them, 'Amen, I say to you, what you did not do for one of these least ones, you did not do for me.' And these will go off to eternal punishment, but the righteous to eternal life."

1209   OUR LORD JESUS CHRIST, KING OF THE UNIVERSE / B

READING I   *Daniel 7:13–14 / 161*

As the visions during the night continued,
I saw
  one like a Son of man coming,
    on the clouds of heaven;
  when he reached the Ancient One
    and was presented before him,
  the one like a Son of man received
    dominion, glory, and kingship;
all peoples, nations, and
    languages serve him.
His dominion is an everlasting
    dominion
  that shall not be taken away,
  his kingship shall not be
    destroyed.

RESPONSORIAL PSALM   *Psalm 93:1ab, 1c–2, 5*

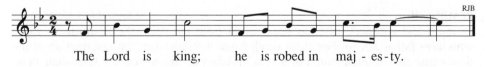

RJB

The Lord is king; he is robed in maj - es - ty.

The LORD is king, with majesty enrobed.
  The LORD has robed himself with
    might;
  he has girded himself with power. ℟.

The world you made firm, not to be
    moved;
  your throne has stood firm from of
    old.
  From all eternity, O LORD, you are. ℟.

Truly your decrees are to be trusted.
    Holiness is fitting to your house,
    O LORD, until the end of time. ℟.

READING II   *Revelation 1:5–8*

Jesus Christ is the faithful witness, the firstborn of the dead and ruler of the kings of the earth. To him who loves us and has freed us from our sins by his blood, who has made us into a kingdom, priests for his God and Father, to him be glory and power forever and ever. Amen.

    Behold, he is coming amid the clouds,
        and every eye will see him,
        even those who pierced him.
    All the peoples of the earth will lament him.
        Yes. Amen.

    "I am the Alpha and the Omega," says the Lord God, "the one who is and who was and who is to come, the almighty."

GOSPEL   *John 18:33b–37*

Pilate said to Jesus, "Are you the King of the Jews?" Jesus answered, "Do you say this on your own or have others told you about me?" Pilate answered, "I am not a Jew, am I? Your own nation and the chief priests handed you over to me. What have you done?" Jesus answered, "My kingdom does not belong to this world. If my kingdom did belong to this world, my attendants would be fighting to keep me from being handed over to the Jews. But as it is, my kingdom is not here." So Pilate said to him, "Then you are a king?" Jesus answered, "You say I am a king. For this I was born and for this I came into the world, to testify to the truth. Everyone who belongs to the truth listens to my voice."

OUR LORD JESUS CHRIST, KING OF THE UNIVERSE / C   1210

READING I   *2 Samuel 5:1–3 / 162*

In those days, all the tribes of Israel came to David in Hebron and said: "Here we are, your bone and your flesh. In days past, when Saul was our king, it was you who led the Israelites out and brought them back. And the LORD said to you, 'You shall shepherd my people Israel and shall be commander of Israel.'" When all the elders of Israel came to David in Hebron, King David made an agreement with them there before the LORD, and they anointed him king of Israel.

RESPONSORIAL PSALM   *Psalm 122:1–2, 3–4ab, 4cd–5*

Let us go re-joic-ing to the house, to the house of the Lord.

I rejoiced when they said to me,   And now our feet are standing
    "Let us go to the house of the LORD."   within your gates, O Jerusalem. ℟.

Jerusalem is built as a city
    bonded as one together.
It is there that the tribes go up,
    the tribes of the LORD. ℟.

For Israel's witness it is
    to praise the name of the LORD.
There were set the thrones for
    judgment,
    the thrones of the house of
    David. ℟.

READING II   *Colossians 1:12–20*

Brothers and sisters: Let us give thanks to the Father, who has made you fit to share in the inheritance of the holy ones in light. He delivered us from the power of darkness and transferred us to the kingdom of his beloved Son, in whom we have redemption, the forgiveness of sins.

He is the image of the invisible God,
    the firstborn of all creation.
For in him were created all things in heaven and on earth,
    the visible and the invisible,
    whether thrones or dominions or principalities or powers;
    all things were created through him and for him.
He is before all things,
    and in him all things hold together.
He is the head of the body, the church.
He is the beginning, the firstborn from the dead,
    that in all things he himself might be preeminent.
For in him all the fullness was pleased to dwell,
    and through him to reconcile all things for him,
    making peace by the blood of his cross
    through him, whether those on earth or those in heaven.

GOSPEL   *Luke 23:35–43*

The rulers sneered at Jesus and said, "He saved others, let him save himself if he is the chosen one, the Christ of God." Even the soldiers jeered at him. As they approached to offer him wine they called out, "If you are King of the Jews, save yourself." Above him there was an inscription that read, "This is the King of the Jews."

Now one of the criminals hanging there reviled Jesus, saying, "Are you not the Christ? Save yourself and us." The other, however, rebuking him, said in reply, "Have you no fear of God, for you are subject to the same condemnation? And indeed, we have been condemned justly, for the sentence we received corresponds to our crimes, but this man has done nothing criminal." Then he said, "Jesus, remember me when you come into your kingdom." He replied to him, "Amen, I say to you, today you will be with me in Paradise."

Other Feasts and Celebrations

Forty days after the celebration of Christmas, this feast tells of how Mary and Joseph brought the child to the Temple. There the aged Simeon took the baby in his arms and proclaimed that Jesus would be "a light to the Gentiles, the glory of Israel." These words have been sung for centuries on February 2 as Christians have blessed and carried lighted candles in procession.

BLESSING OF CANDLES AND PROCESSION

As the candles are lighted, this antiphon (with optional verses) may be sung:

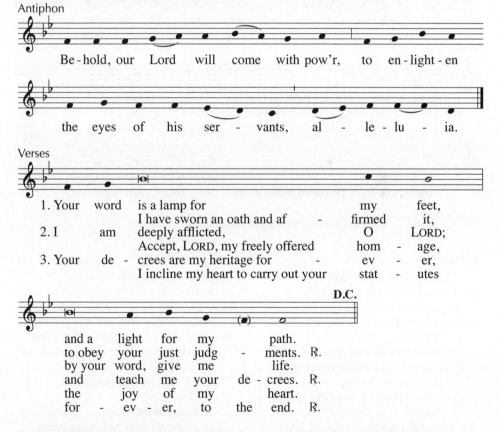

Antiphon

Be - hold, our Lord will come with pow'r, to en - light - en

the eyes of his ser - vants, al - le - lu - ia.

Verses

1. Your	word	is a lamp for		my	feet,
		I have sworn an oath and af -		firmed	it,
2. I	am	deeply afflicted,		O	LORD;
		Accept, LORD, my freely offered		hom -	age,
3. Your	de -	crees are my heritage for -		ev -	er,
		I incline my heart to carry out your		stat -	utes

D.C.

and a	light	for	my		path.	
to obey	your	just	judg -		ments.	℞.
by your	word,	give	me		life.	
and		teach	me	your	de - crees.	℞.
the		joy	of	my	heart.	
for -		ev - er,	to	the	end.	℞.

Text: Psalm 119:105–108, 111–112, *The Revised Grail Psalms*, © 2010, Conception Abbey and The Grail, admin. by GIA Publications, Inc.; antiphon, ICEL, © 2010
Music: Chant Mode VIII; acc. by Richard Proulx, © 1985, GIA Publications, Inc.; antiphon, ICEL, © 2010

When the candles have been blessed, the priest sings:

Let us go in peace   to   meet   the   Lord.

Or:

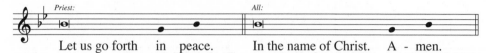

Let us go forth   in   peace.   In the name of Christ.   A - men.

1212 *During the procession, the following may be sung:*

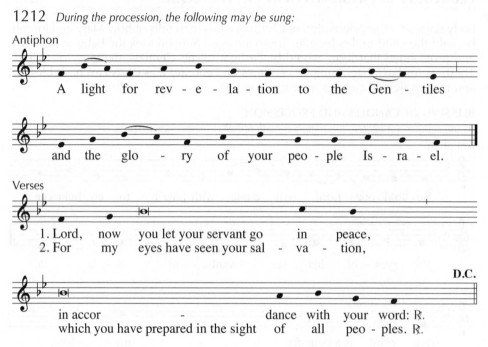

Antiphon

A   light   for   rev - e - la - tion   to   the   Gen - tiles

and   the   glo - ry   of   your   peo - ple   Is - ra - el.

Verses

1. Lord,   now   you let your servant go   in   peace,
2. For   my   eyes have seen your sal - va - tion,

D.C.

in accor -   dance with   your   word: ℟.
which you have prepared in the sight   of   all   peo - ples. ℟.

Text: Luke 2:29–32, trans. ICEL, © 2010
Music: Chant Mode VIII; acc. by Richard Proulx, © 1985, GIA Publications, Inc.; antiphon, ICEL, © 2010

READING I   *Malachi 3:1–4 / 524*

Thus says the Lord God:
Lo, I am sending my messenger
   to prepare the way before me;
And suddenly there will come to the
    temple
   the Lord whom you seek,
And the messenger of the covenant
    whom you desire.
   Yes, he is coming, says the Lord of
    hosts.
But who will endure the day of his
    coming?
   And who can stand when he appears?

For he is like the refiner's fire,
   or like the fuller's lye.
He will sit refining and purifying silver,
   and he will purify the sons of Levi,
Refining them like gold or like silver
   that they may offer due sacrifice to
    the Lord.
Then the sacrifice of Judah and
    Jerusalem
   will please the Lord,
   as in the days of old, as in years
    gone by.

RESPONSORIAL PSALM
Psalm 24:7, 8, 9, 10

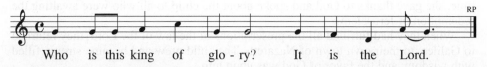

Who   is   this   king   of   glo - ry?   It   is   the   Lord.

O gates, lift high your heads;
  grow higher, ancient doors.
  Let him enter, the king of glory! ℟.

O gates, lift high your heads;
  grow higher, ancient doors.
  Let him enter, the king of glory! ℟.

Who is this king of glory?
  The LORD, the mighty, the valiant;
  the LORD, the valiant in war. ℟.

Who is this king of glory?
  He, the LORD of hosts,
  he is the king of glory. ℟.

READING II
Hebrews 2:14–18

Since the children share in blood and flesh, Jesus likewise shared in them, that through death he might destroy the one who has the power of death, that is, the Devil, and free those who through fear of death had been subject to slavery all their life. Surely he did not help angels but rather the descendants of Abraham; therefore, he had to become like his brothers and sisters in every way, that he might be a merciful and faithful high priest before God to expiate the sins of the people. Because he himself was tested through what he suffered, he is able to help those who are being tested.

GOSPEL
Luke 2:22–40 or 2:22–32

For short form, read only the part in brackets.

[When the days were completed for their purification according to the law of Moses, Mary and Joseph took Jesus up to Jerusalem to present him to the Lord, just as it is written in the law of the Lord, *Every male that opens the womb shall be consecrated to the Lord,* and to offer the sacrifice of *a pair of turtledoves or two young pigeons,* in accordance with the dictate in the law of the Lord.

Now there was a man in Jerusalem whose name was Simeon. This man was righteous and devout, awaiting the consolation of Israel, and the Holy Spirit was upon him. It had been revealed to him by the Holy Spirit that he should not see death before he had seen the Christ of the Lord. He came in the Spirit into the temple; and when the parents brought in the child Jesus to perform the custom of the law in regard to him, he took him into his arms and blessed God, saying:
  "Now, Master, you may let your servant go
    in peace, according to your word,
  for my eyes have seen your salvation,
    which you prepared in sight of all the peoples,
  a light for revelation to the Gentiles,
    and glory for your people Israel."]
The child's father and mother were amazed at what was said about him; and Simeon blessed them and said to Mary his mother, "Behold, this child is destined for the fall and rise of many in Israel, and to be a sign that will be contradicted —and you yourself a sword will pierce— so that the thoughts of many hearts may be revealed." There was also a prophetess, Anna, the daughter of Phanuel, of the tribe of Asher. She was advanced in years, having lived seven years with her husband after her marriage, and then as a widow until she was eighty-four. She never left the temple, but

worshipped night and day with fasting and prayer. And coming forward at that very time, she gave thanks to God and spoke about the child to all who were awaiting the redemption of Jerusalem.

When they had fulfilled all the prescriptions of the law of the Lord, they returned to Galilee, to their own town of Nazareth. The child grew and became strong, filled with wisdom; and the favor of God was upon him.

1213   MARCH 19: JOSEPH, HUSBAND OF MARY

READING I   *2 Samuel 7:4–5a, 12–14a, 16 / 543*

The LORD spoke to Nathan and said: "Go, tell my servant David, 'When your time comes and you rest with your ancestors, I will raise up your heir after you, sprung from your loins, and I will make his kingdom firm. It is he who shall build a house for my name. And I will make his royal throne firm forever. I will be a father to him, and he shall be a son to me. Your house and your kingdom shall endure forever before me; your throne shall stand firm forever.'"

RESPONSORIAL PSALM   *Psalm 89:2–3, 4–5, 27 and 29*

The Son of Da - vid will live for ev - er.

I will sing forever of your mercies,
   O LORD;
   through all ages my mouth will
     proclaim your fidelity.
I have declared your mercy is
   established forever;
   your fidelity stands firm as the
     heavens. ℞.

"With my chosen one I have made a
   covenant;
   I have sworn to David my servant:

I will establish your descendants forever,
   and set up your throne through all
     ages." ℞.

"He will call out to me, 'You are my
   father,
   my God, the rock of my salvation.'
I will keep my faithful love for him
   always;
   with him my covenant shall last." ℞.

READING II   *Romans 4:13, 16–18, 22*

Brothers and sisters: It was not through the law that the promise was made to Abraham and his descendants that he would inherit the world, but through the righteousness that comes from faith. For this reason, it depends on faith, so that it may be a gift, and the promise may be guaranteed to all his descendants, not to those who only adhere to the law but to those who follow the faith of Abraham, who is the father of all of us, as it is written, *I have made you father of many nations.* He is our father in the sight of God, in whom he believed, who gives life to the dead and calls into being what does not exist. He believed, hoping against hope, that he would become *the father of many nations,* according to what was said, *Thus shall your descendants be.* That is why *it was credited to him as righteousness.*

GOSPEL *Matthew 1:16, 18–21, 24a*

Jacob was the father of Joseph, the husband of Mary. Of her was born Jesus who is called the Christ.

Now this is how the birth of Jesus Christ came about. When his mother Mary was betrothed to Joseph, but before they lived together, she was found with child through the Holy Spirit. Joseph her husband, since he was a righteous man, yet unwilling to expose her to shame, decided to divorce her quietly. Such was his intention when, behold, the angel of the Lord appeared to him in a dream and said, "Joseph, son of David, do not be afraid to take Mary your wife into your home. For it is through the Holy Spirit that this child has been conceived in her. She will bear a son and you are to name him Jesus, because he will save his people from their sins." When Joseph awoke, he did as the angel of the Lord had commanded him and took his wife into his home.

Or:

GOSPEL *Luke 2:41–51a*

Each year Jesus' parents went to Jerusalem for the feast of Passover, and when he was twelve years old, they went up according to festival custom. After they had completed its days, as they were returning, the boy Jesus remained behind in Jerusalem, but his parents did not know it. Thinking that he was in the caravan, they journeyed for a day and looked for him among their relatives and acquaintances, but not finding him, they returned to Jerusalem to look for him. After three days they found him in the temple, sitting in the midst of the teachers, listening to them and asking them questions, and all who heard him were astounded at his understanding and his answers. When his parents saw him, they were astonished, and his mother said to him, "Son, why have you done this to us? Your father and I have been looking for you with great anxiety." And he said to them, "Why were you looking for me? Did you not know that I must be in my Father's house?" But they did not understand what he said to them. He went down with them and came to Nazareth, and was obedient to them.

MARCH 25: ANNUNCIATION OF THE LORD 1214

READING I *Isaiah 7:10–14; 8:10 / 545*

The LORD spoke to Ahaz, saying: Ask for a sign from the LORD, your God; let it be deep as the nether world, or high as the sky! But Ahaz answered, "I will not ask! I will not tempt the LORD!" Then Isaiah said: Listen, O house of David! Is it not enough for you to weary people, must you also weary my God? Therefore the Lord himself will give you this sign: the virgin shall conceive, and bear a son, and shall name him Emmanuel, which means "God is with us!"

RESPONSORIAL PSALM *Psalm 40:7–8a, 8b–9, 10, 11*

Here am I, Lord; I come to do your will.

You delight not in sacrifice and offerings, but in an open ear.

You do not ask for holocaust and victim. Then I said, "See, I have come." ℞.

In the scroll of the book it stands
   written of me:
"I delight to do your will, O my God;
  your instruction lies deep within
  me." ℟.

Your justice I have proclaimed
  in the great assembly.
My lips I have not sealed;

you know it, O LORD. ℟.

Your saving help I have not hidden in
  my heart;
of your faithfulness and salvation I
  have spoken.
I made no secret of your merciful love
  and your faithfulness to the great
  assembly. ℟.

READING II   *Hebrews 10:4–10*

Brothers and sisters: It is impossible that the blood of bulls and goats takes away sins.
For this reason, when Christ came into the world, he said:

"Sacrifice and offering you did not desire,
   but a body you prepared for me;
in holocausts and sin offerings you took no delight.
Then I said, 'As is written of me in the scroll,
behold, I come to do your will, O God.'"

First Christ says, "Sacrifices and offerings, holocausts and sin offerings, you neither
desired nor delighted in." These are offered according to the law. Then he says, "Behold,
I come to do your will." He takes away the first to establish the second. By this "will,"
we have been consecrated through the offering of the Body of Jesus Christ once for all.

GOSPEL   *Luke 1:26–38*

The angel Gabriel was sent from God to a town of Galilee called Nazareth, to a virgin
betrothed to a man named Joseph, of the house of David, and the virgin's name was
Mary. And coming to her, he said, "Hail, full of grace! The Lord is with you." But she
was greatly troubled at what was said and pondered what sort of greeting this might
be. Then the angel said to her, "Do not be afraid, Mary, for you have found favor with
God. Behold, you will conceive in your womb and bear a son, and you shall name
him Jesus. He will be great and will be called Son of the Most High, and the Lord
God will give him the throne of David his father, and he will rule over the house of
Jacob forever, and of his Kingdom there will be no end." But Mary said to the angel,
"How can this be, since I have no relations with a man?" And the angel said to her
in reply, "The Holy Spirit will come upon you, and the power of the Most High will
overshadow you. Therefore the child to be born will be called holy, the Son of God.
And behold, Elizabeth, your relative, has also conceived a son in her old age, and
this is the sixth month for her who was called barren; for nothing will be impossible
for God." Mary said, "Behold, I am the handmaid of the Lord. May it be done to me
according to your word." Then the angel departed from her.

1215 JUNE 24: NATIVITY OF ST. JOHN THE BAPTIST—VIGIL MASS

READING I   *Jeremiah 1:4–10 / 586*

In the days of King Josiah, the word of
the LORD came to me, saying:
  Before I formed you in the womb I
   knew you,

before you were born I dedicated you,
a prophet to the nations I appointed
  you.

"Ah, Lord GOD!" I said,
  "I know not how to speak; I am too
    young."
But the LORD answered me,
Say not, "I am too young."
  To whomever I send you, you shall
    go;
  whatever I command you, you shall
    speak.
Have no fear before them,
  because I am with you to deliver

you, says the LORD.

Then the LORD extended his hand and
touched my mouth, saying,

See, I place my words in your mouth!
  This day I set you
  over nations and over kingdoms,
  to root up and to tear down,
  to destroy and to demolish,
  to build and to plant.

RESPONSORIAL PSALM   *Psalm 71:1–2, 3–4a, 5–6ab, 15ab and 17*

Since my moth-er's womb,   you have been my strength.

In you, O LORD, I take refuge;
  let me never be put to shame.
In your justice, rescue me, free me;
  incline your ear to me and save me. ℟.

Be my rock, my constant refuge,
  a mighty stronghold to save me,
for you are my rock, my stronghold.
  My God, free me from the hand
    of the wicked. ℟.

It is you, O Lord, who are my hope,
  my trust, O LORD, from my youth.
On you I have leaned from my birth;
  from my mother's womb, you have
    been my help. ℟.

My mouth will tell of your justice,
  and all the day long of your salvation.
O God, you have taught me from my youth,
  and I proclaim your wonders still. ℟.

READING II   *1 Peter 1:8–12*

Beloved: Although you have not seen Jesus Christ you love him; even though you do not see him now yet believe in him, you rejoice with an indescribable and glorious joy, as you attain the goal of your faith, the salvation of your souls.

Concerning this salvation, prophets who prophesied about the grace that was to be yours searched and investigated it, investigating the time and circumstances that the Spirit of Christ within them indicated when he testified in advance to the sufferings destined for Christ and the glories to follow them. It was revealed to them that they were serving not themselves but you with regard to the things that have now been announced to you by those who preached the good news to you through the Holy Spirit sent from heaven, things into which angels longed to look.

GOSPEL   *Luke 1:5–17*

In the days of Herod, King of Judea, there was a priest named Zechariah of the priestly division of Abijah; his wife was from the daughters of Aaron, and her name was Elizabeth. Both were righteous in the eyes of God, observing all the commandments and ordinances of the Lord blamelessly. But they had no child, because Elizabeth was barren and both were advanced in years. Once when he was serving as priest in his division's turn before God, according to the practice of the priestly service, he was chosen by lot to enter the sanctuary of the Lord to burn incense. Then, when the whole assembly of the people was praying outside at the hour of the incense offering, the angel of the Lord appeared to him, standing at the right of the altar of incense. Zechariah was troubled by what he saw, and fear came upon him. But the angel said to him, "Do not be afraid, Zechariah, because your prayer has been heard. Your wife Elizabeth will bear you a son, and you shall name him John. And you will have joy and gladness, and many will rejoice at his birth, for he will be great in the sight of the Lord. John will drink neither wine nor strong drink. He will be filled with the Holy Spirit even from his mother's womb, and he will turn many of the children of Israel to the Lord their God. He will go before him in the spirit and power of Elijah to turn their hearts toward their children and the disobedient to the understanding of the righteous, to prepare a people fit for the Lord."

1216 JUNE 24: NATIVITY OF ST. JOHN THE BAPTIST–MASS DURING THE DAY

READING I *Isaiah 49:1–6 / 587*

Hear me, O coastlands
    listen, O distant peoples.
The LORD called me from birth,
    from my mother's womb he gave
        me my name.
He made of me a sharp-edged sword
    and concealed me in the shadow of
        his arm.
He made me a polished arrow,
    in his quiver he hid me.
You are my servant, he said to me,
    Israel, through whom I show my
        glory.

Though I thought I had toiled in vain,
    and for nothing, uselessly, spent my
        strength,

yet my reward is with the LORD,
    my recompense is with my God.
For now the LORD has spoken
    who formed me as his servant from
        the womb,
that Jacob may be brought back to him
    and Israel gathered to him;
and I am made glorious in the sight of
        the LORD,
    and my God is now my strength!
It is too little, he says, for you to be my
        servant,
    to raise up the tribes of Jacob,
    and restore the survivors of Israel;
I will make you a light to the nations,
    that my salvation may reach to the
        ends of the earth.

RESPONSORIAL PSALM *Psalm 139:1–3, 13–14ab, 14c–15*

I praise you, O Lord, for I am won‑der‑ful‑ly made.

O LORD, you search me and you know
        me.
    You yourself know my resting and
        my rising;
    you discern my thoughts from afar.
You mark when I walk or lie down;
    you know all my ways through and
        through. ℟.

For it was you who formed my inmost
        being,
    knit me together in my mother's
        womb.
I thank you who wonderfully made me;
    how wonderful are your works,
    which my soul knows well! ℟.

My frame was not hidden from you,
    when I was being fashioned in
      secret

and molded in the depths of the
    earth. ℟.

READING II   *Acts 13:22–26*

In those days, Paul said: "God raised up David as their king; of him he testified, *I have found David, son of Jesse, a man after my own heart; he will carry out my every wish.* From this man's descendants God, according to his promise, has brought to Israel a savior, Jesus. John heralded his coming by proclaiming a baptism of repentance to all the people of Israel; and as John was completing his course, he would say, 'What do you suppose that I am? I am not he. Behold, one is coming after me; I am not worthy to unfasten the sandals of his feet.'

"My brothers, children of the family of Abraham, and those others among you who are God-fearing, to us this word of salvation has been sent."

GOSPEL   *Luke 1:57–66, 80*

When the time arrived for Elizabeth to have her child she gave birth to a son. Her neighbors and relatives heard that the Lord had shown his great mercy toward her, and they rejoiced with her. When they came on the eighth day to circumcise the child, they were going to call him Zechariah after his father, but his mother said in reply, "No. He will be called John." But they answered her, "There is no one among your relatives who has this name." So they made signs, asking his father what he wished him to be called. He asked for a tablet and wrote, "John is his name," and all were amazed. Immediately his mouth was opened, his tongue freed, and he spoke blessing God. Then fear came upon all their neighbors, and all these matters were discussed throughout the hill country of Judea. All who heard these things took them to heart, saying, "What, then, will this child be?" For surely the hand of the Lord was with him.

The child grew and became strong in spirit, and he was in the desert until the day of his manifestation to Israel.

JUNE 29: STS. PETER & PAUL, APOSTLES—VIGIL MASS   1217

READING I   *Acts 3:1–10 / 590*

Peter and John were going up to the temple area for the three o'clock hour of prayer. And a man crippled from birth was carried and placed at the gate of the temple called "the Beautiful Gate" every day to beg for alms from the people who entered the temple. When he saw Peter and John about to go into the temple, he asked for alms. But Peter looked intently at him, as did John, and said, "Look at us." He paid attention to them, expecting to receive something from them. Peter said, "I have neither silver nor gold, but what I do have I give you: in the name of Jesus Christ the Nazorean, rise and walk." Then Peter took him by the right hand and raised him up, and immediately his feet and ankles grew strong. He leaped up, stood, and walked around, and went into the temple with them, walking and jumping and praising God. When all the people saw the man walking and praising God, they recognized him as the one who used to sit begging at the Beautiful Gate of the temple, and they were filled with amazement and astonishment at what had happened to him.

RESPONSORIAL PSALM   *Psalm 19:2–3, 4–5*

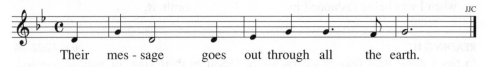

Their mes - sage goes out through all the earth.

The heavens declare the glory of God,	No speech, no word, whose voice goes

The heavens declare the glory of God,
and the firmament proclaims the
work of his hands.
Day unto day conveys the message,
and night unto night imparts the
knowledge. ℟.

No speech, no word, whose voice goes
unheeded;
their sound goes forth through all
the earth,
their message to the utmost bounds
of the world. ℟.

READING II   *Galatians 1:11–20*

I want you to know, brothers and sisters, that the gospel preached by me is not of human origin. For I did not receive it from a human being, nor was I taught it, but it came through a revelation of Jesus Christ.

For you heard of my former way of life in Judaism, how I persecuted the church of God beyond measure and tried to destroy it, and progressed in Judaism beyond many of my contemporaries among my race, since I was even more a zealot for my ancestral traditions. But when God, who from my mother's womb had set me apart and called me through his grace, was pleased to reveal his Son to me, so that I might proclaim him to the Gentiles, I did not immediately consult flesh and blood, nor did I go up to Jerusalem to those who were apostles before me; rather, I went into Arabia and then returned to Damascus.

Then after three years I went up to Jerusalem to confer with Cephas and remained with him for fifteen days. But I did not see any other of the apostles, only James the brother of the Lord. — As to what I am writing to you, behold, before God, I am not lying.

GOSPEL   *John 21:15–19*

Jesus revealed himself to his disciples and, when they had finished breakfast, said to Simon Peter, "Simon, son of John, do you love me more than these?" He answered him, "Yes, Lord, you know that I love you." Jesus said to him, "Feed my lambs." He then said to him a second time, "Simon, son of John, do you love me?" He answered him, "Yes, Lord, you know that I love you." He said to him, "Tend my sheep." He said to him the third time, "Simon, son of John, do you love me?" Peter was distressed that Jesus had said to him a third time, "Do you love me?" and he said to him, "Lord, you know everything; you know that I love you." Jesus said to him, "Feed my sheep. Amen, amen, I say to you, when you were younger, you used to dress yourself and go where you wanted; but when you grow old, you will stretch out your hands, and someone else will dress you and lead you where you do not want to go." He said this signifying by what kind of death he would glorify God. And when he had said this, he said to him, "Follow me."

1218 JUNE 29: STS. PETER & PAUL, APOSTLES–MASS DURING THE DAY

READING I   *Acts 12:1–11 / 591*

In those days, King Herod laid hands upon some members of the church to harm them. He had James, the brother of John, killed by the sword, and when he saw that this was pleasing to the Jews he proceeded to arrest Peter also. —It was the feast of Unleavened Bread.— He had him taken into custody and put in prison under the guard of four squads of four soldiers each. He intended to bring him before the people after Passover. Peter thus was being kept in prison, but prayer by the church was fervently being made to God on his behalf.

On the very night before Herod was to bring him to trial, Peter, secured by double chains, was sleeping between two soldiers, while outside the door guards kept watch on the prison. Suddenly the angel of the Lord stood by him and a light shone in the cell. He tapped Peter on the side and awakened him, saying, "Get up quickly." The chains fell from his wrists. The angel said to him, "Put on your belt and your sandals." He did so. Then he said to him, "Put on your cloak and follow me." So he followed him out, not realizing that what was happening through the angel was real; he thought he was seeing a vision. They passed the first guard, then the second, and came to the iron gate leading out to the city, which opened for them by itself. They emerged and made their way down an alley, and suddenly the angel left him. Then Peter recovered his senses and said, "Now I know for certain that the Lord sent his angel and rescued me from the hand of Herod and from all that the Jewish people had been expecting."

RESPONSORIAL PSALM   *Psalm 34:2–3, 4–5, 6–7, 8–9*

The an-gel of the Lord will res-cue those who fear him.

I will bless the LORD at all times;
  praise of him is always in my mouth.
In the LORD my soul shall make its boast;
  the humble shall hear and be glad. ℟.

Glorify the LORD with me;
  together let us praise his name.
I sought the LORD, and he answered me;
  from all my terrors he set me free. ℟.

Look toward him and be radiant;

let your faces not be abashed.
This lowly one called; the LORD heard,
  and rescued him from all his
  distress. ℟.

The angel of the LORD is encamped
  around those who fear him,
  to rescue them.
Taste and see that the LORD is good.
  Blessed the man who seeks refuge
  in him. ℟.

READING II   *2 Timothy 4:6–8, 17–18*

I, Paul, am already being poured out like a libation, and the time of my departure is at hand. I have competed well; I have finished the race; I have kept the faith. From now on the crown of righteousness awaits me, which the Lord, the just judge, will award to me on that day, and not only to me, but to all who have longed for his appearance.

The Lord stood by me and gave me strength, so that through me the proclamation might be completed and all the Gentiles might hear it. And I was rescued from the lion's mouth. The Lord will rescue me from every evil threat and will bring me safe to his heavenly kingdom. To him be glory forever and ever. Amen.

GOSPEL *Matthew 16:13–19*

When Jesus went into the region of Caesarea Philippi he asked his disciples, "Who do people say that the Son of Man is?" They replied, "Some say John the Baptist, others Elijah, still others Jeremiah or one of the prophets." He said to them, "But who do you say that I am?" Simon Peter said in reply, "You are the Christ, the Son of the living God." Jesus said to him in reply, "Blessed are you, Simon son of Jonah. For flesh and blood has not revealed this to you, but my heavenly Father. And so I say to you, you are Peter, and upon this rock I will build my Church, and the gates of the netherworld shall not prevail against it. I will give you the keys to the Kingdom of heaven. Whatever you bind on earth shall be bound in heaven; and whatever you loose on earth shall be loosed in heaven."

1219 JULY 4: INDEPENDENCE DAY

RESPONSORIAL PSALM *Psalm 85:9ab and 10, 11–12, 13–14*

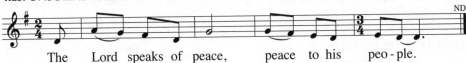

The Lord speaks of peace, peace to his peo-ple.

I will hear what the LORD God speaks;
  he speaks of peace for his people
    and his faithful.
His salvation is near for those who fear
    him,
  and his glory will dwell in our
    land. ℟.

Merciful love and faithfulness have met;
  justice and peace have kissed.

Faithfulness shall spring from the earth,
  and justice look down from
    heaven. ℟.

Also the LORD will bestow his bounty,
  and our earth shall yield its increase.
Justice will march before him,
  and guide his steps on the way. ℟.

1220 AUGUST 6: TRANSFIGURATION OF THE LORD

READING I *Daniel 7:9–10, 13–14 / 614*

As I watched:
  Thrones were set up
    and the Ancient One took his throne.
  His clothing was snow bright,
    and the hair on his head as white as wool;
  his throne was flames of fire,
    with wheels of burning fire.
  A surging stream of fire
    flowed out from where he sat;
  Thousands upon thousands were ministering to him,
    and myriads upon myriads attended him.
The court was convened and the books were opened.

As the visions during the night continued, I saw
One like a Son of man coming,
on the clouds of heaven;
When he reached the Ancient One
and was presented before him,
The one like a Son of man received dominion, glory, and kingship;
all peoples, nations, and languages serve him.
His dominion is an everlasting dominion
that shall not be taken away,
his kingship shall not be destroyed.

RESPONSORIAL PSALM *Psalm 97:1–2, 5–6, 9*

The Lord is king, the Most High o-ver all the earth.

The LORD is king, let earth rejoice;
let the many islands be glad.
Cloud and darkness surround him;
justice and right are the foundation
of his throne. ℟.

The mountains melt like wax
before the face of the LORD,

before the face of the Lord of all the
earth.
The skies proclaim his justice;
all peoples see his glory. ℟.

For you indeed are the LORD,
most high above all the earth,
exalted far above all gods. ℟.

READING II *2 Peter 1:16–19*
Beloved: We did not follow cleverly devised myths when we made known to you the power and coming of our Lord Jesus Christ, but we had been eyewitnesses of his majesty. For he received honor and glory from God the Father when that unique declaration came to him from the majestic glory, "This is my Son, my beloved, with whom I am well pleased." We ourselves heard this voice come from heaven while we were with him on the holy mountain. Moreover, we possess the prophetic message that is altogether reliable. You will do well to be attentive to it, as to a lamp shining in a dark place, until day dawns and the morning star rises in your hearts.

GOSPEL / A *Matthew 17:1–9*
Jesus took Peter, James, and his brother, John, and led them up a high mountain by themselves. And he was transfigured before them; his face shone like the sun and his clothes became white as light. And behold, Moses and Elijah appeared to them, conversing with him. Then Peter said to Jesus in reply, "Lord, it is good that we are here. If you wish, I will make three tents here, one for you, one for Moses, and one for Elijah." While he was still speaking, behold, a bright cloud cast a shadow over them, then from the cloud came a voice that said, "This is my beloved Son, with whom I am well pleased; listen to him." When the disciples heard this, they fell prostrate and were very much afraid. But Jesus came and touched them, saying, "Rise, and do not be afraid." And when the disciples raised their eyes, they saw no one else but Jesus alone.

As they were coming down from the mountain, Jesus charged them, "Do not tell the vision to anyone until the Son of Man has been raised from the dead."

GOSPEL / B   *Mark 9:2–10*

Jesus took Peter, James, and John and led them up a high mountain apart by themselves. And he was transfigured before them, and his clothes became dazzling white,
such as no fuller on earth could bleach them. Then Elijah appeared to them along
with Moses, and they were conversing with Jesus. Then Peter said to Jesus in reply,
"Rabbi, it is good that we are here! Let us make three tents: one for you, one for
Moses, and one for Elijah." He hardly knew what to say, they were so terrified. Then
a cloud came, casting a shadow over them; from the cloud came a voice, "This is my
beloved Son. Listen to him." Suddenly, looking around, they no longer saw anyone
but Jesus alone with them.

   As they were coming down from the mountain, he charged them not to relate what
they had seen to anyone, except when the Son of Man had risen from the dead. So
they kept the matter to themselves, questioning what rising from the dead meant.

GOSPEL / C   *Luke 9:28b–36*

Jesus took Peter, John, and James and went up a mountain to pray. While he was
praying his face changed in appearance and his clothing became dazzling white. And
behold, two men were conversing with him, Moses and Elijah, who appeared in glory
and spoke of his exodus that he was going to accomplish in Jerusalem. Peter and his
companions had been overcome by sleep, but becoming fully awake, they saw his
glory and the two men standing with him. As they were about to part from him, Peter
said to Jesus, "Master, it is good that we are here; let us make three tents, one for you,
one for Moses, and one for Elijah." But he did not know what he was saying. While
he was still speaking, a cloud came and cast a shadow over them, and they became
frightened when they entered the cloud. Then from the cloud came a voice that said,
"This is my chosen Son; listen to him." After the voice had spoken, Jesus was found
alone. They fell silent and did not at that time tell anyone what they had seen.

1221   AUGUST 15: ASSUMPTION OF MARY—VIGIL MASS

READING I   *1 Chronicles 15:3–4, 15–16; 16:1–2 / 621*

David assembled all Israel in Jerusalem to bring the ark of the LORD to the place that
he had prepared for it. David also called together the sons of Aaron and the Levites.

   The Levites bore the ark of God on their shoulders with poles, as Moses had
ordained according to the word of the LORD.

   David commanded the chiefs of the Levites to appoint their kinsmen as chanters,
to play on musical instruments, harps, lyres, and cymbals, to make a loud sound of
rejoicing.

   They brought in the ark of God and set it within the tent which David had pitched
for it. Then they offered up burnt offerings and peace offerings to God. When David
had finished offering up the burnt offerings and peace offerings, he blessed the people
in the name of the LORD.

RESPONSORIAL PSALM   *Psalm 132:6–7, 9–10, 13–14*

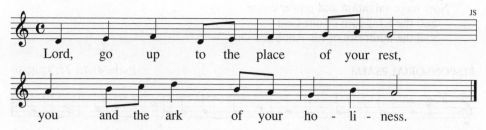

Lord, go up to the place of your rest, you and the ark of your ho - li - ness.

At Ephrata we heard of it;
    we found it in the plains of Yearim.
"Let us go to the place of his dwelling;
    let us bow down at his footstool." ℟.

Your priests shall be clothed with justice;
    your faithful shall ring out their joy.
For the sake of David your servant,

do not reject your anointed. ℟.

For the LORD has chosen Sion;
    he has desired it for his dwelling:
"This is my resting place from age to
    age;
here have I chosen to dwell." ℟.

READING II   *1 Corinthians 15:54b–57*

Brothers and sisters: When that which is mortal clothes itself with immortality, then the word that is written shall come about:

> Death is swallowed up in victory.
> Where, O death, is your victory?
> Where, O death, is your sting?

The sting of death is sin, and the power of sin is the law. But thanks be to God who gives us the victory through our Lord Jesus Christ.

GOSPEL   *Luke 11:27–28*

While Jesus was speaking, a woman from the crowd called out and said to him, "Blessed is the womb that carried you and the breasts at which you nursed." He replied, "Rather, blessed are those who hear the word of God and observe it."

AUGUST 15: ASSUMPTION OF MARY—MASS DURING THE DAY 1222

READING I   *Revelation 11:19a; 12:1–6a, 10ab / 622*

God's temple in heaven was opened, and the ark of his covenant could be seen in the temple.

A great sign appeared in the sky, a woman clothed with the sun, with the moon beneath her feet, and on her head a crown of twelve stars. She was with child and wailed aloud in pain as she labored to give birth. Then another sign appeared in the sky; it was a huge red dragon, with seven heads and ten horns, and on its heads were seven diadems. Its tail swept away a third of the stars in the sky and hurled them down to the earth. Then the dragon stood before the woman about to give birth, to devour her child when she gave birth. She gave birth to a son, a male child, destined to rule all the nations with an iron rod. Her child was caught up to God and his throne. The woman herself fled into the desert where she had a place prepared by God.

Then I heard a loud voice in heaven say:
"Now have salvation and power come,
    and the Kingdom of our God
    and the authority of his Anointed One."

RESPONSORIAL PSALM   *Psalm 45:10, 11, 12ab, 16*

The queen stands at your right hand, ar - rayed in gold.

The daughters of kings are those whom
    you favor.
On your right stands the queen in
    gold of Ophir. ℟.

Listen, O daughter; pay heed and give ear:
    forget your own people and your
    father's house. ℟.

So will the king desire your beauty.
He is your lord, pay homage to
    him. ℟.

They are escorted amid gladness and
    joy;
they pass within the palace of the
    king. ℟.

READING II   *1 Corinthians 15:20–27*

Brothers and sisters: Christ has been raised from the dead, the firstfruits of those
who have fallen asleep. For since death came through man, the resurrection of the
dead came also through man. For just as in Adam all die, so too in Christ shall all
be brought to life, but each one in proper order: Christ the firstfruits; then, at his
coming, those who belong to Christ; then comes the end, when he hands over the
Kingdom to his God and Father, when he has destroyed every sovereignty and every
authority and power. For he must reign until he has put all his enemies under his feet.
The last enemy to be destroyed is death, for "he subjected everything under his feet."

GOSPEL   *Luke 1:39–56*

Mary set out and traveled to the hill country in haste to a town of Judah, where she
entered the house of Zechariah and greeted Elizabeth. When Elizabeth heard Mary's
greeting, the infant leaped in her womb, and Elizabeth, filled with the Holy Spirit,
cried out in a loud voice and said, "Blessed are you among women, and blessed is
the fruit of your womb. And how does this happen to me, that the mother of my Lord
should come to me? For at the moment the sound of your greeting reached my ears,
the infant in my womb leaped for joy. Blessed are you who believed that what was
spoken to you by the Lord would be fulfilled."

And Mary said:
    "My soul proclaims the greatness of the Lord;
        my spirit rejoices in God my Savior
        for he has looked upon his lowly servant.
    From this day all generations will call me blessed:
        the Almighty has done great things for me,
        and holy is his Name.

He has mercy on those who fear him
  in every generation.
He has shown the strength of his arm,
  and has scattered the proud in their conceit.
He has cast down the mighty from their thrones,
  and has lifted up the lowly.
He has filled the hungry with good things,
  and the rich he has sent away empty.
He has come to the help of his servant Israel
  for he has remembered his promise of mercy,
  the promise he made to our fathers,
  to Abraham and his children for ever."

Mary remained with her about three months and then returned to her home.

FIRST MONDAY IN SEPTEMBER: LABOR DAY   1223

RESPONSORIAL PSALM   *Psalm 90:2, 3–4, 12–13, 14 and 16*

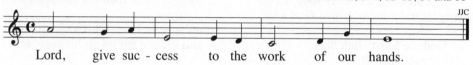

Lord, give suc - cess to the work of our hands.

Before the mountains were born,
  or the earth or the world were
    brought forth,
  you are God, from age to age. ℟.

You turn man back to dust,
  and say, "Return, O children of men."
To your eyes a thousand years
  are like yesterday, come and gone,
  or like a watch in the night. ℟.

Then teach us to number our days,
  that we may gain wisdom of heart.
Turn back, O Lord! How long?
  Show pity to your servants. ℟.

At dawn, fill us with your merciful love;
  we shall exult and rejoice all our
    days.
Let your deed be seen by your servants,
  and your glorious power by their
    children. ℟.

SEPTEMBER 14: EXALTATION OF THE HOLY CROSS   1224

READING I   *Numbers 21:4b–9 / 638*

With their patience worn out by the journey, the people complained against God and Moses, "Why have you brought us up from Egypt to die in this desert, where there is no food or water? We are disgusted with this wretched food!"

In punishment the Lord sent among the people saraph serpents, which bit the people so that many of them died. Then the people came to Moses and said, "We have sinned in complaining against the Lord and you. Pray the Lord to take the serpents from us." So Moses prayed for the people, and the Lord said to Moses, "Make a saraph and mount it on a pole, and if any who have been bitten look at it, they will live." Moses accordingly made a bronze serpent and mounted it on a pole, and whenever anyone who had been bitten by a serpent looked at the bronze serpent, he lived.

RESPONSORIAL PSALM   *Psalm 78:1bc–2, 34–35, 36–37, 38*

Do not for - get   the   works of   the   Lord.

Give ear, my people, to my teaching;
    incline your ear to the words of my
        mouth.
I will open my mouth in a parable
    and utter hidden lessons of the
        past. ℟.

When he slew them, then they sought
        him,
    repented and earnestly sought God.
They would remember that God was
        their rock,
    God the Most High their
        redeemer. ℟.

Yet they deceived him with their
        mouths;
    they lied to him with their tongues.
For their hearts were not steadfast
        toward him;
    they were not faithful to his
        covenant. ℟.

Yet he who is full of compassion
    forgave them their sin and spared
        them.
So often he held back his anger,
    and did not stir up all his rage. ℟.

READING II   *Philippians 2:6–11*

Brothers and sisters:
    Christ Jesus, though he was in the
        form of God,
        did not regard equality with God
           something to be grasped.
    Rather, he emptied himself,
        taking the form of a slave,
        coming in human likeness;
        and found human in appearance,
    he humbled himself,
        becoming obedient to the point
           of death,

        even death on a cross.
    Because of this, God greatly exalted
        him
        and bestowed on him the name
        which is above every name,
        that at the name of Jesus
        every knee should bend,
        of those in heaven and on earth
           and under the earth,
        and every tongue confess that
        Jesus Christ is Lord,
        to the glory of God the Father.

GOSPEL   *John 3:13–17*

Jesus said to Nicodemus: "No one has gone up to heaven except the one who has come down from heaven, the Son of Man. And just as Moses lifted up the serpent in the desert, so must the Son of Man be lifted up, so that everyone who believes in him may have eternal life."

For God so loved the world that he gave his only Son, so that he who believes in him might not perish but might have eternal life. For God did not send his Son into the world to condemn the world, but that the world might be saved through him.

NOVEMBER 1: ALL SAINTS

READING I

Revelation 7:2–4, 9–14 / 667

I, John, saw another angel come up from the East, holding the seal of the living God. He cried out in a loud voice to the four angels who were given power to damage the land and the sea, "Do not damage the land or the sea or the trees until we put the seal on the foreheads of the servants of our God." I heard the number of those who had been marked with the seal, one hundred and forty-four thousand marked from every tribe of the children of Israel.

After this I had a vision of a great multitude, which no one could count, from every nation, race, people, and tongue. They stood before the throne and before the Lamb, wearing white robes and holding palm branches in their hands. They cried out in a loud voice:

"Salvation comes from our God,
who is seated on the throne,
and from the Lamb."

All the angels stood around the throne and around the elders and the four living creatures. They prostrated themselves before the throne, worshipped God, and exclaimed:

"Amen. Blessing and glory, wisdom and thanksgiving,
honor, power, and might
be to our God forever and ever. Amen."

Then one of the elders spoke up and said to me, "Who are these wearing white robes, and where did they come from?" I said to him, "My lord, you are the one who knows." He said to me, "These are the ones who have survived the time of great distress; they have washed their robes and made them white in the Blood of the Lamb."

RESPONSORIAL PSALM

Psalm 24:1bc–2, 3–4ab, 5–6

Lord, this is the peo-ple that longs to see your face.

The LORD's is the earth and its fullness,
the world, and those who dwell in it.
It is he who set it on the seas;
on the rivers he made it firm. R̟.

Who shall climb the mountain of the
LORD?
Who shall stand in his holy place?
The clean of hands and pure of heart,

whose soul is not set on vain
things. R̟.

Blessings from the LORD shall he receive,
and right reward from the God who
saves him.
Such are the people who seek him,
who seek the face of the God of
Jacob. R̟.

READING II

1 John 3:1–3

Beloved: See what love the Father has bestowed on us that we may be called the children of God. Yet so we are. The reason the world does not know us is that it did not know him. Beloved, we are God's children now; what we shall be has not yet been revealed. We do know that when it is revealed we shall be like him, for we shall see him as he is. Everyone who has this hope based on him makes himself pure, as he is pure.

GOSPEL　　　　　　　　　　　　　　　　　　　　　　*Matthew 5:1–12a*

When Jesus saw the crowds, he went up the mountain, and after he had sat down, his disciples came to him. He began to teach them, saying:

"Blessed are the poor in spirit,
　　for theirs is the Kingdom of heaven.
Blessed are they who mourn,
　　for they will be comforted.
Blessed are the meek,
　　for they will inherit the land.
Blessed are they who hunger and thirst for righteousness,
　　for they will be satisfied.
Blessed are the merciful,
　　for they will be shown mercy.
Blessed are the clean of heart,
　　for they will see God.
Blessed are the peacemakers,
　　for they will be called children of God.
Blessed are they who are persecuted for the sake of righteousness,
　　for theirs is the Kingdom of heaven.
Blessed are you when they insult you and persecute you and utter every kind of evil against you falsely because of me. Rejoice and be glad, for your reward will be great in heaven."

1226　NOVEMBER 2: ALL SOULS' DAY

RESPONSORIAL PSALM　　　　　　　　　　　*Psalm 23:1–3a, 3b–4, 5, 6 / 668*

The Lord is my shep-herd; there is noth-ing I shall want.

or:

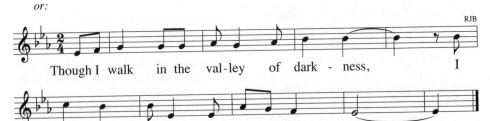

Though I walk in the val-ley of dark - ness, I fear no e-vil, for you are with me.

The LORD is my shepherd;
　　there is nothing I shall want.
Fresh and green are the pastures
　　where he gives me repose.
Near restful waters he leads me;
　　he revives my soul. ℟.

He guides me along the right path,
　　for the sake of his name.
Though I should walk in the valley of
　　the shadow of death,
　　no evil would I fear, for you are
　　with me.
　Your crook and your staff will give
　　me comfort. ℟.

You have prepared a table before me
in the sight of my foes.
My head you have anointed with oil;
my cup is overflowing. ℟.

Surely goodness and mercy shall follow
me
all the days of my life.
In the LORD's own house shall I dwell
for length of days unending. ℟.

Or:

RESPONSORIAL PSALM   *Psalm 25:6–7bc, 17–18, 20–21*

To you, O Lord, I lift my soul.

or:

No one who waits for you, O Lord, will ev-er be put to shame.

Remember your compassion, O LORD,
and your merciful love,
for they are from of old.
In your merciful love remember me,
because of your goodness, O LORD. ℟.

See my lowliness and suffering,
and take away all my sins. ℟.

Relieve the anguish of my heart,
and set me free from my distress.

Preserve my life and rescue me.
Let me not be put to shame,
for in you I trust.
May integrity and virtue protect me,
for I have hoped in you, O LORD. ℟.

Or:

RESPONSORIAL PSALM   *Psalm 27:1, 4, 7 and 8b and 9a, 13–14*

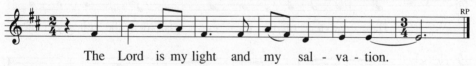

The Lord is my light and my sal - va - tion.

or:

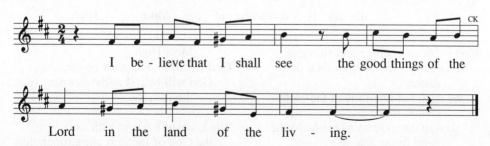

I be - lieve that I shall see the good things of the

Lord in the land of the liv - ing.

The LORD is my light and my salvation;
whom shall I fear?

The LORD is the stronghold of my life;
whom should I dread? ℟.

There is one thing I ask of the LORD,
    only this do I seek:
to live in the house of the LORD
    all the days of my life,
to gaze on the beauty of the LORD,
    to inquire at his temple. ℟.

O LORD, hear my voice when I call;
    have mercy and answer me.

It is your face, O LORD, that I seek;
    hide not your face from me. ℟.

I believe I shall see the LORD's
    goodness
    in the land of the living.
Wait for the LORD; be strong;
    be stouthearted, and wait for the
    LORD! ℟.

1227 NOVEMBER 9: DEDICATION OF THE LATERAN BASILICA

READING I   *Ezekiel 47:1–2, 8–9, 12 / 671*

The angel brought me back to the entrance of the temple, and I saw water flowing out from beneath the threshold of the temple toward the east, for the façade of the temple was toward the east; the water flowed down from the southern side of the temple, south of the altar. He led me outside by the north gate, and around to the outer gate facing the east, where I saw water trickling from the southern side. He said to me, "This water flows into the eastern district down upon the Arabah, and empties into the sea, the salt waters, which it makes fresh. Wherever the river flows, every sort of living creature that can multiply shall live, and there shall be abundant fish, for wherever this water comes the sea shall be made fresh. Along both banks of the river, fruit trees of every kind shall grow; their leaves shall not fade, nor their fruit fail. Every month they shall bear fresh fruit, for they shall be watered by the flow from the sanctuary. Their fruit shall serve for food, and their leaves for medicine."

RESPONSORIAL PSALM   *Psalm 46:2–3, 5–6, 8–9*

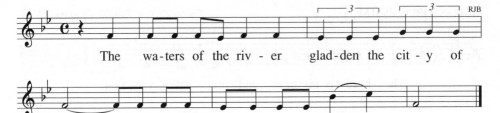

The waters of the river gladden the city of God the holy dwelling of the Most High.

God is for us a refuge and strength,
    an ever-present help in time of
        distress:
so we shall not fear though the earth
        should rock,
    though the mountains quake to the
        heart of the sea. ℟.

The waters of a river give joy to God's
    city,
    the holy place, the dwelling of the

    Most High.
God is within, it cannot be shaken;
    God will help it at the dawning of
    the day. ℟.

The LORD of hosts is with us:
    the God of Jacob is our stronghold.
Come and behold the works of the
    LORD,
    the awesome deeds he has done on
    the earth. ℟.

READING II
1 Corinthians 3:9c–11, 16–17

Brothers and sisters: You are God's building. According to the grace of God given to me, like a wise master builder I laid a foundation, and another is building upon it. But each one must be careful how he builds upon it, for no one can lay a foundation other than the one that is there, namely, Jesus Christ.

Do you not know that you are the temple of God, and that the Spirit of God dwells in you? If anyone destroys God's temple, God will destroy that person; for the temple of God, which you are, is holy.

GOSPEL
John 2:13–22

Since the Passover of the Jews was near, Jesus went up to Jerusalem. He found in the temple area those who sold oxen, sheep, and doves, as well as the money changers seated there. He made a whip out of cords and drove them all out of the temple area, with the sheep and oxen, and spilled the coins of the money changers and overturned their tables, and to those who sold doves he said, "Take these out of here, and stop making my Father's house a marketplace." His disciples recalled the words of Scripture, *Zeal for your house will consume me.* At this the Jews answered and said to him, "What sign can you show us for doing this?" Jesus answered and said to them, "Destroy this temple and in three days I will raise it up." The Jews said, "This temple has been under construction for forty-six years, and you will raise it up in three days?" But he was speaking about the temple of his body. Therefore, when he was raised from the dead, his disciples remembered that he had said this, and they came to believe the Scripture and the word Jesus had spoken.

THANKSGIVING DAY
1228

RESPONSORIAL PSALM
Psalm 138:1–2a, 2bc and 3, 4–5

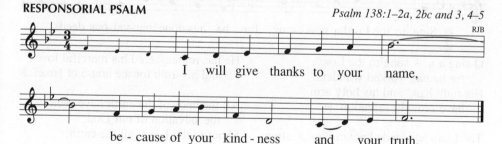

I will give thanks to your name, be-cause of your kind-ness and your truth.

I thank you, LORD, with all my heart;
   you have heard the words of my
      mouth.
In the presence of the angels I praise you.
   I bow down toward your holy
      temple. ℟.

I give thanks to your name
   for your merciful love and your
      faithfulness.
On the day I called, you answered me;

you increased the strength of my
   soul. ℟.

All earth's kings shall thank you,
   O LORD,
when they hear the words of your
   mouth.
They shall sing of the ways of the LORD,
   "How great is the glory of the
      LORD!" ℟.

1229 DECEMBER 8: IMMACULATE CONCEPTION

READING I   *Genesis 3:9–15, 20 / 689*

After the man, Adam, had eaten of the tree, the LORD God called to the man and asked him, "Where are you?" He answered, "I heard you in the garden; but I was afraid, because I was naked, so I hid myself." Then he asked, "Who told you that you were naked? You have eaten, then, from the tree of which I had forbidden you to eat!" The man replied, "The woman whom you put here with me— she gave me fruit from the tree, and so I ate it." The LORD God then asked the woman, "Why did you do such a thing?" The woman answered, "The serpent tricked me into it, so I ate it."

> Then the LORD God said to the serpent:
> "Because you have done this, you shall be banned
>   from all the animals
>   and from all the wild creatures;
> on your belly shall you crawl,
>   and dirt shall you eat
>   all the days of your life.
> I will put enmity between you and the woman,
>   and between your offspring and hers;
> he will strike at your head,
>   while you strike at his heel."

The man called his wife Eve, because she became the mother of all the living.

RESPONSORIAL PSALM   *Psalm 98:1, 2–3ab, 3cd–4*

Sing to the Lord a new song, for he has done mar-vel-ous deeds.

O sing a new song to the LORD,
    for he has worked wonders.
His right hand and his holy arm
    have brought salvation. ℟.

The LORD has made known his salvation,
    has shown his deliverance to the
        nations.

He has remembered his merciful love
    and his truth for the house of Israel. ℟.

All the ends of the earth have seen
    the salvation of our God.
Shout to the LORD, all the earth;
    break forth into joyous song,
    and sing out your praise. ℟.

READING II   *Ephesians 1:3–6, 11–12*

Brothers and sisters: Blessed be the God and Father of our Lord Jesus Christ, who has blessed us in Christ with every spiritual blessing in the heavens, as he chose us in him, before the foundation of the world, to be holy and without blemish before him. In love he destined us for adoption to himself through Jesus Christ, in accord with the favor of his will, for the praise of the glory of his grace that he granted us in the beloved.

In him we were also chosen, destined in accord with the purpose of the One who accomplishes all things according to the intention of his will, so that we might exist for the praise of his glory, we who first hoped in Christ.

GOSPEL *Luke 1:26–38*

The angel Gabriel was sent from God to a town of Galilee called Nazareth, to a virgin betrothed to a man named Joseph, of the house of David, and the virgin's name was Mary. And coming to her, he said, "Hail, full of grace! The Lord is with you." But she was greatly troubled at what was said and pondered what sort of greeting this might be. Then the angel said to her, "Do not be afraid, Mary, for you have found favor with God. Behold, you will conceive in your womb and bear a son, and you shall name him Jesus. He will be great and will be called Son of the Most High, and the Lord God will give him the throne of David his father, and he will rule over the house of Jacob forever, and of his Kingdom there will be no end." But Mary said to the angel, "How can this be, since I have no relations with a man?" And the angel said to her in reply, "The Holy Spirit will come upon you, and the power of the Most High will overshadow you. Therefore the child to be born will be called holy, the Son of God. And behold, Elizabeth, your relative, has also conceived a son in her old age, and this is the sixth month for her who was called barren; for nothing will be impossible for God." Mary said, "Behold, I am the handmaid of the Lord. May it be done to me according to your word." Then the angel departed from her.

1230   Acknowledgments

Acknowledgments/*continued*

Acknowledgments/*continued*

589 Text: © 1992, GIA Publications, Inc.

590 Text: © 1969, James Quinn, SJ. Selah Publishing Co., Inc., North American agent. www.selahpub.com

591 © 1986, Bernadette Farrell. Published by OCP. 5536 NE Hassalo, Portland, OR 97213

592 Text: © 1953, ren. 1981, The Hymn Society (Admin. Hope Publishing Company, Carol Stream, IL 60188). All rights reserved. Used by permission.

593 Text: © 1986, Hope Publishing Company, Carol Stream, IL 60188. All rights reserved. Used by permission. Harm.: © 1938, ren., The H. W. Gray Company. Used by permission of Alfred Publishing Co., Inc.

594 Text: © 1995, 2003, GIA Publications, Inc.

595 Text: © 2011, GIA Publications, Inc. Harm.: © Christian Education

596 English tr. and Harm.: © 2005, GIA Publications, Inc.

597 © 1976, Daniel L. Schutte and OCP. 5536 NE Hassalo, Portland, OR 97213

598 © 1997, Christopher Walker. Published by OCP. 5536 NE Hassalo, Portland, OR 97213

599 Text: © 1982, The Jubilate Group (Admin. Hope Publishing Company, Carol Stream, IL 60188). All rights reserved. Used by permission.

600 © 1972, OCP. 5536 NE Hassalo, Portland, OR 97213

602 Text: © 1969, Hope Publishing Company, Carol Stream, IL 60188. All rights reserved. Used by permission.

603 © 1998, Les Presses de Taizé, GIA Publications, Inc., agent

605 Text: © 1982, Hope Publishing Company, Carol Stream, IL 60188. All rights reserved. Used by permission. Harm.: © 1978, GIA Publications, Inc.

606 Text: © 1974, Hope Publishing Company, Carol Stream, IL 60188. All rights reserved. Used by permission.

608 Text: © 1972, Hope Publishing Company, Carol Stream, IL 60188. All rights reserved. Used by permission.

609 © 1979, Les Presses de Taizé, GIA Publications, Inc., agent

613 © 1979, Les Presses de Taizé, GIA Publications, Inc. agent

615 Text: © 2011, GIA Publications, Inc. Tune: © 2001, Hope Publishing Company, Carol Stream, IL 60188. All rights reserved. Used by permission.

618 © 1979, 2011, Manuel José Alonso and José Pagán. Published by OCP. 5536 NE Hassalo, Portland, OR 97213

619 © 1979, Les Presses de Taizé, GIA Publications, Inc., agent.

620 Harm.: © 1986, GIA Publications, Inc.

621 © 1999, GIA Publications, Inc.

622 © 2007, 2011, Les Presses de Taizé, GIA Publications, Inc., agent

623 © 1958, GIA Publications, Inc.

624 © 1990, GIA Publications, Inc.

625 © 1980, Les Presses de Taizé, GIA Publications, Inc., agent

626 Text: © 1991; Harm.: © 1986, GIA Publications, Inc.

627 Text: © 1982, The Jubilate Group (Admin. Hope Publishing Company, Carol Stream, IL 60188). All rights reserved. Used by permission.

629 Text: © 1973, Hope Publishing Company, Carol Stream, IL 60188. Tune: © 1973, The Jubilate Group (Admin. Hope Publishing Company). All rights reserved. Used by permission.

631 Text: © 1940, The Church Pension Fund. Used by permission of Church Publishing, Inc., New York.

633 Text: © 2000, GIA Publications, Inc.

635 © 1982, 1991, 2011, Les Presses de Taizé, GIA Publications, Inc., agent

636 Text: © 1939, 1966, E. C. Schirmer Music Co., Boston Massachusetts. Harm.: © The Royal School of Church Music, 19 The Close, Salisbury SP1 2EB, UK.

638 Text: © 1992, Hope Publishing Company, Carol Stream, IL 60188. All rights reserved. Used by permission. Tune: © 2001, GIA Publications, Inc.

639 © 1986, 1991, 2011, Les Presses de Taizé, GIA Publications, Inc. agent

640 Text: © 2000, GIA Publications, Inc.

641 Harm.: © 1975, GIA Publications, Inc.

643 Text: © 1982, 1990, Hope Publishing Company, Carol Stream, IL 60188. All rights reserved. Used by permission. Tune: © 1987, Estate of Skinner Chávez-Melo

644 Text: © 1998, Selah Publishing Co., Inc. www.selahpub.com All rights reserved. Used by permission. Harm.: © 2011, GIA Publications, Inc.

646 Acc.: © 1987, GIA Publications, Inc.

647 Text: © 1993, GIA Publications, Inc.

648 © 2008, GIA Publications, Inc.

649 Text: © 1993, John Thornburg. Tune: © 1983, GIA Publications, Inc.

650 Harm.: © 1982, The Jubilate Group (Admin. Hope Publishing Company, Carol Stream, IL 60188). All rights reserved. Used by permission.

651 © 1965, 1966, World Library Publications, Franklin Park, IL wlpmusic.com 800-566-6150. All rights reserved. Used by permission.

652 © 2006, GIA Publications, Inc.

653 © 2007, 2011, Les Presses de Taizé, GIA Publications, Inc., agent

654 © 2009, GIA Publications, Inc.

655 Text: © 1974, The Hymn Society (Admin. Hope Publishing Company, Carol Stream, IL 60188). All rights reserved. Used by permission. Tune: © Mrs. Alfred M. Smith

656 Text: © 1982, The Jubilate Group (Admin. Hope Publishing Company, Carol Stream, IL 60188.) All rights reserved. Used by permission. Tune: © 1986, GIA Publications, Inc.

657 © 1953, ren., arr. © 2011, Doris M. Akers. All rights administered by Chappell & Co., Inc. Used by permission of Alfred Publishing Co., Inc.

658 Text: © 2000, GIA Publications, Inc.

659 Text: © 2009, GIA Publications, Inc.

660 Text: © 1985, Oxford University Press. Assigned to Oxford University Press 2010. Reproduced by permission. All rights reserved.

661 Text: © 2000; Tune: © 1984; Acc.: 2006, GIA Publications, Inc.

663 © 1972, Universal Music - Brentwood Benson Publishing (ASCAP) / Calvary Chapel Costa Mesa Inc., dba CCCM Music (ASCAP). All rights for the world on behalf of CCCM Music admin. by Universal Music - Brentwood Benson Publishing. (Admin. by Music Services) All rights reserved. Used by permission.

664 Text: © 1989, Iona Community, GIA Publications, Inc., agent. Tune: © 1994, Hope Publishing Company, Carol Stream, IL 60188. All rights reserved. Used by permission.

665 Text: © 2004, 2009; Tune: © 2004, GIA Publications, Inc.

666 Text: © 1986, Oxford University Press. Assigned to Oxford University Press 2010. Reproduced by permission. All rights reserved.

667 © 1982, 2011, Les Presses de Taizé, GIA Publications, Inc., agent

668 Text: © 2002, Oxford University Press. Assigned to Oxford University Press 2010. Reproduced by permission. All rights reserved. Tune: © 1998, GIA Publications, Inc.

669 Text: © 2009, 2010; Tune: © 1998, GIA Publications, Inc.

670 Text: © 1996, The Pilgrim Press. Tune: ©1998, GIA Publications, Inc.

671 Tune Adapt.: © 1983, Abingdon Press (Admin. The Copyright Company, Nashville, TN) All rights reserved. International copyright secured. Used by permission. Acc.: © 2011, GIA Publications, Inc.

673 Text: © 1996, Hope Publishing Company, Carol Stream, IL 60188. All rights reserved. Used by permission.

674 Tune: © 1984; Acc.: © 2006, GIA Publications, Inc.

675 Text: © 1984, Hope Publishing Company, Carol Stream, IL 60188. All rights reserved. Used by permission.

676 Text: sts. 2–4, © 1981, Joseph R. Alfred

677 Text: © 1990, Hope Publishing Company, Carol Stream, IL 60188. All rights reserved. Used by permission. Tune: © 2009, GIA Publications, Inc.

678 Text: Verses, © 1963, 1993, The Grail, GIA Publications, Inc., agent; refrain, © 1985, Paul Inwood. Tune: © 1985, Paul Inwood. Published by OCP. 5536 NE Hassalo, Portland, OR 97213

679 Text: © 1991, GIA Publications, Inc. Harm.: © 1938, ren., The H. W. Gray Company. Used by permission of Alfred Publishing Co., Inc.

680 © 1975, 1978, Robert J. Dufford, SJ, and OCP. 5536 NE Hassalo, Portland, OR 97213

681 Text: © 2001, 2002, 2005, The Jubilate Group (Admin. Hope Publishing Company, Carol Stream, IL 60188). All rights reserved. Used by permission.

682 Tune: © 1984, GIA Publications, Inc.

683 Text: © 1997, GIA Publications, Inc.

684 Harm.: © 1988, GIA Publications, Inc.

685 © 2001, GIA Publications, Inc.

686 Text: © 1931, Oxford University Press, from *Enlarged Songs of Praise*, Reproduced by permission. All rights reserved. Harm.: © 1975, Hope Publishing Company, Carol Stream, IL 60188. All rights reserved. Used by permission.

687 Harm.: © 1975, GIA Publications, Inc.

688 Text tr.: © 1978, *Lutheran Book of Worship*. Admin. Augsburg Fortress. Used by permission.

690 © 1979, OCP. 5536 NE Hassalo, Portland, OR 97213

691 Text: © 1994, Selah Publishing Co., Inc. www.selahpub.com All rights reserved. Used by permission.

692 Text: © 1991, GIA Publications, Inc.

Acknowledgments/*continued*

909 Text: Tr. and st. 3 © 1965, FEL Publications, Inc. Assigned 1991 to The Lorenz Corporation.

910 Text: © 1976, Peter J. Scagnelli. Harm.: © 1969, Concordia Publishing House

911 Text: © 2011, GIA Publications, Inc. Tune: © 1967, Concordia Publishing House

912 Text: © 2005, Hope Publishing Company, Carol Stream, IL 60188. All rights reserved. Used by permission.

913 Text: © 1999, World Library Publications, Franklin Park, IL wlpmusic.com 800-566-6150 All rights reserved. Used by permission.

914 Harm.: © Downside Abbey

915 Text: © 1980, Augsburg Fortress

916 Refrain Text: © 1969, ICEL; verses © 1965, 1966, 1968, 1973. Music © 2004, World Library Publications, Franklin Park, IL wlpmusic.com 800-566-6150 All rights reserved. Used by permission.

917 © 1982, GIA Publications, Inc.

918 Text: © 1970, Judith Beatrice O'Neill. Harm.: © 1982, The Jubilate Group (Admin. Hope Publishing Company, Carol Stream, IL 60188). All rights reserved. Used by permission.

919 Text: © 1982, The Jubilate Group (Admin. Hope Publishing Company, Carol Stream, IL 60188). All rights reserved. Used by permission. Acc.: © Downside Abbey

920 © 2002, GIA Publications, Inc.

921 © 1984, 2007, Les Presses de Taizé, GIA Publications, Inc., agent

922 Text: © 1991, GIA Publications, Inc. Harm.: © 1979, assigned by Church of the Redeemer, Houston, to George E. Mims 2011

923 Vss. 1–3, 5–9: © 2008; Harm.: © 1986, GIA Publications, Inc.

924 © 2008, GIA Publications, Inc.

925 © 1988, Bob Hurd and Pia Moriarty. Published by OCP. 5536 NE Hassalo, Portland, OR 97213

926 Text: © 1971, 1995, Hope Publishing Company, Carol Stream, IL 60188. All rights reserved. Used by permission. Harm.: © 1989, The United Methodist Publishing House (Admin. The Copyright Company, Nashville, TN) All rights reserved. International copyright secured. Used by permission.

927 © 2008, GIA Publications, Inc.

928 Text for refrain and Tune: © 2000, GIA Publications, Inc.

929 Acc.: © 2011, GIA Publications, Inc.

930 © 1976, GIA Publications, Inc.

931 ©1978, John B. Foley, SJ, and OCP. 5536 NE Hassalo, Portland, OR 97213

932 Text: © 2002, Birnamwood Publications, a div. of MorningStar Music Publishers, Inc.

933 © 2008, GIA Publications, Inc.

934 © 1995, John Schiavone. Published by OCP. 5536 NE Hassalo, Portland, OR 97213

935 Music © 1992, World Library Publications, Franklin Park, IL wlpmusic.com 800-566-6150 All rights reserved. Used by permission.

936 © 2009, Sumerset Recordings and GIA Publications, Inc.

937 Text: © 1931, Oxford University Press, from *Enlarged Songs of Praise*. Reproduced by permission. All rights reserved. Tune: © 1957, The H. W. Gray Co., Inc.; Harm.: © Chalice Press

938 © 1980, GIA Publications, Inc.

939 © 1977, Archdiocese of Philadelphia. Published by International Liturgy Publications, PO Box 50476, Nashville, TN, 37205. www.ILPmusic.org. All rights reserved. Used with permission.

940 Verse text: © 1969, James Quinn, SJ. Selah Publishing Co., Inc., North American agent. www.selahpub.com. Tune and refrain text: © 1989, GIA Publications, Inc.

941 Harm.: © 1986, GIA Publications, Inc.

942 © 1995, Ricky Manalo, CSP. Published by OCP. 5536 NE Hassalo, Portland, OR 97213

943 © 1984, 2005, Les Presses de Taizé, GIA Publications, Inc., agent

944 © 2008, GIA Publications, Inc.

945 © 1983, GIA Publications, Inc.

946 Refrains, English verses, and Tune: © 2007, GIA Publications, Inc.

948 © 2001, GIA Publications, Inc.

949 © 1998, Iona Community, GIA Publications, Inc., agent

950 © 1966, 1970, 1986, 1993, 2005, GIA Publications, Inc.

951 © 1991; Tune: © 1993, GIA Publications, Inc.

952 Text: Verses © 2010, Conception Abbey and The Grail. Admin. GIA Publications, Inc.; refrain © 1969, 1981, 1997, ICEL. Tune: © 2002, GIA Publications, Inc.

955 Text: © 2008; Tune: © 1998, GIA Publications, Inc.

956 © 1987, GIA Publications, Inc.

957 © 1965, 1966, 1968, 1973, World Library Publications, Franklin Park, IL wlpmusic.com 800-566-6150 All rights reserved. Used by permission.

958 Text: © 2010, GIA Publications, Inc. Tune: © Mrs. Alfred M. Smith

959 Sp. text, Tune: © 1988, GIA Publications, Inc. Eng. tr.: © 1992, The Pilgrim Press

960 Text: © 1990, Hope Publishing Company, Carol Stream, IL 60188. All rights reserved. Used by permission.

961 Text: © 2011, GIA Publications, Inc.

962 Harm.: © 1979, assigned by Church of the Redeemer, Houston, to George E. Mims 2011

963 Text: © 1980, ICEL

964 © 1965, 1966, 1973, World Library Publications, Franklin Park, IL wlpmusic.com 800-566-6150 All rights reserved. Used by permission.

965 © 1987, GIA Publications, Inc.

967 Text: © Oxford University Press. Reproduced by permission. All rights reserved. Harm.: © The Royal School of Church Music, 19 The Close, Salisbury SP1 2EB, UK.

968 Text: © 1965; Harm.: © 1986, GIA Publications, Inc.

969 Text: © 1997, GIA Publications, Inc. Harm.: © The Royal School of Church Music

970 Text: © 1992; Tune: © 1994, GIA Publications, Inc.

971 Text: © 1991, GIA Publications, Inc. Tune: © 1978, Lutheran Book of Worship. Admin. Augsburg Fortress

972 Text alt.: © 1986, GIA Publications, Inc.

973 Text: © 2002, GIA Publications, Inc.

974 Text: © 1974, Hope Publishing Company, Carol Stream, IL 60188. All rights reserved. Used by permission. Harm.: © 1975, GIA Publications, Inc.

975 Text: © 1997; Acc.: © 2011, GIA Publications, Inc.

976 Text: © 1982, Hope Publishing Company, Carol Stream, IL 60188. All rights reserved. Used by permission. Arr.: © 1989, Iona Community, GIA Publications, Inc., agent

977 Text: © 2005, GIA Publications, Inc. Harm.: © 1978, *Lutheran Book of Worship*. Admin. Augsburg Fortress

978 Text: © 1969, Hope Publishing Company, Carol Stream, IL 60188. All rights reserved. Used by permission. Harm.: © 2011, GIA Publications, Inc.

979 Text: © 1993, GIA Publications, Inc.

980 © 1938, ren., arr. © 1994, Warner-Tamerlane Publishing Corp. Used by permission of Alfred Publishing Co., Inc.

981 Text: © 2006, GIA Publications, Inc.

982 Text and Harm.: © 1983, Hope Publishing Company, Carol Stream, IL 60188. All rights reserved. Used by permission.

983 Text: © 2011, GIA Publications, Inc.

984 Text: © 1989, Iona Community, GIA Publications, Inc., agent. Harm.: © 1975, Hope Publishing Company, Carol Stream, IL 60188. All rights reserved. Used by permission.

985 Text: © 2010, GIA Publications, Inc.

986 Text: © 1992, Hope Publishing Company, Carol Stream, IL 60188. All rights reserved. Used by permission.

987 Text: © 2008, GIA Publications, Inc.

988 Text: © 2011, GIA Publications, Inc.

989 Text: © 1982, Hope Publishing Company, Carol Stream, IL 60188. All rights reserved. Used by permission. Music: © 1987, GIA Publications, Inc.

990 Text: Order of Christian Funerals, © 1985, ICEL. Music: © 1990, GIA Publications, Inc.

991 Text: © 1970, ICEL. Tune: © 1977, ICEL

992 © 1996, Iona Community, GIA Publications, Inc., agent

994 Text: © 1970, ICEL. Tune: © 1977, ICEL

997 Text: St. 3 © 1964, Lorenz Publishing Co.

999 Text tr.: © 1969, Concordia Publishing House. Tune: © 1990, Selah Publishing Co., Inc. www.selahpub.com All rights reserved. Used by permission.

1043 Acc.: © 1985, 2011, GIA Publications, Inc.

1048 Acc.: © 1983, GIA Publications, Inc.

1056 Text tr.: © 1969, James Quinn, SJ. Selah Publishing Co., Inc., North American agent. www.selahpub.com. Acc.: © 1964, GIA Publications, Inc.

1058 © 1979, Les Presses de Taizé, GIA Publications, Inc., agent

1071 © 2010, ICEL

1073 Text: © 1969, ICEL, Music: © 1977, ICEL

1080 Text tr.: © 1983, Peter J. Scagnelli. Acc.: © 1975, GIA Publications, Inc.

1100 Text: ©1983, Peter J. Scagnelli. Acc.: © Interkerkelijke Stichting voor het Kerklied

1106 Text tr.: © 2000, World Library Publications, Franklin Park, IL wlpmusic.com 800-566-6150 All rights reserved. Used by permission. Acc.: © 1964, GIA Publications, Inc.

1231   Hymns for the Church Year

Hymns for the Church Year/*continued*

EASTER V
A – You Are the Way   682
   Christ, the Way We're Called to Follow   762
B – God, Bless Your Church with Strength!   791
   I Am the Vine   823
C – Lord of All Nations, Grant Me Grace   697

EASTER VI
A – This Is a Day of New Beginnings   508
   Alleluia! Sing to Jesus   953
B – Love Divine, All Loves Excelling   642
   No Greater Love   698
C – Love Divine, All Loves Excelling   642
   Unless a Grain of Wheat   759

ASCENSION OF THE LORD
See nos. 529–532

EASTER VII
A – Jesus Promises Communion   817
   Lord, Who at Your First Eucharist   954
B – Jesus Promises Communion   817
   Lord, Who at Your First Eucharist   954
C – Jesus Promises Communion   817
   Lord, Who at Your First Eucharist   954

PENTECOST SUNDAY
See nos. 533–547

MOST HOLY TRINITY
See nos. 548–555

BODY AND BLOOD OF CHRIST
See nos. 556–557

SACRED HEART OF JESUS
See nos. 558–560

ORDINARY TIME

SECOND SUNDAY
A – The Baptist Bore Witness   765
B – The Baptist Bore Witness   765
   Here I Am, Lord.   783
C – Jesus, Come! For We Invite You   656

THIRD SUNDAY
A – You Call to Us, Lord Jesus   775
   Two Fishermen   774
B – You Walk along Our Shoreline   766
   Two Fishermen   774
C – A Year of God's Favor   594

FOURTH SUNDAY
A – O Blest Are You   742
B – Silence! Frenzied, Unclean Spirit   666
C – God Has Spoken by the Prophets   592
   Not for Tongues of Heaven's Angels   701

FIFTH SUNDAY
A – Build Your City on the Hill   741
B – Your Hands, O Lord, in Days of Old   972
C – From Shallow Waters Call Us, Lord   758

SIXTH SUNDAY
A – Your Ways Are Not Our Own   695
   Eye Has Not Seen   713
B – Your Hands, O Lord, in Days of Old   972
C – God, Your Knowing Eye Can See   747

SEVENTH SUNDAY
A – To Love Just Those Who Love You   743
B – When Jesus Came Preaching the Kingdom
   of God   723
   Your Hands, O Lord, in Days of Old   972
C – Your Ways Are Not Our Own   695

EIGHTH SUNDAY
A – As the Birds of the Air   796
B – Who Is This Who Breaches Borders   829
C – Deliver Us, O Lord of Truth   751

NINTH SUNDAY
A – Deliver Us, O Lord of Truth   751
B – When You, Lord, Walked   582
C – Surely It Is God Who Saves Me   643
   Sing Praise to God for Friends   889

TENTH SUNDAY
A – How Shocking Were the People   845
   Come, You Sinners, Poor and Needy   962
B – If Christ Is Charged with Madness   746
C – O Christ, Who Shared Our Mortal Life
   (stanzas 2b, 3b)   706

ELEVENTH SUNDAY
A – O Christ, Who Called the Twelve   768
B – The Reign of God   722
C – A Woman Knelt Where Jesus Sat to Eat
   958

TWELFTH SUNDAY
A – Jesus, Lead the Way   715
B – The Storm Is Strong   692
C – Let Kings and Prophets Yield Their Name
   562
   Take Up Your Cross   761

THIRTEENTH SUNDAY
A – Take Up Your Cross   761
   The Summons   773
B – O Christ, Who Shared Our Mortal Life
   (stanzas 2a, 3a)   706
C – O Christ, Who Called the Twelve   768

FOURTEENTH SUNDAY
A – Come to Me, O Weary Traveler   717
B – God Has Spoken by the Prophets   592
C – Not Alone, but Two by Two   769

FIFTEENTH SUNDAY
A – In This Place Your Word Is Planted   595
B – Not Alone, but Two by Two   769
C – We Sing Your Praise, O Christ   804

Hymns for the Church Year/*continued*

SIXTEENTH SUNDAY
A – The Reign of God 722
B – Lord Christ, the People Flocked to You 830
C – Lord, Grant Us Grace to Know the Time 750

SEVENTEENTH SUNDAY
A – The Reign of God 722
B – We Come with Joy in Jesus Christ 832
C – Lord, Teach Us How to Pray 658

EIGHTEENTH SUNDAY
A – They Came, a Milling Crowd 838
B – Shepherd of Souls 941
    Eat This Bread 943
C – Lord, Whose Then Shall They Be 807

NINETEENTH SUNDAY
A – Your Hand, Though Hidden, Guides Us 703
    How Firm a Foundation 687
B – I Am the Bread of Life / Yo Soy el Pan de Vida 950
    Shepherd of Souls 941
C – God, Whose Giving Knows No Ending 805

TWENTIETH SUNDAY
A – Here, Master, in This Quiet Place 974
B – I Am the Bread of Life / Yo Soy el Pan de Vida 950
    All Who Hunger, Gather Gladly 844
C – God, Whose Purpose Is to Kindle 797

TWENTY-FIRST SUNDAY
A – Let Kings and Prophets Yield Their Name 562
B – To Whom, Lord, Shall We Go? 683
C – Let Us Come Now to the Kingdom 724

TWENTY-SECOND SUNDAY
A – Take Up Your Cross 761
B – As a Chalice Cast of Gold 660
C – If Life Is Like a Wedding Feast 737

TWENTY-THIRD SUNDAY
A – Help Us Accept Each Other 818
B – Your Hands, O Lord, in Days of Old 972
C – For God Risk Everything! 778

TWENTY-FOURTH SUNDAY
A – Forgive Our Sins 967
B – Let Kings and Prophets Yield Their Name 562
    Take Up Your Cross 761
C – Shepherd, Do You Tramp the Hills 640
    Our Father, We Have Wandered 963

TWENTY-FIFTH SUNDAY
A – Called to Labor in God's Vineyard 722

B – Lord, Help Us Walk Your Servant Way 779
C – The Word of God 752

TWENTY-SIXTH SUNDAY
A – My Elder Son, Go Work Today! 739
B – Where Christ Is, His Church Is There 728
C – God, Your Knowing Eye Can See 747

TWENTY-SEVENTH SUNDAY
A – The Keeper of a Vineyard 745
B – When Love Is Found 982
C – Faith Begins by Letting Go 673
    The Church of Christ, in Every Age 785
    If You Have Faith / Si Tienen Fe 719
    Lord, Help Us Walk Your Servant Way 779

TWENTY-EIGHTH SUNDAY
A – As We Gather at Your Table 831
B – For God Risk Everything! 778
C – Banned and Banished by Their Neighbors 975

TWENTY-NINTH SUNDAY
A – Baited, the Question Rose 740
B – Lord, Help Us Walk Your Servant Way 779
    Since Our Great High Priest, Christ Jesus 531
C – Eternal Spirit of the Living Christ 655

THIRTIETH SUNDAY
A – Love Is the Law That Jesus Taught 699
B – A Blind Man Sat beside the Road 979
C – Two People Came to Church to Pray 757

THIRTY-FIRST SUNDAY
A – The Virtue of Humility 756
B – Love Is the Law That Jesus Taught 699
C – When Jesus Passed through Jericho 647

THIRTY-SECOND SUNDAY
A - Sleepers, Wake! 409
    Awaken, Sleepers 393
B – The Temple Rang with Golden Coins 809
    Since Our Great High Priest, Christ Jesus 531
C – Jesus, Lead the Way 715
    The God of Abraham Praise 601

THIRTY-THIRD SUNDAY
A – With Gifts That Differ by Your Grace 810
B – From the Father's Throne on High 865
C – From the Father's Throne on High 865
    How Can I Keep from Singing? 684

CHRIST THE KING
A – To Be Your Presence 794
B – O Christ, What Can It Mean for Us 567
C – O Christ, What Can It Mean for Us 567

Scripture Passages Related to Hymns/*continued*

Scripture Passages Related to Hymns/*continued*

Scripture Passages Related to Hymns/*continued*

Scripture Passages Related to Hymns/*continued*

Scripture Passages Related to Hymns/*continued*

Scripture Passages Related to Hymns/*continued*

Psalms and canticles found in the hymnal apart from the lectionary section, arranged according to liturgical use.

LITURGY OF THE HOURS

INVITATORY
Psalm 67 (bilingual)   61
Psalm 95 (with seasonal antiphons)   72
Psalm 95   71
Psalm 100   77
Psalm 100: We Are God's People   78

SUNDAY MORNING PRAYER
Week I
Psalm 63   58
Psalm 63: My Soul Is Thirsting   57
Daniel 3:57–88, 56   118
Psalm 149   112

Week II
Psalm 118   94
Daniel 3:52–57   117
Psalm 150   113

Week III
Psalm 93   70
Daniel 3:57–88, 56   118
Psalm 148   111

Week IV
Psalm 118   94
Daniel 3:52–57   117
Psalm 150   113

SUNDAY EVENING PRAYER II
Week I
Psalm 110:1–5, 7 with Ant. I   84
Psalm 114   88
Revelation 19:1–7   131
1 Peter 2:21–24   130

Week II
Psalm 110:1–5, 7 with Ant. I   84
Psalm 115   89
Revelation 19:1–7   131
1 Peter 2:21–24   130

Week III
Psalm 110:1–5, 7 with Ant. I   84
Psalm 111   85
Revelation 19:1–7   131
1 Peter 2:21–24   130

Week IV
Psalm 110:1–5, 7 with Ant. I   84
Psalm 112   86
Revelation 19:1–7   131
1 Peter 2:21–24   130

NIGHT PRAYER
Sundays & Solemnities, after Evening Prayer I
Psalm 4   26
Psalm 134   104

Sundays & Solemnities, after Evening Prayer II
Psalm 91 with Ant. III   69
Psalm 91: Be with Me, Lord   68

Monday
Psalm 86 with Ant. II   64

Tuesday
Psalm 143:1–11 with Ant. II   106

Wednesday
Psalm 31:1–6 with Ant. I   44
Psalm 130 with Ant. I   103

Thursday
Psalm 16   31
Psalm 16: You Will Show Me the Path of Life
   with Ant. II   30

Friday
Psalm 88   65

OFFICE FOR THE DEAD
Morning Prayer
Psalm 51 with Ant. III   55
Isaiah 38:10–14, 17–20   116
Psalm 146   109
Psalm 150   113

PASCHAL TRIDUUM
Holy Thursday, Night Prayer (Use night prayer for Sundays and Solemnities, after Evening Prayer II)
Psalm 91 with Ant. III   69
Psalm 91: Be with Me, Lord   68

Good Friday, Morning Prayer
Psalm 51 with Ant. III   55
Habakkuk 3:2–4, 13a, 15–19   119
Psalm 147:12–20   110

Good Friday, Night Prayer (Use night prayer for Sundays and Solemnities, after Evening Prayer II)
Psalm 91 with Ant. III   69
Psalm 91: Be with Me, Lord   68

Holy Saturday, Morning Prayer
Psalm 64   59
Isaiah 38:10–14, 17–20   116
Psalm 150   113

Index of Psalms and Canticles/*continued*

Index of Psalms and Canticles/*continued*

Index of Psalms and Canticles/*continued*

Index of Psalms and Canticles/*continued*

METRICAL PSALMS AND CANTICLES

ADDITIONAL PSALMS AND CANTICLES NOT LISTED ELSEWHERE

1234 Liturgical Index

Liturgical Index/*continued*

Topical Index/*continued*

Topical Index/*continued*

987 This Is a Miracle-Moment
949 This Is the Body of Christ
543 Veni Creátor Spíritus
664 We Cannot Measure How You Heal
981 We Come to You for Healing, Lord
918 We Praise You, Lord, for Jesus Christ
938 We Remember
723 When Jesus Came Preaching the Kingdom of God
647 When Jesus Passed through Jericho
670 When Painful Memories Haunt Each Day
395 When the King Shall Come Again
977 When We Must Bear Persistent Pain
771 Who Follows Jesus?
590 Word of God, Come Down on Earth
704 You Are Mine / Contigo Estoy
775 You Call to Us, Lord Jesus
703 Your Hand, Though Hidden, Guides Us
972 Your Hands, O Lord, in Days of Old

HEAVEN
907 Around the Throne a Glorious Band
887 As Stars Adorn the Night-Veiled Sky
470 At the Cross Her Station Keeping
890 By All Your Saints Still Striving
496 Christ the Lord Is Risen Today (LLANFAIR)
628 Come, Christians, Join to Sing
858 Come, You Thankful People, Come
852 Day Is Done
988 Dwellers in the Holy City
4 Father, We Praise You
891 For All the Saints
892 For All the Saints Who've Shown Your Love
623 Heaven Is Singing for Joy / El Cielo Canta Alegría
614 Holy God, We Praise Thy Name
894 How Blessed Is This Place
950 I Am the Bread of Life / Yo Soy el Pan de Vida
527 I Know That My Redeemer Lives! (DUKE STREET)
994 I Know That My Redeemer Lives (Hughes)
585 I Want to Walk as a Child of the Light
497 If Christ Had Not Been Raised from Death
200 In Paradísum / May Choirs of Angels
867 Jerusalem, My Happy Home
715 Jesus, Lead the Way
800 Jesus, Our Divine Companion
869 Jesus, Remember Me
611 Joyful, Joyful, We Adore You
642 Love Divine, All Loves Excelling
868 Martha, Mary, Waiting, Weeping
201 May Saints and Angels Lead You On
991 May the Angels Lead You into Paradise
708 My Shepherd, You Supply My Need
718 Nada Te Turbe / Nothing Can Trouble
637 Now Thank We All Our God

813 O God of Love, O King of Peace
162 O Saving Victim / O Salutaris
440 Once in Royal David's City
980 Precious Lord, Take My Hand
564 Rejoice, the Lord Is King!
517 Rise to Sing! The Light Is Breaking
990 Saints of God (Janco)
198 Saints of God (Proulx)
882 Salve Regína / Hail, Queen of Heaven
866 Shall We Gather at the River
896 Sing We of the Blessed Mother
526 Sing with All the Saints in Glory / Canten con Gloriosos Fieles
409 Sleepers, Wake!
861 Soon and Very Soon
736 The Church's One Foundation
709 The Living God My Shepherd Is
992 There Is a Place
955 To the Wedding Feast
674 We Walk by Faith
694 Where True Love and Charity Are Found / Ubi Cáritas
936 Where Two or Three Are Gathered
888 Who Are These, Like Stars Appearing?
704 You Are Mine / Contigo Estoy

HOLINESS
660 As a Chalice Cast of Gold
901 As a Star on Cloudless Evenings / Como Estrella en Claro Cielo
887 As Stars Adorn the Night-Veiled Sky
721 Blest Are They / Benditos los Pobres
860 Christ Is Surely Coming
733 Church of God, Elect and Glorious
534 Come Down, O Love Divine
439 Come, Sing a Home and Family
537 Come, Spirit Blest / Ven, Creador
892 For All the Saints Who've Shown Your Love
836 Gather Us In
553 Holy, Holy, Holy! Lord God Almighty!
1070 Litany of the Saints
914 O Breathe on Me, O Breath of God
978 O Christ, the Healer
903 O Sanctíssima / O Most Holy One
442 Our Savior's Infant Cries Were Heard
889 Sing Praise to God for Friends
535 Spirit Divine, Inspire Our Prayer
900 Stainless the Maiden / Serdeczna Matko
878 The Great Forerunner of the Morn
910 This Is the Feast Day of the Lord's True Witness
754 When We Are Living / Pues Si Vivimos
700 Where Charity and Love Prevail
888 Who Are These, Like Stars Appearing?
771 Who Follows Jesus?
729 You Strode within the Temple, Lord

HOLY SPIRIT
503 Alleluia! Jesus Is Risen!
919 Baptized in Water
917 Blessed Be God, Who Chose You in Christ
730 Christ, You Formed the Church, Your Body
534 Come Down, O Love Divine
544 Come, Holy Ghost

549 Come Now, Almighty King
537 Come, Spirit Blest / Ven, Creador
806 Come to Us, Creative Spirit
922 Crashing Waters at Creation
842 Diverse in Culture, Nation, Race
655 Eternal Spirit of the Living Christ
555 Father, Lord of All Creation
533 Fire of God, Undying Flame
463 From Ashes to the Living Font
835 God Is Here! As We His People
797 God, Whose Purpose Is to Kindle
957 Grant to Us, O Lord
524 Hail Thee, Festival Day!
665 Have Mercy, Lord
965 Healer of Our Every Ill
540 Holy Spirit, Come to Us
541 Holy Spirit, Lord Divine
926 I Come with Joy
803 If You Believe and I Believe
893 Immaculate Mary
539 Laus Tibi Sancte Spíritus
545 Living Spirit, Holy Fire
914 O Breathe on Me, O Breath of God
551 O God, Almighty Father
546 O Holy Spirit, by Whose Breath
536 O Spirit All-Embracing
542 Praise the Spirit in Creation
596 Sing Praise to the Lord / Cantad al Señor
535 Spirit Divine, Inspire Our Prayer
547 Spirit of God within Me
787 The Spirit Sends Us Forth to Serve
455 The Strong and Gentle Voice
508 This Is a Day of New Beginnings
457 To Jordan Jesus Humbly Came
543 Veni Creátor Spíritus
538 Veni Sancte Spíritus
822 We Are Many Parts / Muchos Miembros Hay
664 We Cannot Measure How You Heal
832 We Come with Joy in Jesus Christ
456 When Jesus Came to Jordan
458 When John Baptized by Jordan's River
654 When My Soul Is Sore and Troubled

HOMECOMING
650 Amazing Grace!
399 Are You the Coming One
975 Banned and Banished by Their Neighbors
733 Church of God, Elect and Glorious
717 Come to Me, O Weary Traveler
988 Dwellers in the Holy City
923 I Receive the Living God
867 Jerusalem, My Happy Home
715 Jesus, Lead the Way
397 Like a Bird
826 Making Their Way
708 My Shepherd, You Supply My Need
980 Precious Lord, Take My Hand
989 Rest in Peace, Earth's Journey Ended
640 Shepherd, Do You Tramp the Hills
712 The King of Love My Shepherd Is
709 The Living God My Shepherd Is
395 When the King Shall Come Again
704 You Are Mine / Contigo Estoy

HOMELESS
796 As the Birds of the Air
584 Christ, Be Our Light!
735 Living Stones
475 Return to God / Volvamos Hoy a Nuestro Dios

Topical Index/*continued*

Topical Index/*continued*

Topical Index/*continued*

Topical Index/*continued*

Topical Index/*continued*

Topical Index/*continued*

870 Long-Awaited Holy One
120 Luke 1:46–53 / My Soul Gives Glory
121 Luke 1:46–55 / Canticle of Mary
122 Luke 1:46–55 / Holy Is Your Name
124 Luke 1:46–55 / Magníficat 3
123 Luke 1:46–55 / Proclaim the Greatness of God
125 Luke 1:68–79 / Now Bless the God of Israel
126 Luke 2:29 / Nunc Dimíttis
127 Luke 2:29–32 / Canticle of Simeon
613 Magníficat (Taizé)
897 Mary, First among Believers
872 Now Let Your Servant Go in Peace
834 O Christ, within These Walls
557 O Food of Exiles Lowly / O Esca Viatórum
677 O God, Who Gives Us Life and Breath
871 O Light of Gentile Nations
415 Of the Father's Love Begotten
925 Pan de Vida
604 Praise the Lord! You Heavens, Adore Him
518 Regína Caeli / Mary, Heaven's Queen
960 Sovereign Maker of All Things
878 The Great Forerunner of the Morn
644 The One Who Longs to Make Us Whole
513 They Disbelieved for Joy
949 This Is the Body of Christ
396 Though Famed in Israel's Royal History
407 Unexpected and Mysterious
543 Veni Creátor Spíritus
581 We Are Known and Not Unnumbered
674 We Walk by Faith

PROPHECY

474 Again We Keep This Solemn Fast
402 Comfort, Comfort, O My People
592 God Has Spoken by the Prophets
881 How Good, Lord, to Be Here!
562 Let Kings and Prophets Yield Their Name
438 Lo, How a Rose E'er Blooming
125 Luke 1:68–79 / Now Bless the God of Israel
872 Now Let Your Servant Go in Peace
387 O Come, Divine Messiah!
871 O Light of Gentile Nations
415 Of the Father's Love Begotten
392 On Jordan's Bank
591 Praise to You, O Christ, Our Savior
876 Praise We the Lord This Day
875 The Angel Gabriel from Heaven Came
878 The Great Forerunner of the Morn
877 The Moon with Borrowed Light
448 What Star Is This
390 Wild and Lone the Prophet's Voice

PROVIDENCE

676 A Living Faith
688 A Mighty Fortress Is Our God
837 All People That on Earth Do Dwell
953 Alleluia! Sing to Jesus!
796 As the Birds of the Air
470 At the Cross Her Station Keeping
890 By All Your Saints Still Striving

717 Come to Me, O Weary Traveler
962 Come, You Sinners, Poor and Needy
858 Come, You Thankful People, Come
852 Day Is Done
555 Father, Lord of All Creation
631 Father, We Thank You, Who Have Planted
891 For All the Saints
857 For the Fruits of All Creation
836 Gather Us In
579 Go Down, Moses
862 God Is Working His Purpose Out
995 God of Our Fathers
805 God, Whose Giving Knows No Ending
687 How Firm a Foundation
707 I Heard the Voice of Jesus Say
527 I Know That My Redeemer Lives! (DUKE STREET)
572 I Sing the Mighty Power of God
719 If You Have Faith / Si Tienen Fe
630 Immortal, Invisible, God Only Wise
715 Jesus, Lead the Way
801 Lift Every Voice and Sing
686 Lord of All Hopefulness
847 Morning Has Broken
998 My Country, 'Tis of Thee
708 My Shepherd, You Supply My Need
685 Nothing Is Impossible with God
637 Now Thank We All Our God
559 O Christ, Your Heart Compassionate
689 O God, Our Help in Ages Past
580 O God, You Search Me
856 Praise and Thanksgiving / Te Damos Gracias
610 Praise, My Soul, the King of Heaven
616 Praise to the Lord, the Almighty
941 Shepherd of Souls
617 Sing Praise to God Who Reigns Above
643 Surely It Is God Who Saves Me
952 Taste and See (Luckner)
945 Taste and See (Moore)
853 The Day You Gave Us, Lord, Is Ended
565 The King of Glory
712 The King of Love My Shepherd Is
709 The Living God My Shepherd Is
838 They Came, a Milling Crowd
850 This Day God Gives Me
581 We Are Known and Not Unnumbered
634 We Praise You, O God
648 What Love and Deep Devotion / Porque de Tal Manera
582 When You, Lord, Walked

RECONCILIATION

958 A Woman Knelt Where Jesus Sat to Eat
833 All Are Welcome
734 As a Fire Is Meant for Burning
831 As We Gather at Your Table
915 Awake, O Sleeper, Rise from Death
975 Banned and Banished by Their Neighbors
919 Baptized in Water
501 Be Joyful, Mary
568 Christ Is the King!
855 Christ, Mighty Savior
496 Christ the Lord Is Risen Today (LLANFAIR)

520 Christ the Lord Is Risen Today (SURGIT IN HAEC DIES)
528 Christ the Lord Is Risen Today (VICTIMAE PASCHALI)
962 Come, You Sinners, Poor and Needy
402 Comfort, Comfort, O My People
821 Creator of the Intertwined
842 Diverse in Culture, Nation, Race
631 Father, We Thank You, Who Have Planted
770 Fishermen Are Sailing Homeward
967 Forgive Our Sins
463 From Ashes to the Living Font
653 God Is Forgiveness
782 God the Spirit, Guide and Guardian
913 God, Who at the Font Once Named Us
957 Grant to Us, O Lord
665 Have Mercy, Lord
966 Have Mercy, Lord, on Us
965 Healer of Our Every Ill
473 Hear Us, Almighty Lord / Atténde Dómine
818 Help Us Accept Each Other
969 Help Us Forgive, Forgiving Lord
894 How Blessed Is This Place
687 How Firm a Foundation
819 How Good and Pleasant, Lord, It Is
845 How Shocking Were the People
926 I Come with Joy
971 In All Our Grief
611 Joyful, Joyful, We Adore You
625 Laudáte Dóminum
905 Let All on Earth Their Voices Raise
755 Lord, Make Us Servants of Your Peace
697 Lord of All Nations, Grant Me Grace
954 Lord, Who at Your First Eucharist
642 Love Divine, All Loves Excelling
708 My Shepherd, You Supply My Need
811 O Day of Peace
812 O God of Every Nation
471 O Sun of Justice
392 On Jordan's Bank
963 Our Father, We Have Wandered
970 Out of the Depths
469 Parce Dómine / Spare Us, Gracious Lord
820 Peace with the Father
610 Praise, My Soul, the King of Heaven
616 Praise to the Lord, the Almighty
591 Praise to You, O Christ, Our Savior
989 Rest in Peace, Earth's Journey Ended
476 Restore in Us, O God
640 Shepherd, Do You Tramp the Hills
679 Show Me Your Hands, Your Feet, Your Side
629 Sing a New Song to the Lord
462 Somebody's Knockin' at Your Door
960 Sovereign Maker of All Things
745 The Keeper of a Vineyard
712 The King of Love My Shepherd Is
720 The Kingdom of God
709 The Living God My Shepherd Is
968 The Master Came to Bring Good News
644 The One Who Longs to Make Us Whole

Topical Index/*continued*

422 Sing We Now of Christmas
896 Sing We of the Blessed Mother
526 Sing with All the Saints in Glory / Canten con Gloriosos Fieles
621 Soli Deo Glória
525 Surréxit Christus
848 The Earth Is Turning toward the Sun
997 This Is My Song
515 This Is the Feast of Victory
851 Through Silver Veils of Morning Mist
846 To You, O God, We Sing / Cantemos al Señor
799 We Are Called
586 We Are Marching / Siyahamba
634 We Praise You, O God
641 What Wondrous Love Is This
608 When in Our Music God Is Glorified
849 When Morning Gilds the Sky
886 Ye Watchers and Ye Holy Ones
964 Yes, I Shall Arise
784 You Are Called to Tell the Story

SORROW *See Grief*

STEWARDSHIP
740 Baited, the Question Rose
806 Come to Us, Creative Spirit
858 Come, You Thankful People, Come
815 Everything That Has Voice
895 For Builders Bold
857 For the Fruits of All Creation
798 For the Healing of the Nations
859 God, Whose Farm Is All Creation
805 God, Whose Giving Knows No Ending
747 God, Your Knowing Eye Can See
999 Greet Now the Swiftly Changing Year
807 Lord, Whose Then Shall They Be
856 Praise and Thanksgiving / Te Damos Gracias
809 The Temple Rang with Golden Coins
808 Touch the Earth Lightly
802 We Cannot Own the Sunlit Sky
748 What Does the Lord Require
810 With Gifts That Differ by Your Grace

STRANGER *See Alienation*

STRENGTH
583 Arise, Your Light Has Come!
22 Before the Ending of the Day
890 By All Your Saints Still Striving
855 Christ, Mighty Savior
662 Come, My Way, My Truth, My Life
537 Come, Spirit Blest / Ven, Creador
717 Come to Me, O Weary Traveler
852 Day Is Done
655 Eternal Spirit of the Living Christ
891 For All the Saints
597 Glory and Praise to Our God
791 God, Bless Your Church with Strength!
633 God, Our Father, You Have Granted
500 Goodness Is Stronger than Evil
684 How Can I Keep from Singing?
687 How Firm a Foundation
639 In the Lord I'll Be Ever Thankful
657 Lead Me, Guide Me
909 Let Us with Joy Our Voices Raise

461 Lord, Who throughout These Forty Days
685 Nothing Is Impossible with God
711 O God, You Are My God Alone
873 Saint Joseph, Mary's Faithful Spouse
761 Take Up Your Cross
467 The Glory of These Forty Days
850 This Day God Gives Me
410 Wait for the Lord
982 When Love Is Found
506 Who Are You Who Walk in Sorrow
710 With a Shepherd's Care
704 You Are Mine / Contigo Estoy

STRUGGLE
688 A Mighty Fortress Is Our God
996 America the Beautiful
907 Around the Throne a Glorious Band
906 Blessed Feasts of Blessed Martyrs
498 Christ Is Risen! Shout Hosanna!
520 Christ the Lord Is Risen Today (SURGIT IN HAEC DIES)
528 Christ the Lord Is Risen Today (VICTIMAE PASCHALI)
717 Come to Me, O Weary Traveler
891 For All the Saints
749 God Made from One Blood
687 How Firm a Foundation
715 Jesus, Lead the Way
459 Jesus, Tempted in the Desert
801 Lift Every Voice and Sing
658 Lord, Teach Us How to Pray
718 Nada Te Turbe / Nothing Can Trouble
866 Shall We Gather at the River
480 Stations of the Cross
484 Stay with Me
736 The Church's One Foundation
692 The Storm Is Strong
511 The Strife Is O'er
664 We Cannot Measure How You Heal
521 We Walk His Way / Ewe, Thina
654 When My Soul Is Sore and Troubled
670 When Painful Memories Haunt Each Day
754 When We Are Living / Pues Si Vivimos
710 With a Shepherd's Care

SUFFERING
676 A Living Faith
492 All You Who Pass This Way
907 Around the Throne a Glorious Band
796 As the Birds of the Air
721 Blest Are They / Benditos los Pobres
717 Come to Me, O Weary Traveler
713 Eye Has Not Seen
466 Forty Days and Forty Nights
597 Glory and Praise to Our God
668 God Weeps with Us Who Weep and Mourn
687 How Firm a Foundation
777 I Danced in the Morning
959 If I Have Been the Source of Pain / Si Fui Motivo de Dolor
971 In All Our Grief
659 Jesus, Show Us How to Pray
897 Mary, First among Believers
495 Now the Green Blade Rises
738 O Blessed Are the Poor in Spirit

742 O Blest Are You
489 O Sacred Head Surrounded / Oh Rostro Ensangrentado
477 Once We Sang and Danced with Gladness
925 Pan de Vida
882 Salve Regína / Hail, Queen of Heaven
652 Shall Tribulation or Distress
896 Sing We of the Blessed Mother
480 Stations of the Cross
761 Take Up Your Cross
776 The Love of the Lord
488 Were You There
654 When My Soul Is Sore and Troubled
670 When Painful Memories Haunt Each Day
754 When We Are Living / Pues Si Vivimos
977 When We Must Bear Persistent Pain
704 You Are Mine / Contigo Estoy

SUNDAY
512 At the Lamb's High Feast We Sing
505 Christ Has Risen
498 Christ Is Risen! Shout Hosanna!
800 Jesus, Our Divine Companion
826 Making Their Way
825 On This Day, the First of Days
827 Prepare a Room for Me
838 They Came, a Milling Crowd
508 This Is a Day of New Beginnings
515 This Is the Feast of Victory

TEACHING
740 Baited, the Question Rose
741 Build Your City on the Hill
747 God, Your Knowing Eye Can See
746 If Christ Is Charged with Madness
737 If Life Is Like a Wedding Feast
750 Lord, Grant Us Grace to Know the Time
658 Lord, Teach Us How to Pray
699 Love Is the Law that Jesus Taught
739 My Elder Son, Go Work Today!
738 O Blessed Are the Poor in Spirit
742 O Blest Are You
485 So You Must Do
745 The Keeper of a Vineyard
756 The Virtue of Humility
743 To Love Just Those Who Love You
744 What Is the World Like
723 When Jesus Came Preaching the Kingdom of God
582 When You, Lord, Walked
728 Where Christ Is, His Church Is There
771 Who Follows Jesus?
443 Within the Father's House
784 You Are Called to Tell the Story
682 You Are the Way
695 Your Ways Are Not Our Own

TEMPTATION
563 At the Name of Jesus (Noel)
466 Forty Days and Forty Nights
959 If I Have Been the Source of Pain / Si Fui Motivo de Dolor
595 In This Place Your Word Is Planted
715 Jesus, Lead the Way
459 Jesus, Tempted in the Desert
461 Lord, Who throughout These Forty Days
455 The Strong and Gentle Voice

Topical Index/*continued*

Index of Composers, Authors and Sources/*continued*

PASSION CHORALE (HERZLICH TUT MICH
VERLANGEN) 489 812 963
ST. THEODULPH (VALET WILL ICH DIR GEBEN)
483 890
TEMPUS ADEST FLORIDUM 446

7 6 7 6 WITH REFRAIN
GLORIA, LAUS ET HONOR 1048
GO TELL IT ON THE MOUNTAIN 428
GOTT VATER SEI GEPRIESEN 551
ROYAL OAK 574

7 7 7 7
HEINLEIN 466 865
HOLY FIRE 545
LÜBECK (GOTT SEI DANK) 825
NUN KOMM DER HEIDEN HEILAND 388 533 870
PUER NOBIS NASCITUR 429 741
THE CALL 659 662

77 77 D
SALZBURG 451 512 728
ST. GEORGE'S WINDSOR 858
VICTIMAE PASCHALI 528

77 77 WITH ALLELUIAS
EASTER HYMN 516
LLANFAIR 496 529
SURGIT IN HAEC DIES 520

7 7 7 7 WITH REFRAIN
BREAKING BREAD 944
GLORIA 417
LIVING GOD 923

7 7 7 7 77
CÂMARA 747
DIX 450 632 660 673

8 6 8 66
DOVE OF PEACE 819 926
WIDOW'S GOLD 795 809

8 7 8 7
DUNSTAN 717
JEFFERSON 394
KAS DZIEDAJA 477 975
RESTORATION 922
ST. COLUMBA 712
STUTTGART 595 672 859

8 7 8 7 WITH REFRAIN
CABRERA 946
COMFORT 701
GRACIOUS GIFT 933
GREENSLEEVES 454
HANSON PLACE 866
ICH GLAUB AN GOTT 570 968
RESTORATION 962

8 7 8 7 77
ALL SAINTS 531 888
IRBY 440

8 7 8 7 8 7
BEST GIFT 656
FORTUNATUS NEW 491 730 911
JULION 542 649 904
LAUDA ANIMA 581 610 988
PANGE LINGUA GLORIOSI 1056 1106
PICARDY 620 626 880

REGENT SQUARE 425 633 762 913
ST. THOMAS (Wade) 164
WESTMINSTER ABBEY 732 798

8 7 8 7 8 7 WITH REFRAIN
GLORY IN THE CROSS 486
GRACE ETERNAL 951

8 7 8 7 8 7 7
CWM RHONDDA 784
DIVINUM MYSTERIUM 415

8 7 8 7 D
ABBOT'S LEIGH 733 788 790 835
ALLE TAGE SING UND SAGE 896
ANITA 505 638
BEACH SPRING 734 854 868
DOMHNACH TRIONOIDE 407
EBENEZER 459 666 797
GENEVA 555 793
GIFTS 615
GREENSBURG 840
HOLY MANNA 506 724 831 844
HOSANNA 498
HOW CAN I KEEP FROM SINGING 684 802
HYFRYDOL 604 642 953 985
HYMN TO JOY 526 611 770 983
IN BABILONE 645 772 780 906
NETTLETON 599 727 735 817
PETHEL 517
PLEADING SAVIOR 444 800 897
RAQUEL 643 901
RUSTINGTON 558 592 805
SHALLOWFORD 782 955
SUO GAN 408 479
TREMONT 465

8 7 8 7 88 7
LOBT GOTT DEN HERREN 573
MIT FREUDEN ZART 617

8 8 7
PERILYPOS PSYCHE 654
STABAT MATER 470

888 WITH ALLELUIAS
GELOBT SEI GOTT 568

888 WITH ALLELUIA AND REFRAIN
O FILII ET FILIAE 507 539
VICTORY 511

8 8 8 8 8 8
HICKORY HILL 562 739
ST. CATHERINE 676 912

9 8 9 8
ST. CLEMENT 853
VINE AND BRANCHES 823

10 10 WITH REFRAIN
CRUCIFER 885
WERE YOU THERE 488

10 10 10 10
NATIONAL HYMN 995
NEW WORLD 744
SLANE 984
SURSUM CORDA 468 655 958

Metrical Index/*continued*

10 10 10 10 WITH REFRAIN
BERTOLINO   518
CORPUS DOMINI   940
NEALE   935
ST. MALACHY   928

11 11 11 5
CHRISTE SANCTORUM   4
ISTE CONFESSOR   839 910
MIGHTY SAVIOR   588 771 855

11 11 11 11
ADORO TE DEVOTE   556
APPALACHIAN FALL   920
CRADLE SONG   437
FOUNDATION   687 749 765
PADERBORN   441 691
ST. DENIO   594 630 681
VEN CREADOR   537

ONE OF A KIND

CMD WITH REFRAIN
LEAVE ALL THINGS   774

LM WITH REPEAT
LAMBILLOTTE   544

IRREGULAR WITH ALLELUIAS
ALEGRÍA   623

4 4 6 WITH REFRAIN
ONE BREAD, ONE BODY   931

44 7 44 7 4444 7
W ŻŁOBIE LEŻY   416

4 5 4 5 WITH REFRAIN
NOAH'S SONG   436

4 5 10 D WITH REFRAIN
EARTH AND ALL STARS   503

55 2 55 2
GARU   523

5 5 6 WITH REFRAIN
BREAD BROKEN   924

55 7 55 7
O DU FRÖLICHE (SICILIAN MARINERS) 903

5 5 8 D
BUNESSAN   919

55 88 55
ROCHELLE (SEELENBRÄUTIGAM)   715

55 10 D
TENDERNESS   808

6 33 6 33 77 6 3
SING FOR PEACE   815

6 5 6 5 D
KING'S WESTON   563 860

6 6 6 6 WITH REFRAIN
DARWALL'S 148TH   564

6 6 6 6 4 44 4
LOVE UNKNOWN   490

666 66 WITH REFRAIN
PERSONENT HODIE   605

66 6 D
LAUDES DOMINI   849

6 6 6 6 66 6 6
MADRID (SPANISH HYMN)   628

66 77 78 55
IN DULCI JUBILO   427

6 6 8 4 D
LEONI (YIGDAL)   601

66 89 66
STILLE NACHT   413

66 10 66 10 14 14 66 10
ANTHEM   801

66 11 D
DOWN AMPNEY   534

66 11 66 11 D
ASH GROVE   636

6 7 6 7 WITH REFRAIN
VREUCHTEN   502

6 7 6 7 6 6 6 6
NUN DANKET   637

6 7 6 8 D WITH REFRAIN
ROSAS   846

7 5 7 5 WITH REFRAIN
HEAVENLY FEAST   936

7 6 7 6
DE EERSTEN ZIJN DE LAATSTEN   879

7 6 7 6 6 7 6
ES IST EIN' ROS' ENTSPRUNGEN   438

7 6 7 6 777 6
KELVINGROVE   773

7 6 8 6 8 6 8 6
WILLOW RIVER   547

77 6 77 8
INNSBRUCK   557

7 7 7
VENI SANCTE SPIRITUS   1100

77 7 4 D WITH REFRAIN
HERE I AM, LORD   783

77 77 WITH REFRAIN
VIA CRUCIS   480

77 7 D
WEBBE   541

7 7 7 7 D
ABERYSTWYTH   390 640 769 960

77 77 D WITH REFRAIN
MENDELSSOHN   414

Index of Settings with Foreign Languages/*continued*

Index of Service Music/*continued*

A light will shine on us this day: the Lord is born for us.   1015

All power is yours, Lord God, our mighty King, alleluia!   131

All the ends of the earth have seen the power of God.   75

All the ends of the earth have seen the saving power of God.   76

All the ends of the earth have seen the saving power of God, the saving power of God.   1016

Alleluia, alleluia, alleluia!   70 77 92 113 1069

And holy is your name through all generations! Everlasting is your mercy to the people you have chosen, and holy is your name.   122

Arise, come to your God, sing him your songs of rejoicing.   77

Be merciful, O Lord, for we have sinned.   1026 1027

Be merciful, O Lord, for we have sinned; be merciful, O Lord, for we have sinned.   54

Be with me, Lord, when I am in trouble.   69 1029

Be with me, Lord, when I am in trouble, be with me Lord, I pray.   68

Blessed are they who follow the law of the Lord!   1124

Blessed are they who hope, who hope in the Lord.   1126

Blessed are those who fear the Lord.   1205

Blessed be God who chose you in Christ.   128

Blessed be the Lord, for he has come to his people and set them free.   6

Blessed, blessed are they who dwell in your house, O Lord.   63 1019

Blessed the people the Lord has chosen to be his own.   1103 1165

Blessed the poor in spirit; the kingdom of heaven is theirs!   1118

Blest are those who love you, happy those who follow you, blest are those who seek you, O God.   101

Blest are you, O Virgin Mary, blest are you for your great faith. All that the Lord promised you will come to pass through you, alleluia, alleluia.   121

Bring an offering and enter God's courts: in his temple worship the Lord.   73

By your wounds, O Christ, we have been healed.   130

Call upon the Lord and he will hear you.   69

Cantaré, cantaré eternamente las misericordias del Señor.   66

Cantemos al Señor, sublime es su victoria.   115

Christ is born for us; Christ is born for us; come, let us adore him.   72

Christ is the light of the nations, to bring salvation to the ends of the earth.   53

Come, let us worship the Lord, come, let us worship the Lord, the King who is to come.   72

Create a clean heart, a clean heart in me, O God.   1040 1068

Cry out with joy and gladness: for among you is the great and Holy One of Israel.   1009

Cry out with joy to the Lord, all the earth; serve the Lord with gladness, serve the Lord with gladness.   72

Day and night I cry to you, my God.   65

Dichoso el pueblo que el Señor se escogió como heredad.   45

Do not forget the works of the Lord.   1224

Do not hide your face from me; in you I put my trust.   106

El cáliz que bendecimos es la comunión de la sangre de Christo.   91

El Señor es mi pastor, nada me falta. El Señor es mi pastor, nada mi falta.   38

Father, into your hands I commend my spirit.   43

Father, into your hands I commend my spirit, my spirit.   1057

Fill us with your love, O Lord, and we will sing for joy!   67 1191

For ever I will sing the goodness of the Lord.   66 1011 1013 1145

For the sake of your name, O Lord, save my life.   106

From the voices of children, Lord, comes the sound of your praise.   28

Give back to me the joy of your salvation.   55

Give peace, O Lord, in our days; may all who love you dwell secure.   97

Give thanks to the Lord for he is good, his love is everlasting.   94 1081

Give thanks to the Lord, his love is everlasting.   1143

Give the Lord glory, glory and honor.   1193

Go out to all the world, and tell the Good News.   1135 1171

Go out to the world and teach all nations. Go out to the world. Alleluia, alleluia.   188

God has freed us and redeemed us with his mighty arm.   88

God, in your goodness, you have made a home for the poor.   1174

God mounts his throne to shouts of joy; a blare of trumpets for the Lord.   52 1094

God mounts his throne to shouts of joy, to shouts, to shouts of joy.   53

God, my Lord, is my strength.   119

God, you are merciful and gracious; turn to me and have mercy.   64

Great is the Lord, worthy of praise; tell all the nations "God is King"; spread the news of his love.   73

Guard us, O Lord, while we sleep, and keep us in peace.   127

Hail, Mary, full of grace, the Lord is with you. Blessed are you among women and blessed is the fruit of your womb. Hail, Mary.   121

Psalm Refrains Set to Music/*continued*

Happy are the people the Lord has chosen, chosen to be his own. 45

Happy are those who do what the Lord commands. 86

Have mercy, Lord, and hear my prayer. 26

Have mercy, Lord; cleanse me from all my sins. 55

Have mercy on me, Lord; my strength is gone. 27

Here am I, Lord; I come to do your will. 1112 1113 1214

His goodness shall follow me always to the end of my days. 37

How can I repay the Lord for his goodness to me? 90

How great is your name, O Lord our God, through all the earth! 28

How lovely is your dwelling place, O Lord of hosts. 63

I am the living bread come down from heaven; anyone who eats this bread will live for ever, alleluia. 37

I believe that I shall see the good things of the Lord in the land of the living. 41 1095 1226

I hope in the Lord, I trust in his word. 103

I love you, I love you, Lord, my strength. 1196 1200

I place all my trust in you, my God; all my hope is in your saving word. 103

I praise you, O Lord, for I am wonderfully made. 1216

I rejoiced when they said to me, "Let us go to the house of the Lord." 97

I shall live in the house of the Lord all the days of my life. 1190

I thank you, Lord, for your faithfulness and love. 85

I turn to you, O Lord, in time of trouble, and you fill me with the joy of salvation. 1125

I will bless the Lord at all times. 49

I will give thanks to your name, because of your kindness and your truth. 1228

I will praise my God all the days of my life, all the days of my life. 109

I will praise you, Lord, for you have rescued me. 1065 1084 1138 1146

I will praise you, Lord, in the assembly of your people. 1089

I will praise your name for ever, Lord. 108

I will praise your name for ever, my king and my God. 107 1090 1148 1201

I will rise and go to my father. 1180

I will sing, I will sing, I will sing, I will sing, I will sing of your salvation. 62 1120

I will sing, I will sing to the God who sets me free! Pharaoh's army and his chariots God cast into the sea! 114

I will sing to the Lord all the days of my life. 116

I will take the cup of salvation, and call on the name of the Lord. 1107

I will walk before the Lord, in the land of the living. 1031 1179

I will walk in the presence of the Lord in the land of the living. 90

If today you hear his voice, harden not your hearts. 1033 1119 1162 1175 1189

If today you hear the voice of God, harden not your hearts, harden not your hearts. 71

If you, O Lord, should mark our sins, Lord, who would survive? 103

In every age, O Lord, you have been our refuge. 67 1177

In the morning I will sing, will sing glad songs of praise to you. 58

In the sight of the angels, I will sing your praises, O Lord. 1123

In the silent hours of night, bless the Lord. 104

In you, Lord, in you, Lord, in you, Lord, I have found my peace. 1199

In you, my God, my body will rest in hope. 31

Incline your ear, O Lord, and answer me. 64

Jesus Christ is Lord! 129

Justice shall flourish in his time, and fullness of peace for ever. 1004

Keep me safe, O God, I take refuge in you. 30

La misericordia de nuestro Dios llena la tierra. 45

La tierra ha dado su fruto, nos benice el Señor, nuestro Dios. 61

Let all praise the name of the Lord. 111

Let all the earth cry out, cry out to God with joy. 1091 1150

Let everything that breathes give praise, give praise, give praise to the Lord. 113

Let heaven rejoice and earth be glad: the Lord has come. 73

Let my tongue be silenced, if I ever forget you! 1037

Let the clouds rain down the just one; and the earth bring forth a Savior. 33

Let the Lord enter; he is king of glory. 1010

Let us bow down before the Lord, the God who made us. 72

Let us come before the Lord our God singing songs of praise, singing songs of praise. 71

Let us go rejoicing to the house of the Lord; Let us go rejoicing to the house of the Lord. 96

Let us go rejoicing to the house, to the house of the Lord. 1001 1210

Let us sing to the Lord; he has covered himself in glory. 115

Let us sing to the Lord, let us sing to the Lord; he has covered himself in glory. 1064

Let your mercy be on us, O God, as we place our trust in you. 45

Let your servant now go in peace, O Lord, according to your word. 126

Like a deer that longs for running streams, my soul longs for you, my God. 50 1068

Look to God and be filled with radiant joy. Lift up your heads for God hears our prayer, lift up your heads for God hears our prayer. 47

Look to him, look to him, that you may be radiant with joy! 49

Lord, come and save us. Lord, come and save us. 1007

Lord, come to my aid! 1168

Lord, every nation on earth will adore you. 1021

Lord, forgive the wrong I have done. 1141

Lord, give success to the work of our hands. 1223

Lord, go up to the place of your rest, you and the ark of your holiness. 1221

Lord God, be my refuge and strength. 44

Lord, heal my soul, for I have sinned against you. 1128

Lord, I love your commands. 1157

Lord, if you will, you can make me clean. 55

Lord, in your great love, answer me. 1142

Lord, it is good to give thanks to you. 1132, 1140

Lord, let us see your kindness, and grant us your salvation. 1005 1152 1163

Lord, let your face shine on us, your face shine on us. 1083

Lord, let your mercy be on us, as we place our trust in you. 1030 1088 1194

Lord, Lord, be my rock of safety. 1133

Lord, make us turn to you; let us see your face and we shall be saved. 1002 1012

Lord, on the day I called for help, you answered me. 1159

Lord, send out your Spirit, and renew the face of the earth. 82 152 1062 1098 1099

Lord, send out your Spirit on us; renew the face of the earth. 81

Lord, this is the people that longs to see your face. 1225

Lord, when your glory appears, my joy will be full. 1204

Lord, you are good and forgiving. 1154

Lord, you are great and do marvelous deeds: you alone are God. 64

Lord, you have the words of everlasting life. 32 33 1034 1067

Lord, you will show us the path of life. 1082

Lord, your love is eternal; do not forsake the work of your hands. 1169

Los que miran a Dios refulgerán. Sobre sus rostros no habrá amargura. Sobre sus rostros no habrá amargura. 47

Magníficat anima mea Dóminum. 124

May God bless us in his mercy, may God bless us in his mercy. 1020

May the Lord bless and protect us all the days of our lives. 1188

May the Lord bless us, may the Lord protect us, all the days, all the days of our life. 101

May the Lord watch over this house, and keep us in peace. 100

Misericordia, Señor, hemos pecado. Be merciful, O Lord, for we have sinned. 56

My God, my God, come quickly to help me. 62 176

My God, my God, O why have you abandoned me? 35

My God, my God, why have you abandoned me? 34 1049

My prayers rise like incense, my hands like the evening offering. 105

My refuge, my stronghold, my God in whom I trust! 69

My shepherd is the Lord, nothing indeed shall I want. 37

My soul, give thanks to the Lord, and bless God's holy name. 79

My soul is thirsting for the Lord: when shall I see God face to face? 50

My soul is thirsting for you, O Lord, thirsting for you, my God. 58 1144 1172 1202

My soul is thirsting, my soul is thirsting, my soul is thirsting for you, O Lord my God. 57

My soul rejoices, my soul rejoices in my God. 121 1008

My spirit exults and rejoices in the Lord. 124

Night holds no terrors for me sleeping under God's wings. 69

No one who waits for you, O Lord, will ever be put to shame. 40 1226

Now and forevermore God's name be exalted. Praised be God's holy name, Alleluia. 87

Nunc dimíttis servum tuum, Dómine, secúndum verbum tuum in pace, Dómine. 126

O bless the Lord, bless the Lord, my soul, O my soul. 83 1024

O bless the Lord, O bless the Lord, my soul. 79

O blessed are those who fear the Lord and walk in his ways. 1017

O come, let us worship the Lord. 72

O God, let all the nations praise you! O God, let all the nations praise you! 61

O God, O God, let all the nations praise you! 1093 1166

O Jubiláte Deo omnis terra! O Alleluia, alleluia! 60

O Lord, hear my prayer, hear my prayer, O Lord. 106

O Lord, our God, how wonderful your name in all the earth! 1104

O Lord, our God, unwearied is your love for us. 64

O praise the Lord, Jerusalem! Sion, praise your God! 110

O Shout to God with joy, all peoples of the earth! O Alleluia, alleluia! 60

Oh Dios, que te alaben los pueblos, que todos los pueblos te alaben. 61

Our blessing-cup is a communion with the Blood of Christ. 91 1054

Our eyes are fixed on the Lord, pleading for his mercy. 98 1149

Our help is from the Lord, who made heaven and earth. 95 1195

Out of the depths I cry to you, O Lord. 103

Padre, a tus manos encomiendo mi espíritu. 43

Praise the Lord, Jerusalem. Praise the Lord, Jerusalem. 1105

Praise the Lord, my soul! Praise the Lord! 1176 1186 1203

Praise the Lord, praise the Lord, who heals the brokenhearted. 1122

Praise the Lord, praise the Lord who lifts up the poor. 1183

Precious in the eyes of the Lord is the death of his friends. 90

Proclaim God's marvelous deeds to all the nations. 73

Proclaim his marvelous deeds to all the nations. 1114

Proclaim the greatness of God; rejoice in God, my Savior! 123

Proclama mi ser lagrandeza del Señor. 124

Protect us, Lord, as we stay awake; watch over us as we sleep, that awake we may keep watch with Christ, and, asleep, rest in his peace. 24

Put your hope in the Lord; take courage and be strong. 41

Qui regarde vers Dieu resplendira, sur son visage, plus d'amertume, sur son visage, plus d'amertume. 47

Remember your mercies, O Lord; remember your mercies, O Lord. 1184

Rest in God alone, rest in God alone, my soul, my soul. 1130

Return, O Lord, and rescue my soul. 27

Señor, que tu misericordia venga sobre nosotros. 45

Shepherd me, O God, beyond my wants, beyond my fears, from death into life. 36

Since my mother's womb, you have been my strength. 1215

Sing a new song to the God of salvation. 112

Sing a new song to the Lord, sing a new song to the Lord: praise him from the ends of the earth, alleluia, alleluia. 76

Sing praise to our king, sing praise: for God is king of all the earth. 53

Sing to the Lord a new song, for God has done wonderful deeds. 75

Sing to the Lord a new song, for he has done marvelous deeds. 1229

Sing to the Lord and bless his name, sing to the Lord and bless his name, alleluia. Alleluia, alleluia. 73

Sing with joy to God! Sing to God our help! 1134

Sit nomen Dómini sit benedíctum. Nunc et in saécula benedíctum. 87

Taste and see, taste and see that the Lord is good, the Lord is good. 48

Taste and see, taste and see the goodness of the Lord. 49

Taste and see the goodness of the Lord. 49 183 1038 1164 1167 1170

Teach me to do your will, my God. 106

Teach me your ways, O Lord, teach me your ways. 1116

The Almighty has done great things for me, and holy is his name. 16

The angel of the Lord will rescue those who fear him. 1218

The earth has yielded its fruit; the Lord our God has blessed us. 61

The earth is full of the goodness of God, the goodness of our God. 45

The earth is full of the goodness, the goodness of the Lord. 1062

The hand of the Lord feeds us; God answers all our needs. 107

The hand of the Lord feeds us; he answers all our needs. 1158 1160

The just man is a light in darkness to the upright. 1121

The just will live in the presence of the Lord. 29

The just will rejoice in the Lord; all upright hearts will glory. 59

The Lord comes to rule the earth, to rule with justice. 1207

The Lord gave them bread from heaven. The Lord gave them bread from heaven. 1161

The Lord has done great things for us; we are filled with joy, we are filled with joy. 99 1006 1041 1197

The Lord has revealed to the nations his saving power. 1092 1192

The Lord has set his throne in heaven. 1096

The Lord hears the cry of the poor. 1198

The Lord hears the cry of the poor. Blessed be the Lord. 46

The Lord is close to the brokenhearted. 49

The Lord is compassionate to every creature. 107

The Lord is compassionate toward all his works. 108

The Lord is kind and merciful. 79 1035 1127 1129 1131

The Lord is kind and merciful, slow to anger, and rich in compassion. 79 1178

The Lord is kind and merciful, the Lord is kind and merciful. 80

The Lord is King for evermore. 70

The Lord is king; he is robed in majesty. 1209

The Lord is king, the Most High over all the earth. 1097 1220

The Lord is my light and my salvation. 41 142 1032 1115 1226

The Lord is my light and my salvation, of whom should I be afraid, of whom should I be afraid? 42

The Lord is my shepherd, nothing shall I want: he leads me by safe paths, nothing shall I fear. 37

The Lord is my shepherd; there is nothing I shall want. 37 194 1036 1085 1111 1155 1208 1226

The Lord is my shepherd; there is nothing I shall want. The Lord is my shepherd; nothing shall I fear. 38

The Lord is near to all who call on him. 1181

The Lord is near to all who call, the Lord is near. 107

The Lord is risen, the Lord is risen, alleluia, alleluia. 72

The Lord of hosts is with us; the God of Jacob is our stronghold. 51

The Lord remembers his covenant for ever. 1018

The Lord said to my lord: "Sit at my right hand." 84

The Lord speaks of peace, peace to his people. 1219

The Lord upholds my life. The Lord upholds my life. 1182

The Lord will bless his people with peace. 1022

The Lord will bless those who fear him, the little no less than the great. 89

The Lord's kindness is everlasting to those who fear him. 1109

The one who does justice will live in the presence of the Lord. 1156 1173

The precepts of the Lord give joy to the heart. 33 1185

The queen stands at your right hand, arrayed in gold. 1222

The seed that falls on good ground will yield a fruitful harvest. 1151

The son of David will live for ever. 1213

The stone rejected by the builders has become the cornerstone. 1086

The vineyard of the Lord is the house of Israel. 1187

The waters of the river gladden the city of God, the holy dwelling of the Most High. 1227

The whole world is filled with the Spirit of the Lord, alleluia. 83

Their message goes out through all the earth. 33 1217

This is the day the Lord has made; let us rejoice and be glad. 92 93

This is the day the Lord has made; let us rejoice, let us rejoice, let us rejoice and be glad. 1079

Though I walk in the valley of darkness, I fear no evil, for you are with me. 37 1226

To God be highest glory and praise for ever. 118

To the upright I will show the saving power of God. 1136

To you, glory and praise for evermore. 117 1102

To you, O Lord, I lift my soul. 40 1003 1226

To you, O Lord, I lift my soul, to you, I lift my soul. 39

Today if you hear the voice of the Lord, harden not your hearts, harden not your hearts. 72

Today is born our Savior, Christ the Lord. Hoy nos ha nacido un Salvador. Born our Savior, Christ the Lord. El Mesías, el Señor. 74

Today is born our Savior, Christ the Lord. Today is born our Savior, Christ the Lord. 1014

Turn to me, Lord, and have mercy. 40

Turn to the Lord in your need, and you will live. 1153

We are God's people, the flock of the Lord. 78

We are his people, the sheep of his flock. 1087 1139

We shall go up with joy to the house of our God. 97

When the Holy Spirit comes to you, you will be my witnesses! 34

Who is this king of glory? It is the Lord. 1212

With the Lord there is mercy, and fullness of redemption. 103 1039 1137

With the Lord there is mercy and the fullness of redemption, call to him in your trials, he will answer whenever you call. 102

With the Lord, with the Lord there is mercy, and fullness of redemption. 168

You are a priest for ever, in the line of Melchizedek. 84 1108

You are my inheritance, O Lord. 30

You are my inheritance, O Lord, O Lord. 1063 1147 1206

You have given your people bread from heaven, (alleluia, alleluia). 63

You have redeemed us, Lord, God of truth. 44

You will draw water joyfully from the springs of salvation. 1023 1066 1068 1110

You will show me the path of life, you, my hope and my shelter. In your presence is endless joy, at your side is my home forever. 30

Your kingdom is everlasting; you shall reign for ever. 108

Your ways, O Lord, are love and truth, to those who keep your covenant. 1028

Your words, O Lord, are Spirit and life, Spirit and life. 1117 1153

Index of First Lines and Common Titles/*continued*

Index of First Lines and Common Titles/*continued*

Index of First Lines and Common Titles/*continued*

Index of First Lines and Common Titles/*continued*

Index of First Lines and Common Titles/*continued*

Index of First Lines and Common Titles/*continued*